ENVIRONMENTAL LAW

**CONTEMPORARY
LEGAL EDUCATION SERIES**

Environmental Law

CASES AND MATERIALS

Second Edition

WILLIAM MURRAY TABB
Professor of Law
University of Oklahoma College of Law

LINDA A. MALONE
Marshall-Wythe Foundation Professor of Law
Marshall-Wythe School of Law
College of William and Mary

LEXIS® LAW PUBLISHING
CHARLOTTESVILLE, VIRGINIA

1328511

Preface

The past twenty-five years have been marked by a tremendous expansion in federal regulation dealing with a vast array of topics ranging from air and water pollution control to programs regarding the cleanup of toxic waste. The diversity and complexity of the common law and legislative solutions aimed at ensuring a clean and safe environment and the numerous public and private interests at stake present unique pedagogical problems in teaching a course in environmental law. Recognizing the breadth and dynamic nature of these developments, we oriented the focus of this book to a mainstream national approach examining the major areas of environmental protection and remediation. The central goal of the book is to offer a balanced, current, and comprehensive study of the field in a traditional format.

Organization and Coverage

The book is organized in six parts: (1) introductory materials, (2) environmental litigation, (3) National Environmental Policy Act, (4) federal pollution control regulation, (5) federal regulation of toxic substances, and (6) environmental regulation of land use. The environmental litigation section covers a broad range of issues, including the study of common law measures regarding protecting and compensating for harm to natural resources, constitutional limits on state action, and the role of citizens' suits, courts, and agencies in environmental disputes. The book is designed to address each of the significant topics in a conventional study of environmental law.

There were several guiding principles which are reflected in the thematic approach and organizational design of the book. The first principle was to provide a thorough, balanced treatment of all the major federal environmental statutes and common law topics with emphasis on significant developments The materials are structured to provide a suitable mix of cases, notes, problems, and charts. The notes have been written to further class discussion of the principles of the main cases and supplementary issues of importance, rather than to address every issue in an encyclopedic manner. The book is intended for primary use as a casebook for teaching a survey course in environmental law rather than as a reference guide or treatise.

A major objective of our organizational philosophy was to make the book "user-friendly" for students and professors. One structural feature incorporated throughout the book is the study of the principal topics in a self-contained fashion. In other words, the major federal statutes are covered as independent units rather than piecemeal in various places throughout the text. This design permits the study of the major statutes as "stand-alone" units. Also, each section is introduced by a discussion of the significant topics which will be examined.

Since environmental law today is a patchwork of complex statutes and common law developments, these introductory materials hopefully will provide a contextual background to understand the materials better and to grasp their importance.

The internal organization of the book is designed to provide maximum flexibility and selectivity of material. Most sections include three or four cases and accompanying notes to reflect an appropriate amount of coverage for a typical class period. Also, the most important topics in each chapter are covered first, and collateral but interesting issues are generally placed at the end. Some professors may desire to cover just the "core" material at the beginning of the chapter and move along to other topics. Others may opt to spend more time in examining a particular area in greater detail. Our approach will accommodate those individual choices while preserving the overall integrity of the book.

Case Selection and Editing

We had two principal goals in the selection of cases. First, we sought to use current cases to illustrate points whenever possible. This reflects the significant developments which have taken place recently in the field of environmental law. Some of the older "classic" cases have been included where appropriate. Second, we tried to choose cases representing the majority position on a topic. In certain instances portions of the dissenting opinion will be included to provide a more complete picture of the respective sides of a particular issue. The note materials often will be used to examine minority views on a subject which are not adequately addressed in the main case.

We have adopted several "conventions" in our editing which should enhance the instructional value of the cases. Our main goal was to focus on the key material that makes the case significant and merits inclusion in the book. In that regard, we have sought to limit the cases to a manageable length by summarizing extensive factual backgrounds where appropriate and deleting long string cites which do not add to the educational value of the opinion.

The study of environmental law offers an interesting and exciting challenge because of the diversity and significance of the interests and policies involved. Any book, by necessity, merely represents a sampling of the many provocative and often controversial issues facing Congress, courts, agencies, business, and the public. The materials presented hopefully will generate thoughtful analysis and a deeper understanding of this rapidly changing field.

Acknowledgments

The second edition of this book is the culmination of years of labor and reflects the tangible and intangible contributions of many friends and colleagues who deserve recognition. Professor Tabb especially acknowledges the constant support, love and encouragement of his wife, Diane, and his children, Brian, Wilson and Emily. He also wants to thank his brother and friend, Professor Charles Tabb. Professor Michael Scaperlanda, a valued colleague, deserves thanks for his encouragement and perspective. Finally, he wants to express appreciation to Peter Graves, for his gift of laughter and tireless support over the years.

Professor Malone acknowledges her deepest thanks to Erin and Corey — the best daughters a mother could ever have — for their kindness, love, and understanding. She also wishes to express special appreciation to Della Harris for her invaluable assistance and friendship in the completion of this manuscript.

Summary Table of Contents

Table of Contents

Page

Part I.
Introduction

Chapter 1

PERSPECTIVES ON ENVIRONMENTAL LAW AND POLICY

INTRODUCTION

The study of environmental law involves a rich mixture of ethics, economics, and public interest issues — all related to a common goal of ensuring protection of human health and the environment from harmful effects of pollution. Unlike many areas of law which have evolved slowly, environmental law — particularly on the federal level — has developed and expanded geometrically over the past two decades. The explosion of federal legislation in the 1970s was fueled by a growing recognition of the inadequacies of the private market system of nuisance law as an effective mechanism for land use regulation of property rights and environmental protection. The public called for state and federal governments to move quickly to address the health and environmental consequences of the release of hazardous and non-hazardous substances into the environment. Although common law retains certain vitality in the overall landscape of environmental law, the effects of federal legislation have widespread significance throughout the public and private sectors.

The principal federal environmental protection statutes, although influenced by common law, reflect a fundamental dissatisfaction with the solutions to the pollution problem offered under a private law system. Among the perceived shortcomings of nuisance law were difficulties in balancing investment and development costs to industry — in the traditional sense of a free enterprise market economy — with the potential health and environmental risks from exposure to materials produced and discarded in the manufacturing and distribution process. Additional problems inherent in the private law structure included remedial and enforcement limitations such as restrictions on standing, ascertaining and tracing the sources of pollution where multiple parties were involved over an extended period of time, and jurisdictional differences in standards of liability. Finally, concerns developed about the need for a comprehensive solution to minimize and control the entry of toxic pollutants into the environment, where in some instances any level of human exposure presented an unacceptable degree of risk.

Through comprehensive national standards Congress could force a different balancing of interests in decisionmaking by industry, government agencies, and the judiciary. Direct regulation requiring nationally uniform pollution control measures offered several apparent advantages in the systematic treatment, consideration and balancing of various interests and concerns. The difficulties faced by Congress, however, in crafting a regulatory model also were considerable. The mission of Congress to decide upon an approach which would most directly and efficiently solve the multi-faceted pollution problem was far from clear. The legislative problems were compounded by the varied perspectives of the different "players" on the environmental scene: government agencies, public interest groups, private citizens, industry, and the courts all had different interests and expectations with respect to the nature and rigor of any legislative solutions.

Moreover, the effectiveness of any regulatory structure turns on the reliability and sufficiency of the supporting data. Immediately, Congress faced an apparently intractable dilemma: the public clamored for swift steps to protect health and the environment yet the information necessary to determine appropriate standards often was unavailable or imprecise. Questions such as what constitutes a "safe" level of exposure presented difficulties for legislative line-drawing, particularly where incomplete or often contradictory scientific data led to disagreements even in the scientific community. Hopes for any legislative panacea were quickly dispelled when critics pointed out the high administrative costs involved in gathering information, setting standards and monitoring compliance. A forward-looking regulatory scheme, although potentially beneficial with respect to changing future behavior, fails to correct the existing problems attributable to past occurrences of pollution. In determining the effective date of legislative mandates, should Congress adopt a scheme of gradual or phased compliance or instead select a target date and require uniform adherence?

The course that Congress chose with respect to these and other difficult policy questions was itself varied and often fell short of unrealistic expectations. The principal federal environmental protection statutes may perhaps best be viewed as an amalgamation of different methodologies or a reconciliation of numerous competing interests — in short, a political compromise. Several unifying principles behind federal legislative efforts, though, are evident: facilitating government acquisition of information about the dangers presented by the myriads of hazardous chemicals and other substances regularly entering the environment, creating regulatory and technological standards to limit and control the release of pollutants by industry, imposing responsibility on those accountable for the harms associated with pollution, and giving government the necessary tools to ensure compliance with the statutory directives.

The need for a statutory scheme to develop pertinent information regarding the potential environmental impacts of a proposed federal project became the cornerstone of the National Environmental Policy Act of 1969 ("NEPA") which was signed into law by President Nixon on January 1, 1970. NEPA's mandate was simple: to force all federal agencies to consider environmental values in their planning and decisionmaking processes and to engage public opinion on proposed projects with significant environmental effects. Congress chose to carry out that goal by crafting NEPA in philosophical terms — where agencies were directed to balance environmental values with other interests — rather than by setting particular standards or regulating specific pollutants. NEPA centers on promoting environmental awareness and information-gathering, then, as opposed to focusing efforts to achieve a particular substantive result. Although NEPA's effectiveness has fostered sharp debate, it survives as an important statute in environmental law. Coverage of the principal issues in NEPA are addressed in Chapter 5.

The Clean Air Act of 1970 reflects an entirely different approach through its scheme of establishing national standards to attain a particular quality of ambient air. The Clean Air Act, in its area-wide plan methodology, emphasized a health-based system carried out by a cooperative system between state and federal governments. The Environmental Protection Agency met with technical and scientific difficulties in setting standards and in implementing the Act, particularly with respect to correcting existing air quality problems in certain densely populated areas of the country. The Act was dramatically overhauled in 1990, reflecting a toughened stance on toxic pollutants and adding a technology-based component. Chapter 6 explores the principal areas of controversy and concern with respect to the Clean Air Act.

The Federal Water Pollution Control Act of 1972 radically changed previous federal measures which emphasized state responsibility for water quality by placing primary authority for water pollution controls in the hands of the federal government. Although states continued to play a key role with respect to water quality, the focus shifted toward nationally uniform, technology-based standards on individual "point sources" where specific limitations were placed on discharges of effluent into the nation's waters. The distinguishing mark of the revitalized Clean Water Act was its scheme of phased compliance with technological standards through a permitting system. The Act generally met with greater administrative success than its pollution control counterpart, the beleaguered Clean Air Act, primarily due to the emphasis on technology and mandatory permit system. The Clean Water Act is discussed in Chapter 7.

Other somewhat dormant statutes which involved labelling and testing of chemical substances also received Congressional attention and revision in the 1970s, including the Toxic Substances Control Act ("TSCA") (Chapter 10) and the Federal Insecticide, Fungicide & Rodenticide Act ("FIFRA") (Chapter 11). TSCA's policy was to develop data on the environmental effects of the thousands of new and existing chemicals distributed in commerce in the United States. The data could then be used by the federal government to prevent unreasonable risks of injury to health or the environment. FIFRA's focus was narrower in that its field was limited to registration of pesticides. Both statutes centrally reflect a tension of risk-benefit analysis where the Environmental Protection Agency balances the interests of industry and the public in administration of the Acts.

Despite the significant changes brought by these federal environmental statutes, certain issues remained unresolved. The primary area of public concern involved the dangers presented by the release of toxic pollutants into the environment. Although hazardous pollutants were regulated in certain respects pursuant to several other acts, no comprehensive statutory mechanism existed to deal with the problems of toxic chemicals. The Resource Conservation and Recovery Act of 1976 (Chapter 8) filled this gap by creating a system to identify and track hazardous waste from its generation until ultimately disposed. The Comprehensive Environmental Response, Compensation and Liability Act ("CERCLA") (Chapter 9) directed federal energy and resources specifically toward the cleanup of hazardous waste sites. Interestingly, these statutes had characteristics of tort law in their backward-looking remedial emphasis.

The following materials are some of the seminal works which have strongly influenced the environmental movement over the past few decades. The infusion of economic considerations in the legislative process has been a major factor in the design and implementation of federal environmental laws. Apart from pecuniary concerns, ethical and ecological issues have foundational significance in affecting the nature of the statutory approaches adopted and their implementation. Environmental law reflects a changing synergy of competing policies and views of what restrictions society is willing to impose upon its members in exchange for living in a healthy environment.

A. THE ROLE OF ECONOMICS

The creation of a legislative model aimed at abating or minimizing the release of pollutants into the ambient environment necessarily must consider the attendant costs. The question of evaluating costs and corresponding benefits, though, is not a precise science. From an economist's perspective, the notion of allocating resources efficiently to maximize total production is the touchstone of analytical thought. The market functions well, however, only if prices accurately reflect the costs and benefits to society. Technical and political problems are implicated when evaluating environmental issues in a traditional economics framework. First, any regulatory structure — including one that purports to balance costs and risks — assumes that the standards are predicated on reliable information. The technical problems with respect to developing an environmental law system are that it is often difficult to place values on or obtain substitutes for sensitive, non-renewable natural resources. The real "value" of such resources is not reflected nor easily quantifiable in commercial terms but instead lies in recognition of the interrelationship of the resource to a wider ecosystem and the human environment.

The political dilemma is equally complex. How should Congress accurately balance costs and benefits of regulation, taking into account differences per industry and locale? What if one industry uniformly falls short of economic and technologically feasible requirements? Should Congress shut down an entire industry, or favor only the largest companies? What if the result of regulation leads to widespread unemployment in a particular sector of the economy or region of the country? Should regulation "force" an industry to find technological solutions which did not currently exist nor were even contemplated in order to survive?

BOULDING, THE ECONOMICS OF THE COMING SPACESHIP EARTH
in Environmental Quality in a Growing Economy 3-14
(H. Jarrett ed. 1966)*

We are now in the middle of a long process of transition in the nature of the image which man has of himself and his environment. Primitive men, and to a large extent also men of the early civilizations, imagined themselves to be living on a virtually illimitable plain. There was almost always somewhere beyond the known limits of human habitation, and over a very large part of the time that man has been on earth, there has been something like a frontier. That is, there was always some place else to go when things got too difficult, either by reason of the deterioration of the natural environment or a deterioration of the social structure in places where people happened to live. The image of the frontier is probably one of the oldest images of mankind, and it is not surprising that we find it hard to get rid of.

. . . .

The closed earth of the future requires economic principles which are somewhat different from those of the open earth of the past. For the sake of picturesqueness, I am tempted to call the open economy the "cowboy economy," the cowboy being symbolic of the illimitable plains and also associated with reckless, exploitative, romantic, and violent behavior, which is characteristic of open societies. The closed economy of the future might similarly be called the "spaceman" economy, in which the earth has become a single spaceship, without unlimited reservoirs of anything, either for extraction or for pollution, and in which, therefore, man must find his place in a cyclical ecological system which is capable of continuous reproduction of material form even though it cannot escape having inputs of energy. The difference between the two types of economy becomes most apparent in the attitude towards consumption. In the cowboy economy, consumption is regarded as a good thing and production likewise; and the success of the economy is measured by the amount of the throughput from the "factors of production," a part of which, at any rate, is extracted from the reservoirs of raw materials and noneconomic objects, and another part of which is output into the reservoirs of pollution. If there are infinite reservoirs from which material can be obtained and into which effluvia can be deposited, then the throughput is at least a plausible measure of the success of the economy. The gross national product is a rough measure of this total throughput....

By contrast, in the spaceman economy, throughput is by no means a desideratum, and is indeed to be regarded as something to be minimized rather than maximized. The essential measure of the success of the economy is not production and consumption at all, but the nature, extent, quality, and complexity of the total capital stock, including in this the state of the human bodies and

---

minds included in the system. In the spaceman economy, what we are primarily concerned with is stock maintenance, and any technological change which results in the maintenance of a given total stock with a lessened throughput (that is, less production and consumption) is clearly a gain. This idea that both production and consumption are bad things rather than good things is very strange to economists, who have been obsessed with the income-flow concepts to the exclusion, almost, of capital-stock concepts.

    ....

    It may be said, of course, why worry about all this when the spaceman economy is still a good way off (at least beyond the lifetimes of any now living), so let us eat, drink, spend, extract and pollute, and be as merry as we can, and let posterity worry about the spaceship earth. It is always a little hard to find a convincing answer to the man who says, "What has posterity ever done for me?" and the conservationist has always had to fall back on rather vague ethical principles postulating identity of the individual with some human community or society which extends not only back into the past but forward into the future. Unless the individual identifies with some community of this kind, conservation is obviously "irrational." Why should we not maximize the welfare of this generation at the cost of posterity? *"Apres nous, le deluge"* has been the motto of not insignificant numbers of human societies. The only answer to this, as far as I can see, is to point out that the welfare of the individual depends on the extent to which he can identify himself with others, and that the most satisfactory individual identity is that which identifies not only with a community in space but also with a community extending over time from the past into the future. If this kind of identity is recognized as desirable, then posterity has a voice, even if it does not have a vote; and in a sense, if its voice can influence votes, it has votes too. This whole problem is linked up with the much larger one of the determinants of the morale, legitimacy, and "nerve" of a society, and there is a great deal of historical evidence to suggest that a society which loses its identity with posterity and which loses its positive image of the future loses also its capacity to deal with present problems, and soon falls apart.

    ....

    It may be complained that the considerations I have been putting forth relate only to the very long run, and they do not much concern our immediate problems. There may be some justice in this criticism, and my main excuse is that other writers have dealt adequately with the more immediate problems of deterioration in the quality of the environment. It is true, for instance, that many of the immediate problems of pollution of the atmosphere or of bodies of water arise because of the failure of the price system, and many of them could be solved by corrective taxation. If people had to pay the losses due to the nuisances which they create, a good deal more resources would go into the prevention of nuisances. These arguments involving external economies and diseconomies are familiar to economists, and there is no need to recapitulate them. The law of torts is quite inadequate to provide for the correction of the price system which is required, simply because where damages are widespread and their incidence on any particular person is small, the ordinary remedies of the civil law are quite inadequate and inappropriate. There needs, therefore, to be special legislation to cover these cases, and though such legislation seems hard to get in practice, mainly because of the widespread and small personal incidence of the injuries, the technical problems involved are not insuperable. If we were to adopt in principle a law for tax penalties for social damages, with an apparatus for making assessments under it, a very large proportion of current pollution and deterioration of the environment would be prevented. There are tricky problems of equity involved, particularly where old established nuisances create a kind of "right by purchase" to perpetuate themselves, but these are problems again which a few rather arbitrary decisions can bring to some kind of solution.

... Our success in dealing with the larger problems, however, is not unrelated to the development of skill in the solution of the more immediate and perhaps less difficult problems. One can hope, therefore, that as a succession of mounting crises, especially in pollution, arouse public opinion and mobilize support for the solution of the immediate problems, a learning process will be set in motion which will eventually lead to an appreciation of and perhaps solutions for the larger ones....

NOTES AND QUESTIONS

1. Boulding suggests that society needs to recognize that society's patterns of consumption and exploitation of resources must be reshaped to take into account the limited supply of those resources. Assuming that the focus should shift toward maintenance and preservation, how should those policies be specifically integrated into a legislative scheme? What should be the role of the courts in applying common law protections to fill in the gaps where Congress has not yet acted?

2. Do Boulding's views also suggest heightened individual accountability with respect to conservation and cleanup of our environment? In what ways should individuals alter their existing behavior to ensure a healthier environment for the community? The Resource Conservation and Recovery Act contains narrow exclusions from regulation for certain reclaimed and recycled materials. *See* 40 C.F.R. § 261.1(c); § 261.2(c), (e). Many recycling activities are not exempted from the statutory scope, however. Approximately thirty states have enacted comprehensive laws designed to encourage recycling. Many of these laws focus on market development for recycled products, government procurement programs, and establishing tax credits for businesses engaged in recycling activities. Although most of the state acts operate through incentives to stimulate voluntary compliance, some have imposed mandatory obligations on citizens and businesses. Compare Or. Rev. Stat. §§ 459.005, 459.015, 459.165-.200 (1989) (Oregon Recycling Opportunities Act, establishing a comprehensive state-wide program for solid waste management promoting recycling through public education and economic incentives) and N.J.S.A. § 13:1E-99.11 (New Jersey Statewide Mandatory Source Separation and Recycling Act). *See generally* Kovacs, *The Coming Era of Conservation and Industrial Utilization of Recyclable Materials*, 15 ECOLOGY L.Q. 537 (1988); Parker, *Oregon's Pioneer Recycling Act*, 15 ENVTL. L. 387 (1985).

HARDIN, THE TRAGEDY OF THE COMMONS, 162 Science 1243-45, 1248 (1968)*

....

What Shall We Maximize?

Population, as Malthus said, naturally tends to grow "geometrically," or, as we would now say, exponentially. In a finite world this means that the per capita share of the world's goods must steadily decrease. Is ours a finite world?

A fair defense can be put forward for the view that the world is infinite; or that we do not know that it is not. But, in terms of the practical problems that we must face in the next few generations with the foreseeable technology, it is clear that we will greatly increase human misery if we do not, during the immediate future, assume that the world available to the terrestrial human population is finite....

We want the maximum good per person; but what is good? To one person it is wilderness, to another it is ski lodges for thousands. To one it is estuaries to nourish ducks for hunters to shoot; to another it is factory land. Comparing one good with another is, we usually say, impossible because goods are incommensurable. Incommensurables cannot be compared.

Theoretically this may be true; but in real life incommensurables *are* commensurable. Only a criterion of judgment and a system of weighting are needed. In nature the criterion is survival. Is it better for a species to be small and hideable, or large and powerful? Natural selection commensurates the incommensurable. The compromise achieved depends on a natural weighting of the values of the variables.

Man must imitate this process....

We can make little progress in working toward optimum population size until we explicitly exorcise the spirit of Adam Smith in the field of practical demography. In economic affairs, *The Wealth of Nations* (1776) popularized the "invisible hand," the idea that an individual who "intends only his own gain," is, as it were, "led by an invisible hand to promote ... the public interest." Adam Smith did not assert that this was invariably true, and perhaps neither did any of his followers. But he contributed to a dominant tendency of thought that has ever since interfered with positive action based on rational analysis, namely, the

---

*Copyright 1968 by the American Association for the Advancement of Sciences. Reprinted with permission of the AAAS.

tendency to assume that decisions reached individually will, in fact, be the best decisions for an entire society....

Tragedy of Freedom in a Commons

The tragedy of the commons develops in this way. Picture a pasture open to all. It is to be expected that each herdsman will try to keep as many cattle as possible on the commons. Such an arrangement may work reasonably satisfactorily for centuries because tribal wars, poaching, and disease keep the numbers of both man and beast well below the carrying capacity of the land. Finally, however, comes the day of reckoning, that is, the day when the long-desired goal of social stability becomes a reality. At this point, the inherent logic of the commons remorselessly generates tragedy.

As a rational being, each herdsman seeks to maximize his gain. Explicitly or implicitly, more or less consciously, he asks, "What is the utility *to me* of adding one more animal to my herd?" This utility has one negative and one positive component.

1) The positive component is a function of the increment of one animal. Since the herdsman receives all the proceeds from the sale of the additional animal, the positive utility is nearly $+1$.

2) The negative component is a function of the additional overgrazing created by one more animal. Since, however, the effects of overgrazing are shared by all the herdsmen, the negative utility for any particular decision-making herdsman is only a fraction of -1.

Adding together the component partial utilities, the rational herdsman concludes that the only sensible course for him to pursue is to add another animal to his herd. And another; and another.... But this is the conclusion reached by each and every rational herdsman sharing a commons. Therein is the tragedy. Each man is locked into a system that compels him to increase his herd without limit — in a world that is limited. Ruin is the destination toward which all men rush, each pursuing his own best interest in a society that believes in the freedom of the commons. Freedom in a commons brings ruin to all.

. . . .

In an approximate way, the logic of the commons has been understood for a long time, perhaps since the discovery of agriculture or the invention of private property in real estate. But it is understood mostly only in special cases which are not sufficiently generalized. Even at this late date, cattlemen leasing national land on the western ranges demonstrate no more than an ambivalent understanding, in constantly pressuring federal authorities to increase the head count to the point where overgrazing produces erosion and weed-dominance. Likewise, the oceans of the world continue to suffer from the survival of the philosophy of the commons. Maritime nations still respond automatically to the shibboleth of the "freedom of the seas." Professing to believe in the "inexhaustible resources of the oceans," they bring species after species of fish and whales closer to extinction.

The National Parks present another instance of the working out of the tragedy of the commons. At present, they are open to all, without limit. The parks themselves are limited in extent — there is only one Yosemite Valley — whereas population seems to grow without limit. The values that visitors seek in the parks are steadily eroded. Plainly, we must soon cease to treat the parks as commons or they will be of no value to anyone.

What shall we do? We have several options. We might sell them off as private property. We might keep them as public property, but allocate the right to enter them. The allocation might be on the basis of wealth, by the use of an auction system. It might be on the basis of merit, as defined by some agreed upon standards. It might be by lottery. Or it might be on a first-come, first-served basis, administered to long queues. These, I think, are all the reasonable possibilities. They are all objectionable. But we must choose — or acquiesce in the destruction of the commons that we call our National Parks.

Pollution

In a reverse way, the tragedy of the commons reappears in problems of pollution. Here it is not a question of taking something out of the commons, but of putting something in — sewage, or chemical, radioactive, and heat wastes into water; noxious and dangerous fumes into the air; and distracting and unpleasant advertising signs into the line of sight. The calculations of utility are much the same as before. The rational man finds that his share of the cost of the wastes he discharges into the commons is less than the cost of purifying his wastes before releasing them. Since this is true for everyone, we are locked into a system of "fouling our own nest," so long as we behave only as independent, rational, free-enterprisers.

The tragedy of the commons as a food basket is averted by private property, or something formally like it. But the air and waters surrounding us cannot readily be fenced, and so the tragedy of the commons as a cesspool must be prevented by different means, by coercive laws or taxing devices that make it cheaper for the polluter to treat his pollutants than to discharge them untreated. We have not progressed as far with the solution of this problem as we have with the first. Indeed, our particular concept of private property, which deters us from exhausting the positive resources of the earth, favors pollution. The owner of a factory on the bank of a stream — whose property extends to the middle of the stream — often has difficulty seeing why it is not his natural right to muddy the waters flowing past his door. The law, always behind the times, requires elaborate stitching and fitting to adapt it to this newly perceived aspect of the commons.

The pollution problem is a consequence of population. It did not much matter how a lonely American frontiersman disposed of his waste. "Flowing water purifies itself every 10 miles," my grandfather used to say, and the myth was near enough to the truth when he was a boy, for there were not too many people. But as population became denser, the natural chemical and biological recycling processes became overloaded, calling for a redefinition of property rights.

Recognition of Necessity

....

Every new enclosure of the commons involves the infringement of somebody's personal liberty. Infringements made in the distant past are accepted because no contemporary complains of a loss. It is the newly proposed infringements that we vigorously oppose; cries of "rights" and "freedom" fill the air. But what does "freedom" mean? When men mutually agreed to pass laws against robbing, mankind became more free, not less so. Individuals locked into the logic of the commons are free only to bring on universal ruin; once they see the necessity of mutual coercion, they become free to pursue other goals....

NOTES AND QUESTIONS

1. According to Hardin, what is the "tragedy" with respect to the environment? In a free market economy can this problem be avoided?

2. A "rational" manufacturer, when seeking to maximize production efficiencies, will try to externalize its operation costs (but not benefits) down the distribution chain and onto the public. Industry will not install expensive pollution control equipment, then, which does not increase production efficiencies absent sufficient market incentives or government coercion. Congress, as demonstrated in the Clean Air Act and the Clean Water Act, has sought to force industry to "internalize" the costs of pollution abatement by establishing technological standards applicable to the discharge or release of pollutants into the environment. Society is collectively indirectly benefitted by these pollution minimization expenditures yet does not directly share in the costs. Certainly to an extent, manufacturers are often able to pass along the added costs of pollution control equipment through increases in the prices of its products. In some instances, though, industry cannot recoup its expenditures and may find that consumers switch to substitute products if the price becomes too high. Should environmental law concern itself with marketplace factors of supply and demand, cross-elasticity of demand, and competitive advantage? *See* Clean Water Act § 301(m)(1)(B),(I), 42 U.S.C. § 1311(m)(1)(B),(I).

SAGOFF, ECONOMIC THEORY AND ENVIRONMENTAL LAW, 79 Mich. L. Rev. 1393-1401, 1410-17, 1419 (1981)*

Many economists take the view that environmental problems are economic problems. They believe that market failure causes these problems: private and social costs diverge; profit-maximizing decisions, therefore, are socially inefficient. Economists would correct this market failure by requiring private decision makers to internalize externalities, that is, to make the price of goods reflect all the economic and social costs of producing them, including the pollution costs. When this is done, they argue, pollution will be controlled, endangered species will be saved, and pristine areas will be preserved, but only to the extent that the benefits therefrom exceed the costs. Any increase in environmental protection from an "optimal" level "would cost more than it is worth," while any decrease would "reduce benefits more than it would save in costs."

Although this economic approach purports to allow us to choose the best among available policies, in fact it makes economic efficiency our only goal. Economic efficiency has traditionally been understood to require the maximum satisfaction of the preferences that markets reveal. These are typically self-regarding or self-interested preferences, that is, preferences that reflect a person's idea of his or her individual welfare. Preferences of this sort may be contrasted with preferences that express what the individual believes is in the public interest or in the interest of a group or community to which he or she belongs. Political activity is supposed, in theory at least, to provide a vehicle for airing, criticizing, and settling upon interests or opinions of this group-regarding kind.

The search for economic efficiency might take us to the best public policies if we were a nation of individualists competing each for his or her own welfare with no regard for or conception of the collective good. Then an efficient market might lead us to satisfy as well as possible all of our interests. In such a situation, government might best be conceived as a prophylactic on markets, and public policies might be considered irrational if they could not be construed as reasonable responses to market failures. But we are not simply a group of consumers, nor are we bent on satisfying only self-regarding preferences. Many of us advocate ideals and have a vision of what we should do or be like as a nation. And we would sacrifice some of our private interests for those public ends.

There may be individuals who believe that our nation as a whole should dedicate itself entirely to the interests that individuals pursue as individuals. This belief comes into question, however, when we distinguish what people want for themselves and what they think is best for the community. Why should we believe that the right policy goal is the one that satisfies only the self-interested preferences of consumers? Why should we not take into account the community-regarding values that individuals seek through the political process as well?

In Part I of this essay, I argue that environmental legislation, at least during the past twenty years, fails to make economic "common sense," that is, it fails to maximize the satisfaction of consumer demand over the long run. Laws like the Endangered Species Act flout this conception of economic efficiency. This is how most Americans would have it: most Americans reject the notion that the natural environment should be made over to serve the wants of the self-interested consumer. Part II describes the way that economists have attempted to take account of citizen- or community-regarding preferences. I suggest that they do this primarily by giving these convictions and beliefs shadow or surrogate prices as if they were market externalities. In Part II, I argue briefly that this shadow pricing of political, moral, and cultural convictions vitiates cost-benefit analysis. Shadow pricing allows the analyst to justify virtually any policy by assigning the appropriate prices to the opinions of the political constituency that favors it. There is, then, no popular public policy that cannot then be justified on "economic" grounds.

In Part III of this essay, I extend my criticism of cost-benefit analysis to show that it confuses statements of principle or opinion with wants and interests of the kind that are properly revealed in and satisfied by markets. I argue that it is a mistake to treat views or convictions that merit the dignity of a hearing as if they were only wants or interests deserving of a price. I conclude that attempts to base environmental law on economic theory must fail.

I

Anyone who believes that government ought to be primarily interested in correcting market failure must find puzzling much of our environmental legislation. Environmentalist groups, not famous for their economic "common sense," successfully backed much of this legislation in the 1970s. It is not surprising, therefore, that environmental protection goes beyond the mere correction of market deficiencies. Congress designed the Clean Air and Clean Water Acts to improve the quality of our air and water. It passed the Endangered Species Act to protect threatened species, even if the economic costs of protection outweigh the benefits. Similarly, the Occupational Safety and Health Act seeks to make the workplace safe and healthful, a goal that is not always consistent with market efficiency. These laws attempt to correct perceived environmental, rather than economic, problems. Congress did not limit itself to providing economically optimal solutions.

....

One reason for these laws is that Americans have moral convictions about the environment that have nothing to do with economic "common sense." A majority of Americans strongly prefer environmental laws that are not economically efficient. The Endangered Species Act remains popular, even though people must recognize that the benefits of preserving Lange's metalmark, the snail darter, or the furbish lousewort may not equal the costs. We choose to save the metalmark to prove to ourselves that we are not motivated solely by economic self-interest. Rather, we act upon moral values and a sense of national responsibility to the land that we inhabit.

Our environmental laws illustrate that we are governed by legislatures, not by markets. There are currently before the courts a variety of cases in which industry has requested relief from economically burdensome regulations promulgated by administrative agencies. Industry argues that regulations imposing costs far in excess of their benefits are unreasonable, and that courts interpreting these regulations should consider economic factors. That benefits exceed costs, however, is not a constitutional requirement for congressional regulation of commerce. A legislative majority voted for the Clean Water and Clean Air Acts, the Endangered Species Act, and other environmental legislation. Courts should enforce regulations that conform to the statutes, even if consumers as a result have to pay more than they receive in benefits.

....

Although economic approaches to public policy may purport to weigh both consumer and citizen values, we may, as citizens, believe that certain public values or collective goals (e.g., that an innocent person not be convicted) supersede the values that we pursue as self-seeking individuals (e.g., security from crime). Moreover, we might decide to sacrifice economic optimality for cleaner air and water. Once legislatures, responding to political pressure, have made this choice, is it defensible for economists to insist that our policymaking process include the very consumer values that we have decided to sacrifice? Shall economic analysts, rather than legislatures, determine the balance to be struck between our preferences as consumers and our opinions as citizens?...

III

Economic methods cannot supply the information necessary to justify public policy. Economics can measure the intensity with which we hold our beliefs; it cannot evaluate those beliefs on their merits. Yet such evaluation is essential to political decision making. This is my greatest single criticism of cost-benefit analysis. The many problems involved in applying the concept of shadow pricing are secondary, because the concept itself rests on a mistake.

To recognize this mistake, we must first understand what it is that economists attempt to measure. If they measure consumer interests, market data are appropriate and relevant. The pricing mechanism can suggest when resources used to satisfy certain wants might be more efficiently employed to satisfy others. When economists approach issues that concern us as citizens, however, they do not, as they should, abandon the pricing mechanism. They believe that they can account for citizen-preferences as well as consumer-preferences by determining their dollar value. They do this, for example, by asking citizens what they would pay for a certain level of environmental protection. But this attempt to measure the convictions or values of citizens by pricing them as market externalities confuses what the individual wants as an individual and what he or she, as a citizen, believes is best for the community.

....

Private and public preferences also belong to different logical categories. Public "preferences" do not involve desires or wants, but opinions or beliefs. They state what a person believes is best or right for the community or group as a whole. These opinions or beliefs may be true or false, and we may meaningfully ask the individual for the reasons that he or she holds them. But an economist who asks how much citizens would pay for opinions that they advocate through political association commits a category-mistake. The economist asks of objective beliefs a question that is appropriate only to subjective wants.

When an environmentalist argues that we ought to preserve wilderness areas because of their cultural importance and symbolic meaning, he or she states a *conviction* and not a *desire*. When an economist asserts that we ought to attain efficient levels of pollution, he or she, too, states a belief. Both beliefs are to be supported by arguments, not by money. One cannot establish the validity of these beliefs by pricing them, nor can that mechanism measure their importance to society as a whole. One can judge how strongly people hold their beliefs by asking how much they would pay to see them implemented, but that is not how we make policy decisions.... When a person advocates a policy as being right or appropriate for society as a whole, however, the intensity of the desire is no longer relevant. Rather, advocates must present arguments that convince the public or its representatives to adopt a policy. Political decision makers judge ideas on their merits, and make decisions based on what is good for us all. These policymakers may consider economic factors, but they should not use the economic method to evaluate competing beliefs.

The distinction between public and private interests is indispensable to the study of political philosophy. "To abolish the distinction," as one commentator has written, "is to make a shambles of political science by treating things that are different as if they were alike." Markets are the appropriate arena for the competition of private interests. This competition may best be understood and regulated in terms of individual willingness to pay. When one advocates not a special or private interest but what one describes as the public interest or the interest of all, however, the framework of debate completely changes. Public discussion must then be carried on in public terms. The issue is no longer to measure the stake that the individual has in his proposal; indeed, the larger the individual's private stake, the more suspect is his public pretension. What matters is whether the argument that he or she offers is sound.

This is not to say that economic data are irrelevant in public decision making. It is to argue that the satisfaction of revealed preferences is only one goal among others that policymakers must take into account. And willingness to pay, as opposed to ability to argue, is not a method for making this choice. Costs and benefits, of course, are important — there are economic constraints. But this does not show that cost-benefit analysis provides an appropriate framework for testing the legitimacy of law.

The blurring of the distinction between public and private interest — and, therefore, between the competition of preferences and the contradiction of ideas — produces results that we should do well to avoid. First, the policymaker, employing the willingness-to-pay criterion, attempts to remain neutral among contending positions. As a result, the analyst must grant equal credibility to every position, no matter how bizarre or preposterous. This approach, indeed, may favor the silliest views over the more sensible ones since extreme opinions often generate the most emotion. An analyst can avoid this result only by abandoning neutrality, e.g., by screening the political opinions to which he or she is willing to assign a price.

Second, the willingness-to-pay approach to public policy removes the basis of legitimacy from the political process. I do not mean merely that it crushes the "cherished illusion" that policy comes from the minds of elected officials in Congress rather than from the computers of economists in the back room. I refer, rather, to the fact that cost-benefit approaches deal only with values or preferences already extant in society. A political process — a process of debate and compromise — is supposed to be creative. The ability of the political process to change values and to rise above self-interest is crucial to its legitimacy. Political leaders are supposed to educate and elevate public opinion; they are not supposed merely to gratify preexisting desires.

A third likely consequence in public policy may be the most disastrous. Economic analysis limits conflict to those parties who have something at stake for which they are willing to pay. This approach would prevent the socialization of conflict that is crucial to the functioning of a democracy. Consider an example. Suppose a corporation proposes and an environmentalist group opposes the building of a shopping center in a rural area just outside of town. An economist might make a recommendation based upon prices assigned to the various wants or preferences of relevant interest groups. This would effectively limit conflict to the immediate parties. The genius of democracy, however, is to let the conflict spread to a larger audience. The institutions of democratic government — legislatures, agencies, parties, courts, and the press — depend and thrive on the potential for conflicts of this kind to widen beyond their original bounds. This happens when one side — usually the side that otherwise would be defeated — finds a public issue (e.g., a "snail darter") and moves the conflict into the press, the legislature, and the courts. The shopping center may then never be built because it takes so long to work through the resulting political process.

This might seem grossly inefficient to economists, and perhaps it is, but it is what democratic government is all about. An alternative — technocracy — quarantines or localizes conflict so that it may be resolved by the application of some mechanical rule or decision procedure. Cost-benefit approaches to public policy, if taken to their extreme, would do this, and thus they would make useless the institutions of democratic government. Cost-benefit analysis localizes conflict among affected individuals and prevents it from breaking open into the public realm. This suggests that the reason that industry favors economic approaches to public policy is not necessarily the obvious one, namely, that cost-benefit analysis is sensitive to the costs of regulation. The deeper reason may be that cost-benefit analysis defines a framework for conflict that keeps the public *qua* public and the citizen *qua* citizen out.

....

Economic efficiency is usually defined in terms of maximum satisfaction of the wants or preferences of individuals in the order that those individuals rank them. A market in which competition is perfect, in theory, achieves this kind of efficiency. Under this approach, the market would determine optimal policies, and the government would be concerned primarily with market failure. Cost-benefit analysis, insofar as it reflects or shadows markets, provides a technique by which society may attempt to determine policies that are economically efficient. But why should we think economic efficiency is an important goal? Why should we take wants or preferences more seriously than beliefs and opinions? Why should we base public policy on the model of a market transaction rather than the model of a political debate?

What many economists do not understand is that efficiency is one value among many and is not a meta-value that comprehends all others. Economists as a rule do recognize one other value, namely, justice or equality, and they speak, therefore, of a "trade-off" between efficiency and equality. They do not speak, as they should, however, about the trade-off between efficiency and our aesthetic and moral values. What about the trade-off between efficiency and dignity, efficiency and self-respect, efficiency and magnificence of our natural heritage, efficiency and the quality of life? These are the trade-offs that are important in setting environmental policy.

....

The role of the policymaker and of the legislature may be to balance what we believe in and stand for as a community with what we want and need as a functioning economy. We must devise some way to relate to each other as citizens in search of common ideals and, at the same time, to compete with each other in a market to satisfy individual interests. The future of environmental policy rests on the resolution of this conflict. A solution must do more than merely allow us to balance interests with interests; it must facilitate the balancing interests with morality and one morality with another morality. Economists would do well to show us how *this* sort of balancing is to be done.

NOTES AND QUESTIONS

1. What are Sagoff's views regarding economic efficiency and its value-based model? To what extent should public interest figure into the equation affecting legislative decisionmaking? How can meaningful distinctions be made in a

statutory scheme between private preferences, moral convictions, and wider
environmental protection interests?

2. One of the seminal works considering the role of economics in environmental law was written by R.H. Coase, *The Problem of Social Cost*, 3 J.L. & ECON.
1 (1960). Coase suggested that the marketplace would function to establish
certain tolerable levels of pollution, and that the solutions offered in a private
market system would parallel results through a governmentally-developed
regulatory scheme. Coase argued that the same amount of pollution would occur
irrespective of whether the polluter were held liable for damages (assuming the
transaction costs were zero). Consider the following excerpt:

> The question is commonly thought of as one in which A inflicts harm on B
> and what has to be decided is: how should we restrain A? But this is wrong.
> We are dealing with a problem of a reciprocal nature. To avoid the harm to
> B would inflict harm on A. The real question that has to be decided is:
> should A be allowed to harm B or should B be allowed to harm A? The
> problem is to avoid the more serious harm.... [An] example is afforded by
> the problem of straying cattle which destroys crops on neighboring land. If
> it is inevitable that some cattle will stray, an increase in the supply of meat
> can only be obtained at the expense of a decrease in the supply of crops.
> The nature of the choice is clear: meat or crops. What answer should be
> given is, of course, not clear unless we know the value of what is obtained
> as well as the value of what is sacrificed to obtain it. [Another example
> involves] the contamination of a stream. If we assume that the harmful
> effect of the pollution is that it kills the fish, the question to be decided is:
> is the value of the fish lost greater or less than the value of the product
> which the contamination of the stream makes possible?

Coase contended that the allocation of resources will remain the same irrespective
of whether the damaging business is held legally accountable in damages for the
harm caused by its actions. In cases involving interference with protectable legal
interests by pollution, the private parties involved would reach a bargain rather
than either shutting down. For example, if the manufacturer responsible for
discharging the pollutants were held liable, the company would choose to pay
damages for the harm caused. If not held liable, the injured party would pay off
the polluter to the extent necessary to maintain their property interests. Coase
conceded that the transaction costs must be less than the increase in the value of
production for the system to function properly. Government regulation will work
more effectively when a large number of people would be affected by the
pollution, and therefore the administrative costs of handling the problem in the
marketplace would be high.

What is your assessment of Coase's thesis? Do the realities of transaction costs
in a private market system preclude effective controls of pollution? What about
the problems presented by exposure to toxic pollutants? Should the damaging
business be allowed to bargain away its responsibility to public health? What

about the interests of third parties who are not directly affected by the conduct of the business, yet who would sustain harm indirectly?

B. ECOLOGICAL VALUES AND THE POLITICAL RESPONSE

COUNCIL ON ENVIRONMENTAL QUALITY, ENVIRONMENTAL QUALITY 1970-1990: TWENTIETH ANNUAL REPORT 4-13 (1990)

Of all the signal environmental events of 1970, the one that most involved the public was Earth Day, April 22, 1970. On that day millions of Americans actively expressed their concerns for the quality of the environment. Through teach-ins, protests, speeches, and neighborhood cleanups, people all across the country conveyed their sense that something had to be done. Many members of Congress took part in Earth Day activities, responding, as *The Washington Post* described it, "to what they sense as the national mood for cleanup by embracing the environmental issue like motherhood."

... During the 1960s large public demonstrations intended to shape public policy had been common; the American public had witnessed a succession of demonstrations over poverty, civil rights, and the war in Vietnam. The public protests against environmental degradation may have been difficult to differentiate from other kinds of well-publicized civil demonstrations.

Moreover, the environmental movement in 1970 was demanding something that no nation had ever done before: the enactment of comprehensive, national legislation to protect the environment. Implicit in that goal — whether explicitly stated or not — was a call for fundamental change in the American economic calculus. More and more people were beginning to appreciate clean air and clean water as precious resources that were neither free nor inexhaustible. Consequently, no person or business or community could appropriate those resources for their personal use to the detriment of others.

The economic implications of those early calls for environmental protection were not overlooked. In fact, the potentially huge economic costs of pollution control — postulated in terms of jobs lost and economic growth foregone — may have been a major reason why some people wondered whether the environmental movement would persist. In 1970 it was not unusual to hear arguments postulating irrevocable links between economic growth and the generation of pollution, and warning that environmental protection would cost jobs....

One way to measure the nation's environmental progress since 1970 would be to look at 20-year data trends in those areas. Trends in pollutant emissions, biodiversity, and human health clearly are important measures of the relative success or failure of national efforts to protect the environment.

However, such trend data give only partial answers, and even those partial answers tell an inconsistent story. The nation's success at fulfilling the promise of 1970 — as measured by environmental trends data — has been mixed. After two decades of unprecedented environmental activism, some facets of the environment show remarkable improvement, while the quality of others has deteriorated sharply.

For example, in response to the Clean Air Act of 1970, the Environmental Protection Agency (EPA) set national standards for the six most prevalent air pollutants: sulfur dioxide, nitrogen oxides, carbon monoxide, particulates, hydrocarbons, and lead. The federal and state governments then took a range of actions designed to reduce emissions of those pollutants so that the national health standards would be met nationwide.

For some of those common air pollutants, the 20-year record has been extraordinarily successful, especially in the case of lead. Between 1970 and 1987, total annual emissions of lead nationwide declined by 96 percent, from 203.8 million to 8.1 million tons, mainly due to the gradual phase-out of leaded gasoline. Today virtually all areas in the United States meet the national health standard for lead.

The United States also has made substantial progress in controlling sulfur dioxide (SO_2) and particulate matter (PM). Prior to 1970, emissions of SO_2 and PM had been increasing rapidly. But, between 1970 and 1987, total annual national emissions of SO_2 dropped by 28 percent, from 28.2 million to 20.4 million tons; particulate emissions declined by 61 percent, from 18.1 million to 7.0 million tons. As of 1987, most areas of the country met the national health standards for SO_2 and particulates.

The nation's record in controlling nitrogen oxides (NO_x), ozone, and carbon monoxide (CO) is mixed. For example, total national emissions of NO_x increased almost 8 percent between 1970 and 1987, rising from 18.1 million to 19.5 million tons, while the pre-1970 rate of growth dropped sharply. Despite the increase in total NO_x emissions, almost all areas in the country meet the national health standard for NO_x.

Total national hydrocarbon and CO emissions, which also had been growing rapidly, dropped by 28 percent and 38 percent, respectively, over the same period. Yet national health standards for both pollutants are still being exceeded in many U.S. cities. During 1989 EPA reported that approximately 110 U.S. urban areas failed to meet the national ozone standard, and about 50 areas did not meet the CO standard.

Despite continued air pollution problems in many places, primarily cities, the country's efforts to protect air quality have been substantial. Not only have total annual emissions of the most common air pollutants declined or remained fairly constant over the past two decades, but they have done so in spite of strong economic and population growth.

Since 1970 the population of the United States has grown by almost 22 percent. In 1970 the U.S. population totalled 205 million. Sometime during 1990, it will pass 250 million.

Over the same period, the U.S. economy has grown more than three times as fast as the population. In 1970 U.S. gross national product (GNP) was $2.42

trillion (measured in 1982 dollars). The Council of Economic Advisors estimates that U.S. GNP in 1989 was $4.17 trillion (measured in 1982 dollars), an increase of 72 percent. At least as far as the six most common air pollutants are concerned, the United States clearly has severed the linkage between economic growth and pollution growth, a linkage that seemed obvious and unbreakable to many people in 1970.

The nation's progress in controlling air pollution is especially noteworthy when evaluated in the context of skyrocketing growth in automobile use over the past 20 years. In 1970 the number of automobiles registered for use on U.S. roads was 89.2 million; by 1989 that number had jumped 56 percent to 139 million. Moreover, those automobiles were being driven many more miles. Between 1970 and 1987, the total vehicle miles traveled annually in this country rose from 920 billion to 1,313 billion, an increase of almost 48 percent.

....

If, on the other hand, the viability of wetlands and estuarine ecosystems is used to measure environmental progress, the nation's track record over the past two decades is less impressive. In 1970 the United States contained about 99 million acres of wetlands. No one knows exactly how many acres have been lost since then, but it is estimated that between the mid-1950s and mid-1970s losses exceeded 450,000 acres per year. Even though annual losses probably dropped after that time, wetlands destruction has continued at an unacceptable rate....

Moreover, the quality of some coastal waters and estuaries apparently has declined over the last two decades. Between 1971 and 1985, shellfish harvest restrictions resulting from environmental contamination increased 14 percent to 7.5 million acres; by 1985 approximately 40 percent of the nation's shellfish beds were closed for some or all of the season. Closures were caused by environmental pollution ranging from inadequate or overwhelmed sewage treatment plants to urban water runoff to contamination from feedlots and other agricultural operations. Most recently, coastal beach closing and oil spills have focused public attention on coastal water quality.

Trends in waterfowl populations, which rely upon wetlands during breeding and migration, indicate the declining health of wetlands. Populations of mallard ducks have dropped by about 40 percent during the past 20 years. Mallards generally use a wide range of habitat for breeding, but filling, draining, and encroachment on wetlands has overtaxed even that species' ability to adapt. In short, both the quantity and quality of U.S. wetlands appear to have declined over the past two decades.

Population growth along U.S. coasts contributes to pressures on water quality and the decline of wetlands in many areas. In 1989, in fact, approximately 80 percent of the U.S. population lived in coastal counties (including those bordering the Great Lakes). Population growth usually leads to more polluted water runoff, the filling or draining of wetlands for development, and overtaxed wastewater treatment systems. Thus population growth — together with associated economic growth — contributes not only to direct wetlands losses, but also to a deterioration in water quality and the health of those wetlands that remain.

....

Taken as a whole, environmental trends data suggest that over the past two decades the United States has been fairly successful in protecting and improving environmental quality when the existence of a problem has been widely recognized and the sources of the problem well defined. In cases where general recognition of a problem were emerged slowly over time, or where the sources of a problem were diverse and widely dispersed, progress has been slow and painful, at best.

Despite the mixed success indicated by environmental trends data, the environmental ethic of the American people clearly has evolved dramatically since 1970. Over the past 20 years the nation's attitude toward environmental pollution and the tools it uses to control it have changed in some extraordinary and fundamental ways.

....

Twenty years ago many Americans were convinced that environmental pollution needed to be controlled, but the science and technology needed to identify, assess, and control such pollution was almost nonexistent. Scientific and technological advances over the past 20 years have changed the way Americans live, and such progress has been especially notable in the environmental arena.

Unlike 1970 environmental pollution today is considered not only harmful and irresponsible, but — in many instances — criminal as well. Environmental laws are enforced now at every level of government, by a number of federal, state, and local agencies, and with a much-expanded array of tools. Although violations of environmental laws continue to present problems, law enforcement officials today are much better equipped to address them.

One of the most fundamental changes that has occurred over the past 20 years is the response of American businesses to their environmental responsibilities. Many corporations today are interested not simply in their legal responsibilities to control pollution before it escapes to the environment, but in the broad corporate benefits that attend efforts to reduce pollution at its source. Widespread efforts to redesign manufacturing processes, substitute less harmful production materials, and recycle wastes are beginning to play a major role in protecting the environment.

In 1970 the need for international cooperation to solve emerging global pollution problems was becoming apparent. Since then, international efforts to assess and respond to problems like stratospheric ozone depletion, global climate change, desertification, transboundary air pollution, loss of species and habitats, and international transportation of hazardous wastes have proliferated.

....

The environmental changes that have occurred in this country over the past 20 years do not suggest that a pollution-free world is in sight. If recent history is any indication, the United States — and the rest of the world — may very well be worrying in 2010 about environmental problems unforeseen today.

Yet the experience of the past two decades also suggests that Americans in 2010 will respond to environmental problems with energy, creativity, and a deep-seated sense of responsibility for future generations. Americans believe strongly that environmental quality is an essential component of their long-term health and economic prosperity. They have demonstrated that they have the will to protect environmental quality and the capacity to act. The lessons of the past 20 years can give all Americans hope for the future.

J. MUIR, WILDERNESS ESSAYS 235-37 (1980)*

No dogma taught by the present civilization seems to form so insuperable an obstacle in the way of a right understanding of the relations which culture sustains to wildness as that which regards the world as made especially for the uses of man. Every animal, plant, and crystal controverts it in the plainest terms. Yet it is taught from century to century as something ever new and precious, and in the resulting darkness the enormous conceit is allowed to go unchallenged.

I have never yet happened upon a trace of evidence that seemed to show that any one animal was ever made for another as much as it was made for itself. Not that Nature manifests any such thing as selfish isolation. In the making of every animal the presence of every other animal has been recognized. Indeed, every atom in creation may be said to be acquainted with and married to every other, but with universal union there is a division sufficient in degree for the purposes of the most intense individuality; no matter, therefore, what may be the note which any creature forms in the song of existence, it is made first for itself, then more and more remotely for all the world and worlds.

Were it not for the exercise of individualizing cares on the part of Nature, the universe would be felted together like a fleece of tame wool. But we are governed more than we know, and most when we are wildest. Plants, animals, and stars are all kept in place, bridled along appointed ways, *with* one another, and *through the midst* of one another — killing and being killed, eating and being eaten, in harmonious proportions and quantities. And it is right that we should thus reciprocally make use of one another, rob, cook, and consume, to the utmost of our healthy abilities and desires. Stars attract one another as they are able, and harmony results. Wild lambs eat as many wild flowers as they can find or desire, and men and wolves eat the lambs to just the same extent.

---

*Copyright 1980 by Peregrine Smith, Inc. Reprinted with permission.

A. LEOPOLD, A SAND COUNTY ALMANAC 201-05, 207-15, 221, 223-26 (Oxford Univ. Press, 1989)*

The Land Ethic

When god-like Odysseus returned from the wars in Troy, he hanged all on one rope a dozen slave-girls of his household whom he suspected of misbehavior during his absence.

This hanging involved no question of propriety. The girls were property. The disposal of property was then, as now, a matter of expediency, not of right and wrong.

Concepts of right and wrong were not lacking from Odysseus' Greece: witness the fidelity of his wife through the long years before at last his black-prowed galleys clove the wine-dark seas for home. The ethical structure of that day covered wives, but had not yet been extended to human chattels. During the three thousand years which have since elapsed, ethical criteria have been extended to many fields of conduct, with corresponding shrinkages in those judged by expediency only.

The Ethical Sequence

This extension of ethics, so far studied only by philosophers, is actually a process in ecological evolution. Its sequences may be described in ecological as well as in philosophical terms. An ethic, ecologically, is a limitation on freedom of action in the struggle for existence. An ethic, philosophically, is a differentiation of social from anti-social conduct. These are two definitions of one thing. The thing has its origin in the tendency of interdependent individuals or groups to evolve modes of co-operation. The ecologist calls these symbioses. Politics and economics are advanced symbioses in which the original free-for-all competition has been replaced, in part, by co-operative mechanisms with an ethical content.

The complexity of co-operative mechanisms has increased with population density, and with the efficiency of tools. It was simpler, for example, to define the anti-social uses of sticks and stones in the days of the mastodons than of bullets and billboards in the age of motors.

The first ethics dealt with the relation between individuals; the Mosaic Decalogue is an example. Later accretions dealt with the relation between the individual and society. The Golden Rule tries to integrate the individual to society; democracy to integrate social organization to the individual.

There is as yet no ethic dealing with man's relation to land and to the animals and plants which grow upon it. Land, like Odysseus' slave-girls, is still property. The land-relation is still strictly economic, entailing privileges but not obligations.

The extension of ethics to this third element in human environment is, if I read the evidence correctly, an evolutionary possibility and an ecological necessity. It is the third step in a sequence. The first two have already been taken. Individual thinkers since the days of Ezekiel and Isaiah have asserted that the despoliation of land is not only inexpedient but wrong. Society, however, has not yet affirmed their belief. I regard the present conservation movement as the embryo of such an affirmation.

An ethic may be regarded as a mode of guidance for meeting ecological situations so new or intricate, or involving such deferred reactions, that the path of social expediency is not discernible to the average individual. Animal instincts are modes of guidance for the individual in meeting such situations. Ethics are possibly a kind of community instinct in-the-making.

The Community Concept

All ethics so far evolved rest upon a single premise: that the individual is a member of a community of interdependent parts. His instincts prompt him to compete for his place in that community, but his ethics prompt him also to co-operate (perhaps in order that there may be a place to compete for).

The land ethic simply enlarges the boundaries of the community to include soils, waters, plants, and animals, or collectively: the land.

This sounds simple: do we not already sing our love for and obligation to the land of the free and the home of the brave? Yes, but just what and whom do we love? Certainly not the soil, which we are sending helter-skelter downriver. Certainly not the waters, which we assume have no function except to turn turbines, float barges, and carry off sewage. Certainly not the plants, of which we exterminate whole communities without batting an eye. Certainly not the animals, of which we have already extirpated many of the largest and most beautiful species. A land ethic of course cannot prevent the alteration, management, and use of these "resources," but it does affirm their right to continued existence, and, at least in spots, their continued existence in a natural state.

In short, a land ethic changes the role of *Homo sapiens* from conqueror of the land-community to plain member and citizen of it. It implies respect for his fellow-members, and also respect for the community as such.

In human history, we have learned (I hope) that the conqueror role is eventually self-defeating. Why? Because it is implicit in such a role that the conqueror knows, *ex cathedra*, just what makes the community clock tick, and just what and who is valuable, and what and who is worthless, in community life. It always turns out that he knows neither, and this is why his conquests eventually defeat themselves.

In the biotic community, a parallel situation exists. Abraham knew exactly what the land was for: it was to drip milk and honey into Abraham's mouth. At the present moment, the assurance with which we regard this assumption is inverse to the degree of our education.

The ordinary citizen today assumes that science knows what makes the community clock tick; the scientist is equally sure that he does not. He knows that the biotic mechanism is so complex that its workings may never be fully understood.

....

The Ecological Conscience

Conservation is a state of harmony between men and land. Despite nearly a century of propaganda, conservation still proceeds at a snail's pace; progress still consists largely of letterhead pieties and convention oratory. On the back forty we still slip two steps backward for each forward stride.

The usual answer to this dilemma is "more conservation education." No one will debate this, but is it certain that only the *volume* of education needs stepping up? Is something lacking in the *content* as well?

It is difficult to give a fair summary of its content in brief form, but, as I understand it, the content is substantially this: obey the law, vote right, join some organizations, and practice what conservation is profitable on your own land; the government will do the rest.

Is not this formula too easy to accomplish anything worth-while? It defines no right or wrong, assigns no obligation, calls for no sacrifice, implies no change in the current philosophy of values. In respect of land-use, it urges only enlightened self-interest. Just how far will such education take us?...

No important change in ethics was ever accomplished without an internal change in our intellectual emphasis, loyalties, affections, and convictions. The proof that conservation has not yet touched these foundations of conduct lies in the fact that philosophy and religion have not yet heard of it. In our attempt to make conservation easy, we have made it trivial.

Substitutes for a Land Ethic

When the logic of history hungers for bread and we hand out a stone, we are at pains to explain how much the stone resembles bread. I now describe some of the stones which serve in lieu of a land ethic.

One basic weakness in a conservation system based wholly on economic motives is that most members of the land community have no economic value. Wildflowers and songbirds are examples. Of the 22,000 higher plants and animals native to Wisconsin, it is doubtful whether more than 5 per cent can be sold, fed, eaten or otherwise put to economic use. Yet these creatures are members of the biotic community, and if (as I believe) its stability depends on its integrity, they are entitled to continuance.

When one of these non-economic categories is threatened, and if we happen to love it, we invent subterfuges to give it economic importance. At the beginning of the century songbirds were supposed to be disappearing. Ornithologists jumped to the rescue with some distinctly shaky evidence to the effect that insects would eat us up if birds failed to control them. The evidence had to be economic in order to be valid.

It is painful to read these circumlocutions today. We have no land ethic yet, but we have at least drawn nearer the point of admitting that birds should continue as a matter of biotic right, regardless of the presence or absence of economic advantage to us.

....

Lack of economic value is sometimes a character not only of species or groups, but of entire biotic communities: marshes, bogs, dunes, and "deserts" are examples. Our formula in such cases is to relegate their conservation to government as refuges, monuments, or parks. The difficulty is that these communities are usually interspersed with more valuable private lands; the government cannot possibly own or control such scattered parcels. The net effect is that we have relegated some of them to ultimate extinction over large areas. If the private owner were ecologically minded, he would be proud to be the custodian of a reasonable proportion of such areas, which add diversity and beauty to his farm and to his community.

....

There is a clear tendency in American conservation to relegate to government all necessary jobs that private landowners fail to perform. Government ownership, operation, subsidy, or regulation is now widely prevalent in forestry, range management, soil and watershed management, park and wilderness conservation, fisheries management, and migratory bird management, with more to come. Most of this growth in governmental conservation is proper and logical, some of it is inevitable. That I imply no disapproval of it is implicit in the fact that I have spent most of my life working for it. Nevertheless the question arises: What is the ultimate magnitude of the enterprise? Will the tax base carry its eventual ramifications? At what point will governmental conservation, like the mastodon, become handicapped by its own dimensions? The answer, if there is any, seems to be in a land ethic, or some other force which assigns more obligation to the private landowner.

....

To sum up: a system of conservation based solely on economic self-interest is hopelessly lopsided. It tends to ignore, and thus eventually to eliminate, many elements in the land community that lack commercial value, but that are (as far as we know) essential to its healthy functioning. It assumes, falsely, I think, that the economic parts of the biotic clock will function without the uneconomic parts. It tends to relegate to government many functions eventually too large, too complex, or too widely dispersed to be performed by government.

An ethical obligation on the part of the private owner is the only visible remedy for these situations.

The Land Pyramid

An ethic to supplement and guide the economic relation to land presupposes the existence of some mental image of land as a biotic mechanism. We can be ethical only in relation to something we can see, feel, understand, love, or otherwise have faith in.

The image commonly employed in conservation education is "the balance of nature." For reasons too lengthy to detail here, this figure of speech fails to describe accurately what little we know about the land mechanism. A much truer image is that one employed in ecology: the biotic pyramid. I shall first sketch the pyramid as a symbol of land, and later develop some of its implications in terms of land-use.

Plants absorb energy from the sun. This energy flows through a circuit called the biota, which may be represented by a pyramid consisting of layers. The bottom layer is the soil. A plant layer rests on the soil, an insect layer on the plants, a bird and rodent layer on the insects, and so on up through various animal groups to the apex layer, which consists of the larger carnivores.

The species of a layer are alike not in where they came from, or in what they look like, but rather in what they eat. Each successive layer depends on those below it for food and often for other services, and each in turn furnishes food and services to those above. Proceeding upward, each successive layer decreases in numerical abundance. Thus, for every carnivore there are hundreds of his prey, thousands of their prey, millions of insects, uncountable plants. The pyramidal form of the system reflects this numerical progression from apex to base. Man shares an intermediate layer with the bears, raccoons, and squirrels which eat both meat and vegetables.

The lines of dependency for food and other services are called food chains. Thus soil-oak-deer-Indian is a chain that has now been largely converted to soil-corn-cow-farmer. Each species, including ourselves, is a link in many chains. The deer eats a hundred plants other than oak, and the cow a hundred plants other than corn. Both, then, are links in a hundred chains. The pyramid is a tangle of chains so complex as to seem disorderly, yet the stability of the system proves it to be a highly organized structure. Its functioning depends on the co-operation and competition of its diverse parts.

....

A land ethic, then, reflects the existence of an ecological conscience, and this in turn reflects a conviction of individual responsibility for the health of the land. Health is the capacity of the land for self-renewal. Conservation is our effort to understand and preserve this capacity.

....

In all of these cleavages, we see repeated the same basic paradoxes: man the conqueror *versus* man the biotic citizen; science the sharpener of his sword *versus* science the searchlight on his universe; land the slave and servant *versus* land the collective organism. Robinson's injunction to Tristram may well be applied, at this juncture, to *Homo sapiens* as a species in geological time:

> Whether you will or not
> You are a King, Tristram, for you are one
> Of the time-tested few that leave the world,
> When they are gone, not the same place it was.
> Mark what you leave.

The Outlook

It is inconceivable to me that an ethical relation to land can exist without love, respect, and admiration for land, and a high regard for its value. By value, I of course mean something far broader than mere economic value; I mean value in the philosophical sense.

Perhaps the most serious obstacle impeding the evolution of a land ethic is the fact that our educational and economic system is headed away from, rather than toward, an intense consciousness of land. Your true modern is separated from the land by many middlemen, and by innumerable physical gadgets. He has no vital relation to it; to him it is the space between cities on which crops grow. Turn him loose for a day on the land, and if the spot does not happen to be a golf links or a "scenic" area, he is bored stiff....

The "key-log" which must be moved to release the evolutionary process for an ethic is simply this: quit thinking about decent land-use as solely an economic problem. Examine each question in terms of what is ethically and esthetically right, as well as what is economically expedient. A thing is right when it tends to preserve the integrity, stability, and beauty of the biotic community. It is wrong when it tends otherwise.

It of course goes without saying that economic feasibility limits the tether of what can or cannot be done for land. It always has and it always will. The fallacy the economic determinists have tied around our collective neck, and which we now need to cast off, is the belief that economics determines *all* land-use. This is simply not true. An innumerable host of actions and attitudes, comprising perhaps the bulk of all land relations, is determined by the land-users' tastes and predilections, rather than by his purse. The bulk of all land relations hinges on investments of time, forethought, skill, and faith rather than on investments of cash. As a land-user thinketh, so is he.

....

The evolution of a land ethic is an intellectual as well as emotional process. Conservation is paved with good intentions which prove to be futile, or even dangerous, because they are devoid of critical understanding either of the land, or of economic land-use. I think it is a truism that as the ethical frontier advances from the individual to the community, its intellectual content increases.

The mechanism of operation is the same for any ethic: social approbation for right actions: social disapproval for wrong actions.

By and large, our present problem is one of attitudes and implements. We are remodeling the Alhambra with a steam-shovel, and we are proud of our yardage. We shall hardly relinquish the shovel, which after all has many good points, but we are in need of gentler and more objective criteria for its successful use.

NOTES AND QUESTIONS

1. What factors determine the "value" of something? When calculating the value of property or life for purposes of legal liability, we necessarily work with artificial and rough-hewn tools, yet the law requires that measurements be made. In the field of personal injury law, for example, the trier-of-fact routinely must make determinations such as the diminished earning capacity of an injured party, pain and suffering, emotional distress, and discounting to present value. Although expert testimony may be used as a guide, such calculations necessarily involve imprecise methodologies. Value, then, perhaps functions as a shorthand way of expressing what society believes is an amount of money which adequately compensates for the injury to a protected interest. Several variables tend to play key roles in that assessment: the amount and credibility of information about the affected interest, the importance of the item in its function, whether the object can be replaced or restored to its previous condition, and whether the destruction of the item would have serious adverse consequences on the ability of other objects to perform their ordinary functions.

2. Leopold suggests that the traditional common law methodology for valuation of property and life interests operates inadequately with respect to natural resources and species of animals and plants. The typical common law approach would tend to undervalue — and thus underprotect — such resources because they often lack "commercial" value and have no ready substitutes. Leopold argues for a new valuation perspective of resources and ecosystems which considers their interrelationship and interdependence with other species in the food chain. Does this "community concept" conflict with a purely economic or utilitarian treatment of land? Does Leopold suggest that conservation and preservation preclude the use, management and development of land and resources?

3. Assuming that Leopold's "land ethic" results in limiting the consumption of land and resources, what should be the appropriate institutional response? How optimistic is Leopold that government will find and carry out satisfactory solutions to ensure the protection of natural resources? Some of the more recent federal legislation establishes a distinct preference for restoration and rehabilitation of injured resources, as opposed to awarding diminution in value. *See Ohio v. United States Department of the Interior*, reprinted in Chapter 9, page 851. Other statutes, such as the Endangered Species Act directly mandate protections for certain species, irrespective of the reasonableness of associated valuations. *See TVA v. Hill*, reprinted in this chapter, page 34. Leopold published *A Sand*

County Almanac in 1949. Consider the following commentary on the treatment of the "land ethic" over the course of the next four decades in the United States.

LITTLE, HAS THE LAND ETHIC FAILED IN AMERICA? AN ESSAY ON THE LEGACY OF ALDO LEOPOLD, U. Ill. L. Rev. 313, 315-18 (1986)*

... The despoliation of land — Leopold's word — cannot be gainsaid. Everywhere, *everywhere*, the rate of despoliation increases: stripmine gashes, kudzu-covered junkyards, billboards, antennae sprouting like asparagus, Stygian milltowns, "condomania" on the coastlines from Jersey to the Keys; asphalted National Parks, Forests, Recreation Areas, Wildlife Refuges, Monuments, and Historic Places that make up the leisure world trailer hook-up that is America; the so-called grey suburbs of Archie Bunkerland in the rustbelt, the ticky-tacky of "the Valley," the sad swaybacked shotgun houses of the southern fields, empty now, occupants fled before giant machines that crawl monstrously on the land like battle tanks; the farmbelt fields washing down to become shoals in the Mississippi, farmsteads deserted, a handful of dust in the high plains; the outer city high-rises commingling with the cows, and in one place near my home a new office building with primrose-colored windows that looks for all the world as if it were filled with pink cold cream.

Despite fifty years of exposure — with some special emphasis during the last twenty five courtesy of organized religion and academic philosophy — the land ethic has not really made a dent nationally. Had policy makers caught some glimmer of it we might now have some significant national legislation. But we do not. And that failure is at least prima facie evidence that a land ethic simply does not exist in the United States of America....

Ignoring Leopold, the conservation community responds with poor imitations of its adversaries. Saving the open space, saving the marsh, saving the farmland — all of these save money, they claim, and are Red, White, and Blue, too. Cool economic analysis replaces outrage. And so, arguably the conservation movement, far from being the embryo for the land ethic, becomes its destroyer. The movement does exactly what Aldo Leopold warned against: it trivializes conservation by reducing its ethical imperatives to mere dollars and cents. "[T]he logic history hungers for bread," he wrote, "and we hand out a stone."

Ethical behavior of any sort — which is to say choosing between social and anti-social conduct between individuals, between individuals and society, or between society and land — is never a matter of dollars and cents except coincidentally....

In our unsuccessful efforts to codify the land ethic in policy — such as for development planning, the stewardship of resource lands, and the protection of

---

critical environmental areas — we have proposed two criteria for establishing the terms of ethical, land-use decision making: ecology and equity. In the case of the first of these, we can identify an unethical decision through ecological analysis, such as a decision to clear a forest in a way that would destabilize the ecological balance between plants and animals. In the case of the second, equity, we can identify an unethical decision through socio-economic analysis, such as inappropriate consolidating land for stripmining and consequently depriving individuals of their rights to ownership, safety, and economic use of land.

If we read our Leopold, however, *three* decision-making criteria exist, not two. The third criterion is the *esthetics* of the land. In the case of esthetics, we need not hire an ecologist who, in fact, may be "callous as an undertaker to the mysteries at which he officiates," nor a social scientist to survey the consequences of diseconomic land use. We need only open our eyes to the esthetic despoliation all around us. The clearcuts, the stripmines, the outer city buildings with pink windows require no statistics to produce outrage. They are outrageous at first sight.

There can be no hierarchy among the three criteria of the land ethic — ecology, equity, esthetics — and I propose none. I do propose that we do not ignore esthetics, for it is the most universally apprehended of all the criteria, and therefore the best means by which we can understand and implement the land ethic as a whole. When despoliation offends our esthetic sensibility, outrage follows. We should allow outrage to flourish. It is the most human defense there is against the despoliation of land.

NOTES AND QUESTIONS

What is your opinion of Little's views? Does the author suggest that Leopold's land ethic was ill-conceived, that legislative actions have been inadequate, or that society lacks the political will to alter behavior to halt the despoliation of the environment? Consider the Supreme Court's application of the Endangered Species Act in the following landmark case and the observations about the role of courts and exercise of equitable discretion in protecting environmentally sensitive species.

TENNESSEE VALLEY AUTHORITY v. HILL
437 U.S. 153 (1978)

MR. CHIEF JUSTICE BURGER delivered the opinion of the Court.

The questions presented in this case are (a) whether the Endangered Species Act of 1973 requires a court to enjoin the operation of a virtually completed federal dam — which had been authorized prior to 1973 — when, pursuant to authority vested in him by Congress, the Secretary of the Interior has determined that operation of the dam would eradicate an endangered species....

... [T]he Tennessee Valley Authority, a wholly owned public corporation of the United States, began constructing the Tellico Dam and Reservoir Project in

1967, shortly after Congress appropriated initial funds for its development. Tellico is a multipurpose regional development project designed principally to stimulate shoreline development, generate sufficient electric current to heat 20,000 homes, and provide flatwater recreation and flood control, as well as improve economic conditions in "an area characterized by underutilization of human resources and outmigration of young people." [Citation.] Of particular relevance to this case is one aspect of the project, a dam which TVA determined to place on the Little Tennessee, a short distance from where the river's waters meet with the Big Tennessee. When fully operational, the dam would impound water covering some 16,500 acres — much of which represents valuable and productive farmland — thereby converting the river's shallow, fast-flowing waters into a deep reservoir over 30 miles in length.

The Tellico Dam has never opened, however, despite the fact that construction has been virtually completed and the dam is essentially ready for operation. Although Congress has appropriated monies for Tellico every year since 1967, progress was delayed, and ultimately stopped, by a tangle of lawsuits and administrative proceedings....

... [A] discovery was made in the waters of the Little Tennessee which would profoundly affect the Tellico Project. Exploring the area around Coytee Springs, which is about seven miles from the mouth of the river, a University of Tennessee ichthyologist, Dr. David A. Etnier, found a previously unknown species of perch, the snail darter, or *Percina (Imostoma) tanasi*. This three-inch, tannish-colored fish, whose numbers are estimated to be in the range of 10,000 to 15,000, would soon engage the attention of environmentalists, the TVA, the Department of the Interior, the Congress of the United States, and ultimately the federal courts, as a new and additional basis to halt construction of the dam.

Until recently the finding of a new species of animal life would hardly generate a cause celebre. This is particularly so in the case of darters, of which there are approximately 130 known species, 8 to 10 of these having been identified only in the last five years. The moving force behind the snail darter's sudden fame came some four months after its discovery, when the Congress passed the Endangered Species Act of 1973 (Act), 87 Stat. 884, 16 U.S.C. § 1531 *et seq.* (1976 ed.). This legislation, among other things, authorizes the Secretary of the Interior to declare species of animal life "endangered" and to identify the "critical habitat" of these creatures....

... After receiving comments from various interested parties, including TVA and the State of Tennessee, the Secretary formally listed the snail darter as an endangered species on October 8, 1975. 40 Fed. Reg. 47505-47506; *see* 50 CFR § 17.11(i) (1976). In so acting, it was noted that "the snail darter is a living entity which is genetically distinct and reproductively isolated from other fishes." 40 Fed. Reg. 47505. More important for the purposes of this case, the Secretary determined that the snail darter apparently lives only in that portion of the Little Tennessee River which would be completely inundated by the reservoir created as a consequence of the Tellico Dam's completion....

In February 1976, pursuant to § 11(g) of the Endangered Species Act, 87 Stat. 900, 16 U.S.C. § 1540(g) (1976 ed.), respondents filed the case now under review, seeking to enjoin completion of the dam and impoundment of the reservoir on the ground that those actions would violate the Act by directly causing the extinction of the species *Percina (Imostoma) tanasi*. The District Court denied respondents' request for a preliminary injunction and set the matter for trial....

Trial was held in the District Court on April 29 and 30, 1976, and on May 25, 1976, the court entered its memorandum opinion and order denying respondents their requested relief and dismissing the complaint. The District Court found that closure of the dam and the consequent impoundment of the reservoir would "result in the adverse modification, if not complete destruction, of the snail darter's critical habitat," making it "highly probable" that "the continued existence of the snail darter" would be "jeopardize[d]." Despite these findings, the District Court declined to embrace the plaintiffs' position on the merits: that once a federal project was shown to jeopardize an endangered species, a court of equity is compelled to issue an injunction restraining violation of the Endangered Species Act.

In reaching this result, the District Court stressed that the entire project was then about 80% complete and, based on available evidence, "there [were] no alternatives to impoundment of the reservoir, short of scrapping the entire project." The District Court also found that if the Tellico Project was permanently enjoined, "some $53 million would be lost in nonrecoverable obligations," meaning that a large portion of the $78 million already expended would be wasted. The court also noted that the Endangered Species Act of 1973 was passed some seven years after construction on the dam commenced and that Congress had continued appropriations for Tellico, with full awareness of the snail darter problem. Assessing these various factors, the District Court concluded:

> "At some point in time a federal project becomes so near completion and so incapable of modification that a court of equity should not apply a statute enacted long after inception of the project to produce an unreasonable result.... Where there has been an irreversible and irretrievable commitment of resources by Congress to a project over a span of almost a decade, the Court should proceed with a great deal of circumspection."...

Less than a month after the District Court decision, the Senate and House Appropriations Committees recommended the full budget request of $9 million for continued work on Tellico.

    ....

Thereafter, in the Court of Appeals, respondents argued that the District Court had abused its discretion by not issuing an injunction in the face of "a blatant statutory violation." The Court of Appeals agreed, and on January 31, 1977, it reversed, remanding "with instructions that a permanent injunction issue halting all activities incident to the Tellico Project which may destroy or modify the critical habitat of the snail darter." The Court of Appeals directed that the injunction "remain in effect until Congress, by appropriate legislation, exempts Tellico from compliance with the Act or the snail darter has been deleted from the list of endangered species or its critical habitat materially redefined."

....

We begin with the premise that operation of the Tellico Dam will either eradicate the known population of snail darters or destroy their critical habitat.... By § 4(d) Congress has authorized — indeed commanded — the Secretary to "issue such regulations as he deems necessary and advisable to provide for the conservation of such species." 16 U.S.C. § 1533(d) (1976 ed.). As we have seen, the Secretary promulgated regulations which declared the snail darter an endangered species whose critical habitat would be destroyed by creation of the Tellico Reservoir....

Starting from the above premise, two questions are presented: (a) would TVA be in violation of the Act if it completed and operated the Tellico Dam as planned? (b) if TVA's actions would offend the Act, is an injunction the appropriate remedy for the violation? For the reasons stated hereinafter, we hold that both questions must be answered in the affirmative.

It may seem curious to some that the survival of a relatively small number of three-inch fish among all the countless millions of species extant would require the permanent halting of a virtually completed dam for which Congress has expended more than $100 million. The paradox is not minimized by the fact that Congress continued to appropriate large sums of public money for the project, even after congressional Appropriations Committees were apprised of its apparent impact upon the survival of the snail darter. We conclude, however, that the explicit provisions of the Endangered Species Act require precisely that result.

One would be hard pressed to find a statutory provision whose terms were any plainer than those in § 7 of the Endangered Species Act. Its very words affirmatively command all federal agencies "to *insure* that actions *authorized, funded,* or *carried out* by them do not *jeopardize* the continued existence" of an endangered species or "*result* in the destruction or modification of habitat of such species...." 16 U.S.C. § 1536 (1976 ed.). (Emphasis added.) This language admits of no exception. Nonetheless, petitioner urges, as do the dissenters, that the Act cannot reasonably be interpreted as applying to a federal project which was well under way when Congress passed the Endangered Species Act of 1973. To sustain that position, however, we would be forced to ignore the ordinary meaning of plain language.

....

Concededly, this view of the Act will produce results requiring the sacrifice of the anticipated benefits of the project and of many millions of dollars in public funds. But examination of the language, history, and structure of the legislation under review here indicates beyond doubt that Congress intended endangered species to be afforded the highest of priorities.

[The Court examined in detail the legislative history of the Endangered Species Act.] ... [T]he totality of congressional action makes it abundantly clear that the result we reach today is wholly in accord with both the words of the statute and the intent of Congress. The plain intent of Congress in enacting this statute was to halt and reverse the trend toward species extinction, whatever the cost. This is reflected not only in the stated policies of the Act, but in literally every section of the statute....

It is not for us to speculate, much less act, on whether Congress would have altered its stance had the specific events of this case been anticipated. In any event, we discern no hint in the deliberations of Congress relating to the 1973 Act that would compel a different result than we reach here....

One might dispute the applicability of these examples to the Tellico Dam by saying that in this case the burden on the public through the loss of millions of unrecoverable dollars would greatly outweigh the loss of the snail darter. But neither the Endangered Species Act nor Art. III of the Constitution provides federal courts with authority to make such fine utilitarian calculations. On the contrary, the plain language of the Act, buttressed by its legislative history, shows clearly that Congress viewed the value of endangered species as "incalculable." Quite obviously, it would be difficult for a court to balance the loss of a sum certain — even $100 million — against a congressionally declared "incalculable" value, even assuming we had the power to engage in such a weighing process, which we emphatically do not.

        ....

Having determined that there is an irreconcilable conflict between operation of the Tellico Dam and the explicit provisions of § 7 of the Endangered Species Act, we must now consider what remedy, if any, is appropriate. It is correct, of course, that a federal judge sitting as a chancellor is not mechanically obligated to grant an injunction for every violation of law. This court made plain in *Hecht Co. v. Bowles*, 321 U.S. 321, 329 (1944), that "[a] grant of *jurisdiction* to issue compliance orders hardly suggests an absolute duty to do so under any and all circumstances." As a general matter it may be said that "[s]ince all or almost all equitable remedies are discretionary, the balancing of equities and hardships is appropriate in almost any case as a guide to the chancellor's discretion." [Citation.] Thus, in *Hecht Co.* the court refused to grant an injunction when it appeared from the District Court findings that "the issuance of an injunction would have 'no effect by way of insuring better compliance in the future' and would [have been] 'unjust' to [the] petitioner and not 'in the public interest.'"

But these principles take a court only so far. Our system of government is, after all, a tripartite one, with each branch having certain defined functions delegated to it by the Constitution. While "[i]t is emphatically the province and duty of the judicial department to say what the law is," *Marbury v. Madison*, 1 Cranch 137, 177 (1803), it is equally — and emphatically — the exclusive province of the Congress not only to formulate legislative policies and mandate programs and projects, but also to establish their relative priority for the Nation.

Once Congress, exercising its delegated powers, has decided the order of priorities in a given area, it is for the Executive to administer the laws and for the courts to enforce them when enforcement is sought.

Here we are urged to view the Endangered Species Act "reasonably," and hence shape a remedy "that accords with some modicum of common sense and the public weal." But is that our function? We have no expert knowledge on the subject of endangered species, much less do we have a mandate from the people to strike a balance of equities on the side of the Tellico Dam. Congress has spoken in the plainest of words, making it abundantly clear that the balance has been struck in favor of affording endangered species the highest of priorities, thereby adopting a policy which it described as "institutionalized caution."

Our individual appraisal of the wisdom or unwisdom of a particular course consciously selected by the Congress is to be put aside in the process of interpreting a statute. Once the meaning of an enactment is discerned and its constitutionality determined, the judicial process comes to an end. We do not sit as a committee of review, nor are we vested with the power of veto. The lines ascribed to Sir Thomas More by Robert Bolt are not without relevance here:

> "The law, Roper, the law. I know what's legal, not what's right. And I'll stick to what's legal.... I'm *not* God. The currents and eddies of right and wrong, which you find such plain-sailing, I can't navigate, I'm no voyager. But in the thickets of the law, oh there I'm a forester.... What would you do? Cut a great road through the law to get after the Devil?... And when the last law was down, and the Devil turned round on you — where would you hide, Roper, the laws all being flat?... This country's planted thick with laws from coast to coast — Man's laws, not God's — and if you cut them down ... d'you really think you could stand upright in the winds that would blow them?... Yes, I'd give the Devil benefit of law, for my own safety's sake." R. Bolt, A Man for All Seasons, Act I, p. 147 (Three Plays, Heinemann ed. 1967).

We agree with the Court of Appeals that in our constitutional system the commitment to the separation of powers is too fundamental for us to pre-empt congressional action by judicially decreeing what accords with "common sense and the public weal." Our Constitution vests such responsibilities in the political branches.

Affirmed.

MR. JUSTICE POWELL, with whom MR. JUSTICE BLACKMUN joins, dissenting.

The Court today holds that § 7 of the Endangered Species Act requires a federal court, for the purpose of protecting an endangered species or its habitat, to enjoin permanently the operation of any federal project, whether completed or substantially completed. This decision casts a long shadow over the operation of even the most important projects, serving vital needs of society and national defense, whenever it is determined that continued operation would threaten extinction of an endangered species or its habitat. This result is said to be required by the "plain intent of Congress" as well as by the language of the statute.

In my view § 7 cannot reasonably be interpreted as applying to a project that is completed or substantially completed when its threat to an endangered species is discovered. Nor can I believe that Congress could have intended this Act to produce the "absurd result" — in the words of the District Court — of this case. If it were clear from the language of the Act and its legislative history that Congress intended to authorize this result, this Court would be compelled to enforce it. It is not our province to rectify policy or political judgments by the Legislative Branch, however egregiously they may deserve the public interest. But where the statutory language and legislative history, as in this case, need not be construed to reach such a result, I view it as the duty of this Court to adopt a permissible construction that accords with some modicum of common sense and the public weal.

....

NOTES AND QUESTIONS

1. The Supreme Court had an opportunity prior to *TVA v. Hill*, in *Hecht Co. v. Bowles*, 321 U.S. 321 (1944), to address the issue of whether the violation of the Emergency Price Control Act of 1942 mandated issuance of an injunction or whether the Court retained its equitable discretion to grant or withhold relief. The Act regulated the maximum price control of commodities and services during World War II. It provided that the Administrator could "make application to the appropriate court for an order enjoining [acts or practices violating the Act]", and an injunction "or other such order shall be granted without bond."

The Administrator discovered numerous violations of the prices and records provisions of the Act during a spot check of the defendant's department store and sought an injunction. The district court found that the defendant had attempted to comply in good faith but the regulations under the Act were complex and confusing to apply. The court declined to enjoin because the store had corrected its mistakes under the Act and undertook measures to prevent future violations. The Court of Appeals reversed on the basis that the Act required issuance of an injunction or other compliance order as a matter of course if violations were found.

The Administrator argued that the "shall be granted" language of the Act was not permissive but required issuance of an injunction when violations occurred. The Supreme Court disagreed and held that the statute left room for remedial discretion. The inclusion of the phrase "other order" in the Act suggested that alternatives to injunctive relief were appropriate in certain instances.

The Court reasoned that it was unlikely that Congress would intend to depart from the traditions of equity practice by removing the discretion in issuing injunctive relief absent an unequivocal statement of its purpose. Justice Douglas, writing for the Court, observed:

> The historic injunctive process was designed to deter, not to punish. The essence of equity jurisdiction has been the power of the Chancellor to do equity and to mould each decree to the necessities of the particular case. Flexibility rather than rigidity has distinguished it. The qualities of mercy and practicality have made equity the instrument for nice adjustment and reconciliation between the public interest and private needs as well as between competing private claims. We do not think that such a major departure from that long tradition as is here proposed should be lightly implied.

Does the analysis in *TVA v. Hill* follow *Hecht?* Does the language of the Endangered Species Act, that federal agencies must insure that actions "do not jeopardize" the existence of an endangered species, require issuance of an injunction where the habitat of a listed species is threatened?

2. The Supreme Court has had several occasions after *TVA v. Hill* to address the question whether the violation of an environmental protection statute mandated issuance of injunctive relief or if the court retained its traditional equitable discretion to grant or deny an equitable remedy. In *Weinberger v. Romero-Barcelo*, 456 U.S. 305 (1982) the Navy, in the course of weapons training, had dropped bombs into the sea off the Puerto Rico coast. The plaintiffs sought to enjoin the Navy's operations claiming that the discharge of ordinance without a permit violated the Federal Water Pollution Control Act. The district court found that the operations did violate the Act but refused to issue an injunction. Instead, the court ordered the Navy to seek a permit. The court reasoned that the Navy's "technical violations" were not causing "appreciable harm" to the environment and that an injunction would unduly interfere with the Navy's military preparedness. The Court of Appeals, relying on *TVA v. Hill*, reversed and ordered the Navy to cease its operations until it had complied with its absolute statutory duty to obtain a permit.

The Supreme Court reversed, holding that the Act did not require a federal court to immediately enjoin all discharges that did not comply with the permit requirements. The Court emphasized that the "integrity of the Nation's Waters" rather than the "permit process" was the main purpose of the Act. The statutory goals could be achieved by means other than issuance of an injunction since the Act contained other remedies and contemplated a scheme of phased compliance. Justice White writing for the majority observed, "The grant of jurisdiction to ensure compliance with a statute hardly suggests an absolute duty to do so under any and all circumstances, and a federal judge sitting as a chancellor is not mechanically obligated to grant an injunction for every violation of law." Rather, the principal basis for injunctive relief in federal court has been demonstration of irreparable injury and inadequacy of legal remedies. The Court cautioned that a "major departure from the long tradition of equity practices should not be lightly implied." *TVA v. Hill* was distinguished on the basis that the Endangered Species Act contained a "flat ban" on violations of its provisions, thereby foreclosing the exercise of the court's equitable discretion. Did the Court truly distinguish *Hill* or implicitly overrule its decision? What is the significance of *Hill* after *Romero-Barcelo*?

3. Several years after *Romero-Barcelo*, the Supreme Court revisited the issue of whether the potential violation of an environmental protection statute necessitated equitable relief as a matter of course or if the court retained its traditional discretion to balance the competing interests and hardships. In *Amoco Production Co. v. Village of Gambell*, 480 U.S. 531 (1987) the plaintiff sought to enjoin the sale by the Secretary of the Interior of oil and gas leases on federally owned lands on Alaska's continental shelf as violating the Alaska National Interest Lands Conservation Act. The plaintiff Alaska Native Villages claimed that the lease operation would adversely affect their aboriginal hunting and fishing rights and that natural resources used for subsistence were protected within the scope of the Act. The district court denied a preliminary injunction but the Court of Appeals reversed, concluding that the balance of irreparable harm favored the Villages and that the lower court failed to properly consider the public interest in protecting the subsistence culture of the Alaskan Natives.

The Supreme Court reversed, following the analysis in *Romero-Barcelo*. The Court recognized that although the purpose of the Act was to protect Alaskan subsistence resources from unnecessary destruction, it did not prohibit all federal land use projects. Instead, the Act simply set forth a procedure to take potential adverse environmental effects into consideration and to minimize them. Thus, the Court reasoned that the message of *Romero-Barcelo* was to focus on the "underlying substantive policy the process was designed to effect" rather than on the statutory procedure. The Court found that an injunction was inappropriate because the plaintiffs had not established a probable injury to the subsistence resources and the balance of hardships favored the defendants.

4. *Compare United States v. Odessa Union Warehouse Co-Op.*, 833 F.2d 172 (9th Cir. 1987), where the government had discovered numerous violations of the food contamination and adulteration standards of the Food, Drug, and Cosmetic Act in the course of inspections of the defendant's grain elevators. The government subsequently sought an injunction to restrain the movement and sale of wheat by the defendant corporation until the defendant complied with the Act. The court held that where the government seeks injunctive relief pursuant to statutory authorization, it does not need to establish irreparable injury where the statutory grounds were satisfied. The court was careful to leave some room for the court's discretion, however, by recognizing that the sole fact of a statutory violation did not automatically require an injunction. In sum, the presence of the statutory remedial scheme narrowed the exercise of the court's traditional exercise of equitable discretion to issue injunctions, but the power to deny relief was preserved.

The defendant contended that an injunction was improper because it had taken steps to remedy the statutory violations. The court acknowledged that the efforts to improve the sanitary conditions were relevant with respect to whether violations were likely to occur in the future. However, the court observed that "Courts must beware of attempts to forestall injunctions through remedial efforts and promises of reform that seem timed to anticipate legal action, especially when there is the likelihood of recurrence." Accordingly, it was appropriate to evaluate the history of past violations, and the cessation of violations did not immunize the defendant from injunctive relief.

5. The Court in *Hill* looked to the legislative history of the Endangered Species Act as demonstrating a Congressional determination that the extinction of any species was intolerable, finding the statutory protections couched in absolute and mandatory terms. Language from early versions of the Endangered Species Act (ESA) such as "insofar as is practicable and consistent with primary purposes" was dropped from the version which ultimately passed. The *Hill* case was unusual because, in spite of the urgency of the ESA, Congress had continued to appropriate millions of dollars to the Tellico Dam project with knowledge of the snail darter controversy.

Congress amended the ESA after the *Hill* decision by including a procedure for exempting certain projects by a newly established Endangered Species Committee. *See* 16 U.S.C. 1536(7)(e)-(p). The exceptional federal project will take precedence over an endangered species when the two irreconcilably conflict, but there is a strong presumption in favor of the species. The Committee may grant an exemption only if it determines that: (1) there are no reasonable and prudent alternatives to the agency action; (2) the benefits of the action are in the public interest and clearly outweigh those of compliance with the ESA; and (3) the action is of regional or national significance. An agency may proceed with a project only after demonstrating good faith compliance with the ESA and a willingness to minimize the potential harm to the species. The consultation and approval process were also given definition by the amendments to decrease the possibility of another "snail darter" situation.

Interestingly, the Committee denied an exemption for the Tellico Dam, finding that the balance of benefits and harms favored protection of the species. Congress then specifically legislated to allow completion of the dam. For additional commentary on *Hill* and its progeny see the following references: Plater, *In the Wake of the Snail Darter*, 19 U. MICH. J.L. REF. 805 (1986); Coggins & Russell, *Beyond Shooting Snail Darters in Pork Barrels: Endangered Species and Land Use in America*, 70 GEO. L.J. 1433 (1982); Houck, *The "Institutionalization of Caution" Under Section 7 of the Endangered Species Act: What Do You Do When You Don't Know?*, 12 ENVTL. L. REP. (Envtl. L. Inst.) 15001 (1982); Erdheim, *The Wake of the Snail Darter: Insuring the Effectiveness of Section 7 of the Endangered Species Act*, 9 ECOLOGY L.Q. 629 (1981).

6. Courts have been reluctant to find, in the spirit of *TVA v. Hill*, that an environmental protection statute forecloses the exercise of their traditional equitable discretionary powers. In *Friends of the Earth v. United States Navy*, 841 F.2d 927 (9th Cir. 1988), however, the court reached precisely that result. The plaintiffs requested a preliminary injunction to halt the construction of a homeport facility by the Navy, alleging that commencement of proposed dredge and fill operations prior to obtaining necessary permits would contravene the National Defense Authorization Act. The court, relying on *Hill*, held that an injunction should issue because the permit requirement was mandatory. The court distinguished *Romero-Barcelo* by pointing out that the NDAA provided the withholding of funds for construction until permits were acquired as the only method for achieving its aims. Also, unlike the Clean Water Act at issue in *Romero-Barcelo*, the NDAA did not contain alternative remedies to ensure compliance. Finally, the court observed that compliance by the Navy could not be achieved by a less drastic means other than enjoining construction until a permit was obtained.

In a different vein, a statute may limit the availability of injunctive relief. In such instances, the courts are similarly constrained by principles of separation of powers and Congressional intent to awarding equitable orders. For example, in *State of Colorado v. Idarado Mining Co.*, 916 F.2d 1486 (10th Cir. 1990) the state sought to obtain a mandatory injunction under CERCLA requiring private defendants to implement a cleanup program of a hazardous waste site. The court determined that since the applicable provision of the statute expressly limited injunctive relief to federal government plaintiffs, the court's inherent equitable power to issue an injunction was circumscribed.

7. Public interest may play a significant role in the court's discretion regarding entitlement and nature of equitable relief. In *Romero-Barcelo* the Court observed:

> In exercising their sound discretion, courts of equity should pay particular regard for the public consequences in employing the extraordinary remedy of injunction. Thus, ... "[t]he award of an interlocutory injunction by courts of equity has never been regarded as strictly a matter of right, even though irreparable injury may otherwise result to the plaintiff," and "where an injunction is asked which will adversely affect a public interest for whose impairment, even temporarily, an injunction bond cannot compensate, the court may in the public interest withhold relief until a final determination of the rights of the parties, though the postponement may be burdensome to the plaintiff." [*Id.* at 456 U.S. 312-13, *quoting Yakus v. United States*, 321 U.S. 414, at 440 (1944).]

Courts often have the difficult task of reconciling competing public concerns and fashioning an appropriate order in light of incompatible interests. *See Stow v. United States*, 696 F. Supp. 857 (W.D.N.Y. 1988) (Court recognized public interest in compliance with environmental statutes but also identified a competing interest in avoiding economic waste). In *Village of Gambell*, the Court recognized public interests in preservation of subsistence resources as well as in the development of natural resources. The Court looked to Congressional expressions of intent to determine the proper weight to balance those competing values. In *Steubing v. Brinegar*, 511 F.2d 489 (2d Cir. 1975) the plaintiffs sought to enjoin the continued construction of a bridge alleging the violation of NEPA by the responsible government agencies. The court recognized the strong public interest in carrying out the intent of Congress in effecting compliance with the federal environmental protection statutes as a significant factor in its equitable consideration. Although the court acknowledged that certain costs could have been saved had the citizen's group instituted their challenge in a more timely manner, the court evaluated whether the public interest could still be served through protection of the environment should an injunction issue.

8. For additional commentary on the role of environmental statutes affecting the exercise of equitable discretion of courts see the following references: Axline, *Constitutional Implications of Injunctive Relief Against Federal Agencies in Environmental Cases*, 12 HARV. ENVTL. L. REV. 1 (1988); Twitchell, *Amoco Production Co. v. Village of Gambell: Federal Subsistence Protection Ends at Alaska's Border*, 18 ENVTL. L. 635 (1988); Plater, *In the Wake of the Snail Darter*, 19 U. MICH. J.L. REF. 805 (1986); Farber, *Equitable Discretion, Legal Duties, and Environmental Injunctions*, 45 U. PITT. L. REV. 513 (1984); Shreve, *Federal Injunctions and the Public Interest*, 51 GEO. WASH. L. REV. 382 (1983); Coggins & Russell, *Beyond Shooting Snail Darters in Pork Barrels: Endangered Species and Land Use in America*, 70 GEO. L.J. 1433 (1982); Plater, *Statutory Violations and Equitable Discretion*, 70 CALIF. L. REV. (1982).

Part II.
Environmental Litigation

Chapter 2

COMMON LAW

INTRODUCTION

This chapter will examine concepts and policies underlying remedies for injuries to natural resources under normative common law doctrines. The areas of emphasis include damages for the total or partial destruction of natural resources and equitable orders to shape future conduct to preserve environmentally sensitive areas.

The principles developed in this chapter also find application throughout environmental laws. The significant health and safety problems posed by releases of hazardous substances necessarily call for comprehensive and sometimes drastic remedial solutions. In certain instances — such as presented by exposure to toxic chemicals — traditional common law may fail to provide satisfactory prevention and remediation. Legislative dissatisfaction with common law methodologies often finds expression in the types of remedies authorized to abate and correct harm to the environment.

A. DAMAGES

The materials in this section explore the policies and principles underlying awards of damages for injuries to natural resources according to traditional common law doctrines. The starting point for evaluation of entitlement and measurement of damages is recognition that the overarching goal is to compensate for the injuries sustained by placing the injured party in the same position as if the harm had not occurred.

The traditional common law approach for calculating damages for injuries to realty compares diminution in value with the cost to restore or rehabilitate the affected property. RESTATEMENT (SECOND) OF TORTS § 929(1)(a) (1977). Determination of which alternative is selected depends on several factors, including the usage of the property, available substitutes, economic efficiencies, and the public interest. Apart from recovery for harm to the land, an injured party may seek damages for loss of use of the realty and for personal inconvenience, discomfort, annoyance, or mental anguish. RESTATEMENT (SECOND) OF TORTS § 920; *French v. Ralph E. Moore, Inc.*, 661 P.2d 844 (Mont. 1983).

Injuries to real property often are characterized as either "temporary" or "permanent" for purposes of determining the measure of damages and the applicable statute of limitations. Despite the apparent simplicity of this approach, application of the terms often proves troublesome. An injury to land is classified as permanent where the harm is considered irremediable; the damages will reflect the diminution in the market value of the property or the loss in its productivity. In contrast, a temporary harm would be considered reparable without unreasonable difficulty or economic waste. The measure of damages would be the reasonable cost of repairing the property, including the loss of use during the period of the harm or the diminution in rental value plus any special damages to crops or improvements.

The common law model for measuring damages has sparked considerable debate, however. Foremost of concern is that natural resources typically do not have a readily ascertainable commercial market value, and traditional valuation methods fail to take into account the interrelationship of ecological systems. The task of courts in awarding fair compensation is further compounded by difficulties in obtaining sufficiently reliable information on the long term significance of the affected resources and inability to procure suitable substitutes if the realty is effectively destroyed. As a result, injuries to valuable resources may be significantly under-valued and consequently under-compensated through application of the common law approach. Also, even if the compensatory damages awarded fully value the harm caused, restoration may not be possible or successful or may not be accomplished within a reasonable period of time. In such cases, violators may not be sufficiently deterred from future destruction of natural resources, and the public interest is not served by restoration of vital ecosystems.

In response to these concerns, legislatures at the state and federal levels have included valuation provisions in environmental protection statutes which modify the normative common law measurement rules. These statutory provisions typically reflect a recognition that because of the unique character of natural resources, their preservation, restoration and remediation is in the public interest. Common law still plays a vital role in ensuring protection of the environment and compensating victims of pollution, however, because even the most stringent federal statutory schemes typically do not provide private rights of recovery. In circumstances where legal remedies will not adequately compensate for the harm threatened, courts may award equitable relief to prevent the injury from occurring. The protection afforded through imposition of equitable remedies will be examined in Section B of this chapter.

STERLING v. VELSICOL CHEMICAL CORP.
855 F.2d 1188 (6th Cir. 1988)

GUY, JR., CIRCUIT JUDGE, on rehearing.

A number of persons, including these plaintiffs, who either lived or owned property near defendant's landfill, brought a class action for personal injuries and property damage resulting from hazardous chemicals leaking from the landfill and contaminating the local water supply. The district court held the corporation liable upon legal theories of strict liability, common law negligence, trespass, and nuisance. The court awarded five representative members of the class compensatory damages for their personal injuries, as well as property damages, plus prejudgment interest on the entire award. The district court further held the corporation liable to the class as a whole for punitive damages.

Upon a review of the lengthy record in this difficult case, we find that the district court properly held Velsicol liable to the five representative plaintiffs but erred in the nature and amount of the damage awards. Accordingly, we affirm in part, reverse in part, and remand with directions for recalculation of some of the damages.

....

Proximate Causation

The main thrust of Velsicol's argument on appeal is that there was insufficient evidence to support a finding of causation between its disposal of toxic chemicals and plaintiffs' injuries. Velsicol further argues that the various types of injuries identified by the district court were based upon impermissible speculative and conjectural evidence.

....

Velsicol argues that proof of the plaintiffs' exposure to its chemicals and the causal connection between that exposure, if any, and their subsequent injuries impermissibly was based upon insufficient evidence. Specifically, the defendant asserts that there was no evidence that two known carcinogens (carbon tetrachloride and chloroform) were in the plaintiffs' wells in the late 1960's and early 1970's when they allegedly were consuming the contaminated water. To overcome this lack of evidence, Velsicol contends that the plaintiffs introduced into evidence an invalid water computing model that erroneously concluded that the plaintiffs were exposed to significant levels of contaminants as early as 1970. By extrapolation, the plaintiffs' model purported to show that dramatically high concentrations of carbon tetrachloride and chloroform were in the plaintiffs' wells as early as 1970 and, therefore, that the plaintiffs had been exposed to the chemical contaminants in sufficiently high dosages for a prolonged period of time sufficient to cause their resultant injuries.

On appeal, the defendant not only questions the validity of ground water modeling techniques in general, but also argues that plaintiffs' particular model fatally failed to utilize all of the relevant data. We reject both of Velsicol's arguments. Numerous courts have validated water modeling techniques to predict past levels of contamination in drinking water where the model was both properly conceived and constructed. [Citation.] The plaintiffs carefully devised, calibrated, and tested their model, based upon physical data generated by Velsicol's own consultants, to determine the physical and chemical characteristics beneath the landfill. They properly formulated the various components of the model (the determination of transmissivity, the infiltration rate, the water table configuration, the porosity, the dispersion coefficient, and the ground water velocity) and utilized all relevant data....

Next, Velsicol argues there was insufficient evidence to prove causation between plaintiffs' ingestion, if any, of Velsicol's chemicals and their alleged resultant injuries.... On the basis of expert testimony (consisting of treating physicians, medical specialists, scientists, psychiatrists, clinical psychologists, engineers, hydrologists, and the plaintiffs themselves), numerous studies, and extensive literature, the district court concluded that Velsicol's chemicals and the duration of the plaintiffs' exposure to them were *capable* of causing the types of injuries alleged by the plaintiffs. The court also concluded that all of the five representative plaintiffs' presently ascertainable and reasonably anticipated future injuries were proximately caused by ingesting or otherwise using the contaminated water.

Thus, the court, as is appropriate in this type of mass tort class action litigation, divided its causation analysis into two parts. It was first established that Velsicol was responsible for the contamination and that the particular contaminants were *capable* of producing injuries of the types allegedly suffered by the plaintiffs. Up to this point in the proceeding, the five representative plaintiffs were acting primarily in their representative capacity to the class as a whole. This enabled the court to determine a kind of generic causation — whether the combination of the chemical contaminants and the plaintiffs' exposure to them had the capacity to cause the harm alleged. This still left the matter of *individual* proximate cause to be determined. Although such generic and individual causation may appear to be inextricably intertwined, the procedural device of the class action permitted the court initially to assess the defendant's potential liability for its conduct without regard to the individual components of each plaintiff's injuries. However, from this point forward, it became the responsibility of each individual plaintiff to show that his or her specific injuries or damages were proximately caused by ingestion or otherwise using the contaminated water. We cannot emphasize this point strongly enough because generalized proofs will not suffice to prove individual damages. The main problem on review stems from a failure to differentiate between the general and the particular. This is an understandably easy trap to fall into in mass tort litigation. Although many common issues of fact and law will be capable of resolution on a group basis, individual particularized damages still must be proved on an individual basis.

To the extent that the plaintiffs seek damages for their bodily injuries, they must prove to a "reasonable medical certainty," though they need not use that specific terminology, that their ingestion of the contaminated water caused each of their particular injuries. [Citations.] This standard implicates the qualifications of the witnesses testifying, the acceptance in the scientific community of their theories, and the degree of certainty as to their conclusions. This standard is of particular importance when dealing with injuries or diseases of a type that may inflict society at random, often with no known specific origin.... Medical testimony that ingesting the contaminated water "possibly," "may have," "might have," or "could have" caused the plaintiffs' presently ascertainable or anticipated injuries does not constitute the same level of proof as a conclusion by a reasonable medical certainty. Although it is argued that a lesser standard of proof allocates loss on a socially acceptable basis, it is the province of the state legislatures to make such changes as they have done in some areas by establishing "no-fault" or other alternate systems.

While upon review of the record in its entirety we cannot say that the district court abused its discretion in making its determination of the proximate causation between Velsicol's chemical dumping operations, the resultant contamination of the plaintiffs' water supply and the capacity of the contaminated water to cause the harm alleged, we find the district court erred in attributing all of the representative plaintiffs' alleged injuries to drinking or otherwise using the contaminated water. We, therefore, address each category of the district court's damage award.

....

Increased Risk of Cancer and Other Diseases

Plaintiffs sought to recover damages for the prospect that cancer and other diseases may materialize as a result of their exposure. The district court awarded the five representative plaintiffs damages predicated upon their being at risk for, or susceptible to, future disease.

Where the basis for awarding damages is the potential risk of susceptibility to future disease, the predicted future disease must be medically reasonably certain to follow from the existing present injury. While it is unnecessary that the medical evidence conclusively establish with absolute certainty that the future disease or condition will occur, mere conjecture or even possibility does not justify the court awarding damages for a future disability which may never materialize. Tennessee law requires that the plaintiff prove there is a reasonable medical certainty that the anticipated harm will result in order to recover for a future injury. [Citations.] Therefore, the mere increased risk of a future disease or condition resulting from an initial injury is not compensable. While neither the Tennessee courts, nor this court, has specifically addressed damage awards for increased risks or susceptibility to cancer and kidney and liver diseases, numerous courts have denied recovery where plaintiffs alleged they might suffer from these future diseases or conditions as a result of existing injuries. For example, in *Ayers v. Jackson*, 189 N.J. Super. 561, 461 A.2d 184 (1983), 325 county residents alleged that toxic wastes leaked through the municipal landfill and contaminated their well water. Plaintiffs' expert testified the ground water was contaminated with numerous known carcinogenic chemicals including benzene, acetone, and chloroform. Plaintiffs argued they suffered from a present condition of enhanced risk of kidney and liver disease and cancer from ingesting the contaminated well water. The *Ayers* court held that damages were not recoverable for such prospective consequences where the plaintiffs' proofs did not establish that they would in the future, to a reasonable medical certainty, suffer from such injury. The court observed that all individuals who were exposed to the well water contamination were at an increased risk of developing cancer and liver and kidney damage. However, the court noted that because plaintiffs' experts could not formulate a quantitative measure to a reasonable medical certainty of excess kidney, liver, and cancer risk, it was left to speculation as to possible consequences of the ingestion of the alleged carcinogens on the future health of each plaintiff....

In the instant case, the district court found an increased risk for susceptibility to cancer and other diseases of only twenty-five to thirty percent. This does not constitute a reasonable medical certainty, but rather a mere possibility or speculation. Indeed, no expert witnesses ever testified during the course of trial that the five representative plaintiffs had even a probability — i.e., more than a fifty percent chance — of developing cancer and kidney and liver disease as a result of the exposure to defendant's chemicals.

For the foregoing reason, the district court's award of compensatory damages to each of the five representative plaintiffs is remanded for recalculation to exclude that portion of the damage award attributed to increased susceptibility to cancer and other diseases.

Fear of Increased Risk of Cancer and Other Diseases

Velsicol next argues that the district court erroneously awarded the five representative plaintiffs compensatory damages or, in the alternative, excessive damages for fear of increased risk of contracting cancer and other diseases. Mental distress, which results from fear that an already existent injury will lead to the future onset of an as yet unrealized disease, constitutes an element of recovery only where such distress is either foreseeable or is a natural consequence of, or reasonably expected to flow from, the present injury. [Citations.] However, damages for mental distress generally are not recoverable where the connection between the anxiety and the existing injury is either too remote or tenuous. [Citation.] While there must be a reasonable connection between the injured plaintiff's mental anguish and the prediction of a future disease, the central focus of a court's inquiry in such a case is not on the underlying odds that the future disease will in fact materialize. To this extent, mental anguish resulting from the chance that an existing injury will lead to the materialization of a future disease may be an element of recovery even though the underlying future prospect for susceptibility to a future disease is not, in and of itself, compensable inasmuch as it is not sufficiently likely to occur. In the context of certain types of injuries and exposures to certain chemicals, cancerphobia has been one basis of claims for mental anguish damages.[24]

In Tennessee, damages for fear arising from an increased risk of disease are recoverable. *Laxton v. Orkin Exterminating Co.*, 639 S.W.2d 431 (Tenn. 1982). In *Laxton*, the plaintiffs' water supply was contaminated by the carcinogens chlordane and heptachlor when defendant's serviceman sprayed the exterior of

---

[24]Cancerphobia is merely a specific type of mental anguish. [Citations.]

plaintiffs' house for termites. The Department of Water Quality Control told plaintiffs to cease using the water for any purpose and to obtain a new water source. As a result of ingesting the contaminated water for over a period of eight months, the plaintiffs worried about their health and the health of their children. The court awarded the plaintiffs $6,000 each for their mental suffering resulting from their reasonable apprehension of the harmful effects to their own and their children's health due to consuming or otherwise using the contaminated water. The *Laxton* court noted that the period of "mental anguish" deserving compensation was confined to the time between the discovery of ingestion of toxic substances and the determination that puts to rest the fear of future injury.

In the instant case, the plaintiffs' fear clearly constitutes a present injury. Each plaintiff produced evidence that they personally suffered from a reasonable fear of contracting cancer or some other disease in the future as a result of ingesting Velsicol's chemicals. Consistent with the extensive line of authority in both Tennessee and other jurisdictions, we cannot say that the district court erred in awarding the five representative plaintiffs damages for their reasonable fear of increased risk of cancer and other diseases.

....

NOTES AND QUESTIONS

1. *Certainty.* In the principal case the court denied recovery of compensatory damages for an enhanced risk of toxic chemicals because the plaintiff could not prove to a reasonable medical certainty that the harm would occur. What amount of proof should be required to satisfy this reasonable probability test? *Compare Werlein v. United States*, 746 F. Supp. 887, 901 (D. Minn. 1990), where individuals residing near an army munitions plant sought recovery of damages for increased risk of disease resulting from pollution of their water supply from chemical discharges from the plant. The court noted that although Minnesota state law does not recognize a cause of action generally for increased risk of disease due to exposure to toxic substances, where the plaintiff suffers a present physical injury that itself causes suffering an increased risk of harm in the future, the plaintiff can recover for that risk.

In *Jackson v. Johns-Manville Sales Corp.*, 781 F.2d 394 (5th Cir. 1986) the court allowed recovery of compensatory damages for the increased probability of developing cancer where the plaintiff showed greater than fifty percent chance of manifesting the disease. Would statistical evidence showing forty percent likelihood of developing a disease in the future be disallowed as not meeting the standard of reasonable certainty? Thirty percent? If a plaintiff could show through expert testimony a significant percentage — but less than a preponderance of evidence — of likelihood of contracting future disease, are there any policy justifications for nevertheless allowing some recovery? Would liberalizing the threshold for entitlement to compensatory damages truly "open the floodgates" for unmeritorious claims? How should courts address this complex, developing area of the law?

2. *Medical Monitoring Damages.* In contrast to an action for enhanced risk of future disease which seeks compensation for the anticipated harm itself, some courts have recognized a separate claim in common law for medical surveillance or medical monitoring costs. This action permits recovery of costs of periodic medical examinations to detect and diagnose the onset of disease. In *Mauro v. Raymark Indus., Inc.*, 561 A.2d 257 (N.J. 1989), for example, the court held that evidence of enhanced risk of future disease was properly excluded from the jury where the plaintiff had a present personal injury from exposure to asbestos but could not prove to a reasonable degree of medical certainty that manifesting cancer was more probable than not. The court did find, however, that the plaintiff could recover for medical surveillance damages. The court reasoned that the cost of periodic medical examinations was properly compensable because the plaintiff would not have spent money on the medical tests to monitor the onset of disease absent their exposure to the toxic chemicals. In *In re Paoli Railroad Yard PCB Litig.*, 916 F.2d 829, 852 (3d Cir. 1990) the court set forth the following test for establishing a medical monitoring cause of action:

> 1. Plaintiff was significantly exposed to a proven hazardous substance through the negligent actions of the defendant.
> 2. As a proximate result of exposure, plaintiff suffers a significantly increased risk of contracting a serious latent disease.
> 3. That increased risk makes periodic diagnostic medical examinations reasonably necessary.
> 4. Monitoring and testing procedures exist which make the early detection and treatment of the disease possible and beneficial.

The court explained the policy reasons for recognizing the medical monitoring tort:

> Medical monitoring claims acknowledge that, in a toxic age, significant harm can be done to an individual by a tortfeasor, notwithstanding latent manifestation of that harm. Moreover, ... recognizing this tort does not require courts to speculate about the probability of future injury. It merely requires courts to ascertain the probability that the far less costly remedy of medical supervision is appropriate. Allowing plaintiffs to recover the cost of this care deters irresponsible discharge of toxic chemicals by defendants and encourages plaintiffs to detect and treat their injuries as soon as possible. *Id.*

3. *Causation.* As demonstrated in *Sterling*, establishing a causal nexus between the defendant's conduct and the plaintiff's harm may present a significant obstacle to recovery of damages at common law. In particular, where wastes from multiple polluters commingle and migrate from disposal sites, the identification of sources becomes scientifically difficult and economically infeasible. *United*

States v. Bliss, 667 F. Supp. 1298, 1309 (E.D. Mo. 1987). The difficulty in establishing the causal link between the defendant's conduct and the claimant's harm at common law may be illustrated by *Graham v. Canadian Nat'l Ry.*, 749 F. Supp. 1300 (D. Vt. 1990). Property owners sought recovery for personal injuries and property damages resulting from exposure to chemical herbicides. The toxic chemicals were released into the environment through an accidental leak from a railcar and through improper spraying on a railroad right-of-way located near the plaintiff's farm. The court stated that evidence showing the railroad had failed to comply with statutory safety rules and warning labels established an initial presumption of negligence. The court found, however, that the plaintiffs did not meet their burden of causation because they could not trace their harms to the defendant's conduct in a manner which would eliminate other possible sources of harm. Moreover, the court found that even though the use of poisonous sprays was a dangerous undertaking which involved a special risk of harm to those exposed to the toxic effects of the activity, plaintiffs could not prevail on a strict liability theory without showing that the chemicals were a substantial factor in causing the plaintiff's injuries.

4. *Punitive Damages.* In *Sterling* the court upheld an award of punitive damages for the entire plaintiff class on the grounds that the defendant had operated the landfill disposal site despite knowledge of the highly toxic nature of chemical contaminants and had refused to cease disposal activities after receiving warnings from state and federal agencies. Punitive damages may be awarded in cases involving malice or bad motive, or where the defendant's conduct demonstrates a reckless disregard for the rights of others. *Also see Exxon Corp. v. Yarema*, 69 Md. App. 124, 516 A.2d 990 (1986) (punitive damages imposed where defendant failed to minimize health risks and take corrective action to abate leakage from underground gasoline storage tanks which contaminated groundwater).

Should courts allow assessment of multiple punitive damage awards arising out of the same incident? In *State ex rel. Young v. Crookman*, 290 Or. 61, 618 P.2d 1268 (1980) raw sewage overflowed and polluted a water supply of a national park causing an epidemic of severe illness in visitors to the park. Federal authorities closed the park and lodge for the season as a result of the contamination. The court refused to certify a class action and the individual plaintiffs signed an agreement to prorate and divide any punitive damages recovered by one of the members. The court rejected the so-called "one bit/first comer" approach, finding that sufficient safeguards existed in the judicial system to prevent excessive damages. The court observed that punitive damages perform a utilitarian function of giving an incentive to prosecute anti-social conduct that might otherwise not be sufficiently deterred. Do multiple punitive damage awards accomplish the goals of punishment and deterrence? What if multiple awards ruin the viability of the company? Do punitive damages prevent manufacturers from making a cost-benefit decision to pay damages rather than change the method of conducting business? *See Wangen v. Ford Motor Co.*, 97 Wis. 2d 260, 294 N.W.2d 437 (1980).

5. *Prejudgment Interest.* In *Sterling* the lower court awarded prejudgment interest on the award of compensatory damages for the plaintiff's personal injuries and property damage claims. Courts have recognized that prejudgment interest serves two interrelated functions: (1) it compensates for the loss of use of the compensatory damages for the time period from the accrual of the harm until judgment, and (2) it promotes the timely settlement of controversies by removing any incentive for the defendant to delay litigation.

Despite the apparent benefits of awarding interest as damages for the time period from the accrual of the harm until judgment, problems exist regarding entitlement and measurement of interest awards where the nature and extent, if any, of the defendant's liability is uncertain prior to rendering of judgment. Consequently, it could place the defendant in an unfair dilemma of choosing between settling a contested claim prior to trial in order to stop the running of interest, or waiting until judgment is rendered and then be required to pay prejudgment interest. Absent statute or contract, courts often have resolved this concern by limiting prejudgment interest to those claims which are "liquidated" or ascertainable in amount and for which the date of injury is determinable. *See Hutchinson Utils. Comm'n v. Curtiss-Wright Corp.*, 775 F.2d 231 (8th Cir. 1985).

As a result of these limitations, courts historically have been reluctant to impose prejudgment interest on most tort claims, reasoning that the extent of liability on such claims is inherently difficult to ascertain prior to judgment. The exception, though, is where the nature of the harm to real or personal property would be susceptible to valuation with reasonable certainty prior to trial. *See Brockelsby v. United States*, 767 F.2d 1288 (9th Cir. 1985) (property damage to aircraft sufficiently certain for prejudgment interest where reasonably ascertainable market prices available); RESTATEMENT (SECOND) OF TORTS § 913 (1977). The Court of Appeals in *Sterling* followed this dichotomous treatment of prejudgment interest by finding that the lower court had not erred in awarding interest on compensatory damages for property damage caused by the contamination of the drinking water by the chemical waste, but rejecting interest on the amounts awarded for physical and emotional distress of the claimants. The court remanded for a determination of the date when the public became aware of the property damage. *Also see Columbia Cas. Co. v. Southern Flapjacks, Inc.*, 868 F.2d 1217 (11th Cir. 1989) (prejudgment interest in property damage case runs from time of wrongful deprivation or loss of property).

As a result of the limitations of the traditional common law rule denying prejudgment interest for unliquidated claims, some legislatures have amended statutes to provide for the recovery of such interest. The rationale for these legislative changes is not to punish statutory violators but to provide full compensation for parties seeking to enforce the statutes whether by reimbursement of cleanup expenses or imposition of liability on responsible parties. Section

107(a)(4) of CERCLA [42 U.S.C. § 9607(a)(4)], as amended by the Superfund Amendments and Reauthorization Act of 1986, provides for the recovery of prejudgment interest accruing from the later of: (1) the date payment of a specified amount is demanded in writing, or (2) the date of the expenditure concerned. *See United States v. Mexico Feed & Seed Co.*, 729 F. Supp. 1250, 1254 (E.D. Mo. 1990) (government request for prejudgment interest and enforcement costs held consistent with CERCLA).

6. For additional commentary on the recovery of damages for enhanced risk of future injuries from exposure to hazardous substances see the following references: Stever, *Remedies for Hazardous or Toxic Substance-Related Personal Injuries: A Discussion of the Usefulness of Regulatory Standards*, 25 HOUS. L. REV. 801 (1988); Trauberman, *Statutory Reform of "Toxic Torts": Relieving Legal, Scientific, and Economic Burdens on the Chemical Victim*, 7 HARV. ENVTL. L. REV. 177 (1983); Seltzer, *Personal Injury Hazardous Waste Litigation: A Proposal for Tort Reform*, 10 B.C. ENVTL. AFF. L. REV. 797 (1982); King, *Causation, Valuation, and Chance in Personal Injury Torts Involving Preexisting Conditions and Future Consequences*, 90 YALE L.J. 1353 (1981); Ginsberg & Weiss, *Common Law Liability for Toxic Torts: A Phantom Remedy*, 9 HOFSTRA L. REV. 859 (1981); Comment, *Sterling v. Velsicol Chemical Corp.: Emotional Distress Damages for the Duration of Toxic Exposure*, 1989 UTAH L. REV. 759; Comment, *Increased Risk of Disease from Hazardous Waste: A Proposal for Judicial Relief*, 60 WASH. L. REV. 635 (1985); Gale & Goyer, *Recovery for Cancerphobia and Increased Risk of Cancer*, 15 CUMB. L. REV. 723 (1985); Note, *The Inapplicability of Traditional Tort Analysis to Environmental Risks: The Example of Toxic Waste Pollution Victim Compensation*, 35 STAN. L. REV. 575 (1983).

MILLER v. CUDAHY CO.

858 F.2d 1449 (10th Cir. 1988)

BALDOCK, CIRCUIT JUDGE.

In this diversity action, plaintiffs-appellees claimed that the American Salt Company's (American Salt) salt mining operations caused the pollution of an underground aquifer passing under their farms, resulting in their inability to utilize the water in the aquifer for irrigation. At the time appellees filed their complaint, American Salt was an operating division of defendant-appellant Cudahy Company (Cudahy), which is a wholly-owned subsidiary of defendant-appellant General Host Corporation (General Host). The district court concluded that the pollution emanating from the salt plant constituted a continuing, abatable nuisance causing temporary damages and found appellants liable for $3.06 million in actual damages and $10 million in punitive damages....

In this consolidated appeal, appellants contend that 1) appellees' claims are barred by the statute of limitations, 2) the district court's method of calculating actual damages was erroneous as a matter of Kansas law....

Appellees are owners and lessees of real property located in Rice County, Kansas. The land is used primarily for agricultural production. American Salt, along with its predecessor, has operated a salt manufacturing plant near Lyons, Kansas since 1908.

Located two miles south of Lyons is Cow Creek, which flows in a southeasterly direction and is a minor tributary of the Arkansas River. Below Cow Creek is the Cow Creek Valley Aquifer (the aquifer), an underground fresh-water stratum which occupies a width of one to two miles and lies at depths of between approximately ten and seventy feet. The aquifer also flows in a southeasterly direction, at a rate of between one-and-a-half and five feet per day. The water in the aquifer passes under the land owned or leased by appellees after it has passed under American Salt's brine fields and plant.

Salt concentrations of over 30,000 parts per million have been recorded in water samples drawn from the aquifer. Concentrations of 250 parts per million are sufficient to render water unfit for domestic or irrigation use. As found by the district court, the salt present in the aquifer escaped from the property and control of American Salt. The majority of the salt escaped through subsurface leaks, while the remainder percolated downward from surface spills.

Due to insufficient rainfall, farmers in Rice County are unable to grow corn without irrigating their land. Appellees alleged that because of the salt pollution of the aquifer, they are unable to irrigate and therefore can grow only dryland crops such as wheat and milo, which do not produce the revenues generated by corn crops.

The district court, in commenting on the more than half-century of disputes between American Salt and area farmers, described the historical background of his case as "Dickensian" in nature. [Citation.] Final resolution of this lawsuit itself required nearly a decade....

The district court denied appellants' motion for summary judgment, which was predicated on their contention that appellees' claims were barred by the statute of limitations. The court concluded that appellees' showing was sufficient to categorize the American Salt operation as a continuing, abatable nuisance causing temporary damages and giving rise to a continuing series of causes of action. The court also concluded that the two-year statute of limitations did operate to preclude appellees from recovering for injuries sustained more than two years prior to the filing of their complaint. The court stated that appellees were entitled to attempt to prove and recover their damages accruing between a date two years before the complaint was filed (May 31, 1975) and the date of judgment.

Following a bench trial, the court found appellants liable for temporary damages to annual crops and awarded appellees $3.06 million in actual damages for the period of 1975 through 1983. The court arrived at the amount of lost crop profits by calculating the difference between the net value of corn crops and the net value of the wheat and milo crops which were actually grown. The court also awarded $10 million in punitive damages; however, it retained jurisdiction over the award and held final judgment in abeyance, pending appellants' "good-faith efforts to define and remedy the pollution they have caused." Pursuant to Fed. R. Civ. P. 54(b), the court entered final judgment on the issues of liability and actual damages....

Appellants first argue that appellees' claims are time-barred, the primary thrust of their argument being that the injuries suffered by appellees are permanent in nature and were ascertained long before the statute of limitations began to run....

The applicable Kansas statute of limitations, Kan. Stat. Ann. § 60-513 (1983), provides in pertinent part:

> (a) The following actions shall be brought within two (2) years: (1) An action for trespass upon real property.
>
> ....
>
> (4) An action for injury to the rights of another, not arising on contract, and not herein enumerated.

The crucial question in regard to the applicability of the two-year statute of limitations is whether the injuries sustained by appellees are permanent or temporary in nature. Drawing a distinction between permanent and temporary damages resulting from a nuisance is at best problematical.[3]

The district court, upon surveying Kansas nuisance law from 1876 to the present, noted that the relevant cases addressing the distinction between permanent and temporary injuries are somewhat unclear and inconsistent.

The Kansas Supreme Court likewise has recognized the rather confused state of the law concerning the distinction between permanent and temporary nuisances. [Citations.] The Supreme Court recently indicated that the distinction between temporary and permanent damages remains a viable concept, however, while emphasizing that "no hard and fast rule can be adopted as to when the damages are deemed permanent and when they are deemed temporary." [Citation.] Noting that some cases refer not only to the permanent or temporary nature of the damages, but also to the permanent or temporary nature of the causative factor, the court stressed that "[e]ach case must be considered in its own factual setting."

....

Under Kansas law, the plaintiff has the option of suing for either permanent or temporary damages. [Citation.] If permanent damages are sought, an action claiming such damages must be brought within two years. "Permanent damages are given on the theory that the cause of injury is fixed and that the property will always remain subject to that injury." *McAlister v. Atlantic Richfield Co.*, 233

---

[3]As described in one tort treatise, "[t]here is perhaps no more impenetrable jungle in the entire law than that which surrounds the word 'nuisance.'" W. Keeton, D. Dobbs, R. Keeton & D. Owen, Prosser and Keeton on Torts 616 (5th ed. 1984). In regard to the specific issue presented here, another treatise notes the general confusion surrounding the distinction the courts have drawn between permanent and temporary nuisance. F. Harper, F. James & O. Gray, The Law of Torts § 1.30 (2d ed. 1986).

Kan. 252, 662 P.2d 1203, 1211 (1983). They "are damages for the entire injury done — past, present and prospective — and generally speaking [are] those which are practically irremediable."

If the injury or wrong is classified as temporary, the limitation period starts to run only when the plaintiff's land or crops are actually harmed, and for purposes of the statute of limitations, each injury causes a new cause of action to accrue, at least until the injury becomes permanent. [Citations.] This rule is especially applicable if the situation involves elements of uncertainty, "such as the possibility or likelihood of the alteration or abatement of the causative condition." The rule is predicated upon the defendant's ability and duty to abate the existing conditions which constitute the nuisance. [Citations.]

Appellants rely primarily on *McAlister v. Atlantic Richfield Co.* in arguing that the damages caused by their admitted pollution of the aquifer will last indefinitely (at least 200 years) and therefore are permanent for purposes of the statute of limitations. In *McAlister*, the plaintiff sued for temporary damage to his water well caused by the defendant's oil fields. The plaintiff alleged "that not less than 150 nor more than 400 years will pass before the well water will be once again fit for drinking." Under the circumstances of that case, in which there was no indication that the pollution was abatable and the relevant defendants had discontinued oil well operations in the 1940's, the Kansas Supreme Court held that portion of the claim to be barred by the two-year statute of limitations because the injury was "fixed" and "the property will always remain subject to that injury."

....

The trial evidence indicates that the damage to the aquifer is remediable if the salt pollution is abated. While it is true that no conclusive time frame for the cleansing of the aquifer has been established, it is apparent to this court that, contrary to appellants' contention, the cleanup process can be accelerated by intervention measures and can be achieved within a reasonable time. Further, appellants' argument focusing solely on the nature of the injuries resulting from the salt pollution of the aquifer disregards the fact that we must also look at the nature of the causative factor of the pollution.[7]

---

[7]In pointing out the inconsistent use of the terms "temporary" and "permanent" in the Kansas cases, the district court noted

> that, when realty is damaged by pollution, the terms 'temporary' and 'permanent' can be applied to three quite distinct facets of the situation. First, the *pollution itself*, or the causal chemistry of the injury to the land, may be either temporary or permanent. Second, the *damage* or *loss* caused by the injury may be temporary or permanent. Last, the *source or origin of the pollution*, be it a sewage plant, an oil well, or a salt mine, may be temporary or permanent. The possibilities for inconsistencies are, of course, multiplied when different labels are applied to these facets, such as, for example, calling the source of the pollution a nuisance and then characterizing the nuisance as temporary or permanent.

Appellants do not contend that there is no "possibility or likelihood" that the causative condition, namely American Salt's mining operations, can be altered or abated. The record indicates that the cause of the injuries can be terminated, and indeed appellants state that they have already undertaken measures to do so. Nor do appellants argue that they have no duty to abate the existing conditions which constitute the nuisance. The conclusion that the damages are temporary is bolstered by the evidence that the salt pollution actually continued during the course of this litigation, further indicating the existence of a continuing nuisance.

The damage to the aquifer is remediable and the cause of the damage is abatable. Upon considering all the facts and circumstances, including the nature of the pollution and the nature of the causative factor, as well as the continuing pollution of the aquifer, we conclude, as did the district court, that American Salt's operation constitutes a continuing nuisance causing temporary damages.

Having rejected appellants' assertion that the damages resulting from their pollution of the aquifer are permanent for statute of limitation purposes, we also reject their claim that *all* of appellees' claims are time-barred. The fact that salt pollution has existed in the aquifer for many years does not negate the district court's limitation of appellees' recovery to temporary damages. By limiting their potential recovery to those damages incurred not more than two years prior to the filing of their complaint, the court implicitly determined that the two-year statute of limitations precluded any claims for permanent damages.

. . . .

Arguing that the district court's method of calculating actual damages was erroneous as a matter of law, appellants assert that the amount of temporary damages awarded cannot exceed the potential recovery for permanent damages. They alternatively contend that, assuming the propriety of an award of temporary damages, the proper measure of such damages is the reduced rental value of appellees' land.

. . . .

The temporary-permanent distinction which is determinative in regard to the running of the statute of limitations is also relevant to the question of the proper measure of damages resulting from an actionable nuisance. [Citations.] In Kansas, the measure of damages for permanent injury to real property is the difference in the fair market value of the land before and after the injury. [Citations.] Diminished fair market value is not used as the measure of recovery, however, if an injury to real property is temporary in nature. Temporary damages represent the reasonable cost of repairing the property, "which may include the value of the use thereof during the period covered by the suit, or it

---

Miller I, 567 F. Supp. at 899-900 (emphasis in original). The district court's analysis is helpful to our determination of the legal nature of the nuisance and serves to reinforce our interpretation of the Kansas nuisance cases, namely that appellants' argument is deficient by virtue of focusing solely on the nature of the injuries resulting from the salt pollution of the aquifer.

may be the diminution in the rental value of the property, together with such special damages to crops, improvements, etc." [Citations.]

Appellants' assertion that temporary damages may not exceed the value of the property injured, or essentially that there must be a "cap" on an award of temporary damages, is unsupported by pertinent Kansas authority. Their alternative contention, that the sole measure of such damages is reduced rental value, is likewise unsupported. While reduced rental value of the property injured is indeed one measure of temporary damages, the value of the *use* of the property is also a proper measure of damages. The Kansas Supreme Court has treated the value of the use of property and the diminution of rental value as separate and distinct bases for awarding temporary damages. [Citations.]

The district court found that because irrigated corn crops would be more profitable than the dryland crops appellees were forced to grow because of the salt pollution of the aquifer, appellees "have been damaged by the pollution to the extent of these lost crop profits." In so finding, the court applied the proper legal standard under Kansas law for measuring temporary damages. The court's calculation of actual damages, made upon consideration of the similar formulas presented by the various expert witnesses, was based upon the difference between the net value of the lost corn production and the net value of the wheat and milo crops actually grown. That calculation is supported by the evidence and is not clearly erroneous.

....

NOTES AND QUESTIONS

1. As discussed in the principal case, one of the difficult issues involved in toxic tort cases is determining the appropriate time for accrual of the cause of action for statute of limitation purposes. This question itself has at least two facets: whether the invasion should be characterized as permanent in nature or continuing, and when the claimant should be fairly charged with knowledge of the harm. A continuing or recurring trespass confers on the possessor of land the option to maintain successive actions for each injury; a permanent injury requires the claimant to bring suit within the limitations period running from the time of the initial harm. *See Regan v. Cherry Corp.*, 706 F. Supp. 145, 150 (D.R.I. 1989); RESTATEMENT (SECOND) OF TORTS § 161, comment b (1965).

In *Piccolini v. Simon's Wrecking*, 686 F. Supp. 1063 (M.D. Pa. 1988) plaintiffs sought recovery under state and federal law for injuries to realty resulting from contamination of their property from toxic waste emanating from a landfill. The court noted that ordinarily the statute of limitations for tort cases under Pennsylvania law begins to run when the cause of action accrues, meaning the date when the injury is sustained. The court recognized an exception existed which would toll the statute of limitations for the period during which the plaintiff did not know of the injury or its cause. Plaintiffs contended that this "discovery rule" should be applied to toll the statute during the time period that they could not ascertain in the exercise of reasonable diligence the identity of the parties responsible for generating the waste. The court disagreed and held that the discovery rule exception only tolled the statute until the person realized the immediate physical cause of their injury. Accordingly, once the claimants became aware that toxic chemicals had been illegally deposited at the landfill site and caused damage to their land, they had the burden to determine the identity of the party responsible.

In contrast, in *Allied Corp. v. Frola*, 730 F. Supp. 626, 631 (D.N.J. 1990) the court held that the discovery rule encompassed tolling of the applicable statute of limitations under New Jersey law until the plaintiff became aware both of the injuries and of an identifiable defendant. The court observed that the identification of potentially responsible parties was particularly crucial in environmental contamination cases because frequently numerous actors are involved over a period of years. The court determined that the cause of action would accrue against each defendant when the claimant reasonably could learn of their identity as a potentially liable party.

In CERCLA, actions for recovery of natural resource damages must be brought within three years after the discovery of the loss and its connection with the contamination from the pollutant. 42 U.S.C. § 9613(g)(1)(A).

2. The traditional common law rules governing measurement of damages for harm to realty have been criticized as undercompensating and underprotecting valuable natural resources. At the state and federal level legislatures have responded by altering the common law limitations. For example, in the early leading case *Commonwealth of Puerto Rico v. The SS Zoe Colocotroni*, 628 F.2d 652 (1st Cir. 1980) an oil tanker struck a reef off the coast of Puerto Rico and the captain ordered the dumping of 5,000 tons of crude oil into the surrounding waters in an attempt to refloat the vessel. The resulting oil slick caused severe environmental harm to the plant and marine animal life, including contamination of a mangrove forest which had little commercial market value. The court found that an anti-pollution statute which authorized recovery for the "total value of the damages caused to the environment and/or natural resources" did not limit the Commonwealth to the common law ceiling of market value for destroyed property. The court observed the policy underlying the statute:

> Implicit in this choice of language, we think, is a determination not to restrict the state to ordinary market damages. Many unspoiled natural areas of considerable ecological value have little or no commercial or market value. Indeed, to the extent such areas have a commercial value, it is logical to assume that they will not long remain unspoiled, absent some governmental or philanthropic protection. A strict application of the diminution in value rule would deny the state any right to recover meaningful damages for harm to such areas, and would frustrate appropriate measures to restore or rehabilitate the environment.

... In enacting [the statute] Puerto Rico obviously meant to sanction the difficult, but perhaps not impossible, task of putting a price tag on resources whose value cannot always be measured by the rules of the market place.... No market exists in which Puerto Rico can readily replace what it has lost. The loss is not only to certain plant and animal life but, perhaps more importantly, to the capacity of the now polluted segments of the environment to regenerate and sustain such life for some time into the future.... In recent times, mankind has become increasingly aware that the planet's resources are finite and that portions of the land and sea which at first glance seem useless, like salt marshes, barrier reefs, and other coastal areas, often contribute in subtle but critical ways to an environment capable of supporting both human life and the other forms of life on which we all depend.

628 F.2d at 673-74. The court determined that the appropriate standard for calculating damages should be the cost to restore or rehabilitate the environment to its pre-existing condition without grossly disproportionate expenditures. The court recognized that the calculation of damages could not be accomplished with absolute certainty, but pointed to jury assessments of damages for pain and suffering or mental anguish as a model. 628 F.2d at 675.

For additional commentary on the measurement of damages for harm to natural resources see the following references: Anderson, *Natural Resource Damages, Superfund, and the Courts*, 16 B.C. ENVTL. AFF. L. REV. 405 (1989); Cross, *Natural Resource Damage Valuation*, 42 VAND. L. REV. 269 (1989); and Breen, *CERCLA's Natural Resource Damage Provisions: What Do We Know So Far?*, 14 ENVTL. L. REP. 10, 304 (1984).

3. Concerns that the traditional common law rules may not provide sufficient compensation and protection of natural resources have sparked the enactment of state and federal statutory provisions enhancing the damages awarded for certain types of harms. For example, California Civil Code section 3346 provides for recovery of "twice the sum as would compensate for the actual detriment" for wrongful injuries to timber, trees, or underwood as a result of an involuntary trespass, and Civil Code section 733 provides for treble damages for the wilful or malicious injury to trees or timber.

The diminution in market value rule does not necessarily impose an absolute limitation on damages recoverable for harm to realty even under common law principles. Courts have recognized exceptions in "appropriate cases" where the costs of restoration of land may be awarded even if exceeding the diminution in value of the property. Factors influencing the decision to deviate from the market value standard may include the nature of the owner's use of the property, whether a personal reason exists for restoring the land to its original condition, and whether the injury is considered reparable and at what cost. In *Weld Cty. Bd. of Comm'rs v. Slovek*, 723 P.2d 1309 (Colo. 1986) the court acknowledged that one concern with awarding restoration costs which exceed the diminution in value is that the owner may receive a monetary windfall by deciding not to restore the property and profiting on resale. Nevertheless, the court decided not to place an absolute ceiling on recovery, rejecting a restriction of restoration costs to the land's pre-tort value.

The difficulty in determining an appropriate measure of damages may be illustrated by *Heninger v. Dunn*, 101 Cal. App. 3d 858, 162 Cal. Rptr. 104 (1980). Landowners sought restoration costs of vegetative undergrowth and trees destroyed when adjacent landowners mistakenly bulldozed a portion of their property. The bulldozing of the rough road actually increased the market value of the property $5,000, from $179,000 to $184,000, by increasing its access. Evidence showed that the trees could be replaced at a cost of approximately $200,000 and the undergrowth restored for $20,000. The court noted that limiting an owner of land to the diminution in value rule would be to compel an acceptance of a wrongful change in the physical condition of the property or perform the restoration work at his own expense. Conversely, the court recognized that proposed replacement costs may be excessive in relation to the damage caused, even if a "personal reason" existed which would justify a restoration award. The court remanded with instructions that the trial court should be guided by principles of reasonableness of the restoration costs relative to the value and uses of the property. *Also see Gendreau v. Smith & Co., Inc.*, 497 N.E.2d 16 (Mass. App. Ct. 1986) (damages for diminution in fair market value of land computed by considering values before and after contamination of water supply, taking into account reasonable measures adopted to prevent, reduce or abate the harm caused).

4. Companies faced with the prospect of extensive liability for the cleanup or restoration of environmental degradation have turned to their insurance companies for indemnification. This has resulted in difficult questions for courts in interpreting whether standard form comprehensive liability insurance policies cover costs of remedying environmental harm. In *Maryland Cas. Co. v. ARMCO, Inc.*, 822 F.2d 1348 (4th Cir. 1987) the government brought suit pursuant to several federal environmental protection statutes against certain waste generators seeking to compel them to undertake a comprehensive remedial program to correct harm caused by the seepage of toxic chemicals into surrounding soil and groundwater. The suit also requested that the defendants reimburse the government for its costs related to the investigation and enforcement of the statutes. The defendant's insurance company requested a declaratory judgment that it had no duty to defend the action and to indemnify the insured because the nature of the relief sought by the government did not constitute "damages" within the meaning of its general comprehensive liability policy. The court held in favor of the insurance company, reasoning that the claim for reimbursement for hazardous waste contamination did not constitute damages in the legal sense but was a form of equitable relief.

Courts also have denied coverage on the grounds that the environmental pollution did not constitute an "occurrence" within the meaning of the policy's terms because the harm took place over an extended period of time or the defendant knowingly caused the injury. *Contra Centennial Ins. Co. v. Lumberman's Mut. Cas. Co.*, 677 F. Supp. 3442 (E.D. Pa. 1987).

A number of recent decisions, however, have held that the term "damages" in standard comprehensive liability policies does include environmental cleanup costs. *See Boeing Co. v. Aetna Cas. & Sur. Co.*, 4 Toxics L. Rptr. 920 (1990); *contra Continental Ins. Co. v. Northeastern Pharmaceutical & Chem. Co.*, 842 F.2d 977 (8th Cir. 1988). Some courts have allowed insurance coverage for harm to natural resources by reasoning that the fortuity that the government had decided to clean up the contamination itself and then seek reimbursement rather than initially seek damages should not be determinative regarding insurance coverage. *See United States Aviex Co. v. Travelers Ins. Co.*, 125 Mich. App. 579, 336 N.W.2d 838 (1983). Other courts have found that the insurance company has a duty to defend and indemnify because the asserted harm resulted from invasions which do not fit within the excluded term "pollutants." *Titan Holdings Syndicate v. City of Keene, N.H.*, 898 F.2d 265 (1st Cir. 1990) (gases and particulates, loud and disturbing noises, and bright lights emanating from a sewage treatment plant were not considered pollutants within language of standard from liability policy).

5. For additional commentary on the insurability of damages for injuries to natural resources see the following references: Abraham, *Environmental Liability and the Limits of Insurance*, 88 COLUM. L. REV. 942 (1988); Chesler, Rodburg & Smith, *Patterns of Judicial Interpretation of Insurance Coverage for Hazardous Waste Site Liability*, 18 RUTGERS L.J. 9 (1986); Tyler & Wilcox, *Pollution Exclusion Clauses: Problems in Interpretation and Application Under the Comprehensive General Liability Policy*, 17 IDAHO L. REV. 497 (1981); Hourihan, *Insurance Coverage for Environmental Damage Claims*, 15 FORUM 551 (1980); Soderstrom, *The Role of Insurance in Environmental Litigation*, 11 FORUM 762 (1976).

PRUITT v. ALLIED CHEMICAL CORP.

523 F. Supp. 975 (E.D. Va. 1981)

MERHIGE, DISTRICT JUDGE.

Plaintiffs bring the instant action against Allied Chemical Corporation ("Allied") for Allied's alleged pollution of the James River and Chesapeake Bay with the chemical agent commonly known as Kepone.

. . . .

Plaintiffs allegedly engage in a variety of different businesses and professions related to the harvesting and sale of marine life from the Chesapeake Bay ("Bay").[1]

All claim to have suffered economic harm from defendant's alleged discharge of Kepone into the James River and thence into the Bay....

... All plaintiffs, subject to defendant's motion, claim as damages lost profits resulting from their inability to sell seafood allegedly contaminated by defendant's discharges, and from a drop in price resulting from a decline in demand for seafood coming from areas affected by Kepone. These plaintiffs can generally be described as parties suffering only indirect harm to their property or businesses as the result of Kepone pollution. They or their possessions have not been caused direct, physical damage by defendant. Instead, plaintiffs allege that the stream of profits they previously received from their businesses or employment has been interrupted, and they seek compensation for the loss of the prospective profits they have been denied....

The Virginia Supreme Court has, to the Court's knowledge, never directly considered the question of recovery for loss of prospective economic benefits. It is commonly stated that the general rule both in admiralty and at common law has been that a plaintiff cannot recover for indirect economic harm. The logical basis for this rule is obscure. Although Courts have frequently stated that economic losses are "not foreseeable" or "too remote," these explanations alone are rarely apposite....

Given the conflicting case law from other jurisdictions, together with the fact that there exists no Virginia law on indirect, economic damages, the Court has considered more theoretical sources in order to find a principled basis for its decision. There now exists a considerable amount of literature on the economic rationale for tort law. In general, scholars in the field rely on Judge Learned Hand's classic statement of negligence[11] to argue that a principal purpose of tort law is to maximize social utility: where the costs of accidents exceeds the costs of preventing them, the law will impose liability.

The difficulty in the present case is how to measure the cost of Kepone pollution. In the instant action, those costs were borne most directly by the wildlife of the Chesapeake Bay. The fact that no one individual claims property rights to the Bay's wildlife could arguably preclude liability. The Court doubts, however, whether such a result would be just. Nor would a denial of liability serve social utility: many citizens, both directly and indirectly, derive benefit

---

[1]Plaintiffs include commercial fishermen; seafood wholesalers, retailers, distributors and processors; restauranteurs; marina, boat tackle and baitshop owners; and employees of all the above groups.

[11]See *United States v. Carroll Towing Co.*, 159 F.2d 169, 173 (2d Cir. 1947), in which Judge Hand stated that a person's duty to prevent injuries from an accident "is a function of three variables: (1) The probability that [the accident will occur]; (2) the gravity of the resulting injury, if [it] does; (3) the burden of adequate precautions."

from the Bay and its marine life. Destruction of the Bay's wildlife should not be a costless activity.

In fact, even defendant in the present action admits that commercial fishermen are entitled to compensation for any loss of profits they may prove to have been caused by defendant's negligence. The entitlement given these fishermen presumably arises from what might be called a constructive property interest in the Bay's harvestable species. These professional watermen are entitled to recover despite any direct physical damage to their own property. Presumably, sportsfishermen share the same entitlement to legal redress for damage to the Bay's ecology. The Court perceives no valid distinction between recognition of commercial damages suffered by those who fish for profit and personal harm suffered by those who fish for sport.

The claims now considered by the Court, however, are not those of direct users of the Bay, commercial or personal. Instead, defendant has challenged the right of those who buy and sell to direct users of the Bay, to maintain a suit.

Defendant would have the Court draw a sharp and impregnable distinction between parties who exploited the Bay directly, and those who relied on it indirectly....

None of the plaintiffs here — including commercial fishermen — has suffered any direct damage to his private property. All have allegedly suffered economic loss as a result of harm to the Bay's ecology. Apart from these similarities, the different categories of plaintiffs depend on the Bay in varying degrees of immediacy.... The use that marina and charter-boat owners make of the water, though hardly less legal, is slightly less direct. (And indeed, businesses in similar situations have been entitled to recover in other courts.) Still less direct, but far from nonexistent, is the link between the Bay and the seafood dealers, restauranteurs, and tackle shops that seek relief (as do the employees of these establishments).

One meaningful distinction to be made among the various categories of plaintiffs here arises from a desire to avoid double-counting in calculating damages. Any seafood harvested by the commercial fishermen here would have been bought and sold several times before finally being purchased for consumption. Considerations both of equity and social utility suggest that just as defendant should not be able to escape liability for destruction of publicly owned marine life entirely, it should not be caused to pay repeatedly for the same damage.

The Court notes, however, that allowance for recovery of plaintiffs' lost profits here would not in all cases result in double-counting of damages. Plaintiffs in categories B, C, D, E, and F[20] allegedly lost profits when deprived of supplies of seafood. Those profits represented a return on the investment of each of the plaintiffs in material and labor in their businesses, and thus the independent loss to each would not amount to double-counting. Conversely,

---

[20]Respectively, seafood wholesalers, retailers, processors, distributors and restaurateurs.

defendants could not be expected to pay, as a maximum, more than the replacement value of a plaintiff's actual investment, even if the stream of profits lost when extrapolated into the future, would yield greater damages.

....

The Court thus finds itself with a perceived need to limit liability, without any articulable reason for excluding any particular set of plaintiffs. Other courts have had to make similar decisions.[22]

The Court concludes that plaintiffs who purchased and marketed seafood from commercial fishermen suffered damages that are not legally cognizable, because insufficiently direct. This does not mean that the Court finds that defendant's alleged acts were not the cause of plaintiffs' losses, or that plaintiffs' losses were in any sense unforeseeable. In fact, in part because the damages alleged by plaintiffs here were so foreseeable, the Court holds that those plaintiffs in categories G, H and I[23] have suffered legally cognizable damages.... While commercial fishing interests are protected by allowing the fishermen themselves to recover it, it is unlikely that sportsfishing interests would be equally protected. Because the damages each sportsman suffered are likely to be both small[25] and difficult to establish, it is unlikely that a significant proportion of such fishermen will seek legal redress. Only if some set of surrogate plaintiffs is entitled to press its own claims which flow from the damage to the Bay's sportsfishing industry will the proper balance of social forces be preserved. Accordingly, the Court holds that to the extent plaintiffs in categories G, H and I suffered losses in sales of goods and services to sportsfishermen as a result of defendant's tortious behavior, they have stated a legally cognizable claim.

Defendant hardly has reason to complain of the equity of the Court's holding. First, it benefitted above from the Court's exclusion of the claims of innocent businessmen in categories B through F who are probable victims of their alleged acts. Here, the Court applies different restrictions on liability for reasons of equity and efficiency previously addressed. Second, the "directness" of the harm,

---

[22]*See, e.g.,* Judge Kaufmann's opinion in *Petition of Kinsman Transit Co.*, 388 F.2d 821, 824-25 (2d Cir. 1968) (hereinafter cited as *Kinsman II*), where the court noted that

> in the final analysis, the circumlocution whether posed in terms of "foreseeability," "duty," "proximate cause," "remoteness," etc. seems unavoidable.

and then turned to Judge Andrews' well-known statement in *Palsgraf v. Long I.R. Co.*, 248 N.Y. 339, 162 N.E. 99, 104 (N.Y. 1928):

> It is all a question of expediency ... of fair judgment, always keeping in mind the fact that we endeavor to make a rule in each case that will be practical and in keeping with the general understanding of mankind.

[23]Boat, tackle and bait shop, and marina owners respectively.

[25]The net loss to any sportsman would have to take into account any enjoyment received from natural areas visited as a substitute to the Chesapeake Bay.

at least to plaintiffs in categories G and I,[27] is high here. Both operate on the water or at its edge....

Plaintiffs' Count VIII alleges that defendant may be held liable under the law of admiralty. Defendant moves to dismiss this claim on the same ground previously discussed: that indirect damage to economic expectancies cannot serve as a basis of liability. Defendant argues that this case is governed by the holding of the Supreme Court in *Robins Dry Dock & Repair Co. v. Flint*, 275 U.S. 303 (1927). The Court is not convinced that *Robins* itself is dispositive here. Nevertheless, in light of *Robins* and subsequent cases thereunder, the Court concludes that the challenged claims of plaintiffs should be dismissed.

In *Robins*, a plaintiff had chartered a ship that was negligently damaged while in dry dock. As a result of the damage and consequent delay, plaintiff suffered losses. Rather than sue the ship's owner for breach of contract, the charter-party sued the dry dock. Justice Holmes, for the Court, held that "the law does not spread its protection so far" as to protect a party from economic loss caused by unintentional torts by third parties against those with whom the original party has continued to do business.

Robins is consistent with defendant's position. It is, however, arguably less than dispositive here, because it essentially involved questions of the law of third party contracts not necessarily applicable in the instant case....

NOTES AND QUESTIONS

1. In the principal case the court departed from the traditional rule which precludes recovery for negligently inflicted economic losses absent physical harm to person or property. The court justified recovery of the indirect economic losses of certain commercial enterprises affected by the pollution of the Chesapeake Bay by distinguishing between direct and remote economic losses. This approach, reasoned the court, avoided double-counting of damages, placed reasonable limits on the tortfeasor's potential liability, and maximized social utility. The court held that the boat, bait and tackle shop owners and marina owners had stated legally cognizable claims for the losses they suffered. In contrast, the plaintiffs who had purchased and marketed seafood for commercial fishermen were disallowed recovery on the basis that their damages were not sufficiently direct. What policy reasons support the distinction used by the court?

2. Other courts have rationalized the per se denial of recovery of economic losses unaccompanied by harm to person or property on the grounds that the wrongdoer owed no duty to the claimant. For example, in *PPG Indus. v. Bean Dredging*, 447 So. 2d 1058 (La. 1984) a dredging contractor negligently damaged a pipeline, forcing customers of the pipeline to purchase gas from other sources during the period of repair. The court recognized that the contractor was liable to the pipeline company for the cost of repairs but was not liable to the

---

[27]Generally boat and marina owners.

affected customers because they were outside the scope of duties owed by the contractor.

3. A handful of courts have rejected the per se rule barring recovery of indirect economic losses unaccompanied by property damage or personal injury. In *People Express Airlines v. Consolidated Rail Corp.*, 100 N.J. 246, 495 A.2d 107 (1985) the defendant's railway tank car overturned and dangerous chemicals escaped, resulting in the evacuation of the surrounding area. A commercial airline located in the affected area sought recovery for its losses sustained during the business interruption. The court rejected the traditional rule denying recovery of damages for negligent interference with economic advantage. The court explained that the fortuity of accompanying physical harm should not be determinative of recovery. Instead, the court held that the normative tort concepts of foreseeability, duty, and fault would provide sufficient guidance and predictability. The court stated, however, that the duty owed must be to a particularly foreseeable, identifiable class of plaintiffs.

4. Compare the principal case with the approach taken in *Union Oil Co. v. Oppen*, 501 F.2d 558 (9th Cir. 1974). The court determined that commercial fishermen could recover lost profits when their business was interrupted by an oil spill caused by the defendant oil companies. The court justified its decision in part using an economic analysis, reasoning that the award of compensatory damages would achieve maximum allocation of resources by imposing the loss on the party in the best position to take cost-avoidance measures.

5. For additional commentary on the recovery of damages for indirect economic harms see the following references: Rabin, *Tort Liability for Negligently Inflicted Economic Loss: A Reassessment*, 37 STAN. L. REV. 1513 (1985); McThenia & Ulrich, *A Return to Principles of Corrective Justice in Deciding Economic Loss Cases*, 69 VA. L. REV. 1517 (1983); Rizzo, *The Theory of Economic Loss in the Law of Torts*, 11 J. LEGAL STUD. 281 (1982); Note, *Interference With Business or Occupation — Commercial Fisherman Can Recover Profits Lost as a Result of Negligently Caused Oil Spill — Union Oil Co. v. Oppen, 501 F.2d 558 (9th Cir. 1974)*, 88 HARV. L. REV. 444 (1974); James, *Limitations on Liability for Economic Loss Caused by Negligence: A Pragmatic Appraisal*, 25 VAND. L. REV. 43 (1972).

B. EQUITABLE RELIEF

The preceding materials addressed the function and application of legal remedies for environmental injuries. Correctional or restorative remedies play an important role in environmental protection to compensate for past harms. In contrast, the main province of equity is to prohibit or mandate certain future behavior in order to avoid potentially serious harm to the environment which could not be adequately redressable by legal remedies. The traditional expression for equitable intervention is that the claimant has no adequate remedy at law, the defendant's conduct presents an immediate threat of irreparable harm if unabated, and the balance of hardships favors issuance of an equitable decree. Additionally — and of particular significance in the area of environmental law — the court will consider public interest concerns in assessing the propriety of issuing an equitable order. The strength of equity is that the orders issue *in personam*. Consequently, the contempt powers of the court stands behind equitable decrees to punish or coerce contumacious conduct in disobedience of its orders.

Statutes may affect the application of equitable remedies by providing that certain behavior justifies imposition of injunctive relief without demonstration of the traditional common law requirements of inadequacy of legal remedies and irreparable harm. In rare instances, legislatures have provided that an injunction must issue where the statutory conditions are satisfied. Courts are reluctant to interpret statutes as withdrawing their traditional discretionary powers unless the legislative expression for entitlement to an equitable remedy is stated in unequivocal terms. More typically statutes will enumerate a range of legal and equitable remedies, leaving the determination regarding entitlement and fashioning of relief to the sound discretion of the court.

BOOMER v. ATLANTIC CEMENT CO.

26 N.Y.2d 219, 257 N.E.2d 870, 309 N.Y.S.2d 312 (1970)

BERGAN, JUDGE.

Defendant operates a large cement plant near Albany. These are actions for injunction and damages by neighboring land owners alleging injury to property from dirt, smoke and vibration emanating from the plant. A nuisance has been found after trial, temporary damages have been allowed; but an injunction has been denied.

The public concern with air pollution arising from many sources in industry and in transportation is currently accorded ever wider recognition accompanied by a growing sense of responsibility in State and Federal Governments to control it. Cement plants are obvious sources of air pollution in the neighborhoods where they operate.

But there is now before the court private litigation in which individual property owners have sought specific relief from a single plant operation. The threshold question raised by the division of view on this appeal is whether the court should resolve the litigation between the parties now before it as equitably as seems possible; or whether, seeking promotion of the general public welfare, it should channel private litigation into broad public objectives.

A court performs its essential function when it decides the rights of parties before it. Its decision of private controversies may sometimes greatly affect public issues. Large questions of law are often resolved by the manner in which private litigation is decided. But this is normally an incident to the court's main function to settle controversy. It is a rare exercise of judicial power to use a decision in private litigation as a purposeful mechanism to achieve direct public objectives greatly beyond the rights and interests before the court.

Effective control of air pollution is a problem presently far from solution even with the full public and financial powers of government. In large measure adequate technical procedures are yet to be developed and some that appear possible may be economically impracticable.

It seems apparent that the amelioration of air pollution will depend on technical research in great depth; on a carefully balanced consideration of the economic impact of close regulation; and of the actual effect on public health. It is likely to require massive public expenditure and to demand more than any local community can accomplish and to depend on regional and interstate controls.

A court should not try to do this on its own as a by-product of private litigation and it seems manifest that the judicial establishment is neither equipped in the limited nature of any judgment it can pronounce nor prepared to lay down and implement an effective policy for the elimination of air pollution. This is an area beyond the circumference of one private lawsuit. It is a direct responsibility for government and should not thus be undertaken as an incident to solving a dispute between property owners and a single cement plant — one of many — in the Hudson River Valley.

. . . .

The ground for the denial of injunction, notwithstanding the finding both that there is a nuisance and that plaintiffs have been damaged substantially, is the large disparity in economic consequences of the nuisance and of the injunction. This theory cannot, however, be sustained without overruling a doctrine which has been consistently reaffirmed in several leading cases in this court and which has never been disavowed here, namely that where a nuisance has been found and where there has been any substantial damage shown by the party complaining an injunction will be granted.

The rule in New York has been that such a nuisance will be enjoined although marked disparity be shown in economic consequence between the effect of the injunction and the effect of the nuisance.

. . . .

Although the court at Special Term and the Appellate Division held that injunction should be denied, it was found that plaintiffs had been damaged in various specific amounts up to the time of the trial and damages to the respective plaintiffs were awarded for those amounts. The effect of this was, injunction having been denied, plaintiffs could maintain successive actions at law for damages thereafter as further damage was incurred.

The court at Special Term also found the amount of permanent damage attributable to each plaintiff, for the guidance of the parties in the event both sides stipulated to the payment and acceptance of such permanent damage as a settlement of all the controversies among the parties. The total of permanent damages to all plaintiffs thus found was $185,000....

This result at Special Term and at the Appellate Division is a departure from a rule that has become settled; but to follow the rule literally in these cases would be to close down the plant at once. This court is fully agreed to avoid that immediately drastic remedy; the difference in view is how best to avoid it.[1]

One alternative is to grant the injunction but postpone its effect to a specified future date to give opportunity for technical advances to permit defendant to eliminate the nuisance; another is to grant the injunction conditioned on the payment of permanent damages to plaintiffs which would compensate them for the total economic loss to their property present and future caused by defendant's operations. For reasons which will be developed the court chooses the latter alternative.

If the injunction were to be granted unless within a short period — e.g., 18 months — the nuisance be abated by improved methods, there would be no assurance that any significant technical improvement would occur.

The parties could settle this private litigation at any time if defendant paid enough money and the imminent threat of closing the plant would build up the pressure on defendant. If there were no improved techniques found, there would inevitably be applications to the court at Special Term for extensions of time to perform on showing of good faith efforts to find such techniques.

Moreover, techniques to eliminate dust and other annoying by-products of cement making are unlikely to be developed by any research the defendant can undertake within any short period, but will depend on the total resources of the cement industry nationwide and throughout the world. The problem is universal whenever cement is made.

For obvious reasons the rate of the research is beyond control of defendant. If at the end of 18 months the whole industry has not found a technical solution a court would be hard put to close down this one cement plant if due regard be given to equitable principles.

On the other hand, to grant the injunction unless defendant pays plaintiffs such permanent damages as may be fixed by the court seems to do justice between the contending parties. All of the attributions of economic loss to the properties on which plaintiffs' complaints are based will have been redressed.

The nuisance complained of by these plaintiffs may have other public or private consequences, but these particular parties are the only ones who have sought remedies and the judgment proposed will fully redress them. The limitation of relief granted is a limitation only within the four corners of these actions and does not foreclose public health or other public agencies from seeking proper relief in a proper court.

It seems reasonable to think that the risk of being required to pay permanent damages to injured property owners by cement plant owners would itself be a reasonable effective spur to research for improved techniques to minimize nuisance.

---

[1]Respondent's investment in the event is in excess of $45,000,000. There are over 300 people employed there.

....

The damage base here suggested is consistent with the general rule in those nuisance cases where damages are allowed. "Where a nuisance is of such a permanent and unabatable character that a single recovery can be had, including the whole damage past and future resulting therefrom, there can be but one recovery."...

The orders should be reversed, without costs, and the cases remitted to Supreme Court, Albany County to grant an injunction which shall be vacated upon payment by defendant of such amounts of permanent damage to the respective plaintiffs as shall for this purpose be determined by the court.

JASEN, JUDGE (dissenting).

I agree with the majority that a reversal is required here, but I do not subscribe to the newly enunciated doctrine of assessment of permanent damages, in lieu of an injunction, where substantial property rights have been impaired by the creation of a nuisance.

It has long been the rule in this State, as the majority acknowledges, that a nuisance which results in substantial continuing damage to neighbors must be enjoined. [Citations.] To now change the rule to permit the cement company to continue polluting the air indefinitely upon the payment of permanent damages is, in my opinion, compounding the magnitude of a very serious problem in our State and Nation today.

....

The harmful nature and widespread occurrence of air pollution have been extensively documented. Congressional hearings have revealed that air pollution causes substantial property damage, as well as being a contributing factor to a rising incidence of lung cancer, emphysema, bronchitis and asthma.

....

I see grave dangers in overruling our long-established rule of granting an injunction where a nuisance results in substantial continuing damage. In permitting the injunction to become inoperative upon the payment of permanent damages, the majority is, in effect, licensing a continuing wrong. It is the same as saying to the cement company, you may continue to do harm to your neighbors so long as you pay a fee for it. Furthermore, once such permanent damages are assessed and paid, the incentive to alleviate the wrong would be eliminated, thereby continuing air pollution of an area without abatement.

....

This kind of inverse condemnation may not be invoked by a private person or corporation for private gain or advantage. Inverse condemnation should only be permitted when the public is primarily served in the taking or impairment of property. [Citations.] The promotion of the interests of the polluting cement company has, in my opinion, no public use or benefit.

Nor is it constitutionally permissible to impose servitude on land, without consent of the owner, by payment of permanent damages where the continuing impairment of the land is for a private use. [Citations.] This is made clear by the State Constitution (art. I, § 7, subd. [a]) which provides that "[p]rivate property shall not be taken for *public use* without just compensation" (emphasis added). It is, of course, significant that the section makes no mention of taking for a *private* use.

In sum, then, by constitutional mandate as well as by judicial pronouncement, the permanent impairment of private property for private purposes is not authorized in the absence of clearly demonstrated public benefit and use.

I would enjoin the defendant cement company from continuing the discharge of dust particles upon its neighbors' properties unless, within 18 months, the cement company abated this nuisance.

It is not my intention to cause the removal of the cement plant from the Albany area, but to recognize the urgency of the problem stemming from this stationary source of air pollution, and to allow the company a specified period of time to develop a means to alleviate this nuisance.

. . . .

In a day when there is a growing concern for clean air, highly developed industry should not expect acquiescence by the courts, but should, instead, plan its operations to eliminate contamination of our air and damage to its neighbors.

NOTES AND QUESTIONS

1. In *Boomer* the dissent contends that the majority's refusal to abate the nuisance because of disparate economic hardships effectively licenses a continuing wrong and grants the defendant a power of inverse condemnation. In all requests for injunctive relief the court must balance the respective benefits and burdens which are likely to accrue in the event that the activity is abated or allowed to continue. A court faced with weighing competing interests seldom can entirely avoid imposing burdens on one of the parties. The question, then, is not whether harm can be averted through the vehicle of equity, but which party should be left in the position of sustaining the burden and in what degree.

2. The balancing process is particularly difficult when extremely disparate values are involved. Can health and safety interests be accurately compared with economic costs? Does the concept of "value" vary depending on the perspective of the party? Stated otherwise, could a parcel of property have different values to: the government for eminent domain purposes, to a corporation acquiring the land for construction of a factory, to public interest groups desiring to preserve the land for ecological reasons, and to a private landowner occupying the property and using it for farming?

Congressional dissatisfaction with traditional common law rules for measuring damages to natural resources has led to statutory changes in valuation preferences. For example, in *Ohio v. United States Dep't of Interior*, 880 F.2d 432 (D.C. Cir. 1989), reprinted *infra* Chapter 9, page 851, the court determined that Congress intended to establish a distinct preference for restoration costs as the basic measure of damages for natural resource injuries under CERCLA. Accordingly, regulations promulgated by the Department of the Interior which limited recovery of damages to the "lesser of" restoration or lost use value of the affected resource were held invalid.

3. If harm to environmental resources typically is undervalued and the touchstone of equity is weighing the competing interests, does that give an undue advantage to commercial, pecuniary interests? The landowners, on the other hand, would contend that abatement of the offending conduct is appropriate because there is no adequate remedy at law. "Adequacy" of the legal remedies does not translate to mean that damages are unavailable, but that the harm cannot be accurately measured or that the damages are insufficient compensation for the type of injury suffered. For additional commentary on the role of economics in environmental law and related issues, see Chapter 1, Section A.

4. In those instances where the nature of the potential harm is severe — as in cases involving exposure to toxic chemicals — courts are ill-equipped to employ the traditional mechanism of balancing interests. Should courts exercise a quasi-legislative role to fashion a remedy in such instances or should deference be given to a comprehensive legislative solution? The majority in *Boomer* acknowledges the problem in using a dispute between private parties to accomplish a broader social policy. The call for legislative reform of the environmental problems presented in *Boomer* set the stage for an explosion in legislation at the state and federal level in the 1970s. The Environmental Protection Agency was established in 1970 and charged with the responsibility of promulgating national ambient air quality standards for air pollutants which endanger public health or welfare. Congress also passed significant legislation to address the problems posed by hazardous waste materials. The Resource Conservation Recovery Act of 1976, 42 U.S.C. § 6901 *et seq.* and the Comprehensive Environmental Response, Compensation and Liability Act of 1980 (known as "Superfund"), 42 U.S.C. § 8601 *et seq.*, are two of the most significant pieces of that legislative movement to combat the serious risks to health and safety from toxic substances. The "new breed" of statutes reflect a toughened stance toward environmental degradation by incorporating tort concepts of strict liability and including a wide range of civil and criminal penalties for violators.

5. Compare *Boomer* with *Christopher v. Jones*, 41 Cal. Rptr. 828 (1964), where the plaintiffs owned an orchard located adjacent to the defendant's manufacturing plant. The plaintiff claimed that chlorine gas and fumes originating from the defendant's plant were irreparably injuring the orchard. The defendants contended that the escape of chemicals resulted from a single explosion and that an injunction should not issue to abate a completed act. The court granted the plaintiff's request for a preliminary injunction based on evidence that a leak of chlorine gas escaped from the plant and was detectable on plaintiff's property for two months. The court also rejected the defendant's argument that an injunction was unnecessary because damages would provide an adequate remedy for any harm to the orchard. The court made the following observation:

> It is elementary that injunctive relief will issue only after a clear showing of irreparable injury for which there is no other adequate remedy. However, the right to injunctive relief exists in some cases irrespective of damage and regardless of whether or not the injury is shown to be irreparable. Such is the case where it is sought to restrain a party from wrongfully taking away a part of real property, from continuing acts that might give rise to a prescriptive right or easement against the plaintiff, that would destroy vegetation — such as fruit and ornamental trees and shrubbery — that may be of peculiar value to the owner, that would destroy the substance of land that could not be replaced, that would destroy the plaintiff's growing crops and render his land valueless, or that might in the future hamper the use of or lessen the value of the land.

Is this analysis consistent with the result in *Boomer*? If not, which approach should courts follow?

6. In *Boomer* the court balanced the competing interests and hardships of the parties and determined that an injunction against the offending plant should issue contingent upon payment of permanent damages. What difference would it make if the landowners had acquired their property after the cement plant had already commenced operations? Some courts have denied injunctive relief to parties who located within close proximity to an established business on the theory that the later arriving party either implicitly consented to the enterprise or should have reasonably foreseen that it would constitute a nuisance. The concept of "coming to the nuisance" which effectively barred equitable relief to one who intentionally placed themselves in a position to be interfered with also was rationalized by notions of protecting the reasonable investment expectations of the existing industry. *See Fischer v. Atlantic Richfield*, 774 F. Supp. 616, 619 (W.D. Okla. 1989) (coming to nuisance doctrine applies only where the injury caused is permanent). *Also see* Wittman, *First Come, First Served: An Economic Analysis of "Coming to the Nuisance,"* 9 J. LEGAL STUD. 557 (1980).

In the famous case, *Spur Indus. v. Del E. Webb Dev. Co.*, 108 Ariz. 178, 494 P.2d 700 (1972), the court adopted an unusual and creative solution to a problem created by a residential development located near a large cattle feedlot operation. The developer sought a permanent injunction to force the feedlot to relocate, alleging that it constituted a public and private nuisance. The court granted the injunction but required the developer to pay the costs associated with moving or shutting down the business A significant factor influencing the court's decision was the public interest in protecting the health and welfare of the residents. What was the role of public interest in *Boomer*?

7. The role of common law of nuisance in relation to federal environmental protection statutes has proved troublesome for courts. In *Illinois v. Milwaukee*, 406 U.S. 91 (1972) (*Milwaukee I*) the State of Illinois sought to enjoin public sewage commissions and municipalities in Wisconsin from discharging improperly treated sewage into Lake Michigan on the grounds that the resulting pollution constituted a public nuisance. The Court recognized the province of federal courts to fashion common law remedies, including public nuisance, to address problems dealing with pollution of interstate or navigable waters. The Court prophetically noted as a caveat, however, that a comprehensive federal regulatory scheme could preempt the field of federal common law of nuisance.

Immediately after its decision, Congress enacted sweeping revisions of federal laws governing water pollution in the Federal Water Pollution Control Act Amendments of 1972. In *Milwaukee v. Illinois*, 451 U.S. 304 (1981) (*Milwaukee II*), reprinted in Chapter 3, page 112, the Supreme Court found that the restructured federal statutes had occupied the field of interstate water pollution regulation and thus left no room for federal common law. In *Middlesex County Sewerage Auth. v. National Sea Clammers Ass'n*, 453 U.S. 1 (1981) the Court expanded upon its decision in *Milwaukee II* by determining that federal common law nuisance claims were preempted by federal statutes governing coastal waters and that no private right of action existed under the federal statutes regulating water and ocean pollution.

Interestingly, in *Milwaukee II* the Court found significance in the fact that Congress had provided a forum for an affected state to protect its interests by receiving notice and opportunity to participate in public hearings regarding permitting decisions by a neighboring state. Contrary to the Court's observation, the interstate pollution problem was not completely resolved by the federal statutory scheme. In *International Paper Co. v. Ouellette*, 479 U.S. 481 (1987), reprinted in Chapter 3, page 119, Vermont landowners claimed that the operations of a pulp and paper mill located in New York discharging waste materials into Lake Champlain caused a significant interference with their property interests. The Court held that the federal Clean Water Act precluded the application of Vermont common law against the out-of-state source; however, an action under New York nuisance law was not preempted by the federal regulation. Finally, in *Arkansas v. Oklahoma*, _ U.S. _, 60 U.S.L.W. 4176 (1992), reprinted in Chapter 7, page 595, the Court found that the EPA's regulations conditioning issuance of a Clean Water Act permit upon compliance with applicable water quality standards of affected downstream states constituted a reasonable exercise of the agency's statutory discretion.

8. A statute may affect the balancing of interests process for purposes of determining the availability and nature of equitable relief. In *Harrison v. Indiana Auto Shredders Co.*, 528 F.2d 1107 (7th Cir. 1975) the defendant operated an auto shredding plant adjacent to an urban neighborhood. The neighboring landowners sought to enjoin the facility, alleging that the dust, noise and vibrations generated by the plant constituted a nuisance. The court noted that the plant was operating validly within local zoning ordinance regulations. Although such compliance did not entirely shield the company from injunctive relief, it was a persuasive factor in the balancing of interests. The court stated:

This case presents the very difficult question of how to balance the legitimate demands of an urban neighborhood for clean air and a comfortable environment against the utility and economic enterprise of a beneficial, but polluting, industry....

In recent years, the abandoned and junked automobile has been recognized as one of this country's major solid waste disposal problems. Auto "graveyards" represent not only an aesthetic blight that mars the natural beauty of the land, but also a scandalous waste of energy and resources that produced those cars....

This case is representative of the new breed of lawsuit spawned by the growing concern for cleaner air and water. The birth and burgeoning growth of environmental litigation have forced the courts into difficult situations where modern hybrids of the traditional concepts of nuisance law and equity must be fashioned.... [T]he right of environmentally-aggrieved parties to obtain redress in the courts serves as a necessary and valuable supplement to legislative efforts to restore the natural ecology of our cities and countryside.

Judicial involvement in solving environmental problems does, however, bring its own hazards. Balancing the interests of a modern urban community like Indianapolis may be very difficult. Weighing the desire for economic and industrial strength against the need for clean and livable surroundings is not easily done, especially because of the gradations in quality as well as quantity that are involved. There is the danger that environmental problems will be inadequately treated by the piecemeal methods of litigation. It is possible that courtroom battles may be used to slow down effective policymaking for the environment. Litigation often fails to provide sufficient opportunities for the expert analysis and broad perspective that such policymaking often requires.

As difficult as environmental balancing may be, however, some forum for aggrieved parties must be made available. If necessary, the courts are qualified to perform the task. The courts are skilled at "balancing the equities," a technique that traditionally has been one of the judicial functions. Courts are insulated from the lobbying that gives strong advantages to industrial polluters when they face administrative or legislative review of their operations....

An unusual feature of the case were the factors which the court took into account in balancing the equities of the parties. The court considered both the community's interest in a clean environment as well as the economic benefits provided by the plant to the community through jobs and taxes. The court also recognized, though, that the company's business actually provided an environmental benefit through conserving natural resources by recycling abandoned automobiles. The court decided that immediately shutting down the plant was inappropriate, but that the defendant should have an opportunity to remedy the offensive nature of its operations within a reasonable time.

9. Some jurisdictions have enacted anti-injunction acts which preclude courts from restraining business activities that comport with the standards of zoning ordinances yet would otherwise be considered an actionable nuisance. For example, in *Kornoff v. Kingsburg Cotton Oil Co.*, 45 Cal. 2d 265, 288 P.2d 507 (1955) the court held that a California anti-injunction statute shielded the defendant's operation of its cotton gin from abatement as a nuisance because it complied with local zoning ordinance regulations. The statute did not, however, preclude the plaintiffs from seeking a recovery of damages for harm attributable to the plant.

VILLAGE OF WILSONVILLE v. SCA SERVICES, INC.

86 Ill. 2d 1, 55 Ill. Dec. 499, 426 N.E.2d 824 (1981)

CLARK, JUSTICE.

[The plaintiff, Village of Wilsonville, sought an injunction against the operation of the defendant's hazardous chemical-waste-disposal site as a public nuisance. The materials deposited at the site were extremely toxic; human exposure to the chemicals could result in pulmonary disease, cancer, brain damage, and birth defects. The defendant had obtained all necessary governmental permits to operate the landfill, but conflicting testimony was presented regarding chemical spills and the escape of noxious fumes from the site. The trial court found that the operation of the disposal site constituted a prospective nuisance, and ordered the defendant to remove the toxic waste and to restore and reclaim the site.]

. . . .

The trial court herein concluded that defendant's chemical-waste-disposal site constitutes both a private and a public nuisance. Professor Prosser has defined a private nuisance as "a civil wrong, based on a disturbance of rights in land" (Prosser, Torts sec. 86, at 572 (4th ed. 1971)), and a public nuisance as "an act or omission 'which obstructs or causes inconvenience or damage to the public in the exercise of rights common to all Her Majesty's subjects.'" [Citation.] Prosser has also quoted the following, more precise definition of a public nuisance. "'A common or public nuisance is the doing of or the failure to do something that injuriously affects the safety, health or morals of the public, or works some substantial annoyance, inconvenience or injury to the public.'" [Citation.] It is generally conceded that a nuisance is remediable by injunction or a suit for damages. [Citation.]

The defendant herein argues that "[e]ven if some or all of plaintiffs' evidence is deemed believable, the findings of the courts below that [defendant's] conduct constitutes a prospective nuisance must be reversed for failure to ... balance the reasonableness and utility of the defendant's conduct, the harm to the plaintiff, and the general societal policy toward risk-taking before [a court may] find an actionable nuisance present."... We do not agree, however, with the foregoing characterization of the trial court's statement.... It is reasonably clear that this court and the circuit court meant that where individual rights are unreasonably interfered with, the public benefit from a particular facility will not outweigh the individual right, and the facility's use will be enjoined or curtailed. Such a conclusion presupposes a balancing process with the greater weight being given to the individual's right to use and enjoy property over a public benefit or convenience from having a business operate at a particular location. In such an instance, the individual's right to noninterference takes precedence.

Moreover, the trial court did engage in a balancing process, as is made clear by the following excerpt from the trial court's memorandum opinion.

> ....
>
> "The Court understands as does counsel that there is a need for disposal of industrial hazardous wastes. However, where disposal of wastes create a nuisance said disposal site may be closed through legal action.
>
> Substantial sums of money have been expended by the defendant in developing and operating the Earthline site at Wilsonville. Not only is the site convenient to nearby industries but it is a profit producer for the defendant. All of these elements are relevant to our economic system but notwithstanding the same it is the opinion of the Court that nuisances cannot be justified on such grounds when we have substantial injury to individual rights, community rights, substantial damage to human beings and other living things.
>
> ....
>
> Whether or not a business is useful or necessary or whether or not it contributes to the welfare and/or prosperity of the community are elements to be considered in a serious manner but said elements are not determinative as to whether or not the operation is a nuisance.
>
> The importance of an industry to the wealth and prosperity of an area does not as a matter of law give to it rights superior to the primary of natural rights of citizens who live nearby. *However, such matters may be considered and have been in this case.*"
>
> ....

We think the foregoing indicates that the trial court did carefully engage in a balancing process between the site's social utility and the plaintiffs' right to enjoy their property and not suffer deleterious effects from chemical wastes. Accordingly, the defendant's argument that the trial court did not balance the equities in this case is without merit.

The defendant's next contention is that the courts below were in error when they failed to require a showing of a substantial risk of certain and extreme future harm before enjoining operation of the defendant's site. We deem it necessary to explain that a *prospective* nuisance is a fit candidate for injunctive relief. Prosser states: "Both public and private nuisances require some substantial interference with the interest involved. Since nuisance is a common subject of equity jurisdiction, the damage against which an injunction is asked is often merely threatened or potential; but even in such cases, there must be at least a threat of a substantial invasion of the plaintiff's interests." [Citation.] The defendant does not dispute this proposition; it does, however, argue that the trial court did not follow the proper standard for determining when a prospective nuisance may be enjoined. The defendant argues that the proper standard to be used is that an injunction is proper only if there is a "dangerous probability" that the threatened or potential injury will occur. (*See* Restatement (Second) of Torts sec. 933(1), at 561, comment b (1979).) The defendant further argues that the appellate court looked only at the potential consequences of not enjoining the operation of the site as a nuisance and not at the likelihood of whether harm would occur....

We agree with the defendant's statement of the law, but not with its urged application to the facts of this case. Again, Professor Prosser has offered a concise commentary. He has stated that "[o]ne distinguishing feature of equitable relief is that it may be granted upon the threat of harm which has not yet occurred. The defendant may be restrained from entering upon an activity where it is highly probable that it will lead to a nuisance, although if the possibility is merely uncertain or contingent he may be left to his remedy after the nuisance has occurred."... We agree.

In this case there can be no doubt but that it is highly probable that the chemical-waste-disposal site will bring about a substantial injury. Without again reviewing the extensive evidence adduced at trial, we think it is sufficiently clear that it is highly probable that the instant site will constitute a public nuisance if, through either an explosive interaction, migration, subsidence, or the "bathtub effect," the highly toxic chemical wastes deposited at the site escape and contaminate the air, water, or ground around the site. That such an event will occur was positively attested to by several expert witnesses. A court does not have to wait for it to happen before it can enjoin such a result. Additionally, the fact is that the condition of a nuisance is already present at the site due to the location of the site and the manner in which it has been operated. Thus, it is only the damage which is prospective....

We also disagree with the defendant that since the plaintiffs could seek review from the IEPA's decision to grant permits to the defendant through the Pollution Control Board they have an adequate remedy at law and are unable to obtain relief in a court of equity. First, the plaintiffs are not seeking a review of the issuance of permits. The plaintiffs seek to enjoin a nuisance, a matter which is properly brought in a court of equity. This court has stated that jurisdiction exists in the circuit court "to abate public nuisances which may endanger the general welfare."...

... [T]he gist of this case is that the defendant is engaged in an extremely hazardous undertaking at an unsuitable location, which seriously and imminently poses a threat to the public health. We are acutely aware that the service provided by the defendant is a valuable and necessary one. We also know that it is preferable to have chemical-waste-disposal sites than to have illegal dumping in rivers, streams, and deserted areas. But a site such as defendant's, if it is to do the job it is intended to do, must be located in a secure place, where it will pose no threat to health or life, now, or in the future. This site was intended to be a *permanent* disposal site for the deposit of extremely hazardous chemical-waste materials. Yet this site is located above an abandoned tunneled mine where subsidence is occurring several years ahead of when it was anticipated. Also, the permeability-coefficient samples taken by defendant's experts, though not conclusive alone, indicate that the soil is more permeable at the site than expected. Moreover, the spillage, odors, and dust caused by the presence of the disposal site indicate why it was inadvisable to locate the site so near the plaintiff village.

Therefore, we conclude that in fashioning relief in this case the trial court did balance the relative hardship to be caused to the plaintiffs and defendant, and did fashion reasonable relief when it ordered the exhumation of all material from the site and the reclamation of the surrounding area. The instant site is akin to Mr. Justice Sutherland's observation that "Nuisance may be merely a right thing in a wrong place — like a pig in the parlor instead of the barnyard." [Citations.]

We are also cognizant of *amicus* USEPA's suggestion in its brief and affidavits filed with the appellate court which urge that we remand to the circuit court so that alternatives to closure of the site and exhumation of the waste materials may be considered. The USEPA states: "Heavy equipment may damage drums, releasing wastes and possibly causing gaseous emissions, fires, and explosions. Repackaging and transporting damaged drums also risks releasing wastes. Workers performing the exhumation face dangers from contact with or inhalation of wastes; these risks cannot be completely eliminated with protective clothing and breathing apparatus. Nearby residents may also be endangered." It is ironic the host of horribles mentioned by the USEPA in support of keeping the site open includes some of the same hazards which the plaintiffs have raised as reasons in favor of closing the site.

....

We note, however, that the USEPA does not suggest how the location of the disposal site above an abandoned tunneled mine and the effects of subsidence can be overcome....

... Moreover, it needs to be remembered, as the trial judge pointed out, that the nuisance in this case came to the village. [Citation.] The residents of Wilsonville have a right to enjoy and use their property without being unreasonably interfered with by the defendant's hazardous-waste site. Also, there is evidence in the record that representatives of the defendant told the village board, in response to a question from the water works commissioner, that no toxic materials would be buried at the site, when the truth is precisely the opposite. We view these factors as additional reasons why defendant's conduct is inequitable and why plaintiffs are entitled to a permanent injunction. We conclude therefore that the relief fashioned by the trial court is reasonable under the precise facts of this case and will not be disturbed.

....

Affirmed and remanded.

RYAN, JUSTICE, concurring.

While I agree with both the result reached by the majority and the reasoning employed supporting the opinion, I wish to add a brief comment. In response to the defendant's argument that the trial court failed to apply the proper standard for determining when a prospective nuisance may be enjoined, the majority concluded that the court had in fact applied the correct rule as set out in *Fink v. Board of Trustees* (1966), 71 Ill. App. 2d 276, 218 N.E.2d 240. I am concerned that the holding of *Fink*, quoted by the majority, may be an unnecessarily narrow view of the test for enjoining prospective tortious conduct in general. Any injunction is, by its very nature, the product of a court's balancing of competing interests, with a result equitably obtained. Prosser, in discussing the law of nuisance, quoted by the majority, states:

> "[I]f the possibility [of harm] is merely uncertain or contingent [the plaintiff] may be left to his remedy after the nuisance has occurred." Prosser, Torts sec. 90, at 603 (4th ed. 1971).

Prosser thus recognizes that there are cases in which the possibility of inflicting harm is slight and where the plaintiff may be left to his remedy at law. However, I believe that there are situations where the harm that is potential is so devastating that equity should afford relief even though the possibility of the harmful result occurring is uncertain or contingent. The Restatement's position applicable to preventative injunctive relief in general is that "[t]he more serious the impending harm, the less justification there is for taking the chances that are involved in pronouncing the harm too remote." (Restatement (Second) of Torts sec. 933, at 561, comment b (1979).) If the harm that may result is severe, a lesser possibility of it occurring should be required to support injunctive relief. Conversely, if the potential harm is less severe, a greater possibility that it will happen should be required. Also, in the balancing of competing interests, a court may find a situation where the potential harm is such that a plaintiff will be left to his remedy at law if the possibility of it occurring is slight. This balancing test allows the court to consider a wider range of factors and avoids the anomalous result possible under a more restrictive alternative where a person engaged in an ultrahazardous activity with potentially catastrophic results would be allowed to continue until he has driven an entire community to the brink of certain disaster. A court of equity need not wait so long to provide relief.

Although the "dangerous probability" test has certainly been met in this case, I would be willing to enjoin the activity on a showing of probability of occurrence substantially less than that which the facts presented to this court reveal, due to the extremely hazardous nature of the chemicals being dumped and the potentially catastrophic results.

NOTES AND QUESTIONS

1. In *Wilsonville* the court dealt with the difficult question of determining at what stage a potentially hazardous activity should be enjoined where the conduct is not yet causing serious harm. Recent federal environmental statutes have incorporated the same concept of authorizing injunctive relief upon a reduced showing of likelihood that the offensive conduct will occur. For example, section 7003 (42 U.S.C. § 6973) of the Resource Conservation and Recovery Act provides that the federal government may seek an injunction when the handling, storage, treatment, transportation or disposal of hazardous waste "may present an imminent and substantial endangerment to health or the environment." Courts have held that section 7003 is not limited to abatement of emergency situations, but that "endanger" means the "risk" of injury rather than actual injury. The "imminence" of the harm refers to the nature of the threat rather than the time that the harm may occur. *United States v. Waste Indus.*, 734 F.2d 159 (4th Cir. 1984). This approach expands the equitable powers of courts by authorizing equitable relief under a more lenient standard than requiring irreparable harm. *Also see Environmental Defense Fund v. EPA*, 465 F.2d 528 (D.C. Cir. 1972) (FIFRA authorizes suspension of registration of pesticides upon showing substantial likelihood of serious harm).

2. A party seeking the extraordinary remedy of an injunction must establish a sufficiently serious and immediate threat of an irreparable injury absent equitable intervention. In *Wilsonville* the court applied a liberalized test of imminent and irreparable harm because the potential injury would be so devastating if it occurred. Courts have differed over whether the violation of an environmental protection statute constitutes irreparable harm justifying equitable intervention as a matter of course or if a court retains its traditional discretion to balance the equities.

In *Town of Huntington v. Marsh*, 884 F.2d 648 (2d Cir. 1989) the plaintiffs sought to enjoin the Army Corps of Engineers from dumping dredged materials or from issuing permits for dumping at a marine disposal site. The plaintiffs alleged that an injunction should follow from violations of the Ocean Dumping Act and NEPA, and the trial court agreed. The court issued a permanent injunction on the basis that the public interest in maintaining the physical, chemical and biological balance at the dump site outweighed the potential harm to private interests. The appellate court vacated the injunction and remanded, rejecting the idea that any violation of a statute per se constituted irreparable harm warranting an injunction. The court explained that the proper inquiry for entitlement to equitable relief is a demonstration of actual or threatened injury rather than inferring injury solely from the fact of noncompliance with statutory directives. *Also see Save the Yaak Comm. v. Block*, 840 F.2d 714, 722 (9th Cir.

1988) (rejecting any presumption of irreparable injury under NEPA when an agency fails to properly evaluate the environmental impact of a proposed action).

3. On the other hand, some courts have recognized that because harm to natural resources is often irremediable, equitable protection may be justified on the grounds that damages would be an inadequate remedy. In *Amoco Prod. Co. v. Village of Gambell*, 480 U.S. 531 (1987), the Court cautioned against an automatic presumption of irreparable harm for entitlement to an injunction. The Court explained, however, why such a presumption is unnecessary in environmental litigation, "Environmental injury, but its nature, can seldom be adequately remedied by money damages, and is often permanent or at least of long duration, i.e., irreparable. If such injury is sufficiently likely, therefore, the balance of harms will usually favor issuance of an injunction to protect the environment."

4. Another hurdle facing potential plaintiffs seeking to abate offensive conduct on the grounds of public nuisance is the traditional requirement for standing that the party has sustained a different kind of harm from that suffered by other persons exercising the same public right. *See* RESTATEMENT (SECOND) OF TORTS § 821C(1) (1977); *Philadelphia Elec. Co. v. Hercules, Inc.*, 762 F.2d 303, 315 (3d Cir. 1985) (expenditures by property owner to clean up polluted water were not special harm sufficient to confer standing to bring public nuisance claim).

On the other hand, in *Westwood Pharmaceuticals, Inc. v. National Fuel Gas Distrib. Corp.*, 737 F. Supp. 1272 (W.D.N.Y. 1990) the court recognized that the release of hazardous substances into the environment constituted an unreasonable infringement upon a public right — the linchpin of public nuisance. Moreover, the court stated that public nuisance law should be flexible and liberally applied to meet the growing public need to address the hazards posed to human health and the environment from exposure to toxic wastes. Accordingly, the court determined that a private party would have standing to assert a public nuisance action if they could establish that they incurred response costs to the hazardous waste. *Id.* at 1281. *Also see Anderson v. W.R. Grace & Co.*, 628 F. Supp. 1219, 1233 (D. Mass. 1986) (plaintiffs sustaining personal injuries resulting from exposure to contaminated groundwater had demonstrated sufficient "special and peculiar" harm for standing to maintain public nuisance claim); *State of New York v. SCA Servs.*, 754 F. Supp. 995, 1002 (S.D.N.Y. 1991) (expenditures for engineering and hydrogeological studies performed at site sufficient for standing to assert public nuisance claim provided injuries not common to the entire community exercising the same public right).

5. An important procedural obstacle faced by a private party seeking to enforce a federal environmental protection statute through a preliminary injunction is satisfying F.R.C.P. 65(c), which requires the claimant to post a bond. Since an interlocutory injunction may be granted based upon a showing of probable rights and probable harm, the bond serves an important function in checking overzealous claimants. A private party seeking to challenge a major development on the basis of noncompliance with an environmental statute must not only bear the cost of obtaining a bond but runs the risk of liability should the defendant prevail at

the trial on the merits. A party who is wrongfully enjoined may turn to the bond for compensation of provable actual damages, even if the plaintiff acted in good faith in seeking an injunction. *Coyne-Delany Co. v. Capital Dev. Bd.*, 717 F.2d 385 (7th Cir. 1983). On the other hand, the bond serves as a ceiling on the total exposure of the claimant provided they acted in good faith. Thus, if a party decided not to post a bond, its potential liability for actual damages would be theoretically unlimited. *See Monroe Div., Litton Bus. Sys. v. De Bari*, 562 F.2d 30 (10th Cir. 1977).

In *Cronin v. United States Dep't of Agri.*, 919 F.2d 439 (7th Cir. 1990) a citizen's group sought a preliminary injunction to halt government sales of timber from national forest tracts as in violation of various federal laws. The Forest Service contended that its "reputation" as a manager of the country's national forests would be irreparably harmed by issuance of a preliminary injunction and could not be fully protected by an injunction bond. The court recognized that certain government interests in carrying out its programs could not be sufficiently protected by an injunction bond; those cases could justify denial of the preliminary injunction or the dissolution of a stay. The court further observed, however, that the Forest Service's anticipated revenues from the projected logging operations were the sort of quantifiable pecuniary harms which could be adequately safeguarded by requiring the plaintiff to post an injunction bond or equivalent security.

The court also has considerable discretion in setting the amount of the bond. For example, in *Wilderness Soc'y v. Tyrrel*, 701 F. Supp. 1473 (E.D. Cal. 1988), *rev'd on other grounds*, 918 F.2d 813 (9th Cir. 1990), the court set the bond in the amount of $100, recognizing that the plaintiffs were nonprofit corporations with limited resources attempting to force the federal government to comply with environmental laws. The court observed that if the plaintiffs were required to post substantial bonds, the resulting financial burden might undermine the private enforcement mechanism of environmental protection statutes. *Also see Friends of the Earth, Inc. v. Brinegar*, 518 F.2d 322 (9th Cir. 1975) (bond reduced from $4,500,000 to $1,000 in NEPA case enjoining the expansion of the San Francisco airport); *Environmental Defense Fund v. Army Corps of Eng'rs*, 331 F. Supp. 925 (D.D.C. 1971) (bond set at $1 in suit enjoining the construction of an extensive barge canal); *Natural Resources Defense Council v. Morton*, 337 F. Supp. 167 (D.D.C. 1971) (bond set at $100 in private suit challenging government project involving Outer Continental Shelf — the court justified the nominal bond to allow the private organization an opportunity to obtain judicial review of a matter in the public interest).

Chapter 3

CONSTITUTIONAL LIMITS ON STATE ACTION

INTRODUCTION

The states have considerable authority, in the exercise of their police power, to enact regulatory measures pertaining to the health, safety and welfare of their citizens. Where Congress has legislated directly or comprehensively on a subject pursuant to its constitutional authority, though, conflicting state laws must yield to the federal scheme in accordance with the Supremacy Clause of the Constitution. U.S. Const. art. VI, cl. 2. The determination of whether state laws can co-exist with or are invalidated or preempted by federal legislation involves examination of Congressional intent and evaluation of the purpose and structure of the respective statutes. In the field of environmental law, significant preemption questions have developed during the past two decades, particularly with respect to the remedial objectives and methodologies of the major pollution control statutes. These developments are examined in Section B of this chapter.

Federal environmental protection regulations can, in some instances, impose such extensive restrictions on the usage or development of private property that a "taking" has occurred necessitating just compensation. The struggle of courts to find the line between noncompensable land use restraints for environmental purposes and where the property owner is constitutionally entitled to compensation for the burdens imposed is the principal theme explored in Section C of this chapter.

The interrelationship of state regulatory power and constitutionally reserved federal power also raises conflicts pursuant to the Commerce Clause of the Constitution. Those issues are examined in the following materials.

A. COMMERCE CLAUSE RESTRAINTS ON STATE CONDUCT

The Commerce Clause of the Constitution grants Congress the power "[t]o regulate Commerce with foreign Nations, and among the several States, and with the Indian Tribes." U.S. Const. art. I, § 8, cl. 3. Although the Clause affirmatively grants powers to Congress respecting commerce, courts have long interpreted it as limiting the power of states to erect barriers against interstate trade. Thus, even absent Congressional action, the Commerce Clause operates as a self-executing limitation on the regulatory authority of states.

Certainly all state laws can have some impact on interstate markets; therefore some interference or burdens may be tolerated within the state-federal cooperative framework. Courts look to the Commerce Clause to strike down laws, then, which either have a discriminatory means or effect or impose excessive burdens on interstate or foreign commerce. The question becomes one of degree — evaluating the nature and extent of the interference allowable in light of the purposes implicated and the interests adversely affected. In *Pike v. Bruce Church, Inc.*, 397 U.S. 137, 142 (1970) the Court set forth a three-part test to evaluate whether a state statute violated the Commerce Clause:

> Where the statute regulates evenhandedly to effectuate a legitimate public interest, and its effects on interstate commerce are only incidental, it will be upheld unless the burden imposed on such commerce is clearly excessive in relation to the putative local benefits. [Citation.] If a legitimate local purpose is found, then the question becomes one of degree. And the extent of the burden that will be tolerated will of course depend on the nature of the local interest involved, and on whether it could be promoted as well with a lesser impact on interstate activities.

If a legitimate local purpose is demonstrated, the extent of the burden tolerated will involve balancing the nature of the interest sought to be protected or effectuated in comparison to the detrimental effects on interstate commerce. This balancing process places courts in a difficult posture of quantifying disparate values of health and safety with the economic policy favoring an unrestricted marketplace. The critical inquiry becomes resolution of the tension between principles of state sovereignty and serving the interests of its citizenry versus fostering free trade. The animating principles of the independent limitations of the Commerce Clause on state conduct have both constitutional and pragmatic dimensions. The constitutional inquiry devolves into determining the allowable parameters of state regulation without intruding into the domain reserved to the federal government. The pragmatic considerations include concerns regarding economic protectionism, competitive disadvantage, and potential retaliatory measures by affected states.

The limits on state action pursuant to the "dormant" Commerce Clause have particular relevance in the field of environmental regulation. One significant issue, examined in the following materials, involves the extent to which state and local governments can prevent the shipment or disposal of hazardous waste in their area. The undesirability of waste products has led to the enactment of various measures designed to limit or exclude their passage across jurisdictional lines — the "not in my backyard" syndrome. Additional concerns involve the extent to which states can constitutionally favor their own citizens over non-residents with respect to the management or restricted access to the state's natural resources.

CITY OF PHILADELPHIA v. NEW JERSEY

437 U.S. 617 (1978)

MR. JUSTICE STEWART delivered the opinion of the Court.

A New Jersey law prohibits the importation of most "solid or liquid waste which originated or was collected outside the territorial limits of the State...." In this case we are required to decide whether this statutory prohibition violates the Commerce Clause of the United States Constitution.

The statutory provision in question is ch. 363 of 1973 N.J. Laws, which took effect in early 1974. In pertinent part it provides:

> "No person shall bring into this State any solid or liquid waste which originated or was collected outside the territorial limits of the State, except garbage to be fed to swine in the State of New Jersey, until the Commissioner [of the State Department of Environmental Protection] shall determine that such action can be permitted without endangering the public health, safety and welfare and has promulgated regulations permitting and regulating the treatment and disposal of such waste in this State." N.J. Stat. Ann. § 13:1*I*-10 (West Supp. 1978).

As authorized by ch. 363, the Commissioner promulgated regulations permitting four categories of waste to enter the State. Apart from these narrow exceptions, however, New Jersey closed its borders to all waste from other States.

Immediately affected by these developments were the operators of private landfills in New Jersey, and several cities in other States that had agreements with these operators for waste disposal. They brought suit against New Jersey and its Department of Environmental Protection in state court, attacking the statute and regulations on a number of state and federal grounds. [The New Jersey Supreme Court held that the statute was permissible under the Commerce Clause (art. I, § 8, cl. 3) because it advanced legitimate state health and environmental objectives without economically discriminating against or unduly burdening interstate commerce. The Supreme Court initially agreed with the New Jersey court that the statute was not preempted by federal legislation, then turned to consideration of the Commerce Clause issue.]

Before it addressed the merits of the appellants' claim, the New Jersey Supreme Court questioned whether the interstate movement of those wastes banned by ch. 363 is "commerce" at all within the meaning of the Commerce Clause. Any doubts on that score should be laid to rest at the outset.

....

The state court reached this conclusion in an attempt to reconcile modern Commerce Clause concepts with several old cases of this Court holding that States can prohibit the importation of some objects because they "are not legitimate subjects of trade and commerce." *Bowman v. Chicago & Northwestern R. Co.*, 125 U.S. 465, 489. These articles include items "which, on account of their existing condition, would bring in and spread disease, pestilence, and death, such as rags or other substances infected with the germs of yellow fever or the virus of small-pox, or cattle or meat or other provisions that are diseased or decayed, or otherwise, from their condition and quality, unfit for human use or consumption."...

We think the state court misread our cases, and thus erred in assuming that they require a two-tiered definition of commerce. In saying that innately harmful articles "are not legitimate subjects of trade and commerce," the *Bowman* Court was stating its conclusion, not the starting point of its reasoning. All objects of interstate trade merit Commerce Clause protection; none is excluded by definition at the outset. In *Bowman* and similar cases, the Court held simply that because the articles' worth in interstate commerce was far outweighed by the dangers inhering in their very movement, States could prohibit their transportation across state lines. Hence, we reject the state court's suggestion that the banning of "valueless" out-of-state wastes by ch. 363 implicates no constitutional protection. Just as Congress has power to regulate the interstate movement of these wastes, States are not free from constitutional scrutiny when they restrict that movement. [Citations.]

. . . .

The opinions of the Court through the years have reflected an alertness to the evils of "economic isolation" and protectionism, while at the same time recognizing that incidental burdens on interstate commerce may be unavoidable when a State legislates to safeguard the health and safety of its people. Thus, where simple economic protectionism is effected by state legislation, a virtually *per se* rule of invalidity has been erected. [Citations.] The clearest example of such legislation is a law that overtly blocks the flow of interstate commerce at a State's borders. But where other legislative objectives are credibly advanced and there is no patent discrimination against interstate trade, the Court has adopted a much more flexible approach....

The crucial inquiry, therefore, must be directed to determining whether ch. 363 is basically a protectionist measure, or whether it can fairly be viewed as a law directed to legitimate local concerns, with effects upon interstate commerce that are only incidental.

The New Jersey Supreme Court accepted [the] statement of the state legislature's purpose [regarding protecting public health and the environment]. The state court additionally found that New Jersey's existing landfill sites will be exhausted within a few years; that to go on using these sites or to develop new ones will take a heavy environmental toll, both from pollution and from loss of scarce open lands; that new techniques to divert waste from landfills to other methods of disposal and resource recovery processes are under development, but that these changes will require time; and finally, that "the extension of the lifespan of existing landfills, resulting from the exclusion of out-of-state waste, may be of crucial importance in preventing further virgin wetlands or other undeveloped lands from being devoted to landfill purposes." Based on these findings, the court concluded that ch. 363 was designed to protect, not the State's economy, but its environment, and that its substantial benefits outweigh its "slight" burden on interstate commerce.

The appellants strenuously contend that ch. 363, "while outwardly cloaked 'in the currently fashionable garb of environmental protection,' ... is actually no more than a legislative effort to suppress competition and stabilize the cost of solid waste disposal for New Jersey residents...."

This dispute about ultimate legislative purpose need not be resolved, because its resolution would not be relevant to the constitutional issue to be decided in this case. Contrary to the evident assumption of the state court and the parties, the evil of protectionism can reside in legislative means as well as legislative ends. Thus, it does not matter whether the ultimate aim of ch. 363 is to reduce the waste disposal costs of New Jersey residents or to save remaining open lands from pollution, for we assume New Jersey has every right to protect its residents' pocketbooks as well as their environment. And it may be assumed as well that New Jersey may pursue those ends by slowing the flow of *all* waste into the State's remaining landfills, even though interstate commerce may incidentally be affected. But whatever New Jersey's ultimate purpose, it may not be accomplished by discriminating against articles of commerce coming from outside the State unless there is some reason, apart from their origin, to treat them differently. Both on its face and in its plain effect, ch. 363 violates this principle of nondiscrimination.

....

The New Jersey law at issue in this case falls squarely within the area that the Commerce Clause puts off limits to state regulation. On its face, it imposes on out-of-state commercial interests the full burden of conserving the State's remaining landfill space. It is true that in our previous cases the scarce natural resource was itself the article of commerce, whereas here the scarce resource and the article of commerce are distinct. But that difference is without consequence. In both instances, the State has overtly moved to slow or freeze the flow of commerce for protectionist reasons. It does not matter that the State has shut the article of commerce inside the State in one case and outside the State in the other. What is crucial is the attempt by one State to isolate itself from a problem common to many by erecting a barrier against the movement of interstate trade.

The appellees argue that not all laws which facially discriminate against out-of-state commerce are forbidden protectionist regulations. In particular, they point to quarantine laws, which this Court has repeatedly upheld even though they appear to single out interstate commerce for special treatment. [Citations.] In the appellees' view, ch. 363 is analogous to such health-protective measures, since it reduces the exposure of New Jersey residents to the allegedly harmful effects of landfill sites.

It is true that certain quarantine laws have not been considered forbidden protectionist measures, even though they were directed against out-of-state commerce. [Citations.] But those quarantine laws banned the importation of articles such as diseased livestock that required destruction as soon as possible because their very movement risked contagion and other evils. Those laws thus did not discriminate against interstate commerce as such, but simply prevented traffic in noxious articles, whatever their origin.

The New Jersey statute is not such a quarantine law. There has been no claim here that the very movement of waste into or through New Jersey endangers health, or that waste must be disposed of as soon and as close to its point of generation as possible. The harms caused by waste are said to arise after its disposal in landfill sites, and at that point, as New Jersey concedes, there is no basis to distinguish out-of-state waste from domestic waste. If one is inherently harmful, so is the other. Yet New Jersey has banned the former while leaving its landfill sites open to the latter. The New Jersey law blocks the importation of waste in an obvious effort to saddle those outside the State with the entire burden of slowing the flow of refuse into New Jersey's remaining landfill sites. That legislative effort is clearly impermissible under the Commerce Clause of the Constitution.

Today, cities in Pennsylvania and New York find it expedient or necessary to send their waste into New Jersey for disposal, and New Jersey claims the right to close its borders to such traffic. Tomorrow, cities in New Jersey may find it expedient or necessary to send their waste into Pennsylvania or New York for disposal, and those States might then claim the right to close their borders. The Commerce Clause will protect New Jersey in the future, just as it protects her neighbors now, from efforts by one State to isolate itself in the stream of interstate commerce from a problem shared by all. The judgment is

Reversed.

MR. JUSTICE REHNQUIST, with whom THE CHIEF JUSTICE joins, dissenting.

A growing problem in our Nation is the sanitary treatment and disposal of solid waste. For many years, solid waste was incinerated. Because of the significant environmental problems attendant on incineration, however, this method of solid waste disposal has declined in use in many localities, including New Jersey. "Sanitary" landfills have replaced incineration as the principal method of disposing of solid waste. In ch. 363 of the 1973 N.J. Laws, the State of New Jersey legislatively recognized the unfortunate fact that landfills also present extremely serious health and safety problems. First, in New Jersey, "virtually all sanitary landfills can be expected to produce leachate, a noxious and highly polluted liquid which is seldom visible and frequently pollutes ... ground and surface waters." The natural decomposition process which occurs in landfills also produces large quantities of methane and thereby presents a significant explosion hazard. Landfills can also generate "health hazards caused by rodents, fires and scavenger birds" and, "needless to say, do not help New Jersey's aesthetic appearance nor New Jersey's noise or water or air pollution problems."

The health and safety hazards associated with landfills present appellees with a currently unsolvable dilemma. Other, hopefully safer, methods of disposing of solid wastes are still in the development stage and cannot presently be used. But appellees obviously cannot completely stop the tide of solid waste that its citizens will produce in the interim. For the moment, therefore, appellees must continue to use sanitary landfills to dispose of New Jersey's own solid waste despite the critical environmental problems thereby created.

The question presented in this case is whether New Jersey must also continue to receive and dispose of solid waste from neighboring States, even though these will inexorably increase the health problems discussed above. The Court answers this question in the affirmative. New Jersey must either prohibit *all* landfill operations, leaving itself to cast about for a presently nonexistent solution to the serious problem of disposing of the waste generated within its own borders, or it must accept waste from every portion of the United States, thereby multiplying the health and safety problems which would result if it dealt only with such wastes generated within the State. Because past precedents establish that the Commerce Clause does not present appellees with such a Hobson's choice, I dissent.

... The physical fact of life that New Jersey must somehow dispose of its own noxious items does not mean that it must serve as a depository for those of every other State. Similarly, New Jersey should be free under our past precedents to prohibit the importation of solid waste because of the health and safety problems that such waste poses to its citizens. The fact that New Jersey continues to, and indeed must continue to, dispose of its own solid waste does not mean that New Jersey may not prohibit the importation of even more solid waste into the State. I simply see no way to distinguish solid waste, on the record of this case, from germ-infected rags, diseased meat, and other noxious items.

....

Second, the Court implies that the challenged laws must be invalidated because New Jersey has left its landfills open to domestic waste. But, as the Court notes, *ante*, at 628, this Court has repeatedly upheld quarantine laws "even though they appear to single out interstate commerce for special treatment." The fact that New Jersey has left its landfill sites open for domestic waste does not, of course, mean that New Jersey prohibits importation of solid waste for reasons other than the health and safety of its population. New Jersey must out of sheer necessity treat and dispose of its solid waste in some fashion, just as it must treat New Jersey cattle suffering from hoof-and-mouth disease. It does not follow that New Jersey must, under the Commerce Clause, accept solid waste or diseased cattle from outside its borders and thereby exacerbate its problems.

....

OREGON WASTE SYSTEMS, INC. v. DEPARTMENT OF ENVIRONMENTAL QUALITY OF THE STATE OF OREGON

__U.S.__,114 S. Ct. 1345, 128 L. Ed. 2d 13,
38 ERC 1249 (1994)

JUSTICE THOMAS delivered the opinion of the Court.

Two Terms ago, in *Chemical Waste Management, Inc. v. Hunt*, 112 S.Ct. 2009 (1992), we held that the negative Commerce Clause prohibited Alabama from imposing a higher fee on the disposal in Alabama landfills of hazardous waste from other States than on the disposal of identical waste from Alabama. In reaching that conclusion, however, we left open the possibility that such a differential surcharge might be valid if based on the costs of disposing of waste from other States. Today, we must decide whether Oregon's purportedly cost-based surcharge on the in-state disposal of solid waste generated in other States violates the Commerce Clause.

Like other States, Oregon comprehensively regulates the disposal of solid wastes within its borders. Respondent Oregon Department of Environmental Quality oversees the State's regulatory scheme by developing and executing plans for the management, reduction, and recycling of solid wastes. To fund these and related activities, Oregon levies a wide range of fees on landfill operators. In 1989, the Oregon Legislature imposed an additional fee, called a "surcharge," on "every person who disposes of solid waste generated out-of-state in a disposal site or regional disposal site." § 459.297(1).The amount of that surcharge was left to respondent Environmental Quality Commission (Commission) to determine through rulemaking, but the legislature did require that the resulting surcharge "be based on the costs to the State of Oregon and its political subdivisions of disposing of solid waste generated out-of-state which are not otherwise paid for" under specified statutes. At the conclusion of the rulemaking process, the Commission set the surcharge on out-of-state waste at $2.25 per ton.

In conjunction with the out-of-state surcharge, the legislature imposed a fee on the in-state disposal of waste generated within Oregon. The in-state fee, capped by statute at $0.85 per ton (originally $0.50 per ton), is considerably lower than the fee imposed on waste from other States....

... Petitioners, Oregon Waste Systems, Inc. (Oregon Waste) and Columbia Resource Company (CRC), joined by Gilliam County, Oregon, sought expedited review of the out-of-state surcharge in the Oregon Court of Appeals. Oregon Waste owns and operates a solid waste landfill in Gilliam County, at which it accepts for final disposal solid waste generated in Oregon and in other States. CRC, pursuant to a 20-year contract with Clark County, in neighboring Washington State, transports solid waste via barge from Clark County to a landfill in Morrow County, Oregon. Petitioners challenged the administrative rule establishing the out-of-state surcharge and its enabling statutes under both state law and the Commerce Clause of the United States Constitution. The Oregon Court of Appeals upheld the statutes and rule.

The State Supreme Court affirmed. As to the Commerce Clause, the court recognized that the Oregon surcharge resembled the Alabama fee invalidated in *Chemical Waste Management, Inc. v. Hunt*, 112 S. Ct. 2009 (1992), in that both prescribed higher fees for the disposal of waste from other States. Nevertheless, the court viewed the similarity as superficial only. Despite the explicit reference in § 459.297(1) to out-of-state waste's geographic origin, the court reasoned, the

Oregon surcharge is not facially discriminatory "[b]ecause of [its] express nexus to actual costs incurred [by state and local government]." That nexus distinguished *Chemical Waste*, by rendering the surcharge a "compensatory fee," which the court viewed as "prima facie reasonable," that is to say, facially constitutional. The court read our case law as invalidating compensatory fees only if they are "'manifestly disproportionate to the services rendered.'"…

We granted certiorari, because the decision below conflicted with a recent decision of the United States Court of Appeals for the Seventh Circuit. We now reverse.

II

The Commerce Clause provides that "[t]he Congress shall have Power ... [t]o regulate Commerce ... among the several States." Art. I, § 8, cl. 3. Though phrased as a grant of regulatory power to Congress, the Clause has long been understood to have a "negative" aspect that denies the States the power unjustifiably to discriminate against or burden the interstate flow of articles of commerce....

[W]e have held that the first step in analyzing any law subject to judicial scrutiny under the negative Commerce Clause is to determine whether it "regulates evenhandedly with only 'incidental' effects on interstate commerce, or discriminates against interstate commerce." [Citations] As we use the term here, "discrimination" simply means differential treatment of in-state and out-of-state economic interests that benefits the former and burdens the latter. If a restriction on commerce is discriminatory, it is virtually per se invalid. [Citations] By contrast, nondiscriminatory regulations that have only incidental effects on interstate commerce are valid unless "the burden imposed on such commerce is clearly excessive in relation to the putative local benefits." *Pike v. Bruce Church, Inc.*, 90 S. Ct. 844, 847 (1970).

In *Chemical Waste*, we easily found Alabama's surcharge on hazardous waste from other States to be facially discriminatory because it imposed a higher fee on the disposal of out-of-state waste than on the disposal of identical in-state waste. We deem it equally obvious here that Oregon's $2.25 per ton surcharge is discriminatory on its face. The surcharge subjects waste from other States to a fee almost three times greater than the $0.85 per ton charge imposed on solid in-state waste. The statutory determinant for which fee applies to any particular shipment of solid waste to an Oregon landfill is whether or not the waste was "generated out-of-state." It is well-established, however, that a law is discriminatory if it "'tax[es] a transaction or incident more heavily when it crosses state lines than when it occurs entirely within the State.'" [Citations]

Respondents argue, and the Oregon Supreme Court held, that the statutory nexus between the surcharge and "the [otherwise uncompensated] costs to the State of Oregon and its political subdivisions of disposing of solid waste generated out-of-state," necessarily precludes a finding that the surcharge is discriminatory. We find respondents' narrow focus on Oregon's compensatory aim to be foreclosed by our precedents. As we reiterated in *Chemical Waste*, the purpose of, or justification for, a law has no bearing on whether it is facially discriminatory. [Citations] Consequently, even if the surcharge merely recoups the costs of disposing of out-of-state waste in Oregon, the fact remains that the differential charge favors shippers of Oregon waste over their counterparts handling waste generated in other States. In making that geographic distinction, the surcharge patently discriminates against interstate commerce.

III

Because the Oregon surcharge is discriminatory, the virtually per se rule of invalidity provides the proper legal standard here, not the *Pike* balancing test. As a result, the surcharge must be invalidated unless respondents can "sho[w] that it advances a legitimate local purpose that cannot be adequately served by reasonable nondiscriminatory alternatives." [Citations] Our cases require that justifications for discriminatory restrictions on commerce pass the "strictest scrutiny." The State's burden of justification is so heavy that "facial discrimination by itself may be a fatal defect." [Citations]

At the outset, we note two justifications that respondents have not presented. No claim has been made that the disposal of waste from other States imposes higher costs on Oregon and its political subdivisions than the disposal of in-state waste. Also, respondents have not offered any safety or health reason unique to nonhazardous waste from other States for discouraging the flow of such waste into Oregon. [Citation] Consequently, respondents must come forward with other legitimate reasons to subject waste from other States to a higher charge than is levied against waste from Oregon....

A

Respondents' principal defense of the higher surcharge on out-of-state waste is that it is a "compensatory tax" necessary to make shippers of such waste pay their "fair share" of the costs imposed on Oregon by the disposal of their waste in the State. In *Chemical Waste* we noted the possibility that such an argument might justify a discriminatory surcharge or tax on out-of-state waste. In making that observation, we implicitly recognized the settled principle that interstate commerce may be made to "'pay its way.'" [Citations] "It was not the purpose of the commerce clause to relieve those engaged in interstate commerce from their just share of state tax burden[s]." [Citations] Nevertheless, one of the central purposes of the Clause was to prevent States from "exacting more than a just share" from interstate commerce. [Citations]

At least since our decision in *Hinson v. Lott*, 8 Wall 148, 19 L. Ed. 387 (1868), these principles have found expression in the "compensatory" or "complementary" tax doctrine. Though our cases sometimes discuss the concept of the compensatory tax as if it were a doctrine unto itself, it is merely a specific way of justifying a facially discriminatory tax as achieving a legitimate local purpose that cannot be achieved through nondiscriminatory means. [Citation]

Under that doctrine, a facially discriminatory tax that imposes on interstate commerce the rough equivalent of an identifiable and "substantially similar" tax on intrastate commerce does not offend the negative Commerce Clause. [Citations]

To justify a charge on interstate commerce as a compensatory tax, a State must, as a threshold matter, "identif[y] ... the [intrastate tax] burden for which the State is attempting to compensate." Once that burden has been identified, the tax on interstate commerce must be shown roughly to approximate — but not exceed — the amount of the tax on intrastate commerce. [Citation] Finally, the events on which the interstate and intrastate taxes are imposed must be "substantially equivalent"; that is, they must be sufficiently similar in substance to serve as mutually exclusive "prox[ies]" for each other.

Although it is often no mean feat to determine whether a challenged tax is a compensatory tax, we have little difficulty concluding that the Oregon surcharge is not such a tax. Oregon does not impose a specific charge of at least $2.25 per ton on shippers of waste generated in Oregon, for which the out-of-state surcharge might be considered compensatory. In fact, the only analogous charge on the disposal of Oregon waste is $0.85 per ton, approximately one-third of the amount imposed on waste from other States. Respondents' failure to identify a specific charge on intrastate commerce equal to or exceeding the surcharge is fatal to their claim.

Respondents argue that, despite the absence of a specific $2.25 per ton charge on in-state waste, intrastate commerce does pay its share of the costs underlying the surcharge through general taxation. Whether or not that is true is difficult to determine, as "[general] tax payments are received for the general purposes of the [government], and are, upon proper receipt, lost in the general revenues." Even assuming, however, that various other means of general taxation, such as income taxes, could serve as an identifiable intrastate burden roughly equivalent to the out-of-state surcharge, respondents' compensatory tax argument fails because the in-state and out-of-state levies are not imposed on substantially equivalent events.

... Indeed, the very fact that in-state shippers of out-of-state waste, such as Oregon Waste, are charged the out-of-state surcharge even though they pay Oregon income taxes refutes respondents' argument that the respective taxable events are substantially equivalent. We conclude that, far from being substantially equivalent, taxes on earning income and utilizing Oregon landfills are "entirely different kind[s] of tax[es]."...

B

Respondents' final argument is that Oregon has an interest in spreading the costs of the in-state disposal of Oregon waste to all Oregonians. That is, because all citizens of Oregon benefit from the proper in-state disposal of waste from Oregon, respondents claim it is only proper for Oregon to require them to bear more of the costs of disposing of such waste in the State through a higher general tax burden. At the same time, however, Oregon citizens should not be required to bear the costs of disposing of out-of-state waste, respondents claim. The necessary result of that limited cost-shifting is to require shippers of out-of-state waste to bear the full costs of in-state disposal, but to permit shippers of Oregon waste to bear less than the full cost.

We fail to perceive any distinction between respondents' contention and a claim that the State has an interest in reducing the costs of handling in-state waste. Our cases condemn as illegitimate, however, any governmental interest that is not "unrelated to economic protectionism."... To give controlling effect to respondents' characterization of Oregon's tax scheme as seemingly benign cost-spreading would require us to overlook the fact that the scheme necessarily incorporates a protectionist objective as well. [Citation]

Respondents counter that if Oregon is engaged in any form of protectionism, it is "resource protectionism," not economic protectionism. It is true that by discouraging the flow of out-of-state waste into Oregon landfills, the higher surcharge on waste from other States conserves more space in those landfills for waste generated in Oregon.... Even assuming that landfill space is a "natural resource," "a State may not accord its own inhabitants a preferred right of access over consumers in other States to natural resources located within its borders." As we held more than a century ago, "if the State, under the guise of exerting its police powers, should [impose a burden] ... applicable solely to articles [of commerce] ... produced or manufactured in other States, the courts would find no difficulty in holding such legislation to be in conflict with the Constitution of the United States." [Citation]

IV

... Because respondents have offered no legitimate reason to subject waste generated in other States to a discriminatory surcharge approximately three times as high as that imposed on waste generated in Oregon, the surcharge is facially invalid under the negative Commerce Clause. Accordingly, the judgment of the Oregon Supreme Court is reversed, and the cases are remanded for further proceedings not inconsistent with this opinion.

NOTES AND QUESTIONS

1. In *Philadelphia*, the Court distinguished the New Jersey ban on importation of waste as an invalid protectionist measure from a narrow class of "quarantine" laws directed toward preventing unreasonable health risks. These laws may pass constitutional scrutiny despite facially discriminating against interstate commerce, because they are aimed at protecting public health, not economic protectionism. *See Clason v. Indiana*, 306 U.S. 439 (1939) (upholding state prohibition against the interstate transportation of dead animals to prevent the spread of disease). In *Maine v. Taylor*, 477 U.S. 131 (1986) the Court upheld a state law banning the shipment of live nonnative baitfish into the state. Maine claimed that importation

presented threats to its fisheries through exposure to parasites prevalent in nonnative baitfish, and also that the introduction of certain species could disturb its aquatic ecology. The Court found that ecological preservation constituted a legitimate purpose for the ban, and that no scientifically-acceptable alternatives existed which would have less discriminatory impacts on interstate commerce.

2. The Supreme Court has been quite active in considering negative Commerce Clause challenges to laws seeking to impose various restrictions on the transportation and disposal of hazardous waste within their borders. In *Chemical Waste Management, Inc. v. Hunt*, 504 U.S. 334, 112 S. Ct. 2009, 119 L. Ed. 2d 121 (1992), the Court held that an Alabama law which imposed an additional fee charged for the disposal of hazardous waste generated outside the state at a commercial landfill impermissibly burdened interstate commerce. The Court found that the differential fee both facially discriminated against waste generated outside the state and effectively discouraged the full operation of the facility. Further, the Court noted less discriminatory alternatives were available to meet the state's enunciated objective of protecting health and safety by limiting the volume of waste. The Court stated that the concerns of environmental conservation and health and safety of its citizens "does not vary with the point of origin of the waste."

In *C & A Carbone, Inc. v. Town of Clarkstown, N.Y.*, ___ U.S. ___, 114 S. Ct. 1677, 128 L. Ed. 2d 399 (1994), the Court invalidated on Commerce Clause grounds a municipal "flow control" ordinance which required all solid waste to be processed for a fee at a local transfer station. The Court found that the ordinance had a protectionist effect because it discriminated in favor of a single local proprietor. The purpose of ensuring that the town-sponsored facility would be financially profitable was not the sort of local interest that would justify the discrimination against interstate commerce.

3. Compare *Minnesota v. Clover Leaf Creamery*, 449 U.S. 456 (1981), which involved a challenge to the constitutionality of a state statute banning the sale of milk in plastic nonreturnable, nonrefillable containers, but permitting the sale in paperboard cartons. The stated purpose of the statute was to promote conservation and to ameliorate solid waste disposal problems. Out-of-state milk sellers claimed the statute in actuality was an economic protectionism measure designed to shift business to Minnesota dairy and pulpwood industries. The Court found that the statute did not violate the Commerce Clause because it regulated "even-handedly" and imposed only an incidental effect on interstate commerce. Do you agree? What difference would it make if evidence showed that the pulpwood containers were also nonreturnable and nonrefillable and that the likely substantial beneficiaries of the statute were local industries? The Court observed that the Commerce Clause focuses on protecting the interstate *market* from prohibitive or burdensome regulations, rather than specific businesses. Should the Court nevertheless consider a major shift in business from predominantly out-of-state industry to local industry as probative evidence of the burden of a regulation on interstate commerce?

Also see Evergreen Waste Sys. v. Metropolitan Serv. Dist., 820 F.2d 1482 (9th Cir. 1987), where a municipal ordinance barring disposal of out-of-district waste in its landfill survived a Commerce Clause challenge. The court reasoned that since the ordinance placed the same restrictions on most in-state waste sources as imposed on out-of-state sources, it was distinguishable from the overt economic protectionism found in *City of Philadelphia*. Further, the court determined that the burden on the interstate shipment of waste was minimal in relation to the local benefits since other landfills had available capacity. Do you agree with the court's analysis?

4. Congress, pursuant to the Commerce Clause, has the authority to permit states to impose regulatory burdens on interstate commerce in a manner that would otherwise not be allowable. *White v. Massachusetts Council of Constr. Employers*, 460 U.S. 204 (1983). Courts have been reluctant, however, to find Congressional consent to remove federal constitutional constraints on state laws affecting commerce absent express and "unmistakably clear" statements. *South-Central Timber Dev., Inc. v. Wunnicke*, 467 U.S. 82, 87-88 (1984); *Sporhase v. Nebraska*, 458 U.S. 941, 960 (1982) (Court declined to find Congressional authorization for state burdens on interstate commerce in groundwater despite thirty-seven federal statutes and various interstate compacts showing deference to state water law).

An interesting illustration of this issue in the context of CERCLA was presented in *National Solid Waste Mgt. Ass'n v. Alabama Dep't of Envtl. Mgt.*, 910 F.2d 713 (11th Cir. 1990). The state of Alabama sought to justify its statutory restrictions on accepting for disposal hazardous waste from out-of-state sources by pointing to requirements imposed on states by CERCLA. In particular, section 104(c)(9) [42 U.S.C. § 9604(c)(9)] of CERCLA required states to demonstrate an adequate capacity to dispose of hazardous waste generated in the state for twenty years as a condition to receiving certain federal funds. The court held that CERCLA's provisions did not authorize states to close their borders to the shipment of hazardous waste, finding that alternatives existed to meet the capacity requirements.

5. How should states respond to the dilemma of providing sufficient disposal sites to handle waste produced by its own residents if precluded from excluding waste generated by out-of-state sources? Evidence introduced in *National Solid Waste Management* showed that Alabama industries shipped about 57,000 tons of hazardous waste outside the state for management, but imported approximately 500,000 tons of such waste for treatment and disposal, causing its Governor to lament that it was "becoming the waste dump of the nation." 910 F.2d at 717 n.6. Should Congress enact comprehensive legislation to address the Commerce Clause problems presented by hazardous waste disposal? If so, what sort of policy considerations and practical hurdles would be implicated?

6. For additional commentary on the limitations of Commerce Clause on state regulations affecting shipment and disposal of waste, see the following references: NOWAK & ROTUNDA, CONSTITUTIONAL LAW §§ 8.1-8.11 (4th ed.

1991); Farber, *State Regulation and the Dormant Commerce Clause*, 3 CONST. COMM. 395 (1986); Stone, *Supremacy and the Commerce Clause Issues Regarding State Hazardous Waste Import Bans*, 15 COLUM. J. ENVTL. L. 1 (1990); Sunstein, *Naked Preferences*, 84 COLUM. L. REV. 1689 (1984); Tarlock, *National Power, State Sovereignty and Federalism in the 1980's: Scaling America's Magic Mountain*, 32 U. KAN. L. REV. 111 (1983); Eule, *Laying the Dormant Commerce Clause to Rest*, 91 YALE L.J. 425 (1982); Maltz, *How Much Regulation Is Too Much — An Examination of Commerce Clause Jurisprudence*, 50 GEO. WASH. L. REV. 47 (1981); Tushnet, *Rethinking the Dormant Commerce Clause*, 1979 WIS. L. REV. 125.

HUGHES v. ALEXANDRIA SCRAP CORP.
426 U.S. 794 (1976)

MR. JUSTICE POWELL delivered the opinion of the Court.

[Maryland, in response to growing aesthetic problem of old abandoned automobiles, enacted a statute designed to accelerate the scrap cycle. The statute provided certain financial incentives or "bounties" to licensed scrap processors for the destruction of abandoned autos ("hulks"). The State subsequently amended its statute and required more extensive documentation from out-of-state scrap processors than those located in Maryland as a condition to collect payment. A scrap processor located in Virginia ("Appellee") challenged the constitutionality of the Maryland plan, claiming that it placed an impermissible burden on interstate commerce in contravention of the Commerce Clause.]

[Appellee's] argument starts from the premise, well established by the history of the Commerce Clause, that this Nation is a common market in which state lines cannot be made barriers to the free flow of both raw materials and finished goods in response to the economic laws of supply and demand. [Citation.] Appellee concedes that until the 1974 amendment the Maryland system operated in conformity with the common-market principle. There was free competition among licensed processors for Maryland hulks from unlicensed suppliers and an unimpeded flow of such hulks out of Maryland to appellee and other non-Maryland processors. The only effect of the bounty was to enhance the value of hulks and thus make it more likely that they would be moved to processing plants.

The practical effect of the amendment, however, was to limit the enhanced price available to unlicensed suppliers to hulks that stayed inside Maryland, thus discouraging such suppliers from taking their hulks out of State for processing. The result was that the movement of hulks in interstate commerce was reduced. Appellee contends that this effect of the 1974 amendment is a "burden" on interstate commerce, the permissibility of which must be determined under the test of *Pike v. Bruce Church, Inc.*, 397 U.S. 137, 142 (1970). The Court there stated that "the extent of the burden that will be tolerated will ... depend on the nature of the local interest involved, and on whether it could be promoted as well with a lesser impact on interstate activities."

The District Court accepted appellee's analysis, and concluded that the 1974 amendment failed the *Pike* test. First, the court found that the amendment did impose "substantial burdens upon the free flow of interstate commerce." Moreover, it considered the disadvantage suffered by out-of-state processors to be particularly suspect under previous decisions of this Court, noting that to avoid the disadvantage those processors would have to build new plants inside Maryland to carry on a business which, prior to the amendment, they had pursued efficiently outside the State. [Citations.] Maryland's principal argument in support of the amendment was that, by making it difficult for out-of-state processors to claim bounties on hulks delivered by unlicensed suppliers, the amendment tends to reduce the amount of state funds paid for destruction of Maryland-titled hulks abandoned in the States where those processors are located instead of in Maryland. The District Court acknowledged the validity of this interest, but considered the means employed inappropriate under *Pike* because the same interest could have been furthered, with less impact upon interstate commerce, by amending the statute to condition the bounty upon a hulk's abandonment in Maryland instead of its previous titling there.

This line of reasoning is not without force if its basic premise is accepted. That premise is that every action by a State that has the effect of reducing in some manner the flow of goods in interstate commerce is potentially an impermissible burden. But we are not persuaded that Maryland's action in amending its statute was the kind of action with which the Commerce Clause is concerned.

The situation presented by this statute and the 1974 amendment is quite unlike that found in the cases upon which appellee relies. In the most recent of those cases, *Pike v. Bruce Church*, a burden was found to be imposed by an Arizona requirement that fresh fruit grown in the State be packed there before shipment interstate. The requirement prohibited the interstate shipment of fruit in bulk, no matter what the market demand for such shipments. In *H. P. Hood & Sons v. Du Mond*, 336 U.S. 525 (1949), a New York official denied a license to a milk distributor who wanted to open a new plant at which to receive raw milk from New York farmers for immediate shipment to Boston. The denial blocked a potential increase in the interstate movement of raw milk. Appellee also relies upon *Toomer v. Witsell*, 334 U.S. 385 (1948), in which this Court found interstate commerce in raw shrimp to be burdened by a South Carolina requirement that shrimp boats fishing off its coast dock in South Carolina and pack and pay taxes on their catches before transporting them interstate. The requirement increased the cost of shipping such shrimp interstate....

The common thread of all these cases is that the State interfered with the natural functioning of the interstate market either through prohibition or through burdensome regulation. By contrast, Maryland has not sought to prohibit the flow of hulks, or to regulate the conditions under which it may occur. Instead, it has entered into the market itself to bid up their price. There has been an impact upon the interstate flow of hulks only because, since the 1974 amendment, Maryland effectively has made it more lucrative for unlicensed suppliers to dispose of their hulks in Maryland rather than take them outside the State.

....

We believe, however, that the novelty of this case is not its presentation of a new form of "burden" upon commerce, but that appellee should characterize Maryland's action as a burden which the Commerce Clause was intended to make suspect. The Clause was designed in part to prevent trade barriers that had undermined efforts of the fledgling States to form a cohesive whole following their victory in the Revolution. This aspect of the Clause's purpose was eloquently expressed by Mr. Justice Jackson:

> "Our system, fostered by the Commerce Clause, is that every farmer and every craftsman shall be encouraged to produce by the certainty that he will have free access to every market in the Nation, that no home embargoes will withhold his exports, and no foreign state will by customs duties or regulations exclude them. Likewise, every consumer may look to the free competition from every producing area in the Nation to protect him from exploitation by any. Such was the vision of the Founders; such has been the doctrine of this Court which has given it reality...." [Citation.]

In realizing the Founders' vision this Court has adhered strictly to the principle "that the right to engage in interstate commerce is not the gift of a state, and that a state cannot regulate or restrain it." But until today the Court has not been asked to hold that the entry by the State itself into the market as a purchaser, in effect, of a potential article of interstate commerce creates a burden upon that commerce if the State restricts its trade to its own citizens or businesses within the State.

We do not believe the Commerce Clause was intended to require independent justification for such action. Maryland entered the market for the purpose, agreed by all to be commendable as well as legitimate, of protecting the State's environment. As the means of furthering this purpose, it elected the payment of state funds — in the form of bounties — to encourage the removal of automobile hulks from Maryland streets and junkyards. It is true that the state money initially was made available to licensed out-of-state processors as well as those located within Maryland, and not until the 1974 amendment was the financial benefit channeled, in practical effect, to domestic processors. But this chronology does not distinguish the case, for Commerce Clause purposes, from one in which a State offered bounties only to domestic processors from the start. Regardless of when the State's largesse is first confined to domestic processors, the effect upon the flow of hulks resting within the State is the same: they will tend to be processed inside the State rather than flowing to foreign processors. But no trade barrier of the type forbidden by the Commerce Clause, and involved in previous cases, impedes their movement out of State. They remain within Maryland in response to market forces, including that exerted by money from the State.

Nothing in the purposes animating the Commerce Clause prohibits a State, in the absence of congressional action, from participating in the market and exercising the right to favor its own citizens over others.[20]

....

[Reversed.]

MR. JUSTICE STEVENS concurring.

....

It is important to differentiate between commerce which flourishes in a free market and commerce which owes its existence to a state subsidy program. Our cases finding that a state regulation constitutes an impermissible burden on interstate commerce all dealt with restrictions that adversely affected the operation of a free market. This case is unique because the commerce which Maryland has "burdened" is commerce which would not exist if Maryland had not decided to subsidize a portion of the automobile scrap-processing business.

By artificially enhancing the value of certain abandoned hulks, Maryland created a market that did not previously exist. The program which Maryland initiated in 1969 included subsidies for scrapping plants located in Virginia and Pennsylvania as well as for plants located in Maryland. Those subsidies stimulated the movement of abandoned hulks from Maryland to out-of-state scrapping plants and thereby gave rise to the interstate commerce which is at stake in this litigation.

That commerce, which is now said to be burdened, would never have existed if in the first instance Maryland had decided to confine its subsidy to operators of Maryland plants. A failure to create that commerce would have been unobjectionable because the Commerce Clause surely does not impose on the States any obligation to subsidize out-of-state business. Nor, in my judgment, does that Clause inhibit a State's power to experiment with different methods of encouraging local industry. Whether the encouragement takes the form of a cash subsidy, a tax credit, or a special privilege intended to attract investment capital, it should not be characterized as a "burden" on commerce....

MR. JUSTICE BRENNAN, with whom MR. JUSTICE WHITE and MR. JUSTICE MARSHALL join, dissenting.

....

I first address the question that the Court answers: the question whether a State may restrict its purchases of items of interstate commerce to items produced, manufactured, or processed within its own boundaries. When a State so restricts

---

[20]Appellee and the other licensed non-Maryland processors are free to withdraw from the bounty program should they decide that the benefits they receive from it after the 1974 amendment do not justify the annual license fee. They are not in the position of a foreign business which enters a State in response to completely private market forces to compete with domestic businesses, only to find itself burdened with discriminatory taxes or regulations. [Citations.]

purchases for its own use, it does not affect the total flow of interstate commerce, but rather precludes only that quantum that would otherwise occur if the State were to behave as a private and disinterested purchaser. Nevertheless, it cannot be gainsaid that a State's refusal for purposes of economic protectionism to purchase for end use items produced elsewhere is a facial and obvious "discrimination against interstate commerce" that we have often said "[t]he commerce clause, by its own force, prohibits ..., whatever its form or method." [Citations.] Clearly the "aim and effect" of such a discrimination is "establishing an economic barrier against competition with the products of another state or the labor of its residents." [Citation.]....

Moreover, the particular form of discrimination arising when the State restricts its purchases for use to items produced in its own State is of a kind particularly suspect under our precedents, as it is aimed directly at requiring the relocation of labor and industry within the bounds of the State, thus tending "to neutralize advantages belonging to" other States, and forcing "an artificial rigidity on the economic pattern of the industry." [Citations.] We have "viewed with particular suspicion state statutes requiring business operations to be performed in the home State that could more efficiently be performed elsewhere. *Even where the State is pursuing a clearly legitimate local interest, this particular burden on commerce has been declared to be virtually per se illegal.*" *Pike v. Bruce Church, Inc.*, 397 U.S., at 145. (emphasis supplied). And we have never held protection of a State's own citizens from the burden of economic competition with citizens of other States to be such a "clearly legitimate local interest."...

It is true, as the Court notes, that we have not previously directly addressed the question whether, when a State enters the market as purchaser for end use of items in interstate commerce, it may "[restrict] its trade to its own citizens or businesses within the State." The novelty of the question, however, does not justify the Court's conclusory assertion, without analysis employing established constitutional principles or policies, that "[n]othing in the purposes animating the Commerce Clause prohibits a State ... from participating in the market and exercising the right to favor its own citizens over others." Certainly the Court does not attempt to tell us the source of any such "right."...

I would hold, consistent with accepted Commerce Clause principles, that state statutes that facially or in practical effect restrict state purchases of items in interstate commerce to those produced within the State are invalid unless justified by asserted state interests — other than economic protectionism — in regulating matters of local concern for which "reasonable nondiscriminatory alternatives, adequate to conserve legitimate local interests, are [not] available." [Citations.]

Second, the Court's insistence on viewing this case as qualitatively different under the Commerce Clause merely because the State is in some sense acting as a "purchaser" of the affected items of commerce leads it completely to forgo analysis of another equally vital question. For even those courts and commentators that have concluded that facially restrictive state purchasing statutes are permissible under the Commerce Clause have restricted this conclusion to instances where the State in a "proprietary" capacity is purchasing items of commerce for end use, and have distinguished other modes of regulation burdening interstate commerce. But it is clear that Maryland in the instant case is not "purchasing" scrap processing for end use; rather, by in effect requiring "price enhanced" hulks to be processed within the State of Maryland, it is affecting one link in the chain of interstate commerce that originates prior to Maryland's regulation and continues long past that point. Even if, as the Court concludes, state economic protectionism in "purchasing" items of interstate commerce is not a suspect motive under the Commerce Clause, analysis in this case cannot cease at that point, for by the instant regulation Maryland is allegedly affecting a larger area of commerce by diverting processing of scrap metal in interstate commerce to its own boundaries....

NOTES AND QUESTIONS

1. The Supreme Court, following *Alexandria Scrap*, has had several occasions to consider the market participant doctrine with respect to environmental laws. In *Reeves, Inc. v. Stake*, 447 U.S. 429 (1980) the Court upheld a South Dakota policy of selling cement produced by a state-owned plant to its own residents in preference to out-of-state customers during a cement shortage. The Court characterized the state actions as fitting within the market participant exception to Commerce Clause restrictions, finding no constitutional limitation on states "to operate freely in the free market." The Court drew support for its holding from considerations of state sovereignty acting as trustee for its residents as well as the historical tradition recognizing the right of a business to choose the parties with whom they will deal. 447 U.S. at 438-39.

Several years after *Reeves*, the Court again examined the market participant doctrine in *South-Central Timber Dev., Inc. v. Wunnicke*, 467 U.S. 82 (1984). In *Wunnicke*, a plurality of the Court found that Alaska's requirement that timber taken from state-owned lands be partially processed within the state prior to export. Alaska's program involved charging a significantly lower price for its timber in order to spur development of local industries. The Court found that the state plan failed to comport with the market participant doctrine because of the restrictions on resale:

> The limit of the market-participant doctrine must be that it allows a State to impose burdens on commerce within the market in which it is a participant, but allows it to go no further. The State may not impose conditions, whether by statute, regulation, or contract, that have a substantial regulatory effect outside of that particular market. Unless the "market" is relatively narrowly defined, the doctrine has the potential of swallowing up the rule that States may not impose substantial burdens on interstate commerce even if they act with the permissible state purpose of fostering local industry.

467 U.S. at 97-98. Additionally, the Alaska processing requirement placed a burden on foreign commerce, as some of the purchasers shipped some of the logs to Japan and other countries. The Court observed that state burdens on foreign commerce were subject to a heightened scrutiny because of the potential for interference with federal government programs and negotiations with other countries.

The market participant doctrine, although criticized and its contours unsettled, retains vitality. In *Swin Resource Sys. v. Lycoming County*, 883 F.2d 245 (3d Cir. 1989) a county operated landfill charged a higher rate and limited the volume of waste generated outside the area than for the reception and disposal of waste generated locally. The court upheld the preference given to county residents in the use of the landfill, finding that the county had acted as a market participant rather than as a market regulator. The court found it significant that the county's price and volume conditions did not affect downstream markets nor pertain to the operation of private landfills. Should a state or subdivision be allowed to give preferential treatment to local garbage when a shortage of disposal sites makes landfills scarce? *See generally* Seamon, *The Market Participation Test in Dormant Commerce Clause Analysis — Protecting Protectionism*, 1985 DUKE L.J. 696 (1985).

2. Should a state be permitted to establish a preference system for its residents with respect to allocation and distribution of state-owned natural resources? Does a state's policy favoring its citizens constitute a form of welfare consistent with the market participant doctrine or an impermissible protection of local economic interests which runs afoul of the Commerce Clause? Should a state be allowed to favor its residents with the benefits of minerals, water, and other resources which may be plentiful in one state and not another?

The Supreme Court has not squarely addressed the issue of applicability of the market participant doctrine with respect to natural resources. In *Reeves* the Court suggested that the Commerce Clause limited the ability of states to "hoard" resources which "by happenstance" were found there. The Court carefully noted, however, that such limits were not at issue because cement was an end-use product, not a natural resource. 447 U.S. at 444. In *Sporhase v. Nebraska*, 458 U.S. 941 (1982) the Court upheld most of a state's program to control the sale of groundwater as justifiable conservation efforts rather than protectionism. The Court, following *Reeves*, observed that the continuing availability of groundwater in the state was "not simply happenstance; the natural resource has some indicia of a good publicly produced and owned in which a State may favor its own citizens in times of shortage." 458 U.S. at 957. The Court continued that theme in *Wunnicke* by noting that one of the distinguishing features of the Alaska program which precluded reliance on the market participant doctrine was that natural resources were involved. *But see Swin Resource Sys. v. Lycoming County*, 883 F.2d 245, 252 (3d Cir. 1989) (State conduct restricting access to its natural resources considered consistent with theoretical foundation of market participant doctrine).

Also see Hughes v. Oklahoma, 441 U.S. 322 (1979) where the Court struck down a state statute which prohibited the exportation of minnows for sale outside the state. The Court rejected an exception to traditional Commerce Clause analysis based on a theory of "ownership" or "title" to resources; reasoning instead that the state must exercise its police power over such resources in a nondiscriminatory manner. *But see Baldwin v. Fish & Game Comm'n of Mont.*, 436 U.S. 371, 389-90 (1978) (Montana law charging residents a lower fee than nonresidents for hunting licenses held justified under privileges and immunities clause and equal protection because bore reasonable relation to substantial regulatory interest of state in preservation of wildlife — a finite resource).

For additional references regarding Commerce Clause implications of state conduct respecting its natural resources see NOWAK & ROTUNDA, CONSTITU-TIONAL LAW § 8.9 (4th ed. 1991); Anson & Schenkkan, *Federalism, The Dormant Commerce Clause, and State-Owned Resources*, 59 TEX. L. REV. 71 (1980); Gergen, *The Selfish State and the Market*, 66 TEX. L. REV. 1097 (1988); Note, *The Commerce Clause and Federalism: Implications for State Control of Natural Resources*, 50 GEO. WASH. L. REV. 601 (1982).

B. PREEMPTION OF COMMON LAW REMEDIES

There are three ways in which common law remedies for environmental harm may be preempted. A state statute may preempt state common law, a federal statute may preempt federal common law, and a federal statute may preempt state common law. The first type of preemption is rare; ordinarily, as a matter of state law, courts will find that the state legislature expressly or impliedly preserved common law remedies. Of the two cases which follow, *Milwaukee II* evaluates a federal statute's preemptive effect on federal common law, and *International Paper* evaluates a federal statute's preemptive effect on state common law.

Six months before passage of the 1972 Federal Water Pollution Control Act (FWPCA), a unanimous Supreme Court recognized application of federal common law to interstate water pollution because of the unique federal interests implicated by use of interstate waters and the hazards of subjecting such waters to a multiplicity of state laws. *Illinois v. City of Milwaukee*, 406 U.S. 91 (1972). On remand, the district court and court of appeals required the defendant to meet more stringent discharge limitations than the FWPCA required. *See Illinois v. City of Milwaukee*, 599 F.2d 151 (7th Cir. 1979). The case once again reached the Supreme Court in the following decision.

CITY OF MILWAUKEE v. ILLINOIS AND MICHIGAN
451 U.S. 304 (1981)

JUSTICE REHNQUIST delivered the opinion of the Court.

When this litigation was first before us we recognized the existence of a federal "common law" which could give rise to a claim for abatement of a nuisance caused by interstate water pollution. *Illinois v. Milwaukee*, 406 U.S. 91 (1972). Subsequent to our decision, Congress enacted the Federal Water Pollution Control Act Amendments of 1972. We granted certiorari to consider the effect of this legislation on the previously recognized cause of action.

Petitioners, the city of Milwaukee, the Sewerage Commission of the city of Milwaukee, and the Metropolitan Sewerage Commission of the County of Milwaukee, are municipal corporations organized under the laws of Wisconsin. Together they construct, operate, and maintain sewer facilities serving Milwaukee County, an area of some 420 square miles with a population of over one million people. The facilities consist of a series of sewer systems and two sewage treatment plants located on the shores of Lake Michigan 25 and 39 miles from the Illinois border, respectively. The sewer systems are of both the "separated" and "combined" variety. A separated sewer system carries only sewage for treatment; a combined sewer system gathers both sewage and storm water runoff and transports them in the same conduits for treatment. On occasion, particularly after a spell of wet weather, overflows occur in the system which result in the discharge of sewage directly into Lake Michigan or tributaries leading into Lake Michigan. The overflows occur at discrete discharge points throughout the system.

Respondent Illinois complains that these discharges, as well as the inadequate treatment of sewage at the two treatment plants, constitute a threat to the health of its citizens. Pathogens, disease-causing viruses and bacteria, are allegedly discharged into the lake with the overflows and inadequately treated sewage and then transported by lake currents to Illinois waters. Illinois also alleges that nutrients in the sewage accelerate the eutrophication, or aging, of the lake....

....

Federal courts, unlike state courts, are not general common-law courts and do not possess a general power to develop and apply their own rules of decision. *Erie R. Co. v. Tompkins*, 304 U.S. 64, 78 (1938). The enactment of a federal rule in an area of national concern, and the decision whether to displace state law in doing so, is generally made not by the federal judiciary, purposefully insulated from democratic pressures, but by the people through their elected representatives in Congress....

When Congress has not spoken to a particular issue, however, and when there exists a "significant conflict between some federal policy or interest and the use of state law,"[7] [citation] the Court has found it necessary, in a "few and restricted" instances, [citation] to develop federal common law. [Citation.] Nothing in this process suggests that courts are better suited to develop national policy in areas governed by federal common law than they are in other areas, or

---

[7]In this regard we note the inconsistency in Illinois' argument and the decision of the District Court that both federal and state nuisance law apply to this case. If state law can be applied, there is no need for federal common law; if federal common law exists, it is because state law cannot be used.

that the usual and important concerns of an appropriate division of functions between the Congress and the federal judiciary are inapplicable. [Citation.] We have always recognized that federal common law is "subject to the paramount authority of Congress." [Citation.] It is resorted to "[i]n absence of an applicable Act of Congress," [citation] and because the Court is compelled to consider federal questions "which cannot be answered from federal statutes alone."...

Contrary to the suggestions of respondents, the appropriate analysis in determining if federal statutory law governs a question previously the subject of federal common law is not the same as that employed in deciding if federal law pre-empts state law. In considering the latter question "'we start with the assumption that the historic police powers of the States were not to be superseded by the Federal Act unless that was the clear and manifest purpose of Congress.'" [Citation.] While we have not hesitated to find pre-emption of state law, whether express or implied, when Congress has so indicated, [citation], or when enforcement of state regulations would impair "federal superintendence of the field," [citation], our analysis has included "due regard for the presuppositions of our embracing federal system, including the principle of diffusion of power not as a matter of doctrinaire localism but as a promoter of democracy." [Citation.] Such concerns are not implicated in the same fashion when the question is whether federal statutory or federal common law governs, and accordingly the same sort of evidence of a clear and manifest purpose is not required. Indeed, as noted, in cases such as the present "we start with the assumption" that it is for Congress, not federal courts, to articulate the appropriate standards to be applied as a matter of federal law.[9]

We conclude that, at least so far as concerns the claims of respondents, Congress has not left the formulation of appropriate federal standards to the courts through application of often vague and indeterminate nuisance concepts and maxims of equity jurisprudence, but rather has occupied the field through the establishment of a comprehensive regulatory program supervised by an expert administrative agency. The 1972 Amendments to the Federal Water Pollution Control Act were not merely another law "touching interstate waters" of the sort surveyed in *Illinois v. Milwaukee*, 406 U.S., at 101-103, and found inadequate to supplant federal common law. Rather, the Amendments were viewed by Congress as a "total restructuring" and "complete rewriting" of the existing water pollution legislation considered in that case. [Citation.] Congress' intent in enacting the Amendments was clearly to establish an all-encompassing program of water pollution regulation. Every point source discharge is prohibited unless

---

[9]Since the States are represented in Congress but not in the federal courts, the very concerns about displacing state law which counsel against finding pre-emption of state law in the absence of clear intent actually suggest a willingness to find congressional displacement of federal common law. Simply because the opinion in *Illinois v. Milwaukee* used the term "pre-emption," usually employed in determining if federal law displaces state law, is no reason to assume the analysis used to decide the usual federal-state questions is appropriate here.

covered by a permit, which directly subjects the discharger to the administrative apparatus established by Congress to achieve its goals. The "major purpose" of the Amendments was "to establish a *comprehensive* long-range policy for the elimination of water pollution."... The establishment of such a self-consciously comprehensive program by Congress, which certainly did not exist when *Illinois v. Milwaukee* was decided, strongly suggests that there is no room for courts to attempt to improve on that program with federal common law.[14]

....

It is also significant that Congress addressed in the 1972 Amendments one of the major concerns underlying the recognition of federal common law in *Illinois v. Milwaukee*. We were concerned in that case that Illinois did not have any forum in which to protect its interests unless federal common law were created. [Citation.] In the 1972 Amendments Congress provided ample opportunity for a State affected by decisions of a neighboring State's permit-granting agency to seek redress. Under § 402(b)(3), 33 U.S.C. § 1342(b)(3), a state permit-granting agency must ensure that any State whose waters may be affected by the issuance of a permit receives notice of the permit application and the opportunity to participate in a public hearing. Wisconsin law accordingly guarantees such notice and hearing. Respondents received notice of each of the permits involved here, and public hearings were held, but they did not participate in them in any way. Section 402(b)(5), 33 U.S.C. § 1342(b)(5), provides that state permit-granting agencies must ensure that affected States have an opportunity to submit written recommendations concerning the permit applications to the issuing State and the EPA, and both the affected State and the EPA must receive notice and a statement of reasons if any part of the recommendations of the affected State are not accepted. Again respondents did not avail themselves of this statutory opportunity. Under § 402(d)(2)(A), 33 U.S.C. § 1342(d)(2)(A), the EPA may veto any permit issued by a State when waters of another State may be affected. Respondents did not request such action. Under § 402(d)(4) of the Act, 33 U.S.C. § 1342(d)(4), added in 1977, the EPA itself may issue permits if a stalemate between an issuing and objecting State develops. The basic grievance of respondents is that the permits issued to petitioners pursuant to the Act do not impose stringent enough controls on petitioners' discharges. The statutory scheme

---

[14]This conclusion is not undermined by Congress' decision to permit States to establish more stringent standards, see § 510, 33 U.S.C. § 1370. While Congress recognized a role for the States, the comprehensive nature of its action suggests that it was the exclusive source of *federal* law. Cases recognizing that the comprehensive character of a federal program is an insufficient basis to find pre-emption of state law are not in point, since we are considering which branch of the Federal Government is the source of federal law, not whether that law pre-empts state law. Since federal courts create federal common law only as a necessary expedient when problems requiring federal answers are not addressed by federal statutory law, the comprehensive character of a federal statute is quite relevant to the present question, while it would not be were the question whether state law, which of course does not depend upon the absence of an applicable Act of Congress, still applied.

established by Congress provides a forum for the pursuit of such claims before expert agencies by means of the permit-granting process. It would be quite inconsistent with this scheme if federal courts were in effect to "write their own ticket" under the guise of federal common law after permits have already been issued and permittees have been planning and operating in reliance on them.

Respondents argue that congressional intent to preserve the federal common-law remedy recognized in *Illinois v. Milwaukee* is evident in §§ 510 and 505(e) of the statute, 33 U.S.C. §§ 1370, 1365(e). Section 510 provides that nothing in the Act shall preclude States from adopting and enforcing limitations on the discharge of pollutants more stringent than those adopted under the Act. It is one thing, however, to say that States may adopt more stringent limitations through state administrative processes, or even that States may establish such limitations through state nuisance law, and apply them to in-state dischargers. It is quite another to say that the States may call upon *federal* courts to employ *federal* common law to establish more stringent standards applicable to out-of-state dischargers. Any standards established under federal common law are federal standards, and so the authority of States to impose more stringent standards under § 510 would not seem relevant. Section 510 clearly contemplates state authority to establish more stringent pollution limitations; nothing in it, however, suggests that this was to be done by federal-court actions premised on federal common law.

Subsection 505 (e) provides:

> "Nothing *in this section* shall restrict any right which any person (or class of persons) may have under any statute or common law to seek enforcement of any effluent standard or limitation or to seek any other relief (including relief against the Administrator or a State agency)" (emphasis supplied).

Respondents argue that this evinces an intent to preserve the federal common law of nuisance. We, however, are inclined to view the quoted provision as meaning what it says: that nothing in § 505, the citizen-suit provision, should be read as limiting any other remedies which might exist.

Subsection 505(e) is virtually identical to subsections in the citizen-suit provisions of several environmental statutes. The subsection is common language accompanying citizen-suit provisions and we think that it means only that the provision of such suit does not revoke other remedies. It most assuredly cannot be read to mean that the Act as a whole does not supplant formerly available federal common-law actions but only that the particular section authorizing citizen suits does not do so. No one, however, maintains that the citizen-suit provision pre-empts federal common law.

We are thus not persuaded that § 505(e) aids respondents in this case, even indulging the unlikely assumption that the reference to "common law" in § 505(e) includes the limited *federal* common law as opposed to the more routine state common law.

....

JUSTICE BLACKMUN, with whom JUSTICE MARSHALL and JUSTICE STEVENS join, dissenting.

....

The Court's analysis of federal common-law displacement rests, I am convinced, on a faulty assumption. In contrasting congressional displacement of the common law with federal pre-emption of state law, the Court assumes that as soon as Congress "addresses a question previously governed" by federal common law, "the need for such an unusual exercise of lawmaking by federal courts disappears." This "automatic displacement" approach is inadequate in two respects. It fails to reflect the unique role federal common law plays in resolving disputes between one State and the citizens or government of another. In addition, it ignores this Court's frequent recognition that federal common law may complement congressional action in the fulfillment of federal policies.

....

In my view, the language and structure of the Clean Water Act leave no doubt that Congress intended to preserve the federal common law of nuisance. Section 505(e) of the Act reads:

> "Nothing in this section shall restrict any right which *any person* (or class of persons) may have under *any statute or common law* to seek enforcement of any effluent standard or limitation *or to seek any other relief* (including relief against the Administrator or a State agency)." 33 U.S.C. § 1365(e) (emphasis added).

The Act specifically defines "person" to include States, and thus embraces respondents Illinois and Michigan. § 502(5), 33 U.S.C. § 1362(5). It preserves their right to bring an action against the governmental entities who are charged with enforcing the statute. Most important, as succinctly stated by the Court of Appeals in this case: "There is nothing in the phrase 'any statute or common law' that suggests that this provision is limited to state common law." 599 F.2d, at 163. To the best of my knowledge, every federal court that has considered the issue has concluded that, in enacting § 505(e), Congress meant to preserve federal as well as state common law.

....

NOTES AND QUESTIONS

1. Do you agree with the Court's reading of section 505(e)? How intrusive would preservation of the federal common law have been? Or, to put it another way, how often would a source complying with the FWPCA be found in violation of federal common law? If you agree that Congress did intend with the FWPCA to preempt federal common law, how broad is that preemption? Would the federal common law be preempted for discharges that violate the Act? *See Middlesex County Sewerage Auth. v. National Sea Clammers Ass'n*, 453 U.S. 1 (1981) (yes); *see also Connor v. Aerovox, Inc.*, 730 F.2d 835 (1st Cir. 1984), *cert. denied*, 470 U.S. 1050 (1985) (holding that federal maritime law is preempted by the FWPCA). Would it be preempted for interstate pollution caused by nonpoint sources?

2. Why would a plaintiff want to bring a common law claim, state or federal? What remedies would be available that would not be under a citizen suit? In footnote 7, the Court concludes that if state law can be applied, there is no need for federal common law. Can you think of any reason why there might be a need for federal common law with interstate pollution even if state common law is applicable?

3. What remedies are available under the FWPCA for interstate water pollution? See pages 595-611 *infra*. What remedies are available under the Clean Air Act for interstate air pollution? See pages 439-45 *infra*. Is the federal common law preempted for air pollution by the Clean Air Act as well? *See United States v. Kin-Buc, Inc.*, 532 F. Supp. 699 (D.N.J. 1982) (holding there is preemption); *see also New England Legal Found. v. Costle*, 666 F.2d 30 (2d Cir. 1981) (discusses the issue without conclusion).

In *National Audubon Soc'y v. Department of Water*, 869 F.2d 1196 (9th Cir. 1988), the National Audubon Society sued the Los Angeles Department of Water to enjoin further diversion of water from Mono Lake, a lake wholly situated within California. The plaintiff asserted that the diversions were causing *interstate air pollution* because the exposed lake bed created dust storms that were carried into Nevada. The Ninth Circuit Court of Appeals avoided the preemption issue by holding that the dispute was not one to which the federal common law would apply:

> It appears that the [Supreme] Court considers only those interstate controversies which involve a state suing sources outside of its own territory because they are causing pollution within the state to be inappropriate for state law to control, and therefore subject to resolution according to federal common law.

Id. at 1205. Federal common law continues to be important in a number of other environmental law areas, as with the "common law" of the National Environmental Policy Act, discussed on pages 240-42 *infra*, and liability for hazardous waste under the Comprehensive Environmental Response, Compensation and Liability Act (CERCLA or Superfund), discussed on pages 749-50 *infra*.

4. On remand, the Seventh Circuit Court of Appeals held that Illinois nuisance law could not be applied to the Wisconsin pollution sources, and remanded to the district court for dismissal of Illinois' claim. *Illinois v. City of Milwaukee*, 731 F.2d 403 (7th Cir. 1984), *cert. denied*, 469 U.S. 1196 (1985). Was the court of appeals correct in light of the Supreme Court decision which follows?

INTERNATIONAL PAPER CO. v. OUELLETTE

479 U.S. 481 (1987)

JUSTICE POWELL delivered the opinion of the Court.

This case involves the pre-emptive scope of the Clean Water Act. [Citation.] The question presented is whether the Act pre-empts a common-law nuisance suit filed in a Vermont court under Vermont law, when the source of the alleged injury is located in New York.

Lake Champlain forms part of the border between the States of New York and Vermont. Petitioner International Paper Company (IPC) operates a pulp and paper mill on the New York side of the lake. In the course of its business, IPC discharges a variety of effluents into the lake through a diffusion pipe. The pipe runs from the mill through the water toward Vermont, ending a short distance before the state boundary line that divides the lake.

Respondents are a group of property owners who reside or lease land on the Vermont shore. In 1978 the owners filed a class action suit against IPC, claiming, *inter alia*, that the discharge of effluents constituted a "continuing nuisance" under Vermont common law. Respondents alleged that the pollutants made the water "foul, unhealthy, smelly, and ... unfit for recreational use," thereby diminishing the value of their property. The owners asked for $20 million in compensatory damages, $100 million in punitive damages, and injunctive relief that would require IPC to restructure part of its water treatment system. The action was filed in State Superior Court, and then later removed to Federal District Court for the District of Vermont.

IPC moved for summary judgment and judgment on the pleadings, claiming that the CWA pre-empted respondents' state-law suit....

... [The District Court] denied the motion to dismiss. 602 F. Supp. 264 (1985). The court acknowledged that federal law normally governs interstate water pollution. It found, however, that two sections of the CWA explicitly preserve state-law rights of action. First, § 510 of the Act provides:

"Except as expressly provided ..., nothing in this chapter shall ... be construed as impairing or in any manner affecting any right or jurisdiction of the States with respect to the waters (including boundary waters) of such States." 33 U.S.C. § 1370.

In addition, § 505(e) states:

"Nothing in this section shall restrict any right which any person (or class of persons) may have under any statute or common law to seek enforcement of any effluent standard or limitation or to seek any other relief...." 33 U.S.C. § 1365(e).

The District Court held that these two provisions (together, "the saving clause") made it clear that federal law did not pre-empt entirely the rights of States to control pollution. Therefore the question presented, said the court, was which *types* of state suits Congress intended to preserve. It considered three possibilities: first, the saving clause could be construed to preserve state law only as it applied to waters not covered by the CWA. But since the Act applies to virtually all surface water in the country, the District Court rejected this possibility. Second, the saving clause might preserve state nuisance law only as it applies to discharges occurring within the source State; under this view a claim could be filed against IPC under New York common law, but not under Vermont law.... The District Court nevertheless rejected this option, finding that "there is simply nothing in the Act which suggests that Congress intended to impose such limitations on the use of state law." 602 F. Supp., at 269.

The District Court therefore adopted the third interpretation of the saving clause, and held that a state action to redress interstate water pollution could be maintained under the law of the State in which the injury occurred. The court was unpersuaded by the concern ... that the application of out-of-state law to a point source would conflict with the CWA. It said there was no interference with the procedures established by Congress because a State's "imposition of compensatory damage awards and other equitable relief for injuries caused ... merely *supplement* the standards and limitations imposed by the Act." 602 F. Supp., at 271 (emphasis in original). The court also found that the use of state law did not conflict with the ultimate goal of the CWA, since in each case the objective was to decrease the level of pollution.

The District Court certified its decision for interlocutory appeal, [citation], and the Court of Appeals for the Second Circuit affirmed for the reasons stated by the District Court. 776 F.2d 55, 56 (1985) (*per curiam*). We now affirm the denial of IPC's motion to dismiss, but reverse the decision below to the extent it permits the application of Vermont law to this litigation. We hold that when a court considers a state-law claim concerning interstate water pollution that is subject to the CWA, the court must apply the law of the State in which the point source is located.

....

As we noted in *Milwaukee II*, Congress intended the 1972 Act amendments to "establish an all-encompassing program of water pollution regulation." 451 U.S., at 318. We observed that congressional "views on the comprehensive nature of the legislation were practically universal." *Id.*, at 318, n. 12 (citing legislative history). An examination of the amendments amply supports these views. The Act applies to all point sources and virtually all bodies of water, and it sets forth the procedures for obtaining a permit in great detail. The CWA also provides its own remedies, including civil and criminal fines for permit violations, and "citizen suits" that allow individuals (including those from affected States) to sue for injunctions to enforce the statute. In light of this pervasive regulation and the fact that the control of interstate pollution is primarily a matter of federal law, *Milwaukee I*, 406 U.S., at 107, it is clear that the only state suits that remain available are those specifically preserved by the Act.

Although Congress intended to dominate the field of pollution regulation, the saving clause negates the inference that Congress "left no room" for state causes of action. Respondents read the language of the saving clause broadly to preserve both a State's right to regulate its waters, 33 U.S.C. § 1370, and an injured party's right to seek relief under "any statute *or common law*," § 1365(e) (emphasis added). They claim that this language and selected portions of the legislative history compel the inference that Congress intended to preserve the right to bring suit under the law of any affected State. We cannot accept this reading of the Act.

To begin with, the plain language of the provisions on which respondents rely by no means compels the result they seek. Section 505(e) merely says that "[n]othing *in this section*," i.e., the citizen-suit provisions, shall affect an injured party's right to seek relief under state law; it does not purport to preclude pre-emption of state law by other provisions of the Act. Section 510, moreover, preserves the authority of a State "with respect to the waters (including boundary waters) of such Stat[e]." This language arguably limits the effect of the clause to discharges flowing *directly* into a State's own waters, i.e., discharges from within the State. The savings clause then, does not preclude pre-emption of the law of an affected State.

Given that the Act itself does not speak directly to the issue, the Court must be guided by the goals and policies of the Act in determining whether it in fact pre-empts an action based on the law of an affected State. [Citation.] After examining the CWA as a whole, its purposes and its history, we are convinced that if affected States were allowed to impose separate discharge standards on a single point source, the inevitable result would be a serious interference with the achievement of the "full purposes and objectives of Congress." [Citation.] Because we do not believe Congress intended to undermine this carefully drawn statute through a general saving clause, we conclude that the CWA precludes a court from applying the law of an affected State against an out-of-state source.

In determining whether Vermont nuisance law "stands as an obstacle" to the full implementation of the CWA, it is not enough to say that the ultimate goal of both federal and state law is to eliminate water pollution. A state law also is pre-empted if it interferes with the methods by which the federal statute was designed to reach this goal. [Citation.] In this case the application of Vermont law against IPC would allow respondents to circumvent the NPDES permit system, thereby upsetting the balance of public and private interests so carefully addressed by the Act.

By establishing a permit system for effluent discharges, Congress implicitly has recognized that the goal of the CWA — elimination of water pollution — cannot be achieved immediately, and that it cannot be realized without incurring costs. The EPA Administrator issues permits according to established effluent standards and water quality standards, that in turn are based upon available technology, 33 U.S.C. § 1314, and competing public and industrial uses, § 1312(a). The Administrator must consider the impact of the discharges on the waterway, the types of effluents, and the schedule for compliance, each of which may vary widely among sources. If a State elects to impose its own standards, it also must consider the technological feasibility of more stringent controls. Given the nature of these complex decisions, it is not surprising that the Act limits the right to administer the permit system to the EPA and the source States. See § 1342(b).

An interpretation of the saving clause that preserved actions brought under an affected State's law would disrupt this balance of interests. If a New York source were liable for violations of Vermont law, that law could effectively override both the permit requirements and the policy choices made by the source State. The affected State's nuisance laws would subject the point source to the threat of legal and equitable penalties if the permit standards were less stringent than those imposed by the affected State. Such penalties would compel the source to adopt different control standards and a different compliance schedule from those approved by the EPA, even though the affected State had not engaged in the same weighing of the costs and benefits. This case illustrates the problems with such a rule. If the Vermont court ruled that respondents were entitled to the full amount of damages and injunctive relief sought in the complaint, at a minimum IPC would have to change its methods of doing business and controlling pollution to avoid the threat of ongoing liability. In suits such as this, an affected-state court also could require the source to cease operations by ordering immediate abatement. Critically, these liabilities would attach even though the source had complied fully with its state and federal permit obligations. The inevitable result of such suits would be that Vermont and other States could do indirectly what they could not do directly — regulate the conduct of out-of-state sources.

Application of an affected State's law to an out-of-state source also would undermine the important goals of efficiency and predictability in the permit system. The history of the 1972 amendments shows that Congress intended to establish "clear and identifiable" discharge standards. As noted above, under the reading of the saving clause proposed by respondents, a source would be subject to a variety of common-law rules established by the different States along the interstate waterways. These nuisance standards often are "vague" and "indeterminate."[17]

The application of numerous States' laws would only exacerbate the vagueness and resulting uncertainty....

---

[17]*See Milwaukee II*, 451 U.S., at 317; *see also* W. KEETON, D. DOBBS, R. KEETON, & D. OWEN, PROSSER AND KEETON ON LAW OF TORTS 616 (5th ed. 1984) ("There is perhaps no more impenetrable jungle in the entire law than that which surrounds the word 'nuisance'"). The possibility that a source will have to meet a number of different standards is relatively small in this case, since Vermont is the only State that shares Lake Champlain with New York. But consider, for example, a plant that discharges effluents into the Mississippi River. A source located in Minnesota theoretically could be subject to the nuisance laws of any of the nine downstream States.

Our conclusion that Vermont nuisance law is inapplicable to a New York point source does not leave respondents without a remedy. The CWA precludes only those suits that may require standards of effluent control that are incompatible with those established by the procedures set forth in the Act. The saving clause specifically preserves other state actions, and therefore nothing in the Act bars aggrieved individuals from bringing a nuisance claim pursuant to the law of the *source* State. By its terms the CWA allows States such as New York to impose higher standards on their own point sources, and in *Milwaukee II* we recognized that this authority may include the right to impose higher common-law as well as higher statutory restrictions. 451 U.S., at 328 (suggesting that "States may adopt more stringent limitations ... through state nuisance law, and apply them to in-state dischargers"); [citation].

An action brought against IPC under New York nuisance law would not frustrate the goals of the CWA as would a suit governed by Vermont law. First, application of the source State's law does not disturb the balance among federal, source-state, and affected-state interests. Because the Act specifically allows source States to impose stricter standards, the imposition of source-state law does not disrupt the regulatory partnership established by the permit system. Second, the restriction of suits to those brought under source-state nuisance law prevents a source from being subject to an indeterminate number of potential regulations. Although New York nuisance law may impose separate standards and thus create some tension with the permit system, a source only is required to look to a single additional authority, whose rules should be relatively predictable. Moreover, States can be expected to take into account their own nuisance laws in setting permit requirements.[20]

IPC asks the Court to go one step further and hold that all state-law suits also must be brought in source-state *courts*. As petitioner cites little authority or justification for this position, we find no basis for holding that Vermont is an improper forum. Simply because a cause of action is pre-empted does not mean that judicial jurisdiction over the claim is affected as well; the Act pre-empts laws, not courts. In the absence of statutory authority to the contrary, the rule is settled that a district court sitting in diversity is competent to apply the law of a foreign State.

. . . .

---

[20]Although we conclude that New York law generally controls this suit, we note that the preemptive scope of the CWA necessarily includes all laws that are inconsistent with the "full purposes and objectives of Congress." We therefore do not agree with the dissent that Vermont nuisance law still may apply if the New York choice-of-law doctrine dictates such a result. As we have discussed, supra, the application of affected-state law would frustrate the carefully prescribed CWA regulatory system. This interference would occur, of course, whether affected-state law applies as an original matter, or whether it applies pursuant to the source State's choice-of-law principles. Therefore if, and to the extent, the law of a source State requires the application of affected-state substantive law on this particular issue, it would be pre-empted as well.

JUSTICE BRENNAN, with whom JUSTICE MARSHALL and JUSTICE BLACKMUN join, concurring in part and dissenting in part.

I concur wholeheartedly in the Court's judgment that the Clean Water Act (Act), 33 U.S.C. § 1251 *et seq.*, does not pre-empt a private nuisance suit filed in a Vermont court when the source of the alleged injury is located in New York. I disagree only with the Court's view that a Vermont court must apply New York nuisance law.

        ....

As a threshold matter, the Court's opinion assumes that in enacting the Act, Congress valued administrative efficiency more highly than effective elimination of water pollution. Yet there is no evidence that Congress ever made such a choice. Instead, the Act reflects Congress' judgment that a rational permit system, operating in tandem with existing state common-law controls, would best achieve the Act's primary goal of controlling water pollution. I base this conclusion on four important considerations.

First, since Congress preserved state common-law rights "[e]xcept as *expressly* provided," [citation] the Court's reliance upon pre-emption by *implication* cannot justify its conclusion.

Second, the legislative history of the Act indicates that Congress saw no peril to the Act in permitting the application of traditional principles of state law. The Senate Committee Report noted that Congress meant "specifically [to] preserve any rights or remedies under any other law. Thus, if damages could be shown, other remedies would remain available. *Compliance with requirements under this Act would not be a defense to a common law action for pollution damages.*" S. Rep. No. 92-414, p. 81 (1971), 2 Leg. Hist. 1499 (emphasis added). The majority's concern that tort liability might undercut permit requirements was thus not shared by Congress.

        ....

Third, we have refused to pre-empt a State's law, even when it is contrary to subsidiary objectives concerning administration, if the State's law furthers the federal statute's primary purpose and is consistent with the Act's saving of States' authority in an area traditionally regulated by States....

Finally, the Court overstates any conflict between the affected State's nuisance law and the subsidiary objectives of the Act. The Court contends that applying the affected State's law would violate the source State's right to set effluent standards for in-state polluters. But if traditional conflict-of-law rules require the application of the affected State's nuisance law, there is no "conflict" with the source State's ability to set the *minimum* standards required under the Act. Congress considered state common-law rights to be supplementary to, and not in conflict with, the Act unless they embodied a "less stringent" standard for polluters than the federal effluent standards. See H.R. Rep. No. 92-911, pp. 169-170 (1972), 1 Leg. Hist. 856-857. The application of an affected State's common-law remedies to an out-of-state polluter does not conflict with the Act because it is possible for the polluter to redress the injuries suffered by the victims of the pollution and to obey the source State's effluent standards. By complying with the most stringent requirement — either under the Act or the affected State's law — the polluter necessarily complies with the more lenient standards.

The Court also argues that application of an affected State's law to an out-of-state source would undermine the important goals of efficiency and predictability in the permit system. But Congress set out to establish "clear and identifiable" discharge standards, [citation], it did not intend to reform the "impenetrable jungle" of state nuisance law. As both legislative history and EPA regulations indicate, compliance with effluent standards is not a defense to state tort suits, [citation] and the affected State's nuisance law is no more "vague" and "indeterminate" than the source State's nuisance law. In fact, in the instant case, Vermont and New York nuisance law are apparently identical. [Citation.] While Congress intended to impose identifiable federal discharge standards upon polluters, we must have much more explicit evidence before assuming that in enacting such a provision Congress meant to revolutionize state conflict-of-law or tort law principles.

....

Even if the Court's conclusion that New York *law* should apply is correct, it does not logically follow that New York *nuisance law* must be applied in this case....

Whether New York law requires the application of New York or Vermont nuisance law depends on an interpretation of New York law *pertaining to conflict of laws*. "A state has the same freedom to adopt its own rules of Conflict of Laws as it has to adopt any other rules of law. Conflict of Laws rules, when adopted, become as definitely a part of the law as any other branch of the state's law." Restatement (Second) of Conflict of Laws § 5, Comment *a*, p. 9 (1971). The Court reasons that a source State must have the primary role in regulating its own pollution discharges. Under this logic, nothing prevents a source State's legislature or courts from choosing to impose, under conflict-of-law principles, the affected State's nuisance law in a case such as this. A source State is free to adopt an affected State's standards as its own standards....

....

NOTES AND QUESTIONS

1. Would it be preferable for interstate pollution to be governed by federal common law or state common law? There are not great variations in state common law for air pollution. *See generally* L. MALONE, ENVIRONMENTAL REGULATION OF LAND USE § 10.02 (1997). Do you agree with the Court that subjecting sources only to the common law of the state where located provides greater certainty in potential liability? *See generally* Glicksman, *Federal Preemption and Private Legal Remedies for Pollution*, 134 U. PA. L. REV. 121

(1985); Bleiweiss, *Environmental Regulation and the Federal Common Law of Nuisance*, 7 HARV. ENVTL. L. REV. 41 (1983).

2. After *International Paper*, what other state standards of a downstream state might still apply? *See Arkansas v. Oklahoma*, pages 595-611 *infra*.

3. Does *International Paper* invite states to limit common law remedies against in-state sources causing harm to downstream states? What constitutional restraints might apply to such state actions?

4. Karen Silkwood was a laboratory analyst at a federally licensed nuclear plant in Oklahoma operated by Kerr-McGee. Shortly before her death in an automobile accident, she somehow was contaminated by plutonium from the plant over a three-day period. Her father, as estate administrator, brought a common law tort suit under Oklahoma law to recover for contamination injuries to Silkwood and her property. There was conflicting evidence on the extent of the company's compliance with safety regulations of the Nuclear Regulatory Commission under the Atomic Energy Act; however, the Commission's investigative report of the contamination incident concluded the only regulatory violation was a minor recordkeeping violation. The jury found in Silkwood's favor, awarded compensatory damages of $505,000, and awarded punitive damages of $10 million. Is the award of punitive damages preempted by the comprehensive safety regulation of the Atomic Energy Act? Of what relevance is the Price-Anderson Act which sets a monetary cap on the nuclear industry's liability for any one nuclear accident? *See Silkwood v. Kerr-McGee*, 464 U.S. 238 (1984) (holding the award was not preempted).

C. LIMITATIONS UNDER THE TAKINGS CLAUSE

The fifth amendment provides that private property shall not be "taken for public use without just compensation." U.S. Const. amend. V. This restriction is applicable to states and municipalities through the fourteenth amendment. *See Penn Cent. Transp. Co. v. City of New York*, 438 U.S. 104, 107 (1978). The prohibition on "takings" of private property without just compensation is not limited to physical appropriation of property or seizure of title. Justice Holmes, writing for a majority of the Supreme Court in 1922, concluded:

> The general rule at least is, that while property may be regulated to a certain extent, if regulation goes too far it will be recognized as a taking.

Pennsylvania Coal v. Mahon, 260 U.S. 393, 415 (1922). Justice Holmes in the landmark case of *Pennsylvania Coal* did not shed much light on how far is too far. When a state or federal government regulates property for a valid public purpose, when is such regulation so intrusive or restrictive as to be tantamount to a taking of the property without just compensation?

The Supreme Court found itself squarely confronting this issue in 1978 in *Penn Cent. Transp. Co. v. City of New York*, 438 U.S. 104 (1978). In the *Penn Central* case, the Supreme Court upheld application of New York City's

Landmarks Preservation Law to the Grand Central Terminal, rejecting in the process claims that this application of the law had taken the owners' property without just compensation and had arbitrarily deprived them of their property without due process of law. *See* 438 U.S. at 104; for a discussion of due process concerns in taking cases, see Strong, *On Placing Property Due Process Center Stage in Takings Jurisprudence*, 49 OHIO ST. L.J. 591 (1988).

The Grand Central Terminal had been designated a landmark by the New York City Landmarks Preservation Commission, and, at that time, Penn Central did not seek judicial review of the designation. Penn Central subsequently leased the air rights above the building for construction of an office building. The Commission, however, disapproved two submitted plans for an office building more than fifty stories high because of the plan's adverse effects on the Terminal's historic and aesthetic features. Under New York City's zoning laws, owners of real property who had not developed their property to the full extent permitted under applicable zoning laws were allowed to petition for transfer of their development rights to other designated parcels of property. 438 U.S. at 113-16.

Following the Commission's disapproval of the multistory office plans, the Terminal owners filed suit, claiming an unlawful taking and denial of due process, and seeking a declaratory judgment, injunctive relief, and damages. The damages were for the "temporary taking" which allegedly occurred between the landmark designation date and the date when the restrictions from the landmark law would be lifted following the owners' success in court. The New York Court of Appeals refused to recognize any "regulatory taking" claim and ultimately concluded that there was no due process violation because Penn Central had not been deprived of a "reasonable return on [its] investment in the [property]." *Id.* at 119, 121.

Justice Brennan acknowledged that the Supreme Court had been unable to develop any "set formula" for determining when economic injury caused by governmental action requires compensation, and that each case necessitates "ad hoc, factual inquiries." *Id.* at 124. The Court had little difficulty in determining that the diminution in value of the property did not constitute a taking within the meaning of the fifth and fourteenth amendments, particularly in light of Penn Central's concession that the property was still capable of earning a reasonable return. *Id.* at 128-29. In determining the diminution in value borne by Penn Central, the Court refused to define the affected property as "air rights"; it focused instead on the economic effects on the parcel as a whole, that is, the city tax block designated as the landmark site. *See* 438 U.S. at 130-31. In reaching its holding, the Court addressed only briefly the extent of deprivation necessary to prove a taking:

> [T]o the extent appellants have been denied the right to build above the Terminal, it is not literally accurate to say that they had been denied *all* use of even those pre-existing air rights. Their ability to use these rights has not

been abrogated; they are made transferable to at least eight parcels in the vicinity of the Terminal, one or two of which have been found suitable for the construction of new office buildings. Although appellants and others have argued that New York City's transferable development-rights program is far from ideal, the New York courts here supportably found that, at least in the case of the Terminal, the rights afforded are valuable.

Id. at 137 (footnote omitted) (emphasis in original).

Justice Rehnquist, joined in his dissent by Justice Stevens and then Chief Justice Burger, concluded that the landmark preservation ordinance had taken Penn Central property by restricting use of the property's air rights. *Id.* at 143. By singling out individual landowners, as opposed to the constitutionally acceptable zoning method of prohibiting certain uses over a broad cross section of land, the ordinance failed to guarantee landmark owners the "average reciprocity of advantage" necessary to fall within the traditional "zoning" exception to the taking prohibition. *Id.* at 147 (quoting *Pennsylvania Coal Co. v. Mahon*, 260 U.S. 393, 415 (1922)). In a footnote, Justice Rehnquist sharply criticized the Court's vacillating suggestions that the restrictions must have "an unduly harsh impact upon the owner's use of the property," prevent "a reasonable return" on the landowner's investment, or prohibit the property from being "economically viable" to establish a taking. 438 U.S. at 149 n.18. The dissent was specifically critical of any requirement that the property owner be denied *all* reasonable return on the property. Rehnquist stressed that the Court not only would have to define "reasonable return" for a variety of types of property, but would have to define the particular property unit to be examined. *See* 438 U.S. at 149 n.13. Nevertheless, Rehnquist would have remanded the case to the New York Court of Appeals "for a determination of whether transferable development rights constitute a 'full and perfect equivalent for the property taken.'" *Id.* at 152. The *Penn Central* decision triggered an optimistic flurry of land use regulation. Nevertheless, *Penn Central* provided relatively limited assurances for such zoning, and lower courts were left to grapple with the Court's repeated admission that taking challenges entail essentially ad hoc, factual inquiries. Although *Penn Central* raised the issue of defining the property unit allegedly taken, it did little to resolve the issue. Its broad suggestion that "'[t]aking' jurisprudence does not divide a single parcel into discrete segments and attempt to determine whether rights in a particular segment have been entirely abrogated," *id.* at 130, is easily circumscribed by the facts of the case. The Court's reasoning in this context was addressed to Penn Central's argument that the property in question was air rights, which in turn was a segment of a single parcel — the city tax block designated as the landmark site.

After *Penn Central* there followed a series of cases in which the character of the interference with the property right was outcome-determinative of the taking issue. For example, in *Kaiser Aetna v. United States*, 444 U.S. 164 (1979), the Corps of Engineers claimed the government had a navigational servitude on what had been a private lagoon, which the owners had connected to the Pacific Ocean, with Corps approval, in order to build an exclusive marina-based community. A navigational servitude is a navigational easement giving the public a right of free access. Writing for the majority, Justice Rehnquist stated that the Court would decide the taking issue by examining "the economic impact of the regulation, its interference with reasonable investment backed expectations, and the character of the governmental action." *Id.* at 175. The Court rejected the government's claim that a navigational servitude existed. Finding that public access would result in an actual physical invasion of private property by the government, Justice Rehnquist stated that impairment of the property owner's right to exclude others would frustrate the owner's reasonable investment-backed expectations, and therefore, constitute a taking. *Id.* at 179-80.

The Court's emphasis on the character of the governmental interference reached its peak in *Loretto v. Teleprompter Manhattan CATV Corp.*, 458 U.S. 419 (1982). In an opinion by Justice Marshall, from which Justices Blackmun, Brennan, and White dissented, the physical invasion resulting from a television cable installed on an apartment owner's roof, as authorized under New York law, was held to constitute a taking of the apartment owner's property without compensation. *Id.* at 421. Despite the minimal interference by the cable in the owner's enjoyment of his property, the Court held the physical invasion to be a "per se" taking of property. *Id.* at 434-35. Thus, the character of the governmental action was not merely a factor, but the only factor in finding a taking when the governmental action is a physical invasion of property. These physical intrusion cases, however, provided little direct guidance as to the direction the Court would take after *Penn Central* with regulatory takings. Indeed, the Court took care in *Loretto* to distinguish between land use regulations and physical intrusions in taking cases:

> As *Penn Central* affirms, the Court has often upheld substantial regulation of an owner's use of his own property where deemed necessary to promote the public interest. At the same time, we have long considered a physical intrusion by government to be a property restriction of an unusually serious character for purposes of the Taking Clause. Our cases further establish that when the physical intrusion reaches the extreme form of a permanent physical occupation, a taking has occurred. In such a case, "the character of the government action" not only is an important factor in resolving whether the action works a taking but also determinative.

458 U.S. at 426. Takings jurisprudence took yet another turn in 1987 with three cases, *Keystone Bituminous Coal Ass'n v. DeBenedictis*, 480 U.S. 470 (1987), *First English Evangelical Lutheran Church v. Los Angeles County*, 482 U.S. 304 (1987), and *Nollan v. California Coastal Comm'n*, 483 U.S. 825 (1987), which indicated a shift in the Court's formulation of what constitutes a "regulatory taking."

Lutheran Church unequivocally decided the issue of the appropriate remedy for a temporary taking. *Lutheran Church* involved property located in a watershed area, on which the Church had operated a retreat center and recreational area for handicapped children. After a severe flood destroyed the buildings, Los Angeles County adopted an interim ordinance prohibiting the construction or reconstruction of any structure in an interim flood protection area, which included the Church's land. In one of its claims, the Church sought the remedy of inverse condemnation for the regulatory taking of the Church's property. 482 U.S. at 307. Chief Justice Rehnquist, writing for the majority, determined that mandamus and declaratory relief are inadequate remedies for a regulatory interference substantial enough to constitute a taking under the fifth and fourteenth amendments, and that such a taking requires just compensation (that is, damages for the losses resulting from deprivation of property use from the time that the interference occurs until the legislating entity either amends the offending regulation, withdraws the regulation, or pays compensation for a permanent deprivation of the property from the exercise of eminent domain). *Id.* at 321-22. Because the Court had to accept as true the allegation in the complaint that the Church had been denied *all* use of its property, the Court gave no further delineation of what degree of interference would amount to a taking. *Id.* The Court emphasized that the takings clause "was not designed to limit governmental interference *per se*, but rather to secure *compensation* in the event of a taking." *Id.* at 315 (emphasis in original). As to the frequently asserted argument that providing damages compels eminent domain in derogation of any of the government's other options, the Court pointed out that after having to provide interim damages for the temporary taking, the government may still decide to amend the regulation, withdraw the regulation, or exercise eminent domain. *Id.* at 321. The Court merely decided that "'temporary' takings which ... deny a landowner all use of his property are not different in kind from permanent takings...." *Id.* at 318.

After *Penn Central*, the Supreme Court seemed well on its way to recognizing damages as the appropriate remedy for a temporary taking, so that the decision in *Lutheran Church* to that extent seemed a logical outgrowth of *Penn Central*. The *Nollan* and *Keystone* decisions that term, however, were far less predictable in their outcomes and, some commentators have suggested, inconsistent with the Court's prior decisions under the takings clause and with each other.

KEYSTONE BITUMINOUS COAL ASSOCIATION v. DeBENEDICTIS
480 U.S. 470 (1987)

JUSTICE STEVENS, delivered the opinion of the Court.

....

Based on detailed findings, the [Pennsylvania] legislature enacted the Bituminous Mine Subsidence and Land Conservation Act (Subsidence Act or

Act). Petitioners contend, relying heavily on our decision in *Pennsylvania Coal*, that §§ 4 and 6 of the Subsidence Act and certain implementing regulations violate the Takings Clause. The District Court and the Court of Appeals concluded that *Pennsylvania Coal* does not control for several reasons and that our subsequent cases make it clear that neither § 4 nor § 6 is unconstitutional on its face. We agree.

....

Pennsylvania's Subsidence Act authorizes the Pennsylvania Department of Environmental Resources (DER) to implement and enforce a comprehensive program to prevent or minimize subsidence and to regulate its consequences. Section 4 of the Subsidence Act prohibits mining that causes subsidence damage to three categories of structures that were in place on April 17, 1966: public buildings and noncommercial buildings generally used by the public; dwellings used for human habitation; and cemeteries. Since 1966 the DER has applied a formula that generally requires 50% of the coal beneath structures protected by § 4 to be kept in place as a means of providing surface support. Section 6 of the Subsidence Act, Pa. Stat. Ann., Tit. 52, § 1406.6 (Purdon Supp. 1986), authorizes the DER to revoke a mining permit if the removal of coal causes damage to a structure or area protected by § 4 and the operator has not within six months either repaired the damage, satisfied any claim arising therefrom, or deposited a sum equal to the reasonable cost of repair with the DER as security.

In 1982, petitioners filed a civil rights action in the United States District Court for the Western District of Pennsylvania seeking to enjoin officials of the DER from enforcing the Subsidence Act and its implementing regulations. Petitioners are an association of coal mine operators, and four corporations that are engaged, either directly or through affiliates, in underground mining of bituminous coal in western Pennsylvania. The members of the association and the corporate petitioners own, lease, or otherwise control substantial coal reserves beneath the surface of property affected by the Subsidence Act....

In the portions of the complaint that are relevant to us, petitioners alleged that both § 4 of the Subsidence Act, as implemented by the 50% rule, and § 6 of the Subsidence Act, constitute a taking of their private property without compensation in violation of the Fifth and Fourteenth Amendments....

Petitioners assert that disposition of their takings claim calls for no more than a straightforward application of the Court's decision in *Pennsylvania Coal Co. v. Mahon*. Although there are some obvious similarities between the cases, we agree with the Court of Appeals and the District Court that the similarities are far less significant than the differences, and that *Pennsylvania Coal* does not control this case.

In *Pennsylvania Coal*, the Pennsylvania Coal Company had served notice on Mr. and Mrs. Mahon that the company's mining operations beneath their premises would soon reach a point that would cause subsidence to the surface. The Mahons filed a bill in equity seeking to enjoin the coal company from removing any coal that would cause "the caving in, collapse or subsidence" of their dwelling. The bill acknowledged that the Mahons owned only "the surface or right of soil" in the lot, and that the Coal Company had reserved the right to remove the coal without any liability to the owner of the surface estate. Nonetheless, the Mahons asserted that Pennsylvania's then recently enacted Kohler Act of 1921, which prohibited mining that caused subsidence under certain structures, entitled them to an injunction.

....

... In its argument in this Court, the company contended that the Kohler Act was not a bona fide exercise of the police power, but in reality was nothing more than "'robbery under the forms of law'" because its purpose was "not to protect the lives or safety of the public generally but merely to augment the property rights of a favored few." [Citation.]

Over Justice Brandeis' dissent, this Court accepted the company's argument. In his opinion for the Court, Justice Holmes first characteristically decided the specific case at hand in a single, terse paragraph:

> "This is the case of a single private house. No doubt there is a public interest even in this, as there is in every purchase and sale and in all that happens within the commonwealth. Some existing rights may be modified even in such a case. [Citation.] But usually in ordinary private affairs the public interest does not warrant much of this kind of interference. A source of damage to such a house is not a public nuisance even if similar damage is inflicted on others in different places. The damage is not common or public. [Citation.] The extent of the public interest is shown by the statute to be limited, since the statute ordinarily does not apply to land when the surface is owned by the owner of the coal. Furthermore, it is not justified as a protection of personal safety. That could be provided for by notice. Indeed the very foundation of this bill is that the defendant gave timely notice of its intent to mine under the house. On the other hand the extent of the taking is great. It purports to abolish what is recognized in Pennsylvania as an estate in land — a very valuable estate — and what is declared by the Court below to be a contract hitherto binding the plaintiffs. If we were called upon to deal with the plaintiffs' position alone, we should think it clear that the statute does not disclose a public interest sufficient to warrant so extensive a destruction of the defendant's constitutionally protected rights." 260 U.S., at 413-414.

Then — uncharacteristically — Justice Holmes provided the parties with an advisory opinion discussing "the general validity of the Act." In the advisory portion of the Court's opinion, Justice Holmes rested on two propositions, both critical to the Court's decision. First, because it served only private interests, not health or safety, the Kohler Act could not be "sustained as an exercise of the police power." Second, the statute made it "commercially impracticable" to mine "certain coal" in the areas affected by the Kohler Act.

The holdings and assumptions of the Court in *Pennsylvania Coal* provide obvious and necessary reasons for distinguishing *Pennsylvania Coal* from the case before us today. The two factors that the Court considered relevant, have become integral parts of our takings analysis. We have held that land use regulation can effect a taking if it "does not substantially advance legitimate state interests, ... or denies an owner economically viable use of his land." [Citation.] Application of these tests to petitioners' challenge demonstrates that they have not satisfied their burden of showing that the Subsidence Act constitutes a taking. First, unlike the Kohler Act, the character of the governmental action involved here leans heavily against finding a taking; the Commonwealth of Pennsylvania has acted to arrest what it perceives to be a significant threat to the common welfare. Second, there is no record in this case to support a finding, similar to the one the Court made in *Pennsylvania Coal*, that the Subsidence Act makes it impossible for petitioners to profitably engage in their business, or that there has been undue interference with their investment-backed expectations.

The Public Purpose

Unlike the Kohler Act, which was passed upon in *Pennsylvania Coal*, the Subsidence Act does not merely involve a balancing of the private economic interests of coal companies against the private interests of the surface owners. The Pennsylvania Legislature specifically found that important public interests are served by enforcing a policy that is designed to minimize subsidence in certain areas. Section 2 of the Subsidence Act provides:

> "This act shall be deemed to be an exercise of the police powers of the Commonwealth for the protection of the health, safety and general welfare of the people of the Commonwealth, by providing for the conservation of surface land areas which may be affected in the mining of bituminous coal by methods other than 'open pit' or 'strip' mining, to aid in the protection of the safety of the public, to enhance the value of such lands for taxation, to aid in the preservation of surface water drainage and public water supplies and generally to improve the use and enjoyment of such lands and to maintain primary jurisdiction over surface coal mining in Pennsylvania."

The District Court and the Court of Appeals were both convinced that the legislative purposes set forth in the statute were genuine, substantial, and legitimate, and we have no reason to conclude otherwise.

None of the indicia of a statute enacted solely for the benefit of private parties identified in Justice Holmes' opinion are present here. First, Justice Holmes explained that the Kohler Act was a "private benefit" statute since it "ordinarily does not apply to land when the surface is owned by the owner of the coal." The Subsidence Act, by contrast, has no such exception. The current surface owner may only waive the protection of the Act if the DER consents. Moreover, the Court was forced to reject the Commonwealth's safety justification for the Kohler Act because it found that the Commonwealth's interest in safety could as easily have been accomplished through a notice requirement to landowners. The Subsidence Act, by contrast, is designed to accomplish a number of widely varying interests, with reference to which petitioners have not suggested alternative methods through which the Commonwealth could proceed.

    ....

Thus, the Subsidence Act differs from the Kohler Act in critical and dispositive respects. With regard to the Kohler Act, the Court believed that the Commonwealth had acted only to ensure against damage to some private landowners' homes. Justice Holmes stated that if the private individuals needed support for their structure, they should not have "take[n] the risk of acquiring only surface rights." Here, by contrast, the Commonwealth is acting to protect the public interest in health, the environment, and the fiscal integrity of the area. That private individuals erred in taking a risk cannot estop the Commonwealth from exercising its police power to abate activity akin to a public nuisance. The Subsidence Act is a prime example that "circumstances may so change in time ... as to clothe with such a [public] interest what at other times ... would be a matter of purely private concern."...

    ....

The Court's hesitance to find a taking when the State merely restrains uses of property that are tantamount to public nuisances is consistent with the notion of "reciprocity of advantage" that Justice Holmes referred to in *Pennsylvania Coal*.[20]

Under our system of government, one of the State's primary ways of preserving the public wealth is restricting the uses individuals can make of their property. While each of us is burdened somewhat by such restrictions, we, in turn, benefit greatly from the restrictions that are placed on others. [Citation.] These restrictions are "properly treated as part of the burden of common citizenship." [Citation.] Long ago it was recognized that "all property in this country is held under the implied obligation that the owner's use of it shall not be injurious to the community." *Mugler v. Kansas*, 123 U.S., at 665, and the Takings Clause did not transform that principle to one that requires compensation

---

[20]The special status of this type of state action can also be understood on the simple theory that since no individual has a right to use his property so as to create a nuisance or otherwise harm others, the State has not "taken" anything when it asserts its power to enjoin the nuisance-like activity. Cf. Sax, *Takings, Private Property and Public Rights*, 81 YALE L.J. 149, 155-161 (1971); Michelman, *Property, Utility, and Fairness: Comments on the Ethical Foundations of "Just Compensation" Law*, 80 HARV. L. REV. 1165, 1235-1237 (1967).

However, as the current Chief Justice has explained: "The nuisance exception to the taking guarantee is not coterminous with the police power itself." *Penn Central Transportation Co.*, 438 U.S., at 145 (Rehnquist, J., dissenting). This is certainly the case in light of our recent decisions holding that the "scope of the 'public use' requirement of the Takings Clause is 'coterminous with the scope of a sovereign's police powers.'" See *Ruckelshaus v. Monsanto Co.*, 467 U.S. 986, 1014 (1984) (quoting *Hawaii Housing Authority v. Midkiff*, 467 U.S. 229, 240 (1984)). *See generally* R. EPSTEIN, TAKINGS 108-112 (1985).

whenever the State asserts its power to enforce it.[22] See *Mugler*, 123 U.S., at 664.

....

Diminution of Value and Investment-Backed Expectations

The second factor that distinguishes this case from *Pennsylvania Coal* is the finding in that case that the Kohler Act made mining of "certain coal" commercially impracticable. In this case, by contrast, petitioners have not shown any deprivation significant enough to satisfy the heavy burden placed upon one alleging a regulatory taking. For this reason, their takings claim must fail.

....

... Petitioners have not claimed, at this stage, that the Act makes it commercially impracticable for them to continue mining their bituminous coal interests in western Pennsylvania. Indeed, petitioners have not even pointed to a single mine that can no longer be mined for profit....

Instead, petitioners have sought to narrowly define certain segments of their property and assert that, when so defined, the Subsidence Act denies them economically viable use. They advance two alternative ways of carving their property in order to reach this conclusion. First, they focus on the specific tons of coal that they must leave in the ground under the Subsidence Act, and argue that the Commonwealth has effectively appropriated this coal since it has no other useful purpose if not mined. Second, they contend that the Commonwealth has taken their separate legal interest in property — the "support estate."

Because our test for regulatory taking requires us to compare the value that has been taken from the property with the value that remains in the property, one of the critical questions is determining how to define the unit of property "whose value is to furnish the denominator of the fraction." Michelman, *Property, Utility, and Fairness: Comments on the Ethical Foundations of "Just Compensation" Law*, 80 HARV. L. REV. 1165, 1192 (1967). In *Penn Central* the Court explained:

> "'Taking' jurisprudence does not divide a single parcel into discrete segments and attempt to determine whether rights in a particular segment have been entirely abrogated. In deciding whether a particular governmental action has effected a taking, this Court focuses rather both on the character of the action and on the nature of the interference with rights in the parcel

---

[22]Courts have consistently held that a State need not provide compensation when it diminishes or destroys the value of property by stopping illegal activity or abating a public nuisance. [Citation.] It is hard to imagine a different rule that would be consistent with the maxim *"sic utere tuo ut alienum non laedas"* (use your own property in such manner as not to injure that of another). As Professor Epstein has recently commented: "The issue of compensation cannot arise until the question of justification has been disposed of. In the typical prevention case, this question is resolved against the claimant." EPSTEIN, *supra*, at 199.

as a whole — here the city tax block designated as the 'landmark site.'" 438 U.S., at 130-131.

The Coal in Place

The parties have stipulated that enforcement of the DER's 50% rule will require petitioners to leave approximately 27 million tons of coal in place. Because they own that coal but cannot mine it, they contend that Pennsylvania has appropriated it for the public purposes described in the Subsidence Act.

This argument fails for the reason explained in *Penn Central* and *Andrus*. The 27 million tons of coal do not constitute a separate segment of property for takings law purposes. Many zoning ordinances place limits on the property owner's right to make profitable use of some segments of his property. A requirement that a building occupy no more than a specified percentage of the lot on which it is located could be characterized as a taking of the vacant area as readily as the requirement that coal pillars be left in place. Similarly, under petitioners' theory one could always argue that a set-back ordinance requiring that no structure be built within a certain distance from the property line constitutes a taking because the footage represents a distinct segment of property for takings law purposes. [Citation.] There is no basis for treating the less than 2% of petitioners' coal as a separate parcel of property.

   ....

The Support Estate

Pennsylvania property law is apparently unique in regarding the support estate as a separate interest in land that can be conveyed apart from either the mineral estate or the surface estate. Petitioners therefore argue that even if comparable legislation in another State would not constitute a taking, the Subsidence Act has that consequence because it entirely destroys the value of their unique support estate. It is clear, however, that our takings jurisprudence forecloses reliance on such legalistic distinctions within a bundle of property rights. For example, in *Penn Central*, the Court rejected the argument that the "air rights" above the terminal constituted a separate segment of property for Takings Clause purposes. [Citation.] ...

The Court of Appeals, which is more familiar with Pennsylvania law than we are, concluded that as a practical matter the support estate is always owned by either the owner of the surface or the owner of the minerals....

Thus, in practical terms, the support estate has value only insofar as it protects or enhances the value of the estate with which it is associated. Its value is merely a part of the entire bundle of rights possessed by the owner of either the coal or the surface. Because petitioners retain the right to mine virtually all of the coal in their mineral estates, the burden the Act places on the support estate does not constitute a taking. Petitioners may continue to mine coal profitably even if they may not destroy or damage surface structures at will in the process.

But even if we were to accept petitioners' invitation to view the support estate as a distinct segment of property for "takings" purposes, they have not satisfied their heavy burden of sustaining a facial challenge to the Act. Petitioners have acquired or retained the support estate for a great deal of land, only part of which is protected under the Subsidence Act, which, of course, deals with subsidence in the immediate vicinity of certain structures, bodies of water, and cemeteries. [Citation.] The record is devoid of any evidence on what percentage of the purchased support estates, either in the aggregate or with respect to any individual estate, has been affected by the Act. Under these circumstances, petitioners' facial attack under the Takings Clause must surely fail.

CHIEF JUSTICE REHNQUIST, with whom JUSTICE POWELL, JUSTICE O'CONNOR, and JUSTICE SCALIA join, dissenting.

More than 50 years ago, this Court determined the constitutionality of Pennsylvania's Kohler Act as it affected the property interests of coal mine operators. *Pennsylvania Coal Co. v. Mahon*, 260 U.S. 393 (1922). The Bituminous Mine Subsidence and Land Conservation Act approved today effects an interference with such interests in a strikingly similar manner. The Court finds at least two reasons why this case is different. First, we are told, "the character of the governmental action involved here leans heavily against finding a taking." Second, the Court concludes that the Subsidence Act neither "makes it impossible for petitioners to profitably engage in their business," nor involves "undue interference with [petitioners'] investment-backed expectations." Neither of these conclusions persuades me that this case is different, and I believe that the Subsidence Act works a taking of petitioners' property interests. I therefore dissent.

....

[I]t is clear that the Court has severely understated the similarity of purpose between the Subsidence Act and the Kohler Act. The public purposes in this case are not sufficient to distinguish it from *Pennsylvania Coal*.

The similarity of the public purpose of the present Act to that in *Pennsylvania Coal* does not resolve the question of whether a taking has occurred; the existence of such a public purpose is merely a necessary prerequisite to the government's exercise of its taking power. [Citation.] The *nature* of these purposes may be relevant, for we have recognized that a taking does not occur where the government exercises its unquestioned authority to prevent a property owner from using his property to injure others without having to compensate the value of the forbidden use. See *Goldblatt v. Hempstead*, 369 U.S. 590 (1962); *Hadacheck v. Sebastian*, 239 U.S. 394 (1915); *Mugler v. Kansas*, 123 U.S. 623 (1887). *See generally Penn Central Transportation Co. v. New York City*, 438 U.S., at 144-146 (REHNQUIST, J., dissenting). The Court today indicates that this "nuisance exception" alone might support its conclusion that no taking has occurred....

....

[O]ur cases applying the "nuisance" rationale have involved at least two narrowing principles. First, nuisance regulations exempted from the Fifth Amendment have rested on discrete and narrow purposes. See *Goldblatt v. Hempstead, supra; Hadacheck v. Sebastian, supra; Mugler v. Kansas, supra.* The Subsidence Act, however, is much more than a nuisance statute. The central purposes of the Act, though including public safety, reflect a concern for preservation of buildings, economic development, and maintenance of property values to sustain the Commonwealth's tax base. We should hesitate to allow a regulation based on essentially economic concerns to be insulated from the dictates of the Fifth Amendment by labeling it nuisance regulation.

Second, and more significantly, our cases have never applied the nuisance exception to allow complete extinction of the value of a parcel of property. Though nuisance regulations have been sustained despite a substantial reduction in value, we have not accepted the proposition that the State may completely extinguish a property interest or prohibit all use without providing compensation....

Here, petitioners' interests in particular coal deposits have been completely destroyed. By requiring that defined seams of coal remain in the ground, § 4 of the Subsidence Act has extinguished any interest one might want to acquire in this property, for "'the right to coal consists in the right to mine it.'" *Pennsylvania Coal, supra*, at 414, quoting *Commonwealth ex rel. Keator v. Clearview Coal Co.*, 256 Pa. 328, 331, 100 A. 820, 820 (1917). Application of the nuisance exception in these circumstances would allow the State not merely to forbid one "particular use" of property with many uses but to extinguish *all* beneficial use of petitioners' property.

Though suggesting that the purposes alone are sufficient to uphold the Act, the Court avoids reliance on the nuisance exception by finding that the Subsidence Act does not impair petitioners' investment-backed expectations or ability to profitably operate their businesses. This conclusion follows mainly from the Court's broad definition of the "relevant mass of property," which allows it to ascribe to the Subsidence Act a less pernicious effect on the interests of the property owner. The need to consider the effect of regulation on some identifiable segment of property makes all important the admittedly difficult task of defining the relevant parcel. See *Penn Central Transportation Co. v. New York City*, 438 U.S., at 149, n. 13 (REHNQUIST, J., dissenting)....

....

In this case, enforcement of the Subsidence Act and its regulations will require petitioners to leave approximately 27 million tons of coal in place. There is no question that this coal is an identifiable and separable property interest. Unlike many property interests, the "bundle" of rights in this coal is sparse. "'For practical purposes, the right to coal consists in the right to mine it.'" *Pennsylvania Coal*, 260 U.S., at 414, quoting *Commonwealth ex rel. Keater v. Clearview Coal Co.*, 256 Pa. 328, 331, 100 A. 820, 820 (1917). From the relevant perspective — that of the property owners — this interest has been destroyed every bit as much as if the government had proceeded to mine the coal for its own use. The regulation, then, does not merely inhibit one strand in the bundle, but instead destroys completely any interest in a segment of property. In these circumstances, I think it unnecessary to consider whether petitioners may operate individual mines or their overall mining operations profitably, for they have been denied all use of 27 million tons of coal. I would hold that § 4 of the Subsidence Act works a taking of these property interests.

Petitioners also claim that the Subsidence Act effects a taking of their support estate. Under Pennsylvania law, the support estate, the surface estate, and the mineral estate are "three distinct estates in land which can be held in fee simple separate and distinct from each other...." In refusing to consider the effect of the Subsidence Act on this property interest alone, the Court dismisses this feature of Pennsylvania property law as simply a "legalistic distinctio[n] within a bundle of property rights." "Its value," the Court informs us, "is merely a part of the entire bundle of rights possessed by the owner of either the coal or the surface." This view of the support estate allows the Court to conclude that its destruction is merely the destruction of one "strand" in petitioners' bundle of property rights, not significant enough in the overall bundle to work a taking.

Contrary to the Court's approach today, we have evaluated takings claims by reference to the units of property defined by state law....

....

... In these circumstances, where the estate defined by state law is both severable and of value in its own right, it is appropriate to consider the effect of regulation on that particular property interest.

NOLLAN v. CALIFORNIA COASTAL COMMISSION
483 U.S. 825 (1987)

JUSTICE SCALIA delivered the opinion of the Court.

James and Marilyn Nollan appeal from a decision of the California Court of Appeal ruling that the California Coastal Commission could condition its grant of permission to rebuild their house on their transfer to the public of an easement across their beachfront property....

....

Had California simply required the Nollans to make an easement across their beachfront available to the public on a permanent basis in order to increase public access to the beach, rather than conditioning their permit to rebuild their house on their agreeing to do so, we have no doubt there would have been a taking. To say that the appropriation of a public easement across a landowner's premises does not constitute the taking of a property interest but rather (as JUSTICE BRENNAN contends) "a mere restriction on its use," is to use words in a manner that deprives them of all their ordinary meaning. Indeed, one of the principal uses of the eminent domain power is to assure that the government be able to require conveyance of just such interests, so long as it pays for them.

[Citation.] Perhaps because the point is so obvious, we have never been confronted with a controversy that required us to rule upon it, but our cases' analysis of the effect of other governmental action leads to the same conclusion. We have repeatedly held that, as to property reserved by its owner for private use, "the right to exclude [others is] 'one of the most essential sticks in the bundle of rights that are commonly characterized as property.'" *Loretto v. Teleprompter Manhattan CATV Corp.*, 458 U.S. 419, 433 (1982), quoting *Kaiser Aetna v. United States*, 444 U.S. 164, 176 (1979). In *Loretto* we observed that where governmental action results in "[a] permanent physical occupation" of the property, by the government itself or by others, see 458 U.S., at 432-433, n. 9, "our cases uniformly have found a taking to the extent of the occupation, without regard to whether the action achieves an important public benefit or has only minimal economic impact on the owner," *id.*, at 434-435. We think a "permanent physical occupation" has occurred, for purposes of that rule, where individuals are given a permanent and continuous right to pass to and fro, so that the real property may continuously be traversed, even though no particular individual is permitted to station himself permanently upon the premises.

    ....

    Given, then, that requiring uncompensated conveyance of the easement outright would violate the Fourteenth Amendment, the question becomes whether requiring it to be conveyed as a condition for issuing a land-use permit alters the outcome. We have long recognized that land-use regulation does not effect a taking if it "substantially advance[s] legitimate state interests" and does not "den[y] an owner economically viable use of his land." Our cases have not elaborated on the standards for determining what constitutes a "legitimate state interest" or what type of connection between the regulation and the state interest satisfies the requirement that the former "substantially advance" the latter. They have made clear, however, that a broad range of governmental purposes and regulations satisfies these requirements. [Citation.] The Commission argues that among these permissible purposes are protecting the public's ability to see the beach, assisting the public in overcoming the "psychological barrier" to using the beach created by a developed shorefront, and preventing congestion on the public beaches. We assume, without deciding, that this is so — in which case the Commission unquestionably would be able to deny the Nollans their permit outright if their new house (alone, or by reason of the cumulative impact produced in conjunction with other construction) would substantially impede these purposes, unless the denial would interfere so drastically with the Nollans' use of their property as to constitute a taking. [Citation.]

    The Commission argues that a permit condition that serves the same legitimate police-power purpose as a refusal to issue the permit should not be found to be a taking if the refusal to issue the permit would not constitute a taking. We agree. Thus, if the Commission attached to the permit some condition that would have protected the public's ability to see the beach notwithstanding construction of the new house — for example, a height limitation, a width restriction, or a ban on fences — so long as the Commission could have exercised its police power (as we have assumed it could) to forbid construction of the house altogether, imposition of the condition would also be constitutional. Moreover (and here we come closer to the facts of the present case), the condition would be constitutional even if it consisted of the requirement that the Nollans provide a viewing spot on their property for passersby with whose sighting of the ocean their new house would interfere. Although such a requirement, constituting a permanent grant of continuous access to the property, would have to be considered a taking if it were not attached to a development permit, the Commission's assumed power to forbid construction of the house in order to protect the public's view of the beach must surely include the power to condition construction upon some concession by the owner, even a concession of property rights, that serves the same end. If a prohibition designed to accomplish that purpose would be a legitimate exercise of the police power rather than a taking, it would be strange to conclude that providing the owner an alternative to that prohibition which accomplishes the same purpose is not.

The evident constitutional propriety disappears, however, if the condition substituted for the prohibition utterly fails to further the end advanced as the justification for the prohibition. When that essential nexus is eliminated, the situation becomes the same as if California law forbade shouting fire in a crowded theater, but granted dispensations to those willing to contribute $100 to the state treasury. While a ban on shouting fire can be a core exercise of the State's police power to protect the public safety, and can thus meet even our stringent standards for regulation of speech, adding the unrelated condition alters the purpose to one which, while it may be legitimate, is inadequate to sustain the ban. Therefore, even though, in a sense, requiring a $100 tax contribution in order to shout fire is a lesser restriction on speech than an outright ban, it would not pass constitutional muster. Similarly here, the lack of nexus between the condition and the original purpose of the building restriction converts that purpose to something other than what it was. The purpose then becomes, quite simply, the obtaining of an easement to serve some valid governmental purpose, but without payment of compensation. Whatever may be the outer limits of "legitimate state interests" in the takings and land-use context, this is not one of them. In short, unless the permit condition serves the same governmental purpose as the development ban, the building restriction is not a valid regulation of land use but "an out-and-out plan of extortion." [Citation.]

The Commission claims that it concedes as much, and that we may sustain the condition at issue here by finding that it is reasonably related to the public need or burden that the Nollans' new house creates or to which it contributes. We can accept, for purposes of discussion, the Commission's proposed test as to how close a "fit" between the condition and the burden is required, because we find that this case does not meet even the most untailored standards. The Commission's principal contention to the contrary essentially turns on a play on the word "access." The Nollans' new house, the Commission found, will interfere with "visual access" to the beach. That in turn (along with other shorefront development) will interfere with the desire of people who drive past the Nollans' house to use the beach, thus creating a "psychological barrier" to "access." The Nollans' new house will also, by a process not altogether clear from the Commission's opinion but presumably potent enough to more than offset the effects of the psychological barrier, increase the use of the public beaches, thus creating the need for more "access." These burdens on "access" would be alleviated by a requirement that the Nollans provide "lateral access" to the beach.

Rewriting the argument to eliminate the play on words makes clear that there is nothing to it. It is quite impossible to understand how a requirement that people already on the public beaches be able to walk across the Nollans' property reduces any obstacles to viewing the beach created by the new house. It is also impossible to understand how it lowers any "psychological barrier" to using the public beaches, or how it helps to remedy any additional congestion on them caused by construction of the Nollans' new house. We therefore find that the Commission's imposition of the permit condition cannot be treated as an exercise of its land-use power for any of these purposes. Our conclusion on this point is consistent with the approach taken by every other court that has considered the question, with the exception of the California state courts. [Citation.]

JUSTICE BRENNAN argues that imposition of the access requirement is not irrational. In his version of the Commission's argument, the reason for the requirement is that in its absence, a person looking toward the beach from the road will see a street of residential structures including the Nollans' new home and conclude that there is no public beach nearby. If, however, that person sees people passing and repassing along the dry sand behind the Nollans' home, he will realize that there is a public beach somewhere in the vicinity. The Commission's action, however, was based on the opposite factual finding that the wall of houses completely blocked the view of the beach and that a person looking from the road would not be able to see it at all.

....

We are left, then, with the Commission's justification for the access requirement unrelated to land-use regulation:

> "Finally, the Commission notes that there are several existing provisions of pass and repass lateral access benefits already given by past Faria Beach Tract applicants as a result of prior coastal permit decisions. The access required as a condition of this permit is part of a comprehensive program to provide continuous public access along Faria Beach as the lots undergo development or redevelopment."

That is simply an expression of the Commission's belief that the public interest will be served by a continuous strip of publicly accessible beach along the coast. The Commission may well be right that it is a good idea, but that does not establish that the Nollans (and other coastal residents) alone can be compelled to contribute to its realization. Rather, California is free to advance its "comprehensive program," if it wishes, by using its power of eminent domain for this "public purpose," see U.S. Const., Amdt. 5; but if it wants an easement across the Nollans' property, it must pay for it.

JUSTICE BRENNAN, with whom JUSTICE MARSHALL joins, dissenting.

Appellants in this case sought to construct a new dwelling on their beach lot that would both diminish visual access to the beach and move private development closer to the public tidelands. The Commission reasonably concluded that such "buildout," both individually and cumulatively, threatens public access to the shore. It sought to offset this encroachment by obtaining assurance that the public may walk along the shoreline in order to gain access to the ocean. The Court finds this an illegitimate exercise of the police power, because it maintains that there is no reasonable relationship between the effect of the development and the condition imposed.

The first problem with this conclusion is that the Court imposes a standard of precision for the exercise of a State's police power that has been discredited for the better part of this century. Furthermore, even under the Court's cramped standard, the permit condition imposed in this case directly responds to the specific type of burden on access created by appellants' development. Finally, a review of those factors deemed most significant in takings analysis makes clear that the Commission's action implicates none of the concerns underlying the Takings Clause. The Court has thus struck down the Commission's reasonable effort to respond to intensified development along the California coast, on behalf of landowners who can make no claim that their reasonable expectations have been disrupted. The Court has, in short, given appellants a windfall at the expense of the public.

The Court's conclusion that the permit condition imposed on appellants is unreasonable cannot withstand analysis. First, the Court demands a degree of exactitude that is inconsistent with our standard for reviewing the rationality of a State's exercise of its police power for the welfare of its citizens. Second, even if the nature of the public-access condition imposed must be identical to the precise burden on access created by appellants, this requirement is plainly satisfied.

. . . .

Even if we accept the Court's unusual demand for a precise match between the condition imposed and the specific type of burden on access created by the appellants, the State's action easily satisfies this requirement. First, the lateral access condition serves to dissipate the impression that the beach that lies behind the wall of homes along the shore is for private use only. It requires no exceptional imaginative powers to find plausible the Commission's point that the average person passing along the road in front of a phalanx of imposing permanent residences, including the appellants' new home, is likely to conclude that this particular portion of the shore is not open to the public. If, however, that person can see that numerous people are passing and repassing along the dry sand, this conveys the message that the beach is in fact open for use by the public. Furthermore, those persons who go down to the public beach a quarter-mile away will be able to look down the coastline and see that persons have continuous access to the tidelands, and will observe signs that proclaim the public's right of access over the dry sand. The burden produced by the diminution in visual access — the impression that the beach is not open to the public — is thus directly alleviated by the provision for public access over the dry sand. The Court therefore has an unrealistically limited conception of what measures could reasonably be chosen to mitigate the burden produced by a diminution of visual access.

....

Consideration of the Commission's action under traditional takings analysis underscores the absence of any viable takings claim. The deed restriction permits the public only to pass and repass along a narrow strip of beach, a few feet closer to a seawall at the periphery of appellants' property. Appellants almost surely have enjoyed an increase in the value of their property even with the restriction, because they have been allowed to build a significantly larger new home with garage on their lot. Finally, appellants can claim the disruption of no expectation interest, both because they have no right to exclude the public under state law, and because, even if they did, they had full advance notice that new development along the coast is conditioned on provisions for continued public access to the ocean.

[The dissenting opinions of JUSTICES BLACKMUN and STEVENS are omitted.]

NOTES AND QUESTIONS

1. In *Keystone*, what is the relevance of the purportedly broader purposes of the Act to the taking issue? *See generally* Michelman, *Takings*, 1987, 88 COLUM. L. REV. 1600, 1602 (1988); *see also Hawaii Hous. Auth. v. Midkiff*, 467 U.S. 229 (1984) ("public use" requirement for exercise of eminent domain is coterminous with scope of a sovereign's police powers). Do you find the distinction made between the purposes of the Act in *Pennsylvania Coal* and *Keystone* convincing?

What is the property unit against which the interference must be measured? The support estate? The support estate and the surface estate or mineral estate together? The support estates in the aggregate or with respect to each individual estate? *See generally* Linda A. Malone, *The Coastal Zone Management Act and the Takings Clause in the 1990's: Making the Case for Federal Land Use to Preserve Coastal Areas*, 62 COLO. L. REV. 711, 748-53 (1991); Note, *Houses on the Sand: Takings Issues Surrounding Statutory Restrictions on the Use of Oceanfront Property*, 18 B.C. ENVTL. AFF. L. REV. 125 (1990). Under *Keystone*, if Penn Central was not permitted to utilize the air rights above the terminal *at all* would there be no taking if Penn Central owned other adjoining properties with development rights?

In contrast to the majority, Chief Justice Rehnquist in his dissent finds that the 27 million tons of coal were a separate, identifiable segment of property. If it were only one ton of coal that could not be removed, would the result be the same under his analysis? What makes the coal a separate property segment? Would a prohibition on use of one natural resource be a taking of a separate segment of property as well? For example, if a local ordinance prohibited drainage affecting certain wetlands, thereby precluding any use of water rights on a particular lot, would there be a taking even if other outside water sources were available and there was little or no economic impact on the value or use of the lot? Chief Justice Rehnquist does at times equate the coal with the right to mine it, which is in turn equated with the support estate. Which of these is an identifiable segment of property the destruction of which would be a taking? Is any identifiable use of property a property right? Is the question determined solely by state law so that results would vary from state to state? If state law is not determinative, under Rehnquist's approach would there be a taking if the record demonstrated that the coal company's mining rights were extinguished but it retained other valuable uses of the support estate?

2. What is the standard due process and equal protection test for government regulation that does not involve suspect classes or interference with fundamental rights? Has Justice Scalia created an intermediate level of scrutiny for land use regulation? For permit conditions? Or only for permit conditions that involve public access? *See generally* Eustis, *Between Scylla and Charybdis: Growth Management Act Implementation that Avoids Takings and Substantive Due Process Limitation*, 16 U. PUGET SOUND L. REV. 1181 (1993); Humbach, *Economic Due Process and the Takings Clause*, 4 PACE ENVTL. L. REV. 311 (1987); McGinley, *Regulatory "Takings": The Remarkable Resurrection of Economic Substantive Due Process Analysis in Constitutional Law*, 17 ENVTL. L. RPTR. 10269 (1987); Mitchell, Lucas v. South Carolina Coastal Council: *The Remaking of Takings Law and the Re-Emergence of* Lochner, 9 J. NAT. RESOURCES & ENVTL. L. 105 (1994); Schwartz, *Property Rights and the Constitution: Will the Ugly Duckling Become a Swan?*, 37 AM. U.L. REV. 9 (1987); Sullivan, *Unconstitutional Conditions*, 102 HARV. L. REV. 1413, 1505 (1989); Wolf, Michael Allan, *Takings Term II: New Tools for Attacking and Defending Environmental Land-Use Regulation*, 13 N. ILL. U. L. REV. 469 (1993); Comment, *Private Property Without* Lochner: *Toward a Takings Jurisprudence Uncorrupted by Substantive Due Process*, 142 PA. L. REV. 837 (1993).

3. Fundamentally, are *Keystone* and *Nollan* consistent in their takings analysis? Which case is most consistent with the approach in *Penn Central*?

4. What role, if any, state law will play in defining property rights will necessarily be a recurring issue before the Court. The issue surfaced squarely in a case during the 1990 Term in which the Court avoided resolution of the takings issue altogether. In *Preseault v. Interstate Commerce Comm'n*, 494 U.S. 1 (1990), the petitioners claimed a reversionary interest under state law in an

unused railroad right-of-way. A 1983 amendment to the National Trails System Act provided for conversion of unused railroad rights-of-way to recreational trails subject to approval by the Interstate Commerce Commission (ICC). *Id.* at 919. Under the statute, the interim recreational use cannot be treated for any purpose as abandonment of the right-of-way, thus permitting the ICC to approve conversion from "rails to trails" without regard to reversionary property interests under state law. The Second Circuit Court of Appeals had concluded that state property law was subject to the ICC's plenary authority to regulate so that no revision could occur under state law until the ICC had issued a certificate of abandonment. *Id.* at 921. The majority opinion of the Supreme Court held that the taking claim was premature until the petitioners had pursued their remedies under the Tucker Act, expressing no opinion on the aspect of the ruling by the court of appeals. However, Justice O'Connor, joined by Justices Scalia and Kennedy, concurred separately on the relevance of state law to the taking issue. To determine whether a taking has occurred, Justice O'Connor noted the "basic axiom" that "'[p]roperty interests ... are not created by the Constitution. Rather, they are created and their dimensions are defined by existing rules or understanding that stem from an independent source such as state law.'" *Id.* at 926. The concurring opinion then goes on to conclude that the Preseault's property rights are determined by state law without reference to the ICC's authority or actions. Given the well established and plenary authority of the ICC in railroad regulation, the factual circumstances in *Preseault* presented a more compelling case for definition of property rights under federal law than would normally be the case when a takings challenge is presented. Yet three Justices of the Court concurred separately to recognize the paramount importance of state law in defining property rights for purposes of the takings clause. *Id.* at 926-28. In light of Chief Justice Rehnquist's dissent in *Keystone*, it would appear that at least four Justices would find state law to be dispositive in defining property rights.

5. The Supreme Court trilogy of cases did have an impact on takings cases in the lower courts. According to one commentator, from June 1987 to October 1, 1989, there were 111 state and federal cases reported in which land use regulation was challenged as a taking. Looper-Friedman, *Constitutional Rights as Property?: The Supreme Court's Solution to the "Takings Issue,"* 15 COLUM. J. OF ENVTL. L. 31, 59 (1990). Of these, only fourteen of the sixty-two cases decided on the merits held there was a taking — five federal cases and nine state cases. As of December 31, 1990, there were seven cases awarding damages for a taking against the federal government. The seven cases were *Loveladies Harbor, Inc. v. United States*, 21 Cl. Ct. 153 (1990) *aff'd*, 28 F.3d 1171 (Fed. Cir. 1994); *Florida Rock Indus. v. United States*, 21 Cl. Ct. 161 (1990), *vacated and remanded*, 18 F.3d 1560 (Fed. Cir. 1994), *cert. denied*, 115 S. Ct. 898 (1995); *Shelden v. United States*, 19 Cl. Ct. 247 (1990), *vacated*, 26 Cl. Ct. 375 (1992), *and rev'd*, 7 F.3d 1022 (Fed. Cir. 1993); *Whitney Benefits, Inc. v. United States*, 18 Cl. Ct. 394 (1989), *aff'd*, 926 F.2d 1169 (Fed. Cir. 1991), *cert. denied*, 112 S. Ct. 406 (1991); *Yancey v. United States*, 915 F.2d 1534

(Fed. Cir. 1990); and *Yuba Natural Resources, Inc. v. United States*, 821 F.2d 638 (Fed. Cir. 1987), *appeal after remand*, 904 F.2d 1577 (Fed. Cir. 1990).

By any measurement these cases hardly represented a ground swell of litigation threatening to paralyze land use regulation. To understand fully their significance, however, it is necessary to recall that takings challenges were rarely successful as a matter of federal constitutional law after *Penn Central*. Therefore, even limited success in these challenges, particularly against the federal government, was a significant departure from the trend in prior litigation and enough to engender caution on the part of land use planners when contemplating the regulatory options. It seems only reasonable to assume that takings cases will continue to proliferate.

6. Scholarly analysis of the Supreme Court's decisions in *Keystone*, *First Evangelical Lutheran Church*, and *Nollan* has been extensive. *See, e.g.*, G. HILL, REGULATORY TAKING: THE LIMITS OF LAND USE CONTROLS (1990); Alexander, *Takings, Narratives, and Power*, 88 COLUM. L. REV. 1752 (1988); Burton, *Predatory Municipal Zoning Practices: Changing the Presumption of Constitutionality in the Wake of the "Takings Trilogy,"* 44 ARK. L. REV. 65 (1991); Clarke, *Constitutional Property Rights and the Taking of the Police Power: The Aftermath of* Nollan *and* First English, 20 SW. U. L. REV. 1 (1991); Duncan, *On the Status of Robbing Peter to Pay Paul: The 1987 Takings Cases in the Supreme Court*, 67 NEB. L. REV. 318 (1988); Falik & Shimko, *The Takings Nexus: The Supreme Court Forges a New Direction in Land-Use Jurisprudence*, 23 REAL PROP. PROB. & TR. J. 1 (1988); Epstein, *Takings: Descent and Resurrection*, 1987 SUP. CT. REV. 1; Fischel, *Introduction: Utilitarian Balancing and Formalism in Takings*, 88 COLUM. L. REV. 158 (1988); Fischer, *The Significance of Public Perceptions of the Takings Doctrine*, 88 COLUM. L. REV. 1774 (1988); Kayden, *Land-Use Regulations, Rationality, and Judicial Review: The RSVP in the* Nollan *Invitation (Part I)*, 23 URB. LAW. 301 (1991); Kmiec, *The Original Understanding of the Taking Clause Is Neither Weak Nor Obtuse*, 88 COLUM. L. REV. 1630 (1988); LaRusso, *"Paying for the Change":* First Evangelical Lutheran Church of Glendale v. County of Los Angeles *and the Calculation of Interim Damages for Regulatory Takings*, 17 B.C. ENVTL. AFF. L. REV. 551 (1990); Lunney, *A Critical Reexamination of the Takings Jurisprudence*, 90 MICH. L. REV. 1892 (1992); Michelman, *Takings*, 1987, 88 COLUM. L. REV. 1600 (1988); Michelman, *A Reply to Susan Rose-Ackerman*, 88 COLUM. L. REV. 1712 (1988); Radin, *The Liberal Conception of Property: Cross Currents in the Jurisprudence of Takings*, 88 COLUM. L. REV. 1667 (1988); Rose-Ackerman, *Against Ad Hocery: A Comment on Michelman*, 88 COLUM. L. REV. 1697 (1988); Sterk & Nollan, *Henry George, and Exactions*, 88 COLUM. L. REV. 1731 (1988); Tideman, *Takings, Moral Evolution, and Justice*, 88 COLUM. L. REV. 1714 (1988); Wiseman, *When the End Justifies the Means: Understanding Takings Jurisprudence in a Legal System with Integrity*, 63 ST. JOHN'S L. REV. 433 (1988); Note, *Taking a Step Back: A Reconsideration of the Takings Test of* Nollan v. California Coastal Commission, 102 HARV. L. REV.

448 (1988); Note, *Keystone Bituminous Coal Ass'n v. DeBenedictis*, 2 J. ENVTL.
L. & LITIG. 281 (1987); Comment, *Where Is the Supreme Court Heading in Its
Taking Analysis and What Impact Will This Direction Have on Municipalities?*,
28 NAT. RESOURCES J. 582 (1988); Comment, *Rethinking Regulatory Takings:
A View Toward a Comprehensive Analysis*, 8 N. ILL. U.L. REV. 113 (1987);
Note, *The 1986 Term "Takings" Clause Cases: A Unified Approach to
Regulatory Takings?*, 13 OKLA. CITY U.L. REV. 325 (1988); Note, *First
English: The Fifth Amendment Requires Just Compensation for a Regulatory
Taking*, 33 VILL. L. REV. 925 (1988). Note, *"Take My Teach, Please!": Nollan
v. California Coastal Commission, and a Rational-Nexus Constitutional Analysis
of Development Exactions*, 69 B.U. L. REV. 823 (1989); Comment, *Taking a
Look at the Modern Takings Clause Jurisprudence: Finding Private Property
Protection Under the Federal and Utah Constitutions*, 1994 B.Y.U.L. REV. 893
(1994).

7. Although the Court in *Keystone* and *Nollan* states that there is a taking if
a regulation does not substantially advance legitimate state interests *or* denies an
owner economically viable use of his land, is it an either/or test? Or do both
factors have to be present for there to be a taking so that what would otherwise
be a taking is not treated as such if the regulation advances a substantial state
interest? *See generally* Coletta, *Reciprocity of Advantage and Regulatory Takings:
Toward a New Theory of Takings Jurisprudence*, 40 AM. U. L. REV. 297 (1990);
Coyle, *Takings Jurisprudence and the Political Cultures of American Politics*, 42
CATH. U. L. REV. 817 (1993); Falik & Shimko, *The Takings Nexus: The
Supreme Court Forges a New Direction in Land-Use Jurisprudence*, 23 REAL
PROP. PROB. & TR. J. 1, 4-6 (1988); Kayden, *Land-Use Regulations, Rationali-
ty, and Judicial Review: The RSVP in the* Nollan *Invitation (Part I)*, 23 URV.
LAW. 301 (1991); Lunney, *A Critical Reexamination of the Takings Jurispru-
dence*, 90 MICH. L. REV. 1892 (1992); Wiseman, *When the End Justifies the
Means: Understanding Takings Jurisprudence in a Legal System With Integrity*,
63 ST. JOHNS L. REV. 433 (1989); Comment, *Takings Claims Involving
Pre-Condemnation Land Use Planning: A Proposal for Means-Ends Analysis*, 43
RUTGERS L. REV. 457 (1991). In *First Evangelical Lutheran Church*, Chief
Justice Rehnquist noted that the Court did not have to decide "whether the
ordinance at issue actually denied appellant all use of its property *or whether the
county might avoid the conclusion that a compensable taking had occurred by
establishing that the denial of all use was insulated as a part of the State's
authority to enact safety regulations.*" 482 U.S. at 313 (emphasis added).
Generally, why is the assessment of the state's interest relevant to whether there
is a taking? Is this prong of the test just a restatement of the nuisance exception?
Or is it more relevant to whether the regulation was a proper exercise of the state
or federal government's powers?

The scope of the nuisance exception is not the only puzzling aspect of the
exception that emerges after the 1987 trilogy of cases. If the nuisance exception
applies, is there a taking even if the value of the property is virtually extin-

guished? If so, how can the two-prong test for a taking be an "either/or" test? Or does the nuisance exception simply allow a substantial reduction in value that would otherwise qualify as a taking if the regulation was securing a public benefit and not preventing a public harm? For a general overview of the nuisance exception, see Connors, *Back to the Future: The "Nuisance Exception" to the Just Compensation Clause*, 19 CAP. U. L. REV. 139 (1990); Ferguson, et al., *The Supreme Court and State and Local Government: Small Change for a Changing Court*, 26 URB. LAW. 623 (1994); Humbach, *Envolving Thresholds of Nuisance and the Takings Clause*, 18 COLUM. J. ENVTL. L. 1 (1993); Comment, *Is There a Doctrine in the House?: The Nuisance Exception to the Takings Clause has been Mortally Wounded by* Lucas, 1992 WIS. L. REV. 1299 (1992).

Keep these questions in mind as you read the following case.

LUCAS v. SOUTH CAROLINA COASTAL COUNCIL
505 U.S. 1003 (1992)

JUSTICE SCALIA delivered the opinion of the Court.

In 1986, petitioner David H. Lucas paid $975,000 for two residential lots on the Isle of Palms in Charleston County, South Carolina, on which he intended to build single-family homes. In 1988, however, the South Carolina Legislature enacted the Beachfront Management Act, S.C. Code § 48-39-250 et seq. (Supp. 1990) (Act), which had the direct effect of barring petitioner from erecting any permanent habitable structures on his two parcels. A state trial court found that this prohibition rendered Lucas's parcels "valueless." This case requires us to decide whether the Act's dramatic effect on the economic value of Lucas's lots accomplished a taking of private property under the Fifth and Fourteenth Amendments requiring the payment of "just compensation." U.S. Const., Amdt. 5.

I

A

....

The Supreme Court of South Carolina reversed. It found dispositive what it described as Lucas's concession "that the Beachfront Management Act [was] properly and validly designed to preserve ... South Carolina's beaches." 304 S. Ct. 376, 379, 404 S.E.2d 895, 896 (1991). Failing an attack on the validity of the statute as such, the court believed itself bound to accept the "uncontested ... findings" of the South Carolina legislature that new construction in the coastal zone — such as petitioner intended — threatened this public resource. The Court ruled that when a regulation respecting the use of property is designed "to prevent serious public harm," *id.*, at 383, 404 S.E.2d, at 899 (citing, inter alia, *Mugler v. Kansas*, 123 U.S. 623 (1887)), no compensation is owing under the Takings Clause regardless of the regulation's effect on the property's value.

II

... [The Court initially found that the takings issue was ripe for its determination despite an amendment of the Act during pendency of the state court proceedings which authorized the Council to issue discretionary "special permits" for building construction. The Court acknowledged the unusual posture of the case in that Lucas could still apply for a permit under the 1990 amendment for future construction and challenging, on takings grounds, a denial. Nevertheless, since the state supreme court had determined the takings question on the merits rather than on ripeness grounds, the Court reasoned that Lucas otherwise would be practically and legally precluded from asserting the takings claim with respect to the period pre-dating the amendment.]

III

A

Prior to Justice Holmes' exposition in *Pennsylvania Coal Co. v. Mahon*, 260 U.S. 393 (1922), it was generally thought that the Takings Clause reached only a "direct appropriation" of property, or the functional equivalent of a "practical ouster of [the owner's] possession." [Citations.] Justice Holmes recognized in *Mahon*, however, that if the protection against physical appropriations of private property was to be meaningfully enforced, the government's power to redefine the range of interests included in the ownership of property was necessarily constrained by constitutional limits. If, instead, the uses of private property were subject to unbridled, uncompensated qualification under the police power, "the natural tendency of human nature [would be] to extend the qualification more and more until at last private property disappeared." These considerations gave birth in that case to the oft-cited maxim that, "while property may be regulated to a certain extent, if regulation goes too far it will be recognized as a taking." [Citation.]

Nevertheless, our decision in *Mahon* offered little insight into when, and under what circumstances, a given regulation would be seen as going "too far" for purposes of the Fifth Amendment. In 70-odd years of succeeding "regulatory takings" jurisprudence, we have generally eschewed any "'set formula'" for determining how far is too far, preferring to "engage in ... essentially ad hoc, factual inquiries," [Citations.] We have, however, described at least two discrete categories of regulatory action as compensable without case-specific inquiry into the public interest advanced in support of the restraint. The first encompasses regulations that compel the property owner to suffer a physical "invasion" of his property. In general (at least with regard to permanent invasions), no matter how minute the intrusion, and no matter how weighty the public purpose behind it, we have required compensation. For example, in *Loretto v. Teleprompter Manhattan CATV Corp.*, 458 U.S. 419 (1982), we determined that New York's law requiring landlords to allow television cable companies to emplace cable facilities in their apartment buildings constituted a taking, *id.*, at 435-440, even though the facilities occupied at most only 1½ cubic feet of the landlords' property. [Citations.]

The second situation in which we have found categorical treatment appropriate is where regulation denies all economically beneficial or productive use of land. [Citations.] As we have said on numerous occasions, the Fifth Amendment is violated when land-use regulation "does not substantially advance legitimate state interests *or denies an owner economically viable use of his land.*" [Citation.][7]

We have never set forth the justification for this rule. Perhaps it is simply, as JUSTICE BRENNAN suggested, that total deprivation of beneficial use is, from the landowner's point of view, the equivalent of a physical appropriation. [Citations.] Surely, at least, in the extraordinary circumstance when no productive or economically beneficial use of land is permitted, it is less realistic to indulge our usual assumption that the legislature is simply "adjusting the benefits and burdens of economic life," in a manner that secures an "average reciprocity of advantage" to everyone concerned. [Citations.] And the *functional* basis for permitting the government, by regulation, to affect property values without compensation — that "Government hardly could go on if to some extent values incident to property could not be diminished without paying for every such change in the general law," *id.*, at 413 — does not apply to the relatively rare situations where the government has deprived a landowner of all economically beneficial uses.

On the other side of the balance, affirmatively supporting a compensation requirement, is the fact that regulations that leave the owner of land without economically beneficial or productive options for its use — typically, as here, by requiring land to be left substantially in its natural state — carry with them a

---

[7]Regrettably, the rhetorical force of our "deprivation of all economically feasible use" rule is greater than its precision, since the rule does not make clear the "property interest" against which the loss of value is to be measured. When, for example, a regulation requires a developer to leave 90% of a rural tract in its natural state, it is unclear whether we would analyze the situation as one in which the owner has been deprived of all economically beneficial use of the burdened portion of the tract, or as one in which the owner has suffered a mere diminution in value of the tract as a whole. (For an extreme — and, we think, unsupportable — view of the relevant calculus, see *Penn Central Transportation Co. v. New York City*, 42 N. Y. 2d 324, 333-334, 366 N.E.2d 1271, 1276-1277 (1977), *aff'd*, 438 U.S. 104 (1978), where the state court examined the diminution in a particular parcel's value produced by a municipal ordinance in light of total value of the taking claimant's other holdings in the vicinity.) Unsurprisingly, this uncertainty regarding the composition of the denominator in our "deprivation" fraction has produced inconsistent pronouncements by the Court. [Citations.] The answer to this difficult question may lie in how the owner's reasonable expectations have been shaped by the State's law of property — i.e., whether and to what degree the State's law has accorded legal recognition and protection to the particular interest in land with respect to which the takings claimant alleges a diminution in (or elimination of) value. In any event, we avoid this difficulty in the present case, since the "interest in land" that Lucas has pleaded (a fee simple interest) is an estate with a rich tradition of protection at common law, and since the South Carolina Court of Common Pleas found that the Beachfront Management Act left each of Lucas's beachfront lots without economic value.

heightened risk that private property is being pressed into some form of public service under the guise of mitigating serious public harm. [Citations.]...

We think, in short, that there are good reasons for our frequently expressed belief that when the owner of real property has been called upon to sacrifice all economically beneficial uses in the name of the common good, that is, to leave his property economically idle, he has suffered a taking.[8]

B

....

It is correct that many of our prior opinions have suggested that "harmful or noxious uses" of property may be proscribed by government regulation without the requirement of compensation. For a number of reasons, however, we think the South Carolina Supreme Court was too quick to conclude that that principle decides the present case. The "harmful or noxious uses" principle was the Court's early attempt to describe in theoretical terms why government may, consistent with the Takings Clause, affect property values by regulation without incurring an obligation to compensate — a reality we nowadays acknowledge explicitly with respect to the full scope of the State's police power....

The transition from our early focus on control of "noxious" uses to our contemporary understanding of the broad realm within which government may regulate without compensation was an easy one, since the distinction between "harm-preventing" and "benefit-conferring" regulation is often in the eye of the beholder. It is quite possible, for example, to describe in either fashion the ecological, economic, and aesthetic concerns that inspired the South Carolina legislature in the present case. One could say that imposing a servitude on Lucas's land is necessary in order to prevent his use of it from "harming" South Carolina's ecological resources; or, instead, in order to achieve the "benefits" of an ecological preserve. [Citations.] Whether one or the other of the competing characterizations will come to one's lips in a particular case depends primarily upon one's evaluation of the worth of competing uses of real estate. *See*

---

[8]JUSTICE STEVENS criticizes the "deprivation of all economically beneficial use" rule as "wholly arbitrary," in that "[the] landowner whose property is diminished in value 95% recovers nothing," while the landowner who suffers a complete elimination of value "recovers the land's full value." This analysis errs in its assumption that the landowner whose deprivation is one step short of complete is not entitled to compensation. Such an owner might not be able to claim the benefit of our categorical formulation, but, as we have acknowledged time and again, "the economic impact of the regulation on the claimant and ... the extent to which the regulation has interfered with distinct investment-backed expectations" are keenly relevant to takings analysis generally. *Penn Central Transportation Co. v. New York City*, 438 U.S. 104, 124 (1978). It is true that in at least some cases the landowner with 95% loss will get nothing, while the landowner with total loss will recover in full. But that occasional result is no more strange than the gross disparity between the landowner whose premises are taken for a highway (who recovers in full) and the landowner whose property is reduced to 5% of its former value by the highway (who recovers nothing). Takings law is full of these "all-or-nothing" situations....

Restatement (Second) of Torts § 822, Comment g, p. 112 (1979) ("practically all human activities unless carried on in a wilderness interfere to some extent with others or involve some risk of interference"). A given restraint will be seen as mitigating "harm" to the adjacent parcels or securing a "benefit" for them, depending upon the observer's evaluation of the relative importance of the use that the restraint favors. [Citation.] Whether Lucas's construction of single-family residences on his parcels should be described as bringing "harm" to South Carolina's adjacent ecological resources thus depends principally upon whether the describer believes that the State's use interest in nurturing those resources is so important that any competing adjacent use must yield.

When it is understood that "prevention of harmful use" was merely our early formulation of the police power justification necessary to sustain (without compensation) any regulatory diminution in value; and that the distinction between regulation that "prevents harmful use" and that which "confers benefits" is difficult, if not impossible, to discern on an objective, value-free basis; it becomes self-evident that noxious-use logic cannot serve as a touchstone to distinguish regulatory "takings" — which require compensation — from regulatory deprivations that do not require compensation. *A fortiori* the legislature's recitation of a noxious-use justification cannot be the basis for departing from our categorical rule that total regulatory takings must be compensated. If it were, departure would virtually always be allowed. The South Carolina Supreme Court's approach would essentially nullify *Mahon*'s affirmation of limits to the noncompensable exercise of the police power. Our cases provide no support for this: None of them that employed the logic of "harmful use" prevention to sustain a regulation involved an allegation that the regulation wholly eliminated the value of the claimant's land.

Where the State seeks to sustain regulation that deprives land of all economically beneficial use, we think it may resist compensation only if the logically antecedent inquiry into the nature of the owner's estate shows that the proscribed use interests were not part of his title to begin with. This accords, we think, with our "takings" jurisprudence, which has traditionally been guided by the understandings of our citizens regarding the content of, and the State's power over, the "bundle of rights" that they acquire when they obtain title to property. It seems to us that the property owner necessarily expects the uses of his property to be restricted, from time to time, by various measures newly enacted by the State in legitimate exercise of its police powers; "as long recognized, some values are enjoyed under an implied limitation and must yield to the police power." [Citation.] And in the case of personal property, by reason of the State's traditionally high degree of control over commercial dealings, he ought to be aware of the possibility that new regulation might even render his property economically worthless (at least if the property's only economically productive use is sale or manufacture for sale). In the case of land, however, we think the notion pressed by the Council that title is somehow held subject to the "implied limitation" that the State may subsequently eliminate all economically valuable use is inconsistent with the historical compact recorded in the Takings Clause that has become part of our constitutional culture.

Where "permanent physical occupation" of land is concerned, we have refused to allow the government to decree it anew (without compensation), no matter how weighty the asserted "public interests" involved, — though we assuredly would permit the government to assert a permanent easement that was a pre-existing limitation upon the landowner's title. [Citations.] We believe similar treatment must be accorded confiscatory regulations, i.e., regulations that prohibit all economically beneficial use of land: Any limitation so severe cannot be newly legislated or decreed (without compensation), but must inhere in the title itself, in the restrictions that background principles of the State's law of property and nuisance already place upon land ownership. A law or decree with such an effect must, in other words, do no more than duplicate the result that could have been achieved in the courts — by adjacent landowners (or other uniquely affected persons) under the State's law of private nuisance, or by the State under its complementary power to abate nuisances that affect the public generally, or otherwise.

On this analysis, the owner of a lake bed, for example, would not be entitled to compensation when he is denied the requisite permit to engage in a landfilling operation that would have the effect of flooding others' land. Nor the corporate owner of a nuclear generating plant, when it is directed to remove all improvements from its land upon discovery that the plant sits astride an earthquake fault. Such regulatory action may well have the effect of eliminating the land's only economically productive use, but it does not proscribe a productive use that was previously permissible under relevant property and nuisance principles. The use of these properties for what are now expressly prohibited purposes was always unlawful, and (subject to other constitutional limitations) it was open to the State at any point to make the implication of those background principles of nuisance and property law explicit. [Citation.] In light of our traditional resort to "existing rules or understandings that stem from an independent source such as state law" to define the range of interests that qualify for protection as "property" under the Fifth (and Fourteenth) amendments, this recognition that the Takings Clause does not require compensation when an owner is barred from putting land to a use that is proscribed by those "existing rules or understandings" is surely unexceptional. [Citations.] When, however, a regulation that declares "off-limits" all economically productive or beneficial uses of land goes beyond what the relevant background principles would dictate, compensation must be paid to sustain it.

The "total taking" inquiry we require today will ordinarily entail (as the application of state nuisance law ordinarily entails) analysis of, among other things, the degree of harm to public lands and resources, or adjacent private property, posed by the claimant's proposed activities, see, e.g., Restatement (Second) of Torts §§ 826, 827, the social value of the claimant's activities and their suitability to the locality in question, see, e.g., id., §§ 828(a) and (b), 831, and the relative ease with which the alleged harm can be avoided through measures taken by the claimant and the government (or adjacent private landowners) alike, see, e.g., *id.*, §§ 827(e), 828(c), 830. The fact that a particular use has long been engaged in by similarly situated owners ordinarily imports a lack of any common-law prohibition (though changed circumstances or new knowledge may make what was previously permissible no longer so, see Restatement (Second) of Torts, *supra*, § 827, comment g. So also does the fact that other landowners, similarly situated, are permitted to continue the use denied to the claimant.

It seems unlikely that common-law principles would have prevented the erection of any habitable or productive improvements on petitioner's land; they rarely support prohibition of the "essential use" of land. The question, however, is one of state law to be dealt with on remand. We emphasize that to win its case South Carolina must do more than proffer the legislature's declaration that the uses Lucas desires are inconsistent with the public interest, or the conclusory assertion that they violate a common-law maxim such as *sic utere tuo ut alienum non laedas*. As we have said, a "State, by *ipse dixit*, may not transform private property into public property without compensation...." [Citation.] Instead, as it would be required to do if it sought to restrain Lucas in a common-law action for public nuisance, South Carolina must identify background principles of nuisance and property law that prohibit the uses he now intends in the circumstances in which the property is presently found. Only on this showing can the State fairly claim that, in proscribing all such beneficial uses, the Beachfront Management Act is taking nothing.

[Reversed and remanded.]

JUSTICE KENNEDY, concurring in the judgment.

The case comes to the Court in an unusual posture, as all my colleagues observe. After the suit was initiated but before it reached us, South Carolina amended its Beachfront Management Act to authorize the issuance of special permits at variance with the Act's general limitations. [Citation.] Petitioner has not applied for a special permit but may still do so. The availability of this alternative, if it can be invoked, may dispose of petitioner's claim of a permanent taking. As I read the Court's opinion, it does not decide the permanent taking claim, but neither does it foreclose the Supreme Court of South Carolina from considering the claim or requiring petitioner to pursue an administrative alternative not previously available.

The potential for future relief does not control our disposition, because whatever may occur in the future cannot undo what has occurred in the past. The Beachfront Management Act was enacted in 1988. S.C. Code § 48-39-250 et seq. (Supp. 1990). It may have deprived petitioner of the use of his land in an interim period. If this deprivation amounts to a taking, its limited duration will not bar constitutional relief. It is well established that temporary takings are as protected by the Constitution as are permanent ones. [Citation.]

The issues presented in the case are ready for our decision. The Supreme Court of South Carolina decided the case on constitutional grounds, and its rulings are now before us. There exists no jurisdictional bar to our disposition, and prudential considerations ought not to militate against it. The State cannot complain of the manner in which the issues arose. Any uncertainty in this regard is attributable to the State, as a consequence of its amendment to the Beachfront Management Act. If the Takings Clause is to protect against temporary deprivations as well as permanent ones, its enforcement must not be frustrated by a shifting background of state law.

Although we establish a framework for remand, moreover, we do not decide the ultimate question of whether a temporary taking has occurred in this case. The facts necessary to the determination have not been developed in the record. Among the matters to be considered on remand must be whether petitioner had the intent and capacity to develop the property and failed to do so in the interim period because the State prevented him. Any failure by petitioner to comply with relevant administrative requirements will be part of that analysis.

The South Carolina Court of Common Pleas found that petitioner's real property has been rendered valueless by the State's regulation. The finding appears to presume that the property has no significant market value or resale potential. This is a curious finding, and I share the reservations of some of my colleagues about a finding that a beach front lot loses all value because of a development restriction. While the Supreme Court of South Carolina on remand need not consider the case subject to this constraint, we must accept the finding as entered below. Accepting the finding as entered, it follows that petitioner is entitled to invoke the line of cases discussing regulations that deprive real property of all economic value. [Citation.]

The finding of no value must be considered under the Takings Clause by reference to the owner's reasonable, investment-backed expectations. [Citations.] The Takings Clause, while conferring substantial protection on property owners, does not eliminate the police power of the State to enact limitations on the use of their property. *Mugler v. Kansas*, 123 U.S. 623, 669 (1887). The rights conferred by the Takings Clause and the police power of the State may coexist without conflict. Property is bought and sold, investments are made, subject to the State's power to regulate. Where a taking is alleged from regulations which deprive the property of all value, the test must be whether the deprivation is contrary to reasonable, investment-backed expectations.

There is an inherent tendency towards circularity in this synthesis, of course; for if the owner's reasonable expectations are shaped by what courts allow as a proper exercise of governmental authority, property tends to become what courts say it is. Some circularity must be tolerated in these matters, however, as it is in other spheres. [Citation.] The definition, moreover, is not circular in its entirety. The expectations protected by the Constitution are based on objective rules and customs that can be understood as reasonable by all parties involved.

In my view, reasonable expectations must be understood in light of the whole of our legal tradition. The common law of nuisance is too narrow a confine for the exercise of regulatory power in a complex and interdependent society. [Citation.] The State should not be prevented from enacting new regulatory initiatives in response to changing conditions, and courts must consider all reasonable expectations whatever their source. The Takings Clause does not require a static body of state property law; it protects private expectations to ensure private investment. I agree with the Court that nuisance prevention accords with the most common expectations of property owners who face regulation, but I do not believe this can be the sole source of state authority to impose severe restrictions. Coastal property may present such unique concerns for a fragile land system that the State can go further in regulating its development and use than the common law of nuisance might otherwise permit.

The Supreme Court of South Carolina erred, in my view, by reciting the general purposes for which the state regulations were enacted without a determination that they were in accord with the owner's reasonable expectations and therefore sufficient to support a severe restriction on specific parcels of property. [Citation.] The promotion of tourism, for instance, ought not to suffice to deprive specific property of all value without a corresponding duty to compensate. Furthermore, the means as well as the ends of regulation must accord with the owner's reasonable expectations. Here, the State did not act until after the property had been zoned for individual lot development and most other parcels had been improved, throwing the whole burden of the regulation on the remaining lots. This too must be measured in the balance. [Citation.]

JUSTICE BLACKMUN, dissenting.

Today the Court launches a missile to kill a mouse.

....

IV

A

I first question the Court's rationale in creating a category that obviates a "case-specific inquiry into the public interest advanced," if all economic value has been lost. If one fact about the Court's taking jurisprudence can be stated without contradiction, it is that "the particular circumstances of each case" determine whether a specific restriction will be rendered invalid by the government's failure to pay compensation. [Citation.] This is so because although we have articulated certain factors to be considered, including the economic impact on the property owner, the ultimate conclusion "necessarily requires a weighing of private and public interests." [Citation.] When the government regulation prevents the owner from any economically valuable use of his property, the private interest is unquestionably substantial, but we have never before held that no public interest can outweigh it. Instead the Court's prior decisions "uniformly reject the proposition that diminution in property value, standing alone, can establish a 'taking.'" [Citation.]

This Court repeatedly has recognized the ability of government, in certain circumstances, to regulate property without compensation no matter how adverse the financial effect on the owner may be. More than a century ago, the Court explicitly upheld the right of States to prohibit uses of property injurious to public health, safety, or welfare without paying compensation: "A prohibition simply upon the use of property for purposes that are declared, by valid legislation, to be injurious to the health, morals, or safety of the community, cannot, in any just sense, be deemed a taking or an appropriation of property." *Mugler v. Kansas*, 123 U.S. 623, 668-669 (1887)....

B

Even more perplexing, however, is the Court's reliance on common-law principles of nuisance in its quest for a value-free taking jurisprudence. In determining what is a nuisance at common law, state courts make exactly the decision that the Court finds so troubling when made by the South Carolina General Assembly today: they determine whether the use is harmful. Common-law public and private nuisance law is simply a determination whether a particular use causes harm. [Citation.] There is nothing magical in the reasoning of judges long dead. They determined a harm in the same way as state judges and legislatures do today. If judges in the 18th and 19th centuries can distinguish a harm from a benefit, why not judges in the 20th century, and if judges can, why not legislators? There simply is no reason to believe that new interpretations of the hoary common law nuisance doctrine will be particularly "objective" or "value-free.''...

JUSTICE STEVENS, dissenting.

Today the Court restricts one judge-made rule and expands another. In my opinion it errs on both counts. Proper application of the doctrine of judicial restraint would avoid the premature adjudication of an important constitutional question. Proper respect for our precedents would avoid an illogical expansion of the concept of "regulatory takings."

....

II

The Categorical Rule

As the Court recognizes, *Pennsylvania Coal Co. v. Mahon*, 260 U.S. 393 (1922), provides no support for its — or, indeed, any — categorical rule. To the contrary, Justice Holmes recognized that such absolute rules ill fit the inquiry into "regulatory takings." Thus, in the paragraph that contains his famous observation that a regulation may go "too far" and thereby constitute a taking, the Justice wrote: "As we already have said, this is a question of degree — and therefore cannot be disposed of by general propositions." *Id.* at 416....

In addition to lacking support in past decisions, the Court's new rule is wholly arbitrary. A landowner whose property is diminished in value 95% recovers nothing, while an owner whose property is diminished 100% recovers the land's full value. The case at hand illustrates this arbitrariness well. The Beachfront Management Act not only prohibited the building of new dwellings in certain areas, it also prohibited the rebuilding of houses that were "destroyed beyond repair by natural causes or by fire." [Citations.] Thus, if the homes adjacent to Lucas' lot were destroyed by a hurricane one day after the Act took effect, the owners would not be able to rebuild, nor would they be assured recovery. Under the Court's categorical approach, Lucas (who has lost the opportunity to build) recovers, while his neighbors (who have lost both the opportunity to build and their homes) do not recover. The arbitrariness of such a rule is palpable.

Moreover, because of the elastic nature of property rights, the Court's new rule will also prove unsound in practice. In response to the rule, courts may define "property" broadly and only rarely find regulations to effect total takings. This is the approach the Court itself adopts in its revisionist reading of venerable precedents. We are told that — notwithstanding the Court's findings to the contrary in each case — the brewery in *Mugler*, the brickyard in *Hadacheck*, and the gravel pit in *Goldblatt* all could be put to "other uses" and that, therefore, those cases did not involve total regulatory takings.[3]

On the other hand, developers and investors may market specialized estates to take advantage of the Court's new rule. The smaller the estate, the more likely that a regulatory change will effect a total taking. Thus, an investor may, for example, purchase the right to build a multi-family home on a specific lot, with the result that a zoning regulation that allows only single-family homes would render the investor's property interest "valueless." In short, the categorical rule will likely have one of two effects: Either courts will alter the definition of the "denominator" in the takings "fraction," rendering the Court's categorical rule meaningless, or investors will manipulate the relevant property interests, giving the Court's rule sweeping effect. To my mind, neither of these results is desirable or appropriate, and both are distortions of our takings jurisprudence.

Finally, the Court's justification for its new categorical rule is remarkably thin. The Court mentions in passing three arguments in support of its rule; none is convincing. First, the Court suggests that "total deprivation of feasible use is,

---

[3]Of course, the same could easily be said in this case: Lucas may put his land to "other uses" — fishing or camping, for example — or may sell his land to his neighbors as a buffer. In either event, his land is far from "valueless."

This highlights a fundamental weakness in the Court's analysis: its failure to explain why only the impairment of "*economically* beneficial or productive use," (emphasis added), of property is relevant in takings analysis. I should think that a regulation arbitrarily prohibiting an owner from continuing to use her property for bird-watching or sunbathing might constitute a taking under some circumstances; and, conversely, that such uses are of value to the owner. Yet the Court offers no basis for its assumption that the only uses of property cognizable under the Constitution are developmental uses.

from the landowner's point of view, the equivalent of a physical appropriation." This argument proves too much. From the "landowner's point of view," a regulation that diminishes a lot's value by 50% is as well "the equivalent" of the condemnation of half of the lot. Yet, it is well established that a 50% diminution in value does not by itself constitute a taking. See *Euclid v. Ambler Realty Co.*, 272 U.S. 365, 384 (1926) (75% diminution in value). Thus, the landowner's perception of the regulation cannot justify the Court's new rule.

Second, the Court emphasizes that because total takings are "relatively rare" its new rule will not adversely affect the government's ability to "go on." This argument proves too little. Certainly it is true that defining a small class of regulations that are *per se* takings will not greatly hinder important governmental functions — but this is true of *any* small class of regulations. The Court's suggestion only begs the question of why regulations of *this* particular class should always be found to effect takings.

Finally, the Court suggests that "regulations that leave the owner ... without economically beneficial ... use ... carry with them a heightened risk that private property is being pressed into some form of public service."... [I] agree that the risks of such singling out are of central concern in takings law. However, such risks do not justify a per se rule for total regulatory takings. There is no necessary correlation between "singling out" and total takings: a regulation may single out a property owner without depriving him of all of his property, and it may deprive him of all of his property without singling him out. [Citations.] What matters in such cases is not the degree of diminution of value, but rather the specificity of the expropriating act....

The Nuisance Exception

Like many bright-line rules, the categorical rule established in this case is only "categorical" for a page or two in the U.S. Reports. No sooner does the Court state that "total regulatory takings must be compensated," than it quickly establishes an exception to that rule.

The exception provides that a regulation that renders property valueless is not a taking if it prohibits uses of property that were not "previously permissible under relevant property and nuisance principles." The Court thus rejects the basic holding in *Mugler v. Kansas*, 123 U.S. 623 (1887). There we held that a state-wide statute that prohibited the owner of a brewery from making alcoholic beverages did not effect a taking, even though the use of the property had been perfectly lawful and caused no public harm before the statute was enacted. We squarely rejected the rule the Court adopts today:

> "It is true, that, when the defendants ... erected their breweries, the laws of the State did not forbid the manufacture of intoxicating liquors. But the State did not thereby give any assurance, or come under an obligation, that its legislation upon that subject would remain unchanged. The supervision of the public health and the public morals is a governmental power, 'continuing

in its nature,' and 'to be dealt with as the special exigencies of the moment may require'; ... 'for this purpose, the largest legislative discretion is allowed, and the discretion cannot be parted with any more than the power itself.'" *Id.*, at 669.

Under our reasoning in *Mugler*, a state's decision to prohibit or to regulate certain uses of property is not a compensable taking just because the particular uses were previously lawful. Under the Court's opinion today, however, if a state should decide to prohibit the manufacture of asbestos, cigarettes, or concealable firearms, for example, it must be prepared to pay for the adverse economic consequences of its decision....

The Court's holding today effectively freezes the State's common law, denying the legislature much of its traditional power to revise the law governing the rights and uses of property....

Arresting the development of the common law is not only a departure from our prior decisions; it is also profoundly unwise. The human condition is one of constant learning and evolution — both moral and practical. Legislatures implement that new learning; in doing so they must often revise the definition of property and the rights of property owners. Thus, when the Nation came to understand that slavery was morally wrong and mandated the emancipation of all slaves, it, in effect, redefined "property." On a lesser scale, our ongoing self-education produces similar changes in the rights of property owners: New appreciation of the significance of endangered species, the importance of wetlands, and the vulnerability of coastal lands, shapes our evolving understandings of property rights....

Statement of JUSTICE SOUTER.

I would dismiss the writ of certiorari in this case as having been granted improvidently. After briefing and argument it is abundantly clear that an unreviewable assumption on which this case comes to us is both questionable as a conclusion of Fifth Amendment law and sufficient to frustrate the Court's ability to render certain the legal premises on which its holding rests.

....

Because the questionable conclusion of total deprivation cannot be reviewed, the Court is precluded from attempting to clarify the concept of total (and, in the Court's view, categorically compensable) taking on which it rests, a concept which the Court describes, as so uncertain under existing law as to have fostered inconsistent pronouncements by the Court itself. Because that concept is left uncertain, so is the significance of the exceptions to the compensation requirement that the Court proceeds to recognize. This alone is enough to show that there is little utility in attempting to deal with this case on the merits.

....

NOTES AND QUESTIONS

1. After *Lucas*, when may the nuisance exception still apply? How often do you think a court will find a "total" taking? Why was one found in this case?

2. How is the scope of the nuisance exception to be determined? If a lower court was inclined to uphold environmental regulation within the nuisance exception, what language in Justice Scalia's opinion would be helpful in defining the exception broadly? Narrowly? *See generally* Richard Lazarus, *Putting the Correct "Spin" on* Lucas, 45 STANFORD L. REV. 1411 (1993).

3. *The "Nuisance Exception."* Justice Stevens in *Keystone* suggests that the Pennsylvania Act falls within the "nuisance" exception to the takings clause, a long-standing exception which Chief Justice Rehnquist broadly reaffirmed in his dissent in *Penn Central* and his opinion in *First Evangelical Lutheran Church*. Why does Chief Justice Rehnquist conclude the nuisance exception does not apply to the Pennsylvania Act? The Court was unanimous in *Keystone* in recognizing this exception and emphasizing that the exception not be so broadly construed as to encompass all regulatory takings. Early Supreme Court opinions indicated that when governmental regulation prevents a public harm, it falls within the nuisance exception and is not taking. *See, e.g., Mugler v. Kansas*, 123 U.S. 623 (1887) (prohibition on manufacture and sale of intoxicating liquors); *Hadacheck v. Sebastian*, 239 U.S. 394 (1915) (prohibition on manufacturing of bricks near residents in Los Angeles); *Miller v. Schoene*, 276 U.S. 272 (1928) (destruction of cedar trees to protect apple trees from disease); *Goldblatt v. Hempstead*, 369 U.S. 590 (1962) (restrictions on gravel removal). When the governmental regulation secures a public benefit, however, it must be evaluated as a taking. As Justice Scalia notes in *Nollan*, the line is a difficult one to draw between securing a public benefit and preventing a public harm. The majority and dissenting Justices differed sharply on that issue in *Keystone*.

For example, does a local ordinance take private property without compensation if it limits use of wetlands to uses in its natural state such as fishing and hunting, and requires a permit for all other uses? Consider the following language in *Just v. Marinette County*, 56 Wis. 2d 7, 201 N.W.2d 761 (1972):

> This case causes us to reexamine the concepts of public benefit in contrast to public harm and the scope of an owner's right to use of his property. In the instant case we have a restriction on the use of a citizen's property, not to secure a benefit for the public, but to prevent a harm from the change in the natural character of the citizen's property. We start with the premise that lakes and rivers in their natural state are unpolluted and the pollution which now exists is man made.... What makes this case different from most condemnation or police power zoning cases is the interrelationship of the wetlands, the swamps and the natural environment of shorelands to the purity of the water and to such natural resources as navigation, fishing, and scenic beauty. Swamps and wetlands were once considered wasteland, undesirable, and not picturesque. But as the people became more sophisticat-

ed, an appreciation was acquired that swamps and wetlands serve a vital role in nature, are part of the balance of nature and are essential to the purity of the water in our lakes and streams. Swamps and wetlands are a necessary part of the ecological creation and now, even to the uninitiated, possess their own beauty in nature.

....

This is not a case where an owner is prevented from using his land for natural and indigenous uses. The uses consistent with the nature of the land are allowed and other uses recognized and still others permitted by special permit. The shoreland zoning ordinance prevents to some extent the changing of the natural character of the land within 1,000 feet of a navigable lake and 300 feet of a navigable river because of such land's interrelation to the contiguous water. The changing of wetlands and swamps to the damage of the general public by upsetting the natural environment and the natural relationship is not a reasonable use of that land which is protected from police power regulation. Changes and filling to some extent are permitted because the extent of such changes and fillings does not cause harm. We realize no cause in Wisconsin has yet dealt with shoreland regulations and there are several cases in other states which seem to hold such regulations unconstitutional; but nothing this court has said or held in prior cases indicates that destroying the natural character of a swamp or a wetland so as to make that location available for human habitation is a reasonable use of that land when the new use, although of a more economical value to the owner, causes a harm to the general public.

....

The Justs argue their property has been severely depreciated in value. But this depreciation of value is not based on the use of the land in its natural state but on what the land would be worth if it could be filled and used for the location of a dwelling. While loss of value is to be considered in determining whether a restriction is a constructive taking, value based upon changing the character of the land at the expense or harm to public rights is not an essential factor or controlling.

We are not mindful of the warning in *Pennsylvania Coal Co. v. Mahon* (1922), 260 U.S. 393:

> ... We are in danger of forgetting that a strong public desire to improve the public condition is not enough to warrant achieving the desire by a shorter cut than the constitutional way of paying for the change.

This observation refers to the improvement of the public condition, the securing of a benefit not presently enjoyed and to which the public is not entitled. The shoreland zoning ordinance preserves nature, the environment, and natural resources as they were created and to which the people have a present right. The ordinance does not create or improve the public condition but only preserves nature from the despoilage and harm resulting from the unrestricted activities of humans.

Does all environmental regulation prevent a public harm?

DOLAN v. CITY OF TIGARD

512 U.S. 374 (1994)

CHIEF JUSTICE REHNQUIST delivered the opinion of the Court.

Petitioner challenges the decision of the Oregon Supreme Court which held that the city of Tigard could condition the approval of her building permit on the dedication of a portion of her property for flood control and traffic improvements. We granted certiorari to resolve a question left open by our decision in *Nollan v. California Coastal Comm'n*, 107 S. Ct. 3141 (1987), of what is the required degree of connection between the exactions imposed by the city and the projected impacts of the proposed development.

I

The State of Oregon enacted a comprehensive land use management program in 1973. Ore. Rev. Stat. §§ 197.005-197.860 (1991) The program required all Oregon cities and counties to adopt new comprehensive land use plans that were consistent with the statewide planning goals.... [The city of Tigard] developed a comprehensive plan and codified it in its Community Development Code (CDC). The CDC requires property owners in the area zoned Central Business District to comply with a 15% open space and landscaping requirement, which limits total site coverage, including all structures and paved parking, to 85% of the parcel. After the completion of a transportation study that identified congestion in the Central Business District as a particular problem, the city adopted a plan for a pedestrian/bicycle pathway intended to encourage alternatives to automobile transportation for short trips....

The city also adopted a Master Drainage Plan (Drainage Plan). The Drainage Plan noted that flooding occurred in several areas along Fanno Creek, including areas near petitioner's property. The Drainage Plan suggested a series of improvements to the Fanno Creek Basin, including channel excavation in the area next to petitioner's property.... The Drainage Plan concluded that the cost of these improvements should be shared based on both direct and indirect benefits, with property owners along the waterways paying more due to the direct benefit that they would receive....

Petitioner Florence Dolan owns a plumbing and electric supply store located on Main Street in the Central Business District of the city.... Fanno Creek flows through the southwestern corner of the lot and along its western boundary. The year-round flow of the creek renders the area within the creek's 100-year floodplain virtually unusable for commercial development....

Petitioner applied to the city for a permit to redevelop the site. Her proposed plans called for nearly doubling the size of the store to 17,600 square feet, and paving a 39-space parking lot.... In the second phase of the project, petitioner proposed to build an additional structure on the northeast side of the site for complementary businesses, and to provide more parking....

The City Planning Commission granted petitioner's permit application subject to conditions imposed by the city's CDC.... Thus, the Commission required that petitioner dedicate the portion of her property lying within the 100-year floodplain for improvement of a storm drainage system along Fanno Creek and that she dedicate an additional 15-foot strip of land adjacent to the floodplain as a pedestrian/bicycle pathway. The dedication required by that condition encompasses approximately 7,000 square feet, or roughly 10% of the property. In accordance with city practice, petitioner could rely on the dedicated property to meet the 15% open space and landscaping requirement mandated by the city's zoning scheme....

Petitioner requested variances from the CDC standards. Variances are granted only where it can be shown that, owing to special circumstances related to a specific piece of the land, the literal interpretation of the applicable zoning provisions would cause "an undue or unnecessary hardship" unless the variance is granted.... Petitioner simply argued that her proposed development would not conflict with the policies of the comprehensive plan. The Commission denied the request.

The Commission made a series of findings concerning the relationship between the dedicated conditions and the projected impacts of petitioner's project. First, the Commission noted that "[i]t is reasonable to assume that customers and employees of the future uses of this site could utilize a pedestrian/bicycle pathway adjacent to this development for their transportation and recreational needs."... In addition, the Commission found that creation of a convenient, safe pedestrian/bicycle pathway system as an alternative means of transportation "could offset some of the traffic demand on [nearby] streets and lessen the increase in traffic congestion."

The Commission went on to note that the required floodplain dedication would be reasonably related to petitioner's request to intensify the use of the site given the increase in the impervious surface. The Commission stated that the "anticipated increased storm water flow from the subject property to an already strained creek and drainage basin can only add to the public need to manage the stream channel and floodplain for drainage purposes." [The Tigard City Council approved the Commission's final order.]

Petitioner appealed to the Land Use Board of Appeals (LUBA) on the ground that the city's dedication requirements were not related to the proposed development, and, therefore, those requirements constituted an uncompensated taking of their property under the Fifth Amendment. In evaluating the federal taking claim, LUBA assumed that the city's findings about the impacts of the proposed development were supported by substantial evidence. Given the undisputed fact that the proposed larger building and paved parking area would increase the amount of impervious surfaces and the runoff into Fanno Creek,

LUBA concluded that "there is a 'reasonable relationship' between the proposed development and the requirement to dedicate land along Fanno Creek for a greenway." With respect to the pedestrian/bicycle pathway, LUBA noted the Commission's finding that a significantly larger retail sales building and parking lot would attract larger numbers of customers and employees and their vehicles. It again found a "reasonable relationship" between alleviating the impacts of increased traffic from the development and facilitating the provision of a pedestrian/bicycle pathway as an alternative means of transportation.

The Oregon Court of Appeals affirmed, rejecting petitioner's contention that in *Nollan v. California Coastal Comm'n*, 107 S. Ct. 3141 (1987), we had abandoned the "reasonable relationship" test in favor of a stricter "essential nexus" test. The Oregon Supreme Court affirmed. The court also disagreed with petitioner's contention that the *Nollan* Court abandoned the "reasonably related" test. Instead, the court read *Nollan* to mean that an "exaction is reasonably related to an impact if the exaction serves the same purpose that a denial of the permit would serve." The court decided that both the pedestrian/bicycle pathway condition and the storm drainage dedication had an essential nexus to the development of the proposed site. Therefore, the court found the conditions to be reasonably related to the impact of the expansion of petitioner's business. We granted certiorari, because of an alleged conflict between the Oregon Supreme Court's decision and our decision in *Nollan*.

II

The Takings Clause of the Fifth Amendment of the United States Constitution, made applicable to the States through the Fourteenth Amendment, provides: "[N]or shall private property be taken for public use, without just compensation."... Without question, had the city simply required petitioner to dedicate a strip of land along Fanno Creek for public use, rather than conditioning the grant of her permit to redevelop her property on such a dedication, a taking would have occurred....

[T]he authority of state and local governments to engage in land use planning has been sustained against constitutional challenge as long ago as our decision in *Euclid v. Ambler Realty Co.*, 47 S. Ct. 114 (1926).... A land use regulation does not effect a taking if it "substantially advance[s] legitimate state interests" and does not "den[y] an owner economically viable use of his land." [Citations.]

The sort of land use regulations [previously enumerated by the Court], however, differ in two relevant particulars from the present case. First, they involved essentially legislative determinations classifying entire areas of the city, whereas here the city made an adjudicative decision to condition petitioner's application for a building permit on an individual parcel. Second, the conditions imposed were not simply a limitation on the use petitioner might make of her own parcel, but a requirement that she deed portions of the property to the city. In *Nollan*, we held that governmental authority to exact such a condition was circumscribed by the Fifth and Fourteenth Amendments. Under the well-settled doctrine of "unconstitutional conditions," the government may not require a person to give up a constitutional right — here the right to receive just compensation when property is taken for a public use — in exchange for a discretionary benefit conferred by the government where the property sought has little or no relationship to the benefit. [Citations.]

Petitioner contends that the city has forced her to choose between the building permit and her right under the Fifth Amendment to just compensation for the public easements. Petitioner does not quarrel with the city's authority to exact some forms of dedication as a condition for the grant of a building permit, but challenges the showing made by the city to justify these exactions. She argues that the city has identified "no special benefits" conferred on her, and has not identified any "special quantifiable burdens" created by her new store that would justify the particular dedications required from her which are not required from the public at large.

III

In evaluating petitioner's claim, we must first determine whether the "essential nexus" exists between the "legitimate state interest" and the permit condition exacted by the city. If we find that a nexus exists, we must then decide the required degree of connection between the exactions and the projected impact of the proposed development....

A

We addressed the essential nexus question in *Nollan*. The California Coastal Commission demanded a lateral public easement across the Nollan's beachfront lot in exchange for a permit to demolish an existing bungalow and replace it with a three-bedroom house. The public easement was designed to connect two public beaches that were separated by the Nollan's property. The Coastal Commission had asserted that the public easement condition was imposed to promote the legitimate state interest of diminishing the "blockage of the view of the ocean" caused by construction of the larger house.

We agreed that the Coastal Commission's concern with protecting visual access to the ocean constituted a legitimate public interest. We also agreed that the permit condition would have been constitutional "even if it consisted of the requirement that the Nollans provide a viewing spot on their property for passersby with whose sighting of the ocean their new house would interfere." We resolved, however, that the Coastal Commission's regulatory authority was set completely adrift from its constitutional moorings when it claimed that a nexus existed between visual access to the ocean and a permit condition requiring lateral public access along the Nollan's beachfront lot. How enhancing the public's ability to "traverse to and along the shorefront" served the same governmental purpose of "visual access to the ocean" from the roadway was beyond our ability to countenance. The absence of a nexus left the Coastal Commission in the position of simply trying to obtain an easement through gimmickry, which converted a valid regulation of land use into "an out-and-out plan of extortion."

No such gimmicks are associated with the permit conditions imposed by the city in this case. Undoubtedly, the prevention of flooding along Fanno Creek and the reduction of traffic congestion in the Central Business District qualify as the type of legitimate public purposes we have upheld. It seems equally obvious that a nexus exists between preventing flooding along Fanno Creek and limiting development within the creek's 100-year floodplain. Petitioner proposes to double the size of her retail store and to pave her now-gravel parking lot, thereby expanding the impervious surface on the property and increasing the amount of stormwater run-off into Fanno Creek.

The same may be said for the city's attempt to reduce traffic congestion by providing for alternative means of transportation. In theory, a pedestrian/bicycle pathway provides a useful alternative means of transportation for workers and shoppers: "Pedestrians and bicyclists occupying dedicated spaces for walking and/or bicycling ... remove potential vehicles from streets, resulting in an overall improvement in total transportation system flow."...

B

The second part of our analysis requires us to determine whether the degree of the exactions demanded by the city's permit conditions bear the required relationship to the projected impact of petitioner's proposed development. [Citations.] Here the Oregon Supreme Court deferred to what it termed the "city's unchallenged factual findings" supporting the dedication conditions and found them to be reasonably related to the impact of the expansion of petitioner's business.

The city required that petitioner dedicate "to the city as Greenway all portions of the site that fall within the existing 100-year floodplain [of Fanno Creek] ... and all property 15 feet above [the floodplain] boundary." In addition, the city demanded that the retail store be designed so as not to intrude into the greenway area. The city relies on the Commission's rather tentative findings that increased stormwater flow from petitioner's property "can only add to the public need to manage the [floodplain] for drainage purposes" to support its conclusion that the "requirement of dedication of the floodplain area on the site is related to the applicant's plan to intensify development on the site."

The city made the following specific findings relevant to the pedestrian/bicycle pathway:

> In addition, the proposed expanded use of this site is anticipated to generate additional vehicular traffic thereby increasing congestion on nearby collector and arterial streets. Creation of a convenient, safe pedestrian/bicycle pathway system as an alternative means of transportation could offset some of the traffic demand on these nearby streets and lessen the increase in traffic congestion.

The question for us is whether these findings are constitutionally sufficient to justify the conditions imposed by the city on petitioner's building permit....

In some States, very generalized statements as to the necessary connection between the required dedication and the proposed development seem to suffice. [Citations.] We think this standard is too lax to adequately protect petitioner's right to just compensation if her property is taken for a public purpose.

Other state courts require a very exacting correspondence, described as the "specifi[c] and uniquely attributable" test. The Supreme Court of Illinois first developed this test in *Pioneer Trust & Savings Bank v. Mount Prospect*, 22 Ill. 2d 375, 380, 176 N.E.2d 799, 802 (1961). Under this standard, if the local government cannot demonstrate that its exaction is directly proportional to the specifically created need, the exaction becomes "a veiled exercise of the power of eminent domain and a confiscation of private property behind the defense of police regulations." We do not think the Federal Constitution requires such exacting scrutiny, given the nature of the interests involved.

A number of state courts have taken an intermediate position, requiring the municipality to show a "reasonable relationship" between the required dedication and the impact of the proposed development. Typical is the Supreme Court of Nebraska's opinion in *Simpson v. North Platte*, 206 Neb. 240, 245, 292 N.W.2d 297, 301 (1980), where that court stated:

> The distinction, therefore, which must be made between an appropriate exercise of the police power and an improper exercise of eminent domain is whether the requirement has some reasonable relationship or nexus to the use to which the property is being made or is merely being used as an excuse for taking property simply because at that particular moment the landowner is asking the city for some license or permit.

Thus, the court held that a city may not require a property owner to dedicate private property for some future public use as a condition of obtaining a building permit when such future use is not "occasioned by the construction sought to be permitted." [Citation.]

... Despite any semantical differences, general agreement exists among the courts "that the dedication should have some reasonable relationship to the needs created by the [development]."

We think the "reasonable relationship" test adopted by a majority of the state courts is closer to the federal constitutional norm than either of those previously discussed. But we do not adopt it as such, partly because the term "reasonable relationship" seems confusingly similar to the term "rational basis" which describes the minimal level of scrutiny under the Equal Protection Clause of the Fourteenth Amendment. We think a term such as "rough proportionality" best encapsulates what we hold to be the requirement of the Fifth Amendment. No precise mathematical calculation is required, but the city must make some sort of individualized determination that the required dedication is related both in nature and extent to the impact of the proposed development.

... We turn now to analysis of whether the findings relied upon by the city here, first with respect to the floodplain easement, and second with respect to the pedestrian/bicycle path, satisfied these requirements.

It is axiomatic that increasing the amount of impervious surface will increase the quantity and rate of storm-water flow from petitioner's property. Therefore, keeping the floodplain open and free from development would likely confine the pressures on Fanno Creek created by petitioner's development. In fact, because petitioner's property lies within the Central Business District, the Community Development Code already required that petitioner leave 15% of it as open space and the undeveloped floodplain would have nearly satisfied that requirement. But the city demanded more — it not only wanted petitioner not to build in the floodplain, but it also wanted petitioner's property along Fanno Creek for its Greenway system. The city has never said why a public greenway, as opposed to a private one, was required in the interest of flood control.

The difference to petitioner, of course, is the loss of her ability to exclude others. As we have noted, this right to exclude others is "one of the most essential sticks in the bundle of rights that are commonly characterized as property." [Citation.] It is difficult to see why recreational visitors trampling along petitioner's floodplain easement are sufficiently related to the city's legitimate interest in reducing flooding problems along Fanno Creek, and the city has not attempted to make any individualized determination to support this part of its request.

The city contends that recreational easement along the Greenway is only ancillary to the city's chief purpose in controlling flood hazards. It further asserts that unlike the residential property at issue in *Nollan*, petitioner's property is commercial in character and therefore, her right to exclude others is compromised....

Admittedly, petitioner wants to build a bigger store to attract members of the public to her property. She also wants, however, to be able to control the time and manner in which they enter.... By contrast, the city wants to impose a permanent recreational easement upon petitioner's property that borders Fanno Creek. Petitioner would lose all rights to regulate the time in which the public entered onto the Greenway, regardless of any interference it might pose with her retail store. Her right to exclude would not be regulated, it would be eviscerated.

If petitioner's proposed development had somehow encroached on existing greenway space in the city, it would have been reasonable to require petitioner to provide some alternative greenway space for the public either on her property or elsewhere.... We conclude that the findings upon which the city relies do not show the required reasonable relationship between the floodplain easement and the petitioner's proposed new building.

With respect to the pedestrian/bicycle pathway, we have no doubt that the city was correct in finding that the larger retail sales facility proposed by petitioner will increase traffic on the streets of the Central Business District.... Dedications for streets, sidewalks, and other public ways are generally reasonable exactions to avoid excessive congestion from a proposed property use. But on the record before us, the city has not met its burden of demonstrating that the additional number of vehicle and bicycle trips generated by the petitioner's development reasonably relate to the city's requirement for a dedication of the pedestrian/bicycle pathway easement. The city simply found that the creation of the pathway "could offset some of the traffic demand ... and lessen the increase in traffic congestion."

... No precise mathematical calculation is required, but the city must make some effort to quantify its findings in support of the dedication for the pedestrian/bicycle pathway beyond the conclusory statement that it could offset some of the traffic demand generated.

IV

Cities have long engaged in the commendable task of land use planning, made necessary by increasing urbanization particularly in metropolitan areas such as Portland. The city's goals of reducing flooding hazards and traffic congestion, and providing for public greenways, are laudable, but there are outer limits to how this may be done. "A strong public desire to improve the public condition [will not] warrant achieving the desire by a shorter cut than the constitutional way of paying for the change." [Citation.]

The judgment of the Supreme Court of Oregon is reversed, and the case is remanded for further proceedings consistent with this opinion.

It is so ordered.

NOTES AND QUESTIONS

1. How does *Dolan* clarify the *Nollan* "nexus" test? Examine each of the conditions imposed on Dolan's permit. Which ones were struck down? Why? What would the city have to demonstrate to sustain these conditions?

2. In the federal cases in which a taking has been found, the Court of Claims and Federal Circuit Court of Appeals have found it necessary to address not only how far regulatory interference must go to be a taking, but also how to measure the damages once a taking has been found. Both courts have emphasized in their opinions that no economically viable use of the property in question remained after regulation, often despite apparent conservation, agricultural, and recreational uses for the property. These courts also appear to be utilizing the "before and after" fair market value of the highest and best use of the property to determine damages, an approach which results in higher damages than many alternative formulations such as measuring damages to immediate use values. Although admittedly a very small sampling, these cases suggest that landowners may well be succeeding with takings challenges by showing that no *development* use remains in the property and then may recover for damage done to the *potential* developmental value of the property rather than to the immediate use value of the property.

The "before and after" fair market value test is only a starting point for addressing the diverse, complicated assessments of the compensation due for a temporary taking which the courts must now address. Consider the following facts from *Wheeler v. City of Pleasant Grove*, 833 F.2d 267 (11th Cir. 1987) and 896 F.2d 1347 (11th Cir. 1990). Cliff Development Corporation had a contract to buy land from the Wheelers for $160,000 to build an apartment complex. The city council, due to public opposition to the complex, passed an ordinance prohibiting construction of apartment complexes which was invalidated by the district court sixteen months later as a taking. The property had *appreciated* in value during the period the ordinance was in effect.

The Wheelers claimed that they would have sold their property for $160,000 to Cliff Development but for the enactment of the ordinance. They sought damages in the amount of the interest they would have received on the proceeds of the sale over the sixteen months that the ordinance was in effect, less rental income derived from the property over the same period. The Wheelers also sought damages for mental anguish they allegedly suffered as a result of the lost sale.

Cliff Development claimed that it had suffered damages separate and apart from those claimed by the Wheelers. First, it claimed that it was entitled to compensation for expenditures in excess of $19,000 it had made in preparation for construction before the enactment of the ordinance. Second, it claimed that it had suffered damages to the extent that building costs and temporary and permanent financing costs had increased over the sixteen months that the ordinance was in effect. Third, it claimed it was entitled to the profits it would have made had construction proceeded on schedule. Fourth, it sought damages for injury to its business reputation. Fifth, it sought punitive damages. You are the unfortunate judge deciding this case. What is the "just compensation" due? To whom is it owed?

M & J COAL CO. v. UNITED STATES

47 F.3d 1148 (Fed. Cir. 1995), *cert. denied*,
116 S. Ct. 53 (1995)

LOURIE, CIRCUIT JUDGE.

This regulatory takings case involves the Surface Mining Control and Reclamation Act of 1977 ("SMCRA"), which regulates mining practices and techniques. *See* 30 U.S.C. §§ 1201-1328 (1988). SMCRA authorizes the Department of the Interior to prohibit mining operations that endanger public health and safety or harm the environment....

In this case, we address the question whether the Department of the Interior's Office of Surface Mining Reclamation and Enforcement ("OSM"), acting pursuant to its authority under SMCRA, may regulate coal operations that are endangering the public health or safety without effecting a taking of property requiring the payment of just compensation under the Fifth Amendment....

Between 1904 and 1920, owners of approximately seven hundred acres of land in the mountainous region of Lincoln District, Marion County, West Virginia, sold to various coal companies for valuable consideration the right to mine the Pittsburgh seam of coal beneath the surface of their property....

By 1966, the Consolidated Coal Company, Inc. ("Consolidated") had acquired all the rights to mine the Pittsburgh seam from these coal companies. Consolidated mined fifty to sixty percent of the Pittsburgh seam coal using a technique known as "room-and-pillar" mining, whereby pillars of coal were left standing to support the surface above the mine. Subsequently, Pittsburgh Coal Works, Inc. ("PCW") acquired the right to mine the coal and pillars left by Consolidated.

In July 1981, the Monongah Development Company [M & J Coal Company and Monongah Development Company (collectively "M & J")] acquired from PCW the right to extract the coal that the earlier operators had left in place to support the roof of a mine known as the "Monongah mine."... [T]hey assumed that they could subside the surface above the mine on the properties for which the original owners had conveyed that right. For those surfaces required to be protected by existing state law, they planned to leave coal pillars in place having a 15-degree angle of draw in order to support the surface....

In March 1986, two neighboring residents complained to the West Virginia Department of Energy (WVDOE) that M & J's mining operations had damaged their properties. Following a joint investigation by state and federal inspectors, the state issued a Notice of Violation (NOV) against M & J for mining without a permit and without notifying all affected surface owners of the mining and the possibility of subsidence.

One resident contacted OSM to complain of the subsidence and described extensive damage to his property. The resident reported that the needle on his gas meter was "spinning wildly," that a section of the gas line adjacent to the gas meter had been severed, and that his water line to the public water supply was broken. In addition, the electric wires leading to his house were stretched "as tight as a fiddle string." The resident expressed concern about the possibility of a gas explosion and its effects on the safety of his family and neighbors. Mining operations had caused large cracks to develop in the surface of his property and a neighbor's dog had fallen into a crack to its death. The resident believed that neighborhood children were at risk of similar harm.

OSM officials visited the scene and consulted with the WVDOE, which replied that M & J was in compliance with all applicable state statutes, rules, and regulations, and that the state would not take any enforcement action against M & J. Nevertheless, OSM believed that the public was at risk of injury from large cracks in the ground, collapsing structures, and breaks in gas, water, and electrical lines. Thus, exercising its authority under SMCRA, OSM issued a cessation order against M & J "for a condition, practice, or violation creating an imminent danger to the health and safety of the public." The order required that M & J protect the public from surface cracks, restore the subsided land's pre-subsidence capacity to support structures and previous uses, and mine pursuant to a revised subsidence control plan. OSM approved a plan requiring a greater angle of draw under the protected structures and protection of single family dwellings.

M & J sought administrative review of OSM's order. In June 1988, the Department of the Interior's Office of Hearings and Appeals (OHA) upheld OSM's action as a valid exercise of its authority pursuant to SMCRA on the ground that M & J's mining activities had created an imminent danger to the health or safety of the public. [The Interior Board of Land Appeals (IBLA) affirmed.]...

Despite the new subsidence control plan, M & J's mining operations continued to cause damage in the region. During the next four years, cracks appeared in other residents' properties, the town of Worthington's water tank subsided, and a section of Route 218 subsided. The damage necessitated the excavation of a gas line and the repair of electric lines adjacent to Route 218....

After completing its mining operations, M & J filed suit in the Court of Federal Claims alleging that OSM's enforcement action, which had required M & J to increase the draw angle under protected structures and to protect single family dwellings, deprived it of 99,700 tons of coal it otherwise could have mined, resulting in $580,000.00 in lost profits....

The court determined that M & J's takings claim depended upon whether it could establish a cognizable property right to mine pursuant to a 15-degree subsidence control plan and a right to subside private dwellings. The court denied M & J's claim because M & J failed to establish that it possessed either of those rights. The court ruled that M & J's reasonable expectations concerning its rights were limited by SMCRA's pre-existing prohibition on mining practices that endanger the public health and safety and that the validity of OSM's actions had been conclusively determined by the prior administrative proceedings, which M & J had failed to challenge. M & J now appeals.

....

Invoking this court's recent decision in *Loveladies Harbor, Inc. v. United States*, 28 F.3d 1171 (Fed. Cir. 1994), M & J argues that it had acquired, by means of a state permit, the right to mine pursuant to its 15-degree plan and, under state property law, the right to subside the private dwellings of owners whose predecessors in title had conveyed away that right. Thus, M & J alleges, OSM's requirement that M & J revise its coal mining operations constituted a taking of two categories of coal deposits: (1) deposits under protected surfaces required to be left in place because of the change to a greater than 15-degree angle of draw, and (2) coal under occupied structures that M & J claims it had the right to subside without limitation or liability. We do not agree.

The Fifth Amendment's guarantee "nor shall private property be taken for public use, without just compensation" is "designed to bar Government from forcing some people alone to bear public burdens which, in all fairness and justice, should be borne by the public as a whole." [Citation.] However, property use may be regulated without a compensable taking occurring. [Citation.] Where to draw the line is not always an easy task, but the Supreme Court has stated that if regulation goes "too far" it will constitute a compensable taking. Whether the regulation of property entitling a property owner to compensation has occurred depends upon the particular circumstances of the case. [Citation.] To determine whether a governmental regulation of property has gone so far as to effect a taking, courts have engaged in an "essentially ad hoc, factual inquir[y] [considering such factors as the] economic impact of the regulation on the claimant[,] the extent to which the regulation has interfered with distinct investment-backed expectations[, and] the character of the governmental action." [Citation.]

In *Lucas v. South Carolina Coastal Council,* ___ U.S. ___, 112 S. Ct. 2886, 120 L. Ed. 2d 798 (1992), the Supreme Court explained that the Takings Clause does not require compensation when an owner is barred from putting land to a use that is proscribed by "'existing rules or understandings that stem from an independent source such as state law' [which] define the range of interests that qualify for protection as 'property' under the Fifth (and Fourteenth) amendments." [Citations.] Thus, even when a governmental land use regulation deprives a claimant of all economically beneficial use of his property, the government may avoid compensation if "the logically antecedent inquiry into the nature of the owner's estate shows that the proscribed use interests were not part of his title to begin with." [Citations.]

While *Lucas* involved an alleged "total taking," one in which the land owner was deprived of "all economically beneficial use" of his land, which is not true in the present case, the *Lucas* formulation is useful for analyzing takings claims involving land use restrictions even when deprivation is not complete. Specifically, in analyzing a governmental action that allegedly interferes with an owner's land use, there can be no compensable interference if such land use was not permitted at the time the owner took title to the property.

Thus, we agree with the Court of Federal Claims that precedent indicates a "two-tiered" approach in analyzing a takings claim involving governmental action that results in land use restriction. First, a court should inquire into the nature of the land owner's estate to determine whether the use interest proscribed by the governmental action was part of the owner's title to begin with, i.e., whether the land use interest was a "stick in the bundle of property rights" acquired by the owner. Second, if the claimant can establish the existence of such an interest, the court must then determine whether the governmental action at issue constituted a compensable taking of that "stick." In making the second determination, the court must consider such factors as the character of the governmental action, the economic impact of the action on the claimant, and the extent to which the action has interfered with the claimant's distinct investment backed expectations. Accordingly, before examining the extent of M & J's alleged property deprivation, the content of, and the government's power over, the "bundle of rights" acquired by M & J must be examined to determine whether the proscribed use was part of M & J's "property" within the meaning of the Fifth Amendment. In this case, M & J never acquired the right to mine in such a way as to endanger the public health and safety, and we need not make the second determination.

M & J's acquisition of rights by deed did not give it the right to mine in such a way as to endanger the public health and safety. Substantial precedent supports this conclusion. In a similar case involving state regulations requiring coal miners, *inter alia*, to leave 50% of the coal beneath dwellings in place as a means of providing surface support, the Supreme Court stated: "Long ago it was recognized that 'all property in this country is held under the implied obligation that the owner's use of it shall not be injurious to the community,' ... and the Takings Clause did not transform that principle to one that requires compensation whenever the [government] asserts its power to enforce it." *Keystone Bituminous Coal Ass'n v. DeBenedictis*, 107 S. Ct. 1232, 1245 (1987). The Court noted that, "since no individual has a right to use his property so as to create a nuisance or otherwise harm others, the [government] has not 'taken' anything when it asserts its power to enjoin the nuisance-like activity." [Citations.] Thus, in accordance with settled precedent, M & J could not have acquired under its deed of title the right to cause damage or a substantial risk of damage to the public health or safety.

The fact that M & J had a state permit to mine is also not controlling. The Secretary of the Interior possesses the right to issue federal cessation orders in cases of imminent danger to the health or safety of the public. *See* 30 U.S.C. § 1271. Thus, at the time M & J acquired its mining rights, whatever they were, it knew or should have known that it could not mine in such a way as to endanger public health or safety and that any state authorization it may have received was subordinate to the national standards that were established by SMCRA and enforced by OSM.

It is incontestable that OSM's actions were legitimate exercises under SMCRA to prevent harm to the public health and safety. The IBLA determined as much, specifically finding that OSM's actions were necessary to protect the public health and safety and that M & J's operations were posing a threat, not only to particular residents, but to the public in general. M & J chose not to appeal the IBLA's determination....

M & J further argues that *Pennsylvania Coal Co. v. Mahon*, 43 S. Ct. 158 (1922), mandates a holding in its favor. In *Mahon*, an owner of land containing coal deposits deeded away the surface of the land, while reserving the right to mine coal beneath the surface. According to the deed, the grantees waived any claim to damages that might arise from the mining, which waiver was valid under state law. A later-enacted state statute prohibited mining in such a way as to cause subsidence of dwellings.

The *Mahon* Court determined that the statutory prohibition against mining went "too far" because it completely diminished the value of the property and because the damage sought to be prevented by the statute was that to a single private house, which was not "common or public" and was "not justified as a protection of personal safety." [Citation.]

Relying upon *Mahon*, M & J alleges that OSM used SMCRA as a pretext to impermissibly assist two specific residents, who allegedly possessed no rights to surface support, at the expense of M & J. Unlike *Mahon*, however, the present case does not involve merely a balancing of the private interests of surface owners against the private economic interest of a coal company. It involves the much broader interests of public health and safety. That certain individuals or their predecessors may have unwisely deeded away their rights to surface support cannot estop OSM from exercising its authority to abate an imminent danger to the public health or safety. Nor may a state mining permit compromise the right of the federal government under SMCRA to ensure that the public is free from imminent danger from mining. Despite M & J's focus on the fact that OSM's actions may have benefitted individual residents, OSM's actions were taken to insure that M & J's use of its property did not injure the community at large. Justice and fairness do not require that the community at large bear the "burden" of M & J's inability to mine in a manner that is safe to the public....

An "antecedent" inquiry into the property use interests acquired by M & J thus reveals that M & J never acquired the right to mine in such a way as to endanger the public health and safety. OSM's action to prevent M & J from doing so did not interfere with M & J's property use interests. Because M & J failed to establish that OSM's actions effected a taking of private property for purposes of the Fifth Amendment, the Court of Federal Claims' grant of the government's motion for summary judgment is affirmed.

NOTES AND QUESTIONS

1. Whenever a state or federal government regulates to preserve a natural resource, is a public harm prevented? When would land use regulation with an underlying purpose of preservation *not* be designed to protect against public harm? Would the landmark preservation ordinance in *Penn Central* qualify under the nuisance exception? Is *M & J Coal* consistent with *Keystone*? Is it consistent with *Lucas*? With *Pennsylvania Coal*?

2. On remand from the Supreme Court's decision in *First Evangelical Lutheran Church*, the California Court of Appeals held that the floodplain ordinance was not a taking. In doing so, it remarked that

> [I]t would not be remarkable at all to allow government to deny a private owner "all uses" of his property where there is no use of that property which does not threaten lives and health. So it makes perfect sense to deny compensation for the denial of "all uses" where health and safety are at stake but require compensation for the denial of all uses where the land use regulation advances lesser public purposes.

First English Evangelical Lutheran Church of Glendale v. County of Los Angeles, 210 Cal. App. 3d 1353, 258 Cal. Rptr. 893, 901 (1989). The church had retained some use of the property because the ordinance only prohibited reconstruction of structures damaged or demolished by floods and did not affect eight acres of the landowner's twenty-acre parcel. The court of appeals held that the church had failed to satisfy either prong of the takings test because the church had not been denied all uses of the property and what uses were denied were denied to protect public safety. For additional discussion of the taking issue with respect to floodplain regulation, see pages 970-72 *infra*.

3. The general literature on the takings clause is voluminous. For a sampling of some of the literature, see B. ACKERMAN, PRIVATE PROPERTY AND THE CONSTITUTION (1977); F. BOSSELMAN, D. CALLIES & J. BANTA, THE TAKING ISSUE (1973); R. EPSTEIN, TAKINGS: PRIVATE PROPERTY AND THE POWER OF EMINENT DOMAIN (1985); Berger, *The Accommodation Power in Land Use Controversies: A Reply to Professor Costonis*, 76 COLUM. L. REV. 799 (1976); Bromley, *Regulatory Takings: Coherent Concept or Logical Contradiction?*, 17 VT. L. REV. 647 (1993); Brookshire, *"Taking" the Time to Look Backward*, 42 CATH. U. L. REV. 901 (1993); Burton, *Regulatory Takings and the Shape of Things to Come: Harbingers of a Takings Clause Reconstellation*, 72 OR. L. REV. 603 (1993); Byrne, *Ten Arguments for the Abolition of the Regulatory Takings Doctrine*, 22 ECOLOGY L.Q. 89 (1995); Cook, Comment, Lucas *and Endangered Species Protection: When "Take" and "Takings" Collide*, 27 U.C. DAVIS L. REV. 185 (1993); Costonis, *"Fair Compensation" and the Accommodation Power: Antidotes for the Taking Impasse in Land Use Controversies*, 76 COLUM. L. REV. 1021 (1975); Blumer & Rubinfeld, *Compensation for Takings: An Economic Analysis*, 72 CAL. L. REV. 569 (1984); Coyle, *Takings Jurisprudence and the Political Cultures of American Politics*, 42 CATH. U. L. REV. 817 (1993); Davis, *To the Promised Land: A Century of Wandering and a Final Homeland for the Due Process and Takings Clauses*, 68 OR. L. REV. 393 (1989); Echeverria and Dennis, *The Takings Issue and the Due Process Clause: A Way Out of a Doctrinal Confusion*, 17 VT. L. REV. 695 (1993); Ely, *"That Due Satisfaction May be Made": The Fifth Amendment and the Origins of the Compensation Principle*, 36 AM. J. LEGAL HIST. 1 (1992); Farber, *Economic Analysis and Just Compensation*, 12 INT'L REV. L. & ECON. 125 (1992); Humbach, *"Taking" the Imperial Judiciary Seriously: Segmenting Property Interests and Judicial Revision of Legislative Judgments*, 42 CATH. U. L. REV. 771 (1993); Fischel & Shapiro, *Takings, Insurance, and Michelman: Comments on Economic Interpretations of "Just Compensation" Law*, 17 J. LEGAL STUD. 269 (1988); Humbach, *Economic Due Process and the Takings Clause*, 4 PACE ENVTL. L. REV. 311 (1987); Kadleck, Note, *The Effect of* Lucas v. South Carolina Coastal Council *on the Law of Regulatory Takings*, 68 WASH. L. REV. 415 (1993); Kaplow, *An Economic Analysis of Legal Transitions*, 99 HARV. L. REV. 509 (1986); Kmiec, *The Original Understanding of the Taking Clause Is Neither Weak Nor Obtuse*, 88 COLUM. L. REV. 1630 (1988); Kendall, Note, *The Limits to Growth and the Limits to the Takings Clause*, 11 VA. ENVTL. L.J. 547 (1992); Laitos, *The Public Use Paradox and the Takings Clause*, 13 J. ENERGY, NAT. RESOURCES & ENVTL. L. 9 (1993); Laitos, *The Takings Clause in*

America's Industrial States After Lucas, 24 U. TOL. L. REV. 281 (1993); Lazarus, *Putting the Correct "Spin" on* Lucas, 45 STAN. L. REV. 1411 (1993); Looper-Friedman, *Constitutional Rights as Property: The Supreme Court's Solution to the "Takings Issue"*, 15 COLUM. J. ENVTL. L. 31 (1990); Lunney, *A Critical Reexamination of the Takings Jurisprudence*, 90 MICH. L. REV. 1892 (1992); Lunney, *Compensation for Takings: How Much Is Just?*, 42 CATH. U. L. REV. 721 (1993); Malone, *The Future of Transferable Development Rights in the Supreme Court*, 73 KY. L.J. 759 (1984-85); Martinez, *Statutes Enacting Takings Law: Flying in the Face of Uncertainty*, 26 URB. LAW. 327 (1994); McLaughlin, *Majoritarian Theft in the Regulatory State, or What's a Takings Clause For?*, 19 WM. & MARY ENVTL. L. & POL'Y REV. 161 (1995); Michelman, *Property, Utility and Fairness: Comments on the Ethical Foundations of "Just Compensation" Law* , 80 HARV. L. REV. 1165 (1967); Michelman, *Takings, 1987*, 88 COLUM. L. REV. 1600 (1988); Minda, *The Dilemmas of Property and Sovereignty in the Post-Modern Era: The Regulatory Takings Problem*, 62 U. COLO. L. REV. 599 (1991); Myren, *Growth Control as a Taking*, 25 URB. LAW. 385 (1993); Overstreet, *The Ripeness Doctrine of the Takings Clause: A Survey of Decisions Showing Just How Far Federal Courts Will Go to Avoid Adjudicating Land Use Cases*, 10 J. LAND USE & ENVTL. L. 91 (1994); Peterson, *The Takings Cluase: In Search of Underlying Principles Part I — A Critique of Current Takings Clause Doctrine*, 77 CAL. L. REV. 1301 (1989); Peterson, *The Takings Clause: In Search of Underlying Principles Part II — Takings as Intentional Deprivations of Property Without Moral Justification*, 78 CAL. L. REV. 53 (1990); Runge, *Economic Implications of Wider Compensation for "Takings" or, What if Agricultural Policies Ruled the World?*, 17 VT. L. REV. 723 (1993); Sax, *The Constitutional Dimensions of Property: A Debate*, 26 LOY. L.A. L. REV. 23 (1992); Sax, *Takings and the Police Power*, 44 YALE L.J. 36 (1964); Sax, *Takings, Private Property and Public Rights*, 81 YALE L.J. 149 (1971); Rose, *Mahon Reconstructed: Why the Takings Issue Is Still a Muddle*, 57 S. CAL. L. REV. 561 (1984); Schwartz, *Property Rights and the Constitution: Will the Ugly Duckling Become a Swan?*, 37 AM. U.L. REV. 9 (1987); Van Alstyne, *Taking or Damaging by Police Power: The Search for Inverse Condemnation Criteria*, 42 S. CAL. L. REV. 1 (1970); Washburn, *Land Use Control, the Individual, and Society:* Lucas v. South Carolina Coastal Council, 52 MD. L. REV. 162 (1993); Note, *Houses on the Sand: Takings Issues Surrounding Statutory Restrictions on the Use of Oceanfront Property*, 18 B.C. ENVTL. AFF. L. REV. 125 (1990); Smith, Note, *Private Property Protection Legislation and Original Understandings of the Takings Clause: Can They Co-Exist?*, 21 J. LEGIS. 93 (1995); Comment, *Regulatory Takings and Wetlands: Comments on Public Benefits and Landowner Cost*, 21 OHIO N.U. L. REV. 527 (1994); Comment, *The Origins and Original Significance of the Just Compensation Clause of the Fifth Amendment*, 94 YALE L.J. 694 (1985).

Chapter 4

THE JUDICIAL ROLE IN ENVIRONMENTAL LITIGATION

INTRODUCTION

Private citizens and environmental public interest organizations perform an important public interest function in effectuating the goals of federal environmental laws. Parties acting in the capacity of private attorney general not only supplement government enforcement efforts but also serve as a watchdog on compliance by government agencies with statutory duties. Despite the valuable public benefits which may accrue from such efforts, there are a number of constraints inherent in the litigation process which check the zeal of environmental activists. Doctrines of standing, reviewability, standard of review, ripeness, and mootness combine to ensure that the proper parties are before the court at the proper time with issues precisely drawn for judicial resolution. Since public interest advocates lack the investigative and financial resources of industry and government, it is also critical that the federal environmental statutes provide for awards of attorneys' fees to prevailing parties. This is particularly necessary in environmental litigation because typically the party challenging the unlawful conduct principally seeks injunctive relief rather than damages. The materials in this chapter will explore some of the important current issues in environmental litigation with particular emphasis on the relationship and respective roles of administrative agencies, courts, and private attorneys general.

A. ENTRY INTO COURTS: STANDING AND RELATED DOCTRINES

Parties seeking to challenge conduct for violating federal environmental protection laws must overcome several preliminary barriers which limit access to courts apart from the substantive criteria of the particular statute. One significant limitation derived from Article III of the Constitution that federal courts can only decide "cases or controversies" is often phrased in terms of "standing." The doctrine of standing, rather than inquiring into the merits of the dispute, focuses on ensuring that the proper party is before the court by demanding that only persons who have alleged an "injury" can be heard. Thus, even if claimants believe that an act is unlawful or unconstitutional and have the motivation to pursue redress of the offending conduct, standing will not be granted unless they can show a "personal stake in the outcome." Courts will not decide abstract or hypothetical issues or render advisory opinions, but only concrete disputes between true adversaries where the parties fully and adequately represent the issues. The Supreme Court in *Valley Forge Christian College v. Americans United for Separation of Church and State, Inc.*, 454 U.S. 464, 471-72 (1982) explained that the federal judicial power is not an "unconditioned authority to determine the constitutionality of legislative or executive acts", but rather must be reserved to the determination of a "real, earnest and vital controversy." The Court stated that at "an irreducible minimum" the doctrine of standing contemplates the following elements: (1) the claimant must show an actual or threatened injury as a result of the putatively illegal conduct of the defendant, (2) that the injury may be "fairly traced" to the challenged action, and (3) the asserted harm "is likely to be redressed by a favorable decision." This limitation of judicial power is consistent with a system of separated powers by prohibiting federal courts from unnecessarily encroaching upon the power of the coordinate branches.

In some instances, Congress has provided statutory standing to challenge government action. Specifically, 5 U.S.C. § 702 of the Administrative Procedure Act (APA) authorizes judicial review for a person who has suffered a legal wrong or has been "adversely affected or aggrieved by agency action within the meaning of the relevant statute." In *Association of Data Processing Serv. Orgs., Inc. v. Camp*, 397 U.S. 150, 152-53 (1970) the Court interpreted the APA grant of standing as comprised of two elements: the claimant must still satisfy the requirements of Article III by showing a particularized injury in fact and additionally must be "arguably within the zone of interests" which the statute is designed to regulate or protect. The zone of interests prong of the APA standard, which inquires into Congressional intent regarding the class of persons covered by the statute, generally is easily satisfied in environmental disputes because many federal statutes are couched in broad terms of protecting the public from pollution.

Most of the litigation in environmental disputes brought under the APA has centered around what constitutes an "injury in fact" for standing purposes. The Court in *Sierra Club v. Morton*, 405 U.S. 727, 739-40 (1972), which introduces this Chapter, determined that a mere "value preference" or "intellectual interest" in the problem is not sufficient; however, the range of injuries cognizable for standing is quite broad and can include economic and economic, aesthetic, and recreational harms.

Apart from the issue of standing to challenge agency conduct, important questions remain regarding whether a court possesses the power to review the merits of the agency action for substantive and procedural adherence to the operative statute and, if so, to what extent. The doctrine of "reviewability" essentially involves a determination of whether the issue itself is suitable for judicial resolution. The APA expresses a strong preference favoring the authority of courts to review agency action, with limited exceptions. 5 U.S.C. § 701. Although statutes may preclude judicial review in certain instances, courts will construe such limitations narrowly. Moreover, courts retain the authority to review cases alleging that the agency has exceeded its statutory authority and to hear challenges to the constitutionality of the statute. Also, a statute may enumerate some actions as being beyond judicial review, leaving other matters subject to review.

The more difficult question in environmental litigation, however, has been the standard of review or the extent to which courts are willing to reexamine agency actions. These issues have been controversial because environmental activists historically have sought tougher judicial intervention and oversight over perceived weak agency action in carrying out environmental laws. The problem is complicated by the multi-faceted ways that administrative agencies operate. In a broad variety of circumstances agencies function in a quasi-legislative role by promulgating rules which have general applicability. Ordinary agency rulemaking only requires a "concise general statement" of the basis and purpose of the rules with an informal process of notice and comment. 5 U.S.C. § 553. Courts will give a stronger presumption of correctness to such agency actions and apply an "arbitrary and capricious" standard of review. In other instances agencies function in a quasi-judicial role by adjudicating matters, such as whether a license should issue to a particular applicant. Here the agency behaves more like a court by conducting trial-type hearings on the record with cross examination and other procedural formalities. Less judicial deference is accorded the agency in these situations, as courts will uphold the agency action unless such action is not supported by "substantial evidence" or violates substantive limits on the agency's powers. The lines between the various types of agency actions often become blurred, especially when a single project involves numerous complex decisions by several agencies. In environmental cases the standard of review often reflects an accommodation of two policies — deference to agency expertise in technical matters within its specialized area and the court's duty to ensure fidelity to the statutory requirements. The shorthand expression for the balance drawn of these policies is popularly referred to as the "hard look" standard of review. The following materials will examine these issues of standing, reviewability of agency action, and the appropriate standard of review together with related doctrines affecting the litigation process.

SIERRA CLUB v. MORTON

405 U.S. 727 (1972)

MR. JUSTICE STEWART delivered the opinion of the Court.

The Mineral King Valley is an area of great natural beauty nestled in the Sierra Nevada Mountains in Tulare County, California, adjacent to Sequoia National Park. It has been part of the Sequoia National Forest since 1926, and is designated as a national game refuge by special Act of Congress. Though once the site of extensive mining activity, Mineral King is now used almost exclusively for recreational purposes. Its relative inaccessibility and lack of development have limited the number of visitors each year, and at the same time have preserved the valley's quality as a quasi-wilderness area largely uncluttered by the products of civilization.

[The United States Forest Service approved a plan by Walt Disney Enterprises, Inc. to develop a multimillion-dollar ski resort and recreation area in the Mineral King Valley. The Sierra Club sought a declaratory judgment and injunctive relief that the proposed plan contravened various federal environmental statutes. The Sierra Club sued as a membership organization with a "special interest" in conservation and the sound maintenance of national parks. The District Court issued a preliminary injunction against the project. The Ninth Circuit Court of Appeals reversed, reasoning that the organization's allegations that the contemplated project was "personally displeasing or distasteful" were insufficient to confer standing.]

....

The first question presented is whether the Sierra Club has alleged facts that entitle it to obtain judicial review of the challenged action. Whether a party has a sufficient stake in an otherwise justiciable controversy to obtain judicial resolution of that controversy is what has traditionally been referred to as the question of standing to sue. Where the party does not rely on any specific statute authorizing invocation of the judicial process, the question of standing depends upon whether the party has alleged such a "personal stake in the outcome of the controversy," as to ensure that "the dispute sought to be adjudicated will be presented in an adversary context and in a form historically viewed as capable of judicial resolution." [Citation.] Where, however, Congress has authorized public officials to perform certain functions according to law, and has provided by statute for judicial review of those actions under certain circumstances, the inquiry as to standing must begin with a determination of whether the statute in question authorizes review at the behest of the plaintiff.[3]

The Sierra Club relies upon § 10 of the Administrative Procedure Act (APA), 5 U.S.C. § 702, which provides:

> "A person suffering legal wrong because of agency action, or adversely affected or aggrieved by agency action within the meaning of a relevant statute, is entitled to judicial review thereof."

Early decisions under this statute interpreted the language as adopting the various formulations of "legal interest" and "legal wrong" then prevailing as constitutional requirements of standing. But, in *Data Processing Service v. Camp*, 397 U.S. 150, and *Barlow v. Collins*, 397 U.S. 159, decided the same day, we held more broadly that persons had standing to obtain judicial review of federal agency

---

[3]Congress may not confer jurisdiction on Art. III federal courts to render advisory opinions, or to entertain "friendly" suits, or to resolve "political questions," because suits of this character are inconsistent with the judicial function under Art. III. But where a dispute is otherwise justiciable, the question whether the litigant is a "proper party to request an adjudication of a particular issue," is one within the power of Congress to determine. [Citations.]

action under § 10 of the APA where they had alleged that the challenged action had caused them "injury in fact," and where the alleged injury was to an interest "arguably within the zone of interests to be protected or regulated" by the statutes that the agencies were claimed to have violated.[5]

In *Data Processing*, the injury claimed by the petitioners consisted of harm to their competitive position in the computer-servicing market through a ruling by the Comptroller of the Currency that national banks might perform data-processing services for their customers. In *Barlow*, the petitioners were tenant farmers who claimed that certain regulations of the Secretary of Agriculture adversely affected their economic position *vis-à-vis* their landlords. These palpable economic injuries have long been recognized as sufficient to lay the basis for standing, with or without a specific statutory provision for judicial review. Thus, neither *Data Processing* nor *Barlow* addressed itself to the question, which has arisen with increasing frequency in federal courts in recent years, as to what must be alleged by persons who claim injury of a noneconomic nature to interests that are widely shared. That question is presented in this case.

The injury alleged by the Sierra Club will be incurred entirely by reason of the change in the uses to which Mineral King will be put, and the attendant change in the aesthetics and ecology of the area. Thus, in referring to the road to be built through Sequoia National Park, the complaint alleged that the development "would destroy or otherwise adversely affect the scenery, natural and historic objects and wildlife of the park and would impair the enjoyment of the park for future generations." We do not question that this type of harm may amount to an "injury in fact" sufficient to lay the basis for standing under § 10 of the APA. Aesthetic and environmental well-being, like economic well-being, are important ingredients of the quality of life in our society, and the fact that particular environmental interests are shared by the many rather than the few does not make them less deserving of legal protection through the judicial process. But the "injury in fact" test requires more than an injury to a cognizable interest. It requires that the party seeking review be himself among the injured.

The impact of the proposed changes in the environment of Mineral King will not fall indiscriminately upon every citizen. The alleged injury will be felt directly only by those who use Mineral King and Sequoia National Park, and for whom the aesthetic and recreational values of the area will be lessened by the highway and ski resort. The Sierra Club failed to allege that it or its members would be affected in any of their activities or pastimes by the Disney development. Nowhere in the pleadings or affidavits did the Club state that its members use Mineral King for any purpose, much less that they use it in any way that would be significantly affected by the proposed actions of the respondents.

---

[5]In deciding this case we do not reach any questions concerning the meaning of the "zone of interests" test or its possible application to the facts here presented.

The Club apparently regarded any allegations of individualized injury as superfluous, on the theory that this was a "public" action involving questions as to the use of natural resources, and that the Club's longstanding concern with and expertise in such matters were sufficient to give it standing as a "representative of the public." This theory reflects a misunderstanding of our cases involving so-called "public actions" in the area of administrative law.

....

The trend of cases arising under the APA and other statutes authorizing judicial review of federal agency action has been toward recognizing that injuries other than economic harm are sufficient to bring a person within the meaning of the statutory language, and toward discarding the notion that an injury that is widely shared is *ipso facto* not an injury sufficient to provide the basis for judicial review. We noted this development with approval in Data Processing, in saying that the interest alleged to have been injured "may reflect 'aesthetic, conservational, and recreational' as well as economic values." But broadening the categories of injury that may be alleged in support of standing is a different matter from abandoning the requirement that the party seeking review must himself have suffered an injury.

Some courts have indicated a willingness to take this latter step by conferring standing upon organizations that have demonstrated "an organizational interest in the problem" of environmental or consumer protection. [Citation.] It is clear that an organization whose members are injured may represent those members in a proceeding for judicial review. [Citation.] But a mere "interest in a problem," no matter how longstanding the interest and no matter how qualified the organization is in evaluating the problem, is not sufficient by itself to render the organization "adversely affected" or "aggrieved" within the meaning of the APA. The Sierra Club is a large and long-established organization, with a historic commitment to the cause of protecting our Nation's natural heritage from man's depredations. But if a "special interest" in this subject were enough to entitle the Sierra Club to commence this litigation, there would appear to be no objective basis upon which to disallow a suit by any other bona fide "special interest" organization, however small or short-lived. And if any group with a bona fide "special interest" could initiate such litigation, it is difficult to perceive why any individual citizen with the same bona fide special interest would not also be entitled to do so.

The requirement that a party seeking review must allege facts showing that he is himself adversely affected does not insulate executive action from judicial review, nor does it prevent any public interests from being protected through the judicial process. It does serve as at least a rough attempt to put the decision as to whether review will be sought in the hands of those who have a direct stake in the outcome. That goal would be undermined were we to construe the APA to authorize judicial review at the behest of organizations or individuals who seek to do no more than vindicate their own value preferences through the judicial process.[16] The principle that the Sierra Club would have us establish in this case would do just that.

As we conclude that the Court of Appeals was correct in its holding that the Sierra Club lacked standing to maintain this action, we do not reach any other questions presented in the petition, and we intimate no view on the merits of the complaint. The judgment is

Affirmed.

MR. JUSTICE POWELL and MR. JUSTICE REHNQUIST took no part in the consideration or decision of this case.

MR. JUSTICE DOUGLAS, dissenting.

. . . .

The critical question of "standing" would be simplified and also put neatly in focus if we fashioned a federal rule that allowed environmental issues to be litigated before federal agencies or federal courts in the name of the inanimate object about to be despoiled, defaced, or invaded by roads and bulldozers and where injury is the subject of public outrage. Contemporary public concern for protecting nature's ecological equilibrium should lead to the conferral of standing upon environmental objects to sue for their own preservation. See Stone, *Should Trees Have Standing? — Toward Legal Rights for Natural Objects*, 45 S. Cal. L. Rev. 450 (1972). This suit would therefore be more properly labeled as *Mineral King v. Morton*.

Inanimate objects are sometimes parties in litigation. A ship has a legal personality, a fiction found useful for maritime purposes. The corporation sole — a creature of ecclesiastical law — is an acceptable adversary and large fortunes ride on its cases. The ordinary corporation is a "person" for purposes of the adjudicatory processes, whether it represents proprietary, spiritual, aesthetic, or charitable causes.

So it should be as respects valleys, alpine meadows, rivers, lakes, estuaries, beaches, ridges, groves of trees, swampland, or even air that feels the destructive pressures of modern technology and modern life. The river, for example, is the living symbol of all the life it sustains or nourishes — fish, aquatic, insects,

---

[16]Every schoolboy may be familiar with Alex de Tocqueville's famous observation, written in the 1830's, that "[s]carcely any political question arises in the United States that is not resolved, sooner or later, into a judicial question." 1 Democracy in America 280 (1945). Less familiar, however, is De Tocqueville's further observation that judicial review is effective largely because it is not available simply at the behest of a partisan faction, but is exercised only to remedy a particular, concrete injury.

"It will be seen, also, that by leaving it to private interest to censure the law, and by intimately uniting the trial of the law with the trial of an individual, legislation is protected from wanton assaults and from the daily aggressions of party spirit. The errors of the legislator are exposed only to meet a real want; and it is always a positive and appreciable fact that must serve as the basis of a prosecution." *Id.*, at 102.

water ouzels, otter, fisher, deer, elk, bear, and all other animals, including man, who are dependent on it or who enjoy it for its sight, its sound, or its life. The river as plaintiff speaks for the ecological unit of life that is part of it. Those people who have a meaningful relation to that body of water — whether it be a fisherman, a canoeist, a zoologist, or a logger — must be able to speak for the values which the river represents and which are threatened with destruction.

....

Mineral King is doubtless like other wonders of the Sierra Nevada such as Tuolumne Meadows and the John Muir Trail. Those who hike it, fish it, hunt it, camp in it, frequent it, or visit it merely to sit in solitude and wonderment are legitimate spokesmen for it, whether they may be few or many. Those who have that intimate relation with the inanimate object about to be injured, polluted, or otherwise despoiled are its legitimate spokesmen.

... The suggestion that Congress can stop action which is undesirable is true in theory; yet even Congress is too remote to give meaningful direction and its machinery is too ponderous to use very often. The federal agencies of which I speak are not venal or corrupt. But they are notoriously under the control of powerful interests who manipulate them through advisory committees, or friendly working relations, or who have that natural affinity with the agency which in time develops between the regulator and the regulated....

The voice of the inanimate object, therefore, should not be stilled. That does not mean that the judiciary takes over the managerial functions from the federal agency. It merely means that before these priceless bits of Americana (such as a valley, an alpine meadow, a river, or a lake) are forever lost or are so transformed as to be reduced to the eventual rubble of our urban environment, the voice of the existing beneficiaries of these environmental wonders should be heard.

Perhaps they will not win. Perhaps the bulldozers of "progress" will plow under all the aesthetic wonders of this beautiful land. That is not the present question. The sole question is, who has standing to be heard?

....

Ecology reflects the land ethic; and Aldo Leopold wrote in A Sand County Almanac 204 (1949), "The land ethic simply enlarges the boundaries of the community to include soils, waters, plants, and animals, or collectively: the land."

That, as I see it, is the issue of "standing" in the present case and controversy.

MR. JUSTICE BLACKMUN, dissenting.

... [T]his is not ordinary, run-of-the-mill litigation. The case poses — if only we choose to acknowledge and reach them — significant aspects of a wide, growing, and disturbing problem, that is, the Nation's and the world's deteriorating environment with its resulting ecological disturbances. Must our law be so rigid and our procedural concepts so inflexible that we render ourselves helpless when the existing methods and the traditional concepts do not quite fit and do not prove to be entirely adequate for new issues?

....

Rather than pursue the course the Court has chosen to take by its affirmance of the judgment of the Court of Appeals, I would adopt one of two alternatives:

1. I would reverse that judgment and, instead, approve the judgment of the district Court which recognized standing in the Sierra Club and granted preliminary relief. I would be willing to do this on condition that the Sierra Club forthwith amend its complaint to meet the specifications the Court prescribes for standing. If Sierra Club fails or refuses to take that step, so be it; the case will then collapse. But if it does amend, the merits will be before the trial court once again....

2. Alternatively, I would permit an imaginative expansion of our traditional concepts of standing in order to enable an organization such as the Sierra Club, possessed, as it is, of pertinent, bona fide, and well-recognized attributes and purposes in the area of environment, to litigate environmental issues. This incursion upon tradition need not be very extensive. Certainly, it should be no cause for alarm.... It need only recognize the interest of one who has a provable, sincere, dedicated, and established status. We need not fear that Pandora's box will be opened or that there will be no limit to the number of those who desire to participate in environmental litigation. The courts will exercise appropriate restraints just as they have exercised them in the past....

The Court chooses to conclude its opinion with a footnote reference to De Tocqueville. In this environmental context I personally prefer the older and particularly pertinent observation and warning of John Donne.[2]

NOTES AND QUESTIONS

1. The requirement that "injury in fact" be demonstrably concrete and specific for standing implicates both constitutional and prudential considerations. Article III demands a particularized showing of a personal stake in the resolution of an otherwise justiciable controversy. The prudential policy concerns that a claimant show a direct effect from the challenged conduct enable the parties to understand the contours of the dispute. This animates the settlement process, provides notice to the defendant and interested third parties so that corrective and investigative action can be taken, and serves a fairness function by giving the defendant an opportunity to prepare a defense. From the court's perspective, specificity and clarity of the alleged harm is of vital importance to render a meaningful decision

---

[2]"No man is an Iland, intire of itselfe; every man is a peece of the Continent, a part of the maine; if a Clod bee washed away by the Sea, Europe is the lesse, as well as if a Promontorie were, as well as if a Mannor of thy friends or of thine owne were; any man's death diminishes me, because I am involved in Mankinde; And therefore never send to know for whom the bell tolls; it tolls for thee." Devotions XVII.

or, in appropriate circumstances, to determine that the issue is moot or unripe for consideration.

Despite its holding that the plaintiff environmental interest organization lacked standing in *Sierra Club v. Morton*, the Court's recognition of aesthetic and non-economic injuries actually enlarges the range of potential harms sufficient for standing. *Also see Goos v. ICC*, 911 F.2d 1283, 1290 (8th Cir. 1990) (landowner residing near area potentially affected by environmental injury has sufficient personal stake in outcome for standing); *National Wildlife Fed'n v. Agricultural Stabilization & Conserv. Serv.*, 901 F.2d 673, 677 (8th Cir. 1990) (landowner living in drainage district had standing to challenge potential environmental harm caused by threatened loss of wetlands).

2. *Representational Standing*. Since standing doctrine focuses on whether the claimant can show a personal stake in an otherwise justiciable case or controversy, claimants generally cannot assert the rights of third parties. The policy justifications for disfavoring representational standing are that courts will not adjudicate disputes unnecessarily and the third parties are considered better positioned to argue their own claims.

Representational standing issues often are of particular relevance in environmental disputes, however, because public interest organizations possess the informational, investigative, and financial capability which individuals lack to effectively contest violations by industry or government. In *Hunt v. Washington Apple Adv. Comm'n*, 432 U.S. 333, 343 (1977) the Court set forth the basis for an organization to have standing to sue on behalf of its members: (1) some of its members would otherwise have standing in their own right; (2) the interests it seeks to protect are germane to the organization's purposes; and (3) neither the claim asserted nor the relief requested requires the participation of the individual members in the suit. In *Sierra Club v. Morton*, the Court held that plaintiff's asserted "special interest" in conservation issues was inadequate to justify standing to maintain its public interest lawsuit. Instead, the organization needed to show that the challenged development would affect the club or its members in their "use" of Mineral King.

3. *Informational Standing*. Ordinarily, an organization establishes standing derivatively by pointing to a specific injury to one of its members. A related issue involving representational standing is whether government conduct which allegedly deprives a public interest organization of information or interferes with its educational and activist functions constitutes an "injury in fact" for standing purposes. In *Scientists Inst. for Pub. Information, Inc. v. Atomic Energy Comm'n*, 481 F.2d 1079, 1086-87 n.29 (D.C. Cir. 1973) the court observed that the plaintiff organization's standing might be shown where an agency's failure to provide an impact statement hindered the group's ability to distribute scientific information to the public. *Also see Foundation on Economic Trends v. Lyng*, 943 F.2d 79, 84 (D.C. Cir. 1991) (informational standing in NEPA).

In *Competitive Enters. Inst. v. NHTSA*, 901 F.2d 107, 123 (D.C. Cir. 1990) the court found that allegations of injury to an organization's ability to disseminate information would constitute a cognizable injury where the information was essential to its activities and the organization showed a plausible link between the agency action and how their programmatic activities had been harmed. In that case the consumer organization contended that the agency's failure to discuss the "true costs" associated with its minimum fuel economy standards for passenger cars in safety terms constituted harm to the organization's aim of educating and informing the public about highway safety. The court disagreed and held that the organization had not shown a sufficient connection between the desired information and its activities. In contrast, in *Foundation on Economic Trends v. Watkins*, 731 F. Supp. 530 (D.D.C. Cir. 1990) the plaintiff public interest organization claimed informational injury associated with federal agency action in carrying out programs which contribute to the "greenhouse effect" without properly documenting the environmental effects as required under NEPA. The court found that the organization had shown sufficient informational harm for standing because one of the central purposes of the statute was to inform the public and the plaintiffs had specifically identified the environmental zone, the global atmosphere, as the area adversely affected by the agency conduct.

4. *Public Interest.* In *Sierra Club v. Morton* the Court drew a distinction between an organization which asserted a longstanding special interest in environmental issues and the more particularized showing of a personal stake in the outcome necessary to confer standing. The Court further observed, however, that once individualized personal injury had been established for standing to seek judicial review of a particular issue, claimants could then raise public interest concerns to support their claims. *Also see Sierra Club v. Adams*, 578 F.2d 389, 393 (D.C. Cir. 1978) (organization which established independent basis for standing to challenge final impact statement under NEPA could then argue public interest to support additional inadequacies under the statute). On the other hand, in *Lujan v. National Wildlife Fed.*, 497 U.S. 871, 111 L. Ed. 2d 695, 110 S. Ct. 3177 (1990) the Court noted that wholesale challenges to an agency program typically were outside the province of the courts and were more properly the domain of the legislative branch. *Also see Conservation Law Found. of New England v. Reilly*, 950 F.2d 38 (1st Cir. 1991) (CERCLA's citizen suit provision did not broaden federal court jurisdiction solely to allow vindication of "public interest" absent showing of particularized injury.)

5. Citizens' suits challenging environmental violations also may be precluded from judicial resolution on jurisdictional grounds. *See Hallstrom v. Tillamook County*, 493 U.S. 20 (1989) (failure to satisfy fully the notice requirements under RCRA deprived the court of subject matter jurisdiction and mandated dismissal of citizens' suit.) *See generally* Fletcher, *The Structure of Standing*, 98 YALE L.J. 221 (1988).

6. In *North Shore Gas Co. v. EPA*, 930 F.2d 1239, 1242 (7th Cir. 1991) Judge Posner explained the purpose and policy underlying the doctrine of standing:

... The first, perhaps ill-named but well established in antitrust and other legal contexts and deeply rooted in the common law, is the idea that not everyone injured by the violation of a statute will be permitted to sue to redress the violation. Suppose Corporation *A* incurs a loss in sales as a result of a violation of the antitrust laws by *B*, and Mr. *C*, an employee of *A*, loses a bonus as a result of his employer's sales loss. The law has been violated and *C* has been hurt as a result, but will not be allowed to sue. It just is too difficult to trace out all the ramifications of a violation of law to justify allowing every person conceivably injured by eddies of illegal conduct to bring suit. Pollution can cause all manner of indirect injury. Manufacturers of brass fittings for yachts may incur business losses because sales of yachts decline in northern Illinois as a consequence of pollution in Waukegan Harbor, but it would be absurd to allow them to invoke the environmental laws in an effort to enjoin a measure that they think might aggravate that pollution. Plaintiffs would be tripping over each other on the way to the courthouse if everyone remotely injured by a violation of law could sue to redress it. An important purpose of rules of standing is to identify the best placed plaintiff and give him a clear shot at suit — and by doing so to cut down on the number of suits, which is no trivial consideration in this age of swollen federal caseloads.

An additional consideration is that derivative losers tend to be offset by derivative gainers, who to prevent overdeterrence would have to be forced to make restitution to the violator — which of course is infeasible. In our hypothetical case, the loss to the manufacturers of brass fittings would be offset by gains to suppliers of the inputs into the clean up. What we are calling derivative losers and gainers are persons linked financially to the immediate injurers and victims, and such financial ramifications of an accident or other disaster tend to be offsetting and can therefore safely be ignored. [Citations omitted.]

Is Posner really explaining the concept of redressability as a prudential doctrine to pare access to courts except to the most meritorious cases? Can this view be reconciled with the notion espoused in *Sierra Club v. Morton* that "injury in fact" can include quantitatively small harms so long as the claimant qualitatively fits within the "user" category?

7. The record compiled by an administrative agency performs several important functions: it forms the basis for decisionmaking by the agency; it serves as a vehicle for public comment; and it constitutes the basis for review by a court of agency action. The specific data contained in the record will vary, of course, but essentially it must reflect sufficient factual information for the agency to comply with its statutory duties. The role of the court in reviewing the record, then, is to determined whether the agency has met its statutory obligations and made a reasonable decision among alternatives. This does not mean, however, that the reviewing court sits to substitute its own judgment for that of the agency.

There are several strategic reasons why parties may challenge the sufficiency of the record. The dispute gives additional time for public opinion to pressure the agency to change their action, it delays implementation of the project, and allows an opportunity for a settlement to be reached. *See Scenic Hudson Preserv. Conf. v. Federal Power Comm'n*, 354 F.2d 608 (2d Cir. 1965).

LUJAN v. DEFENDERS OF WILDLIFE

504 U.S. 555, 119 L. Ed. 2d 351,
112 S. Ct. 2130 (1992)

JUSTICE SCALIA delivered the opinion of the Court with respect to Parts I, II, III-A, and IV, and an opinion with respect to Part III-B in which THE CHIEF JUSTICE, JUSTICE WHITE, and JUSTICE THOMAS join.

[Environmental conservation organizations ("respondents") challenged a regulation promulgated by the Secretary of the Interior ("Secretary") interpreting § 7 of the Endangered Species Act of 1973 ("ESA"). Section 7 (a)(2)[16 U.S.C. § 1536(a)(2)] requires all federal agencies to consult with the Secretary to insure that their actions are not likely to jeopardize endangered species. A joint regulation interpreting section 7 initially provided that the obligations extended to actions taken in foreign nations. A revised joint regulation, however, limited the applicability of section 7 to actions within the United States or on the high seas. The Supreme Court granted certiorari to determine whether respondents had standing to seek judicial review of the revised rule.]....

II

While the Constitution of the United States divides all power conferred upon the Federal Government into "legislative Powers," Art. I, § 1, "the executive Power," Art. II, § 1, and "the judicial Power," Art. III, § 1, it does not attempt to define those terms. To be sure, it limits the jurisdiction of federal courts to "Cases and Controversies," but an executive inquiry can bear the name "case" (the Hoffa case) and a legislative dispute can bear the name "controversy" (the Smoot-Hawley controversy). Obviously, then, the Constitution's central mechanism of separation of powers depends largely upon common understanding of what activities are appropriate to legislatures, to executives, and to courts. In The Federalist No. 48, Madison expressed the view that "it is not infrequently a question of real nicety in legislative bodies whether the operation of a particular measure will, or will not, extend beyond the legislative sphere," whereas "the executive power [is] restrained within a narrower compass and ... more simple in its nature," and "the judiciary [is] described by landmarks still less uncertain." The Federalist No. 48, p. 256 (Carey and McClellan eds. 1990). One of those landmarks, setting apart the "Cases" and Controversies" that are of the justiciable sort referred to in Article III — serving to identify those disputes which are appropriately resolved through the judicial process," — is the doctrine of standing. Though some of its elements express merely prudential considerations that are part of judicial self-government, the core component of standing is an essential and unchanging part of the case-or-controversy requirement of Article III. [Citations]

Over the years, our cases have established that the irreducible constitutional minimum of standing contains three elements: First, the plaintiff must have suffered an "injury in fact" — an invasion of a legally-protected interest which is (a) concrete and particularized;[1] and (b) "actual or imminent, not 'conjectural' or 'hypothetical.'" [Citations] Second, there must be a causal connection between the injury and the conduct complained of — the injury has to be "fairly ... traceable to the challenged action of the defendant, and not ... the result [of] the independent action of some third party not before the court." [Citation] Third, it must be "likely," as opposed to merely "speculative," that the injury will be "redressed by a favorable decision."

When the suit is one challenging the legality of government action or inaction, the nature and extent of facts that must be averred (at the summary judgment stage) or proved (at the trial stage) in order to establish standing depends considerably upon whether the plaintiff is himself an object of the action (or forgone action) at issue. If he is, there is ordinarily little question that the action or inaction has caused him injury, and that a judgment preventing or requiring the action will redress it. When, however, as in this case, a plaintiff's asserted injury arises from the government's allegedly unlawful regulation (or lack of regulation) of someone else, much more is needed. In that circumstance, causation and redressability ordinarily hinge on the response of the regulated (or regulable) third party to the government action or inaction — and perhaps on the response of others as well. The existence of one or more of the essential elements of standing "depends on the unfettered choices made by independent actors not before the courts and whose exercise of broad and legitimate discretion the courts cannot presume either to control or to predict," and it becomes the burden of the plaintiff to adduce facts showing that those choices have been or will be made in such manner as to produce causation and permit redressability of injury. [Citation] Thus, when the plaintiff is not himself the object of the government action or inaction he challenges, standing is not precluded, but it is ordinarily "substantially more difficult" to establish. [Citation]

III

We think the Court of Appeals failed to apply the foregoing principles in denying the Secretary's motion for summary judgment. Respondents had not made the requisite demonstration of (at least) injury and redressability.

---

[1]By particularized, we mean that the injury must affect the plaintiff in a personal and individual way.

A

Respondents' claim to injury is that the lack of consultation with respect to certain funded activities abroad "increases the rate of extinction of endangered and threatened species." Of course, the desire to use or observe an animal species, even for purely aesthetic purposes, is undeniably a cognizable interest for purpose of standing. *See, e.g., Sierra Club v. Morton*, 405 U.S., at 734. "But the 'injury in fact' test requires more than an injury to a cognizable interest. It requires that the party seeking review be himself among the injured." To survive the Secretary's summary judgment motion, respondents had to submit affidavits or other evidence showing, through specific facts, not only that listed species were in fact being threatened by funded activities abroad, but also that one or more of respondents' members would thereby be "directly" affected apart from their "'special interest' in the subject." [Citation]

With respect to this aspect of the case, the Court of Appeals focused on the affidavits of two Defenders' members — Joyce Kelly and Amy Skilbred. Ms. Kelly stated that she traveled to Egypt in 1986 and "observed the traditional habitat of the endangered nile crocodile there and intends to do so again, and hopes to observe the crocodile directly," and that she "will suffer harm in fact as a result of [the] American ... role ... in overseeing the rehabilitation of the Aswan High Dam on the Nile ... and [in] developing ... Egypt's ... Master Water Plan." Ms. Skilbred averred that she traveled to Sri Lanka in 1981 and "observed the habitat" of "endangered species such as the Asian elephant and the leopard" at what is now the site of the Mahaweli Project funded by the Agency for International Development (AID), although she "was unable to see any of the endangered species"; "this development project," she continued, "will seriously reduce endangered, threatened, and endemic species habitat including areas that I visited ... [, which] may severely shorten the future of these species"; that threat, she concluded, harmed her because she "intends to return to Sri Lanka in the future and hopes to be more fortunate in spotting at least the endangered elephant and leopard." When Ms. Skilbred was asked at a subsequent deposition if and when she had any plans to return to Sri Lanka, she reiterated that "I intend to go back to Sri Lanka," but confessed that she had no current plans: "I don't know when. There is a civil war going on right now. I don't know. Not next year, I will say. In the future."

We shall assume for the sake of argument that these affidavits contain facts showing that certain agency-funded projects threaten listed species — though that is questionable. They plainly contain no facts, however, showing how damage to the species will produce "imminent" injury to Mss. Kelly and Skilbred. That the women "had visited" the areas of the projects before the projects commenced proves nothing. As we have said in a related context, "'past exposure to illegal conduct does not in itself show a present case or controversy regarding injunctive relief ... if unaccompanied by any continuing, present adverse effects.'" [Citation] And the affiants' profession of an "intent" to return to the places they had visited before — where they will presumably, this time, be deprived of the opportunity to observe animals of the endangered species — is simply not enough. Such "some day" intentions — without any description of concrete plans, or indeed even any specification of when the some day will be — do not support a finding of the "actual or imminent" injury that our cases require.[2]

Besides relying upon the Kelly and Skilbred affidavits, respondents propose a series of novel standing theories. The first, inelegantly styled "ecosystem nexus," proposes that any person who uses *any part* of a "contiguous ecosystem" adversely affected by a funded activity has standing even if the activity is located a great distance away. This approach, as the Court of Appeals correctly observed, is inconsistent with our opinion in *National Wildlife Federation* [*Lujan v. National Wildlife Federation*, 497 U.S. 871, 111 L. Ed. 2d 695, 110 S. Ct. 3177 (1990)], which held that a plaintiff claiming injury from environmental damage must use the area affected by the challenged activity and not an area roughly "in the vicinity" of it. 497 U.S., at 887-889; *see also Sierra Club*, 405 U.S., at 735. It makes no difference that the general-purpose section of the ESA states that the Act was intended in part "to provide a means whereby the ecosystems upon which endangered species and threatened species depend may be conserved," 16 U.S.C. § 1531(b). To say that the Act protects ecosystems is not to say that the Act creates (if it were possible) rights of action in persons who have not been injured in fact, that is, persons who use portions of an ecosystem not perceptibly affected by the unlawful action in question.

Respondents' other theories are called, alas, the "animal nexus" approach, whereby anyone who has an interest in studying or seeing the endangered animals anywhere on the globe has standing; and the "vocational nexus" approach, under which anyone with a professional interest in such animals can sue. Under these theories, anyone who goes to see Asian elephants in the Bronx Zoo, and anyone who is a keeper of Asian elephants in the Bronx Zoo, has standing to sue because the Director of AID did not consult with the Secretary regarding the AID-funded project in Sri Lanka. This is beyond all reason. Standing is not "an ingenious academic exercise in the conceivable," but as we have said requires, at the summary judgment stage, a factual showing of perceptible harm. [Citation] It is clear that the person who observes or works with a particular animal threatened by a federal decision is facing perceptible harm, since the very subject of his interest will no longer exist. It is even plausible — though it goes to the

---

[2] ... Although "imminence" is concededly a somewhat elastic concept, it cannot be stretched beyond its purpose, which is to insure that the alleged injury is not too speculative for Article III purposes — that the injury is "*certainly* impending." It has been stretched beyond the breaking point when, as here, the plaintiff alleges only an injury at some indefinite future time, and the acts necessary to make the injury happen are at least partly within the plaintiff's own control. In such circumstances we have insisted that the injury proceed with a high degree of immediacy, so as to reduce the possibility of deciding a case in which no injury would have occurred at all. [Citation] ....

outermost limit of plausibility — to think that a person who observes or works with animals of a particular species in the very area of the world where that species is threatened by a federal decision is facing such harm, since some animals that might have been the subject of his interest will no longer exist, *see Japan Whaling Assn. v. American Cetacean Soc.*, 478 U.S. 221, 231, n. 4 (1986). It goes beyond the limit, however, and into pure speculation and fantasy, to say that anyone who observes or works with an endangered species, anywhere in the world, is appreciably harmed by a single project affecting some portion of that species with which he has no more specific connection.[3]

B

Besides failing to show injury, respondents failed to demonstrate redressability. Instead of attacking the separate decisions to fund particular projects allegedly causing them harm, the respondents chose to challenge a more generalized level of government action (rules regarding consultation), the invalidation of which would affect all overseas projects. This programmatic approach has obvious practical advantages, but also obvious difficulties insofar as proof of causation or redressability is concerned....

The most obvious problem in the present case is redressability. Since the agencies funding the projects were not parties to the case, the District Court could accord relief only against the Secretary: He could be ordered to revise his regulation to require consultation for foreign projects. But this would not remedy respondents' alleged injury unless the funding agencies were bound by the Secretary's regulation, which is very much an open question....

... Assuming that it is appropriate to resolve an issue of law such as this in connection with a threshold standing inquiry, resolution by the District Court would not have remedied respondents' alleged injury anyway, because it would not have been binding upon the agencies. They were not parties to the suit, and there is no reason they should be obliged to honor an incidental legal determination the suit produced....

A further impediment to redressability is the fact that the agencies generally supply only a fraction of the funding for a foreign project. AID, for example, has provided less than 10% of the funding for the Mahaweli Project. Respondents have produced nothing to indicate that the projects they have named will either be suspended, or do less harm to listed species, if that fraction is eliminated.... [I]t is entirely conjectural whether the nonagency activity that affects respondents

---

[3]... [JUSTICE STEVENS] would allow standing on an apparent "animal nexus" theory to all plaintiffs whose interest in the animals is "genuine." Such plaintiffs, we are told, do not have to visit the animals because the animals are analogous to family members. We decline to join JUSTICE STEVENS in this Linnaean leap. It is unclear to us what constitutes a "genuine" interest; how it differs from a "non-genuine" interest (which nonetheless prompted a plaintiff to file suit); and why such an interest in animals should be different from such an interest in anything else that is the subject of a lawsuit.

will be altered or affected by the agency activity they seek to achieve. There is
no standing.

IV

The Court of Appeals found that respondents had standing for an additional
reason: because they had suffered a "procedural injury." The so-called
"citizen-suit" provision of the ESA provides, in pertinent part, that "any person
may commence a civil suit on his own behalf (A) to enjoin any person, including
the United States and any other governmental instrumentality or agency ... who
is alleged to be in violation of any provision of this chapter." 16 U.S.C.
§ 1540(g). The court held that, because § 7(a)(2) requires interagency consultation, the citizen-suit provision creates a "procedural right" to consultation in all
"persons" — so that *anyone* can file suit in federal court to challenge the
Secretary's (or presumably any other official's) failure to follow the assertedly
correct consultative procedure, notwithstanding their inability to allege any
discrete injury flowing from that failure. 911 F.2d, at 121-122. To understand
the remarkable nature of this holding one must be clear about what it does *not*
rest upon: This is not a case where plaintiffs are seeking to enforce a procedural
requirement the disregard of which could impair a separate concrete interest of
theirs (e.g., the procedural requirement for a hearing prior to denial of their
license application, or the procedural requirement for an environmental impact
statement before a federal facility is constructed next door to them).[7] Nor is it
simply a case where concrete injury has been suffered by many persons, as in
mass fraud or mass tort situations. Nor, finally, is it the unusual case in which
Congress has created a concrete private interest in the outcome of a suit against
a private party for the government's benefit, by providing a cash bounty for the
victorious plaintiff. Rather, the court held that the injury-in-fact requirement had
been satisfied by congressional conferral upon *all* persons of an abstract,
self-contained, noninstrumental "right" to have the Executive observe the
procedures required by law. We reject this view.

We have consistently held that a plaintiff raising only a generally available
grievance about government — claiming only harm to his and every citizen's
interest in proper application of the Constitution and laws, and seeking relief that

---

[7]There is this much truth to the assertion that "procedural rights" are special: The person who
has been accorded a procedural right to protect his concrete interests can assert that right without
meeting all the normal standards for redressability and immediacy. Thus, under our case-law, one
living adjacent to the site for proposed construction of a federally licensed dam has standing to
challenge the licensing agency's failure to prepare an Environmental Impact Statement, even though
he cannot establish with any certainty that the Statement will cause the license to be withheld or
altered, and even though the dam will not be completed for many years. What respondents'
"procedural rights" argument seeks, however, is quite different from this: standing for persons who
have no concrete interests affected — persons who live (and propose to live) at the other end of
the country from the dam.

no more directly and tangibly benefits him than it does the public at large — does not state an Article III case or controversy....

... The question presented here is whether the public interest in proper administration of the laws (specifically, in agencies' observance of a particular, statutorily prescribed procedure) can be converted into an individual right by a statute that denominates it as such, and that permits all citizens (or, for that matter, a subclass of citizens who suffer no distinctive concrete harm) to sue. If the concrete injury requirement has the separation-of-powers significance we have always said, the answer must be obvious: To permit Congress to convert the undifferentiated public interest in executive officers' compliance with the law into an "individual right" vindicable in the courts is to permit Congress to transfer from the President to the courts the Chief Executive's most important constitutional duty, to "take Care that the Laws be faithfully executed," Art. II, § 3. It would enable the courts, with the permission of Congress, "to assume a position of authority over the governmental acts of another and co-equal department," and to become "'virtually continuing monitors of the wisdom and soundness of Executive action.'" [Citations] We have always rejected that vision of our role.... "Individual rights," within the meaning of this passage, do not mean public rights that have been legislatively pronounced to belong to each individual who forms part of the public.

... We hold that respondents lack standing to bring this action and that the Court of Appeals erred in denying the summary judgment motion filed by the United States.

[Reversed and remanded]

JUSTICE KENNEDY, with whom JUSTICE SOUTER joins, concurring in part and concurring in the judgment.

... I also join Part IV of the Court's opinion with the following observations. As government programs and policies become more complex and far-reaching, we must be sensitive to the articulation of new rights of action that do not have clear analogs in our common-law tradition. Modern litigation has progressed far from the paradigm of Marbury suing Madison to get his commission, *Marbury v. Madison*, 1 Cranch 137 (1803), or Ogden seeking an injunction to halt Gibbons' steamboat operations. *Gibbons v. Ogden*, 9 Wheat. 1 (1824). In my view, Congress has the power to define injuries and articulate chains of causation that will give rise to a case or controversy where none existed before, and I do not read the Court's opinion to suggest a contrary view. [Citation] In exercising this power, however, Congress must at the very least identify the injury it seeks to vindicate and relate the injury to the class of persons entitled to bring suit. The citizen-suit provision of the Endangered Species Act does not meet these minimal requirements, because while the statute purports to confer a right on "any person ... to enjoin ... the United States and any other governmental instrumentality or agency ... who is alleged to be in violation of any provision of this chapter," it does not of its own force establish that there is an injury in "any person" by virtue of any "violation." 16 U.S.C. § 1540(g)(1)(A).

The Court's holding that there is an outer limit to the power of Congress to confer rights of action is a direct and necessary consequence of the case and controversy limitations found in Article III. I agree that it would exceed those limitations if, at the behest of Congress and in the absence of any showing of concrete injury, we were to entertain citizen-suits to vindicate the public's nonconcrete interest in the proper administration of the laws. While it does not matter how many persons have been injured by the challenged action, the party bringing suit must show that the action injures him in a concrete and personal way. This requirement is not just an empty formality. It preserves the vitality of the adversarial process by assuring both that the parties before the court have an actual, as opposed to professed, stake in the outcome, and that "the legal questions presented ... will be resolved, not in the rarefied atmosphere of a debating society, but in a concrete factual context conducive to a realistic appreciation of the consequences of judicial action." [Citation] In addition, the requirement of concrete injury confines the Judicial Branch to its proper, limited role in the constitutional framework of government.

... I concur in Parts I, II, III-A, and IV of the Court's opinion and in the judgment of the Court.

JUSTICE STEVENS, concurring in the judgment.

... In my opinion a person who has visited the critical habitat of an endangered species, has a professional interest in preserving the species and its habitat, and intends to revisit them in the future has standing to challenge agency action that threatens their destruction. Congress has found that a wide variety of endangered species of fish, wildlife, and plants are of "aesthetic, ecological, educational, historical, recreational, and scientific value to the Nation and its people." 16 U.S.C. § 1531(a)(3). Given that finding, we have no license to demean the importance of the interest that particular individuals may have in observing any species or its habitat, whether those individuals are motivated by aesthetic enjoyment, an interest in professional research, or an economic interest in preservation of the species. Indeed, this Court has often held that injuries to such interests are sufficient to confer standing, and the Court reiterates that holding today.

The Court nevertheless concludes that respondents have not suffered "injury in fact" because they have not shown that the harm to the endangered species will produce "imminent" injury to them. I disagree. An injury to an individual's interest in studying or enjoying a species and its natural habitat occurs when someone (whether it be the government or a private party) takes action that harms that species and habitat. In my judgment, therefore, the "imminence" of such an injury should be measured by the timing and likelihood of the threatened environmental harm, rather than — as the Court seems to suggest, — by the time that might elapse between the present and the time when the individuals would visit the area if no such injury should occur.

... [W]e have denied standing to plaintiffs whose likelihood of suffering any concrete adverse effect from the challenged action was speculative. [Citations] In this case, however, the likelihood that respondents will be injured by the destruction of the endangered species is not speculative. If respondents are genuinely interested in the preservation of the endangered species and intend to study or observe these animals in the future, their injury will occur as soon as the animals are destroyed. Thus the only potential source of "speculation" in this case is whether respondents' intent to study or observe the animals is genuine.[2] In my view, Joyce Kelly and Amy Skilbred have introduced sufficient evidence to negate petitioner's contention that their claims of injury are "speculative" or "conjectural."...

JUSTICE BLACKMUN, with whom JUSTICE O'CONNOR joins, dissenting.

I part company with the Court in this case in two respects. First, I believe that respondents have raised genuine issues of fact — sufficient to survive summary judgment — both as to injury and as to redressability. Second, I question the Court's breadth of language in rejecting standing for "procedural" injuries. I fear the Court seeks to impose fresh limitations on the constitutional authority of Congress to allow citizen-suits in the federal courts for injuries deemed "procedural" in nature....

... [A] reasonable finder of fact could conclude from the information in the affidavits and deposition testimony that either Kelly or Skilbred will soon return to the project sites, thereby satisfying the "actual or imminent" injury standard.... Kelly's and Skilbred's professional backgrounds in wildlife preservation, also make it likely — at least far more likely than for the average citizen — that they would choose to visit these areas of the world where species are vanishing.

By requiring a "description of concrete plans" or "specification of when the some day [for a return visit] will be," the Court, in my view, demands what is likely an empty formality. No substantial barriers prevent Kelly or Skilbred from

---

[2]As we recognized in *Sierra Club v. Morton*, 405 U.S., at 735, the impact of changes in the aesthetics or ecology of a particular area does "not fall indiscriminately upon every citizen. The alleged injury will be felt directly only by those who use [the area,] and for whom the aesthetic and recreational values of the area will be lessened...." Thus, respondents would not be injured by the challenged projects if they had not visited the sites or studied the threatened species and habitat. But, as discussed above, respondents did visit the sites; moreover, they have expressed an intent to do so again. This intent to revisit the area is significant evidence tending to confirm the genuine character of respondents' interest, but I am not at all sure that an intent to revisit would be indispensable in every case. The interest that confers standing in a case of this kind is comparable, though by no means equivalent, to the interest in a relationship among family members that can be immediately harmed by the death of an absent member, regardless of when, if ever, a family reunion is planned to occur. Thus, if the facts of this case had shown repeated and regular visits by the respondents, proof of an intent to revisit might well be superfluous.

simply purchasing plane tickets to return to the Aswan and Mahaweli projects. This case differs from other cases in which the imminence of harm turned largely on the affirmative actions of third parties beyond a plaintiff's control....

I fear the Court's demand for detailed descriptions of future conduct will do little to weed out those who are genuinely harmed from those who are not. More likely, it will resurrect a code-pleading formalism in federal court summary judgment practice, as federal courts, newly doubting their jurisdiction, will demand more and more particularized showings of future harm. Just to survive summary judgment, for example, a property owner claiming a decline in the value of his property from governmental action might have to specify the exact date he intends to sell his property and show that there is a market for the property, lest it be surmised he might not sell again. A nurse turned down for a job on grounds of her race had better be prepared to show on what date she was prepared to start work, that she had arranged daycare for her child, and that she would not have accepted work at another hospital instead....

The Court also concludes that injury is lacking, because respondents' allegations of "ecosystem nexus" failed to demonstrate sufficient proximity to the site of the environmental harm. To support that conclusion, the Court mischaracterizes our decision in *Lujan v. National Wildlife Federation*, ___ U.S. ___ (1990), as establishing a general rule that "a plaintiff claiming injury from environmental damage must use the area affected by the challenged activity." In *National Wildlife Federation*, the Court required specific geographical proximity because of the particular type of harm alleged in that case: harm to the plaintiff's visual enjoyment of nature from mining activities. One cannot suffer from the sight of a ruined landscape without being close enough to see the sites actually being mined. Many environmental injuries, however, cause harm distant from the area immediately affected by the challenged action. Environmental destruction may affect animals traveling over vast geographical ranges, or rivers running long geographical courses. [Citations] It cannot seriously be contended that a litigant's failure to use the precise or exact site where animals are slaughtered or where toxic waste is dumped into a river means he or she cannot show injury.

The Court also rejects respondents' claim of vocational or professional injury. The Court says that it is "beyond all reason" that a zoo "keeper" of Asian elephants would have standing to contest his government's participation in the eradication of all the Asian elephants in another part of the world. I am unable to see how the distant location of the destruction necessarily (for purposes of ruling at summary judgment) mitigates the harm to the elephant keeper. If there is no more access to a future supply of the animal that sustains a keeper's livelihood, surely there is harm....

The Court concludes that any "procedural injury" suffered by respondents is insufficient to confer standing. It rejects the view that the "injury-in-fact requirement ... [is] satisfied by congressional conferral upon all person of an abstract, self-contained, noninstrumental 'right' to have the Executive observe the procedures required by law." Whatever the Court might mean with that very broad language, it cannot be saying that "procedural injuries" *as a class* are necessarily insufficient for purposes of Article III standing.

Most governmental conduct can be classified as "procedural." Many injuries caused by governmental conduct, therefore, are categorizable at some level of generality as "procedural" injuries. Yet, these injuries are not categorically beyond the pale of redress by the federal courts. When the Government, for example, "procedurally" issues a pollution permit, those affected by the permittee's pollutants are not without standing to sue. Only later cases will tell just what the Court means by its intimation that "procedural" injuries are not constitutionally cognizable injuries. In the meantime, I have the greatest of sympathy for the courts across the country that will struggle to understand the Court's standardless exposition of this concept today.

... To be sure, in the ordinary course, Congress does legislate in black-and-white terms of affirmative commands or negative prohibitions on the conduct of officers of the Executive Branch. In complex regulatory areas, however, Congress often legislates, as it were, in procedural shades of gray. That is, it sets forth substantive policy goals and provides for their attainment by requiring Executive Branch officials to follow certain procedures, for example, in the form of reporting, consultation, and certification requirements....

... There may be factual circumstances in which a congressionally imposed procedural requirement is so insubstantially connected to the prevention of a substantive harm that it cannot be said to work any conceivable injury to an individual litigant. But, as a general matter, the courts owe substantial deference to Congress' substantive purpose in imposing a certain procedural requirement. In all events, "our separation-of-powers analysis does not turn on the labeling of an activity as 'substantive' as opposed to 'procedural.'" [Citation] There is no room for a per se rule or presumption excluding injuries labeled "procedural" in nature.

In conclusion, I cannot join the Court on what amounts to a slash-and-burn expedition through the law of environmental standing. In my view, "the very essence of civil liberty certainly consists in the right of every individual to claim the protection of the laws, whenever he receives an injury." *Marbury v. Madison*, 1 Cranch 137, 163 (1803).

NOTES AND QUESTIONS

1. According to the Court in the principal case, how specific must an allegation of injury in fact be to survive a motion for summary judgment? *Also see Lujan v. National Wildlife Federation*, 497 U.S. 871 (1990) where affidavits alleging recreational use and aesthetic enjoyment of lands in the "vicinity" of areas affected by a Department of Interior program were found insufficient for standing purposes. The Court found the affidavits deficient because they failed to particularize the precise lands affected by the government program. If the parties both understand which geographic areas are in dispute, should the courts allow liberal amendment of pleadings to remedy a perceived shortcoming in alleging injury in fact?

Compare Alaska Center for the Environment v. Browner, 20 F.3d 981, 985 (9th Cir. 1994) (In CWA citizen suit to compel EPA to implement water quality standards for State of Alaska, plaintiff only required to show "representative" number of waters affected by program since all waters of state were "interrelated"). *See generally* Cass Sunstein, *What's Standing After Lujan? Of Citizen Suits, "Injuries", and Article III*, 91 MICH. L. REV. 163 (1992).

2. In *Sierra Club v. Morton*, the Court recognized that standing to challenge federal agency action pursuant to the APA required a showing by the claimant that their "use" of the affected resources would be adversely impacted by the agency conduct. Delimiting standing doctrine by equating injury in fact to use of the subject has inherent limitations of application. How should courts evaluate claims by wildlife conservation or animal rights groups with regard to their interest in or usage of the affected species? Courts have differed, for instance, as to the frequency or nature of use necessary to justify standing. *See DuBois v. United States Dep't of Agriculture*, 102 F.3d 1273, 1283 (1st Cir. 1996) (regular visits to area affected by proposed project and drinks water potentially tainted by pollution sufficient for injury in fact).

In *PETA v. Department of Health & Human Servs.*, 917 F.2d 15, 17 (9th Cir. 1990) animal rights activists alleged that several federal agencies violated NEPA by awarding animal research grants to institutions in the San Francisco area without preparing environmental impact statements. They alleged that they were adversely affected in their use and enjoyment of the San Francisco Bay area because of the transportation and disposal of hazardous materials and other detrimental environmental effects such as increased air pollution, traffic, noise, and negative land uses attributable to the animal research projects. The court held that the allegations of injury were insufficiently specific to withstand summary judgment on standing. Also, in *Animal Welfare Inst. v. Kreps*, 561 F.2d 1002, 1007-10 (D.C. Cir. 1977), environmental groups challenged a decision by the government to waive a moratorium imposed by the Marine Mammal Protection Act in order to permit importation of baby fur seal skins from South Africa. The court held that the plaintiffs' asserted injury was sufficient to confer standing where two members alleged that they had travelled to South Africa in the past to observe the seals and another planned to do so in the future. *Contra Donham v. United States Dep't of Agri.*, 725 F. Supp. 985, 987 (S.D. Ill. 1989) (a single visit by environmentalist to affected national forest inadequate use for standing to challenge proposed timber harvesting plan).

3. In *International Primate Protection League v. Tulane Educ. Fund*, 895 F.2d 1056 (5th Cir. 1990), *rev'd on other grounds*, ___ U.S. ___, 111 S. Ct. 1700 (1991) the court denied standing to an animal rights organization which sought to prevent a federal agency and a university from euthanizing certain monkeys in conducting medical research. The court distinguished the ability of plaintiffs to claim injury to aesthetic interests where government actions might adversely affect animals living in the wild from instances where the plaintiffs lacked a "personal relationship" with privately-owned laboratory animals.

In contrast, in *Japan Whaling Ass'n v. American Cetacean Soc'y*, 478 U.S. 221, 230 n.4 (1986) the Court held that the plaintiffs had alleged a sufficient "injury-in-fact" for standing by claiming that their whale watching and studying would be adversely affected by continued whale harvesting. Do you agree with these distinctions?

4. Can a plaintiff "manufacture" standing by deciding to use a resource simply for the purpose of subsequently challenging agency action affecting that resource area? In *Regional Ass'n of Concerned Environmentalists v. United States Dep't of Agri.*, 765 F. Supp. 502 (S.D. Ill. 1990) the court upheld a magistrate's findings and denied standing to one plaintiff who sought to halt a timber sale by the government even though the individual alleged visiting the area approximately a dozen times in the preceding year. The court explained that the visits were not for "recreational" purposes pursued by other plaintiffs but instead were part of an "ongoing crusade of environmental activism." Should courts make value judgments regarding the subjective motivation of a person in using a resource for purposes of granting or denying standing?

5. *Causation.* The causation prong of the standing test requires a showing that the purported injury be "fairly traced" to the challenged conduct. The policy underlying the element of causation for standing purposes, although not as rigorous as normative tort requirements of causation, is to place reasoned limits on the breadth of persons who are considered properly positioned to contest certain conduct. Thus, standing will be denied to those who are merely "concerned bystanders" or have asserted remote or attenuated links to the alleged harm. *See Florida Audubon Soc'y v. Bensten*, 94 F.3d 658, 664 (D.C. Cir. 1996) (causation analysis for procedural injury requires two links: a reasonable likelihood that if the government had performed the correct procedure it would have reached a different result and that the error affected a particularized interest of plaintiff).

In *United States v. Students Challenging Regulatory Agency Procedures (SCRAP I)*, 412 U.S. 669 (1973) an unincorporated group of law students challenged under NEPA an Interstate Commerce Commission order approving a railroad freight surcharge. The plaintiffs claimed that its members suffered "economic, recreational, and aesthetic harm" as a direct result of the adverse environmental impact of the rate increase. They alleged that the ICC order discouraged recycling because it promoted the use of new raw materials which compete with scrap materials. Consequently, asserted plaintiffs, the expanded use of nonrecyclable commodities would deplete natural resources and result in more waste materials being discarded in national parks which they used. Justice Stewart, although cautioning that "[P]leadings must be something more than an ingenious academic exercise in the conceivable" still recognized that the plaintiffs had demonstrated a sufficient causal connection between the ICC order and their injury to satisfy standing to overcome a motion to dismiss.

In *Public Interest Research Group of New Jersey v. Powell Duffryn Terminals*, 913 F.2d 64 (3d Cir. 1990) environmental organizations instituted a citizens suit under the Clean Water Act seeking penalties and injunctive relief for alleged permit violations by the defendant in operation of a bulk storage facility. The court observed that the causation requirement for standing was not satisfied merely by showing a statutory violation, but necessitated tracing the defendant's wrongful conduct to plaintiff's asserted harms. On the other hand, the court did not demand a showing that plaintiffs establish to a scientific certainty that the unlawful discharge of pollutants by the plant caused the precise harm suffered by plaintiffs. Rather, plaintiffs must show that there was a "substantial likelihood" that the defendant's conduct caused the alleged injuries.

In *Petro-Chem Processing, Inc. v. EPA*, 866 F.2d 433 (D.C. Cir. 1989) a national trade organization of firms engaged in the business of hazardous waste treatment challenged certain EPA decisions affecting the timing and method of disposal of hazardous waste. The plaintiffs contended that, as a result of lax EPA regulation of its competitors, its own members would suffer economic injury either from the loss of customers or from liability incurred for noncompliance with the laws. The court denied the group standing on the basis that the alleged injuries were not fairly traced to the challenged government conduct. The court reasoned that the causal chain was broken where the plaintiffs' injuries were "self-inflicted"; the claimants could avoid the threatened injuries by choosing safer methods of doing business. *Also see State of Alabama v. EPA*, 871 F.2d 1548, 1556 (11th Cir. 1989) (claimed threatened injury to environmental quality not causally related to asserted lack of notice and opportunity to participate in selection of remedial action for waste disposal facility).

6. Timing. In *Defenders of Wildlife*, the Court observed that, in order to reduce the likelihood that the court will decide a case where the injury never materializes, an allegation of future injury must be shown with a "high degree of immediacy" where the acts necessary to cause the harm are partly within the claimant's control. 112 S. Ct. at 2139 n.2. Courts have reached different results in applying the Court's guidance on the issue of timing. *Compare Sierra Club v. Robertson*, 28 F.3d 753, 758 (8th Cir. 1994) (restrictive view denying standing to challenge land and resource management plan for national forest because couldn't show current harm). *Contra Sierra Club v. Marita*, 46 F.3d 606 (7th Cir. 1995).

Consider *Duke Power Co. v. Carolina Envtl. Study Group, Inc.*, 438 U.S. 59 (1978) where a citizen's group challenged the constitutionality of the Price-Anderson Act, which limited liability for nuclear incidents. The plaintiff organization, comprised of individuals living near construction sites for nuclear power plants, alleged that the Act violated due process by allowing injuries without adequate compensation and equal protection by forcing victims of an accident to bear the burden of injury while the public received the benefits of nuclear development. The Court recognized that the asserted environmental and aesthetic harms resulting from thermal pollution were the kinds of injuries which would satisfy the "injury in fact" standard for standing. The Court rejected the power company's contention that any claimed future harm of radiation from a nuclear accident was too speculative and remote to constitute a direct and present injury. Instead, the Court explained that the injury could be considered concrete because of "our generalized concern about exposure to radiation and the apprehension flowing from the uncertainty about the health and genetic consequences of even small emissions like those concededly emitted by nuclear power plants." 438 U.S. at 74. Can this be reconciled with *Defenders of Wildlife*?

7. *Redressability.* Another prudential limitation on standing to sue is commonly referred to as "redressability." *Simon v. Eastern Kentucky Welfare Rights Org.*, 426 U.S. 26, 41 (1976). In contrast to the "fairly traceable" requirement which focuses on the causal connection between the defendant's conduct and the injury asserted, the redressability factor looks at the relationship between the plaintiff's alleged harm and the judicial relief sought. *Allen v. Wright*, 468 U.S. 737, 753 n.19 (1984). The policy underpinning the element of redressability is simply that courts will refrain from expending their resources unless persuaded that the remedy requested would serve a useful purpose if the plaintiff prevailed on the merits.

In *South East Lake View Neighbors v. Department of Hous. & Urb. Dev.*, 685 F.2d 1027 (7th Cir. 1982) neighborhood groups sought to halt the construction of a federally-financed housing project in their community alleging violations of various federal laws. Plaintiffs claimed that they would sustain injury from increased noise and air pollution, crime, and congestion resulting from the building and occupation of the apartment complex. The court denied standing, though, reasoning that because the building was virtually completed and would be occupied regardless of the outcome of the suit, the plaintiff's injuries would not be redressed by a favorable decision. On the other hand, in *Public Interest Research Group of New Jersey v. Powell Duffryn Terminals*, 913 F.2d 64, 73 (3d Cir. 1990) the court held that the redressability prong of the standing test was satisfied in a citizen's group challenge to alleged ongoing violations of the Clean Water Act where the civil penalties sought would deter the defendant from future violations.

8. Federal environmental protection statutes frequently authorize citizen suits as a supplementary enforcement mechanism to challenge conduct violating the Act's provisions. Although new legal rights may be created by the statute, Congress' provision for citizens suits does not establish Article III standing nor dispense with the constitutional requirement of a case or controversy. Consequently, a claimant must satisfy the "injury in fact" test as a constitutional minimum even where no injury would exist without the statute. *See Sierra Club v. Simkins Indus.*, 847 F.2d 1109, 1113 (4th Cir. 1988). Some have contended, however, that certain citizen suit provisions should authorize "universal standing" which nevertheless would pass constitutional muster even without individualized injury. *See* Currie, *Judicial Review Under Federal Pollution Laws*, 62 IOWA L. REV. 1221 (1977). The justification for broadening the concept of standing in such instances is that the claimant indeed suffers an "injury in fact" through violation of the Act, and that without allowing such suits the harm would go unredressed.

BENNETT v. SPEAR

___ U.S. ___, 117 S. Ct. 1154, 137 L. Ed. 2d 281 (1997)

JUSTICE SCALIA delivered the opinion of the Court.

This is a challenge to a biological opinion issued by the Fish and Wildlife Service in accordance with the Endangered Species Act of 1973 (ESA), 87 Stat. 884, as amended, 16 U.S.C. § 1531 et seq., concerning the operation of the Klamath Irrigation Project by the Bureau of Reclamation, and the project's impact on two varieties of endangered fish. The question for decision is whether the petitioners, who have competing economic and other interests in Klamath Project water, have standing to seek judicial review of the biological opinion under the citizen-suit provision of the ESA, § 1540(g)(1), and the Administrative Procedure Act (APA), 80 Stat. 392, as amended, 5 U.S.C. § 701 et seq.

I

The ESA requires the Secretary of the Interior to promulgate regulations listing those species of animals that are "threatened" or "endangered" under specified criteria, and to designate their "critical habitat." 16 U.S.C. § 1533. The ESA further requires each federal agency to "insure that any action authorized, funded, or carried out by such agency ... is not likely to jeopardize the continued existence of any endangered species or threatened species or result in the destruction or adverse modification of habitat of such species which is determined by the Secretary ... to be critical." § 1536(a)(2). If an agency determines that action it proposes to take may adversely affect a listed species, it must engage in formal consultation with the Fish and Wildlife Service, as delegate of the Secretary, *ibid.*; 50 CFR § 402.14 (1995), after which the Service must provide the agency with a written statement (the Biological Opinion) explaining how the proposed action will affect the species or its habitat, 16 U.S.C. § 1536(b)(3)(A). If the Service concludes that the proposed action will "jeopardize the continued existence of any [listed] species or result in the destruction or adverse modification of [critical habitat]," § 1536(a)(2), the Biological Opinion must outline any "reasonable and prudent alternatives" that the Service believes will avoid that consequence, § 1536(b)(3)(A). Additionally, if the Biological Opinion concludes that the agency action will not result in jeopardy or adverse habitat modification, or if it offers reasonable and prudent alternatives to avoid that consequence, the Service must provide the agency with a written statement (known as the "Incidental Take Statement") specifying the "impact of such incidental taking on the species," any "reasonable and prudent measures that the [Service] considers necessary or appropriate to minimize such impact," and setting forth "the terms and conditions ... that must be complied with by the Federal agency ... to implement [those measures]." § 1536(b)(4).

The Klamath Project, one of the oldest federal reclamation schemes, is a series of lakes, rivers, dams and irrigation canals in northern California and southern Oregon. The project was undertaken by the Secretary of the Interior pursuant to the Reclamation Act of 1902, 32 Stat. 388, as amended, 43 U.S.C. § 371 *et seq.*, and the Act of Feb. 9, 1905, 33 Stat. 714, and is administered by the Bureau of Reclamation, which is under the Secretary's jurisdiction. In 1992, the Bureau notified the Service that operation of the project might affect the Lost River Sucker (Deltistes luxatus) and Shortnose Sucker (Chasmistes brevirostris), species of fish that were listed as endangered in 1988, *see* 53 Fed. Reg. 27130-27133 (1988). After formal consultation with the Bureau in accordance with 50 CFR § 402.14 (1995), the Service issued a Biological Opinion which concluded that the "'long-term operation of the Klamath Project was likely to jeopardize the continued existence of the Lost River and shortnose suckers.'" The Biological Opinion identified "reasonable and prudent alternatives" the Service believed would avoid jeopardy, which included the maintenance of minimum water levels on Clear Lake and Gerber reservoirs. The Bureau later notified the Service that it intended to operate the project in compliance with the Biological Opinion.

Petitioners, two Oregon irrigation districts that receive Klamath Project water and the operators of two ranches within those districts, filed the present action against the director and regional director of the Service and the Secretary of the Interior. Neither the Bureau nor any of its officials is named as defendant. The complaint asserts that the Bureau "has been following essentially the same procedures for storing and releasing water from Clear Lake and Gerber reservoirs throughout the twentieth century"; that "there is no scientifically or commercially available evidence indicating that the populations of endangered suckers in Clear Lake and Gerber reservoirs have declined, are declining, or will decline as a result" of the Bureau's operation of the Klamath Project; that "there is no commercially or scientifically available evidence indicating that the restrictions on lake levels imposed in the Biological Opinion will have any beneficial effect on the ... populations of suckers in Clear Lake and Gerber reservoirs"; and that the Bureau nonetheless "will abide by the restrictions imposed by the Biological Opinion."

Petitioners' complaint included three claims for relief that are relevant here. The first and second claims allege that the Service's jeopardy determination with respect to Clear Lake and Gerber reservoirs, and the ensuing imposition of minimum water levels, violated § 7 of the ESA, 16 U.S.C. § 1536. The third claim is that the imposition of minimum water elevations constituted an implicit determination of critical habitat for the suckers, which violated § 4 of the ESA, 16 U.S.C. § 1533(b)(2), because it failed to take into consideration the designation's economic impact. Each of the claims also states that the relevant action violated the APA's prohibition of agency action that is "arbitrary, capricious, an abuse of discretion, or otherwise not in accordance with law." 5 U.S.C. § 706(2)(A).

The complaint asserts that petitioners' use of the reservoirs and related waterways for "recreational, aesthetic and commercial purposes, as well as for their primary sources of irrigation water" will be "irreparably damaged" by the actions complained of, and that the restrictions on water delivery "recommended" by the Biological Opinion "adversely affect plaintiffs by substantially reducing the quantity of available irrigation water." In essence, petitioners claim a competing interest in the water the Biological Opinion declares necessary for the preservation of the suckers.

The District Court dismissed the complaint for lack of jurisdiction. It concluded that petitioners did not have standing because their "recreational, aesthetic, and commercial interests ... do not fall within the zone of interests sought to be protected by ESA." The Court of Appeals for the Ninth Circuit affirmed. *Bennett v. Plenert*, 63 F.3d 915 (1995). It held that the "zone of interests" test limits the class of persons who may obtain judicial review not only under the APA, but also under the citizen-suit provision of the ESA, 16 U.S.C. § 1540(g), and that "only plaintiffs who allege an interest in the preservation of endangered species fall within the zone of interests protected by the ESA," 63 F.3d at 919. We granted certiorari. 517 U.S. (1996).

In this Court, petitioners raise two questions: first, whether the prudential standing rule known as the "zone of interests" test applies to claims brought under the citizen-suit provision of the ESA; and second, if so, whether petitioners have standing under that test notwithstanding that the interests they seek to vindicate are economic rather than environmental. In this Court, the Government has made no effort to defend the reasoning of the Court of Appeals. Instead, it advances three alternative grounds for affirmance: (1) that petitioners fail to meet the standing requirements imposed by Article III of the Constitution; (2) that the ESA's citizen-suit provision does not authorize judicial review of the types of claims advanced by petitioners; and (3) that judicial review is unavailable under the APA because the Biological Opinion does not constitute final agency action.

II

We first turn to the question the Court of Appeals found dispositive: whether petitioners lack standing by virtue of the zone-of-interests test. Although petitioners contend that their claims lie both under the ESA and the APA, we look first at the ESA because it may permit petitioners to recover their litigation costs, *see* 16 U.S.C. § 1540(g)(4), and because the APA by its terms independently authorizes review only when "there is no other adequate remedy in a court," 5 U.S.C. § 704.

The question of standing "involves both constitutional limitations on federal-court jurisdiction and prudential limitations on its exercise." [Citation] To satisfy the "case" or "controversy" requirement of Article III, which is the "irreducible constitutional minimum" of standing, a plaintiff must, generally speaking, demonstrate that he has suffered "injury in fact," that the injury is "fairly traceable" to the actions of the defendant, and that the injury will likely be redressed by a favorable decision. [Citations] In addition to the immutable requirements of Article III, "the federal judiciary has also adhered to a set of prudential principles that bear on the question of standing." *Id.*, at 474-475. Like their constitutional counterparts, these "judicially self-imposed limits on the exercise of federal jurisdiction,"[Citation] are "founded in concern about the proper — and properly limited — role of the courts in a democratic society,"; but unlike their constitutional counterparts, they can be modified or abrogated by Congress. Numbered among these prudential requirements is the doctrine of particular concern in this case: that a plaintiff's grievance must arguably fall within the zone of interests protected or regulated by the statutory provision or constitutional guarantee invoked in the suit.

The "zone of interests" formulation was first employed in *Association of Data Processing Service Organizations, Inc. v. Camp*, 397 U.S. 150, 25 L. Ed. 2d 184, 90 S. Ct. 827 (1970). There, certain data processors sought to invalidate a ruling by the Comptroller of the Currency authorizing national banks to sell data processing services on the ground that it violated, inter alia, § 4 of the Bank Service Corporation Act of 1962, 76 Stat. 1132, which prohibited bank service corporations from engaging in "any activity other than the performance of bank services for banks."... [W]e stated the applicable prudential standing requirement to be "whether the interest sought to be protected by the complainant is arguably within the zone of interests to be protected or regulated by the statute or constitutional guarantee in question." Data Processing, and its companion case, *Barlow v. Collins*, 397 U.S. 159, 25 L. Ed. 2d 192, 90 S. Ct. 832 (1970), applied the zone-of-interests test to suits under the APA, but later cases have applied it also in suits not involving review of federal administrative action. We have made clear, however, that the breadth of the zone of interests varies according to the provisions of law at issue, so that what comes within the zone of interests of a statute for purposes of obtaining judicial review of administrative action under the "'generous review provisions'" of the APA may not do so for other purposes.

Congress legislates against the background of our prudential standing doctrine, which applies unless it is expressly negated. [Citations] The first question in the present case is whether the ESA's citizen-suit provision, set forth in pertinent part in the margin,[2] negates the zone-of-interests test (or, perhaps more

---

[2]"(1) Except as provided in paragraph (2) of this subsection any person may commence a civil suit on his own behalf —

"(A) to enjoin any person, including the United States and any other governmental instrumentality or agency (to the extent permitted by the eleventh amendment to the Constitution), who is alleged to be in violation of any provision of this chapter or regulation issued under the authority thereof; or

....

accurately, expands the zone of interests). We think it does. The first operative portion of the provision says that "any person may commence a civil suit" — an authorization of remarkable breadth when compared with the language Congress ordinarily uses. Even in some other environmental statutes, Congress has used more restrictive formulations, such as "[any person] having an interest which is or may be adversely affected," 33 U.S.C. § 1365(g) (Clean Water Act); *see also* 30 U.S.C. § 1270(a) (Surface Mining Control and Reclamation Act) (same); "any person suffering legal wrong," 15 U.S.C. § 797(b)(5) (Energy Supply and Environmental Coordination Act); or "any person having a valid legal interest which is or may be adversely affected ... whenever such action constitutes a case or controversy," 42 U.S.C. § 9124(a) (Ocean Thermal Energy Conversion Act). And in contexts other than the environment, Congress has often been even more restrictive. In statutes concerning unfair trade practices and other commercial matters, for example, it has authorized suit only by "any person injured in his business or property," 7 U.S.C. § 2305(c); *see also* 15 U.S.C. § 72 (same), or only by "competitors, customers, or subsequent purchasers," § 298(b).

Our readiness to take the term "any person" at face value is greatly augmented by two interrelated considerations: that the overall subject matter of this legislation is the environment (a matter in which it is common to think all persons have an interest) and that the obvious purpose of the particular provision in question is to encourage enforcement by so-called "private attorneys general" — evidenced by its elimination of the usual amount-in-controversy and diversity-of-citizenship requirements, its provision for recovery of the costs of litigation (including even expert witness fees), and its reservation to the

---

"(C) against the Secretary where there is alleged a failure of the Secretary to perform any act or duty under section 1533 of this title which is not discretionary with the Secretary.

The district courts shall have jurisdiction, without regard to the amount in controversy or the citizenship of the parties, to enforce any such provision or regulation, or to order the Secretary to perform such act or duty, as the case may be....

(2)(A) No action may be commenced under subparagraph (1)(A) of this section —

"(i) prior to sixty days after written notice of the violation has been given to the Secretary, and to any alleged violator of any such provision or regulation;
"(ii) if the Secretary has commenced action to impose a penalty pursuant to subsection (a) of this section; or
"(iii) if the United States has commenced and is diligently prosecuting a criminal action ... to redress a violation of any such provision or regulation.

....

"(3)(B) In any such suit under this subsection in which the United States is not a party, the Attorney General, at the request of the Secretary, may intervene on behalf of the United States as a matter of right.
"(4) The court, in issuing any final order in any suit brought pursuant to paragraph (1) of this subsection, may award costs of litigation (including reasonable attorney and expert witness fees) to any party, whenever the court determines such award is appropriate." 16 U.S.C. § 1540(g).

Government of a right of first refusal to pursue the action initially and a right to intervene later. Given these factors, we think the conclusion of expanded standing follows a fortiori from our decision in *Trafficante v. Metropolitan Life Ins. Co.*, 409 U.S. 205, 34 L. Ed. 2d 415, 93 S. Ct. 364 (1972), which held that standing was expanded to the full extent permitted under Article III by a provision of the Civil Rights Act of 1968 that authorized "any person who claims to have been injured by a discriminatory housing practice" to sue for violations of the Act. There also we relied on textual evidence of a statutory scheme to rely on private litigation to ensure compliance with the Act. The statutory language here is even clearer, and the subject of the legislation makes the intent to permit enforcement by everyman even more plausible.

It is true that the plaintiffs here are seeking to prevent application of environmental restrictions rather than to implement them. But the "any person" formulation applies to all the causes of action authorized by § 1540(g) — not only to actions against private violators of environmental restrictions, and not only to actions against the Secretary asserting underenforcment under § 1533, but also to actions against the Secretary asserting overenforcement under § 1533. As we shall discuss below, the citizen-suit provision does favor environmentalists in that it covers all private violations of the Act but not all failures of the Secretary to meet his administrative responsibilities; but there is no textual basis for saying that its expansion of standing requirements applies to environmentalists alone. The Court of Appeals therefore erred in concluding that petitioners lacked standing under the zone-of-interests test to bring their claims under the ESA's citizen-suit provision.

III

A

... The Government's first contention is that petitioners' complaint fails to satisfy the standing requirements imposed by the "case" or "controversy" provision of Article III. This "irreducible constitutional minimum" of standing requires: (1) that the plaintiff have suffered an "injury in fact" — an invasion of a judicially cognizable interest which is (a) concrete and particularized and (b) actual or imminent, not conjectural or hypothetical; (2) that there be a causal connection between the injury and the conduct complained of — the injury must be fairly traceable to the challenged action of the defendant, and not the result of the independent action of some third party not before the court; and (3) that it be likely, as opposed to merely speculative, that the injury will be redressed by a favorable decision.

Petitioners allege, among other things, that they currently receive irrigation water from Clear Lake, that the Bureau "will abide by the restrictions imposed by the Biological Opinion," and that "the restrictions on lake levels imposed in the Biological Opinion adversely affect [petitioners] by substantially reducing the quantity of available irrigation water." The Government contends, first, that these allegations fail to satisfy the "injury in fact" element of Article III standing because they demonstrate only a diminution in the aggregate amount of available water, and do not necessarily establish (absent information concerning the Bureau's water allocation practices) that the petitioners will receive less water. This contention overlooks, however, the proposition that each element of Article III standing "must be supported in the same way as any other matter on which the plaintiff bears the burden of proof, i.e., with the manner and degree of evidence required at the successive stages of the litigation." Thus, while a plaintiff must "set forth" by affidavit or other evidence "specific facts," to survive a motion for summary judgment, Fed. Rule Civ. Proc. 56(e), and must ultimately support any contested facts with evidence adduced at trial, "at the pleading stage, general factual allegations of injury resulting from the defendant's conduct may suffice, for on a motion to dismiss we 'presume that general allegations embrace those specific facts that are necessary to support the claim.'" Given petitioners' allegation that the amount of available water will be reduced and that they will be adversely affected thereby, it is easy to presume specific facts under which petitioners will be injured — for example, the Bureau's distribution of the reduction pro rata among its customers. The complaint alleges the requisite injury in fact.

The Government also contests compliance with the second and third Article III standing requirements, contending that any injury suffered by petitioners is neither "fairly traceable" to the Service's Biological Opinion, nor "redressable" by a favorable judicial ruling, because the "action agency" (the Bureau) retains ultimate responsibility for determining whether and how a proposed action shall go forward. *See* 50 CFR § 402.15(a) (1995) ("Following the issuance of a biological opinion, the Federal agency shall determine whether and in what manner to proceed with the action in light of its section 7 obligations and the Service's biological opinion"). "If the petitioners have suffered injury," the Government contends, "the proximate cause of their harm is an (as yet unidentified) decision by the Bureau regarding the volume of water allocated to petitioners, not the biological opinion itself." This wrongly equates injury "fairly traceable" to the defendant with injury as to which the defendant's actions are the very last step in the chain of causation. While, as we have said, it does not suffice if the injury complained of is "'the result [of] the independent action of some third party not before the court,'" that does not exclude injury produced by determinative or coercive effect upon the action of someone else.[Citation]

By the Government's own account, while the Service's Biological Opinion theoretically serves an "advisory function," 51 Fed. Reg. 19928 (1986), in reality it has a powerful coercive effect on the action agency·

"The statutory scheme ... presupposes that the biological opinion will play a central role in the action agency's decisionmaking process, and that it will typically be based on an administrative record that is fully adequate for the action agency's decision insofar as ESA issues are concerned.... [A] federal

agency that chooses to deviate from the recommendations contained in a
biological opinion bears the burden of 'articulating in its administrative
record its reasons for disagreeing with the conclusions of a biological
opinion,' 51 Fed. Reg. 19,956 (1986). In the government's experience,
action agencies very rarely choose to engage in conduct that the Service has
concluded is likely to jeopardize the continued existence of a listed species."

What this concession omits to say, moreover, is that the action agency must not
only articulate its reasons for disagreement (which ordinarily requires species and
habitat investigations that are not within the action agency's expertise), but that
it runs a substantial risk if its (inexpert) reasons turn out to be wrong. A
Biological Opinion of the sort rendered here alters the legal regime to which the
action agency is subject. When it "offers reasonable and prudent alternatives" to
the proposed action, a Biological Opinion must include a so-called "Incidental
Take Statement" — a written statement specifying, among other things, those
"measures that the [Service] considers necessary or appropriate to minimize [the
action's impact on the affected species]" and the "terms and conditions ... that
must be complied with by the Federal agency ... to implement [such] measures."
16 U.S.C. § 1536(b)(4). Any taking that is in compliance with these terms and
conditions "shall not be considered to be a prohibited taking of the species
concerned." § 1536(o)(2). Thus, the Biological Opinion's Incidental Take
Statement constitutes a permit authorizing the action agency to "take" the
endangered or threatened species so long as it respects the Service's "terms and
conditions." The action agency is technically free to disregard the Biological
Opinion and proceed with its proposed action, but it does so at its own peril (and
that of its employees), for "any person" who knowingly "takes" an endangered
or threatened species is subject to substantial civil and criminal penalties,
including imprisonment. [Citations]

   The Service itself is, to put it mildly, keenly aware of the virtually determinative effect of its biological opinions. The Incidental Take Statement at issue in the
present case begins by instructing the reader that any taking of a listed species
is prohibited unless "such taking is in compliance with this incidental take
statement," and warning that "the measures described below are nondiscretionary, and must be taken by [the Bureau]." Given all of this, and given petitioners'
allegation that the Bureau had, until issuance of the Biological Opinion, operated
the Klamath Project in the same manner throughout the twentieth century, it is
not difficult to conclude that petitioners have met their burden — which is
relatively modest at this stage of the litigation — of alleging that their injury is
"fairly traceable" to the Service's Biological Opinion and that it will "likely" be
redressed — i.e., the Bureau will not impose such water level restrictions — if
the Biological Opinion is set aside.

B

Next, the Government contends that the ESA's citizen-suit provision does not authorize judicial review of petitioners' claims. The relevant portions of that provision provide that

"any person may commence a civil suit on his own behalf —

"(A) to enjoin any person, including the United States and any other governmental instrumentality or agency ... who is alleged to be in violation of any provision of this chapter or regulation issued under the authority thereof; or

. . . .

"(C) against the Secretary [of Commerce or the Interior] where there is alleged a failure of the Secretary to perform any act or duty under section 1533 of this title which is not discretionary with the Secretary." 16 U.S.C. § 1540(g)(1).

The Government argues that judicial review is not available under subsection (A) because the Secretary is not "in violation" of the ESA, and under subsection (C) because the Secretary has not failed to perform any nondiscretionary duty under § 1533.

1

Turning first to subsection (C): that it covers only violations of § 1533 is clear and unambiguous. Petitioners' first and second claims, which assert that the Secretary has violated § 1536, are obviously not reviewable under this provision. However, as described above, the third claim alleges that the Biological Opinion implicitly determines critical habitat without complying with the mandate of § 1533(b)(2) that the Secretary "take into consideration the economic impact, and any other relevant impact, of specifying any particular area as critical habitat." This claim does come within subsection (C)....

2

Having concluded that petitioners' § 1536 claims are not reviewable under subsection (C), we are left with the question whether they are reviewable under subsection (A), which authorizes injunctive actions against any person "who is alleged to be in violation" of the ESA or its implementing regulations. The Government contends that the Secretary's conduct in implementing or enforcing the ESA is not a "violation" of the ESA within the meaning of this provision. In its view, § 1540(g)(1)(A) is a means by which private parties may enforce the substantive provisions of the ESA against regulated parties — both private entities and Government agencies — but is not an alternative avenue for judicial review of the Secretary's implementation of the statute. We agree.

... [I]nterpreting the term "violation" to include any errors on the part of the Secretary in administering the ESA would effect a wholesale abrogation of the APA's "final agency action" requirement. Any procedural default, even one that had not yet resulted in a final disposition of the matter at issue, would form the basis for a lawsuit. We are loathe to produce such an extraordinary regime without the clearest of statutory direction, which is hardly present here.

Viewed in the context of the entire statute, § 1540(g)(1)(A)'s reference to any "violation" of the ESA cannot be interpreted to include the Secretary's maladministration of the Act. Petitioners' claims are not subject to judicial review under § 1540(g)(1)(A).

IV

The foregoing analysis establishes that the principal statute invoked by petitioners, the ESA, does authorize review of their § 1533 claim, but does not support their claims based upon the Secretary's alleged failure to comply with § 1536. To complete our task, we must therefore inquire whether these § 1536 claims may nonetheless be brought under the Administrative Procedure Act, which authorizes a court to "set aside agency action, findings, and conclusions found to be ... arbitrary, capricious, an abuse of discretion, or otherwise not in accordance with law," 5 U.S.C. § 706.

A

No one contends (and it would not be maintainable) that the causes of action against the Secretary set forth in the ESA's citizen-suit provision are exclusive, supplanting those provided by the APA. The APA, by its terms, provides a right to judicial review of all "final agency action for which there is no other adequate remedy in a court," 5 U.S.C. § 704, and applies universally "except to the extent that — (1) statutes preclude judicial review; or (2) agency action is committed to agency discretion by law," § 701(a). Nothing in the ESA's citizen-suit provision expressly precludes review under the APA, nor do we detect anything in the statutory scheme suggesting a purpose to do so. And any contention that the relevant provision of 16 U.S.C. § 1536(a)(2) is discretionary would fly in the face of its text, which uses the imperative "shall."

In determining whether the petitioners have standing under the zone-of-interests test to bring their APA claims, we look not to the terms of the ESA's citizen-suit provision, but to the substantive provisions of the ESA, the alleged violations of which serve as the gravamen of the complaint. The classic formulation of the zone-of-interests test is set forth in *Data Processing*, 397 U.S. at 153: "whether the interest sought to be protected by the complainant is arguably within the zone of interests to be protected or regulated by the statute or constitutional guarantee in question." The Court of Appeals concluded that this test was not met here, since petitioners are neither directly regulated by the ESA nor seek to vindicate its overarching purpose of species preservation. That conclusion was error.

Whether a plaintiff's interest is "arguably ... protected ... by the statute" within the meaning of the zone-of-interests test is to be determined not by reference to the overall purpose of the Act in question (here, species preservation), but by reference to the particular provision of law upon which the plaintiff relies....

In the claims that we have found not to be covered by the ESA's citizen-suit provision, petitioners allege a violation of § 7 of the ESA, 16 U.S.C. § 1536, which requires, inter alia, that each agency "use the best scientific and commercial data available," § 1536(a)(2). Petitioners contend that the available scientific and commercial data show that the continued operation of the Klamath Project will not have a detrimental impact on the endangered suckers, that the imposition of minimum lake levels is not necessary to protect the fish, and that by issuing a Biological Opinion which makes unsubstantiated findings to the contrary the defendants have acted arbitrarily and in violation of § 1536(a)(2). The obvious purpose of the requirement that each agency "use the best scientific and commercial data available" is to ensure that the ESA not be implemented haphazardly, on the basis of speculation or surmise. While this no doubt serves to advance the ESA's overall goal of species preservation, we think it readily apparent that another objective (if not indeed the primary one) is to avoid needless economic dislocation produced by agency officials zealously but unintelligently pursuing their environmental objectives. That economic consequences are an explicit concern of the Act is evidenced by § 1536(h), which provides exemption from § 1536(a)(2)'s no-jeopardy mandate where there are no reasonable and prudent alternatives to the agency action and the benefits of the agency action clearly outweigh the benefits of any alternatives. We believe the "best scientific and commercial data" provision is similarly intended, at least in part, to prevent uneconomic (because erroneous) jeopardy determinations. Petitioners' claim that they are victims of such a mistake is plainly within the zone of interests that the provision protects.

B

The Government contends that petitioners may not obtain judicial review under the APA on the theory that the Biological Opinion does not constitute "final agency action," 5 U.S.C. § 704, because it does not conclusively determine the manner in which Klamath Project water will be allocated.... This confuses the question of whether the Secretary's action is final with the separate question of whether the petitioners' harm is "fairly traceable" to the Secretary's action. As a general matter, two conditions must be satisfied for agency action to be "final": First, the action must mark the "consummation" of the agency's decisionmaking process — it must not be of a merely tentative or interlocutory nature. And second, the action must be one by which "rights or obligations have been determined," or from which "legal consequences will flow," [Citations]. It is uncontested that the first requirement is met here; and the second is met because, as we have discussed above, the Biological Opinion and accompanying Incidental

Take Statement alter the legal regime to which the action agency is subject, authorizing it to take the endangered species if (but only if) it complies with the prescribed conditions....

The Court of Appeals erred in affirming the District Court's dismissal of petitioners' claims for lack of jurisdiction. Petitioners' complaint alleges facts sufficient to meet the requirements of Article III standing, and none of their ESA claims is precluded by the zone-of-interests test. Petitioners' § 1533 claim is reviewable under the ESA's citizen-suit provision, and petitioners' remaining claims are reviewable under the APA.

The judgment of the Court of Appeals is reversed, and the case is remanded for further proceedings consistent with this opinion.

It is so ordered.

NOTES AND QUESTIONS

1. *Zone of Interests.* The second prong of standing to challenge agency action under § 702 of the APA [5 U.S.C. § 702] is that the claimant be adversely affected or aggrieved "within the meaning of the relevant statute." The requirement that the claimant demonstrate an actual or threatened injury in fact is derived from and mirrors Article III demands. In contrast, the "zone of interests" criteria for standing under the APA is a prudential nonconstitutional limitation on the exercise of jurisdiction. The focus is on whether Congress provided the means for redress of the particular injury asserted, not on the nature or merits of the harm itself. *See Simon v. Eastern Ky. Welfare Rights Org.*, 426 U.S. 26, 39 n.19 (1976). This ordinarily does not present a serious obstacle to standing, though, because it only requires a showing that the person "arguably" is within the class of persons that the statutory provision was designed to regulate or protect. *See Clarke v. Securities Indus. Ass'n*, 479 U.S. 388, 400 (1987) (zone of interests test is "at bottom" an inquiry into Congressional intent). Also, the policy goals in certain environmental protection statutes are couched in extremely broad terms. *See City of Los Angeles v. NHTSA*, 912 F.2d 478, 495 (D.C. Cir. 1990) (broad Congressional mandate in NEPA which directs agencies to consider "worldwide and long-range character of environmental problems" encompasses challenge regarding global warming). *See Douglas County v. Babbitt*, 48 F.3d 1495, 1500 (9th Cir. 1995) (zone of interests test requires that 1) claimant's interests are inconsistent with purposes of NEPA and 2) those interests were so inconsistent that it would be unreasonable to assume that Congress intended to permit suit).

2. Despite the facility with which parties may satisfy the zone of interests test, it retains independent vitality to defeat standing in various circumstances. For example, in *Dan Caputo Co. v. Russian River Cty. Sanitation*, 749 F.2d 571, 575 (9th Cir. 1984) a contractor challenged the reallocation of EPA grant funds under the Clean Water Act regulations. The court denied standing, partially because any asserted financial injury resulting from the agency's funding actions was not the sort of vindication of environmental concerns contemplated by the Act. *Also see Association of Significantly Impacted Neighbors v. Livonia*, 765 F. Supp. 389 (E.D. Mich. 1991) (citizens' claims that city's proposed underground sewage retention basin would emit unpleasant odors and thus reduce local property values fell outside the zone of interests protected by NEPA); *Hazardous Waste Treatment Council v. Thomas*, 885 F.2d 918 (D.C. Cir. 1989) (national trade association lacked prudential standing where commercial interests it sought to protect were outside zone of interests which federal environmental protection statute was designed to regulate).

In *Bross v. Turnage*, 889 F.2d 1256 (2d Cir. 1989) a scientist claimed that the failure of government agencies to evaluate and publish conclusions of his scientific studies which purportedly linked ionizing radiation and cancer violated the Veterans' Dioxin and Radiation Exposure Compensation Standards Act. The court held that the plaintiff lacked standing to challenge the government conduct because the harms asserted fell outside the statutory zone of interests. The court reasoned that the plaintiff's interest in professional and governmental recognition of his scientific views was not reasonably connected to the statutory aims which chiefly dealt with procedures for awarding veterans' benefits.

3. A related issue which dovetails with what constitutes "final agency action" is the ripeness of the dispute for judicial resolution. Several competing policies animate the ripeness doctrine: (1) protection of courts from entangling themselves in unnecessary or premature litigation; (2) shielding administrative agencies from untimely judicial interference until their decisions become formalized; (3) consideration of the relative hardship which would potentially accrue to the parties if resolution was delayed; and (4) the fitness or concreteness of the issue for judicial determination. *Abbott Labs. v. Gardner*, 387 U.S. 136, 148-49 (1967).

In *Chemical Waste Mgt., Inc. v. EPA*, 869 F.2d 1526 (D.C. Cir. 1989) plaintiffs challenged rulemaking by the EPA contained in a proposed negotiated settlement regarding treatment and disposal standards for hazardous waste under a federal statute. The court found that the standards were ripe for judicial resolution because the agency had made certain final decisions which would impose immediate regulatory obligations on plaintiffs. Although the most severe consequences would not be sustained by plaintiffs until the agency promulgated certain other standards, the likelihood of occurrence was not speculative. *Also see American Petr. Inst. v. EPA*, 906 F.2d 729 (7th Cir. 1990) (primary concern in evaluating ripeness of a pre-enforcement challenge to an agency action focused on whether the agency would benefit from deferring review until its policies have "crystallized" through application of its policies to the particular facts).

B. ATTORNEYS' FEES

The expense of attorneys' fees in prolonged environmental litigation can be substantial, and their recovery (or possible nonrecovery) can have a significant impact on the willingness of attorneys to represent public interest plaintiffs. Under the prevailing "American Rule," the costs of litigation including attorneys' fees must be borne by each party independently, in contrast to the "English" rule whereby the prevailing party can recover litigation expenses. The principal justification in support of the American Rule is that our judicial system should not impose barriers or penalties on parties for bringing or defending meritorious claims. The assessment of attorneys' fees against the losing party may discourage the legitimate use of courts. On the other hand, if fees are not awarded to the prevailing litigant, they would not be "made whole" even if entirely successful on the merits. The need for fee awards becomes magnified in those circumstances where the nature of the remedy sought is injunctive relief; no fund of damages is produced to offset often staggering litigation costs. Additional complicating factors in environmental litigation are that private citizens challenging government noncompliance or third party violations of statutory responsibilities are not only carrying out an important public function but are at a severe disadvantage in financial resources.

In response to counter the potential inequities in the American Rule, exceptions permitting fee awards have developed through contractual provisions, common law, and statutes. For example, courts may impose reasonable attorneys' fees against a party that brought suit in "bad faith" — a narrow exception for truly frivolous litigation. Courts also may award attorneys' fees pursuant to their inherent equitable powers in circumstances where the interests of justice so require. One particularly important issue in environmental litigation involved whether federal courts should recognize a common law exception justifying fee awards to plaintiffs acting in the capacity of "private attorneys general" in protecting matters of public interest.

In *Alyeska Pipeline Serv. Co. v. Wilderness Soc'y*, 421 U.S. 240 (1975), the Supreme Court held as a matter of federal law that only Congress could authorize recovery of attorneys' fees on a private attorney general theory. In *Alyeska* the federal Court of Appeals had awarded attorneys' fees to environmental organizations which had successfully challenged the issuance of permits necessary for the construction of the trans-Alaska oil pipeline. In response to *Alyeska*, Congress authorized recovery of attorneys' fees in citizen's suits under most major environmental statutes as well as under a number of civil rights statutes. The statutory language of these authorizations for citizens' suits varies although typically the provision authorizes the federal court to award reasonable fees to the "prevailing party" or whenever the court determines that such an award is "appropriate." Not surprisingly, substantial litigation has involved battles over interpretation of the statutory language regarding entitlement to fees.

Once the threshold of entitlement to an award of attorneys' fees is passed, additional problems remain regarding calculating the fee. The typical fee-shifting statute provides that, within the court's discretion, the prevailing party may recover a reasonable fee. A number of courts have measured the reasonableness of the statutory fee according to the "lodestar" method, which takes into account the number of hours spent on the successful issues in litigation multiplied by a reasonable hourly rate. Courts have been quite active in trying to refine the lodestar approach by considering the propriety of adjustments for a variety of factors, such as the results obtained or the contingency of prevailing in the suit. The following materials will explore issues involving both the entitlement and the measurement of attorneys' fees to parties acting as private attorneys' general in environmental litigation.

RUCKELSHAUS v. SIERRA CLUB

463 U.S. 680 (1983)

JUSTICE REHNQUIST delivered the opinion of the Court.

In 1979, following a year of study and public comment, the Environmental Protection Agency (EPA) promulgated standards limiting the emission of sulfur dioxide by coal-burning powerplants. Both respondents in this case — the Environmental Defense Fund (EDF) and the Sierra Club — filed petitions for review of the agency's action in the United States Court of Appeals for the District of Columbia Circuit. EDF argued that the standards promulgated by the EPA were tainted by the agency's *ex parte* contacts with representatives of private industry, while the Sierra Club contended that EPA lacked authority under the Clean Air Act to issue the type of standards that it did. In a lengthy opinion, the Court of Appeals rejected all the claims of both EDF and the Sierra Club.

Notwithstanding their lack of success on the merits, EDF and the Sierra Club filed a request for attorney's fees.... They relied on § 307(f) of the Clean Air Act, 42 U.S.C. § 7607(f) (1976 ed., Supp. V), which permits the award of attorney's fees in certain proceedings "whenever [the court] determines that such award is appropriate." Respondents argued that, despite their failure to obtain any of the relief they requested, it was "appropriate" for them to receive fees for their contributions to the goals of the Clean Air Act. The Court of Appeals agreed with respondents, ultimately awarding some $45,000 to the Sierra Club and some $46,000 to EDF. [Citations.] We granted certiorari, to consider the important question decided by the Court of Appeals.

The question presented by this case is whether it is "appropriate," within the meaning of § 307(f) of the Clean Air Act, to award attorney's fees to a party that achieved no success on the merits of its claims. We conclude that the language of the section, read in the light of the historic principles of fee-shifting in this and other countries, requires the conclusion that some success on the merits be obtained before a party becomes eligible for a fee award under § 307(f).

Section 307(f) provides only that:

> "In any judicial proceeding under this section, the court may award costs of litigation (including reasonable attorney and expert witness fees) *whenever it determines that such award is appropriate.*" 42 U.S.C. § 7607(f) (1976 ed., Supp. V) (emphasis added).

It is difficult to draw any meaningful guidance from § 307(f)'s use of the word "appropriate," which means only "specially suitable: fit, proper." Webster's Third New International Dictionary 106 (1976). Obviously, in order to decide when fees should be awarded under § 307(f), a court first must decide *what* the award should be "specially suitable," "fit," or "proper" *for*. Section 307(f) alone does not begin to answer this question, and application of the provision thus requires reference to other sources, including fee-shifting rules developed in different contexts. As demonstrated below, inquiry into these sources shows that requiring a defendant, completely successful on all issues, to pay the unsuccessful plaintiff's legal fees would be a radical departure from long-standing fee-shifting principles adhered to in a wide range of contexts.

Our basic point of reference is the "American Rule," see *Alyeska Pipeline Co. v. Wilderness Society*, 421 U.S. 240, 247, (1975), under which even "the *prevailing* litigant is ordinarily not entitled to collect a reasonable attorneys' fee from the *loser*." It is clear that generations of American judges, lawyers, and legislators, with this rule as the point of departure, would regard it as quite "inappropriate" to award the "loser" an attorney's fee from the "prevailing litigant." Similarly, when Congress has chosen to depart from the American Rule by statute, virtually every one of the more than 150 existing federal fee-shifting provisions predicates fee awards on *some* success by the claimant; while these statutes contain varying standards as to the precise degree of success necessary for an award of fees — such as whether the fee claimant was the "prevailing party," the "substantially prevailing" party, or "successful" — the consistent rule is that complete failure will not justify shifting fees from the losing party to the winning party.... Finally, English courts have awarded counsel fees to *successful* litigants for 750 years, but they have never gone so far as to force a vindicated defendant to pay the plaintiff's legal expenses.

While the foregoing treatments of fee-shifting differ in many respects, they reflect one consistent, established rule: a successful party need not pay its unsuccessful adversary's fees. The uniform acceptance of this rule reflects, at least in part, intuitive notions of fairness to litigants. Put simply, ordinary conceptions of just returns reject the idea that a party who wrongly charges someone with violations of the law should be able to force that defendant to pay the costs of the wholly unsuccessful suit against it. Before we will conclude Congress abandoned this established principle that a successful party need not pay its unsuccessful adversary's fees — rooted as it is in intuitive notions of fairness and widely manifested in numerous different contexts — a clear showing that this result was intended is required.

... [W]e fail to find in § 307(f) the requisite indication that Congress meant to abandon historic fee-shifting principles and intuitive notions of fairness when it enacted the section. Instead, we believe that the term "appropriate" modifies but does not completely reject the traditional rule that a fee claimant must "prevail" before it may recover attorney's fees. This result is the most reasonable interpretation of congressional intent.

Respondents make relatively little effort to dispute much of the foregoing, devoting their principal attention to the legislative history of § 307(f). Respondents' arguments rest primarily on the following excerpt from the 1977 House Report on § 307(f):

> "The committee bill also contains express authority for the courts to award attorneys' fees and expert witness fees in two situations. The judicial review proceedings under section 307 of the act [and] when the court determines such award is appropriate.
>
> "In the case of the section 307 judicial review litigation, the purposes of the authority to award fees are not only to discourage frivolous litigation, but also to encourage litigation which will assure proper implementation and administration of the act or otherwise serve the public interest. *The committee did not intend that the court's discretion to award fees under this provision should be restricted to cases in which the party seeking fees was the 'prevailing party.'* In fact, such an amendment was expressly rejected by the committee...." H.R. Rep. No. 95-294, p. 337 (1977) (emphasis added).

In determining the meaning of the Senate Report's rejection of the "prevailing party" standard it first is necessary to ascertain what this standard was understood to mean. When § 307(f) was enacted, the "prevailing party" standard had been interpreted in a variety of rather narrow ways. [Citations.] Some courts — although, to be sure, a minority — denied fees to plaintiffs who lacked a formal court order granting relief, while others required showings not just of some success, but "substantial" success....

These various interpretations of the "prevailing party" standard provide a ready, and quite sensible, explanation for the Senate's Report's discussion of § 307(f). Section 307(f) was meant to expand the class of parties eligible for fee awards from prevailing parties to *partially prevailing* parties — parties achieving *some success*, even if not major success. Put differently, by enacting § 307(f), Congress intended to eliminate both the restrictive readings of "prevailing party" adopted in some of the cases cited above and the necessity for case-by-case scrutiny by federal courts into whether plaintiffs prevailed "essentially" on "central issues."

....

We conclude, therefore, that the language and legislative history of § 307(f) do not support respondent's argument that the section was intended as a radical departure from established principles requiring that a fee claimant attain some success on the merits before it may receive an award of fees. Instead, we are persuaded that if Congress intended such a novel result — which would require federal courts to make sensitive, difficult, and ultimately highly subjective determinations — it would have said so in far plainer language than that employed here. Hence, we hold that, absent some degree of success on the merits by the claimant, it is not "appropriate" for a federal court to award attorney's fees under § 307(f). Accordingly, the judgment of the Court of Appeals is

Reversed.

NOTES AND QUESTIONS

1. Given that Congress in a number of federal environmental statutes expressly limited recovery of fees to a "prevailing party" or "prevailing plaintiff," why did Congress not include similar language in the citizen suit provision of the Clean Air Act? Without such language, how can the decision in *Ruckelshaus* be justified? Does it make any difference in your evaluation of the Court's holding that the citizen suit provisions in environmental statutes permit only equitable relief and not damages? Congress has adopted the reasoning of the Supreme Court in *Ruckelshaus* by employing the "prevailing or substantially prevailing" standard rather than the "whenever appropriate" language for fee awards in recent environmental statutes. *See* Clean Water Act, 33 U.S.C. § 1365(d); Resource Conservation and Recovery Act, 42 U.S.C. § 6972(e); and Comprehensive Environmental Response, Compensation, and Liability Act, 42 U.S.C. § 9659(f).

2. A principal justification for legislation authorizing a departure from the American Rule to award attorneys fees is to encourage private enforcement of statutes promulgated to protect matters of significant public importance. Also, the nature of the remedy sought may be an injunction to force compliance with the statute; consequently even a successful action may not produce a pool of damages to reimburse a private attorney general of the costs of bringing the suit.

In *Newman v. Piggie Park Enters.*, 390 U.S. 400 (1968) the petitioners instituted a class action under Title II of the Civil Rights Act of 1964 seeking to enjoin racial discrimination practices at the defendant's restaurants. The Supreme Court held that the statutory language allowing a "prevailing party" to recover a reasonable attorney's fee in the court's discretion did not contemplate an additional showing that the defendant acted in bad faith. Rather, where the class successfully obtained injunctive relief, courts should ordinarily award attorneys' fees unless "special circumstances" existed which would make the award "unjust." The Court explained:

> When the Civil Rights Act of 1964 was passed, it was evident that enforcement would prove difficult and that the Nation would have to rely in part upon private litigation as a means of securing broad compliance with the law. A Title II suit is thus private in form only. When a plaintiff brings an action under that Title, he cannot recover damages. If he obtains an injunction, he does so not for himself alone but also as a "private attorney general," vindicating a policy that Congress considered of the highest priority. If successful plaintiffs were routinely forced to bear their own attorneys' fees, few aggrieved parties would be in a position to advance the

public interest by invoking the injunctive powers of the federal courts. Congress therefore enacted the provision for counsel fees — not simply to penalize litigants who deliberately advance arguments they know to be untenable but, more broadly, to encourage individuals injured by racial discrimination to seek judicial relief under Title II.

The same public policy considerations underlying civil rights enforcement may also justify awards of attorneys' fees to private parties attempting to enforce environmental protection statutes. In both instances the damages, if any, resulting from litigation, may be low, the parties may be of disproportionate economic strength, and the plaintiff is acting to effectuate matters determined to be in the public interest.

3. *Success on the Merits.* What does it mean to require that a claimant for attorneys' fees have "some degree of success on the merits"? *See Hensley v. Eckerhart*, 461 U.S. 424 (1983) (claimant must succeed "on any significant issue in litigation which achieves some of the benefit the parties sought in bringing suit"). *Also see Texas State Teachers Ass'n v. Garland Indep. School Dist.*, 489 U.S. 782 (1989) (key to recovery of attorneys' fees must be whether the legal relationship of the parties was "materially altered" in a manner consistent with the intentions of Congress in the fee-shifting statute.)

Can either party be deemed "successful" if the case is voluntarily settled? In *Atlantic States Legal Found. v. Eastman Kodak*, 933 F.2d 124 (2d Cir. 1991) the court dismissed a citizen's suit after the alleged violator and the appropriate state officials entered into a settlement agreement regarding the Clean Water Act violations. The court held, however, that a reasonable inference could be drawn that the existence of the citizen suit was a "motive" for the settlement; therefore, the plaintiff would be considered a "prevailing party" entitled to an award of attorneys' fees and expenses under the Act.

4. *Prevailing Party.* Although many federal fee-shifting statutes provide for the recovery of reasonable attorneys' fees to the "prevailing party," some courts have applied different standards for awarding fees to victorious plaintiffs than defendants. One justification for applying a stricter standard for awarding attorneys' fees to successful defendants is that the fee-shifting statutes were promulgated to encourage the private enforcement of certain rights in order to further public interest objectives. In *Christianburg Garment Co. v. Equal Emp. Opportunity Comm'n*, 434 U.S. 412, 421-22 (1978) the Court held that fees could be awarded to a prevailing defendant in a Title VII discrimination case where the plaintiff's suit was "frivolous, unreasonable, or without foundation, even though not brought in subjective bad faith."

Similarly, in *Independent Fed'n of Flight Attendants v. Zipes*, 488 U.S. 1029 (1989) the Court held that attorneys' fees could not be awarded against losing intervenors in a Title VII action. *Also see Autorama Corp. v. Stewart*, 802 F.2d 1284 (10th Cir. 1986) (Court denied fees to successful defendant on claim dismissed for lack of federal court jurisdiction, reasoning that bad faith exception to American Rule applied narrowly and was reserved for exceptional circumstances).

5. A significant consequence of characterizing fee-shifting statutes as intended solely for the benefit of litigants is that parties may use the prospective attorneys' fee award as a bargaining chip in the settlement process. In *Evans v. Jeff D.*, 475 U.S. 717 (1986) a class action alleged civil rights violations of emotionally and mentally handicapped children by the State of Idaho. The claimants principally sought injunctive relief to correct state and federal law deficiencies in health care and educational programs. The plaintiff class would have been entitled by statute to reasonable attorneys' fees if successful at trial. The state officials offered a settlement conditioned upon the plaintiffs' waiver of attorneys' fees. The class accepted the offer, but the plaintiff's attorney argued to the district court that the settlement with fee waiver placed him in an ethical dilemma.

The Supreme Court, however, held that the approval of the class action settlement which included a waiver of statutorily authorized fees was within the district court's discretionary power. The Court found that the plaintiff's attorney had no ethical dilemma, reasoning that an attorney is ethically obligated to communicate all offers to the client and to act in the client's best interests. The fee waiver was an appropriate bargaining point that enabled the class to obtain extensive affirmative relief in the settlement, and thus effectuated the vindication of civil rights.

A strong dissent by Justice Brennan, joined by Justices Marshall and Blackmun, argued that fee awards differed from other remedies. The dissenters predicted that the practice of waiver of attorneys' fees in settlement would make civil rights cases less attractive to competent attorneys. *Also see Krause v. Rhodes*, 640 F.2d 214 (6th Cir. 1981) (Court authorized its inherent supervisory power to approve settlement agreement which judicially modified private contingent fee arrangement).

6. *Equal Access to Justice Act.* Where a federal environmental statute does not provide for attorneys' fees for suits brought by or against the United States (including federal agencies), attorneys' fees may be recoverable under the Equal Access to Justice Act ("EAJA"), 28 U.S.C. § 2412. The EAJA authorizes attorneys' fees to a "prevailing party" unless "the position of the United States was substantially justified or that special circumstances make an award unjust." 28 U.S.C. § 2412(d)(1)(A). *See Federal Election Comm'n v. Rose*, 806 F.2d 1081 (D.C. Cir. 1986). *Also see Thomas v. Peterson*, 841 F.2d 332, 335 (9th Cir. 1988) (EAJA creates a presumption in favor of awarding fees to prevailing parties, thereby shifting the burden to the government to demonstrate that its actions were reasonable). In *Animal Lovers Volunteer Ass'n v. Carlucci*, 867 F.2d 1224 (9th Cir. 1989), for example, the court found that the government's refusal to prepare an environmental impact statement under NEPA considering the impact of a project on an endangered species was unreasonable under NEPA, and therefore not "substantially justified" within the meaning of the EAJA. *See* *generally* Hill, *An Analysis and Explanation of the Equal Access to Justice Act*, 19 ARIZ. ST. L.J. 229 (1987).

7. The Supreme Court has distinguished the function of fee-shifting statutes from private contractual arrangements between an attorney and client. In *Venegas v. Mitchell*, 495 U.S. 82 (1990) the Court held that the amount of an award of a reasonable attorneys' fees under 42 U.S.C. § 1988 to a prevailing litigant in a civil rights action was not inconsistent with the contractual obligations between the plaintiff and attorney. The plaintiff had entered into a contingency fee contract which obligated the payment of an attorneys' fee significantly larger than the fees awarded under the statute. The Court observed that the fee-shifting statute was intended to benefit the plaintiff rather than the attorney, but did not operate to override otherwise valid contractual fee obligations. The Court determined that although the purpose of the fee-shifting statute was to facilitate acquisition of competent representation for civil rights plaintiffs, the plaintiff could contract for an attorneys' fee in excess of the statutory amount if necessary to obtain counsel of their choice.

8. Several states as a matter of state common law or legislation authorize recovery of attorneys' fees for private attorneys general in environmental litigation. As an attorney in one of these states, would you choose to bring an environmental claim in state or federal court? What other considerations might enter into your decision? How might your interest as an attorney conflict with those of your client in selecting the preferable forum?

CITY OF BURLINGTON v. DAGUE
505 U.S. 557; 112 S. Ct. 2638;
120 L. Ed. 2d 449 (1992)

JUSTICE SCALIA delivered the opinion of the Court.

This case presents the question whether a court, in determining an award of reasonable attorney's fees under § 7002(e) of the Solid Waste Disposal Act (SWDA), 90 Stat. 2826, as amended, 42 U.S.C. § 6972(e), or § 505(d) of the Federal Water Pollution Control Act (Clean Water Act (CWA)), 86 Stat. 889, as amended, 33 U.S.C. § 1365(d), may enhance the fee award above the "lodestar" amount in order to reflect the fact that the party's attorneys were retained on a contingent-fee basis and thus assumed the risk of receiving no payment at all for their services....

I

Respondent Dague (whom we will refer to in place of all the respondents) owns land in Vermont adjacent to a landfill that was owned and operated by petitioner City of Burlington. Represented by attorneys retained on a contingent-fee basis, he sued Burlington over its operation of the landfill. The District Court ruled, *inter alia*, that Burlington had violated provisions of the SWDA and the CWA, and ordered Burlington to close the landfill by January 1, 1990. It also determined that Dague was a "substantially prevailing party" entitled to an award of attorney's fees under the Acts, *see* 42 U.S.C. § 6972(e); 33 U.S.C. § 1365(d).

In calculating the attorney's fees award, the District Court first found reasonable the figures advanced by Dague for his attorneys' hourly rates and for the number of hours expended by them, producing a resulting "lodestar" attorney's fee of $198,027.50. (What our cases have termed the "lodestar" is "the product of reasonable hours times a reasonable rate," *Pennsylvania v. Delaware Valley Citizens' Council for Clean Air*, 478 U.S. 546, 565 (1986) (*Delaware Valley I*).) Addressing Dague's request for a contingency enhancement, the court looked to Circuit precedent, which provided that "the rationale that should guide the court's discretion is whether "without the possibility of a fee enhancement ... competent counsel might refuse to represent [environmental] clients thereby denying them effective access to the courts.""" [Citation. The District Court accordingly enhanced the attorney's fee by 25% and the Court of Appeals affirmed.]...

II

We first provide some background to the issue before us. Fees for legal services in litigation may be either "certain" or "contingent" (or some hybrid of the two). A fee is certain if it is payable without regard to the outcome of the suit; it is contingent if the obligation to pay depends on a particular result's being obtained. Under the most common contingent-fee contract for litigation, the attorney receives no payment for his services if his client loses. Under this arrangement, the attorney bears a contingent risk of nonpayment that is the inverse of the case's prospects of success: if his client has an 80% chance of winning, the attorney's contingent risk is 20%....

III

Section 7002(e) of the SWDA and Section 505(d) of the CWA authorize a court to "award costs of litigation (including *reasonable attorney ... fees*)" to a "prevailing or substantially prevailing party." 42 U.S.C. § 6972(e) (emphasis added); 33 U.S.C. § 1365(d) (emphasis added). This language is similar to that of many other federal fee-shifting statutes, *see, e.g.*, 42 U.S.C. §§ 1988, 2000e-5(k), 7604(d); our case law construing what is a "reasonable" fee applies uniformly to all of them. [Citation]

The "lodestar" figure has, as its name suggests, become the guiding light of our fee-shifting jurisprudence. We have established a "strong presumption" that the lodestar represents the "reasonable" fee, and have placed upon the fee applicant who seeks more than that the burden of showing that "such an adjustment is necessary to the determination of a reasonable fee." [Citation] The Court of Appeals held, and Dague argues here, that a "reasonable" fee for attorneys who have been retained on a contingency-fee basis must go beyond the lodestar, to compensate for risk of loss and of consequent nonpayment. Fee-shifting statutes should be construed, he contends, to replicate the economic incentives that operate in the private legal market, where attorneys working on a contingency-fee basis can be expected to charge some premium over their ordinary hourly rates. Petitioner Burlington argues, by contrast, that the lodestar fee may not be enhanced for contingency.

We note at the outset that an enhancement for contingency would likely duplicate in substantial part factors already subsumed in the lodestar. The risk of loss in a particular case (and, therefore, the attorney's contingent risk) is the product of two factors: (1) the legal and factual merits of the claim, and (2) the difficulty of establishing those merits. The second factor, however, is ordinarily reflected in the lodestar — either in the higher number of hours expended to overcome the difficulty, or in the higher hourly rate of the attorney skilled and experienced enough to do so. Taking account of it again through lodestar enhancement amounts to double-counting. [Citation]

The first factor (relative merits of the claim) is not reflected in the lodestar, but there are good reasons why it should play no part in the calculation of the award. It is, of course, a factor that *always* exists (no claim has a 100% chance of success), so that computation of the lodestar would never end the court's inquiry in contingent-fee cases. Moreover, the consequence of awarding contingency enhancement to take account of this "merits" factor would be to provide attorneys with the same incentive to bring relatively meritless claims as relatively meritorious ones. Assume, for example, two claims, one with underlying merit of 20%, the other of 80%. Absent any contingency enhancement, a contingent-fee attorney would prefer to take the latter, since he is four times more likely to be paid. But with a contingency enhancement, this preference will disappear: the enhancement for the 20% claim would be a multiplier of 5 (100/20), which is quadruple the 1.25 multiplier (100/80) that would attach to the 80% claim. Thus, enhancement for the contingency risk posed by each case would encourage meritorious claims to be brought, but only at the social cost of indiscriminately encouraging nonmeritorious claims to be brought as well....

[W]e see a number of reasons for concluding that no contingency enhancement whatever is compatible with the fee-shifting statutes at issue. First, just as the statutory language limiting fees to prevailing (or substantially prevailing) parties bars a prevailing plaintiff from recovering fees relating to claims on which he lost, so should it bar a prevailing plaintiff from recovering for the risk of loss. An attorney operating on a contingency-fee basis pools the risks presented by his various cases: cases that turn out to be successful pay for the time he gambled on those that did not. To award a contingency enhancement under a fee-shifting statute would in effect pay for the attorney's time (or anticipated time) in cases where his client does *not* prevail.

Second ... "we have generally turned away from the contingent-fee model" — which would make the fee award a percentage of the value of the relief awarded in the primary action — "to the lodestar model." [Citation] We have done so, it must be noted, even though the lodestar model often (perhaps, generally) results in a larger fee award than the contingent-fee model. [Citation] For example, in *Blanchard v. Bergeron*, 489 U.S. 87 (1989), we held that the lodestar governed, even though it produced a fee that substantially exceeded the amount provided in the contingent-fee agreement between plaintiff and his counsel (which was self-evidently an amount adequate to attract the needed legal services). Contingency enhancement is a feature inherent in the contingent-fee model (since attorneys factor in the particular risks of a case in negotiating their fee and in deciding whether to accept the case). To engraft this feature onto the lodestar model would be to concoct a hybrid scheme that resorts to the contingent-fee model to increase a fee award but not to reduce it. Contingency enhancement is therefore not consistent with our general rejection of the contingent-fee model for fee awards, nor is it necessary to the determination of a reasonable fee.

And finally, the interest in ready administrability that has underlain our adoption of the lodestar approach, and the related interest in avoiding burdensome satellite litigation, counsel strongly against adoption of contingency enhancement. Contingency enhancement would make the setting of fees more complex and arbitrary, hence more unpredictable, and hence more litigable. It is neither necessary nor even possible for application of the fee-shifting statutes to mimic the intricacies of the fee-paying market in every respect.

... [W]e hold that enhancement for contingency is not permitted under the fee-shifting statutes at issue. We reverse the Court of Appeals' judgment insofar as it affirmed the 25% enhancement of the lodestar.

NOTES AND QUESTIONS

1. As noted in the principal case, the standard method for determining fees is the "lodestar" method of multiplying a reasonable hourly rate for each attorney times the number of hours reasonably spent on the litigation. The most critical factor in measuring an award of attorneys' fees is the "degree of success obtained." *Hensley v. Eckerhart*, 461 U.S. 424, 436 (1983). The overarching consideration with respect to fee measurement is "reasonableness" based on all the circumstances of the case. *See Blanchard v. Bergeron*, 489 U.S. 87 (1989). Any adjustments to the lodestar based on the results obtained must be supported by evidence in the record; inadequate documentation will justify a downward reduction of the fee.

2. Problems in calculation of fees arise where several issues are factually intertwined and the plaintiff does not prevail on all claims. In that event, the court may reduce the award to account for the limited success obtained. Alternatively, the court may choose to award the full fees requested based on assessing the significance of the relief obtained and the relationship to the hours expended on litigation. *See Dominic v. Consolidated Edison Co. of New York*, 822 F.2d 1249, 1259 (2d Cir. 1987).

3. In light of *Burlington v. Dague*, for what circumstances other than risk of nonrecovery would compensation over and above the lodestar amount ever be appropriate? Should an attorney receive additional compensation for the preclusion of other valuable employment opportunities? For delay in payment after lengthy litigation? For representing a difficult or unpopular client? Should the compensation, if any, attributable to these factors be determined from the vantage point of when the litigation was accepted or when the fees are determined?

4. Courts typically will calculate fees based upon the customary market rates for attorneys of like competence and experience in the same community doing similar work during the relevant period. Should courts distinguish between commercial for-profit law firms and nonprofit public interest law firms in measuring fees? In *Blum v. Stenson*, 465 U.S. 886 (1984) the Court concluded from legislative history that Congress in the Civil Rights Attorney's Fee Award Act, 42 U.S.C. § 1988, did not intend for fee calculations to vary depending on whether the plaintiff was represented by private counsel or a nonprofit legal services organization.

What should the measure of fees be if a private practicing attorney charges an environmental interest plaintiff a lower rate than their other clients? *See Save Our Cumberland Mountains, Inc. v. Hodel*, 857 F.2d 1516 (D.C. Cir. 1988) (attorney fees under the Surface Mining Control and Reclamation Act based upon the prevailing market rate even though the attorney had charged the environmental interest plaintiff a reduced rate). *Also see Missouri v. Jenkins*, 491 U.S. 274 (1989) (market rates for paralegals and law clerks were the proper measure of costs under 42 U.S.C. § 1988 rather than the cost of their services to the attorney).

5. For additional commentary on the role of attorney fee-shifting statutes in environmental litigation see the following references: Resnick, Curtis & Hensler, *Individuals Within the Aggregate: Relationships, Representation, and Fees*, 71 N.Y.U. L. REV. 296 (1996); Semmel, Ruckelshaus v. Sierra Club: *A Misinterpretation of the Clean Air Act's Attorneys' Fees Provision*, 12 ECOL. L.Q. 399 (1985); Fadil, *Citizen Suits Against Polluters: Picking up the Pace*, 9 HARV. ENVTL. L. REV. 23 (1985); Miller, *Private Enforcement of Federal Pollution Control Laws*, 14 E.L.R. 10407 (1984); Rowe, *The Legal Theory of Attorney Fee Shifting: A Critical Overview*, 1982 DUKE L.J. 651; Leubsdorf, *The Contingency Factor in Attorney Fee Awards*, 90 YALE L.J. 473 (1981); King & Plater, *The Right to Counsel Fees In Public Interest Environmental Litigation*, 41 TENN. L. REV. 27 (1973); Berger, *Court Awarded Attorneys' Fees: What Is "Reasonable"?*, 126 U. PA. L. REV. 281 (1977).

Part III.
National Environmental Policy Act

Chapter 5

NEPA: POLICY AND PRACTICE

INTRODUCTION

COUNCIL ON ENVIRONMENTAL QUALITY, ENVIRONMENTAL QUALITY 1970-1990: Twentieth Annual Report 15-21 (1990)

The enactment of the National Environmental Policy Act of 1969[1] (NEPA) is now seen to be the first step in 20 years of remarkable environmental activism in the United States. It certainly was a major statement of this country's environmental ethic. Yet the real-world contribution of NEPA to environmental quality is sometimes questioned and often misunderstood. Because NEPA was not designed to control specific kinds or sources of pollution, its benefit to society is difficult to quantify. The act was designed primarily to institutionalize in the federal government an anticipatory concern for the quality of the human environment, that is, an attitude, a heightened state of environmental awareness that, unlike pollution abatement, is measurable only subjectively and qualitatively.

Yet NEPA is not simply a mandate for the federal government. It also recognizes that "each person has a responsibility to contribute to the preservation and enhancement of the environment."[2] NEPA's effectiveness, therefore, requires the diligence of both the federal government and society as a whole, and any judgement on its performance is a reflection on the nation's overall environmental ethic.

Over the past 20 years, NEPA has nourished a growing environmental consciousness within this country, often in ways not envisioned by its sponsors in 1969. The act unquestionably has had a profound effect on attitudes within the federal government, and its influence outside the federal government is almost as impressive. And while NEPA is sometimes seen as not having lived up completely to expectations, those expectations may have underestimated the environmental pressures created by economic and population growth within this country since 1970. It may be more useful to measure NEPA in terms of the progress that has been made over the past 20 years. For during that time, the national environmental policy, which seeks to strike "a balance between population and resource use which will permit high standards of living and a wide sharing of life's amenities,"[3] has remained constant.

---

[1] 42 U.S.C. 4321 *et seq.*
[2] 42 U.S.C. 4331(c).
[3] 42 U.S.C. 4331(b)(5).

Prior to 1970 the vast majority of federal agencies claimed to have no authority to consider environmental factors in their planning and decisionmaking. Moreover, consideration of such factors was viewed by most agencies as an impediment to attaining their primary missions, even though those missions caused detrimental effects on the quality of the environment. NEPA changed all that by supplementing the organic charter of every federal agency with an explicit directive. It also provided a deliberative, analytical process, under which environmental values had to be factored into agency actions. As a consequence, federal agencies today almost reflexively incorporate environmental consideration into their primary decisionmaking responsibilities.

Widespread, methodical consideration of environmental values in federal agency planning and decisionmaking, while an improvement over pre-1970 practices, does not by itself fulfill the intentions of NEPA. The motivation underlying such consideration is probably a better indicator of the extent to which federal agencies have institutionalized the NEPA ethic. Motivation is difficult to gauge, but it usually reveals itself in the administrative records of proposed agency actions subject to NEPA requirements. In general, good environmental decisionmaking is characterized by early and pronounced efforts to anticipate potentially disruptive influences on the environment and to avoid them. On the other hand, simple adherence to the established NEPA administrative process does not ensure that federal agencies will confront the difficult choices created by their responsibility to fulfill their primary mission and their responsibility to minimize environmental degradation. NEPA brings its richest rewards when federal agencies focus their energy on the NEPA goal and not its process.

Some administrative process is necessary to stimulate a sense of concern for environmental values, especially among agencies whose traditional mission has not explicitly incorporated such values. And the NEPA process has proven itself over a score of years to be a flexible, effective tool in developing environmental issues for consideration by government decisionmakers and the public. But process is meaningful only insofar as it is oriented toward a goal. Disconnected from its goal, process, whether or not required by law, tends to become mechanical and an end in itself. NEPA is distinguishable, purposefully so, from other environmental statutes. It targets no specific pollution sources or human health risks for treatment, prescribes formulation of no abatement techniques or remedial actions, and establishes neither milestones nor timetables for achieving its goal, a goal "concerned with principle rather than detail."[4] "Cookbook" solutions are not to be found for the difficult choices posed by the NEPA process, which seeks only to provoke thought and promote open and well-informed decisionmaking. And while federal agencies might have been less challenged had Congress refrained from adopting a national environmental policy

---

[4]Senate Rep. No. 91-296, 91st Cong., 1st Sess. 9 (1969).

and instead simply enacted specific laws to shape specific federal government actions, Congress chose not to do so for compelling reasons.

Historical Perspective

In the early 1960s when several committees of Congress began seriously looking into pollution problems, the nature and extent of such problems were not fully understood. In hearings and seminars that spanned several Congresses, legislators learned that pollution was part of a multifaceted problem, having its roots in technologically induced change and "involving natural and social sciences, economics, and governmental and private institutions." Even more vexing was the revelation that no single environmental problem could be considered separately, "that apparently isolated changes interact in unanticipated ways and that the eventual restoration of environmental quality will depend upon the solution of a series of interrelated problems, none of which can be understood in isolation from its fellows." Indeed, the problem appeared so overwhelming that one observer, summarizing the views offered by several experts in the field during a joint committee hearing, was "left with a vaguely uneasy feeling that if we see the continuous complex here as one set of interconnecting realities that have to be understood as a total system, we may be broadening our interests so much that it is impossible to act on it all."

The complexities and interrelatedness of the "pollution problem" caused Congress to reevaluate its practice passing laws in response to specific episodes of environmental degradation, a practice that had led to passage of the Federal Water Pollution Control Act of 1948[9] and the Air Pollution Control Act of 1955.[10]

The single-solution approach typified in those statutes was unworkable, and environmental laws in general were "floundering due to inadequate information, and misinterpretation of existing facts." Many in Congress began to see the need for a comprehensive approach to the environment, one that was capable of anticipating environmentally disruptive activities and avoiding them, rather than just reacting to episodes of pollution with abatement laws.

With a greater sense of purpose and perhaps some frustration, Congress began to look more closely at the federal establishment. The federal government in the 1960s was seen to be both a major cause of environmental degradation and a major source of regulatory authority. Consequently, the federal government itself became the principal focus of further efforts to fashion a comprehensive approach to the environment.

An area where improvements had long been thought necessary, and for which legislation had been introduced as far back as the early 1960s, was the organization of the federal government. In the 1960s environmental responsibili-

---

[9]Ch. 758, 62 Stat. 1155 (1948) (current version at 33 U.S.C. 1251 *et seq.*).

[10]Ch. 360, 69 Stat. 322 (1955) (current version at 42 U.S.C. 7401 *et seq.*).

ties were divided among 15 to 20 federal departments and agencies receiving direction and funding from two dozen different Congressional committees. Reorganization of the government on a large scale, however, was not desired; nor did it "seem practical to remedy the situation by any superimposed 'czar' of environmental quality...." Existing institutions were thought to be up to the task, but there was no "coordinating group capable of systems analysis and broad management of federal projects." The concept of an advisory council that "should exert a preemptive coordinating role and strive to prevent, rather than correct environmental degradation," although not new, took firm hold in Congress in the late 1960s.

A Council on Environmental Quality was the centerpiece of H.R. 12549, introduced by Representative John Dingell of Michigan and others in February 1969. The purpose of the bill was to create "a council which can provide a consistent and expert source of review of national policies, environmental problems and trends, both long-term and short-term. Such a council would act entirely independently of the executive, mission-oriented agencies." The council envisioned in H.R. 12549 would have been composed of five members and located in the Executive Office of the President. With few changes, notably the number of members, the centerpiece of H.R. 12549 became a constituent element of NEPA.

Many in Congress believed that no amount of coordination would be able to overcome the tendency for agencies to pursue their primary missions, few of which at that time included environmental quality. Further, it was apparent that great potential existed for "conflicts when environmental quality is managed by different policies, originating in conservation, agriculture, esthetics, recreation, economic development, human health, and so forth." For this reason, federal agencies needed an "overall policy for the environment ... which integrates these purposes and objectives and which provides for choice when they are incompatible ... [mindful that] [c]hoices are not always quantitative and trade-offs are not systematic."

Given the intricacies and interrelatedness of the human environment, a policy oriented toward very specific goals or objectives was seen as impractical. Thus it was believed that "a comprehensive policy toward the environment cannot help but be philosophical rather than specific."

....

The need for a comprehensive environmental policy was never seriously disputed. It was recognized, however, that the mere declaration of a national environmental policy would not assure pursuit of its objectives. Agencies could very well ignore a statement of policy if not compelled somehow to do otherwise. The concept of self-policing by federal agencies that pollute or license pollution was flatly rejected. A mechanism to implement the policy was needed, an "'action-forcing' process that could be put into operation."

Section 102(2)(C) of NEPA became the embodiment of the policy's "action-forcing" mechanism. The "detailed statement" prescribed in section 102(2)(C) would require "federal agencies, in submitting proposals, to contain within the proposals an evaluation of the effect of these proposals upon the state of the environment...." ... Still, many questions concerning the applicability, scope, and content of the "detailed statement" remained unanswered.

Analyzing federal actions in terms of their eventual effect on the status of the environment was thought to be a difficult undertaking, even for experts. Expectations with respect to nonexpert agencies were not spelled out by Congress but necessarily derived from the two principal functions that the environmental impact assessment process was designed to serve: (1) to provoke thought in directions with which agencies were generally unfamiliar; and (2) to restore public confidence in the government's capacity to balance the total needs of society in its decisionmaking apparatus....

---

40 C.F.R. § 1500.1

Purpose [of NEPA]

(a) The National Environmental Policy Act (NEPA) is our basic national charter for protection of the environment. It establishes policy, sets goals (section 101), and provides means (section 102) for carrying out the policy. Section 102(2) contains "action-forcing" provisions to make sure that federal agencies act according to the letter and spirit of the Act. The regulations that follow implement section 102(2). Their purpose is to tell federal agencies what they must do to comply with the procedures and achieve the goals of the Act. The President, the federal agencies, and the courts share responsibility for enforcing the Act so as to achieve the substantive requirements of section 101.

(b) NEPA procedures must insure that environmental information is available to public officials and citizens before decisions are made and before actions are taken. The information must be of high quality. Accurate scientific analysis, expert agency comments, and public scrutiny are essential to implementing NEPA. Most important, NEPA documents must concentrate on the issues that are truly significant to the action in question, rather than amassing needless detail.

(c) Ultimately, of course, it is not better documents but better decisions that count. NEPA's purpose is not to generate paperwork — even excellent paperwork — but to foster excellent action. The NEPA process is intended to help public officials make decisions that are based on understanding of environmental consequences, and take actions that protect, restore, and enhance the environment. These regulations provide the direction to achieve this purpose.

A. THRESHOLD REQUIREMENTS: THE DUTY TO PREPARE AN IMPACT STATEMENT

In *Calvert Cliffs' Coordinating Comm. v. Atomic Energy Comm'n*, 449 F.2d 1109 (D.C. Cir. 1971) Judge Skelly Wright cogently explained the background and framework of NEPA:

> NEPA, like so much other reform legislation of the last 40 years, is cast in terms of a general mandate and broad delegation of authority to new and old administrative agencies. It takes the major step of requiring all federal agencies to consider values of environmental preservation in their spheres of activity, and it prescribes certain procedural measures to ensure that those values are in fact fully respected....
>
> ... The relevant portion of NEPA is Title I, consisting of five sections. Section 101 sets forth the Act's basic substantive policy: that the federal government "use all practicable means and measures" to protect environmental values. Congress did not establish environmental protection as an exclusive goal; rather, it desired a reordering of priorities, so that environmental costs and benefits will assume their proper place along with other considerations. In Section 101(b), imposing an explicit duty on federal officials, the Act provides that "it is the continuing responsibility of the Federal Government to use all practicable means, consistent with other essential considerations of national policy," to avoid environmental degradation, preserve "historic, cultural, and natural" resources, and promote "the widest range of beneficial uses of the environment without ... undesirable and unintended consequences."
>
> Thus the general substantive policy of the Act is a flexible one. It leaves room for a responsible exercise of discretion and may not require particular substantive results in particular problematic instances. However, the Act also contains very important "procedural" provisions — provisions which are designed to see that all federal agencies do in fact exercise the substantive discretion given them. These provisions are not highly flexible. Indeed, they establish a strict standard of compliance.
>
> NEPA, first of all, makes environmental protection part of the mandate of every federal agency and department. The Atomic Energy Commission, for example, had continually asserted, prior to NEPA, that it had no statutory authority to concern itself with the adverse environmental effects of its actions. Now, however, its hands are no longer tied. It is not only permitted, but compelled, to take environmental values into account. Perhaps the greatest importance of NEPA is to require the Atomic Energy Commission and other agencies to *consider* environmental issues just as they consider other matters within their mandates. This compulsion is most plainly stated in Section 102. There, "Congress authorizes and directs that, to the fullest extent possible: (1) the policies, regulations, and public laws

of the United States shall be interpreted and administered in accordance with the policies set forth in this Act...." Congress also "authorizes and directs" that "(2) all agencies of the Federal Government shall" follow certain rigorous procedures in considering environmental values. Senator Jackson, NEPA's principal sponsor, stated that "[n]o agency will [now] be able to maintain that it has no mandate or no requirement to consider the environmental consequences of its actions." He characterized the requirements of Section 102 as "action-forcing" and stated that "[o]therwise, these lofty declarations [in Section 101] are nothing more than that."

The sort of consideration of environmental values which NEPA compels is clarified in Section 102(2)(A) and (B). In general, all agencies must use a "systematic, interdisciplinary approach" to environmental planning and evaluation "in decisionmaking which may have an impact on man's environment." I order to include all possible environmental factors in the decisional equation, agencies must "identify and develop methods and procedures ... which will insure that presently unquantified environmental amenities and values may be given appropriate consideration in decisionmaking along with economic and technical considerations." "Environmental amenities" will often be in conflict with "economic and technical considerations." To "consider" the former "along with" the latter must involve a balancing process. In some instances environmental costs may outweigh economic and technical benefits and in other instances they may not. But NEPA mandates a rather finely tuned and "systematic" balancing analysis in each instance.

To ensure that the balancing analysis is carried out and given full effect, Section 102(2)(C) requires that responsible officials of all agencies prepare a "detailed statement" covering the impact of particular actions on the environment, the environmental costs which might be avoided, and alternative measures which might alter the cost-benefit equation. The apparent purpose of the "detailed statement" is to aid in the agencies' own decisionmaking process and to advise other interested agencies and the public of the environmental consequences of planned federal action. Beyond the "detailed statement," Section 102(2)(D) requires all agencies specifically to "study, develop, and describe appropriate alternatives to recommended courses of action in any proposal which involves unresolved conflicts concerning alternative uses of available resources." This requirement, like the "detailed statement" requirement, seeks to ensure that each agency decisionmaker has before him and takes into proper account all possible approaches to a particular project (including total abandonment of the project) which would alter the environmental impact and the cost-benefit balance. Only in that fashion is it likely that the most intelligent, optimally beneficial decision will ultimately be made. Moreover, by compelling a formal "detailed statement" and a description of alternatives, NEPA provides evidence that the mandated decisionmaking process has in fact taken place and, most importantly, allows those removed from the initial process to evaluate and balance the factors on their own.

Of course, all of these Section 102 duties are qualified by the phrase "to the fullest extent possible." We must stress as forcefully as possible that this language does not provide an escape hatch for footdragging agencies; it does not make NEPA's procedural requirements somehow "discretionary." Congress did not intend the Act to be such a paper tiger. Indeed, the requirement of environmental consideration "to the fullest extent possible" sets a high standard for the agencies, a standard which must be rigorously enforced by the reviewing courts.

Unlike the substantive duties of Section 101(b), which require agencies to "use all practicable means consistent with other essential considerations," the procedural duties of Section 102 must be fulfilled to the "fullest extent possible."...

Thus the Section 102 duties are not inherently flexible. They must be complied with to the fullest extent, unless there is a clear conflict of *statutory* authority. Considerations of administrative difficulty, delay or economic cost will not suffice to strip the section of its fundamental importance.

We conclude, then, that Section 102 of NEPA mandates a particular sort of careful and informed decisionmaking process and creates judicially enforceable duties. The reviewing courts probably cannot reverse a substantive decision on its merits, under Section 101, unless it be shown that the actual balance of costs and benefits that was struck was arbitrary or clearly gave insufficient weight to environmental values. But if the decision was reached procedurally without individualized consideration and balancing of environmental factors — conducted fully and in good faith — it is the responsibility of the courts to reverse....

Beyond Section 102(2)(C), NEPA requires that agencies consider the environmental impact of their actions "to the fullest extent possible." The Act is addressed to agencies as a whole, not only to their professional staffs. Compliance to the *"fullest"* possible extent would seem to demand that environmental issues be considered at every important stage in the decisionmaking process concerning a particular action — at every stage where an overall balancing of environmental and nonenvironmental factors is appropriate and where alterations might be made in the proposed action to minimize environmental costs....

---

40 C.F.R. § 1502.1

Purpose [of an Environmental Impact Statement]

The primary purpose of an environmental impact statement is to serve as an action-forcing device to insure that the policies and goals defined in the Act are infused into the ongoing programs and actions of the Federal Government. It shall provide full and fair discussion of significant environmental impacts and shall inform decisionmakers and the public of the reasonable alternatives which would avoid or minimize adverse impacts or enhance the quality of the human environment. Agencies shall focus on significant environmental issues and alternatives and shall reduce paperwork and the accumulation of extraneous background data. Statements shall be concise, clear, and to the point, and shall be supported by evidence that the agency has made the necessary environmental analyses. An environmental impact statement is more than a disclosure document. It shall be used by Federal officials in conjunction with other relevant material to plan actions and make decisions.

HANLY v. KLEINDIENST

471 F.2d 823 (2d Cir. 1972)

MANSFIELD, CIRCUIT JUDGE.

This case, which presents serious questions as to the interpretation of the National Environmental Policy Act of 1969, 42 U.S.C. §§ 4331 *et seq.* ("NEPA"), the language of which has been characterized as "opaque" and "woefully ambiguous," is here on appeal for the second time.... [In an earlier opinion, *Hanly v. Mitchell*, 460 F.2d 640 (2d Cir. 1972) ("*Hanly I*"), the court held that the General Services Administration ("GSA") had based its decision-making regarding the proposed construction of a federal jail in Manhattan, the Metropolitan Correction Center ("MCC"), on an inadequate record for NEPA purposes. The court found that the "human environment" under NEPA necessitated consideration of the environmental impacts on the quality of life for urban residents. The court did not mandate that an environmental impact statement ("EIS") be prepared but had remanded for the agency to expand its inquiry by evaluating the potential impact of various socio-economic and aesthetic factors such as potential increased noise, traffic and crime on the neighborhood.]

Following the remand a new threshold determination in the form of a 25-page "Assessment of the Environmental Impact" ("Assessment") was made by the GSA and submitted to the district court on June 15, 1972. This document reflects a detailed consideration of numerous relevant factors. Among other things, it analyzes the size, exact location, and proposed use of the MCC; its design features, construction and aesthetic relationship to its surroundings; the extent to which its occupants and activities conducted in it will be visible by the community; the estimated effects of its operation upon traffic, public transit and parking facilities; its approximate population, including detainees and employees; its effect on the level of noise, smoke, dirt, obnoxious odors, sewage and solid waste removal; and its energy demands. It also sets forth possible alternatives, concluding that there is none that is satisfactory. Upon the basis of this Assessment the Acting Commissioner of the Public Building Service Division of the GSA, who is the responsible official in charge, concluded on June 7, 1972, that the MCC was not an action significantly affecting the quality of the human environment.

....

Upon attempting to interpret the amorphous term "significantly," as it is used in § 102(2)(C), we are faced with the fact that almost every major federal action, no matter how limited in scope has *some* adverse effect on the human environment. It is equally clear that an action which is environmentally important to one neighbor may be of no consequence to another. Congress could have decided that every major federal action must therefore be the subject of a detailed impact statement prepared according to the procedure prescribed by § 102(2)(C). By adding the word "significantly," however, it demonstrated that before the agency in charge triggered that procedure, it should conclude that a greater environmental impact would result than from "any major federal action." Yet the limits of the key term have not been adequately defined by Congress or by guidelines issued by the Council on Environmental Quality ("CEQ") and other responsible federal agencies vested with broad discretionary powers under NEPA. Congress apparently was willing to depend principally upon the agency's good faith determination as to what conduct would be sufficiently serious from an ecological standpoint to require use of the full-scale procedure.

Guidelines issued by the CEQ, which are echoed in rules for implementation published by the Public Buildings Service, the branch of GSA concerned with the construction of the MCC, suggest that a formal impact statement should be prepared with respect to "proposed actions, the environmental impact of which is likely to be highly controversial." [Citation.] However, the term "controversial" apparently refers to cases where a substantial dispute exists as to the size, nature or effect of the major federal action rather than to the existence of opposition to a use, the effect of which is relatively undisputed. This Court in *Hanly I*, for instance, did not require a formal impact statement with respect to the office building portion of the Annex despite the existence of neighborhood opposition to it. The suggestion that "controversial" must be equated with neighborhood opposition has also been rejected by others. [Citation.]

In the absence of any Congressional or administrative interpretation of the term, we are persuaded that in deciding whether a major federal action will "significantly" affect the quality of the human environment the agency in charge, although vested with broad discretion, should normally be required to review the proposed action in the light of at least two relevant factors: (1) the extent to which the action will cause adverse environmental effects in excess of those created by existing uses in the area affected by it, and (2) the absolute quantitative adverse environmental effects of the action itself, including the cumulative harm that results from its contribution to existing adverse conditions or uses in the affected area. Where conduct conforms to existing uses, its adverse consequences will usually be less significant than when it represents a radical change. Absent some showing that an entire neighborhood is in the process of redevelopment, its existing environment, though frequently below an ideal standard, represents a norm that cannot be ignored. For instance, one more highway in an area honeycombed with roads usually has less of an adverse impact than if it were constructed through a roadless public park. [Citation.]

Although the existing environment of the area which is the site of a major federal action constitutes one criterion to be considered, it must be recognized that even a slight increase in adverse conditions that form an existing environmental milieu may sometimes threaten harm that is significant. One more factory polluting air and water in an area zoned for industrial use may represent the straw that breaks the back of the environmental camel. Hence the absolute, as well as comparative, effects of a major federal action must be considered.

Chief Judge Friendly's thoughtful dissent, while conceding that we (and governmental agencies) face a difficult problem in determining the meaning of the vague and amorphous term "significantly" as used in § 102(2)(C), offers no solution other than to suggest that an impact statement should be required whenever a major federal action might be "arguably" or "potentially" significant and that such an interpretation would insure the preparation of impact statements except in cases of "true" insignificance. In our view this suggestion merely substitutes one form of semantical vagueness for another. By failure to use more precise standards it would leave the agency, which admittedly must make the determination, in the very quandary faced in this case and only serve to prolong and proliferate uncertainty as to when a threshold determination should be accepted....

We agree with Chief Judge Friendly that an impact statement should not be required where the impact will be minor or unimportant, or where "there is no sensible reason for making one," and that such a statement should be required where the action may fairly be said to have a potentially significant adverse effect. But these conclusions merely pose the problem which cannot be solved by an interchange of adjectives. In our view such a morass can be avoided only by formulation of more precise factors that must be considered in making the essential threshold determination. This we have attempted to do.

In the absence of such standards we cannot agree that construction of a proposed office building of the type forming part of the Annex would be "obviously insignificant" and hence would not require an impact statement. An office building or, indeed, a jail, may have an adverse impact in an area where such use does not exist and is not permitted by zoning laws whereas the contrary would hold in a location where such uses do exist and are authorized by such laws. [Citation.] Rather than encourage agencies to dispense with impact statements, we believe that application of the foregoing objective standards, coupled with compliance with minimum procedural requirements (specified below), which are designed to assure consideration of relevant facts, will lead agencies in doubtful cases (so-called "grey" areas) to obtain impact statements rather than to risk the delay and expense of protracted litigation.

....

Appellants offer little or no evidence to contradict the detailed facts found by the GSA. For the most part their opposition is based upon a psychological distaste for having a jail located so close to residential apartments, which is understandable enough. It is doubtful whether psychological or sociological effects upon neighbors constitute the type of factors that may be considered in making such a determination since they do not lend themselves to measurement. However we need not decide that issue because these apartments were constructed within two or three blocks of another existing jail, The Manhattan House of Detention for Men, which is much larger than the proposed MCC and houses approximately 1,200 prisoners. Furthermore the area in which the MCC is located has at all times been zoned by the City of New York as a commercial district designed to provide for a whole range of uses, *specifically including "Prisons."*

Despite the GSA's scrupulous efforts the appellants do present one or two factual issues that merit further considerations and findings by the GSA. One bears on the possibility that the MCC will substantially increase the risk of crime in the immediate area, a relevant factor as to which the Assessment fails to make an outright finding despite the direction to do so in *Hanly I.* Appellants urge that the Community Treatment Program and the program for observation and study of non-resident out-patients will endanger the health and safety of the immediate area by exposing neighbors and passersby to drug addicts visiting the MCC for drug maintenance and to drug pushers and hangers-on who would inevitably frequent the vicinity of a drug maintenance center. If the MCC were to be used as a drug treatment center, the potential increase in crime might tip the scales in favor of a mandatory detailed impact statement....

Appellants further contend that they have never been given an opportunity to discuss the MCC with any governmental agency prior to GSA's submission of its Assessment, which raises the question whether the agency acted "without observance of procedure required by law." [Citation.] We do not share the Government's view that the procedural mandates of § 102(A), (B), and (D), 42 U.S.C. § 4332(2)(A), (B), and (D), apply only to actions found by the agency itself to have a significant environmental effect. While these sections are somewhat opaque, they are not expressly limited to "major Federal actions significantly affecting the quality of the human environment." Indeed if they were so limited § 102(D), which requires the agency to develop appropriate alternatives to the recommended course of action, would be duplicative since § 102(C), which does apply to actions "significantly affecting" the environment, specifies that the detailed impact statement must deal with "alternatives to the proposed action." 42 U.S.C. § 4332(2)(C)(iii)....

A more serious question is raised by the GSA's failure to comply with § 102(2)(B), which requires the agency to "identify and develop methods and procedures ... which will insure that presently unquantified environmental amenities and values may be given appropriate consideration in decisionmaking along with economic and technical considerations." 42 U.S.C. § 4332(2)(B).

Since an agency, in making a threshold determination as to the "significance" of an action, is called upon to review in a general fashion the same factors that would be studied in depth for preparation of a detailed environmental impact statement, § 102(2)(B) requires that some rudimentary procedures be designed to assure a fair and informed preliminary decision. Otherwise the agency, lacking essential information, might frustrate the purpose of NEPA by a threshold determination that an impact statement is unnecessary. Furthermore, an adequate record serves to preclude later changes in use without consideration of their environmental significance as required by NEPA.

Where a proposed major federal action may affect the sensibilities of a neighborhood, the prudent course would be for the agency in charge, before making a threshold decision, to give notice to the community of the contemplated action and to accept all pertinent information proffered by concerned citizens with respect to it. Furthermore, in line with the procedure usually followed in zoning disputes, particularly where emotions are likely to be aroused by fears, or rumors of misinformation, a public hearing serves the dual purpose of enabling the agency to obtain all relevant data and to satisfy the community that its views are being considered. However, neither NEPA nor any other federal statute mandates the specific type of procedure to be followed by federal agencies....

Notwithstanding the absence of statutory or administrative provisions on the subject, this Court has already held in *Hanly I* that federal agencies must "affirmatively develop a reviewable environmental record ... even for purposes of a threshold section 102(2)(C) determination." We now go further and hold that before a preliminary or threshold determination of significance is made the responsible agency must give notice to the public of the proposed major federal action and an opportunity to submit relevant facts which might bear upon the agency's threshold decision. We do not suggest that a full-fledged formal hearing must be provided before each such determination is made, although it should be apparent that in many cases such a hearing would be advisable for reasons already indicated. The necessity for a hearing will depend greatly upon the circumstances surrounding the particular proposed action and upon the likelihood that a hearing will be more effective than other methods in developing relevant information and an understanding of the proposed action. The precise procedural steps to be adopted are better left to the agency, which should be in a better position than the court to determine whether solution of the problems faced with respect to a specific major federal action can better be achieved through a hearing or by informal acceptance of relevant data.

In view of the Assessment's failure to make findings with respect to the possible existence of a drug maintenance program at the MCC, the increased risk of crime that might result from the operation of the MCC, and the fact that appellants have challenged certain findings of fact, we remand the case for the purpose of requiring the GSA to make a further investigation of these issues, with directions to accept from appellants and other concerned citizens such further evidence as they may proffer within a reasonable period, to make supplemental findings with respect to these issues, and to redetermine whether the MCC "significantly affects the quality of the human environment." If, as a result of such further investigation, the GSA concludes that a detailed environmental impact statement is required, a preliminary injunction will be granted restraining further construction of the MCC until the agency has complied with the procedures required by § 102(2)(C) of NEPA. In the event that the GSA reaffirms its initial determination, the district court will determine, should a further request be made, whether preliminary injunctive relief is warranted.

....

FRIENDLY, CHIEF JUDGE (dissenting).

The learned opinion of my brother MANSFIELD gives these plaintiffs, and environmental advocates in future cases, both too little and too much. It gives too little because it raises the floor of what constitutes "major Federal actions significantly affecting the quality of the human environment," 42 U.S.C. § 4332(2)(C), higher than I believe Congress intended. It gives too much because it requires that before making a threshold determination that no impact statement is demanded, the agency must go through procedures which I think are needed only when an impact statement must be made. The upshot is that a threshold determination that a proposal does not constitute major Federal action significantly affecting the quality of the human environment becomes a kind of mini-impact statement. The preparation of such a statement under the conditions laid down by the majority is unduly burdensome when the action is truly minor or insignificant. On the other hand, there is a danger that if the threshold determination is this elaborate, it may come to replace the impact statement in the grey area between actions which, though "major" in a monetary sense, are obviously insignificant (such as the construction of the proposed office building) and actions that are obviously significant (such as the construction of an atomic power plant). We would better serve the purposes of Congress by keeping the threshold low enough to insure that impact statements are prepared for actions in this grey area and thus to permit the determination that no statement is required to be made quite informally in cases of true insignificance.

While I agree that determination of the meaning of "significant" is a question of law, one must add immediately that to make this determination on the basis of the dictionary would be impossible. Although all words may be "chameleons, which reflect the color of their environment," [citation] "significant" has that quality more than most. It covers a spectrum ranging from "not trivial" through "appreciable" to "important" and even "momentous." If the right meaning is at the lower end of the spectrum, the construction of the MCC comes within it; *per contra* if the meaning is at the higher end.

The scheme of the National Environmental Policy Act argues for giving "significant" a reading which places it toward the lower end of the spectrum. The statute's objectives, 42 U.S.C. § 4321, were "To declare a national policy which will encourage productive and enjoyable harmony between man and his environment; [and] to promote efforts which will prevent or eliminate damage to the environment...." Section 4332 outlines methods designed to insure that "the policies, regulations, and public laws of the United States shall be interpreted and administered in accordance with the[se] policies." Most of its provisions are hortatory; the only one with teeth is the mandate in subdivision (2)(C) that each agency must "include in every recommendation or report on proposals for legislation and other major Federal actions significantly affecting the quality of the human environment, a detailed statement ..." covering the five items listed in that section, one of which is described in subdivision (D) at greater length....

It is not readily conceivable that Congress meant to allow agencies to avoid this central requirement by reading "significant" to mean only "important," "momentous," or the like. One of the purposes of the impact statement is to insure that the relevant environmental data are before the agency and considered by it prior to the decision to commit Federal resources to the project; the statute must not be construed so as to allow the agency to make its decision in a doubtful case without the relevant data or a detailed study of it. This is particularly clear because of the absence from the statute of any procedural requirement upon an agency in making the threshold determination that an impact statement is not demanded, although the majority has managed to contrive one....

NOTES AND QUESTIONS

1. *Socio-economic Considerations.* After *Hanly II*, to what extent should courts take into account socio-economic considerations in determining the significance of a proposed project on the environment? Some courts have held that socio-economic factors alone would seldom suffice to trigger an agency's obligation to prepare an EIS; a threshold requirement of significant impact on the physical environment must first be shown. *See Panhandle Producers & Royalty Owners Ass'n v. Economic Reg. Admin.*, 847 F.2d 1168 (5th Cir. 1988) (where only effects of agency order authorizing imports of Canadian natural gas were socio-economic, such effects fell outside the scope of NEPA); *Village of Palatine v. United States Postal Serv.*, 756 F. Supp. 1079 (N.D. Ill. 1991) (Court upheld postal regulations implementing NEPA which considered proposed facility's impact on physical environment as threshold matter; effects on human environment were secondary).

2. Several years after *Hanly II*, the Council on Environmental Quality promulgated regulations under NEPA to provide guidance on the threshold determination of whether a proposal constitutes a major federal action. Some of the relevant regulations pertaining to these critical threshold issues follow:

40 C.F.R. § 1508.8 Effects.

"Effects" include:

(a) Direct effects, which are caused by the action and occur at the same time and place.

(b) Indirect effects, which are caused by the action and are later in time or farther removed in distance, but are still reasonably foreseeable. Indirect effects may include growth inducing effects and other effects related to induced changes in the pattern of land use, population density or growth rate, and related effects on air and water and other natural systems, including ecosystems.

Effects and impacts as used in these regulations are synonymous. Effects includes ecological (such as the effects on natural resources and on the components, structures, and functioning of affected ecosystems), aesthetic, historic, cultural, economic, social, or health, whether direct, indirect, or cumulative. Effects may also include those resulting from actions which may have both beneficial and detrimental effects, even if on balance the agency believes that the effect will be beneficial.

40 C.F.R. § 1508.14 Human environment.

"Human environment" shall be interpreted comprehensively to include the natural and physical environment and the relationship of people with that environment. (See the definition of "effects" (§ 1508.8).) This means that economic or social effects are not intended by themselves to require preparation of an environmental impact statement. When an environmental impact statement is prepared and economic or social and natural or physical environmental effects are interrelated, then the environmental impact statement will discuss all of these effects on the human environment.

40 C.F.R. § 1508.18 Major Federal action.

"Major Federal action" includes actions with effects that may be major and which are potentially subject to Federal control and responsibility. Major reinforces but does not have a meaning independent of significantly (§ 1508.27). Actions include the circumstance where the responsible officials fail to act and that failure to act is reviewable by courts or administrative tribunals under the Administrative Procedure Act or other applicable law as agency action.

(a) Actions include new and continuing activities, including projects and programs entirely or partly financed, assisted, conducted, regulated, or approved by federal agencies; new or revised agency rules, regulations, plans, policies, or procedures; and legislative proposals (§§ 1506.8, 1508.17). Actions do not include funding assistance solely in the form of general revenue sharing funds, distributed under the State and Local Fiscal Assistance Act of 1972, 31 U.S.C. 1221 *et seq.*, with no Federal agency control over the subsequent use of such funds. Actions do not include bringing judicial or administrative civil or criminal enforcement actions.

(b) Federal actions tend to fall within one of the following categories:

(1) Adoption of official policy, such as rules, regulations, and interpretations adopted pursuant to the Administrative Procedure Act, 5 U.S.C. 551 *et seq.*; treaties and international conventions or agreements; formal documents establishing an agency's policies which will result in or substantially alter agency programs.

(2) Adoption of formal plans, such as official documents prepared or approved by federal agencies which guide or prescribe alternative uses of federal resources, upon which future agency actions will be based.

(3) Adoption of programs, such as a group of concerted actions to implement a specific policy or plan; systematic and connected agency decisions allocating agency resources to implement a specific statutory program or executive directive.

(4) Approval of specific projects, such as construction or management activities located in a defined geographic area. Projects include actions approved by permit or other regulatory decision as well as federal and federally assisted activities.

40 C.F.R. § 1508.27 Significantly.

"Significantly" as used in NEPA requires considerations of both context and intensity:

(a) *Context.* This means that the significance of an action must be analyzed in several contexts such as society as a whole (human, national), the affected region, the affected interests, and the locality. Significance varies with the setting of the proposed action. For instance, in the case of a site-specific action, significance would usually depend upon the effects in the locale rather than in the world as a whole. Both short- and long-term effects are relevant.

(b) *Intensity.* This refers to the severity of impact. Responsible officials must bear in mind that more than one agency may make decisions about partial aspects of a major action. The following should be considered in evaluating intensity:

(1) Impacts that may be both beneficial and adverse. A significant effect may exist even if the Federal agency believes that on balance the effect will be beneficial.

(2) The degree to which the proposed action affects public health or safety.

(3) Unique characteristics of the geographic area such as proximity to historic or cultural resources, park lands, prime farmlands, wetlands, wild and scenic rivers, or ecologically critical areas.

(4) The degree to which the effects on the quality of the human environment are likely to be highly controversial.

(5) The degree to which the possible effects on the human environment are highly uncertain or involve unique or unknown risks.

(6) The degree to which the action may establish a precedent for future actions with significant effects or represents a decision in principle about a future consideration.

(7) Whether the action is related to other actions with individually insignificant but cumulatively significant impacts. Significance exists if it is reasonable to anticipate a cumulatively significant impact on the environment. Significance cannot be avoided by terming an action temporary or by breaking it down into small component parts.

(8) The degree to which the action may adversely affect districts, sites, highways, structures, or objects listed in or eligible for listing in the National Register of Historic Places or may cause loss or destruction of significant scientific, cultural, or historical resources.

(9) The degree to which the action may adversely affect an endangered or threatened species or its habitat that has been determined to be critical under the Endangered Species Act of 1973.

(10) Whether the action threatens a violation of Federal State, or local law or requirements imposed for the protection of the environment.

3. *Psychological Factors.* NEPA contemplates agency consideration of a wide array of factors that affect the *relationship* of people with the natural and physical environment. 40 C.F.R. § 1508.14. One dilemma facing agencies involves the degree to which subjective considerations, such as psychological impacts or value preferences, should be part of the NEPA process. In an early decision, *Nucleus of Chicago Homeowners Ass'n v. Lynn*, 524 F.2d 225 (7th Cir. 1975) a group opposed location of a HUD low-income housing project in their neighborhood. They claimed that the project would overburden community services and that the public housing tenants would increase crime in the area. The court rejected the fears of "people pollution" and upheld the agency decision, finding that HUD adequately considered the effect of the project on the social fabric of the community.

In *Metropolitan Edison Co. v. People Against Nuclear Energy*, 460 U.S. 766 (1983) an association of residents challenged a decision by the Nuclear Regulatory Commission authorizing the restart of a nuclear reactor at Three Mile Island after a second plant there had malfunctioned. The plaintiffs claimed that the agency violated NEPA by failing to take into account the severe psychological stress suffered by local residents caused by reopening the plant. The Supreme Court recognized that effects on human health were cognizable under NEPA and that human health may include psychological health.

The Court interpreted NEPA as being primarily concerned with potential harms to the *physical* environment. The Court reasoned that an "effect" qualifies as "environmental" only if a reasonably close causal connection or relationship existed to a change in the physical environment. As a result, the statute did not require the agency to consider psychological effects of the existence of a risk before the risk had materialized.

The Court carefully avoided equating its analysis regarding causation for NEPA purposes with the concept of proximate cause in tort, but did suggest that courts should examine the underlying policies in order to draw a "manageable line between those causal changes that may make an actor responsible for an effect and those that do not." In short, the Court stated that the fear arising from a risk of a nuclear accident did not constitute an "effect" requiring consideration under NEPA.

The holding in *Metropolitan Edison* narrowed the scope of what constitutes the "environment" for NEPA purposes from the expansive treatment fashioned by the court in Hanly II. Questions remain, however, regarding the extent to which NEPA requires evaluation of socio-economic values or human interests and impacts in relation to consideration of the effects of a proposed project on the physical environment. *See Olmsted Citizens For a Better Community v. United States*, 793 F.2d 201 (8th Cir. 1986) (EIS not required where impacts associated with proposed conversion of state mental hospital into a federal prison were not connected to physical changes in the environment but were social changes).

In *Bicycle Trails Council of Marin v. Babbitt*, 82 F.3d 1445 (9th Cir. 1996) bicycle associations challenged government restrictions on the use of bicycles within national parks. The court upheld the agency decision not to prepare an EIS, reasoning:

> Defendants argue that plaintiffs have failed to identify any physical impacts to the environment caused by such crowding, and that plaintiffs' concern with crowding is simply a concern with their bicyclists' subjective trail experience and fear of an increased risk of accidents. Plaintiffs counter that impacts on traffic and safety can qualify as impacts on the environment.

> [A]n EIS need only be prepared for a major federal action having a significant impact on the human environment. The Supreme Court has interpreted the human environment to mean the "physical environment — the world around us, so to speak." Thus NEPA does not require that an agency take into account every conceivable impact of its actions, including impacts on citizens' subjective experiences. Rather, it requires agencies to take into account environmental impacts on the physical "world around us." Plaintiffs' argument that bicyclists being crowded onto fewer trails is such an environmental impact is incorrect. An increased risk of accident is not an impact to the physical environment. Thus, plaintiffs here cannot show as a threshold matter that the 1992 trail plan had any significant impact on the physical environment. The closing of certain trails to bicyclists did not mandate an EIS. [Citations omitted]

Id. at 1466-1467.

4. *Cost-Benefit Factors*. In *River Road Alliance, Inc. v. Army Corps of Eng'rs*, 764 F.2d 445 (7th Cir. 1985) groups challenged the decision of the Corps of Engineers to grant a permit for a barge fleeting facility on the Mississippi River. The court upheld the agency decision, noting that if every federal project with potential environmental effects required preparation of a full-scale EIS, government activity would "pretty much grind to a halt." The court observed that pragmatic considerations of costs and administrative delays played important roles in determining the "significance" of information pertaining to a proposed project:

> The statutory concept of "significant" impact has no determinate meaning, and to interpret it sensibly in particular cases requires a comparison that is also a prediction: whether the time and expense of preparing an environmental impact statement are commensurate with the likely benefits from a more searching evaluation than an environmental assessment provides.

Id. at 449.

5. *Aesthetic Considerations*. In *Hanly*, the court noted that the proposed federal jail in Manhattan harmonized architecturally with existing buildings in area and could even enhance the appearance of the neighborhood. Other courts have recognized that aesthetic considerations are cognizable interests for agency evaluation under NEPA, but because of the inherent differences of opinion do not necessarily require certain results in the decisionmaking process:

> That some, or perhaps all, environmental impacts have an esthetic facet, does not mean that all adverse esthetic impacts affect environment. That is neither good logic nor good law. Some questions of esthetics do not seem to lend themselves to the detailed analysis required under NEPA for a § 102(C) impact statement. Like psychological factors they "are not readily translatable into concrete measuring rods." The difficulty in precisely defining what is beautiful cannot stand in the way of expressions of community choice through zoning regulation. But the difficulties have a bearing on the intention of Congress, and whether it contemplated, for example, a requirement of a detailed "environmental impact statement," and concomitant investigation, because of the possibility that each new Federal construction would be ugly to some, or even most, beholders, on such issues as: Is this proposed building beautiful? Or, what is the esthetic effect of placing the "controversial" Picasso statute in front of the Civic Center building in Chicago?

Maryland-National Capital Park & Planning Comm'n v. U.S. Postal Serv., 487 F.2d 1029, 1038 (D.C. Cir. 1973). *Also see River Road Alliance, Inc. v. Army Corps of Eng'rs*, 764 F.2d 445 (7th Cir. 1985) (because aesthetic values are inherently subjective and not susceptible to measurement or analysis, such effects alone would seldom compel the preparation of an EIS); *Havasupai Tribe v.*

United States, 752 F. Supp. 1471, 1500 (D. Ariz 1990) (Agency properly considered cultural, historic, and religious concerns of tribe in EIS).

6. *Federal Actions.* NEPA only applies to actions by federal agencies, not the states. § 102(2)(C). Difficult interpretive issues are presented in delineating the extent to which federal involvement in a project is sufficient to trigger NEPA duties. The project does not need to be entirely federal in order to fall within the scope of NEPA but encompasses situations where the federal government assumes a degree of responsibility with respect to the project. Despite the guidance provided by the CEQ regulations, no bright-line test exists for determining when a nonfederal project possesses sufficient federal involvement to "federalize" the project for NEPA purposes. *See* 40 C.F.R. § 1508.18(b). Federal inaction can be considered "federal action" for purposes of triggering the EIS requirement under NEPA. *See Ramsey v. Kantor*, 96 F.3d 433 (9th Cir. 1996).

In *Sierra Club v. Hodel*, 848 F.2d 1068, 1089-90 (10th Cir. 1988) the court suggested that the "touchstone" of major federal action was the agency's "authority to influence significant nonfederal activity. This influence must be more than the power to give nonbinding advice to the nonfederal actor." Instead, the federal agency must possess actual power to control the nonfederal activity. The court found federal action with respect to a proposed county road construction project where the federal agency had a duty under another statute and regulations to prevent unnecessary degradation of wilderness areas in changes of rights-of-way, even if the agency was reluctant to exercise its regulatory authority.

In *Maryland Conserv. Council v. Gilchrist*, 808 F.2d 1039, 1042 (4th Cir. 1986) the court stated that the critical inquiry for determining whether a non-federal project could be considered a "federal action" for NEPA purposes focused on the agency's "authority to exercise discretion over the outcome," such as where the project could not begin or continue without the prior approval of a federal agency. In that case, the court found federal action because the state needed permits and discretionary approval from federal agencies prior to commencing construction of a proposed highway.

On the other hand, in *Macht v. Skinner*, 916 F.2d 13 (D.C. Cir. 1990) the court held that federal funding for preliminary engineering studies and a required wetlands permit from the Army Corps of Engineers for the state to construct a light rail project did not constitute sufficient federal involvement to bring the project under NEPA. The court reasoned that the decision to fund the preliminary studies did not carry with it a commitment for further financial assistance. The court observed that the Army Corps only had discretion over a minor portion of the entire project — in contrast to *Gilchrist*, where the state could not proceed with any portion of the highway until the federal agencies had complied with NEPA. The court further distinguished the state project from those circumstances where the state has entered into a "partnership" or "joint venture" with the federal government with respect to funding, services, or goods. The court further distinguished the case from situations where the federal government has discretion over a substantial portion of the project.

Also see Almond Hill School v. United States Dep't of Agri., 768 F.2d 1030, 1039 (9th Cir. 1985) (participation of federal officials in California's program involving pesticide spraying to combat a Japanese beetle infestation not sufficient federal involvement for NEPA compliance); *Village of Los Ranchos De Albuquerque v. Barnhart*, 906 F.2d 1477, 1481 (10th Cir. 1990) (eligibility for federal assistance for highway construction project was not enough standing alone to constitute a major federal action); *Ringsred v. City of Duluth*, 828 F.2d 1305 (8th Cir. 1987) (NEPA not implicated where no federal action was a legal condition precedent to construction project).

FOUNDATION ON ECONOMIC TRENDS v. HECKLER

756 F.2d 143 (D.C. Cir. 1985)

J. SKELLY WRIGHT, CIRCUIT JUDGE.

Almost 14 years ago, soon after passage of the National Environmental Policy Act (NEPA), 42 U.S.C. § 4321 *et seq.* (1982), this court faced the challenge of ensuring that the Act's "important legislative purposes, heralded in the halls of Congress, [were] not lost or misdirected in the vast hallways of the federal bureaucracy." *Calvert Cliffs' Coordinating Committee v. USAEC*, 449 F.2d 1109, 1111 (D.C. Cir. 1971). This case poses a no less formidable challenge: to ensure that the bold words and vigorous spirit of NEPA are not similarly lost or misdirected in the brisk frontiers of science.

For this appeal presents an important question at the dawn of the genetic engineering age: what is the appropriate level of environmental review required of the National Institutes of Health (NIH) before it approves the deliberate release of genetically engineered, recombinant-DNA-containing organisms into the open environment? More precisely, in the context of this case, the question is whether to affirm an injunction temporarily enjoining NIH from approving deliberate release experiments without a greater level of environmental concern than the agency has shown thus far.

....

Two fundamental principles underlie NEPA's requirements: federal agencies have the responsibility to consider the environmental effects of major actions significantly affecting environment, and the public has the right to review that consideration. [Citation.] NEPA's dual mission is thus to generate federal attention to environmental concerns and to reveal that federal consideration for public scrutiny.

In passing NEPA Congress emphasized its particular concern with the role of new technologies and their effect on the environment. The statute explicitly enumerates "new and expanding technological advances" as one of the activities with the potential to threaten the environment. 42 U.S.C. § 4331(a). The legislative history reveals an underlying concern with "[a] growing technological power ... far outstripping man's capacity to understand and ability to control its impact on the environment." One of NEPA's main functions was to bolster this capacity to understand and control the effects of new technology. [Citation.]

NEPA thus stands as landmark legislation, requiring federal agencies to consider the environmental effects of major federal actions, empowering the public to scrutinize this consideration, and revealing a special concern about the environmental effects of new technology.

Genetic engineering is an important development at the very cusp of scientific advances. More than a decade ago scientists discovered a method for transplanting deoxyribonucleic acid (DNA), the principal substance of genes. Although exchanges and mutations of DNA occur in nature, genetic engineering provides the ability to control these fundamental processes of life and evolution. DNA segments can be recovered and cloned from one organism and inserted into another. The result is know as "recombinant DNA." [Citations.]

Recombinant DNA technology has been limited primarily to small organisms, usually bacteria. This production of new bacteria through altering genetic material has been confined to the laboratory; organisms with recombinant DNA have never been released into the general environment.

Broad claims are made about both the potential benefits and the potential hazards of genetically engineered organisms. Use of recombinant DNA may lead to welcome advances in such areas as food production and disease control. At the same time, however, the environmental consequences of dispersion of genetically engineered organisms are far from clear....

In 1976 the NIH Director issued "Guidelines for Research on Recombinant DNA Molecules." 41 Fed. Reg. at 27902, JA 230. The Guidelines were an historic development, representing the first major federal effort to oversee genetic research and the culmination of intense scientific attention to the possible hazards of genetic research.

....

Significantly, NIH prepared an EIS to accompany its Guidelines, JA 244 — the only EIS NIH has ever completed on the subject of genetic engineering. The EIS did not specifically refer to deliberate release experiments; such experiments were banned. The EIS did, however, note that dispersion of organisms with recombinant DNA molecules loomed as a potential environmental hazard from permitted experiments.... [The NIH prepared a brief Environmental Assessment — but not an EIS — with respect to subsequent revisions to its Guidelines.]

Although the guidelines have not changed, NIH's role has begun to change dramatically. For, with the maturation of genetic engineering technology, NIH has been faced with applications for approval of deliberate release experiments.

....

On June 1, 1983 the [NIH] Director gave final approval to the experiment at issue on appeal — the request by Drs. Nickolas Panopoulos and Steven Lindow of the University of California at Berkeley to apply genetically altered bacteria to plots of potatoes, tomatoes, and beans in northern California. As discussed in greater detail below, the goal was to increase the crops' frost resistance. Because of the cancellation of the previous two experiments, the Panopoulos-Lindow experiment would be the first NIH approved deliberate release experiment actually to be conducted.

....

In September 1983 three public interest organizations and two individuals filed suit against the three federal officials ultimately responsible for NIH deliberate release decisions; ... [and] the District Court issued an injunction enjoining the University of California experiment and NIH approval of other deliberate release experiments. The District Court found that plaintiffs were likely to succeed in showing that NIH should have completed at least a more complete environmental assessment, and perhaps an EIS, before approving the University of California experiment; it also found them likely to succeed in showing that NIH should have completed an Environmental Impact Statement in connection with both its 1978 policy change and its imminent "program" of deliberate release approvals.

....

NIH's consideration of the Lindow-Panopoulos experiment falls far short of the NEPA requirements. And, despite the government's apparent belief, the deficiency is not a question of which document contains the environmental analysis. Rather, the deficiency rests in NIH's complete failure to consider the possibility of various environmental effects.

Neither the government nor the University seriously disputes that an environmental assessment is necessary. The government has conceded that the approval is a "major action" and that it does not fall into a categorical exclusion to the EIS requirements....

The most glaring deficiency in NIH's review of the Lindow-Panopoulos experiment is its treatment of the possibility of dispersion of recombinant-DNA-containing organisms. As noted, NIH's only EIS on genetic engineering specifically identified dispersion as one of the major environmental concerns associated with recombinant DNA research. The consequences of dispersion of genetically altered organisms are uncertain....

In light of this complete failure to address a major environmental concern, NIH's environmental assessment utterly fails to meet the standard of environmental review necessary before an agency decides not to prepare an EIS. The argument that this consideration would be adequate if contained in a document labelled "Environmental Assessment" simply misconceives the clear requirements of NEPA as articulated by the courts [citations] and by the Council on Environmental Quality, 40 C.F.R. §§ 1501.4, 1508.9. An environmental assessment that fails to address a significant environmental concern can hardly be deemed adequate for a reasoned determination that an EIS is not appropriate. [Citation.]

Appellants also contend that the adequacy of the environmental assessment can be divined from the NIH Director's final approval — and his accompanying statement of "no significant risk," as required by the 1978 revision. This contention also reveals a fundamental misunderstanding about the adequacy of an environmental assessment. Simple, conclusory statements of "no impact" are not enough to fulfill an agency's duty under NEPA....

It should be stressed that this inquiry into the adequacy of an environmental assessment is ultimately relevant to the agency's determination that its proposed federal action will not have a "significant impact" on the environment — and thus no EIS is required. In that connection, it is notable that NIH never directly addressed the question whether an EIS should be prepared. Such an inquiry is, of course, the ultimate purpose of an environmental assessment. [Citation.]

To reiterate, NIH must first complete a far more adequate environmental assessment of the possible environmental impact of the deliberate release experiment than it has yet undertaken. That assessment must "provide sufficient evidence and analysis for determining whether to prepare an environmental impact statement or a finding of no significant impact," 40 C.F.R. § 1508.9(a)(1). Ignoring possible environmental consequences will not suffice. Nor will a mere conclusory statement that the number of recombinant-DNA-containing organisms will be small and subject to processes limiting survival. Instead, NIH must attempt to evaluate seriously the risk that emigration of such organisms from the test site will create ecological disruption. Second, until NIH completes such an evaluation the question whether the experiment requires an EIS remains open. The University of California experiment clearly presents the possibility of a problem identified by NIH in its EIS as a potential environmental hazard. This fact weighs heavily in support of the view that an EIS should be completed, unless NIH can demonstrate either that the experiment does not pose the previously identified danger, or that its assessment of the previously identified danger has changed through a process of reasoned decisionmaking. Nor is it sufficient for the agency merely to state that the environmental effects are currently unknown. Indeed, one of the specific criteria for determining whether an EIS is necessary is "[t]he degree to which the possible effects on the human environment are highly uncertain or involve unique or unknown risks." 40 C.F.R. § 1508.27(b)(5).

Thus we approve the District Court's determination that, as a matter of law, plaintiffs are likely to prevail in showing that NIH's environmental assessment of the University of California experiment — and its discharge of its statutory duty to consider the propriety of an EIS — was wholly inadequate. And, in light of the government's contention, we emphasize as strongly as we can that the problem lay in the adequacy of the assessment itself, not in the document in which the assessment was contained.

....

The University also argues that, whatever plaintiffs' likelihood of success on the merits, the injunction is not justified under the other three criteria that the court must balance in weighing a request for injunctive relief — the threat of irreparable injury to the plaintiffs, the possibility of injury to other interested parties, and the public interest.

The District Court's discretion in balancing these factors is broad. "The nature of the discretion peculiar to the preliminary injunction lies in the latitude given to the District Court to engage in a balancing of the traditional factors...." [Citation.] The District Court's determinations about the harm to the plaintiffs, the harm to other parties, and the public interest were eminently sound, and far from the abuse of discretion that would justify reversal.

One point bears further elucidation. The University seeks to minimize the injury that would result if its experiment proceeds without adequate environmental consideration. In doing so the University fundamentally misconceives the nature and significance of NEPA's requirements. The NEPA duty is more than a technicality; it is an extremely important statutory requirement to serve the public and the agency *before* major federal actions occur. [Citations.] If plaintiffs succeed on the merits, then the lack of an adequate environmental consideration looms as a serious, immediate, and irreparable injury. Although the *balancing* of this harm against other factors is necessarily particularized, the injury itself is clear. [Citation.]

　....

NOTES AND QUESTIONS

1. NEPA requires federal agencies to make numerous judgment calls regarding whether a project presents sufficient environmental impacts to justify preparation of an EIS. In *Coalition on Sensible Transp. v. Dole*, 826 F.2d 60, 66 (D.C. Cir. 1987) the court described the agency task as follows:

> The NEPA process involves an almost endless series of judgment calls. Here we consider ones relating to the detail in which specific items should be discussed and the agencies' treatment of the project's relation to other government activities. It is of course always possible to explore a subject more deeply and to discuss it more thoroughly. The line-drawing decisions necessitated by this fact of life are vested in the agencies, not the courts.

The difficulty of such line-drawing determinations is compounded in that the variety of projects within the scope of NEPA has been described as "broad as the mind can conceive." *Nucleus of Chicago Homeowners Ass'n. v. Lynn*, 524 F.2d 225, 229 (7th Cir. 1975).

2. *Environmental Assessment.* NEPA provides for an abbreviated document — called an environmental assessment — to determine whether a sufficient likelihood of "significant" environmental consequences exists to justify the time and expense of preparing an environmental impact statement. *See* 40 C.F.R. § 1508.9. An environmental assessment has been described as a "rough-cut, low-budget environmental impact statement designed to show whether a full-fledged environmental impact statement — which is very costly and time-consuming to prepare and has been the kiss of death to many a federal project — is necessary." *Cronin v. United States Dep't of Agri.*, 919 F.2d 439, 443 (7th Cir. 1990).

3. Since one of the principal purposes of the EIS process is to inform decisionmakers and the public of the potential environmental consequences of the proposed agency action, the statements must be understandable to a wide audience. The level of "readability" required is complicated by virtue of the complex technical and scientific data often involved. The CEQ regulations provide that the EIS must be "concise, clear and to the point" (40 C.F.R. § 1500.2(b); it should be "analytic rather than encyclopedic" (40 C.F.R. § 1502.2(a); and "written in plain language." 40 C.F.R. § 1502.8; *see also Oregon Envtl. Council v. Kunzman*, 817 F.2d 484, 493-94 (9th Cir. 1987) (EIS must be organized and written so that government decisionmakers and interested nonprofessional laypersons can readily understand the scientific data and analysis).

4. The distinctions between an environmental assessment and an environmental impact statement are substantial. An EA is a "concise" or "brief" document intended for evaluating the environmental impacts and alternatives of a proposal and determining whether an EIS is needed. In contrast, an EIS by definition must be "detailed." One court explained the breadth of an EIS as follows:

> An EIS must include a discussion of not only the expected environmental impact of the proposed action, any adverse environmental effects, and any alternatives to the proposed action, but also more "cosmic" considerations. These considerations include the relationship between short-term and long-term uses of the environment; any irreversible and irretrievable commitments of resources that would follow upon implementation of the proposal; the effects on surrounding cultural, historical, and ecological resources; the degree to which the project might be "controversial"; the extent to which the project might impose "uncertain or unknown risks" upon the environment; whether the action might establish a precedent for future actions; and the degree to which the project, while insignificant in itself, might be significant when considered in connection with other similar actions.

Township of Lower Alloways Creek v. Public Serv. Elec. & Gas Co., 687 F.2d 732, 741 (3d Cir. 1982) (summarizing 42 U.S.C. § 102(2)(C) and 40 C.F.R. § 1508.27).

5. The detailed statement required by section 102(2)(C) provides "full disclosure" of information pertaining to significant environmental impacts of major federal projects for the benefit of the wider audience of the public and other governmental units. *Silva v. Lynn*, 482 F.2d 1282 (1st Cir. 1973). A reviewing court then may ascertain whether the federal agency has made a good faith effort to discharge its obligations under NEPA of investigation, analysis, and reasoning to support its decisionmaking. In *Silva v. Lynn*, the court stated:

Finally, and perhaps most substantively, the requirement of a detailed statement helps insure the integrity of the process of decision by precluding stubborn problems or serious criticism from being swept under the rug. A conclusory statement "unsupported by empirical or experimental data, scientific authorities, or explanatory information of any kind" not only fails to crystallize issues, but "affords no basis for a comparison of the problems involved with the proposed project and the difficulties involved in the alternatives." Moreover, where comments from responsible experts or sister agencies disclose new or conflicting data or opinions that cause concern that the agency may not have fully evaluated the project and its alternatives, these comments may not simply be ignored. There must be good faith, reasoned analysis in response.

Id. at 1284-1285.

6. NEPA requires the circulation of draft impact assessments and statement for comment by appropriate federal agencies with expertise in aspects of the subject matter of the proposal. Where a project implicates several agencies, CEQ regulations provide for the designation of a "lead agency" which assumes primary responsibility for preparing an impact statement and for supervising the process. 40 C.F.R. § 1501.5. The regulations also provide for the participation throughout the process by other agencies with special expertise with respect to an environmental issue implicated in the proposal. 40 C.F.R. § 1501.6.

A disagreement among agencies as to whether a project should proceed or even that an EIS should be prepared is not binding on the lead agency nor is entitled to deference in the ultimate decision reached. Such differences of opinion do not necessarily mean that the project is "controversial," and therefore factored into the equation of whether the impact would be significant for NEPA purposes. *See Roanoke River Basin Ass'n v. Hudson*, 940 F.2d 58, 64 (4th Cir. 1991).

7. *Relationship With Other Laws.* NEPA, despite its action-forcing mandate to federal agencies to consider environmental values in the decisionmaking process, does not expand an agency's substantive powers. Instead, the nature and range of federal agency actions must be derived from the agency's directives set forth in the appropriate organic statute — although imbued with environmental considerations. *See Natural Resources Defense Council v. Environmental Protection Agency*, 859 F.2d 156, 169 (D.C. Cir. 1988) (NEPA does not authorize EPA to impose non-water quality conditions for permit applicant beyond agency's authority under the Clean Water Act).

Although NEPA requirements are superimposed on other duties by federal agencies, it does not abrogate their responsibilities under those other statutes. If a clear conflict of specific statutory obligations is presented, section 104 of NEPA provides that an agency must carry out the other statutory requirements and conflicting NEPA duties will give way. This subordinate role of NEPA was reaffirmed in *Flint Ridge Dev. Co. v. Scenic Rivers Ass'n*, 426 U.S. 776, 791 (1976), where the Supreme Court found a "clear and fundamental conflict of statutory duty" between the Interstate Land Sales Full Disclosure Act and NEPA. The Court held that the federal agency's duty to prepare an impact statement must yield to the agency's directives under the Disclosure Act where compliance with both was impossible. Despite the preference for complying with other statutes, agencies must still follow their NEPA responsibilities "to the fullest extent possible."

8. *Exemptions.* In certain instances, Congress has specifically exempted the EPA from complying with NEPA duties of preparing environmental impact statements. *See* § 511(c)(1) of the Clean Water Act, 33 U.S.C. § 1371(c)(1) (exempts EPA from NEPA compliance except with respect to providing federal financial assistance for construction of publicly owned treatment works and issuance of permits for effluent discharge by new sources).

In addition, federal agencies are excused from NEPA compliance where the requirements imposed upon the agency by another federal statute constitute the "functional equivalence" to the environmental considerations imposed by NEPA. *Western Nebraska Resources Council v. Environmental Protection Agency*, 943 F.2d 867, 871 (8th Cir. 1991) (EPA not required to comply with formal requirements of NEPA where environmental protection functions met under other organic legislation). One rationale for exempting agencies from NEPA obligations is that the more specific statute would receive precedence over a general statute, such as NEPA. In *State of Alabama v. Environmental Protection Agency*, 911 F.2d 499, 505 (11th Cir. 1990), for example, the court held that the EPA did not have to prepare an EIS regarding the issuance of a permit to a hazardous waste management facility where the act conflicted with RCRA. The court reasoned that since RCRA's substantive and procedural requirements mandated a comprehensive evaluation of environmental issues regarding the permit process, it amounted to the functional equivalent to NEPA. The court observed that the principal aims of NEPA — considering environmental factors before acting — were more than accomplished through RCRA's scheme as well.

Some courts have recognized that compliance with NEPA could actually undermine the balance of interests and objectives established in another federal environmental statute's regulatory scheme. *See Merrell v. Thomas*, 807 F.2d 776, 779 (9th Cir. 1986) (application of NEPA to pesticide registration process in FIFRA would unnecessarily increase the regulatory burden on the EPA, would create litigation opportunities, and "would sabotage the delicate machinery that Congress designed" with respect to regulation of pesticides).

9. *Remedies.* Courts have routinely rejected the view that any NEPA violation *per se* constitutes irreparable harm or even that irreparable harm should be *presumed* for statutory noncompliance requiring issuance of an injunction. On the other hand, the Supreme Court in *Amoco Prod. Co. v. Village of Gambell*, 480 U.S. 531, 545 (1987) made the following observations: "Environmental injury, by its nature, can seldom be adequately remedied by money damages and is often permanent or at least of long duration, i.e., irreparable. If such injury is sufficiently likely, therefore, the balance of harms will usually favor the issuance of an injunction to protect the environment." Although the Court was applying the Alaska National Interest Lands Conservation Act, not NEPA, its analysis reflects an appreciation for the view that environmental resources deserve a high degree of protection, including through the equitable powers of courts. This determination results from two principal factors regarding natural resources — the difficulties in measuring or quantifying such harms and that certain resources, once injured, cannot necessarily be replaced or restored. *See Save Our Ecosystems v. Clark*, 747 F.2d 1240, 1250 (9th Cir. 1984) (only in "rare circumstances" should an injunction not issue when an agency fails to comply with substantial procedural duties under NEPA); *Conner v. Burford*, 848 F.2d 1441 (9th Cir. 1988) (agency oil and gas leasing on national forest lands without preparing EIS violated NEPA and constituted an irreversible and irretrievable commitment of resources which would have a significant impact on the environment absent issuance of an injunction); *Sierra Club v. United States Forest Serv.*, 843 F.2d 1190, 1195 (9th Cir. 1988) (ongoing logging operations without the benefit of an EIS with respect to certain timber sales necessitated injunctive relief to prevent further irreparable harm to the environment); *Save the Yaak Comm. v. Block*, 840 F.2d 714, 722 (9th Cir. 1988).

Although the procedural requirements of the statute must be followed rigorously, and increased costs or hardships attendant upon delays will not alone justify noncompliance, the final decision regarding entitlement to equitable relief remains with the court's discretion. Thus, establishing a statutory violation, standing alone, will not mandate injunctive relief. Instead, the court will balance the equities and interests at stake and consider the public interest implicated. *Town of Huntington v. Marsh*, 884 F.2d 648, 653 (2d Cir. 1989).

Courts also have considerable latitude in shaping an injunction to fit the situation and equities of the parties. *See City of Teanakee Springs v. Clough*, 915 F.2d 1308 (9th Cir. 1990) (court entered narrowly tailored preliminary injunction permitting certain continued logging operations but halting others upon finding NEPA violation); *Sierra Club v. Hodel*, 848 F.2d 1068, 1097 (10th Cir. 1988) (construction was still permitted in nonaffected areas but was halted in areas where the costs to comply were minimal because it would have been interrupted during the hot, dry summer period).

10. In *Northern Cheyenne Tribe v. Hodel*, 851 F.2d 1152 (9th Cir. 1988) the plaintiff Tribe sought to enjoin the Secretary of the Interior from proceeding with coal leases on large tracts of land bordering their reservation in Montana. The Tribe contended that the leases should be voided for noncompliance with NEPA because the improper government action would, if unabated, develop its own self-effectuating momentum and rationalization through the government bureaucracy. The court acknowledged that bureaucratic momentum was a "real danger" but determined that suspension of the leases provided sufficient protection. The court stated that its order assumed that the Secretary would comply with the law, and was directed not to consider prior investments by lessees when reconsidering the lease sale.

In contrast, in *Sierra Club v. Marsh*, 872 F.2d 497 (1st Cir. 1989) the plaintiff sought declaratory and injunctive relief alleging that the defendants had violated NEPA by failing to adequately consider the detrimental environmental effects of a proposed development of a marine dry cargo terminal. The court reversed the lower court's decision not to grant a preliminary injunction and, in remanding, observed:

> [To] set aside the agency's action at a later date will not necessarily undo the harm. The agency as well as private parties may well have become committed to the previously chosen course of action, and new information — a new EIS — may bring about a new decision, but it is that much less likely to bring about a different one. It is far easier to influence an initial decision than to change a mind already made up.
>
> The way that harm arises may well have to do with the psychology of decisionmakers, and perhaps a more deeply rooted human psychological instinct not to tear down projects once they are built.... The difficulty of stopping a bureaucratic steamroller, once started, still seems to us ... a perfectly proper factor for a court to take into account in that risk on a motion for a preliminary injunction.

In a similar vein see *Massachusetts v. Watt*, 716 F.2d 946, 952 (1st Cir. 1983) (each government decision "represents a link in a chain of bureaucratic commitment that will become progressively harder to undo the longer it continues").

GREENPEACE ACTION v. FRANKLIN
14 F.3d 1324 (9th Cir. 1992)

HALL, CIRCUIT JUDGE:

... This case arose out of concern over the fate of the Steller sea lion, which inhabits the waters of the northern Pacific Ocean. Between 1960 and 1989, the Steller sea lion's Alaskan population suffered a precipitous decline, resulting in its classification in 1990 as a "threatened species" under the ESA. Though the Steller sea lion's decline has abated over the last three years, it has not stopped. The harvesting of pollock, a groundfish that comprises about half of the Steller sea lion's diet, has been cited as a likely factor in the Steller sea lion's decline.

Greenpeace contends that studies - including the [National Marine Fisheries] Service's own data - demonstrate that pollock fishing is the "leading factor" in the sea lion's decline. Greenpeace emphasizes that the primary danger is not the depletion of the overall biomass of pollock in the Gulf, but rather localized depletion; the Steller sea lion's proximity to its food source is crucial, and fisheries and sea lions often compete for the same stock of pollock. The Secretary's [of Commerce] final rule listing the Steller sea lion as a threatened species takes a less definitive position on the effects of pollock fishing....

Pursuant to section 302(h)(1) of the Fisheries Conservation Management Act ("Magnuson Act"), 16 U.S.C. § 1852(h)(1), the North Pacific Fishery Management Council ("the Council") issued its Fishery Management Plan ("the Plan") and an environmental impact statement (EIS) for the Gulf of Alaska Groundfish Fishery in 1978. An amendment to the Plan established a procedure for setting annual harvest levels for various species. Every September the Council makes public a preliminary Stock Assessment and Fishery Evaluation Report, as well as preliminary specifications for the acceptable biological catch (ABC) and the total allowable catch (TAC). The ABC is a measure of the size of the catch that the ecosystem can sustain. The TAC is the total tonnage of fish that fishermen may retain in a particular year. Preliminary TACs are replaced by final TACs when they are approved by the Secretary.

In September 1990, the Council made its preliminary recommendations for 1991. It recommended a pollock TAC of 73,400 metric tons (mt), the same as the 1990 level. In December 1990, the Council's assessment of the 1991 fishing stock was released, and based on that report, the Council revised its proposed TAC to 130,000 mt, a 41 percent increase over the 1990 level. Greenpeace sent a letter to the Secretary objecting to the proposed TAC, alleging that the 41 percent increase over the 1990 level would violate ESA. Without the preparation of an EIS, Greenpeace alleged, implementing the increase would also violate NEPA. The letter charged that the Council had not adequately considered the effect of its plan on the Steller sea lion and recommended that the 1991 TAC remain at the 1990 level....

[The Service entered into consultation with the Secretary pursuant to the Endangered Species Act, collected and analyzed new data, and issued a biological opinion recommending a TAC which allocated temporally and geographically to prevent local depletions of pollock.] It also recommended the implementation of a ten nautical mile (nm) no-trawl zone around the Steller sea lion rookeries. The opinion concluded that if implemented under the proposed conditions, the 1991 TAC was not likely to jeopardize the Steller sea lion. It stated that the effects of pollock harvesting on the Steller sea lion's ability to obtain food were uncertain, but that the proposed TAC left available a stock of pollock sufficient both to reproduce and to meet the Steller sea lion's annual food needs. It also determined that various measures it proposed were adequate to prevent temporary local depletions that may affect Steller sea lion feeding success. In June, the Service produced an environmental assessment, pursuant to 40 C.F.R. § 1501.4(a)-(c) (1991), analyzing the impact of the TAC on the environment and concluding that an EIS was unnecessary....

NEPA Violations

The district court upheld the Service's decision not to prepare an EIS for the fourth quarter fishery, finding that the record did not support the need for such action. It found that although commercial fishing may have adversely affected the Steller sea lion in the past, the dangers posed by fishing had been diminished in the fourth quarter by the implementation of the mitigation measures. The court also found there to be no significant controversy regarding the effects of the fourth quarter fishery that would warrant an impact statement. Finally, the court found that the Secretary adequately addressed the effects of the 1991 TAC on the Steller sea lion and other species, and adequately explained how the mitigation measures would protect the sea lion.

B.

First, Greenpeace argues that the Service has admitted pollock fishing may have significant adverse effects on the Steller sea lion. An agency must prepare an EIS if "substantial questions are raised as to whether a project ... may cause significant degradation of some human environmental factor." [Citation] "The plaintiff need not show that significant effects will in fact occur, but if the plaintiff raises substantial questions whether a project may have a significant effect, an EIS must be prepared." [Citation]....

Despite its uncertainty, the Service operated from the assumption that localized depletions might be having an adverse impact on the Steller sea lion, and concluded it was best to take precautions. It therefore recommended that the fourth quarter fishery be subject to the management measures described in the June biological opinion and environmental assessment. Although the effectiveness of these measures was unknown, the Service concluded that if the measures were implemented, opening the fourth quarter fishery under the 1991 TAC would not pose a great enough threat to the Steller sea lion to warrant an impact statement. The issue, then, is not whether the uncertainty surrounding the effect of pollock depletions on the Steller sea lion mandated the preparation of an EIS. It is whether, assuming that pollock depletion has had an adverse impact, the 1991 TAC in combination with the mitigation measures formed such an adequate buffer against that depletion that any possible depletion would be too minor to warrant an impact statement.

Greenpeace presented to the district court affidavits raising questions about the Service's analyses and conclusions regarding the impact of the 1991 TAC and the effectiveness of the management measures. These affidavits do not themselves demonstrate that the fourth quarter fishery, as implemented under the Secretary's management measures, posed a danger to the Steller sea lion. Rather, they criticize the Service for failing to assess the effects of the TAC on the availability (as opposed to abundance) of pollock or to refute the evidence of a causal connection between pollock fishing and the decline of the Steller sea lion. They also question the Service's methodology, which they claim ignored hydroacoustic survey estimates measuring the biomass of pollock, and instead employed less reliable methods for estimating biomass.

The Service contends that its decisions were based on a review of adequate scientific data and that the criticisms offered by Greenpeace's affiants merely represent a difference of scientific opinion. We concur in the Service's assessment of Greenpeace's complaints. The Service's conclusions are clearly based on substantial - though not dispositive - scientific data, and not on mere speculation. Moreover, the June 5, 1991 biological opinion reveals that the Service did indeed consider the hydroacoustic survey estimates.

In *Friends of Endangered Species, Inc. v. Jantzen*, 760 F.2d 976 (9th Cir. 1985), we upheld a decision by the Fish and Wildlife Service not to prepare an impact statement in connection with its issuance of a permit allowing the taking of Mission Blue butterflies. In response to Friends' argument that the agency had based its decision on faulty data, we held that "NEPA does not require that we decide whether an [environmental assessment] is based on the best scientific methodology available, nor does NEPA require us to resolve disagreements among various scientists as to methodology." *Id.* at 986.

While Greenpeace cites several instances in which this Circuit has set aside an agency decision not to prepare an EIS, only in *Wild Sheep* [*Foundation for North American Wild Sheep v. USDA*, 681 F.2d 1172, 1177-78 (9th Cir. 1982)] did the court mandate reconsideration after the agency had prepared an environmental assessment. In *Wild Sheep*, the Forest Service's failure to address "certain crucial factors, consideration of which was essential to a truly informed decision whether or not to prepare an EIS," rendered its conclusion that no statement was necessary unreasonable. Unlike *Wild Sheep*, the record in this case reveals no complete failure to consider crucial factors. Contrary to Greenpeace's assertions, its affidavits do not set forth facts demonstrating that the fishery harvest specifications and mitigation measures may have "disastrous effects" on the Steller sea lion. They demonstrate only that there is uncertainty as to how pollack fishing affects the sea lion, which is undisputed, and that the Service did not prove harm to the sea lion was impossible. To set aside the Service's determination in this case would require us to decide that the views of Greenpeace's experts have more merit than those of the Service's experts, a position we are unqualified to take.

C.

Next Greenpeace argues that substantial public controversy over the potential adverse affects of pollock fishing mandate preparation of an EIS. The existence of a public controversy over the effect of an agency action is one factor in determining whether the agency should prepare such a statement. *See* 40 C.F.R. § 1508.27(b)(4) (1991). A federal action is controversial if "'a substantial dispute exists as to [its] size, nature, or effect.'"

Greenpeace argues that the affidavits of scientists it presented to the district court demonstrate "widespread uncertainty and dispute throughout the scientific community concerning the environmental significance of pollock fishing" in the Gulf of Alaska. We agree with the district court that Greenpeace may not establish a scientific controversy post hoc, through the affidavits of its own scientists and the experts it has hired, when at the time of the Service's action, there existed no substantial dispute that should have alerted the Service to the concerns that Greenpeace now raises.

In *Wild Sheep*, we found a substantial dispute where the agency "received numerous responses from conservationists, biologists, and other knowledgable individuals, all highly critical of the [environmental assessment] and all disputing [its] conclusion...." But in *Jantzen*, we recognized that where "virtual agreement exists among local, state, and federal government officials, private parties, and local environmentalists," the criticisms of the plaintiff and its experts are not sufficient to demonstrate the existence of a public controversy.

Public comment was solicited in September, November, and December 1990, when the proposed 1991 TAC was first noticed and recommended for approval by the Secretary, and in June 1991, when the final 1991 TAC, as modified, was approved and mitigating management measures were implemented. Neither occasioned an outpouring of public protest such as that involved in Wild Sheep. Greenpeace did protest, supplying a report by the Aquatic Resources Conservation Group.... Furthermore, the Service was able to develop a consensus among parties who had objected to the original proposed TAC of 130,000 mt that the revised TAC and emergency measures were adequate to preserve the Steller sea lion's food supply. The history of the implementation of the fourth quarter fishing measures is not one of substantial public controversy. Nor is there any merit to the contention that an EIS must be prepared whenever qualified experts disagree, as Greenpeace contends. If this type of disagreement were all that was necessary to mandate an EIS, the environmental assessment process would be meaningless. An agency's careful evaluation of the impact of its proposed action, its collection and review of evidence, and its reasoned conclusions as to what the date reveals would be for naught if by simply filing suit and supplying an affidavit by a hired expert, predicated upon the same facts relied upon by the agency but reaching a different conclusion, a litigant could create a controversy necessitating an EIS.

D.

The district court concluded that whatever harmful impact pollock fishing might have had on the Steller's food supply in the past, the risk of further harm had been adequately diminished by the emergency management measures. Greenpeace argues that the Service's implementation of those measures does not relieve it of the obligation to prepare an EIS. It maintains that because the Service did not know whether these measures would be effective, implementing them could not absolve the Service of its obligation to prepare a statement. Greenpeace's affiants question the effectiveness of these measures, and they contend that the Service has not presented any data or analyses to suggest that these measures will do any good.

The Service does concede that the effectiveness of the mitigation measures is uncertain, but contends that this uncertainty is largely because the cause of the Steller sea lion's decline is itself uncertain. In any case, "so long as significant measures are undertaken to 'mitigate the project's effects,' they need not completely compensate for adverse environmental impacts."...

E.

Finally, Greenpeace argues that even if the Service adequately studied the effects of its actions on the Steller sea lion, it failed to take a "hard look" at the impact of pollock fishing on harbor seals and other species in the Gulf of Alaska. This charge has some merit. The September environmental assessment states: "[The Service] is proceeding under the assumption that due to the similarity in timing and locations of harbor seal and Steller sea lion declines the declines of the two species may have the same causative agent. Thus the discussion that follows may apply equally well to both species." One of Greenpeace's affiants, Anne Hoover-Miller, states that there is evidence suggesting that commercial fishing has caused a decline in the population of the harbor seal and that the Service's report is entirely inadequate to evaluate the effects of its measures on that animal. Indeed, she suggests, the 10 nm no-trawl zone around the sea lion rookeries may divert pollock fishing towards the feeding areas of the harbor seals.

There is no doubt the Service's analysis of the effects of pollock fishing on the harbor seal is far less rigorous than the study of its effects on the Steller sea lion. But it is equally clear that there is little data available to analyze these effects. Hoover-Miller's affidavit discussing the effects is itself highly speculative, and in no way undermines the Service's assumption that its conclusions about the Steller sea lion could be applied to the harbor seal. At the same time, the environmental assessment indicated that the Service had begun a comprehensive assessment of the harbor seals to determine the status of the population. Given the fact that the harbor seal was not a threatened or endangered species, the lack of available data on the harbor seal, and the apparent reasonableness of the Service's assumption that its analyses of the Steller sea lion could be applied to the harbor seal, we cannot regard its failure to take a "harder look" at the effects of the action on the harbor seal to be arbitrary and capricious.

F.

In conclusion, we disagree with Greenpeace that the Service's "Finding of No Significant Impact" was based on speculation and not supported by adequate evidence. The Service took a careful look at the effects of the 1991 fishery on the Steller sea lion. Although Greenpeace has demonstrated that some scientists dispute the Service's analyses and conclusions, such a showing is not a sufficient basis for us to conclude that the Service's action was arbitrary or capricious. If it were, agencies could only act upon achieving a degree of certainty that is ultimately illusory.

NOTES AND QUESTIONS

1. *Controversy.* In the principal case, one of the key factors affecting whether or not the federal action was significant under NEPA was the extent to which the effects of the proposal were deemed "highly controversial." *See* 40 C.F.R.

§ 1508.27(b)(4). Courts have interpreted this factor by requiring a "robust dissent," a "substantial dispute," or controversy of an "extraordinary nature." *Foundation for Global Sustainability v. McConnell*, 829 F. Supp. 147, 153 (W.D.N.C. 1993); *also see Town of Orangetown v. Gorsuch*, 718 F.2d 29, 39 (2d Cir. 1983) (local opposition to expansion of sewage treatment plant not synonymous with high degree of controversy).

2. Although NEPA contemplates public participation in its process, public opposition to a government proposal does not necessarily influence the outcome. As stated by one court, if mere opposition tipped the balance toward mandating preparation of an EIS, "That would be the environmental counterpart to the 'heckler's veto' of the First Amendment law." *River Road Alliance, Inc. v. Army Corps of Eng'rs*, 764 F.2d 445, 451 (7th Cir. 1985). *See* Tabb, *The Role of Controversy in NEPA: Reconciling Public Veto with Public Participation in Environmental Decisionmaking*, 21 WM. & MARY ENVTL. L. REV. 175 (1997).

3. Should courts determine whether a proposal is highly controversial based on the number of persons opposed? If so, how should such lines be drawn? *See Lockhart v. Kenops*, 927 F.2d 1028 (8th Cir. 1991) (eight letters protesting land exchange agreement not considered highly controversial); *West Houston Air Comm. v. FAA*, 784 F.2d 702, 705 (5th Cir. 1986) (120 letters opposing airport expansion not considered so substantial to trigger agency's duty to prepare environmental review). To what extent should courts consider the self-interest in halting a project on the persons raising opposition? Recall that, for purposes of standing, the movant was required to show that the injury fit within the zone of interests which the statute was designed to protect or effectuate. Would a parallel inquiry be relevant in this context or do the statutory goals of NEPA actually promote consideration of such concerns?

4. *Scientific Debate.* The NEPA process may be influenced by controversy within the scientific community, such as disputes over methodology, reliability of information, or environmental impacts of a proposed project. Courts will be the most deferential to agency decisions involving matters on the "frontiers of science," provided that it has a reasoned basis of support. *See Baltimore Gas & Elec. Co. v. Natural Resource Defense Council, Inc.*, 462 U.S. 87, 103 (1983).

In *Jones v. Gordon*, 792 F.2d 821 (9th Cir. 1986) the National Marine Fisheries Service issued a permit to Sea World to take 100 Orca whales, including 10 for permanent captivity. The whales were to undergo numerous tests, including liver biopsies, hearing and respiratory tests, tooth extractions, and blood tests. Sea World also proposed to tag, mark, and attach radio transmitters to the temporarily held whales. The court found that the agency acted unreasonably by not preparing an EA or an EIS. Although issuance of permits for scientific purposes was categorically excluded from NEPA by another federal act, the court found that the public controversy regarding the potential detrimental effects on the whales created extraordinary circumstances warranting an exception. *See also Progressive Animal Welfare Soc'y v. Department of Navy*, 725 F. Supp. 475, 479 (W.D. Wash. 1989) (Navy's controversial decision to take dolphins from the wild for military purposes constituted a major federal action with an effect on the environment); *Foundation for North American Wild Sheep v. United States Department of Agriculture*, 681 F.2d 1172 (9th cir. 1982) (widespread criticism by scientific community of agency decision that proposed project would not have detrimental impact on habitat of Bighorn sheep justified preparation of EIS).

5. The degree of controversy surrounding a proposed project does not necessarily correspond to the potential adverse environmental impacts. One potential drawback to considering the controversial side of a proposal is that interest groups opposed to the government's plans for reasons entirely apart from the merits could seek to obstruct progress by galvanizing public opposition. *See Rucker v. Willis*, 484 F.2d 158, 162 (4th Cir. 1973) (observed danger in letting critics of a project force full-scale review under NEPA in every instance simply by voicing strong complaint).

MARSH v. OREGON NATURAL RESOURCES COUNCIL

490 U.S. 360 (1989)

JUSTICE STEVENS delivered the opinion of the Court.

This case ... arises out of a controversial decision to construct a dam at Elk Creek in the Rogue River Basin in southwest Oregon.... [I]t presents the question whether information developed after the completion of the [Environmental Impact Statement] EIS requires that a supplemental EIS be prepared before construction of the dam may continue.

In the 1930's in response to recurring floods in the Rogue River Basin, federal and state agencies began planning a major project to control the water supply in the basin. In 1961 a multi-agency study recommended the construction of three large dams: the Lost Creek Dam on the Rogue River, the Applegate Dam on the Applegate River, and the Elk Creek Dam on the Elk Creek near its confluence with the Rogue River. The following year, Congress authorized the Army Corps of Engineers (the Corps) to construct the project in accordance with the recommendations of the 1961 study. The Lost Creek Dam was completed in 1977 and the Applegate Dam was completed in 1981.

....

In 1971, the Corps completed its EIS for the Elk Creek portion of the three-dam project and began development by acquiring 26,000 acres of land and relocating residents, a county road, and utilities.... [T]he Corps completed and released its Final Environmental Impact Statement, Supplement No. 1 [FEISS], in December 1980.

Because the Rogue River is one of the Nation's premier fishing grounds, the FEISS paid special heed to the effects the dam might have on water quality, fish production, and angling.... [T]he FEISS predicted that changes in the "turbidity regime" would not have any major effect on fish production, but that the combined effect of the Lost Creek and Elk Creek Dams on the turbidity of the Rogue River might, on occasion, impair fishing.

Other adverse effects described by the FEISS include the displacement of wildlife population — including 100 black-tailed deer and 17 elk — and the loss of forest land and vegetation resulting from the inundation of 1,290 acres of land with the creation of the artificial lake. Most significantly, it is perfectly clear that the dam itself would interfere with the migration and spawning of a large number of anadromous fish, but this effect has been mitigated by the construction of a new hatchery. Finally, the FEISS found that no endangered or threatened species would be affected by the project.

On February 19, 1982, after reviewing the FEISS, the Corps' Division Engineer made a formal decision to proceed with construction of the Elk Creek Dam, "subject to the approval of funds by the United States Congress."... The dam is now about one-third completed and the creek has been rechanneled through the dam.

[In 1985, several groups sought to enjoin construction of the Elk Creek Dam. The groups alleged that the Corps violated NEPA in several respects, including that the agency had failed to prepare a second supplemental EIS to review information developed after 1980. The District Judge denied relief on each of the NEPA claims but the Court of Appeals reversed.]

....

The new information relied upon by respondents is found in two documents. The first, an internal memorandum prepared by two Oregon Department of Fish and Wildlife (ODFW) biologists based upon a draft ODFW study, suggested that the dam will adversely affect downstream fishing, and the second, a soil survey prepared by the United States Soil Conservation Service (SCS), contained information that might be taken to indicate greater downstream turbidity than did the FEISS. As to both documents, the District Judge concluded that the Corps acted reasonably in relying on the opinions of independent and Corps experts discounting the significance of the new information....

The subject of post-decision supplemental environmental impact statements is not expressly addressed in NEPA. Preparation of such statements, however, is at times necessary to satisfy the Act's "action-forcing" purpose. NEPA does not work by mandating that agencies achieve particular substantive environmental results. Rather, NEPA promotes its sweeping commitment to "prevent or eliminate damage to the environment and biosphere" by focusing government and public attention on the environmental effects of proposed agency action. By so focusing agency attention, NEPA ensures that the agency will not act on incomplete information, only to regret its decision after it is too late to correct. Similarly, the broad dissemination of information mandated by NEPA permits the public and other government agencies to react to the effects of a proposed action at a meaningful time. It would be incongruous with this approach to environmental protection, and with the Act's manifest concern with preventing uninformed action, for the blinders to adverse environmental effects, once unequivocally removed, to be restored prior to the completion of agency action simply because the relevant proposal has received initial approval. As we explained in *TVA v. Hill*, 437 U.S. 153, 188, n. 34 (1978), although "it would make sense to hold NEPA inapplicable at some point in the life of a project, because the agency would no longer have a meaningful opportunity to *weigh* the benefits of the project versus the detrimental effects on the environment," up to that point, "NEPA cases have generally required agencies to file environmental impact statements when the remaining governmental action would be environmentally 'significant.'"

This reading of the statute is supported by Council on Environmental Quality (CEQ) and Corps regulations, both of which make plain that at times supplementation is required. The CEQ regulations, which we have held are entitled to substantial deference, [citations] impose a duty on all federal agencies to prepare supplements to either draft or final EISs if there "are significant new circumstances or information relevant to environmental concerns and bearing on the proposed action or its impacts."[16]

Similarly, the Corps' own NEPA implementing regulations require the preparation of a supplemental EIS if "new significant impact information, criteria or circumstances relevant to environmental considerations impact on the recommended plan or proposed action."[17]

The parties are in essential agreement concerning the standard that governs an agency's decision whether to prepare a supplemental EIS. They agree that an agency should apply a "rule of reason," and the cases they cite in support of this standard explicate this rule in the same basic terms. These cases make clear that an agency need not supplement an EIS every time new information comes to light after the EIS is finalized. To require otherwise would render agency decision-

---

[16]The CEQ regulation provides, in part:

"Agencies:

"(1) Shall prepare supplements to either draft or final environmental impact statements if:

"(i) The agency makes substantial changes in the proposed action that are relevant to environmental concerns; or

"(ii) There are significant new circumstances or information relevant to environmental concerns and bearing on the proposed action or its impacts.

"(2) May also prepare supplements when the agency determines that the purposes of the Act will be furthered by doing so." 40 CFR § 1502.9(c) (1987).

[17]The Corps' regulations provide in relevant part:

"*Supplements.* A Supplement to the draft or final EIS on file will be prepared whenever significant impacts resulting from changes in the proposed plan or new significant impact information, criteria or circumstances relevant to environmental considerations impact on the recommended plan or proposed action as discussed in 40 CFR 1502.9(c). A supplement to a draft EIS will be prepared, filed and circulated in the same manner as a draft EIS.... A supplement to a final EIS will be prepared and filed first as a *draft* supplement and then as a *final* supplement...." 33 CFR § 230.11(b) (1987).

making intractable, always awaiting updated information only to find the new information outdated by the time a decision is made. On the other hand, and as the Government concedes, NEPA does require that agencies take a "hard look" at the environmental effects of their planned action, even after a proposal has received initial approval. Application of the "rule of reason" thus turns on the value of the new information to the still pending decisionmaking process. In this respect the decision whether to prepare a supplemental EIS is similar to the decision whether to prepare an EIS in the first instance: If there remains "major Federal actio[n]" to occur, and if the new information is sufficient to show that the remaining action will "affec[t] the quality of the human environment" in a significant manner or to a significant extent not already considered, a supplemental EIS must be prepared.

The parties disagree, however, on the standard that should be applied by a court that is asked to review the agency's decision. The Government argues that the reviewing court need only decide whether the agency decision was "arbitrary and capricious," whereas respondents argue that the reviewing court must make its own determination of reasonableness to ascertain whether the agency action complied with the law. In determining the proper standard of review, we look to § 10(e) of the Administrative Procedure Act (APA), 5 U.S.C. § 706, which empowers federal courts to "hold unlawful and set aside agency action, findings, and conclusions" if they fail to conform with any of six specified standards. We conclude that review of the narrow question before us of whether the Corps' determination that the FEISS need not be supplemented should be set aside is controlled by the "arbitrary and capricious" standard of § 706(2)(A).

Respondents contend that the determination of whether the new information suffices to establish a "significant" effect is either a question of law or, at a minimum, a question of ultimate fact and, as such, "deserves no deference" on review. Apparently, respondents maintain that the question for review centers on the legal meaning of the term "significant" or, in the alternative, the predominantly legal question of whether established and uncontested historical facts presented by the administrative record satisfy this standard. Characterizing the dispute in this manner, they posit that strict review is appropriate under the "in accordance with law" clause of § 706(2)(A) or the "without observance of procedure required by law" provision of § 706(2)(D). We disagree.

The question presented for review in this case is a classic example of a factual dispute the resolution of which implicates substantial agency expertise. Respondents' claim that the Corps' decision not to file a second supplemental EIS should be set aside primarily rests on the contentions that the new information undermines conclusions contained in the FEISS, that the conclusions contained in the ODFW memorandum and the SCS survey are accurate, and that the Corps' expert review of the new information was incomplete, inconclusive, or inaccurate. The dispute thus does not turn on the meaning of the term "significant" or on an application of this legal standard to settled facts. Rather, resolution of this dispute involves primarily issues of fact. Because analysis of the relevant documents "requires a high level of technical expertise," we must defer to "the informed discretion of the responsible federal agencies." [Citations.] Under these circumstance, we cannot accept respondents' supposition that review is of a legal question and that the Corps' decision "deserves no deference." Accordingly, as long as the Corps' decision not to supplement the FEISS was not "arbitrary or capricious," it should not be set aside.[23]

As we observed in *Citizens to Preserve Overton Park, Inc. v. Volpe*, 401 U.S. 402, 416 (1971), in making the factual inquiry concerning whether an agency decision was "arbitrary or capricious," the reviewing court "must consider whether the decision was based on a consideration of the relevant factors and whether there has been a clear error of judgment." This inquiry must "be searching and careful," but "the ultimate standard of review is a narrow one." When specialists express conflicting views, an agency must have discretion to rely on the reasonable opinions of its own qualified experts even if, as an original matter, a court might find contrary views more persuasive. On the other hand, in the context of reviewing a decision not to supplement an EIS, courts should not automatically defer to the agency's express reliance on an interest in finality without carefully reviewing the record and satisfying themselves that the agency has made a reasoned decision based on its evaluation of the significance — or lack of significance — of the new information. A contrary approach would not simply render judicial review generally meaningless, but would be contrary to the demand that the courts ensure that agency decisions are founded on a reasoned evaluation "of the relevant factors."

Respondents' argument that significant new information required the preparation of a second supplemental EIS rests on two written documents. The first of the documents is the so-called "Cramer Memorandum," an intra-office memorandum prepared on February 21, 1985 by two scientists employed by ODFW. The Cramer Memorandum, in turn, relied on a draft ODFW study describing the effects of the Lost Creek Dam on fish production. The second

---

[23]Respondents note that several Courts of Appeals, including the Court of Appeals for the Ninth Circuit as articulated in this and other cases, have adopted a "reasonableness" standard of review, [citations], and argue that we should not upset this well-settled doctrine. This standard, however, has not been adopted by all of the Circuits. *See, e.g., Wisconsin v. Weinberger*, 745 F.2d 412, 417 (CA7 1984) (adopting "arbitrary and capricious" standard). Moreover, as some of these courts have recognized, the difference between the "arbitrary and capricious" and "reasonableness" standards is not of great pragmatic consequence. *See Manasota-88, Inc. v. Thomas*, 799 F.2d 687, 692, n. 8 (CA11 1986) ("As a practical matter, ... the differences between the 'reasonableness' and 'arbitrary and capricious' standards of review are often difficult to discern"); *River Road Alliance, Inc. v. Corps of Engineers of United States Army*, 764 F.2d 445, 449 (CA7 1985) ("we are not sure how much if any practical difference there is between 'abuse of discretion' and 'unreasonable'"), *cert. denied*, 475 U.S. 1055, 106 S. Ct. 1283, 89 L. Ed. 2d 590 (1986). Accordingly, our decision today will not require a substantial reworking of long-established NEPA law.

document is actually a series of maps prepared in 1982 by SCS to illustrate the composition of soil near the Elk Creek shoreline....

The significance of the Cramer Memorandum and the SCS survey is subject to some doubt. Before respondents commenced this litigation in October 1985, no one had suggested that either document constituted the kind of new information that made it necessary or appropriate to supplement the FEISS. Indeed, the record indicates that the Corps was not provided with a copy of the Cramer Memorandum until after the lawsuit was filed. Since the probative value of that document depends largely on the expert qualification of its authors, the fact that they did not see fit to promptly apprise the Corps of their concern — or to persuade ODFW to do so — tends to discount the significance of those concerns....

The Court of Appeals attached special significance to two concerns discussed in the Cramer Memorandum: the danger that an increase in water temperature downstream during fall and early winter will cause an early emergence and thus reduce survival of spring chinook fry and the danger that the dam will cause high fish mortality from an epizootic disease. Both concerns were based partly on fact and partly on speculation.

With respect to the first, the Cramer Memorandum reported that the authors of the draft ODFW study had found that warming of the Rogue River caused by the Lost Creek Dam had reduced the survival of spring chinook fry; however, the extent of that reduction was not stated, nor did the memorandum estimate the extent of warming to be expected due to closure of the Elk Creek Dam ....

The Corp's response to this concern in its Supplemental Information Report ("SIR") acknowledged that the "biological reasoning is sound and has been recognized for some time," but then explained why the concern was exaggerated. The SIR stressed that because the model employed by ODFW had not been validated, its predictive capability was uncertain.... Finally, the SIR observed that the Cramer Memorandum failed to take into account the dam's beneficial effects, including its ability to reduce peak downstream flow during periods of egg incubation and fry rearing and its ability to reduce outflow temperature through use of the multiport structure....

With respect to the second concern emphasized by the Court of Appeals, the Cramer Memorandum reported the fact that "an unprecedented 76% of the fall chinook in 1979 and 32% in 1980 were estimated to have died before spawning" and then speculated that the Lost Creek Dam, which had been completed in 1977, was a contributing cause of this unusual mortality. The Corps responded to this by pointing out that the absence of similar epizootics after the closure of the Applegate Dam and the evidence of pre-spawning mortality in the Rogue River prior to the closing of the Lost Creek Dam were inconsistent with the hypothesis suggested in the Cramer Memorandum....

In thus concluding that the Cramer Memorandum did not present significant new information requiring supplementation of the FEISS, the Corps carefully scrutinized the proffered information....

There is little doubt that if all of the information contained in the Cramer Memorandum and SCS survey was both new and accurate, the Corps would have been required to prepare a second supplemental EIS. It is also clear that, regardless of its eventual assessment of the significance of this information, the Corps had a duty to take a hard look at the proffered evidence. However, having done so and having determined based on careful scientific analysis that the new information was of exaggerated importance, the Corps acted within the dictates of NEPA in concluding that supplementation was unnecessary. Even if another decisionmaker might have reached a contrary result, it was surely not "a clear error of judgment" for the Corps to have found that the new and accurate information contained in the documents was not significant and that the significant information was not new and accurate. As the SIR demonstrates, the Corps conducted a reasoned evaluation of the relevant information and reached a decision that, although perhaps disputable, was not "arbitrary of capricious."

The judgment of the Court of Appeals is accordingly reversed and the case is remanded for further proceedings consistent with this opinion.

It is so ordered.

NOTES AND QUESTIONS

1. *Supplemental Impact Statement.* As stated in *Marsh*, a post-decision supplemental impact statement may be justified where circumstances have changed or where the agency discovers new information pertaining to the project. In either event, two themes underlie the agency's decision regarding updating an EIS: the significance or value of the information and the extent to which decisions affecting the project may be altered as a result. These factors are conjunctive, not disjunctive. Even the discovery of important new information pertinent to the action will not necessarily require preparation of a supplemental impact statement, then, if the project is substantially completed. The overriding purpose of an EIS is to affect decisionmaking. The agency decisions regarding whether to prepare a supplemental statement is accorded considerable deference as a factual determination reviewable under the arbitrary and capricious standard. *See Churchwell v. Robertson*, 748 F. Supp. 768, 782 (D. Idaho 1990).

2. In *Cronin v. United States Dep't of Agri.*, 919 F.2d 439 (7th Cir. 1990) the court held that the Forest Service's decision to employ one method of logging timber in a national forest rather than another did not necessitate preparation of a supplemental impact statement where both methods had been previously considered and the *incremental* adverse effect was negative. The court made the following observation:

> As a general rule, once an environmental impact statement has been issued for a project, the project can be carried out without the agency's having to issue a new statement for every stage of the project. Otherwise, the project could never be completed. It would be the application of Zeno's Paradox

(how can one cross a finite interval in a finite amount of time, when any interval can be divided into an infinite number of segments each of which must be crossed in turn in order to traverse the entire interval?).

919 F.2d at 447.

In *Headwaters, Inc. v. Bureau of Land Mgt.*, 914 F.2d 1174 (9th Cir. 1990) the court held that an alleged sighting of a breeding pair of northern spotted owls in a timber sale area after issuance of a site-specific environmental assessment did not constitute significant new information requiring a supplemental EIS. The agency had previously recognized the possibility that the owls may habitat the affected area and had discussed in a regional EIS the potential impact of cutting on the owl habitat. Following its decision, the owl was designated as an endangered species. The court denied a petition for rehearing, holding that the changed status of the northern spotted owl by virtue of its designation as an endangered species after an environmental impact statement was prepared did not require preparation of a supplemental EIS. 940 F.2d 435, 436 (9th Cir. 1991). Do you agree with the court in light of *Marsh*?

ENVIRONMENTAL DEFENSE FUND, INC. v. MASSEY
986 F.2d 528 (D.C. Cir. 1993)

MIKVA, CHIEF JUDGE:

The Environmental Defense Fund ("EDF") appeals the district court's order dismissing its action seeking declaratory and injunctive relief under the National Environmental Policy Act ("NEPA"). EDF alleges that the National Science Foundation ("NSF") violated NEPA by failing to prepare an environmental impact statement ("EIS") in accordance with Section 102(2)(C) before going forward with plans to incinerate food wastes in Antarctica....

I.

As both parties readily acknowledge, Antarctica is not only a unique continent, but somewhat of an international anomaly. Antarctica is the only continent on earth which has never been, and is not now, subject to the sovereign rule of any nation. Since entry into force of the Antarctic Treaty in 1961, the United States and 39 other nations have agreed not to assert any territorial claims to the continent or to establish rights of sovereignty there. Hence, Antarctica is generally considered to be a "global common" and frequently analogized to outer space.[Citation]

Under the auspices of the United States Antarctica Program, NSF operates the McMurdo Station research facility in Antarctica. McMurdo Station is one of three year-round installations that the United States has established in Antarctica, and over which NSF exercises exclusive control. All of the installations serve as platforms or logistic centers for U.S. scientific research; McMurdo Station is the largest of the three, with more than 100 buildings and a summer population of approximately 1200.

Over the years, NSF has burned food wastes at McMurdo Station in an open landfill as a means of disposal. In early 1991, NSF decided to improve its environmental practices in Antarctica by halting its practice of burning food wastes in the open by October, 1991. After discovering asbestos in the landfill, however, NSF decided to cease open burning in the landfill even earlier, and to develop quickly an alternative plan for disposal of its food waste. NSF stored the waste at McMurdo Station from February, 1991 to July, 1991, but subsequently decided to resume incineration in an "interim incinerator" until a state-of-the-art incinerator could be delivered to McMurdo Station. EDF contends that the planned incineration may produce highly toxic pollutants which could be hazardous to the environment, and that NSF failed to consider fully the consequences of its decision to resume incineration as required by the decision-making process established by NEPA.

Section 102(2)(C) of NEPA requires "all federal agencies" to prepare an EIS in connection with any proposal for a "major action significantly affecting the quality of the human environment. " 42 U.S.C. § 4332(2)(C). The EIS requirement, along with the many other provisions in the statute, is designed to "promote efforts which will prevent or eliminate damage to the environment and biosphere." 42 U.S.C. § 4321. Following the passage of NEPA, NSF promulgated regulations applying the EIS requirement to its decisions regarding proposed actions in Antarctica. Since the issuance of Executive Order 12144, however, NSF has contended that proposed action affecting the environment in Antarctica is governed by the Executive Order, not NEPA. See Exec. Order 12114, 3 C.F.R. 356 (1980) [hereinafter cited as E.O. 12114].

Executive Order 12144 declares that federal agencies are required to prepare environmental analyses for "major Federal actions significantly affecting the environment of the global commons outside the jurisdiction of any nation (e.g., the oceans or Antarctica)." E.O. 12114 § 2-3a. According to the Executive Order, major federal actions significantly affecting the environment of foreign countries may also require environmental analyses under certain circumstances. *Id.* Although the procedural requirements imposed by the Executive Order are analogous to those under NEPA, the Executive Order does not provide a cause of action to a plaintiff seeking agency compliance with the EIS requirement. The Executive Order explicitly states that the requirements contained therein are "solely for the purpose of establishing internal procedures for Federal agencies ... and nothing in [the Order] shall be construed to create a cause of action." E.O. 12144 § 3-1. Thus, what is at stake in this litigation is whether a federal agency may decide to take actions significantly affecting the human environment in Antarctica without complying with NEPA and without being subject to judicial review.

II.

A. *The Presumption Against Extraterritoriality*

As the district court correctly noted, the Supreme Court recently reaffirmed the general presumption against the extraterritorial application of statutes in *Equal Employment Opportunity Commission v. Arabian American Oil Co.*, 113 L. Ed. 2d 274, 111 S. Ct. 1227 (1991) ("*Aramco*"). Extraterritoriality is essentially, and in common sense, a jurisdictional concept concerning the authority of a nation to adjudicate the rights of particular parties and to establish the norms of conduct applicable to events or persons outside its borders. More specifically, the extraterritoriality principle provides that "rules of the United States statutory law, whether prescribed by federal or state authority, apply only to conduct occurring within, or having effect within, the territory of the United States." [Citation] As stated by the Supreme Court in Aramco, the primary purpose of this presumption against extraterritoriality is "to protect against the unintended clashes between our laws and those of other nations which could result in international discord."

An early example of the application of the extraterritoriality principle is *American Banana Co. v. United States Fruit Co.*, 213 U.S. 347, 53 L. Ed. 826, 29 S. Ct. 511 (1909). In that case, the plaintiff alleged that the defendant, a U.S. corporation, had violated United States antitrust laws by inducing a foreign government to take actions within its own territory which were adverse to the plaintiff's business. The Supreme Court refused, in the absence of a clear statement of extraterritorial scope, to infer congressional intent to apply the federal statute to the conduct of a foreign government because enforcement would have interfered with the exercise of foreign sovereignty....

There are at least three general categories of cases for which the presumption against the extraterritorial application of statutes clearly does not apply. First, as made explicit in Aramco, the presumption will not apply where there is an "affirmative intention of the Congress clearly expressed" to extend the scope of the statute to conduct occurring within other sovereign nations.

Second, the presumption is generally not applied where the failure to extend the scope of the statute to a foreign setting will result in adverse effects within the United States. Two prime examples of this exception are the Sherman Anti-Trust Act, 15 U.S.C. §§ 1-7 (1976), and the Lanham Trade-mark Act, 15 U.S.C. § 1051 (1976), which have both been applied extraterritorially where the failure to extend the statute's reach would have negative economic consequences within the United States. [Citations]

Finally, the presumption against extraterritoriality is not applicable when the conduct regulated by the government occurs within the United States. By definition, an extraterritorial application of a statute involves the regulation of conduct beyond U.S. borders. Even where the significant effects of the regulated conduct are felt outside U.S. borders, the statute itself does not present a problem of extraterritoriality, so long as the conduct which Congress seeks to regulate occurs largely within the United States. [Citation]

Despite these well-established exceptions to the presumption against extraterritoriality, the district court below by-passed the threshold question of whether the application of NEPA to agency actions in Antarctica presents an extraterritoriality problem at all. In particular, the court failed to determine whether the statute seeks to regulate conduct in the United States or in another sovereign country. It also declined to consider whether NEPA would create a potential for "clashes between our laws and those of other nations" if it was applied to the decision-making of federal agencies regarding proposed actions in Antarctica. *Aramco*, 111 S. Ct. at 1230. After a thorough review of these relevant factors, we conclude that this case does not present an issue of extraterritoriality.

B. *Regulated Conduct Under NEPA*

NEPA is designed to control the decisionmaking process of U.S. federal agencies, not the substance of agency decisions. By enacting NEPA, Congress exercised its statutory authority to determine the factors an agency must consider when exercising its discretion, and created a process whereby American officials, while acting within the United States, can reach enlightened policy decisions by taking into account environmental effects. In our view, such regulation of U.S. federal agencies and their decisionmaking processes is a legitimate exercise of Congress' territoriality-based jurisdiction, and does not raise extraterritoriality concerns.

Section 102(2)(C) lies at the heart of NEPA and is often considered the "action-forcing" element of the statute. [Citations] This section requires "all agencies of the Federal Government" to prepare a detailed environmental impact statement for every "major Federal action[]" which has the potential to significantly affect the human environment. 42 U.S.C. § 4332(2)(C). Section 102(2)(C) binds only American officials and controls the very essence of the government function: decisionmaking. Because the decisionmaking processes of federal agencies take place almost exclusively in this country and involve the workings of the United States government, they are uniquely domestic.

NEPA, unlike many environmental statutes, does not dictate agency policy or determine the fate of contemplated action. NEPA simply mandates a particular process that must be followed by a federal agency before taking action significantly affecting the human environment. After weighing environmental considerations, an agency decisionmaker remains free to subordinate the environmental concerns revealed in the EIS to other policy concerns. As this Court observed almost two decades ago, the harm against which NEPA's impact statement requirement was directed was not solely or even primarily adverse consequences to the environment; such consequences may ensue despite the fullest compliance. Rather NEPA was intended to ensure that decisions about federal actions would be made only after responsible decisionmakers had fully adverted to the environmental consequences of the actions, and had decided that the public benefits flowing from the actions outweighed their environmental costs. [Citation]....

Moreover, NEPA would never require enforcement in a foreign forum or involve "choice of law" dilemmas. This factor alone is powerful evidence of the statute's domestic nature, and distinguishes NEPA from Title VII as well as the Federal Tort Claims Act — two statutes that have been limited in their effect by the presumption against extraterritoriality. [Citations]

In sum, since NEPA is designed to regulate conduct occurring within the territory of the United States, and imposes no substantive requirements which could be interpreted to govern conduct abroad, the presumption against extraterritoriality does not apply to this case.

C. *The Unique Status of Antarctica*

Antarctica's unique status in the international arena further supports our conclusion that this case does not implicate the presumption against extraterritoriality.... Thus, where the U.S. has some real measure of legislative control over the region at issue, the presumption against extraterritoriality is much weaker. [Citations] And where there is no potential for conflict "between our laws and those of other nations," the purpose behind the presumption is eviscerated, and the presumption against extraterritoriality applies with significantly less force.

... [I]t cannot be seriously suggested that the United States lacks some real measure of legislative control over Antarctica. The United States controls all air transportation to Antarctica and conducts all search and rescue operations there. Moreover, the United States has exclusive legislative control over McMurdo Station and the other research installations established there by the United States Antarctica Program. This legislative control, taken together with the status of Antarctica as a sovereignless continent, compels the conclusion that the presumption against extraterritoriality is particularly inappropriate under the circumstances presented in this case....

Foreign Policy Considerations

Although NSF concedes that NEPA only seeks to regulate the decisionmaking process of federal agencies, and that this case does not present a conflict between U.S. and foreign sovereign law, NSF still contends that the presumption against extraterritoriality controls this case. In particular, NSF argues that the EIS requirement will interfere with U.S. efforts to work cooperatively with other nations toward solutions to environmental problems in Antarctica. In NSF's view, joint research and cooperative environmental assessment would be "placed at risk of NEPA injunctions, making the U.S. a doubtful partner for future international cooperation in Antarctica."

NSF also argues that the Protocol on Environmental Protection to the Antarctic Treaty, which was adopted and opened for signature on October 4, 1991, would, if adopted by all the proposed signatories, conflict with the procedural requirements adopted by Congress for the decisionmaking of federal agencies under NEPA. According to NSF, since NEPA requires the preparation of an EIS for actions with potentially "significant" impacts, while the Protocol requires an environmental analysis even for actions with "minor or transitory" impacts on the Antarctic environment, the two regulatory schemes are incompatible and will result in international discord.

We find these arguments unpersuasive. First, it should be noted that the Protocol is not in effect in any form and is years away from ratification by the United States and all 26 signatories. Second, we are unable to comprehend the difficulty presented by the two standards of review. It is clear that NSF will have to perform fewer studies under NEPA than under the Protocol, and where an EIS is required under NEPA, it would not strain a researcher's intellect to indicate in a single document how the environmental impact of the proposed action is more than "minor" and also more than "significant."

... [T]he government may avoid the EIS requirement where U.S. foreign policy interests outweigh the benefits derived from preparing an EIS. Since NEPA imposes no substantive requirements, U.S. foreign policy interests in Antarctica will rarely be threatened, except perhaps where the time required to prepare an EIS would itself threaten international cooperation, or where the foreign policy interests at stake are particularly unique and delicate. Thus, contrary to NSF's assertions, where U.S. foreign policy interests outweigh the benefits of the EIS requirement, NSF's efforts to cooperate with foreign governments regarding environmental practices in Antarctica will not be frustrated by forced compliance with NEPA.

E. *NEPA's Plain Language and Interpretation*

NSF's final argument is that even if the presumption against extraterritoriality does not apply to this case, the plain language of Section 102(2)(C) precludes its application to NSF's decisionmaking regarding proposed agency action in Antarctica. We read the plain language differently.

Section 102(2)(C), on its face, is clearly not limited to actions of federal agencies that have significant environmental effects within U.S. borders. This Court has repeatedly taken note of the sweeping scope of NEPA and the EIS requirement. [Citations]

Far from employing limiting language, Section 2 states that NEPA is intended to "encourage productive and enjoyable harmony between *man and his environment*" as well as to "promote efforts which will prevent or eliminate damage to the environment and *biosphere*." 42 U.S.C. § 4321 (emphasis added). Clearly, Congress painted with a far greater brush than NSF is willing to apply....

Section 102(2)(F) further supports the conclusion that Congress, when enacting NEPA, was concerned with worldwide as well as domestic problems facing the environment. 42 U.S.C. § 4332(2)(F) (federal agencies required to "recognize the worldwide and long-range character of environmental problems"). NSF acknowledges that Section 102(2)(F) clearly addresses international environmental problems, but argues that this section announces Congress' only requirement for agencies pursuing action in the international arena.

We find nothing in the statute which supports the construction of Section 102 urged by NSF. Apparently, NSF has chosen to ignore the clear interrelationship between the Section 102 subsections and the Section 102 mandate as a whole. Section 102 lists several requirements under NEPA for "all Federal agencies." 42 U.S.C. § 4332(2). Compliance with one of the subsections can hardly be construed to relieve the agency from its duty to fulfill the obligations articulated in other subsections. For example, compliance with Section 102(2)(G), which requires agencies to make environmental information available to the states, does not excuse an agency from preparing an EIS under Section 102(2)(C).

We also note, that prior to the issuance of Executive Order 12144, the Council on Environment Quality ("CEQ") maintained that NEPA applies to the decisionmaking process of federal agencies regarding actions in Antarctica. CEQ is the agency created by Congress to oversee the implementation of NEPA, and its interpretation of that statute is generally entitled to "substantial deference."

Conclusion

Applying the presumption against extraterritoriality here would result in a federal agency being allowed to undertake actions significantly affecting the human environment in Antarctica, an area over which the United States has substantial interest and authority, without ever being held accountable for its failure to comply with the decisionmaking procedures instituted by Congress — even though such accountability, if it was enforced, would result in no conflict with foreign law or threat to foreign policy. NSF has provided no support for its proposition that conduct occurring within the United States is rendered exempt from otherwise applicable statutes merely because the effects of its compliance would be felt in the global commons. We therefore reverse the district court's decision, and remand for a determination of whether the environmental analyses performed by NSF, prior to its decision to resume incineration, failed to comply with Section 102(2)(C) of NEPA.

We find it important to note, however, that we do not decide today how NEPA might apply to actions in a case involving an actual foreign sovereign or how other U.S. statutes might apply to Antarctica. We only hold that the alleged failure of NSF to comply with NEPA before resuming incineration in Antarctica does not implicate the presumption against extraterritoriality.

Reversed and remanded.

NOTES AND QUESTIONS

1. *Global Environment.* Section 102(2)(F) of NEPA provides that federal agencies must recognize and seek to advance initiatives for international cooperation in solving "worldwide" environmental problems. Further, NEPA contains language of purpose to "encourage productive and enjoyable harmony between man and his environment; to promote efforts which will prevent or eliminate damage to his environment and biosphere." Section 2, 42 U.S.C.

§ 4321. However, the Act does not specifically require federal agencies to comply with NEPA with respect to extraterritorial actions by the federal government.

2. In *Greenpeace USA v. Stone*, 748 F. Supp. 749 (D. Haw. 1990) the United States Army planned to transport a stockpile of obsolete chemical munitions in Germany to an unincorporated United States territory, the Johnson Atoll, located in the Pacific Ocean. The Army planned to store and eventually destroy the munitions. The Army prepared several EISs pertaining to the construction and operation of the storage and incineration facilities. The EISs addressed potential environmental impacts associated with the transportation of the munitions within United States territorial waters. Environmental groups challenged the Army's failure to prepare a comprehensive EIS to discuss potential impacts covering movement of the munitions in Germany or their transoceanic shipment. The court held that although Congress intended to encourage agencies to consider global environmental issues, NEPA only applied within the territorial jurisdiction of the United States. Further, the court observed that NEPA must not contravene foreign policy considerations, and that application of domestic laws in another country could offend the sovereignty of the foreign state. Finally, although the same foreign policy concerns were not implicated with regard to the transoceanic shipment of the munitions, the court found that NEPA still did not mandate an EIS for impacts on the global commons.

3. In *Public Citizen v. United States Trade Representative*, 5 F.3d 549 (D.C. Cir. 1993) the court held that the Office of the United States Trade Representative was not required to prepare an environmental impact statement on the North American Free Trade Agreement before the President submitted it to Congress for ratification. The court held that NAFTA was not a "final agency action" subject to judicial review under the Administrative Procedures Act:

> The ultimate destiny of NAFTA has yet to be determined. Recently negotiated side agreements may well change the dimensions of the conflict that Public Citizen sought to have resolved by the courts. More importantly, the political debate over NAFTA in Congress has yet to play out. Whatever the ultimate result, however, NAFTA's fate now rests in the hands of the political branches. The judiciary has no role to play.

> In sum ... the "final agency action" challenged in this case is the submission of NAFTA to Congress by the President. Because the Trade Acts vest in the President the discretion to renegotiate NAFTA before submitting it to Congress or to refuse to submit it at all, his action, and not that of the OTR, will directly affect Public Citizen's members. The President's actions are not "agency action" and thus cannot be reviewed under the APA.

Id. at 553.

B. TIMING AND SCOPE OF THE IMPACT STATEMENT

The process leading to the finalization of an environmental impact statement involves a number of steps and engages a wide range of parties for an opportunity to comment. The CEQ regulations outline specific procedural steps — binding on all federal agencies — guiding them through the environmental impact statement process. 40 C.F.R. § 1500.3. The CEQ regulations provide for simplifying and streamlining the process by directing agencies to develop procedures for placing proposals into different classifications. Agencies are instructed to establish criteria for identifying actions that typically fall into one of the following categories: (1) those which normally require an environmental impact statement; (2) those which ordinarily will not necessitate either an EIS or an environmental assessment ("EA"); and (3) those which normally require an EA but do not necessarily lead to preparation of an EIS. 40 C.F.R. § 1507.3(b)(2). Since many routine agency actions normally do not individually or cumulatively cause significant environmental impacts, these may be excepted from the NEPA process as "categorical exclusions." 40 C.F.R. § 1508.4. *See also National Trust for Historic Preserv. v. Dole*, 828 F.2d 776, 781 (D.C. Cir. 1987) (Court applied arbitrary and capricious standard of review regarding agency decision to invoke categorical exclusion status).

The starting point for the process involves agency preparation of an environmental assessment, which is a "concise public document" used to ascertain whether or not an EIS is necessary. 40 C.F.R. § 1508.9(a). The EA contains evidence and analysis pertaining to the proposal and considers, in abbreviated fashion, alternatives to the proposed action which are required pursuant to section 102(2)(E). 40 C.F.R. 1508.9(b); 40 C.F.R. § 1501.3. An agency then will either proceed with preparation of a draft EIS or make a finding of no significant impact available to the public. 40 C.F.R. § 1501.4(e)(1).

The next stage in the EIS process is called "scoping." 40 C.F.R. § 1501.7. The purpose of scoping is to identify the significant issues raised by the proposed project and to engage participation by other agencies and interested persons in planning the EIS at an early stage. The range of topics for consideration are narrowed in order to focus discussion, timetables are established, and responsibilities are allocated among various agencies. The CEQ regulations provide that the scope of the impact statement must include connected, cumulative, and similar actions. 40 C.F.R. § 1508.25(a). Three types of alternatives are also discussed: taking no action, other reasonable courses of action, and mitigation measures which are not already included in the proposal. 40 C.F.R. § 1508.25(b). Finally, the EIS must examine direct, indirect, and cumulative environmental impacts potentially resulting from the project. 40 C.F.R. § 1508.25(c).

The draft impact statement is then circulated to appropriate agencies with jurisdiction or special expertise and other parties for comment. 40 C.F.R. § 1503.1; § 1503.4. Following the comment period, the lead agency will prepare a final environmental impact statement. The CEQ serves as a clearinghouse to handle and resolve major interagency disagreements. 40 C.F.R. §§ 1504.1-1504.3. The final EIS must address the criteria set forth in section 102(2)(C) of NEPA and respond analytically to comments received regarding alternatives to the proposed action which had not already received serious consideration by the agency. 40 C.F.R. § 1503.4(a). The agency, after reaching a final decision on the proposed project, must prepare a record of decision summarizing and justifying the actions to be undertaken and explaining why alternatives and mitigation measures were rejected. 40 C.F.R. § 1503.3.

An important question with respect to determining the appropriate scope of an EIS involves considering related or interdependent projects concurrently. The policies and purposes of NEPA of addressing in a timely fashion the potential adverse environmental consequences of "significant" government actions would be undermined if an agency were permitted to divide or piecemeal projects into smaller units which individually do not trigger NEPA review. A corollary problem to segmenting a project is determining at what stage, if any, an entire government program should be evaluated in a comprehensive EIS. The following cases and materials explore these important issues of scope and timing of an impact statement.

SCIENTISTS' INSTITUTE FOR PUBLIC INFORMATION v. ATOMIC ENERGY COMMISSION

481 F.2d 1079 (D.C. Cir. 1973)

J. SKELLY WRIGHT, CIRCUIT JUDGE.

Appellant claims that the Atomic Energy Commission's Liquid Metal Fast Breeder Reactor program involves a "recommendation or report on proposals for legislation and other major Federal actions significantly affecting the quality of the human environment ..." under Section 102(C) of the National Environmental Policy Act (NEPA), 42 U.S.C. § 4332(C) (1970), and that the Commission is therefore required to issue a "detailed statement" for the program. The District Court held that no statement was presently required since, in its view, the program was still in the research and development stage and no specific implementing action which would significantly affect the environment had yet been taken. Taking into account the magnitude of the ongoing federal investment in this program, the controversial environmental effects attendant upon future widespread deployment of breeder reactors should the program fulfill present expectations, the accelerated pace under which this program has moved beyond pure scientific research toward creation of a viable, competitive breeder reactor electrical energy industry, and the manner in which investment in this new technology is likely to restrict future alternatives, we hold that the Commission's program comes within both the letter and the spirit of Section 102(C) and that a detailed statement about the program, its environmental impact, and alternatives thereto is presently required....

I. *Factual Background: The Liquid Metal Fast Breeder Reactor Program*

Although more than a superficial understanding of the technology underlying this case is beyond the layman's ken, a brief summary will prove helpful. Nuclear reactors use nuclear fission — the splitting of the atom — to produce heat which may be used to generate electricity in nuclear power plants. Only a few, relatively rare, naturally occurring substances — primarily Uranium-235 — can maintain the nuclear fission chain reaction necessary for operation of these reactors. There are thus severe constraints on the long run potential of nuclear energy for generating electricity unless new nuclear fuel is "artificially" produced. Such fuel can be produced through the process of "breeding" with a "fast breeder reactor."... The Liquid Metal Fast Breeder Reactor (henceforth LMFBR) is simply a fast breeder reactor that uses a liquid metal, sodium, as a coolant and heat transfer agent.

Because the breeding principle makes possible vast expansion of fuel available for nuclear reactors (Uranium-238 is many times more common than Uranium-235), it has been the subject of considerable interest since the earliest days of atomic energy.... In sum, the Commission came to see its program as serving "as the key to effecting the transition of the fast breeder program from the technology development stage to the point of large-scale commercial utilization."

....

The LMFBR's prospects are sufficiently bright to have led President Nixon to say: "Our best hope today for meeting the Nation's growing demand for economical clean energy lies with the fast breeder reactor." And the Commission has recently predicted that by the year 2000 LMFBR capacity will equal total electric generating capacity in the United States today.

II. *Application of NEPA to Technology Development Programs*

NEPA requires federal agencies to include a detailed environmental impact statement "in every recommendation or report on proposals for legislation and other major Federal actions significantly affecting the quality of the human environment...." That the Commission must issue a detailed statement for each of the major test facilities and demonstration plants encompassed by the LMFBR program is conceded by the Commission and not at issue in this case. The Commission has already issued an impact statement for its Fast Flux Test Facility to be constructed in Hanford, Washington, and, at the President's request, has completed a statement for the first demonstration plant prior to the time such a statement would normally be issued. Nor is the adequacy of either of these statements as they pertain to their respective individual facilities an issue on this appeal. The question raised, instead, is basically twofold: whether at some point in time the Commission must issue a statement for the research and development program as a whole, rather than simply for individual facilities, and, assuming an affirmative answer to this question, whether a statement covering the entire program should be drafted now.

... The Commission's basic position seems to be that NEPA requires detailed statements only for particular facilities, and that no separate NEPA analysis of an entire research and development program is required....

The Commission takes an unnecessarily crabbed approach to NEPA in assuming that the impact statement process was designed only for particular facilities rather than for analysis of the overall effects of broad agency programs. Indeed, quite the contrary is true....

We think it plain that at some point in time there should be a detailed statement on the overall LMFBR program. The program comes before the Congress as a "proposal for legislation" each year, in the form of appropriations requests by the Commission. And as the Council on Environmental Quality has noted in its NEPA Guidelines, the statutory phrase "recommendations or report on proposals for legislation" includes "[r]ecommendations or favorable reports relating to legislation *including that for appropriations.*" In addition, the program constitutes "major Federal action" within the meaning of the statute.

The statutory phrase "actions significantly affecting the quality of the environment" is intentionally broad, reflecting the Act's attempt to promote an across-the-board adjustment in federal agency decision making so as to make the quality of the environment a concern of every federal agency....

Application of NEPA to technology development programs is further supported by the legislative history and general policies of the Act. When Congress enacted NEPA, it was well aware that new technologies were a major cause of environmental degradation....

NEPA's objective of controlling the impact of technology on the environment cannot be served by all practicable means, *see* 42 U.S.C. § 4331(b) (1970), unless the statute's action forcing impact statement process is applied to ongoing federal agency programs aimed at developing new technologies which, when applied, will affect the environment. To wait until a technology attains the stage of complete commercial feasibility before considering the possible adverse environmental effects attendant upon ultimate application of the technology will undoubtedly frustrate meaningful consideration and balancing of environmental costs against economic and other benefits. Modern technological advances typically stem from massive investments in research and development, as is the case here. Technological advances are therefore capital investments and, as such, once brought to a stage of commercial feasibility the investment in their development acts to compel their application. Once there has been, in the terms of NEPA, "an irretrievable commitment of resources" in the technology development stage, the balance of environmental costs and economic and other benefits shifts in favor of ultimate application of the technology.... [B]ecause of the long lead times necessary for development of new commercially feasible technologies for production of electrical energy, the decisions our society makes today as to the direction of research and development will determine what technologies are available 10, 20, or 30 years hence when we must apply some new means of producing electrical energy or face the alternative of energy rationing, through higher prices or otherwise. The manner in which we divide our limited research and development dollars today among various promising technologies in effect determines which technologies will be available, and what type and amount of environmental effects will have to be endured, in the future when we must apply some new technology to meet projected energy demand.

In a very practical sense, then, the Commission's LMFBR program affects the quality of the environment. That the effects will not begin to be felt for several years, perhaps over a decade, is not controlling, for the Act plainly contemplates consideration of "both the long- and short-range implications to man, his physical and social surroundings, and to nature, ... in order to avoid to the fullest extent practicable undesirable consequences for the environment."...

We thus tread firm ground in holding that NEPA requires impact statements for major federal research programs, such as the Commission's LMFBR program, aimed at development of new technologies which, when applied, will significantly affect the quality of the human environment. To the extent the Commission's "environmental survey" would not be issued in accordance with NEPA's procedures for preparation and distribution, it is not an adequate substitute for a NEPA statement. These procedural requirements are not dispensable technicalities, but are crucial if the statement is to serve its dual functions of informing Congress, the President, other concerned agencies and the public of the environmental effects of agency action, and of ensuring meaningful consideration of environmental factors at all stages of agency decision making.

It is apparent, however, that the Commission sees to avoid issuing its forthcoming "environmental survey" as an impact statement under Section 102, not out of any desire to circumvent NEPA's procedural requirements, but rather because of a fear that Section 102's requirements as to the contents of an impact statement are so strict, particularly as to the need for "detail" in the statement, that any Commission attempt to issue its environmental survey as a NEPA statement would be doomed to failure. While we do not altogether understand the Commission's fears, we feel they are based on certain misapprehensions as to what NEPA requires.

It is now clear that an agency's duties to issue a statement on a project and to consider environmental factors at each stage of agency decision making as to that project are not inherently flexible or discretionary. But we have also recognized that the statute admits of some degree of flexibility and agency discretion in determining the contents of impact statements. The range of actions covered by NEPA, as we have just seen, is exceedingly broad, ranging from, for example, construction of a particular segment of interstate highway to embarkation upon a broad development program of nationwide significance such as the LMFBR program. The issues, format, length and detail of impact statements for actions as diverse as these must of course differ. NEPA is not a paper tiger, but neither is it a straightjacket. Drafting a proper impact statement involves much more than filling in the blanks on a government form. NEPA statements can and do vary, from relatively short and simple analyses of the environmental effects of smaller projects to complex multi-volume works for projects of multi-billion-dollar dimensions.

Certainly NEPA does not require the Commission to forecast the deployment and effects of LMFBR power reactors in the year 2000 in the same detail or with the same degree of accuracy as another agency might have to forecast the increased traffic congestion likely to be caused by a proposed highway. Conversely, the Commission may well be expected to devote more resources toward preparation of an impact statement for its multi-billion-dollar program than it would for a project involving a federal investment many times smaller.

Similarly, Section 102(C)'s requirement that the agency describe the anticipated environmental effects of proposed action is subject to a rule of reason. The agency need not foresee the unforeseeable, but by the same token neither can it avoid drafting an impact statement simply because describing the environmental effects of and alternatives to particular agency action involves some degree of forecasting. And one of the functions of a NEPA statement is to indicate the extent to which environmental effects are essentially unknown. It must be remembered that the basic thrust of an agency's responsibilities under NEPA is to predict the environmental effects of proposed action before the action is taken and those effects fully known. Reasonable forecasting and speculation is thus implicit in NEPA, and we must reject any attempt by agencies to shirk their responsibilities under NEPA by labeling any and all discussion of future environmental effects as "crystal ball inquiry." "The statute must be construed in the light of reason if it is not to demand what is, fairly speaking, not meaningfully possible ...." But implicit in this rule of reason is the overriding statutory duty of compliance with impact statement procedures to "the fullest extent possible."

Accordingly, if the Commission's environmental survey is prepared and issued in accordance with NEPA procedures, and if the Commission makes a good faith effort in the survey to describe the reasonably foreseeable environmental impact of the program, alternatives to the program and their reasonably foreseeable environmental impact, and the irreversible and irretrievable commitment of resources the program involves, we see no reason why the survey will not fully satisfy the requirements of Section 102(C). The resulting document may look very different from the impact statement the Commission is used to issuing for a particular nuclear power plant, but this variance should be accepted as a healthy reflection of NEPA's broad scope. It should not be twisted into an excuse for not complying with NEPA at all.

So long as the above described NEPA analysis of the overall program is prepared, we think it of little moment whether that analysis is issued as a separate NEPA statement or whether it is included within a NEPA statement on a particular facility. Questions of format such as these properly reside within the discretion of the issuing agency.... The issues discussed in an analysis of the overall program would be quite different from those discussed in an analysis of a particular facility, and the relevant audiences, both in government and outside, would vary for each analysis. It would thus seem to make more sense to issue a separate statement for the overall project....

III. *Timing the NEPA Statement*

Whether a statement on the overall LMFBR program should be issued now or at some uncertain date in the future is the most difficult question presented by this case....

In our view, the timing question can best be answered by reference to the underlying policies of NEPA in favor of meaningful, timely information on the effects of agency action. In the early stages of research, when little is known about the technology and when future application of the technology is both doubtful and remote, it may well be impossible to draft a meaningful impact statement. Predictions as to the possible effects of application of the technology would tend toward uninformative generalities, arrived at by guesswork rather than analysis. NEPA requires predictions, but not prophecy, and impact statements ought not to be modeled upon the works of Jules Verne or H. G. Wells. At the other end of the spectrum, by the time commercial feasibility of the technology is conclusively demonstrated, and the effects of application of the technology certain, the purposes of NEPA will already have been thwarted. Substantial investments will have been made in development of the technology and options will have been precluded without consideration of environmental factors. Any statement prepared at such a late date will no doubt be thorough, detailed and accurate, but it will be of little help in ensuring that decisions reflect environmental concerns. Thus we are pulled in two directions. Statements must be written late enough in the development process to contain meaningful information but they must be written early enough so that whatever information is contained can practically serve as an input into the decision making process.

Determining when to draft an impact statement for a technology development program obviously requires a reconciliation of these competing concerns. Some balance must be struck, and several factors should be weighed in the balance. How likely is the technology to prove commercially feasible, and how soon will that occur? To what extent is meaningful information presently available on the effects of application of the technology and of alternatives and their effects? To what extent are irretrievable commitments being made and options precluded as the development program progresses? How severe will be the environmental effects if the technology does prove commercially feasible?

Answers to questions like these require agency expertise, and therefore the initial and primary responsibility for striking a balance between the competing concerns must rest with the agency itself, not with the courts. At the same time, however, some degree of judicial scrutiny of an agency's decision that the time is not ripe for a NEPA statement is necessary in order to ensure that the policies of the Act are not being frustrated or ignored. Agency decisions in the environmental area touch on fundamental personal interests in life and health, and these interests have always had a special claim to judicial protection.

The first function of judicial review in this area should be to require the agency to provide a framework for principled decision making. Agencies engaging in long-term technology research and development programs should develop either formal or informal procedures for regular, perhaps annual, evaluation of whether the time for drafting a NEPA statement has arrived.

More importantly, when the agency has decided a NEPA statement is not yet necessary, it should state reasons for its decision. The value of such a statement of reasons is becoming generally recognized as courts and agencies grapple with the difficult task of developing procedures for compliance with NEPA....

A statement of reasons will serve two functions. It will ensure that the agency has given adequate consideration to the problem and that it understood the statutory standard. In addition, it will provide a focal point for judicial review of the agency's decision, giving the court the benefit of the agency's expertise....

... Our examination of this record leads us to conclude that the Commission could have no rational basis for deciding that the time is not yet ripe for drafting an impact statement on the overall LMFBR program. Consideration of each of the facts set out in our balancing test point in the direction of drafting an impact statement now.

To begin with, commercial implementation of LMFBR technology is far from speculative. The massive amounts of money being pumped into this program by Congress and the Presidential Energy Policy statement committing the nation to completion of the first commercialized demonstration plant by 1980 both indicate widespread confidence that the program will succeed in its twin goals of demonstrating the commercial feasibility of the breeder reactor and producing an industrial infrastructure ready, willing and able to construct such reactors on a commercial basis....

Secondly, the Commission's own documents indicate that there already exists much meaningful information on the reasonably foreseeable environmental impact of development of LMFBR technology.... We see no reason why the Commission could not, from information already before us, explore in a NEPA statement such vital matters as, for example, the total amounts of radioactive wastes which will be produced by development of this technology and the total amounts of land area needed for long- and short-term storage of these wastes. The Commission's continual references to "crystal ball inquiry" have a hollow ring in light of the fact that the Commission has already prepared a complex cost-benefit analysis of the LMFBR program, involving projections through and beyond the year 2000. This cost-benefit analysis notably lacks any attempt to quantify the environmental costs or benefits associated with the program so that these factors could play a role in the analysis....

Moving to another factor in our balancing test, it is evident that there are sizable irretrievable commitments of resources taking place in the program. As indicated in the introduction, the federal commitment to this program is now over $100 million per year. The Commission itself admits that one of the results of this commitment has been to slow down development of other new technologies, such as alternative breeder reactor concepts, which would also require a large investment to move from the stage of technical and theoretical research into a stage of commercial feasibility.

Finally, we cannot ignore the fact that the anticipated effects of the LMFBR program on the environment are among the most significant, and most controversial, of all federal programs. We deal here with a radical change in the manner in which our entire nation produces electricity. In many respects, no doubt, this new technique of producing electricity will be less harmful to the environment than present fossil fuel generating plants. But it is evident that the program presents unique and unprecedented environmental hazards. The Commission itself concedes it is expected that by the year 2000 some 600,000 cubic feet of high-level concentrated radioactive wastes will have been generated. These wastes will pose an admitted hazard to human health for hundreds of years, and will have to be maintained in special repositories. The environmental problems attendant upon processing, transporting and storing these wastes, and the other environmental issues raised by widespread deployment of LMFBR power plants, warrant the most searching scrutiny under NEPA.

Of course, some of the environmental impacts of the program are still shrouded in uncertainty. But one of the functions of an impact statement is to point up uncertainties where they exist. And whatever statement is drafted by the Commission can be amended to reflect newly obtained information as the program progresses.

IV. *Conclusion*

At this point it is appropriate that we emphasize the limited nature of the issue under review in this case. By our holding we do not intend in any way to question either the wisdom of the Commission's LMFBR program or the Commission's dedication to protection of the public health and safety.... So far as the human environment is concerned, NEPA has provided a means of answering this "basic question" by requiring full disclosure to the public and to other entities within government of all environmental effects likely to stem from agency action.

[Reversed and remanded.]

NOTES AND QUESTIONS

1. Illustrative of the difficulties in pinpointing the precise stage at which complex information, deliberations, and actions coalesce into a proposal is *Blue Ocean Preserv. Soc'y v. Watkins*, 754 F. Supp. 1450 (D. Haw. 1991). The State of Hawaii and the Department of Energy ("DOE") developed plans for a four-stage project for the purpose of providing large quantities of electric power to be generated by geothermal energy plants to be built in the Hawaiian Islands. Phase I contemplated drilling one geothermal well and construction of a small capacity power plant; Phase II involved research, design, and construction of an undersea cable to transmit electricity between islands; Phase III involved drilling additional wells to "verify" the geothermal resource; and Phase IV contemplated construction of several large capacity power plants. The DOE submitted its plans for the project directly to Congress, and the first two phases were completed with joint funding from the state and federal government. When Congress authorized funds for the third stage, environmental groups sought to compel the DOE to prepare an EIS for the entire development. The court observed that although there was not a "bright-line" standard for determining what constitutes a "proposal," an EIS would serve no useful function with respect to the stages already completed. On the other hand, the court determined that the timing for an EIS would be ripe for evaluation of the final stages of the project since further decisions remained which could be influenced by the impact statement.

The court referenced CEQ regulation 40 C.F.R. § 1502.5 which states that the EIS must be prepared at an early enough stage to contribute to the decision-making process — not to rationalize or justify a particular course of action already selected. Implicit in the court's analysis of the agency's conduct is determining that the four-phases of the project were sufficiently "connected" such that they should be evaluated in a single EIS. Following the court's holding that the project constituted a major federal action meriting an EIS, the government sought to "reprogram" the funding for the project and have it applied to a different federal project in order to avoid compliance with NEPA. The court held that the DOE's statement of intent to prepare an EIS and withhold its participation until an EIS was prepared did not render the case moot. Accordingly, the court enjoined the commitment of further federal resources until the EIS was completed. *Also see* 40 C.F.R. § 1501.2, which provides that the NEPA process must be integrated with other planning at the "earliest possible time" in order to insure that the relevant environmental values are considered but also to avoid delays and avert potential conflicts.

2. Several years after *SIPI*, the Supreme Court addressed questions involving the appropriate scope and timing of a regional or programmatic EIS in *Kleppe v. Sierra Club*, 427 U.S. 390 (1976), reprinted following these notes. The case involved the leasing of coal reserves on public lands to private mining companies by the Department of the Interior. The Sierra Club alleged that the existing individual leasing proposals in the affected region involved interrelated environmental effects justifying an EIS for the entire region. Consider the Court's views regarding when a comprehensive EIS may be required on regional development plans. Compare the approach of the Supreme Court to that adopted by the Court of Appeals in *SIPI*.

KLEPPE v. SIERRA CLUB

427 U.S. 390 (1976)

MR. JUSTICE POWELL delivered the opinion of the Court.

....

Respondents, several organizations concerned with the environment, brought this suit in July 1973 in the United States District Court for the District of Columbia. The defendants in the suit, petitioners here, were the officials of the Department and other federal agencies responsible for issuing coal leases, approving mining plans, granting rights-of-way, and taking the other actions necessary to enable private companies and public utilities to develop coal reserves on land owned or controlled by the Federal Government. Citing widespread interest in the reserves of a region identified as the "Northern Great Plains region," and an alleged threat from coal-related operations to their members' enjoyment of the region's environment, respondents claimed that the federal officials could not allow further development without preparing a "comprehensive environmental impact statement" under § 102(2)(C) on the entire region. They sought declaratory and injunctive relief.

....

The Northern Great Plains region identified in respondents' complaint encompasses portions of four States — northeastern Wyoming, eastern Montana, western North Dakota, and western South Dakota. There is no dispute about its richness in coal, nor about the waxing interest in developing that coal, nor about the crucial role the federal petitioners will play due to the significant percentage of the coal to which they control access. The Department has initiated, in this decade, three studies [the North Central Power Study, the Montana-Wyoming Aqueducts Study, and the Northern Great Plains Resources Program (NGPRP)] in areas either inclusive of or included within this region....

While the record does not reveal the degree of concern with environmental matters in the first two studies, it is clear that the NGPRP was devoted entirely to the environment. It was carried out by an interagency, federal-state task force with public participation, and was designed "to assess the potential social, economic and environmental impacts" from resource development in five States — Montana, Wyoming, South Dakota, North Dakota, and Nebraska. Its primary objective was "to provide an analytical and informational framework for policy and planning decisions at all levels of government" by formulating several "scenarios" showing the probable consequences for the area's environment and culture from the various possible techniques and levels of resource development....

In addition, since 1973 the Department has engaged in a complete review of its coal-leasing program for the entire Nation.... The purpose of the program review was to study the environmental impact of the Department's entire range of coal-related activities and to develop a planning system to guide the national leasing program. The impact statement, known as the "Coal Programmatic EIS," went through several drafts before issuing in final form on September 19, 1975 — shortly before the petitions for certiorari were filed in this case....

The major issue remains the one with which the suit began: whether NEPA requires petitioners to prepare an environmental impact statement on the entire Northern Great Plains region. Petitioners, arguing the negative, rely squarely upon the facts of the case and the language of § 102(2)(C) of NEPA. We find their reliance well placed.

As noted [earlier], § 102(2)(C) requires an impact statement "in every recommendation or report on proposals for legislation and other major Federal actions significantly affecting the quality of the human environment." Since no one has suggested that petitioners have proposed legislation on respondents' region, the controlling phrase in this section of the Act, for this case, is "major Federal actions." Respondents can prevail only if there has been a report or recommendation on a proposal for major federal action with respect to the Northern Great Plains region. Our statement of the relevant facts shows there has been none; instead, all proposals are for actions of either local or national scope.

The local actions are the decisions by the various petitioners to issue a lease, approve a mining plan, issue a right-of-way permit, or take other action to allow private activity at some point within the region identified by respondents. Several Courts of Appeals have held that an impact statement must be included in the report or recommendation on a proposal for such action if the private activity to be permitted is one "significantly affecting the quality of the human environment" within the meaning of § 102(2)(C). [Citation.] The petitioners do not dispute this requirement in this case, and indeed have prepared impact statements on several proposed actions of this type in the Northern Great Plains during the course of this litigation. Similarly, the federal petitioners agreed at oral argument that § 102(2)(C) required the Coal Programmatic EIS that was prepared in tandem with the new national coal-leasing program and included as part of the final report on the proposal for adoption of that program. Their admission is well made, for the new leasing program is a coherent plan of national scope, and its adoption surely has significant environmental consequences.

But there is no evidence in the record of an action or a proposal for an action of regional scope. The District Court, in fact, expressly found that there was no existing or proposed plan or program on the part of the Federal Government for the regional development of the area described in respondents' complaint. It found also that the three studies initiated by the Department in areas either included within or inclusive of respondents' region — that is, the Montana-Wyoming Aqueducts Study, the North Central Power Study, and the NGPRP — were not parts of any plan or program to develop or encourage development of the Northern Great Plains. That court found no evidence that the individual coal development projects undertaken or proposed by private industry and public utilities in that part of the country are integrated into a plan or otherwise interrelated. These findings were not disturbed by the Court of Appeals, and they remain fully supported by the record in this Court.

Quite apart from the fact that the statutory language requires an impact statement only in the event of a proposed action, respondents' desire for a regional environmental impact statement cannot be met for practical reasons. In the absence of a proposal for a regional plan of development, there is nothing that could be the subject of the analysis envisioned by the statute for an impact statement. Section 102(2)(C) requires that an impact statement contain, in essence, a detailed statement of the expected adverse environmental consequences of an action, the resource commitments involved in it, and the alternatives to it. Absent an overall plan for regional development, it is impossible to predict the level of coal-related activity that will occur in the region identified by respondents, and thus impossible to analyze the environmental consequences and the resource commitments involved in, and the alternatives to, such activity. A regional plan would define fairly precisely the scope and limits of the proposed development of the region. Where no such plan exists, any attempt to produce an impact statement would be little more than a study along the lines of the NGPRP, containing estimates of potential development and attendant environmental consequences. There would be no factual predicate for the production of an environmental impact statement of the type envisioned by NEPA.[14]

The Court of Appeals, in reversing the District Court, did not find that there was a regional plan or program for development of the Northern Great Plains region. It accepted all of the District Court's findings of fact, but concluded nevertheless that the petitioners "contemplated" a regional plan or program....

Even had the record justified a finding that a regional program was contemplated by the petitioners, the legal conclusion drawn by the Court of Appeals cannot be squared with the Act. The court recognized that the mere "contemplation" of certain action is not sufficient to require an impact statement. But it believed the statute nevertheless empowers a court to require the preparation of an impact statement to begin at some point prior to the formal recommendation or report on a proposal. The Court of Appeals accordingly devised its own four-part "balancing" test for determining when, during the contemplation of a plan or other type of federal action, an agency must begin a statement. The factors to be considered were identified as the likelihood and imminence of the program's coming to fruition, the extent to which information is available on the effects of implementing the expected program and on alternatives thereto, the

---

[14]In contrast, with both an individual coal-related action and the new national coal-leasing program, an agency deals with specific action of known dimensions. With appropriate allowances for the inexactness of all predictive ventures, the agency can analyze the environmental consequences and describe alternatives as envisioned by § 102(2)(C). Of course, since the kind of impact statement required depends upon the kind of "'federal action' being taken," [citation] the statement on a proposed mining plan or a lease application may bear little resemblance to the statement on the national coal-leasing program. Nevertheless, in each case the bounds of the analysis are defined, which is not the case with coal development in general in the region identified by respondents.

extent to which irretrievable commitments are being made and options precluded "as refinement of the proposal progresses," and the severity of the environmental effects should the action be implemented.

....

The Court's reasoning and action find no support in the language or legislative history of NEPA. The statute clearly states when an impact statement is required, and mentions nothing about a balancing of factors. Rather, as we noted last Term, under the first sentence of § 102(2)(C) the moment at which an agency must have a final statement ready "is the time at which it makes a recommendation or report on a proposal for federal action." [Citation.] The procedural duty imposed upon agencies by this section is quite precise, and the role of the courts in enforcing that duty is similarly precise. A court has no authority to depart from the statutory language and, by a balancing of court-devised factors, determine a point during the germination process of a potential proposal at which an impact statement should be prepared. Such an assertion of judicial authority would leave the agencies uncertain as to their procedural duties under NEPA, would invite judicial involvement in the day-to-day decisionmaking process of the agencies, and would invite litigation. As the contemplation of a project and the accompanying study thereof do not necessarily result in a proposal for major federal action, it may be assumed that the balancing process devised by the Court of Appeals also would result in the preparation of a good many unnecessary impact statements.[15]

... Respondents insist that, even without a comprehensive federal plan for the development of the Northern Great Plains, a "regional" impact statement nevertheless is required on all coal-related projects in the region because they are intimately related.

There are two ways to view this contention. First, it amounts to an attack on the sufficiency of the impact statements already prepared by the petitioners on the coal-related projects that they have approved or stand ready to approve. As such, we cannot consider it in this proceeding, for the case was not brought as a challenge to a particular impact statement and there is no impact statement in the record. It also is possible to view the respondents' argument as an attack upon the decision of the petitioners not to prepare one comprehensive impact statement

---

[15]This is not to say that § 102(2)(C) imposes no duties upon an agency prior to its making a report or recommendation on a proposal for action. The section states that prior to preparing the impact statement the responsible official "shall consult with and obtain the comments of any Federal agency which has jurisdiction by law or special expertise with respect to any environmental impact involved." Thus, the section contemplates a consideration of environmental factors by agencies during the evolution of a report or recommendation on a proposal. But the time at which a court enters the process is when the report or recommendation on the proposal is made, and someone protests either the absence or the adequacy of the final impact statement. This is the point at which an agency's action has reached sufficient maturity to assure that judicial intervention will not hazard unnecessary disruption.

on all proposed projects in the region. This contention properly is before us, for the petitioners have made it clear they do not intend to prepare such a statement.

We begin by stating our general agreement with respondents' basic premise that § 102(2)(C) may require a comprehensive impact statement in certain situations where several proposed actions are pending at the same time. NEPA announced a national policy of environmental protection and placed a responsibility upon the Federal Government to further specific environmental goals by "all practicable means, consistent with other essential considerations of national policy." § 101(b), 42 U.S.C. § 4331(b). Section 102(2)(C) is one of the "action-forcing" provisions intended as a directive to "all agencies to assure consideration of the environmental impact of their actions in decisionmaking." [Citation.] By requiring an impact statement Congress intended to assure such consideration during the development of a proposal or — as in this case — during the formulation of a position on a proposal submitted by private parties. A comprehensive impact statement may be necessary in some cases for an agency to meet this duty. Thus, when several proposals for coal-related actions that will have cumulative or synergistic environmental impact upon a region are pending concurrently before an agency, their environmental consequences must be considered together.[20]

Only through comprehensive consideration of pending proposals can the agency evaluate different courses of action.[21]

. . . .

Respondents conceded at oral argument that to prevail they must show that petitioners have acted arbitrarily in refusing to prepare one comprehensive statement on this entire region, and we agree. The determination of the region, if any, with respect to which a comprehensive statement is necessary requires the weighing of a number of relevant factors, including the extent of the interrelationship among proposed actions and practical considerations of feasibility. Resolving these issues requires a high level of technical expertise and is properly left to the informed discretion of the responsible federal agencies. Absent a

---

[20]At some points in their brief respondents appear to seek a comprehensive impact statement covering contemplated projects in the region as well as those that already have been proposed. The statute, however, speaks solely in terms of proposed actions; it does not require an agency to consider the possible environmental impacts of less imminent actions when preparing the impact statement on proposed actions. Should contemplated actions later reach the stage of actual proposals, impact statements on them will take into account the effect of their approval upon the existing environment; and the condition of that environment presumably will reflect earlier proposed actions and their effects. *Cf.* n. 26, *infra.*

[21]Neither the statute nor its legislative history contemplates that a court should substitute its judgment for that of the agency as to the environmental consequences of its actions. [Citation.] The only role for a court is to insure that the agency has taken a "hard look" at environmental consequences; it cannot "interject itself within the area of discretion of the executive as to the choice of the action to be taken." *Natural Resources Defense Council v. Morton*, 458 F.2d 827, 838 (D.C. Cir. 1972).

showing of arbitrary action, we must assume that the agencies have exercised this discretion appropriately. Respondents have made no showing to the contrary.

Respondents' basic argument is that one comprehensive statement on the Northern Great Plains is required because all coal-related activity in that region is "programmatically," "geographically," and "environmentally" related. Both the alleged "programmatic" relationship and the alleged "geographic" relationship resolve, ultimately, into an argument that the region is proper for a comprehensive impact statement because the petitioners themselves have approached environmental study in this area on a regional basis. Respondents point primarily to the NGPRP, which they claim — and petitioners deny — focused on the region described in the complaint. The precise region of the NGPRP is unimportant [because preliminary studies, like the NGPRP, simply provide a data base that agencies can use in deciding whether to take specific actions which would require preparation of an impact statement.] ... As for the alleged "environmental" relationship, respondents contend that the coal-related projects "will produce a wide variety of cumulative environmental impacts" throughout the Northern Great Plains region. They described them as follows: Diminished availability of water, air and water pollution, increases in population and industrial densities, and perhaps even climatic changes. Cumulative environmental impacts are, indeed, what require a comprehensive impact statement. But determination of the extent and effect of these factors, and particularly identification of the geographic area within which they may occur, is a task assigned to the special competency of the appropriate agencies. Petitioners dispute respondents' contentions that the interrelationship of environmental impacts is region-wide[25] and, as respondents' own submissions indicate, petitioners appear to have determined that the appropriate scope of comprehensive statements should be based on basins, drainage areas, and other factors. We cannot say that petitioners' choices are arbitrary. Even if environmental interrelationships could be shown conclusively to extend across basins and drainage areas, practical considerations of feasibility might well necessitate restricting the scope of comprehensive statements.

In sum, respondents' contention as to the relationships between all proposed coal-related projects in the Northern Great Plains region does not require that

---

[25]For example, respondents assert that coal mines in the region are environmentally interrelated because opening one reduces the supply of water in the region for others. Petitioners contend that the water supply for each aquifer or basin within the region — of which there are many — is independent.

Moreover, petitioners state in their reply brief that few active or proposed mines in respondents' region are located within 50 miles of any other mine, and there are only 30 active or proposed mines in the entire 90,000 square miles of the region.

petitioners prepare one comprehensive impact statement covering all before proceeding to approve specific pending applications.[26]

As we already have determined that there exists no proposal for regionwide action that could require a regional impact statement, the judgment of the Court of Appeals must be reversed, and the judgment of the District Court reinstated and affirmed.

NOTES AND QUESTIONS

1. The *Kleppe* decision has been widely characterized as a more mechanical application of NEPA's action-forcing measures on federal agencies in contrast to the balancing of factors methodology articulated by Judge Skelly Wright in *SIPI*. Given that the EIS is used in the decisionmaking process, environmentalists expressed concern that the formalistic approach of the Court in *Kleppe* would undermine the broad policy directives of NEPA section 101.

2. *Proposal.* With respect to the question of timing of the EIS, the *Kleppe* Court held that NEPA required a "proposal" for regional action by the agency — not just that the agency "contemplated" such action or that local or national proposals existed. The CEQ promulgated regulations in 1978 to clarify the meaning of a number of key terms under NEPA, including what constitutes a "proposal" for purposes of the § 102(2)(C) threshold duty to prepare an EIS. The regulation states:

> "Proposal" exists at that stage in the development of an action when an agency subject to the Act has a goal and is actively preparing to make a decision on one or more alternative means of accomplishing that goal and the effects can be meaningfully evaluated. Preparation of an environmental impact statement on a proposal should be timed (§ 1502.5) so that the final statement may be completed in time for the statement to be included in any recommendation or report on the proposal. A proposal may exist in fact as well as by agency declaration that one exists. 40 C.F.R. § 1508.23.

Would this definition have led the Court to a different conclusion in *Kleppe*?

3. *Programmatic EIS.* The CEQ has established guidelines for determining whether related agency activities should be required to be evaluated in a single, comprehensive or "programmatic" impact statement. The guidelines provide that a "major federal action" can include the "concerted actions to implement a

---

[26]Nor is it necessary that petitioners always complete a comprehensive impact statement on all proposed actions in an appropriate region before approving any of the projects. As petitioners have emphasized, and respondents have not disputed, approval of one lease or mining plan does not commit the Secretary to approval of any others; nor, apparently, do single approvals by the other petitioners commit them to subsequent approvals. Thus, an agency could approve one pending project that is fully covered by an impact statement, then take into consideration the environmental effects of that existing project when preparing the comprehensive statement on the cumulative impact of the remaining proposals. *Cf.* n. 20, *supra.*

specific policy or plan" and also "systematic and connected" agency conduct. 40 C.F.R. § 1508.18(B)(3). The guidelines further provide that a programmatic EIS is necessary where the proposals for federal action are closely related such that they effectively constitute a "single course of action." 40 C.F.R. § 1502.4(a).

In *Foundation on Economic Trends v. Lyng*, 817 F.2d 882 (D.C. Cir. 1987) the court addressed the question of whether the Department of Agriculture was required to prepare a programmatic impact statement with respect to its animal productivity research. The court found that since the research projects were discrete and independent, they should not be considered in the aggregate under a single EIS. The court explained that it was insufficient to show a commonality of objective; instead, the critical inquiry should be whether the projects were interrelated.

4. Cumulative Impacts. The Court in *Kleppe* recognized that a comprehensive EIS may be required when several proposals are concurrently pending before an agency which would have "cumulative or synergistic" environmental impacts upon a region. The significance of a proposed project for NEPA purposes is partly determined by assessing the cumulative impacts on the environment. 40 C.F.R. § 1508.25(a)(2). The CEQ regulations further amplify "cumulative impacts" to mean:

> [T]he impact on the environment which results from the incremental impact of the action when added to other past, present, and reasonably foreseeable future actions regardless of what agency (Federal or non-Federal) or person undertakes such other actions. Cumulative impacts can result from individually minor but collectively significant actions taking place over a period of time. 40 C.F.R. § 1508.7.

In *Natural Resources Defense Council v. Hodel* 865 F.2d 288, 297 (D.C. Cir. 1988) the court found that an impact statement should have considered the cumulative impacts of simultaneous inter-regional offshore oil and gas development on several migratory species, particularly whales and salmon. The final impact statements only had considered the effects of the project on species within each particular area, and any inter-regional analysis simply repeated the same "boilerplate" language.

5. The question of the timing of a programmatic EIS still has presented difficulties of application for courts. The Court in *Kleppe* was concerned that interjecting judicial scrutiny of agency evaluation of a project at an early stage of the decisionmaking process could create uncertainty, invite litigation, and essentially undermine the agency's ability to carry out its duties. Moreover, until the scope of issues are sufficiently drawn with some degree of substance, the agency itself has an inadequate factual basis for evaluating the merits of the project. In contrast to the problem of ripeness, though, is the competing NEPA policy of engaging a wide audience at a sufficiently early stage that comments and suggestions can be considered and the project either modified or even scrapped by the agency accordingly. Thus, agencies — and reviewing courts —

must confront the equal danger of mootness where the EIS process for a program or other project may be started too late to affect the decisionmaking process. Because the timing issue involves a trade-off of those competing policies, courts typically will give considerable latitude to the agency in picking the right time for preparing an EIS. *See Public Citizen, Inc. v. Nuclear Reg. Comm'n*, 940 F.2d 679, 684 (D.C. Cir. 1991).

THOMAS v. PETERSON

753 F.2d 754 (9th Cir. 1985)

SNEED, CIRCUIT JUDGE.

....

This is another environmental case pitting groups concerned with preserving a specific undeveloped area against an agency of the United States attempting to obey the commands given it by a Congress which is mindful of both environmentalists and those who seek to develop the nation's resources. Our task is to discern as best we can what Congress intended to be done under the facts before us.

Plaintiffs — landowners, ranchers, outfitters, miners, hunters, fishermen, recreational users, and conservation and recreation organizations — challenge actions of the United States Forest Service in planning and approving a timber road in the Jersey Jack area of the Nezperce National Forest in Idaho. The area is adjacent to the Salmon River, a congressionally-designated Wild and Scenic River, and is bounded on the west by the designated Gospel Hump Wilderness and on the east by the River of No Return Wilderness. The area lies in a "recovery corridor" identified by the U.S. Fish & Wildlife Service for the Rocky Mountain Gray Wolf, an endangered species.

....

After the passage of the Central Idaho Wilderness Act, the Forest Service, in keeping with its earlier expressed intention, proceeded to plan timber development in the Jersey Jack area. In November, 1980, the Forest Service solicited public comments and held a public hearing on a proposed gravel road that would provide access to timber to be sold. The Forest Service prepared an environmental assessment (EA), *see* 40 C.F.R. § 1508.9 (1984), to determine whether an EIS would be required for the road. Based on the EA, the Forest Service concluded that no EIS was required, and issued a Finding of No Significant Impact (FONSI), *see* 40 C.F.R. § 1508.13. The FONSI and the notice of the Forest Supervisor's decision to go ahead with the road were issued in a single document on February 9, 1981. The decision notice stated that "no known threatened or endangered plant or animal species have been found" within the area, but the EA contained no discussion of endangered species.

The EA for the road discussed only the environmental impacts of the road itself; it did not consider the impacts of the timber sales that the road was designed to facilitate. Subsequently, on November 23, 1981, and on June 30,

1982, the Forest Service issued EAs for, and approved, two of the timber sales. An EA for a third timber sale was also issued prior to the commencement of this action in district court. Each EA covered only the effects of a single timber sale; none discussed cumulative impacts of the sales or of the sales and the road. Each EA resulted in a FONSI, and therefore no environmental impact statements were prepared.

[The plaintiffs alleged that NEPA required the Forest Service to prepare an EIS that analyzes the combined effects of the proposed road and the timber sales that the road is designed to facilitate. The district court granted summary judgment for the Forest Service on all claims.]

....

The central question that plaintiffs' NEPA claim presents is whether the road and the timber sales are sufficiently related so as to require combined treatment in a single EIS that covers the cumulative effects of the road and the sales. If so, the Forest Service has proceeded improperly. An EIS must be prepared and considered by the Forest Service before the road can be approved. If not, the Forest Service may go ahead with the road, and later consider the environmental impacts of the timber sales.

Section 102(2)(C) of NEPA requires an EIS for "major Federal actions significantly affecting the quality of the human environment." 42 U.S.C. § 4332(2)(C) (1982). While it is true that administrative agencies must be given considerable discretion in defining the scope of environmental impact statements, *see Kleppe v. Sierra Club*, 427 U.S. 390, 412-415 (1976), there are situations in which an agency is required to consider several related actions in a single EIS. Not to require this would permit dividing a project into multiple "actions," each of which individually has an insignificant environmental impact, but which collectively have a substantial impact.

Since the Supreme Court decided the *Kleppe* case, the Council on Environmental Quality (CEQ) has issued regulations that define the circumstances under which multiple related actions must be covered by a single EIS. The regulations are made binding on federal administrative agencies by Executive Order. The CEQ regulations and this court's precedents both require the Forest Service to prepare an EIS analyzing the combined environmental impacts of the road and the timber sales.

A. *CEQ Regulations*

1. *Connected actions*

The CEQ regulations require "connected actions" to be considered together in a single EIS. *See* 40 C.F.R. § 1508.25(a)(1) (1984). "Connected actions" are defined, in a somewhat redundant fashion, as actions that

> "(i) Automatically trigger other actions which may require environmental impact statements.

(ii) Cannot or will not proceed unless other actions are taken previously or simultaneously.

(iii) Are interdependent parts of a larger action and depend on the larger action for their justification."

The construction of the road and the sale of the timber in the Jersey Jack area meet the second and third, as well as perhaps the first, of these criteria. It is clear that the timber sales cannot proceed without the road, and the road would not be built but for the contemplated timber sales. This much is revealed by the Forest Service's characterization of the road as a "logging road," and by the first page of the environmental assessment for the road, which states that "[t]he need for a transportation route in the assessment area is to access the timber lands to be developed over the next twenty years." Moreover, the environmental assessment for the road rejected a "no action" alternative because that alternative would not provide the needed timber access. The Forest Service's cost-benefit analysis of the road considered the timber to be the benefit of the road, and while the Service has stated that the road will yield other benefits, it does not claim that such other benefits would justify the road in the absence of the timber sales. Finally, the close interdependence of the road and the timber sales is indicated by an August 1981 letter in the record from the Regional Forester to the Forest Supervisor. It states, "We understand that sales in the immediate future will be dependent on the early completion of portions of the Jersey Jack Road. It would be advisable to divide the road into segments and establish separate completion dates for those portions to be used for those sales."

We conclude, therefore, that the road construction and the contemplated timber sales are inextricably intertwined, and that they are "connected actions" within the meaning of the CEQ regulations.

2. Cumulative Actions

The CEQ regulations also require that "cumulative actions" be considered together in a single EIS. 40 C.F.R. § 1508.25(a)(2). "Cumulative actions" are defined as actions "which when viewed with other proposed actions have cumulatively significant impacts." The record in this case contains considerable evidence to suggest that the road and the timber sales will have cumulatively significant impacts. The U.S. Fish & Wildlife Service, the Environmental Protection Agency, and the Idaho Department of Fish & Game have asserted that the road and the timber sales will have significant cumulative effects that should be considered in an EIS. The primary cumulative effects, according to these agencies, are the deposit of sediments in the Salmon River to the detriment of that river's population of salmon and steelhead trout, and the destruction of critical habitat for the endangered Rocky Mountain Gray Wolf. These agencies have criticized the Forest Service for not producing an EIS that considers the cumulative impacts of the Jersey Jack road and the timber sales. For example, the Fish & Wildlife Service has written, "Separate documentation of related and cumulative potential impacts may be leading to aquatic habitat degradation unaccounted for in individual EAs (i.e., undocumented cumulative effects).... Lack of an overall effort to document cumulative impacts could be having present and future detrimental effects on wolf recovery potential." These comments are sufficient to raise "substantial questions" as to whether the road and the timber sales will have significant cumulative environmental effects. Therefore, on this basis also, the Forest Service is required to prepare an EIS analyzing such effects. [Citations.]

B. *Ninth Circuit Precedents*

The conclusion that NEPA requires a single EIS that considers both road and sales is supported by our precedents. In *Trout Unlimited v. Morton*, 509 F.2d 1276 (9th Cir. 1974), we addressed the issue of when subsequent phases of development must be covered in an environmental impact statement on the first phase. We stated that an EIS must cover subsequent stages when "[t]he dependency is such that it would be irrational, or at least unwise, to undertake the first phase if subsequent phases were not also undertaken." The dependency of the road on the timber sales meets this standard; it would be irrational to build the road and then not sell the timber to which the road was built to provide access.

The same principle is embodied in standards that we have established for determining when a highway may be segmented for purposes of NEPA. In *Daly v. Volpe*, 514 F.2d 1106 (9th Cir. 1975), we held that the environmental impacts of a single highway segment may be evaluated separately from those of the rest of the highway only if the segment has "independent utility." 514 F.2d at 1110. In the light of *Trout Unlimited*, the phrase "independent utility" means utility such that the agency might reasonably consider constructing only the segment in question. The Forest Service has not alleged that the Jersey Jack road has sufficient utility independent from the timber sales to justify its construction. Severance of the road from the timber sales for purposes of NEPA, therefore, is not permissible.

C. *Timing of the EIS*

The Forest Service argues that the cumulative environmental effects of the road and the timber sales will be adequately analyzed and considered in the EAs and/or EISs that it will prepare on the individual timber sales. The EA or EIS on each action, it contends, will document the cumulative impacts of that action and all previous actions.

We believe that consideration of cumulative impacts after the road has already been approved is insufficient to fulfill the mandate of NEPA. A central purpose of an EIS is to force the consideration of environmental impacts in the decisionmaking process. [Citations.] That purpose requires that the NEPA process be integrated with agency planning "at the earliest possible time," 40 C.F.R. § 1501.2, and the purpose cannot be fully served if consideration of the cumulative effects of successive, interdependent steps is delayed until the first step has already been taken.

The location, the timing, or other aspects of the timber sales, or even the decision whether to sell any timber at all affects the location, routing, construction techniques, and other aspects of the road, or even the need for its construction. But the consideration of cumulative impacts will serve little purpose if the road has already been built. Building the road swings the balance decidedly in favor of timber sales even if such sales would have been disfavored had road and sales been considered together before the road was built. Only by selling timber can the bulk of the expense of building the road be recovered. Not to sell timber after building the road constitutes the "irrational" result that *Trout Unlimited*'s standard is intended to avoid. Therefore, the cumulative environmental impacts of the road and the timber sales must be assessed before the road is approved.

The Forest Service argues that the sales are too uncertain and too far in the future for their impacts to be analyzed along with that of the road. This comes close to saying that building the road now is itself irrational. We decline to accept that conclusion. Rather, we believe that if the sales are sufficiently certain to justify construction of the road, then they are sufficiently certain for their environmental impacts to be analyzed along with those of the road. [Citation.] Where agency actions are sufficiently related so as to be "connected" within the meaning of the CEQ regulations, the agency may not escape compliance with the regulations by proceeding with one action while characterizing the others as remote or speculative.

Moreover, the record contains substantial evidence that the timber sales were in fact at an advanced stage of planning by the time that the decision to build the road was made. The Forest Service issued EAs for, and approved, two of the timber sales nine and sixteen months after it issued the road EA, and it had issued an EA for a third sale by the time that this action was filed. In fact, one of the Forest Service's own affidavits shows that the Service was preparing the EA on at least one of the sales at the same time that it was preparing the EA on the road. The record plainly establishes that the Forest Service, in accordance with good administrative practices, was planning contemporaneously the timber sales and the building of the road. Either without the other was impractical. The Forest Service knew this and cannot insist otherwise to avoid compliance with NEPA.

We therefore reverse the district court on the NEPA issue and hold that, before deciding whether to approve the proposed road, the Forest Service is required to prepare and consider an environmental impact statement that analyzes the combined impacts of the road and the timber sales that the road is designed to facilitate.

NOTES AND QUESTIONS

1. The concern about "piecemealing" or "segmenting" a project into several smaller parts — each of which independently may not be considered sufficiently significant to engage NEPA duties — is that an agency may evade compliance with NEPA where the overall environmental effect of the proposal could be substantial. The rule against fractionalizing interrelated projects into less environmentally significant units still presents difficulties in application for courts, however. The CEQ regulations discussed in *Thomas v. Peterson* focus on the concept of interdependence and cumulative nature of the various parts of the plan. 40 C.F.R. § 1508.25(a) (1984).

In *Thomas v. Peterson* the court explained that the nature of the interdependence that must exist between various stages of a project to be considered "connected" was that it would be "irrational, or at least unwise, to undertake the first phase if subsequent phases were not also undertaken." (Quoting from *Trout Unlimited v. Morton*, 509 F.2d 1276 (9th Cir. 1974)). In a related vein, in *Save the Yaak Comm. v. Block*, 840 F.2d 714 (9th Cir. 1988) the court observed that the assessment of connected actions was required by NEPA even if the impact of the proposed action was not significant; the significance or impact of the project involved a separate analysis pertaining to whether to prepare an EIS or just an environmental assessment.

2. The CEQ regulations regarding defining the scope of a project are entitled to substantial deference by courts but are not the exclusive barometers to guide review of agency action. In *Village of Los Ranchos de Albuquerque v. Barnhart*, 906 F.2d 1477, 1483 (10th Cir. 1990) (quoting with approval from *Piedmont Heights Civic Club v. Moreland*, 637 F.2d 430, 439 (5th Cir. 1981)) the court set forth the following factors to determine whether a proposed local project which is closely related physically to a federal project belongs within the scope for an EIS: "(1) has logical termini, (2) has substantial independent utility, (3) does not foreclose the opportunity to consider alternatives, and (4) does not irretrievably commit federal funds for closely related projects."

In a similar vein, consider the following excerpt from *Swain v. Brinegar*, 542 F.2d 364, 369 (7th Cir. 1976) regarding the issue of segmentation of a proposed federal highway:

> 1. Does the proposed segment have a substantial utility independent of future expansion?
>
> 2. Would its construction foreclose significant alternative routes or locations for an extension from the segment?
>
> 3. If, as here, the proposed segment is part of a larger plan, has that plan become concrete enough to make it highly probable that the entire plan will be carried out in the near future?

Which of these tests are the most useful in guiding courts in evaluating the problem of segmenting? What common policies underlie these listed factors?

Recall the multi-factored approach delineated by Judge Skelly Wright in *SIPI* with respect to the proper scope of a programmatic EIS. Do you find similarities with regard to the concern over segmentation?

3. In *Hudson River Sloop Clearwater v. Department of Navy*, 836 F.2d 760 (2d Cir. 1988) conservation groups sought to halt the construction of a Navy battleship homeport pending the filing of an EIS which also considered plans for housing for homeport personnel. The court evaluated whether the two actions were sufficiently "connected" for inclusion in a single EIS by applying the CEQ criteria that the actions would "not proceed unless other actions were taken previously or simultaneously." 40 C.F.R. § 1508.25(a)(1). The court observed that the appropriate inquiry regarding connected actions was whether *both* actions — the construction of the port and the housing — were necessary preconditions to each other. The court rejected the request for a comprehensive EIS because it determined that the Navy planned to build the port even if the housing did not also proceed. Is this the same test as that employed in *Thomas v. Peterson*? Do all portions of agency action need to have mutual dependence in order to consider them related or connected for NEPA purposes?

Similarly, in *Morgan v. Walter*, 728 F. Supp. 1483, 1493 (D. Idaho 1989) the court found that the proposed facility for diversion of a river and a proposed fish hatchery were connected actions because each would not exist without the other. The purpose of the diversion structure was to channel water for support of the hatchery, and the hatchery depended on the water to operate.

4. In *Sylvester v. Army Corps of Eng'rs*, 884 F.2d 394 (9th Cir. 1989) the issue involved whether the Corps was required to issue a comprehensive EIS to consider the impact of an entire resort when issuing a permit for a golf course which would be built on wetlands within the resort. The Corps had considered the impact of the golf course but had not evaluated the environmental effects of the rest of the resort complex in reaching its decision regarding issuance of a conditional permit under the Clean Water Act. The court gave the following colorful description of how to evaluate cumulative impacts of proposed projects under NEPA:

> Environmental impacts are in some respects like ripples following the casting of a stone in a pool. The simile is beguiling but useless as a standard. So employed it suggests that the entire pool must be considered each time a substance heavier than a hair lands upon its surface. That is not a practical guide. A better image is that of scattered bits of a broken chain, some segments of which contain numerous links, while others have only one or two. Each segment stands alone, but each link within each segment does not.

884 F.2d at 400.

The court found that although each portion of the project would derive benefits from the other, they also had independent utility and could exist without the other. Thus, they were not sufficiently "connected" for purposes of inclusion in a single EIS.

WEINBERGER v. CATHOLIC ACTION OF HAWAII
454 U.S. 139 (1981)

JUSTICE REHNQUIST delivered the opinion of the Court.

....

The facts relevant to our decision are not seriously controverted. Pursuant to a decision by the Navy to transfer ammunition and weapons stored at various locations on the island of Oahu, Hawaii, to the West Loch branch of the Luaalualei Naval Magazine, the Navy prepared an Environmental Impact Assessment (EIA) concerning how the plan would affect the environment. The assessment concluded that the necessary construction of 48 earth-covered magazines and associated structures would have no significant environmental impact, and therefore no Environmental Impact Statement (EIS) was prepared at the construction stage. Construction contracts were let in March 1977 and April 1978. Construction of the West Loch facilities has been completed and the magazines are now in use. It is stipulated that the magazines are capable of storing nuclear weapons. Because the information is classified for national security reasons, the Navy's regulations forbid it either to admit or to deny that nuclear weapons are actually stored at West Loch.

In 1978, the Navy prepared a Candidate Environmental Impact Statement (CEIS). This CEIS deals generally with the environmental hazards associated with the storage, handling, and transportation of nuclear weapons, but does not refer to any specific site or storage facility. It concludes that no significant hazards to the environment are present.

[Respondents sought an injunction against the building of new facilities at West Loch, claiming that the Navy's EIA contravened NEPA by failing to address the enhanced risk of a nuclear accident resulting from the potential storage of nuclear weapons at the site. The district court found that the construction of the storage facilities constituted a "major federal action" under NEPA but concluded that the Navy had complied with the Act given its own regulations and the national security provisions of the Atomic Energy Act. The court of appeals held that the Navy was required to prepare and release to the public a "Hypothetical Environmental Impact Statement" regarding the operation of the facility.]

Section 102(2)(C) of NEPA, 42 U.S.C. § 4332(2)(C), provides that, "to the fullest extent possible," all federal agencies shall "include in every recommendation or report on proposals for legislation and other major Federal actions significantly affecting the quality of the human environment, a detailed statement" discussing, *inter alia*, the environmental impact of the proposed action and possible alternatives. Section 102(2)(C) also requires that the EIS be made available to the President, the Council on Environmental Quality (CEQ), and the public, subject to the provisions of the Freedom of Information Act (FOIA), 5 U.S.C. § 552 (1976 ed. and Supp. V).

We have previously noted: "The thrust of § 102(2)(C) is ... that environmental concerns be integrated into the very process of agency decisionmaking. The 'detailed statement' it requires is the outward sign that environmental values and consequences have been considered during the planning stage of agency actions." [Citation.] Section 102(2)(C) thus serves twin aims. The first is to inject environmental considerations into the federal agency's decisionmaking process by requiring the agency to prepare an EIS. The second aim is to inform the public that the agency has considered environmental concerns in its decision-making process. Through the disclosure of an EIS, the public is made aware that the agency has taken environmental considerations into account. Public disclosure of the EIS is expressly governed by FOIA. § 4332(2)(C).

The decisionmaking and public disclosure goals of § 102(2)(C), though certainly compatible, are not necessarily coextensive. Thus, § 102(2)(C) contemplates that in a given situation a federal agency might have to include environmental considerations in its decisionmaking process, yet withhold public disclosure of any NEPA documents, in whole or in part, under the authority of an FOIA exemption. That the decisionmaking and disclosure requirements of NEPA are not coextensive has been recognized by the Department of Defense's regulations, both at the time the West Loch facility was constructed and today.

Congress has thus effected a balance between the needs of the public for access to documents prepared by a federal agency and the necessity of nondisclosure or secrecy....

Since the public disclosure requirements of NEPA are governed by FOIA, it is clear that Congress intended that the public's interest in ensuring that federal agencies comply with NEPA must give way to the Government's need to preserve military secrets. In the instant case, an EIS concerning a proposal to store nuclear weapons at West Loch need not be disclosed. [The information regarding whether nuclear weapons were actually stored at the site was classified and thus exempt from public disclosure under the FOIA.]

If the Navy proposes to store nuclear weapons at West Loch, the Department of Defense's regulations can fairly be read to require that an EIS be prepared solely for internal purposes, even though such a document cannot be disclosed to the public. The Navy must consider environmental consequences in its decisionmaking process, even if it is unable to meet NEPA's public disclosure goals by virtue of [an FOIA exemption].

It does not follow, however, that the Navy is required to prepare an EIS in this case. The Navy is not required to prepare an EIS regarding the hazards of storing nuclear weapons at West Loch simply because the facility is "nuclear capable." As we held in *Kleppe v. Sierra Club*, 427 U.S. 390, 405-406 (1976), an EIS need not be prepared simply because a project is *contemplated*, but only when the project is *proposed*. To say that the West Loch facility is "nuclear capable" is to say little more than that the Navy has contemplated the possibility that nuclear weapons, of whatever variety, may at some time be stored here. It is the proposal to *store* nuclear weapons at West Loch that triggers the Navy's obligation to prepare an EIS. Due to national security reasons, however, the Navy can neither admit nor deny that it proposes to store nuclear weapons at West Loch. In this case, therefore, it has not been and cannot be established that the Navy has proposed the only action that would require the preparation of an EIS dealing with the environmental consequences of nuclear weapons storage at West Loch.

Ultimately, whether or not the Navy has complied with NEPA "to the fullest extent possible" is beyond judicial scrutiny in this case. In other circumstances, we have held that "public policy forbids the maintenance of any suit in a court of justice, the trial of which should inevitably lead to the disclosure of matters which the law itself regards as confidential, and respecting which it will not allow the confidence to be violated." [Citations.] We confront a similar situation in the instant case.

[Reversed and remanded.]

NOTES AND QUESTIONS

1. Although NEPA does not contain an *exception* for projects which implicate national security concerns, *Catholic Action* does provide a shield from public scrutiny with respect to national defense proposals. The military must still comply with NEPA's directive of considering environmental impacts in the decisionmaking process — even where the project may deal with classified information. An internal EIS need not be prepared where a project is merely "contemplated" but only when actually "proposed." In *Catholic Action*, however, the Court recognized that it could not be established that a proposal to deploy nuclear weapons at the site existed until the Navy made such an official disclosure.

Similarly, in *Hudson River Sloop Clearwater v. Department of Navy*, 891 F.2d 414, 423 (2d Cir. 1989) the court disallowed plaintiffs' request to force the military to disclose classified information about nuclear weapon deployment. The court held that the plaintiffs could not "bootstrap" their way to obtaining access to classified documents simply by asserting a reasonable belief of the contents; they must first establish a *prima facie* case regarding the existence of a proposal before litigating the merits.

2. In *No GWEN Alliance of Lane County, Inc. v. Aldridge*, 855 F.2d 1380 (9th Cir. 1988) groups challenged the adequacy of environmental assessments pertaining to the Air Force's proposed construction of a network of emergency radio towers designed to send communications to United States strategic forces even during a nuclear war. As a preliminary matter, the court rejected the Air Force's argument that the claims constituted nonjusticiable political questions. The court held that the claims were not barred from judicial review because NEPA provided sufficient standards for resolving the merits of the case and would not disturb the balance of interests and powers allocated to the coordinate branches of government.

The group contended that the EAs should have considered the environmental impact of nuclear war, arguing that the communications system was destabilizing and increased the likelihood of nuclear war. The court disagreed, finding that the plaintiffs' claims were too speculative. Further, the court observed that since it was commonly understood that the effects of a nuclear exchange would be catastrophic, discussion of those potential impacts would not serve a useful purpose.

3. In *Romer v. Carlucci*, 847 F.2d 445 (8th Cir. 1988) various groups, including the state of Colorado, contested the adequacy of an EIS prepared by the Air Force regarding the proposed deployment of MX missiles. The court held that the scope of the EIS must mirror the scope of the missile program as delimited by Congress. Consequently, claims of environmental groups contending that the EIS should have discussed alternative weapons systems, alternative basing modes, and the proposed wartime use of the missiles were outside the reach of NEPA. On the other hand, claims by Colorado that the EIS should have considered the effect of the MX project on the state's water supply, geological zones, and health and safety of its citizens were proper subjects for consideration on remand.

C. ADEQUACY OF THE EIS: CONSIDERATION OF IMPACTS AND ALTERNATIVES

A central theme in NEPA's structure regards affecting the decisionmaking process and methodology of federal agencies by forcing them to look beyond the contours of their respective principal missions by considering alternatives to proposed actions. By forcing agencies to examine a range of alternatives before committing resources to a project, NEPA attempts to promote more informed — and theoretically leading to more environmentally sound — actions. *See* 102(2)(C)(iii); 102(2)(E). In addition, the inclusion of various options to a given course of action serves to inform Congress, other agencies, and the public about the desirability and potential adverse environmental consequences of a proposal. Although courts consistently have stated that NEPA's principal directives are procedural, there is a corresponding recognition that the process of development and evaluation of alternatives may also improve the substantive decisions made by agencies.

The identification and analysis of alternatives with respect to a proposed action constitutes the "heart" of the environmental impact statement process. 40 C.F.R. § 1502.14. The regulations provide that the potential environmental effects of the proposal and the alternatives must be presented in a comparative fashion. The rationale for that format is to sharply define the issues and thus provide a "clear basis for choice" among the various options by the decisionmaking governmental unit and the public. *See North Buckhead Civic Ass'n v. Skinner*, 903 F.2d 1522,

1541 (11th Cir. 1990). The range of potential alternatives which must be considered, however, is not infinite but rather must be evaluated by a standard of reasonableness. This "rule of reason" operates on two levels: in identifying *which* specific alternatives properly belong in the impact statement and also in ascertaining the *depth* or *degree* to which the agency must analyze those choices. *Natural Resources Defense Council, Inc. v. Hodel*, 865 F.2d 288, 294 (D.C. Cir. 1988). The regulations make clear also that the agency must include the possibility of taking *no* action in a given instance. 40 C.F.R. § 1502.14(e). The following materials explore the adequacy of impact statements, particularly with respect to the issue of determining agency compliance with the duty to identify and consider reasonable alternatives.

CITIZENS AGAINST BURLINGTON, INC. v. BUSEY
938 F.2d 190 (D.C. Cir. 1991)

THOMAS, CIRCUIT JUDGE.

The city of Toledo decided to expand one of its airports, and the Federal Aviation Administration decided to approve the city's plan. In this petition for review of the FAA's order, an alliance of people who live near the airport contends that the FAA has violated several environmental statutes and regulations....

The Toledo Express Airport, object of the controversy in this case, lies about twenty-five miles to the west of downtown Toledo.... The Toledo-Lucas County Port Authority, one of the intervenors, wants to make the city of Toledo a cargo hub. Burlington Air Express, Inc., the other intervenor, wants to move its operations to Toledo. Kasch, Vaughan, Reuter, Van Landingham, and others have formed Citizens Against Burlington, Inc. to stop them.

Citizens Against Burlington first materialized about a year after the Port Authority first commissioned an "Airport Noise Compatibility Planning" study and began to consider the possibility of the airport's expansion. The Port Authority soon heard from Burlington Air Express, which had been flying its planes out of an old World War II hangar at Baer Field, an Air National Guard airport in Fort Wayne. After looking at seventeen sites in four midwestern states, Burlington chose the Toledo Express Airport. Among Burlington's reasons were the quality of Toledo's work force and the airport's prior operating record, zoning advantages, and location (near major highways and close to Detroit and Chicago). For its part, the Port Authority expects the new hub to create one thousand new jobs in metropolitan Toledo and to contribute almost $68 million per year to the local economy after three years of the hub's operation....

The Port Authority submitted its proposal to the FAA on February 2, 1989 and promptly hired Coffman Associates, Inc., a consulting firm, to prepare an environmental assessment and then to convert the environmental assessment into an environmental impact statement (EIS). In December 1989, the FAA sent a draft of the EIS to the Environmental Protection Agency and several state and local agencies. Early the next month, the FAA made the draft public and held a public hearing. Over the following six weeks, Citizens Against Burlington sent the FAA twenty-five letters, commenting on virtually every aspect of the EIS. Individuals sent over three hundred more.

[The FAA published a final EIS and approved the plan to expand the Toledo Express Airport. Citizens sought declaratory and injunctive relief to require the FAA to prepare a new EIS, to enjoin the agency from approving the Port Authority's plan, and to halt construction at Toledo Express pending compliance with applicable laws, including NEPA.]

....

In the National Environmental Policy Act of 1969 (NEPA), Congress resolved "to create and maintain conditions under which man and nature can exist in productive harmony, and fulfill the social, economic, and other requirements of present and future generations of Americans." NEPA § 101(a), 42 U.S.C. § 4331(a). These sweeping policy goals have inspired some commentators to call NEPA an environmentalist Magna Carta. *See, e.g.*, D. Mandelker, NEPA Law and Litigation § 1:01, at 1 (1990); *cf.* 40 C.F.R. § 1500.1(a) ("[NEPA] is our basic national charter for protection of the environment."). But instead of ordering, say, that deforested land be reforested, Congress chose to make NEPA procedural. NEPA commands agencies to imbue their decisionmaking, through the use of certain procedures, with our country's commitment to environmental salubrity. [Citations.] NEPA does not mandate particular consequences.

Just as NEPA is not a green Magna Carta, federal judges are not the barons at Runnymede. Because the statute directs agencies only to look hard at the environmental effects of their decisions, and not to take one type of action or another, federal judges correspondingly enforce the statute by ensuring that agencies comply with NEPA's procedures, and not by trying to coax agency decisionmakers to reach certain results. [Citation.] As the Supreme Court has warned, "once an agency has made a decision subject to NEPA's procedural requirements, the only role for a court is to insure that the agency has considered the environmental consequences; it cannot 'interject itself within the area of discretion of the executive as to the choice of the action to be taken.'" *Strycker's Bay Neighborhood Council, Inc. v. Karlen*, 444 U.S. 223, 227-28 (1980); *see Kleppe v. Sierra Club*, 427 U.S. 390, 410 n.21 (1976) ("Neither [NEPA] nor its legislative history contemplates that a court should substitute its judgment for that of the agency as to the environmental consequences of its actions.").

In short, the obligations that NEPA levies on agencies determine the role of the courts in the statute's enforcement. This case concerns the most important responsibility that NEPA demands — that an agency reviewing proposals for action prepare an environmental impact statement, and, more specifically, that the agency discuss in its statement alternatives to the action proposed. We consider here whether the FAA has complied with NEPA in publishing an environmental impact statement that discussed in depth two alternatives:

approving the expansion of the Toledo Express Airport, and not approving the expansion of the Toledo Express Airport.

Federal agencies must prepare environmental impact statements when they contemplate "major Federal actions significantly affecting the quality of the human environment." NEPA § 102(2)(C), 42 U.S.C. § 4332(2)(C). An EIS must discuss, among other things, "alternatives to the proposed action," NEPA § 102(2)(C)(iii), 42 U.S.C. § 4332(2)(C)(iii), and the discussion of alternatives forms "the heart of the environmental impact statement." 40 C.F.R. § 1502.14.

The problem for agencies is that "the term 'alternatives' is not self-defining." [Citation.] Suppose, for example, that a utility applies for permission to build a nuclear reactor in Vernon, Vermont. Free-floating "alternatives" to the proposal for federal action might conceivably include everything from licensing a reactor in Pecos, Texas, to promoting imports of hydropower from Quebec. If the Nuclear Regulatory Commission had to discuss these and other imaginable courses of action, its statement would wither into "frivolous boilerplate," if indeed the agency were to prepare an EIS at all and not instead just deny the utility a permit. If, therefore, the consideration of alternatives is to inform both the public and the agency decisionmaker, the discussion must be moored to "some notion of feasibility." [Citation.]

Recognizing the harm that an unbounded understanding of alternatives might cause, CEQ regulations oblige agencies to discuss only alternatives that are feasible, or (much the same thing) reasonable. 40 C.F.R. §§ 1502.14(a)-(c), 1508.25(b)(2). But the adjective "reasonable" is no more self-defining than the noun that it modifies. Consider two possible alternatives to our nuclear reactor in Vernon. Funding research in cold fusion might be an unreasonable alternative by virtue of the theory's scientific implausibility. But licensing a reactor in Lake Placid, New York might also be unreasonable, even though it passes some objective test of scientific worth. In either case, the proposed alternative is reasonable only if it will bring about the ends of the federal action — only if it will do what the licensing of the reactor in Vernon is meant to do. [Citations.] If licensing the Vernon reactor is meant to help supply energy to New England, licensing a reactor in northern New York might make equal sense. If licensing the Vernon reactor is meant as well to stimulate the Vernon job market, licensing a reactor in Lake Placid would be far less effective. The goals of an action delimit the universe of the action's reasonable alternatives.

We have held before that an agency bears the responsibility for deciding which alternatives to consider in an environmental impact statement. [Citation.] We have also held that an agency need follow only a "rule of reason" in preparing an EIS, and that this rule of reason governs "both *which* alternatives the agency must discuss, and the extent to which it must discuss them." [Citations.] It follows that the agency thus bears the responsibility for defining at the outset the objectives of an action. [Citation.] As the phrase "rule of reason" suggests, we review an agency's compliance with NEPA's requirements deferentially. We uphold an agency's definition of objectives so long as the objectives that the agency chooses are reasonable, and we uphold its discussion of alternatives so long as the alternatives are reasonable and the agency discusses them in reasonable detail.

We realize, as we stated before, that the word "reasonable" is not self-defining. Deference, however, does not mean dormancy, and the rule of reason does not give agencies license to fulfill their own prophecies, whatever the parochial impulses that drive them. Environmental impact statements take time and cost money. Yet an agency may not define the objectives of its action in terms so unreasonably narrow that only one alternative from among the environmentally benign ones in the agency's power would accomplish the goals of the agency's action, and the EIS would become a foreordained formality. Nor may an agency frame its goals in terms so unreasonably broad that an infinite number of alternatives would accomplish those goals and the project would collapse under the weight of the possibilities.

Instead, agencies must look hard at the factors relevant to the definition of purpose. When an agency is asked to sanction a specific plan, the agency should take into account the needs and goals of the parties involved in the application. [Citations.] Perhaps more importantly, an agency should always consider the views of Congress, expressed, to the extent that the agency can determine them, in the agency's statutory authorization to act, as well as in other congressional directives. [Citations.]

Once an agency has considered the relevant factors, it must define goals for its action that fall somewhere within the range of reasonable choices. We review that choice, like all agency decisions to which we owe deference, on the grounds that the agency itself has advanced. [Citation.]

... [The EIS] describes five alternatives: approving the Port Authority's plan for expanding Toledo Express, approving other geometric configurations for expanding Toledo Express, approving other ways of channelling airplane traffic at Toledo Express, no action by the agency at all, and approving plans for other airports both in the Toledo metropolitan area and out of it, including Baer Field in Fort Wayne. Finally, the EIS briefly explains why the agency eliminated all the alternatives but the first and the fourth. *See* 40 C.F.R. § 1502.14(a).

The FAA's reasoning fully supports its decision to evaluate only the preferred and do-nothing alternatives. The agency first examined Congress's views on how this country is to build its civilian airports. As the agency explained, Congress has told the FAA to nurture aspiring cargo hubs. [Citation.] At the same time, however, Congress has also said that the free market, not an ersatz Gosplan for aviation, should determine the siting of the nation's airports. [Citations.] Congress has expressed its intent by statute, and the FAA took both of Congress's messages seriously.

The FAA also took into account the Port Authority's reasons for wanting a cargo hub in Toledo. In recent years, more than fifty major companies have left the Toledo metropolitan area, and with them, over seven thousand jobs. The Port Authority expects the cargo hub at Toledo Express to create immediately more than two hundred permanent and six hundred part-time jobs with a total payroll value of more than $10 million. After three years, according to the Port Authority, the hub should create directly more than one thousand permanent jobs at the airport and one hundred and fifty other, airport-related jobs. The University of Toledo estimates that the new Toledo Express will contribute at least $42 million to the local economy after one full year of operation and nearly $68 million per year after three. In addition, the Port Authority expects the expanded airport, and Burlington's presence there, to attract other companies to Toledo. All of those factors, the Port Authority hopes, will lead to a renaissance in the Toledo metropolitan region.

Having thought hard about these appropriate factors, the FAA defined the goal for its action as helping to launch a new cargo hub in Toledo and thereby helping to fuel the Toledo economy. The agency then eliminated from detailed discussion the alternatives that would not accomplish this goal. Each of the different geometric configurations would mean technological problems and extravagant costs. So would plans to route traffic differently at Toledo Express, or to build a hub at one of the other airports in the city of Toledo. None of the airports outside of the Toledo area would serve the purpose of the agency's action. The FAA thus evaluated the environmental impacts of the only proposal that might reasonably accomplish that goal — approving the construction and operation of a cargo hub at Toledo Express. It did so with the thoroughness required by law. *See* 40 C.F.R. § 1502.16.

We conclude that the FAA acted reasonably in defining the purpose of its action, in eliminating alternatives that would not achieve it, and in discussing (with the required do-nothing option) the proposal that would. The agency has therefore complied with NEPA.

Citizens agree that the FAA need only discuss reasonable, not all, alternatives to Toledo Express. Relying on *Van Abbema v. Fornell*, 807 F.2d 633 (7th Cir. 1986), however, Citizens argues that "the evaluation of 'alternatives' mandated by NEPA is to be an evaluation of alternative means to accomplish the *general* goal of an action; it is not an evaluation of the alternative means by which a particular applicant can reach his goals." According to Citizens, the "general goal" of the Port Authority's proposal is to build a permanent cargo hub for Burlington. Since, in Citizen's view, Fort Wayne (and perhaps Peoria) will accomplish this general goal just as well as Toledo, if not better, Baer Field is a reasonable alternative to Toledo Express, and the FAA should have discussed it in depth. Since it did not, this court should force the FAA to prepare a new (or supplemental) environmental impact statement.

We see two critical flaws in *Van Abbema* and therefore in Citizens' argument. The first is that the *Van Abbema* court misconstrued the language of NEPA. *Van Abbema* involved a private businessman who had applied to the Army Corps of Engineers for permission to build a place to "transload" coal from trucks to barges. The panel decided that the Corps had to survey "feasible alternatives ... to the applicant's proposal," or alternative ways of accomplishing "the general goal [of] deliver[ing] coal from mine to utility." [Citation.] In commanding agencies to discuss "alternatives to the proposed action," however, NEPA plainly refers to alternatives to the "major *Federal* actions significantly affecting the quality of the human environment," and not to alternatives to the applicant's proposal. An agency cannot redefine the goals of the proposal that arouses the call for action; it must evaluate alternative ways of achieving *its* goals, shaped by the application at issue and by the function that the agency plays in the decisional process. Congress did expect agencies to consider an applicant's wants when the agency formulates the goals of its own proposed action. Congress did not expect agencies to determine for the applicant what the goals of the applicant's proposal should be.

The second problem with *Van Abbema* lies in the court's assertion that an agency must evaluate "alternative means to accomplish the general goal of an action," 807 F.2d at 638 (emphasis deleted) — a statement that troubles us even if we assume that the panel was alluding to the general goals of the federal action instead of to the goals of the private proposal. Left unanswered in *Van Abbema* and Citizens' brief (and at oral argument) is why and how to distinguish general goals from specific ones and just who does the distinguishing. Someone has to define the purpose of the agency action. Implicit in *Van Abbema* is that the body responsible is the reviewing court. As we explained, however, NEPA and binding case law provide otherwise.

In chiding this court for having over-reached in construing NEPA, a unanimous Supreme Court once wrote that Congress enacted NEPA "to ensure a fully informed and well-considered decision, not necessarily a decision the judges of the Court of Appeals or of this Court would have reached had they been members of the decisionmaking unit of the agency." We are forbidden from taking sides in the debate over the merits of developing the Toledo Express Airport; we are required instead only to confirm that the FAA has fulfilled its statutory obligations. Events may someday vindicate Citizens' belief that the FAA's judgment was unwise. All that this court decides today is that the judgment was not uninformed.

The regulations of the Council on Environmental Quality provide that an environmental impact statement "shall [contain] a full and fair discussion of significant environmental impacts" and that "[i]mpacts shall be discussed in proportion to their significance." 40 C.F.R. §§ 1502.1, 1502.2(b); *see* NEPA § 102(2)(C)(i), (ii), 42 U.S.C. § 4332(2)(C)(i), (ii). The EIS in this case discusses more than twenty impacts that the expanded Toledo Express would have on the environment, including the airport's effects on people's homes and neighborhoods; on the quality of the air, the water, and the earth; on architectural, archeological, and cultural resources; on sewage disposal; on traffic patterns; on swamps, marshes, bogs, and rivers; and on bats, butterflies, grass, flowers, and trees. The EIS also states flatly that "[a]ircraft sound emissions" — noise, in a word — are often the most noticeable environmental effect[s] an airport will produce on the surrounding community." In all, the FAA devotes about half of its discussion on environmental consequences to the effects of an increase in noise. Although Citizens does not argue that the FAA failed to discuss the impacts of noise in rough proportion to the effects' importance, it does argue that the discussion is incomplete and unfair. We disagree....

In examining the impacts of noise on the environment, the FAA relies on wisdom and experience peculiar to the agency and alien to the judges on this court. We have thus held consistently that the rule of reason guides every aspect of the FAA's approach, including its choice of scientific method. Employing here a method that we have previously endorsed, the FAA proceeded to mold a body of data, dissect it, and display it in comprehensible forms. The agency's choice of method was obviously not capricious. Nor were the factual conclusions that followed. [Citations.]

The EPA's criticisms of the FAA, and the agencies' subsequent deal, do not change our view of the FAA's findings. Congress wants the EPA to participate when other agencies prepare environmental impact statements. The EPA participated here. But the FAA, not the EPA, bore the ultimate statutory responsibility for actually preparing the environmental impact statement, and under the rule of reason, a lead agency does not have to follow the EPA's comments slavishly — it just has to take them seriously. The FAA considered the EPA's criticisms in this case and decided that enough had been done. That the FAA sensibly resolved to avoid any interagency disputes in the future does not make its decision in this case unreasonable. We uphold the FAA's discussion of the impacts of increased noise.

The regulations of the Council on Environmental Quality require that an environmental impact statement "be prepared directly by or by a contractor selected by the lead agency." 40 C.F.R. § 1506.5(c). If the agency decides to contract out the work on the EIS, the agency must choose the contractor "to avoid a conflict of interest," and the contractor must "execute a disclosure statement prepared by the lead agency ... specifying that [it has] no financial or other interest in the outcome of the project." Citizens argues that the FAA violated the regulations by publishing an EIS prepared for the most part by a contractor (Coffman Associates) that the agency did not itself select and that did not in any event fill out the necessary disclosure forms. The FAA maintains that it (the FAA), and not Coffman, prepared the EIS, that even if Coffman did prepare the EIS, it (the FAA), and not the Port Authority, selected Coffman, and that even though Coffman did not fill out the disclosure statement, its (Coffman's) failure to do so was harmless error.

We reject each of the FAA's contentions. Offered the choice of preparing the environmental impact statement in-house, the FAA chose the other permissible option and hired consultants, including Coffman. The FAA then wrote the consultants' names and qualifications, including Coffman's, in a chapter of the EIS entitled "List of Preparers," a gesture that undermines the agency's current litigating position — that Coffman did *not* prepare the EIS, but that the FAA did instead, mostly by commenting actively on Coffman's drafts. Ultimately, however, the agency's theory founders on the plain meaning of the regulations. Although the CEQ regulations do not define the word "prepare," the dictionary does; in context, it means here "to put into written form: draw up...." *Webster's Third New Int'l Dictionary* 1790 (unabridged ed. 1981). That is just what Coffman did, as the agency freely admits. We need not decide whether the FAA's active editing of Coffman's drafts — behavior consistent with the agency's obligation to "furnish guidance" to consultants and "participate in the preparation [of] and ... independently evaluate the statement prior to its approval," 40 C.F.R. § 1506.5(c) — made it, too, a preparer of the EIS. We are certain, however, that Coffman's initial drafts and responses to the FAA's comments made Coffman more than the agency's amanuensis.

Once the FAA decided not to prepare the environmental impact statement directly, it was obliged to pick a contractor itself, and not to delegate the responsibility. The EIS states that the Port Authority, not the agency, chose Coffman to work on the environmental assessment, and later, on the environmental impact statement. The EIS also states that the agency "concurred" in Coffman's selection. The FAA argues that its concurrence in the Port Authority's choice satisfied its duty under the regulations. We need not page through the dictionary at length to decide that concurring in someone else's choice of consultant is not the same as choosing a consultant of one's own.

By failing to select the consultant that prepared the environmental impact statement, the FAA violated CEQ regulations. Citizens urges us to remedy this breach by invalidating the EIS. We see no reason to do so, however, at least not solely on the ground that the FAA neglected to search on its own for a competent contractor. This particular error did not compromise the "objectivity and integrity of the NEPA process." [Citations.]

The more serious infraction, in our view, was Coffman's failure to fill out the disclosure form exacted of consultants that prepare environmental impact statements. *See id.* § 1506.5(c).... Moreover, the CEQ regulations prohibit broadly any "financial *or other interest* in the outcome of the project." The FAA promised the petitioners in a letter that "Coffman does not have an undisclosed stake in the project that would potentially disqualify it." That *ipse dixit* does not reassure us. We therefore order the FAA to have Coffman execute an appropriate disclosure statement, and, should the agency find that a conflict exists, to decide — promptly — on the measures to take in response.

....

We hold that the FAA has fulfilled the requirements of NEPA, ... and all the CEQ regulations but one. We therefore grant the petition for review and remand to the agency so that it may comply with 40 C.F.R. § 1506.5(c). We affirm the FAA's decision in all other aspects. Given the limited nature of what remains for the agency to do, we decline to enjoin the continuing development of Toledo Express or to grant any other of the equitable relief that the petitioners have asked for. [Citations.]

It is so ordered.

BUCKLEY, CIRCUIT JUDGE, dissenting in part.

....

The majority would limit the consideration of alternatives to those available to the Toledo-Lucas County Port Authority. As the majority sees it, the FAA "defined the goal for its action as helping to launch a new cargo hub in Toledo and thereby helping to fuel the Toledo economy." As a consequence, airports outside the Toledo area were not to be considered because "[n]one ... would serve the purpose of the agency's action." I read the EIS differently. Recognizing that Burlington is an essential party to the Port Authority's application, the FAA understands that the EIS must consider any reasonable alternative to Toledo Express Airport that might be available to Burlington, whether it lies within the Toledo area or outside it.

....

The FAA takes a broader view of its responsibilities because it acknowledges that the proposed project is intended to serve several purposes. Toledo seeks the substantial economic benefits that will accrue from the establishment of an air cargo hub in its metropolitan area. Burlington seeks a home for its air cargo operations, one that will be tailored to its specifications. For its part, the FAA is conscious of its mandate, under the Airport and Airway Improvement Act ("AAIA"), 49 U.S.C. App. § 2201(a)(7) (1988), to encourage the development of a national system of air cargo hubs.

I cannot fault the FAA for the attention given Burlington and its preferences. While both Toledo and Burlington are indispensable to the enterprise, Burlington is plainly the dominant partner; its requirements and desires shaped the project from the start. As the agency points out in its Record of Decision ("ROD"), "[t]he demand for this project is clearly based on a business decision by Burlington Air Express and the interest of a local airport sponsor, the Toledo-Lucas County Port Authority, in accommodating and facilitating this decision."

I do fault the agency for failing to attend to its own business, which is to examine all alternatives "that are practical or feasible from the technical and economic standpoint ... rather than simply desirable from the standpoint of the applicant." [Citation.] As far as I can tell, the FAA never questioned Burlington's assertions that of the ones considered, Toledo Express is the only airport suitable to its purposes. Instead, the agency simply accepted Burlington's "Toledo-or-bust" position.... The FAA thus accepts at face value Burlington's assertion that it had no second choice.

....

I do not suggest that Burlington is untrustworthy, only that the FAA had the duty under NEPA to exercise a degree of skepticism in dealing with self-serving statements from a prime beneficiary of the project. It may well be that none of the sixteen other alternatives examined by Burlington and its consultants could be converted into a viable air cargo hub at acceptable cost. That, however, was something that the FAA should have determined for itself instead of accepting as a given. Under NEPA, "the federal agency must itself determine what is reasonably available." [Citations.] By allowing the FAA to abandon this requirement, the majority establishes a precedent that will permit an applicant and a third-party beneficiary of federal action to define the limits of the EIS inquiry and thus to frustrate one of the principal safeguards of the NEPA process, the mandatory consideration of reasonable alternatives.

. . . .

Even if the FAA had correctly concluded that the only reasonable alternative was "No Action," its EIS would still be flawed. By viewing the no-action alternative exclusively through Toledo's eyes, it failed to appreciate that that city's gains must necessarily be Fort Wayne's losses. Thus the EIS informs us that whereas the proposed project would produce 750 new jobs and $17 million for the Toledo economy during the first full year of operation, "the no-action alternative would mean foregoing ... [these] economic benefits."

This analysis suggests that the jobs and dollars will arise spontaneously from the Toledo soil. In reality, Toledo's gains will come at Fort Wayne's expense. Burlington's Fort Wayne payroll is $8 million; its Toledo payroll will begin at $9 million. If the project were canceled, Toledo would forego "substantial economic benefits," but, unless Burlington were to shut down entirely, which it has asserted it will not, Toledo's loss would be offset by jobs and economic activity in Fort Wayne, or whatever other city ultimately served as Burlington's permanent hub.

. . . .

The FAA was probably free to disregard economic effects in the EIS. *See* CEQ Regulations, 40 C.F.R. § 1508.14 (1990) (requiring discussion of economic effects only if they are "interrelated" with natural environmental effects). Once it undertook to discuss them, however, it was obliged to be impartial; an EIS "must be objectively prepared and not slanted to support the choice of the agency's preferred alternative." Because the FAA's no-action analysis failed to recognize the impact on the Fort Wayne economy, it failed to meet the standard of objectivity required by NEPA.

The EIS requirement "seeks to ensure that each agency decision maker has before him and takes into proper account all possible approaches to a particular project ... which would alter the environmental impact and the cost-benefit balance." [Citation.] With its uncritical dismissal of alternatives and its myopic view of economic consequences, the EIS here fell short of this objective. As a result we cannot be confident that in approving Toledo's application, the FAA took the pertinent environmental as well as economic and technical considerations into the balance. And that, of course, is the purpose of the National Environmental Policy Act.

By sanctioning the FAA's approach, the majority in effect allows a non-federal party to sort out alternatives based entirely on economic considerations, and then to present its preferred alternative as a take-it-or-leave-it proposition. If allowed to stand, today's decision will undermine the NEPA aim of "inject[ing] environmental considerations into the federal agency's decisionmaking process." [Citation.] The discussion of reasonable alternatives — "the heart of the environmental impact statement," 40 C.F.R. § 1502.14 — becomes an empty exercise when the only alternatives addressed are the proposed project and inaction.

In our first encounter with NEPA twenty years ago, we spoke of the duty to ensure that "important legislative purposes, heralded in the halls of Congress, are not lost or misdirected in the vast hallways of the federal bureaucracy." Because I believe that the court today shirks that duty, I respectfully dissent.

DUBOIS v. UNITED STATES DEPARTMENT OF AGRICULTURE

102 F.3d 1273 (1st Cir. 1996)

BOWNES, SENIOR CIRCUIT JUDGE.

The defendant-intervenor Loon Mountain Recreation Corporation ("Loon Corp.") operates a ski resort in the White Mountain National Forest in Lincoln, New Hampshire. In order to expand its skiing facilities, Loon Corp. sought and received a permit to do so from the United States Forest Service. Appellant Roland Dubois sued the Forest Service alleging violations of the National Environmental Policy Act ("NEPA"), 42 U.S.C. § 4321, *et seq.*, [and other federal statutes].... The district court granted the Forest Service's motion for summary judgment and denied the other motions. We affirm in part, reverse in part, and remand.

I. *Statement of the Case*

A. *Facts*

The White Mountain National Forest ("WMNF") is a public resource managed by the United States Forest Service for a wide range of competing public uses and purposes, including "outdoor recreation, range, timber, watershed, ... wildlife and fish purposes," and skiing. Pursuant to the National Forest Management Act of 1976, the Forest Service makes long-term plans to coordinate these competing uses, and issues "special use" permits authorizing private recreational services on national forest land....

Loon Pond is located in the WMNF at an elevation of 2,400 feet. It has a surface area of 19 acres, with shallow areas around the perimeter and a central bowl 65 feet deep. It is unusual for its relatively pristine nature. There is virtually no human activity within the land it drains except skiing at the privately owned Loon Mountain Ski Area.... It ranks in the upper 95th percentile of all lakes and ponds in northern New England for low levels of phosphorus, which results in limited plant growth and therefore high water clarity and higher total biological production. The pond supports a rich variety of life in its ecosystem. Loon Pond also constitutes a major source of drinking water for the town of Lincoln 1,600 feet below it. A dam across the outlet of the Pond regulates the flow of water from the Pond to Lincoln's municipal reservoir.

Loon Corp., defendant-intervenor herein, owns the Loon Mountain Ski Area, which has operated since the 1960s not far from Loon Pond. Prior to the permit revision that gave rise to this litigation, Loon Corp. held a special use permit to operate on 785 acres of WMNF land. That permit allowed Loon Corp. to draw water ("drawdown") for snowmaking from Loon Pond, as well as from the East Branch of the Pemigewasset River ("East Branch") and from nearby Boyle Brook....

In 1986, Loon Corp. applied to the Forest Service for an amendment to its special use permit to allow expansion of its facilities within the WMNF. Pursuant to NEPA, 42 U.S.C. § 4332, the Service developed a draft EIS, and a supplement to the draft. Responding to criticism of the adequacy of those documents, the Forest Service issued a revised draft EIS ("RDEIS"), which was published for public comment. The RDEIS set forth five alternatives to meet the perceived demand for additional alpine skiing. All five were located at the Loon Mountain site....

During the EIS process, Ron Buso, a hydrologist for the WMNF, expressed concern to another Forest Service hydrologist that the proposed drawdown of Loon Pond by twenty feet was likely to have a severe impact on the Pond. He explained that natural snowmelt in New Hampshire is extremely acidic and that, as a result of the planned drawdown, a substantial amount of acidic snowmelt would remain in Loon Pond, increasing the Pond's acidity by a factor of two to three times what it would be without the planned drawdown. Without the drawdown, Loon Pond would be relatively full in the spring, and much of the snowmelt from surrounding higher elevations would glide over the surface of the Pond and down the mountain without significantly mixing with other Loon Pond water. According to Buso and a number of scientists whose affidavits were submitted to the district court, the increase in the Pond's acidity due to the planned drawdown would change the chemistry of the Pond, cause toxic metals to be released from the sediment, and kill naturally occurring organisms.

Without addressing the issues raised in the Buso memorandum or in the comments suggesting artificial storage ponds, the Forest Service prepared a Final EIS ("FEIS"). The FEIS added a sixth alternative, also on the Loon Mountain site. The new alternative provided for expansion of Loon Corp.'s permit area by 581 acres and for the construction of one new lift and approximately 70 acres of new ski trails, changes designed to accommodate 3,200 additional skiers per day (from the current 5,800 per day). The Forest Service deemed Alternative 6 as the preferred alternative. Under it, Loon Corp. would more than double the amount of water used for snowmaking, from 67 million gallons per year to 138 million gallons. Seventeen million gallons of the increase would be drawn from the East Branch, and 54 million gallons from Loon Pond. In addition, Loon Corp. was authorized to draw the Pond down for snowmaking by fifteen feet, compared to the current eighteen inches. The Forest Service assumed that the Town of Lincoln would need up to an additional five feet of Pond water, making a total of twenty feet that the Pond was expected to be drawn down each year. This would constitute approximately 63% of the Pond's water. In March 1993, the Forest Service published a Record of Decision (ROD) adopting Alternative 6.

.. ... NEPA requires that the agency take a "hard look" at the environmental consequences of a project before taking a major action. [Citation] It is the role of the courts on judicial review to ensure "that this legal duty is fulfilled." [Citation]

Congress, in enacting NEPA, meant "to insure a fully informed and well-considered decision." But NEPA "does not mandate particular results"; it "simply prescribes the necessary process." [Citation] "If the adverse environmental effects of the proposed action are adequately identified and evaluated, the agency is not constrained by NEPA from deciding that other values outweigh the environmental costs." Thus, "the role of the courts is simply to ensure that the agency has adequately considered and disclosed the environmental impact of its actions and that its decision is not arbitrary or capricious."...

IV. *The NEPA/EIS Issue*

The National Environmental Policy Act (NEPA), 42 U.S.C. § 4321 *et seq.*, declares a broad national commitment to protecting and promoting environmental quality. The primary mechanism for implementing NEPA is the Environmental Impact Statement (EIS). 42 U.S.C. § 4332 (1994). The EIS is an "action-forcing" procedure, designed "to ensure that this commitment is infused into the ongoing programs and actions of the Federal Government."

NEPA requires that an agency considering any action that would have a significant impact on the environment prepare an EIS. The EIS must contain a "*detailed* statement" including, *inter alia*, the environmental impacts of the proposed project, and all reasonable alternatives to the project. 42 U.S.C. § 4332(C) (emphasis added). We previously emphasized the word "detailed" because "it connotes the careful, reasoned and fully explained analysis which we think Congress intended." [Citation] Thus, the EIS helps satisfy NEPA's "twin aims": to ensure that the agency takes a "hard look" at the environmental consequences of its proposed action, and to make information on the environmental consequences available to the public, which may then offer its insight to assist the agency's decision-making through the comment process. The EIS thus "helps insure the integrity of the process of decision," providing a basis for comparing the environmental problems raised by the proposed project with the difficulties involved in the alternatives.

A. *Consideration of Environmental Impacts*

In its EIS, the agency must "consider every significant aspect of the environmental impact of a proposed action," and "evaluate different courses of action." The EIS's discussion of environmental impacts "forms the scientific and analytic basis for the comparisons" of alternatives, 40 C.F.R. § 1502.16 (1995), which are "the heart" of the EIS, id. at § 1502.14. The discussion of impacts must include both "direct and indirect effects (secondary impacts) of a proposed project." 40 C.F.R. § 1502.16(b). The agency need not speculate about all conceivable impacts, but it must evaluate the reasonably foreseeable significant effects of the proposed action. In this context, reasonable foreseeability means that "the impact is sufficiently likely to occur that a person of ordinary prudence would take it into account in reaching a decision." Id. An environmental effect would be considered "too speculative" for inclusion in the EIS if it cannot be described at the time the EIS is drafted with sufficient specificity to make its consideration useful to a reasonable decision-maker. Nevertheless, "reasonable forecasting ... is ... implicit in NEPA, and we must reject any attempt by agencies to shirk their responsibilities under NEPA by labeling any and all discussion of future environmental effects as 'crystal ball inquiry.'"...

B. *Consideration of Alternatives*

"One important ingredient of an EIS is the discussion of steps that can be taken to mitigate adverse environmental consequences" of a proposed action. As one aspect of evaluating a proposed course of action under NEPA, the agency has a duty "to study all alternatives that appear reasonable and appropriate for study ..., as well as significant alternatives suggested by other agencies or the public during the comment period." [Citations]

As stated in the Council on Environmental Quality ("CEQ") regulations implementing NEPA, the consideration of alternatives is "the heart of the environmental impact statement." 40 C.F.R. § 1502.14. These implementing regulations are entitled to substantial deference. [Citation] The regulations require that the EIS "rigorously explore and objectively evaluate all reasonable alternatives, and for alternatives which were eliminated from detailed study, briefly discuss the reasons for their having been eliminated." 40 C.F.R. § 1502.14(a). It is "absolutely essential to the NEPA process that the decision-maker be provided with a detailed and careful analysis of the relative environmental merits and demerits of the proposed action and possible alternatives, a requirement that we have characterized as 'the linchpin of the entire impact statement.'" [Citation] "The 'existence of a viable but unexamined alternative renders an environmental impact statement inadequate.'" [Citations] Because of the importance of NEPA's procedural and informational aspects, if the agency fails to properly circulate the required issues for review by interested parties, then the EIS is insufficient even if the agency's actual decision was informed and well-reasoned. [Citation]

C. *The Requisite Level of Detail*

One purpose of the EIS requirement is to "provide decisionmakers with sufficiently detailed information to aid in determining whether to proceed with the action in light of its environmental consequences." [Citation] What level of detail is sufficient depends on the nature and scope of the proposed action. The discussion of environmental effects of alternatives need not be exhaustive. "What is required is information sufficient to permit a reasoned choice of alternatives as far as environmental aspects are concerned," information sufficient for the agency to "rigorously explore and objectively evaluate" all reasonable alternatives. 40 C.F.R. § 1502.14(a).

The courts have applied "a rule of reason in determining whether an EIS contains a reasonably thorough discussion of the significant aspects of the probable environmental consequences." One aspect of this determination is whether the agency has gone "beyond mere assertions and indicated its basis for them." The agency "must 'explicate fully its course of inquiry, its analysis and its reasoning.'" The court must determine whether, in the context of the record, the agency's decision — and the analysis on which it is based — is too unreasonable for the law to permit it to stand. We apply a rule of reason because courts should not "fly speck" an EIS and hold it insufficient based on inconsequential or technical deficiencies. "The statute must be construed in the light of reason if it is not to demand what is, fairly speaking, not meaningfully possible.... But implicit in this rule of reason is the overriding statutory duty of compliance with impact statement procedures to the fullest extent possible." The agency must "squarely turn[]" all "procedural corners" in its EIS. The question whether a particular deficiency or combination is sufficient to warrant holding it legally inadequate, or constitutes merely a "fly speck," is essentially a legal question, reviewable de novo.

Applying these standards to the instant case, we conclude that the Forest Service has not rigorously explored all reasonable alternatives, in particular the alternative that Loon Corp. be required to build artificial water storage ponds, instead of withdrawing water for snowmaking from, and discharging water into, an "outstanding resource water" like Loon Pond. The adverse environmental impacts of using Loon Pond were before the agency, and more than one commenter proposed building artificial water storage ponds, a proposal that would, on its face, avoid some of those adverse impacts....

Instead of "rigorously exploring" the alternative of using artificial water storage units instead of Loon Pond, the Forest Service's Final EIS did not respond to these comments at all. The agency did not in any way explain its reasoning or provide a factual basis for its refusal to consider, in general, the possibility of alternatives to using Loon Pond for snowmaking, or LCCC's reasonably thoughtful proposal in particular. This failure violated the Forest Service's EIS obligation under NEPA. *See* 40 C.F.R. § 1502.9(b) (1995); 42 U.S.C. § 4332(C)(iii) (1994)....

Our conclusion is buttressed by NEPA's requirement that an agency consider and an EIS discuss "steps that can be taken to mitigate the adverse environmental consequences" of a proposed project. Even though there is no requirement that the agency reach a particular substantive result, such as actually formulating and adopting a complete mitigation plan, the agency must discuss "the extent to which adverse effects can be avoided," i.e., by mitigation measures, "in sufficient detail to ensure that environmental consequences have been fairly evaluated." This duty — coupled with the comments alerting the agency to the environmental consequences of using Loon Pond for snowmaking and suggesting the containment pond solution — required the Forest Service to seriously consider this alternative and to explain its reasoning if it rejected the proposal.

Nor can the Forest Service claim that its failure to consider an alternative to using Loon Pond for snowmaking was a de minimis or "fly speck" issue. The record indicates serious adverse consequences to Loon Pond if it is used "as a cistern," to use EPA's words, and at least a reasonable probability that the use of artificial storage ponds could avoid those consequences. The existence of this non-de minimis "viable but unexamined alternative renders [the Loon EIS] inadequate."

After the matter had proceeded to court, counsel for the Forest Service argued that constructing artificial storage ponds large enough to serve as an alternative to using Loon Pond would not be a viable alternative for reasons that were conclusorily stated. The district court accepted this argument. But this "post hoc rationalization of counsel" cannot overcome the agency's failure to consider and address in its FEIS the alternative proposed by commenters. Such post hoc rationalizations are inherently suspect, and in any event are no substitute for the agency's following statutorily mandated procedures. As noted supra, even if the agency's actual decision was a reasoned one, the EIS is insufficient if it does not properly discuss the required issues.

In sum, how "probing" an investigation NEPA requires of alternatives depends on the circumstances, including the nature of the action at issue. Thus, the reviewing court must be flexible in evaluating the depth of analysis to require in an EIS, because, while NEPA "does not mandate particular results," it does require that the agency have adequately identified and evaluated a project's environmental consequences. "NEPA's success in large part arises from the use of legal concepts [that are flexible] such as 'reasonableness' and 'adequacy' that permit courts to adapt it successfully to so many different kinds of circumstances surrounding so many different kinds of governmental decisions."

... The agency has discretion to balance competing concerns and to choose among alternatives, but it must legitimately assess the relative merits of reasonable alternatives before making its decision.

After a searching and careful review of the record in the instant case, we are not convinced that the Forest Service's decision was founded on a reasoned evaluation of the relevant factors, or that it articulated a rational connection between the facts found and the choice made. Hence, it acted arbitrarily and capriciously in granting Loon Corp.'s special use permit for the expanded ski resort. Moreover, because the Forest Service did not satisfy the requirement that it "rigorously explore and objectively evaluate" all reasonable alternatives, 40

C.F.R. § 1502.14(a), its decision was not in accordance with law. *See* 5 U.S.C. § 706(2)(A).

V. *Supplemental EIS*

Plaintiffs also appeal the district court's conclusion that the Forest Service was not required, under NEPA, to prepare a supplemental EIS. The question of a supplemental EIS is premised on the dual purposes of the EIS: to assure that the public who might be affected by the proposed project be fully informed of the proposal, its impacts and all major points of view; and to give the agency the benefit of informed comments and suggestions as it takes a "hard look" at the consequences of proposed actions. *See* 40 C.F.R. §§ 1502.1, 1502.9(a) (1995).

An agency "shall" prepare a supplemental EIS if, after issuing its latest draft EIS, "the agency makes substantial changes in the proposed action that are relevant to environmental concerns." 40 C.F.R. § 1502.9(c)(1)(i) (1995). The use of the word "shall" is mandatory, not precatory. It creates a duty on the part of the agency to prepare a supplemental EIS if substantial changes from any of the proposed alternatives are made and the changes are relevant to environmental concerns. Thus, as explained by CEQ, an additional alternative that has not been disseminated previously in a draft EIS may be adopted in a final EIS, without further public comment, only if it is "qualitatively within the spectrum of alternatives that were discussed" in the prior draft; otherwise a supplemental draft is needed. *See Forty Most Asked Questions Concerning CEQ's NEPA Regulations*, 46 Fed. Reg. 18026, #29b (1981).

We conclude, based on the record in this case, that a supplemental EIS was required.... In the instant case, however, nothing in the FEIS indicates that any such technically complex scientific analysis would be required in order for this court to determine that Alternative 6 involves a "substantial change" from the prior proposals at Loon Mountain.

Alternative 6, adopted by the Forest Service as its preferred alternative in the final EIS, does not fall "within the spectrum of alternatives" that were considered in previous drafts, even if Phase II of Alternative 2 had been adequately analyzed prior to the FEIS. Alternative 6 entails a different configuration of activities and locations, not merely a reduced version of a previously-considered alternative. Phase II of Alternative 2 proposed expanding the ski area primarily on land that is not within the current permit area; in contrast, Alternative 6 squeezes much of its expansion into that current permit area. To accomplish this, Alternative 6 widens existing trails so as to eliminate buffers that currently separate the trails. It also envisions a 28,500-square-foot base lodge facility within the existing permit area. And it develops ski trails, access roads and lifts on land that the prior alternatives had left as a woodland buffer between the old ski area and the proposed expansion area. These are substantial changes from the previously-discussed alternatives, not mere modifications "within the spectrum" of those prior alternatives. It would be one thing if the Forest Service had adopted a new alternative that was actually within the range of previously considered alternatives, e.g., simply reducing the scale of every relevant particular. It is quite another thing to adopt a proposal that is configured differently, in which case public commenters might have pointed out, if given the opportunity — and the Forest Service might have seriously considered — wholly new problems posed by the new configuration (even if some of the environmental problems present in the prior alternatives have been eliminated).

... We conclude, based on the record in this case, that Alternative 6 entails substantial changes from the previously proposed actions that are relevant to environmental concerns, and that the Forest Service did not present those changes to the public in its FEIS for review and comment. Accordingly, the Forest Service's failure to prepare a supplemental EIS was arbitrary and capricious.

NOTES AND QUESTIONS

1. An early influential case dealing with the evaluation of alternatives to proposed agency actions under NEPA is *Natural Resources Defense Council v. Morton*, 458 F.2d 827 (D.C. Cir. 1972). The Secretary of the Interior, as part of President Nixon's energy program, engaged in leasing tracts of submerged land off the coast of Louisiana for oil and gas exploration. The NRDC sued to enjoin the leasing pending compliance with NEPA, alleging that the EIS failed to consider alternatives to the nation's energy problems. The court rejected the agency's argument that alternatives outside its jurisdiction to implement — such as changing oil import quotas — were still proper subjects for inclusion in an EIS. The alternative had to be reasonably available, but did not have to be within the province of the agency making the proposal. The court reasoned that one of the principal functions of an EIS, through its circulation to the executive and legislative branches, is as a tool in the decisionmaking process of government. The impact statement must provide a basis for comparing the overall benefits of a project with the potential environmental risks. The court also explained that the EIS requirement of assessing alternatives must be delimited by notions of reasonableness. Consequently, the alternative must be reasonably available, and those options which are simply remote or speculative can be excluded. The extent of discussion of an alternative is determined by a sliding scale where the less likely that an alternative is to be implemented, the less discussion is required.

2. Several years after *NRDC v. Morton*, the Supreme Court had an opportunity to consider the question of alternatives under NEPA in *Vermont Yankee Nuclear Power Corp. v. Natural Resources Defense Council*, 435 U.S. 519 (1978). The NRDC challenged the agency's issuance of a license for a nuclear reactor, claiming that the licensing commission failed to consider energy conservation issues as an alternative to constructing the power plant. The Court acknowledged that the definition of alternatives is an "evolving one," but found that the phrase "energy conservation" was overly broad and thus could suggest innumerable possible actions. The Court rejected NRDC's contentions and upheld the agency's actions.

Interestingly, although the Court quoted with apparent approval portions of the analysis in *Morton*, its own holding reflects a narrowing of what constitutes a reasonable alternative for NEPA purposes. The Court also intimated that upholding the agency's action was also justified because the NRDC had failed to participate adequately in administrative proceedings at an earlier stage to specify alternatives. Justice Rehnquist, writing for the Court, made the following observations about the concept of alternatives under NEPA:

> [A]s should be obvious even upon a moment's reflection, the term "alternatives" is not self-defining. To make an impact statement something more than an exercise in frivolous boilerplate the concept of alternatives must be bounded by some notion of feasibility.... Common sense also teaches us that the "detailed statement of alternatives" cannot be found wanting simply because the agency failed to include every alternative device and thought conceivable by the mind of man. Time and resources are simply too limited to hold that an impact statement fails because the agency failed to ferret out every possible alternative, regardless of how uncommon or unknown that alternative may have been at the time the project was approved.
> ... [T]he concept of "alternatives" is an evolving one, requiring the agency to explore more or fewer alternatives as they become better known and understood.
> ... [A]dministrative proceedings should not be a game or a forum to engage in unjustified obstructionism by making cryptic and obscure reference to matters that "ought to be" considered and then, after failing to do more to bring the matter to the agency's attention, seeking to have that agency determination vacated on the ground that the agency failed to consider matters "forcefully presented."

435 U.S. at 551-54.

3. The meaningful exploration and examination of reasonable alternatives to a proposed agency action — including taking no action — is central to effectuating the NEPA process. The CEQ regulation provides:

40 C.F.R. § 1502.14 Alternatives including the proposed action

This section is the heart of the environmental impact statement. Based on the information and analysis presented in the sections on the Affected Environment (§ 1502.15) and the Environmental Consequences (§ 1502.16), it should present the environmental impacts of the proposal and the alternatives in comparative form, thus sharply defining the issues and providing a clear basis for choice among options by the decisionmaker and the public. In this section agencies shall:

(a) Rigorously explore and objectively evaluate all reasonable alternatives, and for alternatives which were eliminated from detailed study, briefly discuss the reasons for their having been eliminated.

(b) Devote substantial treatment to each alternative considered in detail including the proposed action so that reviewers may evaluate their comparative merits.

(c) Include reasonable alternatives not within the jurisdiction of the lead agency.

(d) Include the alternative of no action.

(e) Identify the agency's preferred alternative or alternatives, if one or more exists, in the draft statement and identify such alternative in the final statement unless another law prohibits the expression of such a preference.

(f) Include appropriate mitigation measures not already included in the proposed action or alternatives.

4. In *Citizens Against Burlington*, one of the principal differences between the majority and the dissent centered on how broadly or narrowly to interpret the purpose of the proposal. Once the purpose is delineated, the range of reasonable alternatives to carry out the project's goals will necessarily follow and certain choices, by definition, will fall outside the options to be realistically considered.

The CEQ regulation defining "proposal" merely equates the term with a "goal" but does not explicate its parameters. *See* 40 C.F.R. § 1508.23. The Supreme Court has held that the scope of a project is shaped by the proposal itself. *Aberdeen & Rockfish R.R. v. Students Challenging Reg. Agency Procedures*, 422 U.S. 289 (1975). Can an agency evade meaningful NEPA review of alternatives to a project simply by declaring that the proposal is aimed at accomplishing a particular result, and thus limit the field of choices for the decisionmaker?

5. An interesting comparison of views of a project's purpose may be found in *City of Angoon v. Hodel*, 803 F.2d 1016 (9th Cir. 1986). The case involved a challenge to the adequacy of an impact statement for a proposed timber harvesting facility. A private enterprise which stood to benefit from the plans argued for a narrow construction of the purpose — that a specific log transfer facility be built at a designated location. The government agency, the Army Corps of Engineers, couched the purpose and need for the facility in terms of providing a "safe and cost effective means of transferring timber harvested on [the land] to market." Finally, the district court viewed the purpose in the broadest sense of promoting a generic public benefit through "commercial timber harvesting." The court of appeals sided with the formulation advanced by the Corps, but also observed that the consequence of so defining the purpose necessarily made certain suggested alternatives too speculative for consideration.

In a similar vein, in *North Buckhead Civic Ass'n v. Skinner*, 903 F.2d 1533, 1541 (11th Cir. 1990) a group sought to enjoin the construction of multi-lane highway with a mass transit component. The plaintiffs claimed that the agencies had defined the purpose of the project in such a manner that it would conclusively presume that the highway should be built as planned. The plaintiffs argued that other alternatives — such as not building or only constructing the mass transit portion — were perfunctorily dismissed for failing to accomplish the stated objectives. The court acknowledged that NEPA requires an assessment of alternatives which may meet only a *portion* of the stated needs and purposes behind a project. Whether those alternatives are actually selected, however, depends on if the decisionmaker determines that satisfying just part of a goal with less environmental effects is worth the tradeoff with a preferred alternative that would cause greater environmental impacts. The court found that the administrative record supported the agencies' actions. Does the court's analysis fully address the concern regarding narrowly defining a project's purpose and thereby foreclosing consideration of otherwise reasonable alternatives?

6. One court stated that when evaluating whether an agency had adequately studied all reasonable alternatives, a reviewing court may consider "the extent and sincerity of the opponents' participation." *Seacoast Anti-Pollution League v. Nuclear Reg. Comm'n*, 598 F.2d 1221, 1231 (1st Cir. 1979) ("played dog in the manger with respect to alerting the agency" to his views regarding alternatives, in an effort to "scuttle" the project).

ROBERTSON v. METHOW VALLEY CITIZENS COUNCIL
490 U.S. 332 (1989)

JUSTICE STEVENS delivered the opinion of the Court.

We granted certiorari to decide ... whether the National Environmental Policy Act requires federal agencies to include in each environmental impact statement: (a) a fully developed plan to mitigate environmental harm; and (b) a "worst case" analysis of potential environmental harm if relevant information concerning significant environmental effects is unavailable or too costly to obtain.

... This case arises out of the Forest Service's decision to issue a special use permit authorizing the development of a major destination alpine ski resort at Sandy Butte in the North Cascades mountains.

Sandy Butte is a 6,000-foot mountain located in the Okanogan National Forest in Okanogan County, Washington. At present Sandy Butte, like the Methow Valley it overlooks, is an unspoiled, sparsely populated area that the district court characterized as "pristine."...

In 1978, Methow Recreation, Inc. (MRI) applied for a special use permit to develop and operate its proposed "Early Winters Ski Resort" on Sandy Butte and a 1,165 acre parcel of land it had acquired adjacent to the National Forest. The proposed development would make use of approximately 3,900 acres of Sandy Butte; would entice visitors to travel long distances to stay at the resort for several days at a time; and would stimulate extensive commercial and residential growth in the vicinity to accommodate both vacationers and staff.

In response to MRI's application, the Forest Service, in cooperation with state and county officials, prepared an EIS known as the Early Winters Alpine Winter Sports Study (Early Winters Study or Study)....

... The Study considered the effect of each level of development on water resources, soil, wildlife, air quality, vegetation and visual quality, as well as land use and transportation in the Methow Valley, probable demographic shifts, the economic market for skiing and other summer and winter recreational activities in the Valley, and the energy requirements for the ski area and related developments. The Study's discussion of possible impacts was not limited to on-site effects, but also, as required by Council on Environmental Quality (CEQ) regulations, see C.F.R. § 1502.16(b) (1987), addressed "off-site impacts that each alternative might have on community facilities, socio-economic and other environmental conditions in the Upper Methow Valley.".... [The study also considered various on-site and off-site measures to mitigate the adverse effects of the project on wildlife and air quality. The Washington Department of Game, in response to the draft EIS, voiced particular concern about potential losses to the state's largest migratory deer herd which uses the Methow Valley as a winter range and migration route. The state agency estimated that the total population of deer likely to be affected exceeded 30,000 animals and that the ultimate impact on the herd could exceed a 50 percent reduction in numbers.]

Section 101 of NEPA declares a broad national commitment to protecting and promoting environmental quality. 42 U.S.C. § 4331. To ensure that this commitment is "infused into the ongoing programs and actions of the Federal Government, the act also establishes some important 'action-forcing' procedures."...

The statutory requirement that a federal agency contemplating a major action prepare such an environmental impact statement serves NEPA's "action-forcing" purpose in two important respects. [Citations.] It ensures that the agency, in reaching its decision, will have available and will carefully consider detailed information concerning significant environmental impacts; it also guarantees that the relevant information will be made available to the larger audience that may also play a role in both the decisionmaking process and the implementation of that decision.

Simply by focusing the agency's attention on the environmental consequences of a proposed project, NEPA ensures that important effects will not be overlooked or underestimated only to be discovered after resources have been committed or the die otherwise cast. Moreover, the strong precatory language of § 101 of the Act and the requirement that agencies prepare detailed impact statements inevitably bring pressure to bear on agencies "to respond to the needs of environmental quality."

Publication of an EIS, both in draft and final form, also serves a larger informational role. It gives the public the assurance that the agency "has indeed considered environmental concerns in its decisionmaking process," and, perhaps more significantly, provides a springboard for public comment. [Citations.] Thus, in this case the final draft of the Early Winters Study reflects not only the work of the Forest Service itself, but also the critical views of the Washington State Department of Game, the Methow Valley Citizens Council, and Friends of the

Earth, as well as many others, to whom copies of the draft Study were circulated.[13]

Moreover, with respect to a development such as Sandy Butte, where the adverse effects on air quality and the mule deer herd are primarily attributable to predicted off-site development that will be subject to regulation by other governmental bodies, the EIS serves the function of offering those bodies adequate notice of the expected consequences and the opportunity to plan and implement corrective measures in a timely manner.

The sweeping policy goals announced in § 101 of NEPA are thus realized through a set of "action-forcing" procedures that require that agencies take a "'hard look' at environmental consequences," and that provide for broad dissemination of relevant environmental information. Although these procedures are almost certain to affect the agency's substantive decision, it is now well settled that NEPA itself does not mandate particular results, but simply prescribes the necessary process. *See Strycker's Bay Neighborhood Council, Inc. v. Karlen*, 444 U.S. 223, 227-228 (1980); *Vermont Yankee Nuclear Power Corp. v. Natural Resources Defense Council, Inc.*, 435 U.S. 519, 558 (1978). If the adverse environmental effects of the proposed action are adequately identified and evaluated, the agency is not constrained by NEPA from deciding that other values outweigh the environmental costs. *See ibid.; Strycker's Bay Neighborhood Council, Inc., supra*, 444 U.S., at 227-28; *Kleppe*, 427 U.S., at 410 n.21. In this case, for example, it would not have violated NEPA if the Forest Service, after complying with the Act's procedural prerequisites, had decided that the benefits to be derived from downhill skiing at Sandy Butte justified the issuance of a special use permit, notwithstanding the loss of 15 percent, 50 percent, or even 100 percent of the mule deer herd. Other statutes may impose substantive environmental obligations on federal agencies, but NEPA merely prohibits uninformed — rather than unwise — agency action.

To be sure, one important ingredient of an EIS is the discussion of steps that can be taken to mitigate adverse environmental consequences.[15]

---

[13]The CEQ regulations require that, after preparing a draft EIS, the agency request comments from other federal agencies, appropriate state and local agencies, affected Indian tribes, any relevant applicant, the public generally, and, in particular, interested or affected person or organizations. 40 CFR § 1503.1 (1987). In preparing the final EIS, the agency must "discuss at appropriate points ... any responsible opposing view which was not adequately discussed in the draft statement and [must] indicate the agency's response to the issue raised." § 1502.9. *See also* § 1503.4.

[15]CEQ regulations define "mitigation" to include:

"(a) Avoiding the impact altogether by not taking a certain action or parts of an action.

"(b) Minimizing impacts by limiting the degree or magnitude of the action and its implementation.

"(c) Rectifying the impact by repairing, rehabilitating, or restoring the affected environment.

The requirement that an EIS contain a detailed discussion of possible mitigation measures flows from both the language of the Act and, more expressly, from CEQ's implementing regulations. Implicit in NEPA's demand that an agency prepare a detailed statement on "any adverse environmental effects which cannot be avoided should the proposal be implemented," 42 U.S.C. § 4332(C)(ii), is an understanding that the EIS will discuss the extent to which adverse effects can be avoided. [Citation.] More generally, omission of a reasonably complete discussion of possible mitigation measures would undermine the "action-forcing" function of NEPA. Without such a discussion, neither the agency nor other interested groups and individuals can properly evaluate the severity of the adverse effects. An adverse effect that can be fully remedied by, for example, an inconsequential public expenditure is certainly not as serious as a similar effect that can only be modestly ameliorated through the commitment of vast public and private resources. Recognizing the importance of such a discussion in guaranteeing that the agency has taken a "hard look" at the environmental consequences of proposed federal action, CEQ regulations require that the agency discuss possible mitigation measures in defining the scope of the EIS, 40 CFR § 1508.25(b) (1987), in discussing alternatives to the proposed action, § 1502.14(f), and consequences of that action, § 1502.16(h), and in explaining its ultimate decision, § 1505.2(c).

There is a fundamental distinction, however, between a requirement that mitigation be discussed in sufficient detail to ensure that environmental consequences have been fairly evaluated, on the one hand, and a substantive requirement that a complete mitigation plan be actually formulated and adopted, on the other. In this case, the off-site effects on air quality and on the mule deer herd cannot be mitigated unless nonfederal government agencies take appropriate action. Since it is those state and local governmental bodies that have jurisdiction over the area in which the adverse effects need be addressed and since they have the authority to mitigate them, it would be incongruous to conclude that the Forest Service has no power to act until the local agencies have reached a final conclusion on what mitigating measures they consider necessary. Even more significantly, it would be inconsistent with NEPA's reliance on procedural mechanisms — as opposed to substantive, result-based standards — to demand the presence of a fully developed plan that will mitigate environmental harm before an agency can act. [Citation.]

We thus conclude that the Court of Appeals erred, first, in assuming that "NEPA requires that 'action be taken to mitigate the adverse effects of major federal actions,'" and, second, in finding that this substantive requirement entails the further duty to include in every EIS "a detailed explanation of specific

---

"(d) Reducing or eliminating the impact over time by preservation and maintenance operations during the life of the action.

"(e) Compensating for the impact by replacing or providing substitute resources or environments." 40 CFR § 1508.20 (1987)."

measures which *will* be employed to mitigate the adverse impacts of a proposed action." [Citation.]

The Court of Appeals also concluded that the Forest Service had an obligation to make a "worst case analysis" if it could not make a reasoned assessment of the impact of the Early Winters project on the mule deer herd. Such a "worst case analysis" was required at one time by CEQ regulations, but those regulations have since been amended. Moreover, although the prior regulations may well have expressed a permissible application of NEPA, the Act itself does not mandate that uncertainty in predicting environmental harms be addressed exclusively in this manner. Accordingly, we conclude that the Court of Appeals also erred in requiring the "worst case" study.

In 1977, President Carter directed that CEQ promulgate binding regulations implementing the procedural provisions of NEPA. Exec. Order No. 11991, 3 CFR 123 (1977 Comp.). Pursuant to this presidential order, CEQ promulgated implementing regulations. Under [40 CFR] § 1502.22 of these regulations — a provision which became known as the "worst case requirement" — CEQ provided that if certain information relevant to the agency's evaluation of the proposed action is either unavailable or too costly to obtain, the agency must include in the EIS a "worst case analysis and an indication of the probability or improbability of its occurrence." In 1986, however, CEQ replaced the "worst case" requirement with a requirement that federal agencies, in the face of unavailable information concerning a reasonably foreseeable significant environmental consequence, prepare "a summary of existing credible scientific evidence which is relevant to evaluating the ... adverse impacts" and prepare an "evaluation of such impacts based upon theoretical approaches or research methods generally accepted in the scientific community." 40 CFR § 1502.22(b) (1987). The amended regulation thus "retains the duty to describe the consequences of a remote, but potentially severe impact, but grounds the duty in evaluation of scientific opinion rather than in the framework of a conjectural 'worst case analysis.'" 50 Fed. Reg. 32237 (1985).

The Court of Appeals recognized that the "worst case analysis" regulation has been superseded, yet held that "[t]his rescission ... does not nullify the requirement ... since the regulation was merely a codification or prior NEPA case law." This conclusion, however, is erroneous in a number of respects. Most notably, review of NEPA case law reveals that the regulation, in fact, was not a codification of prior judicial decisions.... As CEQ recognized at the time it superseded the regulation, case law prior to the adoption of the "worst case analysis" provision did require agencies to describe environmental impacts even in the face of substantial uncertainty, but did not require that this obligation necessarily be met through the mechanism of a "worst case analysis." *See* 52 Fed. Reg. 15625 (1986). CEQ's abandonment of the "worst case analysis" provision, therefore, is not inconsistent with any previously established judicial interpretation of the statute.

Nor are we convinced that the new CEQ regulation is not controlling simply because it was preceded by a rule that was in some respects more demanding. In *Andrus v. Sierra Club*, 442 U.S. 347, 358 (1979) we held that CEQ regulations are entitled to substantial deference. In that case we recognized that although less deference may be in order in some cases in which the "'administrative guidelines'" conflict "'with earlier pronouncements of the agency,'" substantial deference is nonetheless appropriate if there appears to have been good reason for the change. Here, the amendment only came after the prior regulation had been subjected to considerable criticism.[17]

Moreover, the amendment was designed to better serve the twin functions of an EIS — requiring agencies to take a "hard look" at the consequences of the proposed action and providing important information to other groups and individuals. CEQ explained that by requiring that an EIS focus on reasonably foreseeable impacts, the new regulation "will generate information and discussion on those consequences of greatest concern to the public and of greatest relevance to the agency's decision," rather than distorting the decisionmaking process by overemphasizing highly speculative harms. In light of this well-considered basis for the change, the new regulation is entitled to substantial deference. Accordingly, the Court of Appeals erred in concluding that the Early Winters Study is inadequate because it failed to include a "worst case analysis."

. . . .

In sum, we conclude that NEPA does not require a fully developed plan detailing what steps *will* be taken to mitigate adverse environmental impacts and does not require a "worst case analysis." In addition, we hold that the Forest Service has adopted a permissible interpretation of its own regulations. The judgment of the Court of Appeals is accordingly reversed and the case is remanded for further proceedings consistent with this opinion.

It is so ordered.

---

[17]As CEQ explained:

> "Many respondents to the Council's Advance Notice of Proposed Rulemaking pointed to the limitless nature of the inquiry established by this requirement; that is, one can always conjure up a worse 'worst case' by adding an additional variable to a hypothetical scenario. Experts in the field of risk analysis and perception stated that the 'worst case analysis' lacks defensible rationale or procedures, and that the current regulatory language stands 'without any discernible link to the disciplines that have devoted so much thought and effort toward developing rational ways to cope with problems of uncertainty. It is, therefore, not surprising that no one knows how to do a worst case analysis.... [Citation.] Moreover, in the institutional context of litigation over EIS(s) the 'worst case' rule has proved counterproductive, because it has led to agencies being required to devote substantial time and resources to preparation of analyses which are not considered useful to decisionmakers and divert the EIS process from its intended purpose." 50 Fed. Reg. 32236 (1985).

NOTES AND QUESTIONS

1. *Mitigation.* As recognized by the Court in *Methow Valley*, mitigation measures associated with a proposed project help shape the scope of the proposal, illuminate possible alternatives and potential adverse consequences, and may affect an agency's selection and explanation of a course of action. Thus, information regarding mitigation assists the decisionmakers in selecting a course of action or non-action — and stimulates public comment about the proposal. Conditions mitigating the environmental consequences of a proposed action may justify an agency's conclusion that a project's potential effects would not be "significant" enough to require preparation of an EIS. *Jones v. Gordon*, 792 F.2d 821, 829 (9th Cir. 1986). An agency still must independently analyze and explain how the mitigation measures would minimize the project's environmental impact. *See LaFlamme v. FERC*, 852 F.2d 389, 399-400 (9th Cir. 1988). Courts will review the administrative record to evaluate whether an agency has set forth specific reasons why mitigation measures render potential environmental impacts insignificant. *See The Steamboaters v. FERC*, 759 F.2d 1382, 1393 (9th Cir. 1985).

2. In *Friends of the Earth v. Hintz*, 800 F.2d 822 (9th Cir. 1986) groups challenged an agency's decision to issue a permit to a logging company for discharging fill material into a wetlands area without preparing an EIS. The agency had determined that the adverse effects of the loss of wetlands were mitigated by a plan whereby the company transferred title to a substitute parcel of land which would be converted into a wetlands area. The court, noting that the CEQ regulations defined "mitigation" as including providing for substitute resources (40 C.F.R. § 1508.20(e)), upheld the "off-site" mitigation measure as within the agency's reasoned discretion. Compare *Morgan v. Walter*, 728 F. Supp. 1483, 1491 (D. Idaho 1989) (mitigation plan involving establishing preservation zone to offset proposed water diversion project lacked adequate support to justify agency conclusion not to prepare EIS).

3. *Worst Case Analysis.* The current CEQ regulation which supersedes the "worst case analysis" provision states:

40 C.F.R. § 1502.22 Incomplete or unavailable information

When an agency is evaluating reasonably foreseeable significant adverse effects on the human environment in an environmental impact statement and there is incomplete or unavailable information, the agency shall always make clear that such information is lacking.

(a) If the incomplete information relevant to reasonably foreseeable significant adverse impacts is essential to a reasoned choice among alternatives and the overall costs of obtaining it are not exorbitant, the agency shall include the information in the environmental impact statement.

(b) If the information relevant to reasonably foreseeable significant adverse impacts cannot be obtained because the overall costs of obtaining it are exorbitant or the means to obtain it are not known, the agency shall include within the environmental impact statement: (1) A statement that such information is incomplete or unavailable; (2) a statement of the relevance of the incomplete or unavailable information to evaluating reasonably foreseeable significant adverse impacts on the human environment; (3) a summary of existing credible scientific evidence which is relevant to evaluating the reasonably foreseeable significant adverse impacts on the human environment, and (4) the agency's evaluation of such impacts based upon theoretical approaches or research methods generally accepted in the scientific community. For the purposes of this section, "reasonably foreseeable" includes impacts which have catastrophic consequences, even if their probability of occurrence is low, provided that the analysis of the impacts is supported by credible scientific evidence, is not based on pure conjecture, and is within the rule of reason.

(c) The amended regulation will be applicable to all environmental impact statements for which a Notice of Intent (40 CFR 1508.22) is published in the Federal Register on or after May 27, 1986. For environmental impact statements in progress, agencies may choose to comply with the requirements of either the original or amended regulation.

4. *Judicial Review*. NEPA contains no specific provision for judicial enforcement; however, courts have interpreted its procedural requirements as establishing a "strict standard of compliance" judicially reviewable under the Administrative Procedure Act. *Calvert Cliffs Coordinating Comm. v. Atomic Energy Comm'n*, 449 F.2d 1109, 1112 (D.C. Cir. 1971). Does NEPA merely set forth procedural obligations on federal agencies, though, or does its "action-forcing" character also allow for judicial scrutiny of substantive decisions made by agencies? When NEPA was initially enacted, some lower courts found the authority to undertake substantive review of agency actions by finding Congressional intent to effect substantive changes in agency decisionmaking. *Environmental Defense Fund v. Army Corps of Eng'rs*, 470 F.2d 289, 297-98 (8th Cir. 1972) (NEPA was more than "an environmental full-disclosure law"). In *Vermont Yankee Nuclear Power Corp. v. Natural Resources Defense Council*, 435 U.S. 519, 551, 558 (1978) the Court recognized that although NEPA had altered the statutory balance and set forth substantive goals regarding considering environmental values, the mandate for federal agencies was "essentially procedural."

Several years later, in *Strycker's Bay Neighborhood Council v. Karlen*, 444 U.S. 223 (1980) the Supreme Court evaluated a decision by the court of appeals overturning the selection of a site by HUD for a proposed low income housing project. The Court held that once an agency had complied with its duties under NEPA, the role of the reviewing court was limited to insuring that the agency actually considered environmental matters — not to substitute its judgment for the agency's on the merits. The reviewing court could not "interject itself within the area of discretion of the executive as to the choice of action to be taken." 444 U.S. at 227 (quoting *Kleppe v. Sierra Club*, 427 U.S. 390, 410 n.21 (1976)). Moreover, a reviewing court cannot elevate environmental considerations over other legitimate factors when determining agency compliance with NEPA. Courts must insure that the agency has met its statutory obligations in a bona fide manner, but their function is not to "fly speck" an impact statement searching for technical or inconsequential inadequacies. *Lathan v. Brinegar*, 506 F.2d 677, 693 (9th Cir. 1974). Finally, courts will accord particular deference to agency decisions predicated upon matters within the special expertise of the agency, such as involving scientific uncertainties. *See Baltimore Gas & Elec. Co. v. Natural Resources Defense Council*, 426 U.S. 87, 103 (1983) (Court most deferential when evaluating agency predictions at the frontiers of science).

5. The Court in *Robertson* apparently further limits the narrow window of substantive overview of agency action by characterizing the Act's policy in section 101 as "precatory" and stating that the nature of NEPA is to prescribe a "process" for considering environmental values rather than to mandate any particular results. By couching NEPA's reach solely in procedural terms, does the Court fail to give suitable consideration to the statutory policy in section 101 "to use all practicable means" to carry out the Act and in section 102 that "to the fullest extent possible" agencies must consider NEPA in conducting their business? Can reconciliation of the substantive-procedural debate be accomplished by viewing the arbitrary and capricious standard of review as sufficiently rigorous to give agencies appropriate deference yet not unbounded discretion in decisionmaking? Finally, recognition should be given to the statement in *Robertson* that the procedural obligations of NEPA will invariably influence the substantive decisions by agencies.

Part IV.

Federal Pollution Control Regulation

Chapter 6

AIR POLLUTION

INTRODUCTION

After studying the problem of air pollution for fifteen years, Congress in 1970 passed a comprehensive Clean Air Act to regulate pollution. Pub. L. No. 91-604, 84 Stat. 1676. This Clean Air Act (CAA), 42 U.S.C. §§ 7401-7671, was the first of many comprehensive federal pollution control laws to follow the environmental awakening of the 1970s. Although the CAA includes a number of provisions for improving air quality through federal subsidies, technical assistance, studies, training, and other methods, the bulk of the CAA and the focus of this chapter is the regulatory program for controlling air pollution.

The history of air pollution controls in the United States can be traced back to the early 1800s, although it was not until the late 1800s and early 1900s that state and local governments took an active role in regulating the air and water pollution from industrial expansion. *See generally* Laitos, *Legal Institutions and Pollution: Some Intersections Between Law and History*, 15 NAT. RESOURCES J. 423, 426-29 (1975). Private remedies were confined to case-by-base resolution through common law causes of action, such as trespass and nuisance. Although state and local regulation was not entirely ineffective, *see* Currie, *State Pollution Statutes*, 48 U. CHI. L. REV. 27 (1981), common law remedies were of only limited usefulness in rectifying problems of air pollution. Litigation, by not necessarily addressing the most serious or most common problems of air pollution, is a hit-and-miss strategy for control of any widespread environmental problem. In the few cases in which the polluter was compelled to pay for the damage caused, the common law was poorly equipped to handle the difficult financial assessment and scientific issues related to impairment of health and aesthetic values or the risk of catastrophic illness. More importantly, in the guise of balancing the equities, courts gave polluters what was sometimes seen as a license to pollute; rarely were the polluters compelled to cease polluting so long as they were willing to pay damages to continue production. *See, e.g., Chicago v. Commonwealth Edison Co.*, 24 Ill. App. 3d 624, 321 N.E.2d 412 (1974); *but see Reserve Mining Co. v. EPA*, 514 F.2d 492 (8th Cir. 1975) (public nuisance found). As in many areas of environmental law, requirements of standing, causation, and proof of damages made even limited success in common law litigation difficult at best.

In 1955 the federal government tentatively addressed the air pollution problem with research and technical assistance under the 1955 Air Pollution Control Act, but left control responsibility to the states. Pub. L. No. 84-159, 69 Stat. 322. In 1963 the Secretary of HEW was given limited jurisdiction over interstate pollution. Pub. L. No. 88-206, 77 Stat. 392. The Air Quality Act of 1967 did create a federal regulatory program based on ambient air quality standards, Pub. L. No. 90-148, 81 Stat. 485, but it was not until 1970 that regulatory controls could be imposed at the federal level when states failed to satisfy their obligations to control air pollution.

"Air pollutant" for purposes of the Clean Air Act is broadly defined as "any air pollutant agent or combination of such agents, including any physical, chemical, biological, radioactive (including source material, special nuclear material, and byproduct material) substance or matter which is emitted into or otherwise enters the ambient air." CAA § 302(g), 42 U.S.C. § 7602(g). The following excerpt gives a brief explanation of the sources and effects of the principal pollutants which have been regulated under the CAA:

> Suspended particulates (TSPs) are solid particles or liquid droplets which remain suspended in the air. Approximately two-thirds of such particulates come from stationary industrial sources, 18 percent from motor vehicles, and about 5 percent from solid waste disposal. Smaller particulates present more of a health risk than larger, more visible particles. TSPs can be significantly reduced through the use of electrostatic precipitators, scrubbers, or fabric filters, which in essence "clean" emissions by removing particles from emissions before their release into the ambient air. Particulates irritate the human respiratory system, and cause or exacerbate asthma and other respiratory and cardiovascular illnesses. In addition TSPs damage building materials, reduce visibility, contribute to cloud formation, and interfere with plant growth.
>
> Sulfur dioxide [SO_2], in conjunction with TSPs, increases death rates and worsens heart and lung disease. Approximately 80 percent of sulfur dioxide originates with combustion of fossil fuel, particularly by electric utilities, with the remaining sulfur dioxide originating with smelting of ores such as lead and copper. Sulfur dioxide can be reduced through use of low sulfur fuels, removal of sulfur from fuels before use, removal of sulfur by cleaning or "scrubbing" emissions before release, and by catalytic conversion to sulfuric acid. Sulfur dioxide has recently been identified as a major source of visibility problems and of acid rain.
>
> Nitrogen dioxide [NO_2] also causes or contributes to respiratory problems, and contributes to smog. Approximately half of the nitrogen dioxide in the United States comes from automobile emissions; the rest comes from power plant emissions. Nitrogen dioxide also aggravates cardiovascular disease, causes kidney inflammation, impairs visibility, injures paints and dyes, and interferes with plant growth. The pollutant is also believed to contribute to acid rain. Nitrogen dioxide can be reduced by reducing combustion temperatures and "scrubbing" emissions.
>
> Carbon monoxide [CO], an odorless and colorless gas, forms from the incomplete combustion of fossil fuels. Seventy-five percent of carbon

monoxide comes from motor vehicle emissions. Carbon monoxide impairs the blood's hemoglobin, mental functions, and fetal development, and contributes to cardiovascular disease. The pollutant is best controlled through motor vehicle tuning and the use of catalytic converters or thermal exhaust gas conversion on motor vehicles.

Ozone [O_3] is the principal component of smog. Ozone is not produced directly but is the result of a complex photochemical reaction between nitrogen dioxide and volatile organic compounds (VOCs). Industrial processes account for approximately one-half of man-made VOCs and motor vehicles are responsible for another third. Photochemical oxidants such as ozone aggravate respiratory and cardiovascular diseases, impair visibility, corrode rubbers, textiles, and paints, and interfere with plant reproduction. Ozone must be controlled indirectly through reductions in nitrogen dioxide, sulfur dioxide, and hydrocarbons.

Hydrocarbons (HCs) are formed from the incomplete combustion of fossil fuels, as is carbon monoxide. Motor vehicles are the major source, but HCs also originate with manufacture and handling of asphalt, rubber, and petroleum products, decomposition of organic materials, home fireplaces, and forest fires. Hydrocarbons contribute to smog and impair health and visibility, and some hydrocarbons cause cancer. Hydrocarbon controls are similar to those for carbon monoxide. Carbon monoxide, hydrocarbons, and nitrogen dioxide are the three pollutants most commonly associated with motor vehicle pollution.

A more recent addition to the major regulated pollutants is lead, a naturally occurring substance. Lead is also released into the air from motor vehicle combustion of leaded gasoline, lead smelting and processing, manufacture of lead products, combustion of coal and waste, and use of pesticides. Lead accumulates in the body, impairing bone growth and the nervous, circulatory, and renal systems. Lead is controlled through removal of lead from gasoline and paint, cleaning of lead emissions, dietary controls, and removal of lead soldering from cans.

L. MALONE, ENVIRONMENTAL REGULATION OF LAND USE § 10.01 (1991) citing CONSERVATION FOUNDATION, STATE OF THE ENVIRONMENT 1982 (1982) and F. ANDERSON, D. MANDELKER & A. TARLOCK, ENVIRONMENTAL PROTECTION: LAW AND POLICY 119-24 (1990).

The 1970 Act, with much political fanfare, called for nationwide compliance with health-based standards for all major pollutants in less than a decade. In 1977 a more subdued Congress with more experience in environmental issues grappled with conflicting concerns for economic growth, technological capability, and air quality. Pub. L. No. 95-95, 91 Stat. 385. The basic deadlines for compliance were extended in 1977 as they would be once again in the 1990 amendments. Why do you think the extensions were necessary — was Congress too stringent in 1970 or too lax in 1977 and 1990? *See generally* Elliott, Ackerman & Millian,

Toward a Theory of Statutory Evolution: The Federalization of Environmental Law, 1 J.L., EC. & ORG. 313, 337 (1985). The 1990 amendments, Pub. L. No. 101-549, 104 Stat. 2399, were 313 pages long, with a level of regulatory and technical detail which makes the comprehensive 1970 Act seem almost terse and simplistic by comparison. After twenty years, many cities were still experiencing poor, even unhealthy air quality. It remains to be seen whether the next decade will usher in a new phase of compliance with air quality standards, or another round of amendments and deadline extensions. *See generally* Howard Latin, *Regulatory Failure, Administrative Incentives, and the New Clean Air Act*, 21 ENVTL. L. 1647 (1991); Craig N. Oren, *The Clean Air Act Amendments of 1990: A Bridge to the Future?*, 21 ENVTL. L. 1817 (1991); Arnold W. Reitze, Jr., *A Century of Air Pollution Control Law: What's Worked; What's Failed; What Might Work*, 21 ENVTL. L. 1549 (1991); Henry A. Waxman, *An Overview of the Clean Air Act Amendments of 1990*, 21 ENVTL. L. 1721 (1991).

A. NATIONAL AMBIENT AIR QUALITY STANDARDS

In general, the 1970 Clean Air Act (CAA), as amended in 1977 and 1990, utilizes two different types of regulatory controls and regulates two different types of pollutant sources. The two different types of regulatory controls are health-based standards which are set by determining the "safe" level of a pollutant in the ambient air, and technology-based standards which are set primarily by determining the amount of pollutant reduction within an industry's economic and technology capabilities. The two different types of sources that are regulated are: stationary sources and mobile sources. In addition, the CAA authorizes the setting of emission limitations at the federal level and at the state level, so long as certain federal requirements for state standards are met. The final variable is that the emission limitations a source will have to meet will vary depending upon whether the source is located in an area with "dirty" air or "clean" air.

The foundation of the CAA is the establishment of National Ambient Air Quality Standards (NAAQSs). EPA is required to establish "primary" and "secondary" national ambient air quality standards (NAAQSs) for "criteria" pollutants. CAA § 109, 42 U.S.C. § 7409. Criteria pollutants are pollutants which EPA has determined may endanger the public health or welfare and which result from numerous and diverse sources. *Id.* § 108(a), 42 U.S.C. § 7408(a). The primary NAAQS is the acceptable concentration of a pollutant in the ambient air measured over a designated averaging time that will protect the public health with an "adequate margin of safety." *Id.* § 109(b)(1), 42 U.S.C. § 7409(b)(1). The secondary NAAQS is set at a level to protect the public welfare, encompassing environmental and economic interests such as soil and water quality, recreational interests and industrial concerns. *Id.* § 109(b)(2), 42 U.S.C. § 7409(b)(2). The current criteria pollutants are sulfur dioxide, carbon monoxide, nitrogen dioxide, ozone, particulates, and lead. 40 C.F.R. Part 50. The NAAQS for hydrocarbons was rescinded in 1982. 48 Fed. Reg. 628 (1983). Until 1987, the particulate standard was measured in terms of total suspended particulates. EPA replaced this standard with a new standard, the "PM-10" standard, a measurement for particles of 10 micrometers or less which are small enough to be breathed into the lungs. 52 Fed. Reg. 24,634 (1987).

The fundamental goal of the CAA is nationwide attainment and maintenance of these ambient air quality standards. Because the NAAQSs are a measurement of the acceptable level of a pollutant in the air, they must be translated into specific limitations on the amount of a pollutant that an individual source may emit. Before turning to how and when the NAAQSs are to be achieved, the next three cases examine how the NAAQSs are set, revised, and challenged in federal court.

NATURAL RESOURCES DEFENSE COUNCIL v. TRAIN

411 F. Supp. 864 (S.D.N.Y. 1976), *aff'd*, 545 F.2d 320 (2d Cir. 1976)

STEWART, DISTRICT JUDGE.

Natural Resources Defense Council, Inc. ("NRDC") and other named plaintiffs bring this action against the Environmental Protection Agency ("EPA") and its administrator Russell Train for failure to list lead as a pollutant under § 108 of the Clean Air Act of 1970....

Section 304 of the Clean Air Act provides in pertinent part:

> Any person may commence a civil action on his own behalf (2) against the Administrator where there is alleged a failure of the Administrator to perform any act or duty under this chapter which is not discretionary with the Administrator.

Defendants argue that the listing of pollutants under § 108 is a discretionary function and therefore no jurisdiction is vested in this court by virtue of § 304. While § 304 does not provide jurisdiction over distinctly discretionary functions of the Administrator, it does permit jurisdiction to decide whether a function is mandatory or discretionary. We therefore do not need to consider plaintiffs' other asserted jurisdictional grounds.

... Section 108 provides that the Administrator shall publish, and from time to time revise, a list including each air pollutant

> (A) which in his judgment has an adverse effect on public health or welfare;
> (B) the presence of which in the ambient air results from numerous or diverse mobile or stationary sources; and
> (C) for which ... he plans to issue air quality criteria under this section.

Plaintiffs contend that the statutory language, legislative history and purpose, as well as current administrative interpretation of the 1970 Clean Air Act, all militate in favor of finding that the Administrator's function to list pollutants under § 108 is mandatory, once it is determined by the Administrator that a pollutant "has an adverse effect on public health or welfare" and comes from the requisite numerous or diverse sources. Defendants concede in this action that lead comes from the requisite sources and that the Administrator has found lead to have the required "adverse effect." Defendants argue, however, that the language of § 108(a)(1)(C) "for which ... [the Administrator] plans to issue air quality criteria" is a separate and third criterion to be met before § 108 requires placing a pollutant on the list. This construction of § 108(a) leaves the initial decision to list a pollutant within the sole discretion of the Administrator. Defendants contend such discretion is required because the Administrator must choose between alternative remedies provided in various sections of the Act and that any decision to utilize the remedies provided by §§ 108-110 "involves complex considerations."

....

... There is no language anywhere in the statute which indicates that the Administrator has discretion to choose among the remedies which the Act provides. Rather, the language of § 108 indicates that upon certain enumerated conditions, one factual and one judgmental, the Administrator "shall" list a pollutant which triggers the remedial provisions of §§ 108-110. The statute does not provide, as defendants would have it, that the Administrator has authority to determine whether the statutory remedies which follow a § 108 listing are appropriate for a given pollutant.

....

With specific reference to the lead pollution at issue here and in support of their position that the Administrator should have discretion under the Act to choose among remedies provided by various sections, defendants point us to the Administrator's decision to regulate lead in gasoline under § 211(c)(1) [42 U.S.C. § 1857f-6c(c)(1)]. Defendants assert that the EPA considered regulating lead pollution either by setting national ambient air standards under § 108 or by establishing standards for the lead content of motor vehicle gasoline under § 211. However, as we read the two statutory sections, § 108 and § 211, they are neither mutually exclusive nor alternative provisions. Defendants' argument is premised upon the misconception, as discussed above, that the statutory scheme provides alternative remedies for pollutants. We think the misconception becomes clear through analysis of the specific case of lead pollution regulation.

Defendants state the reasons for the Administrator's decision to regulate lead under § 211.

> It was the Administrator's judgment that (a) uniform standards would make industry compliance simpler than a proliferation of differing state standards, (b) federal controls at the refinery level would be more efficient than state or local controls directed at thousands of distributors and retailers, and (c) the states were hard-pressed to implement the six existing ambient air quality standards and should not be assigned another major regulatory task when equally effective alternatives were available.

These reasons could have no bearing upon a policy decision, if one were permissible under the Act, of whether or not to establish national standards under § 108. The benefits of uniform standards, of federal controls and of averting "another major regulatory task" for the states can all accrue from regulations under § 211 when lead is listed under § 108. If the Administrator sets standards under § 211 which effectively decrease the level of lead in the ambient air by taking lead out of gasoline, then the decrease in pollution brought about by the § 211 regulations will be taken into account by each state when it submits its plan to meet the national standard set under § 110....

Finally, we turn to an additional argument of defendants that the Administrator needs discretion not to list lead under § 108 because the data which would be necessary to support an ambient air standard for lead is arguably lacking. Defendants concede, however, that such a potential lack of data did not enter into the Administrator's decision not to list lead at the time it was made. We do not think that the potential lack of data would have been an appropriate consideration prior to listing a pollutant under § 108 in any event. Under the statutory scheme, the listing of a pollutant is no more than a threshold to the remedial provisions. Before a listing, the statute provides for the Administrator to exercise his judgment concerning whether or not a pollutant, here lead, has an adverse effect upon the public health. Once he has made that judgment, however, the Administrator does not have discretion not to list lead as a pollutant because necessary data — data other than that necessary to make the initial decision as to "adverse effect" — is unavailable. The statute appears to assume that, for each pollutant which must be listed, criteria and a national standard can be established. A twelve month period is provided for that purpose. However, Congress cannot require the impossible. It may be that a pollutant exists which meets the listing requirements of § 108 but for which no criteria or national standard is possible. That issue is not before this court. The only question here is the threshold one of whether lead must be listed according to § 108 and we have determined that it must.

... We are convinced that the Administrator has considerable, and sufficient, discretion. Not only does he exercise his judgment over the initial determination of whether a pollutant "has an adverse effect upon health," but also he must set the national standard "which in [his] judgment ... is requisite to protect the public health." (§ 109(b)(1)). Finally, the Administrator must approve the implementation plans of the states. We think that these provisions give the Administrator all the discretion which Congress contemplated that he have.

... [T]he Administrator has conceded that, in his judgment, lead "has an adverse effect on health" and comes from "numerous or diverse mobile or stationary sources." The two statutory criteria having been met and this court having determined that a duty thereafter arises, it is

Ordered that the Administrator place lead on the list of pollutants, in accordance with the mandate of § 108, within 30 days from the date of this decision.

So ordered.

ENVIRONMENTAL DEFENSE FUND v. THOMAS
870 F.2d 892 (2d Cir. 1989)

WINTER, CIRCUIT JUDGE.

... The [Clean Air] Act provides that suits to compel the Administrator to perform non-discretionary duties may be brought only in district courts, while petitions seeking review of the Administrator's discretionary actions must be brought in the Court of Appeals for the District of Columbia. Jurisdiction under the Act thus turns on the threshold question of whether the Administrator's challenged action (or inaction) is discretionary or non-discretionary.

....

... In Section 307 of the Act, the 1970 amendments vested the Court of Appeals for the District of Columbia with exclusive jurisdiction to review a variety of rule promulgations and other "final actions" by the Administrator. 42 U.S.C. § 7607(b). In addition, Section 304 of the Act, the so-called "Citizen Suits" provision, permits any person to bring a civil action in a district court "against the Administrator where there is alleged a failure of the Administrator to perform any act or duty under this chapter which is not discretionary with the Administrator...." 42 U.S.C. § 7604(a)(2).

... [The 1977] amendments added Section 109(d) concerning the "review and revision" of NAAQS, which provides that:

> [n]ot later than December 31, 1980, and at five-year intervals thereafter, the Administrator shall complete a thorough review of the criteria published under Section 108 ... and promulgate such new standards as may be appropriate.... The Administrator may review and revise criteria or promulgate new standards earlier or more frequently than required under this paragraph.

42 U.S.C. § 7409(d). It is this section that plaintiffs seek to enforce by this action under Section 304.

The pollutants involved in this appeal, SO_x [sulfur oxides], are causative of acid deposition and belong to the class of pollutants for which criteria had been issued before the 1970 amendments. In 1971, the Administrator promulgated primary and secondary NAAQS for SO_x. The secondary NAAQS were reviewed by the Court of Appeals for the District of Columbia and were thereafter remanded to the Administrator with instructions to elaborate on their justification. *Kennecott Copper Corp. v. EPA*, 149 App. D.C. 231, 462 F.2d 846 (D.C. Cir. 1972). On that remand, the Administrator modified the secondary NAAQS. The secondary NAAQS as modified were not designed to protect against the deleterious effects of SO_x associated with acid rain and dry acid deposition — deleterious effects on water quality, wildlife, soils and forests, and corrosive effects of SO_x on building materials, monuments and products. Neither the primary SO_x NAAQS as promulgated in 1971, nor the modified secondary SO_x NAAQS of 1973, have been revised since.

In 1979, the Administrator undertook a review of the air quality criteria for SO_x in response to the passage of Section 109(d)(1) in 1977. 44 Fed. Reg. 56731 col. 2 (1979). In 1982, that review resulted in the publication of new criteria both for SO_x and for particulate matter, another pollutant, which includes forms of SO_x, listed under Section 108. The new criteria described in some detail the ill effects associated with acid deposition. The Administrator did not, however, issue revised NAAQS for SO_x. Indeed, the Administrator took no official public action, neither revising the existing standards nor formally declining to revise them. In 1984 and 1985, the EPA issued a three-volume "Critical Assessment" on the acid deposition effects of SO_x. This did not constitute a formal revision of the SO_x criteria, and the Administrator again took no action in conjunction with the issuance of this "Critical Assessment."

In 1985, appellants brought the instant case in the District Court for the Southern District of New York, pursuant to Section 304, the "Citizen Suits" provision of the Act, to compel the Administrator to promulgate revised NAAQS for SO_x. Their complaint alleged that the revised criteria of 1982 and the "Critical Assessment" of 1984 and 1985 constituted a formal finding that SO_x caused acid deposition threatening to the public health and welfare. Appellants claimed that those findings imposed on the Administrator a non-discretionary duty to revise the NAAQS for SO_x, pursuant to Sections 109(b) and 109(d), in order to combat such health and welfare effects. Judge Edelstein disagreed. Looking to the language of Section 109(d), he concluded that the section created a mandatory duty only to revise pollutant criteria — an action the Administrator had taken in 1982. The Administrator, he held, had discretion not to revise the SO_x NAAQS if he so chose. Because the duty to revise the NAAQS was discretionary, he concluded that the district court lacked jurisdiction over the dispute and dismissed the complaint.

One week after Judge Edelstein's decision, the EPA issued a "Proposed Decision Not To Revise the National Ambient Air Quality Standards for Sulfur Oxides (Sulfur Dioxide)." 53 Fed. Reg. 14926 (April 26, 1988). In that "Proposed Decision," the Administrator announced that he was formally "propos[ing] not to revise [the primary and secondary] standards" for sulfur oxides, and invited comments. However, the Administrator expressly excluded the problem of acid deposition from the list of welfare effects for which no revision of the secondary SO_x NAAQS was necessary:

> 1. Based upon the current scientific understanding of the acid deposition problem, it would be premature and unwise to prescribe any regulatory control program at this time.

2. When the fundamental scientific uncertainties have been reduced through ongoing research efforts, EPA will craft and support an appropriate set of control measures.

In light of this EPA action, appellants have narrowed their claim on appeal. Rather than challenging both the primary and secondary NAAQS, they abandoned the challenge to the primary NAAQS, which the Administrator has formally proposed not to revise in his "Proposed Decision," and limited their appeal to a challenge to the secondary NAAQS, the revision of which the Administrator has declared to be "premature and unwise."

Section 304 grants jurisdiction to district courts to compel the Administrator to perform non-discretionary statutory duties. Section 307 grants exclusive jurisdiction to the Court of Appeals for the District of Columbia over "final" and other actions of the EPA....

Appellants take the position that the district court has jurisdiction and must order the Administrator to revise the secondary NAAQS. Appellees argue that the Administrator may stand pat, deciding neither to revise the NAAQS nor to make a public decision that revision is unnecessary. In their view, such a non-decision is unreviewable by the Court of Appeals for the District of Columbia under Section 307 because it involves no decision or other agency "action" and is also invulnerable to challenge in district courts under Section 304 because it is discretionary. We disagree with both parties.

In view of the revised criteria and "Critical Assessment," we believe the Administrator must make *some* decision regarding the revision of the NAAQS that is thereafter reviewable under Section 307 in the Court of Appeals for the District of Columbia. Because the duty to make *some* decision is non-discretionary, it is enforceable under Section 304 in the district courts. Appellants argue that in the present case a revision is mandatory and should be ordered by the district court. The substance of the Administrator's decision is beyond the power of the district court, however, its authority being limited to ordering the Administrator to make a formal decision. Were we to order a revision, we would have to set out criteria governing that revision, and the district court would potentially have to apply those criteria in an enforcement proceeding. An order to revise would thus plunge the district court into the merits, matters that are the exclusive province of the District of Columbia Circuit. We appreciate that this distinction is somewhat artificial but believe it is necessary to confine the district court's authority and to defer to the authority of the District of Columbia Circuit. The April 26, 1988 "Proposed Decision Not To Revise," however, has begun the formal process of decisionmaking, and we remand for entry of an order directing that process to continue.

Our analysis begins with an examination of the jurisdiction of the Court of Appeals for the District of Columbia. In *Oljato Chapter of Navajo Tribe v. Train*, 169 App. D.C. 195, 515 F.2d 654 (D.C. Cir. 1975), that court held that "a challenge to the Administrator's refusal to revise a standard of performance is in effect a challenge to the standard itself and so can be brought only in this court under Section 307(b)(1) of the Clean Air Act...." *Id.* at 656. This language suggests that the District of Columbia Circuit has exclusive jurisdiction over the instant matter. The categorical language of *Oljato* is, however, misleading. *Oljato* involved Section 111 of the Act, which, at that time, included language permitting, but not requiring, the Administrator to revise the "standards of performance" for new stationary sources of air pollution. Because the statute included no stated deadlines for revision of the standards in question, the *Oljato* court could reasonably treat the decision to revise or not to revise as one wholly within the discretion of the Administrator. Since *Oljato*, however, the District of Columbia Circuit has distinguished between those revision provisions in the Act that include stated deadlines and those that do not, holding that revision provisions that do include stated deadlines should, as a rule, be construed as creating non-discretionary duties. *Sierra Club v. Thomas*, 264 App. D.C. 203, 828 F.2d 783, 791 (D.C. Cir. 1987). Section 109(d), the provision at issue here, includes a stated deadline of "[n]ot later than December 31, 1980, and at five-year intervals thereafter." *Oljato* thus does not apply.

The District of Columbia Circuit has also held that it may review agency inaction under the Administrative Procedure Act where the agency has unreasonably delayed in performing a duty over which the District of Columbia Circuit would have jurisdiction after final action under the Act. *Sierra Club*, 828 F.2d at 795-96. Thus, the District of Columbia Circuit arguably has jurisdiction on the grounds that the EPA has unreasonably delayed its decision whether or not to revise the secondary NAAQS for SO_x. The District of Columbia Circuit was careful in *Sierra Club*, however, to limit its exclusive jurisdiction to cases involving "a right the denial of which we would have jurisdiction to review upon final agency action but the integrity of which might be irreversibly compromised by the time such review would occur." *Id.* at 796. Appellants' claimed right in the instant case is not one whose integrity is likely to be "irreversibly compromised." We therefore conclude that the instant action does not raise a claim within the exclusive grant of jurisdiction to the District of Columbia Circuit under Section 307.[1]

---

[1]Our dissenting colleague argues that the District of Columbia Circuit has exclusive jurisdiction pursuant to the petitioning procedure outlined by way of dictum in *Oljato Chapter of Navajo Tribe v. Train*, 169 App. D.C. 195, 515 F.2d 654, 666 & 667 n.20 (D.C. Cir. 1975). We disagree. Because *Oljato* was decided before the enactment of Section 109(d), the *Oljato* court was interpreting a version of the Act that included no provision for the revision of NAAQS. The *Oljato* court thus first determined that Section 307 was the relevant jurisdictional provision, and then outlined a petitioning procedure for satisfying the requirements of that section. We, by contrast, have determined that Section 304 is now the relevant statutory provision. The dictum in *Oljato* was made obsolete after the statutory overhaul that produced Section 109(d). Because the statute now expressly provides for the revision of standards, the problem of "new information ... [which] may dictate a revision or modification" has now been addressed by Congress and the Act includes mandatory language that necessarily alters the jurisdictional scheme.

Having determined that the District of Columbia Circuit does not have exclusive jurisdiction, we now address what mandatory or, as the case may be, discretionary duties are created by the following language of Section 109(d) of the Act. To repeat, that section states in pertinent part:

> [n]ot later than December 31, 1980, and at five-year intervals thereafter, the Administrator shall complete a thorough review of the criteria published under section 108 ... and promulgate such new standards as may be appropriate.... The Administrator may review and revise criteria or promulgate new standards earlier or more frequently than required under this paragraph.

Clearly this section includes both mandatory ("shall complete," "required") and non-mandatory language ("as may be appropriate"). Appellees rely on the phrase "as may be appropriate," arguing that Judge Edelstein was correct in holding that that language confers on the Administrator a wholly discretionary authority to revise the NAAQS, not to revise them, or simply not to address the issue with a formal public opinion. Appellants argue that, as a matter of statutory construction, Section 109(d) must be interpreted in light of the mandatory language of Sections 109(a) and (b). Section 109(a), which requires the initial promulgation of NAAQS, contains clearly mandatory language directing the Administrator to issue NAAQS within 120 days for those pollutants for which criteria had been published before 1970 and to issue proposed NAAQS simultaneously with the publication of criteria for newly identified pollutants. Appellants argue that Section 109(d) should be read in light of this clearly mandatory language.

We find this argument unpersuasive. Section 109(d) contains no cross-reference to Section 109(a). Moreover, it is difficult to perceive why the standard

---

We also note here our disagreement with our colleague's reading of *Sierra Club v. Thomas*, 264 App. D.C. 203, 828 F.2d 783 (D.C. Cir. 1987). While it is true that *Sierra Club* states that "a duty of timeliness must 'categorically mandate' that *all* specified action be taken by a date-certain deadline," *id.* at 791 (quoting *National Resources Defense Council, Inc. v. Train*, 166 App. D.C. 312, 510 F.2d 692, 712 (D.C. Cir. 1975)), that holding is not at odds with our ruling in this case. The statutory provision at issue here, Section 109(d), reads: "[n]ot later than December 31, 1980, and at five-year intervals thereafter, the Administrator shall complete a thorough review of the criteria ... and promulgate such new standards as may be appropriate...." Our colleague argues that this provision does not require that *all* specified action be completed within the stated deadline — i.e., the Administrator is left to exercise his "appropriate" discretion as to whether or not to revise. This argument is, however, not inconsistent with our holding. We believe that the "specified action" under this section is the making of some decision within the stated deadlines, whether to revise new standards or not to revise. To the extent that the "specified action" is simply the making of *some* decision, *all* specified action is required to be completed within a stated deadline — and, indeed, a stated deadline very close in language and meaning to the stated deadline in the *Train* case, in which the D.C. Circuit first announced its rule. *See Train*, 510 F.2d at 697 (interpreting statutory language requiring promulgation of regulations and guidelines "within one year of enactment of this title....").

for the promulgation of initial NAAQS should be identical to that for revised NAAQS. Congress could have repeated the mandatory language of Section 109(a) in Section 109(d), but did not do so. Appellants also argue that Section 109(d) should be read in light of Section 109(b)(2), which declares that secondary NAAQS "shall specify a level of air quality the attainment and maintenance of which in the judgment of the Administrator ... is requisite to protect the public welfare...." Section 109(d) does include a cross-reference to Section 109(b). Because Section 109(b)(2) expressly entrusts the substance of secondary NAAQS to the "judgment of the Administrator," it is difficult to read it as imposing non-discretionary duties. Furthermore, that section adds that secondary NAAQS "*may* be revised in the same manner as promulgated" (emphasis added). This permissive language suggests that, contrary to appellants' contention, the Administrator has discretion not to follow the procedures for issuing initial NAAQS when revising NAAQS. Harmonizing Section 109(d) with Section 109(b) thus does nothing to further appellants' case.

Appellants also contend that language of Section 109(d) itself, read in isolation, imposes a mandatory duty to revise the NAAQS. The phrase "as may be appropriate," they argue, is subject to the section's command that the Administrator "*shall* make ... revisions." Under this view, the district court has jurisdiction to order the Administrator to make appropriate revisions in the NAAQS — power in short to issue orders affecting the substance of revised NAAQS. Again we disagree. The words "as may be appropriate" clearly suggest that the Administrator must exercise judgment and the presence of "shall" in the section implies only that the district court has jurisdiction to order the Administrator to make some *formal* decision whether to revise the NAAQS, the content of that decision being within the Administrator's discretion and reviewable only in the District of Columbia Circuit.

Appellants advance a final argument, based on our caselaw. Conceding *arguendo* that the "as may be appropriate" language creates only discretionary authority, they contend that the district court has jurisdiction to compel the Administrator to revise its secondary NAAQS, the content of the revision being left to the Administrator. Under this view, the Administrator does not have power to decide not to revise. This argument is based on *Natural Resources Defense Council v. Train*, 545 F.2d 320 (2d Cir. 1976), which involved Section 108 of the Act....

... They observe that the EPA's revised criteria of 1982 and its "Critical Assessment" of 1984-1985 both acknowledge the adverse effects of SO_x-caused acid deposition. The published acknowledgments of those adverse effects are, appellants argue, the equivalent of the EPA's explicit concession in *Train* concerning the adverse effects of lead. The 1982 criteria and the "Critical Assessment" constitute, in effect, a formal declaration that revision of the SO_x NAAQS is "appropriate" according to the terms of Section 109(d). In their view, the Administrator has thus already exercised his discretion, impliedly found revision to be "appropriate," and now has a non-discretionary duty, enforceable in the district court, to revise the NAAQS in line with his revised criteria.

This argument did not persuade Judge Edelstein, and it does not persuade us. Even if we were to treat the EPA's revised criteria of 1982 and its "Critical Assessment" of 1984-1985 as equivalent to the concession of the harmful effects of lead that underlay our holding in *Train* — and it is far from clear that we should do so — *Train* is still distinguishable from the present case. The duty at issue in *Train* was a thoroughly ministerial one. We did no more than affirm an order compelling the EPA to include "lead" on a list and to issue some NAAQS for lead. We did not, however, specify the content of those NAAQS. *Train*, 545 F.2d at 328. *Train* thus stands solely for the proposition that the district court has jurisdiction, under Section 304, to compel the Administrator to perform purely ministerial acts, not to order the Administrator to make particular judgmental decisions.

However, if *Train* does not justify all of the relief that appellants seek, that is not to say that it does not justify any relief at all. Although the district court does not have jurisdiction to order the Administrator to make a particular revision, we cannot agree with appellees that the Administrator may simply make no formal decision to revise or not to revise, leaving the matter in a bureaucratic limbo subject neither to review in the District of Columbia Circuit nor to challenge in the district court. No discernible congressional purpose is served by creating such a bureaucratic twilight zone, in which many of the Act's purposes might become subject to evasion. The 1982 criteria and the 1984-1985 "Critical Assessment" triggered a duty on the part of EPA to address and decide whether and what kind of revision is necessary. The district court thus does have jurisdiction to compel the Administrator to make some formal decision as to whether or not to revise the secondary NAAQS.

....

Accordingly, we hold that, while the district court did not have jurisdiction to compel the Administrator to revise the NAAQS, it did have jurisdiction to compel the Administrator to take some formal action, employing rulemaking procedures, *see Thomas v. State of New York*, 256 App. D.C. 49, 802 F.2d 1443 (D.C. Cir. 1986), either revising the NAAQS or declining to revise them.

However, the Administrator's "Proposed Decision Not To Revise" of April 26, 1988, inviting comments on his determination that a decision as to the advisability of revising the secondary NAAQS for acid deposition "would be premature and unwise," is a required procedure in the course of reaching a formal decision. If this process continues, and a formal decision is rendered, appellants will have obtained all the relief to which they are entitled in a Section 304 action. Whether the decision when reached is wrong on the merits — even egregiously wrong — will be for the District of Columbia Circuit to resolve. We remand so the district court can enter an order directing the Administrator to continue the rulemaking to formal decision.

LEAD INDUSTRIES ASSOCIATION v. ENVIRONMENTAL
PROTECTION AGENCY

647 F.2d 1130 (D.C. Cir.), *cert. denied*, 449 U.S. 1042 (1980)

J. SKELLY WRIGHT, CHIEF JUDGE.

I. *Background*

Acting pursuant to authority conferred on it by Congress in the Clean Air Act, EPA has been involved in regulation of lead emissions almost since the Agency's inception. Its initial approach to controlling the amount of lead in the ambient air was to limit lead emissions from automobiles by restricting the amount of lead in gasoline.... However, in 1975 the Natural Resources Defense Council, Inc. (NRDC), and others brought suit against EPA claiming that the Agency was required by Section 108 of the Clean Air Act, 42 U.S.C. § 7408, to list lead as a pollutant for which an air quality criteria document would be prepared, and for which national ambient air quality standards should be promulgated under Section 109 of the Act, 42 U.S.C. § 7409. The District Court agreed with NRDC and directed the Administrator to list lead as a pollutant under Section 108 of the Act, by March 31, 1976. *Natural Resources Defense Council, Inc. v. Train*, 411 F. Supp. 864 (S.D.N.Y. 1976). The Second Circuit affirmed, 545 F.2d 320 (1976), and EPA initiated the proceedings outlined in the statute which are under review here.

The first step toward establishing national ambient air quality standards for a particular pollutant is its addition to a list, compiled by EPA's Administrator, of pollutants that cause or contribute to air pollution "which may reasonably be anticipated to endanger public health or welfare[.]" Section 108(a)(1), 42 U.S.C. § 7408(a)(1). Within twelve months of the listing of a pollutant under Section 108(a) the Administrator must issue "air quality criteria" for the pollutant. Section 108 makes it clear that the term "air quality criteria" means something different from the conventional meaning of "criterion"; such "criteria" do not constitute "standards" or "guidelines," but rather refer to a document to be prepared by EPA which is to provide the scientific basis for promulgation of air quality standards for the pollutant. This criteria document must "accurately reflect the latest scientific knowledge useful in indicating the kind and extent of all identifiable effects on public health or welfare which may be expected from the presence of such pollutant in the ambient air, in varying quantities." Section 108(a)(2), 42 U.S.C. § 7408(a)(2).

At the same time as he issues air quality criteria for a pollutant, the Administrator must also publish proposed national primary and secondary air quality standards for the pollutant. Section 109(a)(2), 42 U.S.C. § 7409(a)(2).... The Administrator is required to submit the proposed air quality standards for public comment in a rulemaking proceeding, the procedure for which is prescribed by Section 307(d) of the Act, 42 U.S.C. § 7607(d).

Within six months of publication of the proposed standards the Administrator must promulgate final primary and secondary ambient air quality standards for the pollutant. Section 307(d)(10), 42 U.S.C. § 7607(d)(10)....

The scope of judicial review of the Administrator's decisions and actions is delineated by Section 307(d) of the Act, 42 U.S.C.§ 7607(d). We must uphold the Administrator's actions unless we find that they were: (1) "arbitrary, capricious, an abuse of discretion, or otherwise not in accordance with law"; (2) "contrary to constitutional right, power, privilege, or immunity"; (3) "in excess of statutory jurisdiction, authority, or limitations, or short of statutory [right.]" Section 307(d)(9), 42 U.S.C. § 7607(d)(9). In addition, we may set aside any action found to be "without observance of procedure required by law," if (i) the failure to follow the prescribed procedure was arbitrary or capricious, (ii) the procedural objection was raised during the public comment period, or there were good reasons why it was not, and (iii) the procedural errors "were so serious and related to matters of such central relevance to the rule that there is a substantial likelihood that the rule would have been significantly changed if such errors had not been made." *Id.* Section 307(d)(8), 42 U.S.C. § 7607(d)(8).

. . . .

The petitioners' first claim is that the Administrator exceeded his authority under the statute by promulgating a primary air quality standard for lead which is more stringent than is necessary to protect the public health because it is designed to protect the public against "subclinical" effects which are not harmful to health. According to petitioners, Congress only authorized the Administrator to set primary air quality standards that are aimed at protecting the public against health effects which are known to be clearly *harmful*. They argue that Congress so limited the Administrator's authority because it was concerned that excessively stringent air quality standards could cause massive economic dislocation.

In developing this argument St. Joe contends that EPA erred by refusing to consider the issues of economic and technological feasibility in setting the air quality standards for lead....

This argument is totally without merit. St. Joe is unable to point to anything in either the language of the Act or its legislative history that offers any support for its claim that Congress, by specifying that the Administrator is to allow an "adequate margin of safety" in setting primary air quality standards, thereby required the Administrator to consider economic or technological feasibility. To the contrary, the statute and its legislative history make clear that economic considerations play no part in the promulgation of ambient air quality standards under Section 109.

. . . .

The legislative history of the Act also shows the Administrator may not consider economic and technological feasibility in setting air quality standards; the absence of any provision requiring consideration of these factors was no accident; it was the result of a deliberate decision by Congress to subordinate such concerns to the achievement of health goals. Exasperated by the lack of significant progress toward dealing with the problem of air pollution under the Air Quality Act of 1967, 81 Stat. 485, and prior legislation, Congress abandoned the approach of offering suggestions and setting goals in favor of "taking a stick to the States in the form of the Clean Air Amendments of 1970...." [*Train v. Natural Resources Defense Council, Inc., supra*, 421 U.S. at 64 (1975)]; see *Union Electric Co. v. EPA*, 427 U.S. 246, 256-257 (1976). Congress was well aware that, together with Sections 108 and 110, Section 109 imposes requirements of a "technology-forcing" character.

For its part, LIA maintains that its claim that the Administrator exceeded the bounds of his statutory authority does not depend on the supposition that he is required, or even permitted, to consider economic and technological feasibility in setting air quality standards. LIA contends that, instead, its argument is based on the fact that Congress itself was concerned about the question of the economic feasibility of compliance with air quality standards, a concern which was reflected in the statute it enacted. According to LIA, Congress was mindful of the possibility that air quality standards which are too stringent could cause severe economic dislocation. For this reason it only granted the Administrator authority to adopt air quality standards which are "designed to protect the public from adverse health effects that are clearly harmful[.]"...

... LIA then argues that the Administrator based the lead air quality standards on protecting children from "subclinical" effects of lead exposure which have not been shown to be harmful to health, that in so doing the Administrator ignored the clear limitation that Congress imposed on his standard-setting powers, and that the Administrator's action will in fact cause the very result that Congress was so concerned about avoiding.

LIA's argument appears to touch on two issues. The first concerns the type of health effects on which the Administrator may base air quality standards, i.e., the point at which the Administrator's regulatory authority may be exercised. This issue, as LIA suggests, does concern the limits that the Act, and its legislative history, may place on the Administrator's authority. The second issue appears to be more in the nature of an evidentiary question: whether or not the evidence in the record substantiates the Administrator's claim that the health effects on which the standards were based do in fact satisfy the requirements of the Act. Although these two issues are closely related, they are conceptually distinct, and they are best examined separately.

... LIA argues that the legislative history of the Act indicates that Congress only intended to protect the public against effects which are known to be clearly *harmful* to health, maintaining that this limitation on the Administrator's statutory authority is necessary to ensure that the standards are not set at a level which is more stringent than Congress contemplated. The Administrator, on the other hand, agrees that primary air quality standards must be based on protecting the public from "adverse health effects," but argues that the meaning LIA assigns to that phrase is too limited. In particular, the Administrator contends that LIA's interpretation is inconsistent with the precautionary nature of the statute, and will frustrate Congress' intent in requiring promulgation of air quality standards.

....

... [I]t is not immediately clear why LIA expects this court to impose limits on the Administrator's authority which, so far as we can tell, Congress did not. The Senate Report explains that the Administrator is to set standards which ensure that there is "an absence of adverse effects." The Administrator maintains that the lead standards are designed to do just that, a claim we will examine in due course. But LIA would require a further showing — that the effects on which the standards were based are clearly harmful or clearly adverse. We cannot, however, find the source of this further restriction that LIA would impose on the Administrator's authority. It may be that it reflects LIA's view that the Administrator must show that there is a "medical consensus that [the effects on which the standards were based] are harmful...." If so, LIA is seriously mistaken. This court has previously noted that some uncertainty about the health effects of air pollution is inevitable. And we pointed out that "[awaiting] certainty will often allow for only reactive, not preventive [regulatory action]." [Citation.] Congress apparently shares this view; it specifically directed the Administrator to allow an adequate margin of safety to protect against effects which have not yet been uncovered by research and effects whose medical significance is a matter of disagreement. This court has previously acknowledged the role of the margin of safety requirement. In *Environmental Defense Fund v. EPA*, 598 F.2d 62, 81 (1978), we pointed out that "[if] administrative responsibility to protect against unknown dangers presents a difficult task, indeed, a veritable paradox — calling as it does for knowledge of that which is unknown — then, the term 'margin of safety' is Congress's directive that means be found to carry out the task and to reconcile the paradox." Moreover, it is significant that Congress has recently acknowledged that more often than not the "margins of safety" that are incorporated into air quality standards turn out to be very modest or nonexistent, as new information reveals adverse health effects at pollution levels once thought to be harmless. Congress' directive to the Administrator to allow an "adequate margin of safety" alone plainly refutes any suggestion that the Administrator is only authorized to set primary air quality standards which are designed to protect against health effects that are known to be clearly harmful.

Furthermore, we agree with the Administrator that requiring EPA to wait until it can conclusively demonstrate that a particular effect is adverse to health before it acts is inconsistent with both the Act's precautionary and preventive orientation and the nature of the Administrator's statutory responsibilities. Congress provided that the Administrator is to use his judgment in setting air quality standards precisely to permit him to act in the face of uncertainty. And as we read the statutory provisions and the legislative history, Congress directed the Administrator to err on the side of caution in making the necessary decisions. We see no reason why this court should put a gloss on Congress' scheme by requiring the Administrator to show that there is a medical consensus that the effects on which the lead standards were based are *"clearly harmful to health."* All that is required by the statutory scheme is evidence in the record which substantiates his conclusions about the health effects on which the standards were based. Accordingly, we reject LIA's claim that the Administrator exceeded his statutory authority and turn to LIA's challenge to the evidentiary basis for the Administrator's decisions.

. . . .

[The court concluded that there was adequate support for each of the Administrator's conclusions about the health effects of lead exposure and, consequently, rejected LIA's challenges to the evidentiary support for these findings.]

Both LIA and St. Joe argue that the Administrator erred by including multiple allowances for margins of safety in his calculation of the lead standards. Petitioners note that the statute directs the Administrator to allow an "adequate margin of safety" in setting primary air quality standards, and they maintain that as a matter of statutory construction the Administrator may not interpret "margin" of safety to mean "margins" of safety. In petitioners' view, the Administrator in fact did just this insofar as he made allowances for margins of safety at several points in his analysis. They argue that margin of safety allowances were reflected in the choice of the maximum safe individual blood lead level for children, in the decision to place 99.5 percent of the target population group below that blood lead level, in the selection of an air lead/blood lead ratio of 1:2, and in the Administrator's estimate of the contribution to blood lead levels that should be attributed to non-air sources. The net result of these multiple allowances for margins of safety, petitioners contend, was a standard far more stringent than is necessary to protect the public health. St. Joe suggests that EPA should have adopted an approach which required decisions on:

> 1) The maximum level of lead in air which is protective of health; i.e., a threshold beyond which the public health is not protected; and
>
> 2) An adequate margin of safety by which the level which is protective of health must be reduced.

EPA responds by maintaining that allowances for a margin of safety were made only at two points in its analysis: in the selection of a maximum safe individual blood lead level of 30 ug Pb/dl and in the decision to set a standard designed to keep 99.5 percent of the target population below that blood lead level. It argues that the statutory requirement of a margin of safety does not mandate adoption of the method suggested by St. Joe. Rather, EPA suggests, it indicates the precautionary orientation the Administrator is to bring to bear on the task of setting air quality standards. How conservative he must be in making particular judgments must, the Agency maintains, depend on such factors as the amount of uncertainty involved, the size of the population affected, and the severity of the effect. EPA argues that petitioners' claims about multiple allowances for margins of safety indicate that they have failed to recognize the difference between providing for a margin of safety and making a scientific judgment in the face of conflicting evidence.

We agree with the Administrator that nothing in the statutory scheme or the legislative history requires him to adopt the margin of safety approach suggested by St. Joe. Adding the margin of safety at the end of the analysis is one approach, but it is not the only possible method. Indeed, the Administrator considered this approach but decided against it because of complications raised by the multiple sources of lead exposure. The choice between these possible approaches is a policy choice of the type that Congress specifically left to the Administrator's judgment. This court must allow him the discretion to determine which approach will best fulfill the goals of the Act.

NOTES AND QUESTIONS

1. Basically, there are three steps to promulgation of an ambient air quality standard. The first step is the inclusion of a pollutant on the section 108 list. CAA § 108(a), 42 U.S.C. § 7408. The second step is the preparation of the "criteria document," which is a scientific study of the injury to the public health and welfare the pollutant may cause. CAA § 108(a)(2), 42 U.S.C. § 7408(a)(2). The third step is the publication for public comment of the criteria document with the proposed primary and secondary ambient standards. CAA § 109(a)(2), 42 U.S.C. § 7409(a)(2). NAAQSs are required for pollutants included by the EPA Administrator on the list prepared under section 108, 42 U.S.C. § 7408. What pollutants are to be included in the section 108 list? The requirement of an "adverse effect" on public health or welfare was changed in 1977 to the requirement that the emissions "endanger" public health or welfare. According to *NRDC v. Train*, when does inclusion on the list become mandatory, and thus enforceable in a citizens' suit under section 304, 42 U.S.C. § 7604?

After inclusion on the list, what are the procedures EPA must follow to promulgate the NAAQS? *See* CAA §§ 109(a)(2)-(b), 307(d), 42 U.S.C. §§ 7409(a)(2)-(b), 7607(d). Notice that the procedures set out in section 307 supplant the general rulemaking provisions that would normally govern agency rulemaking under the Administrative Procedure Act (APA), 5 U.S.C. §§ 551-559. CAA § 307(d)(1), 42 U.S.C. § 7607(d)(1). The rulemaking procedure of the CAA allows for greater public participation in rulemaking than would the APA.

2. EPA had to review and revise air quality criteria and NAAQSs by December 31, 1980 and do so every five years thereafter, as *EDF v. Thomas* points out. CAA § 109(d)(1), 42 U.S.C. § 7409(d)(1). EPA has been very slow to review and revise the NAAQSs. *See generally* Oren, *Prevention of Significant Deterioration: Control-Compelling vs. Site-Shifting*, 74 Iowa L. Rev. 1 (1988). Section 122, enacted in 1977, requires EPA to determine, after notice and opportunity for a public hearing, whether the radioactive pollutants cadmium, arsenic, and polycyclic organic matter should be listed under section 108. When

EPA reviewed the primary and secondary NAAQSs for ozone, it promulgated more lenient NAAQSs. Its action was promptly opposed by environmental groups challenging the standards as too lenient and by industry groups challenging the standards as too stringent. *American Petr. Inst. v. Costle*, 665 F.2d 1176 (D.C. Cir. 1981), *cert. denied*, 455 U.S. 1034 (1982) (upholding the revised NAAQSs for ozone). The only NAAQS of those originally proposed under the 1970 Clean Air Act to be challenged in court successfully (for inadequate documentation) was the secondary NAAQS for sulfur dioxide (SO_2). *Kennecott Copper Corp. v. EPA*, 462 F.2d 846 (D.C. Cir. 1972). In response to the litigation EPA withdrew the secondary NAAQS for SO_2 but ultimately decided to retain the secondary standard for sulfur dioxide in April 1993. For all of the criteria pollutants except sulfur dioxide, the secondary NAAQS is the same as the primary NAAQS or no secondary NAAQS has been promulgated at all. Congress ordered a report on the secondary NAAQSs to be done by EPA by November 15, 1993. Clean Air Act Amendments of 1990, Pub. L. No. 101-549, § 817. Despite years of study, EPA decided in May 1996 not to revise the primary or secondary NAAQS for sulfur dioxide. As a result of litigation, EPA was ordered to review and, if necessary, revise its NAAQS for particulates by January 1997. *American Lung Association v. Browner*, 884 F. Supp. 345 (D. Ariz. 1994). In subsequent negotiations with the American Lung Association, EPA agreed to propose revision of the NAAQSs for particulates and ozone by November 29, 1996, with a final decision on both standards by mid-1997. Its proposed revisions sparked immediate controversies and the possibility of numerous legal challenges to any final standards. EPA submitted a proposed and hotly debated rule on December 13, 1996. 61 Fed. Reg. 65780.

3. According to *Lead Industries*, what role, if any, do consideration of cost and technological feasibility for the industry have in setting the NAAQS?

REVIEW PROBLEMS

1. Assume that there is no NAAQS for an air pollutant called "haze." As an attorney for an environmental group, could you bring a suit to compel EPA to promulgate a primary or secondary NAAQS? In what court and pursuant to what section of the CAA? What would you have to demonstrate to succeed under *NRDC v. Train*?

2. Assume that there are primary and secondary NAAQSs for haze, but EPA has not revised the standards since they were promulgated ten years earlier. Could you bring a lawsuit challenging EPA's inaction? In what court and pursuant to what section of the CAA? What will you have to demonstrate to succeed under *EDF v. Thomas*? According to *Thomas*, what is the only relief available should you succeed? If EPA should decide not to revise the haze standards, can that decision be challenged? Again, in what court and pursuant to what section of the CAA? What substantive and procedural challenges can be made in that lawsuit? *See* CAA § 307(d)(8)-(9), 42 U.S.C. § 7607(d)(8)-(9).

Notice that the answers to these questions are the same regardless of whether you are an attorney for an environmental group seeking more stringent standards or an attorney for industry seeking more lenient standards.

A petition for review under section 307 must be brought within sixty days "from the date notice of such promulgation, approval or action appears in the Federal Register." CAA § 307(b)(1), 42 U.S.C. § 7607(b)(1). Action of the Administrator for which review could have been obtained is not subject to judicial review in civil or criminal enforcement proceedings. CAA § 307(b)(2), 42 U.S.C. § 7607(b)(2). As with the judicial review provision of the Federal Water Pollution Control Act, discussed on pages 576-80 *infra*, costs and fees may be awarded whenever "appropriate." CAA § 307(f), 42 U.S.C. § 7607(f).

B. GENERAL REQUIREMENTS FOR STATE IMPLEMENTATION PLANS

The primary and secondary NAAQSs are only a measure of the acceptable level of a criteria pollutant in the ambient air. Somehow, each NAAQS must be translated into emission limitations on individual sources of the criteria pollutant. Once EPA has set a NAAQS, the responsibility for its implementation shifts to the state governments. Each state must devise a state implementation plan (SIP) to achieve the NAAQS by the statutory deadline and maintain it thereafter, through emission limitations on stationary sources and such other measures as may be necessary to meet the NAAQS. Although the nationwide, technology-forcing emission limitations on mobile sources and new sources may indirectly contribute toward achievement of a NAAQS, the state implementation planning process directly determines how and when the NAAQSs will be attained.

1. CONTENTS OF THE STATE IMPLEMENTATION PLAN

The entire nation is divided into air quality control regions, frequently with several regions within a single state. CAA § 107, 42 U.S.C. § 7407. Although the statutory requirements for state plans vary depending upon the classification of the region, see pages 383-427 *infra*, every SIP generally must contain: (1) enforceable emission limitations and such other measures, schedules and timetables necessary to attain and maintain the NAAQSs; (2) methods for obtaining air quality data for the state; (3) an enforcement program for the SIP; (4) provisions to control interstate and international pollution; (5) measures to ensure adequate personnel, funding and authority to carry out the SIP; (6) requirements for sources in the state to monitor and report their emissions; (7) state authority to restrict pollutants that present an imminent and substantial danger; (8) provisions for revisions of the plan after public hearings; (9) provisions for air quality modeling as EPA may subscribe; (10) provisions for a permit program as required by the CAA; (11) provisions for consultation with local political subdivisions affected by the SIP; and (12) a program for technical assistance to small sources. CAA § 110(a)(2)(A)-(H), (K)-(M), 42 U.S.C. § 7410(a)(2)(A)-(H), (K)-(M). States promulgate SIPs pursuant to their own state administrative procedures. Section 110 of the CAA specifies only that states must adopt SIPs "after reasonable notice and public hearings." CAA § 110(a)(1), 42 U.S.C. § 7410(a)(1).

EPA's regulations impose special SIP requirements on Air Quality Maintenance Areas (AQMAs). An AQMA is an area which is in attainment but which, due to current air quality and projected growth, has the potential to exceed the NAAQS within a ten-year period. For such areas, the SIP must include control measures to ensure that emissions from projected growth and development "will be compatible with maintenance of the national standards." 40 C.F.R. 51.40(c).

After EPA promulgates or revises a NAAQS, each state has at least three years after promulgation or revision (or three years after designation of the area as nonattainment for nonattainment areas) to prepare or revise an SIP specifying how the NAAQS will be met. CAA § 110(a), 42 U.S.C. § 7410(a), *as amended by* Clean Air Act Amendments of 1990, Pub. L. No. 101-549, § 101(d)(8). The 1990 amendments require EPA to promulgate minimum criteria for completeness of plan submission. The Administrator of the EPA has six months from receipt of the submitted plan to determine if it is complete; failure to act within the six months is equivalent to a determination that the submission is complete. CAA § 110(k)(1), 42 U.S.C. § 7410(k)(1). An incomplete submission is treated the same as failure to submit a plan. EPA has twelve months from a determination of completion (or twelve months from submission of plans to which no completeness criteria apply) to reach a decision on whether the SIP meets the CAA's requirements. CAA § 110(k)(2), 42 U.S.C. § 7401(k)(2).

The 1990 amendments allow EPA's action upon review of a state plan to be full approval, partial approval, conditional approval, or disapproval, thus officially authorizing the range of approval options, discussed on pages 380-82 *infra*, which EPA had developed administratively to deal with states failing to submit satisfactory SIPs. CAA § 110(k)(3)-(4), 42 U.S.C. § 7410(k)(3)-(4), *as added by* Clean Air Act Amendments of 1990 Pub. L. No. 101-549, § 101(c). A partially approved plan or revision is not treated as meeting the requirements of the CAA, until EPA approves the whole plan. CAA § 110(k)(3), 42 U.S.C. § 7410(k)(3). After a conditional approval, the state must meet any conditions set by the Administrator for full approval within one year, or the conditional approval will be treated as a disapproval. CAA § 110(k)(4), 42 U.S.C. § 7410(k)(4). Any time that the Administrator determines a plan is "substantially inadequate" and so notifies the state, the state will be given up to eighteen months to revise the plan. CAA § 110(k)(5), 42 U.S.C. § 7410(k)(5).

2. SANCTIONS FOR FAILURE TO COMPLY WITH SIP REQUIREMENTS

If a state fails to make a required SIP submission, makes only an incomplete submission, or has a SIP disapproved in whole or in part, EPA will promulgate its own plan for the state. CAA § 110(c)(1), 42 U.S.C. § 7410(c)(1). EPA has two years to promulgate its own federal implementation plan for the state unless the state corrects the deficiency and has its plan approved by EPA before the federal plan is promulgated. CAA § 110(c)(1), 42 U.S.C. § 7410(c)(1). "Federal implementation plan" is defined as

> a plan (or portion thereof) promulgated by the Administrator to fill all or a portion of a gap or otherwise correct all or a portion of an inadequacy in a State implemention plan, and which includes enforceable emission limitations or other control measures, means or techniques (including economic incentives, such as marketable permits or auctions of emissions allowances), and provides for attainment of the relevant national ambient air quality standard. CAA § 302(y), 42 U.S.C. § 7602(y).

The sanctions of section 179(b), 42 U.S.C. § 7509(b), are also available to EPA if: (1) the State has failed to submit one or more of the elements required for a state implementation plan (SIP), or such submission does not meet the minimum criteria in section 110(k)(1); (2) EPA disapproves a SIP element submitted by the State; (3) the State has failed to make any other required submission (including a maintenance plan), or EPA has disapproved such other required submission; or (4) any requirement of an approved plan is not being implemented. *Id.* § 179(a), 42 U.S.C. § 7509(a). EPA must establish criteria for applying the sanctions to ensure that they are not applied statewide if only certain areas are "principally responsible" for the deficiency. CAA § 110(m), 42 U.S.C. § 7410(m). EPA's authority to impose these sanctions has withstood constitutional challenges by states. *Virginia v. Browner*, 80 F.3d 869 (1996), *cert. denied*, 117 S. Ct. 764 (1997); *Missouri v. United States*, 918 F. Supp. 1320 (E.D. Mo. 1996), *vacated on jurisd. grounds and remanded*, 109 F.3d 440 (8th Cir. 1997).

EPA has a mandatory duty to impose the section 179(b) sanctions for nonattainment areas. *See* CAA § 179(a), 42 U.S.C. § 7509(a). EPA is authorized to cut off federal highway funding (other than for safety projects and a few other limited projects) and to require emissions offsets of at least two-to-one for new or modified sources seeking permits in nonattainment areas. CAA § 179(b)-(1)-(2), 42 U.S.C. § 7509(b)(1)-(2). The state has a grace period of eighteen months to correct its deficiency. After that time has elapsed, the Administrator shall either cut off highway funds or impose the offset requirement until the state complies. If the Administrator finds that the state has not acted in good faith, or the deficiency is not corrected within six months after one of the sanctions is imposed, both sanctions shall apply until the state is in compliance. As an additional sanction for nonattainment areas, EPA may withhold support grants for air pollution planning and control programs. CAA § 179(a), 42 U.S.C. § 7509(a).

Revision of a SIP, however minor the change might be, is a time-consuming, cumbersome process. Plan revisions must go through both the state and federal administrative processes for adoption. Note that EPA approves or disapproves of a SIP; it is not given statutory authority to revise the SIP on its own initiative. *Riverside Cement Co. v. Thomas*, 843 F.2d 1246, 1248 (9th Cir. 1988) (EPA could not approve SIP revision that was contingent upon conclusion of a state hearing, in effect deleting the contingency; *see also Bethlehem Steel Corp. v. Gorsuch*, 742 F.2d 1028 (7th Cir. 1984) (EPA could approve parts of revised SIP and disapprove other parts only if EPA's partial approval/disapproval did not have effect of making state plan more stringent than the state itself had intended). Is it necessary to have this dual approval process? *See generally* Pedersen, *Why the Clean Air Act Works Badly*, 129 U. PA. L. REV. 1059 (1981). What factors can EPA consider under section 110 in deciding whether to approve or disapprove a SIP? After a SIP has been approved at the state and federal levels, can it be challenged in court? By whom and on what grounds? The following Supreme Court case addresses these issues.

UNION ELECTRIC CO. v. ENVIRONMENTAL PROTECTION AGENCY

427 U.S. 246 (1976)

MR. JUSTICE MARSHALL delivered the opinion of the Court.

After the Administrator of the Environmental Protection Agency (EPA) approves a state implementation plan under the Clean Air Act, the plan may be challenged in a court of appeals within 30 days, or after 30 days have run if newly discovered or available information justifies subsequent review. We must decide whether the operator of a regulated emission source, in a petition for review of an EPA-approved state plan filed after the original 30-day appeal period, can raise the claim that it is economically or technologically infeasible to comply with the plan.

. . . .

Petitioner is an electric utility company servicing the St. Louis metropolitan area, large portions of Missouri, and parts of Illinois and Iowa. Its three coal-fired generating plants in the metropolitan St. Louis area are subject to the sulfur dioxide restrictions in the Missouri implementation plan. Petitioner did not seek review of the Administrator's approval of the plan within 30 days, as it was entitled to do under § 307(b)(1) of the Act, but rather applied to the appropriate state and county agencies for variances from the emission limitations affecting its three plants. Petitioner received one-year variances, which could be extended upon reapplication. The variances on two of petitioner's three plants had expired and petitioner was applying for extensions when, on May 31, 1974, the Administrator notified petitioner that sulfur dioxide emissions from its plants violated the emission limitations contained in the Missouri plan. Shortly thereafter petitioner filed a petition in the Court of Appeals for the Eighth Circuit for review of the Administrator's 1972 approval of the Missouri implementation plan.

Section 307(b)(1) allows petitions for review to be filed in an appropriate court of appeals more than 30 days after the Administrator's approval of an implementation plan only if the petition is "based solely on grounds arising after such 30th day." Petitioner claimed to meet this requirement by asserting, inter alia, that various economic and technological difficulties had arisen more than 30 days after the Administrator's approval and that these difficulties made compliance with the emission limitations impossible....

We reject at the outset petitioner's suggestion that a claim of economic or technological infeasibility may be considered upon a petition for review based on new information and filed more than 30 days after approval of an implementation plan even if such a claim could not be considered by the Administrator in approving a plan or by a court in reviewing a plan challenged within the original 30-day appeal period....

Regardless of when a petition for review is filed under § 307(b)(1), the court is limited to reviewing "the Administrator's action in approving ... [the] implementation plan...." Accordingly, if new "grounds" are alleged, they must be such that, had they been known at the time the plan was presented to the Administrator for approval, it would have been an abuse of discretion for the Administrator to approve the plan. To hold otherwise would be to transfer a substantial responsibility in administering the Clean Air Act from the Administrator and the state agencies to the federal courts.

Since a reviewing court — regardless of when the petition for review is filed — may consider claims of economic and technological infeasibility only if the Administrator may consider such claims in approving or rejecting a state implementation plan, we must address ourselves to the scope of the Administrator's responsibility. The Administrator's position is that he has no power whatsoever to reject a state implementation plan on the ground that it is economically or technologically infeasible, and we have previously accorded great deference to the Administrator's construction of the Clean Air Act. After surveying the relevant provisions of the Clean Air Amendments of 1970 and their legislative history, we agree that Congress intended claims of economic and technological infeasibility to be wholly foreign to the Administrator's consideration of a state implementation plan.

As we have previously recognized, the 1970 Amendments to the Clean Air Act were a drastic remedy to what was perceived as a serious and otherwise uncheckable problem of air pollution. The Amendments place the primary responsibility for formulating pollution control strategies on the States, but nonetheless subject the States to strict minimum compliance requirements. These requirements are of a "technology-forcing character," and are expressly designed to force regulated sources to develop pollution control devices that might at the time appear to be economically or technologically infeasible.

This approach is apparent on the face of § 110(a)(2). The provision sets out eight criteria that an implementation plan must satisfy, and provides that if these criteria are met and if the plan was adopted after reasonable notice and hearing, the Administrator "shall approve" the proposed state plan. The mandatory "shall" makes it quite clear that the Administrator is not to be concerned with factors other than those specified, and none of the eight factors appears to permit consideration of technological or economic infeasibility. Nonetheless, if a basis is to be found for allowing the Administrator to consider such claims, it must be among the eight criteria, and so it is here that the argument is focused.

It is suggested that consideration of claims of technological and economic infeasibility is required by the first criterion — that the primary air quality standards be met "as expeditiously as practicable but ... in no case later than three years ..." and that the secondary air quality standards be met within a "reasonable time." § 110(a)(2)(A). The argument is that what is "practicable" or "reasonable" cannot be determined without assessing whether what is proposed is possible. This argument does not survive analysis.

Section 110(a)(2)(A)'s three-year deadline for achieving primary air quality standards is central to the Amendments' regulatory scheme and, as both the language and the legislative history of the requirement make clear, it leaves no room for claims of technological or economic infeasibility. The 1970 congressional debate on the Amendments centered on whether technology forcing was necessary and desirable in framing and attaining air quality standards sufficient to protect the public health, standards later termed primary standards. The House version of the Amendments was quite moderate in approach, requiring only that health-related standards be met "within a reasonable time." The Senate bill, on the other hand, flatly required that, possible or not, health-related standards be met "within three years."

. . . .

The Conference Committee and, ultimately, the entire Congress accepted the Senate's three-year mandate for the achievement of primary air quality standards, and the clear import of that decision is that the Administrator must approve a plan that provides for attainment of the primary standards in three years even if attainment does not appear feasible. In rejecting the House's version of reasonableness, however, the conferees strengthened the Senate version. The Conference Committee made clear that the States could not procrastinate until the deadline approached. Rather, the primary standards had to be met in less than three years if possible; they had to be met "as expeditiously as practicable." § 110(a)(2)(A). Whatever room there is for considering claims of infeasibility in the attainment of primary standards must lie in this phrase, which is, of course, relevant only in evaluating those implementation plans that attempt to achieve the primary standard in less than three years.

It is argued that when such a state plan calls for proceeding more rapidly than economics and the available technology appear to allow, the plan must be rejected as not "practicable." Whether this is a correct reading of § 110(a)(2)(A) depends on how that section's "as expeditiously as practicable" phrase is characterized. The Administrator's position is that § 110(a)(2)(A) sets only a minimum standard that the States may exceed in their discretion, so that he has no power to reject an infeasible state plan that surpasses the minimum federal requirements — a plan that reflects a state decision to engage in technology forcing on its own and to proceed more expeditiously than is practicable. On the other hand, petitioner and amici supporting its position argue that § 110(a)(2)(A) sets a mandatory standard that the States must meet precisely, and conclude that the Administrator may reject a plan for being too strict as well as for being too lax. Since the arguments supporting this theory are also made to show that the Administrator must reject a state plan that provides for achieving more than the secondary air quality standards require, we defer consideration of this question in order to outline the development and content of the secondary standards provision of § 110(a)(2)(A).

Secondary air quality standards, those necessary to protect the public welfare, were subject to far less legislative debate than the primary standards.... The final Amendments ... separated welfare-related standards from health-related standards, labeled them secondary air quality standards, and adopted the ... requirement that they be met within a "reasonable time." §§ 109(b), 110(a)(2)(A). Thus, technology forcing is not expressly required in achieving standards to protect the public welfare.

It does not necessarily follow, however, that the Administrator may consider claims of impossibility in assessing a state plan for achieving secondary standards. As with plans designed to achieve primary standards in less than three years, the scope of the Administrator's power to reject a plan depends on whether the State itself may decide to engage in technology forcing and adopt a plan more stringent than federal law demands.[7]

Amici Appalachian Power Co. et al. argue that the Amendments do not give such broad power to the States. They claim that the States are precluded from submitting implementation plans more stringent than federal law demands by § 110(a)(2)'s second criterion — that the plan contain such control devices "as may be necessary" to achieve the primary and secondary air quality standards. § 110(a)(2)(B). The contention is that an overly restrictive plan is not "necessary" for attainment of the national standards and so must be rejected by the Administrator.

  ....

---

[7]A different question would be presented if the Administrator drafted the plan himself pursuant to § 110(c). Whether claims of economic or technical infeasibility must be considered by the Administrator in drafting an implementation plan is a question we do not reach.

We read the "as may be necessary" requirement of § 110(a)(2)(B) to demand only that the implementation plan submitted by the State meet the "minimum conditions" of the Amendments.[13] [Citation.] Beyond that if a State makes the legislative determination that it desires a particular air quality by a certain date and that it is willing to force technology to attain it — or lose a certain industry if attainment is not possible — such a determination is fully consistent with the structure and purpose of the Amendments, and § 110(a)(2)(B) provides no basis for the EPA Administrator to object to the determination on the ground of infeasibility.

In sum, we have concluded that claims of economic or technological infeasibility may not be considered by the Administrator in evaluating a state requirement that primary ambient air quality standards be met in the mandatory three years. And, since we further conclude that the States may submit implementation plans more stringent than federal law requires and that the Administrator must approve such plans if they meet the minimum requirements of § 110(a)(2), it follows that the language of § 110(a)(2)(B) provides no basis for the Administrator ever to reject a state implementation plan on the ground that it is economically or technologically infeasible. Accordingly, a court of appeals reviewing an approved plan under § 307(b)(1) cannot set it aside on those grounds, no matter when they are raised.

III

Our conclusion is bolstered by recognition that the Amendments do allow claims of technological and economic infeasibility to be raised in situations where consideration of such claims will not substantially interfere with the primary congressional purpose of prompt attainment of the national air quality standards. Thus, we do not hold that claims of infeasibility are never of relevance in the formulation of an implementation plan or that sources unable to comply with emission limitations must inevitably be shut down.

Perhaps the most important forum for consideration of claims of economic and technological infeasibility is before the state agency formulating the implementation plan. So long as the national standards are met, the State may select whatever mix of control devices it desires, [citation] and industries with particular economic or technological problems may seek special treatment in the plan itself. Moreover, if the industry is not exempted from, or accommodated by, the original plan, it may obtain a variance, as petitioner did in this case; and the variance, if granted after notice and a hearing, may be submitted to the EPA as

---

[13]Economic and technological factors may be relevant in determining whether the minimum conditions are met. Thus, the Administrator may consider whether it is economically or technologically possible for the state plan to require more rapid progress than it does. If he determines that it is, he may reject the plan as not meeting the requirement that primary standards be achieved "as expeditiously as practicable" or as failing to provide for attaining secondary standards within "a reasonable time."

a revision of the plan.[15] § 110(a)(3)(A). Lastly, an industry denied an exemption from the implementation plan, or denied a subsequent variance, may be able to take its claims of economic or technological infeasibility to the state courts.

....

... [T]echnological and economic factors may be considered in at least one other circumstance. When a source is found to be in violation of the state implementation plan, the Administrator may, after a conference with the operator, issue a compliance order rather than seek civil or criminal enforcement. Such an order must specify a "reasonable" time for compliance with the relevant standard, taking into account the seriousness of the violation and "any good faith efforts to comply with applicable requirements." § 113(a)(4). Claims of technological or economic infeasibility, the Administrator agrees, are relevant to fashioning an appropriate compliance order under § 113(a)(4).[18]

In short, the Amendments offer ample opportunity for consideration of claims of technological and economic infeasibility. Always, however, care is taken that consideration of such claims will not interfere substantially with the primary goal of prompt attainment of the national standards. Allowing such claims to be raised by appealing the Administrator's approval of an implementation plan, as petitioner suggests, would frustrate congressional intent. It would permit a proposed plan to be struck down as infeasible before it is given a chance to work, even though Congress clearly contemplated that some plans would be infeasible when proposed. And it would permit the Administrator or a federal court to reject a State's legislative choices in regulating air pollution, even though Congress plainly left with the States, so long as the national standards were met, the power to determine which sources would be burdened by regulation and to what extent. Technology forcing is a concept somewhat new to our national experience and it necessarily entails certain risks. But Congress considered those risks in passing the 1970 Amendments and decided that the dangers posed by uncontrolled air pollution made them worth taking. Petitioner's theory would render that considered legislative judgment a nullity, and that is a result we refuse to reach.[19]

---

[15]A variance approved as a revision of a plan under § 110(a)(3)(A) will be honored by the EPA as part of an applicable implementation plan, § 110(d), a matter of no little import to those granted variances. *See* n. 3, *supra*.

[18]If he chooses not to seek a compliance order, or if an order is issued and violated, the Administrator may institute a civil enforcement proceeding. § 113(b). Additionally, violators of an implementation plan are subject to criminal penalties under § 113(c) and citizen enforcement suits under § 304. Some courts have suggested that in criminal or civil enforcement proceedings the violator may in certain circumstances raise a defense of economic or technological infeasibility. *See Buckeye Power, Inc. v. EPA*, 481 F.2d 162, 173 (6th Cir. 1973); *Indiana & Michigan Electric Co. v. EPA*, 509 F.2d 839, 847 (7th Cir. 1975). We do not address this question here.

[19]Petitioner has briefed its contention that the Due Process Clause of the Fifth Amendment demands that at some time it be afforded the opportunity to raise before a court claims of economic and technological impossibility. This claim was neither presented to, nor considered by, the Court

MR. JUSTICE POWELL, with whom THE CHIEF JUSTICE joins, concurring.

I join the opinion of the Court because the statutory scheme and the legislative history, thoroughly described in the Court's opinion, demonstrate irrefutably that Congress did not intend to permit the Administrator of the Environmental Protection Agency to reject a proposed state implementation plan on the grounds of economic or technological infeasibility. Congress adopted this position despite its apparent awareness that in some cases existing sources that cannot meet the standard of the law must be closed down.

....

... [T]he shutdown of an urban area's electrical service could have an even more serious impact on the health of the public than that created by a decline in ambient air quality. The result apparently required by this legislation in its present form could sacrifice the well-being of a large metropolitan area through the imposition of inflexible demands that may be technologically impossible to meet and indeed may no longer even be necessary to the attainment of the goal of clean air.

I believe that Congress, if fully aware of this Draconian possibility, would strike a different balance.

NOTES AND QUESTIONS

1. *Union Electric* stands for the principle that EPA must approve a plan that contains the elements required in section 110 and that will attain the NAAQSs by the deadline. EPA may not reject a plan as too stringent to be feasible. Can a state use the SIP to regulate air quality problems unrelated to NAAQSs, for example, impose controls to regulate odors? *See Concerned Citizens of Bridesburg v. EPA*, 836 F.2d 777 (3d Cir. 1987) (EPA's disapproval of odor regulations in SIP was a revision of SIP subject to statutory procedures for SIP revisions). States do have discretion as to the mix of controls imposed on sources under the SIP to attain and maintain the NAAQSs. *See, e.g., Virginia v. EPA*, 108 F.3d 1397 (D.C. Cir. 1997) (EPA cannot condition SIP approval upon adoption by ozone nonattainment areas of Claifornia's Low Emission Vehicle program). The CAA requires SIPs to contain emission limitations and such other measures as may be necessary, with a 1990 amendment specifying that permissible measures include economic incentives such as fees, marketable permits and auction of emission rights. CAA § 110(a)(2)(A), 42 U.S.C. § 7410(a)(2)(A). Prior to the 1977 amendments, a controversy raged between environmentalists and industry, EPA and other federal agencies over the use of dispersion and intermittent control techniques in SIPs. Intermittent control and

---

of Appeals, and we declined to grant certiorari on the question. In any case, we could not resolve petitioner's claim here, for there has been no showing that a § 307(b)(1) appeal would be the only opportunity for petitioner to raise before a court its claims of economic and technological impossibility.

dispersion techniques give the appearance of reducing emissions, but in fact they do not reduce in absolute terms the volume of emissions. Intermittent controls periodically reduce emissions but are less effective than continuous controls because at times there is little or no reduction in emissions. Dispersion techniques, such as the use of tall stacks, result in lower readings of pollution at the point of emission, but do so by simply causing the pollution to go elsewhere. For what constitutes a dispersion technique, see *Kamp v. Hernandez*, 752 F.2d 1444, *opinion modified*, 778 F.2d 527 (9th Cir. 1985). The courts of appeals favored the environmentalists' position, generally concluding that the CAA required SIPs to impose continuous emission limitations, with resort to intermittent and dispersion techniques only when continuous controls were not feasible. *See, e.g.*, *NRDC v. EPA*, 489 F.2d 390 (5th Cir. 1974), *rev'd on other grounds*, *NRDC v. EPA*, 421 U.S. 60 (1975) (rejecting dispersion techniques); *Big Rivers Elec. Corp. v. EPA*, 523 F.2d 16 (6th Cir. 1975), *cert. denied*, 425 U.S. 934 (1976); *Kennecott Copper Corp. v. Train*, 526 F.2d 1149 (9th Cir. 1975) (rejecting intermittent controls), *cert. denied*, 425 U.S. 935 (1976); *see also Bunker Hill Co. v. EPA*, 572 F.2d 1286 (9th Cir. 1977) (state's determination of the reduction feasible through control is not binding on EPA in reviewing the SIP).

In 1977, Congress also adopted the environmentalists' position. An emission limitation was defined as a requirement that "limits the quantity, rate, or concentration of emissions of air pollutants on a *continuous* basis." CAA § 302(k), 42 U.S.C. § 7602(k) (emphasis added). A new section 123 was also added. Section 123 mandates that the degree of emission limitation required under an SIP "shall not be affected in any manner" by as much of the stack height of a source that "exceeds good engineering practice" or by any other dispersion technique. CAA § 123(a), 42 U.S.C. § 7423(a). "Good engineering practice" is defined as "the height necessary to insure that emissions from the stack do not result in excessive concentrations of any air pollutant in the immediate vicinity of the source." CAA § 123(c), 42 U.S.C. § 7423(c). The CAA clarifies that generally, for purposes of what constitutes good engineering practice, the stack height shall not exceed two and a half times the height of the source. *Id.*

Section 123 does not entirely prohibit the use of tall stacks, but merely limits the "credit" a source can get for emission reductions achieved through the use of tall stacks. The use of this dispersion technique continues to be controversial because the tall stacks of fossil fuel burning power plants may contribute to the interstate problem of acid rain. *See Sierra Club v. EPA*, 719 F.2d 436 (D.C. Cir. 1983), *cert. denied*, 468 U.S. 1204 (1984); *NRDC v. Thomas*, 838 F.2d 1224 (D.C. Cir. 1988), *cert. denied*, 488 U.S. 888 (1988) (challenges, generally unsuccessful, to EPA's tall stack regulations). *See also* Note, *Good Engineering Practice and the Tall Stack Rules: Judicial Disregard of the EPA's Delegated Duties*, 36 WASH. U.J. URB. & CONTEMP. L. 213 (1989). One court has held that the 1977 amendments require that the NAAQSs be met by continuous controls, precluding the use of intermittent controls even when continuous controls are infeasible. *Dow Chem. Co. v. EPA*, 635 F.2d 559 (6th Cir. 1980), *cert. denied*, 452 U.S. 939 (1981).

2. In *Union Electric*, the company did not challenge the Administrator's approval of the SIP, as it was entitled to do under the judicial review provisions of section 307(b)(1), 42 U.S.C. § 7607(b)(1). In addition to promulgation of a NAAQS, as discussed earlier, and approval of SIPs, what other actions of the Administrator may be challenged under section 307(b)(1)? *See also Bethlehem Steel Corp. v. EPA*, 782 F.2d 645 (7th Cir. 1986) (questioning whether disapproval of a SIP is reviewable without approval of at least parts of the SIP); and the discussion in note 2, page 501 *infra*.

3. Instead of challenging the Administrator's approval of the SIP, Union Electric choose to apply for variances from the state. In *Train v. NRDC*, 421 U.S. 60 (1975), the Supreme Court concluded that section 110(a)(3), 42 U.S.C. § 7410(a)(3), allows a state to grant individual variances from emission standards in the SIP so long as the variance does not prevent attainment or maintenance of the NAAQSs. Thus, if a source lobbies unsuccessfully for a feasible limitation when the SIP is formulated, it may seek a variance from the state under whatever procedures are prescribed by state law. A variance is considered an amendment of the SIP, and as such triggers the state and federal administrative processes and dual review at the state and federal level for any SIP revision, as discussed on pages 369-71 *supra*. How demanding can EPA be in its review of a state-granted variance? Should the stringency of the review vary depending upon whether the source is seeking more time to comply with the applicable standard, or is seeking a relaxation of the standard? *See Navistar Int'l Transp. Co. v. EPA*, 941 F.2d 1339 (6th Cir. 1991). Can economic and technological feasibility be grounds for a variance according to *Union Electric*? At what other point in the state process of promulgating or revising an SIP might such claims be brought? *See Union Electric, supra; Commonwealth Edison Co. v. Pollution Control Bd.*, 62 Ill. 2d 494, 343 N.E.2d 459 (1976); *Wells Mfg. Co. v. Pollution Control Bd.*, 73 Ill. 2d 226, 383 N.E.2d 148 (1978). Can such claims be brought in a federal enforcement proceeding? *See* note 18 in *Union Electric* and *Navistar Internat'l Transp. Corp. v. EPA*, page 502 *infra*. The role of economic and technological infeasibility in enforcement proceedings is discussed on pages 495-504 *infra*. If a state fails to prepare an acceptable plan, can EPA consider claims of economic and technological feasibility in formulating a federal implementation plan for the state? *See Cleveland Elec. Illuminating Co. v. EPA*, 572 F.2d 1150, 1164-65 (6th Cir. 1978) (suggesting that EPA may not), *cert. denied*, 439 U.S. 910 (1978).

4. In order to set emission limitations, the emissions of a source must be measured somehow and a projection made of the reduction necessary to achieve or maintain the NAAQSs. EPA has had to develop air modeling techniques to make these determinations. Although the accuracy of the modeling techniques utilized by EPA has been challenged with some frequency, most challenges have been unsuccessful. *Compare Cleveland Elec. Illuminating Co. v. EPA*, 572 F.2d

1150 (6th Cir. 1978) (unsuccessful challenge), *cert. denied*, 439 U.S. 910 (1978); *Ohio v. EPA*, 784 F.2d 224 (6th Cir. 1986) (successful challenge). *See generally* Kramer, *Air Quality Modeling: Judicial, Legislative and Administrative Reactions*, 5 COLUM. J. ENVT. L. 236 (1979); McMahon & Hinkle, State of Ohio v. EPA: *Does the Sixth Circuit Have a New Standard for Its Review of the EPA's Use of Air Quality Monitoring?*, 18 U. TOLEDO L. REV. 569 (1987).

REVIEW PROBLEM

Assume that you represent a trade association of widget plants, the principal source of the pollutant haze. EPA has just proposed a primary NAAQS for haze which the association members claim will be technologically and economically infeasible for most of the industry to meet. With the guidance of *Union Electric*, at what point in the state and federal administrative processes could you participate? Could you raise claims of technological and economic infeasibility? How could you raise the association's claims in state or federal court? In framing your answer, explore all possible forums for the infeasibility claims from the time the NAAQS is proposed up to and including any proceedings that might be brought to enforce an SIP limitation implementing the NAAQS against an individual source.

C. DEADLINES FOR SIP SUBMISSIONS, ATTAINMENT, AND THE NONATTAINMENT AREAS

1. DEADLINES PRIOR TO THE 1990 AMENDMENTS

The 1970 Act required that the primary NAAQSs be met by 1975, with extensions available until 1977 for carbon monoxide and ozone, and that the secondary NAAQSs be met within "a reasonable time" of promulgation. Congress optimistically did not address what would happen if the deadlines were not met. By the first round of amendments in 1977, it was clear that many air quality control regions had not achieved one or more of the NAAQSs as required. To expedite compliance, regions were to be classified as attainment areas, nonattainment areas, and areas that could not be classified for lack of reliable air quality data. CAA § 107(d)(1), 42 U.S.C. § 7407(d)(1). The 1977 amendments also added a new "prevention of significant deterioration" (PSD) program, discussed on pages 389-415 *infra*, for unclassifiable areas and areas with air quality exceeding that required by a NAAQS. For the nonattainment areas, the deadline for attainment of the primary NAAQSs was extended to 1982, with the deadline for photochemical oxidants (measured primarily by ozone levels) and carbon monoxide extended to 1987. Pub. L. No. 95-95, 91 Stat. 685 (1977); *see also* Pub. L. No. 100-202, 101 Stat. 1329 (1987) (extending the 1987 deadline to August 31, 1988). The extension to 1987 for the automobile related pollutants was available to states assuming limited conditions were met, including a specific schedule set by the state for implementation of a vehicle emission control inspection and maintenance program. CAA § 172(b)(11)(B), 42 U.S.C. § 7502(b)(11)(B), *deleted by* Clean Air Act Amendments of 1990, Pub. L. No. 101-549, § 102(b). The nonattainment areas that had failed to meet a NAAQS by 1977 were subject to additional requirements to expedite attainment.

By July 1, 1979, all SIPs for nonattainment areas subject to the 1982 deadline were to have been approved by EPA, and by July 1, 1982, all SIPs for nonattainment areas subject to the 1987 deadline were to have been approved. When only one state had met the first deadline of July 1, 1979, EPA began a policy of "conditional approval" for the SIPs. 44 Fed. Reg. 38583 (1979). *See also City of Seabrook v. EPA*, 659 F.2d 1349 (5th Cir. 1981) (upholding EPA's conditional approval policy), *cert. denied*, 459 U.S. 822 (1982). When a plan was in "substantial compliance" with the requirements of Part D (the nonattainment section of the Clear Air Act), EPA would conditionally approve the SIP and negotiate with the state a schedule for remedying any deficiencies in the plan. EPA, at the time, was authorized by the CAA to impose a construction ban on the construction or modification of major stationary sources unless a plan meeting the Part D requirements had been promulgated. CAA § 110(a)(2)(I), 42 U.S.C. § 7410(a)(2)(I), *deleted by* Clean Air Act Amendments of 1990, Pub. L. No. 101-549, § 101(b). Rather than impose the construction ban in those areas, however, EPA only required that states with approved but ineffective Part D plans revise their plans within set time limits. Only nonattainment areas that did not meet the 1982 deadline and did not have Part D plans approved within the revised administrative schedule were subject to any sanctions, with EPA reserving the construction ban only for those states that never had Part D SIPs approved. *See* 48 Fed. Reg. 50,686, 50,691 (1983) and 51 Fed. Reg. 2,732 (1986). EPA drafted federal implementation plans for states without a satisfactory SIP only when compelled to do so in litigation. *See, e.g.*, 55 Fed. Reg. 36,458 (1990) (EPA proposes FIP for Los Angeles pursuant to court action); 55 Fed. Reg. 41,204 (1990) (EPA proposes FIPs for Phoenix and Tucson in response to court order). In large part as a result of these de facto extensions, the ultimate 1982 deadline for compliance with the primary NAAQSs was not met in many nonattainment areas.

The conditional approval policy was also applied to the 1982 deadline for submission of SIPs to meet the 1987 deadline for compliance with the NAAQSs for ozone and carbon monoxide. After California submitted a plan that it conceded would not achieve attainment by 1987, the Ninth Circuit Court of Appeals held that EPA could not approve the SIP if the state could not demonstrate that the NAAQS would be met by the 1987 deadline. *Abramowitz v. EPA*, 832 F.2d 1071 (9th Cir. 1987). Shortly before *Abramowitz* was decided, however, EPA had already announced that it would disapprove of SIPs that would not demonstrate attainment by 1987 and impose the construction ban, but that it would not impose federal implementation plans so long as a state was making "reasonable efforts" toward attainment. 52 Fed. Reg. 26,404 (1987). EPA was forced again by litigation to begin drafting federal plans for some areas. *See, e.g., Delaney v. EPA*, 20 ENVTL. L. REP. (Envtl. L. Inst.) 20460 (9th Cir. 1990) (EPA forced to develop FIPs for Phoenix and Tucson); *Wisconsin v. Thomas*, 29 ERC 1077 (E.D. Wis. 1989) (EPA forced to develop FIPs for Illinois and Indiana covering the Chicago metropolitan area). Under the 1990 amendments, any construction ban in effect in a nonattainment area due to failure to submit a new source permit program in a SIP, or due to failure to submit an approvable SIP providing for attainment of the sulfur dioxide NAAQS by December 31, 1982, remains in effect until EPA approves a plan correcting the deficiency. CAA § 110(n)(3), 42 U.S.C. § 7410(n)(3). As the 1987 deadline for attainment approached, Congress enacted a moratorium on sanctions until September of 1988. Pub. L. No. 100-202, 101 Stat. 1329 (1987). The Clean Air Act Amendments of 1990 substantially restructured the requirements for nonattainment areas and the sanctions for failures to comply with the Act's requirements. Despite the 1990 Amendments, EPA continued to be responsible for promulgation of FIPs where required under the earlier version of the Act. *Coalition for Clean Air v. United States EPA*, 971 F.2d 219 (9th Cir. 1992), *cert. denied*, 507 U.S. 950 (1993); *but see Sierra Club v. EPA*, 99 F.3d 1551 (10th Cir. 1996) (EPA does not have to wait until an area has been redesignated before it can exempt that area from compliance with some nonattainment area requirements).

2. DESIGNATION OF AIR QUALITY CONTROL REGIONS AFTER THE 1990 AMENDMENTS

One way in which states have attempted to avoid the statutory requirements for nonattainment areas is by gerrymandering attainment areas out of larger nonattainment areas. Because EPA has the power to review and disapprove of state designations, these attempts have been generally unsuccessful. *See, e.g., Illinois State Chamber of Commerce v. EPA*, 775 F.2d 1141 (7th Cir. 1985); *State of Arizona v. Thomas*, 824 F.2d 745 (9th Cir. 1987); *State of Ohio v. Ruckelshaus*, 776 F.2d 1333 (6th Cir. 1985), *cert. denied*, 476 U.S. 1169 (1986). *See also Western Oil & Gas Ass'n v. EPA*, 633 F.2d 803, 807 (9th Cir. 1980) (EPA promulgation of designations is reviewable under section 307); Comment, *When Is an Area that Is In Attainment Not an Attainment Area?*, 16 ENVTL. L. REP. (Envtl. L. Inst.) 10041 (1986). A more troublesome issue before the 1990 amendments was whether EPA could revise designations on its own initiative. Although EPA had taken the position that it could redesignate areas on its own motion, its position was rejected in *Bethlehem Steel Corp. v. EPA*, 723 F.2d 1303 (7th Cir. 1983); EPA subsequently acknowledged that it would not modify designations without a state request to do so. 53 Fed. Reg. 38,724 (1988).

The 1990 amendments require that a state classify every area in it as either an attainment area, a nonattainment area, or an unclassified area as to each criteria pollutant. CAA § 107(d)(1)(A), 42 U.S.C. § 7407(d)(1)(A). Any area which was so designated prior to the enactment date of the 1990 amendments retains its designation by operation of law, CAA § 107(d)(1)(C), 42 U.S.C. § 7407(d)(1)-(C), while initial designations with respect to a new or revised NAAQS must be made by the state within one year of the promulgation of such a standard. CAA § 107(d)(1)(A), 42 U.S.C. § 7407(d)(1)(A). EPA then has one year to promulgate the designation of the area, with a one year extension available if the Administrator has insufficient information to make the designation. In promulgating the designation, the Administrator can make whatever modifications are deemed "necessary." CAA § 107(d)(1)(B), 42 U.S.C. § 7407(d)(1)(B). Generally, a nonattainment area is defined as an area that does not meet the primary or secondary NAAQS or contributes to the failure of a nearby area to meet the primary or secondary NAAQS. CAA § 107(d)(1)(A)(i), 42 U.S.C. § 7407(d)(1)(A)(i).

In response to *Bethlehem Steel*, Congress added section 107(d)(3), which allows the Administrator to redesignate an area on his or her own initiative. CAA § 107(d)(3), 42 U.S.C. § 7407(d)(3). States still may seek redesignation of air quality control regions, subject to EPA's review and approval. CAA § 107(e), 42 U.S.C. § 7407(e). A state which requests redesignation of a nonattainment area as to any air pollutant as an area which has attained the primary NAAQS must submit to EPA a SIP revision providing for maintenance of the primary NAAQS in that area for at least ten years. Until the SIP revision is approved and the area is redesignated as attainment by EPA, the nonattainment area SIP provisions continue to be in effect. CAA § 175A, 42 U.S.C. § 7505a.

3. DEADLINES FOR SIP SUBMISSIONS FOR NAAQSs PROMULGATED OR REVISED AFTER THE 1990 AMENDMENTS

Upon promulgation or revision of a primary or secondary NAAQS after November 15, 1990, states have one year to designate every air quality control region within the state under the designation provisions discussed above. Each state has three years (or such shorter period as EPA may prescribe) after promulgation of a primary or secondary NAAQS to prepare or revise a SIP specifying how the new or revised NAAQS will be met. CAA § 110(a), 42 U.S.C. § 7410(a), *as amended by* Clean Air Act Amendments of 1990, Pub. L. No. 101-549, § 101(d)(8).

SIPs and SIP revisions for nonattainment areas must be submitted to EPA within three years of the area's designation as a nonattainment area. CAA § 172(b), 42 U.S.C. § 7502(b). Areas which are classified as nonattainment must meet the special SIP requirements and attainment deadlines for nonattainment areas. The SIP for other areas need only satisfy the basic SIP requirements of section 110 in order to maintain compliance with the NAAQS.

4. ATTAINMENT DEADLINES AND SIP REQUIREMENTS FOR NONATTAINMENT AREAS FOR NAAQSs PROMULGATED OR REVISED AFTER THE 1990 AMENDMENTS

Generally nonattainment areas must meet primary NAAQSs "as expeditiously as practicable," but not later than five years from designation of the area as nonattainment. The Administrator may extend the five-year deadline an additional five years based on the "severity of nonattainment and the availability and feasibility of pollution control measures." CAA § 172(a)(2)(A), 42 U.S.C. § 7502(a)(2)(A). Nonattainment areas for secondary NAAQSs are only directed to achieve attainment "as expeditiously as practicable." CAA § 172(a)(2)(B), 42 U.S.C. § 7502(a)(2)(B). EPA may grant up to two one-year extensions for attainment of a primary or secondary NAAQS, if the relevant NAAQS has been exceeded only a minimal number of times and the state has otherwise complied with all the other requirements for nonattainment areas. CAA § 172(a)(2)(C), 42 U.S.C. § 7502(a)(2)(C). Notice that the statute allows four years from designation of an area as nonattainment for the state to submit and EPA to act on a SIP, but only allows five years for full attainment. If a nonattainment area fails to meet its attainment deadline the state must submit to EPA within one year of the deadline a SIP revision including any additional measures which EPA may reasonably prescribe. The state then has an additional five to ten years from the date of notice of the failure to attain to achieve attainment. CAA § 179(d), 42 U.S.C. § 7509(d).

Section 110 requires the states to adopt SIP revisions to incorporate the detailed requirements for nonattainment areas set out in Part D of the CAA. CAA §§ 171-178, 42 U.S.C. §§ 7501-7508. Sources are required to use, at a minimum, reasonably available control technology (RACT) "as expeditiously as practicable" to limit emissions, and to demonstrate "reasonable further progress" toward attainment by the applicable deadline. "Reasonable further progress" is defined in section 171(1) as:

> [s]uch annual incremental reductions in emissions of the relevant air pollutant as are required by this part or may reasonably be required by the Administrator for the purpose of ensuring attainment of the applicable national ambient air quality standard by the applicable date.

CAA § 171(1), 42 U.S.C. § 7501(1), *as amended by* Clean Air Act Amendments of 1990, Pub. L. No. 101-549, § 102(a)(2)(B). The 1990 amendments require that every nonattainment SIP include contingency measures that take effect automatically if any "reasonable further progress" milestone or attainment deadline is missed. CAA § 172(c)(9), 42 U.S.C. § 7502(c)(9), *as added by* Clean Air Act Amendments of 1990, Pub. L. No. 101-549, § 102(b). RACT is defined as those "devices, systems process modifications, or other apparatus or techniques," the application of which will permit attainment of emission limits established by EPA for existing sources. 40 C.F.R. § 51.100(o). *See also*

Bethlehem Steel Corp. v. EPA, 723 F.2d 1303 (7th Cir. 1983) (upholding EPA's interpretation of what constitutes RACT); *National Steel Corp. v. Gorsuch*, 700 F.2d 314 (6th Cir. 1983); *Michigan v. Thomas*, 805 F.2d 176 (6th Cir. 1986) (interpreting RACT).

There are also preconstruction review requirements for new major sources and modifications introduced into a nonattainment area. CAA § 173, 42 U.S.C. § 7503. Every operator of a "new" "major stationary source" or "modification" of a major stationary source must obtain a permit to operate, demonstrating that: (1) the source will use the lowest achievable emissions rate (LAER) *for each nonattainment pollutant;* (2) its emissions have been offset by reductions in emissions *of such nonattainment pollutant* in the area so as to represent "reasonable further progress" toward attainment; (3) all sources owned or controlled by the operation meet the requirements of the SIP; (4) the SIP for the nonattainment area is being carried out by the state, and (5) the benefits of the proposed source will significantly outweigh the environmental and social costs of its location, construction, or modification. CAA § 173(a), 42 U.S.C. § 7503(a), *as amended by* Clean Air Act Amendments of 1990, Pub. L. No. 101-549, § 102(c). Emissions of nonattainment pollutants which are not "major" in amount are exempt from preconstruction review. 45 Fed. Reg. 52,711 (1980). LAER is defined as the rate of emissions which reflects either the most stringent emission limitations contained in an implementation plan of any state for such class or category of source (unless the owner demonstrates the limit is not achievable), or the most stringent emission limitations achieved in practice by that category or class, whichever is more stringent. LAER cannot be less stringent than any new source performance standard applicable to the source. CAA § 171(3), 42 U.S.C. § 7501(3). To help states assess LAER, EPA is authorized to issue guidance documents defining LAER. CAA § 178, 42 U.S.C. § 7508. The 1990 amendments also require EPA to make available to the states and the public a database called the RACT/BACT/LAER clearinghouse with information on control technologies obtained from the states. CAA §§ 108(h), 173(d), 42 U.S.C. §§ 7408(h), 7503(d).

The emission offset requirement is discussed on pages 427-39 *infra.*

5. ATTAINMENT DEADLINES AND SIP REQUIREMENTS FOR PRIMARY NAAQSs IN EFFECT BEFORE NOVEMBER 15, 1990

For the primary NAAQSs in effect on November 15, 1990, currently approved SIP provisions remain in effect until EPA approves a revision. If a state submits a SIP or SIP revision for an area that is designated attainment or unclassifiable to attain a primary NAAQS in effect before the 1990 amendments, the SIP must provide for attainment by November 15, 1993. If a state received notification that its SIP for such an area was substantially inadequate, then the SIP revision "in response to that finding must provide for attainment within five years of the finding of inadequacy." CAA § 110(n)(2), 42 U.S.C. § 7410(n)(2). *See also* H.R. Rep. No. 490, 101st Cong., 2d Sess., part 1, at 221 (1990).

A separate set of SIP requirements and attainment deadlines applies to nonattainment areas for the primary NAAQSs which were in effect before November 15, 1990. Nonattainment areas for ozone, carbon monoxide, and particulates have anywhere from five to twenty years to achieve attainment, depending upon a classification of the area reflecting the severity of its air quality problem with the nonattainment pollutant. The time allowed for attainment and the strength of the control measures required in the SIP increase the "higher" the classification (and the more severe the pollution) for that area. For example, a nonattainment area for ozone classified as "Serious" must include in its SIP the general control measures required for every nonattainment area, all the measures required for a Moderate Area, plus the additional control measures required for Serious Areas, but it also has nine years rather than six to achieve attainment. If a nonattainment area fails to achieve attainment by the extended deadlines, additional pollution control measures are automatically imposed, and the area is "bumped up" to the next classification. The additional control measures also vary depending upon the area's classification.

The most extensive classification system and requirements under this graduated control program are for ozone nonattainment areas. Every ozone nonattainment area is classified by its "design value" (a measurement of the ozone level) as either a Marginal Area (up to 15% over the NAAQS), Moderate Area (15-33% over the NAAQS), Serious Area (33%-50% over the NAAQS) Severe Area (50-233% over the NAAQS), or Extreme Area (233% or more over the NAAQS). CAA § 181(a)(1), 42 U.S.C. § 7511(a)(1). *See generally* 2 S. NOVICK, LAW OF ENVIRONMENTAL PROTECTION § 11.02[5][d]. The extended deadlines for attainment of the primary NAAQS for ozone are set out in the statute as follows:

Area Class	Design value*	Primary standard attainment date**
Marginal	0.121 up to 0.138	3 years after November 15, 1990
Moderate	0.138 up to 0.160	6 years after November 15, 1990
Serious	0.160 up to 0.180	9 years after November 15, 1990
Severe	0.180 up to 0.280	15 years after November 15, 1990***
Extreme	0.280 and above	20 years after November 15, 1990

*The design value is measured in parts per million (ppm).
**The primary standard attainment date is measured from November 15, 1990.

***Notwithstanding table 1, in the case of a severe area with a 1988 ozone design value between 0.190 and 0.280 ppm, the attainment date shall be 17 years (in lieu of 15 years) after November 15, 1990.

CAA § 181(a)(1)-(2), 42 U.S.C. § 7511(a)(1)-(2).

The amendments specify in great detail the substantive requirements for SIPs for each classification. For example, the SIP for a moderate nonattainment area for ozone must include such measures as RACT for all major stationary sources and a vehicle inspection and maintenance program. The SIP for a Serious Area must impose all the control measures required for a Moderate Area and additional statutory requirements, including transportation control measures and a program to make use of clean, alternative fuels in clean-fuel vehicles. CAA § 182(c), 42 U.S.C. § 7511a(c).

If a Marginal, Moderate, or Serious Area fails to attain the ozone NAAQS by its deadline, it will be reclassified by operation of law to either the next higher classification or the classification applicable to the area's design value as measured within six months of its missed deadline, whichever is higher. CAA § 181(b)(2), 42 U.S.C. § 7511(b)(2). The reclassified area must then meet the requirements applicable to its new, higher classification, although EPA may adjust deadlines other than attainment dates to the extent that adjustment is necessary or appropriate. CAA § 182(i), 42 U.S.C. § 7511a(i).

A Severe or Extreme Area must provide in its SIP that, if it does not meet its attainment deadline, each major stationary source of volatile organic compounds "VOCs" (a precursor to ozone) in the area must pay a $5,000 fee to the state as a penalty for each ton of VOCs in excess of 80 percent of the baseline amount emitted by the source during the year. CAA §§ 182(d)(3), 185, 42 U.S.C. § 7511a(d)(3), § 7511d. The baseline amount is the lowest amount of actual VOC emissions allowed under the source's permit, or, if the source has no permit for the deadline year, the amount of VOC emissions allowed by the SIP during the deadline year. CAA § 185(b)(2), 42 U.S.C. § 7511d(b)(2). Any area with a population of less than 200,000 which has met all its requirements but fails to meet the attainment deadline is exempted from these sanctions if it can demonstrate that attainment was prevented as a result of the transport of ozone or VOCs or nitrous oxide from other areas. CAA § 185(e), 42 U.S.C. § 7511d(e). In addition to the fee provision, a Severe Area which fails to attain and has a design value over .140 ppm in the deadline year, or which failed to achieve its most recent milestone, will be subject to the new source review requirements. It will also be subject to the definition of "major source" and "major stationary source" applicable to an Extreme Area if it does not achieve attainment by the end of a three year grace period. CAA § 181(b)(4), 42 U.S.C. § 7511(b)(4). A state containing an ozone nonattainment area which anticipates that the area may miss its attainment deadline may apply to EPA for up to two one-year extensions if the state has complied with all the requirements and commitments in the area's SIP and the ozone NAAQS has been exceeded no more than one time during the year preceding the Extension Year. CAA § 181(a)(5), 42 U.S.C. § 7511(a)(5).

A nonattainment area for carbon monoxide is classified as either a Moderate or Serious Area, again based upon its design value. CAA § 186(a), 42 U.S.C. § 7512(a). The deadline for attainment of the primary NAAQS for a Moderate Area is December 31, 1995, and December 31, 2000 for Serious Areas. CAA § 186(a), 42 U.S.C. § 7512(a).

By mid-1991, EPA was to have designated all nonattainment areas for particulates. CAA § 188(a), 42 U.S.C. § 7513(a). Any such area that cannot meet the primary NAAQS by December 31, 1994 is to be classified as a Serious nonattainment area for particulates. CAA § 188(b)(1), 42 U.S.C. § 7513(b)(1). EPA was to have proposed areas to be reclassified by June 30, 1991, and take final action on the reclassification by December 31, 1991. *Id.* The attainment deadline for Moderate Areas is December 31, 1994, or, for any area designated nonattainment after the initial designations made before March 15, 1991, six years after the area's designation as nonattainment. CAA § 188(c)(1), 42 U.S.C. § 7513(c)(1). The state containing the area may apply to EPA for up to two one-year extensions if the state has completed all SIP requirements, the area has only exceeded the NAAQS on one day in the preceding year, and the annual average particulate concentration in the area is less than or equal to the NAAQS level. CAA § 188(d), 42 U.S.C. § 7513(d). Serious Areas must be in attainment no later than 10 years after the area's designation as nonattainment, but areas designated as nonattainment under section 107(d)4 have no later than December 31, 2001. CAA § 188(c)(2), 42 U.S.C. § 7513(c)(2). EPA may grant a deadline extension of up to five years for a Serious Area with a SIP including the most stringent measures included in any SIP or achieved in practice in any state if the state in which the area is located has complied with all the SIP requirements. CAA § 188(e), 42 U.S.C. § 7513(e). To be granted such an extension, the state must submit a SIP revision including a demonstration of attainment by the earliest practicable date. *Id.*

Nonattainment areas for sulfur dioxide, nitrogen dioxide, or lead are for the most part controlled by the general provisions for nonattainment areas. The attainment deadline for such areas designated after November 15, 1990 is five years after the area's nonattainment designation, CAA § 192(a), 42 U.S.C. § 7514a(a), and a SIP revision for such an area, including this deadline and the general nonattainment area requirements, must be submitted within 18 months of the area's designation as nonattainment. CAA § 191(a), 42 U.S.C. § 7514(a). If the state containing an area designated before November 15, 1990 does not already have an approved SIP, the state must submit a SIP for the area by May 15, 1992, specifying an attainment deadline no later than November 15, 1995. CAA § 191(b), 42 U.S.C. § 7514(b). For a nonattainment area as to sulfur dioxide or nitrogen dioxide with a SIP approved by EPA before November 15, 1990, but subsequently found by EPA to be substantially inadequate, a new or revised SIP specifying an attainment deadline of five years from EPA's finding of inadequacy must be submitted for the area. CAA § 192(c), 42 U.S.C. § 7514a(c) *as added by* Clean Air Act Amendments of 1990, Pub. L. No. 101-549, § 106.

D. PREVENTION OF SIGNIFICANT DETERIORATION

In 1970 Congress did not address what special requirements, if any, should apply to areas that had better air quality than that mandated by a NAAQS. Were states free to permit air quality in such areas to degrade to the level of the NAAQS? Concerned in part with protection of superior air quality in the national parks, the Sierra Club brought suit in 1972 to compel EPA to prevent significant deterioration in areas with high air quality. The Sierra Club's principal argument was that such a program was mandated by the language in section 101(b), 42 U.S.C. § 7401(b), that the purpose of the CAA is to "protect and enhance the quality of the Nation's air resources." The district court held that EPA had a nondiscretionary duty to impose measures to improve air quality and prevent significant deterioration of air quality in these areas. The circuit court of appeals affirmed without opinion, as did the Supreme Court, dividing 4 to 4 on the decision. *Sierra Club v. Ruckelshaus*, 344 F. Supp. 253 (D.D.C.), *aff'd per curiam without opinion*, 2 Envtl. L. Rep. (Envtl. L. Inst.) 20656 (1972), *aff'd sub nom. Fri v. Sierra Club*, 412 U.S. 541 (1973). *See generally* Hines, *A Decade of Nondegradation Policy in Congress and the Courts: The Erratic Pursuit of Clean Air and Clean Water*, 62 Iowa L. Rev. 643 (1977); Barr, *The PSD Program and Its Impacts on Natural Resource Development*, 26 Rocky Mtn. Min. L. Inst. 475 (1981). Before EPA had implemented such a program, Congress intervened. *See generally Citizens to Save Spencer County v. EPA*, 600 F.2d 844 (D.C. Cir. 1979) (regarding the awkward transaction from the EPA regulatory PSD program to that mandated by the 1977 amendments).

In 1977, Congress added a new part C to the Clean Air Act designating areas in which the ambient air quality was better than that required by the NAAQS (or for which there could be no classification due to insufficient information) as "prevention of significant deterioration" (PSD) areas. CAA §§ 160-169B, 42 U.S.C. §§ 7470-7492. Every SIP must contain the measures necessary to prevent significant deterioration of air quality. CAA §§ 110(a)(2)(J), 161, 42 U.S.C. §§ 7410(a)(2)(J), 7471. The air quality in PSD areas is primarily maintained through preconstruction review of proposed land uses. The PSD preconstruction permit program applies to any construction or modification of a "major emitting source" for any pollutant regulated under the CAA that would be located in an attainment or unclassifiable area. Every area of the country is designated as an attainment area or unclassifiable area for at least one criteria pollutant.

The following case, *Alabama Power v. Costle*, evaluates EPA's first set of regulations for the PSD program mandated by Congress. Only a brief excerpt from this massive opinion (nearly ninety pages) written by three judges is included. The opinion is a manual on the PSD program (complete with a table of contents). EPA amended its PSD regulations in response to *Alabama Power*. The regulations continue to be especially significant in refining the statutory PSD program.

ALABAMA POWER CO. v. COSTLE

636 F.2d 323 (D.C. Cir. 1979)

LEVENTHAL, CIRCUIT JUDGE.

....

I. *Background of PSD Program and Regulations Under Review*

....

The central focus of this case is Part C of title I (sections 160-169) added to the Clean Air Act by the 1977 Amendments. Section 161 of the Act now provides an express directive that state plans include measures to prevent the significant deterioration of air quality in areas designated by the states under section 107(d)(1)(D) & (E) of the Act as having ambient air quality better than the applicable national primary or secondary ambient air quality standard, or for which there is insufficient data to make a determination of the air quality. An area so designated has commonly been referred to in the legislative history and in the literature that has developed as a "clean air area," a description often contrasted with the term "non-attainment area," which is defined by section 171(2) of the Act as an area that has been demonstrated to exceed an NAAQS for a given pollutant. We wish to alert the reader that the phrase "clean air area" is a generalization that may be confusing when employed in technical usages. A so-called clean air area for a given air pollutant may include an area that for the same pollutant would be classified as a non-attainment area if sufficient data existed. Further, since classification of areas is pollutant-specific, the same area may be a clean air area due to the air quality with respect to one pollutant, yet be a non-attainment area with respect to another pollutant. Finally, the areas of the country subject to regulation under the PSD provisions of the Act include areas other than those commonly referred to as clean air areas....

Under the provisions of the 1977 Amendments, areas subject to PSD regulation are divided into three classes; increments are set for each class; new major facilities to be located in such areas must meet technology-based emission limitations reflecting BACT ["best available control technology"]; these facilities cannot commence construction if their emissions would cause or contribute to a violation of the applicable increments in a Class I, II or III area; and demonstrations that new facility emissions would not violate the applicable increments are to be based on both monitoring and diffusion modeling. The list of 19 major sources which emit, or have the potential to emit, 100 tons per year or more of any pollutant are subject to PSD review. In addition, any other source having the potential to emit 250 tons per year or more of any pollutant is also covered. As in the 1974 regulations, "modifications" of such major sources are also subject to PSD review....

Following several notices of proposed rulemaking, comment periods, and public hearings, EPA promulgated two sets of final PSD regulations on June 19, 1978. One set amended 40 C.F.R. Part 51 to provide guidance to the states on the development of revised state implementation plans. The other set amended 40 C.F.R. Part 52 to incorporate the immediately effective changes required by the 1977 Amendments.

The regulations require that each major stationary source and each modification covered by the regulations undergo a detailed preconstruction review and obtain a permit prior to the commencement of construction. The PSD review process contains a number of steps:

1) *Control Technology Review.* Each new major source must meet all applicable new source performance standards promulgated under section 111 of the Act, all emission standards for hazardous pollutants under section 112 of the Act, and all applicable state implementation plan requirements. In addition, each such source must apply best available control technology (BACT) for sulfur dioxide and particulates....

2) *Air Quality Review.* At the time an application for a PSD permit is submitted, the owner or operator of the proposed source must demonstrate that allowable emissions from the source will not cause or contribute to a violation of any NAAQS or the applicable increments. Estimates of ambient concentrations that must be provided in order to determine compliance with these requirements must "be based on the applicable air quality models, data bases, and other requirements" specified in EPA's modeling guidelines....

3) *Monitoring Requirements.* Two types of monitoring requirements are imposed on sources submitting PSD applications after August 7, 1978. An application must include a full year of continuous monitoring data for any pollutant emitted by the source for which there is an ambient standard. This monitoring data, along with the required modeling results, will form the basis for the permitting authority's determination of whether the proposed source would cause or contribute to a violation of a primary or secondary NAAQS. The second requirement is for post-construction monitoring, to be used as the state or EPA feels necessary to determine actual impact of the source on primary or secondary ambient standards.

4) *Source Information.* The PSD permit application must include, at a minimum, information on the location, design, and planned operating schedule of the proposed facility, a detailed construction schedule, and a description of the control technology that is proposed as BACT. In addition, the applicant must provide an "analysis of impairment to visibility, soils, and vegetation" in the area, and an analysis of the air quality impacts of the expected growth associated with the proposed source....

5) *Processing Applications.* The regulations establish a complex process for handling the permit application. Within 30 days of receipt of the application, EPA must inform the applicant of any additional information required. EPA or the state must make a final determination on the application within one year after the application is complete. During that time, EPA or the state must: (a) make a preliminary determination whether the proposed source will be approved, disapproved, or approved with conditions; (b) give public notice of the preliminary determination, provide opportunity for comment and public hearing and the applicant's responses, and give the applicant and the public notice of the final determination.

The regulations also require that, even after the PSD review process is completed and permit issued, the state plan must be revised — and individual source emissions reduced — if the state or EPA determines that an applicable increment or maximum permissible concentration is being violated.

II. *Potential to Emit*

At the heart of the PSD provisions lies a definition that is jurisdictional in nature. We refer to the section 169(1) definition of "major emitting facility," which identifies sources of air pollution that are subject to the preconstruction review and permit requirements of section 165. The definition is not pollutant-specific, but rather identifies sources that emit more than a threshold quantity of *any* air pollutant. Once a source has been so identified, it may become subject to section 165's substantial administrative burdens and stringent technological control requirements for each pollutant regulated under the Act, even though the air pollutant, emissions of which caused the source to be classified as a "major emitting facility," may not be a pollutant for which NAAQS have been promulgated or even one that is otherwise regulated under the Act. As will become apparent from consideration of the ramifications of this definition, Congress's intention was to identify facilities which, due to their size, are financially able to bear the substantial regulatory costs imposed by the PSD provisions and which, as a group, are primarily responsible for emission of the deleterious pollutants that befoul our nation's air. Such facilities are defined in section 169(1) as those stationary sources of air pollutants from among 28 listed categories which "emit, or have the potential to emit" 100 tons per year or more of any air pollutant plus any other stationary source with the "potential to emit" 250 tons per year or more of any air pollutant.

EPA has interpreted the phrase "potential to emit" as referring to the measure of a source's "uncontrolled emissions" — i.e., the projected emissions of a source when operating at full capacity, with the projection increased by hypothesizing the absence of air pollution control equipment designed into the source. Yet, the language and comprehensive scheme of the statute reveal that an emitting facility is "major" within the meaning of section 169(1), only if it either (1) actually emits the specified annual tonnage of any air pollutant, or (2) has the potential, when operating at full design capacity, to emit the statutory amount. The purpose of Congress was to require preconstruction review and a permit before major amounts of emissions were released into the air. When determining a facility's potential to emit air pollutants, EPA must look to the facility's "design capacity" — a concept which not only includes a facility's maximum productive capacity (a criterion employed by EPA) but also takes into account the anticipated functioning of the air pollution control equipment designed into the facility.

IV. *Protection of the Increments*

The regulations provide that once it is determined that a state implementation plan "is substantially inadequate to prevent significant deterioration or that an applicable increment is being violated," then the SIP must "be revised to correct the inadequacy or the violation." We rule that EPA has authority under the statute to prevent or to correct a violation of the increments, but the agency is without authority to dictate to the States their policy for management of the consumption of allowable increments.

....

V. *Sources Located in Non-attainment Areas*

Section 165 (a) provides that a PSD permit is required before a major emitting facility "may be constructed in any area to which this part applies." Industry petitioners contend that this language limits the application of the PSD review requirements to sources constructed in certain locations, and that those locations are the statutorily defined "clean air areas." On this premise, industry petitioners argue that section 165 does not apply to sources located in the so-called "non-attainment" areas. EPA, on the other hand, takes the position that the identification of "clean air" and "non-attainment" areas in section 107(d) of the Act is only a starting point for the planning process that will lead to revised state implementation plans, that these identifications do not shape the "area" to which the PSD review requirements apply, and that preconstruction review must precede the construction anywhere of a major emitting facility which will adversely affect the air quality of an area to which this part applies. EPA's regulations extend the permit requirements of section 165 to all sources, wherever located, if the emissions from the source have an *impact* on any clean air area. The issue, then, is whether a source becomes subject to the PSD review process because of its *location* within an area to which this part applies, or because of its *impact* upon the air quality of one.

....

After careful consideration of the statute and the legislative history, we must accept the contention of the industry petitioners that the phrase "constructed in any area to which this part applies" limits the application of Section 165 to major emitting facilities to be constructed in certain *locations*. But, we reject the proposition that the only statutory means available to fulfill the purposes of Part C are the permit provisions of § 165.

The plain meaning of the inclusion in section 165 of the words "any area to which this part applies" is that Congress intended location to be the key determinant of the applicability of the PSD review requirements. That this is the correct interpretation is underscored by the inclusion of the same words in section 165(a)(3)(A), and by the precise language employed by Congress in those provisions where its concern was more source (rather than area) specific.

....

Our review of the petitions for reconsideration submitted by both the industry petitioners and EPA has led us to conclude that sections other than section 165 are available to fulfill that congressional objective of need to cope with the problem of interstate pollution.

Section 110(a)(2)(E)(i) provides a vehicle for implementing the congressional objective of abating substantial interstate air pollution. That provision requires that an SIP shall contain "adequate provisions ... prohibiting any stationary source within the State from emitting any air pollutant in amounts which will ... interfere with *measures required to be included in the applicable implementation plan for any other state* under [the PSD part]." The phrase "measures required to be included" in an SIP clearly incorporates at least (1) the absolute emissions limitation for each pollutant for which increment limitations have been set under section 163 or 166, (2) the monitoring and modeling requirements of section 165(e), and (3) "such other measures as may be necessary, as determined by regulations promulgated under [part C]," as provided in section 161. EPA's authority, under § 110(a)(2)(E)(i), to prevent interstate interference with these measures — to prevent, in other words, the industry of one state from interfering with the PSD program of another — is clear. And, it does not depend upon the permit process of section 165 for its effectiveness.

So also, section 126 of the Act is a vehicle for abating substantial interstate air pollution independent of permitting. That provision allows that, upon petition by a state or political subdivision, the EPA may determine that a source in a neighboring state "emits or would emit any air pollutant in violation of the prohibition of section 110(a)(2)(E)(i)." If such a violation is found, the remedy provided by section 126(c) — which remedy is applicable "[notwithstanding] any permit which may have been granted by the State" — is not denial or revocation of a permit, but a prohibition against construction or operation for a new source and a prohibition against continued operation for an existing source, unless EPA authorizes continued operation for up to three years while the source is being brought into compliance with § 110(a)(2)(E)(i). We hold that both section 110(a)(2)(E)(i) and section 126(c) give EPA the authority to require that SIPs contain provisions sufficient to address the problem of interstate air pollution. We find that section 126(a) gives the agency the authority to require that SIPs include notice provisions designed to trigger the mechanisms required by section 110(a)(2)(E)(i) or section 126(c). And we find that section 126(b) is an additional means to activate those mechanisms by permitting any state or political subdivision to petition the Administrator for a finding that *"any* major source emits or would emit *any* air pollutant in violation of the prohibition of section 110(a)(2)(E)(i)."

....

Section 161 provides still another vehicle for implementing the congressional objective of abating substantial interstate air pollution.... [T]he authority granted to the EPA by the plain language of section 161 — "each [SIP] shall contain emission limitations *and such other measures as may be necessary, as determined under regulations promulgated under this part*, to prevent significant deterioration of air quality [in clean air areas]" — grants to the Administrator the power to promulgate rules requiring that SIPs adequately address the problem. We hold that the Administrator may promulgate rules to require the inclusion of such provisions in the SIP of the state whose clean air area is affected, of the state which is the source of the adverse impact, or of both.

....

ROBINSON, CIRCUIT JUDGE.

....

I. *Baseline Date*

A central feature of the statutory program for the prevention of significant deterioration of air quality in attainment areas, with respect to sulfur dioxide and particulate matter at least, is the establishment of maximum allowable increases, known as increments, in concentrations of pollutants. The increment concept incorporates the idea of a baseline from which deterioration is calculated, by models or monitors, to determine whether it is permissible. Congress has defined with specificity the time and manner in which the baseline for an attainment area is to be determined. The first sentence of Section 169(4), the part now relevant, provides:

> The term "baseline concentration" means, with respect to a pollutant, the ambient concentration levels which exist at the time of the first application for a permit in an area subject to [Part C], based on air quality data available in the Environmental Protection Agency or a State air pollution control agency and on such monitoring data as the permit applicant is required to submit.

EPA has acknowledged that the literal purport of the statutory definition is that the starting point for determining the baseline in a particular clean air region is the existing ambient pollution level in that area at the time of the first application for a permit by a major emitting facility....

WILKEY, CIRCUIT JUDGE.

....

I. *Source Definition*

Pollution control measures enacted under the Clean Air Act's PSD program apply to major pollution-emitting facilities, which are defined as certain types of "stationary sources" that emit or could emit 100 tons of pollutants per year, or "any other source" that could emit 250 tons. The terms "stationary source" and "any other source," however, are not specifically defined in the PSD provisions of the Act. To fill this statutory definitional breach, EPA as part of comprehensive Clean Air Act regulations promulgated for the purposes of PSD the following definition:

> "Source" means any structure, building, facility equipment, installation or operation (or combination thereof) which is located on one or more contiguous or adjacent properties and which is owned or operated by the same person (or by persons under common control)....

We consider first whether EPA erred in defining "source" to include "any structure, building, facility, *equipment*, installation *or operation (or combination thereof)....*"

....

We find this definitional issue to be governed by the definition of "source" provided in Clean Air Act section 111(a)(3), pertaining to the Act's new source performance standards (NSPS). Section 111(a)(3) provides that for the purposes of NSPS "[the] term 'stationary source' means any building, structure, facility, or installation which emits or may emit any air pollutant." In addition, section 111(a)(2) provides that for NSPS "[the] term 'new source' means any stationary source, the construction or modification of which is commenced after [a specified time]," thus incorporating into the term "source" the components of the term "stationary source." For NSPS the two terms become essentially interchangeable.

We find no support in the statute for the notion that Congress intended its definition of the term "source" as used in the PSD provision of the Act to differ from that provided for NSPS in section 111(a)(3). Though "stationary source" is not defined expressly for PSD in the Act, it had at the time of the 1977 Amendments a well-established meaning, which included the four terms "structure," "building," "facility," and "installation," but not "equipment," "operation," or "combination thereof."...

... EPA has discretion to define the terms reasonably to carry out the intent of the Act, but not to go clear beyond the scope of the Act, as it has done here. Section 169(1) clearly does mean that a plant is to be viewed as a source; the section lists many types of plants as stationary sources. But EPA has discretion to define statutory terms reasonably so as to carry out the expressed purposes of the Act. We view it as reasonable, for instance, to define "facility" and "installation" broadly enough to encompass an entire plant.

....

EPA regulations provide that the term "source" shall mean any industrial unit "which is located on one or more contiguous or adjacent properties and which is owned or operated by the same person (or by persons under common control)."

....

Because of the limited scope afforded the term "source" in section 111(a)(3), however, EPA cannot treat contiguous and commonly owned units as a single source unless they fit within the four permissible statutory terms. To allow an entire plant or other appropriate grouping of industrial activity to be subject as a single unit to PSD, as Congress clearly intended, EPA should devise regulatory definitions of the terms "structure," "building," "facility," and "installation" to provide for the aggregation, where appropriate, of industrial activities according to considerations such as proximity and ownership....

EPA has latitude to adopt definitions of the component terms of "source" that are different in scope from those that may be employed for NSPS and other clean air programs, due to differences in the purpose and structure of the two programs. The reasonableness of EPA's contiguity and common ownership criteria, in light of the new source definitions required, must await review until their application in specific circumstances.

....

II. *"Major Modification" and "Bubble"*

....

EPA's Regulatory Definition of "Modification"

Standards for PSD review of construction of facilities apply also to the "modification" of any source or facility, as defined by section 111(a)(4). That section of the Act defines "modification" as "any physical change in, or change in the method of operation of, a stationary source which increases the amount of any air pollutant emitted by such source or which results in the emission of any air pollutant not previously emitted."

....

EPA does have discretion, in administering the statute's "modification" provision, to exempt from PSD review some emission increases on grounds of *de minimis* or administrative necessity....

An important issue under the Act arises from the problem of determining what types of industrial changes will be construed as "modifications" subject to PSD review requirements. Under the Act, the PSD permit and review process applies to construction and modification of major emitting facilities. As discussed in the previous section, the Act defines "modification" as any physical or operational change in a stationary source which "increases the amount of any air pollutant emitted by such source." There are two possible ways to construe the term "increases." First, one can look at any change proposed for a plant, and decide whether the net effect of all the steps involved in that change is to increase the emission of any air pollutant — this is commonly termed the "bubble" concept. Second, one can inspect the individual units of a plant, which are affected by an operational change, and determine whether any of the units will consequently emit more of a pollutant. In its regulations, EPA has adopted a qualified form of the "bubble" concept for defining modifications subject to PSD review.

Congress did not, in any pertinent part of legislative history, specify which of these two constructions was to be controlling; but an analysis of the implications of the two possible interpretations shows the second to be unreasonable and contrary to the expressed purposes of the PSD provisions of the Act.

The intent of the relevant portion, Part C, of the Clean Air Act as amended in 1977, is succinctly stated by the title of that part: "Prevention of Significant Deterioration of Air Quality" — in areas that currently attain air quality standards. According to their stated purposes, the PSD provisions seek "to assure that any decision to permit increased air pollution in any area to which this section applies is made only after careful evaluation of all the consequences of such a decision and after adequate procedural opportunities for informed public participation in the decisionmaking process."

....

... [T]he PSD provisions express a purpose of ensuring that economic growth occurs in a manner consistent with preservation of clean air. The bubble concept is precisely suited to preserve air quality within a framework that allows cost-efficient, flexible planning for industrial expansion and improvement....

III. *Pollutants Subject to PSD Regulation and the "Major Emitting Facility" Threshold*

Several sections of the Clean Air Act apply PSD review and best available control technology to emissions by major emitting facilities of each pollutant subject to regulation under the Clean Air Act. In this part we review two regulations of EPA that define which pollutants are subject to PSD and BACT review. One regulation exempts from PSD and BACT each pollutant not emitted in sufficient amounts to qualify a source as a major emitting facility. The other applies PSD and BACT immediately to each type of pollutant regulated for any purpose under any provision of the Act, not limited to sulfur dioxide and particulates. We reverse EPA on the first regulation and affirm on the second.

Section 165 of the Act provides in pertinent part:

(a) No major emitting facility on which construction is commenced after [7 August 1977] may be constructed ... unless —....

(3) the owner or operator of such facility demonstrates that emissions from construction or operation of such facility will not cause, or contribute to, air pollution in excess of any (A) maximum allowable increase or maximum allowable concentration for any pollutant in any area to which [PSD] applies more than one time per year, ... or (C) any

other applicable emission standard or standard of performance under this Act;

(4) the proposed facility is subject to the best available control technology for each pollutant subject to regulation under this Act emitted from, or which results from, such facility....

....

(e)(1) The review provided for in subsection (a) shall be preceded by an analysis ... of the ambient air quality at the proposed site ... for each pollutant subject to regulation under this Act which will be emitted from such facility.

....

(3) The Administrator shall ... promulgate regulations ... which ...

(B) shall require an analysis of the ambient air quality, climate and meteorology, terrain, soils and vegetation, and visibility at the site of the proposed major emitting facility ... for each pollutant regulated under this Act which will be emitted from ... such facility....

Also section 169(3), for the purposes of PSD, defines BACT as "an emission limitation based on the maximum degree of reduction of each pollutant subject to regulation under this Act emitted from or which results from any major emitting facility."

....

The first regulation states that PSD requirements, including BACT, "shall apply to a proposed source or modification only with respect to those pollutants for which the proposed construction would be a major stationary source or major modification." This provision exempts from PSD all pollutants not emitted in quantities of at least 100 tons per year by a major emitting facility of one of the twenty-eight types specified in the first sentence of section 169(1), and 250 tons per year by all other sources....

... We find the regulation to be contrary to clear statutory language. Section 165 states that no major emitting facility may be constructed unless it is subject to BACT "for each pollutant subject to regulation under this Act emitted from ... such facility." The statute, then, does not exempt pollutants emitted at quantities of less than 100 tons per year by the twenty-eight types of sources specified in the first sentence of section 169(1), or less than 250 tons per year by any other source. There is no statutory basis for applying the 100- and 250-ton thresholds directly to the BACT requirement for all pollutants from a major emitting facility....

We understand that the application of BACT requirements to the emission of all pollutants from a new facility, no matter how miniscule some may be, could impose severe administrative burdens on EPA, as well as severe economic burdens on the construction of new facilities. But the proper way to resolve this difficulty is to define a de minimis standard rationally designed to alleviate severe administrative burdens, not to extend the statutory 100- or 250-ton threshold to a context where Congress clearly did not apply it....

Industry groups argue that the Act's provisions which apply PSD to each pollutant subject to regulation under this Act, require that controls be imposed immediately for only two types of pollutants: sulfur dioxide and particulates....

... Section 165, in a litany of repetition, provides without qualification that each of its major substantive provisions shall be effective after 7 August 1977 with regard to each pollutant subject to regulation under the Act, or with regard to any "applicable emission standard or standard of performance under" the Act. As if to make the point even more clear, the definition of BACT itself in section 169 applies to each such pollutant. The statutory language leaves no room for limiting the phrase "each pollutant subject to regulation" to sulfur dioxide and particulates.

... Therefore we uphold this Agency regulation.

NOTES AND QUESTIONS

1. The core of the prevention of significant deterioration programs is the preconstruction review requirement in section 165, 42 U.S.C. § 7475. No "major emitting facility" may be constructed or modified *in* a PSD area (*see Alabama Power*) without undergoing preconstruction review.

Section 169(1), 42 U.S.C. § 7479(1), defines "major emitting facility" as any of 26 categories of "sources" that emits, or has the potential to emit, more than 100 tons per year of any air pollutant or any other "source" that has the potential to emit more than 250 tons per year of any air pollutant. Congress has exempted some non-profit institutions. *See, e.g., Town of Brookline v. Gorsuch*, 667 F.2d 215 (1st Cir. 1981) (exemption for Harvard University power plant). EPA, by regulation, defines "major source" as a source that exceeds the 100/250 tons per year threshold for any *regulated* pollutant under the Act. 40 C.F.R. § 51.166(b)-(1)(i). In determining a source's "potential to emit," EPA regulations had adopted *Alabama Power's* measurement of potential to emit as the potential emissions of the facility when operating at full design capacity, taking into account reductions from air pollution control equipment designed into the facility — but under the regulations only if such reductions were federally enforceable. 40 C.F.R. § 51.166(b)(4). These regulations and similar ones defining "potential to emit" for purposes of the nonattainment preconstruction review program were vacated and remanded to EPA by the D.C. Circuit Court of Appeals in light of its *National Mining* decision. *Chemical Manufacturers Assoc. v. EPA*, 70 F.3d 637 (D.C. Cir. 1995). In *National Mining Assoc. v. EPA*, 59 F.3d 1351 (D.C. Cir. 1995), the court held that in assessing a source's potential to emit, "effective" controls should be taken into account even if they are not federally enforceable. The court noted that the "EPA is clearly not obliged to take into account controls that are only chimeras and do not really restrain an operator from emitting pollution." Rather, the court stressed the need for controls to be "unquestionably" and "demonstrably" effective in order to be taken into account. In addition, these controls must stem from state or local government regulations, and not from "operational restrictions that an owner might voluntarily adopt." *See also Ogden Projects Inc. v. New Morgan Landfill Co.*, 911 F. Supp. 863 (E.D. Pa. 1996). Are "fugitive emissions" that do not get released through a chimney or smokestack to be considered in determining if a source is a major source? *See* 40 C.F.R. § 51.166(i)(4)(ii) (categories of sources for which they must be considered). *See also NRDC v. EPA*, 937 F.2d 641 (D.C. Cir. 1991) (EPA properly excluded surface coal mines from the list on the grounds that the costs of inclusion would outweigh the environmental benefits).

"Source" is not specifically defined in the statute for purposes of the PSD program. If a source has several emission points, none of which emits 100 tons or has the potential to emit 250 tons, is the source subject to preconstruction review if emissions from all the points added together cross either threshold? The broader the definition of the source, the more likely that a source will be subject to review. EPA now defines "source" as any "building, structure, facility, or installation." 40 C.F.R. § 51.166(b)(5). In response to *Alabama Power's* guidance on how EPA reasonably could define source with respect to contiguous and commonly owned units, the regulations also provide that all emission points within the same industrial grouping under the United States Standard Industrial Classification, located on one or more contiguous or adjacent properties, and under the same ownership or control must be added together. 40 C.F.R. § 51.166(b)(6). Thus, for purposes of determining whether the 100/250 tons threshold for preconstruction review has been met, the regulations authorize EPA to determine whether the cumulative emissions cross the threshold.

The "bubble" concept and its use under the CAA are discussed in detail on pages 427-28 *infra*. For now, it is important to note the most important context in which the bubble applies in the PSD program. Preconstruction review is necessary for any major emitting facility exceeding the 100/250 tons threshold which is "constructed" in a PSD area. "Construction" is defined to include "modification" of a source or facility. CAA § 169(2)(C), 42 U.S.C. § 7479(2)-(C). "Modification" is in turn defined as

> any physical change in, or change in the method of operation of, a stationary source which *increases the amount of any air pollutant emitted by such source or which results in the emission of any air pollutant not previously emitted.*

CAA § 111(a)(4), 42 U.S.C. § 7411(a)(4) (emphasis added). Judge Wilkey's opinion in *Alabama Power* expressly authorized use of the plant-wide bubble in determining whether there has been a modification. In this context, use of the bubble makes it *less* likely that a source will be subject to preconstruction review. Assume that a Portland cement plant which has been operating for twenty years in a PSD area plans to change its plant processes. It presently has two smokestacks, each emitting sixty tons per year of particulates. After the change in processes, stack A will be emitting 110 tons per year of particulates and stack B will be emitting 10 tons per year. Without the bubble, stack A will trigger preconstruction review because it was emitting 60 tons per year and with the change it would be emitting 110 tons per year. With the plant-wide bubble, however, the plant is still emitting 120 tons per year of particulates so there is no increase triggering preconstruction review. *See generally* Note, *The EPA's Bubble Concept After* Alabama Power, 32 STAN. L. REV. 943 (1980). EPA by regulation has exempted from PSD review some emission increases as *de minimis*. Increases of up to 100 tons per year, depending upon the pollutant, are exempt from review as a modification. *See* 40 C.F.R. § 51.166(b)23(i).

2. Assuming that the threshold requirements for preconstruction review are met, what must the source demonstrate to qualify for a PSD permit? Review the summary of the permit requirements in *Alabama Power* and section 165, 42 U.S.C. § 7475. The most significant requirements of PSD review are that the facility must demonstrate: (1) that it will utilize the best available control technology (BACT) to control *every pollutant regulated under the CAA;* (2) that it will not cause or contribute to the ambient air quality exceeding the allowable increment or violating any NAAQS in the baseline area; and (3) that it will not violate any other applicable emission limit under the CAA. CAA § 165(a)(3)-(4), 42 U.S.C. § 7475 (a)(3)-(4). By regulation, EPA exempts from PSD review pollutants emitted in *de minimis* amounts, using the same *de minimis* test for BACT as for modifications. *See* 40 C.F.R. §§ 51.166(b)(23), 52.21(b)(23), discussed in note 1 above. Also exempt from PSD review are any pollutants for which the area is designated nonattainment. 40 C.F.R. § 51.166(i)(5). "Best Available Control Technology" (BACT) is defined as an emission limitation "based on the maximum degree of reduction of each pollutant ... which the permitting authority, on a case-by-case basis, taking into account energy, environmental, and economic impacts and other costs, determines is achievable." CAA § 169(3), 42 U.S.C. § 7479(3). BACT must be at least as stringent as the new source performance standard in section 111, 42 U.S.C. § 7411, and the toxic pollutant standard in section 112, 42 U.S.C. § 7412. CAA § 169(3), 42 U.S.C. § 7479(3). If there is no applicable limitation to guide the determination of BACT, how lax can the standard be?

A very thorough and illuminating overview of the PSD program is provided in Oren, *Prevention of Significant Deterioration: Control-Compelling Versus Site-Shifting*, 74 IOWA L. REV. 1 (1988). The article says that in practice BACT has been markedly more stringent than the section 111 new source performance standard. Moreover, EPA has implemented a so-called "top down" policy which presumes a source must use the most stringent technology available unless significant, local economic factors make such technology too costly. *See generally* Wilson, Martin & Friedland, *A Critical Review of the Environmental Protection Agency's Standards for "Best Available Control Technology" under the Clean Air Act*, 20 ENVTL. L. RPTR. 10067 (1990).

3. As *Alabama Power* indicates, PSD areas are divided into three classes with a baseline ambient air quality and allowable increment over that baseline set for each class. Class I areas, which include national parks and wilderness areas, are subject to the strictest limitations. The ambient air in Class I areas cannot exceed a narrow allowable increment above the baseline; Class II areas are allowed a moderate increment above the baseline; and Class III areas are given an allowable increment approaching the level of the NAAQS. All PSD areas not classified as Class I are Class II areas unless redesignated to Class I or Class III under section 164, 42 U.S.C. § 7474. Read section 164 carefully. Major national parks are mandatory Class I areas and cannot be redesignated. In practice, almost no redesignations have been made. *But see Nance v. EPA*, 645 F.2d 701 (9th Cir. 1981) (redesignation of Indian reservation from Class II to Class I), *cert. denied*, 454 U.S. 1081 (1981). EPA may only disapprove a state's redesignation of an area for procedural deficiencies. 40 C.F.R. § 51.166(g)(5).

4. *Alabama Power* also established that the baseline level from which the increments are measured is determined as of the date of the first application for a major emitting facility in the PSD area. In setting the ambient baseline concentration levels, EPA must take into account all projected emissions from any major emitting facility on which construction commenced prior to January 6, 1975. However, sulfur dioxide and particulate emissions from these facilities are not included in the baseline and therefore are computed against the maximum allowable increases in pollution concentrations. CAA § 169(4), 42 U.S.C. § 7479(4). Increments for sulfur dioxide and particulates were set in section 163(b). The 1990 amendments allow EPA to substitute the PM-10 standard for particulates. CAA § 166(f), 42 U.S.C. § 7476(f). The increments for nitrogen dioxide are discussed on pages 410-15.

The setting of the baseline and the allowable increment over that baseline are critical because they determine the amount of industrial growth the state can allow into the PSD area. How does a state decide how to allot the increment? By giving priority to sources which will create the most jobs? To sources which produce the least pollution? First come, first served? Notice that the increment is consumed by sources that do not have to undergo PSD review as well as those that do. *See generally* Comment, *Increment Allocation Under Prevention of Significant Deterioration: How to Decide Who Is Allowed to Pollute*, 74 Nw. U.L. REV. 936 (1980). Could a "market" be established in rights to consume the increment?

5. The provisions of the Clean Air Act relevant to the problem of interstate pollution are discussed on pages 439-45 *infra*.

6. Judge Wilkey's portion of the opinion addresses in the abstract when a "new source" or "modification" must undergo preconstruction review under the statute and implementing regulations. Keep these requirements in mind while reading the following case, which evaluates whether a specific plant must go through preconstruction review.

PUERTO RICAN CEMENT CO. v. ENVIRONMENTAL PROTECTION AGENCY

889 F.2d 292 (1st Cir. 1989)

BREYER, CIRCUIT JUDGE.

The Puerto Rican Cement Co. (the "Company") wishes to build a new cement kiln, replacing older kilns that it now operates at about 60 percent of their capacity. If operated to achieve about the same level of production, the new kiln will pollute far less than the older kilns; but, if the Company operates the new kiln at significantly higher production levels, it will emit more pollutants than did the older kilns. The Environmental Protection Agency, noting that it is *possible* that the new kiln will produce more pollution, has held that the Company cannot build it without obtaining a special kind of EPA approval, required when one wishes to "construct" a "major emitting facility" in a place where the air is particularly clean. (The facility must meet "prevention of significant deterioration" ("PSD") requirements. *See* 42 U.S.C. § 7475.) The Company appeals. We find that EPA's determination is lawful.

I. *Factual*

The Company's cement plant contains six kilns, which produce a fine powder called "clinker." In 1987 the Company decided to convert Kiln No. 6 from a "wet," to a "dry," cement-making process, and to combine that kiln with Kiln No. 3. At that time, Kilns 3 and 6 were operating at about 60 percent of their combined capacity, producing about 424,000 tons of clinker per year. The converted kiln would have a total capacity of 961,000 tons of clinker per year, or about 35 percent more than the 705,000 ton capacity of Kilns 3 and 6. At any given level of production, the new kiln would emit less air polluting substance than the two older kilns combined, and would use less fuel to boot. However, if the Company decided to operate the new kiln close to its capacity, it might produce both more clinker and more pollution than the old kilns produced when operated at 60 percent of their capacity. In particular, information submitted by the Company suggests the following:

Pounds of Emissions Per Ton of Clinker Produced

Old (Wet) Process	4.9	6.32	0.234
New (Dry) Process	2.6	4.01	0.133

Fig. 1: Comparative Emissions Rates

	Tons of Emissions Per Year		
	NO$_x$	SO$_2$	PM
Old (Wet) Process			
/**Actual** (operated at about 60% of capacity)	**1100**	**1340**	**49.6**
/Potential	1745	2230	82.6
New (Dry) Process			
/Actual	578	850	28.2
/**Potential** (operated at full capacity)	**1250**	**1927**	**64.0**

Fig. 2: Comparative Emissions Amounts

These charts show the rate and amount of emissions of three pollutants: nitrogen oxides, sulfur dioxide, and particulate matter. The "Actual" rate of production is the average rate for Kilns 3 and 6 for the years 1985-86, or 424,000 tons; the "Potential" rate equals 705,000 tons of clinker per year for the old wet process and 911,000 tons of clinker per year for the new dry process. The emboldened numbers are those used by EPA in comparing *actual* emissions of the old kilns with *potential* emissions of the proposed new kiln. The charts make clear that emissions will increase only if the company operates the new kiln at significantly higher production levels.

II. *Legal*

Since the cement plant is located near Ponce, Puerto Rico, where the air quality is better than national ambient air quality standards, new construction is subject to PSD provisions contained in Part C of Title I of the Clean Air Act. That part of the Act says that "[n]o major emitting facility ... *may be constructed* in any [such] area" without various specified studies, reviews, demonstrations of compliance with certain substantive standards, and the issuance of a permit. *See* 42 U.S.C. § 7475 (emphasis added). The Act defines "major emitting facility" as a "stationary source[] of air pollutants," including Portland Cement plants that "emit, or have the potential to emit, one hundred tons per year or more of any air pollutant" (such as the facilities at issue here). 42 U.S.C. § 7479(1). It defines "construction" to include "modification," which it says

> means any physical change in, or change in the method of operation of, a stationary source which increases the amount of any air pollutant emitted by such source or which results in the emission of any air pollutant not previously emitted.

42 U.S.C. §§ 7411(a)(4), 7479(2)(C). The Act also provides that EPA itself must review the construction proposal and provide the necessary approvals where, as

here, no EPA-approved "state implementation plan" is in effect. *See* 42 U.S.C. § 7478; 40 C.F.R. 52.21(a).

Because the permitting process is costly and time-consuming, EPA has developed an informal system for determining whether or not a particular construction proposal does, or does not, fall within the scope of the PSD permit law. If EPA decides that PSD review is unnecessary, it issues a "non-applicability determination" (known as a "NAD").

III. *Proceedings*

On July 9, 1987, the Company asked EPA for a NAD. It submitted information to EPA over an eight-month period. On August 30, 1988, EPA denied the Company the NAD. The Company has appealed EPA's determination to this court. Subsequent to the docketing of this appeal the Company and EPA agreed that, if the Company loses this appeal, it will operate its new facility at a sufficiently low capacity to prevent any actual increase in emissions levels. EPA will then issue a NAD, *see* 40 C.F.R. 52.21(b)(4) (federally enforceable limitations on emissions will be taken into consideration in determining "potential to emit"), but the Company will lose its right to ask for a PSD permit, thereby giving up the possibility of obtaining EPA's approval for an increase of emissions.

The Company can appeal the EPA's decision denying a NAD only if that decision is a "final action of the administrator." 42 U.S.C. § 7607(b)(1)....

... [T]he EPA determination before us is sufficiently "final" to warrant review under 42 U.S.C. § 7607(b)(1). *See Hawaiian Elec. Co.*, 723 F.2d at 1442-44 (holding that the determination that a proposed change is a "major modification" requiring PSD review is a "final action" under § 7607(b)(1)).

The statute applies its PSD requirements to the Company's proposed modification of its kilns only if the modification will "increase[] the amount of any air pollutant emitted." 42 U.S.C. §§ 7411(a)(4), 7479(2)(C). In deciding whether or not the kiln conversion would result in such an increase, EPA calculated the *actual* historical amount of pollutants that Kilns 3 and 6 emitted in the past (which, under the regulations, equals the average emissions over the past two years, *see* 40 C.F.R. § 52.21(b)(21)(ii)) and compared that with the amount of pollutants that the converted kiln would be *capable* of emitting in the future. Since the Company operated the kilns at only 60 percent of their capacity in 1985-86, the new kiln, though cleaner and more efficient, is obviously *capable* of emitting significantly more pollutants.

The Company argues that the EPA's application of this "actual/potential" method of measurement to its proposed kiln modification represents an improper, arbitrary, and contradictory interpretation of EPA's own regulations. After reading the regulations themselves, we disagree.

First, the language and expressed intent of the regulations both support EPA's interpretation. The regulations provide that a "major modification," subject to PSD review, includes "any physical change in or change in the method of operation of a major stationary source that would result in a significant *net emissions increase* of any pollutant...." 40 C.F.R. § 52.21(b)(2)(i) (emphasis added). They go on to define "net emissions increase" as the amount by which the "sum of ... any increase in *actual emissions*" (plus or minus other "contemporaneous" changes in emissions) "exceeds zero." 40 C.F.R. § 52.21(b)(3) (emphasis added). And, most importantly for present purposes, they define the words *"actual emissions"* in a special way.

They state that

> "[actual] emissions" means the actual rate of emissions of a pollutant from an emissions unit, *as determined in accordance with paragraphs ... (ii) through (iv) [below].*

40 C.F.R. § 52.21(b)(21)(i) (emphasis added). Paragraph (ii) says that

> [i]n general, actual emissions as of a particular date shall equal the average rate, in tons per year, at which the unit actually emitted the pollutant during [the preceding] two-year period.

40 C.F.R. § 52.21(b)(21)(ii). But, paragraph (iv) adds that

> *[f]or any emissions unit which has not begun normal operations on the particular date, actual emissions shall equal the potential to emit of the unit on that date.*

40 C.F.R. § 52.21(b)(21)(iv) (emphasis added). The regulations also define "emissions unit" to include *"any part* of a stationary source which ... would have the potential to emit any pollutant." 40 C.F.R. § 52.21(b)(7) (emphasis added).

The Company's proposed modified kiln is "part of a stationary source" and it has the "potential to emit" a pollutant. 40 C.F.R. § 52.21(b)(7). EPA considered it to be an "emissions unit which has not begun normal operations." 40 C.F.R. § 52.21(b)(21)(iv). It therefore counted as its "actual emissions," the modified kiln's "potential to emit" pollution, *id.*, namely, in the case of SO[2], 1927 tons per year. It counted the "actual emissions" of the existing kilns as "the average rate ... at which" they "actually emitted the pollutant during the [preceding] two year period," 40 C.F.R. § 52.21(b)(21)(ii), namely, in the case of SO[2], 1340 tons per year. It therefore found an increase in what the regulations call "actual emissions" (1927 minus 1340 equals 587 tons per year). And, after setting off allowable contemporaneous changes, it found that the net increase was significantly greater than zero. *See* 40 C.F.R. §§ 52.21(b)(2)(i), 52.21(b)(3)(i).

....

... [T]he Company argues that EPA's interpretation of the regulation is arbitrary — that the interpretation makes little sense because it would significantly discourage the Company, and others like it, from installing more efficient machinery that, at any production level, emits significantly less pollution. But we cannot agree. EPA has simply taken account of, and given controlling weight to, a different consideration: the fact that a firm's decision to introduce new, more efficient machinery may lead the firm to decide to *increase the level of production*, with the result that, despite the new machinery, overall emissions will increase. Indeed, EPA points out that a firm introducing such machinery can escape PSD review simply by promising that it will ensure its actual emissions do not in fact increase (that is, by promising that it will not run the machinery at such a rate as to create an actual increase in emissions levels.) *See* 40 C.F.R. 52.21(b)(4) (federally enforceable physical or operational limitations which effect emissions will be taken into consideration in determining "potential to emit").

....

Finally, the Company points to another regulation with which, it argues, EPA's interpretation conflicts. That regulation says that

> a physical change or change in the method of operation shall not include ... an increase in the hours of operation or in the production rate.

40 C.F.R. § 52.21(b)(2)(iii)(f). The Company notes that, given this regulation, it could increase production at its old kilns to 100 percent of capacity, thereby vastly increasing actual emissions; why, it argues, should it not be permitted to do the same by building a more efficient kiln and then increasing output?

The answer to this question likely lies in the statute itself, for the statute refers to the *"construction"* of facilities, not to *increased use of existing facilities. See* 42 U.S.C. § 7479(2)(C). It may also lie in a prediction that, as a general rule, new building will more likely lead to increased emissions levels. Regardless, there is no logical contradiction in rules that, on the one hand, permit firms using *existing* capacity simply to increase their output and, on the other, use the potential output of new capacity as a basis for calculating an increase in emissions levels. And, we can find no policy conflict sufficiently serious for a court to override the policymaking authority that Congress has entrusted to the agency.

....

The regulations, as we have previously mentioned, measure any increase in emissions by, first, calculating the "actual" increase in emissions, and second, offsetting any "contemporaneous" decrease in emissions, due, say, to other changes the firm has made at the plant. The Company undertook a coal conversion project in 1982-1983, which led to a significant decrease in emissions. The EPA refused to credit the Company with this decrease because, it found, the decrease was not "contemporaneous" with the present proposed project. The Company now argues that the EPA is wrong.

The EPA's regulations, however, make clear that the coal project was not "contemporaneous." They say that a decrease is "contemporaneous" if it occurs between

> the date five years before construction on the particular change commences[,] and ... the date that the increase from the particular change occurs.

40 C.F.R. § 52.21(b)(3)(iii). Since construction on the kiln modification has not yet "commence[d]," and since more than five years has passed since the coal conversion, the Company cannot bring itself within this "contemporaneous" window. The Company says that it *filed its NAD application* within five years of the time it converted to coal, but that fact is irrelevant; the regulation speaks of "*construction* on the [kiln] ... change," not of an *application* to make the change. 40 C.F.R. § 52.21(b)(3)(iii).

NOTES AND QUESTIONS

1. In *Puerto Rican Cement Co.* the court rejects the company's argument that EPA's regulatory approach would discourage companies from installing more efficient machinery that would emit less pollution. In what circumstances might EPA's approach have that effect? What other changes in a plant's processes might constitute a modification? Would a change to fuel with a higher sulfur content qualify as a modification? *See Hawaiian Elec. Co. v. EPA*, 723 F.2d 1440, 1448 (9th Cir. 1984) (is a modification). Would capital investment in an aging plant with replacement of components, upgrades and other improvements be a modification? *Wisconsin Elec. Power Co. (WEPCO) v. Reilly*, 893 F.2d 901 (7th Cir. 1990) (yes). In addition, the Seventh Circuit Court of Appeals rejected EPA's "actual-to-potential" method for measuring increases upheld in *Puerto Rican Cement Co.*, at least when the modification involves the "like-kind" replacement of equipment. In response to *Puerto Rican Cement Co.* and *WEPCO*, EPA adopted a rule that would allow electric utilities to make many modifications without triggering new source review.

2. Upon receipt of a complete PSD application, the reviewing agency has one year to approve (with or without conditions) or to deny the permit. CAA § 165(c), 42 U.S.C. § 7475(c). Almost every state has assumed responsibility from EPA for PSD preconstruction review and permit issuance, either under a state program that is incorporated into the SIP or under authorization from EPA to administer the federal regulations. 2 S. NOVICK, LAW OF ENVIRONMENTAL REGULATION § 11.05[3]. The practical effect of this division of authority is that the procedures for permits sought directly from EPA or from a state with delegated authority are governed by the federal regulations, but the procedures for permits from states with their own approved programs are governed primarily by state law. Can issuance of a PSD permit be challenged under the judicial review provisions of section 304 or section 307? Does it matter whether the permit was issued by EPA, a state administering the federal regulations, or a state administering its own PSD program in its SIP? What authority does EPA have to review a state-issued permit? *See* CAA § 167, 42 U.S.C. § 7477. One district court has ruled that EPA has a nondiscretionary duty to take necessary measures to prevent the construction of a major emitting facility which does not comply with the CAA, that duty being enforceable by a citizen suit under section 304, 42 U.S.C. § 7604. *Save the Valley, Inc. v. Ruckelshaus*, 565 F. Supp. 709

(D.D.C. 1983). Can EPA bring an enforcement action against a source operating in accordance with an improperly issued permit? *See United States v. Solar Turbines Inc.*, 732 F. Supp. 535 (M.D. Pa. 1989) (suggesting EPA's only recourse is against the state).

3. EPA was required by section 166 to set increments for pollutants other than sulfur dioxide and particulates by 1979. When it failed to do so, litigation resulted in EPA being ordered to set increments for nitrogen oxides by October of 1988. *Sierra Club v. California*, 658 F. Supp. 165 (N.D. Cal. 1987). The following case examines EPA's decisionmaking process in this second phase of PSD regulation.

ENVIRONMENTAL DEFENSE FUND v. ENVIRONMENTAL PROTECTION AGENCY

898 F.2d 183 (D.C. Cir. 1990)

STEPHEN F. WILLIAMS, CIRCUIT JUDGE.

I.

In its 1977 amendments to the Clean Air Act, Congress ratified a previously established program for the "prevention of significant deterioration of air quality." The stated purpose of these "PSD" provisions was (roughly) to protect the air quality in national parks and similar areas of special scenic or recreational value, and in areas where pollution was within the national ambient standards, while assuring economic growth consistent with such protection. For two pollutants, sulfur dioxide and particulate matter ("Set I pollutants"), Congress followed the Environmental Protection Agency's earlier approach, fixing a maximum allowable increase (an "ambient air quality increment") over baseline concentrations. For several other pollutants ("Set II pollutants"), including nitrogen oxides, Congress took no immediate action. Instead it provided the EPA with general guidance as to regulations that it was to promulgate within two years. CAA § 166, 42 U.S.C. § 7476. We deal here with the regulations governing nitrogen oxides, the only Set II pollutant that EPA has yet regulated. The case turns on the meaning, and above all the interrelationship, of the two main guides, § 166(c) and (d):

> (c) Such regulations shall provide specific numerical measures against which permit applications may be evaluated, a framework for stimulating improved control technology, protection of air quality values, and fulfill the goals and purposes set forth in section 7401 of this title [statement of purposes of Clean Air Act] and section 7470 of this title [statement of purposes of the PSD provisions].
>
> (d) The regulations ... shall provide specific measures at least as effective as the increments established in section 7473 of this title [the Set I rules] to fulfill such goals and purposes, and may contain air quality increments, emission density requirements, or other measures.

§ 166(c), (d), 42 U.S.C. § 7476(c), (d). Because the EPA did not adequately consider the requirements of subsection (c), we reverse.

Although in 1980 the EPA noted ten possible strategies for Set II, it ultimately decided to mimic Congress's approach for Set I. The first step, not here controverted, was the use of the same three-tiered scheme for classifying protected areas....

EPA's second step, again not controverted here, was its decision to base the nitrogen oxide PSD program on "ambient air quality increments" similar to those for the Set I pollutants. Though Congress contemplated that EPA might use increments for the Set II program, it did not require their use. See § 166(d), 42 U.S.C. § 7476(d)....

EPA's third step was to formulate the permissible increments "by reference to" the National Ambient Air Quality Standards ("NAAQS" or "ambient standards") established under § 109 of the Clean Air Act, 42 U.S.C. § 7409. In so doing, it rested on its view that Congress had used the ambient standards "as the benchmark for determining what constitutes 'significant deterioration'" for Set I pollutants and that the ambient standards were "the basic measure of air quality under the Act." The three challenged aspects of the nitrogen oxide PSD program stem directly from this decision.

First, though by its terms § 166 demands that the regulations cover "nitrogen oxides," the EPA regulated only one nitrogen oxide compound, nitrogen dioxide or NO_2, as this is the only compound for which it had established ambient standards. Second, as its ambient standard for NO_2 imposes direct limits only for the annual average concentration, EPA defined the permissible increments only in terms of an annual average. Short-term concentrations, which are only indirectly and incompletely limited by an annual average, may have adverse health and welfare effects, but EPA at present appears to believe the evidence too uncertain to justify including a short-term limit among the ambient standards for NO_2. Third, and most sharply contested, the EPA set the permissible increments of nitrogen dioxide at the same percentage of the nitrogen dioxide ambient standard as the percentage that the Set I increments were of their annual ambient standards (at the lower of the two percentages when they varied). The table below sets forth the lower of the primary and secondary national ambient air quality standards for Set I and II pollutants at the time the increments for each were created (date in parentheses), and the increments for the pollutants both as absolute concentrations and as percentages of the ambient standards (in parentheses). Both standards and increments are expressed in micrograms per cubic meter.

Ambient Standards:

Particulate Matter:
  Annual 75 (1977)
  Twenty-four hour 150 (1977)
Sulfur Dioxide:
  Annual 80 (1977)
  Twenty-four hour 365 (1977)
  Three hour 1300 (1977)
Nitrogen Dioxide
  Annual 100 (1988)

Class I Increment (and percentage of ambient standards):

Particulate Matter:
  Annual 5 (6.7%)
  Twenty-four hour 10 (6.7%)
Sulfur Dioxide:
  Annual 2 (2.5%)
  Twenty-four hour 5 (1.4%)
  Three hour 25 (1.9%)
Nitrogen Dioxide
  Annual 2.5 (2.5%)

Class II Increment (and percentage of ambient standards):

Particulate Matter:
  Annual 19 (25%)
  Twenty-four hour 37 (25%)
Sulfur Dioxide
  Annual 20 (25%)
  Twenty-four hour 91 (25%)
  Three hour 512 (39%)
Nitrogen Dioxide
  Annual 25 (25%)

Class III Increment (and percentage of ambient standards):

Particulate Matter:
  Annual 37 (50%)
  Twenty-four hour 75 (50%)
Sulfur Dioxide:
  Annual 40 (50%)
  Twenty-four hour 182 (50%)
  Three hour 700 (54%)
Nitrogen Dioxide
  Annual 50 (50%)

II. *The Interrelation of Subsections (c) and (d)*

EDF's most critical objection is that EPA's construction of § 166 collapsed subsection (c)'s general "goals and purposes" standard into subsection (d)'s requirement that the Set II restrictions be "at least as effective ... to fulfill such goals and purposes" as the ones adopted by Congress for Set I. The agency's logic was that by virtue of the "at least as effective" test, the percentages implicit in the Set I restrictions could serve "as a proxy for all the PSD purposes set forth in the statute."...

First, there are at least three possible meanings to subsection (d)'s "at least as effective" test. The EPA, with some hesitation, appears to have read it as requiring that the Set II rules be at least as *stringent* as those for Set I, i.e., that increments be set no lower, as percentages of a pollutant's ambient standards, than the Set I increments were as percentages of their respective ambient standards. A second possible meaning is that the Set II rules must be at least as *protective* of the various environmental values threatened as the Set I increments were of the environmental values threatened by those pollutants. Finally, there is a literal interpretation, for the most part overlooked by both parties, under which the Set II rules would have to achieve as *optimal* a balancing of the environmental and economic growth values made relevant by § 160 as Congress achieved for the Set I pollutants. The agency recognized that the PSD program necessarily involved a balancing of goals, and to a degree assessed its NO_2 increments in terms of effectiveness in "avoiding unreasonable economic impacts" on adversely affected industries, but it did not attempt to use optimality as an ultimate measuring stick.

....

... The practical problems of the "protective" and "optimal" readings arise from the need to compare the "effectiveness" of regulations across pollutants. When we consider both the practical problems and the legislative history, we believe EPA's choice of the percentage stringency test permissible for purposes of subsection (d)....

As a reading of § 166 as a whole, however, EPA's approach overlooks both the language of subsection (c) and the vector of forces represented by the Senate bill. The Senate originally wanted more study conducted on the Set II pollutants, with Congress to make the final choice. Subsection (c) appears to manifest much of this intention, merely substituting the EPA for Congress as decisionmaker. Thus, except to the extent that EPA may properly read subsection (d) as limiting subsection (c), a failure to assess a pollutant in terms of the PSD goals breaches the agency's duty to consider all the relevant statutory factors....

Now we must turn to some possible relations between the two subsections, for the moment identifying subsection (d) with EPA's stringency interpretation. First, one might, as EPA evidently did, read the two as providing the agency an absolute safe harbor: if the regulations mirror the Set I restrictions on a percentage basis, the EPA is free to disregard whatever the inquiry under subsection (c) might yield. The difficulty with this reading, seemingly incurable, is that it turns subsection (c) into no more than an EPA option, despite mandatory wording.

Second, while subsection (c) commands a broad weighing of factors, subsection (d) might operate as a limited safe harbor (a presumptive baseline) — authorizing regulations ... if but only if the Administrator determines (without being arbitrary and capricious) that the criteria under subsection (c) do not call for a more, or a less, stringent standard. EDF appeared at oral argument to endorse this view, and, while we by no means regard the position as any kind of binding concession, we do find it at least superficially conformable to the statutory language.

If we relax the assumption that subsection (d) imposes a simple stringency test, further alternatives open up. For example, if EPA should read subsection (d)'s "at least as effective" test in terms of optimality, it could function as a refinement of subsection (c)'s mandate to fulfill the specified "goals and purposes," telling EPA how to balance the competing environmental and economic goals. At one time EPA appears to have contemplated such a melding of the two sections, though recognizing some of its formidable difficulties.

While we read the ambiguities and perplexities of the statute as delegating to the agency a broad interpretive authority, as we must under *Chevron U.S.A. Inc. v. NRDC*, 467 U.S. 837, 843-44 (1984), we cannot affirm the agency's action on the current record. The reading that we have hypothesized of § 166(d) as a contingent safe harbor requires the agency first to adopt that view, then to determine that the inquiry under subsection (c) does not require a more stringent standard. It has done neither. We cannot sustain an action merely on the basis of interpretive theories that the agency might have adopted and findings that (perhaps) it might have made.

III. *EPA's Use of the National Ambient Standards*

EDF attacks not only EPA's conclusory decision to allow § 166(d) to supplant subsection (c), but also its choice of the ambient standards under sections 108 and 109 of the Clean Air Act, 42 U.S.C. §§ 7408-09, as the sole basis for deriving permissible increments. That choice resulted in EPA's defining increments for only one compound of nitrogen oxides (NO_2) and defining them only in terms of annual averages....

... For subsection (d), we have already held that EPA's use of the Set I percentages of ambient standards was permissible. Thus, EDF cannot prevail on the argument that the NO_2 increments are not "as effective as" (or "as stringent as") the sulfur dioxide increments just because the NO_2 increments do not include short-term increments while the sulfur dioxide increments do. Subsection (c), however, commands the Administrator to inquire into a pollutant's relation to the goals and purposes of the statute, and we find nothing in the language or legislative history suggesting that this duty could be satisfied simply by referencing the ambient standards. EDF may still, therefore, make the argument on remand that under subsection (c) short-term increments or increments for other nitrogen oxide compounds are needed to "protect[] air quality values, and fulfill the goals and purposes" of the statute. Obviously EPA's resolution of the issue will depend on the interpretation it selects for harmonizing subsections (c) and (d).

IV. *Remedy*

... Accordingly we remand the case for the EPA to develop an interpretation of § 166 that considers both subsections (c) and (d), and if necessary to take new evidence and modify the regulations. While EDF asks that the remand include imposition of an immediate deadline of two years, based on the original deadline created by statute in 1977, cf. *Sierra Club v. Thomas*, 658 F. Supp. at 175, we refrain from any current ruling on this request.

NOTES AND QUESTIONS

1. Review the relief ordered by the court at the end of the opinion. What was EPA required to do upon remand? The increments are still in effect as promulgated by EPA in 1988. How were the increments to be implemented in PSD programs? *See* CAA § 166(b), 42 U.S.C. § 7476(b). By the targeted implementation date of November 17, 1990 the increments were effective in only one state. 2 S. NOVICK, LAW OF ENVIRONMENTAL PROTECTION § 11.05 -[3][b][iii][B] n.191.1 (1991).

2. What are the three methods suggested by the court to satisfy the requirements of section 166(d) for future PSD regulation of other pollutants? Is EPA free to follow whichever of those methods it chooses?

E. VISIBILITY PROTECTION

The Clean Air Act has two mechanisms for protection of visibility. First, a PSD permit may not be issued to a source with emissions within the allowable increment if its emissions would have an adverse impact on air quality related values in a Class I area, such as visibility. On the other hand, a source with emissions that would exceed the allowable increment may be issued a permit if it can demonstrate that it will have no adverse impact on air quality related values in a Class I area, including visibility. CAA § 165(d)(2)(C)(ii)-(iii), 42 U.S.C. § 7475(d)(2)(C)(ii)-(iii). There is no statutory definition of "adverse impact" or "air quality related values." *See generally* Robert L. Glicksman, *Pollution on the Federal Lands I: Air Pollution Law*, 12 UCLA J. ENVTL. L. & POL'Y 1 (1993); Oren, *The Protection of Parklands from Air Pollution: A Look at Current Policy*, 13 HARV. ENVTL. L. REV. 313, 372 (1989); Steven H. Bergman, Comment, *To See or Not to See: The Viability of Visibility of the Grand Canyon*, 13 UCLA J. ENVTL. L. & POL'Y 127 (1994-95); David R. Everett, Note, *The Hazy Future: Are State Attempts to Reduce Visibility Impairment in Class I Areas Caught Between Scylla and Charybdis: The Effects of the Clean Air Act Amendments of 1990 on Visibility Protection*, 8 PACE ENVTL. L. REV. 115 (1990). Federal land managers also have a duty to protect visibility in federal Class I areas, CAA § 165(d)(2)(B), 42 U.S.C. § 7475(d)(2)-(B). Section 165, however, gives little or no guidance on what that duty entails. *Id.*

A second provision addressing visibility was added in 1977. CAA § 169A, 42 U.S.C. § 7491. The Secretary of the Interior is required to review all mandatory federal Class I areas and identify those in which visibility is an important value. CAA § 169A(a)(2), 42 U.S.C. § 7491(a)(2). Such areas have been identified in thirty-five states, the Virgin Islands and New Brunswick, Canada. 40 C.F.R. Part 81, Subpart D. Major stationary sources which adversely affect visibility in mandatory federal Class I areas and which began operation after August 7, 1962 must utilize, as expeditiously as practicable, "best available retrofit technology" (BART). CAA § 169A(b)(2)(A), 42 U.S.C. § 7491(b)(2)(A). "Major stationary source" in this context is a source in any of 26 categories of plants that emits more than 250 tons of any pollutant. CAA § 169A(g)(7), 42 U.S.C. § 7491(g)-(7). New and existing sources that would affect visibility in mandatory Class I areas are also subject to visibility review, regardless of whether they are located in a PSD area. 40 C.F.R. § 51.307.

SIPs for states with designated Class I areas and for states with emissions contributing to "visibility impairment" of such areas must include a long-term strategy to ensure "reasonable progress" toward visibility goals. CAA § 169A(b)-(2), 42 U.S.C. § 7491(b)(2). "Visibility impairment" is defined as a "reduction in visual range and atmospheric discoloration." CAA § 169A(g)(6), 42 U.S.C. § 7491(g)(6). States are also required to provide a long-term strategy in their SIPs for protection of "integral vistas." 40 C.F.R. § 51.304, .307. An "integral vista" is "a view perceived from within the mandatory Class I Federal area of a specific landmark or panorama located outside the boundary of the mandatory Class I Federal area." *Id.* § 51.301(n). Despite these restrictions, states are permitted by regulation to consider a wide range of factors, including economic development, in deciding whether to issue a permit to a source affecting visibility. *See, e.g., id.* § 51.307(c).

Clean Air Act § 169A has been as ineffective as section 165. *See generally* Glicksman, *supra*; Oren, *supra*; Everett, *supra*. In evaluating why the program has been so ineffective, consider the following materials.

VERMONT v. THOMAS

850 F.2d 99 (2d Cir. 1988)

ALTIMARI, CIRCUIT JUDGE.

Petitioners, the State of Vermont, Conservation Law Foundation of New England, Inc., and Vermont Natural Resources Council, seek review, pursuant to 42 U.S.C. § 7607(b)(1), of a final ruling of respondent, the Environmental Protection Agency ("EPA"), taking "no action" on those portions of Vermont's state implementation plan ("state implementation plan" or "SIP") addressing "regional haze" submitted under section 169A of the Clean Air Act of 1970, as amended (the "Clean Air Act" or the "Act"), 42 U.S.C. § 7491 (1982). Because we agree with respondent Lee Thomas, Administrator of the EPA (the "Administrator"), that current regulations do not encompass federally enforceable measures to alleviate "regional haze," we deny the petition for review.

. . . .

At issue in this case are the 1977 amendments to the Act which directed EPA, in pertinent part, to adopt regulations protecting visibility in certain national parklands and wilderness areas, designated as "class I Federal areas." CAA § 169A, 42 U.S.C. § 7491; *see id.* § 162(a), 42 U.S.C. § 7472(a) (defining class I areas to include international parks, national wilderness areas exceeding 5,000 acres, national memorial parks exceeding 5,000 acres, and national parks exceeding 6,000 acres). Class I areas were singled out by Congress as requiring special protection in view of the aesthetic importance of visibility to the continued enjoyment and preservation of the country's scenic vistas. Accordingly, Congress set as a "national goal the prevention of any future, and the remedying of any existing, impairment of visibility … result[ing] from manmade air pollution" in class I areas, *id.* § 7491(a)(1), and directed EPA to provide guidelines for the states in order "to assure … reasonable progress toward meeting the national goal" of visibility enhancement in those areas. *Id.* § 7491(a)(4), (b).

Pursuant to its authority under section 169A of the Act, EPA promulgated regulations in 1980 designed to "establish long-range goals, a planning process, and implementation procedures" toward achieving the national visibility goal. 45 Fed. Reg. 80,084 (codified at 40 C.F.R. § 51,300 *et seq.*). Specifically, EPA determined that visibility impairment is of two types: 1) "plume blight," i.e., traceable streams of smoke, dust or colored gas emanating from single sources or small groups of sources; and 2) "regional haze," i.e., widespread, homogeneous haze from a multitude of sources which impairs visibility in large areas, often for hundreds of miles from the sources of the pollution. Of the two types of air pollution, EPA recognized that plume blight obviously was more susceptible to identification, measurement and thus control. The more vexing problem of how to alleviate regional haze was, in EPA's view, subject to certain scientific and technical limitations. Consequently, the 1980 regulations adopted a "phased approach to visibility protection." *Id.* at 80,085. Under "Phase I" of the program, EPA regulations targeted plume blight while deferring for "future phases" the complexities of regional haze and urban plumes. *Id.* at 80,085-86. "Phase II" would address regional haze once monitoring and other scientific techniques progressed to a point that EPA could develop a regulatory program for that type of impairment.

The effect of the 1980 regulations was to require the 36 states containing class I areas to revise their SIP's to implement a visibility protection program, consistent with the new regulations, to assure reasonable progress toward section

169A's national visibility goal. The regulations mandated that each of the affected states' SIP's contain, *inter alia*, a "long-term (10-15 years) strategy" to combat visibility impairment in each class I area. 40 C.F.R. § 51.306(a) (1987).

In April 1986, Vermont submitted to EPA its proposed plan addressing visibility impairment at the Lye Brook National Wilderness Area, a 12,000 acre mountain plateau in the southern portion of the Green Mountain National Forest and the state's only class I area. As indicated in Vermont's 300-page SIP, the Lye Brook area is afflicted with summertime haze that has drastically reduced visibility by as much as 40 percent since the mid 1950s. The Vermont plan contained extensive technical analysis demonstrating that Lye Brook's visibility impairment is due primarily to sulfur dioxide pollution originating from out-of-state sources, e.g., power plants and coal and oil company factories. Vermont found that sulfate particle emissions from a multitude of sources located in 8 upwind states — Ohio, Pennsylvania, West Virginia, Kentucky, Tennessee, Illinois, Indiana, and Michigan — were principally responsible for the haze blanketing Lye Brook during the summer months.

Vermont's SIP concluded that while adequate in-state measures to prevent plume blight were already in place, a reduction program aimed at out-of-state sulfate emissions would be necessary to assure reasonable progress toward the national visibility goal. Consequently, Vermont proposed a federally enforceable "long-term strategy" to combat the effects of regional haze at Lye Brook. The long-term strategy included a summertime ambient sulfate standard and a 48-state emissions reduction plan in order to meet the air quality standard by 1995. In addition, Vermont asked EPA to disapprove and revise the SIP's of the eight upwind states which were the major contributors to visibility impairment at Lye Brook, *see* CAA § 110(c)(1)(B), 42 U.S.C. § 7410(c)(1)(B) ("[t]he Administrator shall ... set[] forth an implementation plan ... for a State if ... the plan ... submitted for such State is determined by the Administrator not to be in accordance with the requirements of this section"), and also asked that four of these states not containing class I areas (Ohio, Illinois, Indiana, and Pennsylvania) be added to the list of 36 states required to submit visibility plans.

....

In July 1987, EPA issued its final ruling on Vermont's proposal. While EPA approved limited portions of Vermont's SIP complying with existing plume blight regulations under section 169A of the Act, EPA decided to take "no action" on those parts of the SIP aimed at controlling regional haze. EPA also denied Vermont's request to disapprove the SIP's of the eight upwind states as well as its request to add four states to the list of states required to submit visibility protection plans for class I areas. In explaining its "no action" ruling, EPA concluded that Vermont's proposal establishing an ambient sulfate standard and its long-term strategy for emissions reduction throughout the continental United States were outside the scope of EPA's existing regulations. EPA viewed as federally enforceable only those portions of a state implementation plan submitted in response to regulations promulgated by the agency. According to EPA,

Vermont's regional haze measures could not become federal rules "until such time as EPA decides to promulgate a national regional haze program." *Id.* at 26,974.

. . . .

Petitioners argue that EPA's refusal to approve Vermont's SIP in its entirety violates both EPA's own regulations and the Clean Air Act, and accordingly seek reversal of EPA's ruling as an administrative action "not in accordance with law." 42 U.S.C. § 7607(d)(9)(A); 5 U.S.C. § 706(2)(A). Specifically, petitioners contend that the 1980 regulations encompass measures to alleviate regional haze and that EPA's contrary interpretation of its regulations is inconsistent with the terms and the underlying purposes of the Clean Air Act.

. . . .

We begin with the statute itself. Section 169A of the Clean Air Act directs EPA to promulgate regulations requiring states containing class I areas to adopt through their SIP's long-term strategies assuring reasonable progress toward meeting the national visibility goal. 42 U.S.C. § 7491(b). Pursuant to this legislative mandate, in 1980 EPA issued regulations providing that each SIP include a long-term strategy designed to remedy any existing, and prevent any future, impairment of visibility in class I areas. 40 C.F.R. § 51.306(a) (1987).

Vermont claims that its long-term strategy addressing regional haze fits within the purview of the 1980 regulations and must be approved by EPA. *See* CAA § 110(a)(2)(J), 42 U.S.C. § 7410(a)(2)(J) ("Administrator shall approve [the SIP] ... if he determines that ... it meets the requirements" of, *inter alia*, section 169A). The Administrator responds by arguing that the 1980 regulations do not cover regional haze impairment and that measures addressing that type of impairment are not *required* by section 169A and therefore cannot be part of a federally enforceable SIP. *See id.* § 110(d), § 7410(d) (federally enforceable SIP is one which "implements the *requirements*" of the statute) (emphasis added).

In support of its interpretation of the 1980 regulations, EPA cites the preamble to the final regulations in which EPA explained its adoption of a "phased approach" to visibility protection in class I areas. The preamble indicates that "Phase I" of the program "[r]equire[s] control of impairment that can be traced to a single existing stationary facility or small group of ... facilities" while "[f]uture phases will ... address[] more complex problems such as regional haze and urban plumes." 45 Fed. Reg. 80,085-86. Although petitioners concede that action on regional haze was deferred for future phases of the visibility program, they nonetheless argue that the 1980 regulations were intended to allow, as technologies improved, for the evolution of long-term strategies combating regional haze. We disagree.

It is one thing to recognize that the regulatory mechanism put into place by the 1980 regulations *anticipated* long-term strategies designed to alleviate regional haze, *see* 45 Fed. Reg. 34,764 ("[e]ven though we are calling these ... regulations 'Phase I of the visibility protection program,' the basic structure ... will remain constant for all phases"); it is quite another to suggest that the 1980 regulations actually *authorized* states containing class I areas to implement regional haze measures through federally enforceable SIP's. Petitioners would have us ignore the preamble language in favor of the "plain meaning" of the regulations. [Citation.] Respondents correctly note, however, that no "plain meaning" to regulate regional haze can be discerned from the face of the regulations. Consequently, having looked to the preamble to determine the scope of the 1980 regulations, [citation] we find that EPA intended to limit the regulations to plume blight.

Petitioners also contend that even in the absence of EPA regulatory "guidelines" addressing regional haze, CAA § 169A(b)(1), 42 U.S.C. § 7491(b)(1), the Act imposes upon states an independent duty to develop visibility protection standards to assure "reasonable progress" toward achieving the national visibility goal. While it is certainly true that the actual implementation of visibility protection measures is the responsibility of the states, the statute and its legislative history make clear that Congress charged EPA with the responsibility through its rulemaking power to ensure attainment of the national goal. *Id.* § 169A(a)(4), § 7491(a)(4); H.R. Rep. No. 294, 95th Cong., 1st Sess. 206, reprinted in 1977 U.S. Code Cong. & Admin. News 1077, 1285. Without EPA rulemaking on regional haze, therefore, Vermont's proposed interstate measures are outside the scope of the regulations and thus are not subject to federal enforcement under the Act.

Since Vermont's regional haze measures were not required to be included in its SIP, we believe that EPA's "no action" response was appropriate. Petitioners maintain, however, that EPA's "no action" ruling deprives Vermont of a definitive decision on the merits of its proposal and violates section 110 of the Act. *See* 42 U.S.C. § 7410(a)(2) (Administrator "shall ... approve or disapprove" proposed SIP). We have held previously that the Clean Air Act should not be read to permit only outright approval or disapproval of state plans so long as EPA's action was reasonable. *Connecticut Fund for the Environment, Inc. v. EPA*, 672 F.2d 998, 1006-07 (2d Cir.), *cert. denied*, 459 U.S. 1035 (1982). In this case, the effect of EPA's ruling was to "keep [Vermont's] measures out of the Federally enforceable SIP." 52 Fed. Reg. 26,976 (1987). EPA explained its action in this regard as an attempt to "avoid the appearance of a premature judgment as to [the measures'] ultimate approvability, and [to] prevent confusion regarding their present enforceability as a matter of state law." *Id.* Given that Vermont was free to adopt within its borders air quality standards more stringent than federal law requires, 42 U.S.C. § 7416, it is evident that EPA's "no action" ruling — as opposed to outright rejection of Vermont's regional haze measures — was more than reasonable.

We recognize, of course, that without federal enforcement of Vermont's plan, little, if any, progress will be made on regional haze at Lye Brook. While this is indeed lamentable, until such time as a federal regional haze program is in place, Vermont may not impose its standards on upwind states. *See Air Pollution Control Dist. v. EPA*, 739 F.2d 1071, 1087-88 (6th Cir. 1984) (downwind state's air quality standards that are more stringent than national standards do not require upwind state to alter its otherwise valid SIP); *Connecticut v. EPA*, 656 F.2d 902, 909 (2d Cir. 1981) (same); *see also* CAA § 110(a)(2)(E)(i), 42 U.S.C. § 7410(a)(2)(E)(i). Consequently, we find that EPA's denial of Vermont's request to disapprove the SIP's of the eight upwind states contributing to visibility impairment at Lye Brook was in accordance with federal law, *see* CAA § 110(c)(1)(B), 42 U.S.C. § 7410(c)(1)(B) (providing that EPA may revise SIP if it is not in compliance with requirements of the Act), and likewise that EPA's refusal to add four regional haze producing states to those now required to develop class I visibility protection programs was reasonable in view of the limited scope of the 1980 regulations.

Finally, we note that, more than ten years after the enactment of section 169A, there still is no national program addressing regional haze. We are sympathetic to petitioners' argument that something must be done soon. EPA's assurances of future action on regional haze are little comfort to Vermont and visitors to Lye Brook. We can only hope that EPA will act quickly in furtherance of the national visibility goal. In the meantime, Vermont can pursue an alternative remedy, namely, the filing with EPA of a petition for rulemaking under the Administrative Procedure Act, 5 U.S.C. § 553(e), with eventual judicial review in the D.C. Circuit. 42 U.S.C. § 7607(b)(1). In any event, we are convinced that the issues raised by the petition in the instant case are best left to the national rulemaking process rather than to an SIP approval proceeding.

For all of the foregoing reasons, the petition for review is denied.

NOTES AND QUESTIONS

1. How clear does EPA's duty have to be for it to be an enforceable, mandatory duty? Recall *NRDC v. Train*, page 351 *supra*. Was EPA's duty in that case, or its duty to establish a PSD program before the 1977 amendments, any more definite than the duty asserted by Vermont?

2. The 1990 amendments include measures to improve consideration of visibility impairment. EPA is directed to: (1) identify sources and regions with visibility impairment as well as regions with predominantly clean air in Class I areas; (2) assess visibility in Class I areas every five years; and (3) consider establishment of visibility transport regions which "contribute significantly to visibility impairment in Class I areas located in affected States." CAA § 169B, 42 U.S.C. § 7492. *See generally* Robert L. Glicksman, *Pollution on the Federal Lands I: Air Pollution Law*, 12 UCLA J. ENVTL. L. & POL'Y 127 (1994-95); David R. Everett, Note, *The Hazy Future: Are State Attempts to Reduce Visibility Impairment in Class I Areas Caught Between Scylla and Charybdis: The Effects of the Clean Air Act Amendments of 1990 on Visibility Protection*, 8 PACE ENVTL. L. REV. 115 (1990). Upon creation of any visibility transport region, EPA must establish a commission of state and federal officials to report within four years on measures to remedy visibility impairment. The Administrator of

EPA, upon receipt of the report, must "carry out the Administrator's regulatory responsibilities [under section 169A] including criteria for measuring 'reasonable progress' toward the national goal." CAA § 169B(e)(1), 42 U.S.C. § 7492(e)(1). EPA is required by this section to establish a visibility transport region for Grand Canyon National Park. CAA § 169B(f), 42 U.S.C. § 7492(f). *See, e.g.*, Steven H. Bergman, Comment, *To See or Not to See: The Viability of Visibility of the Grand Canyon*, 13 UCLA J. ENVTL. & POL'Y 127 (1994-95).

CENTRAL ARIZONA WATER CONSERVATION DISTRICT v. ENVIRONMENTAL PROTECTION AGENCY

990 F.2d 1531 (9th Cir.), *cert. denied*,
510 U.S. 828 (1993)

GOODWIN, CIRCUIT JUDGE:

Petitioners Central Arizona Water Conservation District ("CAWCD") and four irrigation districts (collectively "Petitioners" or the "Districts") challenge an Environmental Protection Agency ("EPA") Final Rule which requires a 90% reduction in sulfur dioxide (SO_2) emissions at the Navajo Generating Station ("NGS") in order to improve winter average visibility in the Grand Canyon National Park ("Grand Canyon").

Petitioners argue (1) that, because the Final Rule seeks to regulate "regional haze" when EPA has yet to promulgate Phase II implementing regulations addressing regional haze, EPA exceeded the scope of its regulatory authority by issuing the Final Rule, and (2) that the Final Rule constitutes arbitrary and capricious agency action.

....

This case involves regulations promulgated by EPA in an attempt to remedy, at least partially, visibility impairment at the Grand Canyon. In a final rule entitled "Approval and Promulgation of Implementation Plans: Revision of the Visibility FIP for Arizona," 56 Fed. Reg. 50,172 (1991) (codified at 40 C.F.R. § 52) ("Final Rule"), EPA required a 90% reduction in SO_2 emissions at NGS, a power plant situated approximately twelve miles from the Grand Canyon, near Page, Arizona. The Final Rule limits SO_2 emissions from NGS to 0.10 pound per million British thermal units (lb/MMBtu), with an estimated 7% winter average visibility improvement in the Grand Canyon. The estimated cost of the improvement, following an initial capital cost estimated at $430 million, is $89.6 million per year.

....

The Act defines class I Federal areas as international parks, national wilderness areas or memorial parks which exceed 5,000 acres in size, and national parks which exceed 6,000 acres in size. 42 U.S.C. § 7472(a). The Grand Canyon has been classified as a class I Federal area. *See* 44 Fed. Reg. 69,122 (1979). Congress recorded its concern with the visibility impairment at the Grand Canyon caused by NGS.

....

In 1980, EPA promulgated visibility regulations under section 169A of the Act. 45 Fed. Reg. 80,084 (1980) (codified at 40 C.F.R. §§ 51.300-.307). The regulations adopted a "phased approach to visibility protection." *Id.* at 80,085. Phase I was directed at controlling visibility impairment "that can be traced to a single existing stationary facility or small group of existing stationary facilities." *Id.* EPA refers to this type of impairment as "reasonably attributable" impairment. 45 Fed. Reg. 34,762, 34,779 (1980) (codified at 40 C.F.R. § 51). EPA deferred addressing other types of impairment such as "regional haze" for future phases due to the heightened complexity and the scientific and technical limitations inherent in attempts to identify, measure, and control such broadscale visibility impairment. *See* 45 Fed. Reg. at 80,086; *see also id.* at 80,085 (defining regional haze as "widespread, regionally homogeneous haze from a multitude of sources which impairs visibility in every direction over a large area").

Generally, EPA's "Phase I" regulations require affected states to coordinate the development of SIPs with the appropriate Federal land managers, to develop programs to assess and remedy visibility impairment from new and existing sources, and to develop a long-term strategy to assure reasonable progress toward section 169A's national visibility goal. *See* 40 C.F.R. §§ 51.300-.307. The regulations specifically require states to identify those existing sources "which may reasonably be anticipated to cause or contribute" to any visibility impairment which is "reasonably attributable to that existing stationary facility." 40 C.F.R. § 51.302(c)(4)(i). Once the source is identified, the affected state is required to take such measures as are required to attain "reasonable progress"; such measures generally include determination of emissions limitations for that source under BART and the development of a long-term strategy. 40 C.F.R. §§ 51.302(c)(1), (2).

The regulations define the term "visibility impairment" as "any humanly perceptible change in visibility (visual range, contrast, coloration) from that which would have existing under natural conditions." 40 C.F.R. § 51.301(x). The term "reasonably attributable" is defined as "attributable by visual observation or any other technique the State deems appropriate." 40 C.F.R. § 51.301(s). The states, or EPA under § 7410(c), thus have broad discretion in determining how and whether impairment may be attributed to an individual source. *See* 45 Fed. Reg. at 80,094, 80,085.

....

In November 1987, EPA disapproved the SIPs of twenty-nine states, including Airzona, for failing to comply with the visibility regulations.

....

In the Final Rule, dated October 3, 1991, EPA issued its final determination that certain visibility impairment episodes at the Grand Canyon were "traceable to NGS and that NGS is a dominant contributor to certain visibility impairment episodes." and promulgated revisions to the Arizona visibility FIP to address the impairment. *Id.* The revisions adopted a regulatory approach consistent with the memorandum of understanding's proposal, reducing SO_2 emissions 90% to a level of 0.10 lb/MMBtu. *Id.* EPA determined that this approach would more adequately achieve "reasonable progress" toward the national visibility goal under section 169A(b)(2) of the Act, 42 U.S.C. § 7491(b)(2), than would the alternative provided by BART analysis.

....

Petitioners rely on *Vermont v. Thomas*, 850 F.2d 99 (2d Cir. 1988), where EPA reaffirmed that it was without authority to regulate "regional haze" and that measures addressing that type of impairment are outside the scope of EPA's jurisdiction. This reliance is misplaced. In *Thomas*, the state of Vermont submitted to EPA and SIP which "proposed a federally enforceable 'long-term strategy' to combat the effects of regional haze" at the Lye Brook National Wilderness Area. *Id.* at 101. The court held that without EPA rulemaking addressing regional haze, the state's regional haze measures were "outside the scope" of EPA's statutory and regulatory authority. *Id.* at 103-04. Here, EPA properly promulgated its Final Rule under its Phase I regulations directed at "reasonably attributable" impairment. *Thomas* is thus distinguishable since it involved a direct and explicit attempt to regulate "regional haze."

EPA has acknowledged that "NGS is not the only source of visibility impairment" at the Grand Canyon, and that regional haze also adversely affects visibility there. Nonetheless, these mere facts hardly mean that EPA is without statutory authority to remedy the impairment attributable to NGS. Even if Final Rule addresses only a small fraction of the visibility impairment at the Grand Canyon, EPA still has the statutory authority to address that portion of the visibility impairment problem which is, in fact, "reasonably attributable" to NGS. Congress mandated an extremely low triggering threshold, requiring the installment of stringent emission controls when an individual source "emits any air pollutant which may reasonably be anticipated to cause or contribute to any impairment of visibility" in a class I Federal area. 42 U.S.C. § 7491(b)(2)(A). The National Academy of Sciences correctly noted that Congress has not required ironclad scientific certainty establishing the precise relationship between a source's emission and resulting visibility impairment:

> The phase "may reasonably be anticipated" suggests that Congress did not intend to require EPA to show a precise relationship between a source's emissions and all or a specific fraction of the visibility impairment within a Class I area. Rather, EPA is to assess the risk in light of policy consider-ations regarding the respective risks of overprotection and underprotection.

Haze in the Grand Canyon at 5.

....

We conclude that the technical, scientific record more than adequately supports EPA's reasonable conclusion that visibility impairment in the Grand Canyon is "reasonably attributable" to NGS....

Petitioners proffer various arguments that the Final Rule is not the product of "reasoned decisionmaking."... At bottom, however, Petitioners' real complaint appears to be that the Final Rule will most likely lead to minimal visibility improvement at the Grand Canyon while imposing a substantial financial burden on them. Nonetheless, we find unsupported Petitioners' legal claim that EPA acted arbitrarily and capriciously in promulgating the Final Rule. The Final Rule makes "reasonable progress" toward the national goal of remedying visibility impairment at the Grand Canyon, and is the product of reasoned decisionmaking.

....

In the Act, Congress directed EPA to promulgate regulations to assure "reasonable progress toward meeting the national goal" of preventing future, and remedying existing visibility impairment in Class I federal areas like the Grand Canyon. *See* 42 U.S.C. §§ 7491(a)(4), (a)(1), (b)(2), (b)(2)(B). Congress chose not to define the term "reasonable progress," but instead set forth several factors for the agency to consider:

> In determining reasonable progress there shall be taken into consideration the costs of compliance, the time necessary for compliance, the time necessary for compliance, and the energy and nonair quality environmental impacts of compliance, and the remaining useful life of any existing source subject to such requirements[.]

42 U.S.C. § 7491(g)(1). In promulgating the Final Rule, EPA relied on the "reasonable progress" provisions as its statutory authority. *See* 56 Fed. Reg. at 50,177 (noting that EPA adopts the "reasonable progress" provisions of section 169A(b)(2), 42 U.S.C. § 7491(b)(2) as the "legal rationale" for the Final Rule).

Generally, the Act and its regulations require the application of BART once it has been determined that visibility impairment is "reasonably attributable" to an existing source like NGS. *See* 42 U.S.C. § 7491(b)(2); 40 C.F.R. § 51.302-(c)(4)(i). Under the unique circumstances of this case, however, EPA chose not to adopt the emission control limits indicated by BART analysis, but instead to adopt an emission limitations standard that would produce greater visibility improvement at a lower cost. Congress's use of the term "including" in § 7491(b)(2) prior to its listing BART as a method of attaining "reasonable progress" supports EPA's position that it has the discretion to adopt implementation plan provisions other than those provided by BART analyses in situations where the agency reasonably concludes that more "reasonable progress" will thereby be attained. Since the Act itself is ambiguous on the specific issue, we apply the Supreme Court's deferential standard from *Chevron* and hold that the agency's reliance on the "reasonable progress" provisions is a "permissible construction of the statute," 467 U.S. at 843, 104 S. Ct. at 2782, since "reasonable progress" is the overarching requirement that implementation plan revisions under 42 U.S.C. § 7491(b)(2) must address.

....

In the final analysis, Petitioners simply adhere to a different interpretation of the rather disparate and equivocal scientific data in the record. While Petitioners may not be satisfied with EPA's responses, it is not EPA's duty to satisfy all of the concerns of potentially affected or aggrieved parties.... Petitioners' arguments afford no reason for this court disruptively to interject itself into the picture. Because Congress delegated to EPA the power to "regulate on the borders of the unknown," this court will not interfere with the agency's "reasonable interpretations of equivocal evidence." *Public Citizen Health Research Group v. Tyson*, 796 F.2d at 1505. Even if this case highlights how hard it is to engage in "reasoned decisionmaking" in cases involving scientific uncertainty, EPA's actions in promulgating the Final Rule were reasonable and within the bounds of its statutory authority, and not arbitrary and capricious.

NOTES AND QUESTIONS

1. Why is it so difficult to implement an effective program to improve visibility? With respect to the above case, consider the following excerpt:

Visibility problems in Class I areas are predominantly the result of regional haze from many sources, rather than individual plumes caused by a few sources at specific sites. Therefore, a strategy that relies only on influencing the location of new sources, although perhaps useful in some situations, would not be effective in general. Moreover, such a strategy would not remedy the visibility impairment caused by existing sources until these sources are replaced.

....

Because most visibility impairment in Class I areas results from the transport by winds of emissions and secondary airborne particles over great distances, focusing only on sources immediately adjacent to Class I areas — as under the current program — is unlikely to improve visibility effectively.

Nonetheless, the assessment of the contribution of individual sources to haze will remain important in some situations. For instance, a regional emissions management approach to haze could be combined with a strategy to assess whether locating a new source at a particular location would have especially deleterious effects on visibility....

The committee doubts, however, that such attributions could be the basis for a workable visibility protection program. It would be extremely time-consuming and expensive to try to determine the percent contribution of individual sources to haze one source at a time. For instance, the efforts to trace the contribution of the Navajo Generating Station to haze in the Grand Canyon National Park took several years and cost millions of dollars without leading to quantitatively definitive conclusions. Moreover, there are (and probably will continue to be) considerable uncertainties in ascertaining precise relationships between individual sources and the spatial pattern of regional haze.

NATIONAL RESEARCH COUNCIL, PROTECTING VISIBILITY IN NATIONAL PARKS AND WILDERNESS AREAS 240-41 (National Academy Press 1993).

2. For further discussion of visibility protection, *see generally* Glicksman, *supra*; Oren, *The Protection of Parklands from Air Pollution: A Look at Current Policy*, 13 HARV. ENVTL. L. REV. 313 (1989); Ostrov, *Visibility Protection Under the Clean Air Act: Preserving Scenic and Parkland Areas in the Southwest*, 10 ECOL. L.Q. 397 (1982); Walker, *The Seriousness of the Visibility Impairment Rules*, 107 PUB. UTIL. FORTNIGHTLY 104 (Apr. 9, 1981); Bergman, *supra*; Everett, *supra*; Note, *Protecting Visibility Under the Clean Air Act: EPA Establishes Modest "Phase" I Program*, 11 ENVTL. L. REP. (Envtl. L. Inst.) 10053 (1981); Note, *EPA Issues Final Rules on Visibility Protection*, 107 PUB. UTIL. FORTNIGHTLY 31 (Jan. 1, 1981).

F. BUBBLES AND OFFSETS IN NONATTAINMENT AREAS

There are a number of situations in which application of the Clean Air Act requirements will depend upon what constitutes a "source." For example, PSD review, nonattainment requirements and new source performance standards (NSPS) have potential application to any "new" source or "modification." "Modification" in all three contexts is defined to include an increase in emissions. *See* CAA § 169(2)(C), 42 U.S.C. § 7479(2)(C) (utilizing the NSPS definition of modification for the PSD program); CAA § 171(4), 42 U.S.C. § 7501(4) (utilizing the NSPS definition for nonattainment requirements); CAA § 111(a)(4), 42 U.S.C. § 7411(a)(4) (NSPS definition of modifications). If there is a substantial increase in emissions from one stack in a plant, but the emissions from the plant as a whole are not increased, is there a modification? Can a plant-wide "bubble" be put over the plant, "netting" all emissions and thus treating the entire plant as a single source? Plant-wide netting in this case would allow a plant to compensate for an increase at one emission point with a decrease at another. So long as there is no net increase, the plant can avoid application of a more stringent technological standard.

Recall that in *Alabama Power*, page 390 *supra*, the D.C. Circuit Court of Appeals upheld EPA's regulation authorizing use of a plant-wide bubble for defining modifications subject to PSD review. Previously, in *ASARCO, Inc. v. EPA*, 578 F.2d 319 (D.C. Cir. 1978), the court had held that EPA had to use a "dual" definition of source for new source performance standards, treating an increase in emissions from the plant as a whole or an increase from a single emission point as a modification. In *Alabama Power* the court distinguished *ASARCO*, on the grounds that the purpose of the NSPS is to *improve* air quality (thus justifying the more inclusive definition of "source"), but that the purpose of the PSD program is simply to *maintain* existing air quality. In the following case, the Supreme Court found it necessary to address use of the plant-wide bubble to avoid new source review in a nonattainment area.

CHEVRON, U.S.A., INC. v. NRDC
467 U.S. 837 (1984)

JUSTICE STEVENS delivered the opinion of the Court.

In the Clean Air Act Amendments of 1977, Congress enacted certain requirements applicable to States that had not achieved the national air quality standards established by the Environmental Protection Agency (EPA) pursuant to earlier legislation. The amended Clean Air Act required these "nonattainment" States to establish a permit program regulating "new or modified major stationary sources" of air pollution. Generally, a permit may not be issued for a new or modified major stationary source unless several stringent conditions are met. The EPA regulation promulgated to implement this permit requirement allows a State to adopt a plantwide definition of the term "stationary source."[2] Under this definition, an existing plant that contains several pollution-emitting devices may install or modify one piece of equipment without meeting the permit conditions if the alteration will not increase the total emissions from the plant. The question presented by these cases is whether EPA's decision to allow States to treat all of the pollution-emitting devices within the same industrial grouping as though they were encased within a single "bubble" is based on a reasonable construction of the statutory term "stationary source."

When a court reviews an agency's construction of the statute which it administers, it is confronted with two questions. First, always, is the question whether Congress has directly spoken to the precise question at issue. If the intent of Congress is clear, that is the end of the matter; for the court, as well as the agency, must give effect to the unambiguously expressed intent of Congress. If, however, the court determines Congress has not directly addressed the precise question at issue, the court does not simply impose its own construction on the statute, as would be necessary in the absence of an administrative interpretation. Rather, if the statute is silent or ambiguous with respect to the specific issue, the question for the court is whether the agency's answer is based on a permissible construction of the statute.

....

---

[2]"(i) 'Stationary source' means any building, structure, facility, or installation which emits or may emit any air pollutant subject to regulation under the Act.

"(ii) 'Building, structure, facility, or installation' means all of the pollutant emitting activities which belong to the same industrial grouping, are located on one or more contiguous or adjacent properties, and are under the control of the same person (or persons under common control) except the activities of any vessel." 40 C.F.R. §§ 51.18(j)(1)(i) and (ii) (1983).

In light of these well-settled principles it is clear that the Court of Appeals misconceived the nature of its role in reviewing the regulations at issue. Once it determined, after its own examination of the legislation, that Congress did not actually have an intent regarding the applicability of the bubble concept to the permit program, the question before it was not whether in its view the concept is "inappropriate" in the general context of a program designed to improve air quality, but whether the Administrator's view that it is appropriate in the context of this particular program is a reasonable one. Based on the examination of the legislation and its history which follows, we agree with the Court of Appeals that Congress did not have a specific intention on the applicability of the bubble concept in these cases, and conclude that the EPA's use of that concept here is a reasonable policy choice for the agency to make.

The Clean Air Act Amendments of 1977 are a lengthy, detailed, technical, complex, and comprehensive response to a major social issue. A small portion of the statute — 91 Stat. 745-751 (Part D of Title I of the amended Act, 42 U.S.C. §§ 7501-7508) — expressly deals with nonattainment areas. The focal point of this controversy is one phrase in that portion of the Amendments.

... [T]he statute provided that each plan shall

> "(6) require permits for the construction and operation of new or modified major stationary sources in accordance with section 173...." *Id.*, at 747.

Before issuing a permit, § 173 requires the state agency to determine that (1) there will be sufficient emissions reductions in the region to offset the emissions from the new source and also to allow for reasonable further progress toward attainment, or that the increased emissions will not exceed an allowance for growth established pursuant to § 172(b)(5); (2) the applicant must certify that his other sources in the State are in compliance with the SIP, (3) the agency must determine that the applicable SIP is otherwise being implemented, and (4) the proposed source complies with the lowest achievable emission rate (LAER).

The 1977 Amendments contain no specific reference to the "bubble concept." Nor do they contain a specific definition of the term "stationary source," though they did not disturb the definition of "stationary source" contained in § 111(a)(3), applicable by the terms of the Act to the NSPS program. Section 302(j), however, defines the term "major stationary source" as follows:

> "(j) Except as otherwise expressly provided, the terms 'major stationary source' and 'major emitting facility' mean any stationary facility or source of air pollutants which directly emits, or has the potential to emit, one hundred tons per year or more of any air pollutant (including any major emitting facility or source of fugitive emissions of any such pollutant, as determined by rule by the Administrator)."

....

In this Court respondents expressly reject the basic rationale of the Court of Appeals' decision. That court viewed the statutory definition of the term "source" as sufficiently flexible to cover either a plantwide definition, a narrower definition covering each unit within a plant, or a dual definition that could apply to both the entire "bubble" and its components. It interpreted the policies of the statute, however, to mandate the plantwide definition in programs designed to maintain clean air and to forbid it in programs designed to improve air quality. Respondents place a fundamentally different construction on the statute. They contend that the text of the Act requires the EPA to use a dual definition — if either a component of a plant, or the plant as a whole, emits over 100 tons of pollutant, it is a major stationary source. They thus contend that the EPA rules adopted in 1980, insofar as they apply to the maintenance of the quality of clean air, as well as the 1981 rules which apply to nonattainment areas, violate the statute.

Statutory Language

The definition of the term "stationary source" in § 111(a)(3) refers to "any building, structure, facility, or installation" which emits air pollution. This definition is applicable only to the NSPS program by the express terms of the statute; the text of the statute does not make this definition applicable to the permit program. Petitioners therefore maintain that there is no statutory language even relevant to ascertaining the meaning of stationary source in the permit program aside from § 302(j), which defines the term "major stationary source." We disagree with petitioners on this point.

The definition in § 302(j) tells us what the word "major" means — a source must emit at least 100 tons of pollution to qualify — but it sheds virtually no light on the meaning of the term "stationary source." It does equate a source with a facility — a "major emitting facility" and a "major stationary source" are synonymous under § 302(j). The ordinary meaning of the term "facility" is some collection of integrated elements which has been designed and constructed to achieve some purpose. Moreover, it is certainly no affront to common English usage to take a reference to a major facility or a major source to connote an entire plant as opposed to its constituent parts. Basically, however, the language of § 302(j) simply does not compel any given interpretation of the term "source."

Respondents recognize that, and hence point to § 111(a)(3). Although the definition in that section is not literally applicable to the permit program, it sheds as much light on the meaning of the word "source" as anything in the statute. As respondents point out, use of the words "building, structure, facility, or installation," as the definition of source, could be read to impose the permit conditions on an individual building that is a part of a plant. A "word may have a character of its own not to be submerged by its association." *Russell Motor Car Co. v. United States*, 261 U.S. 514, 519 (1923). On the other hand, the meaning of a word must be ascertained in the context of achieving particular objectives, and the words associated with it may indicate that the true meaning of the series is to convey a common idea. The language may reasonably be interpreted to impose the requirement on any discrete, but integrated, operation which pollutes. This gives meaning to all of the terms — a single building, not part of a larger operation, would be covered if it emits more than 100 tons of pollution, as would any facility, structure, or installation. Indeed, the language itself implies a bubble concept of sorts: each enumerated item would seem to be treated as if it were encased in a bubble. While respondents insist that each of these terms must be given a discrete meaning, they also argue that § 111(a)(3) defines "source" as that term is used in § 302(j). The latter section, however, equates a source with a facility, whereas the former defines source as a facility, among other items.

We are not persuaded that parsing of general terms in the text of the statute will reveal an actual intent of Congress. We know full well that this language is not dispositive; the terms are overlapping and the language is not precisely directed to the question of the applicability of a given term in the context of a larger operation. To the extent any congressional "intent" can be discerned from this language, it would appear that the listing of overlapping, illustrative terms was intended to enlarge, rather than to confine, the scope of the agency's power to regulate particular sources in order to effectuate the policies of the Act.

Legislative History

In addition, respondents argue that the legislative history and policies of the Act foreclose the plantwide definition, and that the EPA's interpretation is not entitled to deference because it represents a sharp break with prior interpretations of the Act.

Based on our examination of the legislative history, we agree with the Court of Appeals that it is unilluminating. The general remarks pointed to by respondents "were obviously not made with this narrow issue in mind and they cannot be said to demonstrate a Congressional desire...." [Citation.] We find that the legislative history as a whole is silent on the precise issue before us. It is, however, consistent with the view that the EPA should have broad discretion in implementing the policies of the 1977 Amendments.

More importantly, that history plainly identifies the policy concerns that motivated the enactment; the plantwide definition is fully consistent with one of those concerns — the allowance of reasonable economic growth — and, whether or not we believe it most effectively implements the other, we must recognize that the EPA has advanced a reasonable explanation for its conclusion that the regulations serve the environmental objectives as well. Indeed, its reasoning is supported by the public record developed in the rulemaking process, as well as by certain private studies.

Our review of the EPA's varying interpretations of the word "source" — both before and after the 1977 Amendments — convinces us that the agency primarily responsible for administering this important legislation has consistently interpreted it flexibly — not in a sterile textual vacuum, but in the context of implementing policy decisions in a technical and complex arena. The fact that the agency has from time to time changed its interpretation of the term "source" does not, as respondents argue, lead us to conclude that no deference should be accorded the agency's interpretation of the statute. An initial agency interpretation is not instantly carved in stone. On the contrary, the agency, to engage in informed rulemaking, must consider varying interpretations and the wisdom of its policy on a continuing basis. Moreover, the fact that the agency has adopted different definitions in different contexts adds force to the argument that the definition itself is flexible, particularly since Congress has never indicated any disapproval of a flexible reading of the statute.

Significantly, it was not the agency in 1980, but rather the Court of Appeals that read the statute inflexibly to command a plantwide definition for programs designed to maintain clean air and to forbid such a definition for programs designed to improve air quality. The distinction the court drew may well be a sensible one, but our labored review of the problem has surely disclosed that it is not a distinction that Congress ever articulated itself, or one that the EPA found in the statute before the courts began to review the legislative work product. We conclude that it was the Court of Appeals, rather than Congress or any of the decision-makers who are authorized by Congress to administer this legislation, that was primarily responsible for the 1980 position taken by the agency.

Policy

The arguments over policy that are advanced in the parties' briefs create the impression that respondents are now waging in a judicial forum a specific policy battle which they ultimately lost in the agency and in the 32 jurisdictions opting for the bubble concept, but one which was never waged in the Congress. Such policy arguments are more properly addressed to legislators or administrators, not to judges.

In these cases the Administrator's interpretation represents a reasonable accommodation of manifestly competing interests and is entitled to deference: the regulatory scheme is technical and complex, the agency considered the matter in a detailed and reasoned fashion, and the decision involves reconciling conflicting policies. Congress intended to accommodate both interests, but did not do so itself on the level of specificity presented by these cases. Perhaps that body consciously desired the Administrator to strike the balance at this level, thinking that those with great expertise and charged with responsibility for administering the provision would be in a better position to do so; perhaps it simply did not consider the question at this level; and perhaps Congress was unable to forge a coalition on either side of the question, and those on each side decided to take their chances with the scheme devised by the agency. For judicial purposes, it matters not which of these things occurred.

Judges are not experts in the field, and are not part of either political branch of the Government. Courts must, in some cases, reconcile competing political interests, but not on the basis of the judges' personal policy preferences. In contrast, an agency to which Congress has delegated policy making responsibilities may, within the limits of that delegation, properly rely upon the incumbent administration's views of wise policy to inform its judgments. While agencies are not directly accountable to the people, the Chief Executive is, and it is entirely appropriate for this political branch of the Government to make such policy choices — resolving the competing interests which Congress itself either inadvertently did not resolve, or intentionally left to be resolved by the agency charged with the administration of the statute in light of everyday realities.

When a challenge to an agency construction of a statutory provision, fairly conceptualized, really centers on the wisdom of the agency's policy, rather than whether it is a reasonable choice within a gap left open by Congress, the challenge must fail. In such a case, federal judges — who have no constituency — have a duty to respect legitimate policy choices made by those who do. The responsibilities for assessing the wisdom of such policy choices and resolving the struggle between competing views of the public interest are not judicial ones: "Our Constitution vests such responsibilities in the political branches." *TVA v. Hill*, 437 U.S. 153, 195 (1978).

. . . .

NOTES AND QUESTIONS

1. If EPA were to decide tomorrow to preclude use of the plant-wide bubble for nonattainment review, and the industry challenged the regulation in federal court, what result under *Chevron*? Has the D.C. Circuit Court of Appeals decision in *ASARCO* been overruled by *Chevron*? EPA to date has not adopted the plant-wide bubble in the NSPS program. 2 S. NOVICK, LAW OF ENVIRONMENTAL PROTECTION § 11.03[1][c][ii].

2. Use of the bubble concept does not necessarily allow a source to avoid more stringent requirements. Recall the discussion of the 100/250 tons per year threshold for PSD review, page 400 *supra*. Netting of plant-wide emissions makes it more likely that a plant will cross the threshold and be subject to PSD review.

3. Totally aside from *Chevron*'s importance to the CAA, the case is also a landmark in administrative law. From that perspective, *Chevron* raises difficult issues about allocations of responsibility between the executive and legislative branches. Is an agency free to decide an issue whenever Congress is silent, so long as the agency's approach satisfies some minimal test for rationality? If not, what are the parameters of the agency's authority when Congress is silent? If a statute attempts to reconcile conflicting policy goals, can an agency regulate to serve only one of those goals? What were Congress' policy concerns behind the 1977 amendments? With respect to the nonattainment provisions? Were any or all of these goals served by EPA's adoption of the bubble? *Compare* Hirshman, *Postmodern Jurisprudence and the Problem of Administrative Discretion*, 82 Nw.

U.L. REV. 646 (1988) *with* Pierce, *Chevron and Its Aftermath: Judicial Review of Agency Interpretations of Statutory Provisions*, 41 VAND. L. REV. 301 (1988).

4. EPA has authorized the use of the bubble to enable sources to meet limitations imposed by the state in its SIP. In this context, a source with several emission points, each subject to specific limitations in the SIP, may seek amendment of the SIP to allow the source to choose the most efficient and least costly mix of controls, so long as the total plant emissions are equal to or less than the emissions allowable under the individual emission control strategies set by the SIP. 51 Fed. Reg. 43,814 (1986). One study has concluded that the bubble is not often used by existing sources. Hahn & Hester, *Where Did All the Markets Go? An Analysis of EPA's Emissions Trading Program*, 6 YALE J. ON REG. 109 (1989); *but see NRDC v. EPA*, 33 Env't Rep. Cas. (BNA) 1657 (4th Cir. 1991) (upholding EPA approval of bubble under SIP).

5. The bubble is an *intra*-source offset. The CAA specifically authorizes use of an *inter*-source offset in nonattainment areas. Recall the basic requirements for new sources and modifications for nonattainment areas discussed on pages 384-85 *supra*. The following case illustrates application of these requirements to a specific source and the difficult evaluations that must be made in satisfying the offset requirement.

CITIZENS AGAINST REFINERY'S EFFECTS v. ENVIRONMENTAL PROTECTION AGENCY
643 F.2d 183 (4th Cir. 1981)

K. K. HALL, CIRCUIT JUDGE.

Citizens Against the Refinery's Effects (CARE) appeals from a final ruling by the Administrator of the Environmental Protection Agency (EPA) approving the Virginia State Implementation Plan (SIP) for reducing hydrocarbon pollutants. The plan requires the Virginia Highway Department to decrease usage of a certain type of asphalt, thereby reducing hydrocarbon pollution by more than enough to offset expected pollution from the Hampton Roads Energy Company's (HREC) proposed refinery. We affirm the action of the administrator in approving the state plan.

The Act

....

[Before the 1977 Amendments] the Clean Air Act created a no-growth environment in areas where the clean air requirements had not been attained. EPA recognized the need to develop a program that encouraged attainment of clean air standards without discouraging economic growth. Thus the agency proposed an Interpretive Ruling in 1976 which allowed the states to develop an "offset program" within the State Implementation Plans. 41 Fed. Reg. 55,524 (1976). The offset program, later codified by Congress in the 1977 Amendments to the Clean Air Act, permits the states to develop plans which allow construction of new pollution sources where accompanied by a corresponding reduction in an existing pollution source. 42 U.S.C. § 7502(b)(6) and § 7503. In effect, a new emitting facility can be built if an existing pollution source decreases its emissions or ceases operations as long as a positive net air quality benefit occurs.

If the proposed factory will emit carbon monoxide, sulfur dioxide, or particulates, the EPA requires that the offsetting pollution source be within the immediate vicinity of the new plant. The other two pollutants, hydrocarbons and nitrogen oxide, are less "site-specific," and thus the ruling permits the offsetting source to locate anywhere within a broad vicinity of the new source.

The offset program has two other important requirements. First, a base time period must be determined in which to calculate how much reduction is needed in existing pollutants to offset the new source. This base period is defined as the first year of the SIP or, where the state has not yet developed a SIP, as the year in which a construction permit application is filed. 41 Fed. Reg. 55,529 (1976). Second, the offset program requires that the new source adopt the Lowest Achievable Emissions Rate (LAER) using the most modern technology available in the industry. 41 Fed. Reg. 55,528-9 (1976).

The Refinery

HREC proposes to build a petroleum refinery and off-loading facility in Portsmouth, Virginia. Portsmouth has been unable to reduce air pollution enough to attain the national standard for one pollutant, photochemical oxidants, which is created when hydrocarbons are released into the atmosphere and react with other substances. Since a refinery is a major source of hydrocarbons, the Clean Air Act prevents construction of the HREC plant until the area attains the national standard.

In 1975, HREC applied to the Virginia State Air Pollution Control Board (VSAPCB) for a refinery construction permit. The permit was issued by the VSAPCB on October 8, 1975, extended and reissued on October 5, 1977 after a full public hearing, modified on August 8, 1978, and extended again on September 27, 1979. The VSAPCB, in an effort to help HREC meet the clean air requirements, proposed to use the offset ruling to comply with the Clean Air Act.

On November 28, 1977, the VSAPCB submitted a State Implementation Plan to EPA which included the HREC permit. The Virginia Board proposed to offset the new HREC hydrocarbon pollution by reducing the amount of cutback asphalt used for road paving operations in three highway districts by the Virginia Department of Highways. By switching from "cutback" to "emulsified" asphalt, the state can reduce hydrocarbon pollutants by the amount necessary to offset the pollutants from the proposed refinery.

EPA requested some changes in the state plan, including certain monitoring changes and verification from the Virginia Attorney General that the offset program was legally enforceable.... The EPA administrator ... approved the Virginia offset plan on January 31, 1980.

CARE raises four issues regarding the state plan. First, they argue that the geographic area used as the base for the offset was arbitrarily determined and that the area as defined violates the regulations. Second, CARE contends that EPA should have used 1975 instead of 1977 as the base year to compare usage of cutback asphalt. Third, CARE insists that the offset plan should have been disapproved since the state is voluntarily reducing usage of cutback asphalt anyway. Fourth, CARE questions the approval of the plan without definite Lowest Achievable Emissions Rate (LAER) as required by the statute. We reject the CARE challenges to the state plan.

The Geographic Area

CARE contends that the state plan should not have been approved by EPA since the three highway-district area where cutback usage will be reduced to offset refinery emissions was artificially developed by the state. The ruling permits a broad area (usually within one AQCR) to be used as the offset basis.

The ruling does not specify how to determine the area, nor provide a standard procedure for defining the geographic area. Here the Virginia Board originally proposed to use four highway districts comprising one-half the state as the offset area. When this was found to be much more than necessary to offset pollution expected from the refinery, the state changed it to one highway district plus nine additional counties. Later the proposed plan was again revised to include a geographic area of three highway districts.

The agency action in approving the use of three highway districts was neither arbitrary, capricious, nor outside the statute. First, Congress intended that the states and the EPA be given flexibility in designing and implementing SIP's. Such flexibility allows the states to make reasoned choices as to which areas may be used to offset new pollution and how the plan is to be implemented. Second, the offset program was initiated to encourage economic growth in the state. Thus a state plan designed to reduce highway department pollution in order to attract another industry is a reasonable contribution to economic growth without a corresponding increase in pollution. Third, to be sensibly administered the offset plan had to be divided into districts which could be monitored by the highway department. Use of any areas other than highway districts would be unwieldy and difficult to administer. Fourth, the scientific understanding of ozone pollution is not advanced to the point where exact air transport may be predicted. Designation of the broad area in which hydrocarbons may be transported is well within the discretion and expertise of the agency.

The Base Year

Asphalt consumption varies greatly from year to year, depending upon weather and road conditions.... To calculate consumption of a material where it constantly varies, a base year must be selected. In this case, EPA's Interpretive Ruling establishes the base year as the year in which the permit application is made....

Considering all of the circumstances, including the unusually high asphalt consumption in 1977, the selection by EPA of that as the base year was within the discretion of the agency. Since the EPA Interpretive Ruling allowing the offset was not issued until 1976, 1977 was the first year after the offset ruling and the logical base year in which to calculate the offset. Also, the permit issued by the VSAPCB was reissued in 1977 with extensive additions and revisions after a full hearing. Under these circumstances, 1977 appears to be a logical choice of a base year.

The Legally Binding Plan

For several years, Virginia has pursued a policy of shifting from cutback asphalt to the less expensive emulsified asphalt in road-paving operations. The policy was initiated in an effort to save money, and was totally unrelated to a State Implementation Plan. Because of this policy, CARE argues that hydrocarbon emissions were decreasing independent of this SIP and therefore are not a proper offset against the refinery. They argue that there is not, in effect, an actual reduction in pollution.

The Virginia voluntary plan is not enforceable and therefore is not in compliance with the 1976 Interpretive Ruling which requires that the offset program be enforceable. The EPA, in approving the state plan, obtained a letter from the Deputy Attorney General of Virginia in which he stated that the requisites had been satisfied for establishing and enforcing the plan with the Department of Highways. Without such authority, no decrease in asphalt-produced pollution is guaranteed. In contrast to the voluntary plan, the offset plan guarantees a reduction in pollution resulting from road-paving operations.

The Lowest Achievable Emissions Rate

Finally, CARE argues that the Offset Plan does not provide adequate Lowest Achievable Emission Rates (LAER) as required by the 1976 Interpretive Ruling because the plan contains only a 90% vapor recovery requirement, places an excessive 176.5 ton limitation on hydrocarbon emissions, and does not require specific removal techniques at the terminal. EPA takes the position that the best technique available for marine terminals provides only a 90% recovery and that the 176.5 ton limit may be reduced by the agency after the final product mix at the terminal is determined.

Since the record shows no evidence of arbitrary or capricious action in approving the HREC emissions equipment, the agency determination of these technical matters must be upheld. [Citation.]

NOTES AND QUESTIONS

1. As a practical matter, an owner or operator can satisfy the offset requirement by reducing emissions at the proposed source, by reducing emissions at other sources under the same ownership, or by paying a source in the area under different ownership to reduce its emissions. With the exception of ozone nonattainment areas, no specific offset ratio is required by the CAA. The 1990 amendments added a "proximity" requirement for emissions trading. Generally a source can only offset emissions within the source or with other sources in the same nonattainment area. However, the offset requirement can be satisfied by obtaining emissions reductions in another nonattainment area within the same state, so long as "the other area has an equal or higher nonattainment classification than the area in which the source is located" and emissions from the other area contribute to a NAAQS violation in the area in which the source is located. CAA § 173(c)(1), 42 U.S.C. § 7503(c)(1), *as added by* Clean Air Act Amendments of 1990, Pub. L. No. 101-549, § 102(c)(10). Why was the proximity requirement added?

2. Since 1979, EPA has also permitted "banking" of unused emission reduction with the state governing ownership and sale of the banked emission offsets. *See generally* 51 Fed. Reg. 43,814 (1986) (EPA's emission offset banking and trading policy); Dudek & Palmisano, *Emissions Trading: Why Is This Thoroughbred Hobbled?* 13 COLUM. J. ENVTL. L. 217 (1988); Note, *Emissions Trading and Banking Under the Clean Air Act After* NRDC v. Gorsuch, 34 SYRACUSE L. REV. 803 (1983); Note, *Emission-Offset Banking: Accommodating Industrial Growth with Air-Quality Standards*, 128 U. PA. L. REV. 937 (1980); Meidinger, *On Explaining the Development of "Emissions Trading" in U.S. Air Pollution Regulation*, 7 LAW & POL'Y 447 (1985). EPA has approved a number of state and local emissions banks. Who "owns" an unused offset or emission reduction credit (ERC)? For how long? If a company goes bankrupt, is the ERC an asset of the company or does it "revert" to the state? If the state underestimates the reductions necessary to allow new growth, can it increase the offset ratio, dramatically reducing the value of unused credits, or extinguish unused credits altogether? Would that be an unconstitutional taking of private property without just compensation? Is a company free to refuse a competitor's offer to purchase an ERC under the CAA? Under the antitrust laws?

3. What are the advantages to emissions trading over the command-and-control approach of mandated emissions reduction? *See generally* J.P. Dwyer, *The Use of Market Incentives in Controlling Air Pollution: California's Marketable Permits Program*, 20 ECOLOGY L.Q. 103 (1993); L. HINES, THE MARKET, ENERGY AND THE ENVIRONMENT 62, 65 (1988). Larry B. Parker, et al., *Clean Air Act Allowance Trading*, 21 ENVTL. L. 2021 (1991); Matthew Polesetsky, Comment, *Will a Market in Air Pollution Clean the Nation's Dirtiest Air? A Study of the South Coast Air Quality Management District's Regional Clean Air Incentives Market*, 22 ECOLOGY L.Q. 359 (1995). *But see, e.g.*, Jeanne M. Dennis, Comment, *Smoke for Sale: Paradoxes and Problems of the Emissions Trading Program of the Clean Air Act Amendments of 1990*, 40 UCLA L. REV. 1101 (1993); Adam J. Rosenberg, Note, *Credit Futures Contracts on the Chicago Board of Trade: Regional and Rational Challenges to the Right to Pollute*, 13 VA. ENVTL. L.J. 501 (1994).

REVIEW PROBLEM

The following review problem highlights the interlocking coverage of the PSD and nonattainment programs. Every air quality control region is a PSD area for at least one criteria pollutant. It is possible for an area to be an unclassifiable area with respect to one pollutant, a nonattainment area with respect to another pollutant, and in attainment for all other pollutants.

Assume that a newly proposed lime plant will emit 90 tons per year of nitrogen dioxide and sulfur dioxide and 110 tons per year of particulates and carbon monoxide. It would be located in an area that is a nonattainment area for ozone and nitrogen dioxide and a PSD area for all the other criteria pollutants. Would the source have to go through preconstruction review under the PSD program or nonattainment program or both? Assuming it must go through preconstruction review under both programs, what must be demonstrated to obtain the necessary permits? What additional requirements are applicable to the nonattainment area specifically under the 1990 amendments? What other emission limitations under the Act might have to be met? Be sure to refer to specific pollutants when necessary.

G. INTERSTATE AND INTERNATIONAL TRANSBOUNDARY POLLUTION

The emphasis of the Clean Air Act on the state implementation plan belies the fact that air pollution does not respect state boundaries. The inadequacies of SIPs to address transboundary pollution became apparent with growing recognition of the problem of "acid rain." Sulfur dioxide and nitrogen dioxide from fossil-fuel burning power plants, automobiles, ore smelters and other sources can be carried hundreds of miles by prevailing air currents before returning to earth, in precipitation or dry deposition, as sulfuric or nitric acids. The effects of acid rain may include acidification of lakes and other water sources, as well as damage to forests, man-made materials, and health. *See generally* U.S. CONGRESS OFFICE OF TECHNOLOGY ASSESSMENT, ACID RAIN AND TRANSPORTED AIR POLLUTANTS: IMPLICATIONS FOR PUBLIC POLICY (June 1984).

The problem of interstate pollution before 1990 was addressed only in sections 110(a)(2) and 126, 42 U.S.C. §§ 7410(a)(2) and 7426. Section 110 required states in their SIPs to prohibit emissions from stationary sources that "prevent" attainment or maintenance of a NAAQS or "interfere" with measures to prevent significant deterioration or protect visibility in another state. Section 126 required a state to notify other states of sources which may "significantly contribute" to violation of the Act's standards in another state. More importantly, the section authorized states to petition EPA for a finding that a major source would violate the interstate planning requirements of section 110. In the event of a violation, EPA could prevent the construction of a proposed source and the continued operation of an existing source.

The use of tall stacks by midwestern power plants to meet emission limitations, worsening long-range dispersion, led several states to utilize sections 110 and 126 in seeking relief. Both avenues proved unsuccessful. In general, the courts found no immediately effective, statutory duty on the part of EPA to address interstate pollution problems in SIPs. *See, e.g., Connecticut v. EPA*, 656 F.2d 902 (2d Cir. 1981) (EPA could approve revision of New York SIP before finishing section 126 proceedings filed by New Jersey and Connecticut and did not have to consider whether SIP revision would prevent attainment of those states' ambient goals to allow for economic growth which were more stringent than the NAAQSs); *New England Legal Found. v. Costle*, 475 F. Supp. 425 (D. Conn. 1979), *aff'd, in part, rev'd, in part*, 632 F.2d 936 (2d Cir. 1980); *New England Legal Found. v. Costle*, 666 F.2d 30 (2d Cir. 1981) (EPA had no mandatory duty to revise SIPs for New York and New Jersey to abate pollution in Connecticut). *See also State of New York v. United States EPA*, 852 F.2d 574 (D.C. Cir. 1988), *cert. denied sub nom. Maine v. United States EPA*, 489 U.S. 1065 (1989); *State of New York v. Administrator, United States EPA*, 710 F.2d 1200 (6th Cir. 1983); and *New York v. EPA*, 716 F.2d 440 (7th Cir. 1983) (New York and other northeastern states unsuccessfully challenging EPA approval of SIPs permitting increased SO_2 emissions for midwestern states). Section 126 petitions were also unsuccessful, due to the difficulty of identifying the specific sources in the offending state which "significantly contribute" to violation of a NAAQS in the downwind state. *See, e.g., Air Pollution Control Dist. of Jefferson County, Ky. v. United States EPA*, 739 F.2d 1071, 1093 (6th Cir. 1984) ("... [W]e believe that the test probably intended by Congress is whether one state 'significantly contributes' to NAAQS violations in another state"). In each of these cases, EPA persuaded the courts that its inaction was due to its technological inability to measure and identify transboundary pollution. *See generally* Roberts, *Acid Rain Regulation: Federal Failure and State Success*, 8 VA. J. OF NAT. RES. L. 1 (1988). The 1990 Amendments expand the category of sources that may be found guilty of interstate pollution: now a "major source or group of stationary sources" may be subject to a § 126(b) petition, whereas before only a "major source" could be subject to such a petition. CAA § 126(b), 42 U.S.C. § 7426(b), *as amended by* the Clean Air Act Amendments of 1990 § 109(a). The definition of illegal interstate pollution also has been expanded, so that now *contributing significantly* to nonattainment or interfering with maintenance of the NAAQS in another state is prohibited — the interstate polluter need not actually *prevent* attainment or maintenance of NAAQS to be subject to a § 126(b) petition. CAA § 110(a)(2)(D)(i)(I), 42 U.S.C. § 7410(a)(2)(D)(i)(I), *as amended by* the Clean Air Act Amendments of 1990 § 101(b). This last modification might seem to be a relaxation of the old § 110(a)(2)(E) standard, but the "significant contribution" test in the amendments is the test that has been utilized by the courts before the amendments to find that no relief is available under section 126. 2 S. NOVICK, LAW OF ENVIRONMENTAL PROTECTION § 11.02[6][d][i] n.346.

The amendments also authorize EPA to designate interstate transport regions, areas in which the interstate transport of that pollutant from one or more states "contributes significantly" to a NAAQS violation in one or more other states. EPA must establish a transport commission, consisting of representatives of each state involved and of EPA, for each such region to assess the degree of interstate pollution, assess strategies for mitigating the interstate pollution, and recommend to EPA measures to prevent the interstate pollution. CAA § 176A, 42 U.S.C. § 7506A, *as added by* the Clean Air Act Amendments of 1990 § 102(f)(1).

In a multistate ozone nonattainment area (a single ozone nonattainment area which covers more than one state), the states included must coordinate their SIPs. CAA § 182(j)(1). If a state which contains part of a multistate ozone nonattainment area fails to reach attainment by the deadline, it may petition EPA to find that the state would have been able to reach attainment if not for the failure of one or more other states containing portions of the area to implement all of the control measures required for that area, in which case the state making the petition will not be subject to sanctions under section 179. CAA § 182(j)(2).

The northeastern coast of the mainland United States — Maine, Vermont, New Hampshire, Massachusetts, Connecticut, Rhode Island, New York, New Jersey, Pennsylvania, Delaware, Maryland, and the Consolidated Metropolitan Statistical Area that includes the District of Columbia — is established as a single ozone transport region, subject to the requirements of section 176(a)(1) and (2). CAA § 184(a), 42 U.S.C. § 7511c(a). Each state included in this transport region, or any other ozone transport region that may be established, must implement, among other measures, an enhanced vehicle inspection and maintenance program for the area as required for Serious Areas, and implement RACT for all VOC sources in the state, and control major sources of nitrous oxides as set out in section 182(f). CAA § 184(b), 42 U.S.C. § 7511c(b).

Any state included within an ozone transport region may, with a majority vote of the state representatives on the transport region Commission, petition the Commission to develop recommendations for additional control measures, which EPA must approve, partially approve, or disapprove within nine months of receipt. CAA § 184(c), 42 U.S.C. § 7511c(c). If the recommendations are approved or partially approved by EPA, each state within the transport region to which a requirement of the approved plan applies must revise its SIP to include the new measures within one year. *Id.*

The only provision of the Act providing a remedy for international pollution has proven as ineffective as section 126. Section 115 requires the Administrator of EPA to notify the governor of a state from which emissions originate if the Administrator has reason to believe that the pollution "cause[s] or contribute[s] to air pollution which may reasonably be anticipated to endanger public health or welfare in a foreign country." 42 U.S.C. § 7415(a). The state must then revise its SIP "to prevent or eliminate the endangerment." CAA § 115(b), 42 U.S.C. § 7415(b). When the province of Ontario, several states, and a number of environmental groups sought relief under section 115 from acid rain deposition, EPA successfully defended on the grounds it did not have to initiate the procedures until it identified the specific sources responsible, and that it was not able to do so. In *Her Majesty the Queen in Right of Ontario v. United States EPA*, 912 F.2d 1525 (D.C. Cir. 1990). On March 13, 1991, the United States and Canada signed an agreement to set national caps on emissions of SO_2 and to create a system for resolution of transboundary air quality disputes. Wash. Post, March 14, 1991, A33, col. 8. *See generally* Mark L. Glode & Beverly Nelson Glode, *Transboundary Pollution: Acid Rain and United States-Canadian Relations*, 20 B.C. ENVTL. AFF. L. REV. 1 (1993).

The difficulties in formulating a legislative program to control acid rain are illustrative of the complex interrelationship of cost, equity, and technological uncertainty common to so many environmental problems. Opponents of regulation pointed to the scientific uncertainty over which pollutants cause acid rain, the effects of acid rain, and even whether acid rain exists. Effective controls of SO_2 and NO_X (nitrous oxide) would require installation of expensive technology by coal-burning power plants in the midwest, with the spectre of increased electrical rates for consumers of electricity in that region. Who should bear the costs — the sources themselves, the consumers in that region, the beneficiaries of cleaner air in the downwind states, or the nation as a whole? The alternative to technological controls is use of more scarce, low sulfur coal, with decreased emissions of SO_2 from combustion. However, most low sulfur coal is mined in the west, and the less expensive, high sulfur is mined in the east in states with ailing economies very dependent upon the coal industry. Increased mining in the west would also necessitate increased use of scarce water resources, not to mention the possibility of more mining activity on federally protected lands.

After many unsuccessful attempts in Congress to create a legislative program controlling acid rain over White House opposition, Title IV of the 1990 Amendments established a ground-breaking program to control sulfur dioxide and nitrogen oxides. The program utilizes a market-based allowance system to reduce SO_2 emissions from utilities by 50%, with a nationwide cap on emissions of 8.9 million tons on all fossil fuel-burning utilities by the year 2000. CAA § 403(a), 42 U.S.C. § 7651b(a). *See generally* Brian L. Ferrall, Recent Legislation, *The Clean Air Act Amendments of 1990 and the Use of Market Forces to Control Sulphur Dioxide Emissions*, 28 HARV. J. ON LEGIS. 235 (1991); Carlos A. Gavilondo, Note, *Trading Clean Air — The 1990 Acid Rain Rules: How They Will Work and Initial Responses to the Market System*, 67 TUL. L. REV. 749 (1993); John R. Loxterman, Recent Developments, *Acid Rain Provisions of the Clean Air Amendments of 1990: Environmental Responsibility or Political Necessity?*, 10 TEMP. ENVTL. & TECH. J. 201 (1991). *But see, e.g.*, R.C. Byrd, *The Clean Air Act Amendments of 1990. An Innovative, but Uncertain Approach to Acid Rain Control*, 93 W. VA. L. REV. 477 (1991); Larry B. Parker et al., *Clean Air Act Allowance Trading*, 21 ENVTL. L. 2021 (1991); Project, *New Strategies for a New Market: The Electric Industry's Response to the Environ-*

mental Protection Agency's Sulfur Dioxide Emission Allowance Trading Program, 47 ADMIN. L. REV. 469 (1995); Brian L. Ferrall, Note, *Will a Market in Sulphur Dioxide Work? An Evaluation of the Acid Deposition Title of the Clean Air Act Amendments of 1990*, 11 VA. ENVTL. L.J. 309 (1991-92); Adam J. Rosenberg, Note, *Credit Futures Contracts on the Chicago Board of Trade: Regional and Rational Challenges to the Right to Pollute*, 13 VA. ENVTL. L.J. 501 (1994). This free-market approach grants utility sources a designated number of emission "allowances." Each SO_2 allowance grants a source permission to release one ton of sulfur dioxide pollution in a specified calendar year. CAA § 402(3), 42 U.S.C. § 7651a(3). Allowances can be used for current emissions, sold, or held in reserve for future emission increases. CAA § 403(b), 42 U.S.C. § 7651b(b). After the year 2000, it is illegal for any utility unit to release SO_2 for which it does not have an allowance. CAA § 411, 42 U.S.C. § 7651j. Allowances are reviewable in the federal courts of appeals. *Madison Gas & Elec. Co. v. EPA*, 4 F.3d 529 (7th Cir. 1993).

SO_2 emission reductions under the program are achieved in two phases. Phase I calls for a 3 to 4 million ton reduction by the year 1995. Power plants that are large (100 megawatts or greater) and dirty (emitting 2.5 pounds or more of SO_2 per million Btu of fossil fuel consumed) must comply with a 2.5 pound/mBtu standard by 1995, or 1997 for plants using scrubbers. Over a hundred power plants listed in the amendments are affected by Phase I. CAA § 404, 42 U.S.C. § 7651c.

The balance of the SO_2 reductions are achieved by the year 2000 in Phase II. In Phase II, all existing utility units receive allowances and become subject to the prohibition on emitting SO_2 in excess of the allowances. The large, dirty units regulated in phase one must make additional emission reductions; high-pollution units too small to be affected by Phase I must make reductions for the first time. All other utility units are subject to the nationwide cap with sufficient allowances to accommodate 20 percent growth. CAA § 405, 42 U.S.C. § 7651d.

The principal debate in Congress was over allocation of the 8.9 million allowances. Should allowances be awarded to the highly polluting utilities to compensate them for the costs of cleanup, or to "cleaner" utilities as a reward for their efforts? The complex allocation scheme defies easy description. The basic formula for allocation is riddled with exceptions that are only explicable as the result of successful lobbying.

The allocation scheme is complicated by allowance "reserves," allowances within the cap that are not allocated. There are three principal reserves: (1) bonus allowances for utilities which utilize scrubbers in order to encourage markets for high-sulfur coal, CAA § 404(a)(2)(D), 42 U.S.C. § 7651c(a)(2)(D); (2) a reserve to fund special exceptions from the limitations in phase II, CAA § 405(a)(2), 42 U.S.C. § 7651d(a)(2); and (3) a reserve to fund annual auctions of allowances, CAA § 416, 42 U.S.C. § 7651o. It should be kept in mind that, although allowances are tradeable, they cannot be used if emissions would violate any other provision of the Act.

Title IV also requires the Administrator to set emission limitations to reduce NO_X emissions from coal-fired utilities. These standards should reduce NO_X emissions by 2 million tons annually from 1980 levels. CAA § 407, 42 U.S.C. § 7651f. Section 182(f) requires existing sources to use reasonably available control technology, and new sources to meet the lowest emission rates achievable and offset emissions in ozone nonattainment areas and transport regions. CAA § 182(f), 42 U.S.C. § 7511(a). *See, e.g.*, Paul J. Miller, *Cutting Through the Smog: The 1990 Clean Air Act Amendments and a New Direction Towards Reducing Ozone Pollution*, 12 STAN. ENVTL. L.J. 124 (1993).

In addition, reasonably available control measures are required on major NO_X sources in moderate PM-10 nonattainment areas, CAA § 189(a)(1)(C), 42 U.S.C. § 7513a(a)(1)(C), and the best available control measures are required for major NO_X sources in serious PM-10 nonattainment areas. CAA § 189(b)(1)(B), 42 U.S.C. § 7513a(b)(1)(B). New major NO_X sources in these areas are also subject to the general new source preconstruction review requirements for nonattainment areas. CAA §§ 189(e), 173, 42 U.S.C. §§ 7513a(e), 7503.

The literature on interstate and international transboundary pollution is voluminous. *See, e.g.*, BRUCE A. ACKERMAN & WILLIAM T. HASSLER, CLEAN COAL/DIRTY AIR: OR HOW THE CLEAN AIR ACT BECAME A MULTIBILLION DOLLAR BAIL-OUT FOR HIGH-SULFUR COAL PRODUCERS AND WHAT SHOULD BE DONE ABOUT IT (1981); UNITED NATIONS, AIR BORNE SULPHUR POLLUTION: EFFECTS AND CONTROL (a report prepared in conjunction with the Convention on Long-Range Transboundary Air Pollution) (1984); American Society of International Law, *Transfrontier Environmental Damage*, AM. SOC. INT'L L. PROC. ANN. 12 (1990); Bankes & Saunders, *Acid Rain: Multilateral and Bilateral Approaches to Transboundary Pollution Under International Law*, U.N.B.L.J. ANN. 155 (1984); Chaves, *Acid Rain*, 6 HOUS. J. INT'L L. 197 (1984); Erwin, *Resolving Transboundary Air Pollution Disputes in North America: The Case for a Quasi-judicial Remedy*, 1984 WIS. INT'L L.J. ANN. 202 (1984); Fischer, *Acid Rain: Deploying Private Damage Actions Against Transboundary Polluters*, 19 TRIAL 56 (April 1983); Florence, *Using the Interstate Compact to Control Acid Deposition*, 6 J. ENERGY L. (1985); Fraenkel, *The Convention on Long-Range Transboundary Air Pollution: Meeting the Challenge of International Cooperation*, 30 HARV. INT'L L.J. 447 (1989); Gaines, *Taking Responsibility for Transboundary Environmental Effects*, 14 HASTINGS INT'L & COMP. L. REV. ANN. 279 (1991); Gallob, *Birth of the North American Transboundary Environmental Plaintiff: Transboundary Pollution and the 1979 Draft Treaty for Equal Access and Remedy*, 15 HARV. ENVTL. L. REV. 85 (1991); Garland, *Acid Rain Over the United States and Canada: The D.C. Circuit Fails to Provide Shelter Under Section 115 of the Clean Air Act While State Action Provides a Temporary Umbrella*, 16 B.C. ENVTL. AFF. L. REV. 1 (1988); Mark L. Glode & Beverly Nelson Glode, *Transboundary Pollution: Acid Rain and United States-Canadian Relations*, 20 B.C. ENVTL. AFF. L. REV. 1 (1993); Keith, *The EPA's Discretion to Regulate Acid Rain: A Discussion of the*

Requirements for Triggering Section 115 of the Clean Air Act, 36 CLEV. ST. L. REV. 133 (1987); Knapp, *Our Neighbor's Keeper? The United States and Canada: Coping with Transboundary Air Pollution*, 9 FORDHAM INT'L L.J. 159 (1986); McMahon & Fischer, *Point-Counterpoint: Perspectives on Acid Rain*, 19 TRIAL 80 (August 1983); Meltzer, *The Environmental Policy of the European Economic Community to Control Transnational Pollution — Time to Make Critical Choices*, 12 LOY. L.A. INT'L & COMP. L.J. 579 (1990); Moller, *The United States-Canadian Acid Rain Crisis: Proposal for an International Agreement*, 36 UCLA L. REV. 1207 (1989); Pallemaerts, *Judicial Recourse Against Foreign Air Polluters: A Case Study of Acid Rain in Europe*, 9 HARV. ENVTL. L. REV. 143 (1985); Rivera, *Resolving Air Resource Disputes on a Transfrontier Basis: El Paso and Ciudad Juarez*, 10 HOUS. J. INT'L L. 133 (1987); Rosencranz, *The ECE Convention of 1979 on Long-range Transboundary Air Pollution*, 75 AM. J. INT'L L. 975 (1981); Scott, *The Canadian-American Problem of Acid Rain*, NAT. RESOURCES J. 337 (1986); Smith, *Playing the Acid Rain Game: A State's Remedies*, 16 ENVTL. L. 255 (1986); Stein, Comment, *Acid Rain: The Clean Air Act Cannot Handle the Problem*, 56 UMKC L. REV. 139 (1987); Talkington, *Interstate Air Pollution Abatement and the Clean Air Act Amendments of 1990: Balancing Interests*, 64 COLO. L. REV. 957 (1991); Wetstone & Rosencranz, *Transboundary Air Pollution: The Search for an International Response*, 8 HARV. ENVTL. L. REV. 89 (1984); Williams, *Public International Law Governing Transboundary Pollution*, INT'L BUS. LAW. 243 (1984).

H. FEDERAL EMISSION LIMITATIONS

To this point, the materials have addressed emission limitations imposed through the state planning process to achieve the national ambient air quality goals. The Clean Air Act also establishes three types of uniform, nationwide emission limitations to be promulgated by EPA: (1) new source performance standards (NSPSs); (2) emission limitations on hazardous air pollutants (HAPs); and (3) motor vehicle emission standards. Why do you think Congress chose to utilize nationally uniform standards in these three situations? New source performance standards and motor vehicle emission standards are technology-based standards, that is, the statutory standard is expressed in terms of the technology to be employed which EPA must then translate into the amount of a pollutant that may be emitted utilizing such technology. The National Emission Standards for Hazardous Air Pollutants started out in 1970 as health-based standards. The limitation had to be set at a level to protect human health, whatever the cost of the necessary technology and regardless of its availability. Dissatisfaction with this approach to hazardous pollutants led Congress in 1990 to replace this standard with a very stringent, technology-based standard.

1. NEW SOURCE PERFORMANCE STANDARDS

Section 111 directs the Administrator to promulgate lists of categories of sources that "cause[], or contribute[] significantly to, air pollution which may reasonably be anticipated to endanger public health or welfare." CAA § 111(b)-(1)(A), 42 U.S.C. § 7411(b)(1)(A). Within one year after inclusion of a category of sources on the list, EPA must propose a "standard of performance" for "new" sources in that category. CAA § 111(b)(1)(B), 42 U.S.C. § 7411(b)(1)(B). "Standard of performance" is defined as:

> ... a standard for emissions of air pollutants which reflects the degree of emission limitation achievable through the application of the best system of emission reduction which (taking into account the cost of achieving such reduction and any nonair quality health and environmental impact and energy requirements) the Administrator determines has been adequately demonstrated.

CAA § 111(a)(1), 42 U.S.C. § 7411(a)(1). The standard applies to any "new" source, which is any stationary source constructed or modified after publication of the standard. CAA § 111(a)(2), 42 U.S.C. § 7411(a)(2). To spur EPA to promulgate more NSPSs, section 111(f) requires EPA to propose NSPSs, by November 15, 1996, for all categories of major stationary sources listed before November 15, 1990. CAA § 111(f)(1), 42 U.S.C. § 7411(f)(1).

Review of the Administrator's promulgation of a NSPS must be in the federal Court of Appeals for the District of Columbia. CAA § 307(b)(1), 42 U.S.C. § 7607(b)(1). In the early landmark case of *Portland Cement Ass'n v. Ruckelshaus*, 486 F.2d 375 (D.C. Cir. 1973), *cert. denied*, 417 U.S. 921 (1974), that court concluded that a technology did not have to be in routine use to be adequately demonstrated. The court also rejected industry's assertion that the costs of the standard must be outweighed by the environmental benefits, holding that costs are only a factor to be considered in setting the standard. Looking at the definition of "standard of performance," is the NSPS a technology-forcing standard in the sense that it pushes industry to achieve a level of control that new sources would not otherwise meet through ordinary technological development? *See generally* Currie, *Direct Federal Regulation of Stationary Sources under the Clean Air Act*, 128 U. PA. L. REV. 1389 (1980). Keep this question in mind as you read the following cases.

NATIONAL ASPHALT PAVEMENT ASSOCIATION v. TRAIN

539 F.2d 775 (D.C. Cir. 1976)

McGOWAN, CIRCUIT JUDGE.

Section 111 of the Clean Air Act (1970 and Supp. IV, 1974), directs the Administrator of the Environmental Protection Agency (EPA) to maintain a list of stationary sources which "may contribute significantly to air pollution which causes or contributes to the endangerment of public health or welfare." *Id.*

§ 1857c-6(b)(1)(A). Within 120 days after the Administrator designates a particular source category as a "significant contributor," he must publish proposed standards of performance for sources within that category....

On June 11, 1973 the Administrator published a notice in the Federal Register indicating that he had amended his list of "significant contributors" to include asphalt concrete plants. On that same day he also published proposed standards of performance for new or modified asphalt concrete plants. *Id.* at 15406. After considering written comments on the proposed standards, the Administrator published final standards of performance on March 8, 1974.

....

... [T]he Clean Air Act, and section 111 in particular, was also designed to prevent new pollution problems, especially the deterioration of air quality in areas where existing air quality levels exceed the promulgated air quality standards. The House reported that the provision for control over new stationary sources was enacted to "prevent the occurrence anywhere in the United States of significant new air pollution problems...."

... [T]he Conference Committee eventually recommended what is now section 111(b)(1), which authorizes the Administrator to promulgate standards of performance for new stationary sources which "may contribute significantly to air pollution which causes or contributes to the endangerment of public health or welfare." 42 U.S.C. § 1857c-6(b)(1).

That provision obviously contemplates an evaluation by the Administrator of the risk that certain types of air pollution will "endanger" public health and welfare, and the risk that allowing construction of new stationary sources, even subject to existing state and local regulation, will contribute "significantly" to that air pollution. In our view, the Administrator's evaluation of those risks involves questions which are "particularly prone to uncertainty," and as a result "the statute accords the [Administrator] flexibility to assess [those] risks and make essentially legislative policy judgments...." [Citation.] These policy choices "are not susceptible to the same type of verification or refutation by reference to the record as are some factual questions," [Citation] and consequently are not subject to review with the "substantive rigor proper for questions of fact," [citation]. Instead, our "paramount objective is to see whether the agency, given an essentially legislative task to perform, has carried it out in a manner calculated to negate the dangers of arbitrariness and irrationality in the formulation of rules for general application in the future." [Citation.]

The Administrator has concluded that "in the case of particulate matter — a pollutant for which national ambient air quality standards have been promulgated — ... all sources ... contribute to the endangerment of public health or welfare." App. at 134. Petitioners and various commentators on the "significant contributor" designation do not really challenge the Administrator's conclusion in this regard, and we would be hard pressed to find a reason for overturning this aspect of the Administrator's determination....

Petitioners' primary attack on the Administrator's designation concerns his conclusion that the asphalt concrete industry contributes "significantly" to particulate matter pollution. The Administrator concluded that it is "meaningless" to develop a firm definition of "significant" contribution to be applied nation-wide; as a result of variations in topography, distribution of sources, height from which the pollutant is emitted, and meteorological conditions, a new source may be "significant" in one area and insignificant in another. To achieve the overall objectives of the Act — reduction in existing levels of pollution and prevention of deterioration — the Administrator concluded that construction of new asphalt concrete plants will contribute enough additional particulate matter pollution to warrant regulation as a significant contributor. That determination is based on the Administrator's examination of the rate of emissions of particulate matter from uncontrolled plants, the stringency of existing state and local regulations limiting emissions from these plants, the number of existing plants, and the expected rate of growth in the number of plants.

Petitioners argue that, in determining whether the asphalt cement industry is a "significant contributor," the Administrator relied on a study conducted in 1967 which estimated that in 1967 total particulate emissions from the asphalt concrete industry amounted to 243,000 tons, and that the amount would increase to 403,000 tons in 1977 if the 1967 control level of ninety-five percent were maintained. By the time the Administrator made the designation and promulgated proposed standards, however, a large number of asphalt concrete plants had installed various control devices, especially in response to state and local regulations....

We see no merit in petitioners' argument. First, the Administrator never relied on the disputed study to estimate the level of *controlled* emissions; to the contrary, the Administrator specifically noted that one of the factors he considered was the rate of *uncontrolled* emissions. Moreover, the Administrator also stated that he was aware of and took into account the stringency of existing local and state limitations on emissions from asphalt concrete plants. The Administrator has thus determined that given the number of existing plants, the expected rate of growth in the number of plants, the rate of uncontrolled emissions, and the level of emissions currently tolerated, potential emissions from new asphalt concrete plants would contribute "significantly" enough to warrant additional regulation to prevent deterioration of clean air. Petitioners have pointed to nothing in the record that indicates that the Administrator was arbitrary and capricious in reaching that determination.

We also find a fundamental flaw in the contention that once an industry complies with regulations designed to *reduce* air pollution to the level established by national primary and secondary air quality standards, it is no longer a "significant contributor" subject to new source regulation. Compliance with existing regulations may well enable the states to achieve the national standards, but it does not mean that the Administrator is precluded from exercising regulatory authority to *prevent* deterioration of clean areas. Given the Administrator's statement that he examined current state and local emission limitations, we take his decision to be that construction of new plants subject only to current emission limitations would "significantly contribute" to future air pollution problems. For that reason he promulgated standards of performance that are more stringent than typical state and local regulations, and we can find no basis to upset that determination.

We turn next to petitioners' contention that the Administrator acted in an arbitrary and capricious manner in promulgating the ... standards of performance for new or modified asphalt concrete plants....

Those standards were promulgated pursuant to section 111(a)(1) of the Act.... We have indicated that "[it] is the system which must be adequately demonstrated and the standard which must be achievable." [Citation.] "Adequately demonstrated" does not mean that existing asphalt concrete plants must be capable of meeting the standard; to the contrary, "[section] 111 looks toward what may fairly be projected for the regulated future, rather than the state of the art at present...." *Portland Cement Association v. Ruckelshaus*, 486 F.2d 375, 391 (D.C. Cir. 1973), *cert. denied*, 417 U.S. 921 (1974). And an "achievable standard" is one "within the realm of the adequately demonstrated system's efficiency and which, while not at a level that is purely theoretical or experimental, need not necessarily be routinely achieved within the industry prior to its adoption." [Citation.] Moreover, the system must be one "which can reasonably be expected to serve the interests of pollution control without becoming exorbitantly costly in an economic or environmental way."

The standard of review of actions of the Administrator in setting standards of performance is an appropriately deferential one, and we are to affirm the action of the Administrator unless it is "arbitrary, capricious, an abuse of discretion, or otherwise not in accordance with law," 5 U.S.C. § 706(2)(A). Since this is one of those "highly technical areas, where our understanding of the import of the evidence is attenuated, our readiness to review evidentiary support for decisions must be correspondingly restrained." [Citation.] "Our 'expertise' is not in setting standards for emission control, but in determining if the standards as set are the result of reasoned decisionmaking." [Citation.]

....

... [W]e cannot say that the Administrator's actions are either arbitrary or capricious. On the basis of our evaluation of the record evidence on these issues and the Administrator's responses thereto, we are unable to say that he did not engage in reasoned decision-making....

We recognize that, for a variety of reasons, the Administrator conducted tests on only four plants. But we think that the record evidence with respect to those tests, and tests conducted by others, ... preclude us from overturning the action of the Administrator....

Some of these tests admittedly failed to comply strictly with prescribed testing procedures, but we do not think that the departures were substantial enough to warrant reversal. Moreover, we think the record undercuts petitioners' claim that the Administrator "ignored" or "completely overlooked" relevant factors such as particle size and shape; we think the Administrator's statements indicate an awareness of and a willingness to adjust for such factors....

Petitioners also challenge the final standards on the ground that the Administrator gave inadequate consideration to economic costs. We noted in *Essex Chemical Corporation v. Ruckelshaus*, supra, that "[it] is not unlikely that industry and the EPA will disagree on the economic costs of these various control techniques" and that "[we] have no desire or special ability to settle such a dispute." 486 F.2d at 437. In the case before us we have no difficulty in concluding that the Administrator gave adequate attention to the costs involved, especially in light of petitioner Warren Brothers' statement that the control technologies at issue "can be installed and operated at reasonable cost," and that "petitioners are prepared to install the pollution control equipment the Administrator has determined to be the best demonstrated — and indeed have already largely done so." The record evidence indicates that the Administrator gave consideration to the relevant cost factors, and we have no cause to disturb his judgment.

NATIONAL LIME ASSOCIATION v. ENVIRONMENTAL PROTECTION AGENCY
627 F.2d 416 (D.C. Cir. 1980)

WALD, CIRCUIT JUDGE.

The National Lime Association (NLA), representing ninety percent of this country's commercial producers of lime and lime hydrate (the industry), challenges the new source performance standards (NSPS) for lime manufacturing plants issued by the Environmental Protection Agency (EPA, Administrator or Agency) under § 111 of the Clean Air Act (the Act), 42 U.S.C. § 7411 (Supp. I 1977). The standards limit the mass of particulate that may be emitted in the exhaust gas from all lime-hydrating and from certain lime-manufacturing facilities and limit the permitted visibility of exhaust gas emissions from some facilities manufacturing lime. We find inadequate support in the administrative record for the standards promulgated and therefore remand to the Administrator.

....

The process by which commercially valuable lime is produced is relatively simple. Limestone is quarried, crushed, sized and fed into a kiln where it is subjected to high temperatures (1100 degree C/2000 degree F). By a process known as "calcination," the heating ("burning") of limestone produces quicklime, a soft, porous, highly reactive material commonly used in industry. As might be expected, the process generates a substantial quantity of dust, or in the language of the Agency, particulate matter, sufficiently lightweight to be carried off in the hot exhaust gas and emitted from the kiln. The particulate matter thus released is composed of partially burned limestone, raw limestone feed, deadburned lime and quicklime. Typically, the process also releases sulfur dioxide (SO_2).

....

... 42 U.S.C. § 7411 authorizes the Administrator to limit the air pollutants that can lawfully be emitted from newly constructed or modified plants. This the Administrator can do by promulgating new source performance standards requiring new or modified plants to meet standards which can be met through application of the best system of emission reduction (considering costs) which has been "adequately demonstrated." The purpose is to assure that new or modified plants will not create significant new air pollution problems.

On May 3, 1977, EPA added lime manufacturing plants to the list of sources that "may contribute significantly to air pollution which causes or contributes to the endangerment of public health or welfare" pursuant to section 111(b) of the Clean Air Act. At the same time, EPA proposed NSPS for lime plants....

Although lime plants were determined to be sources of nitrogen oxides, carbon monoxide and sulfur dioxide as well as particulates, standards of performance were proposed and ultimately promulgated only with respect to particulate matter. Furthermore, of the various types of kilns that may be used in the calcination of limestone, only rotary kilns are regulated by the standards.

....

... As the court of exclusive review for NSPS, we have examined section 111 standards on several prior occasions or ... [citing among other cases *Portland Cement Association v. Ruckelshaus*, 486 F.2d 375 (D.C. Cir. 1973), *cert. denied*, 417 U.S. 921 (1974) (*Portland Cement I*)].

These decisions, viewed independently, have established a rigorous standard of review under section 111. We have not deviated from the approach applied to the first NSPS to reach this court. In that case, *Portland Cement I*, we acknowledged that

> [w]hile we remain diffident in approaching problems of this technical complexity, ... the necessity to review agency decisions, if it is to be more than a meaningless exercise, requires enough steeping in technical matters to determine whether the agency "has exercised a reasoned discretion."...
> We cannot substitute our judgment for that of the agency, but it is our duty to consider whether "the decision was based on a consideration of the relevant factors and whether there has been a clear error of judgment."...
> Ultimately, we believe, that the cause of a clean environment is best served by reasoned decision-making.

486 F.2d at 402 (citations omitted).

....

The issue presented here is primarily one of the adequacy of EPA's test data on which the industry standards are based. NLA disagrees with EPA's conclusion that the standards are achievable under the "best technological system of continuous emission reduction which ... the Administrator determines has been adequately demonstrated." Specifically, NLA claims that the test data underlying the development of the standards do not support the Administrator's conclusion that the promulgated emission levels are in fact "achievable" on a continuous basis. Promulgation of standards based upon inadequate proof of achievability would defy the Administrative Procedure Act's mandate against action that is "arbitrary, capricious, an abuse of discretion, or otherwise not in accordance with law." 5 U.S.C. § 706.

Our review has led us to conclude that the record does not support the "achievability" of the promulgated standards for the industry as a whole.[46] This conclusion is a cumulative one, resulting from our assessment of the many points raised by the industry at the administrative level and in this court; no one point made is so cogent that remand would necessarily have followed on that basis alone.[48]

In the analysis that follows, common threads will be discerned in our discussions of individual points. Chief among these common threads is a concern that the Agency consider the representativeness for the industry as a whole of the tested plants on which it relies, at least where its central argument is that the

---

[46]An achievable standard need not be one already routinely achieved in the industry. But, to be achievable, we think a uniform standard must be capable of being met under most adverse conditions which can reasonably be expected to recur and which are not or cannot be taken into account in determining the "costs" of compliance.

....

The EPA has expressly built some flexibility into the enforcement end of the new source performance standards, 40 C.F.R. § 60.8(c) (relating to startup, shutdown, and malfunction), and is vested with a more general enforcement discretion, but the flexibility appropriate to enforcement will not render "achievable" a standard which cannot be achieved on a regular basis, either for the reasons expressly taken into account in compliance determination regulations (here startup, shutdown and malfunction), or otherwise.

Because we remand for the development of a more adequate rationale for the promulgated standards we do not now specify the kinds of variations in conditions — not accounted for in the Agency's cost analysis — which might render a uniform standard "unachievable" or so "unachievable" as to represent an arbitrary or capricious exercise of the Administrator's discretion under the Act.

[48]In addition to the points made in connection with the achievability of the standard, NLA disputes EPA's determination that lime manufacturing plants "may contribute significantly to air pollution which causes or contributes to the endangerment of public health or welfare." [Citation.]

We think the danger of particulate emissions' effect on health has been sufficiently supported in the Agency's (and its predecessor's) previous determinations to provide a rational basis for the Administrator's finding in this case. Moreover, whatever its impact on public health, we cannot say that a dust "nuisance" has no impact on public welfare. Congress has provided that with respect to the Clean Air Act:

> All language referring to effects on welfare includes, but is not limited to, effects on soils, water, crops, vegetation, manmade materials, animals, wildlife, weather, visibility, and climate, damage to and deterioration of property, and hazards to transportation, as well as effects on economic values and on personal comfort and wellbeing.

42 U.S.C. § 7602(h) (Supp. I 1977). Thus, we could not say that the Administrator's determination is arbitrary, even if the dust were shown innocuous to public health.

....

standard *is* achievable because it *has* been achieved (at the tested plants). The Agency's failure to consider the representativeness — along various relevant parameters — of the data relied upon is the primary reason for our remand. The locus of administrative burdens of going forward or of persuasion may shift in the course of a rulemaking proceeding, but we think an initial burden of promulgating and explaining a non-arbitrary, non-capricious rule rests with the Agency and we think that by failing to explain how the standard proposed is achievable under the range of relevant conditions which may affect the emissions to be regulated, the Agency has not satisfied this initial burden.

Bearing this initial burden will involve first, identifying and verifying as relevant or irrelevant specific variable conditions that may contribute substantially to the amount of emissions, or otherwise affect the efficiency of the emissions control systems considered. And second, where test results are relied upon, it should involve the selection or use of test results in a manner which provides some assurance of the achievability of the standard for the industry as a whole, given the range of variable factors found relevant to the standards' achievability.

EPA itself acknowledged in this case that "standards of performance ... must ... meet these conditions for *all variations of operating conditions being considered* anywhere in the country."...

The showing we require does not mean that EPA must perform repeated tests on every plant operating within its regulatory jurisdiction. It does, however, mean that due consideration must be given to the possible impact on emissions of recognized variations in operations and some rationale offered for the achievability of the promulgated standard given the tests conducted and the relevant variables identified....

We must remand to the Agency for a more adequate explanation or, if necessary, for supplementary data to justify the standard in terms of the "representativeness" of the sources tested....

NOTES AND QUESTIONS

1. Both the *National Asphalt* and *National Lime* cases found the designation of an industry as a significant contributor to be judicially reviewable under section 307(b)(1), 42 U.S.C. § 7607(b)(1). Note also that *National Lime* suggests that an industry may be a significant contributor if it significantly contributes to pollution endangering the public welfare, whatever its effect may or may not be on public health.

2. The same court of appeals decided both cases. Do the cases utilize the same standard of review? If so, do you think they apply the standard in the same manner?

3. In 1977, the definition of "standard of performance" in section 111(a)(1), 42 U.S.C. § 7411(a)(1), was amended by the addition of "continuous" before "emission reduction." The addition was intended to preclude the use of intermittent controls. H.R. Conf. Rep. No. 564, 95th Cong., 1st Sess. 129

(1977). In 1990 the word "continuous" was deleted from the definition. Aside from increased utilization of intermittent controls, what flexibility is provided to EPA in setting the standard by the deletion? *See* CAA §§ 111(a)(7) and 111(b)(5), 42 U.S.C. §§ 7411(a)(7) and 7411(b)(5).

4. A NSPS applies to any source on which construction or modification is commenced after publication of the standard. CAA § 111(a)(2), 42 U.S.C. § 7411(a)(2). As to when construction is commenced, see *Potomac Elec. Power Co. v. EPA*, 650 F.2d 509 (4th Cir. 1981), *cert. denied*, 455 U.S. 1016 (1982); *Sierra Pac. Power v. EPA*, 647 F.2d 60 (9th Cir. 1981); and *United States v. City of Painesville*, 644 F.2d 1186 (6th Cir. 1981), *cert. denied*, 454 U.S. 894 (1981). "Modification" is defined as

> ... any physical change in, or change in the method of operation of, a stationary source which increases the amount of any air pollutant emitted by such source or which results in the emission of any air pollutant not previously emitted.

CAA § 111(a)(4), 42 U.S.C. § 7411(a)(4). In determining whether there has been an increase in any air pollutant, measurement is based on atmospheric emissions, not pre-controlled emissions. *National-Southwire Aluminum Co. v. EPA*, 838 F.2d 835 (6th Cir. 1988), *cert. denied*, 488 U.S. 955 (1988). Could turning off or removing obsolete or ineffective pollution control equipment at a plant be a "modification" if emissions substantially increase? *See id.* (concluding that it is a modification unless, under the regulations, the equipment is replaced with equipment more environmentally beneficial).

5. Recall the earlier discussion on pages 427-28 *supra*, of the use of the bubble to avoid new source review. The only statutory definition of "stationary source" is in section 111(a)(3), 42 U.S.C. § 7411(a)(3), which defines the term as "any building, structure, facility, or installation which emits or may emit any air pollutant." The D.C. Court of Appeals held that the bubble may not be used to avoid compliance with a NSPS. The court concluded that the definition focuses on a single building, structure, facility or installation, precluding combination of such units under the bubble concept. Moreover, the court found use of the bubble would undermine the NSPS's purpose to *enhance* air quality, not merely maintain it. *Asarco, Inc. v. EPA*, 578 F.2d 319 (D.C. Cir. 1978). *Asarco* was decided before *Chevron*, pages 428-34 *supra*. Could EPA today authorize use of the bubble in determining whether there has been a modification for purposes of a NSPS?

6. Recall that the PSD and nonattainment provisions of the Act require preconstruction review of new sources and that every area of the country is a PSD or nonattainment area for at least one NAAQS. What, then, is the purpose of the NSPS? When would it apply when preconstruction review for PSD and nonattainment purposes would not?

Although major new sources are subject to overlapping regulatory requirements, major existing sources in some cases may escape regulation altogether.

If such a source emits pollutants for which there are no NAAQSs or hazardous air pollutant standards (HAPs) and the SIP does not limit emissions, the source may be free to pollute. To address this possibility, section 111(d) requires states to have plans to control emissions by existing sources of pollutants that are covered by a NSPS but not by a NAAQS or HAP. CAA § 111(d)(1), 42 U.S.C. § 7411(d)(1). EPA has only recently begun to do much to enforce this requirement. 2 S. NOVICK, LAW OF ENVIRONMENTAL PROTECTION § 11.03[1][c].

7. States may assume responsibility from EPA for implementation and enforcement of NSPSs, although EPA continues to have enforcement authority. CAA § 111(c), 42 U.S.C. § 7411(c). Every state has been delegated at least enforcement authority for the NSPS. *See* 40 C.F.R. § 60.4(b).

2. HAZARDOUS AIR POLLUTANTS (HAPs)

The 1970 version of section 112 authorized EPA to set uniform emission limitations for hazardous pollutants at a level that would provide an "ample margin of safety" to protect public health. CAA § 112(b)(2)(B), 42 U.S.C. § 7412(b)(1)(B). This health-based standard could be read to preclude consideration of cost and technological feasibility, and to require, in cases of scientific uncertainty about the level of safe exposure to a pollutant, that emissions be set at a zero-risk level. EPA moved very slowly in promulgating the standards, and what standards were promulgated were targets for challenges by industry for being too stringent and from environmentalists as too lax. By 1980 EPA had regulated only four pollutants. 1983 CEQ Ann. Rep. 35. In 1984 EPA took a new approach to regulation, incorporating risk assessment and limited consideration of costs and technological feasibility in the decisionmaking process. This approach was promptly challenged in court as inconsistent with the statutory standard. *Natural Resources Defense Council v. EPA*, 824 F.2d 1146 (D.C. Cir. 1987) (the Administrator must first determine what is a "safe" level of exposure without regard to cost and technological feasibility; then may consider these factors in the second step of determining what is an "ample margin of safety"). In 1990 Congress abandoned the health-based standard for an approach similar to that which EPA had adopted in 1984. The few standards adopted under the old section 112 continue in effect until modified under new section 112, 42 U.S.C. § 7412. *See generally* Robert L. Munroe, Comment, *The Clean Air Act Amendments of 1990: Will Hazardous Air Pollutants Finally Be Regulated?* 5 ADMIN. L.J. 161 (1991).

Section 112, as amended, establishes a statutory list of 189 hazardous air pollutants; requires EPA to list all categories of major sources and area sources of each listed pollutant; mandates a standard of "maximum achievable control technology" (MACT) for all new and existing major sources in accordance with a statutory schedule; and requires a second phase of regulation to protect the public health with an ample margin of safety from any residual risks remaining after application of MACT. CAA § 112, 42 U.S.C. § 7412. *See generally* Munroe, *supra*.

a. Listing of Hazardous Pollutants

EPA may add to the statutory list pollutants which present or may present a threat of adverse human health effects or adverse environmental effects. CAA § 112(b)(2), 42 U.S.C. § 7412(b)(2). Upon petition to EPA from any person the list may also be modified by either adding or deleting a substance. CAA § 112(b)(3), 42 U.S.C. § 7412(b)(3). EPA is to add a substance upon either the petitioner's showing or EPA's determination that the substance is an air pollutant and that as "emissions, ambient concentrations, bioaccumulation, or deposition," the substance is known or might "reasonably be anticipated to cause adverse effects" to human health or to the environment. *Id.* Hence a pollutant need not already have been proven to cause adverse health effects to be listed, as the possibility that it poses such a threat is sufficient to subject it to regulation.

To delete a substance from the list, the petitioner must show or EPA must determine that there is enough data on the effects of the pollutant to demonstrate that neither its emission, its ambient concentration, its bioaccumulation, nor its deposition may reasonably be expected to cause any adverse health or environmental effects. CAA § 112(b)(3)(C), 42 U.S.C. § 7412(b)(3)(C). On June 18, 1996, EPA published a final rule amending the list of HAPs in § 112(b)(1) by removing one substance, 61 Fed. Reg. 30,816 (1996).

b. Source Categories

By November 15, 1991, EPA was to publish a list of all categories and subcategories of major sources and area sources of listed hazardous air pollutants, consistent as far as practicable with the list of source categories developed in the context of new source performance standards, and to revise the list at least once every eight years thereafter. CAA § 112(c)(1), 42 U.S.C. § 7412(c)(1). The list of area source categories had to include by November 15, 1995 enough area source categories to ensure that ninety percent of the area source emissions of the thirty hazardous air pollutants posing the greatest threat to public health in the largest number of urban areas are subject to section 112 regulation. CAA § 112(c)(3), 42 U.S.C. § 7412(c)(3). General provisions for administration of the program under 40 C.F.R. pt. 61 were promulgated on March 16, 1994. The initial list of 174 categories of source was published on July 16, 1992.

A "major" source is

> any stationary source or group of stationary sources located within a contiguous area and under common control that emits or has the potential to emit considering controls, in the aggregate, 10 tons per year or more of any hazardous air pollutant or 25 tons per year or more of any combination

of hazardous air pollutants. The Administrator may establish a lesser quantity, or in the case of radionuclides different criteria, for a major source than that specified in the previous sentence, on the basis of the potency of the air pollutant, persistence, potential for bioaccumulation, other characteristics of the air pollutant, or other relevant factors.

CAA § 112(a)(1), 42 U.S.C. § 7412(a)(1). "Area source" is simply defined as any stationary source that is not a major source, other than motor vehicles. CAA § 112(a)(2), 42 U.S.C. § 7412(a)(2). The legislative history indicates that area sources were meant to include small, diverse sources that substantially contribute to emissions of hazardous pollutants, such as dry cleaners, wood stoves, and service stations. S. Rep. No. 228, 101st Cong., 1st Sess. 186 (1989). Adding a pollutant to the list and listing of a source category or subcategory are *not* judicially reviewable until the emission standard has been promulgated. CAA § 112(e)(4), 42 U.S.C. § 7412(e)(4). Why would Congress delay review until the standard is promulgated?

A source category may be deleted from the list if it was included solely because of its emission of a single listed substance which has since been deleted from the list of hazardous air pollutants. CAA § 112(c)(9)(A), 42 U.S.C. § 7412(c)(9)(A). Upon petition or EPA's own motion, a category may be deleted if EPA finds either that no source in a category of sources of carcinogens emits the hazardous air pollutants in quantities posing a lifetime cancer risk of over one in a million to the individual most exposed to the pollutants; or, for sources of non-carcinogenic hazardous air pollutants, that no source in the category emits the pollutant at a higher level than the maximum level which will protect public health with an adequate margin of safety and prevent any adverse environmental effects. CAA § 112(c)(9)(B), 42 U.S.C. § 7412(c)(9)(B). EPA must take action on a petition for deletion of a source category from the list within one year of the petition's being filed. *Id.*

c. Emission Standards

(1) Technology-Based Standards

The foundation for the new approach to regulation of HAPs is the technology-based MACT standard. Emission standards for hazardous air pollutants must require the maximum degree of emission reductions that EPA determines to be achievable, including, if necessary, a prohibition on emissions. CAA § 112(d)(2), 42 U.S.C. § 7412(d)(2). In making this determination, EPA is to consider the cost of achieving the emission reduction and "any non-air quality health and environmental impacts and energy requirements." *Id.* Where a health threshold has been established for a pollutant, EPA may consider the threshold level, with an ample margin of safety, when establishing emission standards. CAA § 112(d)(4), 42 U.S.C. § 7412(d)(4). If EPA thinks it infeasible to establish or to enforce an emission standard for control of a hazardous air pollutant or pollutants, EPA may instead promulgate any one or a combination of "design, equipment, work practice, or operational standard[s]" to meet the emission standard. CAA § 112(h)(1), 42 U.S.C. § 7412(h)(1). For an emission standard to be infeasible, EPA must determine that a hazardous air pollutant cannot be emitted through a conveyance designed to emit or capture the pollutant, or that use of such a conveyance would be illegal, or that the application of measurement methodology to a particular class of sources is technologically or economically impracticable. CAA § 112(h)(2), 42 U.S.C. § 7412(h)(2).

For a new source, emission standards must require controls at least as stringent as the emission control "achieved in practice by the best controlled similar source." CAA § 112(d)(3), 42 U.S.C. § 7412(d)(3). Emission standards for existing sources may be less stringent than those for new sources, but must require at least the average emission limitation achieved by the best performing twelve percent of the existing sources in the same category, or, for categories with fewer than thirty sources, by the best performing five sources. *Id.* With area sources, the Administrator may choose to impose a standard based on generally available control technologies or practices rather than MACT or a health-based standard. CAA § 112(d)(5), 42 U.S.C. § 7412(d)(5). Categorization of sources is, therefore, quite important because the MACT standard is evaluated by the performance of other sources in the same category or subcategory.

EPA is given a timetable of several years for regulation of hazardous air pollutant source categories. CAA § 112(e), 42 U.S.C. § 7412(e). By November 15, 1992, emission standards for at least 40 source categories and subcategories other than coke oven batteries had to be promulgated, and standards for coke oven batteries had to be promulgated by December 31, 1992. CAA § 112(e)(1), 42 U.S.C. § 7412(e)(1). Twenty-five percent of the listed categories and subcategories must be regulated by November 15, 1994; another 25 percent had to be regulated by November 15, 1997. All categories and subcategories must be regulated by November 15, 2000. *Id.* When determining its priorities for regulating categories under the timetable provided by Congress, EPA is to consider the known or anticipated adverse effects of the listed pollutants on public health and the environment, the quantity and location of emissions or reasonably anticipated emissions of listed pollutants that are produced by each category or subcategory, and the efficiency of grouping categories or subcategories according to the pollutants emitted or according to the processes or technologies used. CAA § 112(e)(2), 42 U.S.C. § 7412(e)(2). EPA announced its schedule for promulgating the MACT rules on November 15, 1993. 58 Fed. Reg. 63,941 (1993).

(2) Residual Risk Management

The new structure for hazardous air pollutant regulation does make some provision for health-based standards under section 112(f) after the bulk of technology-based standards have been promulgated. CAA § 112(f), 42 U.S.C.

§ 7412(f). *See generally* Bradford C. Mank, *What Comes After Technology: Using and "Exceptions Process" to Improve Residual Risk Regulation of Hazardous Air Pollution*, 13 STAN. ENVTL. L.J. 263 (1994); Janet L. McQuaid, Note, *Risk Assessment of Hazardous Air Pollutants Under the EPA's Final Benzene Rules and the Clean Air Act Amendments of 1990*, 70 TEX. L. REV. 427 (1991). By November 15, 1996, EPA was to report to Congress on methods of calculating the remaining risk to public health after application of the technology-based standards to sources subject to hazardous air pollutant regulation, the public health significance of the estimated remaining risk, technologically and commercially available methods of reducing that risk, the actual health effects for persons living near the sources, any available epidemiological or other health studies, risks presented by background concentrations of the listed pollutants, any uncertainties in risk assessment methodology or any other health assessment technique, any negative health or environmental consequences to the community of efforts to reduce public health risks, and, finally, recommendations for legislation regarding the remaining risk. CAA § 112(f)(1), 42 U.S.C. § 7412 (f)(1). EPA complied in 1993. 58 Fed. Reg. 42760 (1993).

If Congress itself does not legislate to control residual risks, within eight years after the promulgation of the technology-based standards for each source category or subcategory EPA must determine whether additional standards are necessary to provide an ample margin of safety to protect public health. The residual risk emission standard promulgated must provide an ample margin of safety to protect public health. An even *more stringent* standard may be promulgated if necessary to prevent adverse environmental effects, taking into consideration costs, energy, safety, and other relevant factors. CAA § 112(f)(2)(A), 42 U.S.C. § 7412 (f)(2)(A). Adverse environmental effects is broadly defined in section 112(a)(7), 42 U.S.C. § 7412(a)(7). EPA must make such a determination for each regulated category and subcategory of major sources listed under section 112(d), 42 U.S.C. § 7412(d), and promulgate additional standards if necessary to prevent adverse environmental effects or protect public health. For known, probable or possible human carcinogens, if the MACT standard still poses a lifetime excess cancer risk of one in one million or greater to the individual most exposed to the emission, the Administrator *must* promulgate a residual risk emission standard that will provide an ample margin of safety. *Id.*

(3) Compliance

Deadlines for compliance with the standards depends upon the source's classification as a "new" or "existing" source and whether the standard is the technology-based MACT standard or the health-based, residual risk standard. "New source" is defined to include reconstruction of a source. CAA § 112(a)(4), 42 U.S.C. § 7412(a)(4). After the effective date of a hazardous emission standard, whether a MACT or a residual risk standard, no major source subject to the standard may be constructed or reconstructed unless EPA, or a state with a Title V permit program, determines that the source will comply with the standard. CAA § 112(i)(1), 42 U.S.C. § 7412(i)(1). A new source commencing construction or reconstruction after either type of standard is proposed and before it is promulgated may delay compliance for three years after final promulgation, however, if the promulgated standard is more stringent than the proposed standard, and the source complies with the proposed standard during the three-year period. CAA § 112(i)(2), 42 U.S.C. § 7412(i)(2). If a source commences construction after a technology-based emission standard is proposed but before a health-based standard is proposed, the source has ten years from the date construction is commenced in which to comply with the health-based standard. CAA § 112(i)(7), 42 U.S.C. § 7412(i)(7).

A residual risk standard is effective as soon as it is promulgated. CAA § 112(f)(3), 42 U.S.C. § 7412(f)(3). An existing source, however, has 90 days from the effective date to come into compliance with the standard, and may be granted a waiver allowing it two years to come into compliance if EPA finds that the extra time is necessary for the source to install controls and that during the period of the waiver steps will be taken to protect the health of all affected persons from imminent endangerment. CAA § 112(f)(4), 42 U.S.C. § 7412(f)(4).

EPA must establish a compliance date of no later than three years after its promulgation of a new MACT standard for each category or subcategory of existing sources affected by the new standard. CAA § 112(i)(3)(A), 42 U.S.C. § 7412 (i)(3)(A). EPA, or a state with a Title V permit program, may issue a permit granting an extension of up to one additional year to an existing source, if the extra time is necessary for the installation of controls. CAA § 112(i)(3)(B), 42 U.S.C. § 7412(i)(3)(B). A few other limited exemptions and deadline extensions for new and existing sources are provided from MACT and residual risk standards. *See, e.g.*, CAA § 112(i)(4)-(6), 42 U.S.C. § 7412(i)(4)-(6).

If an existing source is modified, however, the deadline for compliance with MACT is accelerated. CAA § 112(g)(2), 42 U.S.C. § 7412(g)(2). After the effective date of a Title V permit program in any state, a modification may only be made in that state where the maximum achievable control technology (MACT) emission limitation for existing sources will be met. *Id.* A "modification" is defined as

> any physical change in, or change in the method of operation of, a major source which increases the actual emissions of any hazardous air pollutant emitted by such source by more than a de minimis amount or which results in the emission of any hazardous air pollutant not previously emitted by more than a de minimis amount.

CAA § 112(a)(5), 42 U.S.C. § 7412(a)(5). Accelerated compliance may be avoided if a modification is offset by a greater or equal decrease in the quantity of emissions of a more hazardous air pollutant. CAA § 112(g)(1)(A), 42 U.S.C. § 7412(g)(1)(A). Moreover, if a source is constructed, reconstructed, or modified after the effective date of a state permit program and before a MACT standard has been promulgated, state permit writers must impose MACT on a case-by-case basis in issuing state permits. CAA § 112(g)(2), 42 U.S.C. § 7412(g)(2). EPA published its final § 112(g) rule on December 27, 1996. 61 Fed. Reg. 68,384 (1996).

EPA was to publish guidance by May 15, 1992 identifying the relative hazard to human health created by emissions of each listed pollutant, in order to allow the owner or operator of a modified source to more easily show that the modification has been offset. CAA § 112(g)(1)(B), 42 U.S.C. § 7412(g)(1)(B). EPA did so nearly two years later. 59 Fed. Reg. 15503, 15549-63 (Apr. 1, 1994) (offset guidance).

If EPA has failed to promulgate a MACT standard for a listed category of sources within 18 months of its deadline to do so, state permit writers must impose MACT on a case-by-case basis in issuing state permits for all sources. CAA § 112(j), 42 U.S.C. § 7412(j); *see also* 40 C.F.R. pt. 63, subpart B. This MACT "hammer" provision ensures that sources emitting HAPs will not be allowed to avoid the MACT standard if EPA fails in its administrative responsibilities.

A few other provisions deserve mention. Section 112(r) establishes a new program for prevention, detention, and response to accidental releases of hazardous air pollutants, such as that which occurred in Bhopal, India on December 3, 1984. CAA § 112(r), 42 U.S.C. § 7412(r), *see also* 61 Fed. Reg. 31,668 (1996) (final rule establishing a three tier program). Other new programs require the Administrator to evaluate the effects of HAPs on the Great Lakes, Chesapeake Bay, and coastal waters (CAA § 112(m), 42 U.S.C. § 7412(m)); to address regulation of radionuclide emissions (CAA § 112(d)(9), 42 U.S.C. § 7412(d)(9)); to control incinerator emissions (CAA § 129, 42 U.S.C. § 7429); and to regulate coke oven emissions (CAA § 112(d)(8), 42 U.S.C. § 7412(d)(8)).

3. MOTOR VEHICLE EMISSION STANDARDS

Motor vehicle emission standards are a regulatory world unto themselves with a complex history of battles waged between Congress, EPA, the courts and the automobile industry. Although motor vehicle emissions have been regulated by Congress since 1965, see Pub. L. No. 89-272, 79 Stat. 992 (1965), the first stringent attempt to control emissions was in the 1970 Clean Air Act when Congress mandated a 90% "rollback" (reduction) of emissions from new light/heavy-duty vehicles of hydrocarbons (HC) and carbon monoxide (CO) within five years and of nitrous oxide (NO_x) within six years. Light duty vehicles are passenger cars; EPA has separate standards based on gross vehicle weight rating (GVWR) for light duty trucks (such as recreational vehicles) and heavy duty vehicles (such as trucks and buses). S. NOVICK, LAW OF ENVIRONMENTAL PROTECTION § 11.07[2]. With the benefit of hindsight, a 90% reduction in emissions from such passenger cars over a five- to six-year period was extraordinarily demanding and, in fact, did not occur. The major domestic and import automobile manufacturers in 1972 requested a one-year statutory extension of the deadlines for HC and CO which was denied by EPA. The denial was promptly challenged in court. In the landmark decision of *International Harvester v. Ruckelshaus*, 478 F.2d 615 (D.C. Cir. 1973), Judge Leventhal remanded the decision to EPA for further proceedings because the manufacturers had demonstrated that the technology would not be available in time to meet the deadline and EPA's conclusion otherwise was inconsistent with a study of the National Academy of Sciences required by the Act for consideration of the extension. On remand EPA not only granted the extensions for HC and CO, but for NO$_X$ as well. Through a series of EPA waivers and Congressional extensions the 90% rollback for HC of 0.41 grams per mile and for CO of 3.4 grams per mile were not implemented until the 1980 and 1981 model year, respectively. S. NOVICK, *supra*, § 11.06[2]. The 90% reduction of NO$_X$ to 0.4 grams per mile would not again be required under the Act until passage of the 1990 amendments. These "technology-forcing" standards did, however, lead to development of the catalytic converter, which converts HC, NO$_X$ and CO into carbon dioxide, water vapor and nitrogen gas, and could be added on to the exhaust system without necessitating fundamental changes in basic engine design. *Id.* § 11.06[4].

EPA had greater success in the court of appeals with its regulation of diesel vehicles and heavy duty vehicles. In *NRDC v. EPA*, 655 F.2d 318 (D.C. Cir.), *cert. denied sub nom. General Motors Corp. v. Gorsuch*, 454 U.S. 1017 (1981), the plaintiffs asserted that EPA had to set emission standards for light-duty diesel vehicles on the basis of the vehicle's capability of meeting the most stringent standard rather than through industry-wide consideration. The court concluded that although section 202 requires emission standards for all motor vehicles for CO, HC, and NO$_X$, standards for particulates are only required for heavy-duty vehicles. Diesel engines, which are more fuel efficient and produce lower emissions of CO and HC than gasoline engines, emit more NO$_X$ and many times more particulates. *See id.* at 322, 340. A similar argument that the standards for heavy-duty vehicles be based on the technological leader failed in *NRDC v. Thomas*, 805 F.2d 410 (D.C. Cir. 1986). In that case, the court of appeals also set out three conditions for assessing the reasonableness of EPA's projection that technology will be available for purposes of section 202(a): (1) EPA must identify the projected technology to be used and respond to objections to utilization of that technology for the standard; (2) EPA must identify the basic steps necessary for development of the technology; and (3) EPA must offer a plausible basis for concluding that these steps can be completed within the lead time necessary for the automobile industry to "retool" with the necessary technology.

There are several major mechanisms for enforcement by EPA of the motor vehicle emission standards of section 202. EPA can review compliance at the prototype, assembly line, and in-use stages. Generally, for prototype testing, manufacturers must test a prototype representing an "engine family." If the prototype's emissions, with a deterioration factor to reflect decreasing efficiency over time, is under the applicable standard after a designated period of usage, EPA issues a certificate of conformity. The manufacturer may not introduce a vehicle into commerce before receiving certification, and, after certification, may not introduce into commerce a vehicle that does not conform to the prototype certified. CAA § 203(a)(1), 42 U.S.C. § 7522(a)(1). To protect against slippage from prototype to mass production, EPA may test vehicles on the assembly line to determine if a prescribed percentage are conforming to applicable standards; if they do not, EPA may revoke the certificate of conformity. CAA § 206(b)(1), 42 U.S.C. § 7525(b)(1). EPA may also recall any class of vehicles if a substantial number, although properly maintained and used, do not conform with applicable standards when in use throughout their "useful life." CAA § 207(c), 42 U.S.C. § 7541(c).

Among other warranties, manufacturers must provide a warranty to owners that guarantees that each new vehicle is designed, built, and equipped to conform with emission standards at the time of sale and that the vehicle is free from defects in materials or workmanship which would cause it to exceed standards within a designated warranty period after sale. If a defect causes the vehicle to exceed emission standards, the manufacturer must make the necessary repairs free of charge. Manufacturers must also guarantee for two years or 24,000 miles that if a vehicle fails a state inspection and maintenance program with sanctions for such failure, the manufacturer will make the repairs free of charge. Warranties are enforceable between the vehicle owner and the manufacturer, but EPA may also enforce warranties and prosecute manufacturers who fail to honor them. CAA § 207(a), 42 U.S.C. § 7541(a).

Manufacturers, as well as auto mechanics, fleet owners, and individuals, are prohibited from tampering knowingly with any device or element for compliance with emission standards. CAA § 203(a)(3), 42 U.S.C. § 7522(a)(3). EPA has other basic enforcement powers, as well as the power to seek injunctions and penalties in court, and to assess administrative penalties. CAA §§ 204-205, 42 U.S.C. §§ 7523-7524.

To a limited extent, emissions have also been controlled through regulation of fuels and fuel additives. Fuels and fuel additives must be registered with EPA before sale or introduction into commerce. CAA § 211(a), 42 U.S.C. § 7545(a). However, EPA also has the power to

> ... regulat[e], control or prohibit the manufacture, introduction into commerce, offering for sale or sale of any fuel or fuel additive ... (A) if in the judgment of the Administration any emission product of such fuel or fuel additive causes, or contributes, to air pollution which may reasonably be anticipated to endanger the public health or welfare, or (B) if emission products of such fuel or fuel additive will impair to a significant degree the performance of any emission control device....

CAA § 211(c), 42 U.S.C. § 7545(c). EPA has focused its regulatory efforts on reduction of lead in gasoline, due to both health effects and its detrimental effect on operation of the catalytic converter. *See, e.g., Amoco Oil Co. v. EPA*, 501 F.2d 722 (D.C. Cir. 1974) and 543 F.2d 270 (D.C. Cir. 1976) (regulation under section 211(c)(1)(B) for interference with emission controls); *Ethyl Corp. v. EPA, 541 F.2d 1 (D.C. Cir. 1976)*, cert. *denied sub nom. DuPont v. EPA*, 426 U.S. 941 (1976) (regulation under section 211(c)(1)(A) for health effects). The phasedown of lead culminates in the 1990 amendments which prohibit the sale of fuel which contains lead or lead additives after December 31, 1995. CAA § 211(n), 42 U.S.C. § 7545(n). The amendments put much more emphasis on fuel and fuel additive regulation than the prior versions of the Act. *See generally* Henry A. Waxman et al., *Cars, Fuels, and Clean Air: A Review of Title II of the Clean Air Act Amendments of 1990*, 21 ENVTL. L. 1947 (1991).

All of this discussion serves as necessary background to the current state of regulation of motor vehicle emissions under the 1990 amendments, as summarized in the following article.

M. WALSH, MOTOR VEHICLES IN THE CLEAN AIR ACT AMENDMENTS (1991)*

As the primary source of hydrocarbons (HC), carbon monoxide (CO), and nitrogen oxides (NO_x) in the atmosphere, motor vehicles received special attention in the Clean Air Act of 1970. Despite progress in controlling emissions of these chemicals, they again were a focal point of the Clean Air Act Amendments of 1990, largely because 50 million more cars are on U.S. highways now than in 1970, and motor vehicles remain the dominant source of such emissions. In addition to more stringent standards for cars, trucks, and buses, the 1990 amendments:

— Require that conventional fuels be substantially modified;
— Increase opportunities for introducing alternative fuels, without mandating them; and
— Extend manufacturer's responsibility for complying with the act's standards for existing autos to 10 years or 100,000 miles, whichever occurs first.

The 1990 amendments' mobile-source provisions:

— Require steady progress on reducing harmful emissions from conventional vehicles and fuels;
— Reflect Congress' decision not to mandate alternative fuels or vehicles that would require them; to adopt standards that can be met with

---

*Reprinted with permission from a 1991 special report: *The Clean Air Act Amendments: BNA's Comprehensive Analysis of the New Law* (BSP-150) published by the Bureau of National Affairs, Inc.

conventional vehicles or flexible-fuel vehicles; and to let vehicle manufacturers decide which to use to comply with the act; and
— Reject efforts to prevent California and other states from adopting requirements necessary to attain clean air goals.

However, the act reduces California's ability to regulate off-road vehicles and authorizes no aid beyond current law to other states that want to adopt controls as stringent as California's.

CONVENTIONAL VEHICLES

Light-Duty Vehicle Tailpipe Standards

Tier 1

In adopting light-duty vehicle standards, Congress considered both near term (Tier 1) and longer term (Tier 2) standards.

Tables 1 and 2 summarize Tier 1 tailpipe standards for light-duty vehicles.

TABLE 1. Emission Standards for Light-Duty Vehicles (Passenger Cars) and Light-Duty Trucks (LDTs) of up to 6000 lbs. GVWR

Vehicle Type	Column A (5 yrs/50,000 mi)				Column B (10 yrs/100,000 mi)			
	NMHC	CO	NO_x	Part.	NMHC	CO	NO_x	Part.
NON-DIESEL								
LDTs (0-3,750 lbs. LVW) and light-duty vehicles	0.25	3.4	0.4	—	0.31	4.2	0.6	—
LDTs (3,751-5,750 lbs. LVW	0.32	4.4	0.7	—	0.40	5.5	0.97	—
DIESEL								
LDTs (0-3,750 lbs. LVW) and light-duty vehicles	0.25	3.4	1.0	0.08	0.31	4.2	1.25	0.20
LDTs (3,751-5,750 lbs. LVW)	0.32	4.4	—	0.08	0.40	5.0	0.97	0.10

TABLE 2. Emission Standards for Light-Duty Trucks of More than 6,000 lbs. GVWR

	Column A (5 yrs/50,000 mi)			Column B (11 yrs/120,000 mi)			
LTD Test Weight	NMHC	CO	NO$_x$	NMHC	CO	NO$_x$	PM
3,751-5,750 lbs.	0.32	4.4	0.7*	0.46	6.4	0.98	0.10
Over 5,750 lbs.	0.39	5.0	1.1*	0.56	7.3	1.53	0.12

Standards are expressed in grams per mile (gpm).

*Not applicable to diesel-fueled LDTs.

Certification standards are those that a prototype of a vehicle must meet before that vehicle can be sold to the public. For the first two years that passenger cars and light-duty trucks are subject to the Tier I certification standards in Table 1 above, less stringent, intermediate in-use emission standards apply for purposes of recall liability, and the useful-life period is only five years or 50,000 miles, whichever occurs first.

....

For certification purposes, the standards in Table 1 will be phased in over a three-year period (applicable to 40 percent of model year [MY] 1994 vehicles, 80 percent of MY 1995 vehicles, and all MY 1996 vehicles). The standards covering NO$_x$ from in-use vehicles will be phased in, with 40 percent of a manufacturer's sales of vehicles required to comply in 1994, 80 percent in 1995, and 100 percent in 1996. For HC, the act requires 40 percent of sales in 1994 to meet the intermediate in-use standard of 0.32 grams per mile (gpm) non-methane hydrocarbon (NMHC), with the remainder achieving the current standard. This will increase to 80 percent in 1995, and in 1996, 60 percent must meet the intermediate standard, with the other 40 percent meeting the final standard (0.25 NMHC). In 1997, 80 percent will be required to meet the 0.25 level, and 100 percent will be required by 1998.

New standards that cover vehicles during the first 100,000 miles they are in use will be phased in, starting in 1996. New vehicles will be tested only through their first 75,000 miles for the purpose of recall liability. The standards allow for 25 percent higher emissions levels between 50,000 and 100,000 miles for HC and CO, and 50 percent higher for NO$_x$. Diesel-powered vehicles will be allowed to emit 1.0 grams of NO$_x$ per mile. Trucks under 3,750 pounds loaded vehicle weight (LVW) will be required to achieve the same standard as cars.

....

For recall purposes, if a vehicle is tested in-use prior to five years or 50,000 miles, the 50,000-mile certification standards apply. If the vehicle is tested after five years or 50,000 miles, the 100,000-mile certification standards apply for passenger cars and light-duty trucks up to 6,000 pounds GVWR, and the

120,000-mile certification standard applies for light-duty trucks over 6,000 pounds GVWR.

Although passenger cars and light-duty trucks must meet in-use standards for their full useful lives, the Environmental Protection Agency may not conduct recall testing on passenger cars and light-duty trucks up to 6,000 pounds that are more than seven years old or have been driven more than 75,000 miles, or on light-duty trucks over 6,000 pounds GVWR that are over seven years old or been driven more than 90,000 miles.

Tier 2 Standards

EPA is required to study and report to Congress no later than June 1, 1997, on the technological feasibility, the need for, and the cost effectiveness of the standards shown in Table 6 for passenger cars and light-duty trucks of 3,750 pounds LVW or less.

Table 6. Tier 2 Emission Standards for
Gasoline- and Diesel-Fueled Passenger Cars
and Light-Duty Trucks, 3,750 Lbs. LVW or Less

Pollutant	Emission Level
NMHC	0.125 gpm
NO_x	0.2 gpm
CO	1.7 gpm

Within three years after reporting to Congress, but not later than Dec. 31, 1999, EPA is required to:

— Promulgate the Tier 2 standards for model years starting not earlier than model year 2003 and not later than model year 2006;

— Promulgate standards different from those shown in Table 6, provided they are more stringent than the Tier 1 standards for model years starting not earlier than Jan. 1, 2003, or later than the 2006 model year; or

— Determine that standards more stringent than the Tier 1 levels are not technologically feasible, needed, or cost-effective. If the EPA administrator fails to act, the Tier 2 standards go into effect with the model years starting after Jan. 1, 2003.

Potential Revision of Standards

EPA retains the authority to revise emission standards for all classes of motor vehicles and engines based on the need to protect the public welfare, except that the administrator may not revise the specific emission standards established in the act for passenger cars, light-duty trucks, and heavy-duty trucks before the 2004 model year.

Cold-Temperature CO Standards

Beginning with the 1994 model year, EPA is required to establish a cold-temperature (20 degrees Fahrenheit) CO standard of 10.0 gpm for passenger cars and a comparable level for light-duty trucks.

....

The useful life for the cold-temperature CO standards is five years or 50,000 miles, but EPA may extend this period if it determines such requirements are technologically feasible.

Trucks and Buses

New Heavy-Duty Vehicles

The 1990 Clean Air Act replaces the statutory standards for HC, CO, and NO_X for heavy-duty vehicles and engines issued under the Clean Air Act of 1977 with a general requirement that standards applicable to emissions of HC, CO, NO_X, and particulates reflect:

> ... the greatest degree of emission reduction achievable throughout the application of technology which the Administrator determines will be available for the model year to which such standards apply, giving appropriate consideration to cost, energy, and safety factors associated with the application of such technology.

Existing EPA standards will remain in effect, and the agency can relax or strengthen them on the basis of information concerning the effects of air pollutants from heavy-duty vehicles and other mobile sources on public health and welfare, taking costs into consideration.

The new act establishes a 4.0 grams per brake horsepower hour (g/BHP-hr) NO_X standard for 1998 and later model-year gasoline-fueled and diesel-fueled heavy-duty trucks.

Standards adopted for heavy-duty vehicles cannot go into effect until four years after they are issued, and they cannot be changed for at least three years after they go into effect.

....

EPA also may establish cold-temperature CO standards for heavy-duty vehicles and engines.

Urban Buses

The act relaxes the existing 1991 model-year 0.1 g/BHP-hr particulate standard for urban buses to 0.25 g/BHP-hr for the 1991 and 1992 model years and sets the particulate standard at 0.1 g/BHP-hr for the 1992 model year.

Starting with the 1994 model year, EPA is required to establish separate emission standards for urban buses, including a particulate standard of 0.05 g/BHP-hr, or 50 percent more stringent than the present 0.1 g/BHP-hr standard. If EPA determines the 50 percent level is not technologically feasible, the agency must increase the allowable level of particulate to no greater than 70 percent of the 0.1 g/BHP-hr level; that is, 0.07 g/BHP-hr.

The act also requires EPA to conduct annual tests on a representative sample of operating urban buses to determine whether they meet the particulate standard over their full useful life. If the agency determines that buses are not meeting the particulate standard, it must require buses sold in areas with populations of 750,000 or more to operate on low-polluting fuels such as methanol, ethanol, or propane natural gas. EPA may extend this requirement to buses sold in other areas if it determines that such action will be a significant benefit to public health. The low-polluting fuel requirement would be phased in over five model years, starting three years after EPA determined that it was needed.

Not later than Nov. 15, 1991, EPA is required to promulgate emission standards or emission control technology requirements that reflect the best retrofit technology and maintenance practices reasonably achievable. These standards will apply to engines replaced or rebuilt after Jan. 1, 1995, for buses operating in areas with populations of 750,000 or more.

Onboard Refueling Control Systems

By Nov. 15, 1991, and after consulting with the Department of Transportation on safety issues, EPA must issue regulations mandating that passenger cars be equipped with vehicle-based ("onboard") systems to control 95 percent of all HC emitted when such vehicles are being refueled. The regulations take effect beginning in the fourth model year after they are adopted, and they will be phased-in over three years: 40 percent of total sales in the first year; 80 percent in the second, and 100 percent in the third year and in subsequent years.

Warranties

The warranty period for 1995 and later model year passenger cars and light-duty trucks for the catalytic converter, electronic emission control unit, onboard diagnostic device, and other emission control equipment designated by EPA as a "specific major emission control component," will be eight years or 80,000 miles, whichever occurs first. To be designated a "specific major emission control component," the device or component must not have been in general use on vehicles and engines prior to the 1990 model year, and it must have a retail cost, excluding installation costs, that exceeds $200.

The warranty for all remaining emission control components is two years or 24,000 miles, whichever occurs first.

The act gives EPA the authority to establish the warranty period for other classes of motor vehicles and engines.

Evaporative Controls

By June 15, 1991, EPA is required to establish evaporative HC emission standards for all classes of gasoline-fueled motor vehicles. The standards, which are to take effect as soon as possible, must require the greatest degree of reduction reasonably achievable of evaporative HC emissions during operation ("running losses") and over two or more days of non-use, under ozone-prone summertime conditions.

Toxic Substances

The act also requires EPA to report by June 15, 1992, on the need for and feasibility of controlling unregulated motor vehicle toxic air pollutants, including benzene, formaldehyde, and 1,3 butadiene.

By June 15, 1995, EPA is required to issue regulations to control hazardous air pollutants to the greatest degree achievable through technology that will be available, considering cost, noise, safety, and the time necessary before the technology can be applied. These regulations must, at a minimum, cover benzene and formaldehyde. The amendments do not specify an effective date for the regulations.

Onboard Diagnostics

EPA must issue regulations that require all passenger cars and light-duty trucks to be equipped with onboard diagnostic systems capable of:

— Accurately identifying emission-related system deterioration or malfunctions including, at a minimum, the catalytic converter and oxygen sensor;
— Alerting vehicle owners that they need to maintain or repair their emission-related component or system; and
— Storing and retrieving diagnostic fault codes that are readily accessible.

The regulations are to be phased in starting in 1994, with the first year covering 40 percent of sales, the second year covering 80 percent, and the third year covering 100 percent, but EPA may delay the rules for up to two years for any class or category of motor vehicles if the technology is not feasible.

EPA also may establish onboard diagnostic control requirements for heavy-duty vehicles, but it is not required to do so.

The new act requires each state to establish programs for inspecting onboard diagnostic systems as part of their periodic inspection and maintenance program requirements.

....

Testing and Certification

By Nov. 15, 1991, EPA must add to its certification procedures a test to determine whether 1994 and later model-year passenger cars and light-duty trucks are capable of passing state inspection emission (I/M) tests.

By June 15, 1992, EPA must review and revise, as necessary, the certification test procedures to ensure that motor vehicles are tested under conditions that reflect actual current driving conditions, including fuel, temperature, acceleration, and altitude.

....

Tampering Ban

The amendments extend to individuals the prohibition against tampering with emission controls. The act also prohibits the manufacture, sale, or installation of emission control defeat devices.

CONVENTIONAL FUELS

Reformulated Gasoline

The amendments will cause conventional gasoline to be modified significantly during the 1990s. The act includes separate sets of requirements for ozone problems and for CO problems.

Ozone Non-Attainment Areas

By Nov. 15, 1991, EPA must establish standards for reformulated gasoline that require the greatest achievable reduction of ozone-forming volatile organic compounds (VOCs) and toxic air pollutants, considering costs and technological feasibility.

Beginning Jan. 1, 1995, cleaner, reformulated gasoline must be sold in the nine worst ozone non-attainment areas — those with "severe" or "serious" levels of ozone — with populations over 250,000. Other ozone non-attainment areas — those with "marginal," "moderate," or "serious" levels — are allowed to participate, but EPA may delay for a limited time requirements for selling reformulated gasoline in them if it determines adequate quantities of such fuel can not be made available.

At a minimum, reformulated gasoline must:

> — Not cause NO_x emissions to increase (EPA may modify other require-ments discussed below if necessary to prevent an increase in NO_x emis-sions);
> — Have an oxygen content of at least 2 percent by weight (EPA may waive this requirement if it would interfere with attaining an air quality standard);
> — Contain no more than 1.0 percent benzene by volume; and
> — Contain no heavy metals, including lead or manganese (EPA may waive the prohibition against heavy metals other than lead if it determines that the metal will not increase toxic air pollution emissions from motor vehicles on an aggregate-mass or cancer-risk basis).

In addition, VOC and toxic emissions must be reduced by 15 percent under 1990 baseline levels beginning in 1995, and by 25 percent beginning in the year 2000. EPA may increase or reduce the 25-percent requirement on the basis of technological feasibility and cost considerations, but the reduction beginning in the year 2000 cannot be less than 20 percent. The act defines toxic air pollutants in terms of the aggregate emissions of benzene, 1,3 butadiene, polycyclic organic matter (POM), acetaldehyde, and formaldehyde.

The act allows fuel refiners and suppliers that reduce emissions more than they are required while producing reformulated gasoline to accumulate credits for their excess reductions and to sell the credits to other firms that cannot reduce emissions as cheaply, or to trade them for other credits.

By Nov. 15, 1991, EPA must establish regulations that prohibit each refiner, blender, and importer from introducing into commerce gasoline that on average results in emissions of VOC, NO_X, or toxic substances greater than gasoline it sold in 1990. These regulations must go into effect by Jan. 1, 1995.

CO Non-Attainment Areas

Areas with ambient CO levels of 9.5 parts per million (ppm) or above for 1988 and 1989 must include in their state implementation plan (SIP) a requirement that during that portion of the year in which the area is prone to high ambient concentrations of CO (usually the winter months), all gasoline sold must contain not less than 2.7 percent oxygen by weight. Such requirements are to take effect no later than Nov. 1, 1992, or another date in 1992 set by the EPA administrator. In areas that exceed the 9.5 CO design target for any two-year period after 1989, the 2.7 percent oxygen requirement must go into effect no later than three years after the end of the two-year period.

Areas classified as "serious" CO non-attainment areas that have not attained the air quality standard by the date specified in the act must require that the oxygen level in gasoline be 3.1 percent by weight.

EPA can waive this requirement for an area for up to two years if the area petitions the agency for a waiver and if EPA determines that:

— The use of oxygenated gasoline would prevent or interfere with the area's attainment with a federal or state ambient air quality standard;
— Mobile sources do not contribute significantly to the area's CO levels; or
— The domestic supply of, or distribution capacity for, oxygenated gasoline that meets the applicable requirements is inadequate.

EPA must act on petitions within six months after they are filed.

Fuel Volatility

By June 15, 1991, EPA must promulgate regulations limiting the volatility of gasoline to no greater than nine pounds per square inch (PSI) Reid vapor pressure (RVP) during the high ozone season. EPA may establish a lower RVP in a non-attainment area if it determines that a lower level is necessary to achieve comparable evaporative emissions on a per-vehicle basis. The fuel volatility requirements are to take effect not later than the high-ozone season for 1992.

For fuel blends containing 10 percent ethanol, the applicable RVP limitation may be one pound PSI greater than for conventional gasoline.

Detergent Requirements

Starting Jan. 1, 1995, any gasoline sold nationwide must contain additives to prevent the accumulation of deposits in engines and fuel supply systems.

Lead Phasedown

After Dec. 31, 1995, it will be unlawful to sell, supply, dispense, transport, introduce into commerce, or use gasoline that contains lead or lead additives for highway use.

Lead-Substitute Gasoline Additives

The act requires EPA to develop a test procedure for evaluating the effectiveness of lead-substitute gasoline additives and to arrange for independent testing and evaluation of each additive proposed to be registered as a lead substitute. EPA may impose a user fee to cover the cost of testing any lead-substitute fuel additive.

Engines Requiring Leaded Fuel Banned

EPA is required to prohibit the manufacture, sale, or introduction into commerce of any motor vehicle or non-road engine that can be operated only on leaded gasoline and that is manufactured after the 1992 model year.

....

Misfueling

The amendments also extend to individuals the prohibition against misfueling with leaded gasoline. After Oct. 1, 1993, individuals are prohibited from fueling a diesel-powered vehicle with fuel containing a sulfur content greater than 0.05 percent by weight or with fuel that fails to meet a cetane index minimum of 40, or such equivalent aromatic level as prescribed by the EPA administrator.

CLEAN ALTERNATIVE FUELS

The amendments define "clean alternative fuel" as any fuel, such as methanol, ethanol, or other alcohols, including any mixture thereof that contains 85 percent or more by volume of such alcohol with gasoline or other fuels (reformulated gasoline, diesel, natural gas, liquefied petroleum gas, and hydrogen) or power source (including electricity) used in a clean-fuel vehicle that complies with the amendments' performance requirements.

Fleet Program

By Nov. 15, 1992, EPA must issue regulations implementing the Clean Fuel Fleet Vehicle Program.

The fleet program applies in serious non-attainment areas to fleets of 10 or more vehicles that are centrally refueled or are capable of being centrally refueled, but not including vehicles parked at personal residences each night under normal circumstances.

The program will mandate California's Low Emission Vehicle (LEV) standards for light-duty vehicles (0.075 gpm non-methane organic material, 3.4 gpm CO, and 0.2 gpm NO_x) and light trucks below 6,000 pounds (0.1 gpm non-methane organic gas (NMOG), 0.4 gpm NO_x, 4.4 gpm CO) by 1998, provided these vehicles are offered for sale in California. By 2001, these vehicles will be required to meet these standards without regard to their availability in California.

Under the act, EPA must establish an equivalent wrap-around standard combining exhaust, evaporative, and refueling emissions for LEVs below 8,500 pounds GVWR. This wrap-around standard is to be based on low-emission vehicles (LEVs) using reformulated gasoline that meets the reformulated gasoline standards for the applicable time period. The act allows the manufacturers to decide which standard to use — the LEV tailpipe standards or the wrap-around standards.

Congress followed California's lead in substituting an NMOG standard for the current total or NMHC standards. The act defines an NMOG as "the sum of nonoxygenated and oxygenated hydrocarbons contained in a gas sample, including, at a minimum, all oxygenated organic gases containing 5 or fewer carbon atoms (i.e., aldehydes, ketones, alcohols, ethers, etc.), and all known alkanes, alkenes, alkynes, and aromatics containing 12 or fewer carbon atoms." The act mandates the use of the California NMOG Test Procedure for measuring NMOG. NMOG is the most appropriate substance to measure to determine the emission performance of vehicles using alternative fuels.

Covered Fleets

Centrally fueled fleets with 10 or more vehicles that are owned or operated by one person and operate in an area covered by this section of the act are subject to the clean vehicle requirements. Several types of vehicle fleets are exempted, including rental fleets, emergency vehicles, enforcement vehicles, and non-road vehicles. Also, vehicles parked at personal residences each night under normal circumstances are not covered.

Covered areas include ozone non-attainment areas with populations of 250,000 or more that have been classified as serious, severe or extreme (about 26 areas as of early 1991), or any CO non-attainment area with a population of 250,000 or more and a CO design value at or above 16.0 ppm.

States are required to implement clean-fuel vehicle phase-in programs....

....

The clean-vehicle and flexible-fueled vehicle standards in the amendments are based on standards recently adopted by California as part of its Low Emission Vehicles and Clean Fuel Program....

....

California Pilot Program

The 1990 Clean Air Act Amendments also contain a clean fuels pilot program for California. Beginning in 1996, 150,000 clean-fuel vehicles must be produced for sale in California; by 1999, this number must rise to 300,000. These vehicles must meet California's TLEV standards (0.125 gpm NMOG, 0.4 gpm NO_x, 3.4 gpm CO and 0.015 gpm formaldehyde) until the year 2000, when they must meet the LEV requirements (0.075 gpm NMOG, 0.2 gpm NO_x, 3.4 gpm CO and 0.015 gpm formaldehyde). California is required to develop a revised implementation plan within one year to assure that sufficient clean fuels are produced, distributed, and made available to ensure that all clean-fuel vehicles required under the program can operate to the maximum extent practicable exclusively on such fuels in the covered area. If California fails to adopt a fuels program that meets the requirements, EPA must establish such a program within three years.

Other states with serious, severe, or extreme ozone non-attainment areas are authorized to participate "voluntarily" in all or part of the program. This option cannot include any production or sales mandate for vehicles or fuels; it must rely on incentives to encourage their sale and use.

Urban Buses

The amendments also set performance criteria which mandate that starting in 1994 buses operating more than 70 percent of the time in large urban areas and using any fuel must reduce particulate emissions by 50 percent compared with conventional heavy-duty vehicles; that is, 0.05 g/BHP-hr particulates. EPA is authorized to relax the control requirements to 30 percent on the basis of technological feasibility. Beginning in 1994, EPA must conduct tests annually to determine whether buses subject to the standard are meeting it in use over their full useful life. If EPA determines that 40 percent or more of the buses are not, it must establish a low-pollution fuel requirement. This provision allows the use of exhaust after-treatment devices to reduce diesel particulate to a very low level if they operate correctly in the field; if they fail, EPA must mandate alternative fuels.

OFF-HIGHWAY ENGINES

By Nov. 15, 1991, EPA must complete a study of the health and welfare effects of non-road engines and vehicles other than locomotives. Within 12 months of completing the study, EPA must determine if HC, CO, or NO_x emissions from new or existing non-road engines and vehicles significantly contribute to ozone or CO concentrations in more than one ozone or CO non-attainment area.

If EPA determines that they do, it must regulate non-road engines or vehicles by requiring the "greatest degree of emission reduction achievable considering technological feasibility, cost, noise, energy, safety, and lead time factors." In setting standards, EPA must consider standards equivalent in stringency to those for non-road vehicles. The act contains no deadline for establishing such standards.

EPA also may regulate other pollutants from non-road engines and vehicles, such as diesel particulates, if it determines such standards are needed to protect the public health and welfare.

Locomotives

By Nov. 15, 1995, EPA must establish locomotive emission standards that require the use of the best technology that will be available, considering cost, energy, and safety. The standards are to take effect at the earliest possible date, considering the lead time needed to develop the control technology.

State Standards

States, including California, are prohibited from setting emissions standards for (a) new engines smaller than 175 horsepower used in construction vehicles or equipment or in farm equipment, and (b) new locomotives or new engines used in locomotives.

CONCLUSIONS

Three broad themes characterize the mobile source provisions of the Clean Air Act Amendments of 1990:

— Steady, significant improvements in conventional vehicles and fuels.
— A decision not to mandate alternative fuels or vehicles that would require using them. Instead, the act requires standards that can be met with conventional vehicles or flexible-fuel vehicles, and allows vehicle manufacturers to decide which will be used to meet them.
— Rejection of efforts to prevent California and other states from adopting requirements necessary to attain clean air goals. However, the act limits California's ability to regulate off-road vehicles and it provides no help beyond current law to other states that want to adopt programs similar to those of California.

The 1990 Clean Air Act Amendments should get the country back to producing vehicles that create less pollution, a process that has been slowed by almost 10 years of debate without action by Congress. The act allows areas to adopt the California requirements if they need more mobile-source pollution control than the national program will provide. [T]his would enable problem states to reduce HC and NO_x emissions much more quickly and to a substantially greater extent than they could under the federal program.

NOTES AND QUESTIONS

Although the basic structure of Title II remains the same after the 1990 amendments, the amendments strengthened emission standards and made provision for a variety of additional measures — stronger I/M programs, anti-tampering sanctions, controls on fuel volatility and evaporative emissions, controls of nonroad vehicles, encouragement of developmental alternative clean fuels and clean vehicles, and more stringent regulation of fuel and fuel additives. *See generally* Henry A. Waxman et al., *Cars, Fuels, and Clean Air: A Review of Title II of the Clean Air Act Amendments of 1990*, 21 ENVTL. L. 1947 (1991).

For the first time, separate new vehicle emission standards are established for two different "useful life" periods — 5 years/50,000 miles and 10 years/100,000 miles, whichever comes first — for light-duty vehicles and the first category of light-duty trucks, and 5 years/50,000 miles and 11 years/120,000 miles for the three other categories of light-duty trucks. Also, separate standards are established for certification (10 years/100,000 miles for light-duty vehicles) and for vehicles in use for purposes of recall liability (7 years/75,000 miles for light-duty vehicles). Why would separate standards be established for certification and recall? Yet another set of time periods is established for warranty requirements — 8 years/80,000 miles for major emissions controls, 2 years/24,000 miles for all other components.

ETHYL CORP. v. ENVIRONMENTAL PROTECTION AGENCY
51 F.3d 1053 (D.C. Cir. 1995)

HARRY T. EDWARDS, CHIEF JUDGE:

At issue in this case is a claim that the Administrator of the Environmental Protection Agency ("EPA" or "Agency") has impermissibly construed a provision of the Clean Air Act ("Act") governing the regulation of fuel additives. Title II of the Act, 42 U.S.C. §§ 7521-7590 (1988 & Supp. V 1993), establishes a comprehensive scheme for regulating motor vehicle emission and fuel standards for the prevention and control of air pollution. Section 211(f)(1) prohibits the introduction into commerce of new fuels or fuel additives which are not "substantially similar" to existing fuels and fuel additives. *Id.* § 7545(f)(1). A manufacturer may, however, under section 211(f)(4), apply to the Administrator of the EPA for a waiver of the section 211(f) prohibition if the manufacturer can show that the fuel additive "will not cause or contribute to a failure of any emission control device or system ... to achieve compliance by the vehicle with the emission standards." *Id.* § 7545(f)(4). In this case, Ethyl Corporation ("Ethyl") attempted to secure a waiver for a fuel additive under section 211(f)(4), and the Administrator denied the waiver request for reasons other than those specified in the applicable statutory provision.

I. *Background*

A. *The Statutory and Regulatory Regime*

In enacting section 211 of the Clean Air Act, 42 U.S.C. § 7545, Congress adopted a preventative approach to the regulation of fuels, banning fuels and fuel additives which were not "substantially similar" to existing products. *See id.*

§ 7545(f)(1). Section 211(a) authorizes the Administrator to prohibit the sale of fuels and fuel additives unless they have been registered with the Administrator under section 211(b). *See id.* § 7545(a), (b). Before registering a fuel additive under section 211(b), the Administrator may require the manufacturer "to conduct tests to determine potential public health effects of such fuel or additive" and to furnish information regarding the fuel additive's effect on "the emission control performance of any vehicle ... or the extent to which such emissions affect the public health or welfare." *Id.* § 7545(b)(2)(A), (B). Under section 211(c), the Administrator may "control or prohibit" the manufacture or sale of any fuel additive, if she determines that "any emission product of such ... fuel additive causes, or contributes, to air pollution which may reasonably be anticipated to endanger the public health or welfare" or "impair to a significant degree the performance of any emission control device or system which is in general use." *Id.* § 7545(c)(1)(A), (B).

Section 211(f)(1) prohibits the introduction into commerce of new fuel additives, stating that "it shall be unlawful for any manufacturer of any fuel or fuel additive to first introduce into commerce" a fuel additive for general use "which is not substantially similar" to those additives already in use. *Id.* § 7545(f)(1)(A). Under that section, however, the Administrator may grant a waiver if the manufacturer demonstrates that the fuel additive will not cause or contribute to a failure of any emission system which ensures compliance with the emission standards. *See id.* § 7545(f)(4).

In 1978, the EPA issued guidelines describing the specific requirements for a waiver under section 211(f)(4). *Guidelines for Fuel Additive Waivers*, 43 Fed. Reg. 11,258 (1978); *Guidelines for Section 211(f) Waivers for Alcohol-Gasoline Blends*, 43 Fed. Reg. 24,131 (1978). Those guidelines explain that "[a] request for a waiver should contain data relating to a fuel additive's emissions effects which are derived from vehicle testing," and describe the testing procedures indicative of effects on emissions. 43 Fed. Reg. at 11,259. The guidelines do not mention a public health criterion or any testing procedures for determining public health effects. Before the waiver decision at issue in this case, the Agency had considered twenty-three applications for waivers under section 211(f)(4), and it never previously relied on public health effects in denying a waiver. *See Waiver Decision* at 42,232, 42,234.

B. *The Waiver Proceedings*

The fuel additive, methylcyclopentadienyl manganese tricarbonyl or MMT, commercially labeled by Ethyl as HiTEC 3000, is to be blended in unleaded gasoline. MMT increases octane when it is added to gasoline to prevent auto-engine knocking. Because Ethyl's additive is less expensive than other octane enhancers, EPA assumed that if a waiver was granted, MMT would likely be used in a large proportion of this country's gasoline. *See Fuels & Fuel Additives; Waiver Application*, 57 Fed. Reg. 2535, 2536, 2547 n. 58 (1992) (*"1992 Waiver Decision"*). In the past, MMT was used in leaded gasoline in the

United States and in unleaded gasoline in Canada. *Id.* at 2536. MMT's principal component is manganese, which has been the subject of a number of health-related studies, the results of which reveal a debate in the scientific community regarding its potential health hazards. *See Waiver Decision* at 42,239-55.

Before the proceedings culminating in this action, Ethyl sought and had been denied waivers for MMT use in unleaded fuel on several occasions.

In May of 1994, Ethyl and EPA agreed once again to extend the deadline for final agency action to July 13, 1994, and on that day, EPA issued the waiver decision which is the subject of this case. *See Waiver Decision* at 42,231. The Administrator "interpret[ed] section 211(f)(4) of the Act as establishing a two-stage process for evaluating waiver applications." *Id.* at 42,259. First, according to the Administrator, a determination must be made "whether an applicant has met its burden of demonstrating that a fuel [additive] does not cause or contribute to a failure to meet regulated emission standards." *Id.* In the "second stage," the Administrator claimed that she had the discretion to "consider other factors [such as the potential health effects resulting from use of a fuel additive] in determining whether granting a waiver is in the public interest and consistent with the objectives of the Clean Air Act." *Id.* The Administrator noted that she had determined in November of 1993 that Ethyl satisfied the first criterion; i.e., that "use of Ethyl's product HiTEC 3000 in unleaded gasoline at the specified concentration will not cause or contribute to a failure to achieve compliance with vehicle emission standards." *Id.* As to "other factors," however, the Administrator found that "there is a reasonable basis for concern about the effects on public health that could result if EPA were to approve use of MMT in unleaded gasoline." *Id.* at 42,260. Thus, the Administrator again denied Ethyl's request for a waiver of section 211(f)'s prohibition of new fuel additives.

II. *Analysis*

The principal dispute in this case involves EPA's interpretation of section 211(f)(4) of the Act. Ethyl contends that EPA has acted contrary to law in denying Ethyl's application for a waiver under section 211(f)(4) on public health grounds. Ethyl argues that the waiver provision contemplates only emissions criteria. EPA, on the other hand, contends that Congress has not directly spoken on the issue of whether the Administrator may consider the public health implications of fuel additives before granting or denying a section 211(f)(4) waiver. Thus, it argues, this court must defer to the Agency's reasonable interpretation of section 211(f)(4) as providing the Administrator with discretionary authority to consider factors "in the public interest" and in accordance with the "objectives of the Clean Air Act" in waiver determinations.

A. *Public Health Determination Under Section 211(f)(4)*

. . . .

Section 211(f)(4) instructs the Administrator to consider a new fuel additive's effects only on emission standards. The language of the provision, allowing for a waiver of the prohibition if the manufacturer can show that its additive "will not cause or contribute to a failure of any emission control device or system ... to achieve compliance ... with the emission standards," 42 U.S.C. § 7545(f)(4), is specific and definite; it does not permit the Administrator to consider other factors "in the public interest." When compared to the language in section 211(c)(1), which authorizes the Administrator to control or prohibit fuel additives if the emission product contributes "to air pollution which may reasonably be anticipated to endanger the public health," *id.* § 7545(c)(1)(A), it is all the more apparent that Congress's definite scheme does not afford the kind of discretion the EPA would find. Finally, the legislative history of section 211(f) also indicates that Congress was concerned with MMT's effects on emissions, not on public health. Given the plain meaning of the statute, we hold that the EPA erred in considering the health effects of MMT in deciding whether to grant Ethyl a waiver for its fuel additive.

....

Another telling indication that the Administrator has misconstrued the meaning of section 211(f)(4), is the plain language of a nearby provision, section 211(c)(1), which explicitly instructs the Administrator to consider a fuel additive's effects on public health. Section 211(c)(1) authorizes the Administrator to "control or prohibit" the manufacture or sale of any fuel additive

> (A) if in the judgement of the Administrator any emission product of such fuel or fuel additive causes, or contributes, to air pollution which may reasonably be anticipated to endanger the public health or welfare, or (B) if emission products of such fuel or fuel additive will impair to a significant degree the performance of any emission control device or system which is in general use....

42 U.S.C. § 7545(c)(1). This provision not only establishes two criteria — public health implications and emission standard problems — for controlling or prohibiting the sale of fuel additives, it also establishes standards by which the Administrator evaluates those criteria. The language of section 211(c)(1) demonstrates that Congress crafted a very definite scheme in which the Administrator was to consider certain criteria before taking certain actions. Specifically, she considers emission effects of fuel additives before granting waivers under section 211(f)(4), and emissions effects as well as public health effects before prohibiting or controlling the manufacture or sale of fuel additives under section 211(c)(1). The language of section 211(c)(1) only underscores our conclusion that Congress did not delegate to the Agency the authority to consider other factors "in the public interest" such as public health when acting under section 211(f)(4).

....

In *Ethyl Corp. v. EPA*, this court reviewed the Administrator's interpretation of the standard required in evaluating the public health implications of lead emissions under section 211(c) and found it reasonable. 541 F.2d at 12. The

Administrator had construed section 211(c)(1)(A)'s "will endanger the public health" language to require a finding that the fuel additive "presents a significant risk of harm," and this court affirmed that construction after analyzing the language of that provision, the language of nearby provisions, and other circuits' interpretations of the Clean Air Act. *See id.* at 12-32. The court concluded that "the Administrator may regulate lead additives under Section 211(c)(1)(A) when he determines ... that lead automobile emissions significantly increase the total human exposure to lead so as to cause a significant risk of harm to the public health." *Id.* at 31-32. In this case, however, the Administrator used a very different standard from the one she uses in section 211(c)(1)(A) proceedings, saying simply that "I have concluded that there is a reasonable basis for concern about the effects on public health that could result if EPA were to approve use of MMT in unleaded gasoline pursuant to Ethyl's application." *Waiver Decision* at 42,260. This is a bizarre departure from existing practice, in complete defiance of the plain terms of the statutory criterion and with no explanation whatsoever for the application of a different standard.

In sum, the Administrator of the EPA clearly misconstrued the criterion by which she grants and denies waivers for fuel additives. The language of section 211(f)(4) is clear and specific; the Administrator is to consider MMT's effects on the ability of "any emission control devise or system ... to achieve compliance by the vehicle with the emission standards." 42 U.S.C. § 7545(f)(4). Should the Administrator wish to consider whether the emission products of MMT "may reasonably be anticipated to endanger the public health," *id.* § 7545(c)(1)(A), she may initiate proceedings under section 211(c)(1). The Administrator plainly oversteps her authority when she considers other factors "in the public interest" such as the public health implications of an additive in section 211(f)(4) waiver proceedings.

....

NOTES AND QUESTIONS

1. Section 211 for regulation of fuel and fuel additives was amended in several significant respects. Provisions are added to deal with specific problems such as fuel volatility and diesel fuel sulfur content. The preemptive effect of section 211 on state regulation of fuel is narrowed so that there is preemption of state regulation of a fuel or fuel additive only when there is federal regulation of that characteristic or component. *Compare Exxon Corp. v. City of New York*, 548 F.2d 1088 (2d Cir. 1977) (city's regulation of lead content and volatility preempted even though not covered by EPA's regulations at the time). The amendments also require EPA to set standards for reformulated gasoline (gasoline with lower emissions which can still be used in conventional engines) and require sale of reformulated gasoline in the most seriously polluted ozone nonattainment areas. Gasoline sold in the most serious carbon monoxide nonattainment areas must meet prescribed oxygen standards.

2. To encourage alternative fuels and alternative fuel vehicles in the most polluted areas, clean fuel emission standards are established and vehicles meeting these standards must be used in commercial fleets. The California pilot program also requires automobile manufacturers to sell clean-fuel vehicles to the public in that state, with the required volume to be apportioned to manufacturers by EPA. In short, the scope of motor vehicle emissions regulation after 1990 is much broader, although many of the new measures are limited to the most heavily polluted areas.

3. After this opinion EPA tried again, unsuccessfully, to keep MMT from being registered. *Ethyl Corp. v. Browner*, 67 F.3d 941 (D.C. Cir. 1995). Ethyl began providing MMT to oil refineries at the end of 1995. Environmental groups continue to claim the use of MMT can cause serious health problems. Is there anything that EPA can do? What is the difficulty under section 211(c)?

AMERICAN PETROLEUM INSTITUTE v. ENVIRONMENTAL PROTECTION AGENCY

52 F.3d 1113 (D.C. Cir. 1995)

....

SENTELLE, CIRCUIT JUDGE:

The American Methanol Institute, the American Petroleum Institute, the National Petroleum Refiners Association, and the Oxygenated Fuels Association, Inc. (hereinafter "petitioners") challenge the promulgation by the Environmental Protection Agency ("EPA") of a renewable oxygenate requirement in its regulations for the reformulated gasoline program under the Clean Air Act.

....

In 1990, Congress established the reformulated gasoline program ("RFG") in section 211(k), 42 U.S.C. § 7545(k), of the Clean Air Act ("CAA"), 42 U.S.C. § 7401 et seq. (1988 & Supp. V 1993), and directed EPA to "promulgate regulations under this section establishing requirements for reformulated gasoline to be used in gasoline-fueled vehicles in specified nonattainment areas." 42 U.S.C. § 7545(k)(1). The section further provided that the regulations "shall require the greatest reduction in emissions of ozone forming volatile organic compounds (during the high ozone season) and emissions of toxic air pollutants (during the entire year) achievable through the reformulation of conventional gasoline, taking into consideration the cost of achieving such emission reductions, any nonair-quality and other air-quality related health and environmental impacts and energy requirements." *Id.* Congress also required that RFG be at least two percent oxygen by weight, not more than one percent benzene by volume, and contain no heavy metals. 42 U.S.C. § 7545(k)(2).

The primary oxygenates added to RFG to make it at least two percent oxygen by weight are ethanol and methyl tertiary butyl ether ("MTBE"). Ethanol, primarily made from corn, is considered renewable since corn can be regrown year after year. By contrast, MTBE is derived primarily from nonrenewable resources such as natural gas and petroleum. A renewable oxygenate that is not yet in common use is ethyl tertiary butyl ether ("ETBE"), which is derived from ethanol.

During the comment period for the RFG program, supporters of ethanol had argued that the volatile organic compound ("VOC") emission standards in the program, 42 U.S.C. § 7545(k)(3)(B)(i), would preclude the use of ethanol in RFG because adding ethanol to gasoline increases its volatility and raises VOC emissions, especially in the summertime. By contrast, the use of MTBE as an oxygenate does not boost a fuel's volatility. In February 1994, EPA promulgated a set of final regulations implementing the RFG program. Regulation of Fuels and Fuel Additives: Standards for Reformulated and Conventional Gasoline, 59 Fed. Reg. 7,716 (1994). Around that time, EPA also proposed another rule requiring that thirty percent of the oxygen required to be used in RFG come from renewable oxygenates. Regulation of Fuels and Fuel Additives: Renewable Oxygenate Requirement for Reformulated Gasoline, 58 Fed. Reg. 68,343 (proposed Dec. 27, 1993).

In August 1994, EPA issued a final renewable oxygenate rule ("ROR") for RFG. Regulation of Fuels and Fuel Additives: Renewable Oxygenate Requirement in Reformulated Gasoline, 59 Fed. Reg. 39,258 (1994). The ROR adopted the proposed requirement that thirty percent of the oxygen in RFG be derived from renewable sources. EPA noted that at the time the ROR was promulgated, the two most common oxygenates were ethanol and MTBE. *Id*. at 39,259. In justification of the rule, EPA stated that the ROR 1) will help conserve fossil energy resources and minimize any detrimental effects the RFG program may have on energy consumption; 2) has the potential to provide global warming benefits by stimulating the market for renewable oxygenates; and 3) will maintain the benefits of the RFG program and increase those benefits through incentives for increased ETBE use in the summer, displacing ethanol use during those months. *Id*. at 39,262.

Specifically, petitioners argue that section 7545(k)(1), which established the RFG program, does not authorize EPA to include a renewable oxygenate mandate in the program. The overriding goal of the RFG program, petitioners assert, is set forth in section 7545(k)(1) as attaining the greatest achievable reduction in VOCs and toxics emissions through the reformulation of conventional gasoline. Because EPA's asserted justification for the ROR, that is, the promotion of renewable oxygenates and related goals, are not the objectives of section 7545(k)(1), petitioners maintain that EPA has impermissibly exceeded its statutory authority. *See Chevron U.S.A. Inc. v. Natural Resources Defense Council, Inc.*, 467 U.S. 837, 842-43, 81 L. Ed. 2d 694, 104 S. Ct. 2778 (1984).

EPA maintains that the ROR is within its authority because it is designed to ensure that the emissions reduction requirements for RFG are achieved in a way that reasonably "optimize[s] the resulting impacts on cost, energy requirements, and other health and environmental impacts." *See* 59 Fed. Reg. at 39,263. Section 7545(k)(1) provides that EPA shall promulgate regulations establishing requirements for RFG, and the CAA, 42 U.S.C. § 7601(a)(1), delegates to EPA the authority to promulgate such regulations as are necessary for it to carry out its functions under the Act. While section 7601(a)(1) does not give EPA carte blanche authority to promulgate any rule relating to the CAA, EPA maintains that it is sufficiently broad to allow the promulgation of rules that are necessary and reasonable to effect the purposes of the Act.

....

We conclude that the plain meaning of section 7545(k)(1) precludes the adoption of RFG rules that are not directed toward the reduction of VOCs and toxics emissions, and, since the statute is unambiguous, EPA improperly interpreted the section as giving it the broader power to adopt the ROR. *See Chevron*, 467 U.S. at 842-43, 104 S. Ct. at 2781-82. The sole purpose of the RFG program is to reduce air pollution, which it does through specific performance standards for reducing VOCs and toxics emissions. EPA admits that the ROR will not give additional emission reductions for VOCs or toxics, *see* 59 Fed. Reg. at 39,283, and has even conceded that use of ethanol might possibly make air quality worse. *Id*. at 39,268.

While EPA relies on the first sentence of section 7545(k)(1) for its broad authority to impose requirements for RFG that are "independent of and in addition to the obligation to require the greatest achievable VOC and toxics emissions reductions under the second sentence of Section [7545(k)(1)]," 58 Fed. Reg. at 68,351, neither that sentence alone nor in conjunction with the rest of the section grants EPA authority to require the use of oxygenates that will not reduce, and may increase, VOCs and toxics emissions.

....

Section 7545(k)(1) authorizes the adoption of regulations to achieve the greatest reduction in emissions of VOCs and toxics and the consideration of nonair-quality factors listed in the section is only to ensure that any emission reduction steps do not have inordinate economic, environmental, or energy effects. The overriding goal is air quality, and the other listed considerations are subordinate to that goal. Once EPA has taken the factors into consideration in the context of attaining the greatest reduction in VOCs and toxics emissions achievable, the statute does not authorize it to use these factors as a basis for imposing any additional restrictions on RFG, even if the additional restrictions would yield some benefit among the factors to be taken into consideration. Accordingly, since EPA must consider factors such as "energy requirements" only as subordinate concerns to clear goals of the RFG program, it lacks the authority to promulgate the ROR, which advances the use of renewable oxygenates not in furtherance of, and perhaps at the expense of, reductions in VOCs and toxics emissions.

NOTES AND QUESTIONS

1. Should EPA or Congress bear the primary responsibility for formulating emission standards for automobiles? Which is most likely to be effective in forcing technology in the face of industry opposition? Has technology-forcing been an effective approach with motor vehicle emissions? Why or why not? Do you think Congress ever intended to shut down the auto industry if standards were not met?

2. The Clean Air Act in 1970 focused reduction of automobile emissions on two methods: restrictions on emissions of new vehicles and "transportation controls." "Transportation controls" include such measures as on-street parking restrictions, exclusive bus and car pool lanes, road user charges, and — critical to control of emissions — state inspection and maintenance programs to identify vehicles in need of maintenance for emission controls. An exhaustive list of possible transportation control measures is set out in section 108(f)(1)(A), 42 U.S.C. § 7408(f)(1)(A). Each SIP at that time under section 110(a)(2)(B) and (G) was to include a transportation control plan to attain and maintain the NAAQSs.

After several extensions by EPA for submission of state transportation control plans, EPA was forced in litigation to require submission of such plans by April 15, 1973. When states were unwilling or unable to submit the plans by this deadline, EPA was forced to devise its own plans with such measures as rationing of gasoline and preconstruction review of all new activities which would exceed a designated number of parking spaces. In 1977, in response to the ongoing controversy, Congress permitted states to remove transportation control measures from their SIPs and, therefore, only a few plans were ever "fully" implemented. S. NOVICK, LAW OF ENVIRONMENTAL PROTECTION § 11.08[3]; *see, e.g.*, Penny Mintz, Note, *Transportation Alternatives Within the Clean Air Act: A History of Congressional Failure to Effectuate, with Recommendations for the Future*, 3 N.Y.U. ENVTL. L.J. 156 (1994). The requirement of state inspection and maintenance programs fared somewhat better. In the 1977 amendments, state plans under section 110(a)(2) were still to contain I/M programs "to the extent necessary and practicable" and were in fact required in the SIPs for nonattainment areas under section 172. Resistance to such programs continued, and states were slow to implement the programs. Why would TCPs and I/M programs encounter such resistance? *See generally* Ostrov, *Inspection and Maintenance of Automotive Pollution Control: A Decade-Long Struggle Among Congress, EPA and the States*, 8 HARV. ENVTL. L. REV. 139 (1984). The last remaining reference to TCPs in section 110(a)(2) was deleted in the 1990 amendments. *See also Environmental Defense Fund v. Browner*, 40 Env't Rep. Cas. (BNA) 1730 (N.D. Cal. 1995) (EPA must promulgate criteria and procedures to determine conformity of transportation plans, programs and projects with SIPs in all areas, including attainment and unclassified areas); *EDF v. EPA*, 82 F.3d 451 (D.C. Cir. 1996), amended by 92 F.3d 1209 (D.C. Cir.

1996) (upholding EPA's transportation and general conformity rules under section 176(c)(4)).

The 1990 amendments delete I/M programs from the list of transportation control measures in section 108(f), from the list of measures to be included in every SIP in section 110, and from the list of additional SIP measures generally required for all nonattainment areas in section 172(c). While states are free to include or continue transportation control plans and I/M programs in their SIPs, these programs are required only in certain nonattainment areas, based upon the classification of the area and the pollutant for which it is designated nonattainment. See pages 386-89 *supra*. *See generally* Arnold W. Reitze, Jr. & Barry Needleman, *Control of Air Pollution From Mobile Sources Through Inspection and Maintenance Programs*, 30 HARV. J. ON LEGIS. 409 (1993); *see, e.g.*, Phillip E. Rothschild, Comment, *The Clean Air Act and Indirect Source Review: 1970-1991*, 10 UCLA J. ENVTL. L. & POL'Y 337 (1992). However, one district judge has concluded that areas which were required to have TCPs in their SIPs before 1990 are still bound by that requirement until they have revised their SIPs in accordance with the 1990 amendments. The court held that the "savings clause" of section 110(n)(1), 42 U.S.C. § 7410(n)(1), meant that SIPs must remain in effect until they are revised. *Citizens for a Better Environment v. Wilson*, 775 F. Supp. 1291 (N.D. Cal. 1991). The trip reduction program requiring employers to implement car pooling programs in some heavily polluted areas was repealed in 1996.

In 1996 EPA finalized several revisions to the I/M program requirements. 61 Fed. Reg. 39,032; 40,940; 49,679 (1996). For additional discussion of transportation controls, see David Bennett, Note, *Zero Emission Vehicles: The Air Pollution Messiah? Northeastern States Mandate ZEVs Without Considering the Alternatives or Consequences*, 20 WM. & MARY ENVTL. L. & POL'Y REV. 333 (1996); Perry S. Goldschein, *Going Mobile: Emissions Trading Gets a Boost From Mobile Source Emission Reduction Credits*, 13 UCLA J. ENVTL. L. & POL'Y 225 (1995); Patricia A. Leonard, *The Clean Air Act's Mandate of Employer Trip-Reduction Programs: Is This a Workable Solution to the Country's Air Pollution Problems?*, 49 U. MIAMI L. REV. 827 (1995); David B. Trinkle, Comment, *Cars, Congress, and Clean Air for the Northeast: A Separation of Powers Analysis of the Ozone Transport Commission*, 23 B.C. ENVTL. AFF. L. REV. 169 (1995); Tara A. Stanton, Comment, *The Battle Over the Electric Car: The Big Three Versus the Northeastern States*, 8 TUL. ENVTL. L.J. 553 (1995).

I. THE PERMIT PROGRAM

Before the 1990 amendments, the only permits required under the Clean Air Act were permits for new sources that met the threshold requirements for new source review in nonattainment and PSD areas. See pages 384-415 *supra*. Title V of the 1990 amendments requires all "major" sources, new or existing, as well as a variety of other sources regulated under specific programs of the Act, to obtain a permit from the authorized state air pollution agencies. CAA § 402(a), 42 U.S.C. § 7661a(a). Generally, a "major" source is a source with annual emissions of 10 or more tons of a hazardous pollutant, and sources with annual emissions of 100 or more tons of any air pollutant. CAA § 501(2), 42 U.S.C. § 7661(2).

In contrast to the permit program for water pollution, states must submit a state permit program to EPA for approval. Failure to do so or inadequate program enforcement by the state subjects the state to sanctions. CAA § 502(d)-(2)(B)(i), 42 U.S.C. § 7661a(d)(2) & (i). By November 15, 1991, EPA was to promulgate regulations establishing the minimum requirements for state programs, including application requirements, annual permit fees and procedures for applications. CAA § 502(b), 42 U.S.C. § 7661a(b); 40 C.F.R. Part 70. 56 Fed. Reg. 21712 (May 10, 1991). By November 15, 1993, each state was to submit a state program to EPA for approval. CAA § 502(d)(1), 42 U.S.C. § 7661a(d)(1). EPA must approve or disapprove programs, in whole or in part, within one year of submission. *Id.* State permit programs become effective upon approval, CAA § 502(h), 42 U.S.C. § 7661a(h), with permits to be issued within no longer than a three-year period. CAA § 503(c), 42 U.S.C. § 7661b(c). If a state fails to submit a program or the program is disapproved in whole or in part, the state may be subject to the sanctions for SIP failures in section 179(b). If the state has not come up with an approved program within two years of the required submission date, EPA will promulgate, administer, and enforce a federal permit program for the state. CAA § 502(d)(2), 42 U.S.C. § 7661a(d)(2). On July 31, 1996, EPA issued a list of ten states and three territories in which EPA would assume permitting authority. 61 Fed. Reg. 39,877 (1996).

EPA may object to a draft state permit if it does not comply with the Act. CAA § 505(b)(1), 42 U.S.C. § 7661d(b)(1). If the state fails to respond to EPA's objections, EPA may assume responsibility for issuance of the permit. *Id.* Public participation in the permitting process is provided at several levels. State permit programs must provide any person with the opportunity to comment on proposed permit actions, to seek review in state court of the state's final action (as discussed in the following case), and to obtain court orders to compel the permitting authority to take final action on an application. CAA § 502(b)(6) & (7), 42 U.S.C. § 7661a(b)(6) & (7). Also, any person may petition EPA to object to a proposed state permit that does not meet the Act's requirements. EPA must reach a decision on the petition within sixty days, and denial of the petition is reviewable in the federal appeals courts. CAA § 505(b)(2), 42 U.S.C. § 7661d-(b)(2).

There are advantages in the permit system for sources as well. A source's compliance with the permit may "shield" it from enforcement. Compliance with the limitations in a permit is deemed to be compliance with the Act's requirements upon which the limitations are based. The source may also be deemed to be in compliance with any of the Act's requirements found by the permit-issuing authority to be inapplicable in the permit or other requirements of the Act not specifically addressed in the permit. CAA § 504(f), 42 U.S.C. § 7661c(f). The precise scope of the enforcement shield was left by Congress in large part to EPA to address in its regulations.

VIRGINIA v. BROWNER

80 F.3d 869 (4th Cir. 1996),
cert. denied, 117 S. Ct. 764 (1997)

M. BLANE MICHAEL, CIRCUIT JUDGE:

The Commonwealth of Virginia petitions for review of the Environmental Protection Agency's final action disapproving Virginia's proposed program for issuing air pollution permits. Specifically, Virginia challenges EPA's finding that Virginia has failed to comply with Title V of the 1990 Amendments to the Clean Air Act (sometimes "CAA" or the "Act"), CAA §§ 501-507, 42 U.S.C. §§ 766-7661f, because Virginia's proposal lacks adequate provisions for judicial review of the Commonwealth's permitting decisions. Virginia also challenges the constitutionality of Title V and its sanctions provisions, CAA §§ 179(b) & 502(d), 42 U.S.C. §§ 7509(b) & 7661a(d). According to Virginia, these provisions improperly commandeer the legislative processes of the states, in violation of the Tenth Amendment and the Spending Clause, U.S. Const. art. I § 8, cl. 1. We have jurisdiction over all of Virginia's claims, *see* CAA § 307(b)(1), 42 U.S.C. § 7607(b)(1), and we find them to be without merit.

. . . .

If a state fails to submit a permit program, or submits a permit program that EPA disapproves for failure to comply with CAA § 502(b), the state becomes subject to sanctions designed to encourage compliance. CAA § 502(d), 42 U.S.C. § 7661a(d).

One sanction deprives states of certain federal highway funds. CAA § 179(b)-(1), 42 U.S.C. § 7509(b)(1). However, the state loses no funds that would be spent in regions that are in "attainment" within the meaning of the Act. CAA § 179(b)(1)(A), 42 U.S.C. § 7509(b)(1)(A). And, even within "nonattainment" areas, funds remain available for highway projects that "resolve a demonstrated safety problem and likely will result in a significant reduction in, or avoidance of, accidents." *Id.*

A second sanction increases the pollution offset requirements already imposed on private polluters within ozone nonattainment areas. Normally, new major stationary sources of pollution may not be operated within nonattainment areas (and existing stationary sources may not be modified if the modification would increase emissions) unless pollution from other sources is reduced to offset increased pollution from the new or modified source. . . . The sanction supersedes these normal ratios by increasing the ratio in all ozone nonattainment areas to 2:1, requiring 200 tons of old pollutants to be eliminated for every 100 tons of new pollutants allowed. CAA § 179(b)(2), 42 U.S.C. § 7509(b)(2). The offset sanction, therefore, could slow the rate of industrial development within a noncomplying state.

A third sanction eliminates the state's ability to manage its own pollution control regime. If the state does not gain approval for its permit program, EPA develops and implements its own Title V permitting program within the noncomplying state. CAA § 502(d)(3), 42 U.S.C. § 7661a(d)(3). The state is not required to do anything to assist EPA in this effort; the federal government becomes wholly responsible.

....

Virginia claims that EPA erroneously determined that Virginia's permit program contained inadequate judicial review provisions (defect (1)). EPA's finding that Virginia submitted a deficient permit program must be upheld unless that finding is "arbitrary, capricious, or otherwise not in accordance with law." 5 U.S.C. § 706(2)(A). We find that EPA correctly determined that Virginia's proposed judicial review provisions do not comply with the Act. Therefore, even if EPA had based its disapproval solely on defect (1), such disapproval would not have been arbitrary and capricious.

CAA § 502(b)(6), 42 U.S.C. § 7661a(b)(6), provides that a state permit program must contain:

> Adequate, streamlined, and reasonable procedures for expeditiously determining when applications are complete, for processing such applications, for public notice, including offering an opportunity for public comment and a hearing, and for expeditious review of permit actions, including applications, renewals, or revisions, and including *an opportunity for judicial review in State court of the final permit action by the applicant, any person who participated in the public comment process, and any other person who could obtain judicial review of that action under applicable law.*

(Emphasis supplied.)

....

Virginia law grants standing to seek judicial review of permitting decisions to "any owner aggrieved by" such decisions. Va. Code § 10.1-1318(A). This provision satisfies CAA § 502(b)(6)'s requirement that the permit "applicant" be allowed to seek judicial review. But § 502(b)(6) also requires that states grant certain standing rights to members of the public, and here is where Virginia's judicial review provision falls short of the mark. Under Virginia's provision, a member of the public "who is aggrieved by a final [permitting decision] who participated, in person or by submittal of written comments, in the public comment process" may only seek judicial review of a permitting decision if he can establish that

> (i) [he] has suffered an actual, threatened, or imminent injury; (ii) such injury is an invasion of an immediate, legally protected, *pecuniary and substantial* interest which is concrete and particularized; (iii) such injury is

fairly traceable to the [permitting decision] and not the result of the action of some third party not before the court; and (iv) such injury will likely be redressed by a favorable decision of the court.

Va. Code § 10.1-1318(B) (emphasis supplied).

According to EPA, this provision is too restrictive: limiting availability of review to those persons with "pecuniary and substantial" interests violates CAA § 502(b)(6). We agree with EPA.

....

EPA's interpretation, if reasonable, must take precedence over any interpretation Virginia could offer or, indeed, even over any alternative interpretation we could formulate. *Chevron, U.S.A., Inc. v. Natural Resources Defense Council,* 467 U.S. 837, 844, 81 L. Ed. 2d 694, 104 S. Ct. 2778 (1984). We defer to EPA's definition of the bounds of the § 502(b)(6) safe harbor because "the power of an administrative agency to administer a congressionally created ... program necessarily requires the formulation of policy and the making of rules to fill any gap left, implicitly or explicitly, by Congress." [Citations]

....

Having determined that EPA had a valid reason to disapprove Virginia's permit program, we now examine whether Title V and its sanctions provisions are constitutional. Virginia claims that Title V and its sanctions provisions are unconstitutional because they impinge upon a fundamental element of state sovereignty, the state's right to articulate its own rules of judicial standing. Even assuming *arguendo* the accuracy of Virginia's assertion that its standing rules are within the core of its sovereignty, we find no constitutional violation because federal law "may, indeed, be designed to induce state action in areas that otherwise would be beyond Congress' regulatory authority." *FERC v. Mississippi,* 456 U.S. 742, 766, 72 L. Ed. 2d 532, 102 S. Ct. 2126 (1982). As we explain below, we believe that if Virginia chooses to change its rules of judicial standing, it will make the change only because the CAA's sanctions provisions induce it to do so, not because they coerce it.

We agree that Congress lacks power to impinge upon "the core of sovereignty retained by the States." *New York v. United States,* 505 U.S. 144, 158-160, 112 S. Ct. 2408, 2419, 120 L. Ed. 2d 120 (1992). We also agree that an important aspect of a state's sovereignty is the administration of its judicial system....

We need not decide whether judicial standing rules fall within the core of sovereignty because we find that the CAA does not compel the states to modify their standing rules; it merely induces them to do so. The CAA is constitutional because although its sanctions provisions potentially burden the states, those sanctions amount to inducement rather than "outright coercion." *See New York* 505 U.S. at 165-67, 112 S. Ct. at 2423. We examine each sanction separately to explain how we reach this conclusion. *See id.* at 2425.

Two sources of Congressional power allow use of the highway sanction. Because the elimination of air pollution promotes the general welfare, Congress may tie the award of federal funds to the states' efforts to eliminate air pollution. "The Congress shall have Power to lay and collect Taxes, Duties, Imposts and Excises, to pay the Debts and provide for the common Defence and general Welfare of the United States." U.S. Const. art. I § 8, cl. 1. Furthermore, the Commerce Clause, U.S. Const. art. I, § 8, cl. 3, gives Congress the power to regulate "activities causing air or water pollution, or other environmental hazards that may have effects in more than one State." *Hodel v. Virginia Surface Mining & Reclamation Ass'n*, 452 U.S. 264, 282, 69 L. Ed. 2d 1, 101 S. Ct. 2352 (1981).

Generally, Congress may use the power of the purse to encourage states to enact particular legislation. *New York*, 505 U.S. at 165-67, 112 S. Ct. at 2423. This power, however, is not limitless. Exercise of the power to the point of "outright coercion" violates the Constitution. *Id.* "[I]n some circumstances the financial inducement offered by Congress might be so coercive as to pass the point at which 'pressure turns into compulsion.'" *South Dakota v. Dole*, 483 U.S. 203, 211, 97 L. Ed. 2d 171, 107 S. Ct. 2793 (1987) (quoting *Steward Machine Co. v. Davis*, 301 U.S. 548, 590, 81 L. Ed. 1279, 57 S. Ct. 883 (1937)). Also, it has been suggested that federal funds may be subject to conditions "only in ways reasonably related to the purpose for which the funds are expended." *South Dakota*, 483 U.S. at 213 (O'Connor, J., dissenting); *see also New York*, 112 S. Ct. at 2426. No court, however, has ever struck down a federal statute on grounds that it exceeded the Spending Power.

. . . .

The highway sanction here does not rise to the level of "outright coercion." First, a state does not lose any highway funds that would be spent in areas of the state that are in attainment. CAA § 179(b)(1)(A), 42 U.S.C. § 7509(b)(1)(A). Second, even within nonattainment areas, federal highway funds may be spent on projects designed to promote safety or designed to reduce air pollution. CAA § 179 (b)(1), 42 U.S.C. § 7509(b)(1). More severe funding restrictions than those at issue here have been upheld.

. . . .

Virginia concedes that it is allowed to spend federal money on safety projects, on projects that will reduce pollution, and on projects within areas that are in attainment. The Commonwealth contends, however, that because it is difficult to shift funds from one transportation project to another, these exemptions do not reduce the sanction's coercive effect. According to Virginia, it simply lacks the time to reallocate funds away from highway projects it has already planned for nonattainment areas. To this argument we can only say that Title V was enacted in 1990, and the states have had more than five years either to comply or to prepare themselves for the consequences of noncompliance.

And contrary to what Virginia claims, the conditions on spending are reasonably related to the goal of reducing air pollution. The CAA as a whole is a comprehensive scheme to cope with the problem of air pollution from all sources. Congress may ensure that funds it allocates are not used to exacerbate the overall problem of air pollution. It is therefore of no consequence that a highway sanction, which will have the effect of reducing emissions from mobile pollution sources, is being used to induce compliance with a portion of the Act designed to reduce emissions from stationary sources.

We hold that the highway sanction, CAA § 179(b)(1), is a valid exercise of the Spending Power. As a valid exercise of that power, it also comports with the requirements of the Tenth Amendment. *New York*, 505 U.S. at 173-75, 112 S. Ct. at 2427. Congress has not overstepped its bounds here.

The offset sanction, CAA § 179(b)(2), 42 U.S.C. § 7509(b)(2), which limits new construction or modification of major stationary sources of air pollution, is constitutional because it regulates private pollution sources, not states.

....

The final sanction, federal permit program implementation, CAA § 502(d)(3), 42 U.S.C. § 7661a(d)(3), also is constitutional. The essence of a Tenth Amendment violation is that the state is commanded to regulate. Here, Virginia is not commanded to regulate; the Commonwealth may choose to do nothing and let the federal government promulgate and enforce its own permit program within Virginia. Because "the full regulatory burden will be borne by the Federal Government," the sanction is constitutional. *Hodel*, 452 U.S. at 288, 101 S. Ct. at 2366.

....

Because Congress may choose to preempt state law completely, it may also take the less drastic step of allowing the states the ability to avoid preemption by adopting and implementing their own plans that sufficiently address congressional concerns....

Finally, the CAA's sanctions provisions maintain unity between regulation and political accountability. If sanctions are imposed, it will be "the Federal Government that makes the decision in full view of the public, and it will be federal officials that suffer the consequences if the decision turns out to be detrimental or unpopular." *New York*, 505 U.S. at 168, 112 S. Ct. at 2424. The sanctions provisions are constitutional.

In sum, we conclude (1) that EPA correctly disapproved Virginia's proposed state permit program because it did not satisfy the provisions of the Clean Air Act and (2) that the sanctions Virginia faces are constitutional. The petition for review is denied.

NOTES AND QUESTIONS

The permit system, modeled in part on the Clean Water Act's NPDES program, is designed to expedite enforcement and implementation of revised emissions limitations. All of the requirements an individual source must meet, along with monitoring and recordkeeping requirements, will be incorporated into the permit. By referring to the permit and the required compliance information, EPA, states, and the public can determine more easily whether a source is in compliance. Permit fees will help to subsidize state administration and enforcement. S. Rep. No. 101-228, 101st Cong., 1st Sess. 346-48 (1989). Because fees are based on plant emission levels, they also create an incentive for emissions reduction. The Conference Committee without explanation deleted provisions in the House and Senate bills for permit modification and renewal, including a provision that would have allowed sources to avoid the cumbersome variance process. *See* H.R. Rep. No. 490, 101st Cong., 2d Sess. 618 (1990), S. Rep. No. 228, 101st Cong., 1st Sess. 660 (1989). As a result, EPA was left to address renewal and modifications in its regulation with little or no statutory guidance. EPA did not promulgate final regulations on the requirements for state programs in 40 C.F.R. pt. 70 until July 21, 1992. It then proposed revisions in August 1994 and reproposed revisions in April 1996, in addition to a pair of guidance documents in July 1995 and August 1996. Most states had received approval for their programs by the end of 1995. Implementation of the new permit promises to be one of the more monumental tasks assigned to EPA and the states by Congress in the 1990 amendments.

J. ENFORCEMENT

For any environmental regulation to be effective, there must be monitoring of compliance and enforcement. The Clean Air Act contains the basic mechanisms for recordkeeping, inspections, monitoring, civil and criminal sanctions, prevention of imminent and substantial endangerment, and citizen suit enforcement found in most environmental statutes. *See, e.g.*, CAA § 113, 42 U.S.C. § 7413 (federal enforcement); CAA § 114, 42 U.S.C. § 7414 (recordkeeping inspections, monitoring, and entry); CAA § 303, 42 U.S.C. § 7603 (imminent and substantial endangerment prevention); and CAA § 304, 42 U.S.C. § 7604 (citizen suit enforcement). Some unique and significant issues of enforcement are presented by the Act, however, given the division of authority between the states and the federal government in implementing the NAAQSs. Enforcement authority is further complicated by the creation of a permit system under the 1990 amendments similar to that under the Federal Water Pollution Control Act, by the sheer number of separate and distinct regulatory programs, and by provisions authorizing EPA to delegate enforcement authority for many of these programs to qualifying states on a program-by-program basis.

Title VII of the 1990 amendments completely revised the federal enforcement provisions of section 113 to strengthen the provisions and increase civil and criminal penalties. H.R. Conf. Rep. No. 952, 101st Cong., 2d Sess. 347 (1990). To detect violations, EPA is given the authority to require sources "on a one-time, periodic, or ongoing basis" to keep records, make reports, monitor emissions, and provide such other information as may be required. CAA § 114(a)(1), 42 U.S.C. § 7414(a)(1). The Administrator also has a right of entry to review records, inspect monitoring, and sample emissions. CAA § 114(a)(2), 42 U.S.C. § 7414(a)(2). The 1990 amendments expanded EPA's information-gathering authority. For the first time EPA may issue administrative subpoenas in enforcement proceedings to obtain information. CAA § 307(a), 42 U.S.C. § 7607(a). EPA is also authorized to pay rewards for information leading to imposition of criminal sanctions or civil penalties. CAA § 113(f), 42 U.S.C. § 7413(f). *See generally* James Miskiewicz & John S. Rudd, *Civil and Criminal Enforcement of the Clean Air Act After the 1990 Amendments*, 9 PACE ENVTL. L. REV. 281 (1992).

The 1990 amendments also added enhanced monitoring and "compliance certification" requirements. Compliance certifications are required from each owner or operator of a major stationary source, and EPA may require them for other sources. The certification must include

> (A) identification of the applicable requirement that is the basis of the certification, (B) the method used for determining the compliance status of the source, (C) the compliance status, (D) whether compliance is continuous or intermittent, (E) such other facts as the Administrator may require.

CAA § 114(a)(3), 42 U.S.C. § 7414(a)(3). These new reporting requirements for compliance certifications and emissions data, similar to those for the Federal Water Pollution Control Act, should facilitate enforcement. In particular, the availability of the data to the public (*see* CAA § 114(e), 42 U.S.C. § 7414(c)) should facilitate citizen suit enforcement of the Act's requirements. In the past EPA evaluated compliance status by on-site inspections or by investigatory letters to a specific source. S. Rep. No. 228, 101st Cong., 1st Sess. 368-69 (1989). EPA's broad inspection and information-gathering authority is subject to statutory and constitutional restraints. Section 114(a) delineates the statutory purposes which circumscribe EPA's investigatory powers, and the Fourth Amendment requires that all searches and seizures be reasonable. *See* CAA § 114(a), 42 U.S.C. § 7414(a); *Dow Chem. Co. v. United States*, 476 U.S. 227 (1986) (aerial search, although not expressly authorized by the Clean Air Act, was within EPA's enforcement authority and was not a "search" due to the "open field" exception to the Fourth Amendment requirement of a warrant). EPA interprets the Supreme Court decision in *Marshall v. Barlow's, Inc.*, 436 U.S. 307 (1978), to require an administrative warrant for its administrative inspections. *See generally* 2 S. NOVICK, LAW OF ENVIRONMENTAL PROTECTION § 11.02[6]-[b][iii].

Thirty days after issuance of a notice of noncompliance to a source, EPA may (1) issue an administrative order requiring compliance; (2) impose administrative penalties under section 113(d); or (3) bring a civil enforcement action for an injunction, civil penalties, or both under section 113(b). CAA § 113(a)(1), (3) & (5), 42 U.S.C. § 7413(a)(1), (3) & (5). The thirty-day delay is to allow the state the opportunity to take action. S. Rep. No. 228, 101st Cong., 1st Sess. 361 (1989). It appears criminal sanctions under section 113(c) may be pursued at any time. CAA § 113(a)(5), 42 U.S.C. § 7413(a)(5). Except for violations of hazardous air pollutant standards, a compliance order does not take effect until the person to whom it is issued has had "an opportunity to confer with the Administrator concerning the alleged violation." CAA § 113(a)(4), 42 U.S.C. § 7413(a)(4). Issuance of an order does not preclude the state or EPA from assessing penalties or otherwise limit the enforcement options of the state or EPA. *Id.* EPA may issue an order with a compliance schedule of up to one year in length. *Id.*

As background to the materials which follow, review the Supreme Court's decision in *Union Electric Co. v. EPA*, pages 371-77 *supra.* In that case, the Supreme Court concluded that EPA approval of a SIP could not be challenged under the judicial review provision of section 307(b)(1), 42 U.S.C. § 7607(b)(1), on grounds of economic or technological feasibility. It noted, however, that such grounds could be raised at the state level in hearings on the SIP, in proceedings for a state-issued variance, and ultimately in the state courts as a challenge to the SIP or the state's denial of a variance. The Court added that technological and economic infeasibility also could be raised before EPA in fashioning a compliance order under section 113(a)(4), 42 U.S.C. § 7413(a)(4). In two footnotes, the Court specifically refused to address: (1) whether a defense of economic or technological infeasibility may be raised in civil or criminal enforcement proceedings; and (2) whether the due process clause requires that a source have had the opportunity at some time to raise such claims before a court. *Union Electric,* page 376 *supra,* nn. 18, 19. The following case sheds some light on these two issues when, three years after the Supreme Court decision, Union Electric was still not in compliance with the SIP and still was awaiting a final state decision on its variance request.

UNION ELECTRIC CO. v. ENVIRONMENTAL PROTECTION AGENCY

593 F.2d 299 (8th Cir. 1979)

HEANEY, CIRCUIT JUDGE.

The Environmental Protection Agency appeals from a judgment of the United States District Court for the Eastern District of Missouri which enjoined the EPA from instituting an enforcement proceeding under the Clean Air Act, 42 U.S.C. § 7401 *et seq.*, against the Union Electric Company or its officers while that Company is actively and in good faith pursuing a revision or variance of the sulfur dioxide (SO_2) regulations of the Missouri Implementation Plan in the administrative agencies and/or courts of the State of Missouri. We reverse the judgment of the District Court and direct that the complaint of Union Electric be dismissed.

. . . .

On August 18, 1974, Union Electric sought review in this Court, contending that the SO_2 emission regulations contained in the Missouri Implementation Plan were economically and technologically infeasible and that its emissions were not interfering with attainment or maintenance of the National Ambient Air Quality Standards (NAAQS). We held that the claims of infeasibility did not afford a basis for review under § 307(b)(1) of the Act, 42 U.S.C. § 1857h-5(b)(1), and dismissed Union Electric's petition for lack of jurisdiction. *Union Electric Co. v. Environmental Pro. Agcy.*, 515 F.2d 206 (8th Cir. 1975).

Our decision was affirmed by the Supreme Court on October 6, 1975. *Union Electric Co. v. EPA*, 427 U.S. 246 (1976)....

In September, 1976, Union Electric filed a petition with the Missouri Air Conservation Commission for a relaxation of the existing regulations for SO_2, or, in the alternative, for a variance from existing regulations for the Company's plants. In April, 1977, the Commission tabled the Company's request to change the existing SO_2 emission limitations and denied the Company's request for a variance for its St. Louis plant. The Commission indicated, however, that it would consider the Company's petition for variances for the Sioux and Labadie plants. A representative of the EPA was present and indicated agreement with that procedure. Variance petitions for the Sioux and Labadie plants were filed by the Company in September, 1977.

On November 11, 1977, the Regional Administrator of the EPA wrote a letter to the Director of the Missouri Division of Environmental Quality which stated, in pertinent part:

> Based on inspections conducted by the Environmental Protection Agency in the Fall of 1976, the Portage Des Sioux and Labadie power plants are both in violation of the SO_2 emission limitation in the approved Missouri Implementation Plan. As you know, Union Electric petitioned the Missouri Air Conservation Commission in the Fall of 1976 for a relaxation of the existing regulation for SO_2 or, in the alternative, for a variance from the existing regulation for the individual Union Electric plants. The Commission voted not to change the SO_2 emission limitations for the St. Louis metropolitan area, but indicated they would consider the company's petition for a variance for the Sioux and Labadie plants.
>
> In a letter to you dated May 31, 1977, Mr. Charles V. Wright, Acting Regional Administrator, stated that since the Commission had voted not to change the SO_2 emission limitation in the St. Louis regulation, the State was expected to act promptly to either bring the Union Electric plants into compliance with the existing limitation or to adopt and justify less stringent limitations in accordance with Federal requirements. Five months have passed and the State has yet to take any action with regard to the Labadie and Sioux power plants.
>
> ....
>
> I have asked my staff to inspect the Union Electric Meremac [sic], Sioux, and Labadie plants within the next forty-five (45) days to verify and formally document their current status of compliance with all applicable emission limitations in the State plan. If these sources are found to be in violation, this office will be required to take appropriate action under

Sections 113(a)(1) and 113(b) of the Act in the absence of any formal action by the Commission on the Union Electric variance petitions.

On January 13, 1978, the EPA notified Union Electric of its alleged violations of the SO_2 and opacity standards of the Missouri Implementation Plan. The EPA stated that Union Electric's Labadie and Sioux power plants were in violation of SO_2 and opacity regulations.... The notice invited Union Electric to a conference to discuss the violations, and set forth the statutory responsibilities of the Agency if the matter was not resolved within thirty days.

On February 3, 1978, the EPA held the conference with Union Electric. At this conference, the EPA indicated that it would commence enforcement proceedings without waiting for the decision of the Missouri Commission on the Company's request for variances for its plants. The EPA indicated that it was required to proceed with enforcement by § 111(b) [sic] of the Clean Air Act Amendments of 1977, 42 U.S.C. § 7413(b)(2)(B).

On February 8, 1978, Union Electric brought this action in federal District Court for the Eastern District of Missouri, seeking a declaratory judgment and temporary and permanent injunctive relief. It simultaneously sought action by the State of Missouri on its variance requests.

On March 16, 1978, the District Court granted the preliminary injunction requested by Union Electric. The court found: (1) that Union Electric was in the unenviable position of having daily penalties for noncompliance with the Missouri Implementation Plan accrue while it sought variances pursuant to the statutorily authorized procedure contained in Mo. Ann. Stat. § 203.110 (Vernon); (2) that the failure of Union Electric to comply with any governmental directive could constitute an act of default under its first mortgage and deed of trust and make its bonds callable, and that a calling of the bonds could force it into bankruptcy; (3) that compliance with the SO_2 regulations is not possible because compliance can be achieved only by installing flue gas desulfurization (FGD) equipment at an initial cost of $713 million and annual operating costs of $137 million, that the FGD equipment could not be relied upon to operate continually or satisfactorily, that the use of low sulfur coal as an alternative was not possible because the annual cost of such coal would be $179 million per year and would require a capital investment of $49 million, resulting in a rate increase of twenty-five percent, assuming that there was no reduction in the use of electricity, and that, in any event, it was impossible to obtain a sufficient supply of low sulfur coal to meet the SO_2 emission regulations; (4) that compliance with SO_2 regulations could be achieved only by a shutdown of the Union Electric plants which would result in a widespread electrical breakdown throughout the Midwest and drastic financial consequences to Union Electric; (5) that the injury to the EPA was not substantial because Union Electric's plants did not violate the National Air Quality Standards for SO_2; and (6) that Union Electric had a substantial likelihood of success on the merits because the Missouri Air Conservation Commission had informally indicated it would approve the variance.

The court concluded that: (1) considerations of procedural due process required that Union Electric be permitted to seek a variance under state procedures for SO$_2$ emissions prior to suffering a grievous loss which may result from an enforcement proceeding by the EPA; (2) that it had the general equitable power to stay an enforcement proceeding to prevent irreparable harm while Union Electric seeks the variances, in good faith, under state procedures; and (3) that the only fair interpretation of the Clean Air Act is to allow the variance proceeding to proceed to completion prior to the initiation of an enforcement action. This appeal was filed on May 15, 1978.

On July 26, 1978, more than two months after this appeal was filed, the Missouri Air Conservation Commission granted the variance in the SO$_2$ standards requested by Union Electric for its Sioux and Labadie plants. A petition to review that variance was subsequently filed in the Circuit Court of Cole County, Missouri, by the Coalition for the Environment and by the State of Illinois. That action is still pending.

....

... Section 7413(b) specifically requires the Administrator to commence a civil action for injunctive relief or for the assessment of civil or criminal penalties thirty days after notice of violation has been given to a major stationary source. One purpose of this section is to require the states to act promptly in granting or denying variance requests. This purpose would be thwarted if federal courts were permitted to remove the pressures that Congress clearly thought necessary to accomplish the objectives of the Clean Air Act....

No case could better illustrate the need for expeditious enforcement than this one. The Missouri Implementation Plan was approved on May 31, 1972. Now, nearly seven years later, Union Electric is still not in compliance with the plan's SO$_2$ emissions limitations at its Labadie or Sioux plants, and the State of Missouri has yet to finally approve or disapprove its request for a variance from existing standards.

This statement of fact is not necessarily intended to point the finger at Union Electric, the State of Missouri or the EPA. All have been responsible in one way or another for the delays that have occurred. It is only to emphasize that we can only be faithful to the mandate of Congress if we require strict adherence to the procedural routes which it established for bringing clean air to the nation.

In *Fry*, [*Lloyd A. Fry Roofing Co. v. EPA*, 554 F.2d 885 (8th Cir. 1977)] we did not consider a contention by Union Electric which was deemed important by the District Court, i.e., that Union Electric has a due process right to contest the validity of the emission standard without necessarily having to face ruinous penalties if it loses its action. The District Court relied on *Ex parte Young*, 209 U.S. 123 (1908), in so holding. In *Young*, the State of Minnesota enacted a number of statutes which established maximum rates which could be charged by railroads within the State and which fixed penalties for the railroads' failure to comply. Railroad officials contended that the statutes were invalid because the penalties imposed were so severe that no company official would run the risk of violating the statutes in order to test their validity. The Supreme Court sustained their contention. It stated:

> Another Federal question is the alleged unconstitutionality of these acts because of the enormous penalties denounced for their violation, which prevent the railway company, as alleged, or any of its servants or employees, from resorting to the courts for the purpose of determining the validity of such acts. The contention is urged by the complainants in the suit that the company is denied the equal protection of the laws and its property is liable to be taken without due process of law, because it is only allowed a hearing upon the claim of the unconstitutionality of the acts and orders in question, at the risk, if mistaken, of being subjected to such enormous penalties, resulting in the possible confiscation of its whole property, that rather than take such risks the company would obey the laws, although such obedience might also result in the end (though by a slower process) in such confiscation.
>
> ....
>
> [When] the penalties for disobedience are by fines so enormous and imprisonment so severe as to intimidate the company and its officers from resorting to the courts to test the validity of the legislation, the result is the same as if the law in terms prohibited the company from seeking judicial construction of laws which deeply affect its rights.
>
> ... Now, to impose upon a party interested the burden of obtaining a judicial decision of such a question (no prior hearing having ever been given) only upon the condition that, if unsuccessful, he must suffer imprisonment and pay fines, as provided in these acts, is, in effect, to close up all approaches to the courts, and thus prevent any hearing upon the question whether the rates as provided by the acts are not too low, and therefore invalid. The distinction is obvious between a case where the validity of the act depends upon the existence of a fact which can be determined only after investigation of a very complicated and technical character, and the ordinary case of statute upon a subject requiring no such investigation, and over which the jurisdiction of the legislature is complete in any event.

Id. at 144-145, 148.

We do not believe *Young* to be applicable here. Union Electric has an opportunity to test the validity of the Missouri Implementation Plan without *necessarily* incurring confiscatory fines and penalties. The Administrator of the EPA ... has two alternatives. He can either seek injunctive relief or can seek to impose civil or criminal penalties. We should not anticipate what the Administrator will seek in advance of his decision. Thus, it cannot be said that confiscatory fines and penalties will *necessarily* be incurred. Indeed, the Administrator apparently feels, in this case, that he has a third alternative — that of staying enforcement until the resolution of Union Electric's variance request.[8]

Union Electric makes a corollary argument that it must, at some point, have a forum in which to raise its contention that compliance with the Missouri Implementation Plan is economically and technologically infeasible, and that denial of such a forum results in its property being taken without due process of law. Without ruling on the merits of this issue, the Supreme Court stated in *Union Electric Co. v. EPA, supra*, that such a forum is available to alleged violators because contentions of economic and technological infeasibility can be raised in state court. *Union Electric Co. v. EPA, supra* 427 U.S. at 266-267. Moreover, this Court held in *Fry* that such issues can be raised as a defense in an enforcement proceeding.[9] *Lloyd A. Fry Roofing Co. v. United States EPA, supra* at 891. The EPA conceded at oral argument that these issues can be raised in an enforcement proceeding. It affirmed that position in a postargument memorandum which states:

> Our position remains that, as was stated in *Union Electric v. Environmental Protection Agcy.*, 427 U.S. 246, 268 (1976), "claims of technological or economic infeasibility ... are relevant to fashioning an appropriate compliance order under § 113(a)(4)." And, of course, when a compliance order becomes the subject of an enforcement proceeding, then those same claims may be considered by the courts. Concededly, the Supreme Court, in footnote 18 of the *Union Electric* decision, *supra* at page 268, expressly declined to address the question whether economic or technological infeasibility may be raised as a defense in civil or criminal enforcement proceedings. In our opinion, however, the correct rule must be that while such matters may not be raised in defense when the purpose of the defense is to contest the validity or constitutionality of an order, they may be raised as matters to be considered where the object of the proceeding is to fashion a schedule and plan which a company can comply with.

We cannot, of course, read more into *Fry* or into the EPA's concession than was intended. We do not now hold that the Clean Air Act will ultimately permit

---

[8]On September 13, 1978, the EPA notified Union Electric that it will not initiate any enforcement proceedings against that Company with respect to its alleged violations of the existing SO_2 emission limitations until the Regional Administrator of the EPA has informed Union Electric, in writing, of its decision regarding a recommended approval or disapproval of the variance. The Company was further notified that if EPA's Regional Office recommended approval, the enforcement stay would be extended until such time as the Administrator of EPA has taken final action on the variance request. This notification would also appear to eliminate any risk that the Company's bonds would be called for failure to follow a governmental directive. We express no opinion as to whether this stay is authorized by the Act.

[9]In *Union Electric Co. v. EPA, supra* at 268 n.18, the Supreme Court declined to decide whether questions of economic and technological infeasibility can be raised in an enforcement proceeding.

a noncomplying polluter to continue operations without change if such change is not technologically or economically feasible. We do hold, however, that this question can be raised in any future enforcement proceeding, and that Union Electric at that time will be able to argue that Congress did not intend that result or that, if it was intended, the statute is unconstitutional.[10]

We reserve our decision on that issue until it is properly presented to us.

NOTES AND QUESTIONS

1. State variance proceedings can take time, as evidenced by *Union Electric.* In the interim, should a company invest resources to comply with a standard from which it may ultimately be excused by a variance, or do nothing and run the risk of enforcement measures by the state or EPA? How might your answer be affected by EPA's imposition of fines in the interim?

2. Union Electric failed in its attempt to obtain what is known as "pre-enforcement judicial review." Section 307 limits challenges to the validity of a SIP to the federal court of appeals for the appropriate circuit within sixty days of the Administrator's approval of the SIP. Attempts to attack a SIP in federal court outside of section 307 by enjoining the Administrator's approval or enforcement of the SIP have been unsuccessful. *See generally* W. RODGERS, JR., ENVIRONMENTAL LAW § 3.9(f) (1984). The courts have been unwilling to open up any opportunities for delay and forum-shopping when Congress has designated an exclusive forum for judicial review of such challenges. As noted in the Supreme Court decision in *Union Electric*, the company did not seek judicial review under section 307 of the Administrator's approval of the SIP within the statutory time period. As a result, any challenges which the company could have made to the Administrator's approval under section 307(b)(1) could not be brought in civil or criminal proceedings for enforcement. CAA § 307(b)(2), 42 U.S.C. § 7607(b)(2). The danger of preclusion of review under section 307(b)(2) is significant given the Supreme Court's broad interpretation of actions reviewable under section 307(b)(1). In *Harrison v. PPG Indus.*, 446 U.S. 578 (1980), the Court held that a determination by an EPA regional administrator in an exchange of letters that a company was subject to a new source performance standard was a "final action of the Administrator ... locally or regionally

---

[10]Mr. Justice Powell, concurring in *Union Electric Co. v. EPA, supra* at 271-272, stated:

Environmental concerns, long neglected, merit high priority, and Congress properly has made protection of the public health its paramount consideration.... But the shutdown of an urban area's electrical service could have an even more serious impact on the health of the public than that created by a decline in ambient air quality. The result apparently required by this legislation in its present form could sacrifice the well-being of a large metropolitan area through the imposition of inflexible demands that may be technologically impossible to meet and indeed may no longer even be necessary to the attainment of the goal of clean air. I believe that Congress, if fully aware of this draconian possibility, would strike a different balance.

applicable" and thus reviewable under section 307(b)(1). What issues must be brought in federal court pursuant to section 307(b)(1)? What issues *can* be raised subsequently in the enforcement proceeding?

What opportunity remained for Union Electric after this decision to raise its claims of economic or technological infeasibility? If the standard is not feasible, does that excuse Union Electric from compliance in the enforcement proceeding? If Congress did not intend for infeasibility to be a defense, is the Act unconstitutional in that respect? Consider these questions in light of the following opinion.

NAVISTAR INTERNATIONAL TRANSPORTATION CORP. v. ENVIRONMENTAL PROTECTION AGENCY

858 F.2d 282 (6th Cir. 1988)

RYAN, CIRCUIT JUDGE.

Petitioner, Navistar International Transportation Corporation (Navistar) (formerly International Harvester), seeks review of the decision of the Administrator of the Environmental Protection Agency finding petitioner liable for violations of the Clean Air Act. We affirm.

Navistar appeals the decision of the Administrator (EPA) finding Navistar liable for violating § 120 of the Clean Air Act, 42 U.S.C. § 7420. Navistar operates a truck assembly facility in Springfield, Ohio.

. . . .

On September 24, 1984, the EPA notified Navistar that it was not in compliance with the Ohio SIP, as its painting lines emitted pollutants beyond the emission limitations.... The notice informed Navistar it could either calculate the penalty owed and a payment schedule, or file a petition for reconsideration.

After three extensions, Navistar filed its petition for reconsideration on March 4, 1985. Navistar raised four issues: (1) that two painting lines were not within the definition of "coating lines," (2) that four painting lines were subject to the SIP refinishing exemption, (3) that four painting lines were not subject to regulation as they paint plastic as well as metallic parts, and (4) that the EPA was without jurisdiction due to insufficiency of the notice of noncompliance. A hearing was held before an Administrative Law Judge (ALJ) on March 4 and 5, 1986. The ALJ excluded evidence of technological and economic infeasibility in that it was irrelevant to the issue of liability. He held that the offer of proof on economic infeasibility evidence could be retained as proof on the penalty phase of the hearing.

The ALJ found Navistar in violation of the Ohio SIP. Navistar appealed to the Administrator, who affirmed the ALJ's decision through the EPA's chief judicial officer. Navistar then sought review in this court.

The court affirmed the Administrator's determination that the SIP had been violated.

. . . .

Prior to the hearing before the ALJ, the EPA filed a motion *in limine* to exclude from the liability hearing evidence by Navistar of the technological and economic infeasibility of compliance with the SIP. The ALJ excluded the evidence from the liability hearing. He found, and the parties had earlier agreed, that the hearing before the ALJ was only to determine whether petitioner was liable for not being in compliance with the Ohio SIP. 40 C.F.R. § 66.41-43. A second hearing would be held to determine what the penalty for noncompliance would be. 40 C.F.R. § 66.41-54. The ALJ ruled that the evidence of infeasibility "may be retained in the record as an offer of proof on the issue of liability for a penalty (second stage of hearing)."

Technological and economic infeasibility arguments were first raised in *Union Electric Co. v. EPA*, 427 U.S. 246 (1976), by a petitioner who was challenging the SIP itself as opposed to that petitioner's compliance with the SIP. In that context, the Court held that technological and economic infeasibility arguments were not to be heard. The Court found that such a requirement would thwart the goals of and legislative intent behind the Clean Air Act. *Id.* at 269. The Court specifically left open the question of whether due process requires the claims of technological and economic infeasibility be heard at some time. *Id.* at 269, n.19.

This court spoke to the due process issue in *United States v. Ford Motor Co.*, 814 F.2d 1099 (6th Cir. 1987). In *Ford*, the company had challenged a SIP provision on infeasibility grounds in state court. This court held that a state court judgment does not preclude federal enforcement of the SIP. The company then argued that due process is violated by such a holding in that the state forum is the only forum in which to raise the infeasibility claims. This court stated:

> Ford's contention can best be answered by noting that the Clean Air Act envisions situations where standards currently economically or technologically infeasible will nonetheless be enforced. *See Union Electric Co. v. EPA*, 427 U.S. 246, 258-59, [citation]. Congress has the authority to demand that "existing sources of pollutants either should meet the standard of the law or be closed down ...", regardless of whether such standards are currently feasible. S. Rep. No. 91-1196, p. 2-3 (1970), quoted in *Union Electric Co., supra*, 427 U.S. at 259.
>
> In addition, we note that meaningful opportunities for raising claims of technological and economic infeasibility have been provided by the Act.
>
> ....
>
> [T]echnical infeasibility coupled with good faith efforts can be considered by the district court as a factor mitigating against the imposition of monetary penalties in the enforcement action.

Ford Motor Co., 814 F.2d at 1103-04.

Given Congress' intent to obtain compliance or require that facilities be shut down, regardless of feasibility, and given that due process concerns are satisfied by allowing infeasibility arguments at the penalty stage, we affirm the ALJ's decision to exclude evidence of technological and economic infeasibility at the liability hearing. As the evidence was retained in the record for purposes of the penalty hearing, any due process requirements were met.

NOTES AND QUESTIONS

1. EPA can bring a civil action for an injunction, civil penalties, or both in the federal district court where the violation occurred, where the defendant resides, or where the defendant's principal place of business is located. CAA § 113, 42 U.S.C. § 7413. A civil action "shall, as appropriate," be brought by the Administrator for certain designated violations if the violator is an "affected source" under the acid deposition controls of Title IV (discussed on pages 441-43 *supra*), a "major emitting facility" under the PSD program, or a "major stationary source" under the nonattainment provisions. CAA § 113(b), 42 U.S.C. § 7413(b). The district court may enjoin the violation, require compliance, assess civil penalties, or "award any other appropriate relief." *Id.* The court may also award litigation costs, including attorney and expert witness fees, to the defendant if the court finds that the action brought was "unreasonable." *Id.*

In fashioning equitable relief, how much discretion does the district court have to delay compliance? Recall the *Weinberger v. Romero-Barcelo* case on page 41 *supra*. In *United States v. Wheeling-Pittsburgh Steel Corp.*, 818 F.2d 1077 (3d Cir. 1987), Wheeling had entered into a consent decree, after being sued by EPA, which gave Wheeling until the relevant statutory deadline to comply with a SIP limitation. Subsequently, Wheeling succeeded in having the decree modified with an indefinite extension for compliance due to its bankruptcy reorganization, a labor strike, and a pending "bubble" application with the state. The court concluded that a district court retains some equitable discretion to modify a statutory deadline in a consent decree, but neither the source's application for state permission to use a bubble or the claimed economic infeasibility of compliance justified delayed compliance beyond the statutory deadline.

2. Assume that Union Electric ultimately prevails in the state court proceedings on its variance. At what point is the variance as a revision of the SIP enforceable as a matter of state law? When does the revised SIP become enforceable by EPA as federal law? Is the "old" SIP enforceable by EPA until the revised SIP becomes enforceable as a matter of federal law?

GENERAL MOTORS CORP. v. UNITED STATES
496 U.S. 530 (1990)

JUSTICE BLACKMUN delivered the opinion of the Court.

This case concerns a Clean Air Act enforcement action by the Environmental Protection Agency (EPA) against petitioner General Motors Corporation (GMC). We are asked to decide whether the 4-month time limit on EPA review of an original state implementation plan (SIP) also applies to its review of a SIP revision, and whether, if EPA fails to complete its review of a SIP revision in a timely manner, EPA is prevented from enforcing an existing SIP.

....

The entire Commonwealth of Massachusetts is a nonattainment area for NAAQS [sic] with respect to ozone. Petitioner GMC owns and operates an automobile assembly plant in Framingham, Mass. The plant's painting operation is a source of volatile organic compounds that contribute to ozone. In 1980, EPA approved Massachusetts' proposed nonattainment area SIP governing volatile organic compound emissions from automobile-painting operations. The SIP permitted GMC to meet emissions limits in stages, but required full compliance by December 31, 1985. In 1981, EPA published a policy statement suggesting that new technology in automobile-painting operations might justify deferral of industry compliance until 1986 or 1987. Three years later, in November 1984, GMC sought an extension from the December 31, 1985, compliance date imposed by the existing SIP, not for the new technology, but rather for additional time to install emission controls on its existing lines. In June 1985, GMC proposed converting to the new technology and requested a summer 1987 deadline. The Commonwealth approved the revision and submitted the proposal to EPA on December 30, 1985, one day before the existing SIP compliance deadline.

GMC began construction of a new painting facility but continued to operate its existing plant. On August 14, 1986, EPA sent GMC a Notice of Violation informing GMC that it was in violation of the applicable SIP. Approximately one year later, on August 17, 1987, respondent filed an enforcement action under § 113(b) of the Act, 42 U.S.C. § 7413(b), alleging violations of the existing SIP's 1985 deadline. On September 4, 1988, the agency made its final decision to reject the revision.

The District Court construed § 110(a)(3) as imposing a 4-month time limit on EPA review of a SIP revision, and concluded that when EPA failed to complete its review within four months, it was barred from enforcing the existing SIP during the interval between the end of the 4-month period and the time EPA finally acted on the revision. Because EPA had not issued a Notice of Noncompliance until well after the 4-month period had elapsed and, at the time of the court's ruling, had yet to make a final decision on the Commonwealth's SIP revision, summary judgment was entered for GMC.

The Court of Appeals for the First Circuit reversed that judgment and remanded the case for further proceedings. The Court of Appeals agreed with the District Court that the Act imposed a 4-month deadline on EPA review of a SIP revision, but concluded that the failure to meet that deadline did not preclude EPA from enforcing the existing SIP.

Reasoning that an enforcement bar was too drastic a remedy for agency delay, the court concluded that the appropriate remedies for agency inaction were those provided by the Act itself: a suit to compel agency action under § 304(a)(2), 42 U.S.C. § 7604(a)(2), or a request pursuant to § 113(b), 42 U.S.C. § 7413(b), for reduction or elimination of penalties during the period in which unreasonable agency delay resulted in prejudice. We granted certiorari because of a disagreement among the Circuits as to whether EPA is barred from enforcing an existing SIP if the agency fails to take action on a proposed SIP revision within four months.

To assure that some form of pollution-control requirements were put in place quickly, the 1970 Amendments established a series of deadlines. One of these was the requirement that EPA act on a proposed SIP within four months after the State submits its plan. § 110(a)(2), 42 U.S.C. § 7410(a)(2). Specifically, the provision requires EPA to act within "four months after the date required for submission of a plan." This seems to us to refer only to the action required on the original SIP. Section 110(a)(2), by its terms, therefore does not impose such a time restraint on EPA review of a SIP *revision*.

Petitioner nevertheless claims that § 110(a)(3) requires EPA to act on a proposed SIP revision within four months. That provision requires the Administrator to approve "any revision of an implemented plan ... if he determines that it meets the requirements of paragraph (2) [§ 110(a)(2)] and has been adopted by the State after reasonable notice and public hearings." Petitioner contends that the reference to § 110(a)(2) was intended to incorporate both the substantive and the procedural requirements of that provision.

[The Court held that the four-month deadline in section 110(a)(2) was not meant to apply to SIP revisions.]

....

Although the 4-month deadline does not apply, EPA remains subject to the Administrative Procedure Act's (APA's) statutory requirements of timeliness. The APA requires agencies to conclude matters "within a reasonable time," 5 U.S.C. § 555(b), and provides a remedy for agency action "unreasonably delayed." 5 U.S.C. § 706(1). Respondent concedes, as we think it must, that its action on a proposed SIP revision is subject to that mandate.

Petitioner's main claim is that any delay over four months is categorically unreasonable because it violates EPA's statutory duty to process a revision within that period. We have rejected that claim above, but we nevertheless must consider petitioner's alternative contention that EPA may not bring an action to enforce an existing SIP if it unreasonably delays in acting on the proposed revision. Without deciding whether the delay in this case was unreasonable, we now address this claim. Because the statute does not reveal any congressional intent to bar enforcement of an existing SIP if EPA delays unreasonably in acting on a proposed SIP revision, we agree with the Court of Appeals that such an enforcement action is not barred.

The language of the Clean Air Act plainly states that EPA may bring an action for penalties or injunctive relief whenever a person is in violation of any requirement of an "applicable implementation plan." § 113(b)(2), 42 U.S.C. § 7413(b)(2). There can be little or no doubt that the existing SIP remains the "applicable implementation plan" even after the State has submitted a proposed revision. The statute states: "For purposes of this chapter, an applicable implementation plan is the implementation plan, or most recent revision thereof, which has been approved under [§ 110(a), 42 U.S.C. § 7410(a)] or promulgated under [110(c), 42 U.S.C. § 7410(c)] and which implements the requirements of this section." § 110(d), 42 U.S.C. § 7410(d). Both this Court and the Courts of Appeals have recognized that the approved SIP is the applicable implementation plan during the time a SIP revision proposal is pending. The commentators agree with this conclusion.

There is nothing in the statute that limits EPA's authority to enforce the "applicable implementation plan" solely to those cases where EPA has not unreasonably delayed action on a proposed SIP revision. Moreover, we find it significant that Congress expressly enacted an enforcement bar elsewhere in the statute. *See* § 113(d)(10); 42 U.S.C. § 7413(d)(10) ("During the period of the order ... no Federal enforcement action pursuant to this section and no action under section 304 of this Act shall be pursued against such owner...."). The fact that Congress explicitly enacted an enforcement bar similar to the one proposed by petitioner in one section of the statute, but failed to do so in the section at issue in this case reinforces our refusal to import such a bar here.[3]

We note that other statutory remedies are available when EPA delays action on a SIP revision. Although these statutory remedies may not appear to be so strong a deterrent to EPA delay as would an enforcement bar, these are the remedies that Congress has provided in the statute. In the absence of a specific provision suggesting that Congress intended to create an enforcement bar, we decline to infer one.

The judgment of the Court of Appeals is affirmed.

It is so ordered.

NOTES AND QUESTIONS

1. What are the statutory remedies available for EPA's failure to act on a revised SIP within the time limit? The 1990 amendments now require that EPA act on SIP revisions within twelve months of submission. CAA § 110(k)(2), 42 U.S.C. § 7410(k)(2). How long could EPA delay action on a revision under *General Motors* before the prior SIP would become enforceable?

2. *General Motors* points out that section 110(d), 42 U.S.C. § 7410(d), recognizes the last approved SIP or revised SIP as the one which is enforceable. Does state court invalidation of a SIP preclude its enforcement by EPA? Does it

---

[3]Our conclusion is further supported by the language of § 110(g), 42 U.S.C. § 7410(g). Section 110(g) grants certain authority to a State's governor to suspend the existing SIP after four months. As the Court of Appeals discerned, there would have been no reason for Congress to add that section if the existing SIP automatically became unenforceable after some period of EPA delay. The existence of this explicit exception indicates that in all other circumstances the existing SIP remains in effect.

matter what the grounds were for the invalidation, or whether the invalidation occurred before or after EPA approval? In *Sierra Club v. Indiana-Kentucky Elec. Corp.*, 716 F.2d 1145 (7th Cir. 1983), the Seventh Circuit Court of Appeals concluded that once a plan is adopted by the state *and* withstands any subsequent procedural challenges in state court, invalidation under the federal statute may occur only in the federal appellate courts. EPA could not enforce a SIP provision that was invalid under state law when EPA approved it. In contrast, a state court consent decree, after EPA approval, invalidating a SIP on grounds of technological infeasibility has been held not to preclude federal enforcement. *United States v. Ford Motor Co.*, 814 F.2d 1099 (6th Cir. 1987). Although the permit system created in the 1990 amendments should help to clarify what limitations a specific source must meet and when, SIPs are still independently enforceable so that the possibilities for conflict between state-approved and federally-approved standards remain.

3. Once EPA has detected a violation, it has a wide range of sanctions that it can pursue. As noted earlier, thirty days after issuance of a notice of noncompliance EPA may issue a compliance order, impose administrative penalties, or bring a civil suit for an injunction or judicially-imposed civil penalties, or both. CAA § 113(a)(1), (3) & (5), 42 U.S.C. § 7413(a)(1), (3) & (5). Issuance of a compliance order does not preclude EPA from assessing administrative penalties or pursuing judicial enforcement. CAA § 113(a)(4), 42 U.S.C. § 7413(a)(4).

Administrative penalties and civil judicial penalties may be assessed in an amount of up to $25,000 per day for each violation. CAA § 113(b) & (d), 42 U.S.C. § 7413(b) & (d). Both types of penalties are calculated using the factors set out in section 113(e), 42 U.S.C. § 7413(e). However, administrative penalties may not exceed $200,000 and may not be imposed if the first alleged date of violation occurred more than twelve months before initiation of administrative proceedings, unless the Administrator and Attorney General jointly determine that such a larger penalty or longer period of violation is appropriate for administrative action. CAA § 173(d)(1), 42 U.S.C. § 7413(d)(1). The Administrator must provide a notice of the proposed assessment of administrative penalties and of the opportunity to request a hearing within thirty days of receipt of the notice. CAA § 113(d)(2)(A), 42 U.S.C. § 7413(d)(2)(A).

There is another type of penalty under the Act that may be assessed by EPA, or a state by delegation from EPA. For certain serious violations, EPA may impose noncompliance penalties equal to the economic benefits derived from delayed compliance. Of the two cases which follow, the first addresses judicial assessment of civil penalties and the second assessment of section 120 noncompliance penalties.

UNITED STATES v. SCM CORP.

667 F. Supp. 1110 (D. Md. 1987)

RAMSEY, DISTRICT JUDGE.

The United States brought this action against the SCM Corporation (hereinafter "defendant" or "SCM") at the request of the Administrator of the Environmental Protection Agency (hereinafter "EPA"). The action, brought pursuant to 42 U.S.C. § 7413(b), seeks injunctive relief and the imposition of civil penalties as a result of defendant's alleged violations of the Clean Air Act [citation] and the State Implementation Plan approved by the EPA pursuant to the Act....

....

SCM is a major corporation with operations in chemicals, coatings and resins, paper products, foods and typewriters. SCM Corporation is one of the four leading world producers of titanium dioxide, a white inorganic pigment widely used as a whitener and opacifier in the manufacture of paint, paper, plastic and rubber products. SCM is a leading producer of chemicals derived from crude sulfate turpentine. It is one of the four largest coatings and resins manufacturers in the United States. Company management believes that SCM's sales of "Smith-Corona" electric and electronic typewriters in the United States were greater than those of any other company during the year ended June 30, 1985. SCM had $2.18 billion in net sales for fiscal 1985. The company paid a cash dividend of $2.00 per share in each of the four years preceding and including 1985. In 1985, total cash dividends equalled $20,000,000.

....

A. *Civil Penalties*

Section 7413(b) provides for a civil penalty of not more than $25,000 per day of violation.

EPA has proven 14 daily violations of the Maryland SIP limits for particulate matter and 16 daily violations of the Maryland SIP limits for sulfuric acid mist during the relevant penalty period. The maximum available civil penalty for the 30 days of proven violations is $750,000 (30 × $25,000).

Having calculated the maximum civil penalty available, other factors must be considered by the court in determining the appropriate penalty to assess. Section 7413(b) directs that the Court take into consideration (in addition to other factors) the size of the business, the economic impact of the penalty on the business, and the seriousness of the violation. In addition to the factors listed in the statute, other Courts have considered technological or economic infeasibility, good faith, or a lack thereof, on the part of the violating source, the violating source's relationship with the state and governmental delay in bringing the action.... [Citation.]

Application of the first two factors, size of the business and economic impact of the penalty, supports the imposition of a substantial penalty. SCM, like Chevron U.S.A., Inc., is a major corporation. "Only a substantial penalty would have any economic impact or serve as any deterrent." *Chevron U.S.A., Inc.*, 639 F. Supp. at 779. Imposition of the entire $750,000 available would result in a penalty equal to less than four percent of the 20 million dollars in cash dividends paid by the company in fiscal 1985.

SCM's violations of the applicable Maryland SIP limits were serious violations. The Court refused to presume, based on the limited test results available, that SCM was in continuous violation of the SIP limits for the purpose of determining days of violation. But, based even on the limited data available, there is little doubt that had stack tests been performed with greater regularity prior to 1986, a substantial number of additional violations might have been identified. The seriousness of SCM's violations is evident, however, even from the relatively few days of violation proved. Test results obtained on the 30 days of proven violations show particulate matter and sulfuric acid mist measurements equal to two, three and four times SIP limits for those pollutants.

The court heard considerable testimony and argument throughout the trial of this matter on the issue of technological infeasibility. It should be noted that technological infeasibility is not a complete defense to Clean Air Act violations. *See United States v. Ford Motor Co.*, 814 F.2d 1099, 1103-04 (6th Cir. 1987); *United States v. Wheeling Pittsburgh Steel Corp.*, 642 F. Supp. 468, 473 (W.D. Pa. 1986). The Clean Air Act, like Maryland's SIP, is intended to be "technology forcing." [Citation.] Technological infeasibility may be considered, however, as a factor mitigating against the imposition of monetary penalties. [Citation.]

In this case, technological infeasibility mitigates, to some extent, against the imposition of a substantial penalty. In its March, 1979, Final Report prepared for EPA, GCA Corporation acknowledged that only one of the four plants in the United States then producing titanium dioxide pigment via the sulfate process employed an emission control system capable of achieving Maryland's 0.03 gr/SCFD standard for particulate matter. The report further notes that "it cannot be unequivocally stated that [SCM] is not using the best available control equipment."

Reference to the GCA report, without more, would suggest that technological infeasibility should be a substantial mitigating factor. But several circumstances, in addition to the many disclaimers and qualifiers in the report itself, counsel against placing great weight on the GCA report. Technological infeasibility cannot be examined without a corresponding inquiry into good faith. "[T]he absence of demonstrable good faith efforts toward compliance should serve to dampen any enthusiasm for technological and economic arguments advanced in defense of a claimed violation." *Ford Motor Co.*, 814 F.2d at 1104 (quoting *Indiana & Michigan Elec. Co. v. E.P.A.*, 509 F.2d 839, 845 (7th Cir. 1975)). It is evident that at least prior to 1977, SCM dragged its feet, and did not work expeditiously toward compliance. The July 28, 1976, memo from Leonard Burgess characterizes the various air pollution plans of compliance SCM negotiated with the State as a "means to buy time." The memo further admits that SCM did not "regard the plan dates as commandments ... and [SCM] worked toward [its] own best interests." SCM made its most impressive efforts to achieve compliance after the State issued its Notice of Violation in January, 1983.

It should also be noted that the GCA report is dated March, 1979. The Court has held that the relevant period for assessment of civil penalties in this case did not begin until January, 1980, five years prior to the filing of this action. Accordingly, it is the period from 1980 to the present that should be examined in connection with any claimed technological infeasibility. In the early 1980's, SCM's efforts at its Adrian Joyce Works were directed more toward the development and installation of its waste heat recycle system than toward achieving compliance with emission limits. SCM demonstrated its ability to be a leader in the development of new and effective technology with the development and installation of its waste heat recycle system. That same creative energy could have been employed to develop an effective emission control system. Later, when it was forced to do so, after the issuance of the State's NOV in January, 1983, SCM was able to develop in a relatively brief period of time an emission control system capable of achieving State limits for particulate matter and sulfuric acid mist. The Court recognizes that SCM developed the waste heat recycle system at a time when energy conservation was a, if not "the," national priority. However, that does not excuse the failure to meet SIP limits.

In an earlier opinion, disposing of one of the pretrial motions filed in this action, the Court recognized that a violator's relationship with the State may be taken into account by the Court when determining the appropriateness of the relief prayed by plaintiff. [Citation.] In this case, however, SCM's relationship with the State is entitled to little weight. SCM cooperated with the State when it had to; when it faced the possibility of a time consuming and potentially expensive enforcement action.

Finally, some mention of governmental delay should be made. EPA suggests that SCM has been in continuous violation of the Maryland SIP provisions for particulate matter and sulfuric acid mist emissions from the effective date of the SIP, May 31, 1972, to the present. But EPA issued its NOV on April 20, 1984, and it filed this action in January, 1985. The Court does not believe that the government's delay in bringing this action should mitigate against imposition of a substantial penalty; nor should it act to enhance the penalty amount. Suffice it to say that the threat of this action has evidently encouraged SCM to develop an emission control system capable of achieving State limits on particulate matter and acid mist. Earlier action on the part of EPA may have eliminated years of potentially hazardous air pollution.

Having considered the relevant factors the Court imposes the following penalties:

> For the five violations of particulate matter of acid mist limits occurring on days during the period from January, 1980, through January, 1983, the Court imposes $20,000 per violation, for a total of $100,000;

For the 25 violations of particulate matter of acid mist limits occurring on days during the period from February, 1983, through May, 1986, the Court imposes $10,000 per violation, for a total of $250,000;

The total civil penalty imposed shall be $350,000.

B. *Equitable Relief*

....

The Clean Air Act permits EPA to commence a civil action for a permanent or temporary injunction and grants this Court jurisdiction to restrain a violation of an applicable implementation plan or to require compliance with the plan. 42 U.S.C. § 7413(b). But "[t]he grant of jurisdiction to ensure compliance with a statute hardly suggests an absolute duty to do so under any and all circumstances, and a federal judge sitting as chancellor is not mechanically obligated to grant an injunction for every violation of law." *Weinberger v. Romero-Barcelo*, 456 U.S. 305, 313 (1982).

SCM argues that where there are no present violations and no cognizable danger of future violations, injunctive relief is inappropriate and should be denied. The Court agrees. "[T]he court's power to grant injunctive relief survives discontinuance of the illegal conduct. The purpose of an injunction is to prevent future violations, and, of course, it can be utilized even without a showing of past wrongs. But the moving party must satisfy the court that relief is needed. The necessary determination is that there exists some cognizable danger of recurrent violation, something more than the mere possibility which serves to keep the case alive." [Citation.]

....

Accordingly, the Court will deny all aspects of injunctive relief requested by EPA.

NOTES AND QUESTIONS

1. The 1990 amendments authorized EPA for the first time to recover administrative and judicial penalties for past violations. CAA § 113(a)(1) & (b), 42 U.S.C. § 7413(a)(1) & (b).

The amendments also allow a presumption for both such penalties that violations continue every day after issuance of a notice of noncompliance, placing a burden to prove otherwise on the noncomplying source. CAA § 113(e)(2), 42 U.S.C. § 7413(e)(2).

2. Yet another sanction created by the 1990 amendments is the field citation. EPA is to establish a field citation program in which penalties not to exceed $5,000 per day of violation may be assessed by officers or employees to be designated by EPA for "appropriate minor violations." The violator may pay the assessment or request a hearing. If a hearing is not requested, the assessment is final. Payment of the penalty is not a defense to further penalty assessments or enforcement "if the violation continues." CAA § 113(d)(3), 42 U.S.C. § 7413-(d)(3).

3. Administrative penalty orders and field citation assessments are judicially reviewable in the district court for the District of Columbia or for the district in which the violation occurred, the alleged violator resides, or the party's principal place of business is located. Review must be sought within thirty days after the order or assessment becomes final. The court will not overturn the order or assessment "unless there is not substantial evidence in the record, taken as a whole, to support the finding of a violation or unless the order or penalty assessment constitutes an abuse of discretion." CAA § 113(d)(4), 42 U.S.C. § 7413(d)(4). Upon failure to pay an assessment or administrative penalty, the Attorney General must sue in district court to recover payment with interest as well as the enforcement expenses of the United States. CAA § 113(d)(5), 42 U.S.C. § 7413(d)(5).

DUQUESNE LIGHT CO. v. ENVIRONMENTAL PROTECTION AGENCY

791 F.2d 959 (D.C. Cir. 1986)

MIKVA, CIRCUIT JUDGE.

I

In *Duquesne Light Co. v. Environmental Protection Agency*, 225 App. D.C. 290, 698 F.2d 456 (D.C. Cir. 1983) (*Duquesne I*), this court considered twenty consolidated petitions for review of regulations promulgated by the Environmental Protection Agency (EPA) pursuant to the Clean Air Act Amendments of 1977. [Citation.] Those regulations provide a model for the assessment of penalties against entities that fail to comply with the Clean Air Act's pollution limitations. The penalties that the model calls for are designed to recoup the economic benefits those entities derive by failing to comply with the Clean Air Act's requirements. In *Duquesne I* we upheld the penalty assessment model's propriety in most respects. However, briefing was deferred on those issues that we hoped the parties would settle through negotiations. *See Duquesne I* at 461 n.1. Two of those deferred issues were settled. Today we decide the remaining issue: the legality of the model used for calculating noncompliance penalties assessed against regulated utilities. Although the question is not entirely free from doubt, we are satisfied that the EPA's regulations comply with the statutory mandate under which they were adopted.

II

The Clean Air Act, 42 U.S.C. § 7401 *et seq.* ("Act"), provides for national standards on the level of air pollutants. Act § 109, 42 U.S.C. § 7409. These standards are implemented through a procedure that limits permissible emissions from stationary sources, including power plants operated by public utilities. Act

§ 110, 42 U.S.C. § 7410. The Act also provides for penalties for noncompliance. Section 120(d)(2) of the Act, added by the 1977 Amendments, authorizes the EPA to sanction polluters by assessing penalties

> designed to alter their economic behavior by changing the costs of emitting pollutants in violation of the applicable air quality standards.... [B]y removing the economic benefits of noncompliance with the Act, Congress hoped to place polluters on the same economic footing as those who had limited their emissions through increased anti-pollution expenditures.

Duquesne I at 463; *see generally id.* at 461-65.

Section 120 of the Act specifically provides that

> The amount of the penalty which shall be assessed and collected with respect to any source under this section shall be equal to — (A) the amount determined by the Administrator ... which is no less than the economic value which a delay in compliance beyond July 1, 1979, may have for the owner of such source, including the quarterly equivalent of the capital costs of compliance and debt service over a normal amortization period, ... operation and maintenance costs foregone as a result of noncompliance, and any additional economic value which such a delay may have for the owner or operator of such source....

42 U.S.C. § 7420(d)(2).

In 1980 the EPA adopted regulations implementing § 120. 45 Fed. Reg. 50,086 (1980) (codified at 40 C.F.R. §§ 66.1 to 67.43 and appendices). The regulations provide that "[a]ll noncompliance penalties shall be calculated in accordance with the Technical Support Document and the Manual." 40 C.F.R. § 66.21(a). That document in turn provides that "[f]or the purposes of noncompliance penalties, the economic value, or savings, from noncompliance is defined to have two components: (1) the return which can be earned on the capital costs of pollution control equipment whose purchase has been delayed, and (2) the operating and maintenance costs avoided as a result of not having installed the equipment and the return on these savings." Noncompliance Penalties, Technical Support Document, 45 Fed. Reg. at 50,123. It is readily apparent that the penalty assessment model set forth in the EPA's regulations is primarily based on the factors mentioned in the authorizing statute.

III

A

Our standard of review is provided by section 307(d)(9) of the Act.... With that standard in mind, we now evaluate the petitioners' challenge to the EPA regulations.

The dispute in this case concerns the propriety of applying the EPA's § 120 penalty assessment model, upheld by this court in its general application, *see*

Duquesne I, to regulated utilities. Petitioners here, regulated public utilities, urge this court to set aside the EPA regulations governing penalty assessment insofar as they apply to them. They claim that the EPA, to comply with § 120's mandate, must devise a special penalty calculation model for public utilities.

Petitioners argue that Congress' overarching desire in enacting § 120 was to ensure that polluters would be economically "indifferent" between polluting and paying the statutory penalty, on the one hand, and installing pollution control equipment, on the other. According to petitioners, penalties under § 120 should equal an amount that will have the same negative economic effect on the polluters as would complying with the Act's requirements. That is, penalties should be equal to the benefit or "economic value" of noncompliance. Petitioners assert that they suffer much more from a penalty than they would from incurring the same amount of pollution-control costs. Thus, they claim that applying a penalty-assessment model that equates economic value with savings frustrates Congress' plan that firms should be indifferent between penalties and compliance, at least with respect to public utilities. Such a penalty-assessment model allegedly misapplies § 120's requirement that penalties be set equal to economic value.

The petitioners' argument turns on the peculiar way in which costs are borne by regulated utilities. Public utility regulators govern the extent and manner in which public utilities are allowed to recover costs from their ratepayers. Petitioners assert that public utility regulatory bodies allow expenditures on pollution control equipment to be included in a utility's rate base and periodic costs to be passed through as expenses. Thus, the financial impact of complying with the Act's emission standards is assertedly very small for public utilities that are permitted to recover their expenditures on pollution control equipment.

The regulatory treatment of fines imposed pursuant to § 120 will, according to petitioners, be very different. Although no such fines have in fact been incurred, petitioners believe that utility regulators will not allow § 120 penalties to be included in the rate base or passed through to the ratepayers as expenses. (The National Association of Regulatory Utility Commissioners, *amicus curiae* here, endorses this prediction.) Based on the disparate regulatory treatment of actual expenditures on pollution-control equipment and fines for noncompliance, petitioners argue that, for public utilities, the economic value of noncompliance is less than the direct cost avoided by noncompliance. Therefore, petitioners assert, a penalty commensurably lower will engender the desired indifference. Petitioners conclude that the differential impact on their finances of fines and costs requires the EPA to develop a special penalty-assessment model for public utilities. Only by using a special model, argue the petitioners, will Congress' goal of "economic indifference" be achieved.

Petitioners' challenge to the § 120 regulations is misconceived. Petitioners go on at great length about Congress' desire to assure, via the § 120 penalties, that firms would be economically indifferent between polluting and complying with the Act. Although petitioners' conclusions about § 120 are incorrect, they are essentially correct in describing its thrust. As we said in *Duquesne I*, "Congress hoped to place polluters on the same economic footing as those who had limited their emissions through increased anti-pollution expenditures." *Id.* at 463. Section 120 itself speaks of the "economic value" of non-compliance. It is not much of a leap to conclude that if the economic value of noncompliance is to be used in setting the noncompliance penalty, Congress desired to render polluters indifferent to obeying or disobeying the Act. If § 120 merely authorized the EPA to come up with penalties that would remove the economic incentive to continue polluting, the utilities might successfully argue that a penalty equal to the full cost avoided by failing to comply exceeds the statutory authorization.

What the petitioners fail to come to terms with, however, is the specific statutory mandate to include certain elements in the calculation of economic value. The statute specifies that "the capital costs of compliance" and "operation and maintenance costs foregone" are to be included in the § 120 penalty. The penalty-assessment model adopted by the EPA specifically includes these costs. We decline to hold that EPA regulations that follow the clear terms of the statute are arbitrary and capricious or contrary to law, even if the results may be more onerous for some polluters than for others.

Even if § 120 were not so clear as to the elements that are properly included in calculating noncompliance penalties, we think the petitioners would have an uphill battle. The legislative history of § 120 makes clear that Congress believed that § 120 penalties would have the sure and certain effect of eliminating any incentive to avoid compliance.

Representative Henry Waxman, a member of the conference committee that produced the Amendments, explained § 120 as follows:

> In order to speed compliance by industry, we are enacting a penalty applicable to each major source which will be equal to the economic value of noncompliance with emission limitations. No longer will ... our major utilities ... be able to reap an economic windfall from polluting the air. No longer will they find it cheaper to send their lawyers into court instead of purchasing and installing the necessary pollution control equipment.

3 A Legislative History of the Clean Air Act Amendments of 1977[,] 335-36 (House Consideration of the Conference Committee Report, Aug. 4, 1977). Assessing a penalty equal to costs foregone will assure that no incentive remains to delay compliance. That a lesser penalty might have done the job is irrelevant; a penalty equal to the cost avoided will always produce at least indifference.

Moreover, § 120 does not say, as the petitioners sometimes seem to argue, that noncompliance penalties should produce economic indifference. Rather, the section states as its general principle the idea that penalties should be "no less" than the "economic value" of noncompliance. It is not all clear that economic value can be equated with the amount by which profits are reduced by incurring compliance expenditures. (Even petitioners do not suggest that this measure of economic value would be appropriate for firms selling in a competitive market. *See infra* part III B.) The calculation of profits is complicated, and the legislative history strongly suggests that economic value was understood as being a measure of costs foregone rather than net loss. That the Congress' use of "economic value" clashes somewhat with its allegedly primary goal of ensuring economic indifference is not a fatal flaw in the legislative scheme.

Thus, we think the penalty-assessment model adopted by the EPA accurately reflects the mandate of the Amendments' legislative history. Bearing in mind that agency interpretations of ambiguous statutes are to be upheld if they are permissible, we do not think the EPA's regulations would be impermissible even if § 120 were less specific. *See Chevron, U.S.A., Inc. v. Natural Resources Defense Council, Inc.*, 467 U.S. 837, 842-45 (1984). It strains credulity to believe that in adopting regulations that not only track the statute's terms so closely but also clearly achieve Congress' desire to assure compliance with the Act the EPA may have acted in an arbitrary or capricious manner or exceeded its statutory authority.

B

We pause to make clear that petitioners' argument about the unique economic circumstances of regulated public utilities has not been lost on us. The court understands clearly that it is the *differential* impact of fines and costs on public utilities that is at the heart of petitioners' complaint. According to the petitioners, economic indifference is achieved for an unregulated firm when fine and cost are equal. Because the unregulated firm can pass through to its customers an *equal proportion* of its various sorts of expenses (i.e., the demand schedule faced by the firm is independent of its costs), it does not matter what that proportion in fact is or how it compares with the proportion of expenses that another firm, perhaps facing a different competitive environment, may be able to pass through.

Put another way, an unregulated monopolistic firm will be able to pass on to its customers a large fraction of any added expenses it is forced to bear. Conversely, a firm selling into a competitive market (a price-taker) will be forced to absorb expenses. Thus, for unregulated firms across the competitive spectrum, the effect of pollution control expenses and § 120 penalties of equivalent amount will be the same. Although the net benefit of noncompliance for a monopolist is not as great as the costs foregone, neither is the net cost of paying a penalty as great as the penalty.

This is not the case with public utilities. If Congress had mandated economic indifference in the sense that petitioners suggest, petitioners would be right that the unique circumstance of public utilities would merit unique treatment. Where petitioners' analysis fails, however, is in premising their argument on an incorrect notion of economic indifference. Congress understood the economic value of noncompliance to be roughly equivalent to the direct costs avoided by failing to comply. It is not for us to rewrite the statute and its legislative history to conform to petitioners' understanding of economics. If public utilities really benefit so little by failing to comply and suffer so much by bearing § 120 fines, it is open to them to comply with the Act and avoid the problem altogether.

Alternatively, petitioners are of course free to seek to have the Act amended to take explicit account of their unique circumstances.

IV

The Amendments and their legislative history make it clear that Congress was not constructing an econometric model when it fashioned § 120. Rather, Congress fashioned a new sanctioning mechanism to push polluters into compliance with the substantive provisions of the Act. That the sanction chosen may have an asymmetric effect on public utilities does not make it less applicable or less suited to furthering Congress' will. Applying the EPA's § 120 noncompliance penalties to public utilities is proper. It is well past time to put into effect the penalty assessment mechanism ordered by Congress. Accordingly, the petitioners' challenge is dismissed and the regulations at issue are affirmed.

It is so ordered.

NOTES AND QUESTIONS

1. *Duquesne I* provides a succinct summary of the purposes, substance, and procedures for section 120 noncompliance penalties.

Section 120 is a unique federal experiment with economic penalties. It is designed to alter economic behavior by changing the costs of emitting pollutants in violation of applicable air quality standards. *See* H.R. Rep. No. 294, 95th Cong., 1st Sess. 72-79 (1977) [hereinafter 1977 House Report], *reprinted in* 4 A LEGISLATIVE HISTORY OF THE CLEAN AIR ACT AMEND-MENTS OF 1977 at 2539-46 (1978) [hereinafter 1977 LEGISLATIVE HISTORY]. Congress added section 120 to the Act because it anticipated that even the augmented civil and criminal penalty scheme would not create sufficient incentives for sources to comply with air quality standards. *Id.* at 72. Congress also hoped that the section 120 penalties would increase administrative flexibility in enforcing the Act, by serving as a middle ground between stiff criminal sanctions or shutdown of noncomplying facilities. *Id.* at 5. Equally important, by removing the economic benefits of noncompliance with the Act, Congress hoped to place polluters on the same economic footing as those who had limited their emissions through increased anti-pollution expenditures. *Id.*

Section 120 begins by specifying the sources made subject to noncompliance penalties. Under section 120(a)(2), penalties may be assessed against any major stationary source — defined as any source that emits or has the potential to emit one hundred or more tons of any pollutant per year, Act § 302(j), 42 U.S.C. § 7602(j) (Supp. IV 1980) — not in compliance with any applicable emission limitation. Such penalties also are to be assessed against other stationary sources not in compliance with federal new source performance standards or standards for hazardous pollutants. Finally, sources operating under certain types of delayed compliance orders allowed by the Act are to be assessed penalties if they fail to comply with the terms of such orders.

Sources meeting certain conditions, however, are to be exempted from the noncompliance penalties. For example, sources converting from petroleum to coal pursuant to orders issued under the Act, and complying with the terms of such orders, are exempt from noncompliance penalties. § 120(a)-(2)(B)(i). So are sources experimenting with innovative technology under the Act, § 120(a)(2)(B)(iii), and certain sources unable to comply with emission limitations for reasons utterly beyond their control. § 120(a)(2)(B)(iv). These exemptions are mandatory, although the burden of demonstrating entitlement to any of them falls on the source. In addition, EPA may exempt sources from penalties for certain instances of noncompliance that are *de minimis* in nature and duration. § 120/y-(a)(2)(C).

Penalties are to be assessed against noncomplying sources either by EPA or by the individual states. Section 120 directs EPA to promulgate regulations implementing the penalties after notice and opportunity for public hearing — the regulations we must evaluate here. Individual states may take over responsibility for administering the noncompliance penalty program if they submit plans approved by EPA, § 120(a)(1)(B)(i), in which case the penalties are paid to the states, § 120(d)(1). To date, however, states have shown little interest in taking responsibility for the program. In any event, the statute does not differentiate substantively between the penalty program as administered by EPA and by the states, and the discussion to follow will for convenience refer principally to EPA as administering the program.

Section 120 sets out carefully the procedures to be followed in assessing the noncompliance penalties. Sources not complying with applicable air quality standards are to be given "a brief but reasonably specific notice of noncompliance." § 120(b)(3). Upon receipt of a notice of noncompliance, a source must either calculate the amount of the penalty owed, which begins to accrue with the issuance of the notice of noncompliance, § 120(d)(3)-(C)(ii), or submit a petition within forty-five days challenging the notice of noncompliance or asserting entitlement to an exemption. EPA is to provide a hearing on the record and to act on the petition within ninety days. § 120(b)(5). Should a source in receipt of a noncompliance notice fail to respond, EPA may contract for calculation of the penalty. § 120(c).

Penalties are to be calculated to reflect the projected economic value of noncompliance to a source. EPA is to promulgate regulations for calculating the penalty, which must include at least the quarterly equivalents of capital costs, operating costs, and maintenance expenses avoided as a result of noncompliance. § 120(d)(2)(A). The penalty is to be paid on a quarterly basis, in equal installments during the entire period of noncompliance, beginning with issuance of the notice of noncompliance and ending when the source comes into full compliance with applicable air quality standards. § 120(d)(3)(B), (C). Expenditures made during a quarter for the purpose of bringing the source into compliance with air quality standards, and not otherwise reflected in the calculation of the penalty amounts, are to be credited against the penalty assessments for that quarter. § 120(d)(2)(B). Credits not taken into account fully in a given quarter may be carried over and offset against the next quarter's penalty assessment. § 120(d)(2). When a source reaches full compliance with air quality standards, the penalty is to be recalculated to take into account the actual — rather than the projected — expenditures required to bring the source into compliance with air quality standards and the length of the actual period of delay in the expenditures. § 120(d)(4). Sources that have overpaid are entitled to reimbursement, at interest rates set by the United States Treasury (or by the state, if the state is administering the penalty program); sources that have underpaid are to be assessed the deficiency, again with interest. § 120(d)(4)(A), (B).

Initial penalty payments are due six months after issuance of the notice of noncompliance. A source may seek judicial review of a determination by EPA that penalizes the source under section 120, but the penalty is not stayed pending the review process. § 120(e). The penalties are in addition to other civil and criminal penalties under the Act, and do not alter a source's other obligations under the Act. § 120(f).

Duquesne Light Co. v. EPA (Duquesne I), 698 F.2d 456, 463-65 (D.C. Cir. 1983).

2. Does EPA *have* to assess a noncompliance penalty if the violation falls within one of the designated categories of section 120? *See generally* Drayton, *Economic Law Enforcement*, 4 HARV. ENVTL. L. REV. 1 (1980); Perellis, *Noncompliance Penalties under Section 120 of the Clean Air Act*, 16 NAT. RESOURCES J. 499 (1983). EPA has taken the position that imposition of the penalty is within EPA's discretion. 45 Fed. Reg. 50088 (1980).

3. The Clean Air Act also provides for criminal sanctions, "blacklisting" of federal contractors convicted of criminal offenses under the Act, and citizen suit enforcement of the Act's requirements. None of these were widely utilized before 1990. However, for reasons to be explained, criminal sanctions and citizen suit enforcement are likely to play a more significant role in the future. *See generally* James Miskiewicz & John S. Rudd, *Civil and Criminal Enforcement of the Clean Air Act After the 1990 Amendments*, 9 PACE ENVTL. L. REV. 281 (1992).

a. Contractor Listings. Federal contracts for goods, materials, or services with persons convicted of any criminal offense in section 113 are prohibited. CAA § 306(a), 42 U.S.C. § 7606(a).

b. Criminal Sanctions. The 1990 amendments significantly broadened and strengthened the criminal enforcement provisions. Persons subject to criminal sanctions include individuals, corporations, state and local governments, federal agencies and departments, and any officer, agent or employee thereof, CAA

§ 302(e), 42 U.S.C. § 7602(e), as well as any "responsible corporate officer." CAA § 113(c)(6), 42 U.S.C. § 7413(c)(6). Generally, criminal sanctions may be sought for knowing violations of the Act's emissions control requirements (CAA § 113(c)(1), 42 U.S.C. § 7413(c)(1)); knowingly false statements or failures to make required reports (CAA § 113(c)(2), 42 U.S.C. § 7413(c)(2)); knowing failures to pay any fees owed to the United States (CAA § 113(c)(3), 42 U.S.C. § 7413(c)(3)); negligent releases of hazardous air pollutants creating imminent danger of death or serious bodily injury (CAA § 113(c)(4), 42 U.S.C. § 7413(c)-(4)); and knowing releases of hazardous air pollutants creating such a danger (CAA § 113(c)(5)(A), 42 U.S.C. § 7413(c)(5)(A)). Each criminal offense is punishable by fines, imprisonment or both. Before the 1990 amendments, only misdemeanor-level sanctions were authorized; section 113(c) as amended authorizes felony-level sanctions for certain knowing violations. H.R. Rep. No. 490, 101st Cong., 2d Sess. 392 (1990); H.R. Cong. Rep. No. 952, 101st Cong., 2d Sess. 347 (1990). All general defenses and bars to criminal prosecution for federal criminal offenses are preserved. CAA § 113(c)(5)(D), 42 U.S.C. § 7413(c)(5)(D).

   c. Citizen Suit Enforcement. Perhaps the most significant reform in enforcement from the 1990 amendments is revised section 304 for citizen suit enforcement. Citizen suits may be brought to enforce any emission standard or permit requirement against a source, or against the Administrator for failure to perform a nondiscretionary duty. CAA § 304(a), 42 U.S.C. § 7604(a). *See also* CAA § 304(f), 42 U.S.C. § 7604(f) (definition of "emission standard or limitation"). Such actions must be brought in district court, with enforcement against a source in the district where the source is located. No action can be brought until 60 days after notice to the Administrator, the state, and the alleged violator, and generally an action is precluded if the Administrator or state is diligently prosecuting a civil action against the violation. Costs, including reasonable attorney and expert witness fees, may be awarded by the court to any party when appropriate. CAA § 304, 42 U.S.C. § 7604.

   In *Fried v. Sungard Recovery Services, Inc.*, 916 F. Supp. 465 (E.D. Pa. 1996), the district court held that the plain language of section 304(a) of the Act, as amended in 1990, overruled *Gwaltney of Smithfield, Ltd. v. Chesapeake Bay Foundation* for purposes of the Clean Air Act to allow citizen suits for wholly past violations, so long as the violations occurred more than once. In response to the defendant's argument that the *Gwaltney* rule disallowing citizen suits for wholly past violations still applies to alleged violations that occurred prior to the effective date of the 1990 Amendments, the court concluded that the 1990 Amendments apply to any actions filed after the effective date of the Amendments, even for violations that predated the Amendments.

   The amendments added authorization of civil penalties to the court's power to order compliance. Penalties will ordinarily be deposited in a special fund in the United States Treasury for compliance and enforcement activities. A court may order that up to $100,000 of civil penalties be directed toward beneficial mitigation projects to enhance public health or the environment. CAA § 304(g), 42 U.S.C. § 7604(g). Also, district court jurisdiction is expanded to include suits brought to compel "agency action unreasonably delayed" and suits for past violations "if there is evidence that the alleged violation has been repeated." CAA § 304(a), 42 U.S.C. § 7604(a). The latter type of suit cannot be brought until two years after enactment of the amendments. Pub. L. No. 101-549, 104 Stat. 2399, § 707(g), *amending* CAA § 304(a)(1) & (3), 42 U.S.C. § 7604(a)(1) & (3).

Citizen suit enforcement is likely to increase given the greater availability of compliance data to the public under the 1990 amendments. See pages 493-95 *supra*. Since 1986 EPA has increased the use of contractor listing as a sanction. Lee & Slaughter, *Government Contractors and Environmental Litigation*, [Current Developments] Env't Rep. (BNA) 2138 (1989). Criminal enforcement of environmental laws generally has been increasing in volume. Air Office of Criminal Enforcement has been established at EPA, as well as Environmental Crimes Unit at the Justice Department. *See generally* Fromm, *Commanding Respect: Criminal Sanctions for Environmental Crimes*, 21 St. MARY'S L.J. 821 (1990); Leon, *Environmental Criminal Enforcement: A Mushrooming Cloud*, 63 St. JOHN'S L. REV. 679 (1989); Buchanan, *Evolving RICO Issues for the Environmental Material Resources Practitioner*, 6 J. MIN. L. & POL'Y 185 (1990). With the extraordinarily complex regulatory infrastructure in place, it may well be that in the future, effectiveness of environmental protection will not be a function of further regulation, but of how effectively what is already in place can be enforced.

Chapter 7

WATER POLLUTION

A. REGULATORY FRAMEWORK FOR POINT SOURCE POLLUTION UNDER THE FEDERAL WATER POLLUTION CONTROL ACT

In the twentieth century the primary responsibility for regulation of water pollution shifted from state and local governments to the federal government, a shift similar to that which occurred with air pollution, as discussed in Chapter 6. Prior to the mid-1940s, private parties and public entities harmed by water pollution were compelled to seek relief through state law governing water rights, if water uses were damaged, or through state common law torts such as nuisance and trespass, if neighboring land uses were impaired. Plaintiffs seeking these state law remedies were confronted with a number of obstacles to success, as discussed in Chapter 2, and the hit-and-miss approach of individual lawsuits failed to protect the public at large from impaired water quality.

In 1950 the federal government tentatively prodded states into adopting water quality standards by promulgating a model state pollution control law. However, it was not until the Water Quality Act of 1965, Pub. L. No. 89-234, 79 Stat. 903, that states were required to submit to the federal government for approval water quality standards for interstate navigable waters. The Act's convoluted enforcement mechanism proved to be ineffective and unworkable. Plans in 1971 during the Nixon Administration to utilize the Rivers and Harbors Act of 1899, 33 U.S.C. § 401 *et seq.*, for a national discharge permit system were sidetracked before implementation by Congress' consideration and eventual passage of a comprehensive water pollution control act.

The Federal Water Pollution Control Act of 1972 (FWPCA, commonly referred to as the Clean Water Act), 33 U.S.C. §§ 1251-1387, was a legislative response to the inadequacy of water quality standards in controlling pollution. Without standards applicable and directly binding on specific sources of pollution, it was difficult, if not impossible, to determine which of many sources discharging into a water body caused or contributed to violation of a water quality standard. As a result, monitoring entailed significant expense with little enforcement accomplished. Under federal water pollution laws prior to 1972, states were relatively free to adopt lax standards; interstate waters received little or no protection; and there was no effective enforcement against municipal dischargers.

Congress responded to these deficiencies in three ways in the 1972 FWPCA. First, the articulated goals of the Act are that all waters be made "fishable" and "swimmable" by 1983 "wherever attainable" and that "the discharge of pollutants into navigable waters be eliminated by 1985." FWPCA § 101, 33 U.S.C. § 1251. These lofty (and yet to be achieved) goals departed significantly from the parameters of water uses by which water quality standards had been defined. Secondly, the federal government was given the primary responsibility for promulgating water pollution controls. States were to continue to maintain water quality based systems of regulation so long as the state standards were at least as stringent as required by federal law. Finally, and most importantly, federal standards were to be nationally uniform, technology-based standards imposed on individual sources through "end-of-the-pipe" restrictions on discharge. These technology-based standards are incorporated into permits under the National Pollutant Discharge Elimination System (NPDES) with which every point source discharge of any pollutant into "navigable waters" must comply. FWCPA § 402, 33 U.S.C. § 1342. "Navigable waters" is simply defined as the "waters of the United States." FWPCA § 502(7), 33 U.S.C. § 1362(7). The Supreme Court has stated that Congress intended to regulate water pollution to the full extent of the commerce clause. *United States v. Riverside Bayview Homes*, 474 U.S. 121 (1985), pages 644-50 *infra*.

"Discharge of a pollutant" is defined broadly as "any addition of any pollutant to navigable waters from any point source, [and] ... any addition of any pollutant to the waters of the contiguous zone or the ocean from any point source other than a vessel or other floating craft." FWPCA § 502(12), 33 U.S.C. § 1362(12). A "pollutant" is "dredged spoil, solid waste, incinerator residue, sewage, garbage, sewage sludge, munitions, chemical wastes, biological materials, radioactive materials, heat, wrecked or discarded equipment, rock, sand, cellar dirt, and industrial, municipal, and agricultural waste discharged into water." FWPCA § 502(6), 33 U.S.C. § 1362(6). The technology-based standards apply only to point source pollution, which is in turn defined as pollution from "any discernable, confined and discrete conveyance, including but not limited to any pipe, ditch, channel, tunnel, conduit, well, discrete fissure, container, rolling stock, concentrated animal feeding operation, or vessel or other floating craft, from which pollutants are or may be discharged." FWPCA § 502(14), 33 U.S.C. § 1362(14). Until 1987 (and some would argue even today) regulation of nonpoint source pollution, such as runoff, was left to the states with only limited incentives for state regulation.

Point source pollution includes discharges of pollutants from industry, sewage from municipal sanitary sewers, animal waste from large feedlots, and stormwater runoff in urban areas collected and discharged from municipal storm sewers. Municipal sewer systems collect not only household wastes, but also wastes from industrial dischargers which discharge into public sewer systems rather than directly into water sources.

In the 1972 version of the FWPCA all discharges of pollutants other than those from publicly owned treatment works (POTWs) were to be treated with the "best practicable control technology" (BPT) by July 1, 1977, and to be treated with the "best available control technology" (BAT) by July 1, 1983. FWPCA § 301(b)(1)-

(A), (b)(2)(A), 33 U.S.C. § 1311(b)(1)(A), (b)(2)(A). "Best practicable control technology" (BPT) is equivalent to the average of the best technology in use at the time the limitation is established. BPT requires consideration of "the total cost of application of technology in relation to the effluent reduction benefit to be achieved from such application, and shall also take into account the age of equipment and facilities involved, the process employed, the engineering aspects of the application of various types of control techniques, process changes, non-water quality environmental impact (including energy requirements), and such other factors as the Administrator deems appropriate." FWPCA § 304(b)(1)-(B), 33 U.S.C. § 1314(b)(1)(B). The "best available control technology" (BAT), a more stringent standard than BPT, is based on consideration of "the age of equipment and facilities involved, the processes employed, the engineering aspects of the application of various types of control techniques, process changes, the cost of achieving such effluent reduction, non-water quality environmental impact (including energy requirements), and such other factors as the Administrator deems appropriate." FWPCA § 304(b)(2)(B), 33 U.S.C. § 1314(b)(2)(B). BAT differs from BPT primarily in that the cost of the limitation is not measured against the benefits of the effluent reduction. Although cost is a consideration in determining BAT, there is no direct cost/benefit comparison in setting the standard because BAT is designed to elevate performance to the best technology adequately demonstrated even if it is not widely in use. Publicly owned treatment works were required to utilize "secondary treatment" by 1977, FWPCA § 301(b)(1)(B), 33 U.S.C. by § 1311(b)(1)(B), and "best practicable waste treatment over the life of the works" by 1983. The second requirement was eliminated in 1981. FWPCA § 301(b)(2)(B), § 1311(b)(2)(B), *repealed*, Pub. L. No. 97-117, § 21(b), 95 Stat. 1632 (1981). However, the FWPCA grant program for sewage treatment plants requires that new construction employ the "best practical waste treatment technology," thus reviving to some extent the standard that was eliminated from the permit program in 1981. FWPCA § 201(b), 33 U.S.C. § 1281(b).

Primary treatment by POTWs basically involves collection of sewage in tanks so that solids settle into a sludge and bacteria and chlorine can be applied to destroy organic matter. Secondary treatment utilizes physical/chemical treatment methods or biological treatment methods (such as oxidation ponds, lagoons, or trickling filters) to remove additional organic matter.

In addition to these effluent limitations for POTWs and all other point source dischargers under section 301, point source discharges have to comply with any applicable limitations under section 302 governing federally set water quality standards, FWPCA § 302, 33 U.S.C. § 1312, and section 303 governing state water quality standards. FWPCA § 303, 33 U.S.C. § 1313. "New sources," sources on which construction is commenced after publication of a new source performance standard, have to meet effluent limitations based on the "best available demonstrated control technology" (BADT). FWPCA § 306, 33 U.S.C. § 1316. Finally, under section 307, EPA is authorized to set effluent limitations for toxic pollutants adequate to provide an "ample margin of safety." FWPCA § 307, 33 U.S.C. § 1317.

The FWPCA was amended in 1977, 1981, and 1987. In the 1977 amendments, the deadline for full compliance with the BPT standard was, in certain situations, extended. FWPCA § 301(i), (j), 33 U.S.C. § 1311(i), (j). However, the 1983 deadline for BAT was replaced with differing deadlines and standards depending upon the type of pollutant regulated. For the second tier of protection after BPT, point source pollutants are classified as either toxic pollutants, conventional pollutants, or nonconventional pollutants. Conventional pollutants are those which traditionally were regulated in discharges from municipal treatment works and include biochemical oxygen demand (BOD), suspended solids, fecal coliform, pH, oil, and grease. Nonconventional pollutants are simply all pollutants that are not classified as either conventional or toxic pollutants. For toxic pollutants, BAT had to be utilized by July 1, 1984 or three years after EPA promulgation of the BAT standard, whichever was later. FWPCA § 301(b)(2)(C) and (D), 33 U.S.C. § 1311(b)(2)(C) and (D). For conventional pollutants, the "best conventional pollutant control technology" (BCT) had to be achieved by July 1, 1984. FWPCA § 301(b)(2)(E), 33 U.S.C. § 1311(b)(2)(E). The "best conventional pollutant control technology" (BCT) is based on consideration of "the reasonableness of the relationship between the costs of attaining a reduction in effluents and the effluent reduction benefits derived, and the comparison of the cost and level of reduction of such pollutants from the discharge from publicly owned treatment works to the cost and level of reduction of such pollutants from a class or category of industrial sources, and shall take into account the age of equipment and facilities involved, the process employed, the engineering aspects of the application of various types of control techniques, process changes, non-water quality environmental impact (including energy requirements), and such other factors as the Administrator deems appropriate." FWPCA § 304(b)(4)(B), 33 U.S.C. § 1314(b)(4)(B). For nonconventional pollutants, BAT had to be achieved by July 1, 1984, or three years after promulgation of the standard, whichever was later. FWPCA § 301(b)(2)(F), 33 U.S.C. § 1311(b)(2)(F). These deadlines for compliance with BAT and BCT would once again be extended in the 1987 amendments.

The definition of BCT in section 304(b)(4)(B), 33 U.S.C. § 1314(b)(4)(B) quoted above, appears on its face (although not by any means clearly) to require a two-step method for setting BCT. First, EPA must consider the costs to the industry of meeting the proposed BCT standard in relation to the benefits that would result from the proposed BCT standard, and then, secondly, compare that industrial cost/benefit ratio to "the cost and level of reduction of such pollutants from the discharge from publicly owned treatment works...." *Id.* In 1979 EPA adopted a method for setting BCT that involved only one step: a comparison of the marginal cost of going from BPT to BCT to the marginal cost for a POTW to go from "secondary treatment" to "advanced secondary treatment." Industry associations challenged the BCT standards set by this method in *American Paper*

Inst. v. EPA, 660 F.2d 954 (4th Cir. 1981). The plaintiffs contended that the language of the statute required EPA to set BCT in a two-step process of, first, an industry cost-effectiveness test and, secondly, a comparison of that cost-effectiveness ratio to the cost-effectiveness of an equivalent discharge limitation for POTWs. The court agreed with the plaintiffs and invalidated the BCT regulations. The issue still remained under the statutory section as to what the levels of discharge reduction for POTWs were with which the proposed BCT standard for an industry should be compared. On that issue the court determined that EPA's decision to compare the cost-effectiveness of industry going from the previous standard to the proposed BCT standard with the cost-effectiveness of a POTW going from secondary treatment to advanced secondary treatment was not arbitrary or capricious. EPA did not adopt a final rule in accordance with *American Paper* for determining BCT until 1986. For the industry cost-effectiveness test, EPA compares the costs per pound of conventional pollutant removed for the industry of going from BPT to BCT to the cost for the industry of going from no treatment at all to BPT. If the cost of going from BPT to BCT appears "reasonable" in comparison to the costs of going from no treatment at all to BPT, the BCT standard has passed the industry cost-effectiveness test and must then go on to pass the POTW test. If the cost per pound of conventional pollutant removed for the industry to go from BPT to BCT is less than the cost per pound for a POTW to go from secondary treatment to advanced secondary treatment, the proposed BCT standard passes the POTW test. The most stringent BCT considered by EPA that can pass both tests is what EPA will designate as the BCT standard for the industry. 51 Fed. Reg. 24,974 (1986).

Also in the 1977 amendments, an extension was given to POTWs. Pursuant to this amendment and an extension granted in 1981, POTWs were entitled to receive an extension of the 1977 deadline for secondary treatment up to July 1, 1988 if delay in implementation was due to lack of federal construction grant funds. FWPCA § 301(i), 33 U.S.C. § 1311(i). The extension was only available to municipalities that had facilities ready for construction prior to July 1, 1977. 40 C.F.R. § 125.93. Requirements of the Act for POTWs are imposed primarily through the National Pollutant Discharge Elimination System (NPDES) permit program and through the conditions which must be met for FWPCA construction grants. Enforcement, however, has been poor at best, with up to 60 percent of POTWs not in compliance with the Act at the time of the 1977 deadlines. H.R. Rep. No. 139, 95th Cong. 1st Sess. 15 (1977).

Under the Water Quality Act of 1987, the deadlines for industrial point source dischargers were extended once again. BPT standards requiring substantially greater control or fundamentally different technology from that previously required had to be met no later than March 31, 1989. FWPCA § 301(b)(3)(A), 33 U.S.C. § 1311(b)(3)(A). Compliance with BAT for nonconventional and toxic pollutants had to be no later than March 31, 1989, and compliance with BCT for conventional pollutants also had to be no later than March 31, 1989. FWPCA § 301(b)(2)(C)-(F), 33 U.S.C. § 1311(b)(2)(C)-(F).

The next two cases were decided within the original regulatory framework before the 1977 amendments, but the issues they address continue to be of fundamental importance to the current statutory scheme.

E.I. du PONT de NEMOURS & CO. v. TRAIN

430 U.S. 112 (1977)

JUSTICE STEVENS delivered the opinion of the Court.

Inorganic chemical manufacturing plants operated by the eight petitioners ... discharge various pollutants into the Nation's waters and therefore are "point sources" within the meaning of the Federal Water Pollution Control Act.... The Environmental Protection Agency has promulgated industry-wide regulations imposing three sets of precise limitations on petitioners' discharges. The first two impose progressively higher levels of pollutant control on existing point sources after July 1, 1977, and after July 2, 1983, respectively. The third set imposes limits on "new sources" that may be constructed in the future.

These cases present three important questions of statutory construction: (1) whether EPA has the authority under § 301 of the Act to issue industrywide regulations limiting discharges by existing plants; (2) whether the Court of Appeals, which admittedly is authorized to review the standards for new sources, also has jurisdiction under § 509 to review the regulations concerning existing plants; and (3) whether the new-source standards issued under § 306 must allow variances for individual plants.

....

The broad outlines of the parties' respective theories may be stated briefly. EPA contends that § 301(b) authorizes it to issue regulations establishing effluent limitations for classes of plants. The permits granted under § 402, in EPA's view, simply incorporate these across-the-board limitations, except for the limited variances allowed by the regulations themselves and by § 301(c). The § 304(b) guidelines, according to EPA, were intended to guide it in later establishing § 301 effluent-limitation regulations. Because the process proved more time consuming than Congress assumed when it established this two-stage process, EPA condensed the two stages into a single regulation.

In contrast, petitioners contend that § 301 is not an independent source of authority for setting effluent limitations by regulation. Instead, § 301 is seen as merely a description of the effluent limitations which are set for each plant on an individual basis during the permit-issuance process. Under the industry view, the § 304 guidelines serve the function of guiding the permit issuer in setting the effluent limitations.

The jurisdictional issue is subsidiary to the critical question whether EPA has the power to issue effluent limitations by regulation. Section 509(b)(1), 33 U.S.C. § 1369(b)(1), provides that "[r]eview of the Administrator's action ... (E) in approving or promulgating any effluent limitation ... under section 301" may be had in the courts of appeals. On the other hand, the Act does not provide for judicial review of § 304 guidelines. If EPA is correct that its regulations are "effluent limitation[s] under section 301," the regulations are directly reviewable in the Court of Appeals. If industry is correct that the regulations can only be considered § 304 guidelines, suit to review the regulations could probably be brought only in the District Court, if anywhere. Thus, the issue of jurisdiction to review the regulations is intertwined with the issue of EPA's power to issue the regulations.

We think § 301 itself is the key to the problem. The statutory language concerning the 1983 limitation, in particular, leaves no doubt that these limitations are to be set by regulation. Subsection (b)(2)(A) of § 301 states that by 1983 "effluent limitations *for categories and classes* of point sources" are to be achieved which will require "application of the best available technology economically achievable *for such category or class*." (Emphasis added.) This is "language difficult to reconcile with the view that individual effluent limitations are to be set when each permit is issued." *American Meat Institute v. EPA*, 526 F.2d 442, 450 (C.A.7 1975). The statute thus focuses expressly on the characteristics of the "category or class" rather than the characteristics of individual point sources. Normally, such classwide determinations would be made by regulation, not in the course of issuing a permit to one member of the class.[17]

Thus, we find that § 301 unambiguously provides for the use of regulations to establish the 1983 effluent limitations. Different language is used in § 301 with respect to the 1977 limitations. Here, the statute speaks of "effluent limitations for point sources," rather than "effluent limitations for categories and classes of point sources." Nothing elsewhere in the Act, however, suggests any radical difference in the mechanism used to impose limitations for the 1977 and 1983 deadlines. [Citation.] For instance, there is no indication in either § 301 or § 304 that the § 304 guidelines play a different role in setting 1977 limitations. Moreover, it would be highly anomalous if the 1983 regulations and the new-source standards were directly reviewable in the Court of Appeals, while the

---

[17]Furthermore, § 301(c) provides that the 1983 limitations may be modified if the owner of a plant shows that "such modified requirements (1) will represent the maximum use of technology within the economic capability of the owner or operator; and (2) will result in reasonable further progress toward the elimination of the discharge of pollutants." This provision shows that the § 301(b) limitations for 1983 are to be established prior to consideration of the characteristics of the individual plant. *American Iron & Steel Institute v. EPA*, *supra*, 526 F.2d, at 1037 n.15. Moreover, it shows that the term "best technology economically achievable" does not refer to any individual plant. Otherwise, it would be impossible for this "economically achievable" technology to be beyond the individual owner's "economic capability."

1977 regulations based on the same administrative record were reviewable only in the District Court.[18]

The magnitude and highly technical character of the administrative record involved with these regulations makes it almost inconceivable that Congress would have required duplicate review in the first instance by different courts. We conclude that the statute authorizes the 1977 limitations as well as the 1983 limitations to be set by regulation, so long as some allowance is made for variations in individual plants, as EPA has done by including a variance clause in its 1977 limitations.[19]

The legislative history supports this reading of § 301.

....

In presenting the Conference Report to the Senate, Senator Muskie, perhaps the Act's primary author, emphasized the importance of uniformity in setting § 301 limitations. He explained that this goal of uniformity required that EPA focus on classes or categories of sources in formulating effluent limitations.

....

Our construction of the Act is supported by § 501(a), which gives the EPA the power to make "such regulations as are necessary to carry out" its functions, and by § 101(d), which charges the agency with the duty of administering the Act. In construing this grant of authority, as Mr. Justice Harlan wrote in connection with a somewhat similar problem:

> "'[C]onsideration of feasibility and practicality are certainly germane' to the issues before us. [Citation.] We cannot, in these circumstances, conclude that Congress has given authority inadequate to achieve with reasonable effectiveness the purposes for which it has acted." *Permian Basin Area Rate Cases*, 390 U.S. 747, 777.

The petitioners' view of the Act would place an impossible burden on EPA. It would require EPA to give individual consideration to the circumstances of each of the more than 42,000 dischargers who have applied for permits [citation], and to issue or approve all these permits well in advance of the 1977 deadline in order to give industry time to install the necessary pollution-control equipment. We do not believe that Congress would have failed so conspicuously to provide EPA with the authority needed to achieve the statutory goals.

....

Language we recently employed in another case involving the validity of EPA regulations applies equally to this case:

---

[18]Section 509(b)(1)(A) makes new-source standards directly reviewable in the court of appeals.... We consider it unlikely that Congress intended such bifurcated review, and even less likely ... that Congress intended regulations governing existing sources to be reviewable in two different forums, depending on whether the regulations require compliance in 1977 or 1983.

[19]We agree with the Court of Appeals, 541 F.2d, at 1028, that consideration of whether EPA's variance provision has the proper scope would be premature.

"We therefore conclude that the Agency's interpretation ... was 'correct,' to the extent that it can be said with complete assurance that any particular interpretation of a complex statute such as this is the 'correct' one. Given this conclusion, as well as the facts that the Agency is charged with administration of the Act, and that there has undoubtedly been reliance upon its interpretation by the States and other parties affected by the Act, we have no doubt whatever that its construction was sufficiently reasonable to preclude the Court of Appeals from substituting its judgment for that of the Agency." *Train v. Natural Resources Def. Council*, 421 U.S. 60, 87.[25]

When, as in this litigation, the Agency's interpretation is also supported by thorough, scholarly opinions written by some of our finest judges, and has received the overwhelming support of the Courts of Appeals, we would be reluctant indeed to upset the Agency's judgment. Here, on the contrary, our independent examination confirms the correctness of the Agency's construction of the statute.

Consequently, we hold that EPA has the authority to issue regulations setting forth uniform effluent limitations for categories of plants.

Our holding that § 301 does authorize the Administrator to promulgate effluent limitations for classes and categories of existing point sources necessarily resolves the jurisdictional issue as well. For, as we have already pointed out, § 509(b)(1) provides that "[r]eview of the Administrator's action ... in approving or promulgating any effluent limitation or other limitation under section 301, 302, or 306, ... may be had by any interested person in the Circuit Court of Appeals of the United States for the Federal judicial district in which such person resides or transacts such business...."

....

The remaining issue in this case concerns new plants....

The Court of Appeals held:

> "Neither the Act nor the regulations contain any variance provision for new sources. The rule of presumptive applicability applies to new sources as well as existing sources. On remand EPA should come forward with some limited escape mechanism for new sources." [Citation.]

---

[25]Petitioners contend that the administrative construction should not receive deference because it was not contemporaneous with the passage of the Act. They base this argument primarily on the fact that EPA's initial notices of its proposed rulemaking refer to § 304(b), rather than § 301, as the source of authority. But this is merely evidence that the Administrator originally intended to issue guidelines prior to issuing effluent limitation regulations.... Finally, the EPA interpretation would be entitled to some deference even if it was not contemporaneous, "having in mind the complexity and technical nature of the statutes and the subjects they regulate, the obscurity of the statutory language, and EPA's unique experience and expertise in dealing with the problems created by these conditions." *American Meat Institute v. EPA, supra,* 526 F.2d, at 450 n.16.

The court's rationale was that "[p]rovisions for variances, modifications, and exceptions are appropriate to the regulatory process."

The question, however, is not what a court thinks is generally appropriate to the regulatory process; it is what Congress intended for *these* regulations. It is clear that Congress intended these regulations to be absolute prohibitions. The use of the word "standards" implies as much. So does the description of the preferred standard as one "permitting *no* discharge of pollutants." (Emphasis added.) It is "unlawful for *any* owner or operator of *any* new source to operate such source in violation of any standard of performance applicable to such source." § 306(e) (emphasis added). In striking contrast to § 301(c), there is no statutory provision for variances, and a variance provision would be inappropriate in a standard that was intended to insure national uniformity and "maximum feasible control of new sources." S. Rep. No. 92-414, p. 58 (1971), Leg. Hist. 1476.

That portion of the judgment of the Court of Appeals [citation] requiring EPA to provide a variance procedure for new sources is reversed. In all other aspects, the judgments of the Court of Appeals are affirmed.

NOTES AND QUESTIONS

1. As *Du Pont* indicates, the first question EPA had to address in setting effluent limitations for point sources under the Act was whether EPA could set uniform effluent limitations applicable nationwide to classes or subclasses of industry, or whether the Act required EPA to set limitations on a source-by-source basis in each individual NPDES permit. Effluent limitations are set as either concentration limits or as "mass limitations" on both concentrations and flow volumes. Which method is more stringent? Limitations may also include treatment and process requirements. Du Pont's argument that these limitations had to be set on an individual basis was based on a straightforward reading of sections 301, 304 and 402. From an administrative law perspective, what difference would it make procedurally in setting effluent limitations whether the limitations were set under section 301 or 402? What difference would it make in terms of the reviewability of those limitations? If the Court is correct in its conclusion that the limitations can be set by regulation under section 301, what is the purpose of section 304 under the Act?

2. Judicial review of EPA action under the FWPCA is governed by section 509(b)(1), 33 U.S.C. § 1369(b)(1). Generally, petitions for review must be filed within 120 days of the challenged action. The section authorizes judicial review of specific administrative actions, which include promulgation of effluent limitations under sections 301, 302, 306 and 307 as well as the issuance or denial of a NPDES permit. Review may be sought by any "interested person" in the Circuit Court of Appeals for the judicial district "in which such person resides or transacts business which is directly affected by such action." *Id.* The court may award costs, including attorney and expert witness fees to "any prevailing or substantially prevailing party whenever it determines that such award is appropriate." FWPCA § 509(b)(3), 33 U.S.C. § 1369(b)(3). For what is meant by a "prevailing or substantially prevailing party," see pages 222-28 *supra*. It is critical that any substantive or procedural challenges to the Administrator's action that can be brought in a section 509(b)(1) suit be brought, because failure to do so precludes bringing such challenge in a civil or criminal proceeding for enforcement. FWPCA § 509(b)(2), 33 U.S.C. § 1369(b)(2).

3. Why does the Court conclude that a variance provision has to be provided from the BPT limitations? Is it statutorily required or required as a matter of constitutional law? Notice that in footnote 19 the Court refuses to decide whether the scope of the variance provided by EPA in its regulations was proper, an issue ultimately addressed in *EPA v. National Crushed Stone Ass'n*, pages 544-49 *infra*.

4. *The Definition of Point Source.* Congress' emphasis on control of point source pollution was not based on an assessment of point source pollution as being more harmful or more extensive than nonpoint source pollution. It is more difficult, practically and politically, to regulate nonpoint source pollution than point source pollution. *See* pages 635-36 *infra*. The definition of point source pollution, in FWPCA § 502(14), 33 U.S.C. § 1362(14), is quite broad. Faced with an incomprehensible number of point sources to regulate after passage of the Act in 1972, EPA sought unsuccessfully to exempt from the permit requirement all silvicultural point sources, confined animal feedlots, and irrigation return flows from less than 3,000 acres. The District of Columbia Court of Appeals struck down the regulatory exemptions, concluding that EPA could not exempt categorically point sources that fell within the statutory definition of point sources. In response to EPA's contention that issuing permits for these sources was administratively impossible, the court of appeals sanctioned a program for issuing general areawide permits for classes of point source discharges. *Natural Resources Defense Council v. Costle*, 568 F.2d 1369 (D.C. Cir. 1977). In 1977 Congress excluded from the statutory definition of point source "return flows from irrigated agriculture," FWPCA § 502(14), 33 U.S.C. § 1362(14), and prohibited the Administrator of EPA from directly or indirectly requiring any state to impose a permit program on irrigation return flows. FWPCA § 402(l)(1), 33 U.S.C. § 1342(l)(1). In 1987 Congress similarly excluded from the definition of point source "agricultural stormwater discharges." FWPCA § 502(14), 33 U.S.C. § 1362(14). *See generally* Davidson, *Little Waters: The Relationship between Water Pollution and Agricultural Drainage*, 17 ENVTL. L. REP. (Envtl. L. Inst.) 10074, 10079 (1987) (questioning the precise meaning of this undefined term). The wisdom of providing these exemptions for agriculture has been questioned as the water quality problems associated with agricultural runoff of pesticides and other toxic chemicals have become more apparent. *But cf.*, Barker, Albert P., & Richard B. Burleigh, *Agricultural Chemicals and Groundwater Protection: Navigating the Computer Web of Regulatory Controls*, 30 IDAHO L. REV. 443-84 (1994) (concluding that the best fashion in which to control groundwater contamination due to agricultural chemicals is not with enforcement actions available under regulatory authority against the users of agricultural chemicals but rather by establishing state programs to control the use and availability of chemicals posing a threat to groundwater).

As to what constitutes a point source, consider the facts in *United States v. Earth Sciences, Inc.*, 599 F.2d 368 (10th Cir. 1979). Earth Sciences operated a gold leaching faculty on the Rito Seco Creek in Colorado. By spraying cyanide over a heap of gold ore, the resulting solution could be collected and the gold extracted. The heap was on a gradual slope, causing the solution to run into a small pool or sump, with a second sump to catch any excess runoff. During a period of excessive runoff from melting snow, both sumps were filled to capacity causing the excess solution to run into the creek for a six-hour period. The Tenth Circuit Court of Appeals held the discharge was a point source discharge. The court reasoned that Congress was classifying nonpoint source pollution as "disparate runoff caused primarily by rainfall around activities that employ or cause pollutants ... and that it would ... contraven[e] the intent of [the Act] and the structure of the statute to exempt from regulation any activity that emits pollution from an identifiable point." *Id.* at 373. *Compare Long Island Soundkeeper Fund v. N.Y. Athletic Club*, 42 Env't Rep. (BNA) 1421 (S.D.N.Y. 1996) (trap shooting range is point source) *with Hudson Riverkeeper Fund, Inc. v. Harbor at Hastings Assoc.*, 917 F. Supp. 251 (S.D.N.Y. 1996) (trash and rainwater from a building not from a point source). *See also Sierra Club v. Abston Constr. Co.*, 620 F.2d 41, 44 (5th Cir. 1980) (runoff from spoil piles in strip mining operation overflowing from sediment basins or discharged through natural ditches and gullies held to be point source pollution whenever surface runoff is "collected or channeled by the operator"); *Quivira Mining Co. v. EPA*, 765 F.2d 126 (10th Cir. 1985), *cert. denied*, 474 U.S. 1055 (1986) (discharges into gullies that reached navigable waters only through seepage into underground aquifers held to be point source discharges); *but see National Wildlife Fed'n v. Gorsuch*, 693 F.2d 156 (D.C. Cir. 1982); *United States ex rel. Tennessee Valley Auth. v. Tennessee Water Quality Bd.*, 717 F.2d 992 (6th Cir. 1983), *cert. denied*, 466 U.S. 937 (1984) (passage of pollutants through dams held not to be point source pollution). The question of what constitutes a point source also arises under the section 404 permit program for wetlands and is discussed in *Avoyelles Sportsmen's League, Inc. v. Marsh*, pages 659-65 *infra*.

5. As in the Clean Air Act, point sources in the FWPCA are divided into new sources and existing sources, with a more stringent technological standard for new source performance standards (NSPSs). The last part of *Du Pont* is addressed to the NSPSs set by EPA. What is the technological standard for new sources? *See* FWPCA § 306(a)(1), 33 U.S.C. § 1316(a)(1). What is it in the statutory language that leads the Court to conclude that Congress did not intend for a variance to be provided from the NSPSs? Given that Congress intended for BPT to be a nationally uniform standard (as concluded in the first part of *Du*

Pont) and that Congress did not provide a statutory variance for BPT, how can the Court conclude that a variance *cannot* be provided from an NSPS but that some variance has to be provided from BPT? Is *Du Pont* internally inconsistent? Under the current statutory scheme, "BAT" is the technology-based standard required for toxic pollutants and nonconventional pollutants. What, if any, difference is there in compliance with that "BAT" standard and the "BADT" standard for new sources? *See Chemical Mfrs. Ass'n v. EPA*, pages 553-71 *infra*. What qualifies as a "new" source? How does the definition differ from the definition of a "new" source in the Clean Air Act? *Compare* FWPCA § 306(a)(2) & (5), 33 U.S.C. § 1316(a)(2) & (5) *with* Clean Air Act § 111(a)(2) & (4), 42 U.S.C. § 7411(a)(2) & (4). The *Du Pont* case notes that it is illegal to *operate* a new source without a permit. An NSPS regulation which prohibited *construction* before obtaining a permit and completing an environmental impact statement was invalidated in *NRDC v. EPA*, 822 F.2d 104 (D.C. Cir. 1987).

6. *Permit Issuance*. NPDES permits incorporate the effluent limitations and deadlines a discharger must meet, as well as compliance schedules and other provisions for compliance and enforcement. *See generally* 40 C.F.R. § 122 (NPDES permit program regulations). Permits may be issued to last up to five years, FWPCA § 402(b)(1)(B), 33 U.S.C. § 1342(b)(1)(B), and issuance of all permits, except those for sewage treatment plant grants and new sources, are exempt from NEPA. FWCPA § 511(c)(1), 33 U.S.C. § 1371(c)(1).

Under section 402(b), 33 U.S.C. § 1342(b), EPA issues section 402 permits only in states that do not have a federally approved program to do so. Most states now have an approved permit program. Section 401(a) requires that applicants for federal licenses or permits to conduct any activity which may result in a discharge into navigable waters (including EPA-issued permits under section 402) provide to the federal entity certification from the state that the discharge will comply with the FWPCA. FWPCA § 401(a), 33 U.S.C. § 1341(a). The certification upon which the 401 permit is conditioned must set out "any effluent limitations and other limitations, and monitoring requirements" necessary for compliance with the FWPCA. FWPCA § 401(d), 33 U.S.C. § 1341(d). State certification decisions can only be challenged, if at all, under state law in state court. *Compare Sun Enters., Ltd. v. Train*, 532 F.2d 280 (2d Cir. 1976) (challenge to EPA administrator's actions in issuing NPDES permit is reviewable only in a U.S. Court of Appeals pursuant to FWPCA § 509(b)(1), 33 U.S.C. § 1369 (b)(1)) *with Power Auth. of New York v. Department of Envtl. Conserv.*, 379 F. Supp. 243 (N.D.N.Y. 1974) (New York's Department of Environmental Conservation has power to hold hearings regarding state certification decisions).

Section 402 requires that there be public notice and an "opportunity for public hearing" before a permit is issued, whether by EPA or by a state with a federally approved program. FWPCA § 402(a)(3), (b)(3), 33 U.S.C. 1342(a)(3), (b)(3). Review of a permit application by EPA has been held to require a full adjudicatory hearing under the Administrative Procedure Act (APA). *Marathon Oil Co. v. EPA*, 564 F.2d 1253 (9th Cir. 1977); *see generally* 40 C.F.R. § 124.71 *et seq.*

(hearing procedures for EPA-issued permits). There is public notice of any proposed issuance, denial, or modification of a permit and a public hearing if the Administrator finds a significant degree of public interest. "Any interested person" may request an adjudicatory hearing after EPA's determination; however, EPA is not required to hold a hearing if it is not requested by an interested party raising a material issue of fact. *Costle v. Pacific Legal Found.*, 445 U.S. 198 (1980). Because the APA does not apply to the states, however, EPA does not require states to provide evidentiary hearings, and state procedures for permit issuance vary. *See* 2 S. NOVICK, LAW OF ENVIRONMENTAL PROTECTION § 12.05[2][d][iii]. Under section 402(d), 33 U.S.C. § 1342(d), EPA may veto state-issued permits for failing to meet the requirements of the FWPCA and issue an acceptable permit itself if the state then fails to do so.

Judicial review of state-issued permits to which EPA does not object is limited to state courts. *NRDC v. Outboard Marine Corp.*, 702 F. Supp. 690 (N.D. Ill. 1988). Review of EPA's objections to a state-issued permit prior to final action by EPA is also limited to state courts. Only when EPA has assumed permitting authority and made a final decision to issue or deny a permit is judicial review of EPA's objections and decision available under section 509(b). *See, e.g., American Paper Inst. v. EPA*, 890 F.2d 869 (7th Cir. 1989); *Champion Int'l Corp. v. EPA*, 850 F.2d 182 (4th Cir. 1988). Issuance or denial of a permit by EPA for states *without* approved permitting programs is reviewable in federal court under section 509(b).

Permits may be modified, or revoked and reissued, depending upon the type of change involved. *See* 40 C.F.R. § 122.62(a)(3). When a permit is modified, only the conditions subject to modification are reopened. If a permit is revoked and reissued, the entire permit is reopened for revision and the permit is issued for a new term. *See generally Texas Municipal Power Agency v. EPA*, 836 F.2d 1482 (5th Cir. 1988). Until 1987 it was unclear whether a permit could be issued with *less* stringent limitations than the previously issued permit. In the first five years of permit issuance after 1972, before many national effluent limitations had been established, effluent limitations for a few pollutants were individually set in permit issuance on the basis of the issuing agency's "best professional judgment" (BPJ) under the authority of section 402(a)(1). Despite subsequent promulgation of national standards, BPJ limitations are still utilized in permit issuance when there is no national standard for a particular industry or pollutant and water quality standards do not mandate any relevant limitations. For example, a source not subject to nationally-issued effluent limitations when its first permit was obtained might find upon seeking a new permit that newly-issued, less stringent national effluent limitations applied. To prevent such "backsliding" in permit requirements, Congress added section 402(o), 33 U.S.C. § 1342(o), in 1987 to permit backsliding from BPJ and water quality standards only in specified, relatively limited situations. See note 4, pages 592-93 *infra*.

7. Prior to the 1977 amendments, what was the only statutory variance included by Congress in the FWPCA, and what did a source have to demonstrate

to qualify for the variance? Congress would go on to add other statutory variances in the 1977, 1981, and 1987 amendments. See pages 543-52 *infra*.

WEYERHAEUSER CO. v. COSTLE
590 F.2d 1011 (D.C. Cir. 1978)

McGOWAN, CIRCUIT JUDGE.

Under the aegis of the Federal Water Pollution Control Act Amendments of 1972 (the Act), the Environmental Protection Agency has embarked upon a step-by-step process of issuing effluent limitations for each industry that discharges pollutants into the waters of the United States. By these consolidated petitions, members of one such industry, American pulp and paper makers, challenge the validity of EPA regulations limiting the 1977-83 effluent discharges of many pulp, paper, and paperboard mills....

....

... As now authoritatively interpreted by the Supreme Court in *Du Pont, supra* 430 U.S. at 126-36, section 301(b) of the Act, 33 U.S.C. § 1311(b),[1] authorizes the Environmental Protection Agency ... to issue two sets of progressively more stringent regulations precisely limiting the effluent discharges of every "category [or] class of [existing] point sources," i.e., generally, every industry that pollutes the Nation's waters. According to section 301(b), the first set of regulations must limit discharges between July 2, 1977 and July 1, 1983, inclusive, to levels characteristic of point sources utilizing "BPCTCA," i.e., the "best practicable control technology currently available." Section 301(b)(1)(A). The second set applies thereafter and is defined in terms of the more restricted levels of discharges from point sources using "BATEA," i.e., the "best available technology economically achievable." Section 301(b)(2)(A).

....

Before turning to the merits of petitioners' challenges to the 1977 effluent limitations, some mention must be made of the appropriate scope of review under the circumstances of this case. Generally, informal rulemaking such as produced

---

[1]In relevant part, i.e., with reference to the 1977-83 set of limitations for private industry, § 301(b) provides:

> In order to carry out the objective of this Act, there shall be achieved —
> (1)(A) not later than July 1, 1977, effluent limitations for point sources, other than publicly owned treatment works, (i) which shall require the application of the best practicable control technology currently available as defined by the Administrator pursuant to section 304(b) of this Act....

Section 42 of the Clean Water Act of 1977, 33 U.S.C.A. § 1311(b) (1978), replaced the 1972 Act's framework for post-1977 standards (1983 standards) with a new one. The 1972 Act's framework for post-1977 standards is well understood, and so we have used it to provide perspective. To avoid discussing issues not presented in this case, we have deliberately not attempted to describe the new Act's post-1977 framework except where necessary.

the regulations involved herein is reviewed under section 10(e)(2) of the Administrative Procedure Act (APA), 5 U.S.C. § 706(2). Pursuant to this provision, we must "set aside" any portion of the 1977 effluent limitations that is "arbitrary, capricious, an abuse of discretion, or otherwise not in accordance with law," is "in excess of statutory ... authority ... or short of statutory right," or is "without observance of procedure required by law." [Citations.]

....

In the case before us, we first must determine whether the EPA regulations involved herein are "not in accordance with law," or, more particularly, whether they are "in excess of statutory ... authority." APA § 10(e)(2)(A), (C), 5 U.S.C. § 706(2)(A), (C). We must also consider whether the process used in arriving at those regulations afforded those affected their procedural due.... Finally, we are charged by section 10(e)(2) of the APA to consider whether the agency "abuse[d its] discretion" (or was "arbitrary" or "capricious") in exercising the quasi-legislative authority delegated to it by Congress, or, on the other hand, whether its "decision was based on a consideration of the relevant factors and [was not the product of] a clear error of judgment." [Citation.]

....

EPA's consideration of the factors bearing on "the best practicable technology currently available" (BPCTCA) has inspired several challenges from petitioners. Some of these challenges concern the Agency's refusal to consider receiving water quality, while others concern EPA's manner of assessing the factors that all agree must be considered: cost and nonwater environmental impacts. We uphold the Agency's interpretation and application of the statute against both sets of challenges.

Some of the paper mills that must meet the effluent limitations under review discharge their effluents into the Pacific Ocean. Petitioners contend that the ocean can dilute or naturally treat effluents, and that EPA must take this capacity of the ocean ("receiving water capacity") into account in a variety of ways. They urge what they term "common sense," i.e., that because the amounts of pollutant involved are small in comparison to bodies of waters as vast as Puget Sound or the Pacific Ocean, they should not have to spend heavily on treatment equipment, or to increase their energy requirements and sludge levels, in order to treat wastes that the ocean could dilute or absorb.[41]

---

[41]Apart from this simple "common sense" version of the argument, there is a more sophisticated economic version called the "optimal pollution" theory. This economic theory contends that there is a level or type of pollution that, while technologically capable of being controlled, is uneconomic to treat because the benefit from treatment is small and the cost of treatment is large. See generally W. Baxter, People or Penguins: The Case for Optimal Pollution (1974); B. Ackerman, S. Rose-Ackerman, J. Sawyer & D. Henderson, The Uncertain Search for Environmental Quality (1974). These economic theories are premised on a view that we have both adequate information about the effects of pollution to set an optimal test, and adequate political and administrative flexibility to keep polluters at that level once we allow any pollution to go untreated. As discussed in this section, it appears that Congress doubted these premises.

EPA's secondary response to this claim was that pollution is far from harmless, even when disposed of in the largest bodies of water. As congressional testimony indicated, the Great Lakes, Puget Sound, and even areas of the Atlantic Ocean have been seriously injured by water pollution. Even if the ocean can handle ordinary wastes, ocean life may be vulnerable to toxic compounds that typically accompany those wastes. In the main, however, EPA simply asserted that the issue of receiving water capacity could not be raised in setting effluent limitations because Congress had ruled it out. We have examined the previous legislation in this area, and the 1972 Act's wording, legislative history, and policies, as underscored by its 1977 amendments. These sources, which were thoroughly analyzed in a recent opinion of the administrator of the Agency, fully support EPA's construction of the Act. They make clear that based on long experience, and aware of the limits of technological knowledge and administrative flexibility, Congress made the deliberate decision to rule out arguments based on receiving water capacity.

The earliest version of the Federal Water Pollution Control Act was passed in 1948 and amended five times before 1972. Throughout that 24 year period, Congress attempted to use receiving water quality as a basis for setting pollution standards. At the end of that period, Congress realized not only that its water pollution efforts until then had failed, but also that reliance on receiving water capacity as a crucial test for permissible pollution levels had contributed greatly to that failure. [Citation.][45]

Based on this experience, Congress adopted a new approach in 1972. Under the Act, "a discharger's performance is ... measured against strict technology-based effluent limitations — specified levels of treatment — to which it must conform, rather than against limitations derived from water quality standards to which it and other polluters must collectively conform." [Citations.]

This new approach reflected developing views on practicality and rights. Congress concluded that water pollution seriously harmed the environment, and that although the cost of control would be heavy, the nation would benefit from controlling that pollution. Yet scientific uncertainties made it difficult to assess the benefits to particular bodies of receiving water....

Moreover, by eliminating the issue of the capacity of particular bodies of receiving water, Congress made nationwide uniformity in effluent regulation possible. Congress considered uniformity vital to free the states from the temptation of relaxing local limitations in order to woo or keep industrial facilities. In addition, national uniformity made pollution clean-up possible without engaging in the divisive task of favoring some regions of the country over others.

---

[45]Only one violator of the water quality regulatory acts was brought to court in the first 22 years of regulation....

More fundamentally, the new approach implemented changing views as to the relative rights of the public and industrial polluters. Hitherto, the right of the polluter was pre-eminent, unless the damage caused by pollution could be proven. Henceforth, the right of the public to a clean environment would be pre-eminent, unless pollution treatment was impractical or unachievable....

The Act was passed with an expectation of "mid-course corrections," [citation] and in 1977 Congress amended the Act, although generally holding to the same tack set five years earlier. [Citation.] Notably, during those five years, representatives of the paper industry had appeared before Congress and urged it to *change* the Act and to incorporate receiving water capacity as a consideration. [Citation.] Nonetheless, Congress was satisfied with this element of the statutory scheme. Except for a provision specifically aimed at discharges from "publicly owned treatment plants," section 301(h) of the Act, 33 U.S.C. § 1311(h), it resolved in the recent amendments to continue regulating discharges into all receiving waters alike.

... Historically, the paper industry itself, and particularly the sulfite process sector, avoided the impact of regulation because of the difficulty of proving that its discharges adversely affected receiving waters.

Under the new statutory scheme, Congress clearly intended us to avoid such problems of proof so that a set of regulations with enforceable impact is possible.... Given the clarity of Congress' desire not to allow the receiving water capacity loophole to engulf its overall regulatory efforts in this area, we affirm the Agency's refusal to consider water quality in setting its limitations.

Petitioners also challenge EPA's manner of assessing two factors that all parties agree must be considered: cost and nonwater quality environmental impacts. They contend that the Agency should have more carefully balanced costs versus the effluent reduction benefits of the regulations, and that it should have also balanced those benefits against the non-water quality environmental benefit conclusion....

In order to discuss petitioners' challenges, we must first identify the relevant statutory standard. Section 304(b)(1)(B) of the Act, 33 U.S.C. § 1314(b)(1)(B), identifies the factors bearing on BPCTCA in two groups.[51] First, the factors shall

> include consideration of the total cost of application of technology in relation to the effluent reduction benefits to be achieved from such application,

and second, they

> shall also take into account the age of equipment and facilities involved, the process employed, the engineering aspects of the application of various

---

[51]Although its meaning is clear, this section's diction is confusing. In substance, it states that "[f]actors" relating to BPTCA (a) "shall include consideration" of cost and benefit and (b) shall "*take into account*" other specified and unspecified "*factors*" (emphasis added).

types of control techniques, process changes, nonwater quality environmental impact (including energy requirements), and such other factors as the Administrator deems appropriate[.]

[Citation.]

The first group consists of two factors that EPA must compare: total cost versus effluent reduction benefits. We shall call these the "comparison factors." The other group is a list of many factors that EPA must "take into account": age, process, engineering aspects, process changes, environmental impacts (including energy), and any others EPA deems appropriate. We shall call these the "consideration factors." Notably, section 304(b)(2)(B) of the Act, 33 U.S.C. § 1314(b)(2)(B), which delineates the factors relevant to setting 1983 BATEA limitations, tracks the 1977 BPCTCA provision before us except in one regard: in the 1983 section, *all* factors, including costs and benefits, are consideration factors, and no factors are separated out for comparison.

Based on our examination of the statutory language and the legislative history, we conclude that Congress mandated a particular structure and weight for the 1977 comparison factors, that is to say, a "limited" balancing test.[52]

In contrast, Congress did not mandate any particular structure or weight for the many consideration factors. Rather, it left EPA with discretion to decide how to account for the consideration factors, and how much weight to give each factor. In response to these divergent congressional approaches, we conclude that, on the one hand, we should examine EPA's treatment of cost and benefit under the 1977 standard to assure that the Agency complied with Congress' "limited" balancing directive. *See* note 52 *supra*. On the other hand, our scrutiny of the Agency's treatment of the several consideration factors seeks to assure that the Agency informed itself as to their magnitude, and reached its own express and considered conclusion about their bearing. More particularly, we do not believe that EPA is required to use any specific structure such as a balancing test in assessing the consideration factors, nor do we believe that EPA is required to give each consideration factor any specific weight.

---

[52]Senator Muskie described the "limited" balancing test:

> The modification of subsection 304(b)(1) is intended to clarify what is meant by the term "practicable." The balancing test between total cost and effluent reduction benefits is intended to limit the application of technology only where the additional degree of effluent reduction is wholly out of proportion to the costs of achieving such marginal level of reduction for any class or category of sources.
>
> The Conferees agreed upon this limited cost-benefit analysis in order to maintain uniformity within a class and category of point sources subject to effluent limitations, and to avoid imposing on the Administrator any requirement to consider the location of sources within a category or to ascertain water quality impact of effluent controls, or to determine the economic impact of controls on any individual plant in a single community.

[Citation.]

NOTES AND QUESTIONS

1. *Weyerhaeuser* demonstrates how the factors set out in section 304(b)(1)(B), 33 U.S.C. § 1314(b)(1)(B) are to be utilized in setting BPT. What were the petitioners' economic and "common sense" arguments that the extent of the discharge's impact on water quality had to be considered? Why does the Court of Appeals find both arguments unpersuasive? Congress in 1977 provided two narrowly tailored variances for discharges into marine waters. *See* note 5, page 551 *infra*.

2. Given that the petitioners and EPA agreed that cost and non-water quality environmental impacts had to be considered, what was their disagreement over how they should be considered? When, if ever, would the consideration factors necessitate invalidation of a BPT standard by EPA or the reviewing court? *See* footnote 52 of the case.

3. The utilization of a plant-wide "bubble," discussed in connection with the Clean Air Act, pages 427-34 *supra*, arises under the Clean Water Act as well as an alternative to effluent limitations on each "outfall," or discharge point. The first bubble was utilized as part of a consent agreement between the Natural Resources Defense Council, Inc., the steel industry and EPA in 1983. *See generally* Krueger, *The Iron and Steel Industry Consent Decree: Implementing the Bubble Policy under the Clean Water Act*, 4 VA. J. NAT. RESOURCES 155 (1984). In 1984 EPA published final regulations for use of the "shrinking bubble" by the iron and steel industry, 49 Fed. Reg. 21,024-21,038. They permit a source with multiple outfalls to exceed effluent limitations at one outfall in exchange for a reduction in discharge at another outfall, so long as there is a net reduction in discharge. The permitting authority determines the appropriate net reduction in discharge, and a discharger cannot qualify for the bubble if its application would result in violation of any state water quality standard. 40 C.F.R. § 420.03.

4. The linchpin for regulation of pollution under the Clean Air Act, as discussed on pages 350-67 *supra*, is the National Ambient Air Quality Standards (NAAQSs). In essence, an acceptable ambient air quality for a criteria pollutant is determined and the states are then given the responsibility of imposing the limitations on sources necessary to achieve that air quality by the designated deadline. In sharp contrast, the focus of the FWPCA is on uniform, nationwide technological standards imposed without regard to water quality. Is there some justification for the differing approaches to control of air pollution and water pollution? Which approach is preferable? What are the justifications for a system of nationally uniform standards which may require a company to expend substantial financial resources for what may be negligible environmental benefit? Evaluate the avenues of relief available to a company finding itself in such a situation in considering the following materials on variances.

B. VARIANCES FOR POINT SOURCE DISCHARGES

Point source dischargers seeking to avoid compliance with a technological standard may do so through three different methods: (1) by challenging generally EPA's promulgation of a standard on substantive or procedural grounds or challenging a variance provision as too limited; (2) by challenging a standard's applicability to an individual source in its NPDES permit; and (3) by seeking any available variance from a standard. The *Du Pont* and *Weyerhaeuser* cases, as well as the *National Crushed Stone* and *Chemical Manufacturers* cases which follow, all fall within the first category.

As noted above, the FWPCA, before the first set of amendments in 1977, contained only one statutory variance from the technological standards for point sources: the section 301(c) variance from the 1983 BAT standard for sources economically unable to comply. 33 U.S.C. § 1311(c). The Supreme Court in *Du Pont*, pages 528-43 *supra*, had concluded that the Act authorized the 1977 BPT and 1983 BAT standards to be set by regulation, so long as some variance was provided for variation in individual plants, as EPA had done by regulation with the so-called "fundamentally different factor" (FDF) for the 1977 BPT standard. The Supreme Court decided, however, that Congress did not intend for any variance to be provided from the new source performance standards (NSPSs).

The 1977 amendments added two important provisions relevant to the variances available for point source dischargers in addition to the nonstatutory FDF variances EPA had been providing. A source discharging a nonconventional pollutant may obtain a waiver of the 1987 deadline for BAT by receiving a section 301(g) waiver. FWPCA § 301(g), 33 U.S.C. § 1311(g). To qualify, the source must first satisfy the EPA "with the concurrence of the State," that it is in compliance with BPT or any more stringent federal or state water quality based standards, whichever is applicable. FWPCA § 301(g)(2)(A), 33 U.S.C. § 1311(g)(2)(A). In addition, the source must demonstrate its waiver will not necessitate additional limitations "on any other point or nonpoint source," will not interfere with the maintenance of water quality, will assure protection of water supplies and aquatic life, will allow recreational activities, and will not result in discharges in "quantities which may reasonably be anticipated to pose an unacceptable risk to human health or the environment because of bioaccumulation, persistency in the environment, acute toxicity, chronic toxicity (including carcinogenicity, mutagenicity or teratogenicity), or synergistic propensities." FWPCA § 301(g)(2)(B)-(C), 33 U.S.C. § 1311/y-(g)(2)(B)-(C). The 1977 amendments also added section 301(*l*), 33 U.S.C. § 1311(*l*), which states: "[T]he Administrator may not modify any requirement of this section as it applies to any specific pollutant which is on the toxic pollutant list under section 1317(a)(1) of this title." A number of significant provisions that would allow modifications and variances from the technology-based standards would also be provided in the 1987 amendments. *See* pages 551-52 *infra*.

ENVIRONMENTAL PROTECTION AGENCY v. NATIONAL CRUSHED STONE ASSOCIATION

449 U.S. 64 (1980)

Justice White delivered the opinion of the Court.

In April and July 1977, the Environmental Protection Agency (EPA), acting under the Federal Water Pollution Control Act (Act), as amended, 33 U.S.C. § 1251 *et seq.*, promulgated pollution discharge limitations for the coal mining industry and for that portion of the mineral mining and processing industry comprising the crushed-stone, construction-sand, and gravel categories. Although the Act does not expressly authorize or require variances from the 1977 limitation, each set of regulations contained a variance provision. Respondents sought review of the regulations in various Courts of Appeals, challenging both the substantive standards and the variance clause. All of the petitions for review were transferred to the Court of Appeals for the Fourth Circuit [which] set aside the variance provision as "unduly restrictive" and remanded the provision to EPA for reconsideration.

To obtain a variance from the 1977 uniform discharge limitations a discharger must demonstrate that the "factors relating to the equipment or facilities involved, the process applied, or other such factors relating to such discharger are fundamentally different from the factors considered in the establishment of the guidelines." Although a greater than normal cost of implementation will be considered in acting on a request for a variance, economic ability to meet the costs will not be considered. A variance, therefore, will not be granted on the basis of the applicant's economic inability to meet the costs of implementing the uniform standard.

The Court of Appeals for the Fourth Circuit rejected this position. It required EPA to "take into consideration, among other things, the statutory factors set out in § 301(c) [33 U.S.C. § 1311(c)]," which authorizes variances from the more restrictive pollution limitations to become effective in 1987 and which specifies economic capability as a major factor to be taken into account....

We granted certiorari to resolve the conflict between the decisions below and *Weyerhaeuser Co. v. Costle*, 590 F.2d 1011 (1978), in which the variance provision was upheld.

We shall first briefly outline the basic structure of the Act, which translates Congress' broad goal of eliminating "the discharge of pollutants into the navigable waters," 33 U.S.C. § 1251(a)(1), into specific requirements that must be met by individual point sources.

Section 301(b) of the Act, 33 U.S.C. § 1311(b) authorizes the Administrator to set effluent limitations for categories of point sources.... The first step, to be accomplished by July 1, 1977, requires all point sources to meet standards based on "the application of the best practicable control technology currently available [BPT] as defined by the Administrator...." § 301(b)(1)(A). The second step, to be accomplished by July 1, 1987, requires all point sources to meet standards based on application of the "best available technology economically achievable [BAT] for such category or class...." § 301(b)(2)(A)....

Section 301(c) of the Act explicitly provides for modifying the 1987 (BAT) effluent limitations with respect to individual point sources. A variance under § 301(c) may be obtained upon a showing "that such modified requirements (1) will represent the maximum use of technology within the economic capability of the owner or operator; and (2) will result in reasonable further progress toward the elimination of the discharge of pollutants." Thus, the economic ability of the individual operator to meet the costs of effluent reductions may in some circumstances justify granting a variance from the 1987 limitations.

No such explicit variance provision exists with respect to BPT standards, but in *E.I. du Pont de Nemours & Co. v. Train*, 430 U.S. 112 (1977), we indicated that a variance provision was a necessary aspect of BPT limitations applicable by regulations to classes and categories of point sources. The issue in this case is whether the BPT variance provision must allow consideration of the economic capability of an individual discharger to afford the costs of the BPT limitation. For the reasons that follow, our answer is in the negative.

The plain language of the statute does not support the position taken by the Court of Appeals. Section 301(c) is limited on its face to modifications of the 1987 BAT limitations. It says nothing about relief from the 1977 BPT requirements. Nor does the language of the Act support the position that although § 301(c) is not itself applicable to BPT standards, it requires that the affordability of the prescribed 1977 technology be considered in BPT variance decisions.[13]

This would be a logical reading of the statute only if the factors listed in § 301(c) bore a substantial relationship to the considerations underlying the 1977 limitations as they do to those controlling the 1987 regulations. This is not the case.

The two factors listed in § 301(c) — "maximum use of technology within the economic capability of the owner or operator" and "reasonable further progress

---

[13]It is true that in *Du Pont* we said there "[was no] radical difference in the mechanism used to impose limitations for the 1977 and the 198[7] deadlines" and that "there is no indication in either § 301 or § 304 that the § 304 guidelines play a different role in setting 1977 limitations." [Citation.] But our decision in *Du Pont* was that the 1977 limitations, like the 1987 limitations, could be set by regulation and for classes of point sources. It dealt with the power of the Administrator and the procedures he was to employ. There was no suggestion, nor could there have been, that the 1977 BPT and the 1987 BAT limitations were to have identical purposes or content. It follows that no proper inference could be drawn from *Du Pont* that the grounds for issuing variances from the 1987 limitations should also be the grounds for permitting individual point sources to depart from 1977 standards. Indeed, our opinion recognized that § 301(c) was designed for BAT limitations, 430 U.S., at 121, 127. Had we thought that § 301(c) governed variances from both the BAT and BPT standards, there would have been no need postpone to another day, as we did in 430 U.S., at 128, n.19, the question whether the variance clause contained in the 1977 regulations had the proper scope. That scope would have been defined by § 301(c).

toward the elimination of the discharge of pollutants" — parallel the general definition of BAT standards as limitations that "require application of the best available technology economically achievable for such category or class, which will result in reasonable further progress toward ... eliminating the discharge of all pollutants ..." § 301(b)(2). A § 301(c) variance, thus, creates for a particular point source a BAT standard that represents for it the same sort of economic and technological commitment as the general BAT standard creates for the class. As with the general BAT standard, the variance assumes that the 1977 BPT standard has been met by the point source and that the modification represents a commitment of the maximum resources economically possible to the ultimate goal of eliminating all polluting discharges. No one who can afford the best available technology can secure a variance.

There is no similar connection between § 301(c) and the considerations underlying the establishment of the 1977 BPT limitations. First, § 301(c)'s requirement of "reasonable further progress" must have reference to some prior standard. BPT serves as the prior standard with respect to BAT. There is, however, no comparable, prior standard with respect to BPT limitations. Second, BPT limitations do not require an industrial category to commit the maximum economic resources possible to pollution control, even if affordable. Those point sources already using a satisfactory pollution control technology need take no additional steps at all. The § 301(c) variance factor, the "maximum use of technology within the economic capability of the owner or operator," would therefore be inapposite in the BPT context. It would not have the same effect there that it has with respect to BAT's, i.e., it would not apply the general requirements to an individual point source.

More importantly, to allow a variance based on the maximum technology affordable by the point source, even if that technology fails to meet BPT effluent limitations, would undercut the purpose and function of BPT limitations. Rather than the 1987 requirement of the best measures economically and technologically feasible, the statutory provisions for 1977 contemplate regulations prohibiting discharges from any point source in excess of the effluent produced by the best practicable technology currently available in the industry. The Administrator was referred to the industry and to existing practices to determine BPT. He was to categorize point sources, examine control practices in exemplary plants in each category, and, after weighing benefits and costs and considering other factors specified by § 304, determine and define the best practicable technology at a level that would effect the obvious statutory goal for 1977 of substantially reducing the total pollution produced by each category of the industry. Necessarily, if pollution is to be diminished, limitations based on BPT must forbid the level of effluent produced by the most pollution-prone segment of the industry, that segment not measuring up to "the average of the best existing performance." So understood, the statute contemplated regulations that would require a substantial number of point sources with the poorest performances either to conform to BPT standards or to cease production. To allow a variance based on economic capability and not to require adherence to the prescribed minimum technology would permit the employment of the very practices that the Administrator had rejected in establishing the best practicable technology currently in use in the industry.

To put the matter another way, under § 304, the Administrator is directed to consider the benefits of effluent reductions as compared to the costs of pollution control in determining BPT limitations. Thus, every BPT limitation represents a conclusion by the Administrator that the costs imposed on the industry are worth the benefits in pollution reduction that will be gained by meeting those limits. To grant a variance because a particular owner or operator cannot meet the normal costs of the technological requirements imposed on him, and not because there has been a recalculation of the benefits compared to the costs, would be inconsistent with this legislative scheme and would allow a level of pollution inconsistent with the judgment of the Administrator.

In terms of the scheme implemented by BPT limitations, the factors that the Administrator considers in granting variances do not suggest that economic capability must also be a determinant. The regulations permit a variance where "factors relating to the equipment or facilities involved, the process applied, or such other factors relating to such discharger are fundamentally different from the factors considered in the establishment of the guidelines." If a point source can show that its situation, including its costs of compliance, is not within the range of circumstances considered by the Administrator, then it may receive a variance, whether or not the source could afford to comply with the minimum standard.[17] In such situations, the variance is an acknowledgement that the uniform BPT limitation was set without reference to the full range of current practices, to which the Administrator was to refer. Insofar as a BPT limitation was determined without consideration of a current practice fundamentally different from those that were considered by the Administrator, that limitation is incomplete. A variance based on economic capability, however, would not have this character: it would allow a variance simply because the point source could not afford a compliance cost that is not fundamentally different from those the

---

[17]Respondents argue that precluding consideration of economic capability in determining whether to grant a variance effectively precludes consideration of the "total costs" for the individual point source. Respondents rely upon a statement by Representative Jones as to the meaning of "total cost" in § 304(b)(1)(B): "internal, or plant, costs sustained by the owner or operator and those external costs such as potential unemployment, dislocation and rural area economic development sustained by the community, area, or region." Unless economic capability is considered, it is argued, it will be impossible to consider the potential external costs of meeting a BPT limitation, caused by a plant closing. Although there is some merit to respondents' contention, we do not believe it supports the decision of the Court of Appeals. The court did not hold that economic capability is relevant only if it discloses "fundamentally different" external costs from those considered by EPA in establishing the BPT limitation; rather, the court held that the factors included in § 301(c) *must* be taken into consideration. Section 301(c) makes economic capability, regardless of its effect on external costs, a ground for a variance. It is this position that we reject.

Administrator has already considered in determining BPT. It would force a displacement of calculations already performed, not because those calculations were incomplete or had unexpected effects, but only because the costs happened to fall on one particular operator, rather than on another who might be economically better off.

Because the 1977 limitations were intended to reduce the total pollution produced by an industry, requiring compliance with BPT standards necessarily imposed additional costs on the segment of the industry with the least effective technology. If the statutory goal is to be achieved, these costs must be borne or the point source eliminated. In our view, requiring variances from otherwise valid regulations where dischargers cannot afford normal costs of compliance would undermine the purpose and the intended operative effect of the 1977 regulations.

The Administrator's present interpretation of the language of the statute is amply supported by the legislative history, which persuades us that Congress understood that the economic capability provision of § 301(c) was limited to BAT variances and that Congress foresaw and accepted the economic hardship, including the closing of some plants, that effluent limitations would cause....

As we see it, Congress anticipated that the 1977 regulations would cause economic hardship and plant closings: "[T]he question ... is not what a court thinks is generally appropriate to the regulatory process; it is what Congress intended for *these* regulations." [Citation.]

It is by now commonplace that "when faced with a problem of statutory construction, this Court shows great deference to the interpretation given the statute by the officers or agency charged with its administration." [Citation.] The statute itself does not provide for BPT variances in connection with permits for individual point sources, and we had no occasion in *Du Pont* to address the adequacy of the Administrator's 1977 variance provision. In the face of § 301(c)'s explicit limitation and in the absence of any other specific direction to provide for variances in connection with permits for individual point sources, we believe that the Administrator has adopted a reasonable construction of the statutory mandate.

In rejecting EPA's interpretation of the BPT variance provision, the Court of Appeals relied on a mistaken conception of the relation between BPT and BAT standards. The court erroneously believed that since BAT limitations are to be more stringent than BPT limitations, the variance provision for the latter must be at least as flexible as that for the former with respect to affordability. The variances permitted by § 301(c) from the 1987 limitations, however, can reasonably be understood to represent a cost in decreased effluent reductions that can only be afforded once the minimal standard expressed in the BPT limitation has been reached.

We conclude, therefore, that the Court of Appeals erred in not accepting EPA's interpretation of the Act. EPA is not required by the Act to consider economic capability in granting variances from its uniform BPT regulations.

[Reversed.]

NOTES AND QUESTIONS

1. *National Crushed Stone* focuses on the permissible scope of the FDF variance as promulgated by EPA from the 1977 BPT standard, a question expressly reserved in footnote 19 of the *Du Pont* opinion. The regulation allowed a "greater than normal cost of implementation" to be grounds for an FDF variance, but not economic inability of the discharger. What is the difference between the two? The legislative history quoted in note 17 of the opinion suggests that "costs" include "external costs" such as potential unemployment and economic disruption in the community from a plant closing. If that is the case, what distinction is there between consideration of "costs" and consideration of a source's economic capability to meet a standard for purposes of an FDF variance?

2. In deciding in *Du Pont* that BPT as well as BAT could be set by regulation for classes and subclasses of industry, the Supreme Court determined that there was no suggestion in the Act of any "radical difference in the mechanism used to impose limitations" for the two standards. *See* page 529 *supra.* Why, then, does economic inability not justify a variance from BPT as well as BAT?

3. The section 301(c) variance allows the Administration to modify the BAT requirements for any point source if the owner or operator demonstrates that the modified requirement "will represent the maximum use of technology within the economic capability of the owner or operator; and ... will result in reasonable further progress toward the elimination of the discharge of pollutants." 33 U.S.C. § 1311(c). This variance was originally provided to allow modification of the 1983 BAT standard. The 1977 amendments replaced the 1983 BAT standard with a BAT standard for toxic and nonconventional pollutants and BCT standard for conventional pollutants, but the language of section 301(c) remained unchanged. For what pollutant standards is the 301(c) variance available after 1977? What is the relevance of section 301(l) in answering this question?

In *Chemical Mfrs. Ass'n v. NRDC*, 470 U.S. 116 (1985), the Supreme Court had to decide whether section 301(l) (which then stated that EPA could not "modify any requirement of this section" for any toxic pollutant) precluded EPA from providing an FDF variance for any toxic pollutant. Justice White for the majority, held that section 301(l) was only intended by Congress to preclude the statutory variances in section 301 then available, not the FDF variance. In so holding, the Court emphasized that the FDF variance was not a true exception from a pollutant standard in the same way as the statutory variances:

The nature of FDF variances has been spelled out both by this Court and by the Agency itself. The regulation explains that its purpose is to remedy categories which were not accurately drawn because information was either not available to or not considered by the Administrator in setting the original categories and limitations. 40 C.F.R. § 403.13(b) (1984). An FDF variance does not excuse compliance with a correct requirement, but instead represents an acknowledgement that not all relevant factors were taken sufficiently into account in framing that requirement originally, and that those relevant factors, properly considered, would have justified — indeed, required — the creation of a subcategory for the discharger in question. As we have recognized, the FDF variance is a laudable corrective mechanism, "an acknowledgement that the uniform ... limitation was set without reference to the full range of current practices, to which the Administrator was to refer." *EPA v. National Crushed Stone Assn.*, 449 U.S. 64. It is, essentially, not an exception to the standard-setting process, but rather a more fine-tuned application of it.

Id. at 130. The Water Quality Act of 1987 codified the FDF variance in section 301(n), 33 U.S.C. § 1311(n), and modified section 301(l) to reflect the availability of the FDF variance for toxic pollutants. Without looking at the variance chart in note 6, for what standards does section 301(n) expressly authorize the FDF variance? Are there any variances available from new source performance standards? Could EPA provide for an FDF variance from an NSPS? *See Du Pont*, page 528 *supra*.

4. EPA in its regulations has authorized FDF variances to modify the requirements of BPT, BAT, BCT, and categorical pretreatment standards. *See* 40 C.F.R. § 125.30-32. The factors which may be considered fundamentally different under the regulations are the nature and quality of pollutants contained in the raw waste load, the volume of the discharger's wastewater, non-water quality environmental impacts, energy requirements in complying with standards, engineering and process differences in applying control technology, and the "cost of compliance with required control technology." *Id.* § 125.31(d)(1)-(6). A fundamental difference from the rest of the industry is grounds for a less stringent limitation only if it causes a "removal cost wholly out of proportion to the removal cost considered during development of the national limits" or "a non-water quality environmental impact (including energy requirements) fundamentally more adverse than the impact considered during development of the national limits." *Id.* § 125.31(b)(3). *See also Georgia-Pac. Co. v. EPA*, 671 F.2d 1235 (9th Cir. 1982) (regarding what makes a difference "fundamental").

Under the *National Crushed Stone* decision, pages 544-49 *supra*, an owner or operator's inability to pay the costs of compliance, as opposed to having costs of compliance fundamentally different from those of the industry, is not grounds for an FDF variance. *See also* 40 C.F.R. § 125.31(e)(3). Can fundamentally different water quality impacts be grounds for a FDF variance? *See Crown*

Simpson Pulp Co. v. Costle, 642 F.2d 323 (9th Cir. 1981), *cert. denied* 454 U.S. 1053 (1981). *See also Chemical Mfrs. Ass'n v. NRDC*, note 3 *supra;* 40 C.F.R. § 125.31(e)(4).

5. *Water Quality Exceptions.* There are only a few provisions in the FWPCA which authorize consideration of water quality in determining compliance with the Act. POTWs could seek waivers for some discharges into marine waters under section 301(h), 33 U.S.C. § 1311(h), one of the few water quality based exceptions under the Act. The definition of marine waters includes only "deep waters of the territorial sea or the waters of the contiguous zone, or ... saline estuarine waters where there is strong tidal movement...." FWPCA § 301(h), 33 U.S.C. § 1311(h). In a 1981 amendment the waiver was limited to municipalities that applied not later than December 29, 1982, FWPCA § 301(j)(1)(A), 33 U.S.C. § 1311(j)(1)(A), with a brief reopening of the application period after the effective date of the Water Quality Act of 1987. *Id.*, as amended by Pub. L. No. 100-4, § 303(b), 101 Stat. 7, 34. A similar, very limited variance is provided for industrial discharges into deep waters of the territorial seas. FWPCA § 301(m), 33 U.S.C. § 1311(m).

Two other "exceptions" based on water quality considerations are the section 301(g) waiver from BAT for nonconventional pollutants and the relaxation of the definition of "secondary treatment" in section 304(d)(4). Under section 304(d)(4), 33 U.S.C. § 1314(d)(4), certain biological treatment facilities can be deemed the equivalent of secondary treatment if receiving water quality will not be "adversely affected." Under section 301(g), 33 U.S.C. § 1311(g), a variance is available from BAT for the nonconventional pollutants chlorine, iron, ammonia, color, total phenols, and any others EPA should designate. To qualify, the discharger must demonstrate to EPA "with the concurrence of the State" that the source is in compliance with BPT or any more stringent water quality effluent limitation, that its variance will not impose additional requirements on any other point or nonpoint source, and that its discharge will not interfere with the maintenance of water quality, will "assure" protection of water supplies and aquatic life, and will not result in the discharge of pollutants in "quantities which may reasonably be anticipated to pose an unacceptable risk to human health or the environment because of bioaccumulation, persistency in the environment, acute toxicity, chronic toxicity (including carcinogenicity, mutagenicity or teratogenicity), or synergistic propensities." *Id.*

6. *Current Variance Chart.* The Water Quality Act of 1987 added another variance to the statutory scheme for facilities experimenting with innovative technology to control discharges. FWPCA § 301(k), 33 U.S.C. § 1311(k). To qualify, a facility must demonstrate that the innovative system has the potential for industry-wide application. The waiver is available for no more than two years after compliance with the standard would have otherwise been required. From what standards is the section 301(k) variance available? Would it be available for a BAT standard for toxic pollutants under the *Chemical Manufacturers* decision?

Also in 1987, the section 301(g) variance from the BAT standard for nonconventional pollutants was limited to the nonconventional pollutants chlorine, iron, ammonia, color, and total phenols with EPA authorized to add additional nonconventional pollutants to those eligible for the variance. The following chart outlines the variances available to non-POTW direct dischargers and the standards from which they are available after the 1987 amendments:

Standard	Pollutant	Variances Available
BPT	any type of pollutant	FDF variance*
BAT	toxic	301(n) [FDF]
		other statutory variances are not available due to section 301(1)
BCT	conventional	301(n) [FDF]
		301(k) [innovative technology]
BAT	nonconventional	301(n) [FDF]
		301(k) [innovative technology]
		301(g) [water quality variance for certain listed pollutants]
		301(c) [economic inability]
NSPS	any type of pollutant	No variances

*Nonstatutory FDF variance.

C. THE INTERRELATIONSHIP BETWEEN THE EFFLUENT STANDARDS, VARIANCES AND STATUTORY DEADLINES

The preceding cases establish the basic framework for point source effluent limitations and the variances from those limitations. The following case is included to illustrate the interrelationship of these limitations and variances, their continuing refinement in the case law, and the role of the statutory deadlines in implementation and enforcement of the standards. The Act is badly out of date, and reauthorization is expected to be a fundamental debate before Congress in 1997-98. The case involves a comprehensive review of the BPT, BAT, NSPS and pretreatment standards for the organic chemicals, plastics, and synthetic fibers industries. The administrative record alone totalled 600,000 pages, and the mammoth court of appeals decision had to be written jointly by the three judges (as was done in *Alabama Power*, page 390 *supra*).

CHEMICAL MANUFACTURERS ASSOCIATION v. ENVIRONMENTAL PROTECTION AGENCY

870 F.2d 177 (5th Cir. 1989), *modified*,
885 F.2d 253 (5th Cir. 1989)

By RUBIN, GARZA and KING, CIRCUIT JUDGES, Jointly.

Acting under the mandate of the Clean Water Act (CWA), the Environmental Protection Agency (EPA) has promulgated final regulations limiting the discharge of pollutants into the nation's navigable waters by manufacturing plants in the organic chemicals, plastics, and synthetic fibers (OCPSF) industries. The regulations, which the statute requires to be implemented beginning March 31, 1989, cover both direct discharge and indirect discharge through publicly-owned treatment works (POTWs). The Chemical Manufacturers Association (CMA) and a number of companies affected by the regulations allege both procedural defects in their promulgation and substantive defects in various provisions, as well as defects in the application of specific provisions to particular plants.

....

[In Part I, the Court held that the EPA did not violate the notice-and-comment requirements of the Administrative Procedure Act (APA) by: (1) utilizing an updated Dun & Bradstreet economic-impact study to supplement data it had previously disclosed without making the new data public either during the notice-and-comment period or in the public record except to this court under seal; or (2) by failing to publish its regulations for the control of toxic metals for public comment prior to final promulgation.]

II. *Best Practicable Technology (BPT) Issues*

BPT limitations are intended to represent the average of the best levels of performance by existing plants of various sizes, ages, and unit processes within the category or subcategory for control of conventional pollutants. In promulgating the regulations, the Agency identified a model technology: biological treatment preceded by appropriate process controls and in-plant treatment followed by secondary clarification as necessary to assure adequate control of solids. CMA argues that the EPA's data indicate that its limitations will require the installation of additional treatment equipment at a cost "wholly out of proportion" to the marginal effluent reduction that the equipment would achieve and that the limitations consequently fail to meet the cost-effectiveness test required by Section 304(b)(1)(B) of the Act and the "best conventional technology" (BCT) test enacted in 1977. The EPA asserts that the total cost of the BPT rules is justified by the total amount of pollutant that would be removed.

The EPA's Consideration of the Industry's Costs of Complying With the BPT Limitations

CMA maintains that the cost-effectiveness of BPT rulemaking should be measured by a "knee-of-the-curve" test to determine the point at which costs rise steeply per pound of pollutant removed and that, under such a test, the BPT rules are not cost-effective.

The CWA contains no specific statutory language establishing a BPT "knee-of-the-curve" test or any other quantitative cost-benefit ratio test for BPT. The statute simply requires that the EPA consider "the total cost of application of technology in relation to the effluent reduction benefits to be achieved from such application." The courts of appeal have consistently held that Congress intended Section 304(b) to give the EPA broad discretion in considering the cost of pollution abatement in relation to its benefits and to preclude the EPA from giving the cost of compliance primary importance.

....

The EPA argues that the Administrator acted well within this broad discretion in concluding that the costs of the OCPSF BPT limitations were justified by the significant quantities of pollutants that would be removed. The EPA notes that the OCPSF industry is currently a national leader in discharging conventional pollutants into our nation's waters. The industry has approximately 300 direct dischargers which annually discharge an estimated 61 million pounds of biochemical oxygen-demanding substances (BODS) and 100 million pounds of total suspended solids (TSS) for a total estimate of approximately 161 million pounds annually. The EPA estimated that the BPT limitations would result annually in the removal of 108 million pounds of conventional pollutants from OCPSF discharges and consequently from our nation's waters at an annualized compliance cost of 76.6 million dollars after a capital investment of 215.8 million dollars. Thus, the EPA concluded that the total cost of BPT is warranted by the total pounds of pollutant removed.

CMA's Challenge Based on the "Knee-of-the-Curve" Cost Effectiveness Test

CMA argues that Congress was concerned generally that the EPA's regulations not require expenditures that would pass the point at which costs escalate rapidly in relation to benefits — the "knee-of-the-curve" on a diagram depicting the cost curve. CMA conceives of the knee-of-the-curve test as a generally applicable cost-effectiveness test with the "knee" defining the most stringent level of regulation permissible. Thus, CMA asserts, whether the EPA labels its regulations BPT or BCT, the EPA is required to consider whether the marginal costs exceed the marginal benefits of the rule. Applying this test, CMA argues that increasing the removal of conventional pollutants from 96 to 99 percent as required by the limitations would cost the OCPSF industry almost twice as much per pound of pollutant removed as current treatment methods: The annual removal of 108 million pounds would cost 76 million dollars per year — 71 cents per pound — whereas industry efforts to date have required an expenditure of only 38 cents per pound. CMA concludes that the cost per pound for removal of pollutants is thus well beyond the knee-of-the-curve and that the regulations are therefore not cost-effective.

The EPA argues, however, that even if the knee-of-the-curve test applies to any of its regulations, the test is applicable only to assess the cost-effectiveness of incremental increases in limitations beyond BPT — that is, only to BCT....

The BCT provisions were intended to establish an intermediate level between BPT and the stricter BAT limitations for conventional pollutants by adding a cost-effectiveness test for incremental technology requirements that exceed BPT technology. Under BCT, additional limitations on conventional pollutants that are more stringent than BPT can be imposed only "to the extent that the increased cost of treatment [would] be reasonable in terms of the degree of environmental benefits."

Thus, Congress intended that cost would occupy a different role in EPA's promulgation of BPT limitations than it would in the promulgation of BCT because of the different aims of the two standards. While Congress did not consider cost to be irrelevant to BPT, it clearly intended it to be a less significant factor than in the promulgation of BCT limitations. The EPA's interpretation of the Act is rational and supported by both the legislative history and the case law insofar as the EPA emphasizes that the BPT limitations are not subject to the type of stringent cost-benefit analysis required for BCT. The relevant inquiry with respect to BPT, as indicated above, is whether the costs are "wholly disproportionate" to the benefits.

To the extent that CMA's claim is that "wholly disproportionate" is to be measured by a knee-of-the-curve test, the EPA responds that CMA misconceives the nature of the test. Rather than displaying the rate at which costs increase relative to pounds of pollutant removed, CMA's curve displays the rate at which the cost-per-pound increases relative to the *percent* of pollutant removed, resulting in a misleadingly steep curve. While both the BPT and BCT tests require a comparison between costs and effluent reduction, neither test requires the comparison of costs to the percentage removed, as implied by CMA's curve.

CMA relies upon legislative history to justify its percent-removal approach to evaluating the reasonableness of costs. However, the statute does not require that a percent-removal approach be used to establish BPT regulations. Almost all of the BPT regulations promulgated by the EPA since the 1972 enactment of the Clean Water Act are based upon either concentration limitations (as in the case of the OCPSF rule) or more stringent "mass limitations" which limit both concentrations and flow volumes. In the current case, the regulation will require a 10% increase above current industry costs to remove 108 million additional pounds. The EPA reasonably concluded that these costs were not "wholly disproportionate" to the benefits.

The BCT Cost-Effectiveness Test

CMA also argues that whether or not BPT rules are, as a general matter, subject to a knee-of-the-curve test, the EPA's BPT limitations for conventional pollutants must pass the BCT cost test which Congress enacted in 1977.

In promulgating BCT limitations, the Act directs the EPA to consider:

> the reasonableness of the relationship between the costs of attaining a reduction in effluents and the effluent reduction benefits derived, and the comparison of the cost and level of reduction of such pollutants from the discharge from publicly owned treatment works to the cost and level of reduction of such pollutants from a class or category of industrial sources....

CMA contends that this test governs the BPT rules because they represent an increase in regulation over the limitations established on a case-by-case basis by NPDES permits issued before 1977. In other words, CMA contends that the permit limitations established BPT for individual plants and that in enacting the BCT requirements in 1977 Congress intended that any subsequent, more stringent regulations must be evaluated according to the BCT standards.

The EPA responds, however, that its authority to promulgate BPT regulations is not abrogated by the fact that, pursuant to Section 402(a)(1), NPDES permits were issued prior to the promulgation of industry-wide BPT regulations. The EPA notes that, since 1977, it has promulgated BPT regulations limiting conventional pollutants in the iron and steel, metal finishing, coal mining, oil and gas, battery manufacturing, plastics molding and forming, metal molding and casting, coil coating, porcelain enameling, aluminum forming, copper forming, electrical and electronic products, and nonferrous metals forming industries — notwithstanding the fact that most of these facilities had previously been regulated by permits. The oil-and-gas-pollutant effluent limitations were promulgated in 1979 and reviewed by this court in 1981 without any reference to the BCT cost test.

The EPA also maintains that Congress did not intend BCT to displace BPT. The EPA notes that Congress has never repealed the BPT factors as a vital and continuing requirement of the Act and has not stripped the EPA of its explicit authority, under Section 304(b) of the Act, to revise or update BPT periodically. Section 304(b) directs the EPA to "publish ... regulations, providing guidelines for effluent limitations, and at least annually thereafter, revise, if appropriate, such regulations." Thus, as the EPA interprets the Act, BCT standards, which place cost-effectiveness constraints on incremental technology requirements that exceed BPT technology, do not displace BPT or override the EPA's authority to promulgate BPT for conventional pollutants....

As evidenced by numerous rulemakings, the EPA has consistently interpreted the Act to allow the promulgation of BPT limitations applicable to facilities operating under NPDES permits despite the enactment of BCT standards in 1977. We must accord "considerable weight" to an agency's construction of a statutory scheme it is entrusted to administer. Finding the EPA's interpretation of the Act to be reasonable, we conclude that CMA's objections do not compel us to remand the limitations.

The EPA's Definition of the BPT Data Base

NRDC claims that the EPA used data from 71 of 99 plants, approximately 72%, as representing the group of "best dischargers" for purposes of promulgating BPT regulations. How can the group of "best" dischargers encompass 72% of the industry, queries NRDC, leading it to argue that the EPA should have further tightened its editing criteria, which would have led to more stringent regulations.

NRDC's argument is misleading, however. Out of 304 direct dischargers in the industry that will be subject to regulation, the EPA chose a particular technology, namely biological treatment with secondary clarification, which is used by 99 plants. Out of these 99 plants, the EPA then chose data from 71 plants to determine the "average of the best" for the purpose of promulgating its BODS regulations. The EPA defends its decision by noting that its *initial* edit reduced the field from 304 to 99. Thus, the NRDC's complaint that the EPA used 71 of 99 plants is mistaken because the edit in question was the second edit, 205 dischargers having already been weeded out.

We hold, therefore, that the EPA's class of performers for determining the "average of the best" was not unreasonably broad.

Another question is whether the CWA requires the EPA to consider the average of the best performers within an *industrial category*, or the average of the best performers that use a particular chosen technology within an industry. We hold that it is appropriate to extract a group of "best" performers from an industry category; this was done in this case when the EPA selected 99 out of 304 plants in its initial edit. In fact, the EPA went further by narrowing the 99 plants down to 71. The EPA was not required to take the average of the best 99 plants using a particular technology, but merely to take the average of the best 304 plants in the industrial category. The legislative history of the 1972 amendments to the CWA specifies that "the administrator should establish the range of 'best practicable' levels based upon the average of the best performance by plants of various sizes, ages, and unit processes within each industrial category." Therefore, we find that the EPA's methods for setting the BPT standards for BODS were in compliance with the CWA....

BPT Subcategorization

CMA challenges the EPA's division of the OCPSF Industry into seven subcategories for the purpose of establishing BPT limitations on the ground that the subcategories are based on [Standard Industrial Classification] SIC-product groupings rather than wastewater characteristics or treatability. CMA argues that the EPA has created an inequity by grouping together plants with substantially different influent concentrations and subjecting them to the same concentration limitations, thereby requiring, in effect, a higher percent removal at plants with higher influent concentrations.

In Section 304(b)(1)(B), Congress listed several factors, in addition to cost, that the EPA shall "take into account" in determining BPT, including the age of equipment, the process employed, engineering aspects of treatment, process changes, and non-water-quality environmental impacts. Based on these factors, the EPA determines whether plants within an industry should be assigned to a subcategory subject to more particularized regulations than the industry as a whole.

However, the EPA is required to create a separate subcategory for a group of plants only when they are so fundamentally different from other plants on which the limitations are based that they cannot practicably achieve the effluent limitations achieved by the average of the best plants in the industry. The EPA has considerable discretion in evaluating these factors; it is enough that the EPA considered the relevant factors and reached a rational conclusion about them. The Agency's task is "to establish numerical standards limiting effluent pollution," and it should concentrate "on grouping plants that could meet the same limitations." If plants can meet the same limitation, they need not be subcategorized simply because they are different.

Plant Specific Challenges to the BPT Limitations and the Availability of Fundamentally Different-Factor Variances

Several petitioners, including Union Carbide, Borg-Warner, DuPont, Monsanto, and Ethyl, claim that the BPT limitations are arbitrary because the EPA failed to account adequately for wastestream characteristics. Petitioners assert that the wastestream characteristics of certain of their plants preclude compliance with the OCPSF industry limitations. These claims are considered together because several of these petitioners raise highly individualized objections to the limitations.

We will address each petitioner's claim in turn. As an initial matter, however, we note that the EPA is not required to consider fundamentally different factors of particular plants in the national BPT rulemaking. Both Congress and the Supreme Court have expressed concern that the process of formulating nationally applicable water-quality standards would be unduly impeded by requiring EPA to address the idiosyncracies of individual plants in the context of a national rulemaking. The Supreme Court has held that the fundamentally-different-factors (FDF) variance procedure provides an entirely acceptable alternative to subcategorizing an industry to account for plant-specific characteristics. [Citing the Supreme Court decision in *Chemical Manufacturers Association v. NRDC*, page 549 *supra*.] Congress has codified the FDF procedures in the CWA, encouraging the EPA not to complicate and delay unduly the promulgation of national effluent-limitation guidelines and standards where the FDF procedure could be employed to address the concerns of individual facilities claiming to be unique.

The Supreme Court held in 1977 that the EPA may establish categorical BPT limitations, "so long as some allowance is made for variations in individual plants, as EPA has done by including a variance clause in its 1977 limitations." Relying heavily on legislative history that demonstrated Congress' intent to replace the site-specific approach to water-quality regulation with technology-based limitations that apply uniformly to categories of dischargers, the unanimous Court reasoned that the alternative view "would place an impossible burden on EPA" contrary to the legislative purpose of the Act.

Addressing the EPA's identical FDF variance procedure for pretreatment standards, the Supreme Court has approved the procedure "as a mechanism for insuring that [EPA's] necessarily rough-hewn categories do not unfairly burden atypical plants." The Court explained:

> EPA and CMA point out that the availability of FDF variances makes bearable the enormous burden faced by EPA in promulgating categories of sources and setting effluent limitations. Acting under stringent timetables, EPA must collect and analyze large amounts of technical information concerning complex industrial categories. Understandably, EPA may not be apprised of and will fail to consider unique factors applicable to atypical plants during the categorical rulemaking process, and it is thus important that EPA's nationally binding categorical pretreatment standards for indirect dischargers be tempered with the flexibility that the FDF variance mechanism offers....

[Citing *Chemical Manufacturers Association v. NRDC*, page 549 *supra*.] The Court stated that the FDF variance procedure was authorized by Congress in significant part to ensure that the national rule would not be overturned simply because of the Agency's failure to consider unique plants. Several courts of appeal have subsequently relied upon the availability of an FDF variance procedure as the basis for rejecting challenges to BPT regulations that are based upon allegedly facility-specific factors.

In codifying the FDF variance procedure in the CWA, Congress specifically emphasized that the procedure serves as a "safety valve" to the categorical statutory scheme, allowing EPA to address plant-specific variations through a separate administrative process, outside of the national rulemaking. The House Report stated:

> There are two approaches for responding to a facility with valid grounds for arguing that it is fundamentally different from other facilities in its category. One possibility is to develop a separate subcategory within the regulation, undertake a separate data collection and analysis effort and then repropose and issue the final rule. The other alternative is to leave the national rule in place and use the FDF determination procedure to establish alternative technology-based limitations for the facility that accurately reflect its situation. The subcategorization approach would add further complications and require potentially substantial additional time in developing what are already extraordinarily complex and detailed national regulations. By

contrast, the FDF determination procedure allows both implementation of the national rule and consideration of individual petitions claiming unique factors.

....

The highly individualized claims of DuPont, Monsanto, and Ethel are more appropriately addressed in an FDF administrative proceeding. DuPont and Ethel have filed for variances, and Monsanto may certainly do so in the near future. Petitioners argue, however, that we may not decline to address their claims because the EPA has not yet ruled on the applications. Thus, petitioners claim that the EPA will leave them in "administrative limbo" while the limitations go into effect. To the extent, however, that petitioners DuPont and Ethyl seek to compel an Agency decision on their FDF applications, such relief is outside the scope of this court's limited jurisdiction under CWA Section 509(b)(1) to review the EPA's effluent limitations guidelines, pretreatment standards, and new source performance standards....

Congress was aware of the difficulty and corresponding delays in processing FDF variance applications for individual plants. Accordingly, Congress attempted to expedite the process by specifically requiring the EPA to determine the merits of applications for FDF variances for individual plants within 180 days of the submission of the application. Thus, the WQA ensures that all FDF applications on which the EPA had not previously ruled would henceforth be subject to the Act's 180-day time limit.

Notwithstanding Congress' 180-day deadline, the EPA admits that historically it has taken, on average, three years to process an FDF application. The EPA believes that it may require more than 180 days to complete the review of these highly technical applications. However, the fact that the Agency has exceeded the statutory time limit for issuing its decision on the OCPSF FDF applications does not permit this court to order the EPA to produce a schedule for rendering its decisions. Congress provided an explicit statutory deadline for these decisions which specifically contemplates that efforts to compel timely Agency action would be heard exclusively in the district courts. Nevertheless, petitioners argue that because of this delay, and because the OCPSF limitations will require them to install costly control technology, this court should stay application of the OCPSF limitations pending the EPA's consideration of their FDF applications.

Section 509(b)(1) of the CWA authorizes the courts of appeal to review the effluent-pollution limitations promulgated by EPA. Only the rulemaking proceedings are subject to this court's review under Section 509(b)(1), however, and the petitioners do not challenge the promulgation of the regulations. Rather, they challenge the implementation or application of the regulations and such a challenge is not subject to this court's review under Section 509(b)(1). The industrial petitioners' claim that the EPA has failed to consider their FDF applications in a timely manner, therefore, even if true, does not undermine the legality of the regulations because an FDF proceeding is collateral to the rulemaking proceedings.

A challenge to the implementation or application of the regulations may be brought in a civil action under CWA Section 505(a)(2), which provides:

> any citizen may commence a civil action ... against the Administrator where there is alleged a failure of the Administrator to perform any act or duty under this Act which is not discretionary with the Administrator.

A civil action under Section 505(a)(2) must be commenced in the district court.

In addition, the relief requested by the petitioners is precluded by the Act. The Act provides:

> An application for an alternative requirement under this subsection [i.e., an FDF application], shall not stay the applicant's obligation to comply with the effluent limitation guideline or categorical pretreatment standard which is the subject of the application. [Citing FWPCA § 301(n)(6), 33 U.S.C. § 1311(n)(6).]

Staying the regulations pending petitioners' FDF applications would be contrary to Congress' expressed intent that the effluent limits be enforced notwithstanding a pending FDF application.

III. *Best Available Technology (BAT) Issues*

Remedy for Unavoidable Exceedances

Petitioners PPG and Dow assert that the EPA's statistical model demonstrates that a well-operated plant using BAT can be expected to perform within the daily effluent limitations only 99 percent of the time and within the monthly effluent limitations only 95 percent of the time. They contend that the regulations are unachievable, hence arbitrary, because the model implies that exceedances, i.e., toxic discharges in excess of the BAT limitations, can be expected to occur an average of one percent of the time on a daily basis and five percent of the time on a monthly basis. The regulations, they assert, do not provide a remedy for such unavoidable exceedances.

....

The industrial petitioners argue that the EPA has not adequately demonstrated that the data points exceeding the 99th and 95th percentiles represent controllable rather than uncontrollable variability. The EPA's conclusion that these data points result from quality-control problems is, however, reasonable because these points are isolated and extreme departures from average performance. "The purpose of these variability factors is to account for routine fluctuations that occur in plant operation, not to allow for poor performance." The data points exceeding the 99th and 95th percentiles, by definition extreme, do not reflect routine performance, and were reasonably excluded.

In any event, the EPA has provided an exception for unavoidable exceedances. The regulations provide that an unavoidable exceedance caused by an "upset" is an affirmative defense in an action for noncompliance. The regulations define an "upset" as:

> an exceptional incident in which there is unintentional and temporary noncompliance with technology-based permit effluent limitations because of factors beyond the reasonable control of the permittee. An upset does not include noncompliance to the extent caused by operational error, improperly designed treatment facilities, inadequate treatment facilities, lack of preventive maintenance, or careless or improper operation.

It is not clear whether upsets were included in the data used by the EPA to calculate the variability factors. At one point the record states that upsets were edited from the data; however, the record also states that the EPA used all data collected from the data-base plants. We need not resolve this discrepancy. The EPA reasonably concluded that the data points exceeding the 99th and 95th percentiles represent either quality-control problems or upsets because there can be no other explanation for these isolated and extremely high discharges. If these data points result from quality-control problems, the exceedances they represent are within the control of the plant. If, however, the data points represent exceedances beyond the control of the industry, the upset defense is available.

. . . .

We reject the petitioners' premise that the limitations are unachievable unless all plants in the data base have met the limitations. The legislative history of the CWA indicates that the "best available technology" refers to the single best performing plant in an industrial field. The EPA urges that because the Act and the legislative history do not provide more particular guidance, it was free to determine the "best" plant on a pollutant-by-pollutant basis. The Supreme Court has stated that "[i]t is by now commonplace that 'when faced with a problem of statutory construction, this Court shows great deference to the interpretation given the statute by the officers or agency charged with its administration.'" This court defers to the EPA's interpretation of the Act. The EPA's interpretation of the Act is rational and is not precluded by the legislative history.

Though PPG plant 913 exceeded the monthly average limitation for chloroform, the petitioners' own data show that Dow plant 415 performed well within the limits. On at least one occasion Dow plant 415 exceeded the daily limit for trichloroethylene; however, the data show that PPG plant 913 performed within the limits. Given the EPA's interpretation of the Act which is entitled to deference, an exceedance by one of the data-base plants is irrelevant so long as another data-base plant demonstrates that the limitations are achievable.

Compliance Deadline

Lack of Sufficient Lead Time for Industry Members to Comply

The Water Quality Act (WQA) Amendments of 1987 directed the EPA to promulgate BAT limitations by December 31, 1986. The WQA Amendments also established March 31, 1989, as the final compliance date for the OCPSF BAT limitations. The EPA promulgated the OCPSF limitations on November 5, 1987. Borg-Warner argues that Congress intended industry to have at least three years' lead time before it would be subject to the limitations and that the EPA's failure to promulgate regulations with sufficient lead time for compliance constitutes a denial of substantive due process.

We first look to Congressional intent. Because the BAT limitations had not been promulgated on February 4, 1987, the date Congress passed the 1987 WQA Amendments, Congress obviously understood that substantially less than three years would elapse before the compliance date. The Act and its legislative history reflect Congress' intention that good faith non-compliance due to the Administrator's failure to promulgate regulations by the prescribed date would be accommodated by the EPA's post-deadline enforcement policy.

The Act, thus interpreted, does not deny industry members due process. Section 309 of the Act provides that, if a discharger fails to comply with a "final deadline," the Administrator shall schedule a "reasonable" time for compliance "taking into account the seriousness of the violation and any good-faith efforts to comply with applicable requirements." The Conference Report accompanying the WQA Amendments further explains:

> With respect to the establishment of an outside date of March 31, 1989, for compliance with technology based requirements, the conferees note that prompt promulgation of the relevant effluent limitations will be essential to allow dischargers sufficient time to come into compliance. Therefore, the conferees direct that the Administrator promulgate such limitations as expeditiously as possible.
>
> If dischargers in an entire category are unable to meet the March 31, 1989, deadline provided in the conference substitute as a result of the Administrator's failure to promulgate effluent limitations in sufficient time to allow for compliance by such date, *non-compliance resulting from the Administrator's delay can be dealt with under EPA's current post-1984 deadline enforcement policy.* That policy calls for the Agency, at the same time a permit containing the statutory deadline is issued, to *issue an administrative order to the non-complying company which specifies a schedule of compliance as expeditiously as practicable, but not later than three years after permit issuance.*

Through Section 309 Congress has adequately dealt with the dilemma that may confront an industry member due to the Administrator's delay in promulgating the limitations.

Borg-Warner argues that reliance on the EPA's prosecutorial discretion is not an adequate remedy for the Administrator's delay in promulgating the regulations because of the risk of selective enforcement. This argument presumes that the EPA will act in bad faith and contrary to congressional intent. If that should occur, an industrial petitioner's remedy is to seek judicial review of the EPA's illegal actions or to invoke that illegality as a defense to an enforcement action.

"Availability" of BAT Technology

Borg-Warner asserts that at least three years' lead time is necessary for the installation of BAT technology and many plants in the industry will not be able to install the technology in time for the compliance deadline. Borg-Warner argues that without sufficient lead time the technology needed to satisfy the BAT limitations is not "available" within the meaning of the Act.

This argument is based on a misreading of the Act. The Act directs the EPA to establish effluent limitations "which shall require application of the best available technology economically achievable for such category or class." It requires that the effluent limitations be based on "available" model technology; it does not require the EPA to consider the temporal availability of the model technology to individual plants. Section 304(b)(2)(B) of the Act lists those factors the EPA should consider in identifying the BAT model technology; these factors do not include consideration of an individual plant's lead time. Moreover, as previously discussed, Congress separately provided an exception under Section 309 for plants without sufficient lead time to comply with the regulations. This exception would be redundant if Congress intended the EPA to consider lead time in determining whether technology is "available."

IV. Pretreatment Standards for Existing Sources (PSES) Issues

The EPA's Definition of "Pass Through"

In addition to authorizing the EPA to regulate the discharge of pollutants directly into the nation's waters, the CWA authorizes the EPA to establish pretreatment standards for "indirect dischargers" — industrial dischargers who release wastes into publicly-owned treatment works (POTWs) rather than directly into navigable waters.

Congress "recognized that the pollutants which some indirect dischargers release into POTWs could interfere with the operation of the POTWs, or could pass through the POTWs without adequate treatment." Accordingly, the Act authorizes the EPA to identify those pollutants which "pass through" POTWs without adequate treatment, or which "interfere with" the operation of POTWs, and to promulgate pretreatment standards which require indirect dischargers to reduce the levels of such pollutants before they are released into public sewage systems.

. . . .

In 1977, when Congress amended the CWA to strengthen the provisions for controlling toxic pollutants, Congress provided that "an indirect discharger ... had to 'pretreat' its waste waters so as to achieve, together with the [POTW] that treated the waste before final discharge into navigable waters, the same level of toxics removal as was required of a direct discharger."

Pursuant to this statutory mandate, the EPA has developed pretreatment standards for specific categories of dischargers that limit the types and amounts of pollutants which may be discharged to POTWs by facilities in each industrial category. These categorical pretreatment standards are technology-based and are analogous to the BAT effluent-limitation guidelines for the removal of toxic pollutants — that is, they are intended to represent the best available technology that is economically achievable by indirect dischargers. In order to determine when a pollutant "passes through" a POTW and should therefore be subject to pretreatment, the EPA has adopted a "BAT comparison" approach. A pollutant is deemed to "pass through" for purposes of the categorical pretreatment standards "if the nation-wide average percentage of the pollutant removed by well-operated POTWs achieving secondary treatment is less than the percent removed by the BAT model treatment system."

. . . .

Specifically, CMA argues that the EPA has established pretreatment standards for some pollutants which are already receiving exemplary treatment by POTWs across the country and that it has furthermore established pretreatment standards for some pollutants which cannot even be detected in the effluent of POTWs by present analytical methods. With respect to this last group of pollutants, CMA contends that the EPA has unlawfully *assumed* pass through, without any evidence that the POTW is actually achieving less effective removal than a direct discharger complying with the BAT standards.

The statute itself simply directs the EPA to promulgate pretreatment standards for pollutants "which are determined" to pass through and does not specify a method by which the EPA is required to make that determination. "Where a statute is silent with respect to the precise question at issue, the question for the reviewing court is whether the agency's interpretation is based on a permissible construction of the statute." As the EPA interprets the statute, the Agency is not required to assume that no pass through takes place in the absence of full-scale data to the contrary. Because we find the EPA's interpretation of the statute to be reasonable and consistent with Congress' intent, we decline to invalidate the OCPSF PSES on the grounds proposed by CMA.

In adopting the "BAT comparison" approach to defining "pass through," the EPA explained that it sought to satisfy two competing congressional objectives:

> That standards for indirect dischargers be equivalent to standards for direct dischargers, and that the treatment capability and performance of the POTW be recognized and taken into account in regulating the discharge of pollutants from indirect dischargers.

The EPA explained that it had determined, after considering alternative methods, that its approach of comparing average percent removal rates to determine pass through was the best solution to the inherent difficulty of measuring the effectiveness of POTWs' treatment of toxic pollutants. The difficulty stems from the fact that the concentration of toxic pollutants in POTWs' influent is much lower than that in industry treatment systems because the industrial dischargers' wastewater mixes in the POTW system with wastewater from other sources that does not contain toxic pollutants. As a result of this dilution, the POTWs' influent concentrations of toxics may already be nearly undetectable by present methods — even though the mass of toxic pollutants has not been reduced. The concentration of toxic pollutants in effluent may therefore be undetected, even if the POTWs' treatment is not, in actuality, very effective in reducing the mass of toxic pollutants....

CMA objects that if the EPA applied this approach, it would find pass through, and therefore impose pretreatment standards, even if POTWs achieved a 96.2% removal rate for a particular toxic pollutant, so long as the EPA predicts that plants complying with BAT can achieve slightly greater removal — even 96.3%.

Given the EPA's well-founded concern that the effects of dilution may cause the effectiveness of POTW treatment to be overstated, we cannot conclude that the EPA's method of determining pass through is arbitrary. As we have stated, "At first blush, it may be unclear why dilution can be a problem. One might believe that the proper goal of a treatment system is to produce water 'so clean' that pollutants are present in only immeasurably small amounts. This is usually, but not always the case. Certain pollutants are dangerous even in immeasurably small concentrations."

... The EPA reasonably concluded that due to the effects of dilution on influent concentrations, the "non-detects or "ND" values (indicating effluent concentrations too low to measure) derived from POTWs with low influent concentrations of priority toxic pollutants did not necessarily demonstrate that the pollutants had been effectively treated and removed from the effluent.

The EPA's Decision Not to Subcategorize on the Basis of POTW Removal Credits

Petitioners argue that it was unlawful for the EPA to refuse to form a subcategory, based on the performance of an individual POTW, because the only other avenue for the consideration of that factor — the removal credits provision — had been foreclosed by Congress, pending the EPA's promulgation of comprehensive sludge regulations. In other words, petitioners claim that the current unavailability of removal credits compels the EPA to consider the effectiveness of individual POTWs' performance in the context of the national rulemaking.

....

As with the FDF variance scheme discussed above, the removal credits provision, together with Section 307(b)(3) which authorizes the Administrator to "designate the category or categories of sources to which such [pretreatment] standard shall apply," provides a coherent statutory scheme: One vehicle for promulgating categorical regulations of national scope and one vehicle to address concerns relating to individual POTWs. Thus petitioners' interpretation of Section 307(b)(3) to require subcategorization based on POTW removal rates is inconsistent with the statutory scheme. It is axiomatic that statutes must be read as an integral whole and that no part should be read to render inoperative another part of the statute. Petitioners' reading of Section 307(b)(3) would render superfluous the removal-credits provision of Section 307(b)(1) and is inconsistent with the aim of the statute to establish uniform pretreatment standards based upon a comparison between the performance of industrial direct dischargers and that of well-operated POTWs.

Petitioners contend, however, that the statutory scheme has been upset by the suspension of the removal-credits program pending EPA's promulgation of sludge regulations. Petitioners argue that the removal-credits provision was intended to prevent the imposition of costly and redundant treatment requirements. Thus, if removal credits — or some means of considering the performance of an individual POTW — are not available, petitioners contend that the imposition of PSES is itself unlawful.

While we recognize that petitioners may feel caught in a catch-22, the trap is of Congress' making, and we may not circumvent Congress' clear intent that removal credits may not be granted until EPA promulgates sludge regulations. The CWA, as amended by the Water Quality Act of 1987, adopted the Third Circuit's decision to prohibit the award of removal credits pending the final promulgation of sludge regulations — with full knowledge of the implications for indirect dischargers. Section 406(e) provides in full:

> The part of the decision of *Natural Resources Defense Council, Inc. v. U.S. Environmental Protection Agency*, [790 F.2d 289] (3d Cir. 1986), which addresses section 405(d) of the Federal Water Pollution Control Act is stayed until August 31, 1987, with respect to (1) those publicly owned treatment works the owner or operator of which received authority to revise pretreatment requirements under section 307(b)(1) of such Act before the date of the enactment of this section, and (2) those publicly owned treatment works the owner or operator of which has submitted an application for authority to revise pretreatment requirements under such section 307(b)(1) which application is pending on such date of enactment and is approved before August 31, 1987. The Administrator shall not authorize any other removal credits under such Act until the Administrator issues the regulations required by paragraph 2(A)(ii) of § 405(d) of such Act, as amended by subsection (a) of this section.

Congress originally intended that the authority to relax pretreatment standards through removal credits would be "available only under certain limited conditions if the sludge from POTWs meets the standards established under section 405(d) of the [Act]. This precaution ensures that disposal of sludge from POTWs would not be contaminated by the added pollutant that POTWs receive when pretreatment standards are relaxed." Were the EPA to create a subcategory for petitioners based on the removal capabilities of the GCWDA or Village of Sauget POTWs, it would in effect be granting the users of those facilities removal credits in the absence of sludge regulations. This result is directly contrary to the Act.

We recognize, as another court has stated, that:

> [T]his may cause economic hardship for Plaintiffs and other indirect dischargers, because they will be required to meet the same standards as direct dischargers. The treatment equipment the dischargers may have to install may become superfluous when the EPA again can approve removal credits. However, Congress and the EPA are the only bodies which can obviate the need for purportedly redundant treatment facilities.

If petitioners wish to challenge EPA's failure to promulgate sludge regulations, they may do so by bringing an action in the district court under the FWPCA's "citizen suit" provision. We do not have jurisdiction in an action brought to review the Agency's promulgation of effluent guidelines to address the Agency's *inaction* in failing to promulgate sludge regulations.

....

V. *New Source Performance Standards (NSPS) Issues*

We now turn to the challenge presented by the NRDC that the EPA violated the Clean Water Act by basing New Source Performance Standards (NSPS) and Pretreatment Standards for New Sources (PSNS) upon BPT for conventional pollutants and upon BAT model technology for toxic discharges.

NRDC argues that effluent limitations for newly constructed dischargers represent the highest level of technology-based treatment under the Clean Water Act. In promulgating the New Source Performance Standards, according to NRDC, Congress intended that new facilities would be required to take advantage of the most current process and treatment innovations, irrespective of whether the cost of the new technologies is justified by any incremental degree of removal achieved by its application. The reason for dropping the cost-benefit analysis from the NSPS, according to NRDC, was the recognition by Congress that new facilities are not limited by cost and engineering constraints inherent in retrofitting existing plants. Congress also recognized that new sources are uniquely situated to push toward the outer envelope of pollution control technology in a way that will further progress toward the national goal of eliminating the discharge of all pollutants.

Instead of establishing effluent guidelines that would tend to achieve these legislative purposes, however, the EPA final rules set out standards for new sources identical to those for existing plants. This, the NRDC urges, violates section 306 of the Clean Water Act.

....

First, NRDC asserts that the EPA used the same cost test for new and existing sources when Congress intended the Agency to use a "stricter cost test" for evaluating the efficacy of treatment technologies for new sources. According to NRDC, the EPA improperly compared "the costs of incremental pollution control technology against water quality benefits," thereby rejecting at least one new treatment technology on the basis of a cost-benefit analysis.

The EPA responds that the Act requires the Agency to "take into consideration the cost of achieving [NSPS] reduction, and any non-water quality environmental impact and energy requirements." This test, the EPA urges, is identical to the cost requirement for establishing BAT. The use of BPT and BAT costing methods to determine the cost of entirely new treatment systems for new sources was, according to EPA, entirely reasonable. The Agency denies that it compared these costs to the benefits accrued from compliance with NSPS.

We are not convinced that the EPA's costing methods for promulgating NSPS violated the Act. With respect to toxic pollutants, we agree that the statutory test for evaluating the costs of NSPS treatment is identical to that required for establishing BAT standards. In both cases, the Administrator must inquire into the initial and annual costs of applying the technology and make an affirmative determination that those costs can be reasonably borne by the industry. Congress may have contemplated that it would cost less to install new technologies in new plants than to retrofit old plants to accommodate new treatment systems. However, the determination whether that contemplation held true, in fact, with respect to any particular technology, was left by statute to the discretion of the Administrator....

For plants that discharge conventional pollutants, the EPA points out that new sources must install secondary clarifiers, biological treatment limits, equalization and other treatment technologies. BPT costing methods, according to the EPA, provide a framework for estimating the capital and operating costs of such systems. Given the legislative grant of discretion vested in the Administrator to determine the economic feasibility of costs under NSPS, we cannot say, on the basis of this record, that the methods used constitute a violation of the Act.

The second reason presented to support NRDC's argument that the NSPS regulations violate the Clean Water Act is the assertion that the EPA failed to give serious consideration to better control technologies that could be used by new sources. Specifically, NRDC points to indications in the record that 26% of OCPSF plants are "zero or alternative discharge" plants and that 36 plants achieve zero discharge through recycling, a technology the EPA allegedly did not consider in its rulemaking.

The EPA argues that new technologies must be "demonstrated" to achieve more stringent limitations and that they must be "available" in the OCPSF industry before such technologies can form the basis for NSPS. The Agency claims to have considered and rejected technologies other than BPT and BAT. It found, for instance, that requiring filtration in addition to biological treatment for conventional pollutants had not been adequately demonstrated to accomplish better effluent results for the OCPSF industry. As another example, the Agency considered requiring the addition of activated carbon for further control of toxic pollutants but rejected it because of its high cost and because it had not been well-demonstrated to enhance treatment.

Intuitively, there is some force to the observation that Congress would not have devised a completely new statutory scheme for regulation of new sources if it intended that the effluent standards for such plants would be identical to those required for existing sources. This is especially true when one considers that the statute provides an exemption from more stringent standards of performance that the EPA may adopt under NSPS in the future.

The EPA asserts that, at this time, there exist no technologies that have been demonstrated to achieve a greater degree of effluent reduction than existing technologies that meet BPT and BAT standards. The key issue is the meaning attributable to the term "demonstrated." The EPA maintains that "best available demonstrated technology" means "those plant processes and control technology which, at the pilot plant, semi-works, or other level, has [sic] demonstrated both technological performance and economic viability at a level sufficient to reasonably justify the making of investments in such new facilities."

The Third Circuit has concluded, and we agree, that Congress did not intend the term "best available demonstrated control technology" to limit consideration of treatment systems only to those widely in use in the industry. Instead, the present availability of a particular technology may be "demonstrated" if even one plant utilizes the technology in question. NRDC asserts that 36 operating facilities achieve zero discharge by the use of recycling and that the EPA failed to consider this technology when it promulgated effluent limitations for new sources.

The EPA's only response is that NRDC failed to urge consideration of recycling during rulemaking and is therefore precluded from raising the issue on appeal. As to this, as we have previously pointed out, the failure of a petitioner to raise an issue before the Agency may cause us to view the contention less favorably but does not bar our consideration of it.

We frequently defer to the expertise of the EPA. We do this for good reason. Congress entertains the legitimate expectation that the various federal agencies, charged as they are with responsibility for promulgating highly detailed and technical regulations, will be aware of the events and breakthroughs on the technological frontiers that lie within the purview of the agencies' respective fields of expertise.

We do not require, however, that the EPA be fully cognizant of every innovation, wherever employed, that has the potential to achieve greater reductions in the discharge of pollutants into our environment. And we recognize that the purpose of a period of notice and comment during rulemaking is, at least in part, to allow interested parties to bring to the attention of the EPA relevant technologies that may assist the Agency in the discharge of its regulatory duties. Nevertheless, we consider that a treatment system employed by 36 plants in the OCPSF industry is sufficiently common that it is not unreasonable to expect the EPA to know about it. The NSPS statute directs that the "Administrator shall, from time to time, as technology and alternatives change," revise effluent standards for new point sources. We should be able to have confidence that the Administrator will do so, especially since he has chosen at this time to require no more stringent guidelines for new plants than for existing sources.

We know from the record that 36 plants in the industry use recycling and some of them achieve zero discharge. Thus, recycling easily fits the definition of an "available demonstrated technology" under § 306 of the Act. The failure of the EPA even to consider recycling, then, was arbitrary and capricious. We therefore remand these limitations to the EPA for consideration of whether zero discharge limits would be appropriate for new plants in the OCPSF industry because of the existence of recycling.

Conclusion

For the reasons assigned, the petitions for review of the EPA's effluent limitations for the OCPSF industries are denied, but specific portions of the regulations, while remaining in force, are remanded to the Administrator for further proceedings consistent with the opinion....

NOTES AND QUESTIONS

1. As the principal case remarks, the courts of appeal have deferred consistently to EPA's assessments of costs of limitations in relation to benefits, as well as its categorization of sources. *See, e.g., Kennecott Copper Corp. v. EPA*, 612 F.2d 1232 (10th Cir. 1979); *American Iron & Steel Inst. v. EPA*, 526 F.2d 1027 (3d Cir. 1975). To set BPT, EPA must compare the costs for the industry to the "effluent reduction benefits" of the standard. According to *Weyerhaeuser*, pages 537-41 *supra*, Congress has precluded consideration of water quality impacts in setting effluent limitations. How, then, are effluent reduction benefits to be measured? In *Chemical Manufacturers*, in order to set BPT for the 304 direct dischargers in the industry, EPA chose a technology in use in 99 plants and then based the standard on the performance of the 71 best plants using that technology. Assume that most of the other plants in the industry use a different technology and that the removal rate for plants using this technology is lower than that for the technology in use in the 99 plants. However, 20 plants using the more common technology have achieved a higher removal rate than the 71 plants using the "better" technology. How should EPA set BPT given this data? How can EPA set BPT for an industry that has made little or no investment in effluent control? Could the agency look to technologies in use in other industries? *See, e.g., California & Hawaiian Sugar Co. v. EPA*, 553 F.2d 280 (2d Cir. 1977); *Tanner's Council of Am., Inc. v. Train*, 540 F.2d 1188 (4th Cir. 1976).

The BCT standard was intended as an intermediate level of control between BPT and BAT, assuming that the cost-effectiveness test is met for control beyond BPT technology. *American Paper Inst. v. Train*, 660 F.2d 954 (4th Cir. 1981). If BPT is the "average of the best" performers in the industrial category, what is BAT? Is it based on the best performers or the best single performer in the category? Could BAT be based on the performance of a pilot plant? *See American Petr. Inst. v. EPA*, 540 F.2d 1023 (10th Cir. 1976). Or based on a technology that is not yet in use in the industry? *See FMC Corp. v. Train*, 539 F.2d 973 (4th Cir. 1976). For purposes of BAT, is a technology "available" even if it is not in use at all in the industry? *See Association of Pac. Fisheries v. EPA*, 615 F.2d 794, 816 (9th Cir. 1980); *Weyerhaeuser Co. v. Costle*, 590 F.2d 1011 (D.C. Cir. 1978) (yes); *cf. American Petr. Inst. v. EPA*, 540 F.2d 1023 (10th Cir. 1976), *cert. denied sub nom. Exxon Corp. v. EPA*, 430 U.S. 922 (1977) (remand on the availability issue when EPA conceded further development was necessary for widespread use).

2. *Indirect Dischargers and Pretreatment Standards.* As the principal case indicates, many industrial facilities discharge into POTWs and not directly into navigable waters. Why might an industrial discharger prefer to discharge into a POTW? *See generally* 2 W. RODGERS, ENVIRONMENTAL LAW 463-64 (1986). These "indirect" dischargers must comply with the "pretreatment" program of section 307(b), which requires EPA to promulgate

> pretreatment standards for introduction ... into [POTWs] for those pollutants which are determined not to be susceptible to treatment by such treatment works or which would interfere with the operation of such treatment works.... Pretreatment standards ... shall be established to prevent the discharge of any pollutant through [POTWs] which pollutant interferes with, passes through, or otherwise is incompatible with such works. FWPCA § 307(b)(1), 33 U.S.C. § 1317(b)(1).

There is no national permit program for indirect dischargers as there is with direct dischargers. Indirect dischargers only comply with such pretreatment standards as are promulgated and standards are set only for pollutants that interfere with or pass through POTWs. Thus, the statutory scheme imposes very different requirements on point source discharges depending upon the type of discharger — direct private discharger, POTW discharger, or indirect discharger.

Pretreatment standards include general pretreatment regulations applicable to all indirect dischargers and categorical technology-based limitations for existing and new sources imposed on an industry-by-industry basis. FWPCA § 307(b), 33 U.S.C. § 1317(b). Pursuant to a consent decree, EPA promulgates the categorical restrictions for classes and categories of industrial sources equivalent to technological standards for new and existing direct dischargers. Restrictions apply to those pollutants that would otherwise pass through or interfere with a POTW, and are based in part on the economic and technological capacity of the industry as a whole.

The FDF variance from categorical pretreatment standards was upheld in *Chemical Mfrs. Ass'n v. Natural Resources Defense Council*, 470 U.S. 116 (1985), *rev'g National Ass'n of Metal Finishers v. EPA*, 719 F.2d 624 (3d Cir. 1983). The Water Quality Act of 1987 amended section 307 to provide an innovative technology extension similar to that for direct dischargers. FWPCA § 307(e), 33 U.S.C. § 1317(e). It also added section 402(m), 33 U.S.C. § 1342(m), limiting EPA's authority to require additional pretreatment of conventional pollutants by facilities discharging into POTWs violating their permits due to inadequate design or operation.

In 1977 an amendment authorized POTWs to grant "removal credits" to dischargers of toxic pollutants to reduce categorical standards for such pollutants by the level of treatment achieved by the POTW, in order to avoid duplicative treatment by the indirect discharger and the POTW. Under section 307(b)(1), 33 U.S.C. § 1317(b)(1), removal credit is precluded if it would prevent sludge use or disposal in accordance with sludge management guidelines EPA is required to promulgate for POTWs under section 405(d), because most toxic metals discharged into POTWs end up in the POTWs' sewage sludge.

While the FWPCA is concerned primarily with regulation of the effluents from POTWs that enter the navigable water areas of the United States, provision is also made under section 405(d), 33 U.S.C. § 1345(d), for regulation of disposal of the sewage sludge that accumulates as a result of waste treatment by POTWs. EPA's regulations for sludge management have been a constant source of litigation. Removal credit regulations promulgated in 1981 were upheld in *National Ass'n of Metal Finishers v. EPA*, 719 F.2d 624 (3d Cir. 1983), *rev'd in part sub nom. Chemical Mfrs. Ass'n v. Natural Resources Defense Council*, 470 U.S. 116 (1985), but the court of appeals did not address the validity of the sludge management provisions of those regulations. When EPA revised the regulations in 1984 to make removal credits easier to obtain, the same Court of Appeals invalidated the revised regulations and held that removal credits could not be granted until EPA had issued acceptable sludge management regulations. *Natural Resources Defense Council v. EPA*, 790 F.2d 289 (3d Cir. 1986). In 1987 Congress required EPA to issue sludge management regulations by August 31, 1987, prohibiting any further authorizations of removal credit until the regulations were promulgated, but EPA failed to meet the deadline. On November 5, 1987, EPA essentially readopted the provisions of the 1981 regulations for sludge management. 40 C.F.R. § 403. The courts continued to hold that removal credits were not available to any POTW until sludge management regulations found to satisfy the requirements of section 405(d) were promulgated. *See generally Chicago Ass'n of Commerce & Indus. v. EPA*, 873

F.2d 1025 (7th Cir. 1989); *Armco, Inc. v. EPA*, 869 F.2d 975 (6th Cir. 1989). In 1993, the D.C. Circuit Court finally found that 1991 revisions to the sludge management guidelines complied with § 405(d) so that removal credits could be granted. *Sierra Club v. EPA*, 992 F.2d 337 (D.C. Cir. 1993).

After unsuccessful attempts at general pretreatment standards, *see, e.g., National Ass'n of Metal Finishers v. EPA*, 719 F.2d 624 (3d Cir. 1983), *rev'd in part sub nom. Chemical Mfrs. Ass'n v. Natural Resources Defense Council*, 470 U.S. 116 (1985), EPA promulgated revised regulations, 40 C.F.R. § 403, establishing a prohibition on introduction into a POTW of pollutants that will "interfere" or "pass through" the POTW. The revised regulations were upheld in *Arkansas Poultry Fed'n v. EPA*, 852 F.2d 324 (8th Cir. 1988). In short, if an indirect discharger causes a POTW to violate its permit or sludge management requirements, it has violated the general pretreatment standards. Among other requirements, the general pretreatment regulations prohibit discharge of pollutants that will create a fire or explosion hazard at a POTW, that will cause corrosive structural damage, that are solid or viscous in amounts that will cause obstruction of flow in the POTW resulting in interference, or that contain heat in amounts to cause interference. 40 C.F.R. § 403.5(b). The pretreatment regulations also require POTWs with a total design flow greater than five million gallons per day and which receive wastes subject to categorical standards, or which receive wastes which may interfere with or pass through the POTW, to develop a localized pretreatment program to assure compliance by indirect dischargers. POTWs must have had an approved program no later than July 1, 1983. Local limits may be developed on an industry or pollutant basis and be included in a municipal ordinance, or developed for a specific facility and included within the municipal contract or permit for that facility. 40 C.F.R. § 403.8(a) and (b). In addition, such POTWs with previous problems of interference and pass through which are likely to recur must develop specific local limits to implement the prohibition on interference and pass through of pollutants. The general pretreatment regulations were strengthened in final rules issued in July of 1990. 55 Fed. Reg. 30,082 (Jul. 24, 1990).

Federal enforcement options against violators of effluent limitations, including indirect dischargers, generally include administrative compliance orders, civil and criminal penalties, and injunctive relief, FWPCA § 309, 33 U.S.C. § 1319, in addition to the possibility of a citizen suit under section 505, 33 U.S.C. § 1365, and state enforcement. *See* note 4 *infra*. However effective these remedies may be against industrial users, they are less so against a publicly owned treatment works. *See* Note, *Regulation of Noncompliant Publicly Owned Treatment Works Under the Clean Water Act*, 10 Wm. Mitchell L. Rev. 901, 924-34 (1984) (evaluating the effectiveness of various remedial measures for NPDES violations when applied to POTWs). In addition to actions against the POTW itself, EPA may prohibit the introduction of pollutants into a noncompliant treatment works by new sources. FWPCA § 402(h), 33 U.S.C. § 1342(h). There are indications that the EPA intends to enforce compliance much more strictly now that the 1988 deadline for compliance with secondary treatment has passed. *See* Peskar, *Clean Water Act Compliance*, 13 CURRENT MUNICIPAL PROBS. 313 (1987) (discussing the EPA's national enforcement initiative regarding municipal pollutants).

3. *Statutory Deadlines*. The opinion in the principal case was issued March 30, 1989, one day before the congressional deadline for compliance with the BAT effluent standards and ten years after BPT was to have been implemented. Effluent limitations necessitated by the remand in the case were not reproposed until December 6, 1991. 56 Fed. Reg. 63,897 (1991). *See also Rybachek v. Alaska Miners Ass'n*, 904 F.2d 1276 (9th Cir. 1990) (BPT for placer mining operations promulgated in 1988). According to the legislative history quoted in the opinion, how did Congress intend for EPA to deal with industry-wide noncompliance due to EPA's failure to promulgate the standards or schedule? How meaningful are the congressional deadlines for compliance? Are they nothing more than target dates? What can be done to compel EPA to issue effluent deadlines? *See NRDC v. EPA*, 32 Envt. Rep. Cas. (BNA) 1969 (D.D.C. 1991) (congressional deadline is not a mere target date, and EPA's failure to issue effluent guidelines on time is a nondiscretionary duty enforceable in a citizen's suit). What relief is available in a citizen's suit? *See id.* at 1976 (the court set a schedule for establishment of a timetable for issuance of the guidelines). When no effluent limitations or guidelines have been set, permits are issued with effluent limitations individually tailored to the source based on the permit-issuing agency's "best professional judgment" (BPJ), discussed on page 536 *supra*.

4. Technological controls sometimes fail and emergencies precluding wastewater treatment can occur. EPA has had to determine how best to make allowances for unavoidable noncompliance without undermining the effectiveness of effluent limitations. The regulations make allowances for "upsets" as defined in the *Chemical Manufacturers* case on page 562, and for "bypass" which is defined as the intentional diversion of waste streams from treatment. Bypass is prohibited except in a few compelling circumstances, as when necessary to prevent personal injury or severe property damage. An upset is an affirmative defense to an action for noncompliance if certain conditions are met, including that the facility was being operated properly at the time. 40 C.F.R. § 122.41(m), (n). Defendants in enforcement actions generally have been unsuccessful in using the bypass or upset defense to excuse recurring noncompliance. *See, e.g., Chesapeake Bay Found. v. Bethlehem Steel Corp.*, 652 F. Supp. 620 (D. Md. 1987); *Student Pub. Interest Research Group of New Jersey v. Jersey Central Power & Light Co.*, 642 F. Supp. 103 (D.N.J. 1986).

REVIEW PROBLEM

Assume that EPA has published a final regulation for a water pollutant, "goo," applicable to all widget producing plants. You are counsel for Acme, Inc., a widget company presently emitting goo directly into the Mississippi River. You have been called into the office of Acme's president. He tells you that no widget company in the country has the technology to meet the standard, that Acme's goo discharges into the Mississippi have no effect on water quality, and that Acme cannot in any event afford whatever equipment would be necessary to comply unless it tries a promising but still experimental technology that would take a year or two to implement. He wants you to prepare a memo explaining all possible ways in which to attack the regulation and, alternatively, all strategies for getting Acme out of having to comply with the regulations. Prepare such a memo, evaluating the likelihood of success of each avenue of attack and how you answer will differ depending upon whether goo is a conventional, nonconventional, or toxic pollutant.

D. ENFORCEMENT AND CITIZEN SUITS

The mechanisms for enforcement of the FWPCA are similar to those for the Clean Air Act, discussed on pages 493-522 *supra*. Section 308 imposes discharge monitoring and recordkeeping requirements on dischargers and authorizes EPA and its authorized representatives to visit sources, inspect and copy records, inspect monitoring equipment and take samples of effluent discharges. FWPCA § 308(a)(4)(A)-(B), 33 U.S.C. § 1318(a)(4)(A)-(B). Records and other information required by the Act are available to the public unless subject to protection as trade secrets. FWPCA § 308(b)(2), 33 U.S.C. § 1318(b)(2). States may have similar inspection, monitoring, and entry authority to that of EPA if their procedures are approved by EPA. FWPCA § 308(c), 33 U.S.C. § 1318(c). EPA may also impose administrative penalties with the procedures, limits, and availability of judicial review dependent upon whether the penalties assessed are per violation (Class I penalties) or per day (Class II penalties). FWPCA § 309(g), 33 U.S.C. § 1319(g). The public has a right of comment on proposed penalties, and may seek judicial review of the penalties assessed. FWPCA § 309(g)(8), 33 U.S.C. § 1319(g)(8).

Whenever EPA determines that a person is violating any requirement, the Administrator may either issue a compliance order requiring the person to comply or bring a civil action in federal district court in the district in which the defendant resides or is located or is doing business. FWPCA § 309(a)(3), (b), U.S.C. § 1319(a)(3), (b). A compliance order must provide a "reasonable" time for compliance, "taking into account the seriousness of the violation and any good faith efforts to comply...." FWPCA § 309(a)(5)(A), 33 U.S.C. § 1319(a)-(5)(A). *See also Monongahela Power Co. v. EPA*, 586 F.2d 318 (4th Cir. 1978) (interpretation of "good faith"). Setting the terms of a compliance order provides the discharger with some opportunity to negotiate with EPA on achieving compliance. Federal courts may order temporary or permanent injunctive relief and impose civil penalties. FWPCA § 309(b), (d), 33 U.S.C. § 1319(b), (d). There is a constitutional right to a jury trial in cases involving civil penalties. *Tull v. United States*, 481 U.S. 412 (1987). The Ninth Circuit Court of Appeals has held that a state is not authorized to seek penalties under section 309(d) in an enforcement action as opposed to a citizen suit brought by the state. *California v. Department of Navy*, 845 F.2d 222 (9th Cir. 1988). There are also provisions for criminal penalties, generally for negligent and knowing violations of discharge limitations, for knowingly false representations in required information, and for knowing endangerment of any person. State enforcement programs vary greatly, but generally they provide for injunctive relief and civil and criminal penalties at least as stringent as those in section 309, 2 S. NOVICK, LAW OF ENVIRONMENTAL PROTECTION § 12.08[2], although state penalties need not be as stringent as those under federal law. *See* FWPCA § 402(b)(7), 33 U.S.C. § 1342(b)(7); *NRDC v. EPA*, 859 F.2d 156 (D.C. Cir. 1988). In *United States v. Cargill, Inc.*, 508 F. Supp. 734 (D. Del. 1981), the court held that EPA can bring an enforcement action concurrently with the state, if the federal government is seeking a different remedy from the state and is not a party to the state enforcement action. On the issue of how much equitable discretion a court retains in fashioning relief for a statutory violation, see the discussion of *Weinberger v. Romero-Barcelo*, pages 41-42 *supra; see also* Farber, *Equitable Discretion, Legal Duties and Environmental Injunctions*, 45 U. PITT. L. REV. 513 (1984).

Under the citizen suit provision, any person whose interest may be "adversely affected" and who can satisfy the constitutional test for standing may bring suit against any person, including the United States and any state (subject to any sovereign immunity limitations), "in violation of" an effluent standard or limitation as defined in section 505(f) or in violation of any order issued by EPA or a state with respect to an effluent standard or limitation. FWPCA § 505(a)(1), 33 U.S.C. § 1365(a)(1). *See also Gwaltney of Smithfield, Ltd. v. Chesapeake Bay Found.*, 484 U.S. 49 (1987), discussed *infra* ("in violation" language requires good faith allegations of continuous or intermittent violation). A suit may also be brought to compel EPA to perform a nondiscretionary duty. FWPCA § 505(a)-(2), 33 U.S.C. § 1365(a)(2). The courts have disagreed over whether a state may sue under the citizen suit provision. *Compare Massachusetts v. United States Vets. Admin.*, 541 F.2d 119 (1st Cir. 1976); *Illinois v. Outboard Marine Corp.*, 619 F.2d 623 (7th Cir. 1980), *vacated and remanded on other grounds*, 453 U.S. 917 (1981); *National Wildlife Fed'n v. Ruckelshaus*, 99 F.R.D. 558, 15 Envtl. L. Rep. (Envtl. L. Inst.) 20845 (D.N.J. 1983) (state can sue), *with United States v. City of Hopewell*, 508 F. Supp. 526 (E.D. Va. 1980); *California v. Department of Navy*, 24 Env't Rep. Cas. (BNA) 1177 (N.D. Cal. 1986) (state cannot sue). Suit against a discharger must be brought in federal district court in which the source is located. FWPCA § 505(c)(1), 33 U.S.C. § 1365(c)(1). Costs including attorney's fees and expert witness fees may be awarded to any "prevailing or substantially prevailing" party if "appropriate." *Ruckelshaus v. Sierra Club* and *Pennsylvania v. Delaware Valley Citizens' Council for Clean Air*, 478 U.S. 546 (1986); *see also Idaho Conserv. League v. Russell*, 946 F.2d 717 (9th Cir. 1991) (in suit to compel EPA to promulgate water quality standards for state which had not done so, which was terminated by settlement between plaintiffs and the *state*, the plaintiffs did not prevail against EPA). Sixty days' notice prior to commencement of the suit must be given to EPA, the alleged violator, and the state where the alleged violation occurred. A citizen suit may not be brought if the United States is "diligently" prosecuting a civil action in the federal courts. FWPCA § 505(b), 33 U.S.C. § 1365(b). The courts have refused to recognize the doctrine of primary jurisdiction in an administrative agency to preclude a citizen suit when a discharger is still pursuing modification of effluent limitations in the administrative process. *See, e.g.*, *NRDC v. Outboard Marine Corp.*, 702 F. Supp. 690 (N.D. Ill. 1988). On whether a state or federal *administrative* enforcement action is a bar to a citizen suit, *compare Friends of the Earth v. Consolidation Rail Corp.*, 768 F.2d 57 (2d Cir. 1985) (not a bar); *with Baughman v. Bradford Coal Co.*, 592 F.2d 215 (3d Cir. 1979), *cert. denied*, 441 U.S. 961 (1979) (may be a bar if administrative proceeding is equivalent to a court action). Under section 309(g), 33 U.S.C. § 1319(g), a final 309(g) order assessing administrative penalties in a proceeding begun before a citizen suit is filed or after 120 days following issuance of the required citizen suit notice by the plaintiff, bars the citizen suit. One commentator suggests that, by implication from section 309(g), any other administrative orders would not bar a citizen suit. NOVICK, *supra*, § 12.08[3][b][ii]. Does the enforcement proceeding have to be brought before filing of the citizen suit to be a bar? In *Atlantic States Legal Found. v. Eastman Kodak Co.*, 933 F.2d 124 (2d Cir. 1991), a consent decree between New York and Kodak was held to bar the citizen suit even though the citizen suit had been filed prior to any state or federal enforcement proceeding. The court of appeals did remand for a determination of whether the consent decree failed to stop the alleged violations. *See also EPA v. Green Forest*, 921 F.2d 1394 (8th Cir. 1990), *cert. denied sub nom. Work v. Tyson Foods, Inc.*, 502 U.S. 956 (1991) (consent decree between United States and alleged violator bars citizen suit that preceded filing of the enforcement action); *New York Coastal Fishermen's Ass'n v. New York City Sanitation Dep't*, 772 F. Supp. 162 (S.D.N.Y. 1991) (two consent orders did not constitute "diligent prosecution" and thus did not bar *subsequently filed* citizens suit).

The only expressly authorized forms of relief in citizen suits are injunctive relief and civil penalties under section 309(d). FWPCA § 505(a)(2), 33 U.S.C. § 1365(a)(2). *See generally Chesapeake Bay Found. v. Gwaltney of Smithfield, Ltd.*, 611 F. Supp. 1542 (E.D. Va. 1985), *aff'd*, 791 F.2d 304 (4th Cir. 1986), *vacated on other grounds*, 484 U.S. 49 (1987) (factors utilized by the court in assessing civil penalties). In order to recover damages, pendent state law and common law claims must be joined. *But see City of Milwaukee v. Illinois*, pages 112-17 *supra* (federal common law for interstate water pollution preempted by the FWPCA despite section 505(e) savings clause) and *International Paper Co. v. Ouellette*, pages 119-25 *supra* (only the state common law of the source state is not preempted). Most citizen suits filed since 1982 have been settled, with a variety of imaginative devices for payments to improve damaged resources or the environment generally. NOVICK, *supra*, § 12.08[3][d]. *See also* Comment, *Polluter-Financed Environmentally Beneficial Expenditures: Effective Use or Improper Abuse of Citizen Suits Under the Clean Water Act*, 21 ENVT'L L. 175 (1991).

In *Gwaltney of Smithfield, Ltd. v. Chesapeake Bay Found.*, 484 U.S. 49 (1987) the Court held that the citizens suit provision of the Clean Water Act did not confer federal jurisdiction to challenge wholly past violations. The Court acknowledged that the applicable statutory language "alleged to be in violation" was ambiguous. The Court held, however, that citizen-plaintiffs must make a good faith allegation of an ongoing or intermittent violation of the Act in order to confer subject matter jurisdiction. *But cf.* Smith, Beverly McQueary, *The Viability of Citizens' Suits Under the Clean Water Act After Gwaltney of Smithfield v. Chesapeake Bay Foundation*, 40 CASE W. RES. L. REV. 1-78 (1989-1990) (arguing that the decision is inconsistent with congressional intent, and that Congress should reverse the Supreme Court by expressly authorizing citizens' suits for purely past violations of the Clean Water Act). Courts have found it necessary since *Gwaltney* to distinguish between allegations of "ongoing" violations and allegations of "wholly past" violations. Unterberger, *Citizen Enforcement Suits: Putting Gwaltney to Rest and Setting Sights on the Clean Air Act*, [Current Developments] Envt. Rep. (BNA) 1631 (Jan. 4, 1991). The Court in *Gwaltney* noted that the defendant bears a heavy burden to prove mootness by requiring evidence that it is "absolutely clear that the alleged wrongful behavior could not reasonably be expected to recur." 484 U.S. at 66. Plaintiffs have had little difficulty in satisfying *Gwaltney*'s requirements. For example, in *Carr v. Alta Verde Indus.*, 931 F.2d 1055, 1063 (5th Cir. 1991) the plaintiffs claimed that unlawful discharge had occurred when heavy rains caused defendant's wastewater holding ponds to overflow. The defendant contended that improvements in its wastewater disposal system mooted the citizen's action. The court disagreed, reasoning that a discharge of pollution could occur in event of future chronic rainfall.

Although citizen suit provisions are common in environmental statutes, a disproportionate share of citizen suit litigation has been brought under the FWPCA. The recordkeeping requirements and permit system have made such suits less difficult to pursue, and the long-standing availability of civil penalties provides greater leverage to citizen-plaintiffs. *See* Unterberger, *supra*, at 1631. Recent amendments to the Clean Air Act along these lines promise greater activity under its citizen suit provision, but for the near future groundbreaking cases of general significance for citizen suit litigation will continue to be under the FWPCA. For example, the Supreme Court, in *United States Department of Energy v. Ohio*, 503 U.S. 607 (1992), denied individual states the power to impose punitive civil fines against federal facilities for past violations of the Clean Water Act. *See generally* Heintz, Rebecca, *Federal Sovereign Immunity and Clean Water: A Supreme Misstep*, 24 ENVTL. L. 263-292 (1994) (arguing that the decision is inconsistent with congressional intent, that it will hinder the states' ability to enforce water pollution control laws, and that Congress should amend the statute to explicitly waive federal sovereign immunity). The Clean Water Act was subsequently amended to waive federal sovereign immunity. 42 U.S.C. § 6961.

For additional discussion of citizen suit enforcement in relation to nonpoint source pollution and section 401 certification, see pages 619-23 *infra*.

VILLAGE OF OCONOMOWOC LAKE v. DAYTON HUDSON CORP.

24 F.3d 962 (7th Cir. 1994)
(*cert. denied*, 115 S. Ct. 322 (1994))

EASTERBROOK, CIRCUIT JUDGE.

Target Stores, a division of Dayton Hudson Corporation, is building a warehouse in the City of Oconomowoc, Wisconsin. It holds all necessary state and local permits. Federal clearance is unnecessary, for the Environmental Protection Agency has authorized Wisconsin to perform the tasks required by the Clean Air and Clean Water Acts. The Village of Oconomowoc Lake, a nearby municipality, wishes the warehouse would disappear....

Warehouses do not spew pollutants, but they have indirect effects. Trucks that carry goods to and from the warehouse emit nitrogen oxides and other gasses. A well-sited warehouse cuts down on wasted movement of goods, and therefore on pollution in the United States as a whole, but increases the volume of emissions nearby. While parked near the warehouse trucks drip oil, which collects in the runoff from a storm. A few inches of rain falling on a large paved surface means many acre-feet of water. This warehouse has a retention pond, from which the water seeps into the ground — carrying hydrocarbons and other unwelcome substances, the Village fears.

State officials concluded that the warehouse would be such a trivial source of pollution that it should not be classified as a "major source" requiring full scrutiny.... The Clean Air Act requires permits only for "stationary sources" of pollution. A definitional provision provides not only that vehicles are not "stationary sources" but also that vehicular emissions are not attributed to the buildings served as points of origin or destination. 42 U.S.C. § 7602(2); *see also* 42 U.S.C. § 7410(a)(5)(C). Whatever requirements the state has added to federal law must be enforced in state court, the judge held. As for the rainwater runoff: the Clean Water Act regulates discharges into "navigable waters from a point source." Parking lots and retention ponds are not exactly "navigable," but another statute defines "navigable waters" as all "waters of the United States." Some water from the pond evaporates into the air, and the rest seeps into the ground. Even though ground water eventually reaches streams, lakes, and oceans, the court held, it is not part of the "waters of the United States." The district court accordingly dismissed the complaint under Fed. R. Civ. P. 12(b)(1).

As a rule, persons wishing to sue under the Clean Air Act must give 60 days' notice to the potential defendant. 42 U.S.C. § 7604(b). Notice provisions pervade environmental statutes, and would-be plaintiffs often appear to be desperate to evade them.... Why plaintiffs are unwilling to wait even 60 days — when an effort to jump the queue may lead to outright dismissal of the case under *Hallstrom* — eludes us. The Village filed suit only three days after giving notice. To justify this expedition, it invoked 42 U.S.C. § 7604(a)(3), which is not subject to the 60-day rule. Although this enabled it to sue 57 days sooner than it could have done had it used § 7604(a)(1) as the foundation for the suit, the strategy does little besides illustrate the adage that haste makes waste. (This saying predates the Clean Air Act and shows that not all waste is within federal jurisdiction.)

Section 7604(a)(3) permits a citizen to file a civil action against:

> any person who proposes to construct or constructs any new or modified major emitting facility without a permit required under ... part D of subchapter I of this chapter (relating to nonattainment) or who is alleged to be in violation of any condition of such permit.

The warehouse is in a "nonattainment" area, and the Village contends that it lacks the permit required for a "major emitting facility." Wisconsin treated the warehouse as a minor rather than a major source. But to use § 7604(a)(3) the Village had to show that "part D of subchapter I of this chapter" requires a major-facility permit, and it is impossible to see how this could be so. Recall that the warehouse itself does not emit pollutants and that the Clean Air Act does not require the attribution of motor-vehicle emissions to stationary sources. "[P]art D of subchapter I" does not require Dayton Hudson to obtain a permit; any such requirement must come from Wisconsin law and therefore cannot serve as the foundation for suit under § 7604(a)(3).

If the Village had waited for the prescribed 60 days, it would have been eligible to use § 7604(a)(1), which authorizes citizen suits against any person ... who is alleged to be in violation of (A) an emission standard or limitation under this chapter or (B) an order issued by the Administrator or a State with respect to such a standard or limitation. If this had been the foundation of the suit, and if we were to assume that the emissions from trucks going to and from the warehouse violate Wisconsin's implementation plan — for the state has elected to regulate such indirect emissions despite the lack of federal compulsion to do so — then it would have been necessary to decide whether a provision of a state plan going beyond the federal minima is "an emission standard or limitation under this chapter." States must clear their implementation plans with the EPA and enforce them faithfully; it is accordingly possible to characterize a state's rules as "an emission standard or limitation under this chapter" in the sense that it is adopted under the chapter and includes rules that satisfy the chapter. It may even be that rules going beyond federal requirements are essential to satisfy federal law. How could that be? Suppose the EPA approved a plan that was less stringent in some respects than the EPA would have demanded, only because in other respects it did more than federal law required and the rules, taken as a whole, would produce the desired cleanliness. Then failure to comply with the "extra" rules would reduce air quality below the federal minimum. The EPA believes that federal courts (and the Administrator) may enforce provisions in state plans. We need not decide whether this means enforcement under § 7604(a)(1), as some courts have held....

The Village's claim under the Clean Water Act does not depend on any state rule or plan. This time the obstacle is the limitation of the Act's coverage to the "waters of the United States." Rainwater runoff from the 110-acre site (including 25 acres of paved parking) will collect in a 6-acre artificial pond. The pond is supposed to retain oil, grease, and other pollutants while "exfiltrating" the water to the ground below. The Clean Water Act is a broad statute, reaching waters and wetlands that are not navigable or even directly connected to navigable waters. *United States v. Riverside Bayview Homes Inc.*, 474 U.S. 121, 88 L. Ed. 2d 419, 106 S. Ct. 455 (1985).... The Agency's regulatory definition of "waters of the United States" includes "intrastate lakes, rivers, streams (including intermittent streams), mudflats, sandflats, wetlands, sloughs, prairie potholes, wet meadows, playa lakes, or natural ponds, the use, degradation or destruction of which could affect interstate or foreign commerce." 40 C.F.R. § 230.3(s)(3). *Hoffman Homes, Inc. v. Administrator*, EPA, 999 F.2d 256, 260-61 (7th Cir. 1993), concluded that the EPA did not exceed its power when promulgating this definition but that even a rule with such broad scope did not cover a one-acre wetland 750 feet from a small creek. A six-acre retention pond, farther from a body of surface water, is an easier case. The EPA's definition speaks of "natural ponds"; Dayton Hudson built an artificial pond.

What of the possibility that water from the pond will enter the local ground waters, and thence underground aquifers that feed lakes and streams that are part of the "waters of the United States"? ... "Waters of the United States" must be a subset of "water"; otherwise why insert the qualifying clause in the statute? ... Neither the Clean Water Act nor the EPA's definition asserts authority over ground waters, just because these may be hydrologically connected with surface waters.

The omission of ground waters from the regulations is not an oversight. Members of Congress have proposed adding ground waters to the scope of the Clean Water Act, but these proposals have been defeated, and the EPA evidently has decided not to wade in on its own.... Congress elected to leave the subject to state law — and Wisconsin has elected to permit Target Stores to build a warehouse that will affect the local ground waters.

Decisions not to enact proposed legislation are not conclusive on the meaning of the text actually enacted. Laws sometimes surprise their authors. But we are confident that the statute Congress enacted excludes some waters, and ground waters are a logical candidate.... The possibility of a hydrological connection cannot be denied, but neither the statute nor the regulations makes such a possibility a sufficient ground of regulation. On several occasions the EPA has noted the potential connection between ground waters and surface waters, but it has left the regulatory definition alone. E.g., Preamble to NPDES Permit Application Regulations for Storm Water Discharges, ("[T]his rule-making only addresses discharges to waters of the United States, consequently discharges to ground waters are not covered by this rulemaking (unless there is a hydrological connection between the ground water and a nearby surface water body.")) By amending its regulations, the EPA could pose a harder question. As the statute and regulations stand, however, the federal government has not asserted a claim of authority over artificial ponds that drain into ground waters.

Affirmed.

NOTES AND QUESTIONS

1. Why was the Village unable to bring a citizen suit under the Clean Air Act? Under the Clean Water Act? Why does an artificial pond connected hydrologically to groundwater not qualify as "waters of the United States"? Is this case consistent with *United States v. Riverside Bayview Homes, Inc.*, page 644 *infra*?

2. EPA has refused to apply the NPDES permit process to groundwater, purportedly due to the legal problems in doing so. The statute's ambiguity as to regulation of groundwater may be traced to the history of the 1972 amendments. An administration bill would have included coverage of groundwater, Federal Water Quality Administration, Department of Interior, Clean Water for the 1970's: A Status Report 16 (1970), and the legislative history includes arguments for a federal groundwater pollution control program. *See, e.g.*, S. Conf. Rep. No. 1236, 92d Cong., 2d Sess. 98, 116 (1972), *reprinted in* 1 COMMITTEE ON PUBLIC WORKS, A LEGISLATIVE HISTORY OF THE WATER POLLUTION CONTROL ACT AMENDMENTS OF 1972, at 281, 299 (1973); S. Rep. No. 414, 92d Cong., 1st Sess. 52-53 (1971). The primary hurdle to explicit regulation of groundwater was the perception that such regulation would constitute federal land use planning. 2 S. NOVICK, LAW OF ENVIRONMENTAL PROTECTION § 13.01[3] (1988). The resulting ambiguity in the 1972 legislation left both sides believing their position had prevailed. *See* S. Rep. No. 414, *supra*, at 98, *reprinted in* 2 LEGISLATIVE HISTORY, *supra*, at 1513.

Nevertheless, EPA does provide funding under section 205(j) to state and local planning agencies which may be utilized for groundwater protection and management. FWPCA § 205(j), 33 U.S.C. § 1285(j). Also, it remains to be seen what emphasis EPA will place on groundwater preservation under the provision for state planning to control nonpoint source pollution in section 205(j)(5), 33 U.S.C. § 1285(j)(5).

This relative dearth of regulation under the Clean Water Act is not entirely the responsibility of EPA. EPA's efforts in the 1970s to control deep-well disposal of wastes met with resistance and litigation with mixed results. For example, in *United States v. GAF Corp.*, 389 F. Supp. 1379 (S.D. Tex. 1975), the court held that EPA lacked authority to regulate deep-well injection or any groundwater pollution not connected with surface water. When EPA responded later by requiring permits for deep-well injection in groundwater "associated" with surface water, its approach was upheld by the Seventh Circuit Court of Appeals in *United States Steel Corp. v. Train*, 556 F.2d 822 (7th Cir. 1977), but invalidated by the Fifth Circuit Court of Appeals in *Exxon Corp. v. Train*, 554 F.2d 1310 (5th Cir. 1977). As a result, EPA's power to regulate groundwater with or without a connection to surface water remains unclear.

3. Can a citizen suit be brought to stop point source discharge of a substance that EPA has not defined as a pollutant and for which there are no applicable effluent limitations? In other words, is the point source discharge of anything which a court finds to be within the meaning of "pollutant," without a permit, subject to citizen suit enforcement? *See Sierra Club, Lone Star Chapter v. Cedar Point Oil Co.*, 73 F.3d 546 (5th Cir. 1996), *cert. denied*, 117 S. Ct. 57 (1997) (discharge of contaminated water from the production of oil and gas without a permit is subject to a citizen suit).

E. WATER QUALITY STANDARDS

The technology-based effluent limitations for point source discharges discussed above are set primarily through consideration of the technological and economic capacity of the industry whose discharge is regulated. The FWPCA also authorizes water quality based limitations, which are the more stringent limitations necessary to achieve the desired water quality even after achievement of technology-based limitations. As point sources come into compliance with the second tier of compliance of the technology-based standards that were to be met in 1989, compliance with water quality-based limitations may become increasingly the focus of regulatory and enforcement efforts. The water quality-based limitations authorized by the FWPCA are state water quality standards under section 303, 33 U.S.C. § 1313, the "ample margin of safety" standard for toxic pollutants in section 307(a), 33 U.S.C. § 1317(a), federal water quality standards under section 302, 33 U.S.C. § 1312, and the ocean discharge limitations of section 403, 33 U.S.C. § 1343. The section 307 standard for toxic pollutants and the section 403 ocean discharge limitations are discussed on pages 624-31 and 636-37 respectively. Of all these water quality-based limitations, the section 303 state water quality standards have been the most significant source of regulation.

States are required to set water quality standards under section 303 of the FWPCA, 33 U.S.C. § 1313. The Act provides for EPA to set minimum criteria for state water quality standards, to review state water quality standards and revisions to those standards, and to apply those standards when issuing permits under the National Pollution Discharge Elimination System (NPDES). The standards themselves are set by state regulatory agencies and applied by those agencies to navigable waters within the states.

The process and content of state water quality standards is succinctly described in *Natural Resources Defense Council v. EPA*, pages 625-31 *infra*:

> The water quality standard for a particular stream segment was to be determined in the following manner. First, the state in which the stream segment was located was to designate the uses to which it wished to put the segment. The designations that the states had made prior to the 1972 Clean Water Act were deemed to be the initial designations under that Act; however, states were thereafter to review their designations at least once every three years. CWA § 303(c)(1), 33 U.S.C. § 1313(c)(1). Pursuant to the statute's policy that the designation of uses "enhance" the quality of water, CWA § 303(c)(2), 33 U.S.C. § 1313(c)(2), EPA enacted regulations setting limits on the states' ability to downgrade previously designated uses. If a state wished to redesignate a use so that the new use did not require water clean enough to meet the statutory goal of fishable, swimmable water, *see* CWA § 101(a)(2), 33 U.S.C. § 1251(a)(2), it had to conduct a "use attainability analysis" as a condition to federal approval of the redesignated use. CWA § 303(c)(3), 33 U.S.C. § 1313(c)(3); 40 C.F.R. §§ 131.10(j), 131.3(g) (1989). If the result of the "use attainability analysis" was that it was feasible to attain fishable, swimmable waters, EPA would reject the redesignated use.
>
> Second, the state was to determine the "criteria" for each segment — the maximum concentrations of pollutants that could occur without jeopardizing the use. These criteria could be either numerical (e.g. 5 milligrams per liter) or narrative (e.g. no toxics in toxic amounts). The criteria, like the uses, were subject to federal review. The EPA was to reject criteria that did not protect the designated use or that were not based on a "sound scientific rationale." 40 C.F.R. § 131.11 (1989).

915 F.2d 1314, 1317 (9th Cir. 1990).

The Administrator of EPA also may set water quality related effluent limitations for waters in which discharges subject to BAT controls still

> interfere with the attainment or maintenance of that water quality in a specific portion of the navigable waters which shall assure protection of public health, public water supplies, agricultural and industrial uses, and the protection and propagation of a balanced population of shellfish, fish and wildlife, and allow recreational activities in and on the water ... [FWPCA] § 302(a), 33 U.S.C. § 1312(a).

The Administrator must hold public hearings on any proposed limitation. FWPCA § 302(b)(1), 33 U.S.C. § 1312(b)(1). A discharger of nontoxic pollutants, however, may obtain a modification of the limitation if the Administrator, with the concurrence of the state, determines there is no reasonable relationship between the costs and benefits to be obtained from the limitation. FWPCA § 302(b)(2)(A), 33 U.S.C. § 1312(b)(2)(A). There is no such escape valve from section 303 state water quality standards. *See Homestake Mining Co. v. EPA*, 477 F. Supp. 1279 (D.S.D. 1979). *See also* S. Rep. No. 50, 99th Cong., 1st Sess. 24 (1985). The Administrator, with the concurrence of the state, may also modify a limitation for toxic pollutants for a single period not to exceed five years if the technology utilized is the maximum degree of control within the economic capability of the discharger and there will be reasonable further progress beyond BAT to the water quality limitation established. FWPCA § 302(b)(2)(B), 33 U.S.C. § 1312(b)(2)(B). Section 302 has never been utilized by EPA and probably will continue to be of limited significance given the modifications allowed based on cost/benefit analysis and the economic capability of the discharger. State water quality standards, therefore, will continue to be the primary method for preserving water quality. *See generally* S. Rep. No. 50, 99th Cong., 1st Sess. 24 (1985).

NATURAL RESOURCES DEFENSE COUNCIL v. ENVIRONMENTAL PROTECTION AGENCY
16 F.3d 1395 (4th Cir. 1993)

BRITT, DISTRICT JUDGE:

This appeal arises out of consolidated suits brought by the Natural Resources Defense Council ("NRDC") and Environmental Defense Fund ("EDF") to challenge the approval by the United States Environmental Protection Agency ("EPA") of state water quality standards implemented by Maryland and Virginia. Specifically, NRDC and EDF contest the approval of these state standards as they relate to dioxin.

....

I. *Facts*

... On 11 September 1989, the Maryland Department of the Environment ("MDE") sought to revise Maryland's water quality standards to allow its waters to contain dioxin in the amount of 1.2 parts per quadrillion ("ppq"), an amount indisputably less protective than EPA's own guidance criterion of .0013 ppq. However, MDE chose this 1.2 ppq criterion because it had been based on the Food and Drug Administration's ("FDA") less conservative cancer potency factor and because MDE felt that EPA's cancer potency factor overestimated the carcinogenic potential of dioxin. After public hearings were held on the matter, Maryland adopted the 1.2 ppq standard and submitted it to EPA for review and approval.

Similar events took place in Virginia. On 11 December 1989, the Virginia State Water Control Board ("VSWCB") proposed to revise its water quality standards to include the 1.2 ppq dioxin standard. After public hearings were held, VSWCB submitted its proposal to EPA for review and approval on 27 September 1990.

EPA approved the Maryland standard on 12 September 1990, and approved the Virginia standard on 25 February 1991. Accompanying each approval, a Technical Support Document ("TSD") was issued by EPA and set out in detail EPA's scientific review of MDE's and VSWCB's analysis in deriving the 1.2 ppq standard. EPA concluded that Maryland's and Virginia's use of the 1.2 ppq standard for dioxin was scientifically defensible, protective of human health, and in full compliance with the CWA.

....

II. *Statutory Scheme*

The main purpose of the CWA is to "restore and maintain the chemical, physical, and biological integrity of the Nation's waters" by reducing, and eventually eliminating, the discharge of pollutants into these waters. 33 U.S.C. § 1251(a) (Supp. 1993). While the states and EPA share duties in achieving this goal, primary responsibility for establishing appropriate water quality standards is left to the states. EPA sits in a reviewing capacity of the state-implemented standards, with approval and rejection powers only. 33 U.S.C. § 1313(c) (1982 & Supp. 1993). Water quality standards are a critical component of the CWA regulatory scheme because such standards serve as a guideline for setting applicable limitations in individual discharge permits.

....

The CWA requires each state to adopt water quality standards for all waters of that state and to review them at least every three years. *Id*. §§ 1313(a), (b), (c)(1) (1982 & Supp. 1993). To adopt these standards, states must first classify the uses for which the water is to be protected, such as fishing and swimming, and then each state must determine the level of water quality necessary to protect those uses. Thus, the following three factors are considered when adopting or evaluating a water quality standard: (1) one or more designated uses of the state waters involved; (2) certain water quality criteria, expressed as numeric pollutant concentration levels or narrative statements representing a quality of water that supports a particular designated use; and (3) an antidegradation policy to protect existing uses and high quality waters. *Id*. § 1313(c)(2)(A) (Supp. 1993); 40 C.F.R. § 131.

States are directed to adopt numerical water quality criteria for specific toxic pollutants, such as dioxin, for which EPA has published numerical criteria guidance under 33 U.S.C. § 1314(a), if that pollutant can reasonably be expected to interfere with the designated uses of the states' waters.

....

EPA regulations also provide that states should develop numerical criteria based on EPA's criteria guidance under § 304(a) of the CWA, EPA's criteria guidance modified to reflect site-specific conditions, or other scientifically defensible methods. 40 C.F.R. § 131.11(b)(1). Alternatively, states should establish narrative criteria or criteria based on biomonitoring methods if numerical criteria cannot be ascertained, or to supplement numerical criteria. *Id.* § 131.11(b)(2).

III. *Discussion*

....

Appellants argue that the district court's affirmance of EPA's approval of the Maryland and Virginia water standards should be reversed primarily for two reasons. First, they assert that EPA's approval was arbitrary and capricious because it was not based on all relevant factors, ignored key aspects of the record before it, and failed to show a rational connection between the facts found and the choices made. Second, they maintain that EPA's action was contrary to law because it did not ensure, as required by § 303(c) of the CWA (33 U.S.C. § 1313(c)), that state standards were consistent with the CWA; that is, that the standard protected all designated water uses.

Specifically, NRDC attacks EPA's assessment of the Maryland and Virginia standards regarding the first four factors used in the numeric dioxin criteria determination, namely: (1) cancer potency, (2) risk level, (3) fish consumption, and (4) bioconcentration factor ("BCF"). Of these four, NRDC emphasizes its challenge with respect to the latter two factors, fish consumption and BCF. NRDC contends that these two factors, when considered together, are important because they determine the ultimate "exposure" of an individual to dioxin, while the remaining factors only involve choices about risk or toxicity.

1. *Fish Consumption*

EPA estimates, on a national average, that an individual eats 6.5 grams of fish per day. Maryland and Virginia used this estimate, *inter alia*, in calculating the 1.2 ppq water quality standard. Appellants argue that by affirming EPA's approval of the states' use of this estimate, the district court failed to require EPA to protect subpopulations with higher than average fish consumption, particularly recreational and subsistence fishers. Specifically, appellants contend that EPA's 6.5 grams per day fish consumption factor underestimates the actual fish consumption of subpopulations in Maryland and Virginia, and therefore is not protective of a designated use. Appellants further contend that EPA's use of the 6.5 grams per day fish consumption factor is unsupported by the record and violates EPA's own policy and regulations. They emphasize that Maryland and Virginia are coastal states and, as such, are entitled — according to EPA recommendations — to higher than average values for fish consumption.

EPA points out that the 6.5 gram per day value is not intended to represent *total* fish consumption but, rather, that *subset* of fish containing the *maximum* residues of dioxin permissible under state law. In setting this value, EPA was establishing a national standard and was well aware that subpopulations might very well consume more than 6.5 *total* grams of fish per day. No evidence was presented that the subpopulations referred to are consuming more than 6.5 grams per day of maximum residue fish.

Appellants argue that the risk is especially high for the Mattaponi and Native American peoples who live near a major paper mill in Virginia and who, it is argued, consume higher-than-average amounts of fish. EPA counters that the fish consumption of these subpopulations is speculative at best, that it is based on anecdotal evidence, and that there is no evidence that the fish that actually are consumed are maximum residue fish. In fact, EPA argues that the Native Americans fish in the streams primarily for shad and herring, both of which are anadromous fish that spend a large part of their lives in the oceans and migrate to the rivers only at certain stages during their lives.

The District Court concluded that the EPA, in exercising its judgment, "relied on scientifically defensible means to reach reasoned judgments regarding fish consumption levels." *NRDC II*, at 1276. We agree.

2. *Bioconcentration Factor (BCF)*

Based on EPA laboratory studies, dioxin is more soluble in fat tissues than it is in water. As a result, it tends to accumulate in fish fat tissues at concentrations higher than those present in the water. By averaging the fat content of fish likely to be eaten by an exposed population, a generic BCF can be calculated that reflects dioxin's presence in fish as some multiple of its concentration in ambient water. In its 1984 dioxin criteria document, EPA calculates a dioxin BCF of 5000 for fish of average (3%) lipid content. Maryland and Virginia used this BCF figure, *inter alia*, to derive their numeric water quality criteria.

Appellants challenge EPA's use and approval of a 5000 BCF. They essentially contend that the 5000 BCF figure is outdated because the latest scientific research suggests that a higher BCF should be used. Citing the administrative record, appellants emphasize that: (1) EPA admits that scientific literature and research has changed significantly since preparation of the 1984 dioxin criteria document; (2) EPA further admits that BCF factors now range from 26,000 to 150,000, depending on test species; (3) Virginia conducted a state-specific study which revealed a BCF calculation of 22,000; and (4) Maryland refused to conduct such a study. Appellants contend that, taking all of these factors into account, EPA ignored all the current scientific data and simply "defaulted" to its old BCF assumption. Appellants argue that EPA acted arbitrarily and improperly in not requiring a higher BCF, especially when Virginia and Maryland chose less stringent factors for cancer potency and risk. We disagree.

Once again, we are confronted with an area dominated by complex scientific inquiry and judgment. Although EPA is aware that some recent BCF studies suggested a higher BCF than 5000, EPA maintains that such results are inconclusive and that no compelling scientific evidence indicates that a 5000 BCF is no longer within the range of scientific defensibility. We simply are not in a position to secondguess this technical decision by administrative experts. A review of the record does indicate that several more recent BCF studies have been conducted and that some have suggested a higher BCF; however, the court concludes that the best course of action is to leave this debate to the world of science to ultimately be resolved by those with specialized training in this field. Upon a careful review of the administrative record, we find no clear evidence showing that the 5000 BCF figure is not supported by sound scientific rationale. Accordingly, we hold that EPA did not act arbitrarily in approving the BCF figure used by Maryland and Virginia, and that EPA has made a rational connection between the facts found in the administrative record and its choice to approve the BCF figure. EPA's approval of the 5000 BCF will not be disturbed.

....

We find that EPA's review of the Maryland and Virginia water quality standards was neither arbitrary nor capricious. Each review conducted by EPA was supported by lengthy, highly scientific, technical support documents explaining in detail EPA's rationale in approving the 1.2 ppq standards. EPA has satisfied this court that substantial evidence exists in the administrative record to support its decision, and that it acted rationally and in accordance with the CWA and its regulations. We therefore refuse to upset either EPA's decision to approve Maryland's and Virginia's adoption of the 1.2 ppq standard or the district court decision affirming the same.

....

NOTES AND QUESTIONS

1. In this case EPA based its review of the state water quality standards solely on the health effects of dioxin. Could it have considered other effects of dioxin in its review? Does EPA's approval of the state standards adequately protect the Native Americans who consume above-average quantities of fish? Consider in that context President Clinton's Executive Order 12,898 on environmental justice which requires federal agencies whenever "practicable and appropriate" to "collect, maintain, and analyze information on the consumption patterns of populations who principally rely on fish and/or wildlife for subsistence" and to incorporate consideration of such patterns into agency decisionmaking.

2. Water quality standards consist of uses and criteria. Designated uses are the functions that the state has given to a designated body of water and are not necessarily the same as the existing uses of the body of water. Criteria are the technical standards as to the pollutant levels compatible with each designated use. A water quality standard must be sufficient to protect the designated uses of the body of water to which it applies. Standards are required at a minimum to include use designations intended to protect the public health and welfare, to enhance water quality, and to serve the purposes of the Act. FWPCA § 303(c)-(2)(A), 33 U.S.C. § 1313(c)(2)(A). The same section of the Act states that the value of the waters as public water supplies, fish and wildlife habitats, recreational areas, and resources for agricultural, industrial, and other purposes are to be taken into account when the uses are established. *Id.* These two directives are not necessarily consistent. The first directive could be read to include the goals of the Act for fishable and swimmable waters by 1983 and no discharges into navigable waters by 1985. The second directive, however, is the lax standard-setting language from the 1965 statute. *See generally* Pedersen, *Turning the Tide on Water Quality*, 15 ECOLOGY L.Q. 69, 79 (1988). EPA has interpreted this section to require that state water quality standards achieve the "fishable" and "swimmable" goals in section 101(a)(2), 33 U.S.C. § 1251(a)(2) wherever such uses are attainable. 40 C.F.R. §§ 131.6(a), 131.10(g). States may downgrade a designated use which is not an existing use only if the designated use is not attainable due to natural or unremediable human causes or because attainment would cause "substantial and widespread economic and social impact." *Id.* § 131.10(g). On the other hand, state standards are not required to conform to current technology for elimination of pollution. Attainability of a designated use is a minimum criteria for the standards, not a maximum. The states are free to "force technology" to catch up with the standards. *United States Steel Corp. v. Train*, 556 F.2d 822, 838 (7th Cir. 1977).

In *Mississippi Comm'n on Nat. Resources v. Costle*, 625 F. 2d 1269 (5th Cir. 1980), the Fifth Circuit Court of Appeals concluded that rigorous review by EPA of state designation of uses would be the federal land use that Congress expressly rejected in section 101(b), 33 U.S.C. § 1251(b), but that EPA was free to engage in such review of the state *criteria* in the water quality standard. It has been suggested that EPA's regulations, particularly those for antidegradation, discussed in note 5 *infra*, actually authorize extensive review of a state's designated uses. *Compare* Gaba, *Federal Supervision of State Water Quality Standards Under the Clean Water Act*, 36 VAND. L. REV. 1167, 1194-1204 (1983) (concluding such review is appropriate), *with* Pedersen, *supra*, at 93-4 n.128 (concluding it is not). Generally, EPA's review of state water quality standards involves determinations of whether the designated water uses are consistent with the Clean Water Act; whether the criteria protect those uses; whether the standards have been legally adopted; whether uses not specified in section 101(a)(2), 33 U.S.C. § 1251(a)(2), are based on appropriate scientific and technical data; and whether the standards meet other minimum criteria established by the EPA such as inclusion of an antidegradation policy. 40 C.F.R. § 131.5.

A major weakness in the statutory scheme is the vacuum within which states may designate water uses. As discussed above, the statutory directives for setting such uses are unclear, with EPA's antidegradation policy providing the most substantive restriction. Guidance at the federal level is necessary to buffer states from pressure to lower acceptable uses for development, yet any effort to do so flies squarely in the face of Congress's reticence at involvement in land use decisionmaking. In addition to this fundamental weakness, many state water quality standards do not apply at all at very low streamflow levels despite the interrelationship between water quantity and quality.

3. In most cases, state criteria are set as a numerical concentration for a specific pollutant. EPA's regulations require that criteria for pollutants in a given body of water be set at the levels necessary to protect the most sensitive use for which that body of water has been designated, and that the standards be based on the recommended national criterion, on the national criterion modified to reflect local conditions using EPA's methodology, or on other scientifically defensible methods. 40 C.F.R. § 131.11(a)(1), (b)(1). In *Mississippi Commission v. Costle*, *supra*, the Court of Appeals endorsed what has become known as the "presumptive applicability" of the recommended national criteria, so that EPA can require states to justify standards not in conformance with the criteria policy set out in the "Red Book." Most states have based their water quality criteria on the guidelines found in the EPA "Red Book" (the most recent version of which is known as the "Gold Book").

When numerical criteria have not been promulgated by EPA, criteria based on biological assessment or monitoring may be utilized. FWPCA § 303(c)(2)(B), 33 U.S.C. § 1313(c)(2)(B). To this end, EPA must develop information on methods for establishing and measuring water quality criteria for toxic pollutants in ways other than pollutant-by-pollutant criteria. FWPCA § 304(a)(8), 33 U.S.C. § 1314(a)(8).

The pollutants for which states must develop criteria, however, are not clearly delineated in the Act. For nontoxic pollutants, states need only to include criteria to "protect the designated use." 40 C.F.R. § 131.11(a)(1). For toxic pollutants, however, a 1987 amendment to section 303(c)(2)(B) requires criteria for all toxic pollutants "the discharge or presence of which in the affected waters could reasonably be expected to interfere with those designated uses adopted by the State, as necessary to support such designated uses." FWPCA § 303(c)(2)(B), 33 U.S.C. § 1313(c)(2)(B). The regulations require states to review water bodies in which toxic pollutants may be "adversely affecting water quality or the attainment of the designated water use or where the levels of toxic pollutants are at a level to warrant concern." 40 C.F.R. § 131.11(a)(2). Although the Act says little about the nontoxic pollutants for which criteria must be set, state water quality standards are very detailed and cover a broad range of pollutants.

4. Once a state has set the uses and criteria in its water quality standards, for meaningful enforcement they must then be translated into specific limits on individual dischargers. The next step is for the state to set the "total maximum daily load" (TMDL) of each criteria pollutant from point and nonpoint sources for a given body of water to meet the designated use and criteria for that use and to incorporate numerical pollutant limitations in the dischargers' NPDES permits to stay within the TMDL. States must set TMDLs for all waters in their jurisdiction that will not meet water quality standards even after application of technology-based limits. FWPCA § 303(d)(1)(C), 33 U.S.C. § 1313(d)(1)(C). The TMDLs must be set at a level to meet water quality standards "with seasonal variations and a margin of safety which takes into account any lack of knowledge concerning the relationship between effluent limitations and water quality." *Id.* A state's failure to set TMDLs triggers a mandatory duty on the part of EPA to promulgate TMDLs for the state and environmental groups have brought many cases to compel EPA to set TMDLs. *Scott v. City of Hammond*, 741 F.2d 992 (7th Cir. 1984); *Alaska Center for the Env't v. EPA*, 762 F. Supp. 1422 (W.D.

Wash. 1991); *Sierra Club v. Hankinson*, 939 F. Supp. 865 and 872 (N.D. Ga. 1996). States are basically free to allocate the total load as they wish among the dischargers on the given water source. *See* 40 C.F.R. § 130. The final, and most difficult, step is to translate each discharger's share of the TMDL into a specific numerical limitation on the source's discharge in drafting the source's section 402 permit. States may also, subject to EPA review, implement standards with regard to mixing zones, low flow requirements, and variances. 40 C.F.R. § 131.13. The designation of the "mixing zone" is critical in determining a source's compliance with water quality standards, and states retain great discretion in setting its boundaries. The larger the mixing zone, the greater the dilution of a discharge and the more likely it is that the discharge will not cause the water quality standard to be violated. For more on this concept, see generally *Marathon Oil Co. v. EPA*, 830 F.2d 1346 (5th Cir. 1987).

Section 303(d), 33 U.S.C. § 1313(d) was amended in 1987 to prohibit downward revisions of TMDLs for water segments not meeting water quality standards unless a designated use not being attained has been removed in accordance with the regulations, discussed in note 2, *supra*, with respect to downgrading of designated uses. Also, there may be no downward revisions of TMDLs for waters with water quality meeting or exceeding water quality standards unless the revision is consistent with EPA's antidegradation policy. FWPCA § 303(d)(4), 33 U.S.C. § 1313(d)(4). The extent to which Congress intended to codify EPA's regulations on antidegradation and downgrading of existing uses is not clear. *See* 2 S. NOVICK, LAW OF ENVIRONMENTAL PROTECTION § 12.05[3][c][i] nn. 309 & 314 (1989).

The revision of section 303(d) must be read in conjunction with the "anti-backsliding" provisions for permits added in 1987 as section 402(o). FWPCA § 402(o), 33 U.S.C. § 1342(o). Generally, section 402(o) prohibits issuance of new permits that are less stringent than existing permits for the same facilities, with limited exceptions. As to water quality-based permit limitations, they may not be relaxed unless several conditions are met under § 402(o)(2), 33 U.S.C. § 1342(o)(2). However, section 402(o)(1) states that a water quality-based permit limitation may be relaxed if the revision is in keeping with EPA's antidegradation policy as set forth in section 303(d)(4). FWPCA § 402(o)(1), 33 U.S.C. § 1342(o)(1). It would appear that section 402(o)(1) and (2) provides alternative avenues for backsliding in water quality-based permits; that is, both the conditions in section 402(o)(2) and the antidegradation policy need not be met. H.R. Conf. Rep. No. 1004, 99th Cong., 2d Sess. 156 (1986).

5. States must adopt antidegradation policies to maintain existing uses and water quality. 40 C.F.R. § 131.12. Existing instream uses and the level of water quality necessary for those uses may not be lowered. *Id.* § 131.12(a)(1). High quality waters with water quality levels exceeding those necessary to achieve the fishable/swimmable goals may be lowered to the levels necessary to protect those uses only to accommodate important economic or social development in the area in which the waters are located. *Id.* § 131.12(a)(2). There can be no such degradation if the waters are an "outstanding National resource such as waters of National and State parks and wildlife refuges and waters of exceptional recreational or biological significance." *Id.* § 131.12(a)(3).

EPA's antidegradation policy and its purported basis in the Act has been very controversial. *See generally* Hines, *A Decade of Nondegradation Policy in Congress and the Courts: The Erratic Pursuit of Clear Air and Clean Water*, 62 IOWA L. REV. 643 (1977). A legal challenge to EPA's policy was dismissed for lack of ripeness, but a dissenting judge found that the policy was unfounded under the Act. *Commonwealth Edison Co. v. Train*, 649 F.2d 481 (7th Cir. 1980).

6. States are permitted to establish stricter water quality standards than those mandated by the EPA. FWPCA § 510, 33 U.S.C. § 1370. Stricter state standards take precedence over the minimum standards prescribed by the EPA in the NPDES permit process. *Hercules, Inc. v. EPA*, 598 F.2d 91 (D.C. Cir. 1978).

One area that is not covered by EPA criteria but is regulated by most states is groundwater. Most state water quality standards apply to both navigable waters and groundwaters, and some states have separate groundwater standards. No centralized federal authority regulates groundwater, despite considerable federal legislation applicable to groundwater. At least eight federal acts address groundwater, Marks, *Toward a National Groundwater Act: Current Contamination and Future Courses of Action*, FLA. B.J., April 1987, at 10, 11, with EPA administering six of the eight statutes. The six programs administered by EPA are under the Safe Drinking Water Act (SDWA), § 1401, 42 U.S.C. § 300f; Resource Conservation and Recovery Act (RCRA), § 1002, 42 U.S.C. § 6901; Comprehensive Environmental Response, Compensation and Liability Act (CERCLA), § 101, 42 U.S.C. § 9601; Clean Water Act (CWA), § 101, 33 U.S.C. § 1251; Federal Insecticide, Fungicide, and Rodenticide Act (FIFRA), § 2, 7 U.S.C. § 136; and Toxic Substances Control Act (TOSCA), § 2, 15 U.S.C. § 2601. Most of the acts attempt to remedy contamination after it has occurred rather than prospectively protect the quantity or quality of groundwater.

Although EPA has some authority under the Clean Water Act to take preventive action against groundwater contamination, EPA has done very little due to conflicting court decisions and EPA's own hesitancy in utilizing the Act's provisions. The Act instructs EPA to develop programs for "preventing, reducing, or eliminating the pollution of the navigable waters and ground waters and improving the sanitary condition of surface and underground waters." FWPCA § 102(a), 33 U.S.C. § 1252(a). The legislative history may also be interpreted as authorizing EPA to regulate both surface and groundwater. Marks, *supra*, at 16 n.6 (*citing* 118 Cong. Rec. H33,766 (1972)). There are specific provisions as well which refer to regulation of groundwater. Water quality standards under section 303, 33 U.S.C. § 1313, establish designated uses for bodies of water in conjunction with section 304, 33 U.S.C. § 1314, which establishes a methodology for criteria and information regarding the "factors necessary to restore and maintain the chemical, physical, and biological integrity of all navigable waters [and] ground waters." FWPCA § 304(a)(2)(A), 33 U.S.C. § 1314(a)(2)(A). However, EPA has not promulgated the criteria or information required in section 304, 33 U.S.C. § 1314, regulated groundwater at the federal level, or required states to do so.

ARKANSAS v. OKLAHOMA

503 U.S. 91 (1992)

JUSTICE STEVENS delivered the opinion of the Court.

Pursuant to the Clean Water Act the Environmental Protection Agency (EPA) issued a discharge permit to a new point source in Arkansas, about 39 miles upstream from the Oklahoma state line. The question presented in this litigation is whether the EPA's finding that discharges from the new source would not cause a detectable violation of Oklahoma's water quality standards satisfied the EPA's duty to protect the interests of the downstream State. Disagreeing with the Court of Appeals, we hold that the Agency's action was authorized by the statute.

I

In 1985, the City of Fayetteville, Arkansas, applied to the EPA, seeking a permit for the City's new sewage treatment plant under the National Pollution Discharge Elimination System (NPDES). After the appropriate procedures, the EPA, pursuant to § 402(a)(1) of the Act, 33 U.S.C. § 1342(a)(1), issued a permit authorizing the plant to discharge up to half of its effluent (to a limit of 6.1 million gallons per day) into an unnamed stream in northwestern Arkansas.[1] That flow passes through a series of three creeks for about 17 miles, and then enters the Illinois River at a point 22 miles upstream from the Arkansas-Oklahoma border.

The permit imposed specific limitations on the quantity, content, and character of the discharge and also included a number of special conditions, including a provision that if a study then underway indicated that more stringent limitations were necessary to ensure compliance with Oklahoma's water quality standards, the permit would be modified to incorporate those limits.

Respondents challenged this permit before the EPA, alleging, *inter alia*, that the discharge violated the Oklahoma water quality standards. Those standards

---

[1]The permit also authorized the plant to discharge the remainder of its effluent into the White River, a river that does not flow into Oklahoma; this aspect of the permit is not at issue in this litigation.

provide that "no degradation [of water quality] shall be allowed" in the upper Illinois River, including the portion of the River immediately downstream from the state line.[2]

Following a hearing, the Administrative Law Judge (ALJ) concluded that the Oklahoma standards would not be implicated unless the contested discharge had "something more than a mere *de minimis* impact" on the State's waters. He found that the discharge would not have an "undue impact" on Oklahoma's waters and, accordingly, affirmed the issuance of the permit.

On a petition for review, the EPA's Chief Judicial Officer first ruled that § 301(b)(1)(C) of the Clean Water Act "requires an NPDES permit to impose any effluent limitations necessary to comply with applicable state water quality standards."[3] He then held that the Act and EPA regulations offered greater protection for the downstream State than the ALJ's "undue impact" standard suggested. He explained the proper standard as follows:

> "[A] mere theoretical impairment of Oklahoma's water quality standards —
> i.e., an infinitesimal impairment predicted through modeling but not
> expected to be actually detectable or measurable — should not by itself
> block the issuance of the permit. In this case, the permit should be upheld

---

[2]Section 5 of the Oklahoma water quality standards provides:

> "All streams and bodies of water designated as (a) are protected by prohibition of any new point source discharge of wastes or increased load from an existing point source except under conditions described in Section 3.
> "All streams designated by the State as 'scenic river areas,' and such tributaries of those streams as may be appropriate will be so designated. Best management practices for control of nonpoint source discharge should be initiated when feasible."

Oklahoma has designated the portion of the Illinois River immediately downstream from the state line as a "scenic river." Okla. Stat., Tit. 82, § 1452(b)(1) (Supp. 1989).

Section 3 of the Oklahoma water quality standards provides, in relevant part:

> "The intent of the Anti-degradation Policy is to protect all waters of the State from quality degradation. Existing instream water uses shall be maintained and protected. No further water quality degradation which would interfere with or become injurious to existing instream water uses shall be allowed. Oklahoma's waters constitute a valuable State resource and shall be protected, maintained and improved for the benefit of all the citizens.
> "No degradation shall be allowed in high quality waters which constitute an outstanding resource or in waters of exceptional recreational or ecological significance. These include water bodies located in national and State parks, Wildlife Refuges, and those designated 'Scenic Rivers' in Appendix A."

[3]Section 301(b)(1)(C) provides, in relevant part, that

> "there shall be achieved —
> "....
> "(C) not later than July 1, 1977, any more stringent limitation, including those necessary to meet *water quality standards ... established pursuant to any State law or regulations ...* or required to implement any applicable water quality standard established pursuant to this chapter." 33 U.S.C. § 1311(b)(1)(C) (emphasis supplied).

if the record shows by a preponderance of the evidence that the authorized discharges would not cause an actual *detectable* violation of Oklahoma's water quality standards."

On remand, the ALJ made detailed findings of fact and concluded that the City had satisfied the standard set forth by the Chief Judicial Officer. Specifically, the ALJ found that there would be no detectable violation of any of the components of Oklahoma's water quality standards. The Chief Judicial Officer sustained the issuance of the permit.

Both the petitioners in No. 90-1262 (collectively Arkansas) and the respondents in this litigation sought judicial review.[4] Arkansas argued that the Clean Water Act did not require an Arkansas point source to comply with Oklahoma's water quality standards. Oklahoma challenged the EPA's determination that the Fayetteville discharge would not produce a detectable violation of the Oklahoma standards.

The Court of Appeals did not accept either of these arguments. The court agreed with the EPA that the statute required compliance with Oklahoma's water quality standards, see 908 F.2d 595, 602-615 (CA10 1990), and did not disagree with the Agency's determination that the discharges from the Fayetteville plant would not produce a detectable violation of those standards. *Id.*, at 631-633. Nevertheless, relying on a theory that neither party had advanced, the Court of Appeals reversed the Agency's issuance of the Fayetteville permit. The court first ruled that the statute requires that "where a proposed source would discharge effluents that would contribute to conditions currently constituting a violation of applicable water quality standards, such [a] proposed source may not be permitted." *Id.*, at 620. Then the court found that the Illinois River in Oklahoma was "already degraded," that the Fayetteville effluent would reach the Illinois River in Oklahoma, and that that effluent could "be expected to contribute to the ongoing deterioration of the scenic [Illinois R]iver" in Oklahoma even though it would not detectably affect the River's water quality. *Id.*, at 621-629.

The importance and the novelty of the Court of Appeals' decision persuaded us to grant certiorari. We now reverse.

II

Interstate waters have been a font of controversy since the founding of the Nation. *E.g.*, *Gibbons v. Ogden*, 9 Wheat. 1 (1824). This Court has frequently resolved disputes between States that are separated by a common river, see, *e.g.*, *Ohio v. Kentucky*, 444 U.S. 335 (1980), that border the same body of water, see, *e.g.*, *New York v. New Jersey*, 256 U.S. 296 (1921), or that are fed by the same river basin, see, *e.g.*, *New Jersey v. New York*, 283 U.S. 336 (1931).

---

[4]The Arkansas petition was filed in the Court of Appeals for the Eighth Circuit and transferred to the Tenth Circuit where it was consolidated with the petition filed by the respondents.

Among these cases are controversies between a State that introduces pollutants to a waterway and a downstream State that objects. See, *e.g.*, *Missouri v. Illinois*, 200 U.S. 496 (1906). In such cases, this Court has applied principles of common law tempered by a respect for the sovereignty of the States. Compare *id.*, at 521, with *Georgia v. Tennessee Copper Co.*, 206 U.S. 230, 237 (1907). In forging what "may not improperly be called interstate common law," *Illinois v. Milwaukee*, 406 U.S. 91, 105-106 (1972) (*Milwaukee I*), however, we remained aware that new federal laws and new federal regulations may in time pre-empt the field of federal common law of nuisance." *Id.*, at 107.

In *Milwaukee v. Illinois*, 451 U.S. 304 (1981) (*Milwaukee II*), we held that the 1972 Amendments to the Federal Water Pollution Control Act did just that. In addressing Illinois' claim that Milwaukee's discharges into Lake Michigan constituted a nuisance, we held that the comprehensive regulatory regime created by the 1972 Amendments pre-empted Illinois' federal common law remedy. We observed that Congress had addressed many of the problems we had identified in *Milwaukee I* by providing a downstream State with an opportunity for a hearing before the source State's permitting agency, by requiring the latter to explain its failure to accept any recommendations offered by the downstream State, and by authorizing the EPA, in its discretion, to veto a source State's issuance of any permit if the waters of another State may be affected. *Milwaukee II*, 451 U.S., 325-326.

In *Milwaukee II*, the Court did not address whether the 1972 Amendments had supplanted *state* common law remedies as well as the federal common law remedy. See *id.*, at 310 n.4. On remand, Illinois argued that § 510 of the Clean Water Act, 33 U.S.C. § 1370, expressly preserved the State's right to adopt and enforce rules that are more stringent than federal standards.[5] The Court of Appeals accepted Illinois' reading of § 510, but held that that section did "no more than to save the right and jurisdiction of a state to regulate activity occurring within the confines of its boundary waters." *Illinois v. Milwaukee*, 731 F.2d 403, 413 (CA7 1984), *cert. denied*, 469 U.S. 1196 (1985).

This Court subsequently endorsed that analysis in *International Paper Co. v. Ouellette*, 479 U.S. 481 (1987), in which Vermont property owners claimed that the pollution discharged into Lake Champlain by a paper company located in New York constituted a nuisance under Vermont law. The Court held the Clean Water Act taken "as a whole, its purposes and its history" pre-empted an action

---

[5]Section 510 provides in relevant part:

"Except as expressly provided in this Act, nothing in this [Act] shall (1) preclude or deny the right of any State or political subdivision thereof or interstate agency to adopt or enforce (A) any standard or limitation respecting discharges of pollutants, or (B) any requirement respecting control or abatement of pollution [with exceptions]; or (2) be construed as impairing or in any manner affecting any right or jurisdiction of the States *with respect to the waters (including boundary waters) of such States*." 33 U.S.C. § 1370 (emphasis supplied).

based on the law of the affected State and that the only state law applicable to an interstate discharge is "the law of the State in which the point source is located." *Id.*, at 493, 487. Moreover, in reviewing § 402(b) of the Act, the Court pointed out that when a new permit is being issued by the source State's permit-granting agency, the downstream state

> "does not have the authority to block the issuance of the permit if it is dissatisfied with the proposed standards. An affected State's only recourse is to apply to the EPA Administrator, who then has the discretion to disapprove the permit if he concludes that the discharges will have an undue impact on interstate waters. § 1342(d)(2).... Thus the Act makes it clear that affected States occupy a subordinate position to source States in the federal regulatory program." *Id.*, at 490-491.[6]

Unlike the foregoing cases, this litigation involves not a State-issued permit, but a federally issued permit. To explain the significance of this distinction, we comment further on the statutory scheme before addressing the specific issues raised by the parties.

III

The Clean Water Act anticipates a partnership between the States and the Federal Government, animated by a shared objective: "to restore and maintain the chemical, physical, and biological integrity of the Nation's waters." 33 U.S.C. § 1251(a). Toward this end, the Act provides for two sets of water quality measures. "Effluent limitations" are promulgated by the EPA and restrict the quantities, rates, and concentrations of specified substances which are discharged from point sources. See 33 U.S.C. §§ 1311, 1314. "[W]ater quality standards" are, in general, promulgated by the States and establish the desired condition of a waterway. See 33 U.S.C. § 1313. These standards supplement effluent limitations "so that numerous point sources, despite individual compliance with effluent limitations, may be further regulated to prevent water quality from falling below acceptable levels." *EPA v. California ex rel. State Water Resources Control Board*, 426 U.S. 200, 205, n. 12 (1976).

The EPA provides States with substantial guidance in the drafting of water quality standards. See generally 40 CFR pt. 131 (1991) (setting forth model

---

[6]This description of the downstream State's role in the issuance of a new permit by a source State was apparently consistent with the EPA's interpretation of the Act at the time. The Government's *amicus curiae* brief in *Ouellette* stated that the affected neighboring state [has] only an advisory role in the formulation of applicable effluent standards or limitations. The affected state may try to persuade the federal government or the source state to increase effluent requirements, but *ultimately possesses no statutory authority to compel that result, even when its waters are adversely affected by out-of-state pollution.* See 33 U.S.C. § 1341(a)(2), 1342(b)(3) and (5)...." Brief for United States as *Amicus Curiae*, O. T. 1986, No. 85-1233, p. 19 (emphasis supplied; footnote omitted).

water quality standards). Moreover, § 303 of the Act requires, *inter alia*, that state authorities periodically review water quality standards and secure the EPA's approval of any revisions in the standards. If the EPA recommends changes to the standards and the State fails to comply with that recommendation, the Act authorizes the EPA to promulgate water quality standards for the State. 33 U.S.C. § 1313(c).

The primary means for enforcing these limitations and standards is the National Pollution Discharge Elimination System (NPDES), enacted in 1972 as a critical part of Congress' "complete rewriting" of federal water pollution law. *Milwaukee II*, 451 U.S., at 317. Section 301(a) of the Act, 33 U.S.C. § 1311(a), generally prohibits the discharge of any effluent into a navigable body of water unless the point source has obtained an NPDES permit. Section 402 establishes the NPDES permitting regime, and describes two types of permitting systems: state permit programs that must satisfy federal requirements and be approved by the EPA, and a federal program administered by the EPA.

Section 402(b) authorizes each State to establish "its own permit program for discharges into navigable waters within its jurisdiction." 33 U.S.C. § 1342(b). Among the requirements the state program must satisfy are the procedural protections for downstream States discussed in *Ouellette* and *Milwaukee II*. See 33 U.S.C. §§ 1342(b)(3), (5).[7] Although these provisions do not authorize the downstream State to veto the issuance of a permit for a new point source in another State, the Administrator retains authority to block the issuance of any state-issued permit that "is outside the guidelines and requirements" of the Act. 33 U.S.C. § 1342(d)(2).[8]

---

[7]Section 402(b) requires state permit programs

"(3) to insure that any other State the waters of which may be affected ... receive notice of each application for a permit and to provide an opportunity for public hearing before a ruling on each such application;

    "....

"(5) to insure that any State (other than the permitting State), whose waters may be affected by the issuance of a permit may submit written recommendations to the permitting State (and the Administrator) with respect to any permit application and, if any part of such written recommendations are not accepted by the permitting State, that the permitting State will notify such affected State (and the Administrator) in writing of its failure to so accept such recommendations together with its reasons for so doing." 33 U.S.C. § 1342(b).

Although § 402(b) focuses on state-issued permits, § 402(a)(3) requires that, in issuing an NPDES permit, the Administrator follow the same procedures required of state permit programs. See 33 U.S.C. § 1342(a)(3); see also 33 U.S.C. § 1341(a)(2).

[8]Section 402(d)(2) provides:

"(2) No permit shall issue (A) if the Administrator within ninety days of the date of his notification under subsection (b) (5) of this section objects in writing to the issuance of such permit, or (B) if the Administrator within ninety days of the date of transmittal of the proposed permit by the State objects in writing to the issuance of such permit as being outside the guidelines and requirements of this chapter. Whenever the Administrator objects

In the absence of an approved state program, the EPA may issue an NPDES permit under § 402(a) of the Act. (In this case, for example, because Arkansas had not been authorized to issue NPDES permits when the Fayetteville plant was completed, the permit was issued by the EPA itself.) The EPA's permit program is subject to the "same terms, conditions, and requirements" as a state permit program. 33 U.S.C. § 1342(a)(3). Notwithstanding this general symmetry, the EPA has construed the Act as requiring that EPA-issued NPDES permits also comply with § 401(a). That section, which predates § 402 and the NPDES, applies to a broad category of federal licenses, and sets forth requirements for "[a]ny applicant for a Federal license or permit to conduct any activity including, but not limited to, the construction or operation of facilities, which may result in any discharge into the navigable waters." 33 U.S.C. § 1341(a). Section 401(a)(2) appears to prohibit the issuance of any federal license or permit over the objection of an affected State unless compliance with the affected State's water quality requirements can be insured.[9]

IV

The parties have argued three analytically distinct questions concerning the interpretation of the Clean Water Act. First, does the Act require the EPA, in crafting and issuing a permit to a point source in one State, to apply the water quality standards of downstream States? Second, even if the Act does not *require* as much, does the Agency have the statutory authority to mandate such compliance? Third, does the Act provide, as the Court of Appeals held, that once a body of water fails to meet water quality standards no discharge that yields effluents that reach the degraded waters will be permitted?

---

to the issuance of a permit under this paragraph such written objection shall contain a statement of the reasons for such objection and the effluent limitations and conditions which such permit would include if it were issued by the Administrator." 33 U.S.C. § 1342(d)(2).

[9]Section 401(a)(2) provides, in relevant part:

"Whenever such a discharge may affect, as determined by the Administrator, the quality of the waters of any other State, the Administrator ... shall so notify such other State, the licensing or permitting agency, and the applicant. If, within sixty days after receipt of such notification, such other State determines that such discharge will affect the quality of its waters so as to violate any water quality requirements in such State, and within such sixty-day period notifies the Administrator and the licensing or permitting agency in writing of its objection to the issuance of such license or permit and requests a public hearing on such objection, the licensing or permitting agency shall hold such a hearing. The Administrator shall at such hearing submit his evaluation and recommendations with respect to any such objection to the licensing or permitting agency. Such agency, based upon the recommendations of such State, the Administrator, and upon any additional evidence, if any, presented to the agency at the hearing, shall condition such license or permit in such manner as may be necessary to insure compliance with applicable water quality requirements. If the imposition of conditions cannot insure such compliance such agency shall not issue such license or permit." 33 U.S.C. § 1341(a)(2).

In this case, it is neither necessary nor prudent for us to resolve the first of these questions. In issuing the Fayetteville permit, the EPA assumed it was obligated by both the Act and its own regulations to ensure that the Fayetteville discharge would not violate Oklahoma's standards. As we discuss below, this assumption was permissible and reasonable and therefore there is no need for us to address whether the Act requires as much. Moreover, much of the analysis and argument in the briefs of the parties relies on statutory provisions that govern not only federal permits issued pursuant to §§ 401(a) and 402(a), but also state permits issued under § 402(b). It seems unwise to evaluate those arguments in a case such as this one, which only involves a federal permit.

Our decision not to determine at this time the scope of the Agency's statutory *obligations* does not affect our resolution of the second question, which concerns the Agency's statutory *authority*. Even if the Clean Water Act itself does not require the Fayetteville discharge to comply with Oklahoma's water quality standards, the statute clearly does not limit the EPA's authority to mandate such compliance.

Since 1973, EPA regulations have provided that an NPDES permit shall not be issued "[w]hen the imposition of conditions cannot ensure compliance with the applicable water quality requirements of all affected States."[10] 40 CFR § 122.4(d) (1991); see also 38 Fed. Reg. 13533 (1973); 40 CFR § 122.44(d) (1991). Those regulations — relied upon by the EPA in the issuance of the Fayetteville permit — constitute a reasonable exercise of the Agency's statutory authority.

Congress has vested in the Administrator broad discretion to establish conditions for NPDES permits. Section 402(a)(2) provides that for EPA-issued permits "[t]he Administrator shall prescribe conditions for such permits to assure compliance with the requirements of [§ 402(a)(1)] and *such other requirements as he deems appropriate*." 33 U.S.C. § 1342(a)(2) (emphasis supplied). Similarly, Congress preserved for the Administrator broad authority to oversee state permit programs:

> "No permit shall issue ... if the Administrator ... objects in writing to the issuance of such permit as being outside the guidelines and requirements of this chapter." 33 U.S.C. § 1342(d)(2).

The regulations relied on by the EPA were a perfectly reasonable exercise of the Agency's statutory discretion. The application of state water quality standards in the interstate context is wholly consistent with the Act's broad purpose, "to restore and maintain the chemical, physical, and biological integrity of the Nation's waters." 33 U.S.C. § 1251(a). Moreover, as noted above, § 301(b)(1)-(C) expressly identifies the achievement of state water quality standards as one

---

[10]This restriction applies whether the permit is issued by the EPA or by an approved state program. See 40 CFR § 123.25 (1991).

of the Act's central objectives. The Agency's regulations conditioning NPDES permits are a well-tailored means of achieving this goal.

Notwithstanding this apparent reasonableness, Arkansas argues that our description in *Ouellette* of the role of affected States in the permit process and our characterization of the affected States' position as "subordinate," see 479 U.S., at 490-491, indicates that the EPA's application of the Oklahoma standards was error. We disagree. Our statement in *Ouellette* concerned only an affected State's input into the permit process; that input is clearly limited by the plain language of § 402(b). Limits on an affected State's direct participation in permitting decisions, however, do not in any way constrain the *EPA's* authority to require a point source to comply with downstream water quality standards.

Arkansas also argues that regulations requiring compliance with downstream standards are at odds with the legislative history of the Act and with the statutory scheme established by the Act. Although we agree with Arkansas that the Act's legislative history indicates that Congress intended to grant the Administrator discretion in his oversight of the issuance of NPDES permits,[11] we find nothing in that history to indicate that Congress intended to preclude the EPA from establishing a general requirement that such permits be conditioned to ensure compliance with downstream water quality standards.

Similarly, we agree with Arkansas that in the Clean Water Act Congress struck a careful balance among competing policies and interests, but do not find the EPA regulations concerning the application of downstream water quality standards at all incompatible with that balance. Congress, in crafting the Act, protected certain sovereign interest of the States; for example, § 510 allows States to adopt more demanding pollution-control standards than those established under the Act. Arkansas emphasizes that § 510 preserves such state authority only as it is applied to the waters of the regulating State. Even assuming Arkansas's construction of § 510 is correct, cf. *id.*, at 493, that section only concerns state authority and does not constrain the EPA's authority to promulgate reasonable regulations requiring point sources in one State to comply with water quality standards in downstream States.

For these reasons, we find the EPA's requirement that the Fayetteville discharge comply with Oklahoma's water quality standards to be a reasonable exercise of the Agency's substantial statutory discretion. Cf. *Chevron U.S.A. Inc. v. Natural Resources Defense Council, Inc.*, 467 U.S. 837, 842-845 (1984).

---

[11]See, *e.g.*, 1 Legislative History of Water Pollution Control Act Amendments of 1972 (Committee Print compiled for the Senate Committee on Public Works by the Library of Congress), Ser. No. 93-1, pp. 322, 388-389, 814 (1973); see also 33 U.S.C. § 1342(d)(3).

V

The Court of Appeals construed the Clean Water Act to prohibit any discharge of effluent that would reach waters already in violation of existing water quality standards.[12] We find nothing in the Act to support this reading.

The interpretation of the statute adopted by the court had not been advanced by any party during the agency or court proceedings. Moreover, the Court of Appeals candidly acknowledged that its theory has apparently never before been addressed by a federal court." 908 F.2d, at 620, n.39. The only statutory provision the court cited to support its legal analysis was § 402(h), see *id.*, at 633, which merely authorizes the EPA (or a state permit program) to prohibit a publicly owned treatment plant that is violating a condition of its NPDES permit from accepting any additional pollutants for treatment until the ongoing violation has been corrected. See 33 U.S.C. § 1342(h).

Although the Act contains several provisions directing compliance with state water quality standards, see, *e.g.*, 33 U.S.C. § 1311(b)(1)(C), the parties have pointed to nothing that mandates a complete ban on discharges into a waterway that is in violation of those standards. The statute does, however, contain provisions designed to remedy existing water quality violations and to allocate the burden of reducing undesirable discharges between existing sources and new sources. See, *e.g.*, 33 U.S.C. § 1313(d). Thus, rather than establishing the categorical ban announced by the Court of Appeals — which might frustrate the construction of new plants that would improve existing conditions — the Clean Water Act vests in the EPA and the States broad authority to develop long-range, area-wide programs to alleviate and eliminate existing pollution. See, *e.g.*, 33 U.S.C. § 1288(b)(2).

To the extent that the Court of Appeals relied on its interpretation of the Act to reverse the EPA's permitting decision, that reliance was misplaced.

VI

The Court of Appeals also concluded that the EPA's issuance of the Fayetteville permit was arbitrary and capricious because the Agency misinterpreted

---

[12]"[W]e hold that the Clean Water Act prohibits granting an NPDES permit under the circumstances of this case (i.e., where applicable water quality standards have already been violated) and reverse EPA's decision to permit Fayetteville to discharge any part of its effluent to the Illinois River Basin." 908 F.2d 595, 616 (CA10 1990).

"Congress cannot reasonably be presumed to have intended to exclude from the CWA's 'all-encompassing program,' 451 U.S., at 318, a permitting decision arising in circumstances such as those of this case. It is even more unfathomable that Congress fashioned a *comprehensive* ... policy for the *elimination* of 'water pollution,' *id.*, which sanctions continued pollution once minimum water quality standards have been transgressed. More likely, Congress simply never contemplated that EPA or a state would consider it permissible to authorize further pollution under such circumstances. We will not ascribe to the Act either the gaping loophole or the irrational purpose necessary to uphold EPA's action in this case." *Id.*, at 632 (*footnotes omitted*).

Oklahoma's water quality standards. The primary difference[13] between the court's and the Agency's interpretation of the standards derives from the court's construction of the Act. Contrary to the EPA's interpretation of the Oklahoma standards, the Court of Appeals read those standards as containing the same categorical ban on new discharges that the court had found in the Clean Water Act itself. Although we do not believe the text of the Oklahoma standards supports the court's reading (indeed, we note that Oklahoma itself had not advanced that interpretation in its briefs in the Court of Appeals), we reject it for a more fundamental reason — namely, that the Court of Appeals exceeded the legitimate scope of judicial review of an agency adjudication. To emphasize the importance of this point, we shall first briefly assess the soundness of the EPA's interpretation and application of the Oklahoma standards and then comment more specifically on the Court of Appeals' approach.

As discussed above, EPA regulations require an NPDES permit to comply "with the applicable water quality requirements of all affected States." 40 CFR § 122.4(d) (1991). This regulation effectively incorporates into federal law those state law standards the Agency reasonably determines to be "applicable." In such a situation, then, state water quality standards — promulgated by the States with substantial guidance from the EPA[14] and approved by the Agency — are part of the federal law of water pollution control.

Two features of the body of law governing water pollution support this conclusion. First, as discussed more thoroughly above, we have long recognized that interstate water pollution is controlled by *federal* law. Recognizing that the system of federally approved state standards as applied in the interstate context constitutes federal law is wholly consistent with this principle. Second, treating state standards in interstate controversies as federal law accords with the Act's

---

[13]The court identified three errors in the EPA's reading of the Oklahoma standards. First, the court correctly observed that the ALJ and the Chief Judicial Officer misinterpreted § 4.10(c) of the standards as governing only the discharge of phosphorus into lakes, rather than the discharge of phosphorus into lakes and into all "perennial and intermittent streams." *Id.*, at 617 (emphasis omitted). This error was harmless because the ALJ found that the discharge into Lake Francis would comply with § 4.10(c) and it is undisputed that that discharge produced a greater threat to the slow-moving water of the Lake than to the rapid flow in the River.

The second flaw identified by the court was the ALJ's mistaken reliance on the 1985, rather than the 1982 version, of the Oklahoma standards. We agree with the Chief Judicial Officer, who also noted this error, that the portions of the two versions relevant to this case "do not differ materially." App. to Pet. for Cert. in No. 90-1262, p. 150a. Therefore, this error was also harmless.

Because these two errors were harmless, we have focused in the text on the major difference between the court's and the EPA's readings of the Oklahoma standards: the "no degradation" provision.

[14]Oklahoma's water quality standards closely track the EPA's model standards in effect at that time. Compare § 3 of the Oklahoma standards with 40 CFR § 35.1550(e)(1) (1981).

purpose of authorizing the EPA to create and manage a uniform system of interstate water pollution regulation.

Because we recognize that, at least insofar as they affect the issuance of a permit in another State, the Oklahoma standards have a federal character, the EPA's reasonable, consistently held interpretation of those standards is entitled to substantial deference. Cf. *INS v. National Center for Immigrants' Rights*, 502 U.S. ___ (1991) (slip op., at 6); *Chevron U.S.A. Inc. v. Natural Resources Defense Council, Inc.*, 467 U.S. 837 (1984). In this case, the Chief Judicial Officer ruled that the Oklahoma standards — which require that there be "no degradation" of the upper Illinois River — would only be violated if the discharge effected an "actually detectable or measurable" change in water quality.

This interpretation of the Oklahoma standards is certainly reasonable and consistent with the purposes and principles of the Clean Water Act. As the Chief Judicial Officer noted, "unless there is some method for measuring compliance, there is no way to ensure compliance." Moreover, this interpretation of the Oklahoma standards makes eminent sense in the interstate context: if every discharge that had some theoretical impact on a downstream State were interpreted as "degrading" the downstream waters, downstream States might wield an effective veto over upstream discharges.

The EPA's application of those standards in this case was also sound. On remand, the ALJ scrutinized the record and made explicit factual findings regarding four primary measures of water quality under the Oklahoma standards: eutrophication,[15] aesthetics,[16] dissolved oxygen,[17] and metals.[18] In each case, the ALJ found that the Fayetteville discharge would not lead to a detectable change in water quality. He therefore concluded that the Fayetteville discharge would not violate the Oklahoma water quality standards. Because we agree with the Agency's Chief Judicial Officer that these findings are supported by substantial evidence, we conclude that the Court of Appeals should have affirmed

---

[15]Eutrophication is the "normally slow aging process by which a lake evolves into a bog or marsh.... During eutrophication the lake becomes so rich in nutritive compounds (especially nitrogen and phosphorus) that algae and other microscopic plant life become superabundant, thereby 'choking' the lake...." With regard to eutrophication, the ALJ found that the Fayetteville plant would discharge 30 pounds of phosphorus per day, only about 6 pounds of which would reach the Arkansas/Oklahoma border, and that such a small amount would not result in an increase in eutrophication.

[16]With regard to aesthetics, the ALJ concluded that the only discharged compound that would affect aesthetics was phosphorus and that, again, the amount of that substance crossing the border would not affect the aesthetic quality of Oklahoma's waters.

[17]With regard to dissolved oxygen, the ALJ found that in the 39 miles between discharge and the border the effluent would experience "complete oxygen recovery" and therefore would not affect the dissolved oxygen levels in the River.

[18]With regard to metals, the ALJ concluded that the concentrations of metals would be so low as not to violate the Oklahoma standards.

both the EPA's construction of the regulations and the issuance of the Fayetteville permit.

In its review of the EPA's interpretation and application of the Oklahoma standards, the Court of Appeals committed three mutually compounding errors.

First, the court failed to give due regard to the EPA's interpretation of its own regulations, as those regulations incorporate the Oklahoma standards. Instead the court voiced its own interpretation of the governing law and concluded that "where a proposed source would discharge effluents that would contribute to conditions currently constituting a violation of applicable water quality standards, such [a] proposed source may not be permitted." 908 F.2d, at 620.... That reading of the law is not supported by the statute or by any EPA regulation. The Court of Appeals sat in review of an agency action and should have afforded the EPA's interpretation of the governing law an appropriate level of deference. See generally *Chevron, supra*, at 842-844.

Second, the court disregarded well-established standards for reviewing the factual findings of agencies and instead made its own factual findings. The troubling nature of the court's analysis appears on the face of the opinion itself: at least four times, the court concluded that "there was substantial evidence before the ALJ to support" particular findings which the court thought appropriate, but which were contrary to those actually made by the ALJ. 908 F.2d, at 620, 625, 627, 629. Although we have long recognized the "substantial evidence" standard in administrative law, the court below turned that analysis on its head. A court reviewing an agency's adjudicative action should accept the *agency's* factual findings if those findings are supported by substantial evidence on the record as a whole. See generally *Universal Camera Corp. v. NLRB*, 340 U.S. 474 (1951). The court should not supplant the agency's findings merely by identifying alternative findings that could be supported by substantial evidence.

Third, the court incorrectly concluded that the EPA's decision was arbitrary and capricious. This error is derivative of the court's first two errors. Having substituted its reading of the governing law for the Agency's, and having made its own factual findings, the Court of Appeals concluded that the EPA erred in not considering an important and relevant fact — namely, that the upper Illinois River was (by the court's assessment) already degraded.

As we have often recognized, an agency ruling is "arbitrary and capricious if the agency has ... entirely failed to consider an important aspect of the problem." *Motor Vehicle Mfrs. Assn. of United States, Inc. v. State Farm Mutual Automobile Insurance Co.*, 463 U.S. 29, 43 (1983). However, in this case, the degraded status of the River is only an "important aspect" because of the Court of Appeals' novel and erroneous interpretation of the controlling law. Under the EPA's interpretation of that law, what matters is not the River's current status, but rather whether the proposed discharge will have a "detectable effect" on that status. If the Court of Appeals had been properly respectful of the Agency's permissible reading of the Act and the Oklahoma standards, the court would not have adjudged the Agency's decision arbitrary and capricious for this reason.

In sum, the Court of Appeals made a policy choice that it was not authorized to make. Arguably, as that court suggested, it might be wise to prohibit any discharge into the Illinois River, even if that discharge would have no adverse impact on water quality. But it was surely not arbitrary for the EPA to conclude — given the benefits to the River from the increased flow of relatively clean water[19] and the benefits achieved in Arkansas by allowing the new plant to operate as designed — that allowing the discharge would be even wiser. It is not our role, or that of the Court of Appeals, to decide which policy choice is the better one, for it is clear that Congress has entrusted such decisions to the Environmental Protection Agency.

Accordingly, the judgment of the Court of Appeals is

Reversed.

NOTES AND QUESTIONS

1. Does the Court hold that the Act *requires* compliance with an affected downstream state's water quality standards? What showing of a violation must be made to preclude issuance of a federal permit? Does the opinion strengthen or weaken the position of downstream states in objecting to permits for upstream sources?

2. As a preliminary matter, does Arkansas have standing to challenge generally EPA's interpretation of the FWPCA as requiring a source to comply with the water quality standards of any downstream states? Arkansas did not challenge any of the terms of the permit itself. In finding that Arkansas did have standing, the Court of Appeals emphasized the broad authorization of judicial review in section 509, 33 U.S.C. § 1369:

> Section 509 of the Clean Water Act provides that "[r]eview of [EPA's] action … in [, *inter alia*,] issuing or denying any permit under section 1342 of this title … may be had *by any interested person*." 33 U.S.C. § 1369(b) (emphasis added). The legislative history corroborates what the language itself suggests — that the Act intended liberal review of EPA's actions in issuing permits and promulgating rules and standards. The Senate Public

---

[19]Justice Holmes recognized this potential benefit years ago:

> "There is no pretence that there is a nuisance of the simple kind that was known to the older common law. There is nothing which can be detected by the unassisted senses — no visible increase of filth, no new smell. On the contrary, it is proved that the great volume of pure water from Lake Michigan which is mixed with the sewage at the start has improved the Illinois River in these respects to a noticeable extent. Formerly it was sluggish and ill smelling. Now it is a comparatively clear stream to which edible fish have returned. Its water is drunk by the fisherman, it is said, without evil results." *Missouri v. Illinois*, 200 U.S. 496, 522 (1906).

Works Committee explained section 509's judicial review provision as follows:

> "*Any person* has standing in court to challenge administratively developed standards, rules and regulations under the Act. The courts are increasingly adapting this test to what administrative actions are reviewable.... The Courts have granted this review to those being regulated and to those who seek "to protect the public interest in the proper administration of a regulatory system enacted for their benefit." Since precluding review does not appear to be warranted or desirable, the bill would specifically provide for such review within controlled time periods...."
>
> "... For review of permits issued under section 402 [33 U.S.C. § 1342] ..., the section places jurisdiction in the U.S. Court of Appeals...."

S. Rep. No. 414, 92d Cong., 2d Sess., *reprinted in* 1972 U.S. Code Cong. & Admin. News 3668, 3750-51 (emphasis added; citation omitted); *see also* Conf. Rep. No. 1236, *reprinted in* 1972 U.S. Code Cong. & Admin. News 3776, 3825. The Supreme Court reiterated the expansive language of the Senate Report in *Middlesex County Sewerage Auth. v. National Sea Clammers Ass'n*, 453 U.S. 1, 14 n.23 (1981) ("review provisions of § 509 are open to '[a]ny person,' S. Rep. No. 92-414, p. 85 (1971)"); *cf. Montgomery Envtl. Coalition v. Costle*, 646 F.2d 568, 576-78 (D.C. Cir. 1981) [sic] (§ 509 "incorporate[s] the injury in fact rule for standing set out in *Sierra Club v. Morton*," 405 U.S. 727 (1972) [sic]).

908 F.2d at 599. The court then concluded that it would "strain the meaning of 'any interested person' to exclude from those eligible to obtain review of an EPA permit action the state in which the publicly owned treatment works seeking the permit is located, which partially financed the facility's construction, and which, among other entities, has review and approval authority over the facility's construction and operation." 908 F.2d at 600. Moreover, the court noted it would have to reach the issue regardless of whether Arkansas had standing to raise it, as part of the court's obligation under the Administrative Procedure Act to determine whether EPA's issuance of the permit was within EPA's statutory authority.

3. In what other contexts might the issue of a source in state A contributing to a violation of water quality standards in state B be raised? To answer that question, consider first that the states are required to establish use designations in their state water quality standards in such a way as to protect water quality standards for downstream bodies of water. 40 C.F.R. § 131.10(b). Secondly, consider the case of *Champion Int'l Corp. v. EPA*, 850 F.2d 182 (4th Cir. 1988). The context in which the *Oklahoma v. EPA* case arose is somewhat unusual because EPA was the permitting authority for Arkansas. Most states have EPA-approved programs which authorize state issuance of NPDES permits. In

Champion, North Carolina had such a program and proposed issuance of a permit to a source in North Carolina without regard to its effect on Tennessee water quality standards. EPA objected and assumed permitting authority under FWPCA § 402(d)(4), 33 U.S.C. § 1342(d)(4) (authorizing EPA to veto state issuance of any permit as not in compliance with the FWPCA). How could EPA's action be challenged and by whom? The district court upheld EPA's authority to issue the permit. *Champion Int'l Corp. v. EPA*, 648 F. Supp. 1390 (W.D.N.C. 1986), *motion for withdrawal of mandate denied*, 652 F. Supp. 1398 (W.D.N.C. 1987). It also held that EPA was reasonable in its conclusion that issuance of the permit by North Carolina without regard to Tennessee's water quality standards might not be in compliance with the FWPCA. Nevertheless, in its subsequent opinion, the district court stated, "Nothing in the regulatory framework surrounding the CWA [FWPCA] would automatically require that a source state comply with the water quality standards of every downstream state." 652 F. Supp. at 1400.

The Fourth Circuit Court of Appeals vacated the district court judgment with instructions to dismiss for lack of subject matter jurisdiction. *Champion Int'l Corp. v. EPA*, 850 F.2d 182 (4th Cir. 1988). The Court of Appeals indicated its general agreement with much of the district court opinion and expressed its conclusion that "EPA's act in assuming the permit issuing authority was consistent with statute and regulation, and the objections it made to the North Carolina permit do not seem to be out of bounds." *Id.* at 187. However, the Court of Appeals held that, until EPA had either granted or denied the permit, the actions of EPA were not subject to review under section 509(b)(1), 33 U.S.C. § 1369(b)(1). Thus, the issue of whether a source must comply with the water quality standards of downstream states was not appropriate for judicial review at that stage in EPA's decisionmaking process.

4. EPA by regulation requires states to formulate a comprehensive "Water Quality Management (WQM) Plan" on a state or areawide basis to coordinate all the requirements the Clean Water Act imposes on states. 40 C.F.R. § 130. The plans encompass implementation of nonpoint source management under section 208, 33 U.S.C. § 1288, the planning process for state water quality standards under section 303(e), 33 U.S.C. § 1313(e), the water quality monitoring requirements of section 305, 33 U.S.C. § 1315, and the planning grant requirements of sections 106 and 205, 33 U.S.C. §§ 1256 and 1285. More specifically, plans must include such elements as: (a) identification and ranking of water quality limited stream segments and formulation of total maximum daily loads for the segments under section 303(d), 33 U.S.C. § 1313(d); (b) identification of necessary industrial and municipal treatment facilities and construction priorities under section 208(b)(2), 33 U.S.C. § 1288(b)(2); (c) description of best management practices for nonpoint source pollution as required by section 319, 33 U.S.C. § 1329; (d) identification of agencies to carry out the plan; and (e) identification and development of programs to control groundwater pollution under section 208(b)(2)(K), 33 U.S.C. § 1288(b)(2)(K).

40 C.F.R. § 130.6(c). The planning process includes the biennial water quality report required by section 305(b) on water quality within the state, 40 C.F.R. § 130.8, and development of the section 303 water quality standards. 40 C.F.R. § 130.3. Any construction grant and permit decisions must be consistent with approved WQM plans. *Id.* § 130.6(f).

PUD NO. 1 OF JEFFERSON COUNTY v. WASHINGTON DEPARTMENT OF ECOLOGY

511 U.S. 700, 114 S. Ct. 1900, 128 L. Ed. 2d 716,
38 ERC 1593, 24 Envtl. L. Rep. 20,945 (1994)

JUSTICE O'CONNOR delivered the opinion of the Court.

Petitioners, a city and a local utility district, want to build a hydroelectric project on the Dosewallips River in Washington State. We must decide whether respondent, the state environmental agency, properly conditioned a permit for the project on the maintenance of specific minimum stream flows to protect salmon and steelhead runs.

I

... [T]he Clean Water Act establishes distinct roles for the Federal and State Governments. Under the Act, the Administrator of the Environmental Protection Agency is required, among other things, to establish and enforce technology-based limitations on individual discharges into the country's navigable waters from point sources. Section 303 of the Act also requires each State, subject to federal approval, to institute comprehensive water quality standards establishing water quality goals for all intrastate waters. These state water quality standards provide "a supplementary basis ... so that numerous point sources, despite individual compliance with effluent limitations, may be further regulated to prevent water quality from falling below acceptable levels." [Citation.]

... In setting standards, the State must comply with the following broad requirements: "Such standards shall be such as to protect the public health or welfare, enhance the quality of water and serve the purposes of this chapter. Such standards shall be established taking into consideration their use and value for public water supplies, propagation of fish and wildlife, recreational [and other purposes.]"

A 1987 amendment to the Clean Water Act makes clear that § 303 also contains an "antidegradation policy" requiring that state standards be sufficient to maintain existing beneficial uses of navigable waters, preventing their further degradation. Specifically, the Act permits the revision of certain effluent limitations or water quality standards "only if such revision is subject to and consistent with the antidegradation policy established under this section." Accordingly, EPA's regulations implementing the Act require that state water quality standards include "a statewide antidegradation policy" to ensure that "[e]xisting instream water uses and the level of water quality necessary to protect the existing uses shall be maintained and protected." At a minimum, state water quality standards must satisfy these conditions. The Act also allows States to impose more stringent water quality controls. [Citations.]

The State of Washington has adopted comprehensive water quality standards intended to regulate all of the State's navigable waters. The State created an inventory of all the State's waters, and divided the waters into five classes. Each individual fresh surface water of the State is placed into one of these classes. The Dosewallips River is classified AA, extraordinary.... The standard identifies the designated uses of Class AA waters as well as the criteria applicable to such waters.[1]

In addition to these specific standards applicable to Class AA waters, the State has adopted a statewide antidegradation policy. That policy provides: "(a) Existing beneficial uses shall be maintained and protected and no further degradation which would interfere with or become injurious to existing beneficial uses will be allowed. "(b) No degradation will be allowed of waters lying in national parks, national recreation areas, national wildlife refuges, national scenic rivers, and other areas of national ecological importance.... "(f) In no case, will any degradation of water quality be allowed if this degradation interferes with or becomes injurious to existing water uses and causes long-term and irreparable harm to the environment. As required by the Act, EPA reviewed and approved the State's water quality standards. Upon approval by EPA, the state standard became "the water quality standard for the applicable waters of that State."

States are responsible for enforcing water quality standards on intrastate waters. In addition to these primary enforcement responsibilities, § 401 of the Act requires States to provide a water quality certification before a federal license or permit can be issued for activities that may result in any discharge into intrastate navigable waters.... Section 401(d) further provides that "[a]ny certification ... shall set forth any effluent limitations and other limitations, and monitoring requirements necessary to assure that any applicant ... will comply with any applicable effluent limitations and other limitations, under section 1311 or 1312 of this title ... and with any other appropriate requirement of State law set forth in such certification." 33 U.S.C. § 1341(d). The limitations included in the certification become a condition on any Federal license.

II

Petitioners propose to build the Elkhorn Hydroelectric Project on the Dosewallips River. If constructed as presently planned, the facility would be located just outside the Olympic National Park on federally owned land within

---

[1]WAC 173-201-045(1) provides in pertinent part: (1) Class AA (extraordinary). (a) General characteristic. Water quality of this class shall markedly and uniformly exceed the requirements for all or substantially all uses. (b) Characteristic uses. Characteristic uses shall include, but not be limited to, the following: (iii) Fish and shellfish: Salmonid migration, rearing, spawning, and harvesting. Other fish migration, rearing, spawning, and harvesting....

the Olympic National Forest. The project would divert water from a 1.2-mile reach of the River (the bypass reach), run the water through turbines to generate electricity and then return the water to the River below the bypass reach. Under the Federal Power Act (FPA), the Federal Energy Regulatory Commission has authority to license new hydroelectric facilities. As a result, the petitioners must get a FERC license to build or operate the Elkhorn Project. Because a federal license is required, and because the project may result in discharges into the Dosewallips River, petitioners are also required to obtain State certification of the project pursuant to § 401 of the Clean Water Act.

The water flow in the bypass reach ranges seasonally between 149 and 738 cubic feet per second. The Dosewallips supports two species of salmon, Coho and Chinook, as well as Steelhead trout. The project was to include a diversion dam which would completely block the river and channel approximately 75% of the River's water into a tunnel alongside the streambed. About 25% of the water would remain in the bypass reach, but would be returned to the original riverbed through sluice gates or a fish ladder. Depending on the season, this would leave a residual minimum flow of between 65 and 155 cfs in the River. Respondent undertook a study to determine the minimum stream flows necessary to protect the salmon and steelhead fisheries in the bypass reach. On June 11, 1986, respondent issued a § 401 water quality certification imposing a variety of conditions on the project, including a minimum stream-flow requirement of between 100 and 200 cfs depending on the season.

A state administrative appeals board determined that the minimum flow requirement was intended to enhance, not merely maintain, the fishery, and that the certification condition therefore exceeded respondent's authority under state law. On appeal, the state Superior Court concluded that respondent could require compliance with the minimum flow conditions. The Superior Court also found that respondent had imposed the minimum flow requirement to protect and preserve the fishery, not to improve it, and that this requirement was authorized by state law.

The Washington Supreme Court held that the antidegradation provisions of the State's water quality standards require the imposition of minimum stream flows. The court also found that § 401(d), which allows States to impose conditions based upon several enumerated sections of the Clean Water Act and "any other appropriate requirement of State law," authorized the stream flow condition. Relying on this language and the broad purposes of the Clean Water Act, the court concluded that § 401(d) confers on States power to "consider all state action related to water quality in imposing conditions on section 401 certificates." We granted certiorari, to resolve a conflict among the state courts of last resort. [Citations.] We now affirm.

III

The principal dispute in this case concerns whether the minimum stream flow requirement that the State imposed on the Elkhorn project is a permissible condition of a § 401 certification under the Clean Water Act. To resolve this dispute we must first determine the scope of the State's authority under § 401. We must then determine whether the limitation at issue here, the requirement that petitioners maintain minimum stream flows, falls within the scope of that authority.

A

There is no dispute that petitioners were required to obtain a certification from the State pursuant to § 401. Petitioners concede that, at a minimum, the project will result in two possible discharges — the release of dredged and fill material during the construction of the project, and the discharge of water at the end of the tailrace after the water has been used to generate electricity. Petitioners contend, however, that the minimum stream flow requirement imposed by the State was unrelated to these specific discharges, and that as a consequence, the State lacked the authority under § 401 to condition its certification on mainte-nance of stream flows sufficient to protect the Dosewallips fishery.

... [Section 401] also contains subsection (d), which expands the State's authority to impose conditions on the certification of a project. Section 401(d) provides that any certification shall set forth "any effluent limitations and other limitations ... necessary to assure that any applicant" will comply with various provisions of the Act and appropriate state law requirements. The language of this subsection contradicts petitioners' claim that the State may only impose water quality limitations specifically tied to a "discharge." The text refers to the compliance of the applicant, not the discharge. Section 401(d) thus allows the State to impose "other limitations" on the project in general to assure compliance with various provisions of the Clean Water Act and with "any other appropriate requirement of State law."...

Our view of the statute is consistent with EPA's regulations implementing § 401. The regulations expressly interpret § 401 as requiring the State to find that "there is a reasonable assurance that the activity will be conducted in a manner which will not violate applicable water quality standards." [Citations.] EPA's conclusion that activities — not merely discharges — must comply with state water quality standards is a reasonable interpretation of § 401, and is entitled to deference. [Citations.]

Although § 401(d) authorizes the State to place restrictions on the activity as a whole, that authority is not unbounded. The State can only ensure that the project complies with "any applicable effluent limitations and other limitations, or certain other provisions of the Act, "and with any other appropriate requirement of State law." The State asserts that the minimum stream flow requirement was imposed to ensure compliance with the state water quality standards adopted pursuant to § 303 of the Clean Water Act. 33 U.S.C. § 1313.

We agree with the State that ensuring compliance with § 303 is a proper function of the § 401 certification. Although § 303 is not one of the statutory provisions listed in § 401(d), the statute allows states to impose limitations to ensure compliance with § 301 of the Act. Section 301 in turn incorporates § 303 by reference. [Citations.] As a consequence, state water quality standards adopted pursuant to § 303 are among the "other limitations" with which a State may ensure compliance through the § 401 certification process. This interpretation is consistent with EPA's view of the statute. Moreover, limitations to assure compliance with state water quality standards are also permitted by § 401(d)'s reference to "any other appropriate requirement of State law." We do not speculate on what additional state laws, if any, might be incorporated by this language. But at a minimum, limitations imposed pursuant to state water quality standards adopted pursuant to § 303 are "appropriate" requirements of state law....

B

Having concluded that, pursuant to § 401, States may condition certification upon any limitations necessary to ensure compliance with state water quality standards or any other "appropriate requirement of State law," we consider whether the minimum flow condition is such a limitation. Under § 303, state water quality standards must "consist of the designated uses of the navigable waters involved and the water quality criteria for such waters based upon such uses." In imposing the minimum stream flow requirement, the State determined that construction and operation of the project as planned would be inconsistent with one of the designated uses of Class AA water, namely "[s]almonid [and other fish] migration, rearing, spawning, and harvesting." The designated use of the River as a fish habitat directly reflects the Clean Water Act's goal of maintaining the "chemical, physical, and biological integrity of the Nation's waters."... Moreover, the Act expressly requires that, in adopting water quality standards, the State must take into consideration the use of waters for "propagation of fish and wildlife."

Petitioners assert, however, that § 303 requires the State to protect designated uses solely through implementation of specific "criteria." According to petitioners, the State may not require them to operate their dam in a manner consistent with a designated "use"; instead, say petitioners, under § 303 the State may only require that the project comply with specific numerical "criteria."

We disagree with petitioners' interpretation of the language of § 303(c)(2)(A). Under the statute, a water quality standard must "consist of the designated uses of the navigable waters involved and the water quality criteria for such waters based upon such uses." The text makes it plain that water quality standards contain two components. We think the language of § 303 is most naturally read to require that a project be consistent with both components, namely the designated use and the water quality criteria. Accordingly, under the literal terms of the statute, a project that does not comply with a designated use of the water does not comply with the applicable water quality standards.

Consequently, pursuant to § 401(d) the State may require that a permit applicant comply with both the designated uses and the water quality criteria of the state standards. In granting certification pursuant to § 401(d), the State "shall set forth any ... limitations ... necessary to assure that [the applicant] will comply with any ... limitations under [§ 303] ... and with any other appropriate requirement of State law." A certification requirement that an applicant operate the project consistently with state water quality standards — i.e., consistently with the designated uses of the water body and the water quality criteria — is both a "limitation" to assure "compliance with ... limitations" imposed under § 303, and an "appropriate" requirement of State law.

EPA has not interpreted § 303 to require the States to protect designated uses exclusively through enforcement of numerical criteria. In its regulations governing state water quality standards, EPA defines criteria as "elements of State water quality standards expressed as constituent concentrations, levels, or narrative statements, representing a quality of water that supports a particular use." The regulations further provide that "[w]hen criteria are met, water quality will generally protect the designated use." Thus, the EPA regulations implicitly recognize that in some circumstances, criteria alone are insufficient to protect a designated use.

... Washington's Class AA water quality standards are typical in that they contain several open-ended criteria which, like the use designation of the River as a fishery, must be translated into specific limitations for individual projects.... We think petitioners' attempt to distinguish between uses and criteria loses much of its force in light of the fact that the Act permits enforcement of broad, narrative criteria based on, for example, "aesthetics."

Petitioners further argue that enforcement of water quality standards through use designations renders the water quality criteria component of the standards irrelevant. We see no anomaly, however, in the State's reliance on both use designations and criteria to protect water quality. The specific numerical limitations embodied in the criteria are a convenient enforcement mechanism for identifying minimum water conditions which will generally achieve the requisite water quality. And, in most circumstances, satisfying the criteria will, as EPA recognizes, be sufficient to maintain the designated use. Water quality standards, however, apply to an entire class of water, a class which contains numerous individual water bodies.... While enforcement of criteria will in general protect the uses of these diverse waters, a complementary requirement that activities also comport with designated uses enables the States to ensure that each activity — even if not foreseen by the criteria — will be consistent with the specific uses and attributes of a particular body of water.

... The criteria components of state water quality standards attempt to identify, for all the water bodies in a given class, water quality requirements generally sufficient to protect designated uses. These criteria, however, cannot reasonably be expected to anticipate all the water quality issues arising from every activity which can affect the State's hundreds of individual water bodies. Requiring the States to enforce only the criteria component of their water quality standards would in essence require the States to study to a level of great specificity each individual surface water to ensure that the criteria applicable to that water are sufficiently detailed and individualized to fully protect the water's designated uses. Given that there is no textual support for imposing this requirement, we are loath to attribute to Congress an intent to impose this heavy regulatory burden on the States.

The State also justified its minimum stream flow as necessary to implement the "antidegradation policy" of § 303. When the Clean Water Act was enacted in 1972, the water quality standards of all 50 States had antidegradation provisions. These provisions were required by federal law....

EPA has promulgated regulations implementing § 303's antidegradation policy, a phrase that is not defined elsewhere in the Act. These regulations require States to "develop and adopt a statewide antidegradation policy and identify the methods for implementing such policy." These "implementation methods shall, at a minimum, be consistent with the ... [e]xisting instream water uses and the level of water quality necessary to protect the existing uses shall be maintained and protected." EPA has explained that under its antidegradation regulation, "no activity is allowable ... which could partially or completely eliminate any existing use." Thus, States must implement their antidegradation policy in a manner "consistent" with existing uses of the stream. The State of Washington's antidegradation policy in turn provides that "[e]xisting beneficial uses shall be maintained and protected and no further degradation which would interfere with or become injurious to existing beneficial uses will be allowed." The State concluded that the reduced streamflows would have just the effect prohibited by this policy. We agree, that the State's minimum stream flow condition is a proper application of the state and federal antidegradation regulations, as it ensures that an "existing instream water us[e]" will be "maintained and protected."

Petitioners also assert more generally that the Clean Water Act is only concerned with water "quality," and does not allow the regulation of water "quantity." This is an artificial distinction.... First, the Act's definition of pollution as "the man-made or man induced alteration of the chemical, physical, biological, and radiological integrity of water" encompasses the effects of reduced water quantity.... Moreover, § 304 of the Act expressly recognizes that water "pollution" may result from "changes in the movement, flow, or circulation of any navigable waters ... including changes caused by the construction of dams." This concern with the flowage effects of dams and other diversions is also embodied in the EPA regulations, which expressly require existing dams to be operated to attain designated uses.

Petitioners assert that two other provisions of the Clean Water Act, §§ 101(g) and 510(2), exclude the regulation of water quantity from the coverage of the Act. Section 101(g) provides "that the authority of each State to allocate quantities of water within its jurisdiction shall not be superseded, abrogated or otherwise impaired by this chapter." Similarly, § 510(2) provides that nothing in the Act shall "be construed as impairing or in any manner affecting any right or jurisdiction of the States with respect to the waters ... of such States."...

This language gives the States authority to allocate water rights; we therefore find it peculiar that petitioners argue that it prevents the State from regulating stream flow. In any event, we read these provisions more narrowly than petitioners. Sections 101(g) and 510(2) preserve the authority of each State to allocate water quantity as between users; they do not limit the scope of water pollution controls that may be imposed on users who have obtained, pursuant to state law, a water allocation.... Moreover, the certification itself does not purport to determine petitioners' proprietary right to the water of the Dosewallips. In fact, the certification expressly states that a "State Water Right Permit must be obtained prior to commencing construction of the project." The certification merely determines the nature of the use to which that proprietary right may be put under the Clean Water Act, if and when it is obtained from the State....

IV

Petitioners contend that we should limit the State's authority to impose minimum flow requirements because FERC has comprehensive authority to license hydroelectric projects pursuant to the FPA, 16 U.S.C. § 791a et seq....

The FPA empowers FERC to issue licenses for projects "necessary or convenient ... for the development, transmission, and utilization of power across, along, from, or in any of the streams ... over which Congress has jurisdiction." § 797(e). The FPA also requires FERC to consider a project's effect on fish and wildlife. §§ 797(e), 803(a)(1). In *California v. FERC, supra,* we held that the California Water Resources Control Board, acting pursuant to state law, could not impose a minimum stream flow which conflicted with minimum stream flows contained in a FERC license. We concluded that the FPA did not "save" to the States this authority.

No such conflict with any FERC licensing activity is presented here. FERC has not yet acted on petitioners' license application, and it is possible that FERC will eventually deny petitioners' application altogether....

Finally, the requirement for a state certification applies not only to applications for licenses from FERC, but to all federal licenses and permits for activities which may result in a discharge into the Nation's navigable waters....

In summary, we hold that the State may include minimum stream flow requirements in a certification issued pursuant to § 401 of the Clean Water Act insofar as necessary to enforce a designated use contained in a state water quality standard. The judgment of the Supreme Court of Washington, accordingly, is affirmed.

So ordered.

NOTES AND QUESTIONS

1. Could the state have simply denied a water rights permit for the dam instead of refusing state certification? After *Jefferson County,* can a state refuse certification because a federal project would impair the recreational use of a stream segment? Because the stream segment was protected by a state scenic river law? To ensure compliance with state and local land use regulations?

2. Water quality standards may not be challenged themselves in proceedings for federally issued permits, but must instead be challenged in an action against the state officers who established the standards. *United States Steel Corp. v. Train*, 556 F.2d 822, 836 (7th Cir. 1977). Pre-enforcement review of state standards may be available against state officials in state court after adoption and in federal court against EPA after federal approval or disapproval of state standards. *See Commonwealth Edison Co. v. Train*, 649 F.2d 481, 486 (7th Cir. 1980). Otherwise, the only recourse is a citizen suit challenging EPA approval of a state water quality standard for failing to meet the federal requirements for state water quality standards.

3. In *Oregon Natural Resources Council v. United States Forest Serv.*, 834 F.2d 842 (9th Cir. 1987), the Ninth Circuit Court of Appeals held that a citizen suit cannot be brought to enforce water quality standards for nonpoint source pollution because a citizen suit under section 505 can only be brought to enforce requirements in NPDES permits governing point source pollution. Drawing on that reasoning, the Ninth Circuit held that water quality standards could not be enforced in a citizen suit unless they had been translated into numerical limits in the specific permit, because otherwise they would not be "effluent limitations" within the meaning of the citizen suit provision. *Northwest Environmental Advocates v. Portland*, 11 F.3d 900 (9th Cir. 1993), *cert. denied*, 116 S. Ct. 2550 (1996). In the following opinion, the Ninth Circuit had to reconsider its earlier opinion in light of the Supreme Court's decision in the *Jefferson County* case.

NORTHWEST ENVIRONMENTAL ADVOCATES v. PORTLAND

56 F.3d 979 (9th Cir. 1995),
cert. denied, 116 S. Ct. 2550 (1996)

OPINION: Pregerson, Circuit Judge:

Northwest Environmental Advocates and Nina Bell ("NWEA") appeal the district court's judgment in favor of Portland on their claims that the City is violating the Clean Water Act ("CWA"), 33 U.S.C. § 1251 *et seq.* On April 16, 1991, NWEA filed suit in the district court alleging that Portland's practice of discharging raw sewage during times of precipitation from 54 outfall points was not covered by a permit and that the practice had caused and was continuing to cause violations of Oregon's water quality standards....

In *Northwest Environmental Advocates v. City of Portland*, 11 F.3d 900 (9th Cir. 1993) (Northwest), we affirmed. We held that the contested discharge points were covered by Portland's pollution permit, *id.* at 903-06, and we held that Northwest Environmental Advocates lacked standing to bring a citizen suit under § 505(a)(1) of the Clean Water Act, 33 U.S.C. § 1365(a)(1), to enforce water quality standards contained in Portland's permit. *Id.* at 906-11. On December 28,

1993, NWEA filed a petition for rehearing with suggestion for rehearing en banc. While this petition was still pending, the Supreme Court decided *PUD No. 1 of Jefferson County v. Washington Department of Ecology*, ...

....

The plain language of CWA § 505 authorizes citizens to enforce *all* permit conditions. That section provides: "[A]ny citizen may commence a civil action ... (1) against any person ... who is alleged to be in violation of (A) an effluent standard or limitation under [the Clean Water Act]...." 33 U.S.C. § 1365(a)(1)-(A). An effluent standard or limitation includes "(2) an effluent limitation or other limitation under section 1311 ... *or* (6) a permit or condition thereof...." 33 U.S.C. § 1365(f)(2), (f)(6) (emphasis added). This language clearly contemplates citizen suits to enforce "a permit or condition thereof." Portland holds a National Pollutant Discharge Elimination System (NPDES) permit, and the water quality standards are conditions of its permit.

....

By introducing effluent limitations into the CWA scheme, Congress intended to improve enforcement, not to supplant the old system....

Ample case law supports our view that Congress intended to confer citizens standing to enforce water quality standards. Most notably, in *PUD No. 1 of Jefferson County v. Washington Department of Ecology*, the Supreme Court held that the Clean Water Act allows States to enforce the broad narrative criteria contained in water quality standards....

....

The county's losing argument in *Jefferson County* is very similar to the argument advanced by Portland in the instant case. Portland argues that citizens may not enforce the broad narrative conditions of state water quality standards, but may enforce only those conditions that have been translated into numeric effluent limitations.

We disagree with Portland's contention that *Jefferson County* is inapposite to the issue before us. Even though *Jefferson County* involved a state's authority to impose conditions under CWA § 401, whereas the present litigation involves citizen suit enforcement of CWA § 402 conditions, both the § 401 certification process and the § 402 permit process require applicants to comply with CWA § 301. As noted above, § 301 incorporates by reference the water quality requirements of § 303.

Moreover, although *Jefferson County* addressed the authority of States, not citizens, to enforce the narrative conditions of CWA § 303 water quality standards, nothing in the language of the Clean Water Act, the legislative history, or the implementing regulations restricts citizens from enforcing the same conditions of a certificate or permit that a State may enforce. To the contrary, as demonstrated above, these sources uniformly support broad citizen enforcement authority, including the authority to enforce water quality standards.

....

Because the statutory language, legislative history, and case law authorize citizens to enforce permit conditions stated in terms of water quality standards, we hold that NWEA has standing to enforce the water quality standards contained in Portland's NPDES permit.

....

In short, NWEA II contradicts the plain language of the Clean Water Act, conflicts with a prior decision of this circuit, and creates a needless intercircuit conflict with all courts of appeals that have addressed the issue. The decision establishes a citizens' cause of action that Congress never intended and that no other circuit has felt compelled to recognize.

NOTES AND QUESTIONS

1. When Portland petitioned for rehearing en banc, the petition was denied. In dissent, four judges explained why the petition should have been granted:

> By failing to rehear this case en banc, we have significantly reshaped federal environmental law, without consent of Congress, to the curious end that any citizen will now be permitted to bring a lawsuit at government expense for the enforcement of state water quality standards that have not been translated into effluent limitations in federal permits. Such unwarranted expansion of citizen standing conflicts with the plain language of the Clean Water Act and with prior decisions of this circuit and others.

74 F.3d 945, 946-948 (9th Cir. 1996) (dissenting opinion), *cert. denied*, 116 S. Ct. 2550 (1996).

No other circuit has recognized a right of citizens to sue for the enforcement of state water quality standards contained in permits. In fact, other circuits have explicitly and implicitly ruled out such suits. *See Save Our Community v. United States Environmental Protection Agency*, 971 F.2d 1155, 1162 (5th Cir. 1992) ("Without the violation of either (1) an effluent standard or limitation under the CWA, or (2) an order issued with respect to these standards and limitations, the district court lacks jurisdiction to act [in a citizen suit]."); *United States v. Hooker Chemicals & Plastics Corp.*, 749 F.2d 968, 979 (2d Cir. 1984) ("'[a]uthority granted to citizens to bring enforcement actions under this section is limited to effluent standards or limitations established administratively under the Act'" (quoting S. Rep. No. 414, 92d Cong., 2d Sess. 80 (1972), *reprinted in* 1972 U.S.C.C.A.N. 3668, 3747)).

Furthermore, the holding in NWEA II directly conflicts with the Second Circuit's decision in *Atlantic States Legal Found. v. Eastman Kodak*, 12 F.3d 353 (2d Cir. 1993), *cert. denied*, ___ U.S. ___, 115 S. Ct. 62, 130 L. Ed. 2d 19, 115 S. Ct. 62 (1994). In *Atlantic States*, the Second Circuit held that "state regulations, including the provisions of SPDES [State Pollutant Discharge Elimination System] permits, which mandate 'a greater scope of coverage than that required' by the federal CWA and its implementing regulations are not enforceable through a citizen suit under 33 U.S.C. § 1365." *Id.* at 359 (citation omitted). In addition, the court noted:

> States may enact stricter standards for wastewater effluents than mandated by the CWA and federal EPA regulations. 33 U.S.C. § 1342(b). These states' standards may be enforced under the CWA by the states or the EPA, 33 U.S.C. § 1342(h), but private citizens have no standing to do so.

Id. at 358.

2. Is the section 401 certification required for nonpoint source discharges as well as point source discharges? In *Oregon Natural Desert Assoc. v. Thomas,* 940 F. Supp. 1534 (D. Ore. 1996), the district court held that the U.S. Forest Service could not issue federal cattle grazing permits without state certification. Appeal to the Ninth Circuit Court of Appeals seems likely, because a 1996 Idaho district court decision reached a conflicting result with respect to a federal permit to build a logging road.

3. The Water Quality Act of 1987 added five programs to the Clean Water Act to improve water quality in the Chesapeake Bay, the Great Lakes region, lakes suffering from eutrophication, national estuaries, and so-called toxic "hot spots." Under section 117, 33 U.S.C. § 1267, for the Chesapeake Bay program a state or combination of states may submit to EPA a proposal to implement "management mechanisms" in a plan which must include a description of proposed methods to reduce pollution and meet water quality standards along with the estimated cost of such measures. FWPCA § 117(b)(2), 33 U.S.C. § 1267(b)(2). If EPA approves the plan as consistent with the policies and goals of the Clean Water Act, grants of up to fifty percent of the costs of implementing the plan's management mechanisms are available. FWPCA § 117(b)(3), 33 U.S.C. § 1267(b)(3). The section also authorizes an authority within the Chesapeake Bay programs of EPA to coordinate state and federal regulation of water quality in the Bay and to determine the impact of sediment deposition and environmental changes on the Bay. FWPCA § 117(a), 33 U.S.C. § 1267(a).

Section 118 primarily authorizes funding for states to control pollution in the Great Lakes area. FWPCA § 118, 33 U.S.C. § 1268. The section gives the Great Lakes National Program Office in EPA the responsibility for developing, in conjunction with the Great Lakes states, a five-year program for reducing the amount of nutrients released into the Great Lakes. FWPCA § 118(c)(2), 33 U.S.C. § 1268(c)(2). The Program Office is also directed to carry out a five-year study and demonstration project on control of toxic pollutants in the Great Lakes. FWPCA § 118(c)(3), 33 U.S.C. § 1268(c)(3). The time periods within which states are to carry out their responsibilities and the resources to be committed are the ultimate responsibility of EPA. FWPCA § 118(c)(4), 33 U.S.C. § 1268(c)(4).

Under the Clean Lakes program established in section 314, 33 U.S.C. § 1324, every state, on a biennial basis, must submit to EPA for approval a program: (a) identifying and classifying all publicly owned lakes within the state based on eutrophication; (b) describing methods, including land use requirements, for controlling pollution and restoring the quality of such lakes; (c) outlining methods and procedures to mitigate high acidity; (d) listing and describing publicly owned lakes for which designated uses are known to be impaired, including those lakes known not to meet water quality standards, those which require implementation of control programs to maintain compliance with water quality standards, and those in which water quality has deteriorated as a result of high acidity that may reasonably be due to acid deposition; and (e) assessing the status and trends of water quality in the state's publicly owned lakes. FWPCA § 314(a)(1), 33 U.S.C. § 1324(a)(1). States may receive grants from EPA for up to seventy percent of the costs of carrying out the methods and procedures for controlling lake pollution which are in any EPA approved state program. FWPCA § 314(b), (c)(1), 33 U.S.C. § 1324(b), (c)(1). EPA is also directed to establish a lake water quality demonstration program which, among other directives, is to develop cost-effective control technologies and control methods for nonpoint source pollution. FWPCA § 314(d), 33 U.S.C. § 1324(d).

Under the national estuary program set out in section 320, 33 U.S.C. § 1330, the governor of a state may nominate estuaries lying entirely or partly within the state to EPA as estuaries of national significance and request a management conference to develop a management plan for the estuaries. FWPCA § 320(a)(1), 33 U.S.C. § 1330(a)(1). The Administrator may also determine that an estuary is of national significance. FWPCA § 320(a)(2)(A), 33 U.S.C. § 1330(a)(2)(A). When the attainment or maintenance of water quality which "assures protection of public water supplies and the protection and propagation of a balanced, indigenous population of shellfish, fish, and wildlife, and allows recreational activities, in and on the water," necessitates additional control of point and nonpoint source pollution, the Administrator of EPA must convene a management conference. *Id.* The basic purposes of a management conference are to assess water quality problems in the estuary and develop a comprehensive plan that includes corrective actions and compliance schedules for point and nonpoint source pollution in order to restore the water quality. FWPCA § 320(b), 33 U.S.C. § 1330(b). Participants in the conference include the Administrator of EPA as well as federal, state, and local officials with interests in or jurisdiction over the estuarine zone. FWPCA § 320(c), 33 U.S.C. § 1330(c). A conference is convened for a period not to exceed five years, although the conference may be extended by the Administrator. FWPCA § 320(e), 33 U.S.C. § 1330(e). Not more than 120 days after an opportunity for public review and comment on a completed plan, the Administrator must approve a plan which meets the section's requirements, if the affected governor or governors concur. FWPCA § 320(f)(1), 33 U.S.C. § 1330(f)(1). Federal grants are available for up to seventy-five percent of the costs of developing and administering an estuarine management plan. FWPCA § 320(f)(2), (g), 33 U.S.C. § 1330(f)(2), (g).

The section 304(*l*), 33 U.S.C. § 1314(*l*) program for control of toxic "hot spots" is discussed in Section F below.

F. TOXIC WATER POLLUTANTS

As mentioned above, pages 525-26 *supra*, the 1972 FWPCA required EPA to set effluent limitations for toxic pollutants adequate to provide an "ample margin of safety." FWPCA § 307, 33 U.S.C. § 1317. Unlike the technology based standards imposed without regard to water quality impacts, this standard for toxic pollutants is designed to preserve the water quality necessary to protect public health and the environment. The standards are promulgated as uniform national restrictions by classes of sources. *See, e.g., Environmental Defense Fund v. EPA*, 598 F.2d 62 (D.C. Cir. 1978). EPA has promulgated standards for only six pollutants under the margin standard since 1972: aldrin/dieldrin, DDT, endrin, toxaphene, benzidene, and PCBs. 40 C.F.R. § 129.4.

In 1977, Congress concluded that the health-based standard in section 307 had been ineffective and introduced another standard for toxic pollutants into the Act. For the second tier of protection after BPT, best available control technology had to be implemented for toxic pollutants by March 31, 1989. FWPCA § 301(b)(2)-(C)-(D), 33 U.S.C. § 1311(b)(2)(C)-(D). A consent decree requiring EPA to apply BAT for sixty-five toxic pollutants discharged by twenty-one industry subcategories was incorporated into the Act. FWPCA § 301(b)(2)(C), 33 U.S.C. § 1311(b)(2)(C). In determining whether to list other pollutants as toxic, the Administrator may consider their toxicity, persistence, degradability, the presence of affected organisms in any waters, the importance of affected organisms, and the nature and extent of the effect of the pollutants on any affected organisms. FWPCA § 307(a)(1), 33 U.S.C. § 1317(a)(1). The ample margin standard for toxic pollutants, however, still remained in effect so that toxic pollutants can be regulated by EPA either through BAT or the ample margin of safety standard. *Hercules, Inc. v. EPA*, 598 F.2d 91, 102 (D.C. Cir. 1978) (quoting Senator Muskie as saying the test for regulating a pollutant under the health-based standard rather than the technology-based standard is whether "there is sufficient information on toxicity to establish a separate nationwide effluent standard for that pollutant").

Prior to the Water Quality Act of 1987, EPA had attempted to identify toxic "hot spots," areas in which water quality was impaired by toxic pollutants even after application of BAT, new source performance standards, and pretreatment standards. *See generally* Gaba, *Federal Supervision of State Water Quality Standards Under the Clean Water Act*, 36 VAND. L. REV. 1167, 1216 (1983). Although EPA regulations required states to review stream segments to determine where toxic discharges warrant concern, EPA had not adopted requirements for controls in toxic hot spots.

The Water Quality Act of 1987 added a new subsection 304(*l*), 33 U.S.C. § 1314(*l*), specifically addressing the problem of toxic hot spots. By February 4, 1989 each state had to submit to EPA for review, approval, and implementation a control strategy for toxic hot spots. FWPCA § 304(*l*)(1), 33 U.S.C. § 1314(*l*)-(1). The strategy had to include: (a) a list of those waters which, after application of the Act's technological controls, cannot reasonably be expected to attain or maintain water quality standards or that water quality necessary to achieve the "fishable" and "swimmable" goals of the Act due to toxic pollution; (b) a determination of the specific point sources discharging toxic pollutants at a level believed to be preventing or impairing water quality in such waters and the amount of toxic pollution from each such source; and (c) an individual control strategy for each segment of such waters to achieve applicable water quality standards "as soon as possible, but not later than three years after the date of the establishment of such strategy." *Id.* The Administrator must approve or disapprove the state's control strategy within 120 days after the deadline for submission. FWPCA § 304(*l*)(2), 33 U.S.C. § 1314(*l*)(2). If the state fails to meet the section's requirements, the Administrator of EPA may impose a control strategy for the state. FWPCA § 304(*l*)(3), 33 U.S.C. § 1314(*l*)(3).

NATURAL RESOURCES DEFENSE COUNCIL v. ENVIRONMENTAL PROTECTION AGENCY

915 F.2d 1314 (9th Cir. 1990)

FLETCHER, CIRCUIT JUDGE.

The Natural Resources Defense Council (NRDC) petitions for review of a final rule issued by the Environmental Protection Agency (EPA). The rule provides that with regard to some, but not all, of the polluted waters listed pursuant to section 304(*l*) of the Clean Water Act, 33 U.S.C. § 1314(*l*), the states must identify the factories and other "point sources" responsible for discharging toxic pollutants into those waters and must develop strategies to control the pollution from those sources in an expedited manner. 40 C.F.R. §§ 123.46, 130.10. The NRDC argues that with regard to *all* of the listed waters, the states must identify "point source" toxic polluters and must develop strategies to control all the sources identified.

....

Prior to 1972, Congress attempted to control water pollution by focusing regulatory efforts on achieving "water quality standards," standards set by the states specifying the tolerable degree of pollution for particular waters....

Congress, in passing the Clean Water Act, ... shifted the focus of the water pollution laws away from the enforcement of water quality standards and toward the enforcement of technological standards. But Congress recognized that even if all the firms discharging pollutants into a certain stream segment were using the best available technology, the stream still might not be clean enough to meet the water quality standards set by the states. To deal with this problem, Congress supplemented the "technology-based" limitations with "water-quality-based" limitations. *See* CWA §§ 302, 303, 33 U.S.C. §§ 1312, 1313.

....

Under sections 301(b)(1)(C) and 402(a)(1), 33 U.S.C. §§ 1311(b)(1)(C), 1342(a)(1), NPDES permit writers were to impose, along with the technology-based limitations, any more stringent limitations on discharges necessary to meet the water quality standards. Although ostensibly they were supposed to impose these more stringent limitations, in practice they often did not.

One explanation for this failure is that the criteria listed by the states, particularly for toxic pollutants, were often vague narrative or descriptive criteria as opposed to specific numerical criteria. These descriptive criteria were difficult to translate into enforceable limits on discharges from individual polluters....

In 1987 Congress reexamined the water pollution laws. It found that the requirement that individual polluters use the best available technology was not sufficient to solve the pollution problem, particularly the problem of toxic pollutants; a renewed emphasis on water quality-based standards was necessary. Congress enacted a number of new provisions....

... Congress enacted new CWA section 304(*l*), 33 U.S.C. § 1314(*l*), the section directly at issue in this petition....

Section 304(*l*) requires the preparation of three lists. The list required by section 304(*l*)(1)(B) (hereinafter the "B list") is the narrowest of the three lists. It consists only of waters that are not expected to meet water quality standards, even after the application of the technology-based limitations, due entirely or substantially to toxic pollution from *point sources*. The list required by section 304(*l*)(1)(A)(i) (hereinafter the "A(i) list") is broader; it includes most of the waters on the B list plus waters expected not to meet water quality standards due to pollution attributable entirely or almost entirely to toxic pollution from *nonpoint sources*. The list required by section 304(*l*)(1)(A)(ii) (hereinafter the "A(ii) list") is the broadest. It includes all the waters on the other two lists plus any waters which, after the implementation of technology-based controls, are not expected to meet the water quality goals of the Act; since the goals of the Act are sometimes higher than the state standards, the A(ii) list includes even some waters expected to comply fully with applicable water quality standards.

The effect of the individual control strategies is simply to expedite the imposition of water-quality-based limitations on polluters — limitations which otherwise would have had to be imposed when the polluters' NPDES permits expired. NPDES permits are issued for periods of no more than five years, although administrative delays can extend *de facto* the duration of the permits.

The EPA has promulgated a number of regulations interpreting the statute; two are particularly important for our purposes. The first regulation, codified at 40 C.F.R. § 130.10(d), interprets sections 304(*l*)(1)(A), (B), and (C). The first two subsections of that regulation, subsections 130.10(d)(1) and (2), simply track the language of subsections 304(*l*)(1)(A) and (B) respectively. The next subsection of the regulation, section 130.10(d)(3), does *not*, however, track subsection 304(*l*)(1)(C); rather it changes the word "lists" in the statute to "list." By referring to list in the singular, it excludes the A(i) and A(ii) lists from the requirement of section 304(*l*)(1)(C) that point sources of toxic pollution and the amount of pollution discharged for each source be identified. Only the B list is subject to the identification requirement.

The second regulation, codified at 40 C.F.R. § 123.46, interprets section 304(l)(1)(D). It provides that individual control strategies (ICS's) must be prepared only for the point sources identified in section 304(l)(1)(C), as interpreted, of course, by the first regulation. Thus, under the regulations, ICS's are required only in connection with waters on the B list. The A(i) and A(ii) lists are not to be consulted in determining which segments require ICS's.

The NRDC petitioned for review of these regulations, arguing they are inconsistent with the statute. We have jurisdiction under CWA § 509(b)(1)(E), 33 U.S.C. § 1369(b)(1)(E).

... In this case, Congress has spoken directly, in unambiguous terms, to the question whether subsection 304(l)(1)(C) requires the identification of point sources discharging toxics into the waters identified on all three lists. By using the plural "lists," Congress foreclosed EPA from restricting the scope of paragraph C to waters on the B list. Since the language of paragraph C is unambiguous, there is no need to resort to extrinsic sources to interpret the statute. [Citation.]

The EPA makes two arguments as to why paragraph C is ambiguous. First, it points to the caption of § 304(l)(1), which says, "State List of Navigable Waters and Development of Strategies." EPA argues that the use of the singular "List" in the caption creates an ambiguity, thus triggering Chevron's requirement of deference. While words in the title of a statute or the heading of a section can shed light on the meaning of an ambiguous word or phrase in the text of a statute, they cannot create an ambiguity where none otherwise would exist....

The EPA's next argument for its interpretation of section 304(l)(1)(C) is more complex. The EPA starts not with the language of paragraph C, but with the language of paragraph D. EPA asserts several propositions concerning paragraph D: that in referring to "effluent limitations under section 402 of this Act," paragraph D necessarily refers only to limitations imposed on *point sources*, since it is only point sources that are subject to the NPDES permitting process described in section 402, that paragraph D requires individual control strategies which will cause a reduction in toxic pollutants "sufficient, in combination with existing controls on point and nonpoint sources of pollution, to achieve the applicable water quality standard ... not later than three years after the date of the establishment of such strategy"; and that since ICS's are not required under paragraph D when they cannot be expected to achieve water quality standards within the specified time, Congress must have intended ICS's to be required only for polluters discharging into streams whose failure to meet standards could be cured by eliminating discharges of toxics from point sources. From these propositions, the validity of which we do not now decide, EPA then arrives at two controversial conclusions: that ICS's are required only for polluters discharging into the streams on the B list, streams whose failure to meet water quality standards is due "entirely or substantially to discharges from point sources"; and that because only B list waters require ICS's under paragraph D, only those waters are subject to the identification requirement of paragraph C.

EPA argues that the prepositional phrase introducing paragraph D, "for each such segment," compels these conclusions because the phrase must refer only to segments that will require ICS's.

We disagree. Even if EPA's interpretation of paragraph D is proper, which we do not decide here, its interpretation of paragraph C cannot stand. In using the phrase, "for each such segment," Congress was simply requiring the states to consult each segment before determining whether an ICS on that segment could achieve water quality standards within the relevant period of time. We acknowledge that if the use of the plural "lists" in paragraph C were treated as a drafting error, the phrase "for each segment" would make paragraphs B, C, and D flow together more smoothly. But a statute is not ambiguous simply because an agency can suggest a change in wording that would make the statute more elegant. Since paragraph C as drafted neither is ambiguous in its terms nor is incoherent when considered together with the other provisions of the statute to which it relates, we do not accord EPA's regulation redrafting paragraph C any special deference on review. [Citation.]

Reviewing the regulation *de novo*, we conclude that EPA reached the wrong interpretation of paragraph C because it started with a faulty premise. EPA assumed that paragraph D, requiring individual control strategies for certain waters, was the only significant provision of section 304(l)(1) and that paragraphs B and C of that section had to be read as having one purpose and one purpose only — to effectuate paragraph D. This assumption has two flaws, one obvious and one more subtle. The obvious flow is that the assumption utterly fails to account for the presence of paragraph A — especially paragraph A(ii). If Congress was interested only in individual control strategies for toxic pollutants, why would it have wanted a list of waters whose failure to meet the goals of the Act was not necessarily traceable to toxic pollutants? One readily can infer from the presence of paragraph A that Congress wanted certain information not necessarily because it would affect the ICS program but because it might subsequently be useful in formulating other statutory or regulatory programs. There are other provisions in the Clean Water Act which require the gathering of information but which do not necessarily require immediate action on the basis of the information. *See, e.g.*, CWA § 305, 33 U.S.C. § 1315; CWA § 303(d), 33 U.S.C. § 1313(d).[9]

The more subtle flaw in EPA's assumption is that it does not account for the purposes that paragraph C might serve. Like paragraph A, paragraph C will produce useful information. It requires the identification of point sources

---

[9]EPA suggests that prior to the enactment of section 304(l), states already were required, albeit without a statutory deadline, to submit the information requested. It cites CWA § 303(d), but that section requires states to identify only those waters for which limitations based on the best *practicable* technology would not be stringent enough to implement the water quality standards. Those waters for which limitations based on the more demanding best *available* technology — the required level of technology to control toxic — were insufficient did *not* have to be listed.

discharging toxic pollutants and the determination of the amount of such pollutants discharged. Such information may prove useful to regulators even if every point source identified does not require an ICS.

In sum, we hold that EPA erred in assuming that paragraph D and paragraph C of subsection 304(*l*) must perfectly interlock. Since the provisions do not serve the identical purpose, there was no need to distort paragraph C in order to make it connect better with paragraph D.

Our determination that EPA erred in interpreting section 304(*l*)(1)(C) does not settle the issue on which the parties have focused most of their attention: which waters are subject to the ICS's required by section 301(l)(1)(D)?

EPA's position is that only waters on the B list, i.e., waters for which the state does not expect water quality standards to be achieved "due entirely or substantially to point sources of any toxic pollutants" are subject to the ICS requirement. EPA interprets "entirely or substantially" broadly:

> If a water meets either of the two conditions listed below the water must be listed [under paragraph B] on the grounds that the applicable standard is not achieved or expected to be achieved due entirely or substantially to discharges from point sources.
>
> (i) Existing or additional water quality-based limits on one or more point sources would result in the achievement of an applicable water quality standard for a toxic pollutant; or
>
> (ii) the discharge of a toxic pollutant from one or more point sources, regardless of any nonpoint source contribution of the same pollutant, is sufficient to cause or is expected to cause an excursion above the applicable water quality standard for the toxic pollutant.

40 C.F.R. § 130.10(d)(5) (1989).

Consider the hypothetical situation of a stream that can absorb a load of 100 pounds per day of a particular toxic substance without violating water quality standards. In June of 1992 (the date by which ICS's are required to achieve their purpose) after existing controls are implemented, it is expected that 105 pounds per day of the toxic will flow through the segment. If six of the expected 105 pounds are to come from point sources, the point source contribution is considered "substantial" under EPA's regulation and ICS's are required for the point sources. If three of the 105 pounds are expected to come from point sources, the contribution is considered "insubstantial" and no ICS's are required. The reason why the six pound contribution is considered substantial is that a reduction of six pounds would be "sufficient, in combination with existing controls on point and nonpoint sources of pollution, to achieve the applicable water quality standard." The language just quoted comes, of course, from paragraph D, which specifies when ICS's are required. EPA thus derived its interpretation of paragraph B essentially by beginning with its interpretation of paragraph D and working backward. That is the same method EPA used to interpret paragraph C. Since we are remanding to the agency to have it promulgate new regulations under paragraph C, we do not decide whether EPA's current interpretation of paragraph D is too restrictive. (It is not too inclusive).[11] Rather we invite EPA to reconsider its interpretation on remand. In the meantime, until EPA promulgates new regulations, the program shall continue.

... On remand, EPA must, pursuant to CWA § 304(*l*)(1)(C), amend its regulations to require the states to identify all point sources discharging any toxic pollutant which is believed to be preventing or impairing the water quality of any stream segment listed under CWA §§ 304(*l*)(1)(A) and (B) and to indicate the amount of the toxic pollutant discharged by each source. EPA shall also reconsider its interpretation of CWA § 304(*l*)(1)(D).

NOTES AND QUESTIONS

1. What are the differences between the so-called A(i) list, A(ii) list, and B list? Which of these lists had EPA in its regulations required states to include in their state strategies under section 301(*l*)? Procedurally, what must EPA do to ensure that states include a list of all the sources in their strategies that must be included under section 304(*l*)(1)(D)? For which waters are individual control strategies required and why?

2. Assume that you represent a company discharging toxic pollutants into a stream segment that fails to meet state water quality standards. At what point, if any, in the process can you challenge inclusion of the company in the list of sources or question the individual control strategies (ICSs) imposed? If the company is not on the state list and EPA disapproves the state strategy in part for that omission, can EPA's decision be challenged in court? When, if at all, could a private citizen or environmental group challenge the *omission* of a source from the list or challenge the ICSs as too lenient? *See generally Boise Cascade Corp. v. EPA*, 942 F.2d 1427 (9th Cir. 1991); *Roll Coater, Inc. v. Reilly*, 932 F.2d 668 (7th Cir. 1991); *Westvaco Corp. v. EPA*, 899 F.2d 1383 (4th Cir. 1990); 40 C.F.R. §§ 130.10, 123.46.

3. The effectiveness of section 304(*l*) in addressing the troublesome problem of toxic pollution remains to be seen. One commentator has noted that such toxicity-based limitations do have advantages over individual pollutant controls. These advantages are: (a) they can restrict complex toxic pollutants which might not be measurable in individual discharges; (b) they include consideration of the

---

[11]EPA's regulations require ICS's not only for stream segments whose point source toxic problem, if eliminated, would bring the segment up to standards, but also for segments not meeting that description but whose point source contribution of a particular toxic is so severe that, standing alone, it would cause an excursion above the applicable water quality standard regardless of any nonpoint source contribution of the toxic. 40 C.F.R. § 130.10(d)(5)(ii). The inclusion of this latter type of stream segment in the ICS program has not been challenged. We note that EPA has ample authority, in addition to CWA § 304(*l*), to require expedited action in such stream segments. See CWA §§ 301(*l*), 401(k), 33 U.S.C. §§ 1311(*l*), 1342(k). To require such action is fully consistent with paragraph D's recognition that triage is necessary.

interaction of pollutants in the waste stream; and (c) they may be tailored to local conditions. 2 S. NOVICK, LAW OF ENVIRONMENTAL PROTECTION § 12.05(3)(c)-(v)(B).

4. On November 6, 1991, EPA announced that it would set water quality standards for toxic pollutants in states that had not yet adopted their own. Only four states and two territories had adopted the required standards. [Current Developments] Env't Rep. (BNA) 1763 (Nov. 15, 1991).

G. NONPOINT SOURCE POLLUTION

The focus of the Clean Water Act from its inception in 1972 has been on point source pollution from industrial and municipal discharges. Nonpoint source pollution, however, is estimated to cause 65 percent of the stream pollution, 76 percent of the lake pollution, and 45 percent of the estuary pollution of the water bodies which EPA has found to be unfit for their designated uses. Env't Rep., Nov. 13, 1987, at 1740. EPA has defined nonpoint source pollution as pollution:

> caused by diffuse sources that are not regulated as point sources and normally ... associated with agricultural, silvicultural and urban runoff, runoff from construction activities, etc. Such pollution results in human-made or human-induced alteration of the chemical, physical, biological, and radiological integrity of water. In practical terms, nonpoint source pollution does not result from a discharge at a specific, single location (such as a single pipe) but generally results from land runoff, precipitation, atmospheric deposition, or percolation. Pollution from nonpoint sources occurs when the rate at which pollutant materials entering waterbodies or ground water exceeds natural levels.

EPA, Office of Water Regulations and Standards Nonpoint Source Guidance (Aug. 1987).

Agriculture is the largest single source of unregulated water pollution, including 3.1 billion tons of topsoil annually. Malone, *A Historical Essay on the Conservation Provisions of the 1985 Farm Bill: Sodbusting, Swampbusting, and the Conservation Reserve*, 34 U. KAN. L. REV. 577, 584-85 (1986). Other sources include urban storm water, construction site and mining runoff, silviculture, and individual waste water disposal systems. Council on Environmental Quality, Environmental Quality — The Tenth Annual Report of the Council on Environmental Quality 118-19 (1978).

Until 1987, nonpoint source regulation was limited to federal funding of areawide management plans under section 208. FWPCA § 208, 33 U.S.C. § 1288, discussed in L. MALONE, ENVIRONMENTAL REGULATION OF LAND USE § 8.06[1][b][iii]. In response to the ineffectiveness of section 208, the Water Quality Act of 1987 created a new program for nonpoint source management under section 319. FWPCA § 319, 33 U.S.C. § 1329, discussed in L. MALONE, *supra*, § 8.06[1][b][ii]. The difficulty of nonpoint source regulation is that nonpoint pollution necessitates land use controls because it is not amenable to technological controls. Given resistance to "federal land use," federal regulation of nonpoint source pollution remains limited to funding of state and regional programs.

Both sections 208 and 319 refer to the use of "best management practices" (BMP) for control of nonpoint pollution. EPA's regulations define best management practices as "methods, measures or practices selected by an agency to meet its nonpoint source control needs." BMPs include but are not limited to structural and nonstructural controls and operation and maintenance procedures. BMPs can be applied before, during, and after pollution-producing activities to reduce or eliminate the introduction of pollutants into receiving waters. 40 C.F.R. § 130.2(m). This generally unhelpful definition provides little guidance to states on what constitutes BMPs. One of the few incentives that states have to implement even moderately stringent BMPs is the regulation which prohibits downgrading of uses in state water quality standards if designated uses can be achieved by point source effluent limitations and "cost effective and reasonable best management practices for nonpoint source control." *Id.* § 131.10(h)(2).

Under section 208, states are to designate areas with substantial water quality control problems from "urban-industrial concentrations or other factors," and select a regional organization to develop and administer waste treatment management plans for such areas. FWPCA § 208(a)(2), 33 U.S.C. § 1288(a)(2). If a state fails to act, local governments by agreement may designate an organization responsible for the areawide plan. FWPCA § 208(a)(4), 33 U.S.C. § 1288(a)(4). Plans must identify necessary waste treatment facilities, establish construction priorities and time schedules for such facilities, and develop a program to assure that municipal waste treatment and industrial pretreatment requirements are met. FWPCA § 108(b)(2)(A)-(C), 33 U.S.C. § 1288(b)-(2)(A)-(C). Agricultural and silvicultural nonpoint sources of pollution and their effects must be identified, along with procedures and methods to control them "to the extent feasible." FWPCA § 208(b)(2)(F), 33 U.S.C. § 1288(b)(2)(F). There are similar requirements for mine-related sources of pollution, FWPCA § 208(b)(2)(G), 33 U.S.C. § 1288(b)(2)(G), and pollution from construction activity, FWPCA § 208(b)(2)(H). Plans must also include processes to control disposal on land to protect surface and groundwater quality. FWPCA § 208(b)-(2)(K), 33 U.S.C. § 1288(b)(2)(K). Any program which includes control of dredge and fill material discharged into navigable waters must be coordinated with the requirements of section 404, 33 U.S.C. § 1344, discussed on pages 644-86 *infra*. No permit may be issued under section 402, 33 U.S.C. § 1342, which is in conflict with a state management plan. FWPCA § 208(b)(4)(B), (e), 33 U.S.C. § 1288(b)(4)(B), (e). Section 208 management programs are subject to approval by EPA, FWPCA § 208(a)(7), 33 U.S.C. § 1288(a)(7), and federal grants of up to 75% of the costs of developing and operating a program are authorized. FWPCA § 208(f), 33 U.S.C. § 1288(f).

The Water Quality Act of 1987 amended the goals of the Clean Water Act to state that "it is the national policy that programs for the control of nonpoint sources of pollution be developed and implemented in an expeditious manner so as to enable the goals of this chapter to be met through the control of both point and nonpoint sources of pollution." FWPCA § 101(a)(7), 33 U.S.C. § 1251(a)-(7). Under section 319, 33 U.S.C. § 1329, the governor of every state, after public notice and comment, must submit a state assessment report to EPA for approval. The report must: (1) identify those waters which, without additional control on nonpoint source pollution, "cannot reasonably be expected to attain or maintain applicable water quality standards" or the goals and requirements of the Clean Water Act; (2) identify categories and subcategories of nonpoint sources as well as individual sources which add "significant pollution" to those waters in amounts which "contribute to such portion not meeting such water quality standards or such goals and requirements"; (3) describe the process for identifying "best management practices and measures" to control these nonpoint sources and to reduce "to the maximum extent practicable" their pollution; and (4) identify and describe state and local programs for controlling such pollution. FWPCA § 319(a)(1), 33 U.S.C. § 1329(a)(1). The governors of every state must then submit to EPA, after public notice and comment, a management program covering the next four fiscal years to control nonpoint source pollution. FWPCA § 319(b)(1), 33 U.S.C. § 1329(b)(1). Each management program must: (1) identify best management practices taking into account impacts on groundwater quality; (2) identify programs to achieve best management practices; (3) contain a schedule with "annual milestones" for implementation of state programs to achieve best management practices "at the earliest practicable date"; (4) have assurances of adequate enforcement of the program; (5) identify sources of funding for implementing the program; and (6) identify applications for federal development projects and federal financial assistance which the state will review for consistency with the state program. FWPCA § 319(b)(2), 33 U.S.C. § 1329(b)(2). The state is to develop the program to the maximum extent practicable on a watershed-by-watershed basis. FWPCA § 319(b)(4), 33 U.S.C. § 1329(b)(4). All reports and management programs had to be submitted to EPA by August of 1988. FWPCA § 319(c)(2), 33 U.S.C. § 1329(c)(2).

Within 180 days after submission of a report or management program, the Administrator of EPA must approve or disapprove it in whole or in part. Any report, program, or portion of a program not disapproved within 180 days is deemed to be approved. FWPCA § 319(d)(1), 33 U.S.C. § 1329(d)(1). If the Administrator determines within six months of receipt of a management program that: (1) the program does not meet the requirements in subsection (b)(2); (2) there is not adequate authority to implement the program; (3) the schedule for implementation is not "sufficiently expeditious"; or (4) the best management practices proposed are not adequate to reduce the level of nonpoint source pollution, then the Administrator must notify the state of revisions necessary for approval. The state then has another three months to submit revisions, which the

Administrator must approve or disapprove within three months of receipt. FWPCA § 319(d)(2), 33 U.S.C. § 1329(d)(2). EPA may not promulgate its own program if the state fails to promulgate a program or does so inadequately.

If a state failed to submit a report by August of 1988, EPA had to identify the nonpoint sources of pollution and water sources threatened by them by August of 1989. After notice and opportunity for comment, the Administrator then reports to Congress on any actions taken by EPA. FWPCA § 319(d)(3), 33 U.S.C. § 1329(d)(3). If a state fails to submit a management program, or if the program is disapproved, a local public agency or organization which "has expertise in, and authority to, control water pollution resulting from nonpoint sources" in any area of the state which EPA determines is of "sufficient geographic size" may receive technical assistance for developing a program for its area. Such an area program must be submitted to EPA for approval. Such a local agency or organization may also receive financial assistance for its program as if it were a state. FWPCA § 319(e), 33 U.S.C. § 1329(e). States may also receive technical assistance to develop a management program. FWPCA § 319 (f), 33 U.S.C. § 1329(f).

If a state is not meeting water quality standards or the Act's requirements due to significant nonpoint source pollution from another state, the state may petition EPA to convene an "interstate management conference." If the Administrator determines that the failure is attributable to another state, the Administrator must so notify the polluting state and may convene the conference not later than 180 days after the notification. The conference is for the purpose of developing an agreement between the states to reduce the pollution and improve the water quality. FWPCA § 319(g)(1), 33 U.S.C. § 1329(g)(1). The agreement then becomes part of the state's management program. FWPCA § 319(g)(2), 33 U.S.C. § 1329(g)(2). Of course, there is no statutory authority to compel agreement among the states, and the convening of a conference is expressly exempted from the citizen suit provision in section 505, 33 U.S.C. § 1365.

To expedite state programs, states may also receive grants of federal financial assistance to implement management programs. FWPCA § 319(h)(1), 33 U.S.C. § 1329(h)(1). Federal assistance may not exceed 60 percent of the state's cost of implementation and is made on condition that the remaining 40 percent does not include other federal assistance. FWPCA § 319(h)(3), 33 U.S.C. § 1329(h)(3). Priority in grants is given to state programs which will: (1) control difficult or serious pollution problems; (2) implement innovative methods or practices of control; (3) control interstate pollution; or (4) carry out groundwater quality protection. FWPCA § 319(h)(5), 33 U.S.C. § 1329(h)(5). No grant may be made to a state that failed in the preceding fiscal year to make "satisfactory progress" toward its schedule for implementation of best management practices. FWPCA § 319(h)(8), 33 U.S.C. § 1329(h)(8). Every state must submit annual reports to EPA on its progress in meeting the "schedule of milestones" and on the level of improvement of water quality. FWPCA § 319(h)(11), 33 U.S.C. § 1329(h)(11).

States may also receive grants for groundwater quality protection activities, including "research, planning, groundwater assessments, demonstration programs, enforcement, technical assistance, education and training to protect the quality of groundwater and to prevent contamination of groundwater from nonpoint sources of pollution." FWPCA § 319(i)(1), 33 U.S.C. § 1329(i)(1).

As mentioned earlier, section 319, 33 U.S.C. § 1329, was passed largely in recognition of the failure of section 208, 33 U.S.C. § 1288. The primary incentive for a state to have a nonpoint source management program is the availability of federal funding. There are no sanctions for a state's failure to develop a plan. Despite the absence of any enforcement mechanisms, however, EPA can withhold federal funding without violating the Tenth Amendment. *See Natural Resources Defense Council v. Costle*, 564 F.2d 573 (D.C. Cir. 1977) (withholding of funding under section 208(f)). As early as 1979, only a few states had section 208 plans certified by EPA, and EPA had stopped issuing grants. Several reasons have been given for the lack of success of section 208. EPA's commitment to the program was equivocal; in fact, EPA was sued for failure to promulgate implementing regulations, *Natural Resources Defense Council v. Train*, 396 F. Supp. 1386 (D.D.C. 1975), *aff'd sub nom. Natural Resources Defense Council v. Costle*, 564 F.2d 573 (D.C. Cir. 1977), and failure to distribute section 208 grant funds. *National Ass'n of Regional Councils v. Costle*, 564 F.2d 583 (D.C. Cir. 1977). Moreover, a planning agency's use of section 208 funds to develop an environmental management plan work program, air quality maintenance plan, and solid waste management plan was approved by EPA and upheld as a lawful diversion of funds. *Gonzales v. Costle*, 463 F. Supp. 335 (N.D. Cal. 1978), *aff'd sub nom. Gonzales v. Gorsuch*, 688 F.2d 1263 (9th Cir. 1982). The approval of regional planning departed from traditional parameters of state and local authority. *See* Wilkins, *The Implementation of Water Pollution Control Measures — Section 208 of the Water Pollution Control Act of Amendments*, 15 LAND & WATER L. REV. 479 (1980). The section 208 program also encountered the practical and political difficulties of controlling nonpoint source pollution generally. *See* Jungman, *Areawide Planning Under the Federal Water Pollution Control Act Amendments of 1972: Intergovernmental and Land Use Implications*, 54 TEX. L. REV. 1047 (1976); Mandelker, *Controlling Nonpoint Source Pollution: Can It Be Done?*, 65 CHI.-KENT L. REV. 479 (1989). It remains to be seen whether section 319 can overcome similar difficulties.

NOTES AND QUESTIONS

1. Why has section 208 been ineffective in controlling nonpoint source pollution? *See generally* Note, *State and Federal Land Use Regulation: An Application to Groundwater and Nonpoint Source Pollution Control*, 95 YALE L.J. 1433 (1986). What resistance is there to any measures that appear to be "federal land use"? Is there any reason to expect that section 319 will be a more successful program? For a general comparison of sections 208 and 319, *see*

Davidson, *Thinking About Nonpoint Sources of Water Pollution and South Dakota Agriculture*, 34 S.D. L. REV. 20 (1989); Gould, *Agriculture, Nonpoint Source Pollution, and Federal Law*, 23 U.C. DAVIS L. REV. 461 (1990); Comment, *Nonpoint Source Pollution, Groundwater, and the 1987 Water Quality Act: Section 208 Revisited?*, 19 ENVTL. L. 807 (1989). If a state fails to submit a management program to EPA for approval, can EPA promulgate one for the state under section 319? Are there any sanctions for a state's failure to devise a management program? What, if any, incentives does a state have to devise such a program?

2. In 1977 a new section (j), FWPCA § 208(j), 33 U.S.C. § 1288(j), was added to section 208 establishing the Rural Clean Water program. The program, administered by the Soil Conservation Service of the Department of Agriculture, provides for cost sharing to owners and operators of "rural land" in areas with approved section 208 plans for "installing and maintaining measures incorporating best management practices to control nonpoint source pollution for improved water quality." FWPCA § 208(j)(1), 33 U.S.C. § 1288(j)(1). As of March 1990, 2,363 Rural Clean Water Program contracts, costing $35 million, had been approved in 21 project areas. *See Summary of Activities of the Soil Conservation Service for Fiscal Year 1989*, SOIL & CONSERV. NEWS 12 (March 1990). Participants in the program were to enter into contracts of between five and ten years by September 31, 1988. In return, the participant receives technical assistance and cost sharing of up to 50 percent of the costs of the pollution control measures required by the contract. FWPCA § 208(j)(2), 33 U.S.C. § 1288(j)(2). Implementation of this program has been impeded by such problems as inconsistent federal funding, the lack of incentive for tenants to install conservation measures and the expense of such measures even with cost sharing. S. BATIE, SOIL EROSION: CRISIS IN AMERICA'S CROPLANDS? 98 (1983).

H. SPECIAL POLLUTANTS: THERMAL POLLUTION, OCEAN DISCHARGES, STORMWATER DISCHARGES, AND OIL SPILLS

Point source discharge of heat, or thermal pollution, is governed by section 316, 33 U.S.C. § 1326, but in fact regulation of thermal pollution has been determined in a history of litigation between EPA and electric utilities. Section 316(b) is predicated on the assumption that closed-cycle cooling, in which water is cooled and then circulated for re-use through such devices as a cooling tower, is the best practicable and best available technology for new and old facilities. FWPCA § 316(b), 33 U.S.C. § 1326(b). EPA's effluent guidelines under this section for BAT were invalidated by the Fourth Circuit Court of Appeals in *Appalachian Power Co. v. Train*, 545 F.2d 1351 (4th Cir. 1976) for EPA's failure to do an adequate comparison of the costs of compliance with the environmental benefits from compliance. To date, EPA has not promulgated BAT regulations for heat but rather sets BAT on an ad hoc basis in each permit on the basis of "best professional judgment" (BPJ), similar to the way in which EPA utilizes BPJ in permitting under the FWPCA before BPT is set for an industry. The regulations for implementation of BPJ are in 40 C.F.R. § 125.3. This standard for control of thermal pollution is rarely utilized, however, because most dischargers of thermal pollution obtain the variance provided by section 316(a). Section 316(a) allows use of alternative effluent limitations (usually "once-through" cooling before discharge of heat) if "such discharge (taking into account the interaction of such thermal component with other pollutants), ... will assure the protection and propagation of a balanced, indigenous population of shellfish, fish and wildlife." FWPCA § 316(a), 33 U.S.C. § 1326(a). *See also* 40 C.F.R. §§ 125.70-.73 (section 316(a) variance regulations). Qualification for the variance must be determined in an adjudicatory hearing. *Seacoast Anti-Pollution League v. Costle*, 572 F.2d 872 (1st Cir. 1978), *cert. denied sub nom. Public Serv. Co. of New Hampshire v. Seacoast Anti-Pollution League*, 439 U.S. 824 (1978).

No permit may be issued for discharge into the territorial sea, contiguous zone, or ocean beyond the contiguous zone without compliance with the largely water quality-based criteria for marine discharges under section 403. FWPCA § 403(a), 33 U.S.C. § 1343(a). Facilities often subject to section 403 include coastal facilities as well as offshore facilities such as oil and gas platforms. EPA's water discharge criteria in 40 C.F.R. §§ 125.120-.124, which prohibit "unreasonable degradation of the marine environment," are sufficiently general that there is a great deal of discretion as to the limitations which may be imposed. *Id.* § 125.123. The term is defined to include "significant adverse changes in ecosystem diversity, productivity and stability of the biological community within the area of discharge and surrounding biological communities," threats to human health through direct exposure to pollutants or through consumption of exposed aquatic organisms, or loss of aesthetic, recreational, scientific, or economic values which is unreasonable in relation to the benefits of the discharge. *Id.* § 125.121(e). If, however, it cannot be determined whether a given discharge will cause unreasonable degradation, the permit must require certain limitations on toxicity and monitoring, and include a clause which allows EPA to modify or prohibit the discharge based on new information. *Id.* § 125.123(d). No permit may be issued "where insufficient information exists ... to make a reasonable judgment on any of the guidelines." FWPCA § 403(c)(2), 33 U.S.C. § 1343(c)(2). EPA's regulations are more equivocal in allowing a permit if there will be no irreparable harm and there are no reasonable alternatives. 40 C.F.R. § 125.123(d). Section 403 does not preclude application of the section 301 technology-based limitations. *Pacific Legal Found. v. Quarles*, 440 F. Supp. 316 (C.D. Cal. 1977), *aff'd sub nom. Kilroy v. Quarles*, 614 F.2d 225 (9th Cir.), *cert. denied*, 449 U.S. 825 (1980).

Requirements for stormwater discharge depend upon whether the discharge is a combined storm and sanitary sewer system or a stormwater-only discharge into surface water. Often stormwater sewers interconnect with sanitary sewers carrying household and industrial wastes. With interconnected systems, heavy storm runoff can overload public treatment plants allowing discharge of raw or partially treated sewage into water sources. For combined systems the design criteria for POTWs federally funded under Title II of the FWPCA requires treatment plants to accommodate wet weather flows without bypass. Municipalities must also do "infiltration and inflow" analyses to be eligible for Title II funding in order to discover leaks in the system and other problems which worsen wet weather flows. The requirement of secondary treatment for combined sewer, publicly owned treatment works is modified to accommodate their difficulty in meeting the percentage of removal required. *See* 40 C.F.R. § 133.103(a).

In 1987 Congress addressed regulation of discharges "entirely of stormwater" in section 402(p), 33 U.S.C. § 1342(p). This term is not defined, but presumably is meant to exclude stormwater containing pollutants. Until 1992, EPA could not require point source permits for such discharges, with the exception of: (a) discharges for which permits had been issued prior to the section's enactment; (b) discharges "associated with industrial activity"; (c) discharges from large and medium-sized municipal separate storm sewers; and (d) discharges that have been identified and designated by the state or EPA as causing a violation of water quality standards or otherwise significantly contributing pollutants to the waters of the United States. FWPCA § 402(p)(2), 33 U.S.C. § 1342(p)(2). EPA had to promulgate permit regulations for discharges associated with industrial activities and from municipalities with a population greater than 250,000 by February 4, 1989. Such dischargers had to complete their permit applications within the following year, with permits issued a year later. FWPCA § 402(p)(4)(A), 33 U.S.C. § 1342(p)(4)(A). EPA had until February 4, 1991 to issue permit regulations for municipalities with a population between 100,000 and 250,000. FWPCA § 402(p)(4)(B), 33 U.S.C. § 1342(p)(4)(B). Discharges not within the four exceptions may not be regulated until a study mandated by section 402(p) is completed, after which regulations designating discharges to be regulated and a program of regulation had to be completed by October 1, 1992. FWPCA § 402(p)(5) and (6), 33 U.S.C. § 1342(p)(5) and (6). *See also Hughey v. JMS Development Corp.*, 78 F.3d 1523 (11th Cir. 1996), *cert. denied*, 117 S. Ct. 482 (1996) (summary judgment for a developer who failed to obtain a permit for stormwater discharges because EPA had delegated permit authority to Georgia which had yet to establish a permit program).

Before enactment of the Oil Pollution Act of 1990, there were four federal and more than twenty state laws relating to oil pollution liability and compensation. The four federal statutes are the FWPCA, specifically section 311, 33 U.S.C. § 1321, the Trans-Alaska Pipeline Authorization Act of 1973, 43 U.S.C. §§ 1651-1655, the Deepwater Port Act of 1974, 33 U.S.C. §§ 1501-1524, and the Outer Continental Shelf Lands Act, 43 U.S.C. §§ 1331-1356. None of the acts provided comprehensive coverage of oil spill liability. Section 311 of the FWPCA has wide geographic and source coverage but compensation is limited to cleanup and mitigation costs with its fund for cleanup supported only by federal appropriation. The other three statutes provide broader compensation and include a cleanup fund supported by industry, but each is limited to coverage of oil spills from a specific origin, that is, the Trans-Alaska Pipeline, deepwater ports, or the outer continental shelf.

Briefly, section 311 of the FWPCA, 33 U.S.C. § 1321, makes the owner or operator of a facility or vessel, from which harmful quantities of oil are discharged into surface water or on land from which the oil is likely to reach surface water, responsible for removal of the oil, including any damage to natural resources. The discharger must clean up the oil even if it is entitled to one of the statutory defenses. FWPCA § 311(b)(5), (6), 33 U.S.C. § 1321(b)(5), (6). An owner or operator has such a defense if the discharge is caused solely by an act of God, an act of war, negligence on the part of the federal government, or an act or omission of a third party without regard to whether the act or omission was or was not negligent. FWPCA § 1311(f), 33 U.S.C. § 1321(f). A discharger with such a defense can seek reimbursement of reasonable costs from the cleanup fund or the person at fault. FWPCA § 1311(g), (i), 33 U.S.C. § 1321(g), (i).

If the discharger fails to clean up the oil, the government may conduct the clean up and seek the costs of removal from the discharger. FWPCA § 311(c), (f)(1), 33 U.S.C. § 1321(c), (f)(1). The government may also seek reimbursement from a nondischarging party who actually caused a spill. FWPCA § 311(i), 33 U.S.C. § 1321(i).

The Oil Pollution Act (OPA) of 1990, Pub. L. No. 101-380, 104 Stat. 484 (codified in scattered titles of U.S.C.), is a major step taken by Congress in addressing liability for oil spills and the prevention of oil spills. The OPA was enacted after fifteen years of unsuccessful attempts to pass similar legislation. Impetus for its eventual passage in 1990 came from the Exxon Valdez disaster and other major oil spills in Narragansett Bay, the Delaware River, and the Houston Ship Channel. In general, its provisions deal with liability arising from oil spill damages, penalties for harmful discharges, preventive measures, and oil removal plans.

The OPA of 1990 stands apart from previous legislation in two significant aspects. The first significant characteristic of the OPA is its comprehensive nature. Passage of the act was intended to simplify and accelerate litigation arising from oil spills. Claimants had previously confronted a somewhat complex and confusing array of federal legislation on oil spills. The second important characteristic of the OPA of 1990 is that it imposes upon the oil and shipping industry substantially increased penalties, increases monetary limits on liability, and broadens the range of compensable damages. For instance, limits on liability which were $150 per gross ton under the FWPCA § 311, 33 U.S.C. § 1321(p), are $1200 per gross ton under the OPA, 33 U.S.C. § 2704(a). Recoverable damages under previous legislation were limited primarily to removal and restoration costs. 33 U.S.C. § 1321(f). Under the OPA a responsible party may also be held liable for damages arising from injury to real or personal property, loss of subsistence use, loss of revenues on use of natural resources, loss of profits and earning capacity, and costs of additional public services. 33 U.S.C. § 2702(b).

The comprehensive and detailed nature of the OPA stands in contrast to the treatment of oil spills in the FWPCA, which is relatively brief. The provisions of the FWPCA deal very generally with penalties for harmful discharges, notification requirements, a National Contingency Plan, equipment requirements and inspection plans, limitations on liability, authorization for Presidential action in removal plans, and requirements of financial responsibility. 33 U.S.C. § 1321. The OPA incorporates similar issues but in much more detail. For example, the FWPCA requires vessels to carry equipment for prevention and containment of hazardous discharges. 33 U.S.C. § 1321(j). The OPA goes significantly further, explicitly requiring double-hulls for all new oil tankers and including a detailed schedule for the retrofitting of existing vessels. The double-hull requirement is a costly one, and the OPA calls for studies to research other viable safety and prevention measures. 46 U.S.C. § 3713.

Other examples of the level of detail in the OPA are the provisions on employment conditions. The OPA imposes specific limitations on the number of hours ship personnel may be on duty within a given period of time. 46 U.S.C. § 8104. The OPA further reflects concern for the quality of the ship personnel, providing access to driving records and criminal records prior to issuance of licenses and certificates of registry. 46 U.S.C. § 7101.

The far reaching scope of the OPA is further evidenced by its concern for specific sensitive geographic areas, its call for numerous studies, and the establishment of an industry-financed fund. An entire title of the OPA pertains solely to Prince William Sound, 33 U.S.C. §§ 2731-2737, and provisions are also designated to oil and gas exploration and development on the Outer Banks of North Carolina, 33 U.S.C. § 2753. There is authorization for numerous studies, ranging from the long-term environmental effects of the Exxon Valdez incident to construction of safer tankers. The OPA also establishes a $1 billion fund to be financed by charging the oil industry a 5 cent per barrel fee. 26 U.S.C. § 9509. This new fund essentially replaces the funds created by the Trans-Alaska Pipeline Act, 43 U.S.C. §§ 1651-1655, the Deepwater Port Act, 33 U.S.C. §§ 1501-1524, and the Outer Continental Shelf Lands Act, 43 U.S.C. §§ 1331-1356. Additionally, it supersedes the contingency fund of the FWPCA § 311, 33 U.S.C. § 1321. The primary purpose of the fund is to provide a source for the immediate costs of cleanup activities and prompt compensation for damage claims, particularly to the extent that such expenses are not being paid by the party responsible for the oil spill. Private parties as well as federal, state, and Indian tribe trustees have access to the fund. 33 U.S.C. § 2712.

The OPA has greater force than the FWPCA, mandating action in instances when the FWPCA had preserved administrative or executive discretion. For example, the FWPCA gives the President discretion in deciding whether to coordinate and direct cleanup plans when there appears to be a substantial hazard and lack of action on the part of the responsible party. 33 U.S.C. § 1321(c). The OPA, on the other hand, leaves little room for discretion, making Presidential action mandatory under similar circumstances. 33 U.S.C. § 1321.

Despite the comprehensive and detailed nature of the OPA, the intent behind it to simplify and accelerate litigation arising from oil spills may fail to become a reality. Although the OPA appears to consolidate various federal provisions, there remains uncertainty over the precise relationship between the newly enacted OPA and previous oil spill legislation. The previous legislation generally remains intact, with the exception of specific areas in which the OPA explicitly amends the prior laws. A second shortcoming is the OPA's failure to preempt state laws. States remain free to enact their own legislation, and the Act expressly permits states to implement stricter standards than those of the OPA. 33 U.S.C. § 2718. Finally, the OPA does not implement international protocols on oil spills. For further discussion of the OPA, *see* Wagner, *The Oil Pollution Act of 1990: An Analysis*, 21 J. MAR. L. & COM. 569 (1990); Rodriguez & Jaffee, *The Oil Pollution Act of 1990*, 15 TUL. MAR. L.J. 1 (1990); Mitchell, *Preservation of State and Federal Authority under the Oil Pollution Act of 1990*, 21 ENVTL. L. 237 (1991) (for discussion of the OPA, state laws, and international protocols); Edelman, *The Oil Pollution Act of 1990*, N.Y.L.J., Sept. 7, 1990, at 3, col. 1 (for discussion of the business ramifications of the OPA).

I. WETLANDS REGULATION

From an environmental perspective, wetlands have only recently been recognized as a valuable natural resource and not merely a problem to be rectified. In part due to this late recognition, regulation of wetlands is divided among federal, state, and local regulation with varying purposes. At the federal level, development of wetlands is controlled through section 10 of the Rivers and Harbors Act, 33 U.S.C. § 403, and section 404 of the FWPCA, 33 U.S.C. § 1344, which are not in and of themselves statutes designed to preserve wetlands. Both of these programs are administered by the Corps of Engineers. 33 C.F.R. § 320.1(a)(6). The focus of the RHA is protection of navigation, while the focus of the Clean Water Act is prevention of water pollution. The authority of the Corps has been upheld against colleagues claiming an unconstitutional delegation of powers, *Avoyelles Sportsmen's League v. Marsh*, 715 F.2d 897 (5th Cir. 1983); *Buttrey v. United States*, 690 F.2d 1170 (5th Cir. 1982), although the wisdom of allowing the Corps to oversee wetlands as a policy matter has been questioned. *See* Power, *The Fox in the Chicken Coop: The Regulatory Program of the U.S. Army Corps of Engineers*, 63 VA. L. REV. 503 (1977) (noting the Corps' own history as a spoiler of the environment). Of these two statutory provisions, the most pervasive regulation for wetlands development is section 404 of the Clean Water Act.

Wetlands include swamps, marshes, bogs, bottom lands, and tundra once thought to be undesirable and valuable only when drained and filled. Wetlands usually occur in depressions or along rivers, lakes, and coastal waters where they are periodically flooded. FISH AND WILDLIFE SERVICE, WETLANDS OF THE UNITED STATES: CURRENT STATUS AND RECENT TRENDS 2 (1984). Wetlands are valuable in an environmental and socioeconomic sense. They are essential habitats for fish, shellfish, plant life, waterfowl, migratory birds, and other wildlife. OFFICE OF TECHNOLOGY ASSESSMENT, WETLANDS: THEIR USE AND REGULATION 39-41 (1984). Wetlands are also essential to water quality improvement. They remove nutrients, process chemical and organic wastes, remove sediment, produce oxygen, and filter pollution. Wetlands produce aquatic vegetation and help to regulate the climate. The socioeconomic value of wetlands includes flood and storm drainage protection, erosion control, and water supply and groundwater recharge. Wetlands are used for timber harvesting, harvesting of fish and shellfish, hunting and trapping, and some energy production from peat. WETLANDS OF THE UNITED STATES: CURRENT STATUS AND RECENT TRENDS, supra, at 13-19. Increasingly, wetlands are being preserved simply as a natural environment for aesthetic enjoyment, recreation, and scientific research. Despite these values, numerous activities annually eliminate wetlands, resulting in the loss of hundreds of thousands of acres. WETLANDS: THEIR USE AND REGULATION, supra, at 5, 39-42.

In the last 200 years, 30 to 50 percent of the wetlands in the continental United States have been converted. Id. at 87. From the 1950s to the 1970s, wetlands were reduced from 101.8 million acres to 99 million acres. COUNCIL ON ENVIRONMENTAL QUALITY, OUR NATION'S WETLANDS: AN INTERAGENCY TASK FORCE REPORT 6 (1978).

Conversion during this twenty-year period averaged about 550,000 acres per year. Ninety-seven percent of the inland losses occurred in inland, freshwater areas, with 80 percent of the conversion resulting from agricultural drainage, clearing, land leveling, groundwater pumping, and surface water conversion. Of the coastal wetland losses, 56 percent were caused by dredging for marinas, canals, port development, and control of shoreline erosion. An additional 22 percent of coastal losses were due to urbanization. WETLANDS: THEIR USE AND REGULATION, supra, at 6-7. Wetlands are also threatened by some natural activities: the rise of the sea level, droughts, storms, erosion, and some biotic effects from muskrat, nutria, and geese.

Conversion rates, like wetland acreage, vary by regions within the United States. Alaska, Louisiana, and Florida have the most wetland acreage, with significant acreage also in Alabama, Arkansas, Georgia, Maine, Michigan, Minnesota, Mississippi, North Carolina, South Carolina, and Wisconsin. WETLANDS OF THE UNITED STATES: CURRENT STATUS AND RECENT TRENDS, supra, at 28, 30. Conversion rates from the mid-1950s to 1970s in the lower Mississippi Valley were almost three times the national average, while conversion on the Atlantic Coast outside of Florida was 30 percent of the national average. WETLANDS: THEIR USE AND REGULATION, supra, at 87.

To a significant degree, conversion of wetlands is related to population density. Over 50 percent of the people living in the United States live within fifty miles of a coastline. In 1981, population density in the coastal zone was six times that in the rest of the county. In addition, there has been a shift of population from northern states to the south and from metropolitan areas to nonmetropolitan areas. WETLANDS OF THE UNITED STATES: CURRENT STATUS AND RECENT TRENDS, *supra*, at 54. These shifts in population indicate that even wetlands in less developed areas are in increasing danger of conversion.

1. JURISDICTION OVER AND COVERAGE OF WETLANDS UNDER THE FWPCA

When Congress regulates to control pollution, it normally does so under the authorization of the commerce clause, U.S. CONST. art. I, § 8. The Supreme Court has held that the broad reach of the commerce clause allows Congress to regulate both interstate and intrastate activities that have a substantial effect on interstate commerce. *Wickard v. Filburn*, 317 U.S. 111 (1942). As a matter of constitutional authority, therefore, congressional regulation of water pollution under the FWPCA is limited only by this easily satisfied requirement of an effect on interstate commerce.

Although Congress has the authority to regulate water pollution to the full extent of the commerce clause, the question remains whether Congress intended in the FWPCA to regulate water pollution to that extent. Historically, in a variety of contexts, Congress has chosen to restrict federal regulation of water sources to "navigable waters." In the landmark case of *The Daniel Ball*, 77 U.S. (10 Wall.) 557, 557 (1870), the Supreme Court determined that waters are "navigable in fact ... when they form in their ordinary condition by themselves, or by uniting with other waters, a continued highway" in the chain of interstate and foreign commerce. The FWPCA states as its goal the elimination by 1985 of the discharge of pollutants into navigable waters, FWPCA § 101(a)(1), 33 U.S.C. § 1251(a)(1), and section 402 refers frequently to discharges into navigable waters. "Navigable waters" are defined only as "the waters of the United States, including the territorial seas." FWPCA § 502(7), 33 U.S.C. § 1362(7). At least one court of appeals has held that Congress did intend in the FWPCA to exercise its authority to regulate water pollution to the full extent of the commerce clause. *United States v. Ashland Oil & Transp. Co.*, 504 F.2d 1317 (6th Cir. 1974). *See also United States v. Phelps Dodge Corp.*, 391 F. Supp. 1181 (D. Ariz. 1975) (the definition of "navigable waters" is not void for vagueness). Plaintiffs continue to question the jurisdictional reach of the FWPCA over remote tributaries of navigable waters in the traditional sense, but with little or no success. *See, e.g., United States v. Phelps Dodge Corp., supra* (scope of FWPCA extends to all pollutants discharged into any waterway, including normally dry arroyos, from which water might flow into any body of water, including groundwater, in which there is public interest); *United States v. Texas*

Pipe Line Co., 611 F.2d 345 (10th Cir. 1979) (waters of unnamed tributary were "navigable" for FWPCA purposes even though stream did not continuously flow into a river navigable in the traditional sense); *Ward v. Coleman*, 598 F.2d 1187 (10th Cir. 1979), *rev'd on other grounds sub nom. United States v. Ward*, 448 U.S. 242 (1980) (where river is navigable in fact, its tributary is also navigable for FWPCA purposes); *Quivira Mining Co. v. EPA*, 765 F.2d 126 (10th Cir. 1985) (substantial evidence supported EPA decision that gully and creek were "waters of the United States" within meaning of FWPCA); *Texas Mun. Power Agency v. EPA*, 836 F.2d 1482 (5th Cir. 1988) (EPA had authority to regulate discharge of pollutants into internal waste streams when wastes at final discharge point were so diluted as to make monitoring impracticable).

A more significant and troublesome issue is how the concept of navigability affects the jurisdictional reach of the FWPCA over wetlands. Section 404(a) of the FWPCA, 33 U.S.C. § 1344(a) requires a permit for all discharges by point sources of dredged or fill materials into "navigable waters." The following Supreme Court decision discusses the Corps' gradual expansion of its jurisdiction over wetlands and the difficulty of assessing when section 404 applies.

UNITED STATES v. RIVERSIDE BAYVIEW HOMES, INC.
474 U.S. 121 (1985)

JUSTICE WHITE delivered the opinion of the Court.

This case presents the question whether the Clean Water Act (CWA), 33 U.S.C. § 1251 *et seq.*, together with certain regulations promulgated under its authority by the Army Corps of Engineers, authorizes the Corps to require landowners to obtain permits from the Corps before discharging fill material into wetlands adjacent to navigable bodies of water and their tributaries.

I

The relevant provisions of the Clean Water Act originated in the Federal Water Pollution Control Act Amendments of 1972, and have remained essentially unchanged [citation] since that time. Under §§ 301 and 502 of the Act, 33 U.S.C. §§ 1311 and 1362, any discharge of dredged or fill materials into "navigable waters" — defined as the "waters of the United States" — is forbidden unless authorized by a permit issued by the Corps of Engineers pursuant to § 404, 33 U.S.C. § 1344. After initially construing the Act to cover only waters navigable in fact, in 1975 the Corps issued interim final regulations redefining "the waters of the United States" to include not only actually navigable waters but also tributaries of such waters, interstate waters and their tributaries, and nonnavigable intrastate waters whose use or misuse could affect interstate commerce. 40 Fed. Reg. 31320 (1975). More importantly for present purposes, the Corps construed the Act to cover all "freshwater wetlands" that were adjacent to other covered waters. A "freshwater wetland" was defined as an area that is "periodically inundated" and is "normally characterized by the prevalence of vegetation that requires saturated soil conditions for growth and reproduction." 33 C.F.R. § 209.120(d)(2)(h) (1976). In 1977, the Corps refined its definition of wetlands by eliminating the reference to periodic inundation and making other minor changes. The 1977 definition reads as follows:

> "The term 'wetlands' means those areas that are inundated or saturated by surface or ground water at a frequency and duration sufficient to support, and that under normal circumstances do support, a prevalence of vegetation typically adapted for life in saturated soil conditions. Wetlands generally include swamps, marshes, bogs and similar areas." 33 C.F.R. § 323.2(c) (1978).

In 1982, the 1977 regulations were replaced by substantively identical regulations that remain in force today. *See* 33 C.F.R. § 323.2 (1985).

Respondent Riverside Bayview Homes, Inc. (hereafter respondent), owns 80 acres of low-lying, marshy land near the shores of Lake St. Clair in Macomb County, Michigan. In 1976, respondent began to place fill materials on its property as part of its preparations for construction of a housing development. The Corps of Engineers, believing that the property was an "adjacent wetland" under the 1975 regulation defining "waters of the United States," filed suit in the United States District Court for the Eastern District of Michigan, seeking to enjoin respondent from filling the property without the permission of the Corps.

The District Court held that the portion of respondent's property lying below 575.5 feet above sea level was a covered wetland and enjoined respondent from filling it without a permit....

... [T]he Sixth Circuit reversed. [Citation.] The court construed the Corps' regulation to exclude from the category of adjacent wetlands — and hence from that of "waters of the United States" — wetlands that were not subject to flooding by adjacent navigable waters at a frequency sufficient to support the growth of aquatic vegetation. The Court adopted this construction of the regulation because, in its view, a broader definition of wetlands might result in the taking of private property without just compensation. The court also expressed its doubt that Congress, in granting the Corps jurisdiction to regulate the filling of "navigable waters," intended to allow regulation of wetlands that were not the result of flooding by navigable waters. [Citation.] Under the court's reading of the regulation, respondent's property was not within the Corps' jurisdiction, because its semiaquatic characteristics were not the result of frequent flooding by the nearby navigable waters. Respondent was therefore free to fill the property without obtaining a permit.

We granted certiorari to consider the proper interpretation of the Corps' regulation defining "waters of the United States" and the scope of the Corps' jurisdiction under the Clean Water Act, both of which were called into question by the Sixth Circuit's ruling. [Citation.] We now reverse.

II

The question whether the Corps of Engineers may demand that respondent obtain a permit before placing fill material on its property is primarily one of regulatory and statutory interpretation: we must determine whether respondent's property is an "adjacent wetland" within the meaning of the applicable regulation, and, if so, whether the Corps' jurisdiction over "navigable waters" gives it statutory authority to regulate discharges of fill material into such a wetland. In this connection, we first consider the Court of Appeals' position that the Corps' regulatory authority under the statute and its implementing regulations must be narrowly construed to avoid a taking without just compensation in violation of the Fifth Amendment.

We have frequently suggested that governmental land-use regulation may under extreme circumstances amount to a "taking" of the affected property. [Citation.] We have never precisely defined those circumstances, [citation] but our general approach was summed up in *Agins v. Tiburon*, 447 U.S. 255, 260 (1980), where we stated that the application of land-use regulations to a particular piece of property is a taking only "if the ordinance does not substantially advance legitimate state interests ... or denies an owner economically viable use of his land." Moreover, we have made it quite clear that the mere assertion of regulatory jurisdiction by a governmental body does not constitute a regulatory taking. [Citation.] The reasons are obvious. A requirement that a person obtain a permit before engaging in a certain use of his or her property does not itself "take" the property in any sense: after all, the very existence of a permit system implies that permission may be granted, leaving the landowner free to use the property as desired. Moreover, even if the permit is denied, there may be other viable uses available to the owner. Only when a permit is denied and the effect of the denial is to prevent "economically viable" use of the land in question can it be said that a taking has occurred.

If neither the imposition of the permit requirement itself nor the denial of a permit necessarily constitutes a taking, it follows that the Court of Appeals erred in concluding that a narrow reading of the Corps' regulatory jurisdiction over wetlands was "necessary" to avoid "a serious taking problem."... [Citation.]

III

Purged of its spurious constitutional overtones, the question whether the regulation at issue requires respondent to obtain a permit before filling its property is an easy one. The regulation extends the Corps' authority under § 404 to all wetlands adjacent to navigable or interstate waters and their tributaries. Wetlands, in turn, are defined as lands that are "inundated or *saturated* by surface or *ground water* at a frequency and duration sufficient to support, and that under normal circumstances do support, a prevalence of vegetation typically adapted for life in saturated soil conditions." 33 C.F.R. § 323.2(c) (1985) (emphasis added). The plain language of the regulation refutes the Court of

Appeals' conclusion that inundation or "frequent flooding" by the adjacent body of water in a *sine qua non* of a wetland under the regulation. Indeed, the regulation could hardly state more clearly that saturation by either surface or ground water is sufficient to bring an area within the category of wetlands, provided that the saturation is sufficient to and does support wetland vegetation.

. . . .

Without the nonexistent requirement of frequent flooding, the regulatory definition of adjacent wetlands covers the property here. The District Court found that respondent's property was "characterized by the presence of vegetation that requires saturated soil conditions for growth and reproduction," [citation] and that the source of the saturated soil conditions on the property was ground water. There is no plausible suggestion that these findings are clearly erroneous, and they plainly bring the property within the category of wetlands as defined by the current regulation. In addition, the court found that the wetland located on respondent's property was adjacent to a body of navigable water, since the area characterized by saturated soil conditions and wetland vegetation extended beyond the boundary of respondent's property to Black Creek, a navigable waterway. Again, the court's finding is not clearly erroneous. Together, these findings establish that respondent's property is a wetland adjacent to a navigable waterway. Hence, it is part of the "waters of the United States" as defined by 33 C.F.R. § 323.2 (1985), and if the regulation itself is valid as a construction of the term "waters of the United States" as used in the Clean Water Act, a question which we now address, the property falls within the scope of the Corps' jurisdiction over "navigable waters" under § 404 of the Act.

IV

A

An agency's construction of a statute it is charged with enforcing is entitled to deference if it is reasonable and not in conflict with the expressed intent of Congress. *Chemical Manufacturers Assn. v. Natural Resources Defense Council, Inc.*, 470 U.S. 116, 125 (1985); *Chevron U.S.A. Inc. v. Natural Resources Defense Council, Inc.*, 467 U.S. 837, 842-845 (1984). Accordingly, our review is limited to the question whether it is reasonable, in light of the language, policies, and legislative history of the Act for the Corps to exercise jurisdiction over wetlands adjacent to but not regularly flooded by rivers, streams, and other hydrographic features more conventionally identifiable as "waters."[8]

On a purely linguistic level, it may appear unreasonable to classify "lands," wet or otherwise, as "waters." Such a simplistic response, however, does justice neither to the problem faced by the Corps in defining the scope of its authority

---

[8]We are not called upon to address the question of the authority of the Corps to regulate discharges of fill material into wetlands that are not adjacent to bodies of open water, see 33 C.F.R. §§ 323.2(a)(2) and (3) (1985), and we do not express any opinion on that question.

under § 404(a) nor to the realities of the problem of water pollution that the Clean Water Act was intended to combat. In determining the limits of its power to regulate discharges under the Act, the Corps must necessarily choose some point at which water ends and land begins. Our common experience tells us that this is often no easy task: the transition from water to solid ground is not necessarily or even typically an abrupt one. Rather, between open waters and dry land may lie shallows, marshes, mudflats, swamps, bogs — in short, a huge array of areas that are not wholly aquatic but nevertheless fall far short of being dry land. Where on this continuum to find the limit of "waters" is far from obvious.

Faced with such a problem of defining the bounds of its regulatory authority, an agency may appropriately look to the legislative history and underlying policies of its statutory grants of authority. Neither of these sources provides unambiguous guidance for the Corps in this case, but together they do support the reasonableness of the Corps' approach of defining adjacent wetlands as "waters" within the meaning of § 404(a). Section 404 originated as part of the Federal Water Pollution Control Act Amendments of 1972, which constituted a comprehensive legislative attempt "to restore and maintain the chemical, physical, and biological integrity of the Nation's waters." CWA § 101, 33 U.S.C. § 1251. This objective incorporated a broad, systemic view of the goal of maintaining and improving water quality: as the House Report on the legislation put it, "the word 'integrity' ... refers to a condition in which the natural structure and function of ecosystems [are] maintained." H.R. Rep. No. 92-911, p. 76 (1972). Protection of aquatic ecosystems, Congress recognized, demanded broad federal authority to control pollution, for "[w]ater moves in hydrologic cycles and it is essential that discharge of pollutants be controlled at the source." S. Rep. No. 92-414, p. 77 (1972).

In keeping with these views, Congress chose to define the waters covered by the Act broadly. Although the Act prohibits discharges into "navigable waters," see CWA §§ 301(a), 404(a), 502(12), 33 U.S.C. §§ 1311(a), 1344(a), 1362(12), the Act's definition of "navigable waters" as "the waters of the United States" makes it clear that the term "navigable" as used in the Act is of limited import. In adopting this definition of "navigable waters," Congress evidently intended to repudiate limits that had been placed on federal regulation by earlier water pollution control statutes and to exercise its powers under the Commerce Clause to regulate at least some waters that would not be deemed "navigable" under the classical understanding of that term. See S. Conf. Rep. No. 92-1236, p. 144 (1972); 118 Cong. Rec. 33756-33757 (1972) (statement of Rep. Dingell).

Of course, it is one thing to recognize that Congress intended to allow regulation of waters that might not satisfy traditional tests of navigability; it is another to assert that Congress intended to abandon traditional notions of "waters" and include in that term "wetlands" as well. Nonetheless, the evident breadth of congressional concern for protection of water quality and aquatic ecosystems suggests that it is reasonable for the Corps to interpret the term "waters" to encompass wetlands adjacent to waters as more conventionally defined. Following the lead of the Environmental Protection Agency, [citation] the Corps has determined that wetlands adjacent to navigable waters do as a general matter play a key role in protecting and enhancing water quality:

> "The regulation of activities that cause water pollution cannot rely on ... artificial lines ... but must focus on all waters that together form the entire aquatic system. Water moves in hydrologic cycles, and the pollution of this part of the aquatic system, regardless of whether it is above or below an ordinary high water mark, or mean high tide line, will affect the water quality of the other waters within that aquatic system.
>
> "For this reason, the landward limit of Federal jurisdiction under Section 404 must include any adjacent wetlands that form the border of or are in reasonable proximity to other waters of the United States, as these wetlands are part of this aquatic system." 42 Fed. Reg. 37128 (1977).

We cannot say that the Corps' conclusion that adjacent wetlands are inseparably bound up with the "waters" of the United States — based as it is on the Corps' and EPA's technical expertise — is unreasonable. In view of the breadth of federal regulatory authority contemplated by the Act itself and the inherent difficulties of defining precise bounds to regulable waters, the Corps' ecological judgment about the relationship between waters and their adjacent wetlands provides an adequate basis for a legal judgment that adjacent wetlands may be defined as waters under the Act.

This holds true even for wetlands that are not the result of flooding or permeation by water having its source in adjacent bodies of open water. The Corps has concluded that wetlands may affect the water quality of adjacent lakes, rivers, and streams even when the waters of those bodies do not actually inundate the wetlands. For example, wetlands that are not flooded by adjacent waters may still tend to drain into those waters. In such circumstances, the Corps has concluded that wetlands may serve to filter and purify water draining into adjacent bodies of water, see 33 CFR § 320.4(b)(2)(vii) (1985), and to slow the flow of surface runoff into lakes, rivers, and streams and thus prevent flooding and erosion, see §§ 320.4(b)(2)(iv) and (v). In addition, adjacent wetlands may "serve significant natural biological functions, including food chain production, general habitat, and nesting, spawning, rearing and resting sites for aquatic ... species." § 320.4(b)(2)(i). In short, the Corps has concluded that wetlands adjacent to lakes, rivers, streams, and other bodies of water may function as integral parts of the aquatic environment even when the moisture creating the wetlands does not find its source in the adjacent bodies of water. Again, we cannot say that the Corps' judgment on these matters is unreasonable, and we therefore conclude that a definition of "waters of the United States" encompassing all wetlands adjacent to other bodies of water over which the Corps has jurisdiction is a permissible interpretation of the Act. Because respondent's property is part of a wetland that actually abuts on a navigable waterway, respondent was required to have a permit in this case.

Following promulgation of the Corps' interim final regulations in 1975, the Corps' assertion of authority under § 404 over waters not actually navigable engendered some congressional opposition. The controversy came to a head during Congress' consideration of the Clean Water Act of 1977, a major piece of legislation aimed at achieving "interim improvements within the existing framework" of the Clean Water Act. H.R. Rep. No. 95-139, pp. 1-2 (1977). In the end, however, as we shall explain, Congress acquiesced in the administrative construction.

....

In both Chambers, debate on the proposals to narrow the definition of navigable waters centered largely on the issue of wetlands preservation. [Citation.] Proponents of a more limited § 404 jurisdiction contended that the Corps' assertion of jurisdiction over wetlands and other nonnavigable "waters" had far exceeded what Congress had intended in enacting § 404. Opponents of the proposed changes argued that a narrower definition of "navigable waters" for purposes of § 404 would exclude vast stretches of crucial wetlands from the Corps' jurisdiction, with detrimental effects on wetlands ecosystems, water quality, and the aquatic environment generally.... [E]fforts to narrow the definition of "waters" were abandoned; the legislation as ultimately passed, in the words of Senator Baker, "retain[ed] the comprehensive jurisdiction over the Nation's waters exercised in the 1972 Federal Water Pollution Control Act."

....

We are thus persuaded that the language, policies, and history of the Clean Water Act compel a finding that the Corps has acted reasonably in interpreting the Act to require permits for the discharge of fill material into wetlands adjacent to the "waters of the United States." The regulation in which the Corps has embodied this interpretation by its terms includes the wetlands on respondent's property within the class of waters that may not be filled without a permit; and, as we have seen, there is no reason to interpret the regulation more narrowly than its terms would indicate. Accordingly, the judgment of the Court of Appeals is reversed.

NOTES AND QUESTIONS

1. As the principal case notes, the Corps originally limited its jurisdiction under section 404 to those waters traditionally regulated under the Rivers and Harbors Act, the so-called "navigable-in-fact" or historically navigable waters. Although some salt water wetlands were historically navigable, most wetlands, and almost all freshwater wetlands, were not. The Corps' limited definition was invalidated as too restrictive in *Natural Resources Defense Council v. Callaway*, 392 F. Supp. 685 (D.D.C. 1975). The court held that Congress had intended to regulate the waters to the full extent of the commerce clause. The final regulations issued in response to *Callaway* included the first definition to encompass wetlands. 40 Fed. Reg. 31,322, 31,324 (1975). Currently, the Corps and EPA accept the following broad definition of navigable waters as:

> (1) All waters which are currently used, or were used in the past, or may be susceptible to use in interstate or foreign commerce, including all waters which are subject to the ebb and flow of the tide;
> (2) All interstate waters including interstate wetlands;
> (3) All other waters such as intrastate lakes, rivers, streams (including intermittent streams), mudflats, sandflats, wetlands, sloughs, prairie potholes, wet meadows, playa lakes, or natural ponds, the use, degradation or destruction of which could affect interstate or foreign commerce including any such waters:
>
> > (i) Which are or could be used by interstate or foreign travelers for recreational or other purposes; or
> > (ii) From which fish or shellfish are or could be taken and sold in interstate or foreign commerce; or
> > (iii) Which are used or could be used for industrial purposes by industries in interstate commerce;
>
> (4) All impoundments of waters otherwise defined as waters of the United States under this definition;
> (5) Tributaries of waters identified in paragraphs (1) through (4) of this [definition;]
> (6) The territorial sea; and
> (7) Wetlands adjacent to waters (other than waters that are themselves wetlands) identified in paragraphs ... (1)-(6) of this [definition.]

33 C.F.R. § 328.3(a); 40 C.F.R. § 230.3(s).

Wetlands separated from waters of the United States by such impediments as man-made ditches or barriers, natural river berms, or beach dunes are deemed to be "adjacent" wetlands. 33 C.F.R. § 328.3(c); 40 C.F.R. § 230.3(b). The adjacency requirement has been very liberally construed. *See, e.g., United States v. Lee Wood Contr'g, Inc.*, 529 F. Supp. 119, 120 (E.D. Mich. 1981); *United States v. Tilton*, 705 F.2d 429 (11th Cir. 1983); *United States v. Carter*, 18 Env't Rep. Cas. (BNA) 1804 (S.D. Fla. 1982).

The Supreme Court was "not called upon to address the question of the authority of the Corps to regulate discharges of fill material into wetlands that are not adjacent to bodies of open water." Does the reasoning of the Court's opinion suggest that the Corps could regulate nonadjacent wetlands under section 404 as well? For a discussion of whether the Corps has such jurisdiction (concluding that it does), see Geltman, *Regulation of Non-Adjacent Wetlands Under Section 404 of the Clean Water Act*, 23 NEW ENG. L. REV. 615 (1988-89). *See also*, Johnson, Stephen M., *Federal Regulation of Isolated Wetlands*, 23 ENVTL. L. 1-42 (1993). *Contra*, Lemon, John A., *The Birds: Regulation of Isolated*

Wetlands and the Limits of the Commerce Clause, 28 U.C. DAVIS L. REV. 1237-1272 (1995). The following case addresses this ongoing controversy.

HOFFMAN HOMES, INC. v. ENVIRONMENTAL PROTECTION AGENCY

999 F.2d 256 (7th Cir. 1993)

WOOD, JR., SENIOR CIRCUIT JUDGE.

A tremendous amount of effort has gone into trying to determine whether a small wetland near Chicago may be regulated under the Clean Water Act. After having issued, then vacated, one opinion on this subject, we hope now to resolve this difficult question.

On March 26, 1986, an employee of the Army Corps of Engineers was driving through the Village of Hoffman Estates, Illinois. The employee happened to see that work had begun in a former soybean field on a new subdivision called "Victoria Crossings." The subdivision would occupy a 43-acre square parcel which is bordered on the west by the Schaumburg Branch of Poplar Creek, on the east by a road, on the north by another subdivision, and on the south by a wetland and a road.

The Corps investigated the site; it determined that the subdivision's owner, Hoffman Homes, Inc. ("Hoffman"), had violated the Clean Water Act ("CWA" or "Act"), 33 U.S.C. § 1251 et seq., when it filled and graded parts of the site in preparation for construction. Specifically, the Corps felt Hoffman illegally filled two wetlands, "Area A" and "Area B."

Area A was a bowl-shaped depression at the northeast border of the tract that covered approximately one-acre. The basin was lined with relatively impermeable clay; before being filled by Hoffman, Area A collected rain water and snow melt and frequently ponded or saturated during wet weather. Area A contained at least four different types of wetland vegetation, including cattails. Area A was not directly connected to any body of water, either on the surface or by groundwater, and lay approximately 750 feet from Poplar Creek. Area B ran along the entire western and most of the southern borders of the tract. This wetland covered 13.3 acres, of which Hoffman had filled 5.9 acres. Area B is part of a 50-acre wetland area adjacent to the Poplar Creek. The creek flows into the Fox River which is a tributary of the Illinois River which empties into the Mississippi River.

Having been designated as wetlands pursuant to 33 C.F.R. § 328.3(b), the sites could not legally be filled unless Hoffman obtained a permit pursuant to 33 U.S.C. § 1342 or § 1344. On May 30, 1986, the Corps issued a cease and desist order to Hoffman. This order instructed Hoffman to stop filling wetlands at the site and to apply for an after-the-fact permit to fill the areas. Hoffman did so. The Environmental Protection Agency ("EPA" or "Agency"), which shares responsibility with the Corps for administering and enforcing the CWA, then objected to Hoffman's plans for mitigating the damage to the wetlands.

Consequently, on November 20, 1987, the Corps denied Hoffman's permit application and referred the matter to the EPA.

The EPA on December 22, 1987, issued a compliance order pursuant to 33 U.S.C. § 1319(a). The order stated that Hoffman had filled wetlands without a permit, thereby violating 33 U.S.C. § 1311. The compliance order directed Hoffman to cease its filling activities and to submit and carry out a plan to restore the wetlands to their original condition. On January 12, 1988, the EPA also issued an administrative complaint against Hoffman, pursuant to 33 U.S.C. § 1319(g), seeking a $125,000 penalty for Hoffman's filling activities. Hoffman answered the complaint, admitting it had filled the two areas but denying they were waters subject to the CWA. On October 24, 1988, hearings commenced before an EPA Administrative Law Judge ("ALJ")....

On August 4, 1988, while the hearings before the ALJ were still proceeding, Hoffman brought an action in district court seeking a declaration of the compliance order's invalidity and an injunction against its enforcement. At that time the EPA had not yet decided whether to enforce its compliance order by bringing an action in a federal court pursuant to 33 U.S.C. § 1319(b). Consequently, the district court dismissed Hoffman's action in January 1989. The district court held that the CWA precluded preenforcement review of the EPA's compliance order. Hoffman appealed the district court's decision and we affirmed. We explained that Hoffman was not entitled to judicial review unless the EPA either assessed administrative penalties against Hoffman or sought judicial enforcement of its compliance order. Until such time, Hoffman was not subject to penalties or an injunction for not obeying the EPA's compliance order.

Shortly after our decision Hoffman became entitled to judicial review. On November 19, 1990, the EPA's Chief Judicial Officer ("CJO") assessed a $50,000 fine against Hoffman for having discharged "dredged or fill material" into Area A without a permit in violation of 33 U.S.C. § 1311 and § 1314 and affirmed another $50,000 penalty against Hoffman for filling Area B.

In fining Hoffman for filling Area A, the CJO was reversing the ALJ. On September 14, 1989, in the ALJ's "Initial Decision," the ALJ had found that although Area A was a wetland it was not subject to the CWA's permit requirements. The ALJ characterized Area A as being "isolated." The EPA had not shown, the ALJ found, that Area A had any surface or groundwater connection with Poplar Creek. In the ALJ's opinion, the Agency also failed to show that Area A performed flood control or sediment trapping in connection with drainage into or the possible flooding of the creek. Instead, the ALJ found that water drained into Area A from the immediately surrounding area, collected there, and then slowly evaporated or dissipated....

The ALJ recognized that under EPA and Corps regulations, Area A would be subject to the CWA permit requirements if the wetland affected interstate commerce, see 40 C.F.R. § 230.3(s)(3), 33 C.F.R. § 328.3(a)(3), and further noted that the EPA and Corps consider a wetland to affect interstate commerce if, for instance, the wetland serves as habitat for migratory birds. The ALJ, however, found the EPA had not presented evidence of actual use by migratory birds of Area A nor of any special characteristics that would attract migratory birds to Area A.

Since there was nothing more "than the theoretical possibility" Area A would be used by migratory birds, the ALJ found the regulations did not apply. The EPA appealed the ALJ's decision to the CJO. The EPA, however, did not challenge the ALJ's findings regarding Area A's hydrological isolation; the Agency only challenged the ALJ's conclusion that given those findings the regulations were inapplicable to Area A.

The CJO held that the EPA could not assert jurisdiction over "an isolated, intrastate water body" unless it could demonstrate "that the destruction of that water body will have an effect on interstate commerce." To satisfy its burden of proof, the CJO required the EPA to "show some minimal, potential effect on interstate commerce." This effect was shown, the CJO concluded, when the EPA demonstrated Area A provided "a suitable habitat for migratory birds before it was filled in." The CJO noted that Area B supported migratory bird habitat and by its proximity Area A could as well.

Hoffman appealed the CJO's decision regarding Area A, but not Area B, to this court. We exercised jurisdiction pursuant to 33 U.S.C. § 1319(g)(8)(B). The developer contended the CWA did not give the EPA regulatory authority over Area A. The EPA maintained it had jurisdiction due to the potential use of Area A by migratory birds. We held the EPA's regulations went beyond the limits of the Clean Water Act and the commerce clause, U.S. Const. art. 1, § 8, cl. 3. Accordingly, on April 22, 1992, we vacated the EPA's $50,000 penalty against Hoffman for filling Area A....

Hoffman Homes does not dispute that the EPA and the Corps have correctly characterized Area A as a wetland pursuant to 33 C.F.R. § 328.3(b) and 40 C.F.R. § 230.3(t). Nor does Hoffman deny having filled Area A. Hoffman disputes only that the small wetland can be regulated under the Clean Water Act.

Congress's objective in enacting the Clean Water Act was "to restore and maintain the chemical, physical, and biological integrity of the Nation's waters." 33 U.S.C. § 1251(a). To that end, the CWA prohibits "the discharge of dredged or fill material into the navigable waters" without a permit. *Id.* § 1344(a). The CWA defines "navigable waters" as meaning "the waters of the United States, including the territorial seas." *Id.* § 1362(7).

The CWA, though, does not define the term "waters of the United States." The EPA and the Corps have done so in two identically worded regulations. According to the EPA and the Corps, "waters of the United States" includes, among other things, bodies of water wholly within a state whose use or misuse could affect interstate commerce:

(s) The term waters of the United States means:

....

(3) All other waters such as intrastate lakes, rivers, streams (including intermittent streams), mudflats, sandflats, wetlands, sloughs, prairie potholes, wet meadows, playa lakes, or natural ponds, the use, degradation or destruction of which could affect interstate or foreign commerce including any such waters:

(i) Which are or could be used by interstate or foreign travelers for recreational or other purposes; or

(ii) From which fish or shellfish are or could be taken and sold in interstate or foreign commerce; or

(iii) Which are used or could be used for industrial purpose by industries in interstate commerce;

40 C.F.R. § 230.3(s)(3) (EPA's definition); 33 C.F.R. § 328.3(a)(3) (Corps' definition).

The EPA's Chief Judicial Officer ruled that the regulation extended to Area A by virtue of the wetland's potential effect on interstate commerce. It was not necessary under the regulation, the CJO held, that the EPA show an actual effect on interstate commerce. The CJO noted the EPA's regulation explicitly forbids the "degradation or destruction" of intrastate wetlands when such actions "could affect" interstate commerce: "The use of the word 'could' means that EPA need not show an actual effect on interstate commerce. Showing a potential effect will suffice."

Our job is to determine whether (i) the EPA properly interpreted 40 C.F.R. § 230.3(s)(3) and (ii) whether the CJO's finding of a violation of the CWA is supported by "substantial evidence." See 33 U.S.C. § 1319(g)(8) (mandating standard of review)....

Hoffman Homes has failed to persuade us the EPA has misread 40 C.F.R. § 230.3(s)(3). The regulation speaks of regulating wetlands and other bodies of water whose use, degradation or destruction "could" affect interstate commerce. This includes waters "which are or could be" used by interstate travellers, "from which fish or shellfish are or could be taken," and which "are used or could be used" for industrial purposes. We agree with the CJO that the use of the word "could" indicates the regulation covers waters whose connection to interstate commerce may be potential rather than actual, minimal rather than substantial.

We also agree with the CJO that it is reasonable to interpret the regulation as allowing migratory birds to be that connection between a wetland and interstate commerce. Throughout North America, millions of people annually spend more than a billion dollars on hunting, trapping, and observing migratory birds. Yet the cumulative loss of wetlands has reduced populations of many bird species and consequently the ability of people to hunt, trap, and observe those birds....

We obviously do not need to examine the EPA's finding that Hoffman filled Area A; Hoffman has admitted this act. We must ask, however, if the EPA's finding that Area A, before being filled, was a suitable or potential habitat for migratory birds is supported by substantial evidence. The ALJ, as noted earlier, found there was no evidence that any migratory birds actually used Area A. The witnesses the EPA presented only testified as to seeing migratory birds at Area B. The ALJ also found the EPA had failed to present any evidence "that Area A contains any characteristic that would render it any more attractive to birds than any other land that at one time or another contains water." Initial Decision at 48. The ALJ concluded: "It has not been shown by the preponderance of the evidence that Area A has characteristics whose use by and value to migratory birds is well established and that it is likely that it will be used by migratory birds."

Despite the ALJ's findings, the CJO concluded that on the same evidence Area A was a site suitable to migratory birds. Final Decision at 26. First, the CJO noted that Area A was located relatively close to Area B which itself was part of a fifty-acre wetland area and bordered Poplar Creek. Five witnesses testified before the ALJ as to the numerous migratory bird species they had spotted at Area B, including white egrets, blue herons, green herons, Canada geese, mallard ducks, red-winged blackbirds, and mourning doves. The CJO reasoned that if Area B would support those migratory birds then Area A would as well.

The CJO based this conclusion in part on the transcripts of testimony of two witnesses, Gerald Bade, a fish and wildlife biologist with the United States Fish and Wildlife Service, and Douglas Ehorn, an EPA water quality specialist. In the CJO's words, "Bade ... testified that the value of Wetland B as a suitable habitat for migratory birds would be replicated at Area A." Ehorn stated it was a "good possibility" migratory birds would use Area A.

Based on our examination of the record, we find the CJO's conclusion that Area A was suitable for migratory bird habitat to be unsupported by substantial evidence on the record as a whole. Bade, for example, testified as to what he had seen at Area B and not Area A. His testimony as to the suitability of Area A was merely speculation based on the assumption that Area A was a wetland similar to Area B. In contrast to Area B, Area A does not border a stream, it does not adjoin a large wetland, its only source of moisture is rainfall, it is only wet part of the year, and it covers approximately one acre instead of fifty....

It is true, of course, that migratory birds can alight most anywhere. As Gerald Bade testified, he has seen mallards in parking lot puddles. The ALJ, however, was in the unique position to view the evidence, to hear the testimony, and to judge the credibility of the witnesses. He concluded that the evidence did not support the conclusion that Area A had characteristics whose use by and value to migratory birds is well established. We agree. The migratory birds are better judges of what is suitable for their welfare than are we, the ALJ or the CJO. Having avoided Area A the migratory birds have thus spoken and submitted their own evidence. We see no need to argue with them....

... We know now that wetlands are not nuisances but instead are vital to the well-being of both humans and wildlife. Nonetheless, it is our conclusion based on the particular facts and findings below that Area A is not subject to regulation under the Clean Water Act. For this reason we vacate the EPA's order requiring Hoffman Homes, Inc. to pay a $50,000 administrative penalty for the filling of Area A.

NOTES AND QUESTIONS

1. The court conspicuously omitted any discussion of the Commerce Clause from its opinion. The limitations of EPA's jurisdiction was expressly based on the regulatory definition of "waters of the United States." *See* 40 C.F.R. § 230.3(s)(3); 33 C.F.R. § 328.3(a)(3). The court's earlier decision, which it vacated, swept more broadly by relying alternatively on the congressional intent of the Clean Water Act and the Commerce Clause to find no jurisdiction. *Hoffman Homes, Inc. v. EPA*, 961 F.2d 1310 (7th Cir.), *vacated*, 975 F.2d 1554 (7th Cir. 1992).

In *Leslie Salt Co. v. United States*, 55 F.3d 1388 (9th Cir.), *cert. denied by Cargill, Inc. v. United States*, 116 S. Ct. 407 (1995), the Ninth Circuit Court of Appeals held that an isolated, seasonally dry intrastate water used only by migrating birds *was* within the regulatory reach of 33 C.F.R. § 328.3(a)(3), the Clean Water Act, *and* the Commerce Clause. *Hoffman Homes* was cited in support of the "migratory bird" rule. *Id.* at 1395.

2. Developers have attempted to avoid Corps jurisdiction by asserting that the wetlands to be developed were artificially created. This defense has generally been rejected by the courts. *See, e.g., Track 12, Inc. v. Army Corps of Eng'rs*, 618 F. Supp. 448 (D. Minn. 1985); *United States v. Akers*, 651 F. Supp. 320 (E.D. Cal. 1987); *Bailey v. United States*, 647 F. Supp. 44 (D. Idaho 1986); *but see United States v. Fort Pierre*, 747 F.2d 464 (8th Cir. 1984) (artificial wetlands defense accepted because the Corps had created the wetland); *Leslie Salt Co. v. United States*, 896 F.2d 354 (9th Cir. 1990) (Corps jurisdiction under FWPCA extended to property which government actions had helped make aquatic so long as the Corps was not directly or solely responsible for flooding property).

3. The courts have rejected other constitutional challenges to the Corps' broadened jurisdiction as well. *See, e.g., United States v. Tull*, 769 F.2d 182 (4th Cir. 1985), *rev'd on other grounds sub nom. Tull v. United States*, 481 U.S. 412 (1987) (appeals court rejected challenge to wetlands definition as unconstitutionally vague). *See also Conant v. United States*, 786 F.2d 1008 (11th Cir. 1986) (rejected challenge based on failure of Clean Water Act to define "Waters of the United States" to include wetlands).

4. Section 10 of the Rivers and Harbors Act forbids excavation or construction in "navigable waters" without approval of the Corps of Engineers. 33 U.S.C. § 403; 33 C.F.R. § 320.1(a)(6) (delegation of authority under the RHA from the Secretary of the Army to the Corps of Engineers). Jurisdiction under the RHA is limited by the historical concept of navigable waters as those waters which were navigable, had been historically navigable, or were susceptible to navigation

with reasonable improvement. 33 C.F.R. § 329.4. With tidal waters, jurisdiction extends up to the mean high water line; with fresh waters, jurisdiction reaches to the ordinary high water mark. 33 C.F.R. §§ 322.2(a), 329.11(a). It is not clear whether the Corps has jurisdiction under the RHA over waters that are navigable in fact but without interstate navigability, *compare Utah v. Marsh*, 740 F.2d 799 (10th Cir. 1984) (the Corps had jurisdiction over lake located entirely within one state, as lake was used by interstate travelers for public recreation, supported commercial fishery which marketed bulk of its products out-of-state, was used to irrigate crops sold in interstate commerce, and was on flyway of migratory waterfowl protected under international treaties) *and United States v. Byrd*, 9 Env't Rep. Cas. (BNA) 1275 (N.D. Ind. 1976) (the Corps had jurisdiction over lake located entirely within one state and used by interstate travelers and seasonal residents for recreational purposes) *with Minnehaha Creek Watershed Dist. v. Hoffman*, 597 F.2d 617 (8th Cir. 1979) (where lake located entirely within one state, with partially navigable creek as its sole connecting waterway, lake and creek were found not subject to Corps jurisdiction because waters did not form a continual highway over which interstate commerce could be conducted); or over waterways that are infrequently navigable. *Compare Miami Valley Conservancy Dist. v. Alexander*, 507 F. Supp. 924, 931 (S.D. Ohio 1981), *aff'd in part, rev'd in part*, 692 F.2d 447 (6th Cir. 1982) *and Buttrey v. United States*, 573 F. Supp. 283, 296 (E.D. La. 1983) (non-navigability based on sporadic past use) *with Illinois v. Army Corps of Eng'rs*, 17 Env't Rep. Cas. (BNA) 2214 (N.D. Ill. 1981) (navigability despite infrequent past use).

Under RHA section 10, 33 U.S.C. § 403, a permit must be obtained from the Corps before obstructing navigable waters, or altering or modifying the "course, location, condition, or capacity" of any navigable waters. The Corps limits its section 10 jurisdiction to activities conducted in navigable waters or which affect its navigability. 33 C.F.R. § 322.3(a). Construction of canals altering the flow of shoreline tidal waters or the condition of navigable waters, *United States v. Sexton Cove Estates*, 526 F.2d 1293 (5th Cir. 1976); *United States v. Moretti*, 526 F.2d 1306 (5th Cir. 1976), lowering of water levels without impairing navigability, *Sierra Club v. Andrus*, 610 F.2d 581 (9th Cir. 1979), *rev'd on other grounds*, 451 U.S. 287, *and vacated*, 451 U.S. 965 (1981), and activities having "reasonably foreseeable" effects on navigable waters in the future, *United States v. Hanna*, 19 Env't Rep. Cas. (BNA) 1068, 1077-78 (D.S.C. 1983), have all been held to trigger section 10 jurisdiction. *But see National Wildlife Fed'n v. Alexander*, 613 F.2d 1054 (D.C. Cir. 1979) (construction of a drainage ditch not connected to navigable waters did not trigger section 10 jurisdiction).

Thus, the jurisdictional reach of section 404 over wetlands is generally much broader than that of the RHA. Moreover, an entire wetland is encompassed under section 404, as compared to the limitations of the mean or ordinary high water mark for RHA jurisdiction. The RHA continues to be important primarily when FWPCA section 404 does not apply due to an exemption under section 404(f)(1) or when activities are covered by RHA section 10 and not FWPCA section 404. Although the Clean Water Act encompasses many more wetlands than does the RHA, the RHA encompasses more development activities because it is not limited to discharges from point sources as is section 404.

AVOYELLES SPORTSMEN'S LEAGUE, INC. v. MARSH

715 F.2d 897 (5th Cir. 1983)

RANDALL, CIRCUIT JUDGE.

This is an appeal from a district court judgment that enjoined the private defendants from any additional clearing, except by permit under 33 U.S.C. § 1344 [citation], of certain lands determined by the district court to be wetlands. The federal defendants contend that the district court should have reviewed the Environmental Protection Agency's ("EPA") final wetlands determination ... on the basis of the administrative record, and that the court erred in adopting its own wetlands determination instead of reviewing the agency's determination under the arbitrary and capricious standard. The federal defendants also dispute the district court's conclusion that the mere removal of vegetation from wetlands constitutes a discharge of a pollutant under section 301(a) of the Clean Water Act ("CWA"), 33 U.S.C. § 1311(a) (1976). The private defendants contest the validity of the district court's determination that approximately ninety percent of their land is a wetland, as well as the court's conclusion that their landclearing activities fall under the CWA's prohibition on the discharge of pollutants into waters of the United States.

For the reasons set forth below, to the extent that the district court's decision that ninety percent of the Lake Long Tract is a wetland is inconsistent with the EPA's determination, the decision of the district court is reversed. The court's determination that the private defendants' actual landclearing activities require permits is affirmed.

This case concerns an approximately 20,000 acre tract of land (the "Lake Long Tract") in Avoyelles Parish, Louisiana. The tract lies within the Bayou Natchitoches basin, an area of approximately 140,000 acres, which, along with the Ouachita, Black and Tensas river basins, makes up the Red River backwater area. The Bayou Natchitoches basin is subject to flooding during the spring months, and it experiences an average rainfall of sixty inches per year.

Much of the basin had been cleared of forest before the private defendants began their landclearing activities, but 80,000 acres were still forested. The Lake Long Tract made up a quarter of this forested area. The topography of the tract itself is uneven, resulting in some areas with permanent water impoundments and other drier areas that support a variety of plant species.

The private defendants own the Lake Long Tract. They decided that the land could be put to agricultural use, specifically soybean production. Consequently, they began a program of large-scale deforestation in June of 1978. Using bulldozers with shearing blades that "floated" along the ground, the defendants cut the timber and vegetation at or just above ground level. The trees were then raked into windrows, burned, and the stumps and ashes were disced into the ground by other machinery. The shearing and raking caused some leveling of the tract, and the defendants dug one drainage ditch.

On August 25, 1978, the Vicksburg District of the Army Corps of Engineers ordered defendant Prevot to halt his activities pending a wetlands determination by the Corps. Thereafter, Dr. Donald G. Rhodes, an expert consultant employed by the Corps, undertook a comprehensive vegetative mapping of the Lake Long Tract and determined that thirty-five percent of it was a wetland. In October, 1978, the Fish and Wildlife Service wrote a letter to the Corps stating that the Service believed that the entire tract was a wetland. After Dr. Rhodes had made his determination, the landowners resumed their activities on the portion of the tract that the Corps had not designated as a wetland.

On November 8, 1978, the plaintiffs brought this citizens' suit against a number of Corps and EPA officials, as well as against the private landowners. The plaintiffs claimed, *inter alia*, that the landclearing activities would result in the discharge of dredged and fill material into the waters of the United States in violation of sections 301(a) and 404 of the CWA, 33 U.S.C. §§ 1311, 1344 [citation], and also result in the discharge of pollutants into the waters of the United States in violation of section 402 of the CWA, 33 U.S.C. § 1342 [citation]. The plaintiffs requested a declaration that the tract was a wetland within the scope of the CWA, that the private defendants could not engage in their landclearing activities without obtaining a permit from the EPA or the Corps, and that the federal defendants had failed to exercise their "mandatory duty" to designate the tract a wetland and to order the private defendants to cease and desist from discharging pollutants and dredged materials. The plaintiffs also sought injunctive relief against the federal defendants to require them to exercise their jurisdiction over the property and to issue cease-and-desist orders until the private defendants obtained the requisite permits. The district court immediately issued a temporary restraining order, preventing the private defendants from engaging in landclearing activities pending the court's action on the plaintiffs' motion for a preliminary injunction.

....

[The district court granted the plaintiff's motion for a preliminary injunction and ordered the Corps and EPA to make a final wetlands determination. In evaluating what land constituted wetlands, the defendants and EPA disagreed over whether the vegetation indicative of wetlands is limited to "obligate hydrophytes" or whether "facultative hydrophytes" are also wetlands indicators. The obligate hydrophytes exist in deep swamp areas or cypress swamp areas, which are inundated and water dominated most of each year. The facultative hydrophytes cannot withstand such extended periods of inundation, but can survive substantially shorter periods of intermittent inundation and saturation. After examining the vegetation, soil conditions and hydrology of the tract, EPA concluded that 80% of the tract was a wetland and specified which activities would require a section 404 permit. However, the district court conducted a *de novo* hearing to determine what portion of the tract qualified as a wetland and substituted its own evaluation for that of EPA. The court of appeals held that the district court erred in substituting its own wetlands determination for EPA's rather than reviewing EPA's determination under the arbitrary and capricious standard. It found that EPA's addition of facultative hydrophytes to the types of vegetation indicating the existence of wetlands was a reasonable interpretation of the regulations implementing section 404. The court of appeals then proceeded to evaluate several procedural and constitutional challenges before reaching the merits of EPA's wetlands determination.]

While the EPA found that approximately eighty percent of the Lake Long Tract was a wetland, the district court found that over ninety percent of the tract was a wetland. The court and the agency reached different conclusions because they held differing beliefs about whether Tensas and Dundee soils were wetlands soils....

While there may have been room for a difference in opinion about the nature of these soils, such a difference does not mean that the agency's decision was arbitrary or capricious. The agency and its expert explained their reasons for concluding that the Dundee and Tensas soils were not wetlands, and their decision is not irrational. Since the courts may not require any more than that, [citation], the district court erred in substituting its judgment about the character of the soils for the agency's.

....

In summary, we hold that the EPA's final wetlands determination was not arbitrary or capricious. Therefore, the district court's determination must be set aside to the extent that it is in conflict with the agency's, and the agency's determination should be reinstated.

....

The district court held that the private defendants' landclearing activities constituted a "discharge of a pollutant" into the waters of the United States, and that engaging in those activities without a section 404 dredge-and-fill permit was a violation of section 301(a) of the CWA. 33 U.S.C. § 1311(a). As the district court did, we must look beyond section 301(a) itself, to the statutory and regulatory definitions, in order to determine whether the district court's holding was correct.

Section 502(12) defines the term "discharge of a pollutant" as "(a) any addition of any pollutant to navigable waters from any point source...." 33 U.S.C. § 1362(12). A "point source" is defined in section 502(14) as "any discernible, confined and discrete conveyance, including but not limited to any ... container, rolling stock, concentrated animal feeding operation, or vessel ... from which pollutants are or may be discharged...." 33 U.S.C. § 1362(14). Section 502(6) defines the term "pollutant" to mean "dredged spoil, solid waste, incinerator residue, sewage, garbage, sewage sludge, munitions, chemical wastes, biological materials, radioactive materials, heat, wrecked or discarded equipment, rock, sand, cellar dirt and industrial, municipal and agricultural waste discharged into water." 33 U.S.C. § 1362(6). The question in this case is whether the landclearing activities were (1) a discharge (2) of a pollutant (3) from a point source (4) into navigable waters. Further, we must determine whether the activities were "normal agricultural activities" exempted from the permit requirements by 33 U.S.C. § 1344(f).

... [T]hese activities did occur in navigable waters, as that term is defined in the statute. Further, we agree with the district court that the bulldozers and backhoes were "point sources," since they collected into windrows and piles material that may ultimately have found its way back into the waters. *See Sierra Club v. Abston Construction Co.*, 620 F.2d 41 (5th Cir. 1980) (mining scrap piles may be point sources even though material may not be carried directly to waters from the piles); *United States v. Holland*, 373 F. Supp. 665, 668 (M.D. Fla. 1974) (bulldozers are point sources). The question then is whether these activities constituted a "discharge" of a "pollutant."

. . . .

The word "addition," as used in the definition of the term "discharge," may reasonably be understood to include "redeposit." As the district court recognized, this reading of the definition is consistent with both the purposes and legislative history of the statute. The CWA was designed to "restore and maintain the chemical, physical and biological integrity of the Nation's waters," 33 U.S.C. § 1251(a), and ... the legislative history indicates that Congress recognized the importance of protecting wetlands as a means of reaching the statutory goals. *See, e.g.*, 3 Legislative History, at 869 (remarks of Sen. Muskie) (quoted by the district court, 473 F. Supp. at 536). There is ample evidence in the record to support the district court's conclusion that the landowners' redepositing activities would significantly alter the character of the wetlands and limit the vital ecological functions served by the tract. Since we have concluded that the term "discharge" covers the redepositing of materials taken from the wetlands, we hold that the district court correctly decided that the landclearing activities on the Lake Long Tract constituted a discharge within the meaning of the Act.

Similarly, we agree with the district court, the plaintiffs and the federal defendants that the material discharged in this case was "fill," if not "dredged," material and hence subject to the Corps' regulation under section 404, as long as the activities did not fall within the section 404(f) exemption. The term "fill material" is defined in the Corps' regulations as

> any material used for the primary purpose of replacing an aquatic area with dry land or of changing the bottom elevation of a waterbody. The term does

not include any pollutant discharged into the water primarily to dispose of waste, as that activity is regulated under Section 402 of the Federal Water Pollution Control Act Amendments of 1972.

33 C.F.R. § 323.2(m). The regulations define the "discharge of fill material" as

the addition of fill material into waters of the United States. The term generally includes, without limitation, the following activities: Placement of fill that is necessary to the construction of any structure in a water of the United States; the building of any structure or impoundment requiring rock, sand, dirt, or other material for its construction; site-development fills for recreational, industrial, commercial, residential, and other uses; causeways or road fills; dams and dikes; artificial islands; property protection and/or reclamation devices such as rip-rap, groins, seawalls, breakwaters, and revetments; beach nourishment; levees; fill for structures such as sewage treatment facilities, intake and outfall pipes associated with power plants and subaqueous utility lines; and artificial reefs. The term does not include plowing, cultivating, seeding and harvesting for the production of food, fiber, and forest products.

33 C.F.R. § 323.2(n).
... [T]he burying of the unburned material, as well as the discing, had the effect of filling in the sloughs on the tract and leveling the land. The landowners insist that any leveling was "incidental" to their clearing activities and therefore the material was not deposited for the "primary purpose" of changing the character of the land. The district court found, however, that there had been significant leveling. The plaintiffs' witnesses testified that sloughs that had contained rainwater in the past had been filled in; thus, the activities were "changing the bottom elevation of the waterbody." Certainly, the activities were designed to "replace the aquatic area with dry land." Accordingly, we hold that the district court correctly concluded that the landowners were discharging "fill material" into the wetlands.
   ....
Finally, the private defendants argue that their activities are normal farming activities exempt under section 404(f) of the Act. 33 U.S.C. § 1344(f) [citation]. Section 404(f)(1) exempts from the permit requirements:

(f)(1) Except as provided in paragraph (2) of this subsection, the discharge of dredged or fill material —
(A) from normal farming, silviculture, and ranching activities such as plowing, seeding, cultivating, minor drainage, harvesting for the production of food, fiber, and forest products, or upland soil and water conservation practices.

33 U.S.C. § 1344(f)(1)(A). The Corps' regulations further implement this limitation by excluding "plowing, cultivating, feeding and harvesting for the

production of food, fiber and forest products" from the definitions of a discharge of dredged or fill material. 33 C.F.R. §§ 323.2(l), (n). While the private defendants' landclearing activities are not those specified in the Act, the defendants insist that the activities are nonetheless "normal" farming practices that should fall within the exemption.

The district court believed that the section 404(f)(1) exemptions were limited to "ongoing" agricultural activities. It reasoned that the word "'normal' connote[d] an established and continuing activity," and that the activities set out as examples in section 404(f)(1)(A) were the kinds of activities that would "only occur on a continuing basis as part of an ongoing farming or forestry operation." *Avoyelles I*, 473 F. Supp. at 535.[44] Because "no farming operation was or could have been contemplated [on the Lake Long Tract] until after the acreage had been cleared," the district court concluded that the activities in this case were not "normal farming activities." *Id.* It added that this conclusion was "buttressed" by the fact that "section 404(f)(2) specifically takes away the exemption for activities that involve changing the use of the land." *Id.* Since we agree with the district court that section 404(f)(2) precludes applying the "normal farming activities" exemption in this case, we affirm the district court's decision on that basis.[45]

Section 404(f)(2) takes away at least some of the exemptions arguably provided by section 404(f)(1):

> (2) Any discharge of dredged or fill material into the navigable waters incidental to any activity having as its purpose bringing an area of the navigable waters into a use to which it was not previously subject, where the flow or circulation of navigable waters may be impaired or the reach of such waters be reduced, shall be required to have a permit under this section.

33 U.S.C. § 1344(f)(2). Read together, the two parts of section 404(f) provide a narrow exemption for agricultural and silvicultural activities that have little or no adverse effect on the nation's waters. This is precisely what Congress intended in enacting the amendment.... As the district court opinion ably demonstrates, the purpose and effect of the landclearing activities on the Lake Long Tract was to bring "an area of the navigable waters into a use to which it was not previously subject." 33 U.S.C. § 1344(f)(2). All of the vegetation was cut down, the land leveled, and at least one ditch dug to increase drainage so that the property could be *changed* from a forest to a soybean field. These changes can hardly be viewed as having a minimal adverse effect on the wetlands. Accordingly, we hold that the district court was correct in concluding that the

---

[44]The district court correctly noted that § 404(f)(1) was designed to be a narrow exemption. *Avoyelles I*, 473 F. Supp. at 535 n. 12 (quoting the statements of Rep. Hersha during the House debates, 3 *Legislative History*, at 420).

[45]The private defendants point out that if the district court is correct that § 404(f)(1) applies only to ongoing activities, § 404(f)(2) would not appear to be necessary.

landclearing activities in this case were not exempt farming activities under section 404(f)(1).

....

With respect to the activities issue, we hold:

(1) that the bulldozers and backhoes were "point sources" within the meaning of the Clean Water Act;

(2) that in filling in the sloughs and leveling the land, the landowners were redepositing fill material into waters of the United States, and that therefore, these activities constituted a "discharge of a pollutant";

(3) that the landclearing activities were not exempt from the Corps' permit requirements under section 404(f)(1) of the CWA because those activities constituted a change in use of wetlands under section 404(f)(2).

Accordingly, we affirm the district court's judgment that these landclearing activities may not be carried out without a section 404 dredge-and-fill permit....

NOTES AND QUESTIONS

1. Would boating activity that uproots seagrass and deposits bottom sediment on a submerged wetland necessitate a permit as a discharge of a pollutant under section 404 of the FWPCA or section 10 of the RHA? *See United States v. M.C.C. of Florida, Inc.*, 772 F.2d 1501 (11th Cir. 1985), *vacated on other grounds*, 481 U.S. 1034. Relying on *Avoyelles*, the court rejected the argument that the deposits were not an "*addition*" of a pollutant on the grounds that redepositing materials is subject to section 404. M.C.C. also argued that the term "work" meant a planned intentional construction or undertaking, and so the unintended dredging and filling caused by the propellors of its tugs was not "work" under RHA section 10. The court rejected this argument on the grounds that M.C.C.'s narrow interpretation of section 10 had been rejected by the Supreme Court in *United States v. Republic Steel Corp.*, 362 U.S. 482 (1980), and that even if the court accepted M.C.C.'s interpretation, M.C.C.'s activities would still fit within those requiring a permit under section 10. 772 F.2d at 1504-5. Although *M.C.C. of Florida* might ostensibly seem to subject any boating that disturbs the bottom of a wetland to the Corps' jurisdiction, it has been suggested that the case may be limited to circumstances in which there is the presence of hydrophytic vegetation, substantial damage, and a major project involving the boating activity. Want, *Federal Wetlands Litigation: 1986 to the Present*, [Current Developments] Env't Rep. (BNA) 2563, 2565 (Apr. 29, 1988).

2. The Corps and EPA have retained the definition adopted in 1977 of wetlands as

those areas that are inundated or saturated by surface or ground water at a frequency and duration sufficient to support, and that under normal circumstances do support, a prevalence of vegetation typically adapted for life in saturated soil conditions.

33 C.F.R. § 328.3(b). The factors to be considered in evaluating section 404 jurisdiction are the type of soils, the type of vegetation, and the degree and frequency of inundation. *Avoyelles Sportsmen's League, Inc. v. Marsh*, 715 F.2d 897, 931 (5th Cir. 1983). Hydrophytic species are not limited to those able to survive their entire life cycle in saturated conditions. *Id.*; *accord United States v. Carter*, 18 Env't Rep. Cas. (BNA) 1804, 1808 (S.D. Fla. 1982). Rainfall alone can be a sufficient source of water to satisfy the inundation requirement. *United States v. Fleming Plantations*, 12 Env't Rep. Cas. (BNA) 1705, 1707 (E.D. La. 1978); *but cf. Bayou St. John Imp. Ass'n v. Sands*, 13 Envtl. L. Rep. (Envtl. L. Inst.) 20,011, 20,013 (E.D. La. 1982) (submerged grassland not a wetland because of constant, not intermittent, inundation). Wetlands which periodically dry out are still subject to regulation, even during a dry period. *See, e.g., United States v. Phelps Dodge Corp.*, 391 F. Supp. 1181 (D. Ariz. 1975).

On January 10, 1989, the Corps of Engineers, EPA, the Fish and Wildlife Service, and the Soil Conservation Service adopted a joint federal manual for identifying and delineating wetlands. The manual utilizes three criteria — wetland hydrology, hydrophytic vegetation, and hydric soils — for making a wetlands determination. Although all three criteria must be satisfied, the satisfaction of one criterion can in some circumstances be presumed from the satisfaction of another. The Federal Manual for Identifying and Delineating Jurisdictional Wetlands met with immediate resistance from farmers and developers for bringing millions of additional acres within the reach of section 404, support from environmentalists, and a flurry of congressional legislation. The four agencies immediately began revising the manual. After prolonged agency infighting, in part over utilization of facultative hydrophytes to evaluate wetlands as in the *Avoyelles* case, President George Bush announced on August 9, 1991 a narrowing of the definition of wetlands that excluded from protection a third of the 100 million acres that would have been covered by the definition of wetlands in the Federal Manual. *Wetlands Policy Shift Announced*, WASH. POST, Aug. 10, 1991, at A1, col. 1.

Environmental groups organized letter writing campaigns in an effort to prevent the proposed redefinition of wetlands from being implemented. EPA received over 80,000 comments on the proposed manual. On November 20, 1992, a White House official said that the Bush administration had decided to abandon efforts to modify the manual. *Administration Abandons Plans to Modify Wetlands Manual Before Bush Leaves Office*, [Current Developments] 23 Env't Rep. (BNA) 1913 (Nov. 27, 1992).

However, while the debate over the proposed redefinition of wetlands was just heating up, the Corps of Engineers announced that it was returning to the 1987 Wetlands Manual. The Corps was required to take this action by language in an appropriations bill which forbade the Corps from using fiscal year 1992 funds for implementation of the 1989 Manual. 19 Land Use Planning Rep. (BPI) 145 (1991). EPA continued to use the 1989 Manual in making jurisdictional determinations, but in judicial actions it adopted the practice of confirming jurisdiction under the 1987 Manual as well. However, the EPA and the Corps were still concerned with the potential for confusion and inconsistencies presented by the use of two different manuals. On January 19, 1993 the EPA and the Corps released a Memorandum of Agreement which provided that the EPA and the Corps wold both use the 1987 Manual in determining wetlands status under § 404. EPA & DOD, *Memorandum of Agreement Concerning the Determination of the Geographic Jurisdiction of the Section 404 Program*, 58 Fed. Reg. 4995 (Jan. 19, 1993).

3. Is it clear that section 505 of the FWPCA allows citizens' suits to be brought to enforce section 404? What is the question of statutory construction as to whether such a citizen suit can be brought? Commentators have disagreed over whether section 505 authorizes citizen suits for violations of section 404. *Compare* Want, *Federal Wetlands Law: The Cases and the Problems*, 8 HARV. ENVTL. L. REV. 1, 24 (1984) (suggesting that citizen suits are authorized), *with* 2 S. NOVICK, LAW OF ENVIRONMENTAL PROTECTION § 12.06[5][a] (suggesting that the issue is at best unresolved). The question of whether section 505 authorizes private enforcement is an issue of statutory construction. In *Avoyelles*, the court's jurisdiction under section 505 was not challenged until after the Fifth Circuit's decision on the merits, when attorney's fees were sought under section 505(d). In an unreported decision the district court rejected the government's argument, and the argument was not raised on appeal. NOVICK, *supra*, at § 12.06[5][a] n.158.2. The Fourth Circuit Court of Appeals has also recognized a citizen suit may be brought to enforce section 404. *National Wildlife Fed. v. Hanson*, 859 F.2d 313 (4th Cir. 1988). For further discussion of the limitations on citizen suits to enforce section 404, *see* Comment, *Wetland Protection Under Section 404 of the Clean Water Act: An Enforcement Paradox*, 27 SAN DIEGO L. REV. 139, 149-50, 166-68 (1990).

4. Section 404 requires a permit for discharge of dredged or fill material by a point source into navigable waters. "Dredged" and "fill" materials are not defined in the Act, but are defined by EPA and the Corps in regulations. Dredged material is material that is excavated or dredged from waters of the United States. 33 C.F.R. § 323.2(c). Fill material has different definitions in the regulations of EPA and the Corps. The Corps defines fill material as

> any material used for the primary purpose of replacing an aquatic area with dry land or of changing the bottom elevation of a waterbody. The term does not include any pollutant discharged into the water primarily to dispose of waste, as that activity is regulated under Section 402 of the Clean Water Act.

Id. § 323.2(e). EPA rejects this "primary purpose" test as too subjective, substituting a definition of fill material as material, the discharge of which has the effect of replacing an aquatic area with dry land or of changing the bottom elevation of a water body. 40 C.F.R. § 232.2(i). Discharges by point sources which are not discharges of dredged or fill material may still be subject to the section 402 permit requirement administered by EPA and the states. The difference in the Corps' and EPA's definitions of fill material can be subject to abuse by applicants evaluating the relative ease in a given situation of obtaining a section 402 permit or a section 404 permit.

5. Exempt from the section 404 permit requirement are discharges from (1) normal farming activities; (2) maintenance or reconstruction of dams, breakwaters, and other similar structures; (3) construction or maintenance of farm ponds or irrigation and drainage ditches; (4) construction of temporary sedimentation basins on a construction site which do not put fill materials into navigable waters; (5) construction or maintenance of farm roads, forest roads or roads for mining equipment constructed in accordance with best management practices; and (6) activity with respect to which a state has an approved nonpoint source management program. FWPCA § 404(f)(1), 33 U.S.C. § 1344(f)(1). However, any discharge of dredged or fill material from an activity which will bring an area of navigable waters into a new use, impair the flow or circulation of the waters, or reduce the reach of the waters must have a permit. FWPCA § 404(f)(2), 33 U.S.C. § 1344(f)(2). The courts, as in *Avoyelles*, have narrowly interpreted these exemptions and placed the ultimate burden of persuasion on the person seeking the exemption. *United States v. Cumberland Farms of Conn., Inc.*, 647 F. Supp. 1166 (D. Mass. 1986), *aff'd on other grounds*, 826 F.2d 1151 (1st Cir. 1987) (noting that at that time the Fifth, Seventh, and Ninth Circuit Courts of Appeals had construed the exemptions narrowly). Who has the ultimate authority to determine whether an exemption applies — the Corps or EPA?

The exemption for farming activities is the most litigated exemption. *See, e.g.*, *United States v. Huebner*, 752 F.2d 1235 (7th Cir. 1985); *United States v. Akers*, 785 F.2d 814 (9th Cir. 1986); *United States v. Cumberland Farms of Conn., Inc.*, 647 F. Supp. 1166 (D. Mass. 1986), *aff'd*, 826 F.2d 1151 (1st Cir. 1987); *United States v. Larkins*, 657 F. Supp. 76 (W.D. Ky. 1987), *aff'd*, 852 F.2d 189 (6th Cir. 1988) (all cases finding 404(f)(2) applicable). *See also Conant v. United States*, 786 F.2d 1008 (11th Cir. 1986) (no exemption because of conversion to new use for fish farming). For a discussion of the *Avoyelles* series of cases and agriculture's impact on wetlands generally, see Torres, *Wetlands and Agriculture: Environmental Regulation and the Limits of Private Property*, 34 U. KAN. L. REV. 539 (1986); Note, *United States v. Larkins: Conflict Between Wetland Protection and Agriculture; Exploration of the Farming Exemption to the Clean Water Act's Section 404 Permit Requirement*, 35 S.D.L. REV. 272 (1990).

On September 26, 1990, the Corps limited its section 404 jurisdiction by exempting wetlands cropped before December 23, 1985, from section 404 permit requirements. *See* Regulatory Guidance Letter, No. 90-7, *Clarification of the Phrase "Normal Circumstances" as it Pertains to Cropped Wetlands*, 21 ENVTL. L. REP. (Envtl. L. Inst.) 35,271 (Sept. 26, 1990). For discussion of the September 26, 1990 regulatory guidance, see *Millions of Acres of Converted Wetlands No Longer Subject to Federal Water Act Permits*, [Current Developments] Env't Rep. (BNA) 1120 (Oct. 5, 1990); *60 Million Farm Acres Lose Wetlands Protection Status*, WASH. POST, Sept. 29, 1990, at A2, col. 5.

2. PERMIT REQUIREMENTS UNDER SECTION 404

Every section 404 permit must be reviewed for compliance with the section 404(b)(1) guidelines. *See* 33 U.S.C. § 1344(b). These guidelines were promulgated by the Administrator of EPA and the Secretary in final form on December 24, 1980. 40 C.F.R. Part 230. There are four substantive restrictions on permit issuance in the guidelines. A permit will be issued if (1) there is no practicable alternative to the proposed project; (2) there will be no significant adverse impacts on aquatic resources; (3) all reasonable mitigation is employed; and (4) there will be no statutory violations by the proposed activity. 40 C.F.R. § 230.10(a)-(d). The final criterion is simply to assure that other state and federal laws, including those for endangered species, coastal zone management, state water quality standards, toxic discharges, and marine sanctuaries are not violated. In addition, the Corps must comply in permit issuance with a number of other statutory requirements including the National Environmental Policy Act, state water quality certification, and consistency certification with state coastal zone management plans.

Even if a permit application satisfies these four criteria, the Corps has taken the position that it can deny a permit for being "contrary to the public interest." *See* 33 C.F.R. § 320.4(a). The Corps' regulations for public interest review require consideration of and substantial weight for wetlands values. 33 C.F.R. § 320.4(b). The public interest review is a wide-ranging assessment of many other factors as well, including economics, aesthetics, historic preservation, fish and wildlife values, floodplain effects, land use, navigation, recreation, energy and water needs, and "the needs and welfare of the people." 33 C.F.R. § 320.4(a)(1). The regulations do not specify, however, the weight to be given non-wetland factors, whether the Corps must consider any indirect effects of the proposed activity, and whether the Corps can consider the effects of the entire project or just the covered activity. One district court has held that the Corps exceeded its authority by denying a section 404 permit on socioeconomic grounds. *Mall Props., Inc. v. Marsh*, 672 F. Supp. 561 (D. Mass. 1987). The First Circuit Court of Appeals held on appeal only that the lower court's order remanding to the Corps for further proceedings was not a final appealable order. 841 F.2d 440 (1st Cir. 1988).

SYLVESTER v. ARMY CORPS OF ENGINEERS

882 F.2d 407 (9th Cir. 1989)

SNEED, CIRCUIT JUDGE.

[The proposed resort in Squaw Valley, California at issue in this case would include a resort village, skiing facilities, and a golf course. The golf course would necessitate filling of eleven acres of wetlands along Squaw Creek.]

Sylvester appeals the district court's denial of a motion for a preliminary injunction. We affirm.

This appeal addresses issues not before this court in an earlier appeal in which we reversed the district court's issuance of a temporary injunction. *See Sylvester v. United States Army Corps of Eng'rs*, 871 F.2d 817 (9th Cir. 1989) (*Sylvester I*).

We review the district court's refusal to grant injunctive relief for abuse of discretion. [Citation.] This court will set aside the Corps' decision only if it is "arbitrary, capricious, an abuse of discretion, or otherwise not in accordance with [the] law." 5 U.S.C. § 706(2)(A) (1982).

Sylvester raises three objections to the district court's decision which we will address in turn. In sum, Sylvester argues that the Corps violated the CWA, the NEPA, and its own regulations in issuing a permit to Perini to fill eleven acres of wetlands in the process of building a golf course.

A. *Practicable Alternative Under the CWA*

First, we turn to Sylvester's claim that the Corps impermissibly accepted Perini's definition of the project as necessitating an on-site, eighteen hole golf course. By accepting this definition, Sylvester contends that the Corps' evaluation of practicable alternatives was skewed in favor of Perini.

The regulations implementing § 404 of the CWA provide that "no discharge of dredged or fill material shall be permitted if there is a *practicable alternative* to the proposed discharge which would have less adverse impact on the aquatic ecosystem, so long as the alternative does not have other significant adverse environmental consequences." 40 C.F.R. § 230.10(a) (1988) (emphasis added). The Corps defines a practicable alternative as an alternative that "is available and capable of being done after taking into consideration cost, existing technology, and logistics *in light of overall project purposes.*" *Id.* § 230.10(a)(2) (emphasis added). Further, because the golf course is not a water dependent activity, the Corps' regulations presume that practicable alternatives are available "unless clearly demonstrated otherwise." *Id.* § 230.10(a)(3); *see also Louisiana Wildlife Fed'n, Inc. v. York*, 603 F. Supp. 518, 527 (W.D. La. 1984), *aff'd in part and vacated in part*, 761 F.2d 1044 (5th Cir. 1985) ("[Classification] of an activity as 'non-water dependent' does not serve as an automatic bar to issuance of a permit ... [it] simply necessitates a more persuasive showing than otherwise concerning the lack of alternatives.").

In its Environmental Assessment (EA), the Corps defined the project's purpose as follows:

> To construct an 18-hole, links style, championship golf course and other recreational amenities in conjunction with the development of the proposed Resort at Squaw Creek. Research conducted for the applicant has indicated that a quality 18-hole golf course is an essential element for a successful alpine destination resort.

Sylvester protests that the use of this definition impermissibly skewed the "practicable alternatives" analysis in favor of Perini. Specifically, Sylvester objects to the Corps' failure to consider off-site locations for the golf course, i.e., a site that was not contiguous to the rest of the resort complex. The Corps rejected consideration of such an alternative because it "did not meet [Perini's] basic purpose and need." The Corps did note, however, that two off-site locations were considered but rejected because of insufficient size and the potential for more severe environmental impacts.

In evaluating whether a given alternative site is practicable, the Corps may legitimately consider such facts as cost to the applicant and logistics. [Citation.] In addition, the Corps has a duty to consider the applicant's purpose. As the Fifth Circuit observed: "[T]he Corps has a duty to take into account the objectives of the applicant's project. Indeed, it would be bizarre if the Corps were to ignore the purpose for which the applicant seeks a permit and to substitute a purpose it deems more suitable." *Louisiana Wildlife Fed'n, Inc. v. York*, 761 F.2d 1044, 1048 (5th Cir. 1985) (per curiam) (footnote omitted).

Obviously, an applicant cannot define a project in order to preclude the existence of any alternative sites and thus make what is practicable appear impracticable. This court in *Hintz* quite properly suggested that the applicant's purpose must be "legitimate." *Id.* at 833. Yet, in determining whether an alternate site is practicable, the Corps is not entitled to reject Perini's genuine and legitimate conclusion that the type of golf course it wishes to construct is economically advantageous to its resort development.

By contrast, an alternative site does not have to accommodate components of a project that are merely incidental to the applicant's *basic* purpose. For example, in *Shoreline Assocs. v. Marsh*, 555 F. Supp. 169, 179 (D. Md. 1983), *aff'd*, 725 F.2d 677 (4th Cir. 1984), the Corps refused to issue a permit to a developer for building a number of waterfront town houses together with a boat storage and launching facility. The developer argued that the Corps' proposed alternative site for the town houses could not accommodate the boat storage and launch area. The court upheld the Corps' denial of the permit, observing that the boat facilities were merely "incidental" to the town house development. *Id.* In this case, it is not the resort buildings that are at issue as were the town houses in *Shoreline*. The location of the resort buildings was fixed by decisions not involving the Corps of Engineers; and we held in *Sylvester I* that the location of the proposed golf course partially on wetlands did not "federalize" the entire development. Rather the issue in this case, *Sylvester II*, is whether this proposed location ignores other reasonable and practicable alternatives, including no golf course at all. Resolution of this issue requires that the relationship of the course to the entire project be considered. The Corps of Engineers did consider this relationship. Doing so was neither arbitrary nor capricious.

In no way does this conclusion conflict with *Sylvester I*. A relationship required to be considered in determining reasonable and practicable alternatives need not be of such significance as would be necessary to "federalize" the entire project. True, the golf course is not incidental to the resort; but then neither is it the compelling force, the centerpiece, of the resort. To illustrate, *Shoreline* would have resembled *Sylvester I* had the only issue been the location of the boat storage and launch sites, the location of the town houses already having been fixed on a site not subject to federal jurisdiction. Obviously the relationship between the town houses and the boat storage and launch sites would be considered in evaluating possible alternative sites of the latter two; equally obvious, this relationship should not "federalize" the entire project.

B. *Evaluation of the Benefits of the Golf Course*

Sylvester next argues that the Corps' analysis of the "reasonable alternatives" under the NEPA to the project was improper. Sylvester contends that the Corps limited its consideration of the impact of the proposed development to only those of the golf course while simultaneously including the benefits from the entire resort complex. Sylvester argues that such an analysis violates the Corps' regulations. Similarly, Sylvester argues that the Corps' CWA "public interest analysis" was likewise skewed in favor of the project.

It is Sylvester's refusal to recognize the difference between a relationship that "federalizes" an entire project and one that is properly considered in evaluating benefits of a proposed federal action that lies at the bottom of his assertions that the Corps violated its regulations and skewed its CWA public interest analysis. The Corps did not, as Sylvester argues, weigh the benefits of the entire project against the environmental impacts of the golf course. The EA makes plain that the Corps followed its regulations and weighed only the benefits of the golf course to the resort.

We conclude, therefore, that the Corps quite properly did measure the benefit of the golf course in terms of its contribution to making the resort an economically viable year-round facility with all of its attendant advantages. This analysis was proper under both the CWA and the NEPA.

....

NOTES AND QUESTIONS

1. The most critical hurdle in the guidelines to permit issuance is the "practicable alternatives" test at issue in *Sylvester*. As the case indicates, practicable alternatives to non-water-dependent projects are presumed to be available unless the applicant can demonstrate otherwise. Moreover, practicable alternatives that do not require discharges into wetlands are presumed to have less adverse impacts on the aquatic ecosystem than projects that do require such discharges, unless the applicant can demonstrate otherwise. These rebuttable presumptions weigh generally against issuance of a permit. However, for an alternative to be practicable the alternative must be both "available" to the applicant and capable of fulfilling the overall purpose of the project "taking into consideration cost, existing technology, and logistics." 40 C.F.R. § 230.10(a)(2). If the Corps determines there are practicable alternatives with a less adverse impact on the aquatic ecosystem, the permit will be denied. If the Corps determines, however, that there are no practicable alternatives, the Corps then proceeds to evaluate whether there are methods for mitigation of any environmental losses caused by the proposal. The relevance of mitigation to permit issuance has been a source of dispute between EPA and the Corps for years. The Corps had indicated its willingness to grant a permit when the applicant offers to create a habitat of equal or greater value in another location. EPA was much more skeptical about mitigation, taking the position that the guidelines do not permit mitigation as a remedy for wetland destruction when other practicable alternatives exist. *See generally* W. WANT, LAW OF WETLANDS REGULATION § 6.10 (1991). The interagency dispute came to a head in the landmark *Bersani* case which follows, and which also explores the issue of when an alternative is "available" to an applicant.

2. Permit applications are handled by the Civil Works division of the Corps, with the initial decision made by district engineers. Evaluation of permits is done through informal rulemaking that includes public notice and comment. *See generally* 33 C.F.R. § 325.3. Despite language in the Clean Water Act which might suggest a formal adjudication is required (section 404(a), 33 U.S.C. § 1344(a) states that the Secretary may issue permits "after notice and opportunity for public hearings."), the courts that have addressed the issue agree that permit proceedings do not have to be conducted as formal adjudicatory hearings under the APA (Administrative Procedure Act) as both a matter of statutory and constitutional law. *Buttrey v. United States*, 690 F.2d 1170 (5th Cir. 1982); *Nofelco Realty Corp. v. United States*, 521 F. Supp. 458 (S.D.N.Y. 1981). The Corps of Engineers may delegate section 404 permitting authority to a state upon approval of a qualified state program under section 404(h), 33 U.S.C. § 1344(h).

3. Under section 404(b)(2), the Corps may issue a permit that violates the guidelines if justified by the economic impact of the site on navigation and anchorage. 33 U.S.C. § 1344(b)(2). Section 404(c), however, gives EPA the right to override the Corps' permit approval if the discharge would have an unacceptable adverse effect on municipal water supplies, shellfish beds and fishery areas, wildlife, or recreational areas. 33 U.S.C. § 1344(c). The following case explores one of the rare instances in which EPA has exercised that veto power.

BERSANI v. ROBICHAUD

850 F.2d 36 (2d Cir. 1988)

TIMBERS, CIRCUIT JUDGE.

....

This case arises out of Pyramid's attempt to build a shopping mall on certain wetlands in Massachusetts known as Sweedens Swamp. Acting under the Clean Water Act, 33 U.S.C. § 1251 *et seq.*, EPA vetoed the approval by the Corps of a permit to build the mall because EPA found that an alternative site had been available to Pyramid at the time it entered the market to search for a site for the mall. The alternative site was purchased later by another developer and arguably became unavailable by the time Pyramid applied for a permit to build the mall.

On appeal, the thrust of Pyramid's argument is a challenge to what it calls EPA's "market entry" theory, i.e., the interpretation by EPA of the relevant regulation, which led EPA to consider the availability of alternative sites at the time Pyramid entered the market for a site, instead of at the time it applied for a permit. Pyramid argues principally (1) that the market entry approach is contrary to the regulatory language and past practice; and (2) that since the Corps, another agency which was jointly responsible with EPA for administering the program in question, interpreted the pertinent regulation in a different way than EPA had, and since the market entry issue does not involve environmental expertise, this Court should not defer to EPA's interpretation of the regulation....

We hold (1) that the market entry theory is consistent with both the regulatory language and past practice; (2) that EPA's interpretation, while not necessarily entitled to deference, is reasonable; and (3) that EPA's application of the regulation is supported by the administrative record. We agree with the district court's conclusion that EPA's findings were not arbitrary and capricious. We also hold that Pyramid's other arguments, and the arguments of one intervenor and the amicus, lack merit.

We affirm.

....

... It is undisputed that Sweedens Swamp is a "navigable water," as defined in 33 U.S.C. § 1362, and that Pyramid's shopping center proposal will involve the discharge of dredged or fill materials.

Section 404 of the Act, 33 U.S.C. § 1344, focusing on dredged or fill materials, provides that the United States Army and EPA will share responsibility for implementation of its provisions. EPA and the Corps also share responsibility for enforcing the Act. 33 U.S.C. §§ 1311, 1319, 1344(n) and (s). Section 404(a) authorizes the Secretary of the Army, acting through the Corps, to issue permits for the discharge of dredged or fill materials at particular sites. 33 U.S.C. § 1344(a). Section 404(b) provides that, subject to § 404(c), the Corps must base its decisions regarding permits on guidelines (the "404(b)(1) guidelines") developed by EPA in conjunction with the Secretary of the Army. 33 U.S.C. § 1344(b).

The 404(b)(1) guidelines, published at 40 C.F.R. Part 230 (1987), are regulations containing the requirements for issuing a permit for discharge of dredged or fill materials. 40 C.F.R. § 230.10(a)[2] covers "non-water dependent

---

[2]Section 230.10(a)(2) and (3) provide:

"(a) Except as provided under section 404(b)(2) [pertaining to navigation] no discharge of dredged or fill material shall be permitted if there is a practicable alternative to the proposed discharge which would have less adverse impact on the aquatic ecosystem, so long as the alternative does not have other significant adverse environmental consequences.

....

activities" (i.e., activities that could be performed on non-wetland sites, such as building a mall) and provides essentially that the Corps must determine whether an alternative site is available that would cause less harm to the wetlands. Specifically, it provides that "no discharge of dredged or fill material shall be permitted if there is a practicable alternative" to the proposal that would have a "less adverse impact" on the "aquatic ecosystem." It also provides that a practicable alternative may include "an area not presently owned by the applicant which could reasonably be obtained, utilized, expanded or managed in order to fulfill the basic purpose of the proposed activity." 40 C.F.R. 230.10(a)(2). It further provides that, "unless clearly demonstrated otherwise," practicable alternatives are (1) "presumed to be available" and (2) "presumed to have less adverse impact on the aquatic ecosystem." 40 C.F.R. 230.10(a)(3). Thus, an applicant such as Pyramid must rebut both of these presumptions in order to obtain a permit. Sections 230.10(c) and (d) require that the Corps not permit any discharge that would contribute to significant degradation of the nation's wetlands and that any adverse impacts must be mitigated through practicable measures.

In addition to following the 404(b)(1) guidelines, the Corps may conduct a "public interest review." 33 C.F.R. § 320.4. This public interest review is not mandatory under § 404, unlike consideration of the 404(b) guidelines. In a public interest review, the Corps' decision must reflect the "national concern" for protection and use of resources but must also consider the "needs and welfare of the people." *Id.*

Under § 404(c) of the Act, 33 U.S.C. § 1344(c), EPA has veto power over any decision of the Corps to issue a permit. It is this provision that is at the heart of the instant case.

Specifically, § 404(c) provides that the Administrator of EPA may prohibit the specification of a disposal site "whenever he determines, after notice and opportunity for public hearings, that the discharge of materials into such area will have an unacceptable adverse effect" on, among other things, wildlife. An "unacceptable adverse effect" is defined in 40 C.F.R. § 231.2(e) as an effect that is likely to result in, among other things, "significant loss of or damage to ...

---

(2) An alternative is practicable if it is available and capable of being done after taking into consideration cost, existing technology, and logistics in light of overall project purposes. If it is otherwise a practicable alternative, an area not presently owned by the applicant which could reasonably be obtained, utilized, expanded or managed in order to fulfill the basic purpose of the proposed activity may be considered.

(3) Where the activity associated with a discharge which is proposed for a special aquatic site [defined in Subpart E to include wetlands] does not require access or proximity to or siting within the special aquatic site in question to fulfill its basic purpose (i.e., is not "water dependent"), practicable alternatives that do not involve special aquatic sites are presumed to be available, unless clearly demonstrated otherwise. In addition, where a discharge is proposed for a special aquatic site, all practicable alternatives to the proposed discharge which do not involve a discharge into a special aquatic site are presumed to have less adverse impact on the aquatic ecosystem, unless clearly demonstrated otherwise."

wildlife habitat." The procedure under § 404(c) begins with the Regional Administrator ("RA") who, under § 231.3(a), must notify the Corps and the applicant when it is possible he will find an "unacceptable adverse effect." If within 15 days the applicant fails to satisfy the RA that no such effect will occur, the RA must publish his proposed determination to veto the grant of a permit. A period for public comment and an optional public hearing follows, after which the RA either withdraws the determination or submits a recommended determination to the national Administrator, whose decision to affirm, modify or rescind the RA's recommendation is the final determination of EPA for purposes of judicial review. The burden of proving that the discharge will have an "unacceptable adverse effect" is on EPA. [Citation.]

In short, both EPA and the Corps are responsible for administering the program for granting permits for discharges of pollutants into wetlands under § 404. The Corps has the authority to issue permits following the 404(b)(1) guidelines developed by it and EPA; EPA has the authority under § 404(c) to veto any permit granted by the Corps. The Corps processes about 11,000 permit applications each year. EPA has vetoed five decisions by the Corps to grant permits.

The effort to build a mall on Sweedens Swamp was initiated by Pyramid's predecessor, the Edward J. DeBartolo Corporation ("DeBartolo").... At the time of this purchase an alternative site was available in North Attleboro (the "North Attleboro site")....

One of the key issues in dispute in the instant case is just when did Pyramid begin searching for a suitable site for its mall. EPA asserts that Pyramid began to search in the Spring of 1983. Pyramid asserts that it began to search several months later, in September 1983. The difference is crucial because on July 1, 1983 — a date between the starting dates claimed by EPA and Pyramid — a competitor of Pyramid, the New England Development Co. ("NED"), purchased options to buy the North Attleboro site. This site was located upland and could have served as a "practicable alternative" to Sweedens Swamp, *if* it had been "available" at the relevant time. Thus, if the relevant time to determine whether an alternative is "available" is the time the applicant is searching for a site (an issue that is hotly disputed), and if Pyramid began to search at a time *before* NED acquired options on the North Attleboro site, there definitely would have been a "practicable alternative" to Sweedens Swamp, and Pyramid's application should have been denied. On the other hand, if Pyramid did not begin its search until *after* NED acquired options on the North Attleboro site, then the site arguably was not "available" and the permit should have been granted. Of course it also is possible that the North Attleboro site remained "available" after NED's acquisition of the options, since Pyramid arguably could have purchased the options from NED. Moreover, since the North Attleboro site indisputably was "available" when Pyramid's predecessor, DeBartolo, purchased Sweedens Swamp, one might argue, as EPA does, that Pyramid should be held to stand in its predecessor's shoes. The district court apparently agreed with Pyramid on the issue of when Pyramid entered the market, stating that "Pyramid initially became interested in developing a shopping mall in the Attleboro area in September 1983."... [*Bersani v. EPA*, 674 F. Supp. 405, 409 (N.D.N.Y. 1987).]

In December 1983, Pyramid purchased Sweedens Swamp from DeBartolo. In August 1984, Pyramid applied under § 404(a) to the New England regional division of the Corps (the "NE Corps") for a permit. It sought to fill or alter 32 of the 49.6 acres of the Swamp; to excavate nine acres of uplands to create artificial wetlands; and to alter 13.3 acres of existing wetlands to improve its environmental quality. Later Pyramid proposed to mitigate the adverse impact on the wetlands by creating 36 acres of replacement wetlands in an off-site gravel pit.

During the review of Pyramid's application by EPA, by the Fish and Wildlife Service ("FWS") and by the Corps, Pyramid submitted information on "practicable alternatives," especially the North Attleboro site. In rejecting that site as an alternative, Pyramid asserted that building a mall there was not *feasible*, not that the site was *unavailable*. In the words of the district court, Pyramid claimed that

> the site lacked sufficient traffic volume and sufficient access from local roads, potential department store tenants had expressed strong doubts about the *feasibility* of the site and previous attempts to develop the site had met with strong resistance from the surrounding community.

Bersani, *supra*, 674 F. Supp. at 410 (emphasis added).

In November 1984, EPA and FWS submitted official comments to the NE Corps recommending denial of the application because Pyramid's proposal was inconsistent with the 404(b)(1) guidelines. Pyramid had failed (1) to overcome the presumption of the availability of alternatives and (2) to mitigate adequately the adverse impact on wildlife. EPA threatened a § 404(c) review. Pyramid then proposed to create additional artificial wetlands at a nearby upland site, a proposal it eventually abandoned.

In January 1985, the NE Corps hired a consultant to investigate the feasibility of Sweedens Swamp and the North Attleboro site. The consultant reported that either site was feasible but that from a commercial standpoint only one mall could survive in the area. On February 19, 1985, the NE Corps advised Pyramid that denial of its permit was imminent. On May 2, 1985, the NE Corps sent its recommendation to deny the permit to the national headquarters of the Corps. Although the NE Corps ordinarily makes the final decision on whether to grant a permit, *see* 33 C.F.R. § 325.8, in the instant case, because of widespread publicity, General John F. Wall, the Director of Civil Works at the national headquarters of the Corps, decided to review the NE Corps' decision. Wall reached a different conclusion. He decided to grant the permit after finding that Pyramid's offsite mitigation proposal would reduce the adverse impacts sufficiently to allow the "practicable alternative" test to be deemed satisfied. He stated:

> In a proper case, mitigation measures can be said to reduce adverse impacts of a proposed activity to the point where there is no 'easily identifiable difference in impact' between the proposed activity (including mitigation) versus the alternatives to that activity.

Although he did not explicitly address the issue, Wall apparently assumed that the relevant time to determine whether there was a practicable alternative was the time of the application, not the time the applicant entered the market. In other words, Wall appears to have assumed that the market entry theory was not the correct approach. For example, while addressing the traditional "practicable alternatives" analysis as an alternative ground for his decision, Wall found that the North Attleboro site was unavailable "because it has been optioned by another developer." Since the site was *not* optioned at the time EPA argues Pyramid entered the market, this language suggests (to Pyramid at least) that Wall could not have been employing the market entry approach.

On May 31, 1985, Wall ordered the NE Corps to send Pyramid, EPA and FWS a notice of its intent to grant the permit. The NE Corps complied on June 28, 1985.

On July 23, 1985, EPA's RA initiated a § 404(c) review of the Corps' decision. Following the procedure set forth in 40 C.F.R. Part 231 (discussed above), EPA published notice of its intent to prohibit the project in the *Federal Register;* held a public hearing on September 26, 1985; and permitted a period for public comment which closed on October 4, 1985. A second hearing was held on November 18, 1985.

On March 4, 1986, the RA recommended that EPA veto the permit because of adverse impacts on wildlife and available "practicable alternatives." In particular, the RA found that Pyramid had not overcome the presumption that an alternative existed, in part because Pyramid had failed to provide information on the availability of the North Attleboro site. After first refusing to provide the information, Pyramid later had claimed "there is no further or more detailed information. It simply does not exist." The RA alternatively reasoned that the North Attleboro site had been available to DeBartolo, and that EPA should attribute this availability to Pyramid because Pyramid had benefitted from DeBartolo's application for state approval.

On May 13, 1986, EPA issued its final determination, which prohibited Pyramid from using Sweedens Swamp. It found (1) that the filling of the Swamp would adversely affect wildlife; (2) that the North Attleboro site could have been available to Pyramid at the time Pyramid investigated the area to search for a site; (3) that considering Pyramid's failure or unwillingness to provide further materials about its investigation of alternative sites, it was uncontested that, at best, Pyramid never checked the availability of the North Attleboro site as an alternative; (4) that the North Attleboro site was feasible and would have a less adverse impact on the wetland environment; and (5) that the mitigation proposal did not make the project preferable to other alternatives because of scientific uncertainty of success. In the second of these findings, EPA used what Pyramid calls the "market entry" approach.

On July 1, 1986, Pyramid commenced the instant action in the district court to vacate EPA's final determination as arbitrary and capricious. After the parties filed cross-motions for summary judgment, the newspapers reported that Pyramid intended to enter a joint venture with NED to build a mall at the North Attleboro site. Affidavits submitted concerning this development did not indicate whether Pyramid planned to continue the Sweedens Swamp project. Since the joint venture agreement was still in draft form, EPA did not take the position that the case was moot.

On October 6, 1987, the court granted EPA's motion for summary judgment. The court stated that, with regard to the market entry theory, EPA's interpretation of its regulations was entitled to deference. This appeal followed.

....

One of Pyramid's principal contentions is that the market entry approach is inconsistent with both the language of the 404(b)(1) guidelines and the past practice of the Corps and EPA.

With regard to the language of the regulations, Pyramid reasons that the 404(b)(1) guidelines are framed in the present tense, while the market entry approach focuses on the past by considering whether a practicable alternative was available at the time the applicant entered the market to search for a site....

First, while it is true that the language is in the present tense, it does not follow that the "most natural" reading of the regulations would create a time-of-application rule. As EPA points out, "the regulations do not indicate *when* it is to be determined whether an alternative 'is' available," (emphasis in original) i.e., the "present" of the regulations might be the time the application is submitted; the time it is reviewed; or any number of other times.... We therefore agree with the district court that the regulations are essentially silent on the issue of timing and that it would be appropriate to consider the objectives of the Act and the intent underlying the promulgation of the regulations. [Citation.]

Second, as EPA has pointed out, the preamble to the 404(b)(1) guidelines states that the purpose of the "practicable alternatives" analysis is "to recognize the special value of wetlands and to avoid their unnecessary destruction, particularly where practicable alternatives *were* available in non-aquatic areas to achieve the basic purpose of the proposal." 45 Fed. Reg. 85,338 (emphasis added). In other words, the purpose is to create an incentive for developers to avoid choosing wetlands when they could choose an alternative upland site. Pyramid's reading of the regulations would thwart this purpose because it would remove the incentive for a developer to search for an alternative site at the time such an incentive is needed, i.e., at the time it is making the decision to select a particular site. If the practicable alternatives analysis were applied to the time of the application for a permit, the developer would have little incentive to search for alternatives, especially if it were confident that alternatives soon would disappear. Conversely, in a case in which alternatives were not available at the time the developer made its selection, but became available by the time of application, the developer's application would be denied even though it could not have explored the alternative site at the time of its decision.

Pyramid attacks this reasoning by arguing that few developers would take the risk that an available alternative site would become unavailable and that EPA's reading improperly considers the motives and subjective state of mind of the applicant. These arguments are wide of the mark. Whether most real-life developers would take such a risk is irrelevant. The point is that Pyramid's time-of-application theory is completely at odds with the expressed intent of the regulations to provide an incentive to avoid choosing wetlands. Similarly, EPA's interpretation does not require courts to investigate the subjective state of mind of a developer. EPA discusses state-of-mind issues only because it is discussing the *purpose* behind the regulations, which is concerned with incentives, and thus in fact is indirectly concerned with the developer's state of mind.

In short, we conclude that a common-sense reading of the statute can lead only to the use of the market entry approach used by EPA.

With regard to the past practice of the Corps and EPA, Pyramid asserts that neither has ever applied a market entry approach....

Our examination of these prior decisions has satisfied us, however, that the issue raised in the instant case simply has not been addressed before....

We turn next to the issue of whether EPA's interpretation of the 404(b)(1) guidelines is entitled to the deference usually accorded an agency with regard to its interpretation of regulations it is charged with administering, *see EPA v. National Crushed Stone Ass' n*, 449 U.S. 64, 83 (1980), and participated in formulating.

Pyramid contends that such deference was unwarranted because two agencies — EPA and the Corps — developed and administered the regulations, and the Corps reached a different conclusion from that of EPA on the market entry issue....

In response, EPA asserts that the Corps did not take a developed opposing policy position on the issue of what time is relevant in the "practicable alternatives" analysis....

Even if we are not thoroughly persuaded that EPA's interpretation was entitled to deference, however, we nevertheless conclude that the district court's decision in its favor must be upheld. As Pyramid itself points out (to the detriment of its argument), the issue of deference is separate from the issue of the standards of review of the district court and of our Court.

....

The standard of review for the district court in this case is that the court shall set aside EPA's findings, conclusions or actions only if they are "arbitrary, capricious, an abuse of discretion, or otherwise not in accordance with law." [Citation.]...

Applying these standards, we are convinced that EPA's market entry interpretation was reasonable, and therefore was neither "arbitrary and capricious" nor "not in accordance with law." We therefore hold that the district court correctly found that EPA's interpretation of the regulations was reasonable.

....

NOTES AND QUESTIONS

1. What are the alternative tests to EPA's market entry theory for determining whether an alternate site is available? If another developer were to purchase the Sweedens Swamp and apply for a section 404 permit, would the second developer be entitled to receive a permit to develop the same site? Could the second developer build the mall and then sell it to Pyramid? When does a developer "enter" the market? If EPA were to adopt a "time of decision" theory for evaluating the ability of alternatives (the time of decision being when EPA decides whether to approve the permit), would that theory be upheld by the *Bersani* court? For further discussion of *Bersani v. EPA*, *see* Klein, *Bersani v. EPA: The EPA's Authority Under the Clean Water Act to Veto Section 404 Wetland-Filling Permits*, 19 ENVTL. L. 389 (1988); Comment, *Bersani v. EPA: Toward a Plausible Interpretation of the 404(b)(1) Guidelines for Evaluating Permit Applications for Wetland Development*, 15 COLUM. J. ENVTL. L. 99 (1990); Comment, *Practicable Alternatives Under Section 404 of the Federal Clean Water Act After Bersani v. Robichaud*, 41 SYRACUSE L. REV. 813 (1990).

2. EPA and the Corps signed a memorandum of agreement that went into effect on February 7, 1990, which covered policy and procedures for review of permits to develop wetlands. The memorandum included a clarification of the environmental criteria to be used in evaluating compliance with the section 404(b) guidelines and essentially adopted EPA's position that mitigation is not a factor in favor of permit issuance but a condition that can be imposed once the criteria for permit issuance are met without regard to mitigation. *See* Harris, *Wetlands Management Under the Clean Water Act: Checking the Balances and Balancing the Checks*, [Current Developments] Env't Rep. (BNA) 828, 830 (Aug. 24, 1990); *Some Wetland Losses Would Not Be Mitigated Under Revised Agreement Signed by Corps, EPA*, [Current Developments] Env't Rep. (BNA) 1756 (Feb. 9, 1990). For circumstances surrounding the development of the agreement see *Administration Delays Key Wetlands Protection Plans*, WASH. POST, Dec. 15, 1989, at A19, col. 1. The United States District Court for the District of Alaska dismissed for lack of ripeness and lack of jurisdiction a challenge charging EPA and the Corps with violating federal environmental and administrative laws in their preparation of the agreement. *Anchorage v. United States*, 32 Envt. Rep. Cas. (BNA) 1199 (D. Alaska 1990).

JAMES CITY COUNTY, VIRGINIA v.
ENVIRONMENTAL PROTECTION AGENCY

12 F.3d 1330 (4th Cir. 1993),
cert. denied, 115 S. Ct. 87 (1994)

SPROUSE, SENIOR CIRCUIT JUDGE:

The United States Army Corps of Engineers in 1988 granted a permit under section 404(b) of the Clean Water Act, 33 U.S.C. §§ 1251-1387, to James City County, Virginia, to construct a dam and reservoir across Ware Creek located within the County. The Environmental Protection Agency ("EPA") "vetoed" the permit under the authority granted it by section 404(c) of the Clean Water Act, 33 U.S.C. § 1344(c). After the County contested that action in the district court, the court granted it summary judgment and ordered the Corps of Engineers to issue the permit. *James City County v. EPA*, 758 F.Supp. 348 (E.D. Va. 1990). In a previous appeal, we affirmed the district court's holding that there was not substantial evidence to support the EPA's finding in its final determination that the County had practicable alternatives to building the Ware Creek·reservoir for its local water supply, but remanded to the EPA to afford it the opportunity to decide whether environmental considerations alone would justify its veto. *James City County v. EPA*, 955 F.2d 254 (4th Cir. 1992) ("*JCC I*"). We instructed the EPA not to revisit the issue of practicable alternatives.

On remand, the EPA considered its administrative record and again vetoed the § 404(b) permit—basing its veto solely on environmental considerations. The County again brought an action in the district court, which again granted summary judgment and ordered issuance of the permit. *James City County v. EPA*, No. 89 156-NN, 1992 WL 315199 (E.D. Va. 1992). The EPA now appeals that judgment to this court. We reverse.

. . . .

Congress obviously intended the Corps of Engineers in the initial permitting process to consider the total range of factors bearing on the necessity or desirability of building a dam in the Nation's waters, including whether the project was in the public interest. For example, as stated earlier, under 40 C.F.R. § 230.10, in deciding whether to issue a permit, the Corps takes into account the availability of practicable alternatives to the proposed project, whether the proposed discharge would violate environmental laws or significantly degrade national waters, and whether adequate measures are taken to minimize harmful effects. In addition to these environmentally-based criteria, the Corps conducts a "public interest review" which, inter alia, takes into account the public and private need for the project, whether the same result could be achieved through other means, and the "extent and permanence" of the benefits and harms the proposed project is likely to produce. 33 C.F.R. § 320.4(a). Ultimately, however, recognizing the EPA's expertise and concentrated concern with environmental matters, Congress gave the final decision whether to permit a project to that agency. Its authority to veto to protect the environment is practically unadorned. It is simply directed to veto when it finds that the discharge "will have an unacceptable adverse effect on municipal water supplies, shellfish beds and fishery areas (including spawning and breeding areas), wildlife, or recreational areas." (Citation). This broad grant of power to the EPA focuses only on the agency's assigned function of assuring pure water and is consistent with the missions assigned to it throughout the Clean Water Act.

We think it significant that the only mention of responsibility for the quantities of water available to communities is contained in section 101(g) entitled "Authority of States over water" which states:

> It is the policy of Congress that the authority of each State to allocate quantities of water within its jurisdiction shall not be superseded, abrogated or otherwise impaired by this chapter. It is the further policy of Congress that nothing in this chapter shall be construed to supersede or abrogate rights to quantities of water which have been established by any State. Federal agencies shall co-operate with State and local agencies to develop comprehensive solutions to prevent, reduce and eliminate pollution in concert with programs for managing water resources.

33 U.S.C. § 1251(g).

In our view, the EPA's only function relating to the quantities of available water is limited to assuring purity in whatever quantities the state and local agencies provide. For these reasons, we think its veto based solely on environmental harms was proper.

Having found that, in this case, the EPA could consider whether adverse environmental effects alone justified a veto, we now review the district court's alternate holding that the factual conclusion of unacceptable adverse effects was not supported by the record....

The EPA noted that construction of the reservoir would result in the loss of 381 acres of vegetated wetlands, forty-four acres of palustrine (related to marshes), estuarine (related to estuaries), or lacustrine (related to lakes) open water systems, and 792 acres of adjacent forested uplands habitat. Some of the short-term effects of the construction of the project would be the loss of small animals and invertebrates that could not escape the construction site and the destruction of over half the vegetated wetland cover-type habitat. Reptile and amphibian populations in the watershed would be harmed by the destruction of overall habitat and particularly breeding habitat. The EPA also found that by blocking the Ware Creek's flow, the project "would severely and adversely alter the current nutrient regime," which transports organic material into the York River and ultimately into the Chesapeake Bay. In discussing the cumulative adverse environmental impact on the Bay to which the Ware Creek project would contribute, the EPA noted "[t]he incremental loss of functional wetland systems which currently contribute to the environmental well-being of the York River and the Chesapeake Bay and which help maintain and protect the environmental integrity of those systems represents a profound cumulative loss."

Although the EPA recognized that the proposed reservoir would increase greatly the freshwater habitat, the agency found that the dam would harm fish species currently living in the Ware Creek watershed because it would convert the vegetated flowing stream system into a lake, possibly resulting in the eventual elimination of some stream species of fish. Also, the likely introduction of forage and game fish into the reservoir by the Virginia Department of Game and Inland Fisheries could alter the abundance and diversity of the current fish populations. Furthermore, construction of the dam, in the EPA's view, would destroy a valuable Great Blue Heron rookery and would eliminate favorable habitat for foraging species such as the Black Duck.

The EPA considered and discussed the County's mitigation plan. The plan includes wetlands creation, wetlands and uplands preservation, creation of potential Great Blue Heron nesting sites in Ware Creek (within the York River watershed), and removal of an existing dam in another watershed. Based on its review of the administrative record, however, the EPA concluded that the proposed mitigation plan would not adequately offset the adverse effects resulting from the local project. For instance, the more than 1600 acres marked for preservation are in another watershed and, for that matter, are already subject to EPA protection. The EPA also considered that less than fifty percent of the vegetated wetlands would be replaced by newly-created wetlands, even if the plan is completely successful. Moreover, the EPA found that the mitigation plan would not adequately replace the types and qualities of wetlands the proposed project would destroy. The lack of knowledge about the habitat needs of the Great Blue Heron also led the agency to decide that it could not assume that the mitigation efforts for the rookery would be successful. Accordingly, the EPA reached the following conclusions about James City County's mitigation plan:

Upon reevaluation of the administrative record, EPA finds that the mitigation plan as proposed by James City County does not adequately offset adverse impacts to aquatic resources resulting from project implementation. EPA finds that the post-project reservoir system in conjunction with preservation and compensatory mitigation efforts proposed by the County would not adequately replace or compensate for the loss of or impacts to aquatic resource functions and values associated with the current Ware Creek wetlands and aquatic ecosystem. EPA therefore concludes that the mitigation proposed by James City County does not render the project acceptable under Section 404(c).

....

The EPA based its veto decision on several factors, including harm to existing fish and wildlife species, damage to the ecosystem, destruction of wetlands, and inadequate mitigation. Its findings are supported by the administrative record, are not arbitrary and capricious, and, for that matter, are supported by substantial evidence. Consequently, the judgment of the district court is reversed.

NOTES AND QUESTIONS

1. Another ongoing saga over EPA's veto power — the Two Forks Dam — drew closer to resolution in *Alameda Water & Sanitation Dist. v. Reilly*, 930 F. Supp. 486 (D. Colo. 1996). The plaintiffs, municipal and quasi-municipal entities responsible for supplying water to metropolitan Denver, did not have standing to challenge EPA's veto of the dam project because the supporting administrative record contained nothing to show that the Two Forks Dam would indeed be constructed if the EPA reversed its decision. In dicta, the court also rejected plaintiff's argument that EPA exceeded its authority by considering water quality, recreational, aquatic life, and fishing conditions, when it exercised its veto. The court found that it was appropriate for the EPA to consider water quality as well as water quantity.

2. At what point can a permit application challenge EPA's exercise of its veto authority? Is EPA's decision to initiate a section 404(c) proceeding reviewable? *See Newport Galleria Group v. Deland*, 618 F. Supp. 1179, 1185 (D.D.C. 1985) (concluding that it is not reviewable). What are the criteria that EPA is to utilize in exercising its veto? *See generally Bersani v. EPA*, 674 F. Supp. 405 (N.D.N.Y. 1987), *aff'd*, 850 F.2d 36 (2d Cir. 1988). Only one court decision has reversed a veto by EPA, and it did so twice, and was twice reversed. *James City County v. U.S. EPA*, 758 F. Supp. 348 (E.D. Va. 1990), *aff'd in part and remanded*, 955 F.2d 254 (4th Cir. 1992), *on remand*, 23 Envtl. L. Rep. (Envtl. L. Inst.) 20,228 (E.D. Va. Aug. 5, 1992), *rev'd*, 12 F.3d 1330 (4th Cir. 1993), *cert. denied*, 115 S. Ct. 87 (1994).

3. Section 404(e) authorizes the Corps to issue general permits for discharges on a state, regional, or nationwide basis for categories of activities that are similar in nature, cause only minimal adverse environmental effects when performed separately, and have only minimal cumulative adverse effect on the environment. 33 U.S.C. § 1344(e)(1). The most important type of general permit is the nationwide permit and the most important and controversial nationwide permit is Permit 26. For most of the nationwide permits, the landowner is not required even to inform the Corps of the activity. *See generally* 33 C.F.R. Part 330. Ultimately, any development is done at the risk of the developer who assumes that a general permit is available. *Orleans Audubon Soc'y v. Lee*, 742 F.2d 901 (5th Cir. 1984). The Corps' regulations also authorize general permits to avoid "unnecessary duplication of regulatory control exercised by another Federal, state, or local agency." 33 C.F.R. § 323.2(h)(2). The Corps has utilized this provision to turn some general permitting authority over to the states.

In December 1996, the Corps issued revised nationwide permits. These revised permits took effect following the expiration of the nationwide permit program in January 1997. The nationwide permit program authorizes projects that have minimal individual and cumulative effect on the aquatic environment and cover over 80 percent of the activities that are undertaken in areas regulated by Section 404 of the Clean Water Act. The Corps reauthorized thirty-seven NWPs, added two new NWPs, and imposed restrictions designed to ensure that activities with more than minimal effects are not covered. The most significant change covers NWP 26, which authorizes discharges into isolated waters (having no connection to surface water systems) and into headwaters (waters with minimal flow). NWP 26 was reauthorized for only two years and will be replaced by activity-specific NWPs. The Corps also scaled back the NWP 26 threshold from ten to three acres and requires preconstruction notification (PCN) for all fills into one-third or more acres of wetlands or waters. The Corps decided to phase out NWP 26 and lower the acreage threshold out of concerns raised about the cumulative loss of wetlands under prior NWP 26. 61 Fed. Reg. 65,874 (1996).

Although the statute authorizes general permits for categories of activities, the Corps has allowed general permitting for certain classes of water bodies. *See United States v. Cumberland Farms of Conn., Inc.*, 826 F.2d 1151 (1st Cir. 1987). Issuance of general permits must be preceded by notice and opportunity for a public hearing. 33 U.S.C. § 1344(e)(1). No permit may last more than five years, and a permit may be revoked or modified after a hearing if the activities authorized have an adverse effect on the environment or are "more appropriately authorized by individual permits." 33 U.S.C. § 1344(e)(2). General permits must be based on the guidelines for section 404 permits and set forth the requirements and standards for the permitted activity. 33 U.S.C. § 1344(e)(1).

4. Section 404 may be enforced under either section 309, 33 U.S.C. § 1319, which provides for enforcement of the Clean Water Act generally, or under section 404(s), 33 U.S.C. § 1344(s), which is limited to enforcement of the section 404 program. Enforcement under section 309 is by EPA; enforcement under section 404(s) is by the Corps of Engineers. Under both provisions, in the event of a violation of section 404 the relevant agency may issue a compliance order or bring a civil action in federal district court in the district in which the defendant is located, resides, or is doing business. Appropriate relief includes permanent or temporary injunctive relief and civil penalties not to exceed $25,000 per day for each violation. Criminal penalties may also be imposed under section 309 for negligent and knowing violations of section 404, violations of section 404 which place another person in imminent danger of death or bodily injury, and knowingly false statements. Either the Corps or EPA may impose administrative penalties upon a finding by the Corps that a permit holder has violated a "limitation or condition" in a permit.

Most enforcement cases are settled upon payment of civil penalties and acceptance of a restoration plan, after which a permit is obtained for that material which was not removed. Courts may require restoration of a damaged wetland pursuant to the injunction provisions of section 309 and the RHA, and the court's general equitable powers. *United States v. Joseph G. Moretti, Inc.*, 478 F.2d 418, 430-31 (5th Cir. 1973) (RHA and court's equitable powers); *United States v. Carter*, 18 Env't Rep. Cas. (BNA) 1810, 1812-13 (S.D. Fla. 1982) (Clean Water Act).

A five year statute of limitations applies to illegal wetlands fills. 28 U.S.C. § 2642. When does the statute begin to run? When the illegal activity occurs? Or is there an ongoing violation as long as the dredge or fill material is in place?

5. From a preservation perspective, the federal government has several statutes authorizing acquisition of wetlands. These statutes include, among others, the Pitman-Robertson Federal Aid to Wildlife Restoration Act, 16 U.S.C. §§ 669a-669i; the Land and Water Conservation Fund Act, 16 U.S.C. §§ 4601-4 to 4601-11; the Water Bank Act, 16 U.S.C. §§ 1301-1311; the Migratory Bird Conservation Act, 16 U.S.C. §§ 715-715k, 715n-715r; and the Emergency Wetlands Resources Act of 1986, 16 U.S.C. §§ 3901-3932. Executive Order Number 11,990, 3 C.F.R. 121 (1978), *reprinted in* 42 U.S.C. § 4321 note, is designed to prevent federal agencies from causing or encouraging unnecessary destruction of wetland areas. To this end the executive order instructs agencies to avoid construction in wetland areas when feasible alternatives exist, requires agencies to give to the public notice of any construction in wetland areas, and requires any leases or sales of agency wetlands to be subject to restrictions designed to preserve those wetlands. In contrast, for many years some federal laws, particularly tax laws and federal subsidies for agriculture, encouraged conversion of wetlands. Amendments to the tax laws and passage of the 1985 Farm Bill have minimized that effect. The wetlands conservation provisions of the 1985 Farm Bill are discussed on pages 980-82 *infra*.

6. Every coastal state in the United States regulates tidal wetlands. Many coastal states also regulate freshwater wetlands, either under separate statutory authority or under a comprehensive statute that regulates both tidal and freshwater wetlands. A few states regulate only freshwater wetlands. In some states wetlands are also regulated indirectly as part of comprehensive land use controls, coastal zone management, critical areas regulation, floodplain zoning, water quality protection, consumptive water use controls, stream protection, or storm water runoff management. Despite their common elements, state wetland regulation varies a great deal from state to state as a result of differing political climates and environmental concerns. Thus, not only do developers have to comply with local zoning laws and state wetland regulations, they also must comply with a potential panoply of regulations which indirectly impact on wetlands, including regional controls on critical environmental areas and local non-zoning controls. Although the Corps' regulations require consideration of state and local determinations before issuance of a permit, 33 C.F.R. § 320.4(a); *see also Hough v. Marsh*, 557 F. Supp. 74, 86 (D. Mass. 1982) (remand for the Corps to consider local requirements), obtaining a necessary state or local permit or federal section 402 permit under the Clean Water Act does not preempt the requirement for a federal wetlands permit. *Minnehaha Creek Watershed Dist. v. Hoffman*, 597 F.2d 617, 627 (8th Cir. 1979); *Sun Enters., Ltd. v. Train*, 394 F. Supp. 211, 224 (S.D.N.Y. 1975). Conversely, failure to obtain necessary state approval of a proposed project may preclude issuance of a section 402 permit. For example, in *United States v. Marathon Dev. Corp.*, 867 F.2d 96 (1st Cir.

1989), Massachusetts refused to certify that the proposed project would comply with state water quality standards. Section 401(a), 33 U.S.C. § 1341(a)(1), prohibits issuance of a federal license or permit if water quality certification has been denied by the state. The court of appeals thus concluded that no federal permit under section 402 could be issued, rejecting the developer's contention that state water quality certification was a prerequisite only for individual permits and not for the general permit for which the project arguably qualified.

FLORIDA ROCK INDUSTRIES v. UNITED STATES
18 F.3d 1560 (Fed. Cir. 1994),
cert. denied, 115 S. Ct. 898 (1995)

PLAGER, CIRCUIT JUDGE.

This is a regulatory taking case. It arose when the plaintiff Florida Rock Industries Inc. (Florida Rock) sought a permit under § 404 of the Clean Water Act from the Army Corps of Engineers (Corps) to mine the limestone which lay beneath a tract of wetlands. The Corps denied the permit on October 5, 1980. On May 25, 1982, Florida Rock filed suit in the United States Court of Federal Claims, seeking monetary compensation from the defendant United States (Government); Florida Rock alleged that the Corps' permit denial constituted an uncompensated taking of private property for public use in violation of the Fifth Amendment. The Court of Federal Claims agreed, and awarded Florida Rock $1,029,000 plus attorney fees and simple interest. On appeal, this court vacated the judgment that a taking had occurred and remanded for further consideration. [Citation.] On remand, the Court of Federal Claims found that the permit denial deprived Florida Rock of all value in its land, and so again concluded that there had been a taking and reinstated the $1,029,000 damages award, this time with compound interest....

... We provide here only a brief overview before proceeding to the heart of the matter: whether the Corps' denial of the § 404 permit effected a regulatory taking, thus requiring the Government to pay just compensation. The answer to that question depends on the impact the regulatory imposition had on the economic use, and hence value, of the property.

In 1972, shortly before the enactment of the Clean Water Act, Florida Rock purchased a 1,560 acre wetlands parcel in Dade County, Florida, to the west of suburban Miami. The purchase price was $2,964,000 (an average of $1,900 per acre). Florida Rock obtained the parcel in order to extract the underlying limestone — a process which destroys the surface wetlands.

During the 1970s, however, the ecological importance of wetlands was increasingly appreciated. The Corps in 1977 enacted regulations requiring owners of wetlands parcels to obtain permits under § 404 of the Clean Water Act before engaging in dredging or filling activities. [Citation.] Not long after, Florida Rock began mining operations on the parcel, without having applied for a § 404 permit. The Corps issued a cease and desist order on September 7, 1978. Florida

Rock stopped mining, restored the area as best it could, and began negotiating with the Corps for the permit.

Initially, Florida Rock sought a permit for the entire 1,560 acres. The Corps responded that permits would be issued only for parcels of a size to suffice for three years of mining; in Florida Rock's case, 98 acres would serve its anticipated needs for three years. Florida Rock acquiesced in the Corps' demand and applied for a permit covering only the 98 acre parcel at issue here. After considering the revised application, the Corps concluded that the proposed mining would cause irremediable loss of an ecologically valuable wetland parcel and would create undesirable water turbidity. The permit application was denied on October 2, 1980.

Florida Rock, conceding the validity of the Corps' actions, filed suit in the United States Court of Federal Claims, alleging that the permit denial was an uncompensated regulatory taking of its land. In *Florida Rock I*, the Court of Federal Claims found that the value of the parcel before the taking was $10,500 per acre and that the value after the taking was negligible because rock mining — in the view of the court, the only viable economic use — had been foreclosed. [Citation.] ... On appeal to this court, that judgment was vacated in *Florida Rock II*. The Federal Circuit held that the Court of Federal Claims in determining the after-taking value of the affected property had erred in focusing on immediate use — the proper focus should instead have been on a determination of "fair market value." The case was remanded to the Court of Federal Claims for further proceedings.

On remand, the Court of Federal Claims entertained evidence seeking to establish the fair market value of the property subsequent to the permit denial. The Government presented two assessors.... Using the standard comparable sales valuation method, one assessor concluded that the property had a fair market value of $4,000 per acre, while the other found a value of $4,615 per acre. In addition, Florida Rock had received actual purchase offers in the range of $4,000 per acre....

How to determine whether a regulatory taking under the Fifth Amendment has occurred is a subject of on-going debate.... One formula that has emerged and has been repeated in several cases requires that the court balance several pragmatic considerations in making its regulatory takings determination. These considerations include: the economic impact of the regulation on the claimant, the extent to which the regulation interferes with investment-backed expectations, and the character of the Government action. [Citation.] In this appeal, it is the economic impact of the regulation that is at issue. The recent Supreme Court decision in *Lucas v. South Carolina Coastal Council*, 505 U.S. 1003, 112 S. Ct. 2886, 120 L. Ed. 2d 798 (1992) (*Lucas*), teaches that the economic impact factor alone may be determinative; in some circumstances, no balancing of factors is required. If a regulation categorically prohibits all economically beneficial use of land — destroying its economic value for private ownership — the regulation has an effect equivalent to a permanent physical occupation. There is, without more, a compensable taking.

If, however, a regulation prohibits less than all economically beneficial use of the land and causes at most a partial destruction of its value, the case does not come within the Supreme Court's "categorical" taking rule.... [W]e reject the trial court's analysis that led to its conclusion that all economically beneficial use of the land was taken by the Government. We remand for determination of what economic use as measured by market value, if any, remained after the permit denial, and for consideration of whether, in light of the properly assessed value of the land, Florida Rock has a valid takings claim.

In *Florida Rock II* this court stated that, with regard to the property at issue, although "there may be a question what knowledgeable buyers would have paid, but that they would have paid some substantial figure seems certain." The trial court on remand was instructed: "if there is found to exist a solid and adequate fair market value (for the 98 acres) which Florida Rock could have obtained from others for that property, that would be a sufficient remaining use of the property to forestall a determination that a taking had occurred or that any just compensation had to be paid by the government." We did not discuss what residual fair market value would be "adequate" to forestall a taking determination.

We did explicitly indicate that the Court of Federal Claims should give consideration to "a relevant market made up of investors who are real but are speculating in whole or major part." [Citation.]...

In short, we understand *Florida Rock II* to hold that purchases which are made by market speculators as well as home builders and other developers are comparable sales, with the caveat that particular sales might be discarded by the assessor if those sales appear questionable in light of the market as a whole.

Florida Rock, and the Court of Federal Claims on remand in *Florida Rock III*, read *Florida Rock II* differently. Our passing reference to buyers being "correctly informed" was read to require a detailed inquiry into the motivation and sophistication of the buyers whose purchases comprised the comparable sales used in the fair market value assessment. The Court of Federal Claims rejected the testimony of Mr. Cantwell — the same testimony which we had noted with approval in *Florida Rock II* — solely because Mr. Cantwell, with little exception, assumed sufficient knowledge on the part of the purchasers. Instead, the court accepted the testimony of Florida Rock's assessor, who rejected all of the comparable sales values on the principle that none of the purchasers were sufficiently sophisticated and knowledgeable. That was error — contrary to our instruction in *Florida Rock II*, contrary to generally accepted understandings of market valuation, and finally, contrary to the working assumptions of a free market.

There is no disagreement as to the facts regarding the existence and nature of the market. Florida Rock's study identified in the immediate vicinity of the 98 acre tract 240 land sales during the period 1971 through 1987. A significant number of those sales occurred in the early 1980s, despite the intervening change in the regulatory environment. The average sales price per acre in 1980 was $6,100. The price per acre varied predominantly as a function of the overall lot size; smaller lots commanded higher per acre prices. Florida Rock's survey indicated that roughly 80% of the buyers had purchased the land for "investment" purposes and that, overall, the purchasers intended to hold the land for an average of 9 to 10 years.

Thus, there was an active though speculative investment market for Florida Rock's land at the time of and following the permit denial. The fair market price which Florida Rock could have commanded at that time remains, still, to be determined, but it was certainly much higher than the nominal $500 per acre value accepted by the Court of Federal Claims.

Florida Rock's survey does indicate that most of the buyers in this market did not have extensive knowledge of the provisions of the Clean Water Act and its impact on the development potential of those properties involving wetlands. It is doubtful that any legal conclusions should be drawn from this. Such broad-based disregard for current land use regulations suggests that, while parties contract in the shadow of the law, long term market trends in real estate values are not necessarily correlated to Government controls. The Government's appraisers testified that detailed knowledge of regulatory constraints was relevant only when the goal of the purchasers was immediate development. And as Mr. Slack testified, "there was not really a demand for property this far out [from Miami] at this time. People were not buying it to do anything with it right then anyway."

A speculative market may exist in land that is regulated as well as in land that is not, and the precise content of regulations at any given time may not be particularly important to those active in the market....

We need not decide such speculative questions here. The uncontroverted evidence of an active real estate market compels the conclusion that the typical "willing buyer-willing seller" requirement of fair market value had been met; it would be inappropriate for a court to substitute its own judgment of value for that of the market. While an assessor might be justified in adjusting the fair market value figure by discarding aberrational values based upon sales between related entities or fraudulent sales to widows and orphans, an assessor may not discard an entire market as aberrational. "Aberrational" means outside the norm established by general activity. The fact that many players in the market chose to disregard the immediate potential for development in favor of a long-term perspective — hardly unusual behavior in Florida's history of real estate investment — does not make the market as a whole "aberrational." When the market provides a well-substantiated value for a property, a court may not substitute its own judgment as to what is a wise investment.

It was error to read *Florida Rock II* as requiring a detailed inquiry into the motivation and sophistication of the buyers of comparable parcels. Dollars are fungible; a speculative market provides a landowner with monetary compensation which is just as satisfactory as that provided by any other market. Should a landowner wish to pick and choose her buyers, that luxury is not chargeable to the federal fisc. To conclude otherwise would be tantamount to concluding that there could never be a market fueled by speculation — a conclusion at odds both with common sense and with our directions in *Florida Rock II*.

Ultimately, the question that must be answered is whether, as a result of the denial of certain economic uses, there was a taking of Florida Rock's property by the Government. This question turns on "the economic impact of the regulation on the claimant," measured by the change, if any, in the fair market value caused by the regulatory imposition. On the state of the record before us we are unable to answer the question. The Court of Federal Claims answered it with a straightforward "yes" when the per acre value of the 98 acre parcel after the permit denial was found to be only a nominal $500 per acre, as compared to the $10,500 found by the trial court to be the per acre value prior to the permit denial. This represented a loss in value of roughly 95%. The court in effect treated the permit denial as essentially a "categorical" taking of all economic use. *See Lucas*.... "The second situation in which we have found categorical treatment appropriate is where regulation denies all economically beneficial or productive use of land." *Id.*

The Court of Federal Claims' analysis was correct in theory, but started from an incorrect premise — that the value of the parcel after denial of the permit was a nominal $500 per acre. When a figure closer to $4,000 per acre is substituted, the correct outcome is no longer clear. On remand, with a fair market value calculated in accordance with this opinion, the Court of Federal Claims must again return to the approach dictated by *Florida Rock II*: [T]he court should consider, along with other relevant matters, the relationship of the owner's basis or investment, and the fair market value before the alleged taking to the fair market value after the alleged taking. In determining the severity of the economic impact, the owner's opportunity to recoup its investment or better, subject to the regulation, cannot be ignored.

The Court of Federal Claims must reconsider the assessments proffered by the parties and other evidence in the record, and determine a fair market value accordingly. Should that determination establish, as the evidence in the record suggests, that there was some (but not a total) reduction in the overall market value of plaintiff's property as a result of the regulatory imposition, the question will then be posed: does that reduction constitute a taking of property compensable under the Fifth Amendment?

To answer this question requires the court to resolve two preliminary issues. The first is whether a regulation must destroy a certain proportion of a property's economic use or value in order for a compensable taking of property to occur. The second is how to determine, in any given case, what that proportion is.

Since the Supreme Court's decision in *Pennsylvania Coal v. Mahon*, 260 U.S. 393 (1922) (*Pennsylvania Coal*), the problem for courts has been to determine the extent to which the Fifth Amendment burdens the exercise of the police power through regulation, that is, to determine when a particular regulation somehow — in the words of Justice Holmes — goes "too far," and therefore effects a taking. It is now clear that a regulation that constitutes a total deprivation of economically beneficial use goes "too far"; such a regulatory imposition results in a "categorical" taking similar to a physical taking of property.

The question remains, does a partial deprivation resulting from a regulatory imposition, that is, a situation in which a regulation deprives the owner of a substantial part but not essentially all of the economic use or value of the property, constitute a partial taking, and is it compensable as such? This question has been much debated in the literature since the Supreme Court's decision announcing that as a general proposition regulatory takings are compensable; the Court's decisions to date have not provided an answer.

Nothing in the language of the Fifth Amendment compels a court to find a taking only when the Government divests the total ownership of the property; the Fifth Amendment prohibits the uncompensated taking of private property without reference to the owner's remaining property interests. In *Lucas*, the Supreme Court touched upon the question of a partial regulatory taking, but, concluding on the facts before it that the case was one in which the owner was called upon "to sacrifice all economically beneficial uses in the name of the common good," the Court found a categorical taking and thus did not have to decide the partial taking question.

JUSTICE STEVENS, writing separately, criticized as arbitrary the notion that "[a] landowner whose property is diminished in value 95% recovers nothing, while an owner whose property is diminished 100% recovers the land's full value." In response, JUSTICE SCALIA, writing for the Court, noted that JUSTICE STEVENS's analysis "errs in its assumption that the landowner whose deprivation is one step short of complete is not entitled to compensation."

No such conceptual problem seems to exist when the taking is by physical occupation....

Courts have held that even relatively minor physical occupations are compensable. [Citation.] Logically, the amount of just compensation should be proportional to the value of the interest taken as compared to the total value of the property, up to and including total deprivation, whether the taking is by physical occupation for the public to use as a park, or by regulatory imposition to preserve the property as a wetland so that it may be used by the public for ground water recharge and other ecological purposes.

The felt need for some kind of a special rule in regulatory takings cases may stem from the difficult line that has to be drawn between a partial regulatory taking and the mere "diminution in value" that often accompanies otherwise valid regulatory impositions. As expressed by Justice Holmes in *Pennsylvania Coal*, "Government hardly could go on if to some extent values incident to property could not be diminished without paying for every such change in the general law. As long recognized, some values are enjoyed under an implied limitation and must yield to the police power. But obviously the implied limitation must have its limits, or the contract and due process clauses are gone." Gone as well, it is almost superfluous to add, would be the constraints imposed on the Government by the takings clause.

One way to avoid this linedrawing problem would be to declare that no regulatory taking is compensable under the Fifth Amendment; the only available remedy for a regulation that goes "too far" is invalidation of the imposition. That was the historic practice in the courts for much of the twentieth century, but the Supreme Court definitively rejected that practice in *First English Evangelical Lutheran Church v. Los Angeles County*, 482 U.S. 304 (1987). The Fifth Amendment "is designed 'not to limit the governmental interference with property rights per se, but rather to secure compensation in the event of otherwise proper interference amounting to a taking.'" [Citation.] Nothing in the Fifth Amendment limits its protection to only "categorical" regulatory takings, nor has the Supreme Court or this court so held. Thus there remains in cases such as this the difficult task of resolving when a partial loss of economic use of the property has crossed the line from a noncompensable "mere diminution" to a compensable "partial taking."

... [R]ecourse to the facts hardly solves the basic problem at hand — there simply is no bright line dividing compensable from noncompensable exercises of the Government's power when a regulatory imposition causes a partial loss to the property owner. What is necessary is a classic exercise of judicial balancing of competing values....

That the purpose and function of the regulatory imposition is relevant to drawing the line between mere diminution and partial taking should not be read to suggest that when Government acts in pursuit of an important public purpose, its actions are excused from liability. To so hold would eviscerate the plain language of the Takings Clause, and would be inconsistent with Supreme Court guidance. It is necessary that the Government act in a good cause, but it is not sufficient. The takings clause already assumes the Government is acting in the public interest: "nor shall private property be taken *for public use* without just compensation" (emphasis added).

It is for the trial court as an initial matter to determine whether the Government acted within its proper role in the circumstances presented by the case of Florida Rock. Marketplace decisions should be made under the working assumption that the Government will neither prejudice private citizens, unfairly shifting the burden of a public good onto a few people, nor act arbitrarily or capriciously, that is, will not act to disappoint reasonable investment-backed expectations. The Government, in a word, must act fairly and reasonably, so that private parties can pursue their interests. At the same time, when Government acts as the intermediary between private interests to provide a mutually beneficial environment from which all benefit and in which all can thrive, the shared diminution of free choice that results may not rise to the level of constitutionally required compensation.

In addition, then, to a demonstration of loss of economic use to the property owner as a result of the regulatory imposition — a fact yet to be properly determined in this case — the trial court must consider: are there direct compensating benefits accruing to the property, and others similarly situated, flowing from the regulatory environment? Or are benefits, if any, general and widely shared through the community and the society, while the costs are focused on a few? Are alternative permitted activities economically realistic in light of the setting and circumstances, and are they realistically available? In short, has the Government acted in a responsible way, limiting the constraints on property ownership to those necessary to achieve the public purpose, and not allocating to some number of individuals, less than all, a burden that should be borne by all?

Admittedly this is not a bright line, simply drawn. Property owners and regulators, attempting to predict whether a governmental regulation has gone too far, will still need to use judgment and exercise care in making decisions. In this sense our decision today continues the tradition of ad hoc judicial decisionmaking in this area. Over time, however, enough cases will be decided with sufficient care and clarity that the line will more clearly emerge.

... [T]he dissent believes that Supreme Court precedent establishes that a Fifth Amendment claim that specific property has been taken is an all or nothing proposition. If taken to mean that a regulatory taking cannot result in less than a taking of the property owner's entire fee estate, we cannot agree. There has never been any question but that the Government can take any kind of recognized estate or interest in property it chooses in an eminent domain proceeding; it is not limited to fee interests. We see no reason or support for a different rule in inverse condemnation cases, and that is true whether the taking results from a physical or regulatory action.

In this case we have concluded that the record does not support a finding that the fee in the land, i.e., all economic use or value, was taken by this regulation, although that question is still an open one to be decided by the facts of valuation properly found. Since loss of economic use and value is the issue in this regulatory taking case, it is not possible, absent a valid determination in the record of the "after imposition" value of the land, to know if a taking occurred, much less what the Government must pay for it. We are compelled, therefore, to remand the matter to the trial court for a determination of that essential piece of information, and for an initial determination as to its significance in order to decide whether there is a compensable taking of property.

NOTES AND QUESTIONS

1. As wetland regulation has become more restrictive, landowners have challenged state and federal restrictions with growing success, as a taking of private property without just compensation. There have been many cases in which landowners have asserted that imposition of governmental restrictions on wetlands development constitutes a regulatory taking of the property without compensation. Of these cases, only a few have succeeded on the taking claim. In the first case challenging application of the RHA to wetlands, *Zabel v. Tabb*, 430 F.2d 199 (5th Cir. 1970), a taking claim was rejected by the Supreme Court because of the paramount federal authority over the navigational servitude. The navigational servitude is the federal interest in the flow of navigable waters pursuant to the Commerce Clause to which any private claims are inferior. *See, e.g., United States v. Twin City Power Co.*, 350 U.S. 222 (1956); *United States v. Chandler-Dunbar Co.*, 229 U.S. 53 (1913); *United States v. Kansas City Life Ins. Co.*, 339 U.S. 799 (1950); *Greenleaf Johnson Lumber Co. v. Garrison*, 237 U.S. 251 (1915). It is clear after the Supreme Court decision in *Kaiser Aetna v. United States*, discussed on pages 128-29 *supra*, however, that the navigational servitude is not an absolute defense to taking challenges.

The extent to which *Kaiser Aetna* undermines judicial reliance on the navigational servitude to preclude taking claims under the RHA is debatable. *Kaiser Aetna* can be distinguished from taking cases involving wetlands. The waterbody at issue in the case was considered by the Court to be fast land not subject to Corps' jurisdiction absent the connection to navigable waters, while wetlands are clearly subject to Corps' jurisdiction under the RHA and Clean Water Act. Second, the Supreme Court acknowledged Corps' jurisdiction over the pond, requiring compensation when that authority was utilized to necessitate public access. Want, *Federal Wetlands Law: The Cases and the Problems*, 8 HARV. ENVT'L L. REV. 1, 35 (1984). In that sense, even if *Kaiser Aetna* raises the application of traditional taking analysis to regulation under the RHA in particular, only intrusive regulation (such as requiring public access) may constitute a taking.

In contrast, taking challenges to section 404 permit denials have utilized the more traditional taking analysis, focusing on whether the regulation substantially advances a legitimate state interest and whether the landowner is deprived of all or almost all of the property considering "the economic impact of the regulation, its interference with reasonable investment backed expectations, and the character of the government action." See discussion on pages 126-30 *supra*.

The most thorough evaluation of a taking claim in the section 404 context is *Deltona Corp. v. United States*, 657 F.2d 1184 (Ct. Cl. 1981). A 404 permit had been denied for a proposal to build a residential community on a 10,000-acre parcel on the coast. *Id.* at 1188-89. The parcel was divided into five construction sites to be developed consecutively, with 404 permits for two sites already obtained from the Corps. *Id.* Of the remaining three sites, only one permit was granted. The plaintiff claimed that denial of the permits for the two remaining sites was a taking without just compensation. *Id.* at 1189.

The Court of Claims declared that zoning and environmental regulation would be a taking only if the restriction did not "substantially advance legitimate state interests ... or deny a[n] owner economically viable use of his land." *Id.* at 1191. The Court had little difficulty in finding that section 404 substantially advanced a legitimate and important federal interest. *Id.* at 1192. In a related case the Corps' denial of a permit was similarly upheld under the Administrative Procedure Act. *Deltona v. Alexander*, 504 F. Supp. 1280 (M.D. Fla. 1981).

2. In addition to the *Florida Rock* case above, the Court of Claims in a companion case ruled that the Corps' denial of a section 404 permit was a taking and awarded just compensation. In *Loveladies Harbor, Inc. v. United States*, 21 Cl. Ct. 153 (1990), the Corps denied a permit to develop residential housing on 11.5 acres of wetlands in a 250-acre parcel, most of which had already been developed. On a summary judgment motion, the court refused to measure the economic impact by the diminution in value of the entire 250 acres. The Court of Claims found for the property's pre-denial value that the highest and best use was a 40-lot residential development with a projected fair market value of $2,658,000. The court held that there was no economically viable use for the property without a permit, even though the post-denial value of the property of $1,000 per acre was based on the remaining conservation and recreational uses of the property. The United States asserted that the property could be adapted for use for hunting, agriculture, a mitigation site, or a marina. The court found these contentions "unsupported" and without any evidence establishing a market for such uses. Similarly, the court found no evidence to demonstrate a market for the one acre of uplands the government claimed could be developed and sold for up to $40,000. The 99 percent diminution in value, coupled with the court's earlier determination of no countervailing substantial state interest, led the court to find a taking. The court ordered payment of the property's full market value at the time of the taking plus interest despite its residual value of $12,500 after the taking.

Following an appeal by the federal government, the Federal Circuit Court of Appeals affirmed the holding of the lower court in *Loveladies*. The court held that the federal government's denial of a permit was a total taking (unlike *Florida Rock*), based on acceptance of the 12.5 acre parcel as the property affected and a finding of no economically feasible use, and that Loveladies was entitled to the compensation awarded by the trial court. The court also concluded that filling the wetlands would not have constituted a nuisance under state law. 28 F.3d 1171 (Fed. Cir. 1994).

Recent Supreme Court decisions under the taking clause, discussed on pages 130-79 *supra*, have created sufficient ambiguity in the area to encourage taking claims when uses of wetlands are substantially restricted.

3. *Mitigation Banking.* The thrust of federal wetlands policy over the last two administrations have been the achievement of "no net loss." To compensate for unavoidable wetland conversion, efforts to restore, create, enhance, or preserve wetlands need to be increased. An innovative concept in the promotion of mitigation has been the establishment of mitigation banks. Mitigation banking enables developers to gain "credits" for mitigation efforts made prior to development. These credits can then be withdrawn as needed to compensate for future wetland projects and impacts. *See generally* Comment, *Taking Wetlands* *to the Bank: The Role of Wetland Mitigation Banking in a Comprehensive Approach to Wetlands Protection*, 22 B.C. ENVTL. AFF. L. REV. 129-62 (1994) (examining the potential of employing mitigation banking to facilitate a comprehensive wetlands policy that is "fair, flexible, and effective."); Veltman, Virginia C., *Banking on the Future of Wetlands Using Federal Law*, 89 Nw. U. L. REV. 654-689 (1995) (arguing that mitigation banking will not achieve its potential unless a comprehensive federal law governing banking is created).

Part V.

Federal Regulation of Toxic Substances

Chapter 8

RESOURCE CONSERVATION AND RECOVERY ACT (RCRA)

INTRODUCTION

In response to mounting public concern about the health and environmental problems of waste disposal, Congress significantly overhauled the Solid Waste Disposal Act of 1965 by enacting the Resource Conservation and Recovery Act of 1976 ("RCRA"), Pub. L. No. 94-580, 90 Stat. 2795, codified as amended, 42 U.S.C. §§ 6901-6987, 9001-9010. The Act provides a comprehensive national regulatory structure for the management of nonhazardous solid wastes and hazardous solid wastes. A number of factors led to the adoption of RCRA: concerns about the "rising tide" of scrap, discarded, and waste materials; the increasing concentration of population in metropolitan areas with inadequate mechanisms to deal with waste disposal; and recognition that existing waste disposal facilities presented health and environmental hazards, particularly with respect to groundwater contamination. § 1002, 42 U.S.C. § 6901.

RCRA serves a role as a "gap-filler" in the federal statutory landscape by addressing the environmental problems regarding both active and inactive waste disposal sites. The Act contains both regulatory standards and remedial provisions to achieve its goals of conservation, reducing waste disposal, and minimizing the present and future threat to human health and the environment.

RCRA contains two main parts with separate provisions governing the management of nonhazardous solid waste (Subtitle D, 42 U.S.C. §§ 6941/y-6949a) and hazardous solid waste (Subtitle C, 42 U.S.C. §§ 6921/y-6939b). The threshold issue to trigger the statute involves determining whether the material constitutes a "solid waste." § 1004(27), 42 U.S.C. § 6903(27). Subtitle D of RCRA sets forth the requirements for the development of solid waste management plans by the states, including requirements for waste disposal in state-licensed landfills and incinerators.

Subtitle C is more important and yet applies to a narrower class of substances — those solid wastes which meet the criteria for classification as "hazardous waste." § 1004(5), 42 U.S.C. § 6903(5). The central purpose of Subtitle C is to establish a comprehensive management system for the "cradle-to-grave" regulation of the generation (section 3002, 42 U.S.C. § 6922), transportation (section 3003, 42 U.S.C. § 6923), and treatment, storage and disposal (section 3004, 42 U.S.C. § 6924) of hazardous wastes. *United Techs. Corp. v. EPA*, 821 F.2d 714, 716 (D.C. Cir. 1987). This is carried out by classifying waste materials, requiring written manifests to track waste shipments from generation until disposal, and certification through a permit system that performance standards are met for safe treatment, storage or disposal. Enforcement of the Act centers on ensuring compliance with the documentation (section 3002, 42 U.S.C. § 6922) and permitting (section 3005, 42 U.S.C. § 6925) obligations imposed on certain parties dealing with covered wastes. Additionally, RCRA contains authorization for civil and criminal penalties (section 3008, 42 U.S.C. § 6928), injunctive relief (section 7003, 42 U.S.C. § 6973), and citizens' suits (section 7002, 42 U.S.C. § 6972).

The following materials examine RCRA's jurisdictional requirements and some of the most pressing regulatory issues facing the EPA in implementing its statutory obligations and selected issues pertaining to enforcement of the statutory requirements.

CONNECTICUT COASTAL FISHERMEN'S ASSOCIATION v. REMINGTON ARMS CO.

989 F.2d 1305; (2d Cir. 1993)

CARDAMONE, CIRCUIT JUDGE:

Critical on this appeal is the meaning of the terms "solid waste" and "hazardous waste," as these terms are defined in the Solid Waste Disposal Act, 42 U.S.C. §§ 6901-6992 (1988), as amended by the Resource Conservation and Recovery Act of 1976 (RCRA), Pub. L. No. 94-580, 90 Stat. 2795 (1976), and the Hazardous and Solid Waste Amendments of 1984, Pub. L. No. 98-616, 98 Stat. 3221 (1984). Defining what Congress intended by these words is not child's play, even though RCRA has an "Alice in Wonderland" air about it. We say that because a careful perusal of RCRA and its regulations reveals that "solid waste" plainly means one thing in one part of RCRA and something entirely different in another part of the same statute.

> "When I use a word," Humpty Dumpty said in a rather scornful tone, "it means just what I choose it to mean — neither more nor less."
>
> "The question is," said Alice, "whether you can make words mean so many different things." "The question is," said Humpty Dumpty, "which is to be master — that's all."

Lewis Carroll, Through the Looking-Glass ch. 6 at 106-09 (Schocken Books 1987) (1872). Congress, of course, is the master and in the discussion that follows, we undertake to discover what meaning Congress intended in its use of the words solid and hazardous waste.

Remington Arms Co., Inc. (Remington or appellant) has owned and operated a trap and skeet shooting club — originally organized in the 1920s — on Lordship Point in Stratford, Connecticut since 1945. Trap and skeet targets are made of clay, and the shotguns used to knock these targets down are loaded with lead shot. The Lordship Point Gun Club (the Gun Club) was open to the public and it annually served 40,000 patrons. After nearly 70 years of use, close to 2,400 tons of lead shot (5 million pounds) and 11 million pounds of clay target fragments were deposited on land around the club and in the adjacent waters of Long Island Sound. Directly to the north of Lordship Point lies a Connecticut state wildlife refuge at Nells Island Marsh, a critical habitat for one of the state's largest populations of Black Duck. The waters and shore near the Gun Club feed numerous species of waterfowl and shorebirds.

Plaintiff, Connecticut Coastal Fishermen's Association (Coastal Fishermen or plaintiff) brought suit against defendant Remington alleging that the lead shot and clay targets are hazardous wastes under RCRA and pollutants under the Clean Water Act (Act), 33 U.S.C. §§ 1251-1387 (1988 & Supp. II 1990). Remington has never obtained a permit under § 3005 of RCRA for the storage and disposal of hazardous wastes, 42 U.S.C. § 6925, or a National Pollutant Discharge Elimination System (pollution discharge) permit pursuant to § 402 of the Clean Water Act, 33 U.S.C. § 1342. Plaintiff insists that Remington must now clean up the lead shot and clay fragments it permitted to be scattered on the land and in the sea at Lordship Point. Because the debris constitutes an imminent and substantial endangerment to health and the environment under RCRA, we agree....

Discussion

II. Resource Conservation and Recovery Act

A. Overview

Turning now to Remington's appeal from the district court's RCRA ruling, plaintiff asserts that Remington has been operating an unpermitted facility for the treatment, storage or disposal of hazardous wastes in violation of 42 U.S.C. § 6925 (a citizens suit claim under § 6972(a)(1)(A)) and has created an "imminent and substantial endangerment" to human health and the environment under § 6972(a)(1)(B). The district court did not distinguish between these causes of action in granting plaintiff summary judgment. Remington, as noted, never obtained a RCRA permit for the operation of its Gun Club facility, but contends that because lead shot and clay target debris are not "solid wastes" — and hence cannot be "hazardous wastes" regulated by RCRA — it is not subject to a permit requirement. In essence, Remington contends that RCRA does not apply to the Gun Club because any disposal of waste that occurred there was merely incidental to the normal use of a product.

RCRA establishes a "cradle-to-grave" regulatory structure for the treatment, storage and disposal of solid and hazardous wastes. Solid wastes are regulated under Subchapter IV §§ 6941-49a; hazardous wastes are subject to the more stringent standards of Subchapter III §§ 6921-39b. [Citation] Under RCRA "hazardous wastes" are a subset of "solid wastes." See 42 U.S.C. § 6903 (5). Accordingly, for a waste to be classified as hazardous, it must first qualify as a solid waste under RCRA. [Citation] We direct our attention initially therefore to whether the lead shot and clay targets are solid waste....

We consider first the statutory definition of solid waste. RCRA defines solid waste as:

> any garbage, refuse, sludge from a waste treatment plant, water supply treatment plant, or air pollution control facility and other discarded material ... resulting from industrial, commercial, mining and agricultural operations, and from community activities ...

42 U.S.C. § 6903(27). Remington admits that its Gun Club is a "commercial operation" or a "community activity"; it challenges the district court's finding that the lead shot and clay target debris are "discarded material." The statute itself does not further define "discarded material," and this creates an ambiguity with respect to the specific issue raised by Remington: At what point after a lead shot is fired at a clay target do the materials become discarded? Does the transformation from useful to discarded material take place the instant the shot is fired or at some later time?

The legislative history does not satisfactorily resolve this ambiguity. It tells us that RCRA was designed to "eliminate[] the last remaining loophole in environmental law" by regulating the "disposal of discarded materials and hazardous wastes." Further, the reach of RCRA was intended to be broad.

It is not only the waste by-products of the nation's manufacturing processes with which the committee is concerned: but also the products themselves once they have served their intended purposes and are no longer wanted by the consumer. For these reasons the term discarded materials is used to identify collectively those substances often referred to as industrial, municipal or post-consumer waste; refuse, trash, garbage and sludge.

Yet, the legislative history does not tell us at what point products have served their intended purposes. The statutory definition of "disposal" as "the discharge, deposit, injection, dumping, spilling, leaking, or placing of any solid waste or hazardous waste into or on any land or water," 42 U.S.C. § 6903(3), while broad, sheds little light on this question. Remington's focus on RCRA as being intended to address only solid waste "disposal" — in the sense of the affirmative acts of collecting, transporting, and treating manufacturing or industrial by-products — clearly is too narrow because it ignores legislative aim and fails to take into account the often non-voluntary acts of depositing, spilling and leaking. The statute and legislative history do not instruct as to how far the reach of RCRA extends. Thus, we proceed to the second step of the Chevron analysis and consider the EPA's interpretation.

The RCRA regulations create a dichotomy in the definition of solid waste. The EPA distinguishes between RCRA's regulatory and remedial purposes and offers a different definition of solid waste depending upon the statutory context in which the term appears. In its amicus brief, the EPA tells us that the regulatory definition of solid waste — found at 40 C.F.R. § 261.2(a) — is narrower than its statutory counterpart. The regulations define solid waste as "any discarded material" and further define discarded material as that which is "abandoned." 40

C.F.R. § 261.2(a). Materials that are abandoned have been "disposed of." 40 C.F.R. § 261.2(b). According to RCRA regulations, this definition of solid waste "applies only to wastes that also are hazardous for purposes of the regulations implementing Subtitle C of RCRA." 40 C.F.R. § 261.1(b)(1). As previously noted, Subtitle C [Subchapter III] contains more stringent handling standards for hazardous waste, and hazardous waste is a subset of solid waste.

The regulations further state that the statutory definition of solid waste, found at 42 U.S.C. § 6903(27), applies to "imminent hazard" lawsuits brought by the United States under § 7003, 42 U.S.C. § 6973. See 40 C.F.R. § 261.1(b)(2)(ii). This statement recognizes the special nature of the imminent hazard lawsuit under RCRA. Currently, RCRA authorizes two kinds of citizen suits. The first, under § 7002(a)(1)(A), 42 U.S.C. § 6972(a)(1)(A), enables private citizens to enforce the EPA's hazardous waste regulations and — according to 40 C.F.R. § 261.1-(b)(1) — invokes the narrow regulatory definition of solid waste. The second type of citizen suit, under § 7002(a)(1)(B), 42 U.S.C. § 6972(a)(1)(B), authorizes citizens to sue to abate an "imminent and substantial endangerment to health or the environment." While the regulations do not specifically mention this second category of citizen suit, regulatory language referring to § 7003 must also apply to § 7002(a)(1)(B) because the two provisions are nearly identical. [Citation] Consequently, the broader statutory definition of solid waste applies to citizen suits brought to abate imminent hazard to health or the environment.

We recognize the anomaly of using different definitions for the term "solid waste" and that such view further complicates an already complex statute. Yet, we believe on balance that the EPA regulations reasonably interpret the statutory language. Hence, we defer to them. Dual definitions of solid waste are suggested by the structure and language of RCRA. Congress in Subchapter III isolated hazardous wastes for more stringent regulatory treatment. Recognizing the serious responsibility that such regulations impose, Congress required that hazardous waste — a subset of solid waste as defined in the RCRA regulations — be clearly identified. The statute directs the EPA to develop specific "criteria" for the identification of hazardous wastes as well as to publish a list of particular hazardous wastes. 42 U.S.C. § 6921 (a) & (b). By way of contrast, Subchapter IV that empowers the EPA to publish "guidelines" for the identification of problem solid waste pollution areas, does not require explanation beyond RCRA's statutory definition of what constitutes solid waste. *Id.* § 6942(a). Hence, the words of the statute contemplate that the EPA would refine and narrow the definition of solid waste for the sole purpose of Subchapter III regulation and enforcement....

D. *Statutory Definition of Solid Waste*

Coastal Fishermen's allegation that the lead shot and clay target debris in Long Island Sound creates an "imminent and substantial endangerment" under § 7002(a)(1)(B) of RCRA need not meet the present violation hurdle. An imminent hazard citizen suit will lie against any "past or present" RCRA offender "who has contributed or who is contributing" to "past or present" solid waste handling practices that "may present an imminent and substantial endangerment to health or the environment." 42 U.S.C. § 6972(a)(1)(B). Therefore, under an imminent hazard citizen suit, the endangerment must be ongoing, but the conduct that created the endangerment need not be.

As already noted, RCRA regulations apply the broader statutory definition of solid waste to imminent hazard suits. The statutory definition contains the concept of "discarded material," 42 U.S.C. § 6903(27), but it does not contain the terms "abandoned" or "disposed of" as required by the regulatory definition. 40 C.F.R. §§ 261.2(a)(2), (b)(1). Amicus interprets the statutory definition of solid waste as encompassing the lead shot and clay targets at Lordship Point because they are "discarded." Specifically, the EPA states that the materials are discarded because they have been "left to accumulate long after they have served their intended purpose." Without deciding how long materials must accumulate before they become discarded — that is, when the shot is fired or at some later time — we agree that the lead shot and clay targets in Long Island Sound have accumulated long enough to be considered solid waste....

E. *Hazardous Waste*

Having resolved that the lead shot and clay targets are discarded solid waste, we next analyze whether they are hazardous waste. RCRA defines "hazardous waste" as

> a solid waste, or combination of solid wastes, which because of its quantity, concentration, or physical, chemical, or infectious characteristics may —
>
> ....
>
> (B) pose a substantial present or potential hazard to human health or the environment when improperly treated, stored, transported, or disposed of, or otherwise managed.

42 U.S.C. § 6903 (5)(B).

Certain wastes have been listed by the EPA as hazardous pursuant to 40 C.F.R. § 261.30. Alternatively, a waste is considered hazardous if it exhibits any of the characteristics identified in 40 C.F.R. §§ 261.20 through 261.24: ignitability, corrosivity, reactivity, or toxicity. The district court granted summary judgment in favor of plaintiff on the issue of whether the lead shot qualified as a hazardous waste, but at the same time stated there were genuine issues of material fact as to whether the clay targets were hazardous waste. Remington objects to both rulings.

1. *Lead Shot*

The district court concluded that the lead shot was hazardous waste as a matter of law because it satisfied the requirements of 40 C.F.R. § 261.24 for toxicity. That regulation provides that a solid waste is toxic, and therefore hazardous if, using appropriate testing methods, an "extract from a representative sample of the waste contains any of the contaminants listed ... at the concentration equal to or greater than" that specified. 40 C.F.R. § 261.24(a). For lead, the concentration threshold is 5.0 mg/L. *Id.* table 1.

The Battelle study commissioned by defendant outlines the test method utilized as in accordance with EPA procedures, and was of the view that

> Forty-five percent of the sediment samples analyzed exceeded the [applicable limits for lead]. On the basis of these results, upland disposal of the sediments as they currently exist in the environment at Lordship Point would require use of a RCRA-certified hazardous waste disposal site.

Remington does not challenge the accuracy or methodology of the Battelle study that clearly demonstrates that both the sediment at Lordship Point and the lead shot itself are toxic within the meaning of 40 C.F.R. § 261.24. The Battelle study further opines that "the accumulation of lead in the tissues of mussels and ducks [is] sufficient to indicate a lead contamination problem requiring remediation at Lordship Point." As a matter of law, the lead shot is a solid waste which, due to its toxicity and the fact that it poses a substantial threat to the environment, is a hazardous solid waste subject to RCRA remediation and regulation....

2. *Clay Targets*

Remington declares the clay targets cannot be hazardous waste merely because they contain hazardous wastes listed in 40 C.F.R. § 261.33(f). Regardless of whether this assertion properly interprets 40 C.F.R. § 261.33(d) (comment), it is irrelevant. The district court did not decide that there was a genuine issue as to whether the clay targets were hazardous because it was not yet determined whether they contain hazardous wastes listed in 40 C.F.R. § 261.33(f). Rather, it ruled this issue remained undecided because the appropriate tests to determine toxicity under 40 C.F.R. § 261.24 had not yet been completed....

Conclusion

For the foregoing reasons, the judgment of the district court is affirmed, in part, and reversed, in part.

NOTES AND QUESTIONS

1. *Solid Waste.* The first question regarding whether a material is subject to control under RCRA is determining whether it fits within the definition of "solid waste":

> any garbage, refuse, sludge from a waste treatment plant, water supply treatment plant, or air pollution control facility and other *discarded* material, including solid, liquid, semisolid, or contained gaseous material resulting from industrial, commercial, mining, and agricultural operations, and from community activities.... (Emphasis supplied.)

Section 1004(27), 42 U.S.C. § 6903(27). Through this broad definition, RCRA potentially applies to a wide range of materials, regardless of its physical form. The term "solid" waste is actually misleading and more expansive than its ordinary meaning might indicate because it includes solids, semi-solids, liquids, and contained gases.

2. The regulations amplify and expand the statutory definition of solid waste by classifying all materials into three groups: (1) garbage, refuse, or sludge; (2) solid, liquid, semi-solid or contained gaseous material; or (3) other substances. Materials in the first category are always considered subject to RCRA, and those in the third group are excluded. The materials in the middle category are solid waste unless excluded from coverage as domestic sewage, industrial wastewater discharges subject to Clean Water Act permits, irrigation return flow, otherwise regulated nuclear materials, or mining wastes. *See* Appendix I to Part 260; 40 C.F.R. § 261.4(a).

3. *Discarded.* RCRA limits its regulatory reach by providing that only solid waste material which is "discarded" comes within its jurisdiction. Section 1004(27), 42 U.S.C. § 6903(27). The focus on material which is discarded, then, modifies and limits which substances qualify as solid wastes under the statute. RCRA does not define "discarded," but the EPA has promulgated a series of definitions organized to progress from the general definition of "solid waste" to increasingly specific terms to explain the criteria for discarded material. *See* 40 C.F.R. § 261.2. Thus, "discarded" means material which is either abandoned or recycled, or is inherently waste-like. 40 C.F.R. § 261.2(a)(2). A material is considered "abandoned" if it is disposed of, burned or incinerated, or accumulated, stored or treated (but not recycled) before or in lieu of disposal, burning or incineration. 40 C.F.R. § 261.2(b). Finally, the meaning of "disposal" requires cross reference to its statutory definition, which includes the "discharge, deposit, injection, dumping, spilling, leaking" of waste into the environment. Section 1004(3), 42 U.S.C. § 6903(3). One court, although upholding certain hazardous regulations as not unconstitutionally vague, conceded that the regulations were "dense, turgid, and a bit circuitous." *United States v. White*, 766 F. Supp. 873, 880 (E.D. Wash. 1991).

4. *Hazardous Waste.* The EPA is charged with the responsibility of promulgating criteria for identifying which "solid wastes" are also considered "hazardous" and therefore subject to management in accordance with the RCRA's Part C requirements. Section 3001(a), 42 U.S.C. § 6921(a). The EPA uses two separate and independent approaches to classify material as hazardous waste: by an administrative listing procedure and where tests show that the waste exhibits certain characteristics. Section 3001(a), 42 U.S.C. § 6921(a); 40 C.F.R. § 261.3(a); *Hazardous Waste Treatment Council v. EPA*, 861 F.2d 270 (D.C. Cir. 1988). A solid waste becomes subject to the statutory hazardous waste requirements if it meets the standards under either approach. *City of New York v. Exxon Corp.*, 766 F. Supp. 177, 184 (S.D.N.Y. 1991).

5. "Hazardous waste" is defined in section 1004(5), 42 U.S.C. § 6903(5) as follows:

> a *solid waste*, or combination of solid wastes, which because of its quantity, concentration, or physical, chemical, or infectious characteristics may —
> (A) cause, or significantly contribute to an increase in mortality or an increase in serious irreversible, or incapacitating reversible, illness; or
> (B) pose a substantial present or potential hazard to human health or the environment when improperly treated, stored, transported, or disposed of, or otherwise managed. (emphasis added).

6. *Hazardous Waste Characteristics.* One method for qualifying as hazardous waste under RCRA is where the material possesses certain characteristics. The EPA has promulgated regulations which provide that any solid waste possessing any one of four characteristics— ignitability, corrosivity, reactivity, or toxicity — will be considered a hazardous waste which must be "managed" when discarded. 40 C.F.R. §§ 261.21-261.24; *American Petr. Inst. v. EPA*, 906 F.2d 729, 733 (D.C. Cir. 1990). The applicable regulation provides:

> (a) The Administrator shall identify and define a characteristic of hazardous waste in subpart C only upon determining that:
> (1) A solid waste that exhibits the characteristic may:
> (i) Cause, or significantly contribute to, an increase in mortality or an increase in serious irreversible, or incapacitating reversible, illness; or
> (ii) Pose a substantial present or potential hazard to human health or the environment when it is improperly treated, stored, transported, disposed of or otherwise managed; and
> (2) The characteristic can be:
> (i) Measured by an available standardized test method which is reasonably within the capability of generators of solid waste or private sector laboratories that are available to serve generators of solid waste; or
> (ii) Reasonably detected by generators of solid waste through their knowledge of the waste.

40 C.F.R. § 261.10.

The toxicity characteristic is determined through a complex "toxicity characteristic leaching procedure" ("TCLP") which tests whether the amount of certain toxins which are contained in the waste exceed maximum allowable concentration levels. *See* 40 C.F.R. § 261.24, Table 1; 40 C.F.R. Part 261, Appendix II. The burden of identification through testing rests on the person handling the waste. Generators must receive an EPA identification number for such wastes and comply with the notification, recordkeeping, and reporting requirements of the Act. 40 C.F.R. §§ 261.20, 262.12.

7. *Listed Hazardous Waste.* The alternate method by which solid wastes are designated as hazardous under RCRA is through listing by the EPA after a rulemaking proceeding. The administrator lists a solid waste as "hazardous" upon meeting any of three criteria. First, the waste may exhibit one of the four characteristics of hazardous waste. 40 C.F.R. § 261.11(a)(1). Second, the substance may be considered "acutely toxic," based upon studies which show that it would be fatal to humans even in low doses or tested laboratory animals exhibit certain effects. 40 C.F.R. § 261.11(a)(2).

Finally, the EPA may determine that it contains any of the toxic constituents listed in Appendix VIII to 40 C.F.R. Part 261 and the waste is capable of posing substantial harm if managed improperly. 40 C.F.R. § 261.11(a)(3). Substances become listed as toxic in Appendix VIII only when scientific studies demonstrate that the substances possess "toxic, carcinogenic, mutagenic, or teratogenic effects on humans or other life forms." *Id.* The EPA must also find that the waste is "capable of posing a substantial present or potential hazard to human health or the environment when improperly treated, stored, transported or disposed of, or otherwise managed," considering certain factors. 40 C.F.R. § 261.11(a)(3). The factors include the nature and concentration of the toxic constituents of the waste, its migratory potential, degree of bioaccumulation in ecosystems, quantities generated, ways that it could be mismanaged, and the actions of other regulatory agencies. *Id.*

In addition, the EPA also has authority to list classes or types of solid waste simply guided by the general statutory definition of hazardous waste in section 1004(5), 42 U.S.C. § 6903(5). 40 C.F.R. § 261.11(b).

8. *Land Disposal of Hazardous Wastes.* RCRA does not purport to eliminate the disposal of hazardous waste, but instead provides for its management by requiring that disposal occur only in specially licensed facilities. RCRA § 3005(a), 42 U.S.C. § 6925(a). The statute, as initially drafted, presented the EPA with an intractable problem of how to accomplish its mission of protecting health and the environment while tolerating continued hazardous waste land disposal practices. The problem faced by the agency had both economic and technological feasibility difficulties since land disposal of hazardous waste was the most common, least expensive method employed by industry, but the substances placed in landfills eventually leaked out and often contaminated surrounding soil and groundwater. *See generally* NOVICK, LAW OF ENVIRONMENTAL PROTECTION § 13.01[5]. No other alternative for disposition of hazardous waste offered a completely satisfactory solution, however. Treatment by incineration, for instance, ran into compliance problems with ambient air quality standards under the Clean Air Act.

The answer to EPA's dilemma came in 1984 with passage of the Hazardous and Solid Waste Amendments ("HSWA") to RCRA. The HSWA established tough new schedules regarding the EPA's administration of its hazardous waste management program, set stringent design and performance standards for landfills to prevent leaking, and contemplated a phasing out of land disposal of hazardous waste. The statutory policy, as amended, flatly stated that landfill and surface impoundment was the "least favored method" for managing hazardous wastes. RCRA § 1002(b)(7), 42 U.S.C. § 6901(b)(7).

Congress's dissatisfaction with EPA implementation of restrictions on land disposal of hazardous wastes led to the creation of a strict statutory schedule in the 1984 Amendments for the gradual phase-out of that methodology, subject to narrow exceptions. RCRA §§ 3004(d)-(g), 42 U.S.C. §§ 6924(d)-(g). The mandated shift away from land disposal to treatment alternatives was accompanied by statutory fallback or "hammer" provisions which trigger automatically to prohibit land disposal with respect to the enumerated waste category if the EPA fails to set treatment standards by the specified deadlines. RCRA § 3004(g), 42 U.S.C. § 6924(g).

Pursuant to the statutory directive, EPA established a schedule dividing hazardous wastes into three groups ("thirds") in order to satisfy the phased compliance requirements. *See Chemical Waste Mgt., Inc. v. EPA*, 869 F.2d 1526 (D.C. Cir. 1989) (agency rulemaking regarding hazardous waste restrictions upheld as reasonable). The categories of wastes subject to the phased land disposal prohibition include solvents (40 C.F.R. § 268.30), dioxins (40 C.F.R. § 268-31), and California listed wastes, such as PCBs (40 C.F.R. § 268.32). *Chemical Waste Mgmt., Inc. v. EPA*, 976 F.2d 2 (D.C. Cir. 1992) (upholding "third-third" rule regarding hazardous waste possessing certain characteristics).

9. *Exemptions.* The Act, as revised, prohibits the land disposal of hazardous wastes except in two instances: where the substances are "treated" prior to disposal in accordance with certain nationally uniform technology requirements (RCRA § 3004(m), 42 U.S.C. § 6924(m)), or the EPA grants an exemption based on a showing by the petitioner that the methodology meets exacting health and safety standards. RCRA § 3004(d)(1), 42 U.S.C. § 6924(d)(1). RCRA's treatment exemption, which was inspired by the technology-forcing provisions of the Clean Air Act and the Clean Water Act, requires that the waste be treated with the "best demonstrated treatment technology" (BDAT). *See* 40 C.F.R. Part 268, Subpart D (Establishing treatment standards for wastes subject to land disposal prohibition). *Also see American Petr. Inst. v. EPA*, 906 F.2d 729, 742 (D.C. Cir. 1990) (EPA correct in determining that hazardous waste treatment provisions preclude comparative risk assessment and consideration of land treatment in setting BDAT).

The exemption procedure requires the applicant to demonstrate that the land disposal prohibition is not necessary to protect human health or the environment for as long as the waste remains hazardous, by taking into account long-term uncertainties, hazardous waste management goals; and the "persistence, toxicity, mobility, and propensity to bioaccumulate" of the subject wastes. RCRA § 3004(d)(1), 42 U.S.C. § 6924(d)(1). Thus, the statute requires the EPA to promulgate prohibitory regulations unless the agency makes a positive determination that a particular method of land disposal is safe. *See Natural Resources Defense Council v. EPA*, 907 F.2d 1146, 1153-54 (D.C. Cir. 1990) (the phased schedule of land-bans were intended to give the EPA sufficient time to declare a "safe harbor" for methods it found merited exemption from the statutory prohibition). The petitioner faces a difficult hurdle to gain an exemption because section 3004 further requires a showing that there will be "no migration" of the waste from the disposal site "as long as the wastes remain hazardous." RCRA § 3004(d)(1), (e) and (g); 42 U.S.C. § 6924(d)(1), (e) and (g); 40 C.F.R. § 268.6(a). *See Natural Resources Defense Council v. EPA*, 907 F.2d 1146, 1158 (D.C. Cir. 1990) (upheld EPA standard requiring no migration of hazardous wastes from deep well injection zone for 10,000 years as reasonable).

UNITED STATES v. ILCO, INC.

996 F.2d 1126 (11th Cir. 1993)

FAY, CIRCUIT JUDGE:

This case is an enforcement action filed by the United States Environmental Protection Agency and the State of Alabama against a secondary lead smelter for violations of federal and state environmental law. The district court held the defendant liable and awarded civil penalties and cleanup costs to the government, and ordered compliance with the law. Although the government received a favorable decision, it has appealed the district court's conclusion that the lead components reclaimed from spent batteries are raw materials. The district court reasoned that because the smelter recycles the components into lead ingots, the components must be raw materials, and not hazardous waste subject to the provisions of the Resource Conservation and Recovery Act. The defendant has cross-appealed the district court's order awarding penalties and cleanup costs to the government....

Background

1. *Industry Overview*

Over the years in the United States there has been a steady increase in the number of vehicle batteries which become useless and subject to disposal. In 1986 the number stood at approximately 70,000,000. Each spent battery is a potential pollutant of the environment and can have serious deleterious effects on people and animals living in the area where the battery may be discarded. Even a small number of batteries thrown into the woods, discarded along roadways or in government designated garbage areas represent a significant threat to the water we drink, the food we eat and under limited circumstances, the air we breathe. The source of this trouble in a battery is lead.... [Because lead is an expensive element, an industry has developed over the years] to reclaim the lead from spent batteries.... [In the mid-Seventies] there were approximately 50 secondary lead smelters in the United States reclaiming the lead from about 90 of all spent batteries. The smelters were themselves a major source of pollution; surface water run-off and process water discharged by the smelters created very real health-threatening problems; on-site and off-site storage or disposition of waste became an increasing risk to the quality of life; and even the air was dangerously polluted by emissions from the smelters. [In response to these problems] all levels of government began to amend existing laws and to enact new laws and regulations placing much greater controls over ownership and operation of such smelters. Compliance with these new environmental laws and regulations ... placed such a financial burden on the operation of secondary lead smelters that about 60 of the smelters operating in 1976 were out of business by 1986, and the approximately 20 smelters remaining were reclaiming only about 70 ... [of all discarded batteries.] Thus in 1986 only 55,000,000 of the available 70,000,000 batteries were reclaimed, leaving the 15,000,000 unreclaimed spent batteries to endanger the health of all persons near the site of their repose. The 55,000,000 reclaimed batteries produced about 60 of all lead used in the United States.... [This brief overview demonstrates the secondary lead smelting industry] is a most vital industry not only to our economy but also to [our] environment.... Without the industry, over 70,000,000 contaminated batteries would be scattered throughout our country annually. [Nevertheless, the heart of this industry centers around the handling of hazardous materials. Exempting the industry from regulation cannot be justified on the theory that its contribution to resolving our environmental problems outweighs the environmental harm caused by its operations.]

2. *Factual and Procedural Background*

The Interstate Lead Company, Inc. ("ILCO") owned and operated a secondary lead smelting facility in Leeds, Alabama, from the 1960's until operations ceased in 1992. As such, it was one of the 20 smelters remaining in the country which reclaimed spent batteries. In 1986 ILCO reclaimed over 2,500,000 batteries, or about 5 of those reclaimed in the United States....

ILCO purchased batteries from various suppliers and placed them in a reclamation process. Incoming batteries were cracked open and drained of sulfuric acid. The rubber or black plastic battery boxes were chipped and washed to remove lead particles. The lead battery components known as "plates and groups" were then removed from the broken batteries and run through ILCO's smelting process to produce lead ingots for sale. The operation produced several waste products which were the subject of litigation in the district court: waste acid, wastewater treatment sludge, broken battery casings or "chips," and emission control dust and blast slag from the smelting process. EPA asserted, and continues to argue on appeal, that the reclaimed lead plates and groups were also waste products. The defendants viewed the plates and groups as raw materials essential to the lead recovery industry.

EPA and the Alabama Department of Environmental Management ("ADEM") initiated this case as an enforcement action against ILCO and its president, Diego Maffei, seeking an injunction to curtail ongoing violations of environmental laws and regulations at ILCO's plant in Leeds and seeking penalties for past violations.... The second and third claims concerned the treatment, storage and disposal of hazardous wastes since 1980 in violation of the Resource Conservation and Recovery Act ("RCRA"), as amended by the Hazardous and Solid Waste Amendments of 1984, 42 U.S.C. §§ 6901-92k. In the second claim EPA charged ILCO with maintaining storage areas, an incinerator and a treatment tank, all containing hazardous waste, in violation of regulations applicable to their status as an interim facility and maintaining other storage facilities and a landfill without the requisite permit. The third claim encompassed the same RCRA violation, alleging that the facility permitted releases of hazardous waste into the environment....

The court found the lead plates and groups to be solid waste as defined in 40 C.F.R. § 261.2 because they exhibit the characteristic of "Extraction Procedure toxicity" for lead and cadmium as defined in that regulation. However, the court also held the plates and groups at the ILCO facility were not "hazardous waste," accepting ILCO's argument that it did not "discard," but rather purchased the plates and groups as raw materials for the purpose of recovering lead values. EPA and ADEM appeal this ruling.

Discussion

The sole question of law raised by EPA on appeal is whether lead parts, which have been reclaimed from spent car and truck batteries for recycling purposes, are exempt from regulation under RCRA. The standard of review is de novo. *Novak v. Irwin Yacht and Marine Corp.*, 986 F.2d 468, 470 (11th Cir. 1993). Reviewing the interpretive decisions of an administrative agency is a two-step process: If Congress has clearly and directly spoken to the precise question at issue, effect must be given to the expressed intent of Congress. If the court finds the statute silent or ambiguous with respect to the specific issue, it must ask whether the agency's regulation is based on a "permissible" or "reasonable" construction of the statute. *Chevron USA, Inc. v. National Resources Defense Council*, 467 U.S. 837, 842-45, 104 S. Ct. 2778, 2781-83, 81 L. Ed. 2d 694 (1984). Considerable weight and deference are afforded an agency's interpretation of a statute entrusted to its administration. *Id.* at 844, 104 S. Ct. at 2782.

Because Congress has not spoken to the precise question at issue, we must decide whether EPA has reasonably construed the RCRA to permit regulation of the recycling of hazardous materials. There is no question that the materials at issue are hazardous; the district court specifically found the plates and groups were "Extraction Procedure toxic" for lead and cadmium. If it is permissible for EPA to determine that "solid waste," as defined by Congress, includes materials that are recycled, then the lead plates and groups were "hazardous waste" and must be managed accordingly. We conclude that EPA's regulations are a reasonable exercise of its authority granted by Congress. For this reason and those to follow, we find the lead plates and groups that ILCO reclaims from spent batteries fall squarely within the law and regulations governing the storage, disposal and treatment of hazardous waste.

The RCRA, as amended, 42 U.S.C. §§ 6901-92k (1988), is a comprehensive environmental statute, which grants EPA authority to regulate solid and hazardous wastes from "cradle-to-grave." *American Petroleum Institute v. EPA*, 285 U.S. App. D.C. 35, 906 F.2d 729, 732 (D.C. Cir.1990). "Congress' 'overriding concern' in enacting RCRA was to establish the framework for a national system to insure the safe management of hazardous waste." *American Mining Congress v. EPA*, 263 U.S. App. D.C. 197, 824 F.2d 1177, 1179 (D.C. Cir. 1987) (*AMC I*). RCRA directs EPA to promulgate regulations establishing a comprehensive management system for hazardous wastes. 42 U.S.C. §§ 6921-39b (1988).

Before a material can be designated and regulated as a "hazardous waste," it must first be determined to be a "solid waste." *See* 42 U.S.C. § 6903(5) (1988). Solid waste includes:

> any garbage, refuse, sludge from a waste treatment plant, water supply treatment plant, or air pollution control facility *and other discarded material*, including solid, liquid, semisolid, or contained gaseous material resulting from industrial, commercial, mining, and agricultural operations, and from community activities....

42 U.S.C. § 6903(27) (1988) (emphasis added). 42 U.S.C. § 6921 directs the Administrator of the EPA to identify those solid wastes which are "hazardous" and whose management should therefore be governed by RCRA. In particular, § 6921 requires the Administrator both to "promulgate criteria for identifying the characteristics of hazardous waste" and, using these criteria, to list "specific hazardous wastes."[9]

Pursuant to its authority, EPA has promulgated regulations which specifically address discarded lead-acid batteries. Without clarifying the meaning of "discarded," Congress defined solid waste as "any discarded material" not otherwise exempted from regulation. EPA has filled the statutory gap by defining "discarded material" as any material which is abandoned, recycled, or inherently wastelike. 40 C.F.R. § 261.2(a)(2) (1992). "Recycled material" refers to, inter alia, spent material which has been reclaimed. 40 C.F.R. § 261.2(c)(3) (1992). A material is "'reclaimed' if it is processed to recover a usable product, or if it is regenerated. Examples are recovery of lead values from spent batteries...." 40 C.F.R. § 261.1(c)(4) (1992). "Reclaimed material" clearly includes lead values derived from the plates and groups at issue here. Furthermore, these battery components fall within the § 261.1(c)(4) definition of recycled material because ILCO runs the plates and groups through a smelting process to recover a usable product, lead, which is then cast into ingots and sold. Thus, having met the

---

[9]Accordingly, the regulations define two categories of hazardous waste: "listed" waste and "characteristic" waste. Listed wastes are produced by a particular type of industrial process and are given a unique identifying code number. 40 C.F.R. § 261.30 (1992). Characteristic wastes are those wastes which exhibit certain characteristics of ignitability, corrosivity, reactivity or Extraction Procedure toxicity. 40 C.F.R. § 261.21-24 (1992).

definition of "recycled," the lead components are discarded material as defined in 40 C.F.R. § 261.2(a)(2).

The regulations also specify those recycled materials which are solid wastes. They include "spent materials" that are recycled by "reclamation," or are "accumulated, stored, or treated before recycling" by reclamation. 40 C.F.R. § 261.2(c) (1992). A "spent material" is "any material that has been used and as a result of contamination can no longer serve the purpose for which it was produced without processing." 40 C.F.R. § 261.1(c)(1) (1992). Thus, the applicable regulations are unambiguous with respect to spent lead components used in a recycling process: spent materials "are solid wastes when reclaimed." 40 C.F.R. § 261.2(c)(3) and Table 1 (1992).

ILCO argues that it has never "discarded" the plates and groups and, therefore, the material it recycles is not "solid waste" as defined in RCRA § 6903(27). The lead plates and groups are, no doubt, valuable feedstock for a smelting process. Nevertheless, EPA, with congressional authority, promulgate regulations that classify these materials as "discarded solid waste." Somebody has discarded the battery in which these components are found. This fact does not change just because a reclaimer has purchased or finds value in the components.

The regulations reflect EPA's policy decision that spent batteries, including their lead components, became "part of the waste disposal problem," when the original consumer discarded the battery. It is unnecessary to read into the word "discarded" a congressional intent that the waste in question must finally and forever be discarded, as ILCO seems to argue. It is perfectly reasonable for EPA to assume Congress meant "discarded once." Were we to rule otherwise, waste such as these batteries would arguably be exempt from regulation under RCRA merely because they are potentially recyclable. Previously discarded solid waste, although it may at some point be recycled, nonetheless remains solid waste. [Citations] Therefore, we find these batteries and their contents are "discarded" within the everyday sense of the word. Their secondary character as recyclable material is irrelevant to that determination.

We have found nothing in the language of the statute, and ILCO has brought forth nothing from the legislative history to show that EPA's policy choice is not one Congress would have sanctioned. On the contrary, application of these regulations to spent batteries and parts generated by consumers comports with Congress' intent in RCRA to address the problems posed by hazardous waste. The House Committee explained:

> It is not only the waste by-products of the nation's manufacturing processes with which the committee is concerned: but also the products themselves once they have served their intended purposes and are no longer wanted by the consumer. For these reasons the term discarded materials is used to identify collectively those substances often referred to as industrial, municipal or post-consumer waste; refuse, trash, garbage and sludge. We,

therefore, will not disturb an agency's policy choice that is reasonably consistent with the purpose of the statute.

Conclusion

For the foregoing reasons, we *reverse* the district court's determination that the lead plates and groups are "raw materials" and hold they are "hazardous waste" subject to regulation under RCRA, but *affirm* its decision in every other respect. The case is *remanded* for proceedings consistent with this opinion.

NOTES AND QUESTIONS

1. *Useful Products and Recycled Materials.* The concept of when materials become "discarded" presents difficulties particularly with respect to materials that are still useful products or which may be reclaimed or recycled. The regulations addressing these categories fail to demarcate precise boundaries for coverage and exclusion. Recycled materials are considered solid wastes subject to RCRA when used in a manner constituting disposal, burned for energy recovery, reclaimed, and accumulated speculatively. 40 C.F.R. § 261.2(c).

2. Other recycled materials are specifically excluded from coverage, including those used or reused as ingredients in an industrial process to make a product, used as a substitute for a commercial product, or returned as a substitute for raw material feedstock. 40 C.F.R. § 261.2(e). *See Catellus Dev. Corp. v. United States*, 34 F.3d 748, 752 (9th Cir. 1994) (reclamation of spent batteries classified as waste subject to RCRA).

3. Courts and the EPA have continued to struggle over drawing guidelines for application of these principles. In *American Mining Congress v. EPA*, 824 F.2d 1177, 1193 (D.C. Cir. 1987) (*AMC I*) secondary materials that were being recycled and reused in an ongoing manufacturing or industrial production process were not treated as RCRA solid wastes because the materials had not been "discarded." The court noted that the materials had "not yet become part of the waste disposal problem" because they were "destined for beneficial reuse or recycling in a continuous process by the generating industry itself." 824 F.2d at 1186.

Several years after *AMC I*, in *American Petr. Inst. v. EPA*, 906 F.2d 729 (D.C. Cir. 1990) industry challenged the EPA's decision not to prescribe treatment standards for K061 slag, even though the material fell within the agency's rules covering products "derived from" hazardous waste. The EPA claimed that it lacked the authority to regulate the slag because the material had ceased to be a "discarded" solid waste when it reached a metals reclamation facility. The court rejected the EPA's ruling as an unreasonable interpretation of RCRA, reasoning that once K061 had been "discarded" it remained so throughout the waste treatment process.

In *American Mining Congress v. EPA*, 907 F.2d 1179 (D.C. Cir. 1990) (*AMC II*), decided just weeks later, industry petitioners contested action by the EPA in relisting as hazardous six wastes generated from primary metal smelting operations. The waste was being deposited in land disposal units which comprised parts of wastewater treatment systems. The court held that the EPA had not exceeded its statutory authority in relisting the wastes because they had already been discarded when stored in the surface impoundments. 907 F.2d at 1186. Since the material might leak from the storage tanks, it posed a sufficient environmental hazard to justify RCRA coverage. The court stated that the possibility that some of the waste eventually might become reclaimed in the future did not preclude its present characterization as solid waste for RCRA regulation. 907 F.2d at 1187.

4. In *Owen Electric Steel Co. of South Carolina v. Browner*, 37 F.3d 146, 150 (4th Cir. 1994) the court found that slag produced as a byproduct in a steel making process which was cured in piles for six months and then sold to contractors for use as a material in road making or other commercial purposes was "discarded" material and therefore "solid waste" under RCRA. The court observed that the "fundamental inquiry in determining whether a byproduct has been 'discarded' is whether the byproduct is *immediately* recycled for use in the same industry." *Also see Zands v. Nelson*, 779 F. Supp. 1254, 1262 (S.D. Cal. 1991) (gasoline leaking from an underground storage tank no longer was considered a useful product but was "abandoned" and therefore "discarded" solid waste under RCRA). *See generally* D. STEVER, LAW OF CHEMICAL REGULATION AND HAZARDOUS WASTE, § 5.02[2][a]; Needleman, *Hazardous Waste Recycling Under the Resource Conservation and Recovery Act: Problems and Potential Solutions*, 24 ENVTL. L. 971 (1994); Gaba, *Solid Wastes and Recycled Materials Under RCRA: Separating the Chaff for Wheat*, 16 ECOLOGY L.Q. 623 (1989).

5. What if the waste material is placed in a storage tank or pipeline, or simply remains on site at a manufacturing plant? Does the regulatory framework contemplate a showing of intent to throw the material away? If so, what criteria would be appropriate? *See* 40 C.F.R. § 261.4(c) (Hazardous waste becomes subject to RCRA upon "exiting" the unit where generated or after 90 days of remaining at a discontinued manufacturing facility.).

6. *Permit.* RCRA requires that facilities storing hazardous wastes obtain an operating permit which ensures adequate compliance with regulatory storage and handling procedures. §§ 42 U.S.C. §§ 6922-25. The permit can be issued by the EPA or a state agency with delegated authority, or it can be satisfied by meeting the statutory criteria established by Congress for "interim status," which is the functional equivalent of a permit. §§ 42 U.S.C. §§ 6925-26. The 1984 Amendments gave existing hazardous waste disposal facilities an opportunity to continue operations pending final administrative disposition of the permit application. RCRA § 3005(e), 42 U.S.C. § 6925(e); 40 C.F.R. §§ 270.2, 270.70-73. These interim disposal requirements do not grandfather existing facilities, nor do they create a vested right to maintain permanent operations at the interim status level. Notably, interim status land disposal facilities are required to certify compliance with the same groundwater monitoring and financial responsibility requirements as are applicable to other facilities. Additionally, such facilities must comply with extensive reporting, record-keeping, security, inspection, closure and post-closure requirements imposed under state and federal law. *See generally* 40 C.F.R. Part 265.

CITY OF CHICAGO v. ENVIRONMENTAL DEFENSE FUND
__ U.S. __, 114 S. Ct. 1588 128 L. Ed. 2d 302 (1994)

JUSTICE SCALIA delivered the opinion of the Court.

We are called upon to decide whether, pursuant to § 3001(i) of the Solid Waste Disposal Act (Resource Conservation and Recovery Act of 1976 (RCRA)), as added, 98 Stat. 3252, 42 U.S.C. § 6921(i), the ash generated by a resource recovery facility's incineration of municipal solid waste is exempt from regulation as a hazardous waste under Subtitle C of RCRA.

I

Since 1971, petitioner the city of Chicago has owned and operated a municipal incinerator, the Northwest Waste-to-Energy Facility, that burns solid waste and recovers energy, leaving a residue of municipal waste combustion (MWC) ash. The facility burns approximately 350,000 tons of solid waste each year and produces energy that is both used within the facility and sold to other entities. The city has disposed of the combustion residue — 110,000 to 140,000 tons of MWC ash per year — at landfills that are not licensed to accept hazardous wastes.

In 1988 respondent Environmental Defense Fund (EDF) filed a complaint against the petitioners, the city of Chicago and its Mayor, under the citizen suit provisions of RCRA, 42 U.S.C. § 6972, alleging that they were violating provisions of RCRA and of implementing regulations issued by the Environmental Protection Agency (EPA). Respondent alleged that the MWC ash generated by the facility was toxic enough to qualify as a "hazardous waste" under EPA's regulations, 40 CFR pt. 261 (1993). It was uncontested that, with respect to the ash, petitioners had not adhered to any of the requirements of Subtitle C, the portion of RCRA addressing hazardous wastes. Petitioners contended that RCRA § 3001(i), 42 U.S.C. § 6921(i), excluded the MWC ash from those requirements. The District Court agreed with that contention, and subsequently granted petitioners' motion for summary judgment.

The Court of Appeals reversed, concluding that the "ash generated from the incinerators of municipal resource recovery facilities is subject to regulation as a hazardous waste under Subtitle C of RCRA." The city petitioned for a writ of certiorari, and we invited the Solicitor General to present the views of the United States. On September 18, 1992, while that invitation was outstanding, the Administrator of EPA issued a memorandum to EPA Regional Administrators, directing them, in accordance with the agency's view of § 3001(i), to treat MWC ash as exempt from hazardous waste regulation under Subtitle C of RCRA.

Thereafter, we granted the city's petition, vacated the decision, and remanded the case to the Court of Appeals for the Seventh Circuit for further consideration in light of the memorandum.

On remand, the Court of Appeals reinstated its previous opinion, holding that, because the statute's plain language is dispositive, the EPA memorandum did not affect its analysis. 985 F.2d 303, 304 (CA7 1993). Petitioners filed a petition for writ of certiorari, which we granted.

II

RCRA is a comprehensive environmental statute that empowers EPA to regulate hazardous wastes from cradle to grave, in accordance with the rigorous safeguards and waste management procedures of Subtitle C, 42 U.S.C. §§ 6921-6934. Under the relevant provisions of Subtitle C, EPA has promulgated standards governing hazardous waste generators and transporters, see 42 U.S.C. §§ 6922 and 6923, and owners and operators of hazardous waste treatment, storage, and disposal facilities (TSDF's). Pursuant to § 6922, EPA has directed hazardous waste generators to comply with handling, record-keeping, storage, and monitoring requirements. TSDF's, however, are subject to much more stringent regulation than either generators or transporters, including a 4-to-5 year permitting process.... "[The] corrective action requirement is one of the major reasons that generators and transporters work diligently to manage their wastes so as to avoid the need to obtain interim status or a TSD permit." [Citation]

RCRA does not identify which wastes are hazardous and therefore subject to Subtitle C regulation; it leaves that designation to EPA. 42 U.S.C. § 6921(a). When EPA's hazardous-waste designations for solid wastes appeared in 1980, see 45 Fed. Reg. 33084, they contained certain exceptions from normal coverage, including an exclusion for "household waste," defined as "any waste material ... derived from households (including single and multiple residences, hotels and motels)," id., at 33120, codified as amended at 40 CFR § 261.4(b)(1) (1992). Although most household waste is harmless, a small portion — such as cleaning fluids and batteries — would have qualified as hazardous waste. The regulation declared, however, that "[h]ousehold waste, including household waste that has been collected, transported, stored, treated, disposed, recovered (e.g., refuse-derived fuel) or reused" is not hazardous waste. Ibid. Moreover, the preamble to the 1980 regulations stated that "residues remaining after treatment (e.g. incineration, thermal treatment) [of household waste] are not subject to regulation as a hazardous waste." 45 Fed. Reg. 33099. By reason of these provisions, an incinerator that burned only household waste would not be considered a Subtitle C TSDF, since it processed only nonhazardous (i.e., household) waste, and it would not be considered a Subtitle C generator of hazardous waste and would be free to dispose of its ash in a Subtitle D landfill.

The 1980 regulations thus provided what is known as a "waste stream" exemption for household waste, ibid., i.e., an exemption covering that category of waste from generation through treatment to final disposal of residues. The regulation did not, however, exempt MWC ash from Subtitle C coverage if the incinerator that produced the ash burned anything in addition to household waste, such as what petitioner's facility burns: nonhazardous industrial waste. Thus, a facility like petitioner's would qualify as a Subtitle C hazardous waste generator if the MWC ash it produced was sufficiently toxic, see 40 CFR §§ 261.3, 261.24 (1993) — though it would still not qualify as a Subtitle C TSDF, since all the waste it took in would be characterized as nonhazardous. (An ash can be hazardous, even though the product from which it is generated is not, because in the new medium the contaminants are more concentrated and more readily leachable, see 40 CFR §§ 261.3, 261.24, and pt. 261, App. II (1993).)

Four years after these regulations were issued, Congress enacted the Hazardous and Solid Waste Amendments of 1984, Pub.L. 98-616, 98 Stat. 3221, which added to RCRA the "Clarification of Household Waste Exclusion" as § 3001(i), § 223, 98 Stat., at 3252. The essence of our task in this case is to determine whether, under that provision, the MWC ash generated by petitioner's facility — a facility that would have been considered a Subtitle C generator under the 1980 regulations — is subject to regulation as hazardous waste under Subtitle C. We conclude that it is.

Section 3001(i), 42 U.S.C. § 6921(i), entitled "Clarification of household waste exclusion," provides:

> "A resource recovery facility recovering energy from the mass burning of municipal solid waste shall not be deemed to be treating, storing, disposing of, or otherwise managing hazardous wastes for the purposes of regulation under this subchapter, if — "(1) such facility — "(A) receives and burns only — "(i) household waste (from single and multiple dwellings, hotels, motels, and other residential sources), and "(ii) solid waste from commercial or industrial sources that does not contain hazardous waste identified or listed under this section, and "(B) does not accept hazardous wastes identified or listed under this section, and "(2) the owner or operator of such facility has established contractual requirements or other appropriate notification or inspection procedures to assure that hazardous wastes are not received at or burned in such facility."

The plain meaning of this language is that so long as a facility recovers energy by incineration of the appropriate wastes, it (the facility) is not subject to Subtitle C regulation as a facility that treats, stores, disposes of, or manages hazardous waste. The provision quite clearly does not contain any exclusion for the ash itself. Indeed, the waste the facility produces (as opposed to that which it receives) is not even mentioned. There is thus no express support for petitioners' claim of a waste-stream exemption.

Petitioners contend, however, that the practical effect of the statutory language is to exempt the ash by virtue of exempting the facility. If, they argue, the facility is not deemed to be treating, storing, or disposing of hazardous waste, then the ash that it treats, stores, or disposes of must itself be considered nonhazardous. There are several problems with this argument. First, as we have explained, the only exemption provided by the terms of the statute is for the facility. It is the facility, not the ash, that "shall not be deemed" to be subject to regulation under Subtitle C. Unlike the preamble to the 1980 regulations, which had been in existence for four years by the time § 3001(i) was enacted, § 3001(i) does not explicitly exempt MWC ash generated by a resource recovery facility from regulation as a hazardous waste. In light of that difference, and given the statute's express declaration of national policy that "[w]aste that is ... generated should be treated, stored, or disposed of so as to minimize the present and future threat to human health and the environment," 42 U.S.C. § 6902(b), we cannot interpret the statute to permit MWC ash sufficiently toxic to qualify as hazardous to be disposed of in ordinary landfills.

Moreover, as the Court of Appeals observed, the statutory language does not even exempt the facility in its capacity as a generator of hazardous waste. RCRA defines "generation" as "the act or process of producing hazardous waste." 42 U.S.C. § 6903(6). There can be no question that the creation of ash by incinerating municipal waste constitutes "generation" of hazardous waste (assuming, of course, that the ash qualifies as hazardous under 42 U.S.C. § 6921 and its implementing regulations, 40 CFR pt. 261 (1993)). Yet although § 3001(i) states that the exempted facility "shall not be deemed to be treating, storing, disposing of, or otherwise managing hazardous wastes," it significantly omits from the catalogue the word "generating." Petitioners say that because the activities listed as exempt encompass the full scope of the facility's operation, the failure to mention the activity of generating is insignificant. But the statute itself refutes this. Each of the three specific terms used in § 3001(i) — "treating," "storing," and "disposing of" — is separately defined by RCRA, and none covers the production of hazardous waste.[2] The fourth and less specific term ("otherwise managing") is also defined, to mean "collection, source separation, storage, transportation, processing, treatment, recovery, and disposal," 42 U.S.C. § 6903(7) — just about every hazardous waste-related activity except generation. We think it follows from the carefully constructed text of section

---

[2]"Treatment" means "any method, technique, or process, including neutralization, designed to change the physical, chemical, or biological character or composition of any hazardous waste so as to neutralize such waste or so as to render such waste nonhazardous, safer for transport, amenable for recovery, amenable for storage, or reduced in volume. Such term includes any activity or processing designed to change the physical form or chemical composition of hazardous waste so as to render it nonhazardous." 42 U.S.C. s 6903(34). "Storage" means "the containment of hazardous waste, either on a temporary basis or for a period of years, in such a manner as not to constitute disposal of such hazardous waste." 42 U.S.C. s 6903(33). "Disposal" means "the discharge, deposit, injection, dumping, spilling, leaking, or placing of any solid waste or hazardous waste into or on any land or water so that such solid waste or hazardous waste or any constituent thereof may enter the environment or be emitted into the air or discharged into any waters." 42 U.S.C. s 6903(3).

3001(i) that while a resource recovery facility's management activities are excluded from Subtitle C regulation, its generation of toxic ash is not.

Petitioners appeal to the legislative history of § 3001(i), which includes, in the Senate Committee Report, the statement that "[a]ll waste management activities of such a facility, including the generation, transportation, treatment, storage and disposal of waste shall be covered by the exclusion." But it is the statute, and not the Committee Report, which is the authoritative expression of the law, and the statute prominently omits reference to generation.... Petitioners point out that the activity by which they "treat" municipal waste is the very same activity by which they "generate" MWC ash, to wit, incineration. But there is nothing extraordinary about an activity's being exempt for some purposes and nonexempt for others. The incineration here is exempt from TSDF regulation, but subject to regulation as hazardous waste generation.

Our interpretation is confirmed by comparing § 3001(i) with another statutory exemption in RCRA. In the Superfund Amendments and Reauthorization Act of 1986, Pub. L. 99-499, § 124(b), 100 Stat. 1689, Congress amended 42 U.S.C. § 6921 to provide that an "owner and operator of equipment used to recover methane from a landfill shall not be deemed to be managing, generating, transporting, treating, storing, or disposing of hazardous or liquid wastes within the meaning of" Subtitle C. This provision, in contrast to § 3001(i), provides a complete exemption by including the term "generating" in its list of covered activities. "[I]t is generally presumed that Congress acts intentionally and purposely" when it "includes particular language in one section of a statute but omits it in another." We agree with respondents that this provision "shows that Congress knew how to draft a waste stream exemption in RCRA when it wanted to."

Petitioners contend that our interpretation of § 3001(i) turns the provision into an "empty gesture," since even under the pre- existing regime an incinerator burning household waste and nonhazardous industrial waste was exempt from the Subtitle C TSDF provisions. If § 3001(i) did not extend the waste-stream exemption to the product of such a combined household/nonhazardous-industrial treatment facility, petitioners argue, it did nothing at all. But it is not nothing to codify a household waste exemption that had previously been subject to agency revision; nor is it nothing (though petitioners may value it as less than nothing) to restrict the exemption that the agency previously provided — which is what the provision here achieved, by withholding all waste-stream exemption for waste processed by resource recovery facilities, even for the waste stream passing through an exclusively household- waste facility.

We also do not agree with petitioners' contention that our construction renders § 3001(i) ineffective for its intended purpose of promoting household/non-hazardous-industrial resource recovery facilities, see 42 U.S.C. §§ 6902(a)(1), (10), (11), by subjecting them "to the potentially enormous expense of managing ash residue as a hazardous waste." It is simply not true that a facility which is (as our interpretation says these facilities are) a hazardous waste "generator," is also deemed to be "managing" hazardous waste under RCRA. Section 3001(i) clearly exempts these facilities from Subtitle C TSDF regulations, thus enabling them to avoid the "full brunt of EPA's enforcement efforts under RCRA."

RCRA's twin goals of encouraging resource recovery and protecting against contamination sometimes conflict. It is not unusual for legislation to contain diverse purposes that must be reconciled, and the most reliable guide for that task is the enacted text. Here that requires us to reject the Solicitor General's plea for deference to the EPA's interpretation, which goes beyond the scope of whatever ambiguity § 3001(i) contains. [Citations] Section 3001(i) simply cannot be read to contain the cost-saving waste stream exemption petitioners seek.

For the foregoing reasons, the judgment of the Court of Appeals for the Seventh Circuit is

Affirmed.

NOTES AND QUESTIONS

1. *Mixtures and "Derived-from" Hazardous Wastes.* The EPA regulations define hazardous waste, for subtitle C management purposes, to include certain mixtures (40 C.F.R. § 261.3(a)(2)(iv)) of hazardous waste as well as materials derived from processing or managing a hazardous waste. 40 C.F.R. § 261.3(c)-(2)(i), (d)(2). The EPA promulgated the "mixture" rule out of concern that industry might avoid RCRA coverage by simply diluting the concentration of a hazardous waste by commingling it with other substances, even though the resulting material posed environmental hazards. Similarly, the "derived-from" rule sought to close a potential loophole where owners and operators of treatment, storage, and disposal facilities could escape regulation through limited processing of a hazardous waste.

2. The mixture rules treat combinations of solid waste with "listed" and "characteristic" hazardous wastes differently. The amalgamation of solid wastes with listed hazardous wastes remains regulated as hazardous irrespective of the constituency or harms presented by the resulting substance, until de-listed. 40 C.F.R. § 261.3(a)(2)(iii). On the other hand, mixtures of a solid waste with a hazardous waste that exhibits one of the four criteria characteristics will continue to be treated as hazardous *unless* the resulting mixture no longer exhibits one of the characteristics. 40 C.F.R. § 261.3(a)(2)(iv). Does this dichotomous approach accomplish the EPA's stated goal of closing the loophole in RCRA coverage that is provided by diluting a hazardous waste? *Compare United States v. Marine Shale Processors*, 81 F.3d 1329, 1345 (5th Cir. 1996) (substance does not lose its character as listed hazardous waste unless materials added to it change its composition in a significant way); *United States v. Bethlehem Steel Corp.*, 38 F.3d 862, 865 (7th Cir. 1994) (mixture of wastewater changed basic composition of substance).

The derived-from rule considered solid waste generated from a listed waste, including sludge, spill residue, ash, emission control dust, or leachate as hazardous waste. The regulations placed on the generator the burden of showing that the mixture or derived-from material was no longer hazardous and therefore should be delisted.

In *Shell Oil Co. v. EPA*, 950 F.2d 741, 765 (D.C. Cir. 1991) the court held that the EPA had failed to provide adequate notice and opportunity for comment with regard to the mixture and derived-from regulations, and vacated and remanded to the agency for reconsideration. In response, the EPA removed and reissued the rules on an interim basis. 57 Fed. Reg. 7628 (Mar. 3, 1992). *See United States v. Goodner Bros. Aircraft, Inc.*, 966 F.2d 380, 385 (8th Cir. 1992) convictions of RCRA violations must be retried where jury based verdict on application of mixture rule invalidated by *Shell Oil*).

3. The HSWA also directly addressed one of the greatest environmental concerns — contamination of groundwater supplies caused by the release of liquids from disposal sites — by outright bans on placement of liquid hazardous wastes in landfills. RCRA § 3004(c), 42 U.S.C. § 6924(c). The technology requirements in the Amendments focused on groundwater monitoring as a means to detect contamination quickly and undertake corrective actions. RCRA § 3004(p), 42 U.S.C. § 6924(p). The EPA regulations implementing the statute provide for three tiers of groundwater monitoring: a basic detection system, more extensive requirements if leachate reaches groundwater, and undertaking corrective action if ambient tolerance levels are exceeded. RCRA § 3004(p), (u), (v); 42 U.S.C. § 6924(p), (u), (v); 40 C.F.R. §§ 264.97-.100. The facility permit requires compliance with established limits of hazardous constituents in the groundwater. 40 C.F.R. §§ 264.92-94. *See In re Consolidated Land Disposal Regulation Litig.*, 938 F.2d 1386 (D.C. Cir. 1991) (EPA detection monitoring regulations upheld).

UNITED STATES v. WASTE INDUSTRIES, INC.

734 F.2d 159 (4th Cir. 1984)

SPROUSE, CIRCUIT JUDGE:

After the Environmental Protection Agency (EPA) investigated the Flemington landfill waste disposal site in New Hanover County, North Carolina (the Flemington landfill) for possible water pollution in the surrounding area, the United States of America for the Administrator of the EPA initiated this action against Waste Industries, Inc.; Waste Industries of New Hanover County, Inc.; the New Hanover County Board of Commissioners; and the individual owner-lessors of land used for the Flemington landfill (all defendants will be referred to collectively as the landfill group). The EPA demanded affirmative action by the landfill group under section 7003 of the Resource Conservation and Recovery Act of 1976 (Act), 42 U.S.C. § 6973, to abate alleged threats to public health and the environment posed by hazardous chemicals leaking from the Flemington landfill, to monitor the area for further contamination, to reimburse the EPA for money spent on the area, and to provide residents with a permanent potable water supply. The district court granted the landfill group's motion to dismiss under Federal Rule of Civil Procedure 12(b)(6) for failure to state a cause of action and the EPA brought this appeal. We reverse.

[The County Board granted Waste Industries, Inc. and Waste Industries of New Hanover County, Inc. (collectively "Waste Industries") an exclusive license to dispose of solid waste generated in the County.]...

... Waste Industries obtained several landfill sites, including the seventy-acre Flemington site leased from private owners. The Flemington leases granted Waste Industries sole use and control of the premises. The landfill Waste Industries then established on the site is situated in a hole from which sand has been removed, known as a "sand barrow pit"; the surrounding soil is composed of highly permeable sand. The Flemington landfill is within a mile of both the Cape New Fear and Northeast Cape New Fear Rivers. During the operation of the landfill, unknown quantities of solid and hazardous waste were buried at the site. These wastes began leaching through the sandy soil beneath them and into the groundwater aquifer below.

Before Waste Industries began operating the landfill, the residents of the Flemington community had high quality groundwater. Flemington area residents first noticed a decline in water quality in Autumn 1977, when their water became foul in color, taste, and smell. Some residents suffered illnesses or side effects such as blisters, boils, and stomach distress they attribute to their use of well water. Residents complained to the County Board and demanded help.

In response to residents' demands, the County in 1978 placed surplus water tanks that it still operates in the Flemington area. Many residents, however, had found it difficult to use these tanks because of infirmity or disability. Many families wash their clothes at laundromats and drive to the homes of friends or relatives elsewhere to bathe. Others have abandoned their homes because of the contaminated water.

In addition to constructing the water tanks, the County in August 1978 referred the question of groundwater quality in and near the Flemington community to the North Carolina Department of Natural Resources and Community Development. The Department directed Waste Industries to cease disposing of waste at the Flemington landfill, which it did on June 30, 1979.

... Analysis of Flemington area groundwater samples taken by the EPA revealed a large number of toxic, organic, and inorganic contaminants, including known carcinogens, resulting from improper disposal of waste at the Flemington landfill.... These chemicals, migrating from the Flemington landfill, have been detected in residential wells at levels sufficient to affect adversely human health and the environment. The presence of chlorides, dichlorophenol, chlorobenzene, iron, manganese, phenol, and zinc has rendered the water in the wells unfit for human consumption because some of these chemicals are suspected carcinogens and all of them are a source of extremely bad taste or odor in water. Concentrations of lead, benzene, tetrachloroethylene, trichlorethylene, 1, 2-dichloroethane, and vinyl chloride found in three residential wells pose an unacceptably high risk of neurological damage in children and cancer in humans of any age.

After conducting its July 1979 tests, the EPA warned many local residents that continued use of their wells for any purpose would endanger their health, and informed the County that additional water tanks were needed to meet local residents' needs. The EPA helped the County obtain commitments for three-quarters of the funds needed to install a permanent water system in the Flemington community — half from the federal government and one-quarter from the state of North Carolina. The County initially approved the plan but later abandoned it. Finally, after the September 1979 testing established the landfill as a source of groundwater contamination, the EPA demanded that the County provide an adequate water supply to Flemington residents. A water system funded with federal, state, and local money is now in operation.

The new water system, however, has not solved the problem of escaping waste. As precipitation infiltrates the landfill waste and transports contaminants through permeable soil, the contaminants reach the local aquifer and move laterally through the aquifer in the direction of groundwater flow to the south and east. Tests indicate that the process of leaching and migration of contaminants will continue indefinitely unless remedial action is taken.

The EPA, in its initial complaint, requested preliminary and permanent injunctive relief requiring the appropriate parties: (1) to supply affected residents with a permanent and potable source of water; (2) to develop and implement a plan to prevent further contamination; (3) to restore the groundwater; (4) to monitor the area for further contamination; and (5) to reimburse the EPA for money spent in connection with the Flemington landfill. The EPA later withdrew its request for preliminary relief when the federal, state, and local governments, as described above, jointly funded the installation of a permanent safe water supply, but it continued to demand in its complaint a plan to prevent further contamination, the restoration of groundwater, site monitoring, and reimbursement.

... [EPA contends that RCRA § 7003 provides authority to abate the leaching of contaminants from the landfill and to require the polluters to correct their past abuses of the environment.]

Section 7003 of the Act provides that:

> [n]otwithstanding any other provision of this chapter, upon receipt of evidence that the handling, storage, treatment, transportation or disposal of any solid waste or hazardous waste may present an imminent and substantial endangerment to health or the environment, the Administrator may bring suit on behalf of the United States in the appropriate District Court to immediately restrain any person contributing to such handling, storage, treatment, transportation or disposal to stop such handling, storage, treatment, transportation, or disposal or to take such other action as may be necessary.

The landfill group contends, and the district court held, that this section does not authorize an action to correct hazardous conditions because it only regulates the wastes themselves before or as they are produced, not the conditions they later create. The fallacy of that contention is demonstrated by the indication of Congress that section 7003 remedies exist apart from the other provisions in the Act's structure. In addition, section 7003 stands apart from the other sections of the Act defining the EPA's regulatory authority. The regulatory scheme for hazardous wastes appears in subtitle C of the Act; the scheme for solid wastes, in subtitle D. In contrast, section 7003 appears in subtitle G, and it is designed to deal with situations in which the regulatory schemes break down or have been circumvented.

... This section is logically placed in the statutory structure to provide a remedy for environmental endangerment by hazardous or solid waste, whether or not those engaging in the endangering acts are subject to any other provision of the Act. Its application "notwithstanding any other provision of this chapter" indicates a congressional intent to include a broadly applicable section dealing with the concerns addressed by the statute as a whole.

The operative language of section 7003 authorizes the administrator to bring an action against any person contributing to the alleged disposal to stop such disposal "*or* to take such other action as may be necessary." 42 U.S.C. § 6973(a) (emphasis added). "Disposal" is defined in 42 U.S.C. § 6903(3) [section 1004(3)] as follows:

> The term "disposal" means the discharge, deposit, injection, dumping, spilling, leaking, or placing of any solid waste or hazardous waste into or on any land or water so that such solid waste or hazardous waste or any constituent thereof may enter the environment or be emitted into the air or discharged into any waters, including ground waters.

The district court held, after a contextual analysis, that this language means only disposal by "active human conduct." We cannot agree. The term "disposal," it is true, is used throughout subtitle C in the sense that the Administrator can regulate current disposal of hazardous waste. In this way, the Act regulates current conduct of would-be polluters. But a strained reading of that term limiting its section 7003 meaning to active conduct would so frustrate the remedial purpose of the Act as to make it meaningless. Section 7003, unlike the provisions of the Act's subtitle C, does not regulate conduct but regulates and mitigates endangerments. The Administrator's intervention authorized by section 7003 is triggered by evidence that the "disposal of ... hazardous waste *may* present an imminent and substantial endangerment." (emphasis added).

The inclusion of "leaking" as one of the diverse definitional components of "disposal" demonstrates that Congress intended "disposal" to have a range of meanings, including conduct, a physical state, and an occurrence. Discharging, dumping, and injection (conduct), hazardous waste reposing (a physical state) and movement of the waste after it has been placed in a state of repose (an occurrence) are all encompassed in the broad definition of disposal. "Leaking" ordinarily occurs when landfills are not constructed soundly or when drums and tank trucks filled with waste materials corrode, rust, or rot. Thus "leaking" is an occurrence included in the meaning of "disposal."

The district court's statutory analysis relied heavily upon the present-tense definition of "disposal" as indicative of an intent to restrain only ongoing human conduct. The Act, however, permits a court to order a responsible party to "stop" activities "*or* to take such other action as may be necessary" (emphasis added) to abate the endangerment. Such grammatical niceties as tense may be useful in arriving at a narrowly-sculpted meaning, but they are of little help in interpreting remedial statutes in which actions such as "may be necessary" are contemplated in order to abate gross dangers to a community. Since the term "disposal" is used throughout the Act, its definition in section 6903(3) must necessarily be broad and general to encompass both routine regulatory and the less common emergency situations. Thus it includes such diverse characteristics as "deposit, injection, dumping, spilling, leaking, or placing" wastes. We must assume that Congress included "leaking" as a definitional component of "disposal" for a purpose. We conclude that Congress made "leaking" a part of the definition of "disposal" to meet the need to respond to the possibility of endangerment, among other reasons.

Congress expressly intended that this and other language of the Act close loopholes in environmental protection. [Citations.] Limiting the government's enforcement prerogatives to cases involving active human conduct would open a gaping hole in the overall protection of the environment envisioned by Congress, a protection designed to be responsive to unpredictable occurrences. Without a means to respond to disasters precipitated by earlier poor planning, our nation's resources could be "conserved" from further harm, as the title of the Resource Conservation and Recovery Act suggests, but never "recovered" to their former wholesome condition.

The landfill group argues that section 7003 was designed to control pollution only in emergency situations. The district court agreed, concluding that it was similar to other statutes designed by Congress solely to eliminate emergency problems. We find this position insupportable, for the section's language stands in contrast to "emergency" type statutes. The language of section 7003 demonstrates that Congress contemplated circumstances in which the disposal of hazardous waste "*may present* an imminent and substantial endangerment" (emphasis added); therefore, the section's application is not specifically limited to an "emergency."

The Third Circuit, in its recent interpretation of the Act's section 7003, reached the same conclusion. It described section 7003 as having "enhanced the courts' traditional equitable powers by authorizing the issuance of injunctions when there is but a risk of harm, a more lenient standard than the traditional requirement of threatened irreparable harm." *United States v. Price*, 688 F.2d 204, 211 (3d Cir. 1982). Thus the Third Circuit's interpretation of section 7003, far from limiting its application to emergency situations, gave full effect to this expansion of the courts' traditional powers.

Although strictly speaking there is little legislative history to assist us in our quest for exact congressional intent, the history of the Act's amendments is enlightening. The legislative history of the Act as originally enacted contains no specific discussion of the reach of section 7003 and no mention of the reasons for its insertion. The hastiness of the Act's passage in the final days of a congressional session has been well-documented.

The focus of our attention, then, is not on the Act's legislative history, but on the legislative history of its 1980 amendments, in which various congressional committees addressed the issues of EPA authority under section 7003 and the purposes of this section. Later congressional ratification of the availability of section 7003 as a tool for abating hazards created by inactive solid and hazardous waste disposal sites such as the Flemington landfill has been consistent and authoritative.... To the extent that the precise intent of the enacting Congress may be obscure, the views of subsequent Congresses should be given greater deference than they would be otherwise entitled to receive.

. . . .

It is true that some confusion has been created in the interpretation of section 7003 by the EPA's own earlier interpretation — since abandoned — of its authority under this section. The EPA at first took the position that because of its present tense language the statute was not intended to apply to inactive disposal facilities. 43 Fed. Reg. 58,984 (December 18, 1978). This narrow reading by the agency led the House Committee on Interstate and Foreign Commerce, one of the committees which had developed the original Act, to rebuke the EPA for its lack of vigor in using section 7003 and admonish the agency that section 7003 "should be used for abandoned sites as well as active ones." [Citation.] Not only did Congress reject the EPA's narrow view of its own authority, but the EPA later reversed its own early interpretation of section 7003. See 45 Fed. Reg. 33,170 (May 19, 1980). The agency's current view is, of course, entitled to substantial deference. [Citation.]

The landfill group next contends, and the district court held, that section 7003 is solely jurisdictional, authorizing remedies or proceedings, not creating liabilities. Those liabilities, in this view, come only from the earlier, regulatory, portions of the Act. The district court took this view of the section for various reasons, some of which we have already discussed and discarded, including the location of section 7003 within the Act and its broad wording. Again, we cannot agree.

Congress intended section 7003 to function both as a jurisdictional basis and a source of substantive liability.

The Eckhart Report states:

> § 7003 is essentially a codification of the common law public nuisance....
>
> However, § 7003 should not be construed solely with respect to the common law. Some terms and concepts, such as persons "contributing to" disposal resulting in a substantial endangerment, are meant to be more liberal than their common law counterparts.

Congress's intent, then, was to establish a standard of liability by incorporating and expanding upon the common law.

The landfill group observes that some courts have held, by analogy to *City of Milwaukee v. Illinois*, 451 U.S. 304 (1981), that the regulatory provisions of the Act and CERCLA are the sole source of substantive standards in the field of solid and hazardous waste disposal. If true, this would leave no room for the application of common-law principles. This, however, misreads the lesson of *City of Milwaukee*, ... [which] disapproved only of the courts' use of federal common law as a source for setting regulatory standards independent of those established by a comprehensive statutory scheme. The Court did not assail Congress's prerogative to empower the courts to apply common law principles as part of an ongoing regulatory scheme.

Section 7003 is a congressional mandate that the former common law of nuisance, as applied to situations in which a risk of harm from solid or hazardous wastes exists, shall include new terms and concepts which shall be developed in a liberal, not a restrictive, manner. This ensures that problems that Congress could not have anticipated when passing the Act will be dealt with in a way minimizing the risk of harm to the environment and the public. [Citations.]

....

Contrary to the district court holding, we conclude on the peculiar facts of this case that permanent mandatory injunctive relief is an appropriate remedy. The landfill group argues that no emergency exists and that CERCLA provides an adequate remedy at law. The EPA need not prove that an emergency exists to prevail under section 7003, only that the circumstances may present an imminent and substantial endangerment....

Finally, the landfill group contends that an injunction cannot issue because CERCLA provides an adequate remedy at law. This lawsuit was not brought in common-law equity, however, but pursuant to an express statutory command giving the EPA an injunctive remedy. Congress chose to enhance the courts' traditional equitable powers in order to protect the public and the environment. Any other decision would, in effect, interpret CERCLA as repealing the Act — a result obviously not intended by Congress.

[Reversed and remanded.]

NOTES AND QUESTIONS

1. The flexibility and scope of section 7003 provides an attractive vehicle for governmental efforts to respond to environmental hazards. Where the environmental problems involved are chronic and recurring, however, government agencies and courts should consider section 7003 as a supplemental tool rather than as a substitute for more comprehensive measures available under other environmental statutory provisions. *See United States v. Reilly Tar & Chem. Corp.*, 546 F. Supp. 1100, 1100-11 (D. Minn. 1982).

2. Courts have characterized RCRA as a remedial statute which should be liberally construed. *See United States v. Conservation Chem. Co.*, 619 F. Supp. 162, 199 (W.D. Mo. 1985). The government must establish the following elements for a *prima facie* case under section 7003: (1) the conditions at the site present an imminent and substantial endangerment; (2) the danger stems from the handling, storage, treatment, transportation, or disposal of any solid or hazardous waste; and (3) the defendant has contributed or is contributing to that handling, storage, treatment, transportation, or disposal. *United States v. Bliss*, 667 F. Supp. 1298, 1313 (E.D. Mo. 1987). Although the term "contributing to" conduct which contravenes the statute is not defined by RCRA, courts have not limited its scope to persons with the authority to control the activities. *See United States v. Aceto Chem. Corp.*, 872 F.2d 1373, 1383 (8th Cir. 1989), reprinted in Chapter 9, page 761. The phrase "imminent and substantial endangerment" also is not defined in the Act. However, guidance can be drawn from similar terminology in several other federal environmental protection statutes.

3. In an early leading decision interpreting section 7003, *United States v. Vertac Chem. Corp.*, 489 F. Supp. 870 (E.D. Ark. 1980), the court relied upon *Reserve Mining Co. v. Environmental Protection Agency*, 514 F.2d 492 (8th Cir. 1975), a case involving section 504 of the Clean Water Act, to determine the meaning of "endangerment." The government in *Vertac* sought injunctive relief to abate a continuing discharge of toxic and hazardous wastes and pollutants into the soil and groundwater from a landfill. The court held that the primary considerations for issuance of injunctive relief were the seriousness of the potential harm — based on assessing the nature and degree of the toxicity of the substances involved — and the likelihood of human or environmental exposure absent issuance of an abatement order. The court stated that the concept of "endangerment" included a risk of harm less than a certainty. Since toxic materials were escaping from the site in quantities that presented a reasonable medical concern over the public health, an abatement order could issue even though no actual harm had yet occurred. The court observed that injunctive relief was particularly appropriate in circumstances involving scientific uncertainties regarding either the significance of the risk or the probability of exposure. With respect to the fashioning of the remedy, the court again looked to *Reserve Mining*, by balancing the benefits conferred with the hazards presented by the facility involved, including: (a) the nature of the anticipated harm, (b) the burden on Vertac and its employees from the issuance of the injunction, (c) the financial ability of Vertac to convert to other methods of waste disposal, and (d) a margin of safety for the public. 489 F. Supp. at 886.

4. In *United States v. Price*, 688 F.2d 204 (3d Cir. 1982) toxic waste escaped from a commercial landfill and contaminated an aquifer which served as the public water supply for Atlantic City, New Jersey. The government, pursuant to RCRA section 7003, sought to require the landfill owners and operators to fund a diagnostic study to assess the nature of the threat to the water supply and also to provide an alternate supply of potable water for the landowners whose private wells had been contaminated. Although the court decided not to issue a preliminary injunction for procedural reasons, the court gave an expansive reading to the purpose and functional utility of section 7003:

> By enacting the endangerment provisions of [RCRA], Congress sought to invoke the broad and flexible powers of the federal courts in instances where hazardous wastes threatened human health. Indeed, these provisions have enhanced the courts' traditional equitable powers by authorizing the issuance of injunctions when there is but a risk of harm, a more lenient standard than the traditional requirement of threatened irreparable harm.
>
> ....
>
> The unequivocal statutory language and legislative history make it clear that Congress, by enacting section 7003, intended to confer upon the courts the authority to grant affirmative equitable relief to the extent necessary to eliminate any risks posed by toxic wastes. Under section 7003, a court could not order the cleanup of a waste site which posed no threat to health or the environment. There is no doubt, however, that it authorizes the cleanup of a site, even a dormant one, if that action is necessary to abate a present threat to the public health or the environment....
>
> Congress, in the endangerment provisions of [RCRA] sought to invoke nothing less than the full equity powers of the federal courts in the effort to protect public health, the environment, and public water supplies from the pernicious effects of toxic wastes. Courts should not undermine the will of Congress by either withholding relief or granting it grudgingly. [Citations omitted.]

688 F.2d at 211-14. The defendants contended that funding the water study constituted a form of damages and therefore was unavailable under the equitable provisions of section 7003. The court disagreed, and stated that funding of the study did not constitute damages in the traditional sense because it was a preventive measure rather than compensatory. Further, although mandatory injunctions should be issued sparingly, equitable relief could include the payment or expenditure of money. 688 F.2d at 212-13. What limits, then, should be placed on the remedial language of section 7003 that courts may "restrain" or "to order such person to take such other action as may be necessary, or both"?

MEGHRIG v. KFC WESTERN, INC.

___ U.S. ___, 116 S. Ct. 1251, 134 L. Ed. 2d 121 (1996)

JUSTICE O'CONNOR delivered the opinion of the Court.

We consider whether § 7002 of the Resource Conservation and Recovery Act of 1976 (RCRA), 42 U.S.C. § 6972 (1988 ed.), authorizes a private cause of action to recover the prior cost of cleaning up toxic waste that does not, at the time of suit, continue to pose an endangerment to health or the environment. We conclude that it does not.

I

Respondent KFC Western, Inc. (KFC), owns and operates a "Kentucky Fried Chicken" restaurant on a parcel of property in Los Angeles. In 1988, KFC discovered during the course of a construction project that the property was contaminated with petroleum. The County of Los Angeles Department of Health Services ordered KFC to attend to the problem, and KFC spent $ 211,000 removing and disposing of the oil-tainted soil.

Three years later, KFC brought this suit under the citizen suit provision of RCRA, 90 Stat. 2825, as amended, 42 U.S.C. § 6972(a) (1988 ed.),[3] seeking to recover these cleanup costs from petitioners.

KFC claimed that the contaminated soil was a "solid waste" covered by RCRA, see 42 U.S.C. § 6903(27) (1988 ed.), that it had previously posed an "imminent and substantial endangerment to health or the environment," see § 6972(a)(1)(B), and that the Meghrigs were responsible for "equitable restitution" of KFC's cleanup costs under § 6972(a) because, as prior owners of the property, they had contributed to the waste's "past or present handling, storage, treatment, transportation, or disposal."

The District Court held that § 6972(a) does not permit recovery of past cleanup costs and that § 6972(a)(1)(B) does not authorize a cause of action for the remediation of toxic waste that does not pose an "imminent and substantial

---

[3]Section 6972(a) provides, in relevant part:

"Except as provided in subsection (b) or (c) of this section, any person may commence a civil action on his own behalf —

. . . .

"(1)(B) against any person, including ... any past or present generator, past or present transporter, or past or present owner or operator of a treatment, storage, or disposal facility, who has contributed or who is contributing to the past or present handling, storage, treatment, transportation, or disposal of any solid or hazardous waste which may present an imminent and substantial endangerment to health or the environment....

. . . .

"... The district court shall have jurisdiction ... to restrain any person who has contributed or who is contributing to the past or present handling, storage, treatment, transportation, or disposal of any solid or hazardous waste referred to in paragraph (1)(B), to order such person to take such other action as may be necessary, or both...."

endangerment to health or the environment" at the time suit is filed, and dismissed KFC's complaint. The Court of Appeals for the Ninth Circuit reversed, finding that a district court had authority under § 6972(a) to award restitution of past cleanup costs, and that a private party can proceed with a suit under § 6972(a)(1)(B) upon an allegation that the waste at issue presented an "imminent and substantial endangerment" at the time it was cleaned up.

The Ninth Circuit's conclusion regarding the remedies available under RCRA conflicts with the decision of the Court of Appeals for the Eighth Circuit in *Furrer v. Brown*, 62 F.3d 1092, 1100-1101 (1995), and its interpretation of the "imminent endangerment" requirement represents a novel application of federal statutory law. We granted certiorari to address the conflict between the Circuits and to consider the correctness of the Ninth Circuit's interpretation of RCRA, and now reverse.

II

RCRA is a comprehensive environmental statute that governs the treatment, storage, and disposal of solid and hazardous waste. [Citation] Unlike the Comprehensive Environmental Response, Compensation and Liability Act of 1980 (CERCLA), RCRA is not principally designed to effectuate the cleanup of toxic waste sites or to compensate those who have attended to the remediation of environmental hazards. [Citation] RCRA's primary purpose, rather, is to reduce the generation of hazardous waste and to ensure the proper treatment, storage, and disposal of that waste which is nonetheless generated, "so as to minimize the present and future threat to human health and the environment." 42 U.S.C. § 6902(b) (1988 ed.).

Chief responsibility for the implementation and enforcement of RCRA rests with the Administrator of the Environmental Protection Agency (EPA), see §§ 6928, 6973, but like other environmental laws, RCRA contains a citizen suit provision, § 6972, which permits private citizens to enforce its provisions in some circumstances.

Two requirements of § 6972(a) defeat KFC's suit against the Meghrigs. The first concerns the necessary timing of a citizen suit brought under § 6972(a)(1)-(B): That section permits a private party to bring suit against certain responsible persons, including former owners, "who have contributed or who [are] contributing to the past or present handling, storage, treatment, transportation, or disposal of any solid or hazardous waste which *may present* an *imminent* and substantial endangerment to health or the environment." The second defines the remedies a district court can award in a suit brought under § 6972(a)(1)(B): Section 6972(a) authorizes district courts "to *restrain* any person who has contributed or who is contributing to the past or present handling, storage, treatment, transportation, or disposal of any solid or hazardous waste ..., *to order such person to take such other action as may be necessary*, or both."

It is apparent from the two remedies described in § 6972(a) that RCRA's citizen suit provision is not directed at providing compensation for past cleanup efforts. Under a plain reading of this remedial scheme, a private citizen suing under § 6972(a)(1)(B) could seek a mandatory injunction, i.e., one that orders a responsible party to "take action" by attending to the cleanup and proper disposal of toxic waste, or a prohibitory injunction, i.e., one that "restrains" a responsible party from further violating RCRA. Neither remedy, however, is susceptible of the interpretation adopted by the Ninth Circuit, as neither contemplates the award of past cleanup costs, whether these are denominated "damages" or "equitable restitution."

In this regard, a comparison between the relief available under RCRA's citizen suit provision and that which Congress has provided in the analogous, but not parallel, provisions of CERCLA is telling. CERCLA was passed several years after RCRA went into effect, and it is designed to address many of the same toxic waste problems that inspired the passage of RCRA.... CERCLA differs markedly from RCRA, however, in the remedies it provides. CERCLA's citizen suit provision mimics § 6972(a) in providing district courts with the authority "to order such action as may be necessary to correct the violation" of any CERCLA standard or regulation. 42 U.S.C. § 9659(c) (1988 ed.). But CERCLA expressly permits the Government to recover "all costs of removal or remedial action," § 9607(a)(4)(A), and it expressly permits the recovery of any "necessary costs of response, incurred by any ... person consistent with the national contingency plan," § 9607(a)(4)(B). CERCLA also provides that "any person may seek contribution from any other person who is liable or potentially liable" for these response costs. See § 9613(f)(1). Congress thus demonstrated in CERCLA that it knew how to provide for the recovery of cleanup costs, and that the language used to define the remedies under RCRA does not provide that remedy.

That RCRA's citizen suit provision was not intended to provide a remedy for past cleanup costs is further apparent from the harm at which it is directed. Section 6972(a)(1)(B) permits a private party to bring suit only upon a showing that the solid or hazardous waste at issue "may present an imminent and substantial endangerment to health or the environment." The meaning of this timing restriction is plain: An endangerment can only be "imminent" if it "threatens to occur immediately," Webster's New International Dictionary of English Language 1245 (2d ed. 1934), and the reference to waste which "may present" imminent harm quite clearly excludes waste that no longer presents such a danger. As the Ninth Circuit itself intimated in *Price v. United States Navy*, 39 F.3d 1011, 1019 (1994), this language "implies that there must be a threat which is present *now*, although the impact of the threat may not be felt until later." It follows that § 6972(a) was designed to provide a remedy that ameliorates present or obviates the risk of future "imminent" harms, not a remedy that compensates for past cleanup efforts. *Cf.* § 6902(b) (national policy behind RCRA is "to minimize the present and future threat to human health and the environment").

Other aspects of RCRA's enforcement scheme strongly support this conclusion. Unlike CERCLA, RCRA contains no statute of limitations, compare § 9613(g)(2) (limitations period in suits under CERCLA § 9607), and it does not require a showing that the response costs being sought are reasonable, compare §§ 9607-(a)(4)(A) and (B) (costs recovered under CERCLA must be "consistent with the national contingency plan"). If Congress had intended § 6972(a) to function as a cost-recovery mechanism, the absence of these provisions would be striking. Moreover, with one limited exception, see *Hallstrom v. Tillamook County*, 493 U.S. 20, 26-27, 107 L. Ed. 2d 237, 110 S. Ct. 304 (1989) (noting exception to notice requirement "when there is a danger that hazardous waste will be discharged"), a private party may not bring suit under § 6972(a)(1)(B) without first giving 90 days' notice to the Administrator of the EPA, to "the State in which the alleged endangerment may occur," and to potential defendants, see §§ 6972(b)(2)(A)(i)-(iii). And no citizen suit can proceed if either the EPA or the State has commenced, and is diligently prosecuting, a separate enforcement action, see §§ 6972(b)(2)(B) and (C). Therefore, if RCRA were designed to compensate private parties for their past cleanup efforts, it would be a wholly irrational mechanism for doing so. Those parties with insubstantial problems, problems that neither the State nor the Federal Government feel compelled to address, could recover their response costs, whereas those parties whose waste problems were sufficiently severe as to attract the attention of Government officials would be left without a recovery.

Though it agrees that KFC's complaint is defective for failing properly to allege an "imminent and substantial endangerment," the Government (as *amicus*) nonetheless joins KFC in arguing that § 6972(a) does not in all circumstances preclude an award of past cleanup costs. The Government posits a situation in which suit is properly brought while the waste at issue continues to pose an imminent endangerment, and suggests that the plaintiff in such a case could seek equitable restitution of money previously spent on cleanup efforts. Echoing a similar argument made by KFC, the Government does not rely on the remedies expressly provided in § 6972(a), but rather cites a line of cases holding that district courts retain inherent authority to award any equitable remedy that is not expressly taken away from them by Congress. [Citations]

RCRA does not prevent a private party from recovering its cleanup costs under other federal or state laws, see § 6972(f) (preserving remedies under statutory and common law), but the limited remedies described in § 6972(a), along with the stark differences between the language of that section and the cost recovery provisions of CERCLA, amply demonstrate that Congress did not intend for a private citizen to be able to undertake a clean up and then proceed to recover its costs under RCRA. As we explained in *Middlesex County Sewerage Authority v. National Sea Clammers Assn.*, 453 U.S. 1, 14, 69 L. Ed. 2d 435, 101 S. Ct. 2615 (1981), where Congress has provided "elaborate enforcement provisions" for remedying the violation of a federal statute, as Congress has done with RCRA and CERCLA, "it cannot be assumed that Congress intended to authorize by implication additional judicial remedies for private citizens suing under" the statute. "'It is an elemental canon of statutory construction that where a statute expressly provides a particular remedy or remedies, a court must be chary of reading others into it.'" [Citation]

Without considering whether a private party could seek to obtain an injunction requiring another party to pay cleanup costs which arise after a RCRA citizen suit has been properly commenced, or otherwise recover cleanup costs paid out after the invocation of RCRA's statutory process, we agree with the Meghrigs that a private party cannot recover the cost of a past cleanup effort under RCRA, and that KFC's complaint is defective for the reasons stated by the District Court. Section 6972(a) does not contemplate the award of past cleanup costs, and § 6972(a)(1)(B) permits a private party to bring suit only upon an allegation that the contaminated site presently poses an "imminent and substantial endangerment to health or the environment," and not upon an allegation that it posed such an endangerment at some time in the past. The judgment of the Ninth Circuit is reversed.

It is so ordered.

NOTES AND QUESTIONS

1. Citizens' suits are expressly barred if the EPA or delegated state has commenced and is diligently prosecuting an enforcement action, although citizens have a right of permissive intervention in government enforcement actions. *See* RCRA § 7002(b)(2), 42 U.S.C. § 9672(b)(2). The remedial options available to private plaintiffs are broader than under many other federal environmental protection statutes, including injunctive relief, civil penalties awards, litigation costs and expert witness fees, and reasonable attorneys' fees. RCRA §§ 7002(a)-(2), 7002(e); 42 U.S.C. §§ 6972(a)(2), 6972(e). Injunctions are not available, however, with respect to the siting of a new hazardous waste treatment, storage or disposal facility and regarding the issuance of a permit. RCRA § 7002(b)(2)-(D), 42 U.S.C. § 6972(b)(2)(D).

2. In *Hallstrom v. Tillamook County*, 493 U.S. 20, 110 S. Ct. 309, 107 L. Ed. 2d 237 (1989) the Court held that compliance with the notice provision constituted a mandatory condition precedent to filing suit a citizen suit under RCRA section 7002. The Court observed that notice served the following functions: (1) the alleged violator, once on notice of the potential statutory violation, would then have an opportunity to halt or correct the offending conduct; (2) government agencies have primary responsibility and authority to enforce the statutory provisions, which could be undermined by interference from hastily filed citizens' suits; and (3) judicial efficiency would be disturbed by multiplicitous suits regarding the same conduct.

3. Section 7003 of RCRA is reserved for governmental enforcement actions; therefore courts lack subject matter jurisdiction over private claims brought pursuant to that section. Section 7002(b)(1) (42 U.S.C. § 6972(b)(1)), though, gives similar abatement authority to private citizens' suits. The waiting period with respect to imminent and substantial endangerment actions, however, is 90 days unless a violation of the hazardous waste management provisions contained in Subtitle C is also implicated. *See Supporters to Oppose Pollution, Inc. v. Heritage Group*, 33 Env. Rep. Cas. 1054, 1057 (N.D. Ind. 1991) (the 90-day pre-suit notice period under RCRA § 7002(b)(2)(A) must be "nonadversarial" in that litigation between the parties involving factually related issues cannot be pending).

4. In *CWWG v. U.S. Dep't of the Army*, 111 F.3d 1485 (10th Cir. 1997) an environmental organization sought to enjoin the proposed operation of a facility to incinerate lethal chemical weapons by the Department of the Army. The court held that RCRA's citizen suit imminent hazard provision did not allow such a collateral attacks on the agency's permit decision. Instead, RCRA contemplated limited judicial review for direct challenge of such permit decisions within a 90 day window and provided the agency with a deferential standard of judicial review.

5. The commentary on the role of citizens' suits and related issues under environmental law is extensive. For representative perspectives see generally Snook, *Citizen Suits After Hallstrom: Can a Plaintiff Avoid Dismissal After Failing to Give Sixty Days' Notice?*, 13 W. NEW ENG. L. REV. 1 (1991); Greve, *The Private Enforcement of Environmental Law*, 65 TUL. L. REV. 339 (1990); Comment, *Pollution-Financed Environmentally Beneficial Expenditures: Effective Use or Improper Abuse of Citizen Suits Under the Clean Water Act*, 21 ENVTL. L. 175 (1991); Smith, *The Viability of Citizens' Suits Under the Clean Water Act After Gwaltney of Smithfield Versus Chesapeake Bay Foundation, Inc.*, 40 CASE W. RES. 1 (1989); Comment, *The Rise of Citizen Suit Enforcement in Environmental Law: Reconciling Private and Public Attorney Generals*, 81 NW. U.L. REV. 220 (1987); Boyer & Meidinger, *Privatizing Regulatory Enforcement: A Preliminary Assessment of Citizen Suits Under Federal Environmental Laws*, 34 BUFFALO L. REV. 833 (1985); Fadil, *Citizen Suits Against Polluters: Picking Up the Pace*, 9 HARV. ENVTL. L. REV. 23 (1985); Cohen & Rubin, *Private Enforcement of Public Policy*, 3 YALE J. ON REG. 167 (1985); Miller, *Private Enforcement of Federal Pollution Control Laws*, 13 ENVTL. L. REP. 10309 (Envtl. L. Inst.) (1983); Feller, *Private Enforcement of Federal Anti-Pollution Laws Through Citizen Suits: A Model*, 60 DEN. U.L. REV. 553 (1983); Stewart & Sunstein, *Public Programs and Private Rights*, 95 HARV. L. REV. 1195 (1982); Note, *Notice by Citizen Plaintiffs in Environmental Litigation*, 79 MICH. L. REV. 299 (1980); DiMento, *Citizen Environmental Litigation and Administrative Process: Empirical Findings, Remaining Issues and a Directive for Further Research*, 1977 DUKE L.J. 409; Landes & Posner, *The Private Enforcement of Law*, 4 J. LEGAL STUD. 1 (1975); Stewart, *The Reformation of American Administrative Law*, 88 HARV. L. REV. 1667 (1975); Jaffe, *The Citizen as Litigant in Public Actions: The Non-Holfeldian or Ideological Plaintiff*, 116 U. PA. L. REV. 1033 (1968).

UNITED STATES v. DEAN

969 F.2d 187 (6th Cir. 1992)

CHARLES W. JOINER, SENIOR DISTRICT JUDGE. Defendant Gale E. Dean appeals his convictions on one count of conspiracy to violate the Resource Conservation and Recovery Act (RCRA), 42 U.S.C. §§ 6901 *et seq.*, in violation of 18 U.S.C. § 371; one count of failure to file documentation of hazardous waste generation, storage, and disposal as required by 42 U.S.C. § 6928(d)(4); and one count of storage of spent chromic acid without a Permit, one count of storage and disposal of chromic acid rinse water and wastewater sludges in a lagoon without a permit, and one count of disposal of paint sludge and solvent wastes in a pit without a permit, all in violation of 42 U.S.C. § 6928(d)(2)(A).

I.

Defendant's convictions arose out of the operation of the General Metal Fabricators, Inc. (GMF) facility in Erwin, Tennessee, which engaged in metal stamping, plating, and painting. The facility utilized hazardous chemicals and generated hazardous waste. The owners of GMF, Joseph and Jean Sanchez; as well as Dean, the production manager; and Clyde Griffith, the plant manager; were indicted for conspiracy to violate RCRA, and, individually, for violations of various sections of the statute....

RCRA provides a comprehensive system of oversight of hazardous materials, a system centered upon requirements that facilities utilizing such materials obtain permits, and maintain proper records of the treatment, storage, and disposal of hazardous substances. No permit was sought for the GMF facility. The hazardous waste disposal practices at GMF were discovered by chance by state waste-management authorities whose attention was caught, while driving to an appointment at another facility, by two 55-gallon drums abandoned among weeds on GMF's property.

As production manager, Dean had day-to-day supervision of GMF's production process and employees. Among his duties was the instruction of employees on hazardous waste handling and disposal. Numerous practices at GMF violated RCRA. GMF's plating operations utilized rinse baths, contaminated with hazardous chemicals, which were drained through a Pipe into an earthen lagoon outside the facility. In addition, Dean instructed employees to shovel various kinds of solid wastes from the tanks into 55-gallon drums. Dean ordered the construction of a pit, concealed behind the facility, into which 38 drums of such hazardous waste were tossed. The contents spilled onto the soil from open or corroded drums. Chemical analyses of soil and solid wastes, entered by stipulation at trial, revealed that the lagoon and the pit were contaminated with chromium. In addition, the pit was contaminated with toluene and xylene solvents. All of these substances are hazardous. Drums of spent chromic acid solution were also illegally stored on the premises.

Defendant was familiar with the chemicals used in each of the tanks on the production lines, and described to authorities the manner in which the contents of the rinse tanks were deposited in the lagoon. Material Safety Data Sheets (MSDS) provided to GMF by the chemical manufacturer clearly stated that various chemicals in use at GMF were hazardous and were subject to state and federal pollution control laws. The MSDS were given to investigators by Dean, who demonstrated his knowledge of their contents. The MSDS delivered with the chromic acid made specific reference to RCRA and to related EPA regulations. Dean informed investigators that he "had read this RCRA waste code but thought it was a bunch of bull____."

II.

A.

... We shall address first a number of contentions going to the scope and elements of RCRA's criminal provisions, which we think of primary importance among the issues raised by defendant. The first of these issues arises in connection with defendant's contention that the trial court erred in denying his motion for an acquittal on Count 4, because there was no evidence that defendant knew of RCRA's permit requirement. Defendant's characterization of the evidence is inaccurate; but moreover, we see no basis on the face of the statute for concluding that knowledge of the permit requirement is an element of the crime. The statute penalizes:

> Any person who —
>
> ....
>
> (2) knowingly treats, stores, or disposes of any hazardous waste identified or listed under this subchapter —
>
> (A) without a permit under this subchapter or pursuant to title I of the Marine Protection, Research, and Sanctuaries Act (86 Stat. 1052); or
>
> (B) in knowing violation of any material condition or requirement of such permit; or
>
> (C) in knowing violation of any material condition or requirement of any applicable interim status regulations or standards....

42 U.S.C. § 6928(d)(2). Defendant was convicted of violating subsection 6928(d)(2)(A).

The question of interpretation presented by this provision is the familiar one of how far the initial "knowingly" travels. Other courts of appeals have divided on this question. In *United States v. Johnson & Towers, Inc.*, 741 F.2d 662 (3d Cir. 1984), *cert. denied, sub nom.*, the Court of Appeals for the Third Circuit concluded that knowledge of the permit requirement was an element of the crime....

The Court of Appeals for the Ninth Circuit disagreed with the Third Circuit in *United States v. Hoflin*, 880 F.2d 1033 (9th Cir. 1989), *cert. denied*, 493 U.S.

1083, 107 L. Ed. 2d 1047, 110 S. Ct. 1143 (1990). The Ninth Circuit noted first the well-established principle of statutory construction that courts will "give effect, if possible, to every clause and word of a statute," pointing out that the Third Circuit's reading of subsection 6928(d)(2)(A) would render mere surplusage the word "knowing" in subsections 6928(d)(2)(B) and (C). The Ninth Circuit also disagreed with the Third Circuit that there was anything illogical about reading subsections 6928(d)(2)(B) and (C) to have a knowledge requirement but subsection 6928(d)(2)(A) to have none. The Ninth Circuit observed that the permit requirement is intended to give the EPA notice that oversight of a facility is necessary (and, by implication, the force of the statutory scheme would be greatly diminished by exempting all who claimed ignorance of the statute's requirements). The difference in mens rea between the subsections signifies the relative importance, in the estimation of Congress, of the twin requirements of obtaining a permit and complying with the permit. This ranking is consistent with the greater likelihood that compliance with the permit will be monitored....

All of the courts to address this question have reasoned by analogy from the holding of the Supreme Court in *United States v. International Minerals & Chemical Corp.*, 402 U.S. 558, 29 L. Ed. 2d 178, 91 S. Ct. 1697 (1971). In that case, the indictment was brought under 18 U.S.C. § 834(f), which penalizes knowing violation of any regulation. The regulation at issue, enacted by the Interstate Commerce Commission, required shipping papers to reflect certain information concerning corrosive liquids being shipped. The question before the Supreme Court was whether knowledge of existence of the regulation was an element of the crime. The Court held that it was not, turning its decision upon the maxim that ignorance of the law is no excuse. The Court concluded its opinion by stating, with equal force here, that when "dangerous or deleterious devices or products or obnoxious waste materials are involved, the probability of regulation is so great that anyone who is aware that he is in possession of them or dealing with them must be presumed to he aware of the regulation."...

We agree with the reasoning of the Court of Appeals for the Ninth Circuit in *Hoflin*. The "knowingly" which begins § 6928(d)(2) cannot be read as extending to the subsections without rendering nugatory the word "knowing" contained in subsections 6928(d)(2)(B) and (C). Subsection 6928(d)(2)(A) requires knowing treatment (or knowing storage, or knowing disposal) of hazardous waste. It also requires proof that the treatment, or storage, or disposal, was done without a permit. It does not require that the person charged have known that a permit was required, and that knowledge is not relevant.

As to subsections 6928(d)(2)(B) and (C), the requirements are different. Here, the statute clearly requires in addition that if one is to be charged under 6928(d)(2)(B) with violating the terms of a permit or under 6928(d)(2)(C) with violating regulations then one must be aware of the additional requirements of the permit or regulation. To us the statute is clear, makes sense and does not contain the ambiguities or inconsistencies found by others.

... Finally, we note that statutes which are designed to protect the public health and safety (as is RCRA) have consistently been distinguished in Supreme Court precedent as more likely candidates for diminished mens rea requirements. *Liparota v. United States*, 471 U.S. 419, 433, 85 L. Ed. 2d 434, 105 S. Ct. 2084 (1985).

We do not agree with the suggestion in *Johnson & Towers* that section 6928(d)(2)(A) is in fact a strict liability crime if knowledge of the permit requirement need not be shown. The provision applies by its terms to any person who "knowingly treats, stores or disposes of hazardous waste." 42 U.S.C. § 6928(d)(2). The Supreme Court's pronouncement in *International Minerals*, quoted above, stands for the proposition that persons involved in hazardous waste handling have every reason to be aware that their activities are regulated by law, aside from the rule that ignorance of the law is no excuse. In this case, the documentation provided by the chemical manufacturer abundantly illustrates one means by which knowledge of hazardous waste laws is communicated. Accordingly, even absent the requirement of proof that the defendant knew of RCRA's permit provisions, the statute does not impose strict liability. The district court did not err in declining to grant defendant's motion for acquittal based on his alleged ignorance of RCRA's permit requirement.

B.

Defendant also contends that the district court should have granted his motion for acquittal because subsection 6928(d)(2)(A) was not intended to reach employees who are not "owners" or "operators" of facilities. By its terms, the provision applies to "any person." "Person" is a defined term meaning "an individual, trust, firm, joint stock company, corporation (including a government corporation), partnership, association, State, municipality, commission, political subdivision of a State, or any interstate body." 42 U.S.C. § 6903(15).

Defendant would be hard pressed to convince the court that he is not an "individual." He argues, however, that because only owners and operators of facilities are required to obtain permits, 42 U.S.C. § 6925, the penalty imposed for hazardous waste handling without a permit by subsection 6928(d)(2)(A) must apply only to owners and operators.

This contention is unpersuasive for numerous reasons. Of primary importance is the fact that it is contrary to the unambiguous language of the statute. [Citation] We agree with the Third Circuit that "had Congress meant in § 6928(d)(2)(A) to take aim more narrowly, it could have used more narrow language. Second, while defendant's argument at first glance has logical appeal in relation to subsection 6928(d)(2)(A), the relevant language "any person" prefaces § 6928(d) generally. A number of separate crimes are set out in § 6928(d), several of them having nothing to do with the permit requirement (e.g., failure to maintain requisite documentation or to comply with regulations). Defendant's argument would accordingly impose a limitation on all of the crimes set out in § 6928(d) on a ground relevant to few of them. Third, even the logical

appeal of the assertion does not withstand scrutiny. The fact that Congress chose to impose the permit requirement upon owners and operators does not undercut the value of further assuring permit compliance by enacting criminal penalties which would lead others to make inquiry into the permit status of facilities. Given that "such wastes typically have no value, yet can only be safely disposed of at considerable cost," facilities generating hazardous waste have a strong incentive to evade the law. [Citation] Moreover, clean-up of the resulting environmental damage almost always involves far greater cost than proper disposal would have, and may be limited to containing the spread of the harm. Defendant argues that employees are the least likely persons to know facilities' permit status. However, employees of a facility are more able to ascertain the relevant facts than the general public, which the statute is intended to protect. In light of these factors, it was entirely reasonable for Congress to have created broad criminal liability. Fourth, it is far from clear that defendant is in fact not an "operator" of GMF, a term defined in the regulations to mean "the person responsible for the overall operation of a facility." 40 C.F.R. § 260.10 (1991)....
We conclude that employees may be criminally liable under § 6928(d).

Defendant assigns as error the enhancement of his sentence on the ground that he had an aggravating role in the crime. His sentence was enhanced pursuant to § 3B1.1(b) of the Guidelines Manual, which applies when the defendant is "a manager or supervisor (but not an organizer or leader) and the criminal activity involved five or more participants or was otherwise extensive ..." United States Sentencing Commission, Guidelines Manual, § 3B1.1(b) (Nov. 1991). Defendant argues that the enhancement was error because there was evidence that, at most, he supervised only two persons.

This contention misses the language of the Guideline, which refers not to "subordinates" but to "participants," thus encompassing those on an equal footing or superior to defendant in a criminal hierarchy as well as those below. In addition to defendant and the two employees concededly involved, the owners and Griffith are also relevant for purposes of the Guideline. Accordingly, there were five or more participants in the offense, and the district court did not err in enhancing defendant's sentence on this ground....

Affirmed.

NOTES AND QUESTIONS

1. RCRA gives a wide range of enforcement options to the federal government to ensure compliance with the hazardous waste management provisions of the Act. RCRA § 3008(a), 42 U.S.C. 6928(a). The EPA is authorized to assess civil penalties for past or current violations, issue compliance orders, revoke permits, and seek temporary or permanent injunctive relief. The penalties may reach $25,000 per day of violation, but the agency is directed to consider the seriousness of the violation and good faith efforts to comply with the Act.

2. RCRA also contains criminal sanctions for "knowing" violations of certain provisions of the Act. RCRA § 3008(d), 42 U.S.C. § 6928(d). The statute provides even stiffer penalties for "knowing endangerment" [$250,000 fine, 15 years imprisonment or both]. § 3008(e), 42 U.S.C. § 6928(e). Courts have split over interpreting the scienter requirement in the statute. The majority trend as reflected in *Dean*, however, holds that knowledge of RCRA's permit requirement is not an essential element of a violation of § 3008(d)(2)(A), [§ 6928(d)(2)(A)]. *Accord United States v. Wagner*, 29 F.3d 264, 266 (7th Cir. 1994). *Compare United States v. Speach*, 968 F.2d 795, 796 (9th Cir. 1992) (government required to prove defendant's knowledge that facility lacked a permit).

3. What persons may be liable under the statute? In *United States v. MacDonald & Watson Waste Oil Co.*, 933 F.2d 35, 55 (1st Cir. 1991) the court held that the responsible corporate officer in a position to ensure compliance with laws could be held criminally responsible. *Also see United States v. Johnson & Towers, Inc.*, 741 F.2d 662, 667 (3d Cir. 1984) (interpreted term "persons" subject to RCRA § 3008 criminal sanctions broadly to include employees — service manager and foreman — other than owners and operators of company).

4. Courts have recognized that knowledge could be inferred from circumstantial evidence, such as the position and responsibility of the officer, information provided on prior occasions, and "willful blindness" to the facts constituting the offense. *United States v. Johnson & Towers, Inc.*, 741 F.2d 662, 667 (3d Cir. 1984). The court in *United States v. Hayes Int'l Corp.*, 786 F.2d 1499, (11th Cir. 1986) observed:

> [T]he government may prove guilty knowledge with circumstantial evidence. In the context of the hazardous waste statutes, proving knowledge should not be difficult. The statute at issue here sets forth certain procedures transporters must follow to ensure that wastes are sent only to permit facilities. Transporters of waste presumably are aware of these procedures, and if a transporter does not follow the procedures, a juror may draw certain inferences. Where there is no evidence that those who took the waste asserted that they were properly licensed, the jurors may draw additional inferences. Jurors may also consider the circumstances and terms of the transaction. It is common knowledge that properly disposing of wastes is an expensive task, and if someone is willing to take away wastes at an unusual price or under unusual circumstances, then a juror can infer that the transporter knows that the wastes are not being taken to a permit facility.
>
> ... Knowledge does not require certainty, and the jurors may draw inferences from all of the circumstances, including the existence of the regulatory scheme.

Id. at 1504-05.

5. The Guidelines applied in the principal case were developed by the Sentencing Commission, an independent agency of the judicial branch, pursuant to the Sentencing Reform Act of 1984. The guidelines establish a complex system of categories of offense behavior and offender characteristics pertaining to a wide array of crimes. The purpose of the guidelines is to create a sentencing methodology which is effective and fair, uniform, and proportional to the nature and severity of the offense. Courts ordinarily select a sentence from the guideline range, with departure allowed in limited circumstances. 18 U.S.C. § 3553(b).

Regulatory statutes, such as RCRA, which are primarily civil in nature yet contain some criminal provisions present particular problems in criminal sentencing. One such difficulty is distinguishing between substantive offenses and technical or administratively-related offenses, such as improper recordkeeping or reporting. The following is an illustrative provision of the Guidelines which applies both to substantive violations of the statute governing the handling of pesticides and toxic and hazardous substances and to recordkeeping offenses.

> 18 U.S.C.§ 2Q1.2. Mishandling of Hazardous or Toxic Substances or Pesticides; Recordkeeping, Tampering, and Falsification; Unlawfully Transporting Hazardous Materials in Commerce
>
> (a) Base Offense Level: 8
> (b) Specific Offense Characteristics
>   (1) (A) If the offense resulted in an ongoing, continuous, or repetitive discharge, release, or emission of a hazardous or toxic substance or pesticide into the environment, increase by 6 levels; or
>   (B) if the offense otherwise involved a discharge, release, or emission of a hazardous or toxic substance or pesticide, increase by 4 levels.
>   (2) If the offense resulted in a substantial likelihood of death or serious bodily injury, increase by 9 levels.
>   (3) If the offense resulted in disruption of public utilities or evacuation of a community, or if cleanup required a substantial expenditure, increase by 4 levels.
>   (4) If the offense involved transportation, treatment, storage, or disposal without a permit or in violation of a permit, increase by 4 levels.
>   (5) If a recordkeeping offense reflected an effort to conceal a substantive environmental offense, use the offense level for the substantive offense.
>   (6) If the offense involved a simple recordkeeping or reporting violation only, decrease by 2 levels.

Also see statutory provisions: 7 U.S.C. § 136j-136l; 15 U.S.C. §§ 2614 and 2615; 33 U.S.C. §§ 1319(c)(1), (2), 1321(b)(5), 1517(b); 42 U.S.C. §§ 300h-2, 6928(d), 7413, 9603(b), (c), (d); 43 U.S.C. §§ 1350, 1816(a), 1822(b) 49 U.S.C. § 1809(b).

6. In *United States v. Sellers*, 926 F.2d 410 (5th Cir. 1991), the court found that an increase in the base level of offense under the Sentencing Guidelines for knowingly and willfully disposing of hazardous waste without a permit was warranted where waste was discovered just one day after being dumped because the court could infer actual environmental contamination had resulted even from one leaking barrel of toxic substance. *See* § 2Q1.2(b)(1)(B),(b)(4). The government was only required to prove that the defendant knew that one substance dumped was a paint solvent which was extremely flammable, not that he knew it was hazardous within meaning of RCRA. *Also see United States v. Bogas*, 920 F.2d 363, 368 (6th Cir. 1990) (offense level should have been increased for municipal officer convicted of not reporting release of ignitable hazardous waste where environmental contamination resulted necessitating substantial expenditures for cleanup).

Chapter 9

COMPREHENSIVE ENVIRONMENTAL RESPONSE, COMPENSATION, AND LIABILITY ACT

INTRODUCTION

The explosion of federal environmental legislation in the 1970s responded to growing public recognition and demand that the federal government take an active role in ensuring a healthy and safe environment. The implicit basis for regulation was that traditional tort law lacked sufficient protective force and scope to deal with the growing harms presented by pollutants released into the environment. The call for uniform, national solutions to address the shortcomings of private law systems initially aimed to set forth extensive regulatory models to change the way that industry and government conducted business. NEPA, for instance, sought to infuse environmental values into the decisionmaking process of government. The principal pollution control statutes, the Clean Air Act and the Clean Water Act, established comprehensive standards directing technological improvements and innovations purposed toward enhancing and protecting the ambient environment. Despite these enactments, though, there was a growing concern that gaps existed in coverage to deal with existing dangers posed by abandoned or inactive hazardous waste sites.

The Comprehensive Environmental Response, Compensation, and Liability Act of 1980 (CERCLA), 42 U.S.C. § 9601 *et seq.*, as amended by the Superfund Amendments and Reauthorization Act of 1986 (SARA), establishes a mechanism for responding to the escalating health and environmental dangers posed by toxic wastes. The Act is distinctive in the spectrum of federal environmental protection legislation in that the principal focus is remedial and corrective rather than regulatory. CERCLA does not set standards for prospective compliance by industry but essentially is a tort-like, backward-looking statute designed to cleanup expeditiously abandoned hazardous waste sites and respond to hazardous spills and releases of toxic waste into the environment. In contrast to RCRA, which provides a "cradle to grave" program for dealing with coverage of *present* hazardous waste activities, CERCLA is directed toward remediation of *past* occurrences. The statute embodies a twofold perspective of giving governmental authorities and private parties the tools to respond to problems presented by hazardous waste sites and to impose liability on responsible parties. The Act does not, however, create a private cause of action to compensate persons for economic or personal injuries resulting from exposure to toxic waste. Instead, the focus of CERCLA is on abating and correcting the harms presented by releases of toxic waste into the environment. The court in *Artesian Water Co. v. Government of New Castle County*, 659 F. Supp. 1269 (D. Del. 1987) made the following observations about the background and purpose of the statute:

> CERCLA was enacted in 1980 during the final months of the 96th Congress as a legislative response to the growing problem of toxic wastes, many of which were disposed of before their dangers were widely known and had contaminated precious land and water resources. The statute attempts to create a coherent answer to two related problems: the emergency abatement of releases of hazardous substances into the environment and the response, both short- and long-term, to the presence of hazardous wastes in existing disposal sites. Many of these sites had been abandoned by any party who could be held liable for the cleanup. Wherever possible, however, CERCLA places the ultimate financial burden of toxic waste cleanup on those responsible for creating the harmful conditions. [Citations.]
>
> Because CERCLA as finally enacted was the product of an unusually arduous process of political compromise, it is hardly a model of concise legislative draftsmanship. In general terms, the statute establishes the Superfund, which is financed primarily through excise tax revenues. The federal government is authorized to use the Superfund to finance governmental response activities, to pay claims arising from the response activities of private parties, and to compensate federal or state governmental entities for damage caused to natural resources. CERCLA § 111(a), 42 U.S.C. 9611(a). In addition to the Superfund claim structure, CERCLA provides that the federal government, state governments, and private parties may sue those responsible for the generation, transportation, or disposal of hazardous substances. CERCLA § 107(a), 42 U.S.C. § 9607(a). Courts have uniformly imposed strict liability in construing the terms of section 107(a). [Citations.] Liability is, however, subject to the defense that the release of a hazardous substance was caused solely by an act of God, an act of war, or an act or omission of a third party unrelated to the defendant. CERCLA § 107(b), 42 U.S.C. § 9607(b).

A. SCOPE OF LIABILITY

The liability scheme of CERCLA, contained in section 107(a), 42 U.S.C. § 9607(a), is the central focus of the Act. The impact of CERCLA's strict liability approach, coupled with its imposition of joint and several liability with limited and narrow defenses, has dramatically affected numerous commercial transactions and shapes the nature and extent of government and private responses to releases of hazardous wastes. The following materials examine the classes of persons covered under the liability provisions of the Act, evaluate the requirements for a *prima facie* case, and consider the range of alternatives and limitations on response activities by governmental authorities and private parties.

UNITED STATES OF AMERICA v. ALCAN ALUMINUM CORP.

964 F.2d 252 (3d Cir. 1992)

GREENBERG, CIRCUIT JUDGE.

Facts and Procedural History

Virtually all of the facts in this case to the extent developed at this point are undisputed. The Butler Tunnel Site (the "Site") is listed on the National Priorities List established by the Environmental Protection Agency ("EPA") under section 105 of CERCLA, 42 U.S.C. § 9605. See 52 Fed. Reg. 27,620 (July 22, 1987). The Site includes a network of approximately five square miles of deep underground mines and related tunnels, caverns, pools and waterways bordering the east bank of the Susquehanna River in Pittston, Pennsylvania. The mine workings at the Site are drained by the Butler Tunnel (the "Tunnel"), a 7500 foot tunnel which feeds directly into the Susquehanna River.

The mines are accessible from the surface by numerous air shafts or boreholes. One borehole (the "Borehole") is located on the premises of Hi-Way Auto Service, an automobile fuel and repair station situated above the Tunnel. The Borehole leads directly into the mine workings at the Site.

In the late 1970's, the owner of Hi-Way Auto Service permitted various liquid waste transport companies, including those owned and controlled by Russell Mahler (the "Mahler Companies"), to deposit oily liquid wastes containing hazardous substances into the Borehole. The Mahler Companies collected the liquid wastes from numerous industrial facilities located in the northeastern United States and, in total, disposed of approximately 2,000,000 gallons of oily wastes containing hazardous substances through the Borehole. Apparently, it was contemplated that the waste would remain at the Site indefinitely.

Alcan is an Ohio corporation which manufactures aluminum sheet and plate products in Oswego, New York. From 1965 through at least 1989, Alcan's manufacturing process involved the hot-rolling of aluminum ingots. To keep the rolls cool and lubricated during the hot-rolling process, Alcan circulated an emulsion through the rolls, consisting of 95% deionized water and 5% mineral oil. At the end of the hot-rolling process, Alcan removed the used emulsion and replaced it with unused emulsion.

During the rolling process, fragments of the aluminum ingots, which also contained copper, chromium, cadmium, lead and zinc, hazardous substances under CERCLA, broke off into the emulsion. In an effort to remove those fragments, Alcan then filtered the used emulsion prior to disposing of it, but the filtering process was imperfect and hence some fragments remained. According to Alcan, however, the level of these compounds in the post-filtered, used emulsion was "far below the EP toxic or TCLP toxic levels and, indeed, orders of magnitude below ambient or naturally occurring background levels. Moreover, the trace quantities of metal compounds in the emulsion [were] immobile...." Appellant's Br. at 4. The Government does not specifically challenge Alcan's assertion that the used emulsion contained only low levels of these metallic compounds, as it contends that this fact is irrelevant to Alcan's liability under CERCLA.

From mid-1978 to late 1979, Alcan contracted with the Mahler Companies to dispose of at least 2,300,950 gallons of used emulsion from its Oswego, New York, facility. During that period, the Mahler Companies disposed of approximately 32,500-37,500 gallons (or five 6500-7500 gallon loads) of Alcan's liquid waste through the Borehole into the Site.

In September 1985, approximately 100,000 gallons of water contaminated with hazardous substances were released from the Site into the Susquehanna River. It appears that this discharge was composed of the wastes deposited into the Borehole in the late 1970's. Between September 28, 1985, and January 7, 1987, EPA incurred significant response costs due to the release and the threatened release of hazardous substances from the Site. According to the Government, EPA's response actions included "containing an oily material on the river through the use of absorbent booms; immediately removing and disposing of 161,000 pounds (over 80 tons) of oil and chemical-soaked debris and soil, monitoring, sampling and analysis of air and water, and conducting hydrogeologic studies." Government's Br. at 10-11.

On December 27, 1985, EPA issued written information requests to potentially responsible parties ("PRPs"),[4] including Alcan, concerning their responsibility for the presence of hazardous substances at the Site. In May and June of 1986, EPA issued letters to the PRPs informing them of their potential liability under CERCLA. Those letters invited the PRPs to conduct a remedial investigation/feasibility study and to enter into an agreement with EPA for the issuance of an administrative order governing the study. Several PRPs conducted these negotiations with EPA in an attempt to settle their liability for removal costs incurred by the Government, but Alcan did not participate in this process.

---

[4]Under 42 U.S.C. § 9607(a), "responsible parties" include:

(1) the owner and operator of a vessel or a facility,

(2) any person who at the time of disposal of any hazardous substance owned or operated any facility at which such hazardous substances were disposed of,

(3) any person who by contract, agreement, or otherwise arranged for disposal or treatment, or arranged with a transporter for transport for disposal or treatment, of hazardous substances owned or possessed by such person, by any other party or entity, at any facility or incineration vessel owned or operated by another party or entity and containing such hazardous substances, and

(4) any person who accepts or accepted any hazardous substances for transport to disposal or treatment facilities, incineration vessels or sites selected by such person, from which there is a release, or a threatened release which causes the incurrence of response costs, of a hazardous substance....

[The district court granted the Government's motion for summary judgment, holding Alcan jointly and severally liable for the removal costs because Alcan's waste contained identifiable levels of hazardous substances and was present at the Site from which there was a release.]

II. *Discussion*

A. *CERCLA Framework:*

In response to widespread concern over the improper disposal of hazardous wastes, Congress enacted CERCLA, a complex piece of legislation designed to force polluters to pay for costs associated with remedying their pollution. [Citation] As numerous courts have observed, CERCLA is a remedial statute which should be construed liberally to effectuate its goals. [Citations]

CERCLA, as amended by the Superfund Amendments and Reauthorization Act of 1986, Pub. L. No. 99-499, 100 Stat. 1613 (Oct. 17, 1986), grants broad authority to the executive branch of the federal government to provide for the clean-up of hazardous substance sites. Specifically, section 104 authorizes the President to respond to a release or substantial threat of a release of hazardous substances into the environment by: (1) removing or arranging for the removal of hazardous substances; (2) providing for remedial action relating to such hazardous substances; and (3) taking any other response measure consistent with the National Contingency Plan that the President deems necessary to protect the public health or welfare or the environment. 42 U.S.C. § 9604(a). The President has delegated most of his authority under CERCLA to EPA.

CERCLA's bite lies in its requirement that responsible parties pay for actions undertaken pursuant to section 104. Under section 107, CERCLA liability is imposed where the plaintiff establishes the following four elements:

(1)   the defendant falls within one of the four categories of "responsible parties";

(2)   the hazardous substances are disposed at a "facility";[8]

---

[8]A facility is defined as:

> any building, structure, installation, equipment, pipe or pipeline (including any pipe into a sewer or publicly owned treatment works), well, pit, pond, lagoon, impoundment, ditch, landfill, storage container, motor vehicle, rolling stock, or aircraft, or (B) any site or area where a hazardous substance has been deposited, stored, disposed of, or placed, or otherwise come to be located; but does not include any consumer product in consumer use or any vessel.

42 U.S.C. § 9601(A). The parties have agreed that the Site is a "facility" within the meaning of CERCLA.

(3) there is a "release" or threatened release of hazardous substances from the facility into the environment;[9]

(4) the release causes the incurrence of "response costs."[10]

Reimbursement for response costs can be obtained in a variety of ways. For example, the Government can clean the sites itself using monies in the Hazardous Substance Response Trust Fund established by section 221 of CERCLA, 42 U.S.C. § 9631 and now the Hazardous Substance Superfund or "Superfund" (*see* 26 U.S.C. § 9507); EPA can then seek reimbursement from responsible parties, as it has done in this case. In addition, section 106(a) permits EPA to request the Attorney General to "secure such relief as may be necessary to abate such danger or threat" by filing a civil action in federal district court. That section also permits EPA to issue administrative orders "as may be necessary to protect public health and welfare and the environment."

Finally, and of great significance in this case, CERCLA imposes strict liability on responsible parties. 42 U.S.C. § 9601(32). *See Dedham Water Co. v. Cumberland Farms Dairy, Inc.*, 889 F.2d at 1150; *New York v. Shore Realty Corp.*, 759 F.2d 1032, 1042 (2d Cir. 1985) ("Congress intended that responsible parties be held strictly liable, even though an explicit provision for strict liability was not included in the compromise....").

---

[9]A release is defined as:

> any spilling, leaking, pumping, pouring, emitting, emptying, discharging, injecting, escaping, leaching, dumping, or disposing into the environment (including the abandonment or discarding of barrels, containers, and other closed receptacles containing any hazardous substance or pollutant or contaminant), but excludes (A) any release which results in exposure to persons solely within a workplace, with respect to a claim which such persons may assert against the employer of such persons, (B) emissions from the engine exhaust of a motor vehicle, rolling stock, aircraft, vessel, or pipeline pumping station engine, (C) release of source, byproduct, or special nuclear material from a nuclear incident, as those terms are defined in the Atomic Energy Act of 1954 [42 U.S.C. § 2011 et seq.] if such release is subject to requirements with respect to financial protection established by the Nuclear Regulatory Commission under section 170 of such Act [42 U.S.C. § 2210], or, for the purposes of section 9604 of this title or any other response action, any release of source byproduct, or special nuclear material from any processing site designated under section 7912(a)(1) or 7942(a) of this title, and (D) the normal application of fertilizer.

42 U.S.C. § 9601. The parties in this suit have also agreed that a "release" has occurred.

[10]Section 9601 provides that the terms "respond" and "response" mean "remove, removal, remedy, and remedial action, all such terms (including the terms 'removal' and 'remedial action') include enforcement actions related thereto." Typically, a "removal" action is an action intended to remove the hazardous waste from the area, whereas a "remedial" action involves a long-term effort to remedy the damaged environment.

B. *CERCLA Contains No Quantitative Requirement in Its Definition of "Hazardous Substance":*

Alcan argues that it should not be held liable for response costs incurred by the Government in cleaning the Susquehanna River because the level of hazardous substances in its emulsion was below that which naturally occurs and thus could not have contributed to the environmental injury. It asserts that we must read a threshold concentration requirement into the definition of "hazardous substances" for the term "hazardous" to have any meaning....

The Government responds that under a plain reading of the statute, there is no quantitative requirement in the definition of "hazardous substance. " Therefore, the Government asserts that Alcan's argument that substances containing below-ambient levels of hazardous substances are not really "hazardous" is properly directed at Congress, not the judiciary....

1. *Plain Meaning:*

Section 9601(14) sets forth CERCLA's definition of "hazardous substance" as:

'hazardous substance' means (A) any substance designated pursuant to section 1321(b)(2)(A) of Title 33, (B) any element, compound, mixture, solution, or substance designated pursuant to section 9602 of this title, (C) any hazardous waste having the characteristics identified under or listed pursuant to section 3001 of the Solid Waste Disposal Act [42 U.S.C.A. § 6921] (but not including any waste the regulation of which under the Solid Waste Disposal Act [42 U.S.C.A. § 6901 et seq.] has been suspended by Act of Congress), (D) any toxic pollutant listed under section 1317(a) of Title 33, (E) any hazardous air pollutant listed under section 112 of the Clean Air Act [42 U.S.C.A. § 7412], and (F) any imminently hazardous chemical substance or mixture with respect to which the Administrator has taken action pursuant to section 2606 of Title 15. The term does not include petroleum, including crude oil or any fraction thereof which is not otherwise specifically listed or designated as a hazardous substance under subparagraphs (A) through (F) of this paragraph....

Hence, the statute does not, on its face, impose any quantitative requirement or concentration level on the definition of "hazardous substances." Rather, the substance under consideration must simply fall within one of the designated categories....

D. *Causation.*

Alcan maintains that, if we decline to construe the determination of "hazardous substance" to encompass a concentration threshold, we must at least require the Government to prove that Alcan's emulsion caused or contributed to the release or the Government's incurrence of response costs. The Government contends, and the district court by adopting the reasoning of Alcan New York agreed, that the statute imposes no such causation requirement, but rather requires that the plaintiff in a CERCLA proceeding establish that the release or threatened release caused the incurrence of response costs; it underscores the difficulty CERCLA plaintiffs would face in the multi-generator context if required to trace the cause of the response costs to each responsible party.

1. *Plain Meaning:*

The plain meaning of the statute supports the Government's position. As noted above, section 107 imposes liability upon a generator of hazardous substances who contracts with another party to dispose of the hazardous substances at a facility "from which there is a *release, or threatened release which causes the incurrence of response costs.*" 42 U.S.C. § 9607 (emphasis supplied). The statute does not, on its face, require the plaintiff to prove that the generator's hazardous substances themselves caused the release or caused the incurrence of response costs; rather, it requires the plaintiff to prove that the release or threatened release caused the incurrence of response costs, and that the defendant is a generator of hazardous substances at the facility.

2. *Legislative History:*

The legislative history also supports the Government's position that CERCLA does not require the plaintiff to establish a specific causal relationship between a generator's waste and the release or the plaintiff's incurrence of response costs. It appears that the early House of Representatives' version of CERCLA imposed liability upon those persons who "caused or contributed to the release or threatened release." H.R. 7020, 96th Cong., 2d Sess. § 3071(a)(D), 126 Cong. Rec. 26,779. However, the version ultimately passed by Congress deleted the causation requirement and instead imposed liability upon a class of responsible persons without regard to whether the person specifically caused or contributed to the release and the resultant response costs. See 126 Cong. Rec. 31,981-82. Moreover, Congress added three limited defenses to liability based on causation which are contained in 42 U.S.C. § 9607(b): acts of God, acts of war, and acts or omissions of a contractually unrelated third party when the defendant exercised due care and took appropriate responses. Imputing a specific causation requirement would render these defenses superfluous.

In sum, the legislative history indicates that Congress considered and rejected a requirement that the plaintiff establish that the defendant's waste caused or contributed to the release or the incurrence of response costs.

... Accordingly, we reject Alcan's argument that the Government must prove that Alcan's emulsion deposited in the Borehole caused the release or caused the Government to incur response costs. Rather, the Government must simply prove that the defendant's hazardous substances were deposited at the site from which there was a release and that the release caused the incurrence of response costs....

F. *Divisibility of Harm:*

The foregoing conclusions that (1) there is no quantitative threshold in the definition of hazardous substances and (2) the plaintiff need not establish a causal connection between a given defendant's waste and the release or the incurrence of response costs would initially appear to lead to unfair imposition of liability. As Alcan asserts, this definition of "hazardous substances" effectively renders everything in the universe hazardous, including, for example, federally approved drinking water. When this definition is read in conjunction with the rule that specific causation is not required, CERCLA seemingly would impose liability on every generator of hazardous waste, although that generator could not, on its own, have caused any environmental harm.[25]

While Alcan's assertion is of considerable strength, the Government's rebuttal is equally forceful. It notes that individual defendants must be held responsible for environmental injury brought about by the actions of multiple defendants, even if no single defendant itself could have produced the harm, for otherwise "each defendant in a multi-defendant case could avoid liability by relying on the low concentrations of hazardous substances in its waste, while the plaintiff is left with the substantial clean-up costs associated with the defendant's accumulated wastes." The Government reasons that this strong public interest in forcing polluters in the multi-generator context to pay outweighs a defendant's interest in avoiding liability even if that defendant has not acted in an environmentally unsound fashion when its actions are viewed without regard to the actions of others....

We find some merit in the arguments advanced by both the Government and Alcan. Accordingly, in our view, the common law principles of joint and several liability provide the only means to achieve the proper balance between Alcan's and the Government's conflicting interests and to infuse fairness into the statutory scheme without distorting its plain meaning or disregarding congressional intent.

Other courts have agreed that Congress' deletion of joint and several liability from the final version of the statute signalled its intent to have the courts determine, in accordance with traditional common law principles, whether such liability is proper under the circumstances. [Citations] In determining whether the

---

[25]Dean Prosser's hornbook highlights the paradox of liability where acts harmless in themselves together cause damage, observing:

> A very troublesome question arises where the acts of each of two or more parties, standing alone, would not be wrongful, but together they cause harm to the plaintiff. If several defendants independently pollute a stream, the impurities traceable to each may be negligible and harmless, but all together may render the water entirely unfit for use. The difficulty lies in the fact that each defendant alone would have committed no tort. There would have been no negligence, and no nuisance, since the individual use of the stream would have been a reasonable use, and no harm would have resulted.

William L. Prosser, Law of Torts, § 52, at 322 (4th ed. 1971).

imposition of joint and several liability upon Alcan is proper, so that it may be held liable for the Government's full response costs less what had been recovered from the settling defendants, we turn to the Restatement (Second) of Torts for guidance.

Section 433A of the Restatement provides that, when two or more joint tortfeasors acting independently cause a distinct or single harm for which there is a reasonable basis for division according to the contribution of each, each is subject to liability only for the portion of the harm that the individual tortfeasor has caused. It states,

> (1) Damages for harm are to be apportioned among two or more causes where
> (a) there are distinct harms, or
> (b) there is a reasonable basis for determining the contribution of each cause to a single harm.
> (2) Damages for any other harm cannot be apportioned among two or more causes.

Similarly, section 881 sets forth the affirmative defense based upon the divisibility of harm rule in section 433A:

> If two or more persons, acting independently, tortiously cause distinct harms or a single harm for which there is a reasonable basis for division according to the contribution of each, each is subject to liability only for the portion of the total harm that he has himself caused.

However, where joint tortfeasors cause a single and indivisible harm for which there is no reasonable basis for division according to the contribution of each, each tortfeasor is subject to liability for the entire harm. Section 875 recites:

> Each of two or more persons whose tortious conduct is a legal cause of a single and indivisible harm to the injured party is subject to liability to the injured party for the entire harm.

Obviously, of critical importance in this analysis is whether a harm is divisible and reasonably capable of apportionment, or indivisible, thereby subjecting the tortfeasor to potentially far-reaching liability.[27]

---

[27]Interestingly, the drafters of the Restatement found that joint pollution of water is typically subject to the divisibility rule. They write:

> There are other kinds of harm which, while not so clearly marked out as severable into distinct parts, are still capable of division upon a reasonable and rational basis, and of fair apportionment among the causes responsible.... *Such apportionment is commonly made in cases of private nuisance, where the pollution of a stream ... has interfered with the plaintiff's use and enjoyment of his land.*

Section 433 A, Comment d (emphasis supplied).

Under the Restatement, where a joint tortfeasor seeks to apportion the full amount of a plaintiff's damages according to that tortfeasor's own contribution to the harm, it is the tortfeasor's burden to establish that the damages are capable of such apportionment.[28] As the comments concerning this issue explain, the burden of proving that the harm is capable of apportionment is placed on the tortfeasor to avoid:

> the injustice of allowing a proved wrongdoer who has in fact caused harm to the plaintiff to escape liability merely because the harm which he has inflicted has combined with similar harm inflicted by other wrongdoers, and the nature of the harm itself has made it necessary that evidence be produced before it can be apportioned. In such a case the defendant may justly be required to assume the burden of producing that evidence, or if he is not able to do so, of bearing full responsibility. As between the proved tortfeasor who has clearly caused some harm, and the entirely innocent plaintiff, any hardship due to lack of evidence as to the extent of the harm should fall upon the former.

Comment on Section 433 B subsection (2).

These provisions underscore the intensely factual nature of the "divisibility" issue and thus highlight the district court's error in granting summary judgment for the full claim in favor of EPA without conducting a hearing. For this reason, we will remand this case for the court to determine whether there is a reasonable basis for limiting Alcan's liability based on its personal contribution to the harm to the Susquehanna River.

Our conclusions on this point are completely consistent with our previous discussion on causation, as there we were concerned with the Government's burden in demonstrating liability in the first instance. Here we are dealing with Alcan's effort to avoid liability otherwise established. We observe in this regard that Alcan's burden in attempting to prove the divisibility of harm to the Susquehanna River is substantial, and the analysis will be factually complex as it will require an assessment of the relative toxicity, migratory potential and synergistic capacity of the hazardous waste at issue. But Alcan should be permitted this opportunity to limit or avoid liability. If Alcan succeeds in this endeavor, it should only be liable for that portion of the harm fairly attributable to it....

In sum, on remand, the district court must permit Alcan to attempt to prove that the harm is divisible and that the damages are capable of some reasonable apportionment. We note that the Government need not prove that Alcan's emulsion caused the release or the response costs. On the other hand, if Alcan

---

[28]Section 433 B(2) provides, "Where the tortious conduct of two or more actors has combined to bring about harm to the plaintiff, and one or more of the actors seeks to limit his liability on the ground that the harm is capable of apportionment among them, the burden of proof as to the apportionment is upon each such actor."

proves that the emulsion did not or could not, when mixed with other hazardous wastes, contribute to the release and the resultant response costs, then Alcan should not be responsible for any response costs. In this sense, our result thus injects causation into the equation but, as we have already pointed out, places the burden of proof on the defendant instead of the plaintiff. We think that this result is consistent with the statutory scheme and yet recognizes that there must be some reason for the imposition of CERCLA liability. Our result seems particularly appropriate in light of the expansive meaning of "hazardous substance." Of course, if Alcan cannot prove that it should not be liable for any response costs or cannot prove that the harm is divisible and that the damages are capable of some reasonable apportionment, it will be liable for the full claim of $473,790.18.

III. *Conclusion*

In conclusion, the district court correctly determined that CERCLA's definition of "hazardous substance" does not include a threshold requirement. This interpretation is fully consistent with the plain language of the statute, the legislative history, EPA regulations and EPA policy. In addition, the court correctly determined that a CERCLA plaintiff need not establish a causal connection between a generator's hazardous substances and the release or the incurrence of response costs....

However, we find that the court should have conducted a hearing to determine the divisibility of harm to the Susquehanna River, and will remand the case for the court to do so. If Alcan can establish in that hearing that the harm is capable of reasonable apportionment, then it should be held liable only for the response costs relating to that portion of harm to which it contributed. Further, if Alcan can establish that the hazardous substances in its emulsion could not, when added to other hazardous substances, have caused or contributed to the release or the resultant response costs, then it should not be liable for any of the response costs....

NOTES AND QUESTIONS

1. *Causation.* In CERCLA Congress adopted a strict liability scheme which implicitly allows recovery based on a weaker showing of causation than the proximate cause required under traditional common law. A party may be held liable under the Act merely by showing that the defendant disposed of hazardous waste at a facility which now contains substances of "the kind" attributable to the defendant and that a release or a threatened release of that or any hazardous substance caused the incurrence of response costs. *City of New York v. Exxon Corp.*, 744 F. Supp. 474, 483 (S.D.N.Y. 1990). The justification for relaxing the traditional common law rules of proximate cause is simply Congress's recognition of the scientific difficulties often presented in showing a causal link between specific waste and the harm, particularly where multiple sources of pollution are potentially implicated over an extended period of time. *See Sterling v. Velsicol Chem. Corp.*, reprinted *supra* Chapter 2, page 50. Thus, the statute does not require the plaintiff to "fingerprint" or trace specific wastes to the defendant in order to impose liability. *United States v. Marisol*, 725 F. Supp. 833, 840 (M.D. Pa. 1989). Moreover, the plaintiff need not show any particular volume, toxicity, form or concentration of the hazardous waste in order to establish liability. *United States v. Carolina Transformer Co.*, 739 F. Supp. 1030, 1035 (E.D.N.C. 1989).

The statute provides limited, narrow defenses which will allow a potentially responsible party to escape liability by showing that the harm was caused "solely" by a third party. *See Violet v. Picillo*, 648 F. Supp. 1283, 1294 (D.R.I. 1986) (common law doctrine of superseding or intervening cause held not applicable to CERCLA). The effect of the liability approach in CERCLA, then, is that the burden of proof of causation shifts to the defendant.

In *Artesian Water Co. v. Government of New Castle County*, 659 F. Supp. 1269 (D. Del. 1987) the plaintiff water company sought to recover its costs to clean up a polluted aquifer under CERCLA. The defendant challenged the existence of the requisite causal link to establish liability because leachate emanating from several nearby landfills could have caused the contamination. The court rejected a "but for" rule of causation where concurrent causes bring about an event. Instead, the court held that causation was satisfied if the release of contaminants from the defendant's landfill site was a substantial factor in producing the plaintiff's injury. *Id.* at 1283.

2. *Release.* Section 104 of CERCLA gives the EPA broad authority to respond to the release or threatened release of hazardous substances irrespective of whether a health or environmental danger is presented, and also to respond where nonhazardous pollutants or contaminants are being released into the environment which "may present an imminent and substantial danger to the public health or welfare." CERCLA § 104(a), 42 U.S.C. § 9604(a).

In *Licciardi v. Murphy Oil U.S.A., Inc.*, 111 F.3d 396 (5th Cir. 1997) the court held that the presence of hazardous substances in soil samples in a quantity exceeding "background levels" did not support a finding that a release by a nearby oil refinery caused response costs. CERCLA liability, reasoned the court, does not necessarily attach to any release of a hazardous substance into the environment, but requires a showing that the release justified the response costs.

UNITED STATES v. ACETO AGRICULTURAL CHEMICALS CORP.

872 F.2d 1373 (8th Cir. 1989)

LARSON, SENIOR DISTRICT JUDGE.

This case arises from efforts by the Environmental Protection Agency (EPA) and the State of Iowa to recover over 10 million dollars in response costs incurred in the clean up of a pesticide formulation facility operated by the Aidex

Corporation in Mills County, Iowa. Aidex operated the facility from 1974 through 1981, when it was declared bankrupt. Investigations by the EPA in the early 1980s revealed a highly contaminated site. Hazardous substances were found in deteriorating containers, in the surface soil, in fauna samples, and in the shallow zone of the groundwater, threatening the source of irrigation and drinking water for area residents. Using funds from the "Hazardous Substance Superfund," see 26 U.S.C. § 9507, the EPA, in cooperation with the State of Iowa, undertook various remedial actions to clean up the site.

The EPA now seeks to recover its response costs from eight pesticide manufacturers who did business with Aidex, in particular, who hired Aidex to formulate their technical grade pesticides into commercial grade pesticides....

CERCLA places the ultimate responsibility for clean up on "those responsible for problems caused by the disposal of chemical poisons," by authorizing suit against four classes of parties: (1) the owners and operators of a facility at which there is a release or threatened release of hazardous substances; (2) the owners or operators of such a facility any time in the past when hazardous substances were disposed of; (3) any person who "arranged for" the treatment or disposal of a hazardous substance at the facility; and (4) the persons who transported hazardous substances to the facility. 42 U.S.C. § 9607(a). Most courts have held CERCLA imposes strict liability and joint and several liability. Only a limited number of statutorily-prescribed defenses are available. See 42 U.S.C. § 9607(b). [Citations.]

CERCLA's sweep, while broad, is more limited than RCRA's in terms of the substances it covers. Tailored particularly to hazardous waste sites, CERCLA liability may attach only to those responsible for "hazardous substances" as defined in the statute. See 42 U.S.C. § 9601(14). Three of the pesticide wastes found at the Aidex site are *not* alleged to be "hazardous substances" under CERCLA. For this reason, plaintiffs have sued only six of the eight defendants under CERCLA. [All of the chemical wastes found at the Aidex site were alleged to be solid or hazardous wastes under RCRA.][3]

... As to each of the six CERCLA defendants, plaintiffs allege they by contract, agreement, or otherwise, "arranged for" the disposal of a hazardous substance when they contracted with Aidex to formulate their technical grade pesticides into commercial grade pesticides. Plaintiffs allege defendants owned the technical grade pesticide alleged to be a "hazardous substance" under CERCLA, the work in process, and the resulting commercial grade product; that is, the defendant retained ownership of its pesticide throughout the formulation and packaging process. Moreover, plaintiffs allege that the generation of wastes containing "hazardous substances" is an "inherent" part of the formulation

---

[3]"Solid waste" includes any "garbage, refuse, sludge ... and other discarded material...." 42 U.S.C. § 6903(27). "Hazardous waste" is defined as a solid waste or combination of solid waste which may increase mortality or illness or pose a health or environmental hazard. *Id.* § 6903(5).

process through spills, cleaning of equipment, mixing and grinding operations, production of batches which do not meet specifications, and other means. Finally, plaintiffs allege Aidex in fact generated such wastes and disposed of them on the Aidex site.

....

Liability Under CERCLA

To establish a prima facie case of liability under CERCLA, plaintiffs must establish

(1) the Aidex site is a "facility";

(2) a "release" or "threatened release" of a "hazardous substance" from the Aidex site has occurred;

(3) the release or threatened release has caused the United States to incur response costs; and

(4) the defendants fall within at least one of the four classes of responsible persons described in section 9607(a). [Citation.]

The complaint adequately alleges facts which would establish the first three elements, and defendants do not challenge these allegations for purposes of this appeal. At issue in this appeal is whether the defendants "arranged for" the disposal of hazardous substances under the Act, and thus fall within the class of responsible persons described in section 9607(a)(3). In finding plaintiffs' allegations sufficient to hold defendants liable as responsible persons, the district court relied on the principle that CERCLA should be broadly interpreted and took guidance from common law rules regarding vicarious liability. In particular, the district court found that defendants could be liable under common law for the abnormally dangerous activities of Aidex acting as an independent contractor, *see* Restatement (Second) of Torts § 427A (1965), holding that the common law was an appropriate source of guidance when the statutory language and legislative history of CERCLA prove inconclusive.

The six CERCLA defendants challenge the district court's decision on appeal, arguing the court's "hazardous activity" analogy is inapplicable to the facts of this case, and that Aidex, not they, "owned the hazardous waste and made the crucial decision how it would be disposed of or treated, and by whom." They argue Aidex was hired "to formulate, not to dispose," and that imposition of liability under CERCLA on these facts would lead to "limitless" liability. Finally, defendants assert the plain meaning of the statute requires an intent to dispose of some waste, or, at the very least, the authority to control the disposal process, and that neither are alleged by plaintiffs here.

The plaintiffs counter that defendants' ownership of the technical grade pesticide, the work in process, and the commercial grade product establishes the requisite authority to control Aidex's operations. Plaintiffs argue that because the generation of pesticide-containing wastes is inherent in the pesticide formulation process, Aidex could not formulate defendants' pesticides without wasting and disposing of some portion of them. Thus, plaintiffs argue, defendants could not have hired Aidex to formulate their pesticides without also "arranging for" the disposal of the waste.

We begin our analysis with the language of the CERCLA statute. Section 9607(a)(3) provides in relevant part:

> Notwithstanding any other provision or rule of law, and subject only to the defenses set forth in subsection (b) of this section —
>
> ....
>
> (3) any person who by contract, agreement, or otherwise arranged for disposal or treatment, or arranged with a transporter for transport for disposal or treatment, of hazardous substances owned or possessed by such person, by any other party or entity, at any facility or incineration vessel owned or operated by another party or entity and containing such hazardous substances ...
>
> ... from which there is a release, or a threatened release which causes the incurrence of response costs, of a hazardous substance, shall be liable for —
>
> (A) all costs of removal or remedial action incurred by the United States Government or a State ... not inconsistent with the national contingency plan.

"Arrange for" is not defined by the statute, but "disposal" is. "Disposal" includes "the discharge, deposit, injection, dumping, spilling, leaking, or placing" of any hazardous substance such that the substance "may enter the environment." 42 U.S.C. § 6903(3). *See* 42 U.S.C. § 9601(29).

Citing dictionary definitions of the word "arrange,"[7] defendants argue they can be liable under section 9607(a)(3) only if they intended to dispose of a waste. Defendants argue further the complaint alleges only an intent to arrange for formulation of a valuable product, and no intent to arrange for the disposal of a waste can be inferred from these allegations. We reject defendants' narrow reading of both the complaint and the statute.

Congress used broad language in providing for liability for persons who "by contract, agreement, *or otherwise arranged for*" the disposal of hazardous substances. While the legislative history of CERCLA sheds little light on the intended meaning of this phrase, courts have concluded that a liberal judicial interpretation is consistent with CERCLA's "overwhelmingly remedial" statutory scheme. [Citations.]

Both the First and Second Circuits have declared they "will not interpret section 9607(a) in any way that apparently frustrates the statute's goals, in the absence of a specific congressional intent otherwise." [Citations.] We thus

---

[7]Defendants contend the word "arrange" means to come to an agreement" or "to make plans, prepare." *See* Webster's Third New International Dictionary 120 (1961).

interpret the phrase "otherwise arranged for" in view of the two essential purposes of CERCLA:

> First, Congress intended that the federal government be immediately given the tools necessary for a prompt and effective response to the problems of national magnitude resulting from hazardous waste disposal. Second, Congress intended that those responsible for problems caused by the disposal of chemical poisons bear the costs and responsibility for remedying the harmful conditions they created.

The second goal — that those responsible should pay for clean up — would be thwarted by acceptance of defendants' argument that the allegations in plaintiffs' complaint do not sufficiently allege they "arranged for" disposal of their hazardous substances. While defendants characterize their relationship with Aidex as pertaining solely to formulation of a useful product, courts have not hesitated to look beyond defendants' characterizations to determine whether a transaction in fact involves an arrangement for the disposal of a hazardous substance. In *Conservation Chemical* [*United States v. Conservation Chem.*, 619 F. Supp. 162 (W.D. Mo. 1985)], for example, the court found defendants' sale of lime slurry and fly ash by-products to neutralize and treat other hazardous substances at a hazardous waste site could constitute "arranging for disposal" of the lime slurry and fly ash. Denying defendants' motions for summary judgment, the court reasoned that defendants contracted with the owner of the site "for deposit or placement" of their hazardous substances on the site, and thus could be found liable under the statute.

Other courts have imposed CERCLA liability where defendants sought to characterize their arrangement with another party who disposed of their hazardous substances as a "sale" rather than a "disposal." [Citations.] In the *G.E.* [*New York v. General Electric Co.*, 592 F. Supp. 291 (N.D.N.Y. 1984)] case, General Electric had sold used transformer oil to a dragstrip, which used the oil for dust control. The oil contained PCBs and other hazardous substances, and the State of New York sought to recover costs for clean up of the site from G.E. In denying G.E.'s motion to dismiss, the court emphasized G.E. allegedly arranged for the dragstrip to take away its used transformer oil with "knowledge or imputed knowledge" that the oil would be deposited on the land surrounding the dragstrip. Stating that CERCLA liability could not be "facilely circumvented" by characterizing arrangements as "sales," the *G.E.* Court cited CERCLA's legislative history: "[P]ersons cannot escape liability by 'contracting away' their responsibility or alleging that the incident was caused by the act or omission of a third party."

Courts have also held defendants "arranged for" disposal of wastes at a particular site even when defendants did not know the substances would be deposited at that site or in fact believed they would be deposited elsewhere. [Citations.]

Courts have, however, refused to impose liability where a "useful" substance is sold to another party, who then incorporates it into a product, which is later disposed of. [Citations.] Defendants attempt to analogize the present case to those cited above, but the analogy fails. Not only is there no transfer of ownership of the hazardous substances in this case (defendants retain ownership throughout), but the activity undertaken by Aidex is significantly different from the activity undertaken by, for example, Florida Power & Light. Aidex is performing a process on products owned by defendants for defendants' benefit and at their direction; waste is generated and disposed of contemporaneously with the process. Florida Power & Light, on the other hand, purchased electrical transformers for approximately 40 years, and then made the decision to dispose of them at the site in question. *Florida Power & Light Co. v. Allis Chalmers Corp.*, 27 Env't Rep. Cas. (BNA) at 1558-60 (S.D. Fla. 1988). Allis Chalmers was thus far more removed from the disposal than the defendants are in this case.

Defendants nonetheless contend they should escape liability because they had no authority to control Aidex's operations, and our *NEPACCO* decision states "[i]t is the authority to control the handling and disposal of hazardous substances that is critical under the statutory scheme." *NEPACCO*, 810 F.2d at 743. In *NEPACCO*, we were confronted with the argument that only individuals who *owned* or *possessed* hazardous substances could be liable under CERCLA. We rejected that notion and imposed liability, in addition, on those who had the authority to control the disposal, even without ownership or possession. Defendants in this case, of course, actually owned the hazardous substances, as well as the work in process....

Plaintiffs alleged defendants contracted with Aidex for the formulation of their hazardous substances — technical grade pesticides — into commercial grade pesticides. Plaintiffs further alleged that inherent in the formulation process was the generation and disposal of wastes containing defendants' hazardous substances. Finally, plaintiffs alleged that defendants retained ownership of their hazardous substances throughout the formulation process. We hold these allegations are sufficient to establish — for purposes of defeating defendants' motion to dismiss — that defendants "arranged for" the disposal of hazardous substances under CERCLA, 42 U.S.C. § 9607(a)(3), and "contributed to" the disposal of hazardous wastes under RCRA, 42 U.S.C. § 6973(a). We affirm the judgment of the district court in part, reverse in part, and remand for further proceedings consistent with this opinion.

NOTES AND QUESTIONS

1. The EPA will often seek to impose liability on a potentially responsible party under both RCRA section 7003, 42 U.S.C. § 6973, and CERCLA section 107(a), 42 U.S.C. § 9607(a) or section 106(a), 42 U.S.C. § 9606(a). Although the same conduct may constitute a violation under both statutes, the requirements for liability vary in a number of respects. The class of persons covered under

RCRA section 7003, which includes those who "contribute" to the offending conduct, is conceptually broader than those who "arrange for" the disposal of hazardous substances under CERCLA section 107(a)(3). On the other hand, CERCLA section 106(a) contains no limitation regarding the class of persons subject to EPA abatement orders. Both RCRA section 7003 and CERCLA section 106(a) are triggered by conduct which "may present an imminent and substantial endangerment" — a broad standard, yet still more rigorous than simply showing a "threat of a release" of a hazardous substance under CERCLA section 107(a). CERCLA also authorizes response actions by the federal government with respect to dangers presented by nonhazardous pollutants or contaminants in certain situations. *See* CERCLA section 104(a), 42 U.S.C. § 9604(a). Citizens seeking to abate potential harms resulting from hazardous substances will be restricted to using RCRA because section 106(a) of CERCLA is available only to the federal government. The only exception is that CERCLA section 310(a), 42 U.S.C. § 9659(a), permits citizens to seek enforcement of a final section 106(a) abatement order, even though they cannot maintain a direct action.

2. *Hazardous Substances*. One of the requisite elements in a prima facie case for recovery of response costs under CERCLA section 107(a) is the presence of a hazardous substance at the site. In *Aceto*, the state and federal government plaintiffs relied upon the same core allegations to support their claims under both CERCLA and RCRA. However, since several of the pesticide wastes found at the site were not "hazardous substances" within the scope of CERCLA section 101(14), only RCRA liability could attach with respect to certain defendants. RCRA, through its expansive regulatory coverage of "solid wastes," applies to a broader class of substances than CERCLA. *See* 42 U.S.C. § 6901; 42 U.S.C. § 6903(5) (defining hazardous waste); 42 U.S.C. § 6903(27) (defining solid waste). The definition of "hazardous substances" in CERCLA, though, incorporates by reference hazardous or toxic substances under RCRA, as well as under the Clean Air Act, Clean Water Act, and the Toxic Substances Control Act. See section 101(14), 42 U.S.C. § 9601(14). The EPA also designates as hazardous additional substances which "may present substantial danger" to public health or the environment; the agency then promulgates regulations setting reportable quantities. *See* 42 U.S.C. § 9602(a). Despite the similarity in terminology, a material that is not a "hazardous waste" under RCRA may still be considered a hazardous "substance" under CERCLA. *See Arizona v. Motorola, Inc.*, 774 F. Supp. 566, 571 (D. Ariz. 1991).

3. CERCLA also gives broad authority to the EPA to respond to "pollutants or contaminants" which have not been designated as hazardous in circumstances which "may present an imminent and substantial endangerment" to health or the environment. *See* 42 U.S.C. § 9604(a)(1)(B); § 9601(33) (defining "pollutant or contaminant"). Private parties are only potentially responsible for cleanup costs and natural resource damages and subject to CERCLA's reporting requirements with respect to hazardous substances, however. Despite the liberal provisions for listing hazardous substances pursuant to CERCLA, questions of application remain. *United States v. Serafini*, 750 F. Supp. 168 (M.D. Pa. 1990) involved whether scrap material, which was not listed as a hazardous substance under CERCLA, could nevertheless implicate statutory liability where the material, when burned, released benzene and hydrogen chloride which were substances on the EPA list promulgated under section 101(14). The plaintiff argued that since the generator defendant knew or should have known that fires at the site were commonplace, the disposal of the scrap material was "tantamount" to disposal of the hazardous substances released. The court disagreed, and held that CERCLA's policy necessitated a determination of hazardous wastes on a substance by substance basis for purposes of statutory liability.

4. *Petroleum Exclusion*. The definition of "hazardous substance" in CERCLA specifically excludes "petroleum, including crude oil or any fraction thereof which is not otherwise specifically listed or designated as a hazardous substance." § 101(14), 42 U.S.C. § 9601(14);[(Also excluded from definition of "pollutants or contaminants" under section 101(33)]. Since the statute fails to amplify the meaning of the petroleum exclusion clause, interpretation of its scope and application has presented difficulties.

Courts generally have found that the clause effectively removes from CERCLA coverage hazardous substances which are inherent in petroleum products but does not extend to subsequent contamination of petroleum. In *Wilshire Westwood Assoc. v. Atlantic Richfield*, 881 F.2d 801, 810 (9th Cir. 1989) the court held that the petroleum exclusion applied to include not only indigenous components of unrefined and refined gasoline but also certain hazardous additives added during the refining process. *Compare Cose v. Getty Oil Co.*, 4 F.3d 700, 704 (9th Cir. 1993) (separated sediment and water found at bottom of crude oil storage tank does not fit within the petroleum exclusion clause). *Also see United States v. Gurley*, 43 F.2d 1188, 1199 (8th Cir. 1994) (refining wastes which contained PCBs and sulfuric acid were not within the scope of the petroleum exclusion because hazardous substances did not naturally occur in the crude oil). The EPA has determined that the exclusion applies to all kinds of petroleum products. *See* 50 Fed. Reg. 13, 460 (April 4, 1985). The EPA can still respond to dangers presented by those substances pursuant to its authority under section 104(a), 42 U.S.C. § 9604(a).

NURAD, INC. v. WILLIAM E. HOOPER & SONS CO.

966 F.2d 837 (4th Cir. 1992)

WILKINSON, CIRCUIT JUDGE:

This is a suit brought by the current owner of a piece of property for reimbursement of costs it incurred in removing from the property some underground storage tanks and their hazardous contents. The current owner sought reimbursement from previous owners and tenants at the site, claiming that they were liable under the Comprehensive Environmental Response, Compensation, and Liability Act (CERCLA) as "owners" or "operators" of the facility at the time of "disposal" of the hazardous substances. 42 U.S.C. § 9607(a)(2). The district court entered summary judgment against the original owner of the tanks and in favor of the other defendants.

We think the district court was correct both in holding that the original owner was liable under CERCLA and in holding that the tenant defendants were not liable as "operators" of the facility in question. We think it erred, however, in absolving certain of the previous owner defendants on the ground that they were not owners "at the time of disposal." By requiring proof of affirmative participation in hazardous waste disposal as a prerequisite to liability under § 9607(a)(2), the district court misconstrued both the statutory definition of "disposal" and a decision of this court interpreting that definition. We think the statute plainly imposes liability on a party who owns a facility at the time hazardous waste leaks from an underground storage tank on the premises. Any other result would substantially undermine CERCLA's goal of encouraging voluntary cleanup on the part of those in a position to do so.

I.

Plaintiff Nurad, Inc., brought this lawsuit to recover the costs it incurred in removing several underground storage tanks (USTs) from a piece of property it owns in Baltimore, Maryland. From 1905 to 1963, Wm. E. Hooper & Sons Co. (the Hooper Co. or the Company) owned the site and adjacent properties, collectively known as Hooperwood Mills. At some point before 1935, the Hooper Co. began to install tanks for the storage of mineral spirits which it used to coat fabrics in its textile finishing plant. The Company continued to use the tanks for that purpose until 1962, when it shut down its finishing operations. At that time, the Hooper Co. abandoned the USTs and did not remove the mineral spirits.

In 1963, the Hooper Co. sold Hooperwood Mills to Property Investors, Inc. Frank Nicoll, as president and principal shareholder of Property Investors and its successor, Monumental Enterprises, Inc., leased several of the buildings on Hooperwood Mills to various tenants, none of which ever used the USTs. Then in 1976, Monumental Enterprises sold Hooperwood Mills to Kenneth Mumaw, who subdivided the property and sold a portion of it to Nurad.

Nurad's operations at the site involve the manufacture of antennae. In all its years at the site, Nurad apparently never used the USTs. In 1987, however, the Maryland Department of the Environment informed Nurad that the tanks had not been properly abandoned and required that they be removed from the ground or filled with sand or concrete within 180 days. Nurad sought assistance with the cleanup from several of the previous owners and tenants of the site, but they all refused. Nurad then hired an environmental consultant and a tank removal contractor to analyze the contents of the tanks and dispose of several of the tanks and the surrounding soil.

In 1990, Nurad filed this CERCLA suit, seeking reimbursement for approximately $226,000 in cleanup costs from former owners of the site (the Hooper

Co., Nicoll, Mumaw, and Monumental Enterprises); from former tenants at the site (Allstates Moving & Storage, Raymond B. McMillan, Universal Laboratory Installations, Inc., and Monumental Millwork); and from James Hooper, Jr., and Lawrence Hooper (the Hooper brothers), who were shareholders and directors of the Hooper Co. ...

II.

Congress enacted CERCLA to address the increasing environmental and health problems associated with inactive hazardous waste sites. The statute encourages private cleanup of such hazards by providing a cause of action for the recovery of costs incurred in responding to a "release" of hazardous substances at any "facility." 42 U.S.C. § 9607; H. Rep. No. 1016, 96th Cong., 2d. Sess. 17, reprinted in 1980 U.S.C.C.A.N. 6119, 6120. Under CERCLA, a person who incurs such cleanup costs is entitled to recover from anyone who qualifies as a "responsible person" under the statute. 42 U.S.C. § 9607. Responsible persons include the current "owner" or "operator" of the facility, *id.* § 9607(a)(1), any person who "owned" or "operated" the facility at the time of "disposal" of a hazardous substance, *id.* § 9607(a)(2), any person who "arranged for disposal or treatment" of hazardous substances at the facility, *id.* § 9607(a)(3), and any person who accepts hazardous substances "for transport to disposal or treatment facilities, incineration vessels or sites," *id.* § 9607(a)(4). Any of these responsible persons is strictly liable for costs incurred in responding to the release of a hazardous substance at the facility, subject only to the defenses set forth in subsection (b)." 42 U.S.C.§ 9607(a). The court has the authority to "allocate response costs among liable parties using such equitable factors as the court determines are appropriate." *Id.* § 9613(f)(1)....

A.

We shall first address Nurad's claims against the former tenants at the site. The district court dismissed Nurad's claims against the tenant defendants on the grounds that they lacked the authority to control the USTs and therefore did not "operate[]" a "facility" under § 9607(a)(2). Nurad raises three objections to this aspect of the district court's ruling. First, Nurad contends that the district court applied the wrong legal standard in interpreting the word "operator." In Nurad's view, the court too narrowly defined that term to include only those persons who actually exercised control over the facility.

We do not agree with Nurad that the district court applied an improper standard. The district court applied the correct standard in holding that the tenant defendants need not have exercised actual control in order to qualify as operators under § 9607(a)(2), so long as the authority to control the facility was present. Although the court did note that the tenant defendants "never actively participated in the disposal of hazardous substances" at the site, the court's decision quite properly turned on the fact that they lacked "authority to control the operations or decisions involving the disposal of hazardous substances at the Site or the contents of the USTs." Indeed, the district court's examination of the terms of the various leases in question indicated that it recognized that authority to control — not actual control — was the appropriate standard. This is the definition of the word "operator" that most courts have adopted, and it is one which properly declines to absolve from CERCLA liability a party who possessed the authority to abate the damage caused by the disposal of hazardous substances but who declined to actually exercise that authority by undertaking efforts at a cleanup. Under this standard, the district court was entitled to consider a defendant's actual conduct as evidence of the authority to control, but it clearly did not inflate that item of evidentiary significance into a dispositive legal requirement. [Citations]

Second, Nurad objects to the district court's interpretation of the word "facility." Liability under § 9607(a)(2) extends to any person who "operated any facility" at which hazardous substances were disposed of, and the district court proceeded on the premise that the "facility" in this case was confined to the USTs. Nurad contends that the "facility" at issue here encompassed the entire Nurad site, so that the proper inquiry is whether the tenant defendants had control over any portion of that site, not just the storage tanks.

We disagree. CERCLA defines "facility" to include a "building, structure, ... storage container" or other "area where a hazardous substance has been deposited, stored, disposed of, or placed, or otherwise come to be located." 42 U.S.C. § 9601(9). In this case, the only "area" where hazardous substances have "come to be located" is in and around the storage tanks, so the relevant "facility" is properly confined to that area. To be sure, the tanks are a part of the larger piece of property that is now the Nurad site. During the relevant period, however, the site was subdivided and separate portions of it were leased out to individual tenants. The fact that those tenants may have had control over a building that was adjacent to the USTs is irrelevant under the statute; a defendant operates a "facility" only if it has authority to control the area where the hazardous substances were located. Thus, while liability under § 9607(a)(2) is strict, it nonetheless extends only to those who have authority over the area where hazardous substances are stored. The statute places accountability in the hands of those capable of abating further environmental harm, while Nurad's proposed definition of "facility" would rope in parties who were powerless to act.

Finally, Nurad contends that even if the court applied the correct legal standard, it erred in its factual determination that the tenant defendants lacked the authority to control the USTs. Nurad contends that as lessees the tenants had a property interest that necessarily included the implicit authority to control the portion of the site that contained the USTs. We agree with the district court, however, that the terms of the tenants' lease agreements conclusively establish that their authority as tenants did not extend to the USTs. Defendant Allstates Moving & Storage, for example, leased parts of several buildings on the Nurad site to conduct its freight transfer and storage operations from 1966 to 1979, but

Allstates' lease agreements never conferred upon it any authority over the USTs, which were under the active management of the landlord. The initial lease demised to Allstates the "1st floor of Building 4C," and limited it to use "as an office and warehouse for the storage of furniture, appliances, and other such equipment and material consistent with the business of the tenant." In addition, the lease demised to Allstates use of the following common areas:

> the lavatory marked I and the parking area marked II and ... the railsiding in the said complex to spot boxcars plus the ... driveways to the siding in order to load and unload goods stored in the demised premises.

Subsequent lease agreements demised to Allstates portions of other buildings on the site, but none expanded its authority to use any common areas other than those specifically identified in the initial agreement, and none purported to give Allstates authority to use the areas where the tanks were situated.

The other tenant defendants also lacked authority to control the USTs. Universal Laboratory Installations, Inc., occupied portions of two of the buildings at Hooperwood Mills under an oral lease for nine months during 1972. Universal used the buildings as an office and storage facility for its cabinet installation business. Under Universal's oral agreement, it had the right to occupy specific portions of the two buildings, rights of ingress and egress to those buildings, and the right to use the loading dock. Monumental Millwork leased a portion of one of the buildings at the site from 1969 to 1978 for use as an office and for the assembly and storage of doors and windows. Nurad makes broad assertions about both Universal's and Millwork's authority over the Nurad site, but has adduced no evidence sufficient to contradict the trial court's conclusion that they had no authority to control the USTs or their contents.

Given the precise language of the lease agreements and the absence of any express authority to use the USTs, we think it would be unreasonable to assume that the tenant defendants possessed any implicit authority to exercise control over the tanks. Indeed, Nurad's suggestion that these tenants had some de facto authority over the USTs is inconsistent with the landlord's actual practice, which required a separate lease agreement when in 1966 the Hooper Co., then a tenant, sought to use one of the tanks. Under the circumstances, the tenant defendants may even have been trespassing if they had attempted to assume the role of "operator" of the USTs. We thus agree with the district court that each of the tenant defendants — Allstates Moving & Storage, Universal Laboratory Installations, and Monumental Millwork — was entitled to summary judgment. Since Nurad's only allegations against McMillan were that he was president and sole shareholder of Allstates, our holding requires that McMillan be granted summary judgment also.

B.

Next we address Nurad's claims against James and Lawrence Hooper. Nurad contends that the district court erred in finding that the Hooper brothers did not qualify as operators. Even if we assume that a corporate officer may be held personally liable as an operator, we agree with the district court that the Hooper brothers lacked the requisite authority to control the USTs or to prevent the disposal of hazardous waste at the site. It is true that the Hooper brothers were vice presidents of the Hooper Co. beginning in the early 1960s. Any authority they possessed was entirely subordinate to that of their father, however, who as president and majority stockholder exercised ultimate authority over the finishing plant. The senior Hooper was not anxious to cede this authority to his sons; an uncontradicted affidavit described him as "a man of strong will and temperament suited to running the entire affairs of the corporation, which he did." Nurad has failed to direct our attention to any evidence that would undermine the district court's conclusion that "James Hooper, Sr., as president during the relevant times, retained all decision-making authority over the company including the daily operations at the finishing plant," and that the younger Hoopers should accordingly not face CERCLA liability.

Finally, we address Nurad's claims against the previous owners of the site, the Hooper Co. and Kenneth Mumaw. Neither the Hooper Co. nor Mumaw appeals from the district court's conclusion that they are prior owners of the facility. At oral argument, Mumaw did direct our attention to the fact that he held legal title to the property for only a short period of time. We do not think, however, that the word "owned" is a word that admits of varying degrees. Such equitable considerations as the duration of ownership may well be relevant at a later stage of the proceedings when the district court allocates response costs among liable parties, see 42 U.S.C. § 9613(f)(1), but we reject any suggestion that a short-term owner is somehow not an owner for purposes of § 9607(a)(2).

Because both the Hooper Co. and Mumaw are prior owners of the facility, we must ask whether recovery against them is nonetheless barred because no "disposal" of hazardous wastes took place on their watch. The district court took a narrow view of the word "disposal," limiting it to disposal by affirmative human conduct. Thus, the court concluded that the Hooper Co. was liable because it actively disposed of hazardous substances and then abandoned them in the USTs. The court held, however, that Mumaw was not liable — even though passive migration of hazardous substances may have occurred during his ownership — since he did not take an active role in managing the tanks or their contents. We think the district court's restrictive construction of "disposal" ignores the language of the statute, contradicts clear circuit precedent, and frustrates the fundamental purposes of CERCLA. The statute defines "disposal" in 42 U.S.C. § 9601(29) by incorporating by reference the definition found in the Resource Conservation and Recovery Act (RCRA). That definition states:

> The term "disposal" means the discharge, deposit, injection, dumping, spilling, leaking, or placing of any solid waste or hazardous waste into or on any land or water so that such solid waste or hazardous waste or any

constituent thereof may enter the environment or be emitted into the air or discharged into any waters, including ground waters.

42 U.S.C. § 6903(3). Some of the words in this definition appear to be primarily of an active voice. [Citation] This is true of "deposit," "injection," "dumping," and "placing." Others of the words, however, readily admit to a passive component: hazardous waste may leak or spill without any active human participation. The district court arbitrarily deprived these words of their passive element by imposing a requirement of active participation as a prerequisite to liability.

Indeed, this circuit has already rejected the "strained reading" of disposal which would limit its meaning to "active human conduct." *United States v. Waste Ind., Inc.*, 734 F.2d 159, 164-65 (4th Cir. 1984). In *Waste Industries*, the court held that Congress intended the 42 U.S.C. § 6903(3) definition of disposal "to have a range of meanings," including not only active conduct, but also the reposing of hazardous waste and its subsequent movement through the environment. Here the district court attempted to distinguish *Waste Industries* on the ground that it involved the authority of the Environmental Protection Agency to demand cleanup by former owners and operators under RCRA. The district court thought that the *Waste Industries* definition was necessary to close a loophole in RCRA's environmental protection scheme, and believed "that the only way for the *Waste Industries* court to preserve the EPA's ability to demand cleanup by the actual former owners and operators was to define 'disposal' in RCRA to cover completely passive repose or movement through the environment." In this CERCLA action, by contrast, the district court noted that the current owner and all prior owners were already defendants and in some cases were liable for cleanup costs.

We think the district court was bound to follow *Waste Industries* in interpreting the term "disposal." It is true that Waste Industries interpreted the definition in the context of RCRA, but Congress expressly provided that under CERCLA the term "shall have the meaning provided in section 1004" of RCRA (42 U.S.C. § 6903(3)). 42 U.S.C. § 9601(29). Moreover, the aim of both RCRA and CERCLA is to encourage the cleanup of hazardous waste conditions. Whether the context is one of prospective enforcement of hazardous waste removal under RCRA or an action for reimbursement of response costs under CERCLA, a requirement conditioning liability upon affirmative human participation in contamination equally frustrates the statutory purpose.

It is easy to see how the district court's requirement of active participation would frustrate the statutory policy of encouraging "voluntary private action to remedy environmental hazards." [Citation] Under the district court's view, an owner could avoid liability simply by standing idle while an environmental hazard festers on his property. Such an owner could insulate himself from liability by virtue of his passivity, so long as he transfers the property before any response costs are incurred. A more conscientious owner who undertakes the task of cleaning up the environmental hazard would, on the other hand, be liable as the current owner of the facility, since "disposal" is not a part of the current owner liability scheme under 42 U.S.C. § 9607(a)(1). The district court's view thus introduces the anomalous situation where a current owner, such as Nurad, who never used the storage tanks could bear a substantial share of the cleanup costs, while a former owner who was similarly situated would face no liability at all. A CERCLA regime which rewards indifference to environmental hazards and discourages voluntary efforts at waste cleanup cannot be what Congress had in mind.

The district court's view of the CERCLA definition of disposal is also at odds with CERCLA's strict liability emphasis. The trigger to liability under § 9607(a)(2) is ownership or operation of a facility at the time of disposal, not culpability or responsibility for the contamination. [Citations] We must decline therefore to engraft onto the statute additional prerequisites to the reimbursement of response costs which Congress did not place there.

Thus, we hold that § 9607(a)(2) imposes liability not only for active involvement in the "dumping" or "placing" of hazardous waste at the facility, but for ownership of the facility at a time that hazardous waste was "spilling" or "leaking." The only remaining question is whether a statutory disposal of hazardous waste occurred during the period of Hooper's and Mumaw's ownership.

We think for the following reasons that it did. Initially, the record supports the conclusion that both the Hooper Co. and Mumaw owned the facility at a time when the mineral spirits were "leaking" from the tanks. Nurad has established that the Hooper Co. began to install the USTs some time before 1935 and that mineral spirits reposed in the tanks until they were removed by Nurad in 1988-89. Nurad has further presented uncontroverted evidence that at the time the tanks were removed the soil around several of the tanks was contaminated with mineral spirits. Indeed, the district court found that the "mineral spirits in the excavated soil show an exact chromatographic match" with those in one tank, and that another of the tanks had "corrosion holes in the bottom and was underlain by discolored soils that emanated solvent odors." Neither the Hooper Co. nor Mumaw has pointed to anything to overcome the presumption that the leaking that has occurred was not a sudden event, but the result of a gradual and progressive course of environmental contamination that included these defendants' period of ownership. We do not think in such circumstances that Congress intended to impose upon a CERCLA plaintiff the onerous burden of pinpointing at what precise point a leakage may have begun....

Finally, we agree with the district court that the Hooper Co.'s claim that there was no statutory disposal is especially insubstantial. The Company disposed of hazardous substances at the site by depositing them in the USTs and abandoning them upon closing its finishing plant in 1962. The statute provides that "disposal" includes the "placing" of any hazardous waste "into or on any land" so that such hazardous waste "may enter the environment," 42 U.S.C. § 6903(3), and courts have specifically held that depositing hazardous waste into enclosed containers fits this definition. [Citation] Even if we accept the Hooper Co.'s argument that the storage of useful mineral spirits for active use as a raw material cannot constitute disposal because it is not "waste," we think there clearly was a disposal in 1962 when the Company closed down the finishing plant and abandoned the tanks. At that point, the mineral spirits clearly became "waste," as they were abandoned and were apparently never again used. *See* 40 C.F.R. § 261.2 (defining waste as any "discarded" material, or material which has been "abandoned"). The Hooper Co. is quick to point out that it later "sold" the USTs and their contents to Property Investors, but we agree with the district court that the sale of the previously abandoned tanks to a real estate investor — who had no use for the mineral spirits or the tanks and apparently never used them — cannot reverse the earlier disposal. A defendant who has abandoned hazardous materials at a site cannot escape CERCLA liability by simply labelling a subsequent transfer of the property as a "sale" of the hazardous waste. [Citation]

III.

In sum, Nurad is entitled to reimbursement from some of the prior occupants of Hooperwood Mills, but not from all. We affirm the district court's dismissal of Nurad's claims against each of the tenant defendants and against the Hooper brothers, and we affirm the entry of summary judgment in Nurad's favor against the Hooper Co. We reverse the district court's denial of Nurad's motion for summary judgment as to Mumaw. We remand the case for further proceedings consistent with this opinion.

NOTES AND QUESTIONS

1. *Disposal.* Liability under section 107(a) of CERCLA requires a showing that the person "disposed of" hazardous substances. Courts have held that statutory liability under section 107(a) will not attach unless the disposal is characterized as an affirmative act to "get rid of" or "dump" the waste, but not for transfers or sales of a useful product which contains a hazardous substance. Merely labelling a transaction to be a "sale" does not exculpate the person from CERCLA liability, however. Since the Act imposes strict liability, courts will examine the character of the transaction rather than the intent or knowledge of the actors.

For example, in *3550 Stevens Creek Assocs. v. Barclays Bank of Cal.*, 915 F.2d 1355, 1363 (9th Cir. 1990) the court held that a private cost recovery action for removal of asbestos in a commercial building was precluded for failure to satisfy the "disposal" requirement in section 107(a)(2) of CERCLA. Further, the court noted that even if the asbestos fibers became "friable," the resulting hazard would be within the building and thus not "entering the environment" or "emitted into the air" within the definition of "disposal." 915 F.2d at 1361. *Also see Prudential Ins. Co. of America v. United States Gypsum*, 711 F. Supp. 1244,

1254 (D.N.J. 1989) (sale of asbestos-containing products used in the construction of a building not considered a "disposal" under CERCLA); *but see CP Holdings, Inc. v. Goldberg-Zoino & Assocs.*, 769 F. Supp. 432 (D.N.H. 1991) (sale of building containing asbestos qualified as "disposal" of hazardous waste under CERCLA where sellers knew that purchasers intended to demolish structure). *See generally* Hartigan & Davis, *Asbestos Abatement Cost Recovery Under the Comprehensive Environmental Response, Compensation, and Liability Act*, 14 HARV. ENVTL. L. REV. 253 (1990).

2. In *United States v. CDMG Realty Co.*, 96 F.3d 706 (3d Cir. 1996) the court held that the passive migration of contamination dumped at a site prior to acquisition by a subsequent owner did not constitute a "disposal" for purposes of CERCLA liability. The court reasoned that "disposal" often involves some affirmative human action such as spilling waste, or at least the leaking of material from barrels as in *Nurad*, rather than simply the gradual natural spreading of waste. The court also noted that "disposal" is a narrower concept than contemplated under the definition of "release" which is the triggering event to prompt a CERCLA response. Is the court's distinction valid? How difficult would it be to demonstrate scientifically whether material escaped from a barrel during a previous ownership rather than simply migrated?

3. *Private Cost Recovery Actions.* Congress enacted CERCLA to provide a mechanism for facilitating the cleanup of leaking hazardous waste sites. The statute carries out its goals through a bifurcated system which equips both governmental and private parties with the authority and means of responding to hazardous releases at abandoned and inactive waste disposal sites. The federal government may look to Superfund for resources in responding to hazardous waste disposal problems. The statute also authorizes private parties to maintain claims for recovery of costs involved in the cleanup of waste sites from the party responsible for the harm. The act is not intended, however, to create a cause of action for toxic torts to compensate for every injury resulting from hazardous waste contamination. *See Exxon v. Hunt*, 475 U.S. 355, 375 (1986); *Artesian Water Co. v. Government of New Castle County*, 650 F. Supp. 1269, 1285 (D. Del. 1987) (CERCLA does not compensate for economic losses or for personal injuries sustained attributable to the release of hazardous waste); *Wehner v. Syntex Corp.*, 681 F. Supp. 651, 653 (N.D. Cal. 1987) (diminished property value of home deemed nonrecoverable type of economic loss); *Piccolini v. Simon's Wrecking*, 686 F. Supp. 1063, 1068 (M.D. Pa. 1988) (no recovery for loss in value of land or lost income). Instead, CERCLA aims to focus its resources on the expeditious cleanup of waste sites in a cost-effective and environmentally sound manner. *See Ambrogi v. Gould, Inc.*, 750 F. Supp. 1233, 1238 (M.D. Pa. 1990). Consequently, private parties are restricted to recovery of "necessary costs of response" which are "consistent with the national contingency plan." *See* CERCLA § 107(a)(4)(B).

Although courts may differ somewhat in their articulation of the requirements for establishing a prima facie case for a private cost recovery action under section 107, the principal elements that a plaintiff must show include:

(1) the waste disposal site is a "facility" within the meaning of § 101(9), 42 U.S.C. § 9601(9);

(2) a "release" (§ 101(14), 42 U.S.C. § 9601(14)) or a "threatened release" of any "hazardous substance" (§ 101(22), 42 U.S.C. § 9601(22)) from that facility has occurred;

(3) which has caused the claimant to incur cleanup and response costs;

(4) the costs sought to be recouped were "necessary";

(5) the actions taken were consistent with the national contingency plan; and

(6) that the defendant is within one of the four classes of "covered persons" subject to the liability provisions of the statute in § 107(a).

See CERCLA § 107(a)(4)(B), 42 U.S.C. § 9607(a)(4)(B); *Ascon Props., Inc. v. Mobil Oil Co.*, 866 F.2d 1149, 1152 (9th Cir. 1989); *Dedham Water Co. v. Cumberland Farms Dairy*, 889 F.2d 1146, 1150 (1st Cir. 1989); *Channel Master Satellite v. JFD Elecs. Corp.*, 748 F. Supp. 373, 381 (E.D.N.C. 1990).

4. *Response.* The term "response" under CERCLA is defined as encompassing two types of actions — short-term cleanup measures called "removal" actions and the more comprehensive long-term "remedial" actions involving permanent containment or disposal programs. CERCLA § 101(25), 42 U.S.C. § 9601(25). The statute provides a partial list of representative removal actions, including security fencing, providing alternative water supplies, temporary evacuation and housing of threatened individuals, and other emergency assistance. CERCLA § 101(23), 42 U.S.C. § 9601(23). Examples of remedial actions listed in the statute include various containment actions, treatment or incineration, provision of alternative water supplies, and monitoring reasonably required to protect public health and welfare and the environment. CERCLA § 101(24), 42 U.S.C. § 9601(24).

The distinction between the two categories of response — although far from clear-cut — has significance in several respects. The cleanup standards governing removal actions are generally more limited and flexible than those pertaining to remedial actions. A remedial action must be both cost-effective and provide a permanent solution to the waste site. Also, a private party undertaking a remedial action cannot seek reimbursement from Superfund unless the site is listed on the National Priorities List, but is limited to seeking recovery from potentially responsible parties. *See generally* NOVICK, LAW OF ENVIRONMENTAL PROTEC-TION § 13.05[3]; *General Elec. Co. v. Litton Indus. Automation Sys.*, 920 F.2d 1415, 1419 (8th Cir. 1990) (excavation of soil and buried drums of waste characterized as removal action). The 1986 SARA amendments narrowed the distinction between the two types of response actions by providing that a removal action should "contribute to the efficient performance of any long term remedial action." CERCLA § 104(a)(2), 42 U.S.C. § 9604(a)(2).

5. *Response Costs.* Although section 107(a)(4)(B) authorizes recovery of "response costs," the statute does not define the term. As a consequence, courts have struggled over determining which claims by private parties should merit compensation. Courts have split, for example, over whether private parties can recover medical monitoring and surveillance expenses attributable to exposure to hazardous waste as proper "response costs" within the meaning of CERCLA § 107(a)(4)(B). *See Lutz v. Chromatex, Inc.*, 718 F. Supp. 413, 419 (M.D. Pa. 1989) (denied recovery for past and future medical monitoring expenses). *But see Brewer v. Ravan*, 680 F. Supp. 1176, 1179 (M.D. Tenn. 1988) (costs of medical testing and screening cognizable under CERCLA).

In *Ambrogi v. Gould, Inc.*, 750 F. Supp. 1233, 1238 (M.D. Pa. 1990) the court gave two justifications for holding that costs for air, soil and water testing and monitoring were within the scope of private response costs recoverable under CERCLA but that medical monitoring, including medical surveillance, health effects studies, and health assessments were not covered. First, in the 1986 SARA amendments, Congress provided for mandatory health assessments for each facility on the National Priority List, and authorized medical testing and monitoring studies of exposed individuals through the Agency for Toxic Substances and Disease Registry. Second, the court observed:

> [T]esting of air, soil, and water for exposure to hazardous wastes serves the purpose of determining if a removal or remedial action is necessary. If such action is required, testing and monitoring will determine if soil needs to be removed, water must be treated, and airborne particles eliminated. With medical testing, however, the primary purpose of the statute is frustrated since hazardous substances are not "removed" in the traditional sense of the word from the human body. Exposure may be reduced by evacuation of the area, but "removal" in terms of CERCLA is not the nature of the solution when it comes to the health concerns of the adjacent population at a particular site. That is why the traditional remedies of state tort actions are available to an aggrieved individual. Since a statute should be construed in harmony with the sphere of legal remedies available, Congress surely did not intend to create an overlap between traditional state tort claims and a "new" CERCLA federal toxic tort action. Thus, the purpose of the Act — i.e., the removal of hazardous waste *from the environment*, would seemingly preclude recovery of medical costs.

750 F. Supp. at 1250.

6. *Liability of Parent Corporations.* Courts have struggled to determine the nature and extent of control necessary to impose liability on a parent corporation for the environmental activities of a wholly owned subsidiary. The *Nurad* court's "authority to control" standard for determining status as an "operator" for CERCLA liability purposes has received mixed treatment in the courts. *Accord Kaiser Aluminum & Chemical Corp. v. Catellus Dev. Corp.*, 976 F.2d 1338, 1341-42 (9th Cir. 1992) (following *Nurad*'s authority to control standard).

Some courts, looking to the broad remedial purposes of CERCLA, have held parent corporations liable as "operators" by virtue of exercising a substantial degree of control over the operations of their subidiaries. *See Kayser-Roth*, 901 F.2d 24, 26-27 (1st Cir. 1990) (parent corporation exerted pervasive control over subsidiary, including environmental matters). In *Redwing Carriers, Inc. v. Saraland Apts.*, 94 F.3d 1489, 1504 (11th Cir. 1996) the court rejected the *Nurad* approach in favor of requiring that limited partners must either (1) actually participated in operating the site or in the activities resulting in disposal of hazardous substances or (2) actually exercised control over or were otherwise intimately involved in operations of the partnership. Similarly, in *United States v. Gurley*, 43 F.3d 1188, 1193 (8th Cir. 1994) the court held that some affirmative conduct was required for operator liability under CERCLA. Otherwise, it would produce the anomalous result of imposing liability as an operator on someone who never in fact operated a facility. Which is the better view?

7. The competing views on liability of parent corporations under CERCLA are summarized in *Lansford-Coaldale Joint Water Auth. v. Tonolli Corp.*, 4 F.3d 1209, 1221-1222 (3d Cir. 1993):

> Courts have fashioned two competing standards for the imposition of operator liability: what we term the "actual control" test and the "authority-to-control" test. Under the actual control standard, a corporation will only be held liable for the environmental violations of another corporation when there is evidence of substantial control exercised by one corporation over the activities of the other. In contrast, under the authority-to-control test, operator liability is imposed as long as one corporation had the capability to control, even if it was never utilized.
>
> We reject the Authority's contention that the authority-to-control standard should govern. We believe that test sweeps too broadly and we thus adopt the actual control standard, which appears to strike the appropriate middle ground, balancing the benefits of limited liability with CERCLA's remedial purposes. Under the actual control standard, while the longstanding rule of limited liability in the corporate context remains the background norm, a corporation cannot hide behind the corporate form to escape liability in those instances in which it played an active role in the management of a corporation responsible for environmental wrongdoing. In contrast, we believe that a rule which imposes liability on a corporation which never exercised its general authority over its subsidiary or sister corporation may unduly penalize the corporation for a decision by that corporation to benefit from one of the well-recognized and salutary purposes of the corporate form: specialization of management.
>
> The determination whether a corporation has exerted sufficient control to warrant imposition of operator liability requires an inherently fact-intensive

inquiry, involving consideration of the totality of the circumstances presented. The factors courts should consider focus on the extent of the corporation's involvement in the other corporation's day-to-day operations and its policy-making decisions. We understand the actual control standard to hold accountable for environmental violations those corporations which are not mere investors in other corporations, but instead have actively and substantially participated in the corporation's management.

8. In a recent decision by the Sixth Circuit Court of Appeals, *United States v. Cordova Chem. Co.*, 113 F.3d 572 (6th Cir. 1997), the court rejected the "middle-ground" approach as too "nebulous" and held that a parent corporation would be directly liable under section 107(a)(2) as an operator for the hazardous waste disposal activities of a wholly owned subsidiary only by piercing the corporate veil as determined by state law or where the parent jointly or independently directly operated the facitility. Also, the parent could be as an "owner" of the facility by piercing the corporate veil. *Also see Joslyn Mfg. Co. v. T.L. James & Co.*, 893 F.2d 80, 82-83 (5th Cir. 1990) (parent corporation could only be held derivatively liable as an owner and operator by piercing the corporate veil.)

9. *Arranger Liability.* In *United States v. TIC Investment Corp.*, 68 F.3d 1082, 1089 (8th Cir. 1995) the court held that direct "arranger" liability may be imposed on a parent corporation for a subsidiary's off-site disposal practices only where the parent had the authority and exercised actual or substantial control, directly or indirectly, over the subsidiary's arrangement for disposal of hazardous substances plus a causal connection or nexus existed between the parent corporation's conduct and the subsidiary's arrangement.

10. The commentary on the subject of corporate responsbility for environmental costs associated with CERCLA has been voluminous. *See generally* Stewart & Campbell, *Lessons from Parent Liability Under CERCLA*, 6 NAT. RESOURCES & ENV'T. 7 (1992); Oswald & Schipani, *CERCLA and the "Erosion" of Traditional Corporate Law Doctrine*, 86 NW. U.L. REV. 259, 301-15 (1992); Menell, *Legal Advising on Corporate Structure in the New Era of Environmental Liability*, 1990 COLUM. BUS. L. REV. 399; Healy, *Direct Liability for Hazardous Substance Cleanups Under CERCLA: A Comprehensive Approach*, 42 CASE W. RES. 65 (1992); Birg, *Redefining "Owner or Operator" Under CERCLA to Preserve Traditional Notions of Corporate Law*, 43 EMORY L.J. 772 (1994); Worden, *CERCLA Liability of Parent Corporations for the Act of Their Subsidiaries*, 93 IDAHO L. REV. 73 (1993).

UNITED STATES v. NORTHEASTERN PHARMACEUTICAL & CHEMICAL CO.

810 F.2d 726 (8th Cir. 1986)

McMILLIAN, CIRCUIT JUDGE.

Northeastern Pharmaceutical & Chemical Co. (NEPACCO), Edwin Michaels and John W. Lee appeal from a final judgment entered in the District Court for the Western District of Missouri finding them and Ronald Mills jointly and severally liable for response costs incurred by the government after December 11, 1980, and all future response costs relative to the cleanup of the Denney farm site that are not inconsistent with the national contingency plan (NCP) pursuant to §§ 104, 107 of the Comprehensive Environmental Response, Compensation, and Liability Act of 1980 (CERCLA), 42 U.S.C. §§ 9604, 9607. For reversal, appellants argue the district court erred in (1) applying CERCLA retroactively, (2) finding Michaels and Lee individually liable, ... (4) awarding response costs absent affirmative proof that the response costs were consistent with the NCP....

I. *Facts*

... Michaels formed NEPACCO, was a major shareholder, and was its president. Lee was NEPACCO's vice-president, the supervisor of its manufacturing plant located in Verona, Missouri, and also a shareholder. Mills was employed as shift supervisor at NEPACCO's Verona plant.

From April 1970 to January 1972 NEPACCO manufactured the disinfectant hexachlorophene at its Verona plant. NEPACCO leased the plant from Hoffman-Taff, Inc.; Syntex Agribusiness, Inc. (Syntex), is the successor to Hoffman-Taff. Michaels and Lee knew that NEPACCO's manufacturing process produced various hazardous and toxic byproducts, including 2, 4, 5-trichlorophenol (TCP), 2, 3, 7, 8-tetrachlorodibenzo-p-dioxin (TCDD or dioxin), and toluene. The waste byproducts were pumped into a holding tank which was periodically emptied by waste haulers. Occasionally, however, excess waste byproducts were sealed in 55-gallon drums and then stored at the plant.

In July 1971 Mills approached NEPACCO plant manager Bill Ray with a proposal to dispose of the waste-filled 55-gallon drums on a farm owned by James Denney located about seven miles south of Verona. Ray visited the Denney farm and discussed the proposal with Lee; Lee approved the use of Mills' services and the Denney farm as a disposal site. In mid-July 1971 Mills and Gerald Lechner dumped approximately 85 of the 55-gallon drums into a large trench on the Denney farm (Denney farm site) that had been excavated by Leon Vaughn. Vaughn then filled in the trench. Only NEPACCO drums were disposed of at the Denney farm site.

In October 1979 the Environmental Protection Agency (EPA) received an anonymous tip that hazardous wastes had been disposed of at the Denney farm. Subsequent EPA investigation confirmed that hazardous wastes had in fact been disposed of at the Denney farm and that the site was not geologically suitable for the disposal of hazardous wastes. Between January and April 1980 the EPA prepared a plan for the cleanup of the Denney farm site and constructed an access road and a security fence. During April 1980 the EPA conducted an on-site investigation, exposed and sampled 13 of the 55-gallon drums, which were found to be badly deteriorated, and took water and soil samples. The samples were found to contain "alarmingly" high concentrations of dioxin, TCP and toluene.

In July 1980 the EPA installed a temporary cap over the trench to prevent the entry and run-off of surface water and to minimize contamination of the surrounding soil and groundwater. The EPA also contracted with Ecology & Environment, Inc., for the preparation of a feasibility study for the cleanup of the Denney farm site. Additional on-site testing was conducted. In August 1980 the government filed its initial complaint against NEPACCO, the generator of the hazardous substances; Michaels and Lee, the corporate officers responsible for arranging for the disposal of the hazardous substances; Mills, the transporter of the hazardous substances; and Syntex, the owner and lessor of the Verona plant, seeking injunctive relief and reimbursement of response costs pursuant to RCRA § 7003, 42 U.S.C. § 6973 (count I). In September 1983 the feasibility study was completed.

In the meantime the EPA had been negotiating with Syntex about Syntex's liability for cleanup of the Denney farm site. In September 1980 the government and Syntex entered into a settlement and consent decree. Pursuant to the terms of the settlement, Syntex would pay $100,000 of the government's response costs and handle the removal, storage and permanent disposal of the hazardous substances from the Denney farm site. The EPA approved Syntex's proposed cleanup plan, and in June 1981 Syntex began excavation of the trench. In November 1981 the site was closed. The 55-gallon drums are now stored in a specially constructed concrete bunker on the Denney farm. The drums as stored do not present an imminent and substantial endangerment to health or the environment; however, no plan for permanent disposal has been developed, and the site will continue to require testing and monitoring in the future.

In August 1982 the government filed an amended complaint adding counts for relief pursuant to CERCLA §§ 104, 106, 107, 42 U.S.C. §§ 9604, 9606, 9607 (counts II and III). CERCLA was enacted after the filing of the initial complaint....

....

III. CERCLA — Retroactivity

A. Application of CERCLA to Pre-1980 Acts

Appellants first argue the district court erred in applying CERCLA retroactively, that is, to impose liability for acts committed before its effective date, December 11, 1980. CERCLA § 302(a), 42 U.S.C. § 9652(a), provides that "[u]nless otherwise provided, all provisions of this chapter shall be effecive on

December 11, 1980." Appellants argue that CERCLA should not apply to pre-enactment conduct that was neither negligent nor unlawful when committed. Appellants argue that all the conduct at issue occurred in the early 1970s, well before CERCLA became effective. Appellants also argue that there is no language supporting retroactive application in CERCLA's liability section, CERCLA § 107, 42 U.S.C. § 9607, or in the legislative history. Appellants further argue that because CERCLA imposes a new kind of liability, retroactive application of CERCLA violates due process and the taking clause. We disagree.

... We acknowledge there is a presumption against the retroactive application of statutes. [Citation.] We hold, however, the CERCLA § 302(a), 42 U.S.C. § 9652(a), is "merely a standard 'effective date' provision that indicates the date when an action can first be brought and when the time begins to run for issuing regulations and doing other future acts mandated by the statute." [Citation.]

Although CERCLA does not expressly provide for retroactivity, it is manifestly clear that Congress intended CERCLA to have retroactive effect. The language used in the key liability provision, CERCLA § 107, 42 U.S.C. § 9607, refers to actions and conditions in the past tense: "any person who at the time of disposal of any hazardous substances owned or operated," CERCLA § 107(a)(2), 42 U.S.C. § 9507(a)(2), "any person who ... arranged with a transporter for transport for disposal," CERCLA § 107(a)(3), 42 U.S.C. § 9607(a)(3), and "any person who ... accepted any hazardous substances for transport to ... sites selected by such person," CERCLA § 107(a)(4), 42 U.S.C. § 9607(a)(4). [Citations.]

Further, the statutory scheme itself is overwhelmingly remedial and retroactive. CERCLA authorizes the EPA to force responsible parties to clean up inactive or abandoned hazardous substance sites, CERCLA § 106, 42 U.S.C. § 9606, and authorizes federal, state and local governments and private parties to clean up such sites and then seek recovery of their response costs from responsible parties, CERCLA §§ 104, 107, 42 U.S.C. §§ 9604, 9607. In order to be effective, CERCLA must reach past conduct. CERCLA's backward-looking focus is confirmed by the legislative history. Congress intended CERCLA "to initiate and establish a comprehensive response and financing mechanism to abate and control the vast problems associated with abandoned and inactive hazardous waste disposal sites."

The district court also correctly found that retroactive application of CERCLA does not violate due process. Appellants argue CERCLA creates a new form of liability that is designed to deter and punish those who, according to current standards, improperly disposed of hazardous substances in the past. We disagree.... Due process is satisfied "simply by showing that retroactive application of the legislation is itself justified by a rational legislative purpose." "Provided that the retroactive application of a statute is supported by a legitimate legislative purpose furthered by rational means, judgments about the wisdom of such legislation remain within the exclusive province of the legislative and executive branches...."

Appellants failed to show that Congress acted in an arbitrary and irrational manner. Cleaning up inactive and abandoned hazardous waste disposal sites is a legitimate legislative purpose, and Congress acted in a rational manner in imposing liability for the cost of cleaning up such sites upon those parties who created and profited from the sites and upon the chemical industry as a whole. [Citation.] We hold retroactive application of CERCLA to impose liability upon responsible parties for acts committed before the effective date of the statute does not violate due process.

[The court then holds that the district court erred in finding that CERCLA did not authorize the government to seek recovery of response costs incurred prior to the enactment of the statute.]

V. *Scope of Liability*

The district court found NEPACCO liable as the "owner or operator" of a "facility" (the NEPACCO plant) under CERCLA § 107(a)(1), 42 U.S.C. § 9607(a)(1), and as a "person" who arranged for the transportation and disposal of hazardous substances under CERCLA § 107(a)(3). The district court found Lee liable as a "person" who arranged for the disposal of hazardous substances under CERCLA § 107(a)(3), and as an "owner or operator" of the NEPACCO plant under CERCLA § 107(a)(1), by "piercing the corporate veil." The district court also found Michaels liable as an "owner or operator" of the NEPACCO plant under CERCLA § 107(a)(1).

Appellants concede NEPACCO is liable under CERCLA § 107(a)(3), 42 U.S.C. § 9607(a)(3), for arranging for the transportation and disposal of hazardous substances at the Denney farm site. Because NEPACCO's assets have already been liquidated and distributed to its shareholders, however, it is unlikely that the government will be able to recover anything from NEPACCO.

. . . .

First, appellants argue the district court erred in finding them liable under CERCLA § 107(a)(1), 42 U.S.C. § 9607(a)(1), as the "owners and operator" of a "facility" where hazardous substances are located. Appellants argue that, regardless of their relationship to the NEPACCO plant, they neither owned nor operated the Denney farm site, and that it is the Denney farm site, not the NEPACCO plant, that is a "facility" for purposes of "owner and operator" liability under CERCLA § 107(a)(1). We agree.

CERCLA defines the term "facility" in part as "any site or area where a hazardous substance has been deposited, stored, disposed of, or placed, or otherwise come to be located." CERCLA § 101(9)(B), 42 U.S.C. § 9601(9)(B). The term "facility" should be construed very broadly to include "virtually any place at which hazardous wastes have been dumped, or otherwise disposed of." [Citations.] In the present case, however, the place where the hazardous substances were disposed of and where the government has concentrated its cleanup efforts is the Denney farm site, not the NEPACCO plant. The Denney farm site is the "facility." Because NEPACCO, Lee and Michaels did not own or operate the Denney farm site, they cannot be held liable as the "owners or operator" of a "facility" where hazardous substances are located under CERCLA § 107(a)(1).

CERCLA § 107(a)(3), imposes strict liability upon "any person" who arranged for the disposal or transportation for disposal of hazardous substances. As defined by statute, the term "person" includes both individuals and corporations and does not exclude corporate officers or employees. See CERCLA § 101(21), 42 U.S.C. § 9601(21). [Citations.] Congress could have limited the statutory definition of "person" but chose not to do so. Moreover, construction of CERCLA to impose liability upon only the corporation and not the individual corporate officers and employees who are responsible for making corporate decisions about the handling and disposal of hazardous substances would open an enormous, and clearly unintended, loophole in the statutory scheme.

First, Lee argues he cannot be held individually liable for having arranged for the transportation and disposal of hazardous substances under CERCLA § 107(a)(3), because he did not personally own or possess the hazardous substances. Lee argues NEPACCO owned or possessed the hazardous substances.

The government argues Lee "possessed" the hazardous substances within the meaning of CERCLA § 107(a)(3), because, as NEPACCO's plant supervisor, Lee had actual "control" over the NEPACCO plant's hazardous substances. We agree. It is the authority to control the handling and disposal of hazardous substances that is critical under the statutory scheme. The district court found that Lee, as plant supervisor, actually knew about, had immediate supervision over, and was directly responsible for arranging for the transportation and disposal of the NEPACCO plant's hazardous substances at the Denney farm site. We believe requiring proof of personal ownership or actual physical possession of hazardous substances as a precondition for liability under CERCLA § 107(a)(3), would be inconsistent with the broad remedial purposes of CERCLA. [Citations.]

Next, Lee argues that because he arranged for the transportation and disposal of the hazardous substances as a corporate officer or employee acting on behalf of NEPACCO, he cannot be held individually liable for NEPACCO's violations. Lee also argues the district court erred in disregarding the corporate entity by "piercing the corporate veil" because there was no evidence that NEPACCO was inadequately capitalized, the corporate formalities were not observed, individual and corporate interests were not separate, personal corporate funds were commingled or corporate property was diverted, or the corporate form was used unjustly or fraudulently.

The government argues Lee can be held individually liable, without "piercing the corporate veil," because Lee personally arranged for the disposal of hazardous substances in violation of CERCLA § 107(a)(3). We agree. As discussed below, Lee can be held individually liable because he personally participated in conduct that violated CERCLA; this personal liability is distinct from the derivative liability that results from "piercing the corporate veil." "The effect of piercing a corporate veil is to hold the owner [of the corporation] liable.

The rationale for piercing the corporate veil is that the corporation is something less than a bona fide independent entity." [Citation.] Here, Lee is liable because he personally participated in the wrongful conduct and not because he is one of the owners of what may have been a less than bona fide corporation. For this reason, we need not decide whether the district court erred in piercing the corporate veil under these circumstances.

We now turn to Lee's basic argument. Lee argues that he cannot be held individually liable for NEPACCO's wrongful conduct because he acted solely as a corporate officer or employee on behalf of NEPACCO. The liability imposed upon Lee, however, was not derivative but personal. Liability was not premised solely upon Lee's status as a corporate officer or employee. Rather, Lee is individually liable under CERCLA § 107(a)(3), because he personally arranged for the transportation and disposal of hazardous substances on behalf of NEPACCO and thus actually participated in NEPACCO's CERCLA violations.

....

VII. *Burden of Proof of Response Costs*

The district court found appellants had the burden of proving the government's response costs were inconsistent with the NCP, and that response costs that are not inconsistent with the NCP are conclusively presumed to be reasonable and therefore recoverable. Appellants argue the district court erred in requiring them to prove the response costs were inconsistent with the NCP, not cost-effective or unnecessary. Appellants further argue the district court erred in assuming all costs that are consistent with the NCP are conclusively presumed to be reasonable. Appellants note that the information and facts necessary to establish consistency with the NCP are matters within the possession of the government.

We believe the district court's analysis is correct. CERCLA § 107(a)(4)(A), 42 U.S.C. § 9607(a)(4)(A), states that the government may recover from responsible parties "all costs of removal or remedial action ... not inconsistent with the [NCP]." The statutory language itself establishes an exception for costs that are inconsistent with the NCP, but appellants, as the parties claiming the benefit of the exception, have the burden of proving that certain costs are inconsistent with the NCP and, therefore, not recoverable. [Citation.] Contrary to appellants' argument, "not inconsistent" is not, at least for purposes of statutory construction and not syntax, the same as "consistent." [Citations.]

The statutory scheme also supports allocation of the burden of proof of inconsistency with the NCP upon the defendants when the *government* seeks recovery of its response costs. As noted above, CERCLA § 107(a)(4)(A), provides that the federal government or a state can recover "all costs of removal or remedial action ... not inconsistent with the [NCP]." In comparison, CERCLA § 107(a)(4)(B), provides that "any other person," referring to any "person" other than the federal government or a state, can recover "any other necessary costs of response ... consistent with the [NCP]." That statutory language indicates that *non* governmental entities must prove that their response costs are consistent with the NCP in order to recover them. The statutory scheme thus differentiates between governmental and nongovernmental entities in allocating the burden of proof of whether response costs are consistent with the NCP. [Citations.]

The statutory language also supports the district court's reasoning that under CERCLA § 107(a)(4)(A), "all costs" incurred by the government that are not inconsistent with the NCP are conclusively presumed to be reasonable. CERCLA does not refer to "all *reasonable* costs" but simply to "all costs." [Citations.]

Appellants also argue the district court erred in requiring them to establish that the government's cleanup actions were not cost-effective and necessary. This argument challenges the government's choice of a particular cleanup method. We note, however, that CERCLA § 105(3), (7), 42 U.S.C. § 9605(3), (7), requires the EPA, as the agency designated by the President, to revise the NCP required by § 311 of the FWPCA, 33 U.S.C. § 1321, to include the "national hazardous substance response plan," which is specifically required by CERCLA to include "methods and criteria for determining the appropriate extent of removal, remedy, and other measures," and "means of assuring that remedial action measures are cost-effective." Consideration of whether particular action is "necessary" is thus factored into the "cost-effective" equation. The term "cost-effective" is defined by regulation as "the lowest cost alternative that is technologically feasible and reliable and which effectively mitigates and minimizes damage to and provides adequate protection of public health, welfare, or the environment." 40 C.F.R. § 300.68(j) (1986).

Because determining the appropriate removal and remedial action involves specialized knowledge and expertise, the choice of a particular cleanup method is a matter within the discretion of the EPA. The applicable standard of review is whether the agency's choice is arbitrary and capricious....

Here, appellants failed to show that the government's response costs were inconsistent with the NCP. Appellants also failed to show that the EPA acted arbitrarily and capriciously in choosing the particular method it used to clean up the Denney farm site.

NOTES AND QUESTIONS

1. *Retroactivity.* In the principal case the court followed the prevailing view and determined that, despite lack of express language in the statute, Congress intended CERCLA to apply retroactively, imposing liability on responsible persons for remediation of hazardous waste sites. *Accord Virginia Properties, Inc. v. Home Ins. Co.*, 74 F.3d 1131, 1132 (11th Cir. 1996) (characterizing CERCLA's statutory scheme as retroactively imposing strict liability for pollution cleanup"). *Also see United States v. Olin Corp.*, 107 F.3d 1506 (11th Cir. 1997). (Observing that Congress has reauthorized CERCLA twice, once with substantive changes, without an indication that courts had misconstrued the statute regarding retroactivity, citing the Omnibus Budget Reconciliation Act of 1990, Pub. L. No.

101-508, 104 Stat. 1388; Superfund Amendment and Reauthorization Act of 1986, Pub. L. No. 99-49, 100 Stat. 1613.)

Oddly, CERCLA itself precludes the recovery of natural resource damages and attendant claims against Superfund if the release of hazardous substances and resulting injury "occurred wholly" before the effective date of the statute. *See* CERCLA § 107(f)(1), 42 U.S.C. § 9607(f)(1); CERCLA § 111(d)(1), 42 U.S.C. § 9611(d)(1). What policy considerations might have persuaded Congress to draw such a distinction with respect to natural resource damage claims?

In another portion of the opinion, the court in *Northeastern* held that RCRA did not apply retroactively because its focus was essentially prospective by imposing liability for the *present and future* conditions resulting from past actions. 810 F.2d at 741. Thus, RCRA § 7003 — although technically not retroactive — still could be utilized to impose strict liability upon past off-site generators and transporters of hazardous waste for the present manifestations of harm attributable to the past activities.

2. *National Contingency Plan.* One of the requisite elements for private recovery actions is demonstrating that the costs incurred were consistent with the National Contingency Plan. The NCP is authorized by section 105 of CERCLA, 42 U.S.C. § 9605, and is designed to establish procedures and standards for preparing for and responding to releases of hazardous substances. *See* 40 C.F.R. § 300.1. The government can recover costs which are "not inconsistent" with the NCP. CERCLA § 107(a)(4)(A), 42 U.S.C. § 9607(a)(4)(A). The difference in the language of the two sections involves more than semantics. The critical distinction, as recognized in *Northeastern Pharmaceutical*, is that all of the government's costs are considered presumptively recoverable unless the defendant proves inconsistency with the NCP, while a private plaintiff can only recover those costs that it shows are consistent with the plan. The private claimant bears the burden of pleading and proving consistency with the NCP by developing a specific factual record. *Commerce Holding Co. v. Buckstone*, 749 F. Supp. 441, 444 (E.D.N.Y. 1990).

A private party response action will be considered consistent with the NCP when in "substantial compliance" with enumerated requirements and "results in a CERCLA-quality cleanup." 40 C.F.R. § 300(c)(3)(i). EPA has defined a "CERCLA-quality cleanup" as a response action that satisfies the following remedy selection requirements contained in section 121(b)(1): (1) the remedial action must be protective of human health and the environment, utilize permanent solutions and alternative treatment technologies or resource recovery technologies to the maximum extent practicable, and be cost-effective; (2) attain applicable and relevant and appropriate requirements; and (3) provide for meaningful public participation. 55 Fed. Reg. at 8793. *See County Line Inv. Co. v. Tinney*, 933 F.2d 1508, 1514 (10th Cir. 1991).

3. The regulations include provisions detailing public comment and participation concerning the response action, compliance with applicable requirements of local, state and federal laws, and require remedial investigation and feasibility studies to assess conditions and evaluate alternatives to select an appropriate response. *See* 40 C.F.R. § 300.700(c)(5)-(6); § 300.430(a)(2). Courts have held that the failure to provide an opportunity for public comment regarding a response action is inconsistent with the NCP and thus bars recovery. *See Channel Master Satellite v. JFD Elec. Corp.*, 748 F. Supp. 373, 389-90 (E.D.N.C. 1990). The regulations also set forth the following criteria to evaluate the appropriateness of privately conducted removal actions:

> (i) Actual or potential exposure to nearby human populations, animals, or the food chain from hazardous substances or pollutants or contaminants;
> (ii) Actual or potential contamination of drinking water supplies or sensitive ecosystems;
> (iii) Hazardous substances or pollutants in drums, barrels, tanks, or other bulk storage containers, that may pose a threat of release;
> (iv) High levels of hazardous substances or pollutants or contaminants in soils largely at or near the surface that may migrate;
> (v) Weather conditions that may cause hazardous substances or pollutants or contaminants to migrate or be released;
> (vi) Threat of fire or explosion; ... and
> (viii) Other situations or factors that may pose threats to public health or welfare or the environment.

40 C.F.R. § 300.415(b)(2).

4. *Jury Trial*. An important question in evaluating the nature of remedies sought for environmental harm is whether the parties have a constitutional right to jury trial. The Seventh Amendment provides that in "suits at common law, where the value in controversy shall exceed twenty dollars, the right of trial by jury shall be preserved." Courts have construed the right to jury to depend on the nature of the issue to be tried rather than the character of the action. The jury right is constitutionally mandated if the relief sought is characterized as a legal action pursuant to common law or statute, but is not recognized for equitable claims. *Ross v. Bernhard*, 396 U.S. 531 (1970).

In *Northeastern Pharmaceutical*, the court characterized the government's recovery of response costs under CERCLA and abatement costs under RCRA as equitable in nature and therefore not implicating the defendant's right to jury trial. The court reasoned that the reimbursement of such costs in effect was in the form of restitution rather than legal damages. *Also see Hatco Corp. v. W.R. Grace & Co.-Conn.*, 59 F.3d 400, 414 (3d Cir. 1995) (no jury trial for contribution claim under CERCLA).

On the other hand, in *Acushnet River v. New Bedford Harbor: Proceedings re Alleged PCB Pollution*, 712 F. Supp. 994 (D. Mass. 1989) the court held that the Seventh Amendment required a jury trial for issues regarding claims for injuries to natural resources brought by the government under CERCLA. The court noted that although the statute was silent with respect to the right to jury trial, the type of relief sought under CERCLA was analogous to common law tort claims for damages for diminution in value and loss of use of the natural resources. In addition, the court found that the claims for recovery of abatement expenses and damages for injury to natural resources were legal issues which gave the defendant the right to jury trial under the Massachusetts Constitution. *Also see Tull v. United States*, 481 U.S. 412 (1987) (Civil penalties under Clean Water Act analogized historically to actions in debt and entitled to jury trial).

5. In *United States v. Buckley*, 934 F.2d 84 (6th Cir. 1991) the court upheld jury instructions given regarding the knowledge required for a conviction under CERCLA's notification requirements pertaining to a release of a reportable quantity of asbestos during a demolition project. Section 103(b)(3), 42 U.S.C. § 9603(b)(3), requires persons "in charge of a facility" to notify appropriate governmental authorities of certain releases "as soon as he has knowledge" of the release. The court interpreted the term "persons in charge" as applicable to supervisory personnel, whether in joint or exclusive control of a facility, who are in a position to detect, prevent and abate a release of hazardous substances. 934 F.2d at 86. The "knowledge" required for conviction under the reporting rules simply meant that one was doing the acts prescribed by the statute, not that the statute or the potential health hazard existed. A defendant is subject to criminal sanctions, then, when aware of the presence of the hazardous waste — not its legal status.

STATE OF NEW YORK v. SHORE REALTY CORP.

759 F.2d 1032 (2d Cir. 1985)

OAKES, CIRCUIT JUDGE.

[Donald LeoGrande incorporated Shore Realty Corp. ("Shore") for the sole purpose of acquiring a small tract of land located in New York for condominium development. LeoGrande, as the only officer and stockholder of the company, made all corporate decisions and directed all its activities. As a result of an environmental consultant's report, LeoGrande was aware that tenants had been illegally operating a hazardous waste storage facility on the site. Although Shore made certain improvements to the property after the tenants were evicted, hundreds of thousands of gallons of hazardous substances remained in deteriorating tanks. The State of New York incurred costs in assessing the conditions at the site and in removing the drums containing hazardous materials. The State brought suit against Shore and LeoGrande under CERCLA and state nuisance law for an injunction and damages. The district court held the defendants liable for the State's response costs under CERCLA and entered a permanent injunction based solely on state public nuisance law.]

... CERCLA was designed "to bring order to the array of partly redundant, partly inadequate federal hazardous substances cleanup and compensation laws." It applies "primarily to the cleanup of leaking inactive or abandoned sites and to emergency responses to spills." And it distinguishes between two kinds of response: remedial actions — generally long-term or permanent containment or disposal programs — and removal efforts — typically short-term cleanup arrangements.

CERCLA authorizes the federal government to respond in several ways. EPA can use Superfund resources to clean up hazardous waste sites and spills. 42 U.S.C. § 9611. The National Contingency Plan ("NCP"), prepared by EPA pursuant to CERCLA, § 9605, governs cleanup efforts by "establish[ing] procedures and standards for responding to releases of hazardous substances." At the same time, EPA can sue for reimbursement of cleanup costs from any responsible parties it can locate, § 9607, allowing the federal government to respond immediately while later trying to shift financial responsibility to others. Thus, Superfund covers cleanup costs if the site has been abandoned, if the responsible parties elude detection, or if private resources are inadequate. In addition, CERCLA authorizes EPA to seek an injunction in federal district court to force a responsible party to clean up any site or spill that presents an imminent and substantial danger to public health or welfare or the environment. 42 U.S.C. § 9606(a). In sum, CERCLA is not a regulatory standard-setting statute such as the Clean Air Act. Rather, the government generally undertakes pollution abatement, and polluters pay for such abatement through tax and reimbursement liability.

Congress clearly did not intend, however, to leave clean up under CERCLA solely in the hands of the federal government. A state or political subdivision may enter into a contract or cooperative agreement with EPA, whereby both may take action on a cost-sharing basis. 42 U.S.C. § 9604(c), (d). And states, like EPA, can sue responsible parties for remedial and removal costs if such efforts are "not inconsistent with" the NCP. § 9607(a)(4)(A). While CERCLA expressly does not preempt state law, § 9614(a), it precludes "recovering compensation for the same removal costs or damages or claims" under both CERCLA and state or other federal laws, § 9614(b), and prohibits states from requiring contributions to any fund "the purpose of which is to pay compensation for claims ... which may be compensated under" CERCLA, § 9614(c). Moreover, "any ... person" who is acting consistently with the requirements of the NCP may recover "necessary costs of response." § 9607(a)(4)(B). Finally, responsible parties are liable for "damages for injury to, destruction of, or loss of natural resources, including the reasonable costs of assessing such injury, destruction, or loss resulting from such a release." 42 U.S.C. § 9607(a)(4)(C).

    ....

Liability for Response Costs Under CERCLA

We hold that the district court properly awarded the State response costs under section 9607(a)(4)(A). The State's costs in assessing the conditions of the site and supervising the removal of the drums of hazardous waste squarely fall within CERCLA's definition of response costs, even though the State is not undertaking to do the removal. *See* §§ 9601(23), (24), (25)....

1. Covered Persons

CERCLA holds liable four classes of persons:

(1) the owner and operator of a vessel (otherwise subject to the jurisdiction of the United States) or a facility,[15]

(2) any person who at the time of disposal of any hazardous substance owned or operated any facility at which such hazardous substances were disposed of,

(3) any person who by contract, agreement, or otherwise arranged for disposal or treatment, or arranged with a transporter for transport for disposal or treatment, of hazardous substances owned or possessed by such person, by any other party or entity, at any facility owned or operated by another party or entity and containing such hazardous substances, and

(4) any person who accepts or accepted any hazardous substances for transport to disposal or treatment facilities or sites selected by such person.

42 U.S.C. § 9607(a). As noted above, section 9607 makes these persons liable, if "there is a release, or a threatened release which causes the incurrence of response costs, of a hazardous substance" from the facility, for, among other things, "all costs of removal or remedial action incurred by the United States Government or a State not inconsistent with the national contingency plan."

Shore argues that it is not covered by section 9607(a)(1) because it neither owned the site at the time of disposal nor caused the presence or the release of the hazardous waste at the facility. While section 9607(a)(1) appears to cover Shore, Shore attempts to infuse ambiguity into the statutory scheme, claiming that section 9607(a)(1) could not have been intended to include all owners, because the word "owned" in section 9607(a)(2) would be unnecessary since an owner "at the time of disposal" would necessarily be included in section 9607(a)(1). Shore claims that Congress intended that the scope of section 9607(a)(1) be no greater than that of section 9607(a)(2) and that both should be limited by the "at the time of disposal" language. By extension, Shore argues that both provisions should be interpreted as requiring a showing of causation. We agree with the State, however, that section 9607(a)(1) unequivocally imposes strict liability on the current owner of a facility from which there is a release or threat of release, without regard to causation.[17]

---

[15]CERCLA defines the term "facility" broadly to include any property at which hazardous substances have come to be located. See 42 U.S.C. § 9601(9).

[17]We pause to note the distinction between whether § 9607(a) imposes strict liability and whether it requires a showing of causation. That is to say, finding that § 9607(a) imposes strict liability does not rebut Shore's causation argument. Traditional tort law has often imposed strict liability while recognizing a causation defense. See W. Prosser, Handbook of the Law of Torts § 79, at 517 (1971).

Shore's claims of ambiguity are illusory; section 9607(a)'s structure is clear. Congress intended to cover different classes of persons differently. Section 9607(a)(1) applies to all current owners and operators, while section 9607(a)(2) primarily covers prior owners and operators. Moreover, section 9607(a)(2)'s scope is more limited than that of section 9607(a)(1). Prior owners and operators are liable only if they owned or operated the facility "at the time of disposal of any hazardous substance"; this limitation does not apply to current owners, like Shore....

Shore's causation argument is also at odds with the structure of the statute. Interpreting section 9607(a)(1) as including a causation requirement makes superfluous the affirmative defenses provided in section 9607(b), each of which carves out from liability an exception based on causation....

Furthermore, as the State points out, accepting Shore's arguments would open a huge loophole in CERCLA's coverage. It is quite clear that if the current owner of a site could avoid liability merely by having purchased the site after chemical dumping had ceased, waste sites certainly would be sold, following the cessation of dumping, to new owners, who could avoid the liability otherwise required by CERCLA. Congress had well in mind that persons who dump or store hazardous waste sometimes cannot be located or may be deceased or judgment-proof....

2. *Release or Threat of Release*

We reject Shore's repeated claims that it has put in dispute whether there has been a release or threat of release at the Shore Road site. The State has established that it was responding to "a release, or a threatened release" when it incurred its response costs. We hold that the leaking tanks and pipelines, the continuing leaching and seepage from the earlier spills, and the leaking drums all constitute "releases." 42 U.S.C. § 9601(22). Moreover, the corroding and deteriorating tanks, Shore's lack of expertise in handling hazardous waste, and even the failure to license the facility, amount to a threat of release.

In addition, Shore's suggestion that CERCLA does not impose liability for threatened releases is simply frivolous. Section 9607(a)(4)(A) imposes liability for "all costs of removal or remedial action." The definitions of "removal" and "remedial" explicitly refer to actions "taken in the event of the threat of release of hazardous substances."

3. *The NPL and Consistency with the NCP*

Shore also argues that, because the Shore Road site is not on the NPL, the State's action is inconsistent with the NCP and thus Shore cannot be found liable under section 9607(a). This argument is not frivolous. Section 9607(a)(4)(A) states that polluters are liable for response costs "not inconsistent with the national contingency plan." And section 9605, which directs EPA to outline the NCP, includes a provision that requires EPA to publish the NPL. Nevertheless, we hold that inclusion on the NPL is not a requirement for the State to recover its response costs.

The State claims that, while NPL listing may be a requirement for the use of Superfund money, it is not a requisite to liability under section 9607. [Citation.] The State relies on the reasoning of several district courts that have held that liability under section 9607 is independent of the scope of section 9611, which governs the expenditure of Superfund monies, and by extension, section 9604, which governs federal cleanup efforts. [Citations.] These courts have reasoned that CERCLA authorizes a bifurcated approach to the problem of hazardous waste cleanup, by distinguishing between the scope of direct federal action with Superfund resources and the liability of polluters under section 9607. While implicitly accepting that Superfund monies can be spent only on sites included on the NPL, they conclude that this limitation does not apply to section 9607. And it is true that the relevant limitation on Superfund spending is that it be "consistent with" the NCP, 42 U.S.C. § 9604(a), while under section 9607(a)(4)-(A), liability is limited to response costs "not inconsistent with" the NCP. This analysis, however, is not so compelling as might be; the distinction between section 9604 and section 9607 blurs for two reasons. First, as we noted above, Congress envisioned section 9607 as a means of reimbursement of monies spent by government on cleanup pursuant to section 9604. The money that the federal government presumably would be spending is Superfund money. That is to say, Congress may have seen section 9607 as equal in scope to sections 9604 and 9611. Second, it is difficult to accept the State's argument that section 9607's statement "[n]otwithstanding any other provision or rule of law" supports the distinction. Shore's argument is not based on implying limitations on the scope of section 9604 into section 9607 but on an interpretation of "not inconsistent with" the NCP under section 9607 itself.

Still, we reject Shore's argument. Instead of distinguishing between the scope of section 9607 and the scope of section 9604, we hold that NPL listing is not a general requirement under the NCP. We see the NPL as a limitation on remedial, or long-term, actions — as opposed to removal, or short-term, actions — particularly federally funded remedial actions. The provisions requiring the establishment of NPL criteria and listing appear to limit their own application to remedial actions. Section 9605(8)(A) requires EPA to include in the NCP "criteria for determining priorities among releases or threatened releases ... for the purpose of taking remedial action and, to the extent practicable taking into account the potential urgency of such action, for the purpose of taking removal action." And section 9605(8)(B), which requires EPA to draw up the NPL, refers to "priorities for remedial action." [Citation.] And section 9604, which authorizes and governs federal response actions, reveals the special role of the NPL for federally sponsored remedial actions. Section 9604(c)(3) states that federal remedial actions can be taken only if "the State in which the release occurs first enters into a contract or cooperative agreement" with the federal government, thus setting up a joint federal-state cost-sharing and cleanup effort.

At the same time, section 9604(d)(1) states that such joint efforts must be taken "in accordance with criteria and priorities established pursuant to section 9605(8)" — the NPL provision. If the NPL criteria and listing were a general requirement for action "consistent with" the NCP, this language would be surplusage.

. . . .

Finally, we reject Shore's argument that the State's response costs are not recoverable because the State has failed to comply with the NCP by not obtaining EPA authorization, nor making a firm commitment to provide further funding for remedial implementation nor submitting an estimate of costs. *See* 40 C.F.R. § 300.62 (1984) (describing the states' role in joint federal-state response actions). EPA designed the regulatory scheme — the NCP — focusing on federal and joint federal-state efforts. *See, e.g.,* § 300.6 (defining "lead agency"). Shore apparently is arguing that EPA has ruled that the State cannot act on its own and seek liability under CERCLA. We disagree. Congress envisioned states' using their own resources for cleanup and recovering those costs from polluters under section 9607(a)(4)(A). We read section 9607(a)(4)(A)'s requirement of consistency with the NCP to mean that states cannot recover costs inconsistent with the response methods outlined in the NCP....

Injunctive Relief Under CERCLA

Having held Shore liable under CERCLA for the State's response costs, we nevertheless are required to hold that injunctive relief under CERCLA is not available to the State. Essentially, the State urges us to interpret the right of action under section 9607 broadly, claiming that "limiting district court relief [under section 9607] to reimbursement could have a drastic effect upon the implementation of Congress's desire that waste sites be cleaned." Conceding that section 9607 does not explicitly provide for injunctive relief, the State suggests that the court has the inherent power to grant such equitable relief, citing *Hecht Co. v. Bowles*, 321 U.S. 321, 329 (1944).

The statutory scheme, however, shows that Congress did not intent to authorize such relief. Section 9606 expressly authorizes EPA to seek injunctive relief to abate "an actual or threatened release of a hazardous substance from a facility." Implying the authority to seek injunctions under section 9607 would make the express injunctive authority granted in section 9606 surplusage. [Citations.] In addition, the scope of injunctive relief under section 9607 would conflict with the express scope of section 9606. The standard for seeking abatement under section 9606 is more narrow than the standard of liability under section 9607. Section 9606 authorizes injunctive relief only where EPA "determines that there may be an imminent and substantial endangerment to the public health or welfare of the environment." Section 9607 contains no such limitation. Finally, we recognize that "it is an elemental canon of statutory construction that where a statute expressly provides a particular remedy or remedies, a court must be chary of reading others into it."...

Common Law of Public Nuisance

Under New York law, Shore, as a landowner, is subject to liability for either a public or private nuisance on its property upon learning of the nuisance and having a reasonable opportunity to abate it.... It is immaterial therefore that other parties placed the chemicals on this site; Shore purchased it with knowledge of its condition — indeed of the approximate cost of cleaning it up — and with an opportunity to clean up the site. LeoGrande knew that the hazardous waste was present without the consent of the State or its DEC, but failed to take reasonable steps to abate the condition. Moreover, Shore is liable for maintenance of a *public* nuisance irrespective of negligence or fault....

We also reject Shore's argument that its maintenance of the Shore Road site does not constitute a public nuisance. We have no doubt that the release or threat of release of hazardous waste into the environment unreasonably infringes upon a public right and thus is a public nuisance as a matter of New York law....

LeoGrande's Personal Liability

We hold LeoGrande liable as an "operator" under CERCLA, 42 U.S.C. § 9607, for the State's response costs. Under CERCLA "owner or operator" is defined to mean "any person owning or operating" an onshore facility, § 9601(20)(A), and "person" includes individuals as well as corporations, § 9601(21). More important, the definition of "owner or operator" excludes "a person, who, without participating in the management of a ... facility, holds indicia of ownership primarily to protect his security interest in the facility." § 9601(20)(A). The use of this exception implies that an owning stockholder who manages the corporation, such as LeoGrande, is liable under CERCLA as an "owner or operator." That conclusion is consistent with that of other courts that have addressed the issue. [Citations.] In any event, LeoGrande is in charge of the operation of the facility in question, and as such is an "operator" within the meaning of CERCLA.

....

[Affirmed.]

NOTES AND QUESTIONS

1. In recognition that the number of potential hazardous waste sites requiring remediation far exceeds the EPA's administrative and financial resources, CERCLA requires the agency to establish a procedure for identifying and ranking which sites warrant the highest priority for remedial action. CERCLA § 105, 42 U.S.C. § 9605. The EPA employs a Hazard Ranking System ("HRS") for determining which waste sites should be placed on the National Priorities List ("NPL"). The HRS assigns a "score" to each site based on various risk assessment criteria such as the potential for contamination of drinking water supplies, the destruction of sensitive ecosystems, and population exposure attributable to migration of hazardous substances from the site.

The EPA can use Superfund resources for undertaking a remedial action only at sites on the NPL. 40 C.F.R. § 300.425(b). Removal actions, however, may be conducted by the government or private parties irrespective of the listing status of the site. Further, as demonstrated in *Shore Realty*, inclusion of a site on the NPL is not a precondition for agency action pursuant to CERCLA § 106 or § 122 or for recovery of non-Fund financed costs under section 107. *See* 40 C.F.R. § 300.425(b)(4).

There are several alternative methods for including a release on the NPL: (1) each state is authorized to designate one site as its highest priority (CERCLA § 105(a)(8)(B), 42 U.S.C. § 9605(a)(8)(B); 40 C.F.R. § 300.425(c)(2)); (2) the release scores sufficiently high according to the HRS criteria; or (3) the Agency for Toxic Substances and Disease Registry issues a health advisory regarding the release, the EPA finds that the release presents a significant threat to public health and a remedial action would be more cost-effective than removal. *See* 40 C.F.R. § 300.425(c).

2. Where EPA determines that an actual or threatened release of hazardous substances presents an "imminent and substantial endangerment" to health or the environment, the EPA may issue the responsible party an abatement order pursuant to section 106(a). 42 U.S.C. § 9606(a). The government has several enforcement options available to ensure prompt compliance with its order. The EPA may bring an action in federal district court to hold the violator in contempt or to impose fines up to $5,000 per day of noncompliance. CERCLA § 106(a)-(b); 42 U.S.C. § 9606(a)-(b). If the EPA determines that the responsible party will not properly and promptly respond, the agency may conduct the cleanup itself using funds from the Superfund. *See* CERCLA § 104(a), 42 U.S.C. § 9604(a) (authorizes the EPA to perform the cleanup); CERCLA § 221, 42 U.S.C. § 9631 (creates the Hazardous Substance Response Trust Fund); CERCLA § 111(a), 42 U.S.C. § 9611(a) (authorizes EPA to use fund resources to pay cleanup costs). The statute also authorizes the EPA to obtain reimbursement of its actual costs incurred in performing the cleanup (§ 107(a)(4)(A)) and also to seek punitive damages. CERCLA § 107(c)(3), 42 U.S.C. § 9607(c)(3). The punitive damages provision states that EPA may recover three times the cleanup costs against a responsible party who failed to comply with the abatement order "without sufficient cause." Further, in order to expedite the cleanup of hazardous waste sites, section 113(h) of CERCLA precludes pre-enforcement judicial review of the merits of its compliance orders.

3. In *Solid State Circuits, Inc. v. EPA*, 812 F.2d 383 (8th Cir. 1987), the parties subject to a cleanup order under section 106 contended that the combination of potential treble damages exposure for noncompliance and the preclusion of judicial review of compliance orders violated due process. Consider their argument as follows:

[The defendant-manufacturers] argue that upon receiving the EPA order they found themselves stuck between a rock and a hard place. They assert that, under the statutory scheme, if they had chosen to comply with the EPA's order and were later found to have a valid defense to liability, they would have been forced to bring an action against the responsible party in order to obtain reimbursement for the clean-up. If the responsible party could not have been located or determined or had turned out to be judgment proof, they would have been forced to bear the cost of a clean-up for which they were not liable. On the other hand, if [the parties] had refused to comply, they would have been exposed to the possibility of treble damage liability under CERCLA § 107(c)(3). In addition, [the parties] contend that even if the EPA did not bring an action for treble damages, they would still have had to carry the potential treble liability on all public financing disclosure for an indefinite period because, at the time the EPA issued its order, there was no statute of limitations on EPA cost recovery actions.... [They] contend this "Hobson's choice" between compliance and potential treble liability effectively prevents a challenge to an EPA order.

812 F.2d at 389. The parties argued that the phrase "sufficient cause" in section 107(c)(3) embodied a good faith defense; punitive damages could be imposed only where the government could show bad faith refusal to comply with its order. The EPA, conversely, argued for an objective test regarding treble damages. The court responded:

As a matter of constitutional law, we believe that the label "objective" or "subjective" is not as important as the functional significance of the standard. To put it another way, to pass constitutional requirements, the standard must provide parties served with EPA clean-up orders a real and meaningful opportunity to test the validity of the order. [Citation.] At the same time, the standard must protect the government's interest in encouraging parties to conduct clean-ups promptly and in promoting settlements once the EPA has performed clean-ups itself so as to avoid using resources necessary to respond to threats posed by hazardous waste on litigation to replenish the Superfund. We are, therefore, convinced that "sufficient cause" as used in CERCLA § 107(c)(3) may be constitutionally interpreted to mean that treble damages may not be assessed if the party opposing such damages had an objectively reasonable basis for believing that the EPA's order was either invalid or inapplicable to it.

Under this standard, a court assessing the objective reasonableness of a party's challenge to a clean-up order must keep in mind that the EPA is presumed to have acted correctly, and its decision to issue such an order may be found erroneous only if it acted arbitrarily or capriciously.

812 F.2d at 391-92. Is this virtually an impossible task for parties seeking to challenge section 106 orders? Courts have also recognized that section 107(c)(3)

allows the government to recover treble damages *in addition* to its response costs. *See United States v. Parsons*, 936 F.2d 526, 529 (11th Cir. 1991). The statute now provides for a six year statute of limitations on cost recovery actions and a three year limitations period for claims for natural resource damages. *See* § 112(d), 42 U.S.C. § 9612(d).

4. A partial solution to the dilemma illustrated in Solid State Circuits is found in section 106(b)(2). If a party complies with a section 106 order, they may petition the EPA for reimbursement from Superfund using the section 112 claims procedure. Section 112(c), 42 U.S.C. § 9612(c), allows the government to acquire subrogation rights to proceed against a party responsible for hazardous waste dumping when an innocent party cleans up the site and is reimbursed by the Superfund. Judicial review of the agency's order would be available under section 113 if the EPA denied the relief requested. The petitioner could obtain reimbursement to the extent that the remedy selected by the EPA was excessive under the arbitrary and capricious standard, and could be completely reimbursed if able to show a defense to liability for the response costs. *See* CERCLA § 106(b)(2)(C)-(D), 42 U.S.C. § 9606(b)(2)(C)-(D).

5. *Pre-enforcement Judicial Review.* Courts have upheld the validity of section 113(h) by recognizing the public interest in the prompt cleanup of hazardous waste sites. Thus, the EPA must have the ability to conduct clean-up operations prior to a final judicial determination of the rights and the potential liabilities of parties affected. In *Schalk v. Reilly*, 900 F.2d 1091 (7th Cir. 1990) citizens brought suit challenging a consent decree entered into between the EPA and a corporation providing for cleanup of hazardous waste under CERCLA. The district court dismissed the suit for lack of subject matter jurisdiction and the court of appeals affirmed. The court found that the plain language of section 113(h) of CERCLA, 42 U.S.C. § 9613, precluded federal court jurisdiction to review an action under the Act at the stage when a cleanup plan had been selected but not yet completed. The court observed that CERCLA's scheme of precluding preenforcement judicial review reflected an intent by Congress to prevent delays in the implementation of hazardous waste cleanup. The court pointed out that the citizens had an opportunity to participate in the public comment period regarding the proposed decree and would have additional chances to give their input at further stages in the actual implementation of the plan when the corporation applied for permits. *Also see Barmet Aluminum Corp. v. Reilly*, 927 F.2d 289, 292 (6th Cir. 1991) (CERCLA provision prohibiting judicial review prior to enforcement action also foreclosed constitutional challenges to agency action where plaintiff could not demonstrate that bar violated due process).

In *Boarhead Corp. v. Erickson*, 923 F.2d 1011, 1022 (3d Cir. 1991) the court held that section 113(h) also precluded judicial review regarding EPA compliance with a separate federal statute, the National Historic Preservation Act, in conjunction with the agency's pre-cleanup activities under CERCLA. The court conceded that the plaintiff's post-cleanup review would likely be inadequate to redress the irreparable harm which could occur to the archaeological and historical resources during the clean-up. The court noted, however, that the EPA must consider the historic preservation concerns of the site, including the potential impact of the clean-up activities on the artifacts and Indian remains located at the site. What would be the likelihood of maintaining a successful challenge to the remedial plan once work had commenced and expenditures made?

6. *Attorney Fees.* In *Key Tronic Corp. v. United States*, ___ U.S. ___, 114 S. Ct. 1960, 128 L. Ed. 2d 797 (1994) the Court held that attorney's fees were not awardable as "necessary costs of response" in a private cost recovery action under CERCLA. The Court noted that CERCLA does expressly authorize fees for government abatement actions in section 106(b)(2)(E) and for citizen's suits under section 310(f) but does not explicitly provide for fees in private cost recovery suits under section 107.

Accordingly, the Court relied upon the traditional "American Rule" which provides that, absent a contractual or statutory authorization or a showing of bad faith litigation, each side in litigation must bear their own costs. Recall *Alyeska Pipeline Serv. Co. v. Wilderness Soc'y*, 421 U.S. 240 (1975), where the Court denied attorneys' fees to a citizens' group which had obtained success on the merits in challenging government action under federal environmental laws. The Court declined to recognize in its inherent equitable powers a common law exception justifying attorneys' fees even for a prevailing private attorneys' general protecting the public interest.

B. DEFENSES, LIMITATIONS, AND SETTLEMENT

Although liability is strict under CERCLA, it is not absolute. CERCLA contains three narrow, causation-based defenses to liability in section 107(b): that the release of a hazardous substance was caused *solely* by either an act of God, act of war, or was attributable to a third party unaffiliated and unrelated to the defendant. The defendant bears the burden of establishing one of the defenses by a preponderance of the evidence. The Act borrows the most favorable parts of common law of torts with respect to assessing liability strictly, jointly and severally, but relaxes common law rules pertaining to causation. Instead of the traditional concept of limiting accountability to the harms directly traceable to the offending conduct, CERCLA liberalizes the requisite causal showing by dispensing with any "fingerprinting" of the defendant's waste and the release which resulted in the incurrence of response costs. This treatment of causation reflects two policies — one scientific and the other public interest. The scientific rationale undergirding the more generous causation standard is recognition that waste sites often contain chemicals and substances from numerous generators which have commingled, making a specific causal linking of particular waste and the harm virtually impossible. The Act overcomes this dilemma by shifting the burden to the defendant to *disprove* a causal nexus. Second, CERCLA moderated causation requirements in an attempt to impose liability more readily and effectively on the actors responsible. The benefits to this approach are that it stimulates settlement and directs government efforts and resources to cleanup activities rather than litigation over liability. The potential inequities inherent in the statutory methodology spurred amendments to CERCLA in 1986 through the addition of more specific cleanup standards, settlement criteria, and provisions dealing with the relations between jointly responsible parties.

CERCLA litigation typically involves complex technical and scientific issues implicating numerous parties with diverse interests and concerns. Substantial transaction and delay costs often hamper the effectiveness of the statute by impeding the accomplishment of hazardous waste remediation. From government's perspective, settlement through consent decree offers an attractive vehicle to economize limited administrative resources while achieving the statutory goals of expeditiously cleaning up hazardous waste sites and imposing liability on responsible parties. CERCLA contains several provisions which give tremendous incentive to PRPs to forego litigation and agree to settlement even under relatively unfavorable terms, including the statutory scheme of strict liability with limited narrow defenses, imposition of joint and several liability irrespective of relative fault, and the shield given to settling parties from contribution claims. Moreover, the framework of the settlement provisions in CERCLA effectively penalizes non-settlors by leaving them with the risk of bearing a disproportionate amount of liability. Section 122 of CERCLA, 42 U.S.C. § 9622, provides for three distinct types of settlement options: (1) agreements for the cleanup of a hazardous waste site; (2) *de minimis* settlement with small volume generators; and (3) cost recovery settlements. *See City of New York v. Exxon Corp.*, 697 F. Supp. 677, 691 (S.D.N.Y. 1988). The EPA has considerable discretion in deciding which, if any, settlement route to pursue with potentially responsible parties. Nevertheless, the addition of section 122 in SARA clearly evidenced Congress's view that settlement should be pursued where the public interest in cleanup of hazardous waste sites can be accomplished.

STATE OF NEW YORK v. LASHINS ARCADE CO.

91 F.3d 353 (2d Cir. 1996)

MAHONEY, CIRCUIT JUDGE:

[The State of New York brought suit against Lashins Arcade Corporation ("Lashins") under § 107(a) of the Comprehensive Environmental Response, Compensation and Liability Act of 1980, as amended ("CERCLA"), 42 U.S.C. § 9607(a),[2] and various state law claims seeking damages for costs incurred

---

[2]Section 9607(a) provides in pertinent part:

  Notwithstanding any other provision or rule of law, and subject only to the defenses set forth in subsection (b) of this section —
    (1) the owner and operator of a vessel or a facility, [and]

investigating and cleaning up the release of tetrachloroethene, or perchloro-ethylene ("PCE"), and its breakdown compounds, trichloroethene ("TCE"), 1,2-dichloroethene ("DCE"), and vinyl chloride, into the groundwater in the vicinity of the Bedford Village Shopping Arcade (the "Arcade") in Westchester County, New York. The district court awarded Lashins summary judgment based upon the third-party defense provided by § 107(b)(3) of CERCLA, 42 U.S.C. § 9607(b)(3).][3]

Background

This appeal involves the release of hazardous substances at the Arcade, which resulted in groundwater contamination in the area. The Arcade, a 6,800 square foot one-story building housing six retail stores, was built in 1955, and was owned by Holbrook B. Cushman until his death in 1966. The property was then held in trust by Cushman's widow, Beatrice Cushman, and the Bank of New York until 1972. Cushman leased a store in the Arcade to Astrologo from about 1958 to 1963, where Astrologo operated a dry cleaning business. The store was

---

(2) any person who at the time of disposal of any hazardous substance owned or operated any facility at which such hazardous substances were disposed of, ...

....

... shall be liable for —

(A) all costs of removal or remedial action incurred by the United States Government or a State or an Indian tribe not inconsistent with the national contingency plan;

(B) any other necessary costs of response incurred by any other person consistent with the national contingency plan;

(C) damages for injury to, destruction of, or loss of natural resources, including the reasonable costs of assessing such injury, destruction, or loss resulting from such a release; and

(D) the costs of any health assessment or health effects study carried out under section 9604(i) of this title.

[3]Section 9607(b) provides:

There shall be no liability under subsection (a) of this section for a person otherwise liable who can establish by a preponderance of the evidence that the release or threat of release of a hazardous substance and the damages resulting therefrom were caused solely by —

(1) an act of God;

(2) an act of war;

(3) an act or omission of a third party other than an employee or agent of the defendant, or than one whose act or omission occurs in connection with a contractual relationship, existing directly or indirectly, with the defendant (except where the sole contractual arrangement arises from a published tariff and acceptance for carriage by a common carrier by rail), if the defendant establishes by a preponderance of the evidence that (a) he exercised due care with respect to the hazardous substance concerned, taking into consideration the characteristics of such hazardous substance, in light of all relevant facts and circumstances, and (b) he took precautions against foreseeable acts or omissions of any such third party and the consequences that could foreseeably result from such acts or omissions; or

(4) any combination of the foregoing paragraphs.

next leased to defendant Rocco Tripodi (with whom defendant Bedford Village Cleaners, Inc. is affiliated) in 1963, who maintained the dry cleaning business at the Arcade until 1971. During this period, Tripodi dumped powdered wastes from his dry cleaning machines, which contained the volatile organic compound ("VOC") PCE, on the ground outside the Arcade behind his store. In December 1971, Tripodi moved his dry cleaning business out of the Arcade, and no other dry cleaning establishment has operated there since that time. In November 1972, the trust sold the Arcade to Miriam Baygell, who owned the property until her death in 1977, when it was inherited by her husband, Milton Baygell.

In 1978, the Westchester County Department of Health (the "WCDOH") conducted a countywide survey regarding possible groundwater contamination by VOCs. The survey found elevated VOC levels in the hamlets of Katonah, Armonk, and Bedford Village. Further sampling of private wells in Bedford Village conducted by the WCDOH in 1979 revealed groundwater contamination in an area southeast of the Arcade. These samples contained high concentrations of PCE and its breakdown compounds, TCE and DCE. The WCDOH issued "boil water" notices to affected homeowners.

In 1982, the New York State Department of Environmental Conservation (the "NYSDEC") authorized state funds for an investigation and remediation of the groundwater problem at the Arcade and the nearby Hunting Ridge Shopping Mall pursuant to § 27-1301 et seq. of the New York Environmental Conservation Law. [A preliminary investigation] reported that the highest level of contamination in the Arcade was found in the area formerly occupied by the dry cleaning establishment....

Meanwhile, in January 1987, Milton Baygell entered into negotiations with Lashins for the sale of the Arcade after a real estate broker contacted Lashins about the property. In the course of these negotiations, Baygell's attorney, Donald Mazin, wrote Lashins' attorney, Henry Hocherman, on March 20, 1987 to inform him that "there are chemicals in the ground being treated by ultra violet and activated carbon machines situated in the rear of the building to clean the water. Chemicals have to be replaced approximately every 8-9 months." Prior to executing the contract of sale, Lashins contacted the Arcade's water service contractor, Environmental Recovery Co., who advised Lashins that the well on the premises had a water filter, but assured Lashins that the filter was "routine" and had been installed in response to an area-wide groundwater contamination problem, and that the suspected source of the contamination was a nearby Exxon gas station.

In addition, Lashins states that it contacted the Town of Bedford prior to purchasing the Shopping Arcade to determine whether there were any violations or other present or past problems with the property, and was assured that there were none. Lashins further asserts that it interviewed the Arcade's tenants, all of whom spoke enthusiastically about the property. New York contends, however, that Lashins made no inquiry concerning the groundwater contamination (other than the discussion with Environmental Recovery Co.) prior to purchasing the

Arcade. In any event, Lashins executed a contract of sale with Baygell on April 6, 1987, and the transaction closed on June 26, 1987.

Lashins claims that at the time of the closing, it was unaware that the NYSDEC was conducting an administrative proceeding involving the Arcade, or that it had contracted with a firm to conduct the RI/FS concerning the Bedford Village Wells site. Baygell did not transmit any NYSDEC notices to Lashins, no public notice was issued, and the Arcade tenants, the Town of Bedford, and the local bank were allegedly unaware of the situation.

Lashins was first informed that the NYSDEC was conducting a formal investigation of the Arcade by letter dated August 13, 1987. That letter advised Lashins of the impending RI/FS requested by the NYSDEC, and stated that NYSDEC representatives intended to enter the Arcade property "for the purpose of drilling, installing and operating groundwater monitoring wells and taking samples of soil, septage, surface water, and groundwater." [The State notified Lashins and Baygell that it intended to investigate and remediate the site.]...

After purchasing the Arcade, Lashins maintained the existing GAC filter and took water samples which were analyzed by a laboratory for VOC contamination on a semi-annual basis. It also instructed all tenants to avoid discharging any hazardous substances into the waste and septic systems, subsequently incorporated this requirement into the tenant leases, and conducted periodic inspections of the tenants' premises to assure compliance with this obligation....

The district court concluded that all elements for strict liability as to Lashins under § 9607(a), were satisfied in this case, but that Lashins was entitled to summary judgment on its affirmative defense under § 9607(b)(3). In so ruling, the court noted that "Lashins had no direct or indirect contractual relationship with either of the third party dry cleaners who released the VOCs, or with the owners of the Shopping Arcade at the time the dry cleaners operated and when the pollution occurred," and that Lashins had done "everything that could reasonably have been done to avoid or correct the pollution."...

Discussion

... [T]here is no dispute that New York has established a prima facie case against Lashins under § 9607(a), for recovery of expenses incurred investigating and cleaning up the release of PCE at the Arcade. This prima facie case consists of the following elements:

(1) the site in question is a "facility" as defined in [42 U.S.C. § 9601(9)];

(2) the defendant is a responsible person under [§ 9607(a)];

(3) a release or a threatened release of a hazardous substance has occurred; and

(4) the release or threatened release has caused the plaintiff to incur response costs. [Citations]

Since Lashins is a current owner of the Shopping Arcade, it is a potentially responsible defendant under § 9607(a)(1), notwithstanding the fact that it did not own the Arcade at the time of disposal of the hazardous substances. Thus, Lashins may be held strictly liable for New York's response costs unless it can satisfy one of CERCLA's affirmative defenses. We now turn to Lashins' claim that it may avoid such liability under the third-party defense of § 9607(b)(3).

Section 9607(b)(3), provides an affirmative defense for a party who can establish that the offending "release ... of a hazardous substance and the damages resulting therefrom were caused solely by ... an act or omission of a third party," provided that: (1) the third party is not "one whose act or omission occurs in connection with a contractual relationship, existing directly or indirectly, with the defendant," (2) the defendant "took precautions against foreseeable acts or omissions of any such third party and the consequences that could foreseeably result from such acts or omissions," and (3) the defendant "exercised due care with respect to the hazardous substance concerned, taking into consideration the characteristics of such hazardous substance, in light of all relevant facts and circumstances."

The offending release here was clearly caused by third parties (Tripodi, Bedford Village Cleaners, Inc., Astrologo, and (New York contends) Milton Baygell). Although paragraphs (1)-(3) of § 9607(b) speak exclusively in the singular, referring to events and damages "caused solely by — (1) *an* act of God; (2) *an* act of war; [or] (3) *an* act or omission of a third party," § 9607(b) (emphasis added), paragraph (4) of § 9607(b) refers to "any combination of the foregoing paragraphs." We read paragraph (4) as allowing consideration of multiple causes within, as well as among, the several preceding paragraphs. Thus, in our view, damage that resulted from an earthquake and a subsequent flood would fall within paragraph (1) of § 9607(b), and damages caused by a number of acts by a single third party (as typically occurs when pollution is caused by a course of conduct), or a number of acts by several third parties (as in this case), would fall within paragraph (3). One case that involved acts of multiple third parties proceeded on the premise that their joint activities could provide exculpation under § 9607(b)(3), although without explicit analysis of the applicable statutory language. [Citations]

In this case, the only one of the allegedly offending third parties with whom Lashins had a contractual relationship was Milton Baygell. Further, Baygell's allegedly offending conduct did not "occur in connection with a contractual relationship ... with [Lashins]" within the meaning of § 9607(b)(3), and therefore Lashins may not be disqualified from the protection afforded by § 9607(b)(3) because of its contractual relationship with Baygell.

This conclusion is mandated by the following ruling in *Westwood Pharmaceuticals, Inc. v. National Fuel Gas Distribution Corp.*, 964 F.2d 85 (2d Cir. 1992):

> We hold that ... the phrase "in connection with a contractual relationship" in [§ 9607(b)(3)] requires more than the mere existence of a contractual relationship between the owner of land on which hazardous substances are or have been disposed of and a third party whose act or omission was the sole cause of the release or threatened release of such hazardous substances into the environment, for the landowner to be barred from raising the

third-party defense provided for in that section. In order for the landowner to be barred from raising the third-party defense under such circumstances, the contract between the landowner and the third party must either relate to the hazardous substances or allow the landowner to exert some element of control over the third party's activities.

In *Westwood*, the seller of the contaminated site sought exoneration from the buyer's conduct, whereas in this case the buyer seeks exoneration from the seller's activities, but this is surely an immaterial distinction in terms of the *Westwood* rationale. ("[A] landowner is precluded from raising the third-party defense only if the contract between the landowner and the third party somehow is connected with the handling of hazardous substances."). The straightforward sale of the Arcade by Baygell to Lashins clearly did not "relate to hazardous substances" or vest Lashins with authority "to exert some element of control over [Baygell's] activities" within the contemplation of our ruling in *Westwood*.

The second requirement for the successful assertion of a third-party defense demands that the defendant shall have taken adequate precautions against actions by the third party that would lead to a release of hazardous waste. Given that the last release in the instant case happened more than fifteen years before Lashins' purchase of the Arcade, there was obviously nothing Lashins could have done to prevent actions leading to a release.

Thus, the resolution of this appeal turns upon the validity of the district court's ruling that Lashins was entitled to summary judgment on the question whether Lashins "exercised due care with respect to the hazardous substance concerned ... in the light of all relevant facts and circumstances" within the meaning of § 9607(b)(3). This requirement is not defined in the statute. CERCLA's legislative history, however, provides some guidance: "The defendant must demonstrate that he took all precautions with respect to the particular waste that a similarly situated reasonable and prudent person would have taken in light of all relevant facts and circumstances." H.R. Rep. No. 1016, 96th Cong., 2d Sess., pt. 1, at 34 (1980), reprinted in 1980 U.S.C.C.A.N. 6119, 6137. Further, "due care 'would include those steps necessary to protect the public from a health or environmental threat.'" *United States v. A & N Cleaners & Launderers, Inc.*, 854 F. Supp. 229, 238 (S.D.N.Y. 1994) (quoting H.R. Rep. No. 253, 99th Cong., 2d Sess. 187 (1986)); *see also Kerr-McGee Chem. Corp.*, 14 F.3d at 325 & n.3 (due care not established when no affirmative measures taken to control site).

Against this background, New York contends that Lashins inadequately investigated the contamination problem before buying the Arcade despite being notified about it, and after its purchase "did nothing to contain, control or clean up the pollution except to continue to maintain a filter on its own property." New York points to cases such as *A & N Cleaners* and *Kerr-McGee Chemical Corp.* where § 9607(a) liability was imposed because the defendant did not take active measures to address a hazardous waste problem, and adds that *Kerr-McGee*

Chemical Corp. and *United States v. DiBiase Salem Realty Trust*, Civ. A. No. 91-11028-MA, 1993 WL 729662 (D. Mass. Nov. 19, 1993), establish that the "due care" standard does not permit a landowner to remain passive simply because public environmental authorities are addressing a hazardous waste situation.

We are not persuaded by New York's arguments, nor by the authorities that New York cites to us. The pertinent language of § 9607(b)(3) focuses the "due care" inquiry upon "all relevant facts and circumstances" of the case at hand. In this case, the RI/FS by Dvirka and Bartilucci had been commissioned six months before Lashins purchased the Arcade, and before Lashins had even learned that the Arcade was for sale. It would have been pointless to require Lashins to commission a parallel investigation once it acquired the Arcade and became more fully aware of the environmental problem. Pressed at oral argument as to what Lashins might appropriately have been required to do at that juncture, New York contended that Lashins was obligated to pay some or all of the cost of the RI/FS undertaken at the behest of the EPA and the NYSDEC.

This is surely an anomalous proposal. Response costs are assessed when there is liability under § 9607(a). It is counterintuitive to suppose that a defendant is required to pay some or all of those response costs in order to establish the affirmative defense provided by § 9607(b)(3) to liability under § 9607(a), thereby rendering the affirmative defense partly or entirely academic.

Nor do we discern any policy reasons for imposing such a rule. We agree with *HRW Systems, Inc. v. Washington Gas Light Co.*, 823 F. Supp. 318 (D. Md. 1993), that the "due care" mandate of § 9607(b)(3) does not "impose a duty on a purchaser of land to investigate prior to purchase, in order to determine whether there is pollution on the land caused by someone with whom the purchaser is not in contractual privity." No claim is made that Lashins' purchase of the Arcade deprived New York of any remedy available to it against any predecessor owners or operators under § 9607(a); consent decrees were in fact entered against Tripodi and Astrologo. It is surely the policy of CERCLA to impose liability upon parties responsible for pollution, rather than the general taxpaying public, but this policy does not mandate precluding a "due care" defense by imposing a rule that is tantamount to absolute liability for ownership of a site containing hazardous waste....

In sum, we perceive no basis for reversal of the district court's award of summary judgment to Lashins on the basis that Lashins satisfied its obligation to "exercise[] due care" with respect to the Arcade within the meaning of § 9607(b)(3). In so ruling, we proclaim no broad rule of exemption from the liability imposed by § 9607(a). Rather, mindful of the mandate of § 9607(b)(3) that the "due care" inquiry focus upon "all relevant facts and circumstances" of the case presented for decision, we conclude that Lashins' "due care" obligation did not require it to go beyond the measures that it took to address the contamination problem at the Arcade, and to supplant, duplicate, or underwrite the RI/FS previously commissioned by the EPA and NYDESC to address pollution that ensued from activities which occurred more than fifteen years before Lashins purchased the Arcade.

[Affirmed]

NOTES AND QUESTIONS

1. *Innocent Landowner Defense.* A special category of the third-party defense under section 107(b)(3) provides a narrow defense for "innocent landowners." The landowner bears the burden of proving the defense by making the following showings:

> (1) The release or threat of release of a hazardous substance and the resulting damages were caused solely by an act or omission of a third party;
> (2) The third party's act or omission did not occur in connection with a contractual relationship (either direct or indirect) with the defendants;
> (3) The defendants exercised due care with respect to the hazardous substance; and
> (4) The defendants took precautions against the third party's foreseeable acts or omissions and the foreseeable consequences resulting therefrom.

See United States v. Pacific Hide & Fur Depot, Inc., 716 F. Supp. 1341, 1346-1347 (D. Idaho 1989). The essence of the defense, then, is demonstrating a complete absence of responsibility for causation of the harm and exercising due diligence with respect to ownership and operation of the property. *See* CERCLA § 107(b)(3), 42 U.S.C. § 9607(b)(3); CERCLA § 101(35A), 42 U.S.C. § 9601(35A).

2. The landowner must show that the release was caused "solely" by the actions or omissions of a third party — partial fault will bar access to the defense. Further, the landowner cannot be considered affiliated with a responsible third party, such as through a contractual relationship. This qualifier is primarily directed at eliminating any loophole from liability simply through a conveyancing of contaminated real estate. The question of what types of land sale contracts constituted a "contractual relationship," though, was not clarified until the 1986 SARA amendments which added explanatory language in CERCLA § 101(35A), 42 U.S.C. § 9601(35A). That definition includes real estate transactions *unless* the defendant acquired the property *after* the disposal of the hazardous waste and the defendant did not know nor had reason to know of the presence of hazardous waste at the site.

3. *Due Diligence.* One of the principal difficulties in applying the defense involves determining whether the defendant has met exercised due diligence. In *United States v. A & N Cleaners and Launderers, Inc.*, 854 F. Supp. 229, 238-39 (S.D.N.Y. 1994) the court explained:

> To qualify as an Innocent Landowner under CERCLA § 101(35)(A), one must have undertaken "all appropriate inquiry into the previous ownership

and uses of the property, consistent with good commercial or customary practice" at the time of transfer. CERCLA § 101(35)(B), 42 U.S.C. § 9601(35)(B). "Good commercial or customary practice" is not defined in the statute, and the relevant legislative history is vague, indicating that "a reasonable inquiry must have been made in all circumstances, in light of best business and land transfer principles." H.R. Conf. Rep. No. 962, 99th Cong., 2d Sess., at 187 (1986). In deciding whether a defendant has complied with this standard, courts consider any specialized knowledge or expertise the defendant has, whether the purchase price indicated awareness of the presence of a risk of contamination, commonly known or reasonable information about the property, the obviousness of the presence of contamination at the property, and the ability to detect such contamination by appropriate inspection. CERCLA § 101(35)(B), 42 U.S.C. § 9601(35)-(B).

Landowners who meet the requirements of CERCLA § 101(35)(A) will not be found to be in a "contractual relationship" with the party responsible for the release of hazardous substances at the property. To obtain the protection of the Innocent Landowner Defense, they must also meet the Due Care and Precautionary Requirements of CERCLA § 107(b)(3)(a) and (b). See CERCLA § 101(35)(A), 42 U.S.C. 9601(35)(A).

The Due Care Requirement, also undefined in the statute, has been interpreted as requiring that a defendant demonstrate that it took necessary steps to prevent foreseeable adverse consequences arising from the pollution on the site.

The Precautionary Requirement is satisfied by taking precautionary action against the foreseeable actions of third parties responsible for the hazardous substances in question.

Both the Third-Party Defense and the Innocent Landowner Defense are affirmative defenses, requiring the defendant to prove each of the required elements by a preponderance of the evidence. [Citations omitted]

See Lincoln Properties v. Higgins, 823 F. Supp. 1528, 1543-44 (E.D. Cal. 1992) (due care demonstrated where defendant took contaminated wells out of service and removed them to prevent further environmental harms); Kerr-McGee Chem. Corp. v. Lefton Iron & Metal Co., 14 F.3d 321, 325 (7th Cir. 1994) (owner failed to satisfy due care standard where evidence showed that although aware of pollution at site, made no attempt to remove the hazardous substances or take other affirmative steps to reduce the threat at the affected site).

4. A private party who pays CERCLA response costs may bring an action against another party to collect cleanup costs. The statutory scheme permits cost recovery suits by "any person" against a potentially responsible party. Sand Springs Home v. Interplastic Corp., 670 F. Supp. 913 (N.D. Okla. 1987).

Consequently, most courts do not recognize a "clean hands" defense to preclude maintenance of a cost recovery suit by a PRP against another PRP. *See Smith Land & Imp. Corp. v. Celotex Corp.*, 851 F.2d 86 (3d Cir. 1988) (defense of caveat emptor not available in suit by purchaser of land seeking contribution regarding cleanup expenses incurred of hazardous waste site, although could be considered in mitigation of amount due). *But see Mardan Corp. v. C.G.C. Music, Ltd.*, 600 F. Supp. 1049 (D. Ariz. 1984). The claimant in such instances may be an "innocent landowner" who decided to remedy a hazardous site voluntarily rather than expend litigation costs and delays trying to fit within one of the narrow defenses available in section 107(b).

KELLEY v. ENVIRONMENTAL PROTECTION AGENCY

15 F.3d 1100 (D.C. Cir. 1994)

SILBERMAN, CIRCUIT JUDGE:

Petitioners challenge an EPA regulation limiting lender liability under CERCLA. We hold that EPA lacks statutory authority to restrict by regulation private rights of action arising under the statute and therefore grant the petition for review.

I.

Congress enacted the Comprehensive Environmental Response, Compensation, and Liability Act (CERCLA) 42 U.S.C. § 9601 et seq., in 1980 to "provide for liability, compensation, cleanup, and emergency response for hazardous substances released into the environment and the cleanup of inactive hazardous waste disposal sites." The statute provides several mechanisms to further these objectives. Section 105 requires the President to promulgate and publish a National Contingency Plan (NCP) to direct actions in response to a hazardous contamination and to prescribe the procedures for those actions. The President in turn has delegated primary authority under section 105 — and much of CERCLA — to EPA. Under section 104, the President (again, EPA by delegation) may undertake direct remedial actions — either by employing agency personnel or through private contracting — to clean up a contaminated site and may fund the cost of such actions through the Hazardous Waste Superfund. The government may then bring cost recovery actions under section 107 of CERCLA against responsible parties to replenish the funds expended.

Alternatively, where "there may be an imminent and substantial endangerment to the public health or welfare or the environment," EPA may order parties to clean up the hazardous waste and remedy its effects. Those who receive and comply with such orders are entitled to reimbursement of their reasonable costs if they are not liable under section 107, or — even if liable — if they establish on the administrative record that the cleanup action ordered was arbitrary and capricious or otherwise unlawful. EPA also may assess civil penalties for noncompliance with certain CERCLA provisions and bring an action in federal district court to collect such penalties.

CERCLA also authorizes private parties and EPA to bring civil actions independently to recover their costs associated with the cleanup of hazardous wastes from those responsible for the contamination. Section 107 of CERCLA generally imposes strict liability on, among others, all prior and present "owners and operators" of hazardous waste sites. Congress created a safe harbor provision for secured creditors, however, in the definition of "owner or operator," providing that "[s]uch term does not include a person, who, without participating in the management of a vessel or facility, holds indicia of ownership primarily to protect his security interest in the vessel or facility." 42 U.S.C. § 9601(20)-(A).

... In *United States v. Fleet Factors Corp.*, 901 F.2d 1550 (11th Cir. 1990) the court, although adhering to the settled view that Congress intended to protect the commercial practices of secured creditors "in their normal course of business," nevertheless stated that "a secured creditor will be liable if its involvement with the management of the facility is sufficiently broad to support the inference that it could affect hazardous waste disposal decisions if it so chose."

This language, portending as it did an expansion in the scope of secured creditor liability, caused considerable discomfort in financial circles....

EPA, responding to the understandable clamor from the banking community and in light of the federal government's increasing role as a secured creditor after taking over failed savings and loans, instituted a rulemaking proceeding, to define the secured creditor exemption when legislative efforts to amend CERCLA failed. In April 1992, EPA issued the final regulation, which employs a framework of specific tests to provide clearer articulation of a lender's scope of liability under CERCLA. The rule provides an overall standard for judging when a lender's "[p]articipation in [m]anagement" causes the lender to forfeit its exemption. 40 C.F.R. § 300.1100(c)(1)(1992). A lender may, without incurring liability, undertake investigatory actions before the creation of a security interest, monitor or inspect the facility, and require that the borrower comply with all environmental standards. 40 C.F.R. § 300.1100(c)(2) (1992). When a loan nears default, the rule permits the lender to engage in work-out negotiations and activities, including ensuring that the collateral facility does not violate environmental laws. 40 C.F.R. § 300.1100(c)(2)(ii)(B). The rule also protects a secured creditor that acquires full title to the collateral property through foreclosure, as long as the creditor did not participate in the facility's management prior to foreclosure and undertakes certain diligent efforts to divest itself of the property. 40 C.F.R. § 300.1100(d). Lenders still face liability under section 107(a)(3) and (4) — as opposed to liability as an "owner and operator" under section 107(a)(1) and (2) — if they arrange for the disposal of hazardous substances at a facility or accept hazardous waste for transportation and disposal. 40 C.F.R. § 300.1100(d)(3).

In response to comments questioning whether the rule would apply in actions where the United States was not a party, EPA stated that the regulation is "a 'legislative' or 'substantive' rule that has undergone notice-and-comment pursuant to the Administrative Procedure Act" and as such "defines the liability of holders [of security interests] for CERCLA response costs in both the United States' and private party litigation." [Citation] The agency alternatively asserted that even if the rule were read as "a 'mere' interpretation of section 101(20)(A)," it would affect third-party litigation since "EPA guidance and interpretations of laws administered by the Agency are given substantial deference by the courts."

Michigan and the Chemical Manufacturers Association filed petitions for review of the final regulation under section 113(a) of CERCLA, 42 U.S.C. § 9613(a).... Petitioners argue that EPA lacks statutory authority to define, through its regulation, the scope of lender liability under section 107 — an issue that they assert only federal courts may adjudicate. They also urge that the substance of the regulation contradicts the plain meaning of certain statutory language.

II.

Although petitioners bring a general challenge to the authority of EPA to promulgate any substantive regulations under CERCLA, that issue is settled. We held in *Wagner Seed Co., Inc. v. Bush*, 946 F.2d 918, 920 (D.C. Cir. 1991), that the President had broadly delegated his statutory powers to EPA, and it is "the administering agency" for the statute. However, we had previously recognized that with respect to any specific regulation, EPA must demonstrate "either explicit or implicit evidence of congressional intent to delegate interpretive authority." [Citation] EPA, for its part, contends that *Wagner Seed* went further and recognized EPA's general authority under section 115 of CERCLA to promulgate rules that a typical administrative agency would issue, rules that are "reasonably related to the purposes of the enabling legislation." [Citation]

The government overreads *Wagner Seed*. We held there that EPA had authority to interpret certain language in section 106 of CERCLA that applied to EPA's administrative responsibilities. We rejected petitioners' argument, which found some support in a strong dissent, that the entire section 106 referring to liability questions must be interpreted in court, and that EPA therefore had no authority to define that section.... Here we encounter an issue not squarely decided in *Wagner Seed* — whether the EPA can, by regulation, define and limit a party's liability under section 107. But the reasoning of *Wagner Seed*, or at least its dicta, cuts against the government.

EPA looks to several different portions of CERCLA to find the specific authority we have required. The agency points to section 105 of CERCLA, which provides that the agency has responsibility to promulgate the national contingency plan setting forth the actions and procedures to be taken in response to a contamination. It is argued that the broad language of section 105, authorizing EPA "to reflect and effectuate the responsibilities and powers created by this chapter," 42 U.S.C. § 9605(a), gives it power to define section 107 liability — which the agency characterizes as a "responsibility and power" under the chapter. Although the mandate of section 105 does "provide[] the EPA with broad rulemaking authority to craft the NCP," it is hardly a specific delegation of authority to EPA to interpret section 107. [Citation] We must still determine whether defining the scope of liability is among the "responsibilities and powers" Congress delegated to EPA under CERCLA.

EPA points to specific provisions of that section, paragraphs 105(a)(4) and 105(a)(3). The former authorizes the agency to prescribe "appropriate roles and responsibilities ... of nongovernmental entities in effectuating the plan." [Citation] EPA claims that the lender liability rule accomplishes just that by defining the "role" of security creditors. That is an imaginative use of the word role, but EPA's argument is hardly persuasive since section 105 refers to the nature of actions parties must take in response to contamination — not their ultimate liability for the contamination set forth in section 107. If EPA's position were correct, Congress would have had no need to provide for a party's liability in section 107; EPA would have been authorized to develop those standards under section 105. For similar reasons, paragraph 105(a)(3) does not help EPA. That provision obliges the agency to issue "methods and criteria for determining the appropriate extent of removal, remedy, and other measures authorized by [CERCLA]," but it does not speak to liability. As discussed below, a party might be obliged to provide a remedy and be entitled to reimbursement when determined subsequently not to be liable.

EPA also relies on those statutory provisions which grant it authority to seek enforcement. The agency may choose to contract to clean up a contaminated site (financed through the Superfund), and then bring action in federal court under section 107(a)(4)(A) to recover its costs from a liable party. It is argued that the agency must first decide whether a party is actually liable before bringing such an action. That is no different, however, than any government "prosecutor" who must in good faith determine for itself whether a civil action in federal court should be brought — which necessarily includes a judgment whether a potential defendant violated the law or is "liable." The court is, nevertheless, the first body to formally determine liability, and therefore a civil prosecutor typically lacks authority to issue substantive regulations to interpret a statute establishing liability. [Citations]

To be sure, the agency also has authority, when imminent danger of harm exists, to issue administrative orders under section 106(a) requiring private parties to clean up a site. And, if the party refuses, section 106(b)(1) authorizes EPA to seek compliance in federal court. But, under the statute, a respondent must comply with such orders whether or not it is liable. Liability issues are resolved when the party against whom the order was levied seeks reimbursement under section 106(b)(2). The statutory scheme might be described as requiring parties to shoot first (clean up) and ask questions (determine who bears the ultimate liability) later.

That brings us to EPA's strongest argument — that its role in implementing the reimbursement provisions of section 106(b)(2) implies authority to define liability. Under that section, a party that has cleaned up a contaminated site pursuant to an administrative order may petition the EPA for reimbursement of its reasonable costs. If EPA refuses, a federal court may order reimbursement if it determines that the party is not liable or, even if liable, that the party has demonstrated that the cleanup actions it was ordered to take were arbitrary and capricious or otherwise unlawful. 42 U.S.C. § 9606(b)(2)(C)-(D). By implication, EPA argues that it must decide these liability questions when it determines whether or not to reimburse.

A careful reading of that provision, and the entire subsection 106(b), leads us to a contrary view. Although a party must first petition EPA for reimbursement under subparagraph 106(b)(2)(A), that provision is completely silent as to what criteria EPA uses to grant reimbursement. If EPA denies reimbursement because the agency contends the party is liable, the party has a right to bring an action in federal court under subparagraph 106(b)(2)(B); if the party establishes that it is not liable by a preponderance of the evidence, under subparagraph 106(b)(2)-(C) it prevails. EPA is, under that scenario, only a defendant; its preliminary conclusion that the party was liable is entitled to no consideration, let alone the deference afforded to the typical administrative agency adjudication. On the other hand, a petitioner who is liable may nevertheless seek review under subparagraph 106(b)(2)(D) to challenge the reasonableness of EPA's ordered response. In such a case, the party, "a petitioner," must establish on the administrative record that EPA's order was arbitrary and capricious or not in accordance with law, the familiar APA standard of review.

The drafters of subsection 106(b) appear to us to have quite consciously distinguished between EPA's role in determining the appropriate cleanup action (which is entitled to deference under 106(b)(2)(D)) from the agency's position on liability when a party disputes claims. Liability issues are to be decided by the court, and therefore although EPA may well enjoy authority to issue regulations interpreting or implementing subparagraph 106(b)(2)(D), it does not seem that Congress intended the same authority with respect to subparagraphs 106(b)(2)(B) and (C).

That reading of section 106(b)(2) conforms with the provisions of CERCLA that provide for a private right of action in federal court by property owners or states to recover cleanup costs, from those liable for the contamination. [Citations] Questions of liability, accordingly, can be put at issue in federal court by disputing private parties — without any government involvement. Under these circumstances, it cannot be argued that Congress intended EPA, one of many potential plaintiffs, to have authority to, by regulation, define liability for a class of potential defendants.... Congress, by providing for private rights of action under section 107, has designated the courts and not EPA as the adjudicator of the scope of CERCLA liability. And Congress did so quite deliberately. [Citation]

III.

There remains the question of whether the regulation can be sustained as an interpretative rule. The preamble to the final regulation suggests that EPA attempted to straddle two horses — issuing the rule as a legislative regulation but asserting in the alternative that as an interpretative rule, it would still be entitled to judicial deference and therefore affect private party litigation. Although we have admitted that the distinction between legislative and interpretative rules is "enshrouded in considerable smog," it is commonly understood that a rule is legislative if it is "based on an agency's power to exercise its judgment as to how best to implement a general statutory mandate," and has the binding force of law. [Citations] By contrast, an interpretative rule "is based on specific statutory provisions," and represents the agency's construction of the statute that is — while not binding — entitled to substantial judicial deference under *Chevron U.S.A. Inc. v. Natural Resources Defense Council, Inc.*, 467 U.S. 837.

The rule bears little resemblance to what we have traditionally found to be an interpretative regulation. EPA does not really define specific statutory terms, but rather takes off from those terms and devises a comprehensive regulatory regime to address the liability problems facing secured creditors....

In any event, the same reason that prevents the agency from issuing the rule as a substantive regulation precludes judicial deference to EPA's offered "interpretation." If Congress meant the judiciary, not EPA, to determine liability issues — and we believe Congress did — EPA's view of statutory liability may not be given deference....

Petitioners conceded that the regulation could be sustained as a policy statement that would guide EPA's enforcement proceedings across the country, but EPA has not asked that its regulation be so regarded. Furthermore, intervenors point out that if the regulation were to affect only EPA's enforcement proceedings, lenders would still face potentially staggering liability because of the generality of the statutory language and the prospect of private suits. That potential liability would force lenders to behave cautiously even if EPA were to adhere to the regulation as its policy. Given our uncertainty as to EPA's wishes, we think the proper course is to vacate the rule and leave EPA free to take whatever steps it thinks appropriate.

The petition for review is granted and the regulation is hereby vacated.

NOTES AND QUESTIONS

1. Following the decision in *Kelley* vacating the lender liability rule on grounds of lack of agency authority, the EPA reaffirmed its intentions to follow the provisions of the 1992 rule as the basis of its enforcement policy. 60 Fed. Reg. 63517 (December 11, 1995).

2. Court decisions since *Kelley* have interpreted the security interest exemption in a manner generally consistent with the invalidated EPA rule. *See Z & Z Leasing, Inc. v. Graying Reel, Inc.*, 873 F. Supp. 51, 55 (E.D. Mich. 1995) (bank not liable under CERCLA where involvement in financial affairs of mortgagor was part of normal course of business); *Kemp Industries, Inc. v. Safety Light Corp.*, 857 F. Supp. 373, 395 (D.N.J. 1994) (security exemption applied to company which financed construction of industrial facility through sale-leaseback arrangement where company did not actually participate in operations or management of properties).

3. For additional commentary on the security interest exception to liability generally and *Fleet Factors* in particular, see the following references: Malloy, *Equity Participations and Lender Liability Under CERCLA*, 15 COLUM. J. ENVT'L L. 63 (1990); Smith, *The Expansive Scope of Liable Parties Under CERCLA*, 63 ST. JOHN'S L. REV. 821 (1989); Burkhart, *Lender/Owners and CERCLA: Title and Liability*, 25 HARV. J. ON LEGIS. 317 (1988); Grad, *A Legislative History of the Comprehensive Environmental Response, Compensation and Liability ("Superfund") Act of 1980*, 8 COLUM. J. ENVT'L L. 1 (1982).

UNITED STATES OF AMERICA v. R.W. MEYER, INC.

932 F.2d 568 (6th Cir. 1991)

BERTELSMAN, DISTRICT JUDGE.

This appeal involved the construction of the provisions of the Comprehensive Environmental Response, Compensation, and Liability Act (CERCLA) governing contribution actions among responsible parties following a cleanup of a hazardous waste site and an Immediate Removal Action by the Environmental Protection Agency (EPA). 42 U.S.C. §§ 9607, 9613(f)(1).

Background

The facts and background necessary to place this opinion in context were well stated by Chief Judge Hillman in his unpublished opinion awarding contribution, as follows:

> "This matter stems from a suit brought by the United States against Northernaire Plating Company ("Northernaire") for recovery of its costs in conducting an 'Immediate Removal Action' pursuant to the Comprehensive Environmental Response, Compensation & Liability Act (hereinafter, "CERCLA"), 42 U.S.C. § 9601, et seq. Northernaire owned and operated a metal electroplating business in Cadillac, Michigan. Beginning in 1972, it operated under a 10-year lease on property owned by R.W. Meyer, Inc. ("Meyer"). Northernaire continued operations until mid-1981 when its assets were sold to Toplocker Enterprises, Inc. ("Toplocker"). From July of 1975 until this sale, Willard S. Garwood was the president and sole shareholder of Northernaire. He personally oversaw and managed the day-to-day operations of the company.
>
> "Acting upon inspection reports from the Michigan Department of Natural Resources ("MDNR"), the United States Environmental Protection Agency ("EPA") conducted an Immediate Removal Action at the Northernaire site

from July 5 until August 3, 1983. Cleanup of the site required neutralization of caustic acids, bulking and shipment of liquid acids, neutralization of caustic and acid sludges, excavation and removal of a contaminated sewer line, and decontamination of the inside of the building. All of the hazardous substances found at the site were chemicals and by-products of metal electro-plating operations. [The district court found the defendants Garwood, Northernaire, and Meyer jointly and severally liable to plaintiff for the costs of the Immediate Removal Action under Section 107(a) of CERCLA. Each defendant brought cross-claims for contribution against the other.]

"CERCLA specifically allows actions for contribution among parties who have been held jointly and severally liable:

"(1) Contribution

"Any person may seek contribution from any other person who is liable or potentially liable under section 9607(a) of this title, during or following any civil action under section 9606 of this title or under section 9607(a) of this title. Such claims shall be brought in accordance with this section and the Federal Rules of Civil Procedure, and shall be governed by Federal law. In resolving contribution claims, the court may allocate response costs among liable parties using such equitable factors as the court determines are appropriate. Nothing in this sub-section shall diminish the right of any person to bring an action for contribution in the absence of a civil action under section 9606 or section 9607 of this title." 42 U.S.C. 9613(f)(1)."

Apparently, the parties allowed the building to degenerate into a true environmental disaster area. As this court observed in the former appeal:

"In March 1983, officials from the EPA and the Michigan Department of Natural Resources (MDNR) examined the property. Their examination was prompted by earlier reports of MDNR officials indicating that the building had been locked and abandoned and that a child had received chemical burns from playing around discarded drums of electroplating waste that were left outside the building. State tests on samples of the soil, sludge, and drum contents disclosed the presence of significant amounts of caustic and corrosive materials. During their examination of the site, EPA and MDNR officials observed drums and tanks housing cyanide littered among disarray outside the facility. Based on their observations outside the building, the officials determined that Northernaire had discharged its electroplating waste into a "catch" basin and that the waste had seeped into the ground from the bottom of the basin. The waste then entered a pipe that drained into a sewer line that discharged into the sewage treatment plant for the city of Cadillac."

In the former appeal, this court affirmed the decision of the trial court finding that the damage to the site had been "indivisible" and imposing joint and several liability on the present parties to reimburse the EPA for the removal costs for the cleanup of the building.

The total cost of the cleanup plus prejudgment interest was $ 342,823.22. In this subsequent contribution action, the trial court held that two-thirds of the liability should be borne by Northernaire and its principal shareholder, each contributing one-third each. But the court held that the remaining one-third ($114,274.41) should be borne by the appellant property owner.

The appellant attacks this apportionment, arguing strenuously that its responsibility should be limited to an amount apportioned according to the degree that the sewer line mentioned in the above quote contributed to the cleanup costs. Applying this approach, the appellant generously offers to pay $ 1,709.03. Appellees accept the trial court's apportionment....

Analysis

The trial court held that it was within its discretion to apply certain factors found in the legislative history of CERCLA in making its contribution apportionment. Although these factors were originally intended as criteria for deciding whether a party could establish a right to an apportionment of several liability in the EPA's initial removal action, the trial court found "these criteria useful in determining the proportionate share each party is entitled to in contribution from the other."

The criteria mentioned are:

"(1) the ability of the parties to demonstrate that their contribution to a discharge release or disposal of a hazardous waste can be distinguished;

"(2) the amount of the hazardous waste involved;

"(3) the degree of toxicity of the hazardous waste involved;

"(4) the degree of involvement by the parties in the generation, transportation, treatment, storage, or disposal of the hazardous waste;

"(5) the degree of care exercised by the parties with respect to the hazardous waste concerned, taking into account the characteristics of such hazardous waste; and

"(6) the degree of cooperation by the parties with Federal, State, or local officials to prevent any harm to the public health or the environment."

Id. (citing *Amoco Oil Co. v. Dingwell*, 690 F. Supp. 78, 86 (D. Me. 1988), *aff'd sub nom. Travelers Indemnity Co. v. Dingwell*, 884 F.2d 629 (1st Cir. 1989); *United States v. A & F Materials Co., Inc.*, 578 F. Supp. 1249 (S.D. Ill. 1984); H.R. No. 253 (III), 99th Cong., 2d Sess. 19, (1985), *reprinted in* 1986 U.S. Code Cong. & Admin. News 3038, 3042).

The trial court recognized that the lessee was the primary actor in allowing this site to become contaminated. (Appellant argues that the lessee was the *only* actor.) The trial court found, however, that in addition to constructing the defective sewer line which contributed to the contamination, appellant bore significant responsibility "simply by virtue of being the landowner." The trial court observed further that appellant "neither assisted nor cooperated with the EPA officials during their investigation and eventual cleanup of the ... site."

Chief Judge Hillman concluded, "As it is well within the province of this court, I have balanced each of the defendants' behavior with respect to the equitable guidelines discussed." *Id.* at 421. As a result of the balancing, he made the apportionment described above.

The trial judge was well within the broad discretion afforded by the statute in making the apportionment he did.

Congress intended to invest the district courts with this discretion in making CERCLA contribution allocations when it provided, "the court may allocate response costs among the liable parties using such *equitable factors as the court determines are appropriate*." 42 U.S.C. § 9613(f)(1) (emphasis added).

Essentially, appellant argues here that a narrow, technical construction must be given to the term "contribution," so that, as in common law contribution, contribution under the statute is limited to the percentage a party's improper conduct causally contributed to the toxicity of the site in a physical sense. This argument is without merit. On the contrary, by using the term "equitable factors" Congress intended to invoke the tradition of equity under which the court must construct a flexible decree balancing all the equities in the light of the totality of the circumstances.[3] ...

"The hallmark of a court of equity is its ability to frame its decree to effect a balancing of all the equities and to protect the interest of all affected by it, including the public." Congress reemphasized that the trial court should invoke its moral as well as its legal sense by providing that the court use not just "equitable factors," which phrase already implies a large degree of discretion, but "such equitable factors as the court determines are appropriate." This language broadens the trial court's scope of discretion even further.

Thus, under § 9613(f)(1) the court may consider any factor it deems in the interest of justice in allocating contribution recovery. Certainly, the several factors listed by the trial court are appropriate, but as it recognized, it was not limited to them. No exhaustive list of criteria need or should be formulated.

---

[3]The pertinent legislative history reads: "New subsection 113(g)(1) of CERCLA was also amended by the Committee to ratify current judicial decisions that the courts may use their equitable powers to apportion the costs of clean-up among the various responsible parties involved with the site. The Committee emphasizes that courts are to resolve claims for apportionment on a case-by-case basis pursuant to Federal common law, taking relevant equitable considerations into account. Thus, after all questions of liability and remedy have been resolved, courts may consider any criteria relevant to determining whether there should be an apportionment." H.R. 253(III), 99th Cong., 2d Sess. 19, (1985), *reprinted in* 1986 U.S. Code Cong. & Admin. News 3038, 3041-42.

However, in addition to the criteria listed above, the court may consider the state of mind of the parties, their economic status, any contracts between them bearing on the subject, any traditional equitable defenses as mitigating factors and any other factors deemed appropriate to balance the equities in the totality of the circumstances.

Therefore, the trial court quite properly considered here not only the appellant's contribution to the toxic slough described above in a technical causative sense, but also its moral contribution as the owner of the site. Review of the trial court's equitable balancing process is limited to a review for "abuse of discretion." This is in accord with the principle of equity that the chancellor has broad discretion to frame a decree.

This case, even though it involves over $300,000, is but a pimple on the elephantine carcass of the CERCLA litigation now making its way through the court system. Some of these cases involve millions or even billions of dollars in cleanup costs and hundreds or even thousands of potentially responsible parties.

I do not believe Congress intended to require meticulous findings of the precise causative contribution each of several hundred parties made to a hazardous site. In many cases, this would be literally impossible. Rather, by the expansive language used in § 9613(f)(1) Congress intended the court to deal with these situations by creative means, considering all the equities and balancing them in the interests of justice. As recognized by a recent comprehensive scholarly article, this multi-factor approach takes into account more varying circumstances than common law contribution.

"Courts are also following CERCLA Section 113(f) and taking 'equitable factors' into account in apportioning liability for response costs. The equitable factors which courts are examining in order to decide what kind of apportionment to make depend on the actual facts of each case. Nevertheless, many federal courts do consider common law equitable defenses such as unclean hands and caveat emptor as mitigating factors in deciding liability for response costs. This approach is in line with Congressional intent as long as courts do not consider these equitable defenses to be a total bar to a liability action, but merely mitigating factors in awarding damages. Courts are also using a modified comparative fault analysis that takes numerous factors such as culpability and cooperation into account in apportioning damages."

Although such an approach "cannot be applied with mathematical precision, it is the fairest and most workable approach for apportioning CERCLA liability. Such an approach furthers the legislative intent of encouraging the prompt cleanup of hazardous sites by those equitably responsible. The parties actually performing the cleanup can look for reimbursement from other potentially responsible parties without fear that their contribution actions will be bogged down by the impossibility of making meticulous factual determinations as to the causal contribution of each party. Chief Judge Hillman was well within the equitable discretion afforded him by Congress in the way he handled this CERCLA contribution action.

Affirmed.

NOTES AND QUESTIONS

1. The system of joint and several liability in CERCLA may result in certain responsible parties ultimately bearing a disproportionate amount of the cleanup costs than their share of the harm. The potential inequity in CERCLA's liability scheme is partially alleviated by providing settlement alternatives for *de minimis* waste contributors (CERCLA § 122, 42 U.S.C. § 9622) and by providing a statutory cause of action for contribution to settling parties. CERCLA § 113(f), 42 U.S.C. § 9613(f).

2. *Contribution and Settlement.* Prior to the 1986 SARA amendments, CERCLA did not address the issues of contribution, indemnification, and settlement. Courts recognized that the CERCLA scheme imposed joint and several liability where the harm is indivisible, but the effect of settlement on contribution rights of non-settling PRPs was unresolved. The amended contribution provisions promote settlement by giving incentives and protections to parties who have resolved their liability with federal or state entities. *See* CERCLA § 113(f), 42 U.S.C. § 9613(f). One court explained the history as follows:

> Congress passed this provision to encourage settlement of CERCLA cases. Previously, settlors had no statutory assurance that any settlement that they reached with the EPA would end their liability in a case because non-settlors might later seek contribution from them. In an attempt to offset this disincentive to settle, the Environmental Protection Agency ("EPA") adopted a policy of reducing its judgment against non-settlors to the extent necessary to extinguish the settlor's liability to the non-settlors. SARA's contribution provisions eliminates the need for such a policy where the settlement is "administrative or judicially approved."

> The result is a powerful tool — actually a carrot and a stick — placed in the hands of the EPA to obtain settlements. The carrot the EPA can offer potential settlors is that they need no longer fear that a later contribution action by a non-settlor will compel them to pay still more money to extinguish their liability. In addition to this protection, settlors themselves are enabled to seek contribution against non-settlors. 42 U.S.C. sec. 9613(f)(3)(B). As for the stick, if the settlor pays less than its proportionate share of liability, the non-settlors, being jointly and severally liable, must make good the difference. In this respect, the words of the statute are clear: the potential liability of the others is reduced "by the amount of settlement,"

not by the settlor's proportionate share of any damages ultimately determined to have been caused.

In re Acushnet River & New Bedford Harbor: Proceedings re Alleged PCB Pollution, 712 F. Supp. 1019, 1027 (D. Mass. 1989).

3. Section 113(f)(2) thus extinguishes contribution rights of PRPs against parties which have settled with the United States or a state with respect to matters contained in the settlement. Similarly, the statute provides a shield from contribution claims for parties who have entered into a *de minimis* settlement agreement with the government. CERCLA § 122(g)(5), 42 U.S.C. § 9622(g)(5). The government is shielded from contribution claims arising out of its own cleanup activities by virtue of sovereign immunity principles. The exclusive method for a private party to challenge an improper cleanup, then, is to show that the actions taken were inconsistent with the National Contingency Plan. *See* CERCLA § 107(a)(4)(A), 42 U.S.C. 9607(a)(4)(A); *United States v. Azrael*, 33 ERC 1029, 1034-35 (D. Md. 1991).

4. The party which has "resolved" its liability with the government, on the other hand, is empowered to seek contribution from other potentially responsible parties. 42 U.S.C. § 113(f)(3)(B). The government retains its right to seek recovery of response costs against non-settling PRPs if the settlement does not provide complete relief. CERCLA § 113(f)(3), 42 U.S.C. § 113(f)(3). The resolution of liability with the government must be pursuant to an administrative or judicially approved settlement in order to be insulated from contribution actions. CERCLA § 113(f)(2). *See United States v. Alcan Aluminum Corp.*, 990 F.2d 711, 725 (2d Cir. 1993) (government decision not to pursue legal action against PRP did not constitute "administrative settlement" resolving CERCLA liability for purposes of contribution immunity).

5. A private party cannot maintain a suit for recovery of response costs under section 107 nor bring a contribution claim unless the costs incurred were consistent with the National Contingency Plan. *See County Line Inv. Co. v. Tinney*, 933 F.2d 1508, 1516 (10th Cir. 1991) (Congress did not intend CERCLA to create a general federal right of contribution for damages and response costs that would not be otherwise cognizable under the statute).

6. In resolving contribution claims, the statute authorizes the court to allocate costs among the responsible parties using "equitable factors" that it deems appropriate. The "Gore factors" referenced in *Meyer* derive originally from a proposed House amendment to Superfund sponsored by then Congressman Albert Gore. Although the amendment, aimed at providing criteria to determine joint and several liability, did not pass the factors were pickd up by several courts and were cited favorably in legislative history to the amended section 113(f) regarding contribution. *See Environmental Transp. Systems, Inc. v. Ensco, Inc.*, 969 F.2d 503, 508 (7th Cir. 1992). In *United States v. Monsanto Co.*, 858 F.2d 160, 168 n.13. (4th Cir. 1988) the court suggested that the relative degree of fault and involvement by the parties in the generation, transportation, treatment, storage or disposal of hazardous substances were appropriate factors for allocating damages.

7. *Measurement.* A settlement by one joint tortfeasor with the government also affects the measure of liability exposure for remaining non-settlors. In section 113(f)(2), Congress adopted the approach followed by the UCAJTA where the non-settling defendant's liability is reduced only by the amount of the settlement rather than by a proportional share. *See* 42 U.S.C. § 113(f)(2); § 122(g)(5), 42 U.S.C. § 9622(g)(5). *See United States v. Rohm & Haas Co.*, 721 F. Supp. 666, 679 (D.N.J. 1989) (if proposed decree judicially approved, the non-settling PRP only gets credit for the dollar amount of the settlement, not a percentage reduction based on equitable factors).

8. CERCLA's approach is intended to encourage prompt settlements not only by giving protection to early settlors from contribution suits but also by leaving non-settlors bearing the risk of paying more than their equitable share. *See City of New York v. Exxon Corp.*, 697 F. Supp. 677, 693 (S.D.N.Y. 1988); *United States v. Rohm & Haas Co.*, 721 F. Supp. 666, 679 (D.N.J. 1989) (proportionate reduction approach would not decrease government enforcement costs because the parties would seek to litigate what constituted an equitable share). Although a settlement agreement among private parties does not carry protection from contribution claims by joint tortfeasors, the liability of non-settlors may be determined by comparative fault factors for an equitable apportionment of costs — such as embodied in the UCFA. *See Lyncott Corp. v. Chemical Waste Mgt., Inc.*, 690 F. Supp. 1409, 1418 (E.D. Pa. 1988). *Also see* Garber, *Federal Common Law of Contribution Under the 1986 CERCLA Amendments*, 14 ECOLOGY L.Q. 365 (1987).

RUMPKE OF INDIANA, INC. v. CUMMINS ENGINE CO.

107 F.3d 1235 (7th Cir. 1997)

WOOD, CIRCUIT JUDGE.

The net of potential liability under the Comprehensive Environmental Response, Compensation and Liability Act, better known as CERCLA, 42 U.S.C. §§ 9601 *et seq.*, is wide indeed, reflecting the need both to clean up the nation's toxic waste sites and the practical imperative to find the necessary money for the job. The cleanup will be less likely to occur if potentially responsible parties do not come forward, yet the often astronomical sums needed to restore these sites can deter prompt remedial action. CERCLA protects parties who settle claims with the government from liability for contribution in suits relating to "matters addressed" in administratively or judicially settled consent decrees. *See* § 113(f)(2), 42 U.S.C. § 9613(f)(2). In this interlocutory appeal, certified pursuant to 28 U.S.C. § 1292(b), we have been asked to decide several questions relating to the breadth of one of those settlements. The central issue is whether a 1982 consent decree approved in *United States v. Seymour Recycling Corp.*, 554 F. Supp. 1334 (S.D. Ind. 1982), to which Cummins Engine Co. and its fellow appellants were parties (to which we refer as the "Cummins group"), stands in the way of the efforts of Rumpke of Indiana, Inc. ("Rumpke"), either to recover its costs of cleaning up a site arguably not covered by the *Seymour* decree under § 107(a) of the Act, 42 U.S.C. § 9607(a), or to obtain contribution from the Cummins group under § 113(f)(1) of the Act, 42 U.S.C. § 9613(f)(1). We agree with the district court that the *Seymour* decree did not encompass the matters Rumpke is now raising and we accordingly affirm its order.

I

The background facts are relatively straightforward. In 1984, Rumpke bought a 273-acre dump known as the Uniontown Landfill from George and Ethel Darlage. At that time, the Darlages informed Rumpke that the landfill had never accepted hazardous waste. For reasons undisclosed on this record, Rumpke did not conduct its own inspection of the land for environmental hazards prior to the sale. In light of where we are today, it is easy to predict what happened next. In 1990, to its professed surprise, Rumpke discovered that the Darlages' beliefs about the landfill had been quite wrong. In fact, a cocktail of hazardous wastes had been deposited at Uniontown for many years, and volatile organic compounds (VOCs) were migrating to surrounding areas. Looking into the matter, Rumpke determined that much of this material had come from the Seymour Recycling Corporation, which was located about ten miles away in Seymour, Indiana. For many years, Seymour had distilled for reuse acetones, alcohols, paint thinners, chlorinated solvents, and freon materials, all of which had been discarded by various manufacturers. The distilling process yielded both reusable solvents and a toxic sludge. Seymour disposed of the sludge by shoveling it into 55-gallon drums, or on other occasions, incinerating it and storing the resulting ash in similar drums. Rumpke believed that some of those 55-gallon drums made their way to the Uniontown landfill. Because Seymour Recycling was by this time out of the picture, Rumpke brought this action against the manufacturers that used to send materials to Seymour Recycling for processing.

Rumpke's lawsuit opened a Pandora's Box of its own. Whatever one might say about the Uniontown site, it had become clear in the 1980's that the Seymour site was an environmental disaster area. Seymour Recycling had left some 60,000 drums and 98 bulk storage tanks, in various stages of decay, strewn about the site. By 1980, the drums and tanks were leaking, exploding, and sending clouds of toxic chemicals into the air over nearby residential areas. The United States responded with a complaint in May 1980, alleging violations of section 7003 of the Resource Conservation and Recovery Act (RCRA), 42 U.S.C. § 6973, and section 311 of the Clean Water Act, 33 U.S.C. § 1321. In 1982, the United States filed an amended complaint adding allegations under CERCLA, §§ 106 and 107, 42 U.S.C. §§ 9606 and 9607, which had been enacted in the meantime. The amended complaint added 24 new defendants who allegedly had transported hazardous wastes to the Seymour site for handling, storage, disposal, or treatment. At the same time, the State of Indiana and the County of Jackson moved to intervene in the action.

The amended complaint was accompanied by a proposed consent decree that was filed with the court, as required by § 122(d), 42 U.S.C. § 9622(d), which the court accepted in due course. *See Seymour Recycling*, 554 F. Supp. 1334, *supra*. The decree resolved all obligations and responsibilities of the settling companies with respect to "the Seymour site." The companies paid agreed amounts into the Seymour Site Trust Fund, which was then available to trustees to perform the work described in an exhibit to the decree. It provided for penalties in the event the work was not performed satisfactorily; it gave the United States and the State the right to access and inspect the site at all times until the work was completed; and it contained various administrative provisions. The decree also promised, in section XII, that the United States, the State, and the local governments would not bring any more civil actions against the settling companies:

> ... arising out of or related to the storage, treatment, handling, disposal, transportation or presence or actual or threatened release or discharge of any materials at, to, from or near the Seymour site, including any action with respect to surface cleanup and soil or groundwater cleanup at the Seymour site.

Our case arises because the defendants Rumpke wants to pursue — Cummins, Ford Motor Company, International Business Machines Corp., General Motors Corp., and Essex Group, Inc. — were among the Seymour settling parties.

II

After Rumpke filed its action with respect to the contaminated Uniontown site, the Cummins group moved for summary judgment against Rumpke's claims. They argued that Rumpke's suit was blocked by the language just quoted from the 1982 Seymour consent decree, by virtue of CERCLA § 113(f)(2), which reads as follows:

> A person who has resolved its liability to the United States or a State in an administrative or judicially approved settlement shall not be liable for claims for contribution regarding matters addressed in the settlement. Such settlement does not discharge any of the other potentially liable persons unless its terms so provide, but it reduces the potential liability of the others by the amount of the settlement.

The Cummins group reasoned that (1) the Rumpke suit presented "claims for contribution," and (2) the claims were "matters addressed in the settlement" by virtue of section XII of the decree. Specifically, with appropriate ellipses, they argued that section XII covered actions "arising out of ... the ... transportation ... of any materials ... from ... the Seymour site." Rumpke's claim against them alleged that materials from the named manufacturers had been transported from the Seymour site to the Uniontown site; thus, they asserted, it fell squarely within the language of section XII and the claim was barred by § 113(f)(2). Q.E.D.

In the order on interlocutory appeal, the district court did not dwell on the question whether the Rumpke suit presented claims for contribution, evidently for two reasons. First, it noted that Rumpke's suit was in part based on § 107(a) of the Act, which provides for private cost recovery, rather than contribution. It acknowledged that *Akzo Coatings, Inc. v. Aigner Corp.*, 30 F.3d 761 (7th Cir. 1994), held that claims by one potentially responsible party (PRP) (here, Rumpke as present landowner) against another (here, the Cummins group) must normally be brought as contribution claims under § 113(f)(1), but it noted that *Akzo* also recognized an exception to that rule. Under the exception, a landowner may bring a § 107 action to recover for its direct injuries "if the party seeking relief is itself not responsible for having caused any of the hazardous materials to be spilled onto the property."...

III

The central question that concerned the district court was whether the 1982 settlement protects the Cummins defendants from this suit, as a result of the protection afforded by § 113(f)(2). As we noted above, § 113(f)(2) is triggered when several circumstances are present: (1) a person must have resolved liability either to the United States or a State in an administrative or judicially approved settlement, (2) it must be facing "claims for contribution" in the present suit, and (3) those claims must encompass "matters addressed in the settlement." In our view, however, before addressing the specifics of § 113(f)(2), we must decide how Rumpke's § 107(a) theory affects the case.

A. *Claims for Direct Cost Recovery and Contribution*

Rumpke's suit against the Cummins group was based on both the cost recovery theory of § 107(a) and the contribution theory of § 113(f)(1). [We believe] that we should reach the question whether this suit may proceed under § 107(a), or under § 113(f)(1), or both. If § 107(a) is unavailable as a matter of law to Rumpke, we have only the § 113(f)(1) arguments to consider, which in turn requires us to interpret the *Seymour* consent decree. On the other hand, if Rumpke is entitled to proceed under § 107(a), the contribution bar of § 113(f)(2) may not apply at all; if it does not, then the dispute about the scope of the *Seymour* decree might be beside the point. Either way, it appears to us that the proper basis for Rumpke's action is a question fairly comprehended within the order under review.

1. *Rumpke's § 107(a) claim.*

Rumpke pointed out in both its brief and at oral argument that it is not subject to any administrative cleanup order from the Indiana Department of Environmental Management (IDEM), the federal Environmental Protection Agency (EPA), or any other public authority. Thus, Rumpke is not a party that is now or ever has been subject to a civil action under CERCLA § 106, 42 U.S.C. § 9606 (which authorizes the President to bring an action to require responsible parties to clean up sites threatening the environment). It is also undisputed that no party has ever brought a cost recovery action against Rumpke under § 107. Instead, Rumpke has stated that it "intends to act, consistent with the National Contingency Plan, to assure that the VOCs it has discovered outside of the waste disposal area of the Uniontown Landfill, but within the property boundaries of the Landfill, do not become a threat to health or the environment." Furthermore, like the district court, on this review from a grant of summary judgment, we assume that Rumpke did nothing to contribute to the presence of the hazardous substances. Its status as a PRP for CERCLA purposes is based solely on its ownership of the Uniontown site — ownership, we assume at this stage, it acquired without knowledge of the presence of environmental hazards and after all the deposits had been made.

The question is whether our *Akzo* exception applies to Rumpke: may a landowner PRP bring a direct liability suit for cost recovery under § 107(a) against other PRPs (in this case "arrangers"), if it contributed nothing to the hazardous conditions at the site, or is the *Akzo* exception available only to a narrower group of parties, such as the landowner who discovers someone surreptitiously dumping wastes on its land? In this connection, it is useful to review our decision in *Akzo* in somewhat more detail. In that case, Akzo sued Aigner Corporation and a number of other companies seeking contribution for initial cleanup work it had performed at the Fisher-Calo site and the costs it had incurred in studying the long term cleanup of the site with other PRPs. Akzo itself had sent hazardous wastes to the site. 30 F.3d at 764. It argued nevertheless that it was entitled to bring a direct cost recovery action under § 107(a), because the language of § 107(a) broadly permits any "person" to seek recovery of appropriate cleanup costs. *Id.* at 764. We rejected that argument, noting that:

> ... Akzo has experienced no injury of the kind that would typically give rise to a direct claim under section 107(a) — it is not, for example, a landowner forced to clean up hazardous materials that a third party spilled onto its property or that migrated there from adjacent lands. Instead, Akzo itself is a party liable in some measure for the contamination at the FisherCalo site, and the gist of Akzo's claim is that the costs it has incurred should be apportioned equitably amongst itself and the others responsible.... That is a quintessential claim for contribution.

Id. Both the majority and the dissenting judges agreed, therefore, that Akzo's claim was governed solely by the contribution action § 113(f). In other words, when two parties who both injured the property have a dispute about who pays how much — a derivative liability, apportionment dispute — the statute directs them to § 113(f) and only to § 113(f).

... [W]e see nothing in the language of § 107(a) that would make it unavailable to a party suing to recover for direct injury to its own land, under circumstances where it is not trying to apportion costs (i.e., where it is seeking to recover on a direct liability theory, rather than trying to divide up its own liability for someone else's injuries among other potentially responsible parties). It is true that liability under § 107(a) is joint and several, and § 113(f) exists for the express purpose of allocating fault among PRPs. [Citations] Nevertheless, one of two outcomes would follow from a landowner suit under § 107(a): either the facts would establish that the landowner was truly blameless, in which case the other PRPs would be entitled to bring a suit under § 113(f) within three years of the judgment to establish their liability among themselves, or the facts would show that the landowner was also partially responsible, in which case it would not be entitled to recover under its § 107(a) theory and only the § 113(f) claim would go forward. Neither one of those outcomes is inconsistent with the statutory scheme promoting allocation of liability.

The statutes of limitations available for § 107(a) and § 113(f) actions also provide no reason for concern. Superficially, it is true that a cost recovery suit under § 107(a) must be brought within six years (roughly speaking — in some circumstances a shorter 3-year period applies), see 42 U.S.C. § 9613(g)(2), while a seemingly shorter 3-year period applies to contribution actions, see 42 U.S.C. § 9613(g)(3). The question is, however, three years from when? Contribution actions may be brought within three years of either the date of judgment in any cost recovery action or within three years of the date of an administrative order under §§ 9622(g) or (h), or a judicially approved settlement order. In cases like Rumpke's, where no prior cost recovery action or applicable order has been entered, it would therefore be impossible to use § 107(a) as a tool for obtaining an advantage for limitations purposes. The contribution claim would not accrue until one of the events specified in § 9613(g)(2) occurred, at which time three years would be available in which to file an appropriate suit.

The language of § 113(f) also suggests that Rumpke's § 107(a) suit is consistent with the statute as a whole. Section 113(f)(1) begins with the following sentence:

> Any person may seek contribution from any other person who is liable or potentially liable under section 9607(a) [§ 107(a)] of this title, during or following any civil action under section 9606 [§ 106] of this title or under section 9607(a) of this title.

Because neither a § 106 nor a § 107(a) proceeding has been concluded, Rumpke's action obviously does not "follow" such an action. Rumpke has brought its own § 107(a) action, in Count I of its complaint. If it turns out that Rumpke is not the innocent party it portrays itself to be, then Rumpke will not qualify for the *Akzo* exception. It would still be entitled to seek contribution for its expenses from the other PRPs, assuming it met the requirements of § 113(f)(1). (We acknowledge, as other courts have, that this seems to provide a disincentive for parties voluntarily to undertake cleanup operations, because a § 106 or § 107(a) action apparently must either be ongoing or already completed before § 113(f)(1) is available. This appears to be what the statute requires, however.)

If one were to read § 107(a) as implicitly denying standing to sue even to landowners like Rumpke who did not create the hazardous conditions, this would come perilously close to reading § 107(a) itself out of the statute. As one district court in New Jersey recognized, this position would "mean that Section 107(a) private party plaintiffs will be few and far between. Truly innocent private party plaintiffs would be limited to, for example, a neighbor of a contaminated site who has acted to stem threatened releases for which he is not responsible, or a party who can claim one of the complete defenses set forth in 42 U.S.C. § 9607(b)." [Citation] Notwithstanding that observation, the New Jersey district court adopted the narrower approach to § 107(a), relying in part on a rather narrow reading of our *Akzo* opinion. We disagree, however, that *Akzo* requires such a result, or that it would be consistent with the broader purpose and structure of CERCLA. We conclude instead that landowners who allege that they did not pollute the site in any way may sue for their direct response costs under § 107(a). To the extent this looks like an implied claim for contribution, where the landowner is alleging that its share should be zero, we note that dicta in the Supreme Court's decision in *Key Tronic Corp. v. United States*, 511 U.S. 809, 128 L. Ed. 2d 797, 114 S. Ct. 1960 (1994), suggests that the Court was not disturbed by that possibility. *See* 511 U.S. at 816.

Rumpke, as a landowner seeking to recover for direct injury to its property inflicted by the Cummins group, was therefore entitled to sue under § 107(a). Unlike the plaintiff in *Akzo*, Rumpke alleges that it was not responsible for any of the waste at the Uniontown site. On the basis of the present record, we must regard it as a landowner on whose property others dumped hazardous materials, before Rumpke even owned the property. We see no distinction between this situation and a case where a landowner discovers that someone has been surreptitiously dumping hazardous materials on property it already owns, apart from the potentially more difficult question of fact about the landowner's own responsibility in the latter case.

Last, we must consider whether the contribution bar of § 113(f)(2) has any role to play in a direct cost recovery action under § 107(a). We conclude that it does not. The theory of a direct cost recovery action is that other parties must pay Rumpke for the cost of restoring the property. Contribution among the defendants could be of no possible benefit to a party entitled to recover its full direct costs, nor could the settlement carve-out feature of § 113(f)(2) be of any possible benefit to Rumpke as a Uniontown PRP. Cummins conceded at oral argument that its *Seymour* settlement will not and cannot reduce Rumpke's liability as a landowner of Uniontown by as much as a penny. This means that § 113(f)(2) has no role to play insofar as this is a direct liability action under § 107(a)(1).

2. *Rumpke's § 113(f)(1) claim.*

If the facts show, contrary to Rumpke's protestations, that it was partially responsible for the mess at Uniontown, *Akzo* holds that it can proceed only under § 113(f)(1) in a suit for contribution. In that case, the scope of the settlement bar of § 113(f)(2) would become important. We therefore turn to the question whether the 1982 *Seymour* settlement addressed the Cummins defendants' liability for sites other than the Seymour site itself.

B. *Matters Addressed in the Settlement*

The starting point for our analysis of this question is, as we noted in *Akzo*, the language of the consent decree itself. We said there that "the 'matters addressed' by a consent decree must be assessed in a manner consistent with both the reasonable expectations of the signatories and the equitable apportionment of costs that Congress has envisioned." This does not mean that the language of the decree is subject to an ill-defined equitable trump card; the congressional intent was viewed instead as something like a canon of construction for the language of the decree. The *Akzo* majority was especially concerned about the potential for negotiated consent decrees to affect third-party rights, through the contribution bar of § 113(f)(2). The statute itself addresses this problem directly, by making the contribution bar applicable only for administrative and judicially approved settlements, rather than to every private settlement that might be negotiated....

None of the factors found important in *Akzo* suggest that the 1982 *Seymour* decree addressed the settling parties' liability for waste from Seymour Recycling dumped at virtually any or every other spot on the globe, including the Uniontown landfill. Rumpke's Uniontown work is apart in "kind, context, and time" from the Seymour surface cleanup. The decree defined, very specifically, the parties' responsibilities for the Seymour Recycling site in Seymour, Indiana....

We therefore *affirm* the district court's order denying summary judgment based on the 1982 consent decree to Cummins Engine and its co-defendants, and granting partial summary judgment on this issue to Rumpke.

OLIN CORP. v. CONSOLIDATED ALUMINUM CORP.

5 F.3d 10 (2d Cir. 1993)

MESKILL, CIRCUIT JUDGE:

... At issue in this appeal is the proper interpretation of indemnity and release provisions contained in certain agreements entered into by Conalco and Olin. Conalco contends that these contractual provisions, which predated the enactment of CERCLA, are insufficient to relieve Olin of its liability under CERCLA for its pre-CERCLA activities at certain sites because the provisions contain no clear, unequivocal and express transfer of CERCLA liability. We hold that as to the site in Hannibal, Ohio these provisions are broad enough to require Conalco to indemnify Olin for CERCLA liability....

Background

Olin operated an aluminum plant in Ohio (the Hannibal site) from 1955 until December 1973. As part of its aluminum operations, Olin maintained processing equipment utilizing hydraulic fluid (Pydraul) manufactured by Monsanto Industrial Chemicals Company (Monsanto). The Pydraul contained polychlorinated biphenyls (PCBs) which CERCLA defines as a hazardous substance. *See* 42 U.S.C. § 9601(14)(A); 33 U.S.C. § 1321(b)(2)(A); 40 C.F.R. § 116.4 (1992).

The district court found that until 1972 Olin was unaware that Pydraul contained PCBs and was toxic. Olin disposed of the Pydraul and many of its industrial byproducts by depositing them in an impoundment pool on the Hannibal site. Olin periodically set the contents of the pool afire and then drained what remained into a swale.

In 1972, Monsanto sent Olin a letter advising that PCBs were present in Pydraul and that certain prophylactic measures, such as high-heat incineration, were necessary to assure safe disposal. Olin responded by discontinuing use of the impoundment pool; it constructed a liquid waste incinerator to dispose properly of its Pydraul and other hazardous liquids. The district court found, however, that Olin took no action to eliminate contaminants from the impoundment pool or to clean up the surrounding soil.

After deciding to divest itself of all assets and liabilities of its aluminum business, Olin, in 1973, engaged in successful negotiations with Conalco for the sale of Olin's aluminum operations, including the Hannibal site. The parties signed several agreements to effectuate the sale, each of which contained very broad language which required Conalco to indemnify Olin for all post-divestment liabilities associated with Olin's ownership of the Hannibal site and the aluminum operations. However, none of these agreements specifically addressed allocation of environmental liabilities between the parties....

Conalco has owned and operated the aluminum facility located at the Hannibal site since January 1, 1974. In 1986, the Ohio Environmental Protection Agency (Ohio EPA) concluded that the pool, as well as the soil adjacent and subjacent to the pool, was contaminated with PCBs and ordered remediation of this hazard. Conalco complied with this remediation order, incurring substantial cleanup costs. Conalco believed that Olin's disposal practices created the PCB contamination and sought voluntary contribution from Olin. Olin refused to contribute to the cleanup costs and filed this declaratory judgment action seeking, inter alia, a determination that defendants Conalco and Swiss Aluminum, Ltd. (Alusuisse) are "liable to Olin for the costs of defending against, and for all losses in connection with, all claims against, and liabilities of, Olin arising out of its former aluminum business." [Conalco filed a counterclaim.]

Discussion

The primary question we address in this appeal is whether the Agreements at issue, which predate the enactment of CERCLA and which make no mention of environmental liabilities, allocate to Conalco, the buyer, the subsequently created CERCLA obligation to clean up the Hannibal site, which Conalco claims was contaminated by Olin, the seller.

Section 107(e)(1) of CERCLA deals with the contractual allocation of CERCLA liability and contains two seemingly contradictory statements concerning whether a private party can enter into an indemnity agreement absolving itself of CERCLA liability. This section states as follows:

> No indemnification, hold harmless, or similar agreement or conveyance shall be effective to transfer from the owner or operator of any vessel or facility or from any person who may be liable for a release or threat of release under this section, to any other person the liability imposed under this section. Nothing in this subsection shall bar any agreement to insure, hold harmless, or indemnify a party to such agreement for any liability under this section.

42 U.S.C. § 9607(e)(1).

The district court interpreted this section to mean that under CERCLA private parties may contract with respect to indemnification and contribution but that, notwithstanding such contracts, all responsible parties remain fully liable to the government. Conalco does not dispute this holding on appeal. Rather, its main argument is that in order to transfer CERCLA liabilities an agreement must include a clear, express and unequivocal waiver of CERCLA rights. Conalco argues that the Agreements at issue here do not apply to CERCLA liability because they were entered into before CERCLA was enacted and do not contain a specific reference to environmental liabilities.

... [W]e now turn to our task of interpreting the indemnity provisions in question. These Agreements contain extremely broad language. As Judge Edelstein stated: "One would be hard pressed to draft broader or more inclusive indemnification provisions than those entered into by Conalco and Olin." Indeed, we noted at oral argument that it seemed to us that the contractual language at issue was virtually airtight.

Conalco cites a New York case, *Huskission v. Sentry Ins.*, 123 A.D.2d 832, 833, 507 N.Y.S.2d 447, 449 (2d Dep't 1986), for the proposition that the parties had the relevant existing law in mind when they contracted and the contract should not be interpreted to include later statutory enactments that changed the obligations of the parties "absent a clear expression in the contract that such is the parties' intention." We agree. These Agreements, however, do contain such a clear expression of the parties' intent.

The Purchase Agreement requires Conalco to indemnify Olin against "*all liabilities*, obligations and indebtedness of Olin related to [its aluminum business] ... as they exist on the Closing Date *or arise thereafter*." (emphasis added). In the Assumption Agreement executed at the closing, Conalco agreed to "indemnify Olin against, *all liabilities (absolute or contingent)*, obligations and indebtedness of Olin related to [the aluminum business] ... as they exist on the Effective Time *or arise thereafter with respect to actions or failures to act occurring prior to the Effective Time*." (emphasis added). Finally, the Release provides that Conalco "releases and settles *all claims of any nature which Conalco now has or hereafter could have against Olin* ... whether or not previously asserted." (emphasis added).

Notwithstanding the fact that CERCLA did not exist at the time these contracts were executed, we hold that as to the Hannibal site, these contractual provisions are sufficiently broad to encompass CERCLA liability. The language evidences the parties' "clear and unmistakable intent" that Conalco indemnify Olin for all liabilities related to the Hannibal site, even future unknown liabilities. We are not convinced, therefore, by Conalco's argument that "in order to release CERCLA liability, the agreement must include a clear, express and unequivocal waiver of CERCLA rights."

Nevertheless, Conalco presents a very strong equitable argument. Conalco contends that CERCLA, which imposes strict liability and casts a broad liability net, was a previously unimaginable scheme. The district court's decision forces Conalco, an apparently innocent purchaser of land, to assume a liability that did not exist at the time of contract for conditions that it did not create. However, Olin's argument is also not without strong equities in its favor. As to the Hannibal site, Olin contracted to release itself from all liability arising from its previous ownership of its aluminum business. Clearly the inclusion of the broadly worded contractual provisions affected the selling price Olin received. This was a contract between two large, sophisticated companies who hammered out an agreement and expected to be able to rely on its terms.

In resolving a dispute where there are equities in favor of each side, we must respect the unambiguous contractual language. We agree with Olin that this language is broad enough to require Conalco to indemnify Olin for CERCLA liability. We acknowledge that this is a seemingly harsh result for a company that must pay for the cleanup of contamination that it apparently did not cause. However, we are unwilling to ignore the broad inclusive language of agreements freely entered into by two sophisticated parties. Parties should be able to rely on the terms of an agreement arrived at after arduous negotiations....

NOTES AND QUESTIONS

1. Other courts have followed the result in *Olin* and validated pre-CERCLA indemnity provisions to include coverage of costs associated with the statute. *See Kerr-McGee Chem. Corp. v. Lefton Iron & Metal Co.*, 14 F.3d 321, 327 (7th

Cir. 1994); *Joslyn Mfg. Co. v. Koppers Co.*, 40 F.3d 750, 755 (5th Cir. 1995) (the scope of an indemnity agreement entered into prior to the enactment of CERCLA included environmental claims even though potential liability under the statute was not specifically contemplated at the time of contracting).

2. Courts generally construe indemnity provisions pertaining to environmental cleanup liability in accordance with ordinary principles of state contract law. The contractual language must demonstrate a clear and explicit language manifesting an intent to allocate responsibility for environmental obligations. *Lion Oil Co. v. Tosco Corp.*, 90 F.3d 268, 270 (8th Cir. 1996); *Taracorp, Inc. v. NL Indus.*, 73 F.2d 738, 743 (7th Cir. 1996) (Since indemnity agreements are disfavored under Illinois law, they are strictly construed against the indemnitee).

3. Courts have recognized that federal law governs the validity of liability agreements for CERCLA purposes. *Mardan Corp. v. C.G.C. Music, Ltd.*, 804 F.2d 1454, 1457 (9th Cir. 1986). As in *Olin*, courts generally have applied the substantive law of the state rather than fashioing federal common law to interpret contractual provisions that purport to indemnify or release a party from CERCLA liability, provided that it is compatible with the objectives and federal interests underlying CERCLA. *See John S. Boyd Co. v. Boston Gas Co.*, 992 F.2d 401, 406 (1st Cir. 1993).

4. Although CERCLA expressly authorizes a right of contribution among private parties with respect to sharing of response costs, the statute does not grant a right of indemnification. The two concepts are functionally distinct: contribution is a means by which a tortfeasor sues a joint tortfeasor for their share of liability to an injured party, while indemnification is a device for shifting liability entirely to a third party who is the real party responsible for the harm.

Although CERCLA does not abrogate private contracts — such as indemnity, guaranty, or warranty — to shift responsibility for response costs among each other, parties cannot transfer or escape underlying liability to the government or a third party through contractual arrangements. CERCLA § 107(e)(1)-(2), 42 U.S.C. § 9607(e)(1)-(2). *United States v. Hardage*, 985 F.2d 1427, 1433 (10th Cir. 1993); *Hatco Corp. v. W.R. Grace & Co.*, 59 F.3d 400, 404 (3d Cir. 1995) (private agreements cannot nullify CERCLA liability but are effective to shift the ultimate financial loss).

5. Consider the following language from *Harley-Davidson, Inc. v. Minstar, Inc.*, 41 F.3d 341, 343 (7th Cir. 1994) regarding section 107(e):

> It would be extraordinary if the draftsmen had wanted to bar insurance against CERCLA liability (insurance is just a form of indemnification). Public policy does on occasion demand that a wrongdoer be forbidden to shift the cost of liability to another through insurance or some other form of indemnification, but that is in cases of deliberate wrongdoing. Individuals and firms are normally allowed to insure against the consequences of their negligence; what else is automobile liability insurance? Proof of CERCLA liability does not require proof even of negligence, let alone of deliberate

wrongdoing; CERCLA liability is strict. Harley Davidson flinches from the implications of its position, and, fastening on the word "insure" in the subsection's second sentence (it does not appear in the first sentence), argues that contracts of insurance are the one and only form of indemnification that the statute allows. But what sense would that make? Why would rational draftsmen allow a polluter to shift the cost of his liability to an insurance company but not to another polluter? Even the semantic argument is weak, since "insure" does not stand alone; the words are "to insure, hold harmless, or indemnify." Harley-Davidson wants us to strike words from the statute, and it had better have compelling reasons for such disfiguring surgery.

It points out that if indemnification (we would add, in the form of insurance as otherwise) is allowed, potential polluters will have less incentive to take steps to avoid CERCLA liability, since they will be able to hand off all or part of the cost to the indemnitor. That of course is a problem with any form of insurance or indemnification. It is what is called moral hazard. When the problem is especially acute, insurance companies will not write insurance. The law may even, as we noted, bar indemnification, as in cases of deliberate wrongdoing. The venerable requirement that an insured have an "insurable interest," the requirement that for example prevents a person from buying life insurance on the life of a stranger, illustrates the concern with moral hazard. One can imagine, if barely, a decision by Congress that pollution is such an awful menace to society that polluters — even involuntary polluters — should be forbidden to insure.

UNITED STATES v. CANNONS ENGINEERING CORP.

899 F.2d 79 (1st Cir. 1990)

SELYA, CIRCUIT JUDGE.

"Superfund" sites are those which require priority remedial attention because of the presence, or suspected presence, of a dangerous accumulation of hazardous wastes. Expenditures to clean up such sites are specially authorized pursuant to 42 U.S.C. § 9611 (1987). After the federal government, through the United States Environmental Protection Agency (EPA), identified four such sites in Bridgewater, Massachusetts, Plymouth, Massachusetts, Londonderry, New Hampshire, and Nashua, New Hampshire (collectively, the Sites), the EPA undertook an intensive investigation to locate potentially responsible parties (PRPs). In the course of this investigation, the agency created a de minimis classification (DMC), putting in this category persons or firms whose discerned contribution to pollution of the Sites was minimal both in the amount and toxicity of the hazardous wastes involved. See 42 U.S.C. § 9622(g) (1987). The agency staked out the DMC on the basis of volumetric shares, grouping within it entities identifiable as generators of less than one percent of the waste sent to the Sites. To arrive at a PRP's volumetric share, the agency, using estimates, constituted a ratio between the volume of wastes that the PRP sent to the Sites and the total amount of wastes sent there.

The EPA sent notices of possible liability to some 671 PRPs, including generators and nongenerators. Administrative settlements were thereafter achieved with 300 generators (all de minimis PRPs). In short order, the United States and the two host states, Massachusetts and New Hampshire, brought suits in the United States District Court for the District of Massachusetts against 84 of the PRPs who had rejected, or were ineligible for, the administrative settlement. The suits sought recovery of previously incurred cleanup costs and declarations of liability for future remediation under the Comprehensive Environmental Response, Compensation and Liability Act (CERCLA, 42 U.S.C. §§ 9601-9675 (1987)). The actions were consolidated.

With its complaint, the United States filed two proposed consent decrees. The first (the MP decree) embodied a contemplated settlement with 47 major PRPs, that is, responsible parties who were ineligible for membership in the DMC. This assemblage included certain generators whose volumetric shares exceeded the 1% cutoff point and certain nongenerators (like the owners of the Sites and hazardous waste transporters). The second consent decree (the DMC decree) embodied a contemplated settlement with 12 de minimis PRPs who had eschewed participation in the administrative settlement. As required by statute, notice of the decrees' proposed entry was published in the Federal Register. No comments were received.... [The District Court, over the objection of the seven non-settling defendants, approved both consent decrees and dismissed all cross-claims against the settling defendants.]

I

We approach our task mindful that, on appeal, a district court's approval of a consent degree in CERCLA litigation is encased in a double layer of swaddling. In the first place, it is the policy of the law to encourage settlements. [Citations.] That policy has particular force where, as here, a government actor committed to the protection of the public interest has pulled the laboring oar in constructing the proposed settlement....

Respect for the agency's role is heightened in a situation where the cards have been dealt face up and a crew of sophisticated players, with sharply conflicting interests, sit at the table. That so many affected parties, themselves knowledgeable and represented by experienced lawyers, have hammered out an agreement at arm's length and advocate its embodiment in a judicial decree, itself deserves weight in the ensuing balance. The relevant standard, after all, is not whether the settlement is one which the court itself might have fashioned, or considers as ideal, but whether the proposed decree is fair, reasonable, and faithful to the objectives of the governing statute. [Citation.] Thus, the first layer of insulation implicates the trial court's deference to the agency's expertise and to the parties' agreement. While the district court should not mechanistically rubberstamp the agency's suggestions, neither should it approach the merits of the contemplated settlement *de novo*.

The second layer of swaddling derives from the nature of appellate review. Because approval of a consent decree is committed to the trial court's informed discretion, the court of appeals should be reluctant to disturb a reasoned exercise of that discretion. [Citations.] In this context, the test for abuse of discretion is itself a fairly deferential one.... Unless the objectors can demonstrate that the trier made a harmful error of law or has lapsed into "a meaningful error in judgment," a reviewing tribunal must stay its hand. [Citation.] The doubly required deference — district court to agency and appellate court to district court — places a heavy burden on those who purpose to upset a trial judge's approval of a consent decree.

II

....

Originally, the EPA extended an open offer to all de minimis PRPs, including five of the six appellants, proposing an administrative settlement based on 160% of each PRP's volumetric share of the total projected response cost, that is, the price of remedial actions, past and anticipated. The settlement figure included a 60% premium to cover unexpected costs and/or unforeseen conditions. Settling PRPs paid their shares in cash and were released outright from all liability. They were also exempted from suits for contribution, *see* 42 U.S.C. § 9622(g)(5) (1987).

Following consummation of the administrative settlement, plaintiffs entered into negotiations with the remaining PRPs. These negotiations resulted in the proposed MP decree (accepted by 47 "major" defendants) and the DMC decree.... The latter was modelled upon the administrative settlement, but featured an increased premium: rather than allowing de minimis PRPs to cash out at a 160% level, an eligible generator could resolve its liability only by agreeing to pay 260% of its volumetric share of the total projected response cost. The EPA justified the incremental 100% premium as being in the nature of delay damages.

III

... The Superfund Amendments and Reauthorization Act of 1986 (SARA), P.L. 99-499, § 101 *et seq.*, 100 Stat. 1613, authorized a variety of types of settlements which the EPA may utilize in CERCLA actions, including consent decrees providing for PRPs to contribute to cleanup costs and/or to undertake response activities themselves. *See* 42 U.S.C. § 9622 (1987). SARA's legislative history makes pellucid that, when such consent decrees are forged, the trial court's review function is only to "satisfy itself that the settlement is reasonable, fair, and consistent with the purposes that CERCLA is intended to serve."...

A. *Procedural Fairness*

We agree with the district court that fairness in the CERCLA settlement context has both procedural and substantive components. To measure procedural fairness, a court should ordinarily look to the negotiation process and attempt to gauge its candor, openness, and bargaining balance....

Appellants claim that they were relatively close to the 1% cutoff point, and were thus arbitrarily excluded from the major party settlement, avails them naught. Congress intended to give the EPA broad discretion to structure classes of PRPs for settlement purposes. We cannot say that the government acted beyond the scope of that discretion in separating minor and major players in this instance, that is, in determining that generators who had sent less than 1% of the volume of hazardous waste to the Sites would comprise the DMC and those generators who were responsible for a great percentage would be treated as major PRPs. While the dividing line was only one of many which the agency could have selected, it was well within the universe of plausibility. And it is true, if sometimes sad, that whenever government draws lines, some parties fall on what they may perceive as the "wrong" side. [Citation.] There was no cognizable unfairness in this respect. Moreover, having established separate categories for different PRPs, the agency had no obligation to let defendants flit from class to class, thus undermining the rationale and purpose for drawing lines in the first place.

Nor can we say that appellants were entitled to more advance warning of the EPA's negotiating strategy than they received. At the time *de minimis* PRPs were initially invited to participate in the administrative settlement, the EPA, by letter, informed all of them including appellants, that:

> The government is anxious to achieve a high degree of participation in this *de minimis* settlement. Accordingly, the terms contained in this settlement offer are the most favorable terms that the government intends to make available to parties eligible for *de minimis* settlement in this case.

Appellants knew, early on, that they were within the DMC and could spurn the EPA's proposal only at the risk of paying more at a later time. Although appellants may have assumed that they could ride on the coattails of the major parties and join whatever MP decree emerged — the government had, on other occasions, allowed such cafeteria-style settlements — the agency was neither asked for, not did it give, any such assurance in this instance. As a matter of law, we do not believe that Congress meant to handcuff government negotiators in CERCLA cases by insisting that the EPA allow polluters to pick and choose which settlements they might prefer to join. And as a matter of equity, we think that if appellants were misled at all, it was by their own wishful thinking.

The district court found the consent decrees to have been the product of fair play. Given that the decrees were negotiated at arm's length among experienced counsel, that appellants had an opportunity to participate in the negotiations and to join both the first and the second de minimis settlements, and that the agency operated in good faith, the finding of procedural fairness is eminently supportable.

B. *Substantive Fairness*

Substantive fairness introduces into the equation concepts of corrective justice and accountability: a party should bear the cost of the harm for which it is legally responsible. [Citation.] The logic behind these concepts dictates that settlement terms must be based upon, and roughly correlated with, some acceptable measure of comparative fault, apportioning liability among the settling parties according to rational (if necessarily imprecise) estimates of how much harm each PRP has done. [Citations.]

Even accepting substantive fairness as linked to comparative fault, an important issue still remains as to how comparative fault is to be measured. There is no universally correct approach. It appears very clear to us that what constitutes the best measure of comparative fault at a particular Superfund site under particular factual circumstances should be left largely to the EPA's expertise. Whatever formula or scheme EPA advances for measuring comparative fault and allocating liability should be upheld so long as the agency supplies a plausible explanation for it, welding some reasonable linkage between the factors it includes in its formula or scheme and the proportionate shares of the settling PRPs. [Citations.] Put in slightly different terms, the chosen measure of comparative fault should be upheld unless it is arbitrary, capricious, and devoid of a rational basis. *See* 42 U.S.C. § 9613(j) (1987).

Not only must the EPA be given leeway to construct the barometer of comparative fault, but the agency must also be accorded flexibility to diverge from an apportionment formula in order to address special factors not conducive to regimented treatment. While the list of possible variables is virtually limitless, two frequently encountered reasons warranting departure from strict formulaic comparability are the uncertainty of future events and the timing of particular settlement decisions. Common sense suggests that a PRP's assumption of open-ended risks may merit a discount on comparative fault, while obtaining a complete release from uncertain future liability may call for a premium. [Citations.] By the same token, the need to encourage (and suitably reward) early, cost-effective settlements, and to account *inter alia* for anticipated savings in transaction costs inuring from celeritous settlement, can affect the construct. [Citations.] Because we are confident that Congress intended EPA to have considerable flexibility in negotiating and structuring settlements, we think reviewing courts should permit the agency to depart from rigid adherence to formulae wherever the agency proffers a reasonable good-faith justification for departure.

We also believe that a district court should give the EPA's expertise the benefit of the doubt when weighing substantive fairness — particularly when the agency and hence the court, has been confronted by ambiguous, incomplete, or inscrutable information. In settlement negotiations, particularly in the early phases of environmental litigation, precise data relevant to determining the total extent of harm caused and the role of each PRP is often unavailable. Yet, it would disserve a principal end of the statute — achievement of prompt settlement and a concomitant head start on response activities — to leave matters in limbo until more precise information was amassed. As long as the data the EPA uses to apportion liability for purposes of a consent decree falls along the broad spectrum of plausible approximations, judicial intrusion is unwarranted — regardless of whether the court would have opted to employ the same data in the same way. [Citation.]

In this instance, we agree with the court below that the consent decrees pass muster from a standpoint of substantive fairness. They adhere generally to principles of comparative fault according to a volumetric standard, determining the liability of each PRP according to volumetric contribution. And, to the extent they deviate from this formulaic approach, they do so on the basis of adequate justification. In particular, the premiums charged to de minimis PRPs in the administrative settlement, and the increased premium charged in the DMC decree, seem well warranted.

The argument that the EPA should have used relative toxicity as a determinant of proportionate liability for response costs, instead of a strictly volumetric ranking, is a stalking horse. Having selected a reasonable method of weighing comparative fault, the agency need not show that it is the best, or even the fairest, of all conceivable methods. The choice of the yardstick to be used for allocating liability must be left primarily to the expert discretion of the EPA, particularly when the PRPs involved are numerous and the situation is complex. [Citation.] We cannot reverse the court below for refusing to second-guess the agency on this score.

Appellants' next asseveration — that the decrees favor major party PRPs over their less culpable counterparts — is a gross distortion. While the DMC and MP decrees differ to some extent in application of the volumetric share formula, requiring lower initial contributions under the latter, the good-faith justification for this divergence is readily apparent. In return for the premium paid, de minimis PRPs can cash out, thus obtaining two important benefits: reduced transaction costs and absolute finality with respect to the monetization of their overall liability. The major PRPs, on the other hand, retain an open-ended risk anent their liability at three of the Sites, making any comparison of proportionate contributions a dubious proposition. At the very least, assumption of this unquantifiable future liability under the MP decree warranted some discount — and the tradeoff crafted by the government's negotiators seems reasonable. Indeed, the acceptance of the first and second DMC settlement offers by so many of the de minimis PRPs is itself an indication of substantive fairness toward the class to which appellants belong. On this record, the district court did not misuse its discretion in ruling that the decrees sufficiently tracked the parties' comparative fault.

The last point which merits discussion under this rubric involves the fact that the agency upped the ante as the game continued, that is, the premium assessed as part of the administrative settlement was increased substantially for purposes of the later DMC decree. Like the district court, we see no unfairness in this approach. For one thing, litigation is expensive — and having called the tune by their refusal to subscribe to the administrative settlement, we think it not unfair that appellants, thereafter, would have to pay the piper. For another thing, rewarding PRPs who settle sooner rather than later is completely consonant with CERCLA's makeup.

Although appellants berate escalating settlement offers as discriminating among similarly situated PRPs, we think that the government's use of such a technique is fair and serves to promote the explicit statutory goal of expediting remedial measures for hazardous waste sites. *See* 42 U.S.C. § 9622(a) (1987). That the cost of purchasing peace may rise for a laglast is consistent with the method of the statute; indeed, if the government cannot offer such routine incentives, there will be little inducement on the part of any PRP to enter an administrative settlement. Of course, the extent of the differential must be reasonable and the graduation neither unconscionable nor unduly coercive, but these are familiar subjects for judicial review in a wide variety of analogous settings. [Citation.] We believe that the EPA is entitled to make use of a series of escalating settlement proposals in a CERCLA case and that, as the district court ruled, the serial settlements employed in this instance were substantively fair.

C. *Reasonableness*

In the usual environmental litigation, the evaluation of a consent decree's reasonableness will be a multifaceted exercise. We comment briefly upon three such facets. The first is obvious: the decree's likely efficaciousness as a vehicle for cleansing the environment is of cardinal importance. [Citations.] Except in cases which involve only recoupment of cleanup costs already spent, the reasonableness of the consent decree, for this purpose, will be basically a question of technical adequacy, primarily concerned with the probable effectiveness of proposed remedial responses.

A second important facet of reasonableness will depend upon whether the settlement satisfactorily compensates the public for the actual (and anticipated) costs of remedial and response measures. Like the question of technical adequacy, this aspect of the problem can be enormously complex. The actual cost of remedial measures is frequently uncertain at the time a consent decree is proposed. Thus, although the settlement's bottom line may be definite, the proportion of settlement dollars to total needed dollars is often debatable. Once again, the agency cannot realistically be held to a standard of mathematical precision. If the figures relied upon derive in a sensible way from a plausible interpretation of the record, the court should normally defer to the agency's expertise.

A third integer in the reasonableness equation relates to the relative strength of the parties' litigating positions. If the government's case is strong and solid, it should typically be expected to drive a harder bargain. On the other hand, if the case is less than robust, or the outcome problematic, a reasonable settlement will ordinarily mirror such factors. In a nutshell, the reasonableness of a proposed settlement must take into account foreseeable risks of loss. [Citations.] The same variable, we suggest, has a further dimension: even if the government's case is sturdy, it may take time and money to collect damages or to implement private remedial measures through litigatory success. To the extent that time is of the essence or that transaction costs loom large, a settlement which nets less than full recovery of cleanup costs is nonetheless reasonable. [Citations.] The reality is that, all too often, litigation is a cost-ineffective alternative which can squander valuable resources, public as well as private.

In this case, the district court found the consent decrees to be reasonable. We agree. Appellants have not seriously questioned the technological efficacy of the cleanup measures to be implemented at the Sites. Insofar as they contend that the settlements are not designed to assure adequate compensation to the public for harms caused — at times, they seem to argue that the settlements overcompensate — they are whistling past the graveyard. The risks of trial and the desirability for expedition seem to have been blended into the mix....

D. *Fidelity to the Statute*

... [T]he broad settlement authority conferred upon the EPA must be exercised with deference to the statute's overarching principles: accountability, the desirability of an unsullied environment, and promptness of response activities. The bases appear to have been touched in this instance. Appellants concede that the government made a due and diligent search to uncover the identity of PRPs; the classification of perpetrators and the use of a modified volumetric share formula appear reasonably related to assuring accountability; the settlements will unarguably promote early completion of cleanup activities; and the technical efficacy of the selected remedial measures is not in issue. On this basis, the consent decrees seem fully consistent with CERCLA.

One can, of course, conjure up ways in which particular consent decrees, while seemingly fair and reasonable, might nevertheless contravene the aims of the statute. Rather than attempting to catalogue a virtually endless list of possibilities, we address, in terms of what we discern to be the congressional will, certain points raised by the appellants.

1. *De Minimis Settlements.* In the SARA Amendments, Congress gave the EPA authority to settle with a de minimis PRP so long as (i) the agreement involved only a "minor portion" of the total response costs, and (ii) the toxicity and amount of substances contributed by the PRP were "minimal in comparison to the other hazardous substances at the facility." 42 U.S.C. § 9622(g)(1) (1987). The two determinative criteria are not further defined. Appellants, for a variety

of reasons, question the boundaries fixed for the DMC class in this instance, contending that drawing lines so sharply, and adhering to those lines so blindly, thwarts CERCLA's legitimate goals.

... [H]ad Congress meant the agency to employ a purely mechanical taxonomy, it would have so provided. We believe that Congress intended quite the opposite; the EPA was to have substantial discretion to interpret the statutory terms in light of both its expertise and its negotiating strategy in a given case. Therefore, in attempting to gauge a consent decree's consistency with the statute, courts must give a wide berth to the agency's choice of eligibility criteria. In this case, the criteria selected fell well within the ambit of Executive discretion.

2. *Disproportionate Liability.* In the SARA Amendments, Congress explicitly created a statutory framework that left nonsettlors at risk of bearing a disproportionate amount of liability. The statute immunizes settling parties from liability for contribution and provides that only the amount of the settlement — not the pro rata share attributable to the settling party — shall be subtracted from the liability of the nonsettlors.[5] This can prove to be a substantial benefit to settling PRP's — and a corresponding detriment to their more recalcitrant counterparts.

Although such immunity creates a palpable risk of disproportionate liability, that is not to say that the device is forbidden. To the exact contrary, Congress has made its will explicit and the courts must defer. [Citation.] Disproportionate liability, a technique which promotes early settlements and deters litigation for litigation's sake, is an integral part of the statutory plan.

....

As originally enacted, CERCLA did not expressly provide for a right of contribution among parties found jointly and severally liable for response costs. When CERCLA was amended by SARA in 1986, Congress created an express right of contribution among parties found liable for response costs. *See* 41 U.S.C. § 9613(f)(1) (1987). Congress specifically provided that contribution actions could not be maintained against settlors. *See* 42 U.S.C. § 9613(f)(2) (1987). This provision was designed to encourage settlements and provide PRPs a measure of finality in return for their willingness to settle. [Citation.] Congress plainly intended non-settlors to have no contribution rights against settlors regarding matters addressed in settlement. Thus, the cross-claims were properly dismissed; Congress purposed that all who choose not to settle confront the same sticky wicket of which appellants complain.

---

[5]The statute provides:

> A person who has resolved its liability to the United States or a State in an administrative or judicially approved settlement shall not be liable for claims for contribution regarding matters addressed in the settlement. Such settlement does not discharge any of the other potentially liable persons unless its terms so provide, but it reduces the potential liability of the others by the amount of the settlement.

42 U.S.C. § 9613(f)(2) (1987).

The statute, of course, not only bars contribution claims against settling parties, but also provides that, while a settlement will not discharge other PRPs, "it reduces the potential liability of the others by the amount of settlement." 42 U.S.C. § 9613(f)(2) (1987). The law's plain language admits of no construction other than a dollar-for-dollar reduction of the aggregate liability....

4. *Notice.* The appellants also contend that the government's negotiating strategy must be an open book. We disagree. Congress did not send the EPA into the toxic waste ring with one arm tied behind its collective back. Although the EPA may not mislead any of the parties, discriminate unfairly, or engage in deceptive practices, neither must the agency spoon feed PRPs. In the CERCLA context, the government is under no obligation to telegraph its settlement offers, divulge its negotiating strategy in advance, or surrender the normal prerogatives of strategic flexibility which any negotiator cherishes. In short, contrary to the objectors' thesis, the EPA need not tell de minimis PRPs in advance whether they will, or will not, be eligible to join ensuring major party settlements.

5. *Exclusions from Settlements.* The CERCLA statutes do not require the agency to open all settlement offers to all PRPs; and we refuse to insert such a requirement into the law by judicial fiat. Under the SARA Amendments, the right to draw fine lines, and to structure the order and pace of settlement negotiations to suit, is an agency prerogative. After all, "divide and conquer" has been a recognized negotiating tactic since the days of the Roman Empire, and in the absence of a congressional directive, we cannot deny the EPA use of so conventional a tool. So long as it operates in good faith, the EPA is at liberty to negotiate and settle with whomever it chooses.

....

Affirmed.

NOTES AND QUESTIONS

1. *Judicial Review of Consent Decrees.* What should be the proper role of the court in reviewing a consent decree entered into between government and parties undertaking certain responsibilities for environmental remediation? As demonstrated in *Cannons Engineering*, courts favorably view the voluntary settlement of environmental disputes between government agencies and PRPs as effectuating the public interest implicit in CERCLA. The judicial inclination to give significant deference to agency determinations that the proposed consent decree will be in the public interest coupled with an elastic standard of judicial review of "legality, fairness, and reasonableness" present difficult hurdles for parties seeking to challenge settlement terms. Consider the following exposition from the court in *Kelley v. Thomas Solvent Co.*, 717 F. Supp. 507, 514-15 (W.D. Mich. 1989):

A consent decree is in essence "a settlement agreement subject to judicial policing." The decree is, however, not a simple contract. A consent decree has attributes of both a contract and a judicial act. In one sense, a consent decree could be effective on its own as a voluntary settlement agreement. Viewed this way, the decree merely memorializes the bargained-for positions of the parties. A defendant has foregone the possibility of prevailing on the merits in exchange for granting some form of limited relief to plaintiff. A plaintiff has exchanged a right to obtain adjudicatory relief for a known recovery sum. The bargained-for position of the parties should be preserved when possible by strictly construing the terms of the decree....

A consent decree, however, especially one that impacts the interests of the public and specific groups of persons not party to the decree, is more than a simple contract. It is also a judicial order and a continuing decree of injunctive relief. It may be said that "judicial approval of a settlement agreement places the power and prestige of the court behind the compromise struck by the parties." The consent decree will therefore not be approved where the agreement is illegal, a product of collusion, inequitable, or contrary to the public good.

Once the consent decree is approved, the consent decree's prospective provisions operate as an injunction. The court may then retain jurisdiction over the term of the decree's existence; protect the integrity of the decree with its contempt power; and, in addition, modify the decree should changed circumstances subvert its original purpose.

Review of a consent decree is committed to the informed discretion of the trial court. In its exercise of discretion, the trial court should consider the strong policy favoring voluntary settlement of litigation. The consent decree — as a judicial act — requires court approval. It may approve or reject the consent decree and, although it may suggest modifications, it can only approve or reject the consent decree. The controlling criterion is not what might have been agreed upon or what the court believes might have been the optimal settlement. Yet, the court must "eschew any rubber stamp approval" in favor of an independent evaluation. At the same time, a court must avoid the detailed investigation required if the parties were actually trying the case. [Citations omitted.]

Since consent decrees embody injunctive relief, courts will be assuming ongoing supervisory functions to ensure that the cleanup obligations are accomplished within the agreed terms. Consequently, although some savings of government resources may be achieved through settlement, there are costs associated with judicial oversight and agency implementation of a decree. Some courts have applied a higher level of scrutiny for approval of decrees which contemplate long-term response actions — with concomitant extensive judicial involvement — versus those where the proposed remedial plan simply involves the payment of money. *See City of New York v. Exxon Corp.*, 697 F. Supp. 677, 691 (S.D.N.Y. 1988).

Consent decrees submitted for judicial approval under CERCLA are not governed by Rule 23 of the Federal Rules of Civil Procedure applicable to proposed class action settlements. Nevertheless, as recognized by the court in *Cannons Engineering*, courts frequently borrow portions of the common law standard employed in reviewing a class action settlement that the terms be fair, adequate and reasonable.

2. In *Cannons Engineering*, the court stated that its task in reviewing a proposed settlement agreement was not to substitute its judgment for the agency nor to determine whether a better solution might have reached, but whether the decree was fair, reasonable, and corresponded to the statutory purposes. What factors should courts take into account in ascertaining the fairness and reasonableness of a consent decree? The following is a collection of illustrative criteria used by various courts: (1) the strength of the plaintiff's case; (2) the good faith efforts of the arm's-length negotiators; (3) the amount of opposition to the settlement; (4) the opinion of competent counsel; (5) the stage of the proceeding; (6) the complexity, length, expense, and risk of litigation; (7) the nature and extent of potential hazards at the site; (8) the availability and likelihood of implementation of alternatives to the decree; (9) the adequacy of the technical information pertaining to the proposed cleanup; (10) the extent to which the decree furthers the statutory goals; (11) whether the decree safeguards the public interest. *See United States v. Hardage*, 750 F. Supp. 1460, 1491-92 (W.D. Okl. 1990); *City of New York v. Exxon Corp.*, 697 F. Supp. 677, 692 (S.D.N.Y. 1988); *United States v. Seymour Recycling Corp.*, 554 F. Supp. 1334, 1339 (S.D. Ind. 1982). How precise are these factors in guiding courts to discharge their obligations of reviewing proposed decrees?

3. One of the problems with the early version of CERCLA was that the statute contained no specific guidance with respect to the appropriate standards governing cleanup plans. Consequently, PRPs complained that CERCLA improperly allowed the EPA to exercise excessive discretion in demanding inordinate cleanup commitments which varied on a case-by-case basis. Moreover, the EPA had no obligation to enter into settlements with PRPs and the agency's actions with respect to cleanup negotiations were not subject to judicial review outside of enforcement proceedings. In the SARA amendments of 1986 Congress added § 121, 42 U.S.C. § 9621, which set forth uniform national cleanup standards applicable both to fund financed cleanups under § 104 and private operations under § 106. The government is charged to select remedial actions which are "cost-effective" (CERCLA § 121(a)) and assure protection of health and the environment. CERCLA § 121(d)(1). Two key principles emerge in section 121: the permanent treatment of hazardous substances is strongly preferred over containment or disposal remedial actions, and offsite disposal methods are disfavored. *See* CERCLA § 121(b)(1). If any hazardous substances, pollutants, or contaminants remain onsite, the cleanup must meet all "applicable, relevant, and appropriate" state and federal requirements and criteria — of particular importance satisfying the rigorous groundwater protection standards in RCRA.

4. Section 122, 42 U.S.C. § 9622, encourages settlement where "practicable and in the public interest"; however, the ultimate decision regarding settlement rests with EPA discretion and is not subject to judicial review. Consequently, consent decrees often will not resolve the claims against all the PRPs. Section 122 gives EPA discretion to allocate one hundred percent of the response costs among PRPs prior to cleanup by assigning non-binding allocations of responsibility ("NBAR"). CERCLA § 122(e)(3). The NBAR serves a useful purpose as a framework for PRPs to allocate cleanup costs among themselves and to develop settlement offers. Contrary to EPA's pre-SARA policy, there is no requirement in section 122 setting a threshold for percentage of liability which must be assumed. Moreover, EPA can enter into "mixed funding" arrangements where the agency will agree to cover certain portions of the costs (§ 122(a)(1)), use Superfund to pay for "orphan shares" (§ 122(b)(1)), and enter into "partial" consent decrees. Rule 54(b) of the Federal Rules of Civil Procedure authorizes courts to enter a final judgment in actions involving multiple parties where all the claims or parties are not yet determined. *See Consolidated Rail Corp. v. Fore River Ry. Co.*, 861 F.2d 322 (1st Cir. 1988) (Rule 54(b) requires that the decree is a final judgment, no just reason for delay exists, and the court must enumerate the factors and concerns relied upon in making its decision).

5. *Releases and Covenants Not to Sue.* One of the difficult questions involved in entering into a settlement agreement regarding cleanup of a hazardous waste site is whether the government should grant a settling party a release or covenant not to sue with respect to future harms resulting from the contamination. The covenant typically would encompass relief from suit seeking injunctive relief under section 106 of CERCLA and section 7003 of RCRA and cost recovery under CERCLA section 107(a). Certainly from the PRPs viewpoint, there would be little incentive to settle if the agreement did not provide limits on future liability. Conversely, under the initial version of CERCLA, critics charged that government unduly restricted its options by giving violators "sweetheart deals" by agreeing to minimal cleanup arrangements and giving covenants not to sue. In response to these competing concerns, Congress modified and tightened the settlement provisions in CERCLA in 1986. *See* CERCLA § 122, 42 U.S.C. § 9622. The amended version adopts a sliding-scale approach where the completeness of a covenant not to sue corresponds to the permanence of the remedial action undertaken. CERCLA § 122(c)((1), 42 U.S.C. § 9622(c)(1). Natural resource damage claims ordinarily will not be released by the government except in limited circumstances. CERCLA § 122(j)(2).

The EPA may protect itself from the possibility that information supporting cash-out settlement is inaccurate or incomplete by including a reservation of the right to seek further relief in certain instances. This "re-opener" exception to the covenant not to sue in a consent decree need not be exercised only in "exceptional" circumstances. Rather, EPA must determine that the public health and environment will be adequately protected by the present terms of the decree. Factors relevant to the EPA's inquiry include an analysis of the conditions at the site, the nature of the remedies selected, and the volume, toxicity, mobility, strength of evidence, ability to pay, litigation risks, public interest considerations, precedential value, and inequality and aggravating factors. CERCLA § 122(f)-(4)-(6), 42 U.S.C. § 9622(f)(4)-(6).

6. *De Minimis Settlement Agreements.* EPA, under the initial version of CERCLA, followed a stringent practice of declining settlement for less than the total costs of cleanup and refusing to entertain settlement proposals for less than eighty percent of the costs. Although the agency subsequently modified its harsh settlement posture, small quantity waste contributors still found little receptivity from the government to negotiate. In the 1986 SARA amendments Congress added section 122(g) to CERCLA to provide a mechanism to expedite the cleanup process by encouraging the EPA to enter into settlement agreements with minor potentially responsible parties. The *de minimis* classification provides a partial escape hatch from the onerous joint and several liability provisions of the Act, but does not alter the fundamental approach of CERCLA of imposing liability even on small quantity contributors. *O'Neill v. Picillo*, 883 F.2d 176, 179 n.4 (1st Cir. 1989).

Section 122(g) encourages *de minimis* settlement "whenever practicable and in the public interest" in circumstances where only a minor portion of the response costs are involved. Despite the statutory policy favoring increased settlement with minor PRPs, the agency has interpreted its obligations with respect to *de minimis* settlement as largely discretionary. *See* EPA, *Environmental Protection Agency, Interim Guidance on Settlement with De Minimis Waste Contributors Under CERCLA*, 52 FED. REG. 24334, 441 ENV'T REP. (BNA) 3201 (1987).

There are two distinct categories of parties who may qualify for *de minimis* treatment. First, a small volume contributor whose volume and toxicity of waste are minimal compared to the hazardous waste at the site may receive such treatment. CERCLA § 122(g)(1)(A). Alternatively, *de minimis* treatment may be accorded to property owners who did not contribute to the release of hazardous substances through action or omission, provided they acquired the property without actual or constructive knowledge of the existence of the toxic waste. CERCLA § 122(g)(1)(B). The requirements under this classification essentially track the criteria for establishing the third party defense applicable to "innocent landowners" in section 107(b)(3), 42 U.S.C. § 9607(b)(3). The EPA policy provides that *de minimis* settlement normally requires the landowner to provide access to the property and cooperation with the agency in its response activities and due care assurances with respect to the hazardous substances at the site. *See* EPA Guidance on Landowner Liability Under Section 170(a)(1) and De Minimis Settlements Under Section 122(g)(1)(B) of CERCLA and Settlements with Prospective Purchasers of Contaminated Property (June 6, 1989) ("EPA Settlement Guidance").

The settling party benefits in either instance by reducing transaction costs, eliminating litigation risks, and receiving protection from contribution claims. Further, typically the *de minimis* settlor will be allowed to "cash-out" with EPA rather than be required to perform the site cleanup. Government may, however, reserve the right to bring back a *de minimis* settlor into the litigation as a principal if later determined to have contributed more than the one percent ceiling designated by EPA. *See United States v. Alexander*, 771 F. Supp. 830, 834 (S.D. Tex. 1991).

A *de minimis* settlement may be entered as a judicial consent decree or may be embodied in an administrative order, which may be enforced by a district court. *United States v. Rohm & Haas Co.*, 721 F. Supp. 666 (D.N.J. 1989). When incorporated in an administrative order, is the settlement then subject to an arbitrary and capricious (or some other) standard of review pursuant to the Administrative Procedure Act? If so, does this level of review differ substantially from the legality, fairness and reasonableness standard applied generally to consent decrees?

7. An important issue involves determining the appropriate circumstances where courts will allow the modification of the terms of a previously approved consent decree. In *United States v. County of Nassau*, 749 F. Supp. 463, (E.D.N.Y. 1990) the defendants requested a modification of a consent decree and enforcement agreement to delay the implementation schedule for construction and operation of a dewatering plant. The county had entered into the decree to comply with the Ocean Dumping Ban Act of 1988 which prohibited the continued dumping of sewage sludge into the ocean without a permit. The county subsequently complained that the schedule was too "tight" and did not allow sufficient time to complete the construction program. The court rejected the county's request, finding that the Act reflected a clear Congressional intent "to severely limit the equitable discretion of a court to extend the compliance dates of a dumper." Moreover, the court recognized that strict adherence to the Act's requirements was in the public interest based upon the national policy in safeguarding the oceans.

8. For additional commentary on settlement agreements consent, see the following references: Glass, *Superfund and SARA: Are There Any Defenses Left?*, 12 HARV. ENVTL. L. REV. 385 (1988); Strock, *Settlement Policy Under the Superfund Amendments and Reauthorization Act of 1986*, 58 COLO. L. REV. 599 (1988); Cross, *Settlement Under the 1986 Superfund Amendments*, 66 OR. L. REV. 517 (1988); Balcke, *Superfund Settlements: The Failed Promise of the 1986 Amendments*, 74 VA. L. REV. 123 (1988); Mengler, *Consent Decree Paradigms: Models Without Meaning*, 29 B.C. L. REV. 291 (1988).

C. NATURAL RESOURCE DAMAGES

CERCLA contains two separate liability schemes, both of which are set forth in section 107(a), 42 U.S.C. § 9607(a): provisions which authorize recovery of response costs for dealing with contaminated sites, and another which establishes liability for damages for injuries to natural resources. The differences between these sections are more numerous than their similarities. The overall requirements and limitations imposed for asserting natural resource claims are considerably greater, and consequently less utilitarian, than the statutory counterpart for recovery of response costs.

The starting point with respect to claims for natural resources is section 107(a)(4)(C), which provides that liability includes "damages for injury to, destruction of, or loss of natural resources, including the reasonable costs of assessing such injury, destruction, or loss resulting from such a release." The Act defines "natural resources" to include "land, fish, wildlife, biota, air, water, groundwater, drinking water supplies, and other such resources." 42 U.S.C. § 101(16); 40 C.F.R. § 300.5.

The statutory scheme in CERCLA authorizes "trustees" to bring natural resource damage claims on behalf of state and federal governments and Indian tribes. 42 U.S.C. § 107(f)(1). CERCLA does not provide for private recovery of natural resource damages, nor does it authorize private attorney general suits for such claims. Federal trustees for asserting natural resource claims under CERCLA and under section 311(f)(5) of the Clean Water Act are designated in the National Contingency Plan. 40 C.F.R. § 300.600(a). State trustees are designated by the governor of the affected state, and tribal trustees are ordinarily appointed by the tribal chairman. See 40 C.F.R. §§ 300.605, 300.610.

The government is not required to possess title to the affected resources in order to seek damages, but can also recover for harms to resources which it substantially controls, regulates or manages. See Ohio v. Department of Interior, 880 F.2d 432, 461 (D.C. Cir. 1989), reprinted below. By expanding the scope of resources subject to government "control" or management, the Act presents potential problems of overlapping jurisdiction and conflicts where multiple governmental entities assert interests in the same resource. The government cannot, however, recover natural resource damages for harms to privately owned property. The Act requires the government to use any damages recovered to "restore, rehabilitate, or acquire the equivalent of the damaged natural resources." 42 U.S.C. § 107(f)(1).

OHIO v. UNITED STATES DEPARTMENT OF THE INTERIOR
880 F.2d 432 (D.C. Cir. 1989)

WALD, CHIEF JUDGE and ROBINSON and MIKVA, CIRCUIT JUDGES.

Petitioners are 10 states, three environmental organizations ("State and Environmental Petitioners"), a chemical industry trade association, a manufacturing company and a utility company ("Industry Petitioners"), who seek review of regulations promulgated by the Department of the Interior ("DOI" or "Interior") pursuant to § 301(c)(1)-(3) of the Comprehensive Environmental Response, Compensation and Liability Act of 1980 ("CERCLA" or the "Act"), as amended, 42 U.S.C. § 9651(c). The regulations govern the recovery of money damages from persons responsible for spills and leaks of oil and hazardous substances, to compensate for injuries such releases inflict on natural resources.[2]

Damages may be recovered by state and in some cases the federal governments, as trustees for those natural resources.

Petitioners challenge many aspects of those regulations. State and Environmental Petitioners raise ten issues, all of which essentially focus on the regulations' alleged undervaluation of the damages recoverable from parties responsible for hazardous materials spills that despoil natural resources. Industry Petitioners attack the regulations from a different vantage point, claiming they will permit or encourage overstated damages. In addition, three public interest organizations ("Environmental Intervenors") defend the regulations from the attacks of Industry Petitioners, and a collection of corporations and industry groups ("Industry Intervenors") defend the regulations from the attacks of State and Environmental Petitioners.

We hold that the regulation limiting damages recoverable by government trustees for harmed natural resources to "the lesser of" (a) the cost of restoring or replacing the equivalent of an injured resource, or (b) the lost use value of the resource is directly contrary to the clearly expressed intent of Congress and is therefore invalid. We also hold that the regulation prescribing a hierarchy of methodologies by which the lost-use value of natural resources may be measured, which focuses exclusively on the market values for such resources when market values are available, is not a reasonable interpretation of the statute. We remand the record to DOI for a clarification of its interpretation of its own regulations concerning the applicability of the CERCLA natural resource damage provisions to privately owned land that is managed or controlled by a federal, state or local government. We reject all other challenges to Interior's regulations.

... CERCLA provides that responsible parties may be held liable for "damages for injury to, destruction of, or loss of natural resources, including the reasonable costs of assessing such injury, destruction, or loss resulting from such a release." § 107(a)(C), 42 U.S.C. § 9607(a)(C). Liability is to "the United States Government and to any State for natural resources within the State or belonging to, managed by, controlled by, or appertaining to such State." § 107(f)(1), 42 U.S.C. § 9607(f)(1). The Act provides for the designation of federal and state "trustees" who are authorized to assess natural resource damages and press claims for the recovery of such damages, both under CERCLA and under § 311 of the Federal Water Pollution Control Act (commonly referred to as the "Clean Water Act"), 33 U.S.C. § 1321. CERCLA § 107(f)(2), 42 U.S.C. § 9607(f)(2).

Congress conferred on the President (who in turn delegated to Interior) the responsibility for promulgating regulations governing the assessment of damages for natural resource injuries resulting from releases of hazardous substances or

---

[2]The natural resource damage regulations are codified at 43 C.F.R. §§ 11.10-11.93 (1987).

oil, for the purposes of CERCLA and the Clean Water Act's § 311(f)(4)-(5) oil and hazardous substance natural resource damages provisions, 33 U.S.C. § 1321(f)(4)-(5).... CERCLA prescribed the creation of two types of procedures for conducting natural resources damages assessments. The regulations were to specify (a) "standard procedures for simplified assessments requiring minimal field observation" (the "Type A" rules), and (b) "alternative protocols for conducting assessments in individual cases" (the "Type B" rules). § 301(c)(2), 42 U.S.C. § 9651(c)(2). Both the Type A and the Type B rules were to "identify the best available procedures to determine such damages."...

In August 1986, Interior published a final rule containing the Type B regulations for natural resource damage assessments, the subject of this lawsuit. Shortly thereafter, in October 1986, Congress adopted SARA, amending the natural resources damages provisions of CERCLA in several respects. For example, SARA provided that assessments performed by state as well as federal trustees were entitled to a rebuttable presumption, it provided for the recovery of prejudgment interest on damage awards, and it proscribed "double recovery" for natural resources damages. §§ 107(f)(2)(C), 107(a), 107(f)(1), 42 U.S.C. §§ 9607(f)(2)(C), 9607(a), 9607(f)(1). SARA also amended § 301(c) to require Interior to adopt any necessary conforming amendments to its natural resource damage assessment regulations within six months of the effective date of the amendments, "[n]otwithstanding the failure of the President to promulgate the regulations required under this subsection on the required [December 1982] date." § 301(c)(1), 42 U.S.C. § 9651(c)(1).

....

The most significant issue in this case concerns the validity of the regulation providing that damages for despoilment of natural resources shall be "the *lesser of*: restoration or replacement costs; or diminution of use values." 43 C.F.R. § 11.35(b)(2) (1987) (emphasis added).

State and Environmental Petitioners challenge Interior's "lesser of" rule, insisting that CERCLA requires damages to be at least sufficient to pay the cost in every case of restoring, replacing or acquiring the equivalent of the damaged resource (hereinafter referred to shorthandedly as "restoration"). Because in some — probably a majority of — cases lost-use-value will be lower than the cost of restoration, Interior's rule will result in damages awards too small to pay for the costs or restoration....

Interior defends its rule by arguing that CERCLA does not prescribe any floor for damages but instead leaves to Interior the decision of what the measure of damages will be....

Although our resolution of the dispute submerges us in the minutiae of CERCLA text and legislative materials, we initially stress the enormous practical significance of the "lesser of" rule. A hypothetical example will illustrate the point: imagine a hazardous substance spill that kills a rookery of fur seals and destroys a habitat for seabirds at a sealife reserve. The lost use value of the seals and seabird habitat would be measured by the market value of the fur seals' pelts (which would be approximately $15 each) plus the selling price per acre of land comparable in value to that on which the spoiled bird habitat was located. Even if, as likely, that use value turns out to be far less than the cost of restoring the rookery and seabird habitat, it would nonetheless be the only measure of damages eligible for the presumption of recoverability under the Interior rule.

After examining the language and purpose of CERCLA, as well as its legislative history, we conclude that Interior's "lesser of" rule is directly contrary to the expressed intent of Congress.

... [The precise question here is] whether DOI is entitled to treat use value and restoration cost as having equal presumptive legitimacy as a measure of damages.

Interior's "lesser of" rule operates on the premise that, as the cost of a restoration project goes up relative to the value of the injured resource, at some point it becomes wasteful to require responsible parties to pay the full cost of restoration. [Citation.] The logic behind the rule is the same logic that prevents an individual from paying $8,000 to repair a collision-damaged car that was worth only $5,000 before the collision. Just as a prudent individual would sell the damaged car for scrap and then spend $5,000 on a used car in similar condition, DOI's rule requires a polluter to pay a sum equal to the diminution in the use value of a resource whenever that sum is less than restoration cost. What is significant about Interior's rule is the point at which it deems restoration "inefficient." Interior chose to draw the line not at the point where restoration becomes practically impossible, nor at the point where the cost of restoration becomes grossly disproportionate to the use value of the resource, but rather at the point where restoration cost exceeds — by any amount, however small — the use value of the resource. Thus, while we agree with DOI that CERCLA permits it to establish a rule exempting responsible parties *in some cases* from having to pay the full cost of restoration of natural resources, we also agree with Petitioners that it does not permit Interior to draw the line on an automatic "which costs less" basis.

Interior's "lesser of" rule squarely rejects the concept of any clearly expressed congressional preference for recovering the full cost of restoration from responsible parties. The challenged regulation treats the two alternative measures of damages, restoration cost and use value, as though the choice between them were a matter of complete indifference from the statutory point of view: thus, in any given case, the rule makes damages turn solely on whichever standard is less expensive.... [W]e conclude that CERCLA unambiguously mandates a distinct preference for using restoration cost as the measure of damages, and so precludes a "lesser of" rule which totally ignores that preference.

... The Regulations promulgated pursuant to § 107(a)(C) are to identify procedures for measuring damages that "shall take into consideration factors including, but not limited to, replacement value, use value, and ability of the ecosystem or resource to recover." § 301(c)(2), 42 U.S.C. § 9651(c)(2). While CERCLA thus empowers DOI to formulate a measure of damages, several other provisions of the Act make it clear that replacement cost and use value are not to be accorded equal presumptive legitimacy in the process.

The strongest linguistic evidence of Congress' intent to establish a distinct preference for restoration costs as the measure of damages is contained in § 107(f)(1) of CERCLA. That section states that natural resource damages recovered by a government trustee are "for use only to restore, replace, or acquire the equivalent of such natural resources." It goes on to state: "The measure of damages in any action under [§ 107(a)(C)] shall not be limited by the sums which can be used to restore or replace such resources."

. . . .

The same section of CERCLA that mandates the expenditures of all damages on restoration (again a shorthand reference to all three listed uses of damages) provides that the measure of damages "shall not be limited by" restoration costs. § 107(f)(1), 42 U.S.C. § 9607(f)(1). This provision obviously reflects Congress' apparent concern that its restorative purpose for imposing damages not be construed as making restoration cost a damages ceiling. But the explicit command that damages "shall not be limited by" restoration costs also carries in it an implicit assumption that restoration cost will serve as the basic measure of damages in many if not most CERCLA cases. It would be markedly inconsistent with the restorative thrust of the whole section to limit restoration-based damages, as Interior's rule does, to a minuscule number of cases where restoration is cheaper than paying for lost use.

. . . .

3. *Superfund Provisions*

CERCLA's Superfund provisions lend additional weight to our conclusion that Interior's "lesser of" rule is not true to the statute. In CERCLA as originally enacted, public trustees could rely on Superfund money to pay for restoration in cases where they could not recover money from the polluters themselves (for example, where the responsible party had become insolvent, or where the responsible party had engaged in secret dumping and thus could not be identified. SARA cut off the availability of Superfund money for natural resource restoration in 1986, but the statutory provisions governing Superfund remain on the books and provide evidence of Congress' intent to require responsible parties to pay restoration costs. Under CERCLA, Superfund monies can be spent to redress harm to natural resources only to (1) assess the extent of the damages, and to (2) finance government trustees' "efforts in the restoration, rehabilitation, or replacement or acquiring the equivalent of any natural resources injured, destroyed, or lost as a result of a release of a hazardous substance." § 111(c)-(1)-(2), 42 U.S.C. § 9611(c)(1)-(2). The statute, though, bars a trustee from obtaining Superfund money until it has first "exhausted all administrative and judicial remedies to *recover the amount of such claim* from persons who may be liable" under § 107 as responsible parties. § 111(b)(2)(A), 42 U.S.C. § 9611(b)-(2)(A) (emphasis added). Interior's "lesser of" rule, however, means that in the majority of cases, the trustee cannot "recover the amount of such claim" from the responsible parties since use-based damages will be less. So once again, Interior's rule appears to be out of sync with the statutory scheme and with CERCLA's decided emphasis on making polluters pay for restoration of spoiled resources.

CERCLA's settlement provision provides that a federal trustee may settle a natural resource damages case only "if the potentially responsible party agrees to undertake appropriate actions necessary to protect and restore the natural resources damaged by [the] release or threatened release of hazardous substances." § 122(j)(2), 42 U.S.C. § 9622(j)(2). Interior's "lesser of" rule is out of step with this settlement provision as well: taken together, they establish a ragged-edged scheme whereby a responsible party can settle only if it pays restoration costs, but those restoration costs will usually be more than it stands to lose by trying the case, if damages are awarded in court under the "lesser of" rule. Normally, a rational polluter would not settle for an amount larger than its potential liability.[20]

Thus, we should be reluctant to attribute to Congress a Machiavellian intent to allow Interior to undermine its own settlement provision. The fact that Congress insisted on restoration costs as a floor for settlements shows it must have intended a similar measure of damages to operate in the litigation itself.

. . . .

The "lesser of" rule is also inconsistent with § 311(f)(4) and (5) of the Clean Water Act, to which Interior's natural resource damage regulations are applicable in accordance with § 301(c)(1) of CERCLA. Section 311 of the Clean Water Act

---

[20]In bargaining between rational actors, any settlement reached before trial will normally lie between the lower limit of potential liability ($0, which represents a finding of no liability) and the upper limit of potential liability (under DOI's rule, this will be the "lesser of" use value or restoration cost). Each party will thus achieve its goal of averting the risk of an adverse judgment, because the amount paid by the defendant to the plaintiff will lie somewhere between the two possible extremes that could result from a trial. The amount within that range that the parties will settle on depends partly on their prediction as to the likelihood of a verdict relieving the defendant of liability entirely or awarding damages in an amount smaller than the upper limit of potential liability.

Of course, the foregoing analysis omits transaction costs — such as lawyers' fees and down-time caused by litigation — which the defendant will add to the upper limit of its potential liability when deciding whether to make or accept a particular settlement offer. Given this, it is conceivable that a rational defendant would settle for an amount greater than the maximum potential damages award. Yet this would only happen where the defendant foresaw litigation burdens so enormous that, *even after factoring in the likelihood of a verdict relieving him of liability entirely or awarding an amount less than the maximum potential award*, acceding to the high settlement amount would be the least costly avenue for the defendant to take.

Interior's "lesser of" rule, on the other hand, envisions a scheme in which a defendant would accept a settlement figure (i.e., restoration cost) vastly greatly than the amount it stands to lose at trial (i.e., use value). Given that the difference could often run into millions of dollars, it is difficult to see why Congress would construct such a scenario if it wanted to encourage settlement.

provides that damages recoverable for releases of hazardous substances or oil covered by the CWA "shall include any costs or expenses incurred by the Federal Government or any State government in the restoration or replacement of natural resources damaged or destroyed." 33 U.S.C. § 1321(f)(5). Thus, the CWA expressly establishes restoration cost as the standard measure of damages.

... Interior's position of course assumes a conflict between the two statutes. We perceive none; quite the contrary. The CWA provides that damages must "include" restoration cost, while CERCLA provides recovered sums must be spent on restoration and "shall not be limited by" restoration cost. These directives are in harmony: restoration is the basic measure of damages, but damages can exceed restoration cost in some cases. A compatible reading of the two statutes reinforces our view that restoration costs were the intended basis for damages in CERCLA and that there is no authorization for DOI to abandon Congress' strong preference for restoration, clearly expressed in two separate statutes enacted within three years of one another.

The text and structure of CERCLA indicate clearly to us that Congress intended restoration costs to be the basic measure of recovery for harm to natural resources....

Alternatively, Interior justifies the "lesser of" rule as being economically efficient. Under DOI's economic efficiency view, making restoration cost the measure of damages would be a waste of money whenever restoration would cost more than the use value of the resource....

This is nothing more or less than cost-benefit analysis: Interior's rule attempts to optimize social welfare by restoring an injured resource only when the diminution in the resource's value to society is greater in magnitude than the cost of restoring it. And, acknowledgedly, Congress did intend CERCLA's natural resource provisions to operate efficiently. For one thing, the Act requires that the assessment of damages and the restoration of injured resources take place as cost-effectively as possible. Moreover, as we have indicated, there is some suggestion in the legislative history that Congress intended recovery not to encompass restoration cost where restoration is infeasible or where its cost is grossly disproportionate to use value.

The fatal flaw of Interior's approach, however, is that it assumes that natural resources are fungible goods, just like any other, and that the value to society generated by a particular resource can be accurately measured in every case — assumptions that Congress apparently rejected. As the foregoing examination of CERCLA's text, structure and legislative history illustrates, Congress saw restoration as the presumptively correct remedy for injury to natural resources. To say that Congress placed a thumb on the scales in favor of restoration is not to say that it forswore the goal of efficiency. "Efficiency," standing alone, simply means that the chosen policy will dictate the result that achieves the greatest value to society. Whether a particular choice is efficient depends on *how the various alternatives are valued*. Our reading of CERCLA does not attribute to Congress an irrational dislike of "efficiency"; rather, it suggests that Congress was skeptical of the ability of human beings to measure the true "value" of a natural resource. Indeed, even the common law recognizes that restoration is the proper remedy for injury to property where measurement of damages by some other method will fail to compensate fully for the injury. Congress' refusal to view use value and restoration cost as having equal presumptive legitimacy merely recognizes that natural resources have value that is not readily measured by traditional means. Congress delegated to Interior the job of deciding at what point the presumption of restoration falls away, but its repeated emphasis on the primacy of restoration rejected the underlying premise of Interior's rule, which is that restoration is wasteful if its cost exceeds — by even the slightest amount — the diminution in use value of the injured resource.

    ....

Our reading of the complex of relevant provisions concerning damages under CERCLA convinces us that Congress established a distinct preference for restoration cost as the measure of recovery in natural resource damage cases. This is not to say that DOI may not establish some class of cases where other considerations — i.e., infeasibility of restoration or grossly disproportionate cost to use value — warrant a different standard. We hold the "lesser of" rule based on comparing costs alone, however, to be an invalid determinant of whether or not to deviate from Congress' preference.

    ....

The regulations establish a rigid hierarchy of permissible methods for determining "use values," limiting recovery to the price commanded by the resource on the open market, unless the trustee finds that "the market for the resource is not reasonably competitive." 43 C.F.R. § 11.83(c)(1). If the trustee makes such a finding, it may "appraise" the market value in accordance with the relevant sections of the "Uniform Appraisal Standards for Federal Land Acquisition." Only when neither the market value nor the appraisal method is "appropriate" can other methods of determining use value be employed.

Environmental petitioners maintain that Interior's emphasis on market value is an unreasonable interpretation of the statute ... and we agree. While it is not irrational to look to market price as *one* factor in determining the use value of a resource, it is unreasonable to view market price as the *exclusive* factor, or even the predominant one. From the bald eagle to the blue whale and snail darter, natural resources have values that are not fully captured by the market system.... Indeed, many of the materials in the record on which DOI relied in developing its rules regarding contingent valuation expressed the same idea; it is the incompleteness of market processes that gives rise to the need for contingent valuation techniques. Courts have long stressed that market prices are not to be used as surrogates for value "when the market value has been too difficult to find, or when its application would result in manifest injustice to owner or public." [Citations.] As we have previously noted in the context of the "lesser of" rule, market prices are not acceptable as primary measures of the use values of natural resources. [Citation.] We find the DOI erred by establishing "a strong presumption in favor of market price and appraisal methodologies."

We are not satisfied that the problem is solved by the provision in section 11.83(c)(1) permitting nonmarket methodologies to be used when the market for the resource is not "reasonably competitive." There are many resources whose components may be traded in "reasonably competitive" markets, but whose total use values are not fully reflected in the prices they command in those markets. Interior itself provides ample proof of the inadequacy of the "reasonably competitive market" caveat. For example, DOI has noted that "the hierarchy established in the type B regulation" would dictate a use value for fur seals of $15 per seal, corresponding to the market price for the seal's pelt. Another example of DOI's erroneous equation of market price with use value is its insistence that the sum of the fees charged by the government for the use of a resource, say, for admission to a national park, constitutes "the value to the public of recreational or other public uses of the resource," 43 C.F.R. § 11.83(b)(1), because "these fees are what the government has determined to represent the value of the natural resource and represent an offer by a willing seller," 51 Fed. Reg. 27, 719 (1986). This is quite obviously and totally fallacious; there is no necessary connection between the total value to the public of a park and the fees charged as admission, which typically are set not to maximize profits but rather to encourage the public to visit the park. In fact, the decision to set entrance fees far below what the traffic would bear is evidence of Congress's strong conviction that parks are priceless national treasures and that access to them ought to be as wide as possible, and not, as DOI would have it, a sign that parks are really not so valuable after all.

Neither the statute nor its legislative history evinces any congressional intent to limit use values to market prices. On the contrary, Congress intended the damage assessment regulations to capture fully all aspects of loss....

On remand, DOI should consider a rule that would permit trustees to derive use values for natural resources by summing up all reliably calculated use values, however measured, so long as the trustee does not double count. Market valuation can of course serve as one factor to be considered, but by itself it will necessarily be incomplete....

When a natural resource is injured by a discharge of oil or release of a hazardous substance, an authorized official[60] assesses the damages resulting.[61]

DOI has prescribed methodologies for estimating in any such instance the amount of money to be sought as recompense. Either DOI's restoration

---

[60]"Authorized official" means the Federal or State official to whom is delegated the authority to act on behalf of the Federal or State agency designated as trustee, or an official designated by an Indian tribe, pursuant to section 126(d) of CERCLA, to perform a natural resource damage assessment." 43 C.F.R. § 11.14(d) (1988). *See also* CERCLA § 107(f)(2), 42 U.S.C. § 9607(f)(2) (Supp. IV 1986).

[61]43 C.F.R. § 11.80(a)(1) (1988).

methodology or one of its use methodologies must be employed in calculations of damages. The issue we now address concerns one of the latter.

DOI's natural resource damage assessment regulations define "use value" as

> the value to the public of recreational or other public uses of the resource, as measured by changes in consumer surplus, any fees or other payments collectable by the government or Indian tribe for a private party's use of the natural resource, and any economic rent accruing to a private party because the government or Indian tribe does not charge a fee or price for the use of the resource.

The regulations provide several approaches to use valuation. When the injured resource is traded in a market, the lost use value is the diminution in market price. When that is not precisely the case, but similar resources are traded in a market, an appraisal technique may be utilized to determine damages. When, however, neither of these two situations obtains, non-marketed resource methodologies are available. One of these is "contingent valuation" (CV), the subject of controversy here.

The CV process "includes all techniques that set up hypothetical markets to elicit an individual's economic valuation of a natural resource."[69]

CV involves a series of interviews with individuals for the purpose of ascertaining the values they respectively attach to particular changes in particular resources. Among the several formats available to an interviewer in developing the hypothetical scenario embodied in a CV survey are direct questioning, by which the interviewer learns how much the interviewee is willing to pay for the resource; bidding formats, for example, the interviewee is asked whether he or she would pay a given amount for a resource and, depending upon the response, the bid is set higher or lower until a final price is derived; and a "take or leave it" format, in which the interviewee decides whether or not he or she is willing to pay a designated amount of money for the resource. CV methodology thus enables ascertainment of individually-expressed values for different levels of quality of resources, and dollar values of individuals' changes in well-being....

Industry Petitioners point out that at common law there can be no recovery for speculative injuries, and they contend that CV methodology is at odds with that principle. CV methodology, they say, is rife with speculation, amounting to no more than ordinary public opinion polling.

....

The primary argument of Industry Petitioners is that the possibility of bias is inherent in CV methodology, and disqualifies it as a "best available procedure." In evaluating the utility of CV methodology in assessing damages for impairment of natural resources, DOI surveys a number of studies which analyzed the

---

[69]42 U.S.C. § 11.83(d)(5)(i) (1988).

methodology, addressed the shortcomings of various questionnaires, and recommended steps needed to fashion reliable CV assessments....

Industry Petitioners urge, however, that even assuming that questions are artfully drafted and carefully circumscribed, there is such a high degree of variation in size of the groups surveyed, and such a concomitant fluctuation in aggregations of damages, that CV methodology cannot be considered a "best available procedure."[86]

We think this attack on CV methodology is insufficient in a facial challenge to invalidate CV as an available assessment technique. The extent of damage to natural resources from releases of oil and hazardous substances varies greatly, and though the impact may be widespread and severe, it is in the mission of CERCLA to assess the public loss....

We sustain DOI in its conclusion that CV methodology is a "best available procedure." As such, its conclusion in the Natural Resource Damage Assessment regulations was entirely proper.

....

NOTES AND QUESTIONS

1. In the principal case, the court observed that one motivating factor behind the CERCLA natural resource damage provisions was the dissatisfaction of Congress with common law damage rules. The traditional common law approach for measuring damages for injuries to real property provides that the claimant has a choice between two rules: diminution in value or cost to restore. RESTATEMENT (SECOND) OF TORTS § 929(1)(a) (1977). This choice is not absolute, however. The principal objective of compensatory damages, of course, is to place the injured party in the same position as if the harm had not occurred. Other policy considerations factor into the equation as well, including economic efficiency, avoiding waste, and promoting settlement through predictable and objective criteria for calculating damages. As a result, the injured party may ordinarily recover the reasonable cost of restoring land to its original condition provided that it is not "grossly disproportionate" to the diminution in value. RESTATEMENT (SECOND) OF TORTS § 929 comment b; *Williams-Bowman Rubber Co. v. Industrial Main. Welding & Mach. Co.*, 677 F. Supp. 539 (N.D. Ill. 1987).

One criticism of the common law methodology is that certain types of injuries — such as harm to natural resources — are difficult to value. Consequently, absent statutory guidance, courts may tend to undervalue those resources and decide not to award the cost of restoration. In such cases, critics observe that

---

[86]Industry Petitioners cite a study estimating the combined option and existence values to Texas residents of whooping cranes at $109,000,000 (13.9 million Texas residents × $7.13). The estimate rested upon responses to a survey eliciting the amount an individual would pay for a permit to visit the National Wildlife Refuge where the whooping crane winters. Had the survey been nationwide in scope, the estimate would have been $1.58 billion. [Citation.]

violators are not sufficiently deterred from future destruction of natural resources, and the public interest is not served by restoration of vital ecosystems.

2. In a companion case, *Colorado v. Department of Interior*, 880 F.2d 481 (D.C. Cir. 1989), the D.C. Circuit Court of Appeals considered the validity of the scope and content of Type A regulations promulgated by the Interior Department pursuant to CERCLA. The regulations governed assessment of damages caused by minor, short-duration discharges or releases of oil or hazardous substances in coastal and marine environments. Interior developed a computer model with databases containing chemical, biological, and economic information to assess damages.

The court upheld the scope of the regulations, finding that the agency acted reasonably within its rulemaking authority. However, the court found the content flawed in the same manner as in the Type B regulations invalidated in *Ohio* — the agency failed to incorporate restoration and replacement values. The statutory language and legislative history of CERCLA clearly demonstrated that the Type A rules could not be based exclusively on lost use values to measure national resource damage.

3. *Causation.* CERCLA requires the trustee to show that the harm to natural resources *resulted* from a release of hazardous substances. 42 U.S.C. § 107(a)-(4)(C); 42 U.S.C. § 107(f)(1). This requirement of a causal connection between the defendant's conduct and the actual injury to the natural resources is higher than the standard for recovery of response costs under section 107(a)(4)(B). Liability may be imposed for response costs on a slight causal nexus — the claimant does not need to "fingerprint" or trace the release of waste to an actual contamination of the property. *See Dedham Water Co. v. Cumberland Farms Dairy*, 889 F.2d 1146, 1154 n.7 (1st Cir. 1989). *But see In re Acushnet River & New Bedford Harbor*, 722 F. Supp. 893, 897 (D. Mass. 1989) (government needs to show that the releases were a "contributing factor" to injury to natural resources).

4. The trustee bears the burden to prove natural resource damages, in contrast to the scheme for government recovery of response costs which shifts the burden to the potentially responsible party to disprove the government's consistency with the national contingency plan. The natural resource damage provisions also limit the government to recovery of its *reasonable* costs in assessing damages — also a higher standard than for response costs where reasonableness is not mandated. Further, trustees cannot use CERCLA funding to perform damage assessments but can recover costs incurred only by prevailing on a claim or through settlement. *Compare* 42 U.S.C. § 107(a)(4)(A) and (C).

5. In *In re Acushnet River & New Bedford Harbor*, 712 F. Supp. 1019, 1035 (D. Mass. 1989) the court held that natural resource damages should be measured by the "difference between the natural resource in its pristine condition and the natural resource after the cleanup, together with the lost use value and the costs of assessment." CERCLA precludes the double counting of damages; consequently the measure of natural resource damages should be the "residual" determined after considering the effects of response actions. *See* 42 U.S.C. 107(f)(1); 43 C.F.R. § 11.84(c). Different trustees cannot recover damages for injuries to the same resource unless able to show that a different interest was harmed. *See* Marten & McFarland, *Litigating CERCLA Natural Resource Damage Claims*, 22 ENVTL. L. REP. 670, 674 (1991) (gives illustration that burial ground located on federal park land could have separately compensable value to tribal trustee distinct from value as a park to federal trustee).

6. Although private parties cannot directly recover for natural resource damages under CERCLA, such claims may overlap with recovery of costs of remedial action under section 107(a)(4)(B). *Artesian Water Co. v. New Castle County*, 659 F. Supp. 1269, 1288 (D. Del. 1987); *Lutz v. Chromatex, Inc.*, 718 F. Supp. 413, 419 (M.D. Pa. 1989) (individuals claims for loss of use of drinking water wells contaminated by toxic chemicals not recoverable under CERCLA when characterized as suit for natural resource damages). In *Bedford v. Raytheon Co.*, 755 F. Supp. 469 (D. Mass. 1991) the court held that a town could not bring suit under CERCLA § 107(a)(4)(C) for natural resource damages resulting from the contamination of an aquifer which had served as the town's principal drinking water source. The court found that political subdivisions, such as municipalities, cannot bring such claims unless specifically designated in a representative capacity by the state. The court observed that Congress adopted the trustee system partially in order to centralize litigation strategy and settlement decisions, thus reducing the potential divisive influence of "parochial" views and concerns about damaged resources.

In *Alaska Sport Fishing Assoc. v. Exxon Corp.*, 34 F.3d 769 (9th Cir. 1994) the court held that a class action by sport fishermen seeking damages for public loss of use and enjoyment of natural resources resulting from oil spill was barred by res judicata because a consent decree between government trustees and the defendant corporation had previously settled all public claims. The court also recognized that CERCLA's structure provides that government trustees are entitled to recover for all lost use damages on behalf of the public from time of release until restoration.

7. In contrast to other liability provisions of the Act, natural resource damages are not recoverable for injuries which occurred prior to the enactment of CERCLA in 1980. *See* § 107(f)(1), 42 U.S.C. § 9607(f)(1); § 111(d)(1), 42 U.S.C. § 9611(d)(1). Although liability is not imposed retroactively, both the release and the resulting harm to resources must predate the statute. *Idaho v. Bunker Hill Co.*, 635 F. Supp. 665, 674-75 (D. Idaho 1986) (damages occurring after effective date of CERCLA recoverable even if the result of pre-enactment releases). The statute of limitations for natural resource damages provides that suit must be brought within three years after the later of discovery of the loss and its connection with the release of hazardous waste or when regulations were promulgated to assess damages. 42 U.S.C. § 113(g)(1). *See United States v. Seattle*, 33 Env't Rep. Cas. (BNA) 1549 (W.D. Wash. 1991).

8. 43 C.F.R. § 11.83 sets forth a range of possible actions for the applicable trustee to take regarding injuries to natural resource, including: restoration, rehabilitation, replacement and/or acquisition of the equivalent of the injured resources and the *services* the resources provide. 43 C.F.R. § 11.82(a) (emphasis added). When selecting which alternative to pursue, the authorized official is directed to evaluate the following factors:

(1) Technical feasibility, as that term is used in this part.

(2) The relationship of the expected costs of the proposed actions to the expected benefits from the restoration, rehabilitation, replacement, and/or acquisition of equivalent resources.

(3) Cost-effectiveness, as that term is used in this part.

(4) The results of any actual or planned response actions.

(5) Potential for additional injury resulting from the proposed actions, including long-term and indirect impacts, to the injured resources or other resources.

(6) The natural recovery period determined in § 11.73(a)(1) of this part.

(7) Ability of the resources to recover with or without alternative actions.

(8) Potential effects of the action on human health and safety.

(9) Consistency with relevant Federal, State, and tribal policies.

(10) Compliance with applicable Federal, State, and tribal laws.

43 C.F.R. § 11.82(d).

In *Kennecott Utah Copper v. United States Dep't of Interior*, 88 F.3d 1191, 1209 (D.C. Cir. 1996) the court rejected various procedural challenges by industry to the promulgation of final regulations issued by the Department of the Interior regarding Type B natural resource damage assessments. 59 Fed. Reg. 14,262 (March 25, 1994). The court also generally upheld the substantive validity of the regulations except it did grant industry's petition for review of the DOI's interpretation of the statute of limitations and the use "resources and services" in the measurement of damages (43 C.F.R. § 11.80(b). The court invalidated the "resources and services" provision on the basis that the agency had failed to adequately explain its actions.

9. In *State of California v. Montrose Chem. Corp. of Cal.*, 104 F.3d 1507 (9th Cir. 1997) the court held that an action to recover natural resource damages under CERCLA was not barred by the statute of limitations under § 9613(g)(1). The court held that the limitations period begins to run upon the occurrence of the later discovery of the loss or when all applicable regulations are promulgated under section 9651(c).

The court also found that 42 U.S.C. § 9607(c)(1)(D), which limits each owner/operator's liability for "each release of a hazardous substance or incident involving release of a hazardous substance" to the costs of response plus $50 million, applied to each person separately rather than collectively. The court explained its interpretation of the cap:

> For these reasons, we reject the Montrose defendants' argument that "incident" should be interpreted as a term of art, meaning "contaminated site." Instead, we interpret "incident involving release" in accord with its common definition and the legislative history of H.R. 85 to mean an occurrence or series of occurrences of relatively short duration involving a single release or a series of releases all resulting from or connected to the event or occurrence. Thus a series of events that lead up to a spill of hazardous substance would be considered an incident involving release; however, a series of releases over a long period of time might or might not.

Id. at 1520.

10. The statute also provides an exception from liability for harm to resources which had been previously identified as an "irreversible and irretrievable commitment of resources" in an environmental impact statement or comparable document. 42 U.S.C. § 107(f)(1). The exception requires that the permitting or licensing decision authorized the commitment of the particular resources and the terms of the authorization were met. This exception has been interpreted narrowly by courts. In *Idaho v. Hanna Mining Co.*, 882 F.2d 392, 395 (9th Cir. 1989) the state sought damages under CERCLA for the contamination of certain ground and surface waters and harm to wildlife caused by waste produced by a commercial mining operation. The court held that the statutory exception did not excuse the current landowner from liability for damage caused by mining activities of previous operators which occurred prior to the issuance of an environmental impact statement and accompanying permit. Thus, although an EIS might authorize a new project, CERCLA liability could be imposed on the current owners for hazardous waste problems attributable to the prior mining company. The court stated, however, that the terms "irreversible" and "irretrievable" did not have to be recited in the EIS for the exception to apply.

11. The statute provides an exception from liability for injuries to natural resources which result from releases pursuant to a federal permit. 42 U.S.C. § 107(j). The exception for federally permitted activities includes, for instance, discharges complying with a NPDES permit or a section 404 permit for dredge or fill operations under the Clean Water Act, and pursuant to a hazardous waste management facility permit under RCRA. 42 U.S.C. § 101(10). The statute recognizes that recovery of damages may be pursued under other laws, such as state common law of nuisance. The release must be in compliance with the terms of the federal permit in order to assert the exemption. *Idaho v. Bunker Hill Co.*, 635 F. Supp. 665, 674 (D. Idaho 1986) (damage to natural resources caused by releases which exceeded the limitations established by the permits were recoverable by the state).

12. For additional commentary on the recovery of natural resource damages under CERCLA see the following references: Binger, Copple, & Hoffman, *The Use of Contingent Valuation Methodology in Natural Resource Damage Assessments: Legal Fact and Economic Fiction*, 89 Nw. U.L. REV. 1029 (1995); Sunstein, *Incommensurability and Valuation in Law*, 92 MICH. L. REV. 779 (1994); Levy & Friedman, *The Revenge of the Redwoods? Reconsidering Property Rights and the Economic Allocation of Natural Resources*, 61 U. CHI. L. REV. 493 (1994); Marten & McFarland, *Litigating CERCLA Natural Resource Damage Claims*, 22 ENVTL. L. REP. 670 (1991); Woodward & Hope, *Natural Resource Damage Litigation Under the Comprehensive Environmental Response, Compensation, and Liability Act*, 14 HARV. ENVTL. L. REV. 189 (1990); Cross, *Natural Resource Damage Valuation*, 42 VAND. L. REV. 269 (1989); Straube, *Is Full Compensation Possible for the Damages Resulting From the Exxon Valdez Oil Spill?*, 19 ENVTL. L. REP. 10338 (1989); Olson, *Natural Resource Damages in the Wake of the Ohio and Colorado Decisions: Where Do We Go From Here?*, 19 ENVTL. L. REP. 10551 (1989); Habicht, *Expanding Role of Natural Resource Damage Claims Under Superfund*, 7 VA. J. NAT. RESOURCES L. 1 (1987); Menefee, *Recovery for Natural Resource Damages Under Superfund: The Role of the Rebuttable Presumption*, 12 ENVTL. L. REP. 15057 (1982).

Chapter 10

TOXIC SUBSTANCES CONTROL ACT

INTRODUCTION

A significant number of chemical substances and mixtures are manufactured and processed annually in the United States, many of which are socially useful commercial products. Prior to the enactment of the Toxic Substances Control Act (TSCA) in 1976, though, no mechanism existed under federal law to evaluate the potential health risks associated with exposure to these often toxic chemicals. The major federal pollution control statutes, the Clean Air Act and Clean Water Act, regulated the types and quantities of certain pollutants when they entered the environment. Other federal statutes — principally CERCLA and RCRA — were aimed at the cleanup, treatment, storage and disposal of hazardous wastes. An assortment of other federal statutes were limited by being either product-specific (Food, Drug and Cosmetic Act), use specific (FIFRA), or pertained only to certain types of chemical risks, such as OSHA's focus on workplace safety. Consequently, this myriad of statutes comprised a patchwork of regulatory coverage which inadequately addressed the spectrum of human and environmental exposure to toxic substances. Congress envisioned a need, then, to obtain critical information pertaining to the dangers presented by the thousands of chemicals which did not fit within the regulatory scope of existing federal statutes before allowing the introduction of such substances into interstate commerce. In TSCA, Congress gave the EPA considerable latitude to gather and assess such data, yet tempered the statutory regulatory structure with recognition of the potential economic consequences and burdens of regulation on industry.

The principal goals of TSCA essentially are twofold: to gather information regarding chemical toxicity, use and exposure, and then to utilize that data to protect human health and the environment from unreasonable risks. The Act provides various means to generate information production on chemical substances including: (1) granting EPA authority to adopt rules requiring testing by manufacturers for both new and existing chemicals (TSCA § 4, 15 U.S.C. § 2603); (2) requiring industry to submit a premanufacture notification (PMN) before producing a new chemical substance or for making significant new uses of an existing chemical (TSCA § 5(a), 15 U.S.C. § 2604(a)); and (3) imposing extensive reporting and recordkeeping duties on industry and mandating the EPA to compile an inventory of chemicals manufactured and processed in the United States (TSCA § 8, 15 U.S.C. § 2607). These data-generating provisions, although somewhat overlapping, are designed to work in tandem as the inventory list of existing chemicals enables the agency to implement the PMN for new ones. The agency can ascertain gaps in coverage from existing reported toxicological studies and determine what tests would produce the information. The Act also gives the EPA broad authority to take regulatory measures to protect against risks posed by hazardous chemical substances and mixtures (TSCA § 6(a), 15 U.S.C. § 2605(a)).

The TSCA provides for a two-tier system for evaluating and regulating chemical substances to protect against unreasonable risks to human health and to the environment. The Act provides for the EPA to require health and environmental effects testing of chemicals by and at the expense of their manufacturers and processors (TSCA § 4, 15 U.S.C. § 2603) and to regulate substantively the manufacturing and processing of those chemicals (TSCA § 6, 15 U.S.C. § 2605). The EPA is empowered to require testing under section 4 in two instances. The first is where the agency finds that the manufacture, distribution, processing, use or disposal of a particular chemical substance "may present an unreasonable risk of injury to human health or the environment." 15 U.S.C. § 2603(a)(1)(A)(i). Second, testing may be ordered to evaluate substantial human exposure to chemical substances or where chemicals may reasonably be anticipated to enter the environment in substantial quantities. 15 U.S.C. § 2603(a)(1)(B)(i). The underlying premise in both circumstances is that insufficient information exists regarding the health risks associated with such exposure to the chemicals and that data developed through testing would fill those information gaps.

The toxicological data developed pursuant to testing under section 4 provides the EPA with the information necessary to make a decision whether or not to regulate the substance under section 6, 15 U.S.C. § 2605(a). TSCA grants the EPA broader testing than regulatory authority; the level of certainty of risk warranting a section 4 test rule is lower than that warranting a section 6 regulatory rule. The ambivalence of Congress toward regulation under TSCA, though, is reflected in the conflicting instructions given to the EPA to pass rules to "protect adequately" against unreasonable risks yet to do so by using the "least burdensome" means. TSCA § 6(a), 15 U.S.C. § 2605(a). Moreover, the agency is directed to exercise its regulatory powers by taking into account the potential economic consequences on industry and to defer to regulation under other statutes in preference to TSCA. TSCA § 6(c), 15 U.S.C. § 2605(c).

Since TSCA permits the EPA to require testing and to issue regulations of chemicals based on an assessment of "risk" rather than a certainty of harm, manufacturers have been concerned that the EPA might abuse its powers under the Act and require expensive testing too frequently. Congress, mindful of such industry concerns, struck a balance in TSCA between the need for obtaining adequate information on potentially dangerous chemicals and not imposing undue economic barriers to technological innovation. 15 U.S.C. § 2601(b). The history of EPA action under TSCA since its enactment demonstrates that industry fears of excessive testing obligations and regulations were largely unfounded. The effectiveness of TSCA has been hampered partly because of the inherent difficulty in balancing cost factors with information needs, compounded with the EPA's inadequate administrative resources or enthusiasm to conduct rulemaking under the Act. Despite its widely perceived failed promise, TSCA could still prove to be a significant regulatory statute with respect to the control of toxic substances and may assume a more prominent status in the federal environmental protection arena with increased attention by the EPA.

The volume of new and existing chemical substances and mixtures subject to the reach of the TSCA is enormous. In order to carry out the goals of the Act in the most efficient manner, Congress established a committee of representatives from specified federal agencies and federally funded institutions, known as the Interagency Testing Committee (ITC). The principal charge of the ITC is the responsibility for recommending to the EPA a list of no more than the fifty most potentially dangerous chemicals for priority consideration for testing. TSCA § 4(e), 15 U.S.C. § 2603(e). The EPA is required to initiate rulemaking proceedings to require testing of the chemicals designated by the ITC or to publish its reasons for not doing so.

Although TSCA is primarily oriented at developing data through testing of chemicals, it also contains several unique features including provisions regulating asbestos in schools (TSCA §§ 201-215, 15 U.S.C. §§ 2641-2655), indoor radon pollution (TSCA §§ 310-311, 15 U.S.C. §§ 2661-2671), and phasing out the highly toxic chemical polychlorinated biphenyls (PCBs) (TSCA § 6(e), 15 U.S.C. § 2605(e)). The following materials will examine the regulatory framework of TSCA with particular emphasis on the ongoing controversy between industry and the EPA over risk assessment as it pertains to testing responsibilities and regulatory action.

AUSIMONT U.S.A., INC. v. ENVIRONMENTAL PROTECTION AGENCY

838 F.2d 93 (3d Cir. 1988)

WEIS, CIRCUIT JUDGE.

The Environmental Protection Agency adopted a rule requiring petitioner manufacturers to conduct extensive testing of certain chemicals, fluoroalkenes, to determine their potential for producing adverse health effects. The manufacturers have petitioned for judicial review, asserting that the rule is contrary to law and should be set aside. An examination of the record persuades us that the agency action is supported by substantial evidence, and accordingly, we deny review.

The Toxic Substances Control Act, 15 U.S.C. §§ 2601-29, authorizes EPA to promulgate rules directing manufacturers to arrange for testing of chemical substances that "may present an unreasonable risk of injury to health." 15 U.S.C. § 2603(a)(1)(A)(i). Petitioners are the manufacturers of four chemicals, collectively known as fluoroalkenes: vinyl fluoride, vinylidene fluoride, hexafluoropropene, and tetrafluoroethene.

....

The manufacturing and processing of these fluoroalkenes takes place within closed pipes, reaction vessels and other equipment located behind sealed and barricaded areas of the factory.... Several of the fluoroalkenes are highly flammable. The danger of explosion combined with the economic cost of inefficient production act as incentives to guard against release of the gases into the environment.

Five companies produce one hundred percent of the fluoroalkenes: DuPont, Pennwalt, ICI Americas, Allied and American Hoechst. Currently no commercially available substitutes for these monomers exist. Consequently, the inelastic demand permits manufacturers to pass along price increases and testing costs. The major end-use markets include the automotive, chemical-petrochemical, industrial pollution control, hydraulic-pneumatic, and aerospace industries. Growth rates in these markets are favorable.

The parties disagree on the number of workers who may be affected by contact with the chemicals. In their brief, petitioners assert that only fifty workers are "potentially exposed" to vinyl fluoride and that the number potentially exposed to the other fluoroalkenes is less than five hundred. EPA estimates that "between eleven hundred fifty and two thousand ninety-five workers" may be exposed to these substances during their production and use. This numerical disparity may have been caused partly by recounting workers exposed to more than one of the chemicals, and at oral argument EPA conceded that its estimates may have involved some double counting.

Nearly seven million pounds of vinyl fluoride are transported annually by rail in closed tanks from DuPont's production plant in Louisville, Kentucky to its facilities in Buffalo, New York. Although in the event of derailment these movements carry a possibility of leaks and a threat of chemical escape into the atmosphere, EPA believes that human exposure to these chemicals is unlikely to occur outside the workplace.

Petitioners assert that exposure above two parts per million (2 ppm)[1] has occurred only during non-recurring short-term events — operational upsets, atypical work day exposures, reactor plugging problems, and unusual work practices. Petitioners characterize these incidents as "fugitive emissions." Although some workers wear air-supplied respirators, these devices are not used generally where industry considers engineering controls adequate to prevent emissions. An industrial hygiene study by the Fluoroalkene Industry Group (Industry Group) revealed, however, that in the instances where exposure exceeded 2 ppm, workers were not wearing respirators.

---

[1]For purposes of risk assessment, EPA employs standardized dosage scales. Such typical exposure units include parts per million in air, food or water. Petitioners apparently singled out 2 ppm as an arbitrary measure. EPA has not assigned a threshold of toxicity for the fluoroalkenes; however, EPA has established that vinyl chloride, which is molecularly similar to the fluoroalkenes, creates a risk to health at non-zero levels of emission. [Citation.]

The Toxic Substances Control Act created the Interagency Testing Committee, an entity consisting of eight members from various federal agencies whose work focuses on various concerns associated with toxic substances. Represented are such agencies as EPA, the National Cancer Institute, the National Science Foundation and the National Institute for Occupational Safety and Health. *See* 15 U.S.C. § 2603(e)(2)(A). The Committee is charged with preparing a list limited to fifty chemicals to which EPA must give first order scrutiny. In establishing such a list, "the committee shall give priority attention to those chemical substances and mixtures which are known to cause or contribute to or which are suspected of causing or contributing to cancer, gene mutations, or birth defects." § 2603(e)(1)(A).

In November 1980 the Committee listed the fluoroalkenes for priority testing. After a number of conferences with industry groups and an aborted "negotiated testing proposal," EPA issued a notice of proposed rulemaking to require testing. Written and oral comments were submitted. The agency held a public meeting, examined scientific data, and then published a final test rule on June 8, 1987.

... EPA estimates total testing costs to range from $4,783,500 to $6,196,200, for a unit cost of about 2.6 to 3.3 cents per pound of the listed substances. Petitioners expect the expense to be from $5,000,000 to $9,000,000.

In asking for review, petitioners contend that before issuing a testing rule, EPA must demonstrate that humans are actually exposed to the chemicals to such a degree that serious harm could result if the substances are toxic. Petitioners assert that EPA may not base a rule on speculation but must found it on evidence establishing a reasonable likelihood of significant risk. The agency insists that the Act authorizes it to issue a rule based on potential exposure, and that evidence in the rulemaking record supports the testing order here. EPA also contends that scientific uncertainty over the possible harmful effects of the chemicals provides the justification for testing.

In enacting the Toxic Substances Control Act, Congress made a number of preliminary findings. It indicated concern that the manufacture and processing of some chemicals "may present an unreasonable risk of injury to health." § 2601(a)(2). To meet this threat, the government declared its policy that the manufacturers and processors of these substances must develop "adequate data" with respect to "the effect of chemical substances and mixtures on health and the environment." § 2601(b)(1).

Agency authority, however, should be exercised "in such a manner as not to impede unduly or create unnecessary economic barriers to technological innovation," while assuring that those activities do not "present an unreasonable risk of injury to health." § 2601(b)(3). EPA is directed to carry out the provisions of the Act in a "reasonable and prudent manner" and to "consider the environmental, economic, and social impact of any action" taken. § 2601(c).

These themes underlie section 2603(a)(1)(A), which directs that testing be conducted when the EPA Administrator "finds" that "the manufacture, distribution in commerce, processing ... of a chemical substance ... may present an unreasonable risk of injury to health or the environment" and

> "(ii) there are insufficient data and experience upon which the effects of such manufacture ... or ... of such activities on health ... can reasonably be determined or predicted, and
> (iii) testing ... is necessary to develop such data...."

...[T]he statutory language "unreasonable risk of injury" and "may present" are not completely specific. We can agree with petitioners that Congress did not intend EPA to direct expensive experimentation based on mere speculation. We appreciate, too, that with thousands of substances in the marketplace, the agency must be reasonably discriminate in selecting subjects for testing. But section 2603 focuses on investigating areas of uncertainty as a prelude to regulating harmful substances.

Although mere scientific curiosity does not form an adequate basis for a rule, as the seriousness of risk becomes known and the extent of exposure increases, the need for testing fades into the necessity for regulatory safeguards. The issue presented here is where in the spectrum from screening to regulation this rule falls. In most administrative proceedings, we examine the record to see if there is a foundation for an agency determination of fact; however, here we look to see if the Administrator produced substantial evidence to demonstrate not fact, but doubt and uncertainty.

Both parties agree that risk is a critical factor. Risk implicates two concepts — toxicity and exposure. In each instance, quantity is important. Essentially, petitioners argue that neither factor has been shown to exist in sufficiently threatening amounts to justify promulgation of a rule. Petitioners argue that EPA has not pointed to any evidence showing the fluoroalkenes to be "unusually toxic" and has never posited that long-term health effects have been established.

To bolster their argument, petitioners question the necessity of oncological testing for VDF because it has not been shown to cause cancer. The record, however, does refer to published work by scientists Maltoni and Tovoli showing that VDF is a carcinogen. Although skeptical about the scientific conclusions of that work, the Industry Group has not produced evidence strong enough to fully discredit the Maltoni and Tovoli data.

Petitioners also criticize EPA's practice of relying on its information about one harmful substance to assess the danger from another of similar molecular structure. In this case, EPA has identified such a "structure-activity relationship" (SAR) between VDF and vinylidene chloride, which has been suspected, but not definitely established, as a carcinogen. [Citations.] Again, we believe that the petitioners' attempt to transform EPA's concerns about the lack of scientific certainty into mere speculative scouting for data actually strengthens the government's position. These questions broaching the frontiers of scientific knowledge highlight the need for testing.

....

Petitioners principally attack the exposure aspect. They interpret their own study as showing minimal quantities of the chemicals in the plant atmosphere and note the small number of workers exposed to the substance. Although the data support these claims to some extent, EPA calls attention to the results of the Industry Group's industrial hygiene survey indicating that "worker exposure to fluoroalkenes typically takes the form of brief episodes of relatively high exposure followed by extended periods of little or no exposure." For purposes of risk assessment, EPA assumes that a high dose of a carcinogen received over a short period is equivalent to a corresponding low-dose spread over a lifetime.

Moreover, as the agency argues, certain workers because of their jobs are more apt to be present during periods when gases become "fugitive" and thus may experience substantial concentrations of fluoroalkenes over the long term. As we observed above, not all workers who may inhale gases while performing tasks wear respirators routinely.

....

We are not prepared to say, as petitioners urge, that the number of persons potentially exposed to the fluoroalkenes, or the evidence of incidents which have occurred, is such that the element of risk is insignificant. Ultimately, the question in this case is one of degree, and on that issue there is substantial evidence in the record to justify a finding of unreasonable risk.

In construing the statutory phrase "may present," we agree to some extent with both parties. The necessity for testing depends on lack of knowledge. If no doubt existed, testing would not be required and the "actual" risk concept espoused by petitioners would have little meaning. Likewise, if EPA views "potential" exposure as merely a remote possibility founded on the theoretical factual situations, the statutory directive for "reasonable and prudent" agency action would counsel against expensive testing.

Our reading of the statutory phrase falls between the poles staked out by the parties. We believe that this interpretation of the statute prevents a testing rule based on little more than scientific curiosity, yet allows the agency to act when an existing possibility of harm raises reasonable and legitimate causes for concern. So read, the statute expresses the intention of Congress.

The congressional conference committee report on the Act stated that the purpose of the testing provision is to

> "focus the Administrator's attention on those chemical substances and mixtures about which there is a basis for concern, but about which there is inadequate information to reasonably predict or determine their effects on health or the environment. The Administrator need not show that the substance or mixture does or will present a risk." [Citation.]

Congress obviously had serious concerns about toxic substances and made a policy judgment to place the expense of testing on manufacturers who ultimately can transfer the cost to consumers. Although cautioning that the agency must act reasonably and prudently, and take into consideration the economic impact of any action, of necessity Congress granted EPA fairly broad discretion in exercising its expertise to determine when data must be produced.

....

We conclude that the rule promulgated by EPA falls within the statutory authorization and is supported by substantial evidence. Accordingly, the petition for review will be denied.

NOTES AND QUESTIONS

1. A central mission for the EPA under TSCA is to promulgate test rules to develop data to fill information gaps regarding the potential environmental risks associated with new and existing chemical substances and mixtures. Although the responsibility for conducting EPA mandated tests is placed on industry, the EPA is required to walk a statutory tightrope in its testing orders by seeking relevant data while not imposing undue economic burdens on manufacturers. TSCA § 2(b)(3), 15 U.S.C. § 2601(b)(3).

2. *Risk Assessment.* The crux of EPA's testing authority turns on an assessment of whether the chemical substance "may present an unreasonable risk." Although the court in *Ausimont* acknowledged that the EPA cannot mandate expensive testing based on speculative harms, implicit in a testing order is an agency determination that scientific uncertainty exists about the health risks posed by the chemical. Industry bears a difficult burden in challenging agency testing orders for two related reasons: an underlying premise of TSCA is that inadequate information exists about numerous dangerous chemicals, and the agency can require testing merely by finding that the chemical substance "may present" an unreasonable risk of harm. In *Chemical Mfrs. Ass'n v. EPA*, 859 F.2d 977, 984 (D.C. Cir. 1988) the court rejected an industry claim that test rules must be predicated on an agency finding that the risk was "more probable than not," and upheld the EPA view that the statute is satisfied simply by finding a "substantial probability" of harm. The court explained that although the agency must have more than a "theoretical" basis for ordering testing, Congress intended that the agency be authorized to seek data when the degree of risk gave rise to a "solid basis for concern." 859 F.2d at 986.

For additional commentary on the application of the "unreasonable risk" regulatory standard in the face of informational gaps, see Applegate, *The Perils of Unreasonable Risk: Information, Regulatory Policy, and Toxic Substances Control*, 91 COLUM. L. REV. 261 (1991); and Lyndon, *Information Economics and Chemical Toxicity: Designing Laws to Produce and Use Data*, 87 MICH. L. REV. 1795 (1989).

3. The difficulty of balancing the apparently inconsistent statutory policies led to an agency practice of negotiating directly with manufacturers over test programs, or simply accepting voluntary testing programs. In *NRDC v. EPA*, 595 F. Supp. 1255 (S.D.N.Y. 1984) a citizens' group challenged the EPA practice of accepting voluntary testing agreements by manufacturers. The plaintiffs alleged that TSCA § 4, 15 U.S.C. § 2603(a), required EPA to follow statutory rulemaking procedures by promulgating test rules for potentially dangerous chemicals on which insufficient data existed. The court acknowledged that certain benefits could accrue from the agency working with industry to develop effective and meaningful testing protocols rather than "blind, often impractical, bureaucratic blundering." The court also noted, though, that privately negotiated testing arrangements undercut the statutory provisions for public comment in the regulatory process and often lacked an enforcement mechanism if a breach occurred in the negotiated agreement. The court held, therefore, that the EPA could not allow de facto voluntary testing programs to replace statutory rulemaking duties. Moreover, although the statute was silent with respect to the time deadline for publishing final test rules, the EPA must act within a reasonable time in complying with its statutory responsibilities.

The *NRDC* decision prompted a flurry of activity to facilitate the use of testing consent agreements in conjunction with TSCA § 4, 15 U.S.C. § 2603. *See* 40 C.F.R. § 790 (1989) (makes testing consent agreements enforceable to the same extent as a section 4 test rule).

4. *Substantial Quantities*. An interesting feature of TSCA is that the EPA is authorized to require testing either based on an appraisal of risk (TSCA § 4(a)(1)(A)(i), 15 U.S.C. § 2603(a)(1)(A)(i)) or a quantitative assessment of the volume of the substance that may enter the environment or involve significant human exposure. TSCA § 4(a)(1)(B)(i), 15 U.S.C. § 2603((a)(1)(B)(i). In both instances the EPA must determine that data on the effects of the chemical is inadequate and that testing would develop needed information. Since testing often demands significant expenditures and may impede product introduction into the market, industry often is at odds with the EPA regarding the scientific basis for risk assessment and over what amount of a substance potentially entering the environment constitutes "substantial quantities" necessary to trigger the testing authority.

Illustrative of this conflict is *Chemical Mfrs. Ass'n v. EPA*, 899 F.2d 344 (5th Cir. 1990), where an industry group challenged the EPA's rule requiring manufacturers and processors to perform toxicological testing of cumene, one of the top fifty chemicals produced in the United States. The EPA claimed that substantial quantities — three million pounds — of the chemical entered the environment as "fugitive" or escaped emissions from manufacturing operations and a greater amount entered the atmosphere from vehicle exhaust. The EPA estimated that over 700 workers might potentially experience some level of exposure to the chemical and that approximately 13.5 million people lived in the vicinity of the facilities which produced the substance.

The industry-plaintiffs contended that the EPA data regarding quantity and exposure to cumene was exaggerated and that the agency had failed to articulate administrative criteria for the statutory term "substantial quantities." The court rejected the plaintiffs' view that the statutory meaning of "substantial" was limited to chemicals which presented a high degree of risk. Also, the court agreed with the EPA that infrequent or intermittent emissions could be considered substantial for testing purposes; persistence of the chemical in the environment was not required. The court acknowledged that scientific evidence differed regarding emissions and potential exposure but deferred to the agency's findings as supported by substantial evidence. However, the court remanded for the EPA to explain the basis for its determination that the amounts of cumene entering the environment from industrial sources and resulting human exposure were "substantial."

5. *Information.* One of the dominant themes throughout TSCA is the development and evaluation of data regarding the potential health effects of chemical substances. In addition to the EPA's authority under TSCA to require testing to fill information gaps, the agency possesses broad information-gathering authority pursuant to section 8(d), 15 U.S.C. § 2607(d), to obtain health and safety studies performed in the process of research and development of new products for commercial purposes. In *Dow Chem. Co. v. EPA*, 605 F.2d 673 (3d Cir. 1979) the court held that the EPA, pursuant to section 8(d), could require the submission of studies in the hands of a company which was not the manufacturer, processor, or distributor of the chemical that was the subject of the studies. The court acknowledged that forcing disclosure of such unpublished studies to the EPA could create a disincentive to conducting research on hazardous substances, as companies may choose to direct their research efforts in areas beyond agency scrutiny. The court recognized that although granting the EPA extensive powers to obtain such studies could measurably reduce a company's competitive advantage in technological innovation, the statute contemplates just such a trade-off for procuring important, and otherwise unobtainable, information.

6. *Premanufacture Notification.* TSCA's strategy which places the responsibility on industry to develop data on the environmental effects of chemicals and then uses that data as the springboard for government regulation to prevent unreasonable risks of injury to health or the environment centers around the section 5 premanufacture notice ("PMN") requirement. 15 U.S.C. § 2604. Section 5 requires manufacturers to notify the EPA at least 90 days before manufacturing or importing a new chemical substance or before making a significant new use of an existing chemical substance. A "new chemical substance" is one which is subject to the TSCA's statutory scope yet which is not included in the comprehensive Inventory list compiled by the EPA pursuant to section 8(b). *See* 15 U.S.C. 2602(9), 2607(b).

The effectiveness of the regulatory process, though, depends largely on the usefulness of the data disclosed by the manufacturer. Manufacturers must furnish information regarding the chemical identity, molecular formula and structure of the chemical to be manufactured, known impurities, synonyms or tradenames, description of the byproducts, estimated maximum amounts to be produced or imported for each use, categories of projected use, identity of sites where the chemical will be manufactured, estimates of employee exposure, and projected method of disposal. 40 C.F.R. § 720.45.

The PMN process does not mandate that particular studies be performed or data developed; rather the focus is on disclosure of whatever test data is known or reasonably ascertainable by the submitter or is in the submitter's possession and control. The report must indicate what information appears in open scientific literature and also where the data is incomplete. The types of test data on health and safety which must be submitted include:

(i)   Health effects data.
(ii) Ecological effects data.
(iii) Physical and chemical properties data.
(iv) Environmental fate characteristics.
(v)   Monitoring data and other test data related to human exposure to or environmental release of the chemical substance. 40 C.F.R. 720.50(2).

There are various exemptions from the PMN requirement as well, including: small quantities for research and development, test marketing, low volume usage, certain polymers and mixtures, manufacture solely for export 5(h), 15 U.S.C. § 2604(h); 40 C.F.R. § 720.30 723.50.

7. *Relationship with FIFRA.* TSCA shares certain features with FIFRA in that both statutes seek to regulate chemicals which are intended to serve socially beneficial purposes, in contrast to other federal environmental statutes which address the problems presented by the release of harmful waste products into the environment. The statutes differ, however, in a number of important respects. FIFRA regulates chemical products through a licensing system predicated on a risk-benefit balancing analysis which focuses on the particular commercial use contemplated for the pesticide. FIFRA § 3, 7 U.S.C. § 136a. TSCA does not employ a registration scheme, but relies on data supplied through the premanufacture notice (TSCA § 5(a), 15 U.S.C. § 2604(a)), testing (TSCA § 4, 15 U.S.C. § 2603), and reporting (TSCA § 8, 15 U.S.C. § 2607) processes to allow the EPA to determine whether regulation is necessary. TSCA is considerably broader in the scope of chemical substances and mixtures covered and the wide range of commercial and consumer uses potentially impacted. Like FIFRA, a predominant theme of TSCA is balancing the goal of protecting against unreasonable risks without imposing undue economic burdens on manufacturers.

CORROSION PROOF FITTINGS v. ENVIRONMENTAL PROTECTION AGENCY

947 F.2d 1201 (5th Cir. 1991)

SMITH, CIRCUIT JUDGE.

....

Asbestos is a naturally occurring fibrous material that resists fire and most solvents. Its major uses include heat-resistant insulators, cements, building materials, fireproof gloves and clothing, and motor vehicle brake linings. Asbestos is a toxic material, and occupational exposure to asbestos dust can result in mesothelioma, asbestosis, and lung cancer.

....

An EPA-appointed panel reviewed over one hundred studies of asbestos and conducted several public meetings. Based upon its studies and the public comments, the EPA concluded that asbestos is a potential carcinogen at all levels of exposure, regardless of the type of asbestos or the size of the fiber....

... In 1989, the EPA issued a final rule [under section 6 of TSCA, 15 U.S.C. § 2605] prohibiting the manufacture, importation, processing, and distribution in commerce of most asbestos-containing products. Finding that asbestos constituted an unreasonable risk to health and the environment, the EPA promulgated a staged ban of most commercial uses of asbestos. The EPA estimates that this rule will save either 202 or 148 lives, depending upon whether the benefits are discounted, at a cost of approximately $450-800 million, depending upon the price of substitutes.

The rule is to take effect in three stages, depending upon the EPA's assessment of how toxic each substance is and how soon adequate substitutes will be available. The rule allows affected persons one more year at each stage to sell existing stocks of prohibited products. The rule also imposes labeling requirements on stage 2 or stage 3 products and allows for exemptions from the rule in certain cases.

... [The court found that the EPA's rulemaking procedure was flawed in several respects. The agency's failure to allow cross-examination of some witnesses, although in contravention of TSCA section 19(c), 15 U.S.C. § 2618(c)(1)(B)(ii), did not mandate invalidating the asbestos regulations. The EPA's failure to provide timely notice to the public regarding its analysis and methodology, however, deprived the rule of the substantial evidence necessary to survive judicial scrutiny.]

IV. *The Language of TSCA*

A. *Standard of Review*

Our inquiry into the legitimacy of the EPA rulemaking begins with a discussion of the standard of review governing this case. EPA's phase-out ban of most commercial uses of asbestos is a TSCA § 6(a) rulemaking. TSCA provides that a reviewing court "shall hold unlawful and set aside" a final rule promulgated under § 6(a) "if the court finds that the rule is not supported by substantial evidence in the rulemaking record ... taken as a whole." 15 U.S.C. § 2618(c)(1)(B)(i).

Substantial evidence requires "something less than the weight of the evidence, and the possibility of drawing two inconsistent conclusions from the evidence does not prevent an administrative agency's finding from being supported by substantial evidence." [Citation.] This standard requires (1) that the agency's decision be based upon the entire record,[12] taking into account whatever in the record detracts from the weight of the agency's decision; and (2) that the agency's decision be what "'a reasonable mind might accept as adequate to support [its] conclusion.'" [Citation.] Thus, even if there is enough evidence in the record to support the petitioners' assertions, we will not reverse if there is substantial evidence to support the agency's decision. [Citations.]

Contrary to the EPA's assertions, the arbitrary and capricious standard found in the APA and the substantial evidence standard found in TSCA are different standards, even in the context of an informal rulemaking. Congress specifically went out of its way to provide that "the standard of review prescribed by paragraph (2)(E) of section 706 [of the APA] shall not apply and the court shall hold unlawful and set aside such rule if the court finds that the rule is not supported by substantial evidence in rulemaking record ... taken as a whole." 15 U.S.C. § 2618(c)(1)(B)(i). "The substantial evidence standard mandated by [TSCA] is generally considered to be more rigorous than the arbitrary and capricious standard normally applied to informal rulemaking," *Environmental Defense Fund v. EPA*, 636 F.2d 1267, 1277 (D.C. Cir. 1980), and "afford[s] a considerably more generous judicial review" than the arbitrary and capricious test. The test "imposes a considerable burden on the agency and limits its discretion in arriving at a factual predicate." [Citation.]

"Under the substantial evidence standard, a reviewing court must give careful scrutiny to agency findings and, at the same time, accord appropriate deference to administrative decisions that are based on agency experience and expertise." *Environmental Defense Fund*, 636 F.2d at 1277. As with consumer product legislation, "Congress put the substantial evidence test in the statute because it wanted the courts to scrutinize the Commission's action more closely than an 'arbitrary and capricious' standard would allow." [Citation.]

The recent case of *Chemical Mfrs. Ass'n v. EPA*, 899 F.2d 344 (5th Cir. 1990), provides our basic framework for reviewing the EPA's actions. In evaluating whether the EPA has presented substantial evidence, we examine (1) whether the quantities of the regulated chemical entering into the environment are "substantial" and (2) whether human exposure to the chemical is "substantial" or "significant." *Id.* at 359. An agency may exercise its judgment without strictly relying upon quantifiable risks, costs, and benefits, but it must "cogently explain

---

[12]The term "rulemaking record" means: (A) the rule being reviewed; (B) all commentary received in response to the Administrator's notice of proposed rulemaking, and the Administrator's own published statement of the effects of exposure of the substance on health and the environment, the benefits of the substance for various uses and the availability of substitutes for such uses, and "the reasonably ascertainable economic consequences of the rule" on the national economy, small business, technological innovation, the environment, and public health; (C) transcripts of hearings on promulgation of the rule; (D) written submissions of interested parties; and (E) any other information the Administrator deems relevant. *See* 15 U.S.C. § 2618(a)(3) (referring to §§ 2604(f) and 2605(c)(1) in regard to component (B) above).

why it has exercised its discretion in a given matter" and "must offer a 'rational connection between the facts found and the choice made.'" [Citation.]

We note that in undertaking our review, all agency rules are given a presumption of validity, and it is up to the challenger to any rule to show that the agency action is invalid. [Citation.] The burden remains on the EPA, however, to justify that the products it bans present an unreasonable risk, no matter how regulated. [Citations.] ... [B]ecause TSCA instructs the EPA to undertake the least burdensome regulation sufficient to regulate the substance at issue, the agency bears a heavier burden when it seeks a partial or total ban of a substance than when it merely seeks to regulate that product. *See* 15 U.S.C. § 2605(a).

B. *The EPA's Burden Under TSCA*

TSCA provides, in pertinent part, as follows:

(a) Scope of regulation. — If the Administrator finds that there is a *reasonable basis* to conclude that the manufacture, processing, distribution in commerce, use, or disposal of a chemical substance or mixture, or that any combination of such activities, presents or will present an *unreasonable risk of injury* to health or the environment, the Administrator shall by rule apply one or more of the following requirements to such substance or mixture to the extent necessary *to protect adequately* against such risk using the *least burdensome* requirements. 15 U.S.C. § 2605(a). (Emphasis added.)

As the highlighted language shows, Congress did not enact TSCA as a zero-risk statute.[14] The EPA, rather, was required to consider both alternatives to a ban and the costs of any proposed actions and to "carry out this chapter in a reasonable and prudent manner [after considering] the environmental, economic, and social impact of any action." 15 U.S.C. § 2601(c).

We conclude that the EPA has presented insufficient evidence to justify its asbestos ban. We base this conclusion upon two grounds: the failure of the EPA to consider all necessary evidence and its failure to give adequate weight to statutory language requiring it to promulgate the least burdensome, reasonable regulation required to protect the environment adequately. Because the EPA failed to address these concerns, and because the EPA is required to articulate a "reasoned basis" for its rules, we are compelled to return the regulation to the agency for reconsideration.

1. *Least Burdensome and Reasonable*

TSCA requires that the EPA use the least burdensome regulation to achieve its goals of minimum reasonable risk. This statutory requirement can create

---

[14]Cf. *Southland Mower Co. v. CPSC*, 619 F.2d 499, 510 (5th Cir. 1980) ("It must be remembered that '[t]he statutory term "unreasonable risk" presupposes that a real, and not a speculative, risk be found to exist and that the Commission bear the burden of demonstrating the existence of such a risk before proceeding to regulate.'" (Citation omitted.)).

problems in evaluating just what is a "reasonable risk." Congress's rejection of a no-risk policy, however, also means that in certain cases, the least burdensome yet still adequate solution may entail somewhat more risk than other, known regulations that are far more burdensome on the industry and the economy. The very language of TSCA requires that the EPA, once it has determined what an acceptable level of non-zero risk is, choose the least burdensome method of reaching that level.

In this case, the EPA banned, for all practical purposes, all present and future uses of asbestos — a position the petitioners characterize as the "death penalty alternative," as this is the *most* burdensome of all possible alternatives listed as open to the EPA under TSCA. TSCA not only provides the EPA with a list of alternative actions, but also provides those alternatives in order of how burdensome they are. The regulations thus provide for EPA regulation ranging from labeling the least toxic chemicals to limiting the total amount of chemicals an industry may use. Total bans head the list as the most burdensome regulatory option.

By choosing the harshest remedy given to it under TSCA, the EPA assigned to itself the toughest burden in satisfying TSCA's requirement that its alternative be the least burdensome of all those offered to it. Since both by definition and by the terms of TSCA the complete ban of manufacturing is the most burdensome alternative — for even stringent regulation at least allows a manufacturer the chance to invest and meet the new, higher standard — the EPA's regulation cannot stand if there is any other regulation that would achieve an acceptable level of risk as mandated by TSCA.

. . . .

The EPA considered, and rejected, such options as labeling asbestos products, thereby warning users and workers involved in the manufacture of asbestos-containing products of the chemical's dangers, and stricter workplace rules. EPA also rejected controlled use of asbestos in the workplace and deferral to other government agencies charged with worker and consumer exposure to industrial and product hazards, such as OSHA, the CPSC, and the Mine Safety and Health Administration (MSHA). The EPA determined that deferral to these other agencies was inappropriate because no one other authority could address all the risks posed "throughout the life cycle" by asbestos, and any action by one or more of the other agencies still would leave an unacceptable residual risk.

Much of the EPA's analysis is correct, and the EPA's basic decision to use TSCA as a comprehensive statute designed to fight a multi-industry problem was a proper one that we uphold today on review. What concerns us, however, is the manner in which the EPA conducted some of its analysis. TSCA requires the EPA to consider, along with the effects of toxic substances on human health and the environment, "the benefits of such substances or mixtures for various uses and the availability of substitutes for such uses," as well as "the reasonably ascertainable economic consequences of the rule, after consideration for the effect on the national economy, small business, technological innovation, the environment, and public health." § 2605(c)(1)(C-D).

The EPA presented two comparisons in the record: a world with no further regulation under TSCA, and a world in which no manufacture of asbestos takes place. The EPA rejected calculating how many lives a less burdensome regulation would save, and at what cost. Furthermore the EPA, when calculating the benefits of its ban, explicitly refused to compare it to an improved workplace in which currently available control technology is utilized. *See* 54 Fed. Reg. at 29,474. This decision artificially inflated the purported benefits of the rule by using a baseline comparison substantially lower than what currently available technology could yield.

Under TSCA, the EPA was required to evaluate, rather than ignore, less burdensome regulatory alternatives. TSCA imposes a least-to-most-burdensome hierarchy. In order to impose a regulation at the top of the hierarchy — a total ban of asbestos — the EPA must show not only that its proposed action reduces the risk of the product to an adequate level, but also that the actions Congress identified as less burdensome also would not do the job. The failure of the EPA to do this constitutes a failure to meet its burden of showing that its actions not only reduce the risk but do so in the Congressionally-mandated *least burdensome* fashion.

Thus, it was not enough for the EPA to show, as it did in this case, that banning some asbestos products might reduce the harm that could occur from the use of these products. If that were the standard, it would be no standard at all, for few indeed are the products that are so safe that a complete ban of them would not make the world still safer.

This comparison of two static worlds is insufficient to satisfy the dictates of TSCA. While the EPA may have shown that a world with a complete ban of asbestos might be preferable to one in which there is only the current amount of regulation, the EPA has failed to show that there is not some intermediate state of regulation that would be superior to both the currently-regulated and the completely-banned world. Without showing that asbestos regulation would be ineffective, the EPA cannot discharge its TSCA burden of showing that its regulation is the least burdensome available to it.

Upon an initial showing of product danger, the proper course for the EPA to follow is to consider each regulatory option, in the order mandated by Congress, and the costs and benefits of regulation under each option. The EPA cannot simply skip several rungs, as it did in this case, for in doing so, it may skip a less-burdensome alternative mandated by TSCA. Here, although the EPA mentions the problems posed by intermediate levels of regulation, it takes no steps to calculate the costs and benefits of these intermediate levels. Without doing this it is impossible, both for the EPA and for this court on review, to know that none of these alternatives was less burdensome than the ban in fact chosen by the agency.

....

2. The EPA's Calculations

Furthermore, we are concerned about some of the methodology employed by the EPA in making various of the calculations that it did perform....

First, we note that there was some dispute in the record regarding the appropriateness of discounting the perceived benefits of the EPA's rule. In choosing between the calculated costs and benefits, the EPA presented variations in which it discounted only the costs, and counter-variations in which it discounted both the costs and the benefits, measured in both monetary and human injury terms. As between these two variations, we choose to evaluate the EPA's work using its discounted benefits calculations.

Although various commentators dispute whether it ever is appropriate to discount benefits when they are measured in human lives, we note that it would skew the results to discount only costs without according similar treatment to the benefits side of the equation. Adopting the position of the commentators who advocate not discounting benefits would force the EPA similarly not to calculate costs in present discounted real terms, making comparisons difficult. Furthermore, in evaluating situations in which different options incur costs at varying time intervals, the EPA would not be able to take into account that soon-to-be-incurred costs are more harmful than postponable costs. Because the EPA must discount costs to perform its evaluations properly, the EPA also should discount benefits to preserve an apples-to-apples comparison, even if this entails discounting benefits of a non-monetary nature. [Citation.]

When the EPA does discount costs or benefits, however, it cannot choose an unreasonable time upon which to base its discount calculation. Instead of using the time of injury as the appropriate time to discount, as one might expect, the EPA instead used the time of exposure.

The difficulties inherent in the EPA's approach can be illustrated by an example. Suppose two workers will be exposed to asbestos in 1995, with worker X subjected to a tiny amount of asbestos that will have no adverse health effects, and worker Y exposed to massive amounts of asbestos that quickly will lead to an asbestos-related disease. Under the EPA's approach, which takes into account only the time of exposure rather than the time at which any injury manifests itself, both examples would be treated the same. The EPA's approach implicitly assumes that the day on which the risk of injury occurs is the same day the injury actually occurs. Such an approach might be proper when the exposure and injury are one and the same, such as when a person is exposed to an immediately fatal poison, but is inappropriate for discounting toxins in which exposure often is followed by a substantial lag time before manifestation of injuries.

Of more concern to us is the failure of the EPA to compute the costs and benefits of its proposed rule past the year 2000, and its double-counting of the costs of asbestos use. In performing its calculus, the EPA only included the number of lives saved over the next thirteen years, and counted any additional lives saved as simply "unquantified benefits." 54 Fed. Reg. at 29,486. The EPA and intervenors now seek to use these unquantified lives saved to justify calculations as to which the benefits seem far outweighed by the astronomical costs. For example, the EPA plans to save about three lives with its ban of asbestos pipe, at a cost of $128-227 million (i.e., approximately $43-76 million per life saved). Although the EPA admits that the price tag is high, it claims that the lives saved past the year 2000 justify the price.

Such calculations not only lessen the value of the EPA's cost analysis, but also make any meaningful judicial review impossible. While TSCA contemplates a useful place for unquantified benefits beyond the EPA's calculation, unquantified benefits never were intended as a trump card allowing the EPA to justify any cost calculus, no matter how high.

The concept of unquantified benefits, rather, is intended to allow the EPA to provide a rightful place for any remaining benefits that are impossible to quantify after the EPA's best attempt, but which still are of some concern. But the allowance for unquantified costs is not intended to allow the EPA to perform its calculations over an arbitrarily short period so as to preserve a large unquantified portion.

Unquantified benefits can, at times, permissibly tip the balance in close cases. They cannot, however, be used to effect a wholesale shift on the balance beam. Such a use makes a mockery of the requirements of TSCA that the EPA weigh the costs of its actions before it chooses the least burdensome alternative.

We do not today determine what an appropriate period for the EPA's calculations would be, as this is a matter better left for agency discretion. We do note, however, that the choice of a thirteen-year period is so short as to make the unquantified period so unreasonably large that any EPA reliance upon it must be displaced.

Under the EPA's calculations, a twenty-year-old worker entering employment today still would be at risk from workplace dangers for more than thirty years after the EPA's analysis period had ended. The true benefits of regulating asbestos under such calculations remain unknown. The EPA cannot choose to leave these benefits high and then use the high unknown benefits as a major factor justifying EPA action.

We also note that the EPA appears to place too great a reliance upon the concept of population exposure. While a high population exposure certainly is a factor that the EPA must consider in making its calculations, the agency cannot count such problems more than once. For example, in the case of asbestos brake products, the EPA used factors such as risk and exposure to calculate the probable harm of the brakes, and then used, as an *additional* reason to ban the products, the fact that the exposure levels were high. Considering that calculations of the probable harm level, when reduced to basics, simply are a calculation of population risk multiplied by population exposure, the EPA's redundant use of population exposure to justify its actions cannot stand.

3. *Reasonable Basis*

In addition to showing that its regulation is the least burdensome one necessary to protect the environment adequately, the EPA also must show that it has a reasonable basis for the regulation. 15 U.S.C. § 2605(a). To some extent, our inquiry in this area mirrors that used above, for many of the methodological problems we have noted also indicate that the EPA did not have a reasonable basis....

Most problematical to us is the EPA's ban of products for which no substitutes presently are available. In these cases, the EPA bears a tough burden indeed to show that under TSCA a ban is the least burdensome alternative, as TSCA explicitly instructs the EPA to consider "the benefits of such substance or mixture for various uses and the availability of substitutes for such uses." § 2605(c)(1)(C). These words are particularly appropriate where the EPA actually has decided to ban a product, rather than simply restrict its use, for it is in these cases that the lack of an adequate substitute is most troubling under TSCA.

As the EPA itself states, "when no information is available for a product indicating that cost-effective substitutes exist, the estimated cost of a product ban is very high." 54 Fed. Reg. at 29,468. Because of this, the EPA did not ban certain uses of asbestos, such as its use in rocket engines and battery separators. The EPA, however, in several other instances, ignores its own arguments and attempts to justify its ban by stating that the ban itself will cause the development of low-cost, adequate substitute products.

As a general matter, we agree with the EPA that a product ban can lead to great innovation, and it is true that an agency under TSCA, as under other regulatory statutes, "is empowered to issue safety standards which require improvements in existing technology or which require the development of new technology." [Citation.] As even the EPA acknowledges, however, when no adequate substitutes currently exist, the EPA cannot fail to consider this lack when formulating its own guidelines. Under TSCA, therefore, the EPA must present a stronger case to justify the ban, as opposed to regulation, of products with no substitutes.

We note that the EPA does provide a waiver provision for industries where the hoped-for substitutes fail to materialize in time. *See* 54 Fed. Reg. at 29,464. Under this provision, if no adequate substitutes develop, the EPA temporarily may extend the planned phase-out.

The EPA uses this provision to argue that it can ban any product, regardless of whether it has an adequate substitute, because inventive companies soon will develop good substitutes. The EPA contends that if they do not, the waiver provision will allow the continued use of asbestos in these areas, just as if the ban had not occurred at all.

The EPA errs, however, in asserting that the waiver provision will allow a continuation of the status quo in those cases in which no substitutes materialize.

By its own terms, the exemption shifts the burden onto the waiver proponent to convince the EPA that the waiver is justified. As even the EPA acknowledges, the waiver only "may be granted by [the] EPA in very limited circumstances."

The EPA thus cannot use the waiver provision to lessen its burden when justifying banning products without existing substitutes. While TSCA gives the EPA the power to ban such products, the EPA must bear its heavier burden of justifying its total ban in the face of inadequate substitutes. Thus, the agency cannot use its waiver provision to argue that the ban of products with no substitutes should be treated the same as the ban of those for which adequate substitutes are available now.

We also are concerned with the EPA's evaluation of substitutes even in those instances in which the record shows that they are available. The EPA explicitly rejects considering the harm that may flow from the increased use of products designed to substitute for asbestos, even where the probable substitutes themselves are known carcinogens. The EPA justifies this by stating that it has "more concern about the continued use and exposure to asbestos than it has for the future replacement of asbestos in the products subject to this rule with other fibrous substitutes." *Id.* at 29,481. The agency thus concludes that any "regulatory decisions about asbestos which poses well-recognized, serious risks should not be delayed until the risk of all replacement materials are fully quantified."

This presents two problems. First, TSCA instructs the EPA to consider the relative merits of its ban, as compared to the economic effects of its actions. The EPA cannot make this calculation if it fails to consider the effects that alternate substitutes will pose after a ban.

Second, the EPA cannot say with any assurance that its regulation will increase workplace safety when it refuses to evaluate the harm that will result from the increased use of substitute products. While the EPA may be correct in its conclusion that the alternate materials pose less risk than asbestos, we cannot say with any more assurance than that flowing from an educated guess that this conclusion is true.

Considering that many of the substitutes that the EPA itself concedes will be used in the place of asbestos have known carcinogenic effects, the EPA not only cannot assure this court that it has taken the least burdensome alternative, but cannot even prove that its regulations will increase workplace safety. Eager to douse the dangers of asbestos, the agency inadvertently actually may increase the risk of injury Americans face. The EPA's explicit failure to consider the toxicity of likely substitutes thus deprives its order of a reasonable basis. [Citation.]

Our opinion should not be construed to state that the EPA has an affirmative duty to seek out and test every workplace substitute for any product it seeks to regulate. TSCA does not place such a burden upon the agency. We do not think it unreasonable, however, once interested parties introduce credible studies and evidence showing the toxicity of workplace substitutes, or the decreased effectiveness of safety alternatives such as non-asbestos brakes, that the EPA then consider whether its regulations are even increasing workplace safety, and whether the increased risk occasioned by dangerous substitutes makes the proposed regulation no longer reasonable....

In short, a death is a death, whether occasioned by asbestos or by a toxic substitute product, and the EPA's decision not to evaluate the toxicity of known carcinogenic substitutes is not a reasonable action under TSCA. Once an interested party brings forth credible evidence suggesting the toxicity of the probable or only alternatives to a substance, the EPA must consider the comparative toxic costs of each. Its failure to do so in this case thus deprived its regulation of a reasonable basis, at least in regard to those products as to which petitioners introduced credible evidence of the dangers of the likely substitutes.[22]

4. *Unreasonable Risk of Injury*

The final requirement the EPA must satisfy before engaging in any TSCA rulemaking is that it only take steps designed to prevent "unreasonable" risks. In evaluating what is "unreasonable," the EPA is required to consider the costs of any proposed actions and to "carry out this chapter in a reasonable and prudent manner [after considering] the environmental, economic, and social impact of any action." 15 U.S.C. § 2601(c).

....

That the EPA must balance the costs of its regulations against their benefits further is reinforced by the requirement that it seek the least burdensome regulation. While Congress did not dictate that the EPA engage in an exhaustive, full-scale cost-benefit analysis, it did require the EPA to consider both sides of the regulatory equation, and it rejected the notion that the EPA should pursue the reduction of workplace risk at any cost....

Even taking all of the EPA's figures as true, and evaluating them in the light most favorable to the agency's decision (non-discounted benefits, discounted costs, analogous exposure estimates included), the agency's analysis results in figures as high as $74 million per life saved. For example, the EPA states that its ban of asbestos pipe will save three lives over the next thirteen years, at a cost of $128-227 million ($43-76 million per life saved), depending upon the price of substitutes; that its ban of asbestos shingles will cost $23-34 million to save 0.32 statistical lives ($72-106 million per life saved); that its ban of asbestos coatings will cost $46-181 million to save 3.33 lives ($14-54 million per life saved); and

---

[22]We note that at least part of the EPA's arguments rest on the assumption that regulation will not work because the federal government will not adequately enforce any workplace standards that the EPA might promulgate. This is an improper assumption. The EPA should assume reasonable efforts by the government to implement its own regulations. A governmental agency cannot point to how poorly the government will implement regulations as a reason to reject regulation. Rather, the solution to poor enforcement of regulations is better enforcement, not more burdensome alternative solutions under TSCA.

that its ban of asbestos paper products will save 0.60 lives at a cost of $4-5 million ($7-8 million per life saved). *See* 54 Fed. Reg. at 29,484-85....

While we do not sit as a regulatory agency that must make the difficult decision as to what an appropriate expenditure is to prevent someone from incurring the risk of an asbestos-related death, we do note that the EPA, in its zeal to ban any and all asbestos products, basically ignored the cost side of the TSCA equation. The EPA would have this court believe that Congress, when it enacted its requirement that the EPA consider the economic impacts of its regulations, thought that spending $200-300 million to save approximately seven lives (approximately $30-40 million per life) over thirteen years is reasonable.
....

VI. *Conclusion*

In summary, of most concern to us is that the EPA has failed to implement the dictates of TSCA and the prior decisions of this and other courts that, before it impose a ban on a product, it first evaluate and then reject the less burdensome alternatives laid out for it by Congress. While the EPA spent much time and care crafting its asbestos regulation, its explicit failure to consider the alternatives required of it by Congress deprived its final rule of the reasonable basis it needed to survive judicial scrutiny.

Furthermore, the EPA's adoption of the analogous exposure estimates during the final weeks of its rulemaking process, after public comment was concluded, rather than during the ten years during which it was considering the asbestos ban, was unreasonable and deprived the petitioners of the notice that they required in order to present their own evidence on the validity of the estimates and its data bases. By depriving the petitioners of their right to cross-examine EPA witnesses on methodology and data used to support as much as eighty percent of the proposed benefits in some areas, the EPA also violated the dictates of TSCA.

Finally, the EPA failed to provide a reasonable basis for the purported benefits of its proposed rule by refusing to evaluate the toxicity of likely substitute products that will be used to replace asbestos goods. While the EPA does not have the duty under TSCA of affirmatively seeking out and testing all possible substitutes, when an interested party comes forward with credible evidence that the planned substitutes present a significant, or even greater, toxic risk than the substance in question, the agency must make a formal finding on the record that its proposed action still is both reasonable and warranted under TSCA.

... [The court grants the petition for review, vacates the EPA's proposed regulation, and remands to the agency.]

NOTES AND QUESTIONS

1. *"Least Burdensome" Regulation.* One of the principal difficulties in utilizing TSCA as an effective environmental protection statute is the directive to the EPA to regulate in the "least burdensome" manner. Section 6(a), 15

U.S.C. § 2605(a). Once the EPA determines that an unreasonable risk is presented, the agency still must tailor its regulatory approach to correspond to the hierarchy of alternatives set forth in section 6(a).

Why would Congress choose to outline the sliding scale of regulatory alternatives with such specificity? Does the statute reflect a fundamental lack of faith in the EPA's discretion? Does the court unduly focus on the cost side of the balancing test and slight the countervailing consideration of protecting adequately against the risks presented by asbestos? What did the agency do wrong, according to the court? Was its error procedural, substantive, or both? Do you agree with the EPA's view or the court's assessment on the issue of consideration of the availability of substitute products? Which perspective is more likely to give industry an incentive to develop substitute products to replace substances prohibited or restricted in commerce by the agency? The Fifth Circuit Court of Appeals panel issued a clarification of its decision and stated that the EPA could continue to apply its phase I ban on the manufacture, importation, and processing of asbestos products that were no longer being produced in the United States as of July 12, 1989 — the date the EPA issued its final asbestos rules.

2. *Judicial Review.* Judicial review of EPA rulemaking under TSCA is governed by section 19, which provides that agency action will be set aside where not supported by "substantial evidence in the rulemaking record ... taken as a whole." 15 U.S.C. § 2618(c)(1)(B)(i). Unlike the typical deferential record review of administrative decision under the Administrative Procedure Act (5 U.S.C. § 706(2)(E)), Congress contemplated a rigorous standard of review under TSCA involving careful scrutiny of the agency findings contained in the record. *Shell Chem. Co. v. EPA*, 826 F.2d 295, 297 (5th Cir. 1987). Did the court in *Corrosion Proof Fittings* overstep its role in its exacting review of the agency's prohibition of asbestos products?

3. The statutory review system in TSCA is complex. The Act distinguishes, for example, between section 19, 15 U.S.C. § 2618, which provides for direct review of established rules, and section 21(a), 15 U.S.C. § 2620(a), which authorizes citizens to petition the EPA to initiate proceedings for issuance, amendment or repeal of a rule or order under certain provisions of the Act. If the petition under section 21 is denied or the agency fails to act within a designated period, the petitioner may obtain de novo review in federal district court seeking compliance with the request. 15 U.S.C. § 2620(b)(4)(B). The statute reserves de novo review to petitions for issuance of a new rule, however, on the rationale that the agency would not have already addressed the subject matter and compiled a record. *See Environmental Defense Fund v. Reilly*, 909 F.2d 1497 (D.C. Cir. 1990). Even if the petitioner is able to show that insufficient data existed and that the chemical presented an unreasonable risk, the court will not require rulemaking unless persuaded that the rule requested would actually develop the needed data. *Citizens for a Better Env't v. Reilly*, 1991 W.L. 95040 (N.D. Ill.). *Also see Citizens for a Better Env't v. Thomas*, 704 F. Supp. 149 (N.D. Ill.

1989) (TSCA § 21 de novo review of agency refusal to initiate rulemaking proceeding does not contravene separation of powers doctrine).

4. *Regulation of Asbestos.* One of the interesting features of TSCA is a special Title II, added by a 1986 amendment, which specifically addresses the health hazards associated with exposure to asbestos-containing building materials in public and commercial buildings and in schools. TSCA §§ 201-215, 15 U.S.C. §§ 2641-2655. Title II establishes four principal requirements for EPA regulation to combat the asbestos problem: inspection of school buildings (§ 203(b), 15 U.S.C. § 2643(b)); development of asbestos management plans by local educational agencies (§ 203(i), 15 U.S.C. § 2643(i)); determination and implementation of appropriate response actions (§ 203(d), 15 U.S.C. § 2643 (d)); and the training and accreditation of asbestos contractors and laboratories (§ 206, 15 U.S.C. § 2646). Enforcement of Title II's provisions may be carried out through a combination of administrative civil penalties and citizen's suits. Although TSCA does not provide a private right of action for recovery of damages, it does authorize citizens' petitions to the EPA to initiate proceedings for issuance of a rule and suits to compel the administrator to meet deadlines. TSCA §§ 207(d)-(f), 15 U.S.C. §§ 2647(d)-(f). Section 208, 15 U.S.C. § 2648, empowers the EPA to take emergency measures, including seeking injunctive relief, whenever airborne asbestos fibers or friable asbestos in a school building presents an "imminent and substantial endangerment." Also, a special free-standing, revolving Asbestos Trust Fund was created to carry out the goals of asbestos abatement.

Title II provides that the EPA must issue regulations describing appropriate response actions by using the "least burdensome methods which protect human health and the environment." TSCA § 203(i), 15 U.S.C. § 2643(i). The EPA's task in issuing such regulations is complicated, however, because the statute further provides that the administrator must take into account "local circumstances," yet studies estimate that over 30,000 schools in the United States have asbestos problems. In *Safe Buildings Alliance v. EPA*, 846 F.2d 79 (D.C. Cir. 1988) the court recognized the difficult task faced by the EPA in carrying out its regulatory mandate under Title II, particularly in light of scientific uncertainties regarding what constitutes a dangerous level of exposure to asbestos and the varied circumstances of the numerous schools which contain the hazardous material. The court, influenced by such complicating factors, upheld EPA's guidelines as minimum standards against a challenge brought by former manufacturers of asbestos-containing materials. *See generally* Note, *Asbestos in Schools: The Asbestos Hazard Emergency Response Act and School Litigation*, 42 VAND. L. REV. 1685 (1989).

5. *Enforcement.* TSCA contains a wide range of civil remedies for enforcement of the act as well as criminal penalties. TSCA § 16, 15 U.S.C. § 2615. *See Yaffe Iron & Metal Co. v. EPA*, 774 F.2d 1008 (10th Cir. 1985) (assessment of $10,000 administrative civil penalty for company's violation of storage requirements for PCBs upheld); *United States v. Ward*, 676 F.2d 94 (4th Cir.

1982) (federal conviction for unlawful disposal of toxic substances after acquittal of state charges of malicious damage to realty did not violate Double Jeopardy Clause because offenses involved different elements).

TSCA provides for a hearing and judicial review of civil penalties imposed by the EPA. However, if the penalty goes unpaid and the order becomes final, the validity, amount, and appropriateness of a final administrative civil penalty is not reviewable. TSCA § 16(a)(4), 15 U.S.C. § 2615(a)(4). *Also see United States v. Carolina Transformer Co.*, 739 F. Supp. 1030, 1039 (E.D.N.C. 1989), *aff'd*, 978 F.2d 832 (4th Cir. 1992).

Section 16 of TSCA, 15 U.S.C. § 2615(a)(2)(B), requires the agency to consider mitigating factors in determining the amount of the penalty. In *Rollins Envtl. Servs. v. EPA*, 937 F.2d 649 (D.C. Cir. 1991), for example, the court set aside an administrative penalty because the regulation violated contained ambiguous language and the agency acknowledged that its personnel had given conflicting advice to private parties regarding compliance. Accordingly, the uncertainty in meaning constituted a mitigating factor which should have been considered in determining the civil penalty.

Similarly, in *General Elec. Co. v. EPA*, 53 F.3d 1324 (D.C. Cir. 1995), the court vacated a finding of liability and set aside a fine where it found that the EPA's regulations failed to provide fair notice of the agency's interpretations of permissible methods of disposal of PCBs.

In *3M Co. v. Browner*, 17 F.3d 1453 (D.C. Cir. 1994) the court held that the EPA was barred by 28 U.S.C. § 2462 from assessing civil penalties for a company's noncompliance with TSCA's Premanufacture Notice requirements where the agency proceeding was not commenced within five years of the accrual of the violation. The court rejected the EPA's argument that the statute of limitations should commence upon "discovery of violation." Rather, the court observed that "An agency's failure to detect violations ... does not avoid the problems of faded memories, lost witnesses and discarded documents in penalty actions brought decades after alleged violations are finally discovered."

6. Emergency Enforcement Actions. TSCA also provides for emergency enforcement measures where the chemical substance presents an imminent hazard to health or the environment. TSCA § 7, 15 U.S.C. § 2606. In *United States v. Commonwealth Edison Co.*, 620 F. Supp. 1404 (N.D. Ill. 1985) the government sought an emergency cleanup order of several residential sites contaminated by PCBs which were spilled from the utility's malfunctioning electrical equipment. The utility argued that since no precise cleanup standards existed, it would be unreasonable for the agency to force it to clean up every "molecule" of PCBs spilled through a section 7 order. The court found that the presence of the PCBs posed an unusually great health risk which justified an emergency cleanup order. However, the government first had the burden to show how the utility's cleanup efforts had failed to satisfy the agency's disposal standards. The court also explained that existing regulations did not preclude section 7 relief but rather permitted the agency to close regulatory loopholes by taking prompt action against unreasonable health and environmental risks. Emergency orders under TSCA, then, serve two purposes: to complement the ordinary enforcement remedies in the act, and to provide an intermediate solution to abate threats presented by chemical substances until the agency can promulgate appropriate regulations under section 6 (15 U.S.C. § 2605).

7. *Attorney Fees.* An additional incentive to promote the enforcement of TSCA is the Act's provision for awards of attorney fees and costs in "appropriate cases." TSCA § 19(d), 15 U.S.C. § 2618(d). In *Environmental Defense Fund v. EPA*, 672 F.2d 42 (D.C. Cir. 1982), following its partially successful challenge to the EPA's regulation of PCBs, the EDF sought an award of its attorney's fees. The court held that the statutory authorization for attorney's fees allowed awards not only to prevailing parties but permitted fee awards even with respect to issues unsuccessfully litigated because of the public interest served in more fully considering the issues at stake.

ENVIRONMENTAL DEFENSE FUND v. ENVIRONMENTAL PROTECTION AGENCY

636 F.2d 1267 (D.C. Cir. 1980)

EDWARDS, CIRCUIT JUDGE.

In this case the Environmental Defense Fund (EDF) petitions for review of regulations, issued by the U.S. Environmental Protection Agency (EPA) that implement section 6(e) [15 U.S.C. § 2605(e)] of the Toxic Substances Control Act (TSCA). That section of the Act provides broad rules governing the disposal, marking, manufacture, processing, distribution, and use of a class of chemicals called polychlorinated biphenyls (PCBs).

....

Polychlorinated biphenyls (PCBs) have been manufactured and used commercially for fifty years for their chemical stability, fire resistance, and electrical resistance properties. They are frequently used in electrical transformers and capacitors. However, PCBs are extremely toxic to humans and wildlife....

Epidemiological data and experiments on laboratory animals indicate that exposure to PCBs pose carcinogenic and other risks to humans. Experimental animals developed tumors after eating diets that included concentrations of PCBs as low as 100 parts per million (ppm). Experiments on monkeys indicate that diets with PCB concentrations of less than ten ppm reduce fertility and cause stillbirths and birth defects. Other data show that PCBs may adversely affect enzyme production, thereby interfering with the treatment of diseases in humans.

EPA has found that PCBs will adversely affect wildlife as well as humans. Concentrations below one ppb (part per billion) are believed to impair reproductivity of aquatic invertebrates and fish. Some birds suffered "severe reproductive failure" when fed diets containing concentrations of only ten ppm of PCBs. Because PCBs collect in waterways and bioaccumulate in fish, fish-eating mammals run a special risk of adverse effects. Such mammals may have "significantly higher concentrations of PCBs in their tissues than the aquatic forms they feed on."

EPA estimates that by 1975, up to 400 million pounds of PCBs had entered the environment. Approximately twenty-five to thirty percent of this amount is considered "free," meaning that it is a direct source of contamination for wildlife and humans. The rest, "mostly in the form of industrial waste and discarded end use products, is believed to be in landfill sites and thus constitutes a potential source of new free PCBs." Other significant sources of PCBs include atmospheric fallout and spills associated with the use or transportation of PCBs.

....

Responding to the dangers associated with the use of PCBs and other toxic chemicals, Congress in 1976 enacted the Toxic Substances Control Act (TSCA), Pub. L. No. 94-469, 90 Stat. 2003 (1976). Although the Act is generally designed to cover the regulation of all chemical substances, section 6(e) refers solely to the disposal, manufacture, processing, distribution, and use of PCBs. No other section of the Act addresses the regulation of a single class of chemicals.

....

As enacted, section 6(e) of the Act sets forth a detailed scheme to dispose of PCBs, to phase out the manufacture, processing, and distribution of PCBs, and to limit the use of PCBs. Specifically, section 6(e) provides that, within six months of the effective date of the Act (January 1, 1977), EPA must prescribe methods to dispose of PCBs and to require that PCB containers be marked with appropriate warnings. 15 U.S.C. § 2605(e)(1). One year after the effective date of the Act, PCBs can be manufactured, processed, distributed, and used only in a "totally enclosed manner." § 2605(e)(2)(A). One year later, all manufacture of PCBs is prohibited. § 2605(e)(3)(A)(i). Six months after that (i.e., two and one-half years after the effective date of the Act), all processing and distribution of PCBs in commerce is prohibited. § 2605(e)(3)(A)(ii). Thus, today, except for the specified authorizations and exemptions described below, the Act permits PCBs to be used only in a totally enclosed manner, and it completely prohibits the manufacture, processing, and distribution of PCBs.

The statute sets forth only limited exceptions to these broad prohibitions. Subsection 6(e)(B) [15 U.S.C. § 2605(e)(3)(B)] allows the Administrator of EPA to authorize by rule the continued use of PCBs in a non-totally enclosed manner if he finds that the proposed activity "will not present an unreasonable risk of injury to health or the environment." § 2605(e)(2)(B). Under subsection 6(e)(3)(B) [15 U.S.C. § 2605(e)(3)(B)], the Administrator may grant a case-by-case exemption to the prohibitions on manufacture, processing, and distribution of PCBs in subsection 6(e)(3). An exemption, which may be granted for one year subject to conditions set by the Administrator, § 2605(e)(3)(B), must be based on the Administrator's findings that "an unreasonable risk of injury to health or environment would not result, *and* ... good faith efforts have been made to develop a chemical [substitute] which does not present an unreasonable risk of injury to health or the environment." (Emphasis added).

 ....

Criteria for the "Unreasonable Risk" Determination

The Act permits the Administrator to authorize "by rule" non-totally enclosed uses of PCBs if he finds that such uses "will not present an unreasonable risk of injury to health or the environment." 15 U.S.C. § 2605(e)(2)(B). Using the criteria set forth in subsection 6(c)(1),[18] the Administrator found that eleven non-totally enclosed uses did not present an unreasonable risk. On the basis of these findings, EPA authorized the continued use of the eleven non-totally enclosed uses here in dispute.

In attacking these use authorizations, EDF claims that the Administrator employed the wrong criteria in making his determinations concerning "unreasonable risk." In particular, EDF argues that Congress intended to preclude the Administrator from using the subsection 6(c)(1) criteria in promulgating the PCB use authorization rules.

The basis for EDF's argument is found in subsection 6(e)(4) [15 U.S.C. § 2605(e)(4)], which requires the Administrator to promulgate rules in accordance with the procedural provisions in subsections 6(c)(2), (3), and (4); no reference to subsection 6(c)(1) is found in subsection 6(e)(4). EDF claims that this omission evidences a congressional intent to preclude EPA from using the 6(c)(1) criteria in making "unreasonable risk" determinations pursuant to

---

[18]Subsection 6(c)(1) [15 U.S.C. § 2605(c)(1)], which governs the promulgation of rules under § 6(a) for most chemical substances, provides in part that:

> (1) In promulgating any rule under subsection (a) of this section with respect to a chemical substance or mixture, the Administrator shall consider and publish a statement with respect to (A) the effects of such substance or mixture on health and the magnitude of the exposure of human beings to such substance or mixture; (B) the effects of such substance or mixture on the environment and the magnitude of the exposure of the environment to such substance or mixture; (C) the benefits of such substance or mixture for various uses and the availability of substitutes for such uses; and (D) the reasonably ascertainable economic consequences of the rule, after consideration of the effect on the national economy, small business, technological innovation, the environment, and public health.

15 U.S.C. § 2605(c)(1). Subsections 6(c)(2), (3), and (4) list the procedural requirements for promulgating a rule.

Section 6(a) of the Act, which governs the regulations of non-PCB substances, permits the Administrator to issue seven types of regulations whenever he finds

> that there is a reasonable basis to conclude that the manufacture, processing, distribution in commerce, use, or disposal of a chemical substance or mixture, or that any combination of such activities, presents or will present *an unreasonable risk of injury to health or the environment.*

15 U.S.C. § 2605(a) (emphasis added). Once he has made this finding, the Administrator is to choose the "least burdensome" regulation that will "protect adequately against such risk." *Id.*

subsection 6(e)(2)(B). Because the Administrator used those criteria, EDF argues that the unreasonable risk determinations were "fatally flawed ... [placing] disproportionate weight ... on the adverse economic impact of a ban, [and seriously undermining] the Congressional objective of bringing about the development and use of substitutes in existing PCB activities...."

Without more, however, we find that the omission of a reference to subsection 6(c)(1) in 6(e)(4) does not imply that Congress meant to prevent EPA from considering the challenged criteria in making unreasonable risk determinations under 6(e)(2)(B). There is nothing in the wording of the statute or the legislative history that affirmatively supports the position of EDF.

....

Moreover, because the expression "unreasonable risk of injury to health or the environment" is left undefined in section 6(e), the Administrator was required to give some meaning to it. Since the 6(c)(1) criteria obviously pertain to factors of "unreasonable risk," it was entirely appropriate for EPA to consider such criteria in ascribing a meaning to the use authorization provision in 6(e)(2)(B). EDF has shown nothing to indicate otherwise. In fact, EDF does not really contest use of the first three criteria in 6(c)(1) — i.e., the effects on health and on the environment, and the availability of substitutes. Rather, EDF's primary focus is on the fourth criterion in 6(c)(1), relating to the economic consequences of the authorization. Yet EDF's objections to the "economic consequences" criterion cannot stand in the face of section 2(c) [15 U.S.C. § 2601(c)] of the Act, which expressly requires the Administrator to consider such factors.

Furthermore, the particular economic factors that EPA took into account were plainly reasonable. The Administrator did not simply propose to consider the effect of the ban on industry, but also the effects on "the national economy, small business, technological innovation, the environment, and public health." This formulation, which considers a broad range of benefits and costs of the ban and use authorization, is entirely consistent with the section 2(c) requirement that the Administrator consider the economic and social impact on his actions.

Because the 6(c)(1) criteria fulfill an express mandate of the statute and reflect a reasonable interpretation of an ambiguous phrase, we conclude that the Administrator did not err in choosing those criteria to make the unreasonable risk determinations under 6(e)(2)(B).

[The court found that the EPA's classification system and authorization for railroad transformers were supported by substantial evidence.]...

The Fifty Ppm Regulatory Cutoff

As a part of the regulatory scheme for PCBs under section 6(e), EPA limited application of the Disposal and Ban Regulations to materials containing concentrations of at least fifty ppm of PCBs. With one exception, materials with lower concentrations remain unregulated under the TSCA regulations. EDF contends that this limitation contravenes the statutory command in subsections 6(e)(2)(A) and 6(e)(3)(A) to regulate "any polychlorinated biphenyl." While we do not adopt all of EDF's reasoning, we find that, under the applicable standard of judicial review, there is no substantial evidence in the record to support the Administrator's decision to establish a regulatory cutoff at fifty ppm.

....

In the Proposed Ban Regulations, EPA listed four reasons for setting the regulatory cutoff at fifty ppm. First, EPA believed that a fifty ppm limit would "exclude from the rule municipal sludges and other mixtures containing low (less than 50 ppm) levels of PCB's whose presence is due to ambient levels of PCB present in the air or water." As EPA develops in its brief, Congress did not design section 6(e) to regulate ambient sources of PCBs. Second, EPA believed that some industrial chemical processes inevitably produce traces of PCBs, and that careful controls could reduce the concentrations of PCBs only to fifty ppm. Third, EPA felt that it was impractical to regulate the "diffuse and extremely numerous PCB sources" with concentrations below fifty ppm. EPA believed that the proposed cutoff would ensure maximum effectiveness of the regulation by focusing "Agency attention under TSCA upon the most significant and controllable sources of PCB exposure." Fourth, the agency believed that other statutes were available to regulate low concentrations of PCBs, particularly municipal sludges and dredge soils.

In the Final Ban Regulations, EPA adopted the proposed fifty ppm regulatory cutoff. Although industry favored a cutoff of 500 ppm in order to reduce the costs of complying with the regulations, EPA found that industry could comply with more stringent standard. Furthermore, lowering the cutoff from 500 to fifty ppm would "result in substantially increased health and environmental protection."

A cutoff below fifty ppm, on the other hand, would "provide an additional degree of environmental protection but would have a grossly disproportionate effect on the economic impact and would have a serious technological impact on the organic chemicals industry." While it did not have firm data, EPA believed that for some chemical processes, it was technically impossible to eliminate the inadvertent production of PCBs. EPA also feared that because of limited disposal facilities, a lower cutoff would increase disposal requirements and interfere with the disposal of high concentration wastes. In short, EPA believed that the fifty ppm cutoff "provides adequate protection for human health and the environment while defining a program that EPA can effectively implement."

Both EPA and EDF claim that the statutory language and legislative history support their positions on the regulatory cutoff. The statutory language is simple: "no person may ... use any polychlorinated biphenyl in any manner other than in a totally enclosed manner." 15 U.S.C. § 2605(e)(2)(A). Similarly, the prohibitions on manufacture, processing, and distribution refer to "any polychlorinated biphenyl." Taken literally, this language might require EPA to regulate every molecule of PCB. We are reluctant, however, to impose such an extreme interpretation absent support in the legislative history.

... [T]he Administrator chose a regulatory cutoff at a level that he felt would exclude the ambient sources from regulation. We are troubled by this regulation, however, since the purpose of section 6(e) is to prevent the "introduction of additional PCB's into the environment." The selection of a cutoff undermines the congressional intent to regulate non-ambient sources of PCBs if non-ambient sources of contamination remain unregulated. It is equally troubling that the Administrator apparently is not aware of the amount of PCBs excluded from regulation by the fifty ppm or other possible cutoffs. Particularly because the Administrator has found that any exposure to PCBs may have adverse effects, the Administrator's flat exclusion of some industrial sources of contamination must undergo careful scrutiny. While some cutoff may be appropriate, we note that the Administrator did not explain why the regulation could not be designed expressly to exclude ambient sources, thus directly fulfilling congressional intent, rather than achieve that goal indirectly with a cutoff, thereby partly contravening congressional intent. Thus, a desire to exclude ambient sources of contamination, without more, cannot support the regulatory cutoff.

EPA also seeks to justify the regulatory cutoff on the basis of the serious impact a lower cutoff would have on industries that inadvertently produce PCBs during the manufacturing process. As EPA readily concedes, however, the inadvertent commercial production of PCBs is to be regulated under the Act. By providing a blanket exemption for concentrations below fifty ppm, the Administrator has circumvented the authorizations and exemptions requirements provided in the statute. EPA made no finding that the cutoff would involve no unreasonable risk to health or the environment....

Considerations such as the availability of enforcement resources are relevant to the administrative necessity exemption. It appears, however, that EPA is not even aware of the amount of PCBs left unregulated by the cutoff. Having made no showing that it cannot carry out the statutory commands for concentrations of PCBs below fifty ppm, EPA fails to meet its heavy burden. Thus, administrative need, on this record, provides no basis for the fifty ppm cutoff.

... EPA's *ad hoc* consideration of economic impact and disposal requirements, leading to a conclusion that the fifty ppm cutoff "provides adequate protection for human health and the environment," is neither as rigorous nor as strict as the statutorily required unreasonable risk determination based on subsection 6(c)(1) [15 U.S.C. § 2605(c)(1)] criteria. Thus, we remand this part of the record to EPA for further proceedings.

Totally Enclosed Uses

EDF also petitions for review of the Administrator's decision to list several uses, including non-railroad transformers, capacitors, and electromagnets, as totally enclosed uses and therefore exempt from the regulations promulgated under section 6(e)....

There can be no serious doubt that Congress intended to permit the continued use of PCBs in a "totally enclosed manner." The statute defines that expression to mean "any manner which will ensure that any exposure of human beings or the environment to a polychlorinated biphenyl will be insignificant as determined by the Administrator by rule." 15 U.S.C. § 2605(e)(2)(C).

In both the proposed and final Ban Regulations, EPA defines "'insignificant exposure' as no exposure." Because "any release of PCBs into the environment will eventually result in widespread exposure of wildlife, including some of man's major food sources, and humans and that any such exposure may have adverse effects," EPA concluded that there was "no rational basis for selecting any particular exposure level above zero for the purposes of this regulation."

Despite these strict standards, EPA contends that its classifications fulfill the statutory and regulatory mandates. Its designation of totally enclosed uses does not include all transformers, capacitors, and electromagnets, but only the "intact, non-leaking" variety. By definition, if a transformer is leaking, it is not totally enclosed and therefore is not exempt from the Act or the regulations.

This scheme, however, begs the question. Under the current regulations, EPA has no idea which PCB uses are "intact, non-leaking." The current regulatory structure provides no procedures for inspection or even self-reporting of leaks or other forms of contamination. Absent such procedures, EPA's regulations are a blanket exception for transformers, capacitors, and electromagnets, which use the vast majority of all PCBs in commercial use. Without a better justification, the regulation cannot stand.

... Congress left to the Administrator the task of deciding which uses were to be deemed totally enclosed. The statute delegates to the Administrator the duty of ensuring that human environmental exposure is "insignificant," a word that he must define. Second, given Congress' enactment of a special section for regulating PCBs, we cannot believe that Congress meant to leave unregulated leaking transformers, capacitors, and electromagnets. Congress could not have intended to designate, whether explicitly or implicitly, *all* transformers, capacitors, and electromagnets as totally enclosed. Third, references in the congressional debates to "closed uses," do not necessarily refer to "totally enclosed" uses. Put simply, closed systems develop leaks.

....

In light of the record in this case, we find that there is no substantial evidence that the regulations concerning totally enclosed uses "will *ensure* that any exposure of human beings or the environment to a polychlorinated biphenyl will be insignificant." 15 U.S.C. § 2605(e)(2)(C) (emphasis added). This lack of substantial evidence calls into question EPA's implicit finding that it can designate entire classes of uses, rather than individual containers, as totally enclosed. Of course, we are not directing EPA to apply the "totally enclosed" proviso on a more individualized basis. On the present record, however, EPA's findings as to which PCB uses may be classified as totally enclosed cannot stand....

Conclusion

On the basis of the foregoing, we find that there is substantial evidence in the record to support the use authorizations; therefore, we uphold those regulations. However, because we find no substantial evidence in the record to support either the fifty ppm cutoff or the EPA classification of certain PCB uses as totally enclosed, these latter two regulations cannot be upheld. Consequently, we set aside the regulations dealing with the fifty ppm cutoff and classification of certain PCB uses as totally enclosed, and remand those portions of the record for further proceedings consistent with this opinion.

We feel constrained to add one final note to emphasize our concern in this case. Human beings have finally come to recognize that they must eliminate or control life threatening chemicals, such as PCBs, if the miracle of life is to continue and if earth is to remain a living planet. This is precisely what Congress sought to do when it enacted section 6(e) of the Toxic Substances Control Act. Yet, we find that forty-six months after the effective date of an act designed to either totally ban or closely control the use of PCBs, 99% of the PCBs that were in use when the Act was passed are still in use in the United States. With information such as this in hand, timid souls have good reason to question the prospects for our continued survival, and cynics have just cause to sneer at the effectiveness of governmental regulation.

The EPA regulations can hardly be viewed as a bold step forward in the battle against life threatening chemicals. There is no substantial evidence in the record to support certain of the EPA regulatory enactments, and portions of the regulations are plainly contrary to law. Thus, the effort by EPA has, in certain respects, fallen far short of the mark set by the congressional mandate found in section 6(e) of the Toxic Substances Control Act.

On remand, we trust that EPA will act with some sense of urgency to find effective solutions to enforce the Act. We are not so naive as to assume or suggest that hasty responses will ensure effective regulations. However, we are well able to see, from the plain text of the Act, that the deadlines for the enactment of regulations to enforce section 6(e) have passed. We therefore believe that EPA should act with expedition to complete the important task assigned to it by Congress.

So ordered.

NOTES AND QUESTIONS

1. The regulation of PCBs under TSCA charges the EPA with the difficult task of reconciling a host of complex variables, often with incomplete information. The agency's principal charge under section 6(e), 15 U.S.C. § 2605(e), is protecting against potential health hazards, but *EDF v. EPA* adds that the agency also must evaluate the availability of other enforcement resources, the potential economic impact on industries which utilize PCBs in socially useful products, and scientific information gaps such as the toxicity of the chemical at low levels of exposure and transferability through complex food chains.

2. If Congress wanted to ban immediately the manufacture, processing and use of PCBs, why did it include the "totally enclosed" exemption? Is a "leak-proof" enclosure technologically feasible? Do such exemptions undermine the purpose of section 6(e), particularly in view of the court's observation in *EDF* concerning the large percentage of PCBs that remain in the ambient environment? The case highlights the significance of controlling the environmental risks created by PCBs, and yet underscores the difficulty of totally eliminating such substances from the environment in light of their recognized social utility. How should the EPA and the courts strike this balance?

3. Following the principal decision where the court found that the EPA's decision to limit the PCB regulations to materials with concentrations of 50 parts per million ("ppm") or higher, the EPA decided to limit the application of the 50 ppm cutoff to certain storage and disposal procedures. 40 C.F.R. § 761.1(b). PCB handlers also must comply with various record keeping and reporting requirements. 40 C.F.R. §§ 761.180-761.193. The EPA has established specific cleanup procedures for spills releasing PCBs in excess of the 50 ppm limit. 40 C.F.R. §§ 761.120-761.135.

4. In *Lockett v. United States*, 938 F.2d 630 (6th Cir. 1991) residents living near a scrap yard site contaminated with PCBs brought a Federal Tort Claims Act action against the United States, alleging negligence by the EPA in failing to warn them of dangers associated with potential exposure to the site and failing to exercise reasonable care to prevent or decrease risks from continued exposure to the PCBs. The claimants relied upon Congressional intent that the EPA was charged with carrying out TSCA's requirements in a "reasonable and prudent manner" and to "consider the environmental, economic, and social impact" of its actions. 15 U.S.C. § 2601(c). The court found that TSCA's regulatory scheme granted the EPA discretion to formulate a response to evidence of PCB contamination at a particular spill site. Thus, the "discretionary function" exception to the FTCA barred the plaintiff's suit against the government.

5. TSCA provides for the coordination of actions between the EPA and other federal agencies with respect to the health risks presented by chemical substances. TSCA § 9, 15 U.S.C. § 2608. The EPA is charged with various responsibilities under section 9 including consulting with other agencies, recommending action under other laws, deferring to pending enforcement actions, and avoiding duplicative regulatory measures.

Where such coordinating efforts have not been taken, conflicts over compliance standards may develop. In *Environmental Transportation Systems, Inc. v. Ensco, Inc.*, 763 F. Supp. 384 (C.D. Ill. 1991) a trucking company sought contribution under CERCLA for clean up costs incurred when its truck accidentally overturned, causing transformers containing PCBs to rupture. The trucker claimed that the company which had contracted to ship the transformers to a disposal site should bear a portion of the expenses because the PCBs were improperly packaged and loaded in violation of Department of Transportation (DOT) regulations governing the transportation of hazardous substances. The district court found that a statutory conflict existed, but that TSCA controlled because of its specific provisions regulating PCBs. The district court noted that ironically the shipper was exculpated from liability under the supposedly more stringent TSCA regulations yet would have been partially responsible under the DOT approach. On appeal, the Seventh Circuit did not reach the statutory conflict issue but affirmed summary judgment denying contribution based on equitable factors on the basis that the accident was entirely the fault of the trucker. 969 F.2d 503, 512 (7th Cir. 1992).

6. *Preemption.* The comprehensive regulatory scheme of TSCA may preempt local land use control measures, particularly those aimed at PCBs and lead. Section 18 [15 U.S.C. § 2617] provides that federal regulations pursuant to TSCA will preempt similar state and local laws but also provides a mechanism for the EPA to grant an exemption in certain instances.

In *Rollins Environmental Services, Inc. v. Parish of St. James*, 775 F.2d 627 (5th Cir. 1985), for example, the court found that a local ordinance which effectively prohibited the siting of a PCB waste disposal facility contravened TSCA. The court found the local ordinance to be a "sham" attempt to keep the unwanted facility away from a nearby elementary school. Although sympathetic to the concerns of the local citizenry, the court explained its preemption decision as follows:

> This court is not insensitive to the concerns expressed by the Parish of St. James in this case. No one wants a toxic waste disposal facility "in his own back yard" — and for good reason. The uncontrolled chemical emissions that have occurred elsewhere this year lend sober perspective to the sanguine assurances of scientists that such mishaps will not — indeed, cannot — occur. These concerns are rightfully intensified when, as here, a hazardous facility appears to have been located almost deliberately on the most inauspicious possible site, one-quarter mile from a local elementary school.

> Precisely because of such concerns, Congress enacted in the Toxic Substances Control Act a broad national program of measures to prevent and guard against the uncontrolled and hazardous emission of substances such as PCBs. If every locality were able to dodge responsibility for and participation in this program through artfully designed ordinances, the national goal of safe, environmentally sound toxic waste disposal would surely be frustrated....

> The Continental Congress knew that, without a powerful preemption doctrine, its chances of forming a more perfect union of the struggling states, with their variegated philosophies and economies, would have been nil. For this reason a strong Supremacy Clause was inserted in the

Constitution, and it has been justified by the events of the founding years and throughout the history of our country.

In the 1960's, for example, the Civil Rights legislation and the Voting Rights Act were distinctly distasteful to some of the states of the Union. These states responded with an agenda of frustrating and nullifying and eviscerating the benign principles of *Brown v. Board of Education* and the subsequent Civil Rights legislation. Thus, the state legislatures busily engaged in the legislative process, passing bills and convening the legislature in the midnight hours — at times to negate what Congress and the President had put into law the day before. It quickly became obvious that the federal supremacy fostered by the Constitution, and the doctrine of preemption as it applies when federal statutes are involved, were indispensable in assuring that there could be no interdiction of the progress of civil rights through state legislative action.

Preemption is an absolute necessity, an imperative, if the federal government is to be a federal government. To do what is asked for by the appellee in this case is really to change the whole constitutional structure of our country and to bury federalism many feet below the surface of a babbling group of states and an utterly ineffective federal government. The Constitution of the United States prevents the erection of 50 Towers of Babel.

Id. at 637-638.

Also see Environmental Defense Fund v. EPA, 598 F.2d 62 (D.C. Cir. 1978), where the court upheld EPA regulations prohibiting the discharge of PCBs into the nation's waters pursuant to the provisions governing toxic pollutants under the Clean Water Act. The court found that the TSCA provisions regulating PCBs did not repeal by implication the power to regulate the chemical under another federal law, but looked to section 9(b), 15 U.S.C. § 2608(b), as specifically authorizing regulatory authorities the choice of the most effective methods to combat the risks posed by toxic substances.

7. *Whistleblower Protection.* TSCA, like many federal environmental statutes, contains a provision protecting employee "whistleblowers" from discharge or discrimination by employers. *See* 15 U.S.C. § 2622. In an interesting case of first impression, *Coupar v. United States Dep't of Labor*, ___ F.3d ___, 1997 W.L. 33533 (9th Cir. 1997), a prison inmate claimed status as a whistleblower under TSCA. The claimant, who worked for a government corporation which provided work to inmates in federal institutions, alleged that his administrative transfer from a prison facility was in retaliation for filing a complaint with the Labor Department of sewage leaking into a river and improper storage of toxic chemicals. The court denied the claim, finding that the inmate was not an "employee" within the meaning of the whistleblower provision. The court reasoned that the "economic reality" was that the inmate's relationship to the corporation was "penological, not pecuniary" because he was obligated to work at some job pursuant to the prison work program.

8. *Regulation of Radon.* In a 1988 amendment to TSCA, Congress added Title III to address the hazards posed by indoor radon pollution. TSCA §§ 310-311, 15 U.S.C. §§ 2661-2671. The EPA estimates that radon gas may be to blame for 20,000 lung cancer deaths annually, making it a greater health hazard than asbestos. The Clean Air Act does not address the problem of indoor air pollution by radon, though; its focus is the regulation of "ambient" or outdoor air quality. 42 U.S.C. § 7409(a). Radon presents an unusual dilemma for legislative solution, however, because it is an inert radioactive gas which occurs naturally in the environment by the decay of uranium in soil and rock. The health risks posed by radon arise when the gas escapes to the surface and becomes trapped in buildings in large concentrations. The "daughter" products of the gas attach to smoke and dust particles which are inhaled and become lodged in lung tissue. Ironically, the increasing focus on energy efficiency in buildings reduces ventilation which would otherwise mitigate the negative effects of radon by allowing the gas to dissipate into the atmosphere.

Although radon occurs naturally, it also may be produced through the mill tailings left over from mining and processing uranium ore. Throughout the 1950s and 1960s mining companies deposited these mill tailings as landfill over which homes were built. Congress passed the Uranium Mill Tailings Radiation Control Act of 1978 (42 U.S.C. §§ 7911-7925), which appropriated money to decontaminate buildings located over such mill tailing landfills and authorized the EPA to determine what levels of radon exposure would be considered safe.

Recognition of the severity of radon gas as a national environmental and health problem did not develop until the mid-1980s, however, with the discovery of exceptionally high levels of radon contamination in homes located in Pennsylvania. Radon concentrations in one home were measured in excess of 1,000 times greater than the EPA's suggested guideline for residential homes. Experts estimated that the degree of exposure was equivalent to smoking 135 packs of cigarettes per day or being exposed to 455,000 chest x-rays per year. The homes were located on the Reading Prong, a uranium-rich geological formation which stretches from eastern Pennsylvania through northern New Jersey into southern New York.

In 1985 the EPA took the lead in researching and managing radon by establishing the Radon Action Program, principally with the goals of assessing the extent of the problem and developing information about mitigation techniques. In 1986 Congress included several provisions pertaining to radon gas as part of the Superfund Amendments and Reauthorization Act (SARA), which required the EPA to conduct a national assessment of radon gas contamination and to determine appropriate response methods. Pub. L. No. 99-499, § 188, 100 Stat. 1613, 1659 (codified at 42 U.S.C. § 7401 note) (1988). In SARA Congress also created a freestanding statute called The Radon Gas and Indoor Air Quality Research Act of 1986, 42 U.S.C. § 7401 note (1988), which required the EPA to create a research program on the radon threat to human health and to assess appropriate government steps to mitigate the risks posed by indoor air pollution.

Despite the significant health hazards associated with radon exposure, the risks can be largely avoided by various fairly inexpensive mitigation methods. Rather than establishing a comprehensive regulatory scheme, then, TSCA's Title III provisions are principally aimed at providing information to the public describing the health risks associated with radon (TSCA § 303, 15 U.S.C. § 2663) so that detection and mitigation steps can be taken. The amendments require the EPA to develop model construction standards and techniques to control radon levels in new construction (TSCA § 304, 15 U.S.C. 2664), and authorize technical and financial assistance to states for radon programs. TSCA §§ 305-306, 15 U.S.C. §§ 2665-2666. Finally, Title III authorizes certain studies of the radon problem in schools and federal buildings and the establishment of training centers. TSCA §§ 307-309, 15 U.S.C. §§ 2667, 2669.

For additional commentary on the problem of indoor air pollution caused by radon, see the following references: Kirsch, *Behind Closed Doors: Indoor Air Pollution and Governmental Policy*, 6 HARV. ENVTL. L. REV. 339 (1982); Cross & Murray, *Liability for Toxic Radon Gas in Residential Home Sales*, 66 N.C. L. REV. 687 (1988); Kindt, *Radioactive Wastes*, 24 NAT. RESOURCES J. 967 (1984); Note, *Radon's Radioactive Ramifications: How Federal and State Governments Should Address the Problem*, 16 B.C. ENVTL. AFF. L. REV. 329 (1988); Note, *Radon: An Environmental Problem That Is Too Close to Home*, 4 J. CONTEMP. L. POL'Y 415 (1988).

9. *Regulation of Biotechnology.* With the discovery in 1953 of the double stranded helix of deoxyribonucleic acid (DNA) — the principal substance of genes — it became possible to decipher the genetic code. The science of genetic engineering developed processes capable of transferring genetic information from one organism to another. This procedure of gene-splicing, or separating and cloning DNA segments, described as recombinant DNA (RDNA), presented intriguing opportunities to develop new products and processes to benefit society and industry. In the environmental context, illustrations of the varied potential uses for RDNA technology include "ice minus" experiments (genetically altering crops to increase frost resistance and thus yield larger harvests), bacteria potentially capable of destroying hazardous waste in landfills, plants developed to produce their own pesticides, and animal growth hormones. *See generally* Von Oehsen, *Regulating Genetic Engineering in an Era of Increased Judicial Deference: A Proper Balance of the Federal Powers*, 40 ADMIN. L. REV. 317 (1988). Following the decision by the Supreme Court in *Diamond v. Chakrabarty*, 447 U.S. 303 (1980) that a genetically engineered bacterium capable of breaking down components of crude oil was a patentable subject, increased emphasis was placed on the prospects for using biotechnology in commercial industry rather than simply conducting scientific research to gather information.

The substances created through genetic engineering or biotechnology, though, present special regulatory problems because of the scientific uncertainty of potential risks associated with their release into the environment and the question of whether they fit within the regulatory scope of federal laws. A principal concern articulated by environmentalists is that the deliberate release of genetically altered organisms into the environment may potentially disrupt natural ecosystems, causing irreversible and irremediable harm.

In 1984, the President's Office of Science and Technology Policy announced the formation of an interagency working group to assess the biotechnology problem and to encourage cooperation among agencies. The Biotechnology Science Coordinating Committee (BSCC) developed the Coordinated Framework for Regulation of Biotechnology. 51 Fed. Reg. 23,302 (1986). The Framework recognized that no single legislative act governed biotechnology, but placed the responsibility on each agency to develop methods to review and evaluate biotechnology products and processes on an ad hoc basis. Agency jurisdiction was determined by the proposed product's intended use rather than its biological properties.

In *Foundation on Economic Trends v. Johnson*, 661 F. Supp. 107 (D.D.C. 1986) the plaintiff organization challenged the definitions and exemptions contained in the Framework as procedurally defective because they were promulgated without notice and comment and were substantively irrational for failing to take into account certain risks posed by genetically engineered substances. Plaintiffs were concerned that the release of genetically altered microorganisms, without additional scientific knowledge and more effective federal controls, could adversely affect human health and the environment. The court characterized the state of federal regulation governing biotechnology as marked by "confusion, controversy, indecision and delay" but still dismissed the complaint for failure to state a case or controversy. The court found that the agencies involved had not engaged in regulatory rulemaking in drafting the Framework, but simply used the document to guide policymaking. Moreover, the court found that the plaintiffs had failed to meet the injury-in-fact prong of the test for standing because the asserted harm related to future unspecified agency actions which might present unreasonable risks. On the other hand, in *Foundation on Economic Trends v. Heckler*, 756 F.2d 143 (D.C. Cir. 1985) the court held that the National Institutes of Health (NIH) was required to prepare an environmental impact statement pursuant to NEPA before allowing field testing by University of California, Berkeley researchers of ice minus experiments.

The EPA has declared its authority to regulate the deliberate release of genetically engineered commercial microbial products under FIFRA and TSCA. 51 Fed. Reg. 23,313 (1986). The FIFRA licensing scheme and pre-release review system of pesticides provides ample jurisdictional authority for EPA action to consider the environmental risks posed by genetically engineered microorganisms which are intended for use as pesticides. EPA, drawing upon the BSCC definitions, regulates these microorganisms under FIFRA on a case-by-case basis by establishing two levels of review for substances based on the potential degree of risk presented. FIFRA, of course, has serious limitations in scope of coverage because the statute focuses only on licensing substances to be used as pesticides or for significant new uses of the product.

TSCA, on the other hand, provides considerably greater latitude to the EPA to regulate all chemicals irrespective of intended usage and to gather information to fill in the gaps of scientific uncertainty about those substances. Although TSCA's application to genetically engineered organisms is controversial because its jurisdictional grant pertains to "chemical substances" (TSCA § 3(2)(A), § 2602(2)(A)), the EPA has asserted the statutory language encompasses living organisms. The premanufacture notice program provides certain information to the EPA which may provide the basis for establishing regulatory controls by the agency. Moreover, the agency possesses broad information-gathering authority under section 4 of TSCA, 15 U.S.C. § 2603, which authorizes the EPA to mandate additional testing of chemicals, and pursuant to section 8, 15 U.S.C. § 2607, permitting the agency to require reporting and recordkeeping of health and safety studies and incidents. Additionally, since naturally occurring microbes are listed on the inventory of existing chemicals, the EPA can gather additional information and pass new regulations by employing the significant new use regulations. TSCA § 5(a)(1)(B), 15 U.S.C. § 2604(a)(1)(B).

For additional commentary discussing the regulation of genetically engineered microbial organisms see the following references: Shapiro, *Biotechnology and the Design of Regulation*, 17 ECOLOGY L.Q. 1 (1990); McGarity, *Federal Regulation of Agricultural Biotechnologies*, 20 U. MICH. J.L. REF. 1089 (1987); McGarity & Bayer, *Federal Regulation of Emerging Genetic Technologies*, 36 VAND. L. REV. 461 (1983); Schiffbauer, *Regulating Genetically Engineered Microbial Products Under the Toxic Substances Control Act*, 15 ENVTL. L. REP. (Envtl. L. Inst.) 10279 (1985); Note, *Interagency Conflict and Administrative Accountability: Regulating the Release of Recombinant Organisms*, 77 GEO. L.J. 1787 (1989); Note, *The EPA and Biotechnology Regulation: Coping with Scientific Uncertainty*, 95 YALE L.J. 553 (1986); Note, *Genetic Engineering: Innovation and Risk Minimization*, 57 GEO. WASH. L. REV. 100 (1988).

Chapter 11

FEDERAL INSECTICIDE, FUNGICIDE, AND RODENTICIDE ACT

INTRODUCTION

American agriculture is probably the most proficient food enterprise in the world. American farmers have increasingly relied upon chemical pesticides to minimize damage caused by crop disease and pests. The widespread application of these chemicals in the agricultural process, however, also presents collateral risks to human health and the environment. Thus, a difficult balance must invariably be struck between society's needs and demands for adequate food production and protecting environmental quality. This political balance is further complicated by various marketplace factors which include recognition of the economic interests and expectations of manufacturers, distributors, and purchasers of pesticides and the public demand for reasonably priced, high quality foods. Manufacturers and formulators of pesticides face a formidable task of developing products which will be effective in abating harmful pests yet which will not present unreasonable risks to human health or the environment.

The first federal legislation regulating pesticides was the Insecticide Act of 1910 which made it unlawful to manufacture and sell insecticides which were adulterated or improperly labeled. This Act was primarily directed at protecting consumers from ineffective products and deceptive labeling practices, but it had serious shortcomings in its lack of product registration or safety rules. The low priority of regulation of chemical pesticides prior to World War II may be attributable to several factors: the relatively minor usage of pesticides, the lack of understanding about the potential risks to health and the environment resulting from indiscriminate application of toxic chemicals, and the lack of public pressure to expand regulatory controls.

In 1947, Congress enacted the Federal Insecticide, Fungicide, and Rodenticide Act (FIFRA) (7 U.S.C. § 136 *et seq.*) to regulate the expanding use of pesticides in American agriculture. The Act required that all pesticides be registered with the Secretary of Agriculture prior to their distribution in interstate or foreign commerce. The Act also contained rudimentary standards for labeling, declaring that pesticides were "misbranded" if found harmful to people, animals, or vegetation even if properly used. The Act still proved inadequate in addressing the environmental hazards and health risks associated with pesticide usage and exposure, though, because the Secretary had little regulatory authority so long as the product met the labeling requirements of the statute. Subsequent amendments to FIFRA in 1964 allowed the Secretary to refuse or cancel registration, and the applicant had the burden of proof regarding product safety and effectiveness. The Act remained largely ineffective because of inadequate staffing and resources, despite its strengthened registration provisions.

The most significant developments affecting regulation of pesticides did not take place until the early 1970s. The Environmental Protection Agency was established in 1970 and inherited the pesticides division from the Department of Agriculture. In 1972, in response to mounting pressure from environmental interest organizations, Congress drastically amended FIFRA by changing its focus from a labeling law into a comprehensive regulatory statute. EPA administers two separate systems to regulate potentially harmful pesticides: it establishes registration and labeling requirements for "economic poisons" under FIFRA, and sets tolerance limits for pesticide residues in crops shipped in interstate commerce under the Food, Drug and Cosmetic Act.

A. REGULATORY FRAMEWORK

The cornerstone of the regulatory framework remains one of registration with the EPA of pesticide products used in the United States, coupled with provisions for review, suspension, and cancellation of registration in certain circumstances. The primary condition for registering a pesticide under FIFRA involves a determination by the EPA that the product will not cause "unreasonable adverse effects on the environment." This phrase, as defined elsewhere in the Act, takes into account the "economic, social, and environmental costs and benefits" of the pesticide. Centering regulatory approval on a risk-benefit analysis, however, has created considerable controversy. Public interest groups have criticized the statutory consideration of costs as being too lenient to protect human health and the environment from harmful exposure to pesticides. Moreover, the technical, scientific, statutory, administrative, and, in some instances, litigation and delay costs associated with developing research data to support this threshold finding often present formidable obstacles to applicants for registration of a pesticide and to EPA. On the other hand, industry has contended that certain other provisions of FIFRA, such as data sharing and mandatory licensing, fail to protect their investment interests.

Although FIFRA does broadly regulate the use, sale and labeling of pesticides, its detailed regulatory structure has often been assailed for actually frustrating its objectives. Significant transaction and delay costs exist at virtually every level of FIFRA's regulatory structure primarily because of the vast scientific uncertainty and complexity generally surrounding pesticide safety. Several significant but controversial topics which are presently outside the scope of FIFRA will likely draw considerable attention from Congress in the reauthorization process of the statute in 1991. Agenda items of particular interest for regulatory coverage include groundwater contamination, inert chemical ingredients, and farmworker health and safety.

The following materials will explore the regulatory framework of FIFRA and the particular problems presented in the registration, cancellation, and suspension of pesticides.

HUE v. FARMBOY SPRAY CO., INC.
127 Wash. 2d 67; 896 P.2d 682 (1995)

TALMADGE, J. — This case arises out of the use of pesticides in the Horse Heaven Hills and their alleged downwind fall-out in Badger Canyon, Benton County. The plaintiffs allege that pesticides drifted from the Hills down into the Canyon, onto their homes and farms, damaging their crops and plants. Defendant E.I. du Pont de Nemours & Co., Inc. ("DuPont") manufactured the pesticides in question (sulfonylurea herbicides named "Glean," "Harmony" and "Finesse"). Defendant Farmboy Spray Co., Inc. ("Farmboy") aerially sprayed them on wheat farms in the Horse Heaven Hills, at the behest of the other 27 defendants who own the farms ("Wheat Growers").

Holding that the Federal Insecticide, Fungicide, and Rodenticide Act ("FIFRA"), 7 U.S.C. § 136 *et seq.*, preempted plaintiffs' common law inadequate warnings actions,[1] because the products' labels are registered under FIFRA, the trial court dismissed various claims against the defendants....

Facts

Plaintiffs owned 14 farms and/or homes with gardens in Badger Canyon. They grow irrigated crops such as alfalfa, walnuts, fruits, asparagus and other vegetables, and ornamental plants such as "baby's breath." They alleged that their plants were damaged or destroyed by pesticides drifting from the Horse Heaven Hills, an area south, west and above the southern wall of the Canyon.

The Wheat Growers used the pesticides to kill off competitive, moisture-consuming weeds on their dryland (non-irrigated) wheat farms. There is no dispute that, pursuant to FIFRA, DuPont had registered the pesticides and their labels with the Environmental Protection Agency ("EPA"). The labels contain detailed instructions and warnings as to the maximum amount of pesticides to be used, the need for extreme care to avoid drift, and how to safely

---

[1] In this opinion, the term "common law actions" is used to refer to claims for damages brought by private parties, such as tort or breach of contract actions, regardless of whether the law underlying the claim is found today in court decisions or in enactments of the Legislature. *See, e.g.*, RCW 7.72 et seq. (products liability) and RCW Title 62A.2 (sales).

use the pesticides under particular conditions and in particular states.[4] The labels also disclaimed warranty liability.[5]

The plaintiffs claimed that Farmboy sprayed enough farms in a given period that 1 - 3% of each application escaped and collectively contaminated the air, and then would drift into Badger Canyon due to wind patterns, and damage plaintiffs' plants. Under these circumstances, it was allegedly not possible to trace particular plant damage in the Canyon to particular applications of pesticide in the Hills.

Plaintiffs filed an action for damages in the Yakima County Superior Court, asserting a variety of very general claims against various defendants. As against

---

[4]For example, there are 18 pages of warnings for Glean in the 1989 specimen label. The label sets a maximum application in Washington of 1/3 ounce per acre. The label is replete with cautions about drift onto desirable plants:

> Injury to or loss of desirable trees or vegetation may result from failure to observe the following: Do not apply ... on or near desirable trees or other plants, or on areas where their roots may extend, or in locations where the chemical may be washed or moved into contact with roots.... Prevent drift of spray to desirable plants.

One section of the label urges "CAUTION — AVOID SPRAY DRIFT" and states:

> Do not allow spray from either ground or aerial equipment to drift onto adjacent crops or land, as even small amounts will injure other plants. When spraying near adjacent, sensitive crops or plants, do everything possible to reduce spray drift. This includes:
>
> • Stop spraying if wind speed becomes excessive. DO NOT SPRAY IF WIND SPEED IS 10 MPH OR GREATER. Spray drift can occur at wind speeds less than 10 MPH. If sensitive crops or plants are downwind, extreme caution must be used even in relatively low wind conditions! ...

This section also warns that "extreme caution" must be used under certain weather conditions, regardless of wind speed; prohibits an application "when an inversion exists"; indicates methods to diminish drift; and concludes that "Extreme care must be taken to prevent drift to desirable plants or nontarget agricultural land." The label further warns of the need to "reduce the potential for movement of treated soil due to wind erosion," and advises that "Injury to adjacent crops may occur when treated soil is blown onto land used to produce crops other than cereal grains." Despite the foregoing, plaintiffs did not articulate a breach of express warranty claim in this case.

[5]The Glean label, like those of the other pesticides, includes a disclaimer of warranty as follows:

NOTICE OF WARRANTY

> Du Pont warrants that this product conforms to the chemical description on the label thereof and is reasonably fit for purposes stated on such label only when used in accordance with the directions under normal use conditions. It is impossible to eliminate all risks inherently associated with the use of this product. Crop injury ... or other unintended consequences may result because of such factors as weather conditions, presence of other materials, or the manner of use or application ... In no case shall Du Pont be liable for consequential, special or indirect damages resulting from the use or handling of this product. All such risks shall be assumed by the buyer. DU PONT MAKES NO WARRANTIES OF MERCHANTABILI-TY OR FITNESS FOR A PARTICULAR PURPOSE NOR ANY OTHER EXPRESSED OR IMPLIED WARRANTY EXCEPT AS STATED ABOVE. (Emphasis added).

the Wheat Growers and Farmboy, plaintiffs asserted claims for negligence and strict liability. Before trial, the trial court apparently dismissed the negligence claim against the Wheat Growers. Plaintiffs did not appeal this ruling. The court also dismissed a strict liability claim against the Wheat Growers in connection with ground applications or alleged movement of pesticides from the Wheat Growers' land. Plaintiffs did not appeal this ruling. Ultimately, as against the Wheat Growers and Farmboy, only a strict liability claim for drift from aerial applications was tried and submitted to the jury.

Against DuPont, plaintiffs alleged claims for design defect, inadequate warnings/instructions, nonconformity with implied warranties, failure to meet consumer safety expectations, unfair or deceptive acts or practices in marketing the products for use in the Horse Heaven Hills, and negligence.

Before trial, the court dismissed certain claims against DuPont which were based upon alleged inadequate testing and marketing the pesticides for use in the Horse Heaven Hills/Badger Canyon ecosystem. The trial court ruled that FIFRA preempted most of the product claims and the negligence claim to the extent that they were based upon inadequate label warnings. The court also dismissed claims for breach of implied warranties (due to lack of privity), and unfair or deceptive acts under RCW 19.86....

At trial, plaintiffs and defendants introduced expert opinion and other evidence supporting and rebutting the allegations of long distance drift causing damage to plaintiffs' plants. Plaintiffs also introduced evidence supporting what they call "negligence," but which would be better termed "misrepresentation," to the effect that DuPont knew of the long distance drift pattern in the Horse Heaven Hills/Badger Canyon ecosystem, and withheld the relevant information from the EPA, materially affecting the warnings on the labels. At the close of plaintiffs' case, the trial court dismissed this claim because there was no proof that the EPA would have required DuPont to change the labels had DuPont provided the information to the EPA. Plaintiffs did not appeal this ruling, stating this "was not the theory of negligence that the plaintiffs desired to proceed on."

Defendants then moved for dismissal of the remaining claims, contending that there was no evidence that any defendant caused any harm since the proof did not identify the particular pesticides, applications or entities that caused or contributed to the particular injuries. The trial court denied the motion, ruling that plaintiffs did not have to establish proportions of responsibility or establish the effects of individual applications....

Issues

(1) Did the trial court err in holding that FIFRA preempted plaintiffs' claims relating to the adequacy of the pesticide labels?

(2) Did the trial court err in dismissing plaintiffs' claims based on breach of implied warranties? ...

Discussion

The central focus of this case, as argued by the parties and certified by the Court of Appeals, Division III, is the issue of FIFRA preemption....

A. *FIFRA Preemption Analysis*

We adhere to a rigorous analysis of the preemption issue because of this Court's continuing desire to uphold state sovereignty to the maximum extent, tempered only by the mandate of the Supremacy Clause of the United States Constitution. We hold that FIFRA preempts only those state common law actions that are predicated on the allegation that a product label should have had additional or different warnings than those required under FIFRA. This conclusion is mandated by this Court's long-standing support for the presumption against preemption of state law by federal enactments, and the plain meaning of FIFRA's express preemption clause. It also finds compelling support in an overwhelming wave of appellate court decisions interpreting FIFRA, in which Congress has acquiesced.

1. *The Presumption Against Preemption*

The Supremacy Clause of the United States Constitution provides that United States law is supreme, notwithstanding any contrary state law. U.S. Const., Art. VI, cl. 2. Accordingly, state law that conflicts with federal law is "without effect." *Maryland v. Louisiana*, 451 U.S. 725, 746, 68 L. Ed. 2d 576, 101 S. Ct. 2114, 2128 (1981), quoted in *Cipollone v. Liggett Group, Inc.*, 505 U.S. 504, 120 L. Ed. 2d 407, 112 S. Ct. 2608, 2617 (1992).

However, we do not presume that Congress relishes abrogating state authority. Congress is presumed to respect our system of "dual governance." Accordingly, any consideration of preemption issues "'start[s] with the assumption that the historic police powers of the States [are] not to be superseded by ... Federal Act unless that [is] the clear and manifest purpose of Congress.'" Indeed, we have "repeatedly emphasized" that there is a "strong presumption against finding preemption [of State law] in an ambiguous case.... State laws are not superseded by federal law unless that is the clear and manifest purpose of Congress." [Citation] The presumption against preemption is "even stronger with state regulation regarding matters of health and safety," in which states have traditionally exercised their sovereignty.

The meaning of the presumption against preemption is twofold. First, where Congress expressly addresses state authority in a federal law, the preemptive scope of the federal law should not be extended any further by resort to an implied preemption analysis. "Congress' enactment of a provision defining the pre-emptive reach of a statute implies that matters beyond that reach are not pre-empted."

Second, the presumption against preemption has implications for the construction to be given a preemption provision in federal law. In construing such a provision, the court "must in the first instance focus on the plain wording of the clause, which necessarily contains the best evidence of Congress' pre-emptive intent." [Citation] Further, the court should consider whether the preemption clause voids each state law at issue on a case by case basis, giving the clause a "fair but narrow reading" in each case.

2. Effect of Cipollone

This application of the presumption against preemption is illustrated in the *Cipollone* case. There, the Court held that the 1969 amendment to § 5(b) of the 1965 Federal Cigarette Labeling and Advertising Act (15 U.S.C. § 1334(b)) was an express preemption provision. As amended, § 5(b) states:

> No requirement or prohibition based on smoking and health shall be imposed under State law with respect to the advertising or promotion of any cigarettes the packages of which are labeled in conformity with the provisions of this chapter....

After deciding that "requirements and prohibitions" included common law duties, the Supreme Court in *Cipollone* then separately determined whether each common law claim was within the scope of the preemption clause. The Court stated that:

> The central inquiry in each case is straightforward: we ask whether the legal duty that is the predicate of the common law damages action constitutes a "requirement or prohibition based on smoking and health ... imposed under State law with respect to ... advertising or promotion," giving that clause a fair but narrow reading.

The *Cipollone* Court then considered each claim asserted by petitioner. It held that the preemption clause encompassed "failure to warn" claims, because those claims required a showing that the advertising should have included additional or clearer warnings. Significantly, the Court looked to the substance of the claim, and counted both a failure to warn claim and a negligence claim resting on allegations of inadequate testing and marketing as "failure to warn" claims. In contrast, the Court noted that claims that relied "solely" on testing or research or "other actions unrelated to advertising or promotion" would not be preempted. The Court held that other common law actions asserted by petitioner were not preempted because the duties sought to be enforced did not fall wholly within all of the terms and conditions of the preemption clause. For instance, the duty underlying a breach of express warranty claim was held to be voluntarily assumed, not "imposed under State law." The duties underlying fraudulent misrepresentation and conspiracy claims were held to be duties to not deceive and to not conspire to commit fraud, not duties "based on smoking and health." Therefore, the Court held that the preemption clause did not preempt claims for conspiracy, fraudulent misrepresentation or breach of express warranty.

3. *FIFRA's Preemption Provision*

Since its enactment in 1947, FIFRA has provided a comprehensive federal scheme for pesticide labeling. *Wisconsin Public Intervenor v. Mortier*, 501 U.S. 597, 601, 115 L. Ed. 2d 532, 111 S. Ct. 2476, 2486 (1991). FIFRA prohibits the sale of pesticides unless the manufacturer registers the label with the EPA. 7 U.S.C. § 136a(a). To register the pesticide, the manufacturer files information including test descriptions and results, the proposed label, the purpose of the pesticide and "any directions for its use." 7 U.S.C. §§ 136a(c)(1)(B)-(D) (1988); see 40 C.F.R. § 156 (1992). The EPA reviews the filing and the label, 7 U.S.C. § 136a(c)(5), and determines whether the label information is adequate to protect the public from fraud, injury or "unreasonable adverse" environmental effects. *Chemical Specialties Mfrs. Ass'n v. Allenby*, 958 F.2d 941, 944 (9th Cir. 1992) (California initiative requiring point-of-sale warnings not preempted by FIFRA), *cert. denied*, ___ U.S. ___, 121 L. Ed. 2d 44, 113 S. Ct. 80 (1992). 7 U.S.C. § 136a(c)(5) (registration turns on such factors as whether the product composition warrants the proposed claims for it, whether its labeling complies with FIFRA, and whether it will "generally cause unreasonable adverse effects on the environment" when "used in accordance with widespread and commonly recognized practice").

FIFRA preempts any contrary labeling requirements. Section 136v of FIFRA states:

> (a) A State may regulate the sale or use of any federally registered pesticide or device in the State, but only if and to the extent the regulation does not permit any sale or use prohibited by this subchapter.

> (b) Such State shall not impose or continue in effect any requirements for labeling or packaging in addition to or different from those required under this subchapter.

This provision plainly is an express preemption clause. In interpreting this statute, this Court's duty is to focus on its plain wording.

Clearly the words "any requirements" in § 136v(b), like the words, "no requirement or prohibition" in the cigarette labeling act, include positive enactments of state law-making bodies and common law duties enforced in actions for damages. There is no discernible difference in meaning between the phrases because the cigarette label preemption clause refers to "requirement[s] or prohibition[s]," while § 136v(b) of FIFRA refers only to state "requirements." [Citations] It would be anomalous to rule that a state could avoid FIFRA labeling preemption merely by formulating its own labeling law in terms of a "prohibition" rather than a "requirement." The plain wording of § 136v(b) amounts to a Congressional command that no state shall enforce any "requirements" — including duties underlying common law actions — "for labeling or packaging in addition to or different from those required" under FIFRA....

Our conclusion that common law duties and state regulatory commands both may be state "requirements" preempted by the federal labeling law also furthers the policies of uniformity. In the federal labeling law involved here, as in *Cipollone*, Congress has decided that the federal government will determine the appropriate warnings for a product, and that the warnings shall be uniform for the whole nation. This precludes allowing the appropriate warnings to be worked out through private actors and the tort systems of the states. Contrary to arguments of the plaintiffs and WSTLA, common law duties and direct regulatory commands must both be deemed "requirements" for purposes of FIFRA preemption, so that the EPA's decisions as to uniform labeling standards for pesticides are not undermined through decisions by juries in the 50 states....

4. Preemption of Plaintiffs' Claims

Having decided that § 136v(b) preempts common law duties, we must determine which of plaintiffs' claims based upon those duties are preempted. We can do no better than to adapt the United States Supreme Court's approach in *Cipollone*: the central inquiry in each case is whether the legal duty that is the predicate of the common law damages action constitutes a State "requirement[]" for labeling or packaging in addition to or different from" the FIFRA requirements, giving that clause a fair but narrow reading. 7 U.S.C. § 136v(b).

Plaintiffs' claim based upon inadequate warnings or instructions is predicated upon a state duty to provide warnings and instructions that are necessary to make a product reasonably safe. RCW. 7.72.030(1). Clearly, this duty constitutes a requirement for labeling or packaging in addition to or different from the information required under FIFRA. The gist of plaintiffs' case is that pesticides like those at issue here should not be used in an area like the Horse Heaven Hills/Badger Canyon ecosystem, where there is a risk of long distance drift or mass air contamination. Clearly, this sort of caution should go on the label. The labels for the pesticides at issue in this case contain dozens of detailed warnings and instructions, including warnings for specific states, warnings to use "extreme caution" to avoid drift if desirable plants are "downwind," even under low wind conditions, and specific instructions as to how to avoid drift. Therefore, the plaintiffs' inadequate warnings claim was correctly ruled preempted by the trial court.

The trial court also correctly held that plaintiffs' "negligence" claim against DuPont was preempted. The plaintiffs' negligence theory is not clearly articulated. The "negligence" claim against DuPont resting upon alleged improper or inadequate testing or marketing was merely another way of contending that the labels should have warned against use in the Horse Heaven Hills or long distance drift. As the United States Supreme Court ruled in *Cipollone*, the "negligence" claim in this case which was predicated upon the manufacturer's alleged deficiencies in testing and marketing was, in actuality, a "failure to warn" claim, that is preempted....

Contrary to DuPont's view, claims for design defects or products liability that do not attack the label's adequacy under FIFRA are not preempted, as they are predicated upon a manufacturer's duty to make a product that is reasonably safe.... The trial court correctly ruled that plaintiffs' design defect claims were not preempted by FIFRA, although the jury's verdict on that issue was for the defendants.

B. *Implied Warranty Claims*

Citing RCW 7.72.030(2), plaintiffs alleged that the pesticides were not reasonably safe because they failed to conform to the implied warranties under RCW Title 62A. It is uncontested that plaintiffs were not in privity with DuPont. They neither purchased the pesticides from DuPont nor relied upon DuPont with respect to the pesticides. They were not even known to DuPont. On DuPont's motion for summary judgment, the trial court dismissed this claim because there was not a sufficient connection between plaintiffs and DuPont....

However, on appeal and in the proceedings below, plaintiffs failed to specify the alleged nonconformity, or indicate which implied warranty was not honored by DuPont. Plaintiffs do not allege anything "wrong" with the pesticides at all, other than the claim that they should not be used in an area allegedly prone to long distance drift, like the Horse Heaven Hills. As discussed above, this defect or nonconformity, if it is one, is the sort of problem that would be cured by adopting an appropriate warning or instruction on the pesticide label. Plaintiffs' implied warranty claims would again appear to be an attack upon the adequacy of the label warnings, and the dismissal of such claims is proper because they are preempted under FIFRA.

Conclusion

The trial court did not err in its rulings with respect to FIFRA preemption and plaintiffs' warranty theories.... The judgment of the trial court is affirmed, with costs on appeal to respondents.

NOTES AND QUESTIONS

1. As recognized in the principal case, the dichotomy for preemption purposes between "labeling" requirements and "use and sale" requirements potentially impacts upon state common law tort liability. In *Grenier v. Vermont Log Buildings, Inc.*, 96 F.3d 559, 564 (1st Cir. 1996) the court noted that Congress intended the labeling requirements under FIFRA to "bear the primary burden of informing the buyer of dangers and limitations." *Also see MacDonald v. Monsanto Co.*, 27 F.3d 1021 (5th Cir. 1994) (Compliance with FIFRA labeling requirements obviated state common law damage claims based upon a chemical manufacturer's failure to properly label herbicides and warn of dangers associated with their use).

2. Although the distinction between a claim for mislabeling and a claim for a deficient product may be less than clear, one court reasoned that the issue could be resolved by determining whether the deficiency is in the product or in the label, "looking to, as one factor, whether one could reasonably foresee that the manufacturer, in seeking to avoid liability for the error, would choose to alter the product or the label." *Worm v. American Cyanamid Co.*, 5 F.3d 744, 747 (4th Cir. 1993).

3. *Compare Lowe v. Sporicidin Int'l*, 47 F.3d 124 (4th Cir. 1995) where a hospital worker sued the manufacturer of a disinfectant registered under FIFRA for respiratory disorders caused by inhalation of the chemicals. The court found that FIFRA preempted state law failure to warn and express warranty claims based upon EPA-approved labeling of pesticides. However, the statute did not preclude a state from monitoring compliance with labeling or other requirements by FIFRA, such as where a manufacturer's advertisements made claims that substantially differed from statements required by FIFRA registration.

Also see Shaw v. Dow Brands, Inc., 994 F.2d 364, 371 (7th Cir. 1993) (FIFRA preempts common law strict liability and negligence claims against bathroom cleaner manufacturer for failure to warn customers that fumes from cleaner could cause lung damage). *Accord King v. E.I. DuPont De Nemours & Co.*, 996 F.2d 1346 (1st Cir. 1993) (State common law personal injuries claims based upon exposure to herbicides preempted by FIFRA). *Papas v. Upjohn Co.*, 985 F.2d 516 (11th Cir. 1993) (FIFRA expressly preempts state common law actions against manufacturers of EPA-registered pesticides to the extent claims are based upon inadequate labeling or packaging).

4. Local regulations of pesticide usage have encountered constitutional challenges that they are impliedly preempted by the comprehensive regulatory scheme of FIFRA. FIFRA does provide some authority for states to regulate the use of federally registered pesticides and precludes states from imposing labeling or packaging requirements different from the Act. *See* 7 U.S.C. §§ 136v(a) and (b).

In *Wisconsin Pub. Intervenor v. Mortier*, ___ U.S. ___, 111 S. Ct. 2476 (1991) the Court held that FIFRA did not expressly or impliedly preempt a town ordinance which required a permit for certain applications of pesticides to public and private lands. The Court found that although FIFRA is a comprehensive regulatory statute, substantial portions of the field remained for supplemental state and local regulation. The Court viewed the relationship between federal, state and local govenments as a "partnership" of cooperation and joint regulation over a wide range of matters involving pesticides. Recognition by the Court of the authority to regulate on a local level was grounded in traditional notions of state sovereignty, adaptability of restrictions to unique local conditions, and the presumption against preemption.

5. *Registration.* Registration of a pesticide requires a determination by the EPA that the following requirements are satisfied:

(A) its composition is such as to warrant the proposed claims for it;

(B) its labeling and other material required to be submitted comply with the requirements of [FIFRA];

(C) it will perform its intended function without unreasonably adverse effects on the environment; and

(D) when used in accordance with widespread and commonly recognized practice it will not generally cause unreasonably adverse effects on the environment.

7 U.S.C. § 136a(c)(5)(A)-(D) [3a(c)(5)(A)-(D)]. *Also see* 40 C.F.R. § 152.112-(f).

6. *Pesticides and the Federal Food, Drug and Cosmetic Act.* The Federal Food, Drug and Cosmetic Act (FFDCA) ensures the safety of food by prohibiting the sale of food that is "adulterated." *See* 21 U.S.C. § 331(a). Section 409 of the Act, known as the Delaney Clause, provided that no food additive would be deemed safe if it induced cancer. *See* 21 U.S.C. § 348(c)(3). In *Les v. Reilly*, 968 F.2d 985 (9th Cir. 1992), *cert. denied, National Agric. Chems. Ass'n v. Les*, 507 U.S. 950 (1993) the court held that EPA regulations that had permitted the use of pesticides as food additives which presented only a de minimis risk of causing cancer violated the Delaney Clause. The court found that the use of any additive that was carcinogenic could never be deemed "safe" regardless of the degree of risk. The EPA subsequently began a process of revoking all tolerances (maximum allowable levels) that were not consistent with the strict reading of the FFDCA. In the Food Quality Protection Act of 1996, Pub. L. 104-170, Congress amended the FFDCA to establish a single, health-based standard for pesticide residues in all types of foods, thus replacing the Delaney Clause as it applied to some residues in ready-to-eat processed foods. In response, the EPA recently has withdrawn final and proposed rules revoking tolerances for pesticide residues in processed food or animal feed that were predicated on the Delaney Clause. *See generally* Merrill, *FDA's Implementation of The Delaney Clause: Repudiation of Congressional Choice or Reasoned Adaptation to Scientific Progress*, 5 YALE J. ON REG. 1 (1988).

7. The registration process of pesticides under FIFRA does not displace the application of other federal environmental protection statutes. The cost-benefit considerations implicit in registration leave room for more complete evaluation of environmental impact issues, such as are conducted under NEPA. *See Save Our Ecosystems v. Clark*, 747 F.2d 1240, 1248 (9th Cir. 1984). *Also see Oregon Environmental Council v. Kunzman*, 714 F.2d 901, 905 (9th Cir. 1983) (Forest Service program for aerial spraying of registered pesticide to combat the gypsy moth in a populated area satisfied labeling requirements of FIFRA but still necessitated site-specific impact statement under NEPA).

RUCKELSHAUS v. MONSANTO CO.

467 U.S. 986 (1984)

JUSTICE BLACKMUN delivered the opinion of the Court.

In this case, we are asked to review a United States District Court's determination that several provisions of the Federal Insecticide, Fungicide, and Rodenticide Act (FIFRA), 61 Stat. 163, as amended, 7 U.S.C. § 136 *et seq.*, are unconstitutional. The provisions at issue authorize the Environmental Protection Agency (EPA) to use data submitted by an applicant for registration of a pesticide in evaluating the application of a subsequent applicant, and to disclose publicly some of the submitted data.

....

For purposes of this litigation, the most significant of the 1972 amendments pertained to the pesticide-registration procedure and the public disclosure of information learned through that procedure. Congress added to FIFRA a new section governing public disclosure of data submitted in support of an application for registration. Under that section, the submitter of data could designate any portions of the submitted material it believed to be "trade secrets or commercial or financial information." § 10(a), 7 U.S.C. § 136h(a). Another section prohibited EPA from publicly disclosing information which, in its judgment, contained or related to "trade secrets or commercial or financial information." § 10(b). In the event that EPA disagreed with a submitter's designation of certain information as "trade secrets or commercial or financial information" and proposed to disclose that information, the original submitter could institute a declaratory judgment action in federal district court. § 10(c).

The 1972 amendments also included a provision that allowed EPA to consider data submitted by one applicant for registration in support of another application pertaining to a similar chemical, provided the subsequent applicant offered to compensate the applicant who originally submitted the data. § 3(c)(1)(D), 7 U.S.C. § 136a(c)(1)(D). In effect, the provision instituted a mandatory data-licensing scheme. The amount of compensation was to be negotiated by the parties, or, in the event negotiations failed, was to be determined by EPA, subject to judicial review upon the instigation of the original data submitter....

Appellee Monsanto Company (Monsanto) is an inventor, developer, and producer of various kinds of chemical products, including pesticides.... It is one of a relatively small group of companies that invent and develop new active ingredients for pesticides and conduct most of the research and testing with respect to those ingredients.

....

Monsanto, like any other applicant for registration of a pesticide, must present research and test data supporting its application. The District Court found that Monsanto had incurred costs in excess of $23.6 million in developing the health, safety, and environmental data submitted by it under FIFRA. The information submitted with an application usually has value to Monsanto beyond its instrumentality in gaining that particular application. Monsanto uses this information to develop additional end-use products and to expand the uses of its registered products. The information would also be valuable to Monsanto's competitors. For that reason, Monsanto has instituted stringent security measures to ensure the secrecy of the data.

....

Monsanto brought suit in District Court, seeking injunctive and declaratory relief from the operation of the data-consideration provisions of FIFRA's § 3(c)(1)(D), and the data-disclosure provisions of FIFRA's § 10 and the related § 3(c)(2)(A). Monsanto alleged that all of the challenged provisions effected a "taking" of property without just compensation, in violation of the Fifth Amendment. In addition, Monsanto alleged that the data-consideration provisions violated the Amendment because they effected a taking of property for a private, rather than a public, purpose....

In deciding this case, we are faced with four questions: (1) Does Monsanto have a property interest protected by the Fifth Amendment's Taking Clause in the health, safety, and environmental data it has submitted to EPA? (2) If so, does EPA's use of the data to evaluate the applications of others or EPA's disclosure of the data to qualified members of the public effect a taking of that property interest? (3) If there is a taking, is it a taking for a public use? (4) If there is a taking for a public use, does the statute adequately provide for just compensation?

....

[The Court held that to the extent that Monsanto had an interest in its health, safety, and environmental data cognizable as a trade-secret property right under state law, that property right was protected by the Taking Clause of the Fifth Amendment.]

Having determined that Monsanto has a property interest in the data it has submitted to EPA, we confront the difficult question whether a "taking" will occur when EPA discloses those data or considers the data in evaluating another application for registration. The question of what constitutes a "taking" is one with which this Court has wrestled on many occasions....

... The Court, however, has identified several factors that should be taken into account when determining whether a governmental action has gone beyond "regulation" and effects a "taking." Among those factors are: "the character of the governmental action, its economic impact, and its interference with reasonable investment backed expectation." [Citations.] It is to the last of these three factors that we now direct our attention, for we find that the force of this factor is so overwhelming, at least with respect to certain of the data submitted by Monsanto to EPA, that it disposes of the taking question regarding those data.

A "reasonable investment-backed expectation" must be more than a "unilateral expectation or an abstract need." We find that with respect to any health, safety, and environmental data that Monsanto submitted to EPA after the effective date of the 1978 FIFRA amendments — that is, on or after October 1, 1978 —

Monsanto could not have had a reasonable, investment-backed expectation that EPA would keep the data confidential beyond the limits prescribed in the amended statute itself. Monsanto was on notice of the manner in which EPA was authorized to use and disclose any data turned over to it by an applicant for registration.

Thus, with respect to any data submitted to EPA on or after October 1, 1978, Monsanto knew that, for a period of 10 years from the date of submission, EPA would not consider those data in evaluating the application of another without Monsanto's permission. § 3(c)(1)(D)(i). It was also aware, however, that once the 10-year period had expired, EPA could use the data without Monsanto's permission. §§ 3(c)(1)(D)(ii) and (iii). Monsanto was further aware that it was entitled to an offer of compensation from the subsequent applicant only until the end of the 15th year from the date of submission. § 3(c)(1)(D)(iii). In addition, Monsanto was aware that information relating to formulae of products could be revealed by EPA to "any Federal agency consulted and [could] be revealed at a public hearing or in findings of fact" issued by EPA "when necessary to carry out" EPA's duties under FIFRA. § 10(b). The statute also gave Monsanto notice that much of the health, safety, and efficacy data provided by it could be disclosed to the general public at any time. § 10(d). If, despite the data-consideration and data-disclosure provisions in the statute, Monsanto chose to submit the requisite data in order to receive a registration, it can hardly argue that its reasonable investment-backed expectations are disturbed when EPA acts to use or disclose the data in a manner that was authorized by law at the time of the submission.

Monsanto argues that the statute's requirement that a submitter give up its property interest in the data constitutes placing an unconstitutional condition on the right to a valuable Government benefit. But Monsanto has not challenged the ability of the Federal Government to regulate the marketing and use of pesticides. Nor could Monsanto successfully make such a challenge, for such restrictions are the burdens we all must bear in exchange for "'the advantage of living and doing business in a civilized community.'" [Citations.] This is particularly true in an area, such as pesticide sale and use, that has long been the source of public concern and the subject of government regulation. That Monsanto is willing to bear this burden in exchange for the ability to market pesticides in this country is evidenced by the fact that it has continued to expand its research and development and to submit data to EPA despite the enactment of the 1978 amendments to FIFRA.

Thus, as long as Monsanto is aware of the conditions under which the data are submitted, and the conditions are rationally related to a legitimate Government interest, a voluntary submission of data by an applicant in exchange for the economic advantages of a registration can hardly be called a taking....

The situation may be different, however, with respect to data submitted by Monsanto to EPA during the period from October 22, 1972 through September 30, 1978. Under the statutory scheme then in effect, a submitter was given an opportunity to protect its trade secrets from disclosure by designating them as trade secrets at the time of submission.... But the statute also gave Monsanto explicit assurance that EPA was prohibited from disclosing publicly, or considering in connection with the application of another, any data submitted by an applicant if both the applicant and EPA determined the data to constitute trade secrets. Thus, with respect to trade secrets submitted under the statutory regime in force between the time of the adoption of the 1972 amendments and the adoption of the 1978 amendments, the Federal Government had explicitly guaranteed to Monsanto and other registration applicants an extensive measure of confidentiality and exclusive use. This explicit governmental guarantee formed the basis of a reasonable investment-backed expectation....

In summary, we hold that EPA's consideration or disclosure of data submitted by Monsanto to the agency prior to October 22, 1972, or after September 30, 1978, does not effect a taking. We further hold that EPA consideration or disclosure of health, safety, and environmental data will constitute a taking if Monsanto submitted the data to EPA between October 22, 1972 and September 30, 1978; the data constituted trade secrets under Missouri law; Monsanto had designated the data as trade secrets at the time of its submission; the use or disclosure conflicts with the explicit assurance of confidentiality or exclusive use contained in the statute during that period; and the operation of the arbitration provision does not adequately compensate for the loss in market value of the data that Monsanto suffers because of EPA's use or disclosure of the trade secrets.

We must next consider whether any taking of private property that may occur by operation of the data-disclosure and data-consideration provisions of FIFRA is a taking for a "public use." We have recently stated that the scope of the "public use" requirement of the Taking Clause is "coterminous with the scope of a sovereign's police powers." [Citations.] The role of the courts in second-guessing the legislature's judgment of what constitutes a public use is extremely narrow.

The District Court found that EPA's action pursuant to the data-consideration provisions of FIFRA would effect a taking for a private use, rather than a public use, because such action benefits subsequent applicants by forcing original submitters to share their data with later applicants. It is true that the most direct beneficiaries of EPA actions under the data-consideration provisions of FIFRA will be the later applicants who will support their applications by citation to data submitted by Monsanto or some other original submitter. Because of the data-consideration provisions, later applicants will not have to replicate the sometimes intensive and complex research necessary to produce the requisite data. This Court, however, has rejected the notion that a use is a public use only if the property taken is put to use for the general public. [Citations.]

... Congress believed that the provisions would eliminate costly duplication of research and streamline the registration process, making new end-use products available to consumers more quickly. Allowing applicants for registration, upon payment of compensation, to use data already accumulated by others, rather than forcing them to go through the time-consuming process of repeating the research, would eliminate a significant barrier to entry into the pesticide market, thereby allowing greater competition among producers of end-use products....

We therefore hold that any taking of private property that may occur in connection with EPA's use or disclosure of data submitted to it by Monsanto between October 22, 1972 and September 30, 1978, is a taking for a public use.

....

We find no constitutional infirmity in the challenged provisions of FIFRA. Operation of the provisions may effect a taking with respect to certain health, safety, and environmental data constituting trade secrets under state law and designated by Monsanto as trade secrets upon submission to EPA between October 22, 1972, and September 30, 1978. But whatever taking may occur is one for a public use, and a Tucker Act remedy is available to provide Monsanto with just compensation.... The judgment of the District Court is therefore vacated, and the case is remanded for further proceedings consistent with this opinion.

It is so ordered.

NOTES AND QUESTIONS

1. The mandatory licensing scheme in FIFRA which allows subsequent applicants to use previously submitted data from another registrant in exchange for compensation has created controversy since its inception in 1972. The principal criticism has been that the statutory program fails to adequately protect important information acquired at great cost by manufacturers, and therefore operates to stifle research and development of new products. In *Monsanto*, the Court determined that the company could not have had a reasonable investment-backed expectation of confidentiality with respect to data submitted under the pre-1972 and post-1978 versions of FIFRA. However, in the 1972-1978 period a company could have claimed the data to be trade secrets and thus shield its use from "me-too" registrants. This problem was partially alleviated by amendments to FIFRA which added "exclusive use" provisions which allow a registrant of a pesticide containing a new active ingredient to prevent the use of its supporting test data by other applicants for a period of ten years. 7 U.S.C. § 136a(c)(1)(D)-(i).

2. The *Monsanto* Court further determined that a taking could occur where reliance on data protection was a valid expectation. If a registrant believed that the compensation received pursuant to the statutory arbitration mechanism was insufficient, it could seek additional compensation from the United States under the Tucker Act, 28 U.S.C. § 1491 *et seq.* Where FIFRA's data-consideration and data-disclosure provisions constitute a taking of property, what available methodology or mechanism should the Court of Claims use to determine what is "just compensation" for original submitters like Monsanto? What type of evidence should be relevant to this issue?

3. One of the most troublesome aspects of the FIFRA mandatory data-sharing scheme is that it allows follow-on registrants to gain market entry faster than would otherwise be possible, thus removing some of the competitive advantage earned by the original registrant. Also, the later registrant avoids overhead costs of research and development which are expended for products which never prove to be commercially viable. For example, in *Monsanto* the District Court found that development costs of a commercial pesticide range between $5 and $15 million annually for several years, and may take 14 to 22 years to complete the development process. Monsanto, which had a significantly better than average success rate than the industry average, still only commercially marketed one out of every 10,000 chemicals it tested. In *Monsanto*, however, the Court justified the data-sharing system and elimination of barriers to market entry for follow-on registrants by noting that consumers benefitted by the streamlined procedure for introduction of new products and the resulting increase in competition among producers of commercial end-use pesticides. Is that a satisfactory rationale?

4. The trade-off for authorizing the use of test data to support later registrations is that FIFRA requires a follow-on registrant to compensate the original pesticide licensee for the use of test data in support of their application. In the event that the original data submitter and the applicant cannot reach an agreement regarding the terms of compensation, the statute provides that the dispute will be settled by binding arbitration. 7 U.S.C. § 136a (c)(1)(D)(ii). The statute does not specify any particular guidelines or formula which arbitrators are bound to follow in determining the amount of compensation. Instead, Congress decided to leave the decision regarding standards for assessing compensation to the discretion and expertise of the private arbitrators on a case-by-case basis. The lack of specific statutory standards allows for considerable flexibility to fashion awards to individualized circumstances, but it has also fostered sharp disagreement among the affected parties over the varying criteria used by arbitrators in practice. Several key issues of debate have involved whether to base compensation on the cost to produce the data or the value of the benefit to the subsequent applicant, allowances for research and development overhead, awards of royalties for future profits generated from sales of the pesticide, and whether test costs should be divided based on market share or a per capita basis. *See PPG Indus. v. Stauffer Chem. Co.*, 637 F. Supp. 85 (D.D.C. 1986) (court upheld arbitrator's compensation award which included a cost-sharing portion for developing the data relied upon in the application but also included a royalty for a ten-year period).

5. The binding arbitration mechanism of FIFRA for resolving compensation disputes among participants in the registration process was challenged in *Thomas v. Union Carbide Agrl. Prods. Co.*, 473 U.S. 568 (1985) as contravening Article III of the Constitution. Pesticide manufacturers claimed that FIFRA's arbitration scheme constituted an impermissible delegation of federal judicial power to arbitrators because they lacked the constitutional attributes of Article III judges, such as lifetime tenure, yet their decisions were subject to only limited judicial review. The Court upheld the constitutionality of the arbitration procedure, concluding that Congress, pursuant to its powers under Article I, could vest decisionmaking authority in tribunals other than Article III courts. Justice O' Connor, writing for the majority, observed:

> Looking beyond form to the substance of what FIFRA accomplishes, we note several aspects of FIFRA that persuade us the arbitration scheme adopted by Congress does not contravene Article III. First, the right created by FIFRA is not purely a "private right, but bears many of the characteristics of a "public" right. Use of a registrant's data to support a follow-on registration serves a public purpose as an integral part of a program safeguarding public health. Congress has the power, under Article I, to authorize an agency administering a complex regulatory scheme to allocate the costs and benefits among voluntary participants in the program without providing an Article III adjudication. It also has the power to condition an issuance of registrations or licenses on compliance with agency procedures. Article III is not so inflexible that it bars Congress from shifting the task of data evaluation from the agency to the interested parties.
>
> The 1978 amendments represent a pragmatic solution to the difficult problem of spreading the costs of generating adequate information regarding the safety, health, and environmental impact of a potentially dangerous product. Congress, without implicating Article III, could have authorized EPA to charge follow-on registrants fees to cover the cost of data and could have directly subsidized FIFRA data submitters for their contributions of needed data. Instead, it selected a framework that collapses two steps into one, and permits the parties to fix the amount of compensation, with binding arbitration to resolve intractable disputes. Removing the task of valuation from agency personnel to civilian arbitrators, selected by agreement of the parties or appointed on a case-by-case basis by an independent federal agency, surely does not diminish the likelihood of impartial decisionmaking, free from political influence.
>
> The near disaster of the FIFRA 1972 amendments and the danger to public health of further delay in pesticide registration led Congress to select arbitration as the appropriate method of dispute resolution. Given the nature of the right at issue and the concerns motivating the Legislature, we do not think this system threatens the independent role of the Judiciary in our constitutional scheme. [Citations omitted.]

473 U.S. at 593-94.

6. FIFRA provides for the issuance of experimental use permits (EUPs) by EPA to allow testing of unregistered chemicals or for the application of registered pesticides for an unapproved use. 7 U.S.C. § 136c. The grant of an EUP is limited to situations where the applicant needs to develop certain information in order to register a pesticide. Laboratory or greenhouse tests or limited field trials designed to determine a chemical's value for pesticide purposes or to ascertain its toxicity do not require an EUP, however. 40 C.F.R.

§ 172.3(a). Similarly, no EUP is required for substances or mixtures being tested to gather data supporting approval under the Federal Food, Drug, and Cosmetic Act. 40 C.F.R. § 172.3(d).

In *Rohm & Haas Co. v. EPA*, 525 F. Supp. 921 (E.D. Pa. 1981) the plaintiff corporation sought to prevent EPA from issuing an EUP to a competitor, Mobil Oil Corporation, for the purpose of conducting tests on a new pesticide product called "Tackle" it was developing. EPA had determined that an EUP should issue to Mobil based upon evaluation of test data supporting registration of a pesticide manufactured by Rohm & Haas, called "Blaze," which contained the same active ingredient. The plaintiff complained that reliance on its data to obtain the permit without its consent or compensation gave Mobil a "free ride." The court acknowledged that the generation of research and test data required the expenditure of significant resources, and that an EUP played an important part in the registration process. The court upheld EPA's action, though, by recognizing that FIFRA provided for compensation if the "me-too" registrant ultimately registered the pesticide in reliance on a prior data submitter's test results. Also, the court observed that Rohm & Haas would not sustain a competitive harm because an EUP did not permit its holder to market the pesticide. Do you agree that the plaintiff's interests were adequately protected in light of the court's interpretation of FIFRA?

7. In 1988 Congress amended FIFRA in several important respects to remedy perceived shortcomings with the registration scheme. One of the most significant features of the 1988 amendments required the reregistration of approximately 600 older pesticides (registered prior to 1984). Pesticides previously registered under less stringent testing standards must now be tested for health and safety considerations under current standards. Reregistration involves a complex five-phase, nine-year process which contemplates extensive evaluation of scientific data supporting registrations and additional testing to fill in gaps in information regarding the effects of the chemicals. 7 U.S.C. § 136a-1.

8. FIFRA currently does not regulate pesticide contamination of groundwater, despite serious concerns about the significant risks posed by such chemicals to human health and the environment. EPA has undertaken to fill the statutory gap on this issue by regulatory action which would place primary responsibility on states to implement a groundwater management plan. The agency's strategy contemplates protection levels based on the use of the groundwater, giving priority to protecting drinking water and fragile ecosystems. *See generally* Sater, *Pesticides-in-Groundwater Strategy: Agency Action in the Face of Congressional Inaction*, 17 ECOLOGY L.Q. 143 (1990); Day, *Integrated Pest Management: Towards a Greening of American Pesticide Policy*, 8 TEMPLE ENVTL. L. & TECH. J. 93 (1989); and Comment, *Carcinogen Roulette: The Game Played Under FIFRA*, 49 MD. L. REV. 975 (1990).

9. *Export.* FIFRA provides an exemption from registration for pesticides produced solely for export to a foreign country. 7 U.S.C. § 136o(a); 40 C.F.R. § 152.30(d). The rationale for exempting exports is that other countries can weigh the risks and benefits of pesticide usage in light of their own circumstances and needs. Fundamentally different considerations may be involved, for example, in evaluating the propriety of using a dangerous pesticide in an undeveloped Third World economy in contrast to application in a developed industrialized nation. *Environmental Defense Fund v. EPA*, 465 F.2d 528, 535 (D.C. Cir. 1972).

The exemption requires that the pesticide must meet certain labeling standards to avoid being misbranded and be produced by a registered establishment subject to the Act's record keeping and reporting requirements. Also, the foreign purchaser must sign a statement acknowledging restrictions on resale and distribution in the United States. Copies of the statement are then given to foreign government officials informing them that unregistered pesticides are being shipped to their country. FIFRA also provides that EPA, acting through the State Department, is obligated to notify governments of foreign countries and appropriate international organizations when a pesticide registration, cancellation, or suspension becomes effective or is terminated. 7 U.S.C. § 136o(b).

Imports of pesticides into the United States must comply with FIFRA. The Secretary of the Treasury, acting through the Customs Service, is required to notify EPA of the arrival of pesticides and will supply samples upon request of the agency. 7 U.S.C. § 136o(c). The pesticide may be denied entry into the country if EPA determines that the chemical is adulterated, misbranded, or otherwise in violation of the statute.

Substantial controversy has currently centered around the EPA's compliance efforts with the export provisions of FIFRA. The principal concern is that lax observation of the notification requirements may increase the danger to inhabitants of the foreign country and to citizens of the United States when the residue of harmful pesticides contaminates foods. The export of foodstuffs to the United States which exceed allowable tolerances perpetuates the "circle of poison" and undercuts the effectiveness of FIFRA's registration process.

B. CANCELLATION AND SUSPENSION

The registration process in FIFRA, as explored in the previous section, revolves around an agency determination that the pesticide will not present unreasonable adverse risks to human health or the environment when used appropriately. FIFRA contains several mechanisms designed to ensure that the public and environment continues to be protected from dangerous pesticides. The most important measures involve cancellation and suspension of registration of the pesticide.

The trigger for agency action to initiate proceedings to take a product off the market essentially mirrors the type of cost-benefit analysis involved in the original registration process. Complex scientific, technical, economic, and legal considerations are implicated in these determinations. Whether and to what extent EPA acts to cancel or suspend registration of a pesticide presents a difficult balancing of competing public interests. For example, a particular pesticide may prove extremely and uniquely effective at abating pests and diseases which would otherwise harm an important crop in a specific region of the country. What should EPA do, then, if evidence comes to light that application of the pesticide in normal usage may pose a more serious health problem than originally believed? If the farmers in that locale need to use the pesticide immediately in order to achieve a successful crop, should EPA wait for additional studies regarding the safety of the pesticide or issue an order removing the pesticide from the market? Thus, EPA faces a dilemma of imposing economic hardship on a certain segment of the population if it bans usage of the pesticide or risking adverse health effects on the public if it chooses to pursue a more restrained course of action. In addition, EPA must evaluate the health risks to farmworkers and the economic losses faced by manufacturers, dealers, and distributors of the pesticide. Resolution of these sorts of issues involves the relationship and utility of FIFRA's cancellation and suspension procedures.

Cancellation, despite its harsh name, actually is considered less drastic than suspension because it involves often protracted administrative proceedings before a pesticide is actually banned from shipment or use in interstate commerce. Suspension, on the other hand, may be used to remove pesticides more swiftly from the market upon a showing that the product constitutes an "imminent hazard" to man or the environment. The following materials will examine many of the complicated, multifaceted issues involved in pesticide cancellation and suspension proceedings under FIFRA.

NATIONAL COALITION AGAINST MISUSE OF PESTICIDES v. ENVIRONMENTAL PROTECTION AGENCY

867 F.2d 636 (D.C. Cir. 1989)

SILBERMAN, CIRCUIT JUDGE.

The Administrator of the Environmental Protection Agency appeals from an order of the district court permanently enjoining EPA from permitting "sales, commercial use and commercial application of existing stocks" of the termiticides chlordane and heptachlor pursuant to a settlement agreement under which the producers of the chemicals agreed to voluntary cancellation of the chemicals' registrations under the Federal Insecticide, Fungicide and Rodenticide Act ("FIFRA"), 7 U.S.C. §§ 136-136y (1982 & Supp. IV 1986). We think the district court misconstrued the relevant provisions of FIFRA by holding unlawful EPA's determination to permit continued sale and use of existing stocks of the cancelled termiticides. Accordingly, we reverse the district court and remand with instructions to vacate the injunction and thereby allow EPA to fulfill its commitments under the original settlements.

FIFRA provides a comprehensive framework for regulating the sale and distribution of pesticides within the United States. Under the statute, EPA may not approve a pesticide's introduction into commerce unless the Administrator finds that the pesticide "will not generally cause unreasonable adverse effects on the environment" when used in accordance with any EPA-imposed restriction and "with widespread and commonly recognized practice." 7 U.S.C. § 136a(c)(5)(D) (1982). "Unreasonable adverse effects on the environment" are defined to include "any unreasonable risk to man or the environment, taking into account the economic, social, and environmental costs and benefits of the use of any pesticide." § 136(bb). With few exceptions, FIFRA prohibits the sale, distribution, and professional use of unregistered pesticides. §§ 136a(a) & 136j(a)(1).

Once registered, pesticides are still subject to continuing scrutiny by EPA. Indeed, section 6 of FIFRA requires EPA to cancel a pesticide's registration after the first five years in which the registration has been effective (and at the conclusion of subsequent five year periods if the registration is renewed) "unless the registrant, or other interested person with the concurrence of the registrant, ... requests ... that the registration be continued in effect." § 136d(a). And at any time, EPA may propose cancellation of a registration and initiate elaborate cancellation proceedings if "it appears to the Administrator that a pesticide ... does not comply with [FIFRA] or ... generally causes unreasonable adverse effects on the environment...." § 136d(b).

During the pendency of cancellation proceedings, the registration remains in effect unless the Administrator "suspend[s] the registration of the pesticide immediately." § 136d(c). But before suspending, the Administrator must determine that an "imminent hazard" exists — that "continued use of the pesticide during the time required for cancellation proceedings[s] would be likely to result in unreasonable adverse effects on the environment...." § 136(*l*). Even then, FIFRA guarantees registrants the right to an expedited administrative hearing on that issue, and the pesticide's registration remains effective during this latter proceeding. § 136d(c)(2). Only if "the Administrator determines that an emergency exists that does not permit him to hold a hearing before suspending" may he prohibit commerce in the pesticide in advance of administrative proceedings. § 136d(c)(3).

While commerce in unregistered pesticides is generally prohibited, the Administrator may permit continued sale and use of existing stocks of pesticides whose registrations have been cancelled provided "he determines that such sale or use is not inconsistent with the purposes of this subchapter and will not have unreasonable adverse effects on the environment." § 136d(a)(1). It is this last provision — section 6(a)(1), concerning the disposition of existing stocks — that we are called upon to interpret today.

Chlordane and heptachlor (to which we refer simply as "chlordane") are part of a class of chlorinated hydrocarbon insecticides known generally as "cyclodienes," introduced into the marketplace for general use in the late 1940s and early 1950s. In recent years, the chemical has been sold and distributed both by chlordane's sole manufacturer, Velsicol Chemical Company, and a number of so-called "reformulator" companies who acquire chlordane from Velsicol and manufacture derivative products. Until 1987, Velsicol and the reformulators maintained various registrations for these products with EPA.

... [EPA entered into a settlement agreement] whereby Velsicol consented to cancellation of certain registered termiticide uses, to suspension of certain others pending the completion of outstanding "data call-ins," and to a cessation of all manufacture, distribution, and sale of chlordane. In exchange, EPA agreed to permit indefinitely the sale and use of existing stocks of chlordane outside the control of Velsicol, which EPA estimated to amount to a two-months' supply at normal application rates.

Upon publication of the settlement terms, plaintiffs [National Coalition Against the Misuse of Pesticides ("NCAMP")] amended their complaint and moved to restrain EPA from permitting any use of the existing stocks exempted from the EPA-Velsicol agreement, claiming that EPA had arbitrarily and capriciously failed to make the required FIFRA section 6(a)(1) determination that "continued sale and use of [those] existing stocks ... [would] not have unreasonable adverse effects on the environment." 7 U.S.C. § 136d(a)(1) (1982)....

The district court implicitly interpreted section 6(a)(1)[6] to require the Administrator, when he negotiates a voluntary cancellation agreement, to assume hypothetically that he has already issued a cancellation order before he considers the existing stocks question. If a cancellation order formally issued — if cancellation proceedings had concluded — then the Administrator, when he turned to the issue of the existing stocks, would have no reason to consider stock sales made during the pendency of litigation. Those sales or uses would have been accomplished and therefore beyond the regulatory power of the Administrator....

... [I]t is apparent that Congress drafted this provision without the notion of agency cancellation settlements in mind. Section 6(a)(1) does not explicitly contemplate an agreed-upon cancellation order. Rather, it refers only to automatic cancellations after five years' registration and to cancellations pursuant to section 6(b) after the Administrator initiates cancellation proceedings and conducts any requested hearings. 7 U.S.C. § 136d(a)(1) (1982). Since appellees do not deny that Congress implicitly authorized the Administrator to enter into such

---

[6]*(1) Procedure* — ... [T]he Administrator may permit the continued sale and use of existing stocks of a pesticide whose registration is canceled ... to such extent, under such conditions, and for such uses as he may specify if he determines that *such sale or use* is not inconsistent with the purposes of this subchapter and will not have unreasonable adverse effects on the environment.

7 U.S.C. § 136d(a)(1) (1982) (emphasis added). FIFRA further defines "unreasonable adverse effects on the environment" to mean:

(bb) Unreasonable adverse effects on the environment. — The term "unreasonable adverse effects on the environment" means any unreasonable risk to man or the environment, taking into account the economic, social, and environmental costs and benefits of the use of any pesticide.

§ 136(bb).

agreements, we conclude that Congress expressed no specific intent on the statutory construction issues before us. Neither the statutory language nor a single reference in the legislative history is directed to the subject of cancellation settlements. Under *Chevron* [*Chevron USA, Inc. v. NRDC*, 467 U.S. 837 (1984)], then, our responsibility is limited to asking whether the Administrator's construction is a permissible interpretation of the statute.

... If the Administrator were not authorized to enter into settlement agreements containing existing stocks exemptions, registrants would have every incentive to contest cancellation proceedings, both for the prospect of prevailing and to use litigation time to dispose, at minimum, of existing stocks.[7]

In construing statutes that authorize enforcement proceedings, we look with disfavor upon interpretations offered by parties, in opposition to the administering agency, that induce litigation by making settlement impracticable. [Citations.] Yet, this is precisely the sort of construction appellees advance.

Appellees contend that this litigation risk, which the Administrator avoids through settlement, is illusory. They emphasize that the proponent of continued registration bears the burden of persuasion as to whether a given chemical "generally causes unreasonable adverse effects on the environment." But this procedural rule — as important as it may be — hardly eliminates the litigation risk for the Administrator, when acting in his prosecutorial role. Nor do our cases holding that the Administrator satisfies his burden of production by proffering "substantial evidence" of harm from respected scientific sources mean that the Administrator is guaranteed victory if the proceedings are contested by the registrant and the ultimate order challenged subsequently in federal court. [Citations.] In any event, the Administrator *himself*, wearing his adjudicatory hat, might determine after an administrative hearing (involving the expenditure of substantial administrative resources) that scientific uncertainty as to the danger of a particular pesticide (combined perhaps with the economic impact of cancellation on "agricultural commodities, retail food prices and the agricultural economy,") indicates that the registration should not be cancelled.

We cannot see how the statutory purpose is enhanced by interpreting FIFRA's ambiguous language to force the Administrator to litigate aggressively, even where a settlement might avoid administrative costs, litigation imponderables and, perhaps most important, continued sales of the product during administrative proceedings. After all, the Administrator's charge under section 6(a)(1) is to determine whether permission to continue to sell or use existing stocks will have

---

[7]During cancellation proceedings, the registrant may continue producing the subject pesticide and distribute these additional stocks to consumers. Indeed, unless the registrant possesses facts concerning the unsuitability of the pesticide for registration which he is withholding from the Administrator, he has every incentive to persist in his production effort during the pending of cancellation proceedings. In most circumstances, upon final cancellation the Administrator will be obliged to indemnify the registrant in the amount of the production cost of the canceled pesticide in his possession at the time of cancellation. *See* 7 U.S.C. § 136m (1982).

an "*unreasonable* adverse effect" on the environment. § 136d(a)(1). If entering into a settlement provides for less use than would be the case if the Administrator initiated formal cancellation proceedings, it seems rather obvious that the settlement, at minimum, meets the statutory test of reasonableness.

Appellees argue that the Administrator's primary rationale for agreeing to the settlement terms — that more chlordane would have been sold and used during litigation than the small amount that the Administrator allowed to be disposed of as part of the settlement — is a red herring. The Administrator, it is contended, could have issued a notice of intent to cancel *and* proceeded immediately to a suspension order or an emergency order, either of which would have avoided the existing stocks problem. One obvious difficulty with the appellees' argument in this case, however, is that even a suspension order could not have been issued before a hearing was conducted (assuming one was requested), which we are told would likely have lasted six months. Only by use of a draconian emergency order would the Administrator have avoided a hearing delay....

... [T]he EPA reasonably reads the statute to provide different evidentiary thresholds for the three procedures the Administrator is authorized to pursue in defeating an existing registration. Accordingly, we think appellees incorrect in assuming that grounds which may support a cancellation notice automatically warrant the Administrator's recourse to FIFRA's summary procedures.

The language of the statute and the case law amply demonstrate that EPA's reading, even if arguably not compelled by the legislative text, is at least consistent with it. A notice of intent to cancel is called for if it "*appears* to the Administrator that a pesticide ... generally causes unreasonable adverse effects on the environment." 7 U.S.C. § 136d(b) (1982) (emphasis added). We have interpreted this standard as obliging the Administrator to issue such a notice "and thereby initiate the administrative process whenever there is a substantial question about the safety of a registered pesticide." [Citation.] That standard is perhaps even less rigorous than the typical "reason to believe" with which many agencies begin enforcement proceedings. [Citation.] Analytically, a notice of intent to cancel is little more than "a determination ... that adjudicatory proceedings will commence."

By comparison, the Administrator may issue a notice of suspension only if he determines it "is necessary to prevent an imminent hazard" to human health or the environment. 7 U.S.C. § 136d(c)(1) (1982). If the notice is contested, the Administrator must conduct an "expedited" hearing before the suspension can take effect. § 136d(c)(2). We have described that standard as calling for more than a mere "substantial question of safety"; it requires an appraisal that harm to humans or the environment "would be likely to result" during the period required for interagency consultation and cancellation hearings. § 136(*l*). The extraordinary step of emergency suspension is available only if the requisite unreasonable harm would be likely to materialize during the pendency of ordinary suspension proceedings. [Citations.] The Administrator therefore reasonably requires a showing of even more immediate harm before he may halt commerce in a pesticide prior to conducting often lengthy administrative proceedings.

From these different statutory standards it follows that the quality and quantity of evidence of harm to the environment that the Administrator properly requires before choosing one of these three procedural routes will vary along a continuum. The statute authorizes the Administrator to reserve expedited procedures for cases in which the available data reliably demonstrate some sort of immediate threat or where the information before him suggests greater certainty concerning the pesticide's danger to humans than would warrant merely initiating cancellation proceedings....

Under EPA's reasonable reading of the statute, then, the facts placed before the Administrator that might justify issuing a notice of intent to cancel may not necessarily justify suspension or emergency suspension procedures. Perhaps the most important variable in the Administrator's decision, one discounted by appellees, is the degree of certainty the scientific data provide as to the pesticide's danger. In cases such as ours, where the scientific data are uncertain and scientific opinion divided, we do not think Congress intended FIFRA to compel the Administrator to initiate expedited procedures.... Given the difference in these discrete standards, it follows that there is no statutory bar to the Administrator's permitting sale or use of existing stocks in return for a registrant's consent to cancel an active pesticide registration.

... We think the fundamental scientific question concerning the environmental effects of chlordane's termiticide uses was sufficiently unsettled to justify the Administrator's putative determination to seek only an ordinary cancellation. Under these circumstances, we believe it was reasonable for the Administrator to conclude that the settlement he reached, providing as it did for continued sale and use of existing stocks of chlordane, would involve the introduction of more moderate quantities of the chemical into the environment than would have been so if contested proceedings had ensued. Only an emergency suspension order would have resulted in less distribution than the settlement; the Administrator's determination that no emergency existed seems unassailable.

For the reasons stated, we reverse and remand with instructions to the district court to vacate its injunction so that EPA may fulfill the obligations it undertook in eliciting the cancellation settlements.

NOTES AND QUESTIONS

1. In the principal case the court recognized that deference to EPA judgment and expertise in reaching settlement terms advances the purposes of FIFRA by eliminating protracted delays, costs, and litigation risks associated with the cancellation process. Is this simply a reflection that courts may view voluntary cancellation settlements as generally the swiftest and most cost-effective means to protect human health and the environment? Does that justification lose some of its force in light of the emergency suspension provisions of the statute which are specifically intended to provide interim abatement pending resolution of the cancellation process? The court characterized emergency suspension orders as being "draconian," implying that such measures should be sparingly applied and one of last resort. Which approach more closely effectuates the goals of the Act? For a similar holding see *Northwest Food Processors Ass'n v. Reilly*, 886 F.2d 1075 (9th Cir. 1989).

2. In an important early opinion by Judge Leventhal, *Environmental Defense Fund v. EPA*, 465 F.2d 528 (D.C. Cir. 1972), the court addressed the relationship between the cancellation and suspension provisions of FIFRA. EPA issued notices of cancellation of several registered pesticides because of a "substantial question of safety" of the products. The agency did not, however, order an emergency suspension in the interim pending a final determination of the administrative decision on cancellation. The plaintiff environmental public interest organization challenged EPA's decision not to suspend registration, asserting that EPA failed to adequately identify and balance specific benefits of continued usage of the chemicals to offset the potential harms already identified in the cancellation notice.

The court stated that the "imminent hazard" standard for suspension orders was not limited to crisis situations. Instead, the court explained that suspension would be justified if there was a "substantial likelihood that serious harm will be experienced during the year or two required in any realistic projection of the administrative process." Accordingly, once EPA made a determination of harm by issuing a cancellation notice, it triggered responsibilities to evaluate the need for suspension as well. EPA could deny suspension in such instances either by identifying specific benefits of continued usage of the pesticide or by finding that the potential risks did not rise to the level of an imminent hazard. The court remanded for EPA to reexamine whether the projected benefits and harms in continued uses of the products, including the availability and feasibility of alternatives, necessitated an interim suspension order.

3. Judge Leventhal, writing for the court in *Environmental Defense Fund v. EPA*, also provided a thoughtful perspective on the role of courts supervising EPA actions under FIFRA:

> Our own responsibility as a court is as a partner in the overall administrative process — acting with restraint, but providing supervision. We cannot discharge our role adequately unless we hold EPA to a high standard of articulation. [Citation.] The EPA is charged with profoundly important tasks; reclamation and preservation of our environment is a national priority of the first rank. It is not an agency in the doldrums of the routine or familiar. The importance and difficulty of subject matter entail special responsibilities when the EPA undertakes to explain and defend its actions in court.
>
> ... Environmental law marks out a domain where knowledge is hard to obtain and appraise, even in the administrative corridors; in the courtrooms,

difficulties of understanding are multiplied. But there is a will in the courts to study and understand what the agency puts before us. And there is a will to respect the agency's choices if it has taken a hard look at hard problems. We emphasize again the judicial toleration of wide flexibility for response to developing situations.

465 F.2d at 540-41.

4. One of the most controversial provisions in FIFRA requires EPA to indemnify registrants and applicators holding unused stocks of suspended and canceled pesticides. Critics have alleged that the indemnification policy deters rigorous enforcement efforts by EPA since the agency would bear the financial costs of taking unsafe products off the market. In the 1988 amendments to FIFRA, the indemnity provisions were tightened by denying payments to pesticide registrants unless Congress approved a specific line item appropriation of funds. 7 U.S.C. § 136m(a)(4). Consumers may receive indemnification from the government's Judgment Fund instead of necessitating a specific appropriation. Dealers and distributors, on the other hand, will be reimbursed directly by the pesticide sellers in most circumstances. 7 U.S.C. § 136m(b). The amount of indemnification will be based on the cost of the pesticide owned by the person immediately prior to issuance of the suspension notice, limited by its fair market value. 7 U.S.C. § 136m(c). *See generally* Ferguson & Gray, *1988 FIFRA Amendments: A Major Step in Pesticide Regulation*, 19 ENVTL. L. REP. 10070 (1989); Comment, *FIFRA Lite: A Regulatory Solution or Part of the Pesticide Problem?*, 6 PACE ENVTL. L. REV. 615 (1989).

5. *CERCLA Exemption.* CERCLA provides a limited exemption from the recovery of response costs or damages resulting from the application of a pesticide product registered under FIFRA. *See* 42 U.S.C. § 9607(i). In *Redwing Carriers, Inc. v. Saraland Apts.*, 94 F.3d 1489, 1511 (11th Cir. 1996) the court held that a contractor was not liable under CERCLA for the disposal of pesticides that were properly registered at the time of treatment of property for termites. *Also see South Florida Water Mgmt. Dist. v. Montalvo*, 84 F.3d 402, 409 (11th Cir. 1996) (Section 108(i) would insulate landowners from liability for contamination resulting from application of pesticides to their property).

LOVE v. THOMAS

858 F.2d 1347 (9th Cir. 1988)

KOZINSKI, CIRCUIT JUDGE:

Farmers and food processors in the Pacific Northwest brought this lawsuit to enjoin the Environmental Protection Agency from suspending registrations of the pesticide dinoseb. Plaintiffs use products containing dinoseb or its salts in the cultivation of green peas, snap beans, cucurbits and caneberries....

The Federal Insecticide, Fungicide, and Rodenticide Act (FIFRA), 7 U.S.C.A. §§ 136-136y (1980 & Supp. 1987), establishes an elaborate framework for the regulation of pesticide use in the United States. No pesticide may be sold or distributed unless it is registered with the EPA. FIFRA §§ 3(a), 12(a)(1)(A), 7 U.S.C. §§ 136a(a), 136j(a)(1)(A). In order to register a pesticide, an applicant, who may be a manufacturer or user of the product, must demonstrate with sufficient scientific evidence that, "when used in accordance with widespread and commonly recognized practice [the pesticide] will not generally cause unreasonable adverse effects on the environment." FIFRA § 3(c)(5)(D), 7 U.S.C. § 136a(c)(5)(D). After a pesticide has been registered, the EPA Administrator must issue a notice of his intent to cancel its registration or change its classification "'whenever there is a substantial question about the safety of a registered pesticide.'" [Citations.]

Because cancellation or reclassification proceedings may take one or two years to complete, FIFRA authorizes the Administrator to suspend a pesticide's registration pending the outcome of the proceeding if he determines that suspension "is necessary to prevent an imminent hazard." FIFRA § 6(c)(1), 7 U.S.C. § 136d(c)(1). Absent an emergency, the Administrator may not issue a suspension order until he has done two things: (1) notified registrants of the pesticide that he intends to cancel the registration and that he will issue a suspension order based upon "findings pertaining to the question of 'imminent hazard,'" which he must include in the notice; and (2) given registrants an opportunity for an "expedited hearing" on "whether an imminent hazard exists." FIFRA § 6(c)(1), 7 U.S.C. § 136d(c)(1).

Dinoseb is a pesticide registered for use as an herbicide, insecticide, fungicide and desiccant, and has been used in the United States for nearly 40 years. It is applied primarily as a contact herbicide to control broadleaf weeds and as a desiccant on caneberries to suppress growth that would obstruct harvesting.
....

In the spring of 1986, the EPA developed doubts about the safety of dinoseb. Preliminary studies showed that dinoseb may cause serious health risks to persons exposed to it, including sterility in men and birth defects in the unborn children of pregnant women. In October 1986, the EPA began proceedings to cancel all dinoseb registrations. On October 7, the Administrator issued an emergency suspension order under section 6(c)(3) of FIFRA, 7 U.S.C. § 136d(c)(3), prohibiting the sale, distribution and use of dinoseb pending the completion of the cancellation proceedings....

[W]ith the growing season upon them, plaintiffs rushed into district court seeking relief from the EPA's suspension order. The growers' argument was quite straightforward: They simply could not grow their crops without dinoseb. Unlike farmers in other parts of the country, farmers in the Northwest have no substitutes for dinoseb. Climatic conditions and the prevalence of certain pests, black nightshade in particular, make dinoseb the only effective pesticide available on the market. For example, the farmers argued, without dinoseb there would be no caneberry crop in the Pacific Northwest, where 95 percent of the nation's commercial caneberry crop is grown. Potential crops losses would amount to $39.2 million this year.

... [The district court] then preliminarily enjoined enforcement of the suspension order pending completion of the EPA's cancellation proceedings, and allowed use of dinoseb subject to twelve conditions. The court permitted limited sales of dinoseb to growers of certain crops; prohibited uncertified applicators from using the pesticide; barred "[w]omen of child-bearing age, i.e., under the age of 45," from "any aspect of dinoseb application"; restricted the manner and extent of application of dinoseb to crops; and set standards for applicator clothing and exposure....

The EPA may only issue a suspension order if it determines that continued use of the pesticide during cancellation proceedings would pose an "imminent hazard." The statute defines that term as a situation where continued use "would be likely to result in unreasonable adverse effects on the environment or will involve unreasonable hazard to the survival of a species declared endangered or threatened...." FIFRA § 2(*l*) (amended 1973), 7 U.S.C. § 136(*l*). In turn, "unreasonable adverse effects on the environment" means "any unreasonable risk to man or the environment, taking into account *the economic, social, and environmental costs and benefits* of the use of any pesticide." FIFRA § 2(bb), 7 U.S.C. § 136(bb) (emphasis added). Before suspending all dinoseb registrations, the statute thus required the EPA to consider the benefits as well as the risks of its use, including the economic consequences of suspension.[16]

... The EPA's evaluation of the relevant factors under FIFRA was incomplete and rushed and, under the circumstances of this case, simply not adequate to justify the emergency suspension of plaintiffs' use of dinoseb.

First, the EPA gave itself insufficient time to comply with the statutory requirement that it balance risks and benefits....

Given [its] tight schedule, the EPA personnel responsible for evaluating the benefits of dinoseb never quite got around to studying plaintiffs' crops. The agency's standard methodology called for the staff to rank the various sites either by total acreage treated or by total pounds of dinoseb applied. With the information at hand, the EPA staff identified roughly 15 sites. Starting with the largest crops, soybeans, peanuts and potatoes, the staff was supposed to work its way down the list until no other usages could be identified. However, by the sixth and seventh sites, green peas and snap beans (each of which accounted for approximately 2 percent of total dinoseb usage in the United States), the EPA had to stop because it ran out of staff and resources. As economist Holtorf testified, "we flat ran out of resources when we got about halfway down the list which would be roughly peas and beans.... We have a relatively small staff in relation

---

[16]As the court held in *Dow Chem. Co. v. Blum*, 469 F. Supp. 892, 902 (E.D. Mich. 1979), the EPA should examine: "(1) The seriousness of the threatened harm; (2) The immediacy of the threatened harm; (3) The probability that the threatened harm would result; (4) Benefits to the public of the continued use of the pesticides in question during the suspension process; and (5) The nature and extent of the information before the Administrator at the time he made his decision."

to our work load, Your Honor. The Federal has been somewhat on a slide in terms of resources over the last few years."

....

In addition to limited data, the EPA conducted only a cursory evaluation of the availability of alternative pesticides and the consequent economic impact of suspension; it gave no particular attention to the Northwest at all....

In its own defense, the EPA argues that it ordered suspension on a nationwide basis, and was entitled to rely on nationwide findings as to alternatives and economic impact. For example, it found that only a third of the nation's green pea acreage and 20 percent of the snap bean acreage was treated with dinoseb. It therefore extrapolated the costs of suspension likely to be suffered by pea and bean farmers in such states as Wisconsin to all parts of the country and concluded there "would be a minor effect on a national basis." However, as the district court pointed out, there was no pressing need to enter an immediate nationwide ban on dinoseb: "The agency did have the power to suspend registration on a crop by crop and/or area by area basis." The suspension order was entered in October while the spraying season for the crops here at issue was not until the following March or April, some six months later. The EPA therefore had ample time to give the Northwest crops separate and careful attention.

There were good reasons for EPA to have done so. At the time it entered the order suspending dinoseb nationally, the EPA was aware that the Pacific Northwest was subject to unusual conditions that made reliance on national figures tenuous, if not completely arbitrary. For example, Northwest green pea farmers have to contend with black nightshade, a weed that produces a toxic berry about the same size as a pea. The agency was aware that dinoseb was the only pesticide effective against nightshade. Without dinoseb, farmers would be unable to keep nightshade out of the pea harvest, and processors would reject the crops infested with the toxic berries. [Citations.] Although the EPA knew that nightshade posed some problem, it did not follow up on this issue, nor did it specifically evaluate the impact of suspension on the Northwest region.

By extrapolating data from other regions, the EPA also did not consider, as it should have, the particular economic circumstances of farmers in the Pacific Northwest. For example, 95 percent of the commercial raspberry crop is grown in that region, and dinoseb is the only herbicide known to be effective as a chemical pruning agent in suppressing the primocane stage of raspberry growth; this "cane burning" increases crop yield and permits mechanical harvesting. The industry faces strong competition from Canadian producers across the Washington border, where dinoseb is permitted. Without dinoseb, the entire American raspberry crop might prove unprofitable.

In addition, specific crop effects, such as the loss of various caneberries and the contamination of green peas by black nightshade, could have tremendous secondary effects in the Northwest, none of which the EPA considered.... Should the caneberry, pea or bean crops fail or prove unmarketable because of the suspension, the effects might ripple through the Northwest agricultural sector. Buyers would establish sources of supply elsewhere; processor might find it unprofitable to maintain plants in the region without those key crops; producers of other, ancillary, crops may be unable to sell their harvests as well. The effect of crop losses growing from discontinued use of dinoseb thus could seriously harm the entire regional economy.

It may well be that, despite these dire economic effects, the suspension would be justified by the health risks to applicators and other farmworkers. Without any investigation of those economic effects, however, the EPA could not do even a rough and ready balancing.

The EPA claims that the health risks were equivalent for all crops, and that the need to act decisively in removing dangerous pesticides from use justifies its less than exhaustive inquiry at the emergency suspension stage. [Citation.] Complete review of all uses, it claims, is the proper function of the full cancellation proceedings. [Citation.] Because the Pacific Northwest sites represented a relatively small percentage of dinoseb use nationally, the EPA contends that it was not required to prepare a full evaluation of economic consequences.

With all due respect to the EPA and its overworked staff, such insensitivity to the local economic problems caused by its decision is unbecoming and inappropriate. Crop losses of over $39 million may look like small potatoes from Washington, D.C., but, as the district court found, such losses would cause very serious economic hardships to the people of the Northwest who would have to bear them. There may well be very minor uses that are of economically trivial importance and therefore need not be separately studied before a suspension order is entered.... The effects in the Northwest documented here surely do not fall into that category....

The EPA's inattention to the Northwest's special problems might nevertheless have been justified if there had been a genuine emergency that necessitated an immediate suspension of all dinoseb uses and foreclosed consideration of the problems faced by different regions of the country. However, the record does not document any particularly compelling circumstances requiring the EPA's haste. In order to issue a suspension order without notice and prior opportunity for a hearing, the EPA must first find that there is an emergency that justifies immediate suspension. FIFRA § 6(c)(3), 7 U.S.C. § 136d(c)(3)....

... By suspending first and asking questions later — if at all — the EPA acted without due regard to the commands of FIFRA. We therefore agree with the district court that the emergency suspension order was arbitrary and capricious, an abuse of discretion, and was not issued in accordance with the provisions of FIFRA.

....

NOTES AND QUESTIONS

1. The decision in *Love* that the emergency suspension order was arbitrary and capricious did not constitute the final determination regarding the uses of the herbicide dinoseb. There remained, of course, the ultimate issue concerning the cancellation of registration. In *Northwest Food Processors Ass'n v. Reilly*, 886 F.2d 1075 (9th Cir. 1989) the Ninth Circuit upheld a cancellation order which resulted from a voluntary settlement between EPA and the two remaining registrants contesting the proposed cancellation. The settlement agreement provided for cancellation of registrations, specified uses of existing stocks of dinoseb, and the indemnification of certain holders of dinoseb products. The agreement contained special provisions allowing limited use of remaining stocks of dinoseb on designated crops during the 1988 and 1989 growing seasons. This provision was favorably received by the court because it avoided the dire economic consequences that could arise in the Pacific Northwest from the immediate cancellation of the use of dinoseb on all crops.

2. In *Ciba-Geigy Corp. v. EPA*, 874 F.2d 277 (5th Cir. 1989) a pesticide manufacturer challenged EPA's decision to cancel the registration of the pesticide diazinon for use on golf courses and sod farms because of the agency's concern about the effects of the chemical on birds. The case centered on the meaning of the statutory language authorizing cancellation upon finding that the pesticide "generally causes unreasonable adverse effects on the environment." The plaintiff argued that the word "generally" meant that the purported harm was more likely than not to occur. EPA, on the other hand, contended that the cancellation test involved assessing the nature of the harm rather than evaluating the frequency that the risk might result in actual harm. The court adopted a middle-ground approach by stating that both the likelihood of occurrence and the seriousness of the injury were proper factors to take into account in the cancellation determination. The court explained:

> Because FIFRA defines "adverse effects" as "unreasonable risks," the Administrator need not find that use of a pesticide commonly causes undesirable consequences, but only that it commonly creates a significant probability that such consequences may occur. FIFRA therefore does not oblige the Administrator to maintain the registration of a pesticide that might not generally have adverse effects but, say killed children 30% of the occasions on which it was used. A 30% risk that children might be killed is plainly an "unreasonable risk" more than sufficient to justify cancellation of the noxious pesticide. Similarly, a significant risk of bird kills, even if birds are actually killed infrequently, may justify the Administrator's decision to ban or restrict diazinon use.

... If the use of diazinon creates an unreasonable risk of killing birds on only 10% of the golf courses on which it is used, for example, the Administrator should define the class of golf courses on which its use is to be prohibited more narrowly.

874 F.2d at 279-80. *Also see National Grain Sorghum Producers Assoc., Inc. v. EPA*, 1996 U.S. App. LEXIS 10867 (Scientific studies showing adverse effects of pesticide on birds in corn and rice fields supported inference by EPA of unreasonable adverse effects when used in sorghum fields to sufficient to justify denial of reinstatement of certain uses of pesticide).

3. In *Defenders of Wildlife v. EPA*, 882 F.2d 1294 (8th Cir. 1989) plaintiffs brought an action under the citizen suit provision of the Endangered Species Act seeking to enjoin certain uses of strychnine, a pesticide registered under FIFRA, as jeopardizing protected wildlife. The court noted that cancellation of registration of a pesticide must be brought exclusively under FIFRA. The court observed, however, that the EPA must comply with the Endangered Species Act in its administration of FIFRA. Accordingly, plaintiffs could indirectly force cancellation of registration outside the framework of FIFRA by prevailing on the merits of the claim against EPA pursuant to the Endangered Species Act.

4. FIFRA provides a cost allocation formula for the storage and disposal of suspended or canceled pesticides. Once a storage and disposal plan is submitted by the registrant, EPA will pay all the storage costs. 7 U.S.C. § 136q(c)(2)(B). When the plan is approved, EPA will share equally with the registrant the costs for one year. The registrant bears the costs of storage and disposal until the expiration of five years after approval of the plan, then the agency will incur twenty-five percent of such costs. 7 U.S.C. § 136q(c)(2)(E).

ENVIRONMENTAL DEFENSE FUND v. ENVIRONMENTAL PROTECTION AGENCY

548 F.2d 998 (D.C. Cir. 1976)

LEVENTHAL, CIRCUIT JUDGE.

This case involves the pesticides heptachlor and chlordane. Consolidated petitions seek review of an order of the Environmental Protection Agency (EPA) suspending the registration of those pesticides under the Federal Insecticide, Fungicide and Rodenticide Act (FIFRA) for certain uses. [The EPA suspended registration of the two pesticides during the pendency of the more involved cancellation of registration proceedings.] The Administrator of EPA issued an order on December 24, 1975. The order prohibited further production of these pesticides for the suspended uses, but permitted the pesticides' continued production and sale for limited minor uses. Even as to the suspended uses, the Order tempered its impact in certain respects: It delayed until August 1, 1976, the effective date of the prohibition of production for use on corn pests; and it permitted the continued sale and use of existing stocks of registered products formulated prior to July 29, 1975.

One petition to review was filed by Earl L. Butz, Secretary of Agriculture of the United States (U.S.D.A.). Secretary Butz and intervenor Velsicol Chemical Corporation, the sole manufacturer of heptachlor and chlordane, urge that the EPA order as to chlordane be set aside on both substantive and procedural grounds. They contend that substantial evidence does not support the Administrator's conclusion that continued use of chlordane poses an "imminent hazard" to human health, and that the Administrator made critical errors in assessing the burden of proof and in weighing the benefits against the risks of continued use of chlordane.

The other petition, filed by Environmental Defense Fund, urges that the Order did not go far enough to protect against the hazards of heptachlor and chlordane use. EDF sought an injunction against the provisions permitting continued production and use of the pesticides on corn pests until August 1, 1976. EDF also challenges the Administrator's decision to allow continued use of the stocks of the two pesticides existing as of July 29, 1975, contending that EPA should have provided for retrieval and controlled disposal of such stocks. EDF also contends that the Administrator erred in failing to suspend certain "minor uses" of chlordane and heptachlor.

....

The Administrator is authorized to suspend the registration of a pesticide where he determines that an "imminent hazard" is posed by continued use during the time required for cancellation. Section 6(c) of FIFRA, 7 U.S.C. § 136d(c)(1). An "imminent hazard" exists where continued use during the time required for the cancellation proceeding would be likely to result in "unreasonable adverse effects on the environment." Section 2(l) of FIFRA, 7 U.S.C. § 136(l). The term "unreasonable adverse effects on the environment" is, in turn, defined as "any unreasonable risk to man or the environment, taking into account the economic, social, and environmental costs and benefits of the use of any pesticide." Section 2(bb) of FIFRA, 7 U.S.C. § 136(bb).

... [T]he primary challenge raised by Velsicol and USDA goes to the adequacy of the evidentiary basis of EPA's finding that the suspended pesticides present an imminent hazard during the time required for cancellation....

To evaluate whether use of a pesticide poses an "unreasonable risk to man or the environment," the Administrator engages in a cost-benefit analysis that takes "into account the economic, social, and environmental costs and benefits of the use of any pesticide" 7 U.S.C. § 136(bb). We have previously recognized that in the "preliminary assessment of probabilities" involved in a suspension proceeding, "it is not necessary to have evidence on ... a specific use or area in order to be able to conclude on the basis of substantial evidence that the use of [a pesticide] in general is hazardous." [Citation.] "Reliance on general data, consideration of laboratory experiments on animals, etc." has been held a sufficient basis for an order cancelling or suspending the registration of a pesticide. Once risk is shown, the responsibility to demonstrate that the benefits outweigh the risks is upon the proponents of continued registration. Conversely, the statute places a "heavy burden" of explanation on an Administrator who decides to permit the continued use of a chemical known to produce cancer in experimental animals. Applying these principles to the evidence adduced in this case, we conclude that the Administrator's decision to suspend most uses of heptachlor and chlordane and not to suspend others is supported by substantial evidence and is a rational exercise of his authority under FIFRA.

A. *Risk Analysis — Carcinogenicity of Heptachlor and Chlordane*

Velsicol and USDA contend that the laboratory tests on mice and rats do not "conclusively" demonstrate that chlordane is carcinogenic to those animals; that mice are too prone to tumors to be used in carcinogenicity testing in any case; and that human exposure to chlordane is insufficient to create a cancer risk....

1. *Mice and Rat Studies*

An ultimate finding in a suspension proceeding that continued use of challenged pesticides poses a "substantial likelihood of serious harm" must be supported by substantial, but not conclusive, evidence. In evaluating laboratory animal studies on heptachlor and chlordane there was sufficient "respectable scientific authority" upon which the Administrator could rely in determining that heptachlor and chlordane were carcinogenic in laboratory animals.

... [T]he "cancer principles" EPA relied on in structuring its analysis of the mice and rat studies ... accept the use of animal test data to evaluate human cancer risks; consider a positive oncogenic effect in test animals as sufficient to characterize a pesticide as posing a cancer risk to man; recognize the negative results may be explained by the limited number and sensitivity of the test animals as compared to the general human population; note that there is no scientific basis for establishing a no-effect level for carcinogens; and view the finding of benign and malignant tumors as equally significant in determining cancer hazard to man given the increasing evidence that many "benign" tumors can develop into cancers.... Velsicol was properly given an opportunity to put in evidence contesting those principles, but failed to demonstrate anything more than some scientific disagreement with respect to them. Velsicol's principal complaint — that mice are inappropriate test animals — was specifically rejected by the Administrator, citing statements by [numerous scientific organizations]....

2. *Extrapolation of Animal Data to Man*

Human epidemiology studies so far attempted on chlordane and heptachlor gave no basis for concluding that the two pesticides are safe with respect to the issue of cancer. To conclude that they pose a carcinogenic risk to humans on the basis of such a finding of risk to laboratory animals, the Administrator must show a causal connection between the uses of the pesticides challenged and resultant exposure of humans to those pesticides. He made that link by showing that widespread residues of heptachlor and chlordane are present in the human diet and human tissues. Their widespread occurrence in the environment and accumulation in the food chain is explained by their chemical properties of persistence, mobility and high solubility in lipids (the fats contained in all organic substances). Residues of chlordane and heptachlor remain in soils and in air and aquatic ecosystems for long periods of time. They are readily transported by means vaporization, aerial drift, and run-off of eroding soil particles. The residues have been consistently found in meat, fish, poultry and dairy products monitored in the FDA Market Basket Survey and are also frequent in components of animal feeds. This evidence supports a finding that a major route of human exposure is ingestion of contaminated foodstuffs. EPA's National Human Monitoring Survey data shows that heptachlor epoxide and oxychlordane, the principal metabolites of heptachlor and chlordane respectively, are present in the adipose tissue of over 90% of the U.S. population.

The population's exposure to these pesticides, in large part involuntary, can be divided into agricultural and nonagricultural related routes. Seven million pounds of heptachlor and chlordane were used as corn soil insecticide in 1975, producing residues which persist in the soil for several years after application. These residues are taken up by such food, feed, and forage crops as soybeans, barley, oats, and hays typically rotated with corn. By volatilization the pesticides contaminate corn and other plant leaves. And root crops like potatoes, carrots and beets directly absorb the pesticides from the soil. Other sources of agricultural-related residues include exposure to contaminated dust particles and agricultural runoff containing eroded soil particles.

Velsicol urges that the dietary exposure resulting from agricultural uses of the pesticides is insignificant, and that current exposure is well below "safe" dose levels as calculated by the Mantel-Bryan formula, or by the World Health Organization's Acceptable Daily Intake figures. Mantel himself criticized the use of the formula for persistent pesticide, and the Administrator rejected the concept of a "safe" dose level defined by mathematical modeling because of "the incomplete assumptions made by the registrant's witnesses about the sources of human exposure in the environment, the natural variation in human susceptibility to cancer, the lack of any evidence relating the level of human susceptibility to cancer from heptachlor and chlordane as opposed to that of the mouse, and the absence of precise knowledge as to the minimum exposure to a carcinogen necessary to cause cancer." That explanation is within the reasonable bounds of the agency's expertise in evaluating evidence. And it is confirmed by the common sense recognition that reliance on average "safe" dietary levels fail to protect people with dietary patterns based on high proportional consumption of residue-contaminated foods (e.g., children who ingest greater quantities of milk than the general population).

There are several non-agricultural uses which involve a large volume of heptachlor and chlordane as well as significant human exposures. For example, the record shows that approximately six million pounds of chlordane are used annually on home lawns and gardens. The Administrator found that these uses involve high risks of human intake "due to the many avenues which exist for direct exposure, through improper handling and misuse, inhalation, and absorption through the skin from direct contact." Velsicol asserts that the mice studies showing carcinogenic effects after ingestion of chlordane do not warrant an inference about the carcinogenic effects of inhaling it or absorbing it through the skin, and that consequently nonagricultural routes of exposure cannot be considered to present a cancer risk.... [T]he FIFRA statutory scheme mandates explicit relief — the suspension of registration — when an unreasonable risk to health is made out. We have previously held that it is not necessary to have evidence on a specific use to be able to conclude that the use of a pesticide in general is hazardous. Once the initial showing of hazard is made for one mode of exposure in a suspension proceeding, and the pesticide is shown to present in human tissues, the burden shifts to the registrant to rebut the inference that other modes of exposure may also pose a carcinogenic hazard for humans. Velsicol has totally failed to meet that burden here. Although it was put on notice in the Notice to Suspend of EPA's intent to rely on direct inhalation and dermal exposure as reasons to suspend household lawn and turf uses of chlordane, it failed to offer even a medical theory as to why the significant inhalation or dermal exposure associated with such uses would *not* pose a carcinogenic threat.... Nor did Velsicol focus on the individual user's intense inhalation exposure associated with lawn and turf uses in its response to the point made in the EPA Staff's exceptions to the ALJ recommended decision, that the evidence showed that an individual using these chemicals for lawn and turf applications is subjected to a marked intensity of inhalation. Instead Velsicol attacked as inconsistent with the minimal amounts of chlordane and heptachlor normally found in ambient air, the EPA Staff's proposed reliance on inhalation as a major route of human exposure for the general population. However, the Administrator did not proceed on this basis. And if Velsicol hypothesized that chlordane residues are safe so long as they reach the tissue only through inhalation (even intense inhalation) it should have presented witnesses expressing that hypothesis. Instead they argue, in general and procedural terms, that the evidence presented by the Administrator was not sufficient to meet his full burden, and this in our view seeks to impose a broader burden on the Administrator than is appropriate in a suspension proceeding.

....

[The suspension order was affirmed.]

NOTES AND QUESTIONS

1. Did the court's decision reflect some sense of the magnitude and complexity of the regulatory issues facing EPA during a suspension proceeding? The "imminent hazard" test for suspension reflects a preliminary assessment of the relative potential risks and benefits. It functions, then, like an interlocutory injunction by evaluating probabilities, rather than a final resolution of competing scientific evidence. Does the court's analysis unduly focus on safety concerns at the expense of vital economic and social interests associated with the manufacture and sale of the pesticides heptachlor and chlordane? Can the court's deference to EPA's interpretation of certain scientific studies be reconciled with the approach taken in *Love v. Thomas*?

2. Does the court's treatment of the evidentiary burdens and requirements reflect a strong desire to prevent future harm to humans from uncertain, but possibly substantial, health risks during the period required for a cancellation proceeding? In other words, is the court willing to err on the side of public safety in a suspension proceeding in the absence of medical or scientific proof by the registrant demonstrating that the product is safe? If so, is that approach consistent with the policies underlying FIFRA?

3. One court recently noted that the regulatory scope of FIFRA encompasses approximately 40,000 chemicals or mixtures of substances used as pesticides. *Arkansas Platte & Gulf Pt'ship v. Van Waters*, 748 F. Supp. 1474 (D.C. Colo. 1990). When *Environmental Defense Fund v. EPA* was decided in 1976, the regulatory burden may not have been as massive, but it was perhaps sufficiently burdensome to have an adverse impact upon EPA's ability to meet its statutory responsibilities under FIFRA to protect public health and the environment.

Part VI.

Environmental Regulation of Land Use

Chapter 12

PROTECTION OF CRITICAL RESOURCES THROUGH LAND USE CONTROLS

INTRODUCTION

Throughout the 1970s Congress repeatedly confronted and rejected any measures that even approximated what could be considered federal land use controls. From 1970 to 1975, approximately forty national land use bills that would have established planning procedures for states supported by federal funding were rejected by one or both houses of Congress, even though the proposals would have left the actual planning process to the states. *See, e.g.*, Reilly, *Transformation at Work: The Effect of Environmental Law on Land Use Control*, 24 REAL PROPERTY, PROBATE & TRUST J. 33 (1989). The entrenched political resistance to "federal zoning" ignored the fact that the federal government had been involved in land use regulation since the 1700s. R. HYMAN, NATIONAL LAND USE POLICY LEGISLATION: A BIBLIOGRAPHY (1979). *See generally* Johnson, *Land Use Planning and Control by the Federal Government*, in NO LAND IS AN ISLAND 75 (1975); N. LYDAY, THE LAW OF THE LAND: DEBATING NATIONAL LAND USE LEGISLATION 1970-75 (1976); C. LAMB, LAND USE POLITICS AND LAW IN THE 1970'S 36-54 (1975). Even while efforts for a national land use policy were failing in Congress, federal legislation was "federalizing" land use controls. A. REITZE, ENVIRONMENTAL PLANNING: LAW OF LAND AND RESOURCES 1-10 (1974). To avoid the appearance of federal zoning, even the most expansive federal programs affecting land use were limited to funding of state or local programs for land use regulation in accordance with federal standards or withdrawal of federal funding for environmentally destructive activities. Hagman, *A New Deal: Trading Windfalls for Wipeouts*, in NO LAND IS AN ISLAND 169, 173 (1975).

The modern era of state and local government involvement in land use can be traced to the issuance in 1922 by the United States Department of Commerce of the Standard State Zoning Enabling Act, U.S. Department of Commerce, Advisory Committee on Zoning, A Standard State Zoning Enabling Act (rev. ed. 1926), as a model for state delegation of zoning powers, and the 1926 decision of the Supreme Court in *Village of Euclid v. Ambler Realty Co.*, 272 U.S. 365 (1926), upholding the constitutionality of comprehensive zoning. These two events would lead to virtually exclusive control of land use by local governments for nearly fifty years. The counter-revolution in land use was first recognized in 1971 in a seminal book, F. BOSSELMAN & D. CALLIES, THE QUIET REVOLUTION IN LAND USE CONTROL (1971). In that book, the authors illuminated a growing trend in which state legislatures were reallocating land use authority from local governments to regional and statewide entities. This trend was reflected in the American Law Institute's Model Land Development Code (Proposed Official Draft 1975). Adopted in 1975, the Code was the result of a twelve-year study of the Standard Zoning Enabling Act, the Standard City Planning Enabling Act, and state legislation based upon the acts. Article seven of the Model Code provides for an expanded state role in land use regulation through state review of local decisionmaking in critical areas and of major developments. Although the United States Senate passed the Land Use Policy and Planning Assistance Act of 1973, S. 268, 93d Cong., 1st Sess. (1973), based roughly on article seven of the Code, the legislation did not pass in the House of Representatives. The Act would have provided federal funding to states regulating areas of critical state concern, developments of regional benefit, large-scale development, and areas impacted by key facilities such as major airports and highway interchanges.

Undeniably the dissatisfaction with local regulation was in part due to social problems created by fragmented, uncoordinated growth controls. Yet it is questionable whether this quiet revolution would have taken place without the environmental awareness of the late 1960s and 1970s. The growing sophistication in the science of ecology in this period directly led to an understanding of the need for regional and state controls to protect an entire ecosystem. The shift in the concept of property-as-commodity to property-as-resource necessitated a fundamental rethinking of the ultimate goals of all land use regulation. To their credit, states as well as local governments continued to experiment with innovative land use techniques. A number of states adopted legislation based on article seven of the Model Code to protect critical areas and regulate developments of regional impact or benefit. State and regional regulation in most states did not usurp local zoning powers so much as create an additional layer of regulation or oversight for local decisionmaking in accordance with the Model Code approach. Within such a framework, local governments increasingly utilized methods such as planned unit developments, open space zoning, and transferable development rights to preserve natural resources and protect environmental values. *See generally* Callies, *The Quiet Revolution Revisited: A Quarter Century of Progress*, 26 URB. LAW. 197 (1994); Wickersham, *The Quiet Revolution Continues: The Emerging New Model for the State Growth Management Statutes*, 18 HARV. ENVTL. L. REV. 489 (1994); Porter, *Do State Growth Management Acts Make a Difference? Local Growth Management Measures Under Different State Growth Policies*, 24 LOY. L.A. L. REV. 1015 (1991).

Land use controls utilized to improve the quality of air and water resources are discussed within the chapters on federal regulation of air, water, and hazardous waste. This chapter focuses on land use regulation of critical resources to preserve them in their natural state or to limit their development. In no other area of environmental law or land use law are the conflicts so stark, the stakes so high, and the issues so complex. When land use controls become necessary to preserve a critical resource, frequently nothing less than a complete ban on further development can ensure preservation. The legal issues then posed do not involve how much development is permissible, but whether development is permissible at all. It is not surprising, therefore, that the most significant cases under the takings clause in recent years have involved land use regulation to protect the environment. The intensity of the conflict between land development and environmental preservation is further complicated by the uncertainty of what constitutes a "taking," the proliferation of environmental statutes, and the fragmentation of land use regulation among federal, state, and local governments. Even the simplest development project can be subject to an assortment of legal requirements that are at best bewildering and at worst unfathomable to attorneys without substantial experience in both land use and environmental regulation. *See generally* Stone & Seymour, *Regulatinig the Timing of Development: Takings Clause and Substantive Due Process Challenges to Growth Control Regulations*, 24 LOY. L.A. L. REV. 1205 (1991).

A. COASTAL ZONE MANAGEMENT

In 1972, Congress passed the Coastal Zone Management Act (CZMA). The passage of the CZMA created a great sense of achievement in many different quarters because for the first time Congress had declared a national interest in land use decisions previously viewed as local in nature. The CZMA acknowledged that a rapidly growing population endangered the fragility and beauty of the coastal zone. The United States' coastal zone is rich in resources used for transportation, food, water, dilution of waste, and aesthetics. The coastal zone acts as a buffer zone for dispersion of pollutants and sediments. The coasts offer attractive areas for homes and recreation, and are often the site of major ports and industry. Approximately 70% of the total United States commercial fisheries catch consists of species that are dependent upon estuarine environments in their life cycle, and an even greater percentage of the recreational catch is dependent on estuaries. Coastal Zone Management: Hearing before the Nat'l Ocean Pol'y Study of the Comm. on Commerce, Science, and Transp. of the Senate, 100th Cong., 1st Sess. 38, 45, 73 (1987).

These resource values of the coastal zone depend upon preservation of the various coastal zones' natural character. Yet fifty-three percent of the United States' population lives in counties within fifty miles of the coastline or the Great Lakes. *Nat'l Oceanic and Atmospheric Admin., U.S. Dep't of Commerce, The Federal Coastal Programs Review, A Report to the President* (1981). In addition, the United States has jurisdiction and control over 1.8 million square miles of continental shelf and slope under which enormous amounts of energy resources exist. It has been estimated that at least 3.5 billion cubic feet of gas reserves are offshore. Grosso, *Federal Offshore Leasing: States' Concerns Fall on Deaf Ears*, 2 FLA. ST. J. OF LAND USE & ENVTL. L. 249, 250 (1986). Development in the coastal zone could, however, result in toxic contamination, eutrophication, contamination by human pathogens, loss and alteration of habitats critical to living resources, and alterations to circulation and freshwater inflow. In addition, the so-called "greenhouse effect," a steady increase in carbon dioxide in the earth's atmosphere, threatens a rise in global sea level of one to three feet in the next seventy years from the accompanying global climate warming. As a result, the quality of the coastal environment is on the decline. *Hearing, supra*, at 46-47.

Generally, the purpose of the CZMA is to preserve the unique values of coastal lands and waters by encouraging states to devise land and water use plans for coastal protection. The Act provides funds to states that develop programs for management of land and water uses consistent with the Act's standards. The Secretary of Commerce must approve these programs upon finding that they satisfy the requirements of sections 305 and 306 of the CZMA. After approval, the Secretary must award grants to the state for the costs of administration of the approved state management program. 16 U.S.C. §§ 1454-1455. In addition to the grants states obtain for having an approved program, states also benefit from the requirement that federal agencies, permittees, and licensees must show that their proposed developments, including certain oil and gas activities on the outer continental shelf, are consistent with the state's management program. *Id.* § 1456(c).

The CZMA defines "coastal zones" as

> the coastal waters (including the lands therein and thereunder) and the adjacent shorelands (including the waters therein and thereunder), strongly influenced by each other and in proximity to the shorelines of the several coastal states, [which] includes islands, transitional and intertidal areas, salt marshes, wetlands, and beaches.

Id. § 1453(1). In 1990 the definition was amended to limit the seaward boundary to the extent of state ownership and title under the Submerged Lands Act, 43 U.S.C. §§ 1301-1356. The zone now extends inland "to the extent necessary to control shorelands, the uses of which have a direct and significant impact on the coastal waters, and to control those geographical areas which are likely to be affected by or vulnerable to sea level rise." Coastal Zone Act Reauthorization Act Amendments of 1990, Pub. L. No. 101-508, § 6204, 104 Stat. 1388, 1388 (codified as amended at 16 U.S.C. § 1453(1)). To paraphrase, the coastal zone consists of the land affected by the waters and the waters affected by the land. The definition of the coastal zone is purposefully vague, giving states great discretion in setting their own jurisdiction. This discretion is necessary since different types of areas, developed and undeveloped, may exist within a single state's coastal zone.

Excluded from the definition of coastal zone is land "the use of which is by law solely subject to the discretion of or which is held in trust by the Federal government, its officers or agents." In the following case, the Supreme Court sought to clarify state authority over federal lands within the coastal zone.

CALIFORNIA COASTAL COMMISSION v. GRANITE ROCK CO.

480 U.S. 572 (1987)

JUSTICE O'CONNOR delivered the opinion of the Court.

This case presents the question whether Forest Service regulations, federal land use statutes and regulations, or the Coastal Zone Management Act of 1972 (CZMA), 16 U.S.C. § 1451 *et seq.* pre-empt the California Coastal Commission's imposition of a permit requirement on operation of an unpatented mining claim in a national forest.

I

Granite Rock Company is a privately owned firm that mines chemical and pharmaceutical grade white limestone. Under the Mining Act of 1872, 17 Stat. 91, as amended, 30 U.S.C. § 22 *et seq.*, a private citizen may enter federal lands to explore for mineral deposits. If a person locates a valuable mineral deposit on federal land, and perfects the claim by properly staking it and complying with other statutory requirements, the claimant "shall have the exclusive right of possession and enjoyment of all the surface included within the lines of their locations," 30 U.S.C. § 26, although the United States retains title to the land. The holder of a perfected mining claim may secure a patent to the land by complying with the requirements of the Mining Act and regulations promulgated thereunder, and, upon issuance of the patent, legal title to the land passes to the patent holder. Granite Rock holds unpatented mining claims on federally owned lands on and around Mount Pico Blanco in the Big Sur region of Los Padres National Forest.

From 1959 to 1980, Granite Rock removed small samples of limestone from this area for mineral analysis. In 1980, in accordance with federal regulations, Granite Rock submitted to the Forest Service a five-year plan of operations for the removal of substantial amounts of limestone. The plan discussed the location and appearance of the mining operation, including the size and shape of excavations, the location of all access roads, and the storage of any overburden. The Forest Service prepared an Environmental Assessment of the plan. The Assessment recommended modifications of the plan, and the responsible Forest Service Acting District Ranger approved the plan with the recommended modifications in 1981. Shortly after Forest Service approval of the modified plan of operations, Granite Rock began to mine.

Under the California Coastal Act (CCA), Cal. Pub. Res. Code Ann. § 30000 *et seq.*, any person undertaking any development, including mining, in the State's coastal zone must secure a permit from the California Coastal Commission. According to the CCA, the Coastal Commission exercises the State's police power and constitutes the State's coastal zone management program for purposes of the federal CZMA. In 1983 the Coastal Commission instructed Granite Rock to apply for a coastal development permit for any mining undertaken after the date of the Commission's letter.

Granite Rock immediately filed an action in the United States District Court for the Northern District of California seeking to enjoin officials of the Coastal Commission from compelling Granite Rock to comply with the Coastal Commission permit requirement and for declaratory relief. Granite Rock alleged that the Coastal Commission permit requirement was preempted by Forest Service regulations, by the Mining Act of 1872, and by the CZMA....

....

III

Granite Rock does not argue that the Coastal Commission has placed any particular conditions on the issuance of a permit that conflict with federal statutes or regulations. Indeed, the record does not disclose what conditions the Coastal Commission will place on the issuance of a permit. Rather, Granite Rock argues, as it must given the posture of the case, that there is no possible set of conditions the Coastal Commission could place on its permit that would not conflict with federal law — that any state permit requirement is per se pre-empted. The only issue in this case is this purely facial challenge to the Coastal Commission permit requirement.

The Property Clause provides that "Congress shall have Power to dispose of and make all needful Rules and Regulations respecting the Territory or other Property belonging to the United States." U.S. Const., Art. IV, § 3, cl. 2. This Court has "repeatedly observed" that "'[t]he power over the public land thus entrusted to Congress is without limitations.'" [Citation.] Granite Rock suggests that the Property Clause not only invests unlimited power in Congress over the use of federally owned lands, but also exempts federal lands from state regulation whether or not those regulations conflict with federal law.... We agree with Granite Rock that the Property Clause gives Congress plenary power to legislate the use of the federal land on which Granite Rock holds its unpatented mining claim. The question in this case, however, is whether Congress has enacted legislation respecting this federal land that would pre-empt any requirement that Granite Rock obtain a California Coastal Commission permit. To answer this question we follow the pre-emption analysis by which the Court has been guided on numerous occasions:

> [S]tate law can be pre-empted in either of two general ways. If Congress evidences an intent to occupy a given field, any state law falling within that field is pre-empted. [Citation.] If Congress has not entirely displaced state regulation over the matter in question, state law is still pre-empted to the extent it actually conflicts with federal law, that is, when it is impossible to comply with both state and federal law, [citation] or where the state law stands as an obstacle to the accomplishment of the full purposes and objectives of Congress. [Citation.]

Granite Rock and the Solicitor General as *amicus* have made basically three arguments in support of a finding that any possible state permit requirement would be pre-empted. First, Granite Rock alleges that the Federal Government's environmental regulation of unpatented mining claims in national forests demonstrates an intent to pre-empt any state regulation. Second, Granite Rock and the Solicitor General assert that indications that state land use planning over unpatented mining claims in national forests is pre-empted should lead to the conclusion that the Coastal Commission permit requirement is pre-empted. Finally, Granite Rock and the Solicitor General assert that the CZMA, by excluding federal lands from its definition of the coastal zone, declared a legislative intent that federal lands be excluded from all state coastal zone regulation. We conclude that these federal statutes and regulations do not, either independently or in combination, justify a facial challenge to the Coastal Commission permit requirement.

....

Upon examination, however, the Forest Service regulations that Granite Rock alleges pre-empt any state permit requirement not only are devoid of any expression of intent to pre-empt state law, but rather appear to assume that those submitting plans of operations will comply with state laws. The regulations explicitly require all operators within the national forests to comply with state air quality standards, 36 CFR § 228.8(a) (1986), state water quality standards, § 228.8(b), and state standards for the disposal and treatment of solid wastes, § 228.8(c). The regulations also provide that, pending final approval of the plan of operations, the Forest Service officer with authority to approve plans of operation "will approve such operations as may be necessary for timely compliance with the requirements of Federal and *State laws....*" § 228.5(b) (emphasis added). Finally, the final subsection of § 228.8, "[r]equirements for environmental protection," provides:

> "(h) Certification or other approval issued by *State agencies* or other Federal agencies of compliance with laws and regulations relating to mining operations will be accepted as compliance with similar or parallel requirements of these regulations." (emphasis supplied).

It is impossible to divine from these regulations, which expressly contemplate coincident compliance with state law as well as with federal law, an intention to pre-empt all state regulation of unpatented mining claims in national forests. Neither Granite Rock nor the Solicitor General contends that these Forest Service regulations are inconsistent with their authorizing statutes.

....

The second argument proposed by Granite Rock is that federal land management statutes demonstrate a legislative intent to limit States to a purely advisory role in federal land management decisions, and that the Coastal Commission permit requirement is therefore pre-empted as an impermissible state land use regulation.

In 1976 two pieces of legislation were passed that called for the development of federal land use management plans affecting unpatented mining claims in national forests. Under the Federal Land Policy and Management Act of 1976 (FLPMA), 90 Stat. 2744, 43 U.S.C. § 1701 *et seq.*, the Department of the Interior's Bureau of Land Management is responsible for managing the mineral resources on federal forest lands; under the National Forest Management Act (NFMA), 90 Stat. 2949, 16 U.S.C. §§ 1600-1614, the Forest Service under the Secretary of Agriculture is responsible for the management of the surface impacts of mining on federal forest lands. Granite Rock, as well as the Solicitor General, point to aspects of these statutes indicating a legislative intent to limit States to an advisory role in federal land management decisions. For example, the NFMA directs the Secretary of Agriculture to "develop, maintain, and, as appropriate, revise land and resource management plans for units of the National Forest System, coordinated with the land and resource management planning processes of State and local governments and other Federal agencies," 16 U.S.C. § 1604(a). The FLPMA directs that land use plans developed by the Secretary of the Interior "shall be consistent with State and local plans to the maximum extent [the Secretary] finds consistent with Federal law," and calls for the Secretary, "to the extent he finds practical," to keep apprised of state land use plans, and to "assist in resolving, to the extent practical, inconsistencies between Federal and non-Federal Government plans." 43 U.S.C. § 1712(c)(9).

For purposes of this discussion and without deciding this issue, we may assume that the combination of the NFMA and the FLPMA pre-empts the extension of state land use plans onto unpatented mining claims in national forest lands. The Coastal Commission asserts that it will use permit conditions to impose environmental regulation.

While the CCA gives land use as well as environmental regulatory authority to the Coastal Commission, the state statute also gives the Coastal Commission the ability to limit the requirements it will place on the permit.... In the present case, the Coastal Commission has consistently maintained that it does not seek to prohibit mining of the unpatented claim on national forest land. [Citation.]

The line between environmental regulation and land use planning will not always be bright; for example, one may hypothesize a state environmental regulation so severe that a particular land use would become commercially impracticable. However, the core activity described by each phrase is undoubtedly different. Land use planning in essence chooses particular uses for the land; environmental regulation, at its core, does not mandate particular uses of the land but requires only that, however the land is used, damage to the environment is kept within prescribed limits. Congress has indicated its understanding of land use planning and environmental regulation as distinct activities. As noted above, 43 U.S.C. § 1712(c)(9) requires that the Secretary of the Interior's land use plans be consistent with state plans only "to the extent he finds practical." The immediately preceding subsection, however, requires that the Secretary's land use plans "provide for compliance with applicable pollution control laws, including State and Federal air, water, noise, or other pollution standards or implementation plans." § 1712(c)(8).... Congress clearly envisioned that although environmental regulation and land use planning may hypothetically overlap in some instances, these two types of activity would in most cases be capable of differentiation. Considering the legislative understanding of environmental regulation and land use planning as distinct activities, it would be anomalous to maintain that Congress intended any state environmental regulation of unpatented mining claims in national forests to be *per se* pre-empted as an impermissible exercise of state land use planning. Congress' treatment of environmental regulation and land use planning as generally distinguishable calls for this Court to treat them as distinct, until an actual overlap between the two is demonstrated in a particular case.

Granite Rock suggests that the Coastal Commission's true purpose in enforcing a permit requirement is to prohibit Granite Rock's mining entirely. By choosing to seek injunctive and declaratory relief against the permit requirement before discovering what conditions the Coastal Commission would have placed on the permit, Granite Rock has lost the possibility of making this argument in this litigation. Granite Rock's case must stand or fall on the question whether *any possible* set of conditions attached to the Coastal Commission's permit requirement would be pre-empted. As noted in the previous section, the Forest Service regulations do not indicate a federal intent to pre-empt all state environmental regulation of unpatented mining claims in national forests. Whether or not state land use planning over unpatented mining claims in national forests is pre-empted, the Coastal Commission insists that its permit requirement is an exercise of environmental regulation rather than land use planning. In the present posture of this litigation, the Coastal Commission's identification of a possible set of permit conditions not pre-empted by federal law is sufficient to rebuff Granite Rock's facial challenge to the permit requirement. This analysis is not altered by the fact that the Coastal Commission chooses to impose its environmental regulation by means of a permit requirement. If the Federal Government occupied the field of environmental regulation of unpatented mining claims in national forests — concededly not the case — then state environmental regulation of Granite Rock's mining activity would be pre-empted, whether or not the regulation was implemented through a permit requirement. Conversely, if reasonable state environmental regulation is not pre-empted, then the use of a permit requirement to impose the state regulation does not create a conflict with federal law where none previously existed. The permit requirement itself is not talismanic.

Granite Rock's final argument involves the CZMA, 16 U.S.C. § 1451 *et seq.*, through which financial assistance is provided to States for the development of coastal zone management programs.

Granite Rock argues that the exclusion of "lands the use of which is by law subject solely to the discretion of or which is held in trust by the Federal Government, its officers or agents" excludes all federally owned land from the CZMA definition of a State's coastal zone, and demonstrates a congressional intent to pre-empt any possible Coastal Commission permit requirement as applied to the mining of Granite Rock's unpatented claim in the national forest land.

According to Granite Rock, because Granite Rock mines land owned by the Federal Government, the Coastal Commission's regulation of Granite Rock's mining operation must be limited to participation in a consistency review process detailed in the CZMA....

....

Absent any other expression of congressional intent regarding the pre-emptive effect of the CZMA, we would be required to decide, first, whether unpatented mining claims in national forests were meant to be excluded from the § 1453(1) definition of a State's coastal zone, and, second, whether this exclusion from the coastal zone definition was intended to pre-empt state regulations that were not pre-empted by any other federal statutes or regulations. Congress has provided several clear statements of its intent regarding the pre-emptive effect of the CZMA; those statements, which indicate that Congress clearly intended the CZMA not to be an independent cause of pre-emption except in cases of actual conflict, end our inquiry.

Title 16 U.S.C. § 1456(e)(1) provides:

"Nothing in this chapter shall be construed —

"(1) to diminish either Federal or state jurisdiction, responsibility, or rights in the field of planning, development, or control of water resources, submerged lands, or navigable waters; nor to displace, supersede, limit, or modify any interstate compact or the jurisdiction or responsibility of any legally established joint or common agency of two or more states or of two or more states and the Federal Government; nor to limit the authority of Congress to authorize and fund projects...."

....

The clearest statement of congressional intent as to the pre-emptive effect of the CZMA appears in the "Purpose" section of the Senate Report, quoted in full:

"[The CZMA] has as its main purpose the encouragement and assistance of States in preparing and implementing management programs to preserve, protect, develop and whenever possible restore the resources of the coastal zone of the United States. The bill authorizes Federal grants-in-aid to coastal states to develop coastal zone management programs. Additionally, it authorizes grants to help coastal states implement these management programs once approved, and States would be aided in the acquisition and operation of estuarine sanctuaries. Through the system of providing grants-in-aid, the States are provided financial incentives to undertake the responsibility for setting up management programs in the coastal zone. *There is no attempt to diminish state authority through federal preemption.* The intent of this legislation is to enhance state authority by encouraging and assisting the states to assume planning and regulatory powers over their coastal zones." S. Rep. No. 92-753, *supra*, at 1, U.S. Code Cong. & Admin. News 1972, p. 4776 (emphasis supplied).

Because Congress specifically disclaimed any intention to pre-empt pre-existing state authority in the CZMA, we conclude that even if all federal lands are excluded from the CZMA definition of "coastal zone," the CZMA does not automatically pre-empt all state regulation of activities on federal lands.

....

JUSTICE POWELL, with whom JUSTICE STEVENS joins, concurring in part and dissenting in part.

Because I agree that this case is properly before us, I join Parts I and II of the Court's opinion. In Part III, the Court considers the Forest Service's approval of Granite Rock's plan to operate its mine in a national forest. Because I cannot agree with the Court's conclusion that Congress intended to allow California to require a state permit, I dissent from Part III.

....

The Court's analysis of this case focuses on selected provisions of the federal statutes and regulations, to the exclusion of other relevant provisions and the larger regulatory context. First, it examines the Forest Service regulations themselves, apart from the statutes that authorize them. Because these regulations explicitly require the federal permits to comply with specified state environmental standards, the Court assumes that Congress intended to allow state enforcement of any and all state environmental standards. Careful comparison of the regulations with the authorizing statutes casts serious doubt on this conclusion. The regulations specifically require compliance with only three types of state regulation: air quality, see 36 CFR § 228.8(a) (1986); water quality, see § 228.8(b); and solid waste disposal, see § 228.8(c). But the Court fails to mention that the types of state regulation preserved by § 228.8 already are preserved by specific nonpre-emption clauses in other federal statutes. *See* 42 U.S.C. § 7418(a) (Clean Air Act requires federal agencies to comply with analogous state regulations); 33 U.S.C. § 1323(a) (similar provision of the Clean Water Act); 42 U.S.C. § 6961 (similar provision of the Solid Waste Disposal Act). The Forest Service's specific preservation of certain types of state regulation — already preserved by federal law — hardly suggests an implicit intent to allow the States to apply other types of regulation to activities on federal lands. Indeed the maxim *expressio unius est exclusio alterius* suggests the contrary.

The second part of the Court's analysis considers both the NFMA and the FLPMA. The Court assumes, *ante*, at 1427, that these statutes "pre-emp[t] the extension of state land use plans onto unpatented mining claims in national forest lands." But the Court nevertheless holds that the Coastal Commission can require Granite Rock to secure a state permit before conducting mining operations in a national forest. This conclusion rests on a distinction between "land use planning" and "environmental regulation." In the Court's view, the NFMA and the FLPMA indicate a congressional intent to pre-empt state land use regulations, but not state environmental regulations. I find this analysis unsupportable, either as an interpretation of the governing statutes or as a matter of logic.

The basis for the alleged distinction is that Congress has understood land use planning and environmental regulation to be distinct activities. The only statute cited for this proposition is § 202(c)(8) of the FLPMA, 43 U.S.C. § 1712(c)(8), that requires the Secretary of the Interior's land use plans to "provide for compliance with applicable pollution control laws, including State and Federal air, water, noise, or other pollution standards or implementation plans." But this statute provides little support for the majority's analysis. A section mandating consideration of environmental standards in the formulation of land use plans does not demonstrate a general separation between "land use planning" and "environmental regulation." Rather, § 202(c)(8) recognizes that the Secretary's land use planning will affect the environment, and thus directs the Secretary to comply with certain pollution standards.

Nor does this section support the Court's ultimate conclusion, that Congress intended the Secretary's plans to comply with all state environmental regulations. As I have explained other federal statutes require compliance with the listed standards. Also, because the FLPMA requires compliance only with "applicable" standards, it is difficult to treat this one section as an independent and controlling command that the Secretary comply with all state environmental standards. Rather, viewing the complex of statutes and regulations as a whole, it is reasonable to view § 202(c)(8) simply as a recognition that the Secretary's plans must comply with standards made applicable to federal activities by other federal laws.

. . . .

The most troubling feature of the Court's analysis is that it is divorced from the realities of its holding. The Court cautions that its decision allows only "reasonable" environmental regulation and that it does not give the Coastal Commission a veto over Granite Rock's mining activities. But if the Coastal Commission can require Granite Rock to secure a permit before allowing mining operations to proceed, it necessarily can forbid Granite Rock from conducting these operations. It may be that reasonable environmental regulations would not force Granite Rock to close its mine. This misses the point. The troubling fact is that the Court has given a state authority — here the Coastal Commission — the power to prohibit Granite Rock from exercising the rights granted by its Forest Service permit. This abdication of federal control over the use of federal land is unprecedented.

Apart from my disagreement with the Court's characterization of the governing statutes, its pre-emption analysis accords little or no weight to both the location of the mine in a national forest, and the comprehensive nature of the federal statutes that authorized Granite Rock's federal permit.

One important factor in pre-emption analysis is the relative weight of the state and federal interests in regulating a particular matter. The Court recognizes that the mine in this case is located in a national forest, but curiously attaches no significance to that fact. The Property Clause specifically grants Congress "Power to dispose of and make all needful Rules and Regulations respecting the Territory or other Property belonging to the United States." U.S. Const., Art. IV, § 3, cl. 2. This provision may not of its own force pre-empt the authority of a State to regulate activities on federal land, but it clearly empowers Congress to limit the extent to which a State may regulate in this area. In light of this clear constitutional allocation of power, the location of the mine in a national forest should make us less reluctant to find pre-emption than we are in other contexts.

The state regulation in this case is particularly intrusive because it takes the form of a separate, and duplicative, permit system. As the Court has recognized, state permit requirements are especially likely to intrude on parallel federal authority, because they effectively give the State the power to veto the federal project. Although the intrusive effect of duplicative state permit systems may not lead to a finding of pre-emption in all cases, it certainly is relevant to a careful pre-emption analysis.

....

In summary, it is fair to say that, commencing in 1872, Congress has created an almost impenetrable maze of arguably relevant legislation in no less than a half-dozen statutes, augmented by the regulations of two Departments of the Executive. There is little cause for wonder that the language of these statutes and regulations has generated considerable confusion. There is an evident need for Congress to enact a single, comprehensive statute for the regulation of federal lands.

Having said this, it is at least clear that duplicative federal and state permit requirements create an intolerable conflict in decisionmaking. In view of the Property Clause of the Constitution, as well as common sense, federal authority must control with respect to land "belonging to the United States." Yet, the Court's opinion today approves a system of twofold authority with respect to environmental matters. The result of this holding is that state regulators, whose views on environmental and mineral policy may conflict with the views of the Forest Service, have the power, with respect to federal lands, to forbid activity expressly authorized by the Forest Service. I dissent.

JUSTICE SCALIA, with whom JUSTICE WHITE joins, dissenting.

... In my view, the merits of this case must be decided on simpler and narrower grounds than those addressed by the Court's opinion. It seems to me ultimately irrelevant whether state environmental regulation has been pre-empted with respect to federal lands, since the exercise of state power at issue here is not environmental regulation but land use control. The Court errs in entertaining the Coastal Commission's contention that "its permit requirement is an exercise of environmental regulation," and mischaracterizes the issue when it describes it to be whether "any state permit requirement, whatever its conditions, [is] *per se* pre-empted by federal law." We need not speculate as to what the nature of this permit requirement was. We are not dealing with permits in the abstract, but with a specific permit, purporting to require application of particular criteria, mandated by a numbered section of a known California law. That law is plainly a land use statute, and the permit that statute requires Granite Rock to obtain is a land use control device. Its character as such is not altered by the fact that the State may now be agreeable to issuing it so long as environmental concerns are satisfied. Since, as the Court's opinion quite correctly assumes, state exercise of land use authority over federal lands is pre-empted by federal law, California's permit requirement must be invalid.

....

NOTES AND QUESTIONS

1. Is the California permit requirement environmental regulation or land use regulation? How broad is state authority over federal land in the coastal zone after *Granite Rock*? Did Congress intend to exclude all federal lands from the definition of the coastal zone? If so, why does Justice O'Connor conclude the CZMA does not "automatically" preempt all state regulations of activities on federal lands? *Compare Friends of the Earth v. United States Navy*, 841 F.2d 927 (9th Cir. 1988) (state coastal act applied to Navy activities) *with Sierra Club v. Marsh*, 692 F. Supp. 1210 (S.D. Cal. 1988) (no state coastal permit required). To what extent can states regulate activities in the outer continental shelf without creating an impermissible burden on interstate commerce? *See Norfolk Southern Corp. v. Oberly*, 822 F.2d 388 (3d Cir. 1987).

2. *Funding of State Management Programs.* Under the CZMA, coastal states are given grants for the development and administration of federally approved state management programs for coastal zones. Approval of state programs is made through the Assistant Administrator of the Office of Ocean and Coastal Resource Management (OCRM). Every management program must incorporate the following requirements: (1) identification of the boundaries of the coastal zone; (2) a definition of what constitutes permissible land and water uses which have a direct and significant impact on the coastal waters; (3) an inventory and designation of areas of particular concern; (4) identification of the means to exert control over land and water uses, including a listing of relevant constitutional provisions, laws, regulations, and judicial decisions; (5) broad guidelines or priorities of uses in particular areas including specifically those of lowest priority; (6) a description of organizational structure proposed to implement the program, including the responsibilities and interrelationships of local, areawide, state, regional and interstate agencies in the management process; (7) a definition of the term "beach" and a planning process for the protection of, and access to, public beaches and other public coastal areas of environmental, recreational, historical, esthetic, ecological, or cultural value; (8) a planning process for energy facilities likely to be located in, or which may significantly affect, the coastal zone, including, but not limited to, a process for anticipating and managing the impacts from such facilities; and (9) a planning process for assessing the effects of shoreline erosion and studying and evaluating ways to control, or lessen the impact of, such erosion, and to restore areas adversely affected by such erosion. 16 U.S.C. § 1455(d)(2).

The CZMA provides for "management program development grants" under section 305, *id.* § 1454(a), and "administrative grants" under section 306, *id.* § 1455(a). Although the statutory language is confusing, grants are made under section 305 for a state to develop a final management program. When that program is approved by the OCRM, the state is eligible for further grants under section 306 to implement and administer the program.

Grants for administration may be given to the state if the Secretary finds the substantive requirements of section 1455(d)(2) for management programs are met and approves the state's management program. *Id.* § 1455(b). Prior to granting approval, the Secretary must also find that:

> (1) the management program has been adopted in accordance with the applicable regulations after notice and with the opportunity for full participation by the relevant federal agencies, state agencies, local governments, regional organizations, port authorities, and other public and private interested parties;
>
> (2) the state has held public hearings in its development;
>
> (3) the management program and any changes have been reviewed and approved by the Governor;
>
> (4) the Governor of the state has designated a single agency to receive and administer the administrative grants;
>
> (5) the state is organized to implement the management program;
>
> (6) the state has the authority necessary to implement the program;
>
> (7) the management program provides for adequate consideration of the national interest involved in planning for, and in the siting of, facilities (including energy facilities in, or which significantly affect, such state's coastal zone) that are necessary to meet requirements that are not local in nature; and
>
> (8) the management program makes provision for procedures whereby specific areas may be designated for the purpose of preserving or restoring them for their conservation, recreational, ecological, or aesthetic values.

Id. § 1455(d)(1)-(9). In addition, for approval of a management program the state must have coordinated the program with local, area-wide, and interstate plans applicable to areas within the coastal zone. *Id.* § 1455(d)(3)(A)(i). The state also must establish an "effective mechanism" for continuing consultation and coordination between the designated management agency and local governments, interstate agencies, regional agencies, and area-wide agencies within the coastal zone to assure the full participation of such governments and agencies. *Id.* § 1455(d)(3)(b).

The state is given a choice among three methods of regulation in its program. The designated techniques for control of land and water uses are: (1) state establishment of criteria and standards for local implementation, subject to administrative review and enforcement of compliance; (2) direct state land and water use planning and regulation; and (3) state administrative review for consistency with the management program of all development plans, projects, or land and water regulations, including exceptions and variances thereto proposed by any state or local authority or private developer, with power to approve or disapprove after public notice and an opportunity for hearings. *Id.* § 1455(d)(11)-(A)-(C). Approval of a management program is key to receiving the two incentives provided to coastal states in the Act — funding and federal consistency.

3. *Federal Participation and Consistency Review.* There are five categories of federal activities subject to consistency review: (1) activities conducted or supported by a federal agency "affecting any land or water use or natural resource of the coastal zone"; (2) federal development projects "in the coastal zone"; (3) federally licensed and permitted activities "affecting any land or water use or natural resource of the coastal zone"; (4) federally licensed or permitted activities described in detail in OCS plans "affecting any land or water use or natural resource of the coastal zone"; and (5) federal assistance to state and local governments "affecting any land or water use or natural resource of the coastal zone." *Id.* § 1456(c), (d). The requirements for consistency review, as well as when those requirements must be met, vary depending upon the type of federal activity at issue and whether it must affect or be conducted in the coastal zone.

The most controversial consistency determinations have involved oil and gas lease activities in the outer continental shelf. Any plan for the exploration, development, or production in any area leased under the Outer Continental Shelf Lands Act (OCSLA), 43 U.S.C. §§ 1331-1356, that affects any land or water use or natural resource of a coastal zone must have attached a certification that each activity detailed in the plan complies with the enforceable policies of a state's management program and will be carried out consistently with that program. 16 U.S.C. § 1456(c)(3)(B). No federal license or permit can be granted for any such activity until the state or designated agency receives the certification, the plan, and any other necessary information and the state or designated agency concurs with the certification and so notifies the Secretaries of Commerce and the Interior. *Id.* § 1456(c)(3)(B)(i). If the state objects to the certification, the Secretary may nevertheless find that the activity is consistent with the objectives of the chapter or that it is otherwise necessary in the interest of national security. *Id.* § 1456(c)(3)(B)(iii). If a state objects and the Secretary fails to make such a finding or if the applicant fails to comply with the plan as submitted, the applicant must submit an amended or new plan to the Secretary of the Interior.

Prior to the 1990 amendments, section 307(c)(1) of the CZMA required that federal activity "directly affecting" a state's coastal zone must be done "in a manner which is, to the maximum extent practicable, consistent with approved state management programs." In July, 1980, the California Coastal Commission asked the Department of the Interior to submit a consistency determination at the time the Department published its proposed Notice of Sale for Lease off the coast of California. *California v. Watt*, 683 F.2d 1253, 1258-1259 (9th Cir. 1982), *rev'd sub nom. Secretary of the Interior v. California*, 464 U.S. 312 (1984). The Department of the Interior refused to submit a consistency determination because of its view that the proposed notice of sale did not "directly affect" the coastal zone and thus did not require a consistency determination under § 307(c)(1). Both the district court, *California v. Watt*, 520 F. Supp. 1359 (C.D. Cal. 1981), and the Ninth Circuit Court of Appeals, *California v. Watt*, 683 F.2d 1253 (9th Cir. 1982), rejected the Department's position that activities "directly affecting" the coastal zone were only those activities that physically affected the coastal zones so that consistency review was limited to activities during the actual exploration, development, and production stages.

By a 5-4 vote the Supreme Court in *Secretary of the Interior v. California*, 464 U.S. 312 (1984), upheld the Department's position. Justice O'Connor focused on the remaining lease sale in controversy — lease sale 53, which included the Santa Maria Basin, an important habitat of the sea otter. *Id.* at 318. In holding that only federal activities *within* the coastal zone could directly affect the coastal zone, the court relied on the legislative history of the CZMA. Congress's rejection of four proposals to extend the CZMA beyond three miles, and of a specific proposal to make OCSLA leasing subject to consistency review, demonstrated to the Court a congressional intent to exclude OCSLA leasing from review. In addition, the separation of OCSLA development into four stages was interpreted as a congressional decision to separate OCSLA lease sales from the later two stages of development for purposes of consistency review under § 307(c)(3)(B). According to Justice O'Connor, the purchase of an OCS lease entailed no right to explore for, develop, or produce oil or gas resources that would trigger § 307(c)(3)(B) consistency review. Section 307(c)(1) consistency review was not triggered because the phrase "directly affecting" was "aimed at including activities conducted or supported by federal agencies on federal lands physically situated in the coastal zone but excluded from the zone" as defined in the CZMA. Even if OCS lease sales were an activity conducted or supported by a federal agency under § 301(c)(1), lease sales would have no direct effect on the coastal zone because they authorized only very limited "preliminary activities" on the OCS.

The opinion was intensely criticized. *See generally* Fitzgerald, *Outer Continental Shelf Revenue Sharing: A Proposal to End the Seaweed Rebellion*, 5 UCLA J. OF ENVTL. L. & POL'Y 1 (1985); Note, *The Seaweed Rebellion: Federal-State Conflicts Over Offshore Oil and Gas Development*, 18 WILLAMETTE L. REV. 535 (1982); Comment, *The Seaweed Rebellion Revisited: Continuing Federal-State Conflicts in OCS Oil and Gas Leasing*, 20 WILLAMETTE L. REV. 83 (1984); *see also* Yi, *Application of the Coastal Zone Management Act to Outer Continental Shelf Lease Sales*, 6 HARV. ENVTL. L. REV. 159 (1982);

Note, *Federal "Consistency" Under the Coastal Zone Management Act — A Promise Broken by Secretary of the Interior v. California*, 15 ENVTL. L. 153 (1984); Note, *Outer Continental Shelf Leasing Policy Prevails Over the California Coastal Commission*, 24 NAT. RESOURCES J. 1133 (1984); Comment, *Reappraisal of State's Interests in Outer Continental Shelf Lease Sales Under the Coastal Zone Management Act: Secretary of the Interior v. California*, 29 WASH. U.J. URB. & CONTEMP. L. 277 (1985). In the 1990 amendments to the CZMA, section 307(c)(1) was amended to read in its entirety as follows:

(c)(1)(A) Each Federal agency activity within or outside the coastal zone that affects any land or water use or natural resource of the coastal zone shall be carried out in a manner which is consistent to the maximum extent practicable with the enforceable policies of approved State management programs. A Federal agency activity shall be subject to this paragraph unless it is subject to paragraph (2) or (3).

(B) After any final judgment, decree, or order of any Federal court that is appealable under section 1291 or 1292 of title 28, United States Code, or under any other applicable provision of Federal law, that a specific Federal agency activity is not in compliance with subparagraph (A), and certification by the Secretary that meditation under subsection (h) is not likely to result in such compliance, the President may, upon written request from the Secretary, exempt from compliance those elements of the Federal agency activity that are found by the Federal court to be inconsistent with an approved State program, if the President determines that the activity is in the paramount interest of the United States. No such exemption shall be granted on the basis of a lack of appropriations unless the President has specifically requested such appropriations as part of the budgetary process, and the Congress has failed to make available the requested appropriations.

(C) Each Federal Agency carrying out an activity subject to paragraph (1) shall provide a consistency determination to the relevant State agency designated under section 1455(d)(6) of this title at the earliest practicable time, but in no case later than 90 days before final approval of the Federal activity unless both the Federal agency and the State agency agree to a different schedule.

Coastal Zone Act Reauthorization Act Amendments of 1990, Pub. L. No. 101-508, § 6208, 104 Stat. 1388, 1388-307 (codified as amended at 16 U.S.C. § 1456(c)(1). The first subsection of this provision overturns *Secretary of the Interior v. California* by subjecting OCSLA oil and gas lease sales to the consistency requirements of section 307(c)(1). The second subsection is new and authorizes a Presidential exemption if the activity is in the paramount interest of the United States, a standard exemption provided in a number of other environmental statutes. Technical changes in the other consistency provisions of sections 307(c)(3)(A) and 307(d) coupled with the new section 307(c)(1) make it clear that any federal agency activity that affects any natural resources, land uses, or water uses in the coastal zone are subject to consistency review regardless of whether the activity is in or outside the coastal zone. The House conference report states that, in evaluating whether or not the federal agency activity may affect the coastal zone, consideration must be given to effects that the federal agency:

> may reasonably anticipate as a result of its action, including cumulative and secondary effects. Therefore, the term "affecting" is to be construed broadly, including direct effects which are caused by the activity and occur at the same time and place, and indirect effects which may be caused by the activity and are later in time or farther removed in distance, but are still reasonably foreseeable.

H.R. CONF. REP. NO. 964, 101st Cong., 2d Sess. 970-71, *reprinted in* 1990 U.S.C.C.A.N. 2374, 2675-76.

4. *Coastal Zone Enhancement Grants and the Coastal Nonpoint Pollution Control Program.* The 1990 Amendments to the CZMA created the Coastal Zone Enhancement Grant (CZEG) program. Coastal Zone Act Reauthorization Act Amendments of 1990, Pub. L. No. 101-508, § 6210, 104 Stat. 1388, 1388-309 (codified as amended at 16 U.S.C. § 1456b). These grants are to be provided to coastal states for the purpose of attaining any one or more of eight enumerated coastal zone enhancement objectives. 16 U.S.C. § 1456b(b). These objectives are: (1) protection of existing coastal wetlands or creation of new coastal wetlands; (2) minimization or elimination of development in natural hazard areas in order to protect life and property; (3) increased public access to coastal areas having recreational, historical, aesthetic, ecological, or cultural value; (4) reduction of marine debris through increased management of uses and activities which contribute to the presence of such debris in the coastal and ocean environment; (5) development and adoption of procedures to control the cumulative and secondary impacts created by coastal growth and development; (6) preparation and implementation of special area management plans for important coastal areas; (7) planned use of ocean resources; and (8) adoption of enforceable procedures and policies regarding the siting of coastal energy and government facilities having greater than local significance. *Id.* § 1456b(a).

The 1990 amendments also require every state with a federally approved program to develop a program to implement coastal land use management measures for controlling nonpoint source pollution. Coastal Zone Act Reauthorization Act Amendments of 1990, Pub. L. No. 101-508, § 6217, 104 Stat. 1388, 1388-314 (codified as amended at 16 U.S.C. § 1455b). The Administrator of EPA must publish national guidelines on "management measures" to control coastal nonpoint sources. 16 U.S.C. § 1455b(b)(1). "Management measures" are defined as "economically achievable measures" for the control of pollutants from new and existing nonpoint sources that reflect the "greatest degree of pollutant reduction achievable" through application of the best available nonpoint pollution control practices and other methods. *Id.* § 1455b(g)(5). States must submit their programs to the Secretary and the Administrator of EPA within thirty months of publication of the national guidelines. *Id.* § 1455b(a)(1). After approval, the state must implement the program through changes in the state plan for control of nonpoint source pollution approved under section 319 of the Clean Water Act, 33 U.S.C. § 1329, and through changes in the state's coastal zone management program. 16 U.S.C. § 1455b(c)(2). If the state fails to submit an approved program, the Secretary may withhold a percentage of any section 306 grant under the CZMA, and EPA may withhold portions of any section 319 grant under the Clean Water Act. *Id.* § 1455b(c)(3), (4).

5. *The Coastal Barrier Resources Act.* Enacted in 1982, the Coastal Barrier Resources Act (CBRA), 16 U.S.C. §§ 3501-3510, was the first environmental law that coordinated federal fiscal policy with environmental preservation. Coastal barriers, or barrier islands, are long, narrow, low-lying land forms, partially or almost completely surrounded by water, such as New York's Fire Island and North Carolina's Outer Banks. Because barrier islands were largely inaccessible before the 1950s, ninety percent were undeveloped. *Hearings on H.R. 3252 Before the Subcomm. on Fisheries and Wildlife Conservation and the Environment and the Subcomm. on Oceanography of the House Comm. on Merchant Marine and Fisheries*, 97th Cong., 2d Sess. 299 (1982). Recently, however, approximately 5,000 to 6,000 acres of barrier islands were developed each year with approximately one-third of the developable land acreage and over one-third of the shoreline already developed. S. Rep. No. 49, 97th Cong., 2d Sess. 2 (1982), *reprinted in* 1982 U.S.C.C.A.N. 3214. Much of this development had been accomplished through federal subsidies and assistance. *Hearings on H.R. 3252, supra*, at 378, 53-54. The purposes of the CBRA were to minimize danger to human life from poorly located coastal development, to end federal expenditures for such development, and to preserve the natural resources of the coastal barriers. 16 U.S.C. § 3501(b). The CBRA accomplishes these purposes by limiting new federal expenditures or financial assistance within designated coastal barrier areas. *See generally* Jones, *The Coastal Barrier Resources Act: A Common Cents Approach to Coastal Protection*, 21 ENVTL. L. 1015 (1991).

Basically, the CBRA restricts new federal assistance or expenditures, including financial assistance for construction or purchase of structures, roads, bridges, facilities, and related infrastructure, within certain coastal barrier areas. The costs of development, and the costs from the risks of development, thus must be borne by the developer and consumer of coastal barrier property. The CBRA in this manner departs significantly from more traditional forms of land use and environmental protection, such as regulation, acquisition, and land planning. The Act was enacted despite challenges from realtors and developers that the Act was federal land use which failed to distinguish between coastal barriers suitable for development and those which are not.

No new expenditures or new financial assistance may be made available under authority of any federal law for any purpose within the Coastal Barrier Resources

System. *Id.* § 3504(a). Financial assistance includes any form of loan, grant, guarantee, insurance, payment, rebate, subsidy, or any other form of direct or indirect federal assistance. *Id.* § 3502(3). Although this definition is very broad, it is subject to many exemptions. *See id.* §§ 3502(3), 3505(a).

In a district court decision affirmed by the Fourth Circuit Court of Appeals, a general challenge to the validity of the CBRA failed. *Bostic v. United States*, 581 F. Supp. 254 (1984), *aff'd*, 753 F.2d 1292 (1985).

6. *Floodplain Regulation.* Damage caused by flooding has long been a major social policy concern, and substantial regulation of land use, development, construction practices, and insurance coverage in areas prone to flooding exists at the federal, state, and local levels. The federal government is particularly active in flood control in structural terms, through the efforts of agencies such as the Army Corps of Engineers.

In 1968 Congress enacted the National Flood Insurance program (NFIP). 42 U.S.C. §§ 4001-4128. The program was upheld as constitutional in *Texas Landowners Rights Ass'n v. Harris*, 453 F. Supp. 1025 (D.D.C. 1978), *aff'd*, 598 F.2d 311 (D.C. Cir. 1979), *cert. denied*, 444 U.S. 927 (1979). Flood insurance is not widely available through the private insurance market, and thus participation in the federal flood insurance scheme is a practical necessity for the owners of the many residences and businesses erected in floodplain areas. The federal government has in turn used this leverage to exert powerful pressures on state and local governments to enact effective land use measures mitigating the potential damage in areas prone to flooding.

The persons regulated under the NFIP are property owners in flood-prone communities that agree to meet federal requirements for reducing potential flood damage. When state and local governments in flood-prone areas establish plans for mitigating potential losses consistent with federal regulations, owners in those communities become eligible to purchase insurance through the NFIP.

Roughly 20,000 communities have been identified as flood prone. The regulatory measure is the so-called "100 year floodplain," an area exposed to damage from a "100 year flood." A 100 year flood refers to a statistical calculation whereby hydrologists determine that the flood will be equalled or exceeded once in every 100 years on average — thus creating roughly a one percent chance of occupance in any given year. Of the 20,000 flood-prone communities in the United States, over 17,000 have adopted plans that meet federal requirements under the NFIP, thus permitting owners in their areas to participate in the flood insurance program. 3 P. ROHAN, ZONING AND LAND USE CONTROLS § 18.02[2][a] (1989).

The National Flood Insurance Program is administered by the Federal Insurance Administration within the Federal Emergency Management Agency (FEMA). The FEMA works to reduce exposure to flood hazards by encouraging adoption of appropriate land-use and construction regulations. *See* 44 C.F.R. § 205.32(f).

Courts have not been willing to hold the United States government liable for damages arising from floods or the administration of the NFIP. *See, e.g., Baroni v. United States*, 662 F.2d 287 (5th Cir. 1981), *cert. denied*, 460 U.S. 1036 (1983); *Britt v. United States*, 515 F. Supp. 1159 (M.D. Ala. 1981); *Oahe Conservancy Subdistrict v. Alexander*, 493 F. Supp. 1294 (D.S.D. 1980). Congress flatly precluded liability arising from flooding, stating unequivocally: "No liability of any kind shall attach to or rest upon the United States for any damages from or by floods or flood waters at any place." 33 U.S.C. § 702c. The United States Supreme Court has interpreted this prohibition to preclude not only claims of property damage but claims of personal injury as well. *United States v. James*, 478 U.S. 597 (1986), discussed in Note, *"United States v. James: Expanding the Scope of Sovereign Immunity for Federal Flood Control Activities,"* 37 CATH. U.L. REV. 219 (1987).

The Disaster Relief Act of 1974, Pub. L. No. 98-288, codified at 42 U.S.C. § 5121 *et seq.* is primarily designed to provide financial assistance to state and local governments, individuals, and businesses in the event of a Presidentially declared "emergency" or "major disaster." An "emergency" is any natural disaster that occurs or threatens to occur beyond the response capabilities of state and local governments which necessitates federal energy assistance to protect lives, property, health, and safety. 44 C.F.R. § 205.34(a). A "major disaster" is one for which federal assistance is necessary to supplement the efforts and resources of state and local governments and disaster relief organizations. *Id.* § 205.33(a). From a land use perspective, the most significant provision of the Act is section 406, which requires local governments that receive funding to evaluate natural hazards in the area for which the funds are used and formulate a hazard mitigation plan. 42 U.S.C. § 5176.

In May 1977, Executive Order 11988 was promulgated to improve federal policy on floodplain management. 42 Fed. Reg. 26951 (May 24, 1977). *See generally* Holmes, *Federal Participation in Land Use Decisionmaking at the Water's Edge — Floodplains and Wetlands*, 13 NAT. RESOURCES LAW. 351, 364-66 (1980). The order requires federal agencies to avoid direct or indirect support of floodplain development when there is a "practicable" alternative. The order applies to acquisition, disposal, or management of federal land, undertaking, financing, or assisting construction projects, and conducting activities affecting land use, including planning, regulating, and licensing.

7. The Takings Issue in Coastal and Floodplain Regulation. The cumulative effect of the Supreme Court's 1987 trilogy of decisions under the takings clause (discussed on pages 130-79 *supra*), coupled with increasing coastal development is likely to be a resurgence of taking claims to coastal and floodplain regulation. Almost before Hurricane Hugo had dissipated, disgruntled beachfront owners were threatening litigation against South Carolina's Beachfront Management Act, S.C. Code Ann. §§ 48-39-10 to -220. The law as amended in 1988 prohibits the replacement of some buildings and structures in an area twenty feet behind the first row of dunes, and limits rebuilding and new construction in a much larger area. *Id.* §§ 48-39-290, 48-39-300. Real estate developers and private landowners wasted no time in alleging violations of the takings clause. N.Y. Times, D4, col. 4 (Oct. 1, 1989).

At first glance, the landowners' arguments are forceful. Increasingly restrictive floodplain regulations sometimes prohibit all or almost all use of floodplain or coastal property. Moreover, landowners argue that they are willing to self-insure. If they are willing to run the risk of such development, the governmental interest in floodplain management is reduced to an aversion toward self-insurance. These arguments, however, ignore the fact that governmental regulation is often paternalistic and the government has its own compelling interest in protecting the lives and property of beachfront owners, whatever their willingness to risk destruction. From the perspective of takings clause analysis, an even more compelling argument can be made that floodplain regulation falls within the well-established exception for nuisance regulation. Construction and development in high-risk floodplain areas increases the size of the floodway, causing floodwaters and perhaps even the structures themselves to damage property and endanger lives that might otherwise have remained safe. In a more general sense, the disaster relief necessary in floods is a governmental burden that increases in direct proportion to the number of self-insurers within floodplain areas. *See generally* Linda A. Malone, *The Coastal Zone Management Act and the Takings Clause in the 1990s: Making the Case for Federal Land Use to Preserve Coastal Areas,* 62 UNIV. COLO. L. REV. 711 (1991).

8. The Public Trust Doctrine. The public trust doctrine is often implicated in takings clause challenges to governmental regulation or public access rights for wetlands, floodplains, and coastal areas. The most traditional notion of the public trust is a property right authorizing public access to water resources. *Illinois Central R.R. v. Illinois,* 146 U.S 387 (1892) (public rights of navigation and fishing preclude state from granting fee title to submerged lands to private railroad); *Lake Michigan Fed'n v. Corps of Eng'rs,* 742 F. Supp. 441 (N.D. Ill. 1990) (proposed transfer to Loyola University of lands under Lake Michigan violates the public doctrine despite preservation of some rights of public access). *See generally* Sax, *The Public Trust Doctrine in Natural Resource Law: Effective Judicial Intervention,* 68 MICH. L. REV. 473 (1970). The Supreme Court recently gave an expansive interpretation to the waters included within the scope of the public trust. In *Phillips Petr. Co. v. Mississippi,* 484 U.S. 469 (1988) Mississippi had granted oil and gas leases to several acres of submerged land in a non-navigable tidal waterbody to which the state claimed title in public trust. Phillips Petroleum asserted title on the grounds that the public trust did not extend to non-navigable waters. The Supreme Court concluded that upon entering the Union the states gained title to all lands influenced by the tide, whether navigable or non-navigable, and holds such lands in trust for the public. The Court rejected the company's equitable estoppel argument that it had reasonable expectations of ownership based on its record title. The Court recognized "the importance of honoring reasonable expectations in property interests." Because

Mississippi law had consistently held that the public trust included "title to all the land under tidewater," the company was unreasonable in expecting the public trust to be limited to lands under navigable waters. For further discussion of the impact of *Phillips Petroleum*, see Johnson, *Water Pollution and the Public Trust Doctrine*, 19 ENVTL. L. 486 (1989); Watry, *Resolution of the Public Trust Doctrine: Analysis of the Impact of Phillips Petroleum Co. v. Mississippi*, 24 U.S.F. L. REV. 471 (1990); Wilkinson, *The Headwaters of the Public Trust: Some Thoughts on the Source and Scope of the Traditional Doctrine*, 19 ENVTL. L. 425 (1989).

Preexisting public rights, therefore, were held to limit private expectations of ownership which are entitled to protection under the takings and due process clauses. When the state is regulating to resolve land use conflicts, such regulation is likely to encounter resistance based on the takings clause from private landowners. The public trust broadens the parameters of the government's regulatory authority. As *Phillips* suggests, when state law has consistently recognized public rights, private expectations of property rights are less likely to be deemed reasonable under the takings clause.

The public trust doctrine has been extended far beyond the traditional concept of a public right to navigation and fishing in tidal waters. *See, e.g.*, *National Audubon Soc'y v. Superior Court of Alpine County*, 33 Cal. 3d 419, 189 Cal. Rptr. 346, 658 P.2d 709 (1983) (the purposes of the public trust include preservation of tidelands in their natural state for recreational and ecological value and state prior appropriation doctrine of water rights must be reconciled with the public trust); Blumm, *Public Property and the Democratization of Western Water Law: A Modern View of the Public Trust Doctrine*, 19 ENVTL. L. 573 (1989). The potential impact of the doctrine on environmental regulation of land use is immense. The brevity of its treatment in this book, and in casebooks generally, is a function of the elusive parameters of the doctrine and its peripatetic application in property, environmental, and water law which defies adequate treatment in any one area.

B. SOIL CONSERVATION

Soil erosion is a natural process that is constantly occurring. S. BATIE, SOIL EROSION: CRISIS IN AMERICA'S CROPLANDS? 15 (1983). Almost half the total soil loss in the United States occurs on cropland. AMERICAN FARMLAND TRUST, SOIL CONSERVATION IN AMERICA XV (1984). Soil loss on cropland most dramatically affects the anticipated use of the land, to produce agricultural commodities. *See* Smith, *Soil Depletion in the United States: The Relationship Between the Loss of the American Farmer's Independence and the Depletion of the Soil*, 22 ENVTL. L. 1539 (1992).

Soil loss per acre is estimated by either the universal soil loss equation (USLE) or the wind erosion equation (WEE), both of which estimate the average annual tonnage of soil loss from each soil type as a result of climate, topography, cropping systems, and management practices. These losses are compared to loss tolerances ("T-values"), which reflect the maximum annual soil losses that can be sustained without adversely affecting the productivity of the land.

The off-site impacts of soil erosion include damage to air and water quality and toxic contamination from nutrients and pesticides. Agriculture is also considered to be the greatest contributor to nonpoint-source water pollution. Sediment from soil erosion and the water runoff carry pollutants, fertilizer residues, insecticides, herbicides, fungicides, dissolved minerals, and animal-waste-associated bacteria. Although the national average loss of soil and croplands from water erosion, based on the USLE, was estimated at 4.8 tons per acre in 1977, the most serious problems of soil erosion are concentrated on a relatively few acres. Almost 70 percent of the combined erosion over five tons per acre per year was concentrated on 8.6 percent of the cropland. These statistics point out that soil conservation efforts should focus on the highly erodible cropland that is responsible for a disproportionate amount of the total erosion. The concept of concentrating federal funding for soil conservation in problem areas, or "targeting," became the focus of soil conservation "reform" after forty years of federal conservation programs had proven ineffective. *See generally* Malone, *The Renewed Concern Over Soil Erosion: The Current Federal Program and Proposals*, 10 J. AGRIC. TAX'N & L. 310, 315-17 (1989).

There are more than twenty-seven federal programs under eight different agencies that are designed to control soil erosion; however, all are voluntary. As a result, there is limited direction of federal funding or "targeting" of funding for soil conservation toward the soil that needs it most. Until the 1985 Farm Bill, there were no meaningful sanctions of any sort that could be imposed on a landowner guilty of contributing to, or failing to control, excessive erosion. Nevertheless, voluntary programs continue to be of importance in providing technical assistance and cost-sharing for conservation measures. In 1936, the Soil Conservation and Domestic Allotment Act was passed. Pub. L. No. 74-461, 49 Stat. 1148 (1936). The Act created the Agricultural Stabilization and Conservation Service (ASCS) with a network of offices at the national, state, and local levels. The Soil and Water Act of 1935, Pub. L. No. 74-46, 49 Stat. 163 (1935), had previously created the Soil Conservation Service (recently renamed the Natural Resources Conservation Service). Under this act, the Soil Conservation Service was authorized to give technical assistance only for conservation measures. In the 1970s, given the export boom and the direction to farmers to plant "fence row to fence row," soil conservation was viewed as a practical necessity. In 1977, the Comptroller General of the United States criticized federal soil conservation programs in a pivotal report to Congress titled "To Protect Tomorrow's Food Supply, Soil Conservation Needs Priority Attention." Among other criticisms, the report pointed out that federal financial assistance was not directed toward the most erosive land, and cost-sharing practices seemed to be designed to enhance productivity rather than to control erosion. Malone, *supra*, at 326.

The Soil and Water Resources Conservation Act of 1977 (RCA), 16 U.S.C. §§ 2001-2009, was passed by Congress to reform and improve federal conservation programs. It requires the USDA to (1) appraise, on a continuing basis, the soil, water, and other resources along federal land; (2) develop a program for furthering the conservation, protection, and enhancement of those resources; and (3) evaluate annually program performance in achieving conservation objectives.

A study done by the American Farmland Trust (AFT) concluded that highly erodible land on which excessive erosion was concentrated was not being farmed with conservation farming or with traditional USDA conservation programs. Most USDA programs were aimed at production, and even those programs that tried to limit production resulted in farmers removing from production their least productive land, not their most erosive land. A second AFT study recommended, as a solution, legislation that essentially would become the conservation provisions of the 1985 Farm Bill. Despite general dissatisfaction with a purely voluntary approach to soil conservation, a major hurdle remaining to federal conservation legislation was the long-standing aversion to anything approximating "federal land use." Malone, *supra*, at 329-30.

Congress had refused twice before 1985 to pass legislation similar to the conservation title of the 1985 Farm Bill (FSA). The relatively uneventful passage of the conservation programs arguably resulted from a combination of four key developments: the first opportunity since 1981 for a comprehensive revamping of agricultural policy: the spiraling cost of farm programs calling for reduced farm output and government subsidies; the growing recognition of the environmental destructivity of many agricultural policies; and — perhaps most important — the recognition by urban and suburban interests, as well as environmental groups, of their stake in the farm bill debate. Malone, *A Historical Essay on the Conservation Provisions of the 1985 Farm Bill: Sodbusting, Swampbusting, and the Conservation Reserve*, 34 KAN. L. REV. 577, 578 (1986). The 1985 Farm Bill, Food Security Act of 1985, Pub. L. No. 99-198, *codified at* 16 U.S.C. §§ 3801-3845, was signed on December 23, 1985 and contained several conservation provisions that were new to agricultural programs: the so-called sodbuster, swampbuster, conservation compliance, and conservation reserve programs.

The basic purpose of the sodbuster, swampbuster, and conservation compliance provisions is to ensure cross-compliance between conservation programs of the USDA and price and income support programs of the USDA. Under these provisions, a producer will receive no USDA program payments, such as price and income supports, disaster payments, and crop insurance, unless the producer is in compliance with the conservation provisions. The legislation does not, however, make soil and water conservation mandatory. Farmers may still refuse to use conservation measures or preserve wetlands, but, if they do so, they pay the price by being excluded from certain USDA payment programs. *See generally* Malone, *Reflections on the Jeffersonian Ideal of an Agrarian*

Democracy and the Emergence of an Agricultural and Environmental Ethic in the 1990 Farm Bill, 12 STAN. ENVTL. L. REV. 3 (1993); Mudge, *Impact Fees for Conversion of Agricultural Land: A Resource-Based Development Policy for California's Cities and Counties*, 19 ECOLOGY L.Q. 63 (1992).

In 1990, Congress reauthorized the conservation programs created by the 1985 Farm Bill. The conservation title of the 1990 Farm Bill, known as the "Conservation Program Improvements Act," significantly amended the existing programs, expanding the scope of the conservation reserve program while broadening the exemptions in and weakening enforcement of the swampbuster and sodbuster programs. It also created several new conservation programs. *See generally* Malone, *Conservation at the Crossroads: Reauthorization of the 1985 Farm Bill Conservation Provisions*, 8 VA. ENVT'L L.J. 215 (1989) (explaining some of the needed reforms which would be incorporated into the Act). The Federal Agriculture Improvement and Reform Act of 1966, Pub. L. No. 104-127, increased flexibility in program administration and created several new conservation programs.

1. SODBUSTING AND CONSERVATION COMPLIANCE

The sodbusting provision is designed to ensure that no highly erodible land will be placed into production of an agricultural commodity for the first time without full application of a conservation plan. An "agricultural commodity" is (1) any commodity planted and produced by annual tilling of the soil, including tilling by one-trip planters or (2) sugarcane. 16 U.S.C. § 3801(a)(1).

In short, the sodbuster provision requires a conservation plan for highly erodible land which was not in production or set aside any year from 1981 to 1985. For highly erodible land that was in production or set aside in that period, the "conservation compliance" provision requires active application of a conservation plan or system in most cases by January 1, 1990 with full implementation by January 1, 1995. *Id.* §§ 3811, 3812. Farmers with highly erodible land already in production are thus given more time to have a conservation plan implemented because of the greater economic and technological difficulties in implementing a plan for land on which the farmer is already dependent economically. The costs and difficulties of adequate conservation are, however, a factor that should be taken into consideration before a farmer brings previously unfarmed land that is highly erodible into agricultural production.

There are a number of provisions restricting liability in the event that a violation has occurred, most of which were added in the 1990 amendments. *Id.* §§ 3812(a)(4), 3812(e); 7 C.F.R. § 12.9; 16 U.S.C. § 3812(f)(4). Moreover, the conservation compliance requirements as amended in 1990 authorize graduated sanctions for good faith violations. Under these provisions, failure to "actively apply" a conservation plan for conservation compliance will not result in ineligibility for program payments if the person has not violated the highly erodible land requirements within the previous five years and acted in good faith without intent to violate the Act. *Id.* § 3812(f)(1). Instead, the violator's program benefits for that crop year alone will be reduced by not less than $500 nor more than $5,000 depending on the seriousness of the violation, so long as the person actively applies the conservation plan according to schedule in subsequent crop years. *Id.* § 3812(f)(2). Program ineligibility resulting from failure to actively apply a conservation plan is not permanent; eligibility may be regained if, prior to the beginning of a subsequent crop year, the Secretary determines that the individual is actively applying an approved conservation plan according to schedule. *Id.* § 3812(f)(3).

Under the final regulations, highly erodible land is land that has an erodibility index of eight or more. 7 C.F.R. § 12.2(a)(14). The erodibility index is a numerical value that expresses the potential erodibility of the soil in relation to its soil loss tolerance value without consideration of applied conservation practices or management. *Id.* § 12.2(a)(10). Therefore, land that may actually be eroding at an acceptable rate but that has an inherent potential of eroding eight times faster than it is rebuilding will be considered highly erodible land. *See id.*

In 1991 the USDA announced that conservation compliance plans were about 40% implemented. At that time, about 135 million acres had plans, with 54 million of those acres having the plans fully implemented. 54 DOANE'S AGRIC. REP. 8-1 (February 22, 1991). To ensure that farmers continue to make progress, the USDA plans to conduct random status reviews on 5% of them each year. *Id.* A limited study by the Soil and Water Conservation Society released in April of 1991 was less optimistic. The study says many farmers failed to follow their plans, and others were receiving payments in spite of practices that should have made them ineligible, such as breaking out land in native vegetation for crop production. Washington Post, April 22, 1991, at A7, col. 1.

2. THE ENVIRONMENTAL CONSERVATION ACREAGE RESERVE PROGRAM

The 1990 Farm Bill created an umbrella program, the Environmental Conservation Acreage Reserve Program, which consists of the conservation reserve program and a wetlands reserve program. 16 U.S.C. § 3803(a). The stated goals of the ECARP are to assist owners and operators of highly erodible lands, other fragile lands (including land with associated ground or surface water that may be vulnerable to contamination), and wetlands in conserving and improving the soil and water resources of the farms or ranches of such owners and operators. *Id.* During the 1986 through 1995 calendar years, the Secretary must place not less than 40 million nor more than 45 million acres into the ECARP. *Id.* § 3830(b). This acreage threshold includes the 34 million acres already enrolled in the conservation reserve program. *Id.* § 3830(c).

Lands eligible to be placed in the conservation reserve program under the Act include:

(1) highly erodible croplands that —

(A) if permitted to remain untreated could substantially reduce the production capability for future generations; or

(B) cannot be farmed in accordance with a [conservation compliance plan];

(2) marginal pasture lands converted to wetland or established as wildlife habitat prior to November 28, 1990;

(3) marginal pasture lands to be devoted to trees in or near riparian areas or for similar water quality purposes, not to exceed 10 percent of the number of acres of land that is placed in the conservation reserve ... in each of the 1991 through 1995 calendar years;

(4) croplands that are otherwise not eligible —

(A) if the Secretary determines that (i) such lands contribute to the degradation of water quality or would pose an on-site or off-site environmental threat to water quality if permitted to remain in agricultural production, and (ii) water quality objectives with respect to such land cannot be achieved under the water quality incentives program ...;

(B) if such croplands are newly-created, permanent grass sod waterways, or are contour grass sod strips established and maintained as part of an approved conservation plan;

(C) that will be devoted to, and made subject to an easement for the useful life of, newly established living snow fences, permanent wildlife habitat, windbreaks, shelterbelts, or filterstrips devoted to trees or shrubs; or

(D) if the Secretary determines that such lands pose an off-farm environmental threat, or pose a threat of continued degradation of productivity due to soil salinity, if permitted to remain in production.

Id. § 3831(b). Upon application by the appropriate state agency, the Secretary can also designate watershed areas of the Chesapeake Bay region, the Great Lakes region, the Long Island Sound region and other areas of special environmental sensitivity for inclusion in the reserve. *Id.* § 3831(f).

To put eligible land into the conservation reserve program (CRP), the owner must agree by contract: (1) to apply an approved conservation plan removing the land from commodity production to a less intensive use; (2) to place the land in the reserve; (3) not to use the land for agricultural purposes except as permitted by the Secretary; (4) to establish approved vegetative cover, or watercover, on the land; (5) to forfeit the right to receive rental and cost sharing payments and to refund payments received with interest for violation of the terms of the contract warranting termination, or to refund or accept adjustments to rental and cost sharing payments for violations not warranting termination of the contract; (6) to forfeit the right to receive rental and cost sharing payments and to refund such payments as the Secretary considers appropriate upon transfer of the land subject to the contract unless the transferee agrees to assume the contract or the Secretary and the transferee agree to modifications of the contract; (7) not to conduct harvesting, grazing or commercial use of forage except as permitted by the Secretary; (8) not to make commercial use of trees unless expressly permitted in the contract; (9) not to adopt any practice specified by the Secretary in the contract as a practice which would tend to defeat the purposes of the program; (10) to comply with any additional requirements the Secretary might include in the contract; and (11) under a 1990 amendment, not to produce an agricultural commodity on any other highly erodible land purchased after November 28, 1990 that does not have a history of being used to produce an agricultural commodity other than forage crops. *Id.* § 3832(a)(11).

In return for adhering to the contract terms, the owner or operator receives technical assistance and cost sharing for the conservation measures required. *Id.* § 3833. In general, the Secretary shall pay 50% of the cost of establishing water quality and conservation measures and practices required by the contract, and annual rental payments to compensate for the retirement of the land during the period of the contract and any permanent retirement of the cropland base and allotment history. *Id.* §§ 3833(b) and 3834(b)(1).

In determining the annual rental payment, the amount is determined by submission of bids by the owners or operators. *Id.* § 3834(c)(2). In determining the acceptability of contract offers, the Secretary may consider the extent to which the enrollment of the land would improve soil resources, water quality, wildlife habitat, or provide other environmental benefits. *Id.* § 3834(c)(3)(A).

Conservation reserve program contracts under the Act may range in duration from not less than ten years to no more than fifteen years. *Id.* § 3831(e)(1). During the 1996 through 2000 calendar years, the Secretary may extend for up to ten years conservation reserve contracts entered prior to November 28, 1990, or place such land in the environmental easement program, at the option of the owner or operator. Conservation Program Improvements Act, Pub. L. No. 101-624, § 1437. In the case of lands devoted to hardwood trees which are enrolled in the program prior to October 1, 1990, the Secretary may, with the agreement of the owner, extend the contract period for up to five years. *Id.* To further encourage such long-term conserving uses of land, the Act provides for cost-share assistance to persons who wish to convert highly erodible land already enrolled in the CRP to hardwood trees, windbreaks, shelterbelts, or wildlife corridors. *Id.* §§ 3835a(a)(1) and (a)(2)(C). In return, the owner of such land must provide a conservation easement for the useful life of the plantings and agree to participate in the Forest Stewardship Program. *Id.* § 3835a(a)(2)(B) and (d). Land under contract may also be converted to wetlands if the owner or operator agrees to provide the Secretary with a long-term or permanent easement under the wetlands reserve program. *Id.* § 3835a(b). Highly erodible land for purposes of the CRP has a complex definition which differs from the definition of highly erodible land for purposes of the sodbuster and conservation compliance requirements. *Id.* § 1410.3(b). The most significant change in the conservation reserve program in the 1990 amendments was in the expansion of lands eligible for inclusion in the CRP beyond highly erodible land in order to serve broad environmental objectives. *See generally* Watson, *Conservation Reserve Program: What Happens to the Land After the Contracts End?*, 14 N. ILL. U. L. REV. 733 (1994); *The Conservation Reserve Program: 1990 and Beyond*, 69 NEB. L. REV. 697 (1990).

The wetlands reserve program is intended to "assist owners of eligible lands in restoring and protecting wetlands." 1990 Conservation Program Improvements Act, Pub. L. No. 101-624, § 1438, *amending* subtitle D of Title XII of the Food Security Act of 1985, Pub. L. No. 99-198, *codified at* 16 U.S.C. § 3837(a). During the 1991 to 1995 calendar years, approximately one million acres have been enrolled in this reserve. *Id.* § 3837(b). The Secretary may not enroll more than 200,000 acres in 1991, 400,000 acres in the 1991 to 1992 period, 600,000 acres in the 1991 to 1993 period, 800,000 acres in the 1991 to 1994 period, and 1,000,000 acres in the 1991 to 1995 period. *Id.* The 1996 Act set a maximum enrollment of 975,000 acres. 16 U.S.C.A. § 3837(b). Eligible wetlands are farmed wetlands or converted wetlands (along with adjacent lands functionally dependent on such wetlands) if "the likelihood of the successful restoration of such land and the resultant wetland values merit inclusion ... in the program taking into consideration the cost of such restoration." *Id.* § 3837(c). Some other wetlands may be eligible under certain conditions. These lands are farmed wetland and adjoining lands already enrolled in the conservation reserve with high wetland functions and values which are likely to return to production, other wetlands of an owner which would not otherwise be eligible but which would add to the functional value of the easement, and riparian areas that link protected wetlands. *Id.* § 3837(d). To participate in the program, the owner of qualifying wetlands must agree to grant an easement on the land to the Secretary with an appropriately recorded deed restriction and to implement a wetland conservation plan to preserve the wetland values. *Id.* § 3837a(a). The easement must be for thirty years, be permanent, or have the maximum duration allowed under applicable state laws. *Id.* § 3837(a)(e). In return for this easement, the Secretary will provide compensation in cash in an amount not to exceed the difference in the fair market value of the land unencumbered and as encumbered with the easement. *Id.* § 3837a(f). Cost sharing for conservation measures and technical assistance are also provided by the Secretary. *Id.* § 3837c(a). Land subject to a wetlands reserve program easement may be utilized for compatible economic uses if specifically permitted by the plan; such uses include hunting, fishing, managed timber harvest, and periodic grazing. *Id.* § 3837a(d). *See generally* Ogle, *The Ongoing Struggle Between Private Property Rights and Wetlands Regulation: Recent Developments and Proposed Solutions*, 64 COLO. L. REV. 573 (1993).

The 1990 Act also creates a separate Environmental Easement Program with the stated goal of ensuring the continued long-term protection of environmentally sensitive lands or reduction in the degradation of water quality through the continued conservation and improvement of soil and water resources. 1990

Conservation Program Improvements Act, Pub. L. No. 101-624, § 1440, *amending* subtitle D of Title XII of the Food Security Act of 1985, Pub. L. No. 99-198, *codified at* 16 U.S.C. § 3839(a). Under this program, the Secretary may acquire easements on land placed in the conservation reserve, land under the Water Bank Act (16 U.S.C. § 1301), and any other cropland that contains riparian corridors, is a critical habitat, or contains other environmentally sensitive areas. *Id.* § 3839b(b)(1). In determining the acceptability of easement offers, the Secretary may take into consideration the extent to which the purposes of the easement program would be achieved on the land, the productivity of the land, and the on-farm and off-farm environmental threats if the land is used for the production of an agricultural commodity. *Id.* § 3839c(c)(2).

Easements acquired under this program are to be either permanent or of the maximum duration permitted under applicable state law. *Id.* § 3839(a). In return for the easement and implementation of a natural resource conservation management plan, the Secretary will make annual easement payments for a period not to exceed the lesser of $250,000 or the difference in the land's value with and without the easement. *Id.* § 3839b(2). A "natural resources conservation management plan" must set forth the conservation measures and practices to be carried out by the owner, the commercial use, if any, to be permitted on the land during the term of the easement, and must provide for the permanent retirement of any existing cropland base and allotment history. *Id.* § 3839a(b). In addition, the Secretary will provide cost sharing for up to one hundred percent of the cost of establishing the conservation measures and practices called for in the plan, provide technical assistance, and permit the land to be used for wildlife activities, including hunting and fishing. *Id.* § 3839(4).

3. SWAMPBUSTING

Under the swampbuster provision, any person who produces an agricultural commodity on wetlands converted after December 23, 1985, or who, after December 23, 1990, converts a wetland by any means *so as to make possible* the production of an agricultural commodity on such converted wetland, will be ineligible for price and income supports and other USDA payments. *Id.* § 3822. The 1990 amendments changed the "trigger" for ineligibility. Under the 1985 Farm Bill, a person became ineligible upon *production* of an agricultural commodity on a converted wetland. Food Security Act of 1985, Pub. L. 98-198, § 1221. After November 28, 1990, however, a person is ineligible whenever a wetland is converted *so as to make possible the production of an agricultural commodity*, if that was the purpose or the effect of conversion. 16 U.S.C. § 3821(b). Availability and application of a conservation plan to the converted wetlands under the swampbuster provision, unlike the sodbuster and conservation compliance provisions, is irrelevant to the prohibition of financial support. *See id.* § 3822.

A wetland is defined as land that:

(A) has a predominance of hydric soils;
(B) is inundated or saturated by surface or groundwater at a frequency and duration sufficient to support a prevalence of hydrophytic vegetation typically adapted for life in saturated soil conditions; and
(C) under normal circumstances does support a prevalence of such vegetation.

Id. § 3801(a)(16). Converted wetland is wetland that has been drained, dredged, filled, leveled, or otherwise manipulated for the purpose or to have the effect of making the production of an agricultural commodity possible if such production would not have been possible but for the action and, before such action, the land was wetland and was neither highly erodible land nor highly erodible cropland. *Id.* § 3801(a)(4)(A).

There are several exemptions from the requirements of the Act. If conversion of the wetland was commenced or completed before December 23, 1985, no program ineligibility will result due to the production of an agricultural commodity on the land. *Id.* § 3822(b)(1)(A). No ineligibility will result due to production on or conversion of an artificial lake, pond, or wetland created by excavating or diking nonwetland to collect and retain water for purposes such as water for livestock, fish production, irrigation, a settling basin, cooling, rice production, or flood control. *Id.* §§ 3822(b)(1)(B) and (b)(2)(A). An area is considered an artificial wetland if such area was formerly nonwetland or wetland on which conversion was started or completed before December 23, 1985, but meets the wetland criteria "due to the action of man." 7 C.F.R. § 12.31(c)(1). Nor will program ineligibility result due to production on or conversion of a wet area created by a water delivery system, irrigation, or irrigation system. *Id.* §§ 3822 (b)(1)(C) and (b)(2)(B). Production of an agricultural commodity on a wetland using normal farming or ranching techniques will not result in ineligibility "where such production is possible as the result of a natural condition, such as drought, and is without action by the producer that destroys a natural wetland characteristic." *Id.* § 3822(b)(1)(D). Finally, cropland will not be considered a wetland for purposes of the Act if its wetland characteristics result from the actions of "an unrelated person or public entity, outside the control of, and without the prior approval of the landowner or tenant." *Id.* § 3834.

Even if land is found to be subject to the swampbuster prohibitions, the Secretary has discretion to grant certain exemptions. First, the Secretary may exempt a person from program ineligibility as a result of production of an agricultural commodity on a converted wetland or the conversion of a wetland if it is determined that "such action, individually and in connection with all other similar actions authorized by the Secretary in the area, will have a minimal effect on the functional hydrological and biological value of the wetland...." *Id.* § 3822(f)(1). In the comments to the regulations, the USDA indicates that it will continue its practice of considering mitigation of conversion, including restoration, in making a minimal effects determination. 56 Fed. Reg. 18633 (April 23, 1991).

Secondly, under the 1990 Amendments, if the Secretary determines that the wetland has been frequently cropped in the past or that it was converted subsequent to December 23, 1985 but prior to November 28, 1990, no program ineligibility will result if the wetland values, acreage and functions are mitigated by the restoration of another converted wetland which was converted before December 23, 1985. This restoration must be in accordance with a restoration plan, be in advance of or concurrent with the production or conversion being mitigated, not be at the expense of the federal government, be on not greater than a one-for-one acreage basis unless more acreage is necessary for adequate mitigation, be on lands in the same general area of the local watershed as the converted wetland, and be subject to a recorded easement for so long as the other wetland is not returned to its original state. 16 U.S.C. § 3822 (f)(2) and (3). It should be noted that the provisions requiring mitigation with production on frequently cropped or prior converted wetland are a distinct requirement from mitigation or restoration required for the minimal effects exemption. 56 Fed. Reg. 18633 (April 23, 1991).

Impermissible conversion of a wetland does not always result in total ineligibility; there is a provision for graduated sanctions in the case of a good faith violation. A person's payments may be reduced by not less than $750 nor more than $10,000 for the crop year, rather than terminated altogether as the result of the conversion of a wetland if the person is actively restoring the converted wetland under an agreement with the Secretary or if the wetland has been restored, the person has not violated the swampbuster requirements in the previous ten-year period, and the conversion was done in good faith without intent to violate the requirements of the program. *Id.* § 3822(h). These graduated sanctions for good faith violations may be applied retroactively to permit the restoration of portions of benefits withheld for violations which occurred between December 23, 1985 and November 27, 1990. 7 C.F.R. § 12.5(b)(7)(iii). No program benefits may ever be withheld unless there has first been an on-site inspection. 16 U.S.C. § 3821(c). Ineligibility is not permanent; any violator of the swampbuster program can once again become eligible for program payments by fully restoring the illegally converted wetland to its prior wetland state. *Id.* § 3822(i).

4. MANDATORY SOIL CONSERVATION PROGRAMS

WOODBURY COUNTY SOIL CONSERVATION DISTRICT v. ORTNER

279 N.W.2d 276 (Iowa 1979)

LeGrand, Justice.

This appeal involves a dispute concerning the obligation of landowners to comply with the provisions of ch. 467A, The Code, 1975, commonly referred to as the Soil Conservation Districts Law. The trial court found § 467A.44 of the act, the section fixing the rules and regulations under which the soil conservation district operates, unconstitutional. We reverse the trial court and remand the case for further proceedings.

The defendants Ortner and Schrank each own farm land in Woodbury County. In 1974, an adjacent landowner, John C. Matt, filed a complaint with the soil conservation district alleging that his farm was suffering damage from water and soil erosion from defendants' land. This complaint was settled by private agreement among the parties, and no formal action was taken by the district.

The following year Matt filed another complaint, alleging similar damage. An investigation made under § 467A.47 resulted in a finding that the soil loss on the Ortner and Schrank farms was in excess of the established statutory limits. The district issued an administrative order finding defendants in violation of the district soil erosion control regulations and requiring them to remedy the situation within six months.

The order offered defendants two alternatives to bring the soil within acceptable limits. They were directed to either seed the land to permanent pasture or hay or to terrace it. Defendants failed to do either within the time allowed by the commission's order and the district brought this action as authorized by § 467A.49, The Code.

Even with state grants which were available through the Department of Soil Conservation to defray part of the cost, terracing would cost the Ortners more than $12,000.00 and the Schranks approximately $1,500.00. There was also testimony that this process would render a number of acres of each farm untillable. The other alternative — pasture or hay seeding — would be less expensive but would also remove some of each farm from active production. The defendants introduced evidence that either alternative would decrease the value of their land, although there was considerable evidence to the contrary.

The trial court held that § 467A.44, The Code, 1975, is unconstitutional. The court held that this section places an unreasonable burden on the defendants and that it is unduly oppressive. The trial court concluded that the section in question (§ 467A.44) therefore "deprives [defendants] of rights granted by the Fifth and Fourteenth Amendments of the Constitution of the United States and comparable provisions of the state of Iowa."

The two specific issues raised on this appeal are: Did the trial court err in holding § 467A.44 unconstitutional and did the trial court err in finding that the acceptable soil loss limit on the property is ten tons per acre per year? The second of these may be disregarded because the parties admit there is no support in the record for the trial court's finding that the acceptable soil loss is ten tons per acre per year. Actually the testimony shows without dispute that the acceptable loss limit is five tons per acre per year. The Ortners and Schranks concede as much and we give this no further consideration. The only question before us, therefore, is the constitutional one involving both federal and state constitutional provisions.

In considering the constitutionality of legislative enactments, we accord them every presumption of validity and find them unconstitutional only upon a showing that they clearly infringe on constitutional rights and only if every reasonable basis for support is negated. [Citation.]

Important to our decision here is a determination as to whether the restrictions and conditions imposed by ch. 467A, The Code, amount to a taking of property under eminent domain or simply a regulation under the police power of the state. The latter entitles the property owner to no compensation; the former requires that he be paid for the appropriation of his property for public use.

We recognized this distinction in *Hinrichs v. Iowa State Highway Commission*, 260 Iowa 1115, 1126, 152 N.W.2d 248, 255 (1967) as follows:

> "Eminent domain" is the taking of private property for a public use for which compensation must be given. On the other hand "Police Power" controls and regulates the use of property for the public good for which no compensation need be made.

Even the exercise of police power, however, may amount to a taking if it deprives a property owner of the substantial use and enjoyment of his property. The point at which police power regulation becomes so oppressive that it results in a taking is impossible of general definition and must be determined on the circumstances of each case. *Penn Central Transportation Co. v. City of New York*, 438 U.S. 104, 124 (1978); *Iowa Natural Resources Council v. Van Zee*, 261 Iowa 1287, 1294, 158 N.W.2d 111, 116 (1968); *Benschoter v. Hakes*, 232 Iowa 1354, 1361, 8 N.W.2d 481, 485-86 (1943).

In *Van Zee* and *Hakes* we stated that the test is whether the "collective benefits [to the public] outweigh the specific restraints imposed [on the individual]." Factors of particular importance include the "economic impact of the regulation on the claimant and, particularly, the extent to which the regulation has interfered with distinct investment backed expectations." To be considered also is the "character of the governmental action." *See Penn Central*, 437 U.S. at 124. It is important therefore to consider the nature of the public interest involved and the impact of the restrictions placed on defendants' use of their land by ch. 467A, The Code.

It should take no extended discussion to demonstrate that agriculture is important to the welfare and prosperity of this state. It has been judicially recognized as our leading industry.

The state has a vital interest in protecting its soil as the greatest of its natural resources, and it has a right to do so. *Iowa Natural Resources Council v. Van Zee*, 261 Iowa at 1297, 158 N.W.2d at 118. This is the purpose of ch. 467A as is apparent from this declaration of purpose contained in § 467A.2:

> It is hereby declared to be the policy of the legislature to provide for the restoration and conservation of the soil and soil resources of this state and for the control and prevention of soil erosion, floodwater, and sediment damages, and thereby to preserve natural resources, control floods, prevent impairment of dams and reservoirs, assist and maintain the navigability of rivers and harbors, preserve wildlife, protect the tax base, protect public lands, and promote the health, safety and public welfare of the people of this state.

This same subject receives further legislative treatment in § 467A.43 as follows:

> To conserve the fertility, general usefulness, and value of the soil and soil resources of this state, and to prevent the injurious effect of soil erosion, it is hereby made the duty of the owners of real property in this state to establish and maintain soil and water conservation practices or erosion control practices, as required by the regulations of the commissioners of the respective soil conservation districts.

Defendants' argument is two-fold. They assert first that the statute amounts to a taking of private property without just compensation. Next, they say the statute is an unreasonable and illegal exercise of the state's police power.

We hold defendants have failed to establish § 467A.44 is unconstitutional. Its provisions are reasonably related to carrying out the announced legislative purpose of soil control, admittedly a proper exercise of police power.

While this imposes an extra financial burden on defendants, it is one the state has a right to exact. The importance of soil conservation is best illustrated by the state's willingness to pay three-fourths of the cost. In Ortner's case, the state's share is $36,760.50 and in Schrank's it is $4,413.00. The remainder to be paid by defendants ($12,253.50 by Ortner and $1,471.00 by Schrank) is still substantial, but not unreasonably so. A law does not become unconstitutional because it works a hardship. [Citations.] The argument that one must make substantial expenditures to comply with regulatory statutes does not raise constitutional barriers.

There is conflicting testimony concerning the effect which either proposal — permanent seeding or terracing — will have on future farming operations, the necessity for additional equipment, the possibility of other alternatives, diminution in farm income, and decrease in value of the land. This is not the kind of clear and compelling evidence necessary as a premise for holding a statute unconstitutional.

What we have already said is relevant, too, on defendants' claim the regulations established by the soil conservation district amount to a taking of their property without compensation in violation of the federal and state constitutions.

As we have already pointed out, an exercise of police power may be so sweeping in its scope and so all inclusive in its operation that it becomes a taking rather than a regulation. However, this did not happen here. Defendants still have the use and enjoyment of their property, limited only by the necessity to prevent soil erosion beyond allowable standards.

Each case must be determined on its own facts. Our conclusion on the facts here is that the record does not support the trial court's finding of unconstitutionality. We have reviewed the authorities relied on by defendants and have given particular attention to *Penn Central Transportation Co. v. City of New York*, 437 U.S. at 124, where the factors important to deciding if there has been a taking without compensation are discussed. We are unable to agree they help defendants' position.

Defendants raise one other objection. They say the statute is invalid because it is designed "solely as a means of furthering the purely private property interests of a very limited class of landowners" rather than for the benefit of the public generally. This is based on § 467A.47 which, they allege, provides for action by the soil conservation district upon the complaint of one damaged by erosion, rather than upon the initiative of the district itself. We believe this argument ignores other sections of the act under which the soil conservation district is authorized to act. *See* § 467A.44(3), under which the commissioners may require owners to act, and § 467A.52, under which, in limited circumstances, they may take independent action. *See also Miller v. Schoene*, 276 U.S. 272, 281 (1928), where a similar provision was held unobjectionable. We find no merit in this complaint.

The judgment of the trial court is reversed and the case is remanded for such other proceedings as may be appropriate.

NOTES AND QUESTIONS

1. In important dicta in the last paragraph, the court suggested that the soil district, on its own, could enforce the requirements of the Act without first obtaining a neighbor's complaint. In response to *Woodbury County*, the Iowa statute was amended to provide explicitly for enforcement of soil loss tolerances by the district on its own authority. Under the amendments, the soil conservation district officials may inspect a piece of property that they have reasonable grounds to suspect is eroding beyond the statutory limits. If they find that the loss is more than twice the acceptable limit, they must send notice to the owner or operator. The officials may petition the court for an order to comply with the conservation plan if notice is sent to an owner or operator for three consecutive

years. Iowa Code § 467A.61, discussed in Note, *Regulatory Authority to Mandate Soil Conservation in Iowa After Ortner*, 65 IOWA L. REV. 1035 (1980). How much time could elapse between inspection by conservation district officials and enforced compliance with a conservation plan? Do you see any problems with reliance on complaints of neighboring landowners as set out in the statute to ensure compliance? *See generally* L. MALONE, ENVIRONMENTAL REGULATION OF LAND USE § 5.08 (1991). The statute only authorized 50% cost-sharing for voluntarily adopted conservation measures but 75% cost-sharing for measures mandated by the district. Coupled with the procedures for private complaints, is there potential for collusive complaints?

2. Increasingly, landlords and property owners are requiring conservation measures in leases and installment land contracts. For example, in *Moser v. Thorp Sales Corp.*, 312 N.W.2d 881 (Iowa 1981), an action to quiet title was sought by the Mosers who had purchased the farm at an auction. The sellers refused to perform. The issue involving soil erosion was whether the Mosers were entitled to recover for damages to the land for the time while other parties were in possession. The damages were caused by the planting of row crops, particularly corn, in rows on steep hills, and the use of a moldboard plow. Previously, the Mosers had planted the corn in contours with terracing and minimum tillage. Although the majority found no liability or damages, the dissent argued that there was both liability and damage. The basis for liability, given the unusual nature of the case, was trespass (although the court also mentioned implied covenants might be violated). The difficulty with damages in the case was that the usual remedy for trespass was the difference in value of the property or the cost of reparation. The cost of reparation could not be estimated, and therefore it seemed the difference in value had to be utilized for the measure of damages. However, due to inflation, the land value had actually increased during the time the Woods were in possession. The dissent then suggested that the measure of damages should be the difference in the value of the land without the damage and with the damage. *See also* Note, *Moser v. Thorp Sales Corporation: The Protection of Farmland from Poor Farming Practices*, 27 S.D. L. REV. 513 (1982).

The *Moser* case is just one example of the increasing use of measures to control soil erosion in installment land contracts or leases. *See also Buras v. Shell Oil Co.*, 666 F. Supp. 919 (S.D. Miss. 1987) (plaintiffs alleged that the oil company with an easement on their property had negligently constructed a pipeline, resulting in excessive erosion damage to the farmland on which it was constructed; because of an express provision in the easement grant that the company would bury the pipeline "so it will not interfere with the ordinary cultivation of the land," the court held that the company was liable for damage to crops, fences, buildings, and timber, without regard to negligence). As this measure is increasingly used, it seems inevitable that tougher leases will be drafted and more cases will arise in which possessors have abused the land and failed to control soil erosion. Of course, persons may sue others in nuisance for damage caused by excessive erosion. Absent off-site damage, however, litigation poses no hurdle to abuse of the soil. The public trust has yet to be extended to protect the soil from abuse by the landowner absent damage to others' property or health.

C. FARMLAND PRESERVATION

Concern about irreversible conversion of agricultural land to nonagricultural uses in the 1970s led to a wave of farmland preservation measures at the state and local levels. Economists have criticized this concern as alarmist and unjustified by the rate of conversion. *See, e.g.*, C. LITTLE, LAND AND FOOD: THE PRESERVATION OF U.S. FARMLAND (American Land Forum, Washington 1979); M. COTNER, LAND USE POLICY AND AGRICULTURE: A STATE AND LOCAL PERSPECTIVE (USDA. Economic Research Service, Washington 1974); E. ROBERTS, THE LAW AND THE PRESERVATION OF AGRICULTURAL LAND (1982); Urban Land Institute, *Has the "Farmland Crisis" Been Overstated?: Recommendations for Balancing Urban and Agricultural Land Needs*, 1983 ZONING AND PLANNING LAW HANDBOOK 235, 266 (Strom ed. 1983). Nevertheless, state and local governments have adopted and implemented right-to-farm laws, exceptions for agriculture in county zoning, agricultural zoning, agricultural districts, differential assessment, purchases of development rights, and transferable development rights to protect farmland. *See generally* Popp, *A Survey of Agricultural Zoning: State Responses to the Farmland Crisis*, 24 REAL PROP. TR. J. 371 (1989). At the federal level, the Farmland Protection Policy Act of 1981 (FPPA) serves the limited purpose of requiring federal agencies to consider alternatives to projects and financial assistance that would result in conversion of agricultural land. Farmland preservation measures may reduce the relative attractiveness of a farming area for development, offset additional burdens placed on farmers by encroaching development, or directly prevent change from agricultural use to nonagricultural uses. Only those programs in the third category, however, actually prevent conversion of agricultural land.

In 1981, an eighteen-month, two million dollar study of farmland conversion was published as a cooperative venture between the United States Department of Agriculture (USDA) and the Council on Environmental Quality (CEQ). N. SAMPSON, FARMLAND OR WASTELAND: A TIME TO CHOOSE 108 (1981). The National Agricultural Lands Study, NATIONAL AGRICULTURAL LANDS STUDY (NALS), FINAL REPORT (1981), had been commissioned by the USDA and CEQ in 1979, largely due to the defeat of the first proposed federal act for farmland protection, the so-called "Jeffords bill." Fischel, *The Urbanization of Agricultural Land: A Review of the National Agricultural Land Study*, 58 LAND ECON. 236, 237 (May 1981). The focus of the final report of the study is upon the continued adequacy of food and fiber production in the United States. According to the report, that adequacy was threatened by two trends in the 1970s: (1) the increase in world grain prices and the accompanying increase in the demand for exports;

and (2) the "quantum leap" in the rate at which agricultural land was being converted to nonagricultural uses. *Id.* at 237-38.

All agricultural land may be seen as on a continuum from stable rural land to land in imminent danger of urbanization. NATIONAL AGRICULTURAL LANDS STUDY (NALS), THE PROTECTION OF FARMLAND: A REFERENCE GUIDEBOOK FOR STATE AND LOCAL GOVERNMENTS 37-39 (1981). The threat of development has an impact on the farmer-landowner as well, the effect commonly known as the "impermanence syndrome." Due to the multitude of problems created for farmland by surrounding development and the farmer's growing recognition that sale to developers is imminent and unavoidable, a threatened farmer reduces ongoing, long-term investments in land improvements, soil and water conservation, and farm structures. According to farmland preservationists, the impermanence syndrome inevitably leads to sale of the farmland for the financial profits obtainable through commercial or residential development. *Id.* at 35.

To avoid that dilemma, the report urged state and county governments to adopt a variety of farmland preservation techniques, and stated that "the national interest in agricultural land should be articulated by a presidential-level and/or congressional statement of policy" to be implemented by federal agencies. NALS, FINAL REPORT, *supra*, at 88. This suggestion of federal action triggered in 1981 the first federal legislation designed to protect farmland from conversion, the Farmland Protection Policy Act.

1. THE FARMLAND PROTECTION POLICY ACT

In December 1981, ten months after publication of the NALS, the Farmland Protection Policy Act of 1981, 7 U.S.C. §§ 4201-4209, was passed by Congress. In the preamble to the Act, the stated concern of the Act is to preserve the United States' ability "to produce food and fiber in sufficient quantities to meet domestic needs and the demands of our export markets." *Id.* § 4201(a) and (b). The reach of the Act, however, is limited to procedures "to assure that the actions [of federal agencies] do not cause United States farmland to be irreversibly converted to nonagricultural uses in cases in which other national interests do not override the importance of the protection of farmland nor otherwise outweigh the benefits of maintaining farmland resources." *Id.* § 4201(a)(7).

The somewhat general provisions of the Act left meaningful implementation to regulations to be promulgated by the Secretary of Agriculture. The Act says only that the USDA shall develop criteria for identifying the effects of federal programs on the conversion of farmland to nonagricultural uses. *Id.* § 4202(a). The key substantive provision is section 4202(b):

> Departments, agencies, independent commissions, and other units of the Federal Government shall use the criteria established under subsection (a) of this section, to identify the quantity of farmland actually converted by Federal programs, and to identify and take into account the adverse effects

of Federal programs on the preservation of farmland; consider alternative actions, as appropriate, that could lessen such adverse effects; and assure that such Federal programs, to the extent practicable, are compatible with State, unit of local government, and private programs and policies to protect farmland.

Id. § 4202(b). Also, every agency is to review current laws, administrative rules and regulations, policies, and procedures within its authority to determine if any of these will prevent the agency from taking appropriate action to comply with the Act. Each agency must then develop proposals to bring its program's authorities and administrative activities into conformity with the Act. *Id.* § 4203(a) and (b). The Act has two very significant limitations in sections 4208(a) and 4209:

§ 4208. Limitations.

(a) This chapter does not authorize the Federal Government in any way to regulate the use of private or non-Federal land, or in any way affect the property rights of owners of such land.

....

§ 4209. Prohibition on maintenance of actions.

This chapter shall not be deemed to provide a basis for any action, either legal or equitable, by any person or class of persons challenging a Federal project, program, or other activity that may affect farmland: *Provided*, That the Governor of an affected State where a State policy or program exists to protect farmland may bring an action in the Federal district court of the district where a Federal program is proposed to enforce the requirements of section 4202 of this title and regulations issued pursuant thereto.

Id. §§ 4208(a) and 4209.

NOTES AND QUESTIONS

1. Given the limitations in sections 4208 and 4209, how can the requirements of the Act be enforced? Does the Act impose any limitations on an agency's decision to continue or abandon a project? *See also* 7 C.F.R. § 658.3(c). Consider the following discussion of the implementing regulations in your assessment:

Aside from the obvious failure to forbid conversion, the regulations provide many loopholes to even the limited procedural protection provided by the Act; for example:

1. Prime farmland is zoned for agricultural and residential use with large-lot zoning, and the agency fails to follow the procedures as outlined in the Act and regulations. There may not be a violation of the FPPA. Under section 658.2 of the regulations, the farmland may already be

"committed to urban development." The land is zoned for residential use in a zoning ordinance, and the large-lot zoning itself may not have been "intended to protect farmland."

2. A federal agency approves a public utility license for a project on protected farmland, without going through any of the procedures required by the Act and regulations. There is no violation of the FPPA, because the definition of "federal program" does not include federal permitting or licensing for activities on private or nonfederal land.

3. The federal agency sends its request to the SCS for the land evaluation of a project covered by the Act, but the SCS does not respond within forty-five days. The agency may proceed with the project without further compliance with the Act under section 658.4(a), which allows an agency to proceed if it has not received a response from the SCS within forty-five days.

4. Federal land administered by the Bureau of Land Management that is protected farmland is leased for surface mining. There is no need for the agency to follow the procedures of the FPPA, because the comments to the regulations indicate there is no irreversible conversion of the land to nonagricultural use with surface mining.

It should also be noted that, under the site assessment criteria, farmland that is surrounded by nonagricultural uses receives a lower score and less protection under the FPPA than farmland in rural areas. The criteria implicitly assume that farmland should be protected only in rural areas. Also, the criteria do not include assessment of the number of farms affected or the amount of income affected by a proposed project, because "Congress apparently intended to protect farmland per se, not farms as economic units."

L. MALONE, ENVIRONMENTAL REGULATION OF LAND USE § 6.05(5) (1991). The Department of Agriculture has also been extraordinarily slow in implementing the Act through regulations. The first set of regulations to implement the 1981 Act were not published in final form until 1984. Regulations to implement the amendments to the Act in 1985 were not finalized until 1994. *See also* Johnson & Fogelman, *The Farmland Protection Policy Act: Stillbirth of a Policy?*, 1986 U. ILL. L. REV. 563.

2. In 1996, the Farmland Protection Program (the FPP) was included in the Federal Agriculture Improvement and Reform Act. Section 338 directs the Secretary of Agriculture to establish and carry out the FPP. Under this program, the USDA will purchase conservation easements or other interests in land with productive soil that is subject to a pending offer from a state or local government for the purpose of protecting topsoil by limiting non-agricultural uses of the land. *See* Farmland Protection Program, 61 Fed. Reg. 43,226 (1996).

2. RIGHT-TO-FARM LAWS

As urban development begins to surround farmland, conflicts between the competing land uses frequently result in nuisance lawsuits by residents against farmers. Residential neighbors often complain of the odors, flies, animal control problems, noise, dust, chemical spraying, and other necessary incidents of farming operations. The surrounding residential neighbors may bring a nuisance lawsuit against the farming operation to curtail its interference with surrounding development uses. The other possibility is that the residents of the neighborhood may lobby for local ordinances to restrict the farming operation. Both attempts to restrict the farming operation can significantly hamper it or make its operation economically infeasible.

Farmers then find it necessary to defend themselves in court against lawsuits and enforcement of local ordinances. States have responded to remedy the conflict through "right-to-farm" laws. Generally, these statutes codify the "coming to the nuisance defense," providing protection to agricultural operations that were in place before the neighboring residential development. NATIONAL AGRICULTURAL LANDS STUDY (NALS), THE PROTECTION OF FARM-LAND: A REFERENCE GUIDEBOOK FOR STATE AND LOCAL GOVERNMENTS 98 (1981). Almost every state has some form of right-to-farm law. L. MALONE, ENVIRONMENTAL REGULATION OF LAND USE § 6.06[1] n.6 (1991).

LAUX v. CHOPIN LAND ASSOCIATES

550 N.E.2d 100 (Ind. App. 1990)

GARRARD, JUDGE.

The record discloses that in June 1986 Lauxes listed for sale with a local real estate dealer approximately 113 of the 123 acres they owned and farmed in Whitley County, Indiana. They intended to retain the remaining ten acres which surrounded their home.

In late July or early August Lauxes' sons purchased 29 feeder hogs and had them delivered to Lauxes' property. Initially the hogs were raised in a vacant implement shed. The size of the hog raising operation grew and at the time of sale closing in December 1986 Lauxes were feeding between 85 and 90 hogs. In March 1987 Lauxes commenced construction of a hog raising facility which was put into use in late May or early June 1987. During the summer of 1987 the number of hogs increased to between 300 and 350 in a farrow-to-finish operation.

Meanwhile, on August 14, 1986, several individuals had made a proposal to Lauxes to purchase the 113 acres being offered for sale. Negotiations continued through the fall, an agreement was reached and the sale was closed on December 2, 1986. Title was to be placed in the name of Chopin, which was subsequently incorporated in January 1987.

At all pertinent times the entire area was zoned for agricultural uses. While the purchasers advised Lauxes that they intended to use the land for the purpose of developing large residential tracts, the land has been actually used as a grain farm since the sale.

No tracts have been sold nor residences built, but Chopin lost an opportunity to sell a portion of the real estate to a physician because of odors produced by the hog raising operation.

Additionally, the trial court found that Mr. Popp of Chopin first learned of the hogs in late June of 1987 and protested to Lauxes. In August he caused a notice to be served upon them requesting abatement of a nuisance.

Chopin commenced suit on January 19, 1988, to abate the hog operation as a nuisance. Lauxes answered asserting inter alia that they were entitled to the protection of the Right-to-Farm Act, IC 34-1-52-4.

The trial court, after hearing, entered its special findings of fact and conclusions thereon. It determined that the odor generated by the hog raising operation constituted a nuisance, and enjoined the Lauxes from maintaining, assisting or permitting the operation of any feeder hog operation on the 10.673 acres and to refrain from conducting or permitting any livestock raising operation on that real estate. This appeal followed.

In 1981 the Indiana legislature amended IC 34-1-52-1 *et seq.* concerning actions for nuisance by adding a new section often referred to as the Right-to-Farm Act.

This section, IC 34-1-52-4, declares the policy of this state to conserve, protect and encourage the development and improvement of its agricultural land for the production of food and other agricultural products. It further states the purpose of the section to be to reduce the loss to the state of its agricultural resources by limiting the circumstances under which agricultural operations may be deemed to be a nuisance, noting that when non-agricultural land uses extend into agricultural areas, nuisance suits against agricultural uses are often the result.

The critical provisions of the section state:

> (f) No agricultural or industrial operation or any of its appurtenances shall be or become a nuisance, private or public, by any changed conditions in the vicinity of the locality after the agricultural or industrial operation, as the case may be, has been in operation continuously on the locality for more than one year, provided:
>
> > (1) There is no significant change in the hours of operation;
> > (2) There is no significant change in the type of operation; and
> > (3) The operation would not have been a nuisance at the time the agricultural or industrial operation, as the case may be, began on that locality.
>
> (g) This section does not apply whenever a nuisance results from the negligent operation of an agricultural or industrial operation or its appurtenances.

The statute is essentially a non-claim statute. Thus, if the operation was not an actionable nuisance at the time it was begun, and if it is engaged in continuously for more than a year on that locality, then it will not become a nuisance because of any subsequent changed conditions in the vicinity. In other words, activities or uses subsequently "coming to the nuisance" will have no claim for its abatement.

The statute imposes three conditions, or limitations on that bar. Subsection (g) removes from the protection of the statute nuisances which result from negligent operation.

In addition, subsections (f)(1) and (2) remove the bar where there has been either a significant change in the hours of operation or a significant change in the type of operation. Because the language of the statute makes it applicable to any given point in time, the effect of a significant change in either hours of operation or type of operation is to again invoke the statutory conditions and recommence the running of the statutory clock. If then the operation was not an actionable nuisance when the change occurred (i.e., went into effect), it will not become one by virtue of changed conditions in the vicinity which occur more than a year after the operation continuously exists in the changed form. *See* Hand, *Right-to-Farm Laws — Breaking New Ground in the Preservation of Farmland*, 45 U. PITT. L. REV. 289, 308-09.

In *Erbrich Products Co. v. Wills* (1987), Ind. App., 509 N.E.2d 850, our First District considered the statute's application to industrial operations. It determined that the burden of proof as to subsection (f) rested with the party claiming the benefit of that provision. It also determined that subsection (g) concerning negligent operation is an exception to subsection (f)'s application and the burden of proof for the exception rested upon the party opposing the application of the statutory defense. 509 N.E.2d at 858. The court in *Erbrich* was not directly concerned with which party bears the burden of proving the existence or non-existence of the three numbered provisos to subsection (f) that there be no significant change in hours of operation, and that the operation would not have been a nuisance at the time it began on that locality. Nevertheless, the reasoning employed by the court on general principles of evidence involving statutory exceptions clearly indicates that the court would have placed the burden of establishing compliance with the provisos upon the party claiming the benefit of the statute.

We therefore accept *Erbrich* as establishing the allocation of the burden of proof under the statute.

In this case the court made no finding that Lauxes' hog raising operation would have been a nuisance absent any changes in the vicinity or that the facility was being operated negligently. Additionally, we note that Indiana has determined that the raising of hogs is not a nuisance *per se*. *Shatto v. McNulty* (1987), Ind. App., 509 N.E.2d 897; *Yeager and Sullivan, Inc. v. O'Neill* (1975), 163 Ind. App. 466, 324 N.E.2d 846.

In its conclusions the trial court stated that the commencement of the hog raising operation constituted a significant change in the type of operation conducted by Lauxes "and increasing the operation from 29 hogs in August of 1986 to between two and three hundred by the summer of 1987 was another significant change."

In its findings (which were sustained by the evidence) the court determined that prior to August 1986, the land had been used for grain farming and in August the Lauxes commenced a hog raising operation. It also found that hog raising produced a distinctive and unpleasant odor. We agree that the findings sustain the conclusion that within the meaning of IC 34-1-52-4 the original change to a hog raising operation constituted a significant change in the type of operation.

The conclusion concerning a second change is much more troublesome. The requirement for invoking the statute is that there be no significant change in the *type* of operation. Since the statute supplies no definition of that term, we think it must be taken in its ordinary sense, as referring to qualities common to a number of items, individuals or activities which distinguish them as an identifiable class. It follows that merely increasing or decreasing the size or numbers of an operation will not serve to change the type of operation. That is not to say, however, that other changes which occur as a part of or incidental to a change in size may not indeed work a change in the type of an operation. It does say that merely determining that numbers have increased is insufficient to support a conclusion that there has been a significant change in the type of an operation.

Here the only special findings to support the court's conclusion of a second significant change in the type of operation were its findings concerning the increase in the number of pigs and its findings that Lauxes constructed a facility for the hogs in the spring and summer of 1987. Those findings are not sufficient to sustain the conclusion of a significant change in the type of operation.

Another problem arises from the court's determination that IC 34-1-52-4 was inapplicable. The statute provides that no agricultural operation will become a nuisance "by any changed conditions in the vicinity ... after the agricultural [operation] ... has been in operation continuously on the locality for more than one (1) year...."

The question then arises as to what constitutes a changed condition in the vicinity. Clearly, the principal scenario envisioned by the legislature arises when people build and move into residences close by a theretofore permissible agricultural or industrial operation. They then become disturbed over noise, odors, etc. and wish to have the offensive activity abated.

As already noted, the court's findings support the conclusion that there was a significant change in the type of agricultural operation conducted by Lauxes in August 1986. Since the court made no determination that their operation constituted an actionable nuisance at the time it began, we can assume for the purpose of analysis that the injurious effect (*see* IC 34-1-52-1 and 2) occurred because of the impact of the operation's odors on proposed residential development.

Yet during the one year period following August 1986, there were no residences built, no platting of a subdivision or change in the agricultural zoning. The court did find that due to the odor from the activity Chopin lost the opportunity to sell a portion of its real estate to a physician. That finding alone would appear insufficient to ground a determination that there had been such a change in conditions in the vicinity as to make hog raising an actionable nuisance and terminate the running of the statutory one year clock.

The court's other findings concerning the Chopin tract establish that Chopin paid more than the average market price for the land for agricultural purposes; that Lauxes were aware that Chopin was purchasing for residential development and sold the land for development purposes.

Such findings might be indicative of a basis for determining that Lauxes should be equitably estopped from claiming the benefit of the Right-to-Farm statute, but the court entered no findings or conclusions concerning estoppel. Therefore, we may not treat them on that basis. While they demonstrate an intention to change the conditions in the vicinity by beginning a residential development, we believe they are inadequate to demonstrate that such a change has in fact occurred so as to preclude the agricultural operator from establishing the one year continuous operation required by the statute.

We realize that when the hearing was conducted herein neither the trial court nor the parties had available to them any detailed interpretation concerning the application of the Right-to-Farm Act. Under the circumstances it appears that fairness dictates that the parties should be entitled to develop their evidence in the light of our decision today. Therefore, we reverse and remand for a new hearing.

NOTES AND QUESTIONS

1. If a right-to-farm law provides protection against "nuisance" liability, what theories of liability are encompassed within the term "nuisance"? According to RESTATEMENT (SECOND) OF TORTS § 821A (1986), and PROSSER, HANDBOOK OF THE LAW OF TORTS 573 (4th ed. 1971), nuisance is a field of tort liability with reference to interference with land uses, rather than a separate, distinct type of tortious conduct. Under this approach, liability for nuisance may rest upon an intentional invasion of the plaintiff's interest, negligence, or strict liability. In contrast, a more recent edition of Prosser rejects the approach of the Second Restatement and the late William Prosser and characterizes nuisance as encompassing only intentional interference of substantial and unreasonable nature in another's use and enjoyment of land. KEETON ET AL., PROSSER AND KEETON ON THE LAW OF TORTS 622-33 (5th ed. 1984). This scholarly disagreement is of significant practical importance to what causes of action are precluded under right-to-farm laws.

2. There is one case in Indiana in which a right-to-farm law was successfully used to protect an agricultural facility from nuisance liability. In *Shatto v. McNulty*, 509 N.E.2d 897 (Ind. App. 1987) the owners of property adjacent to a farm sued in nuisance for damages and an injunction against the farm. The defendant had purchased his farm in 1956, although the farm had been used to raise pigs for an "indeterminate time." The area was zoned for agricultural use. The plaintiffs, who had purchased their property in 1968, complained of odors and flies from the farm. There was testimony from several witnesses that the farm was not being conducted negligently, and the trial court found that the defendant had not changed his hours or type of operation. The Indiana Court of Appeals concluded the hog farm was not a nuisance and, in any event, the right-to-farm law protected the farm since none of the exemptions were applicable. The court asserted that so long as the human race consumes pork, someone must tolerate the smell. *Cf.* Hodas, *Promote Actions for Public Nuisances: Common Law Citizen Suits for Relief from Environmental Harm*, 16 ECOLOGY L.Q. 883 (1989).

3. There are four models of right-to-farm laws on which most right-to-farm laws have been based. The New York model prohibits local laws that unreasonably restrict agricultural operations. The North Carolina model, the most frequently utilized model and the model for the Indiana act, prohibits nuisance lawsuits that occur as a result of changed conditions in the locality if the agricultural facility has been in operation for one year or more before the changed conditions. The Tennessee model provides the broadest protection, but to the most limited types of agricultural facilities. For feedlots, dairy facilities, and egg production facilities, if the agricultural facility is in compliance with state law and was in operation before the complaining party's ownership or use of the land, the agricultural facility is protected from a nuisance cause of action and exempted from other forms of state and local regulation. In Washington and those states following the Washington model, an agricultural facility is presumed reasonable if it is operated in accordance with good agricultural practices and was established prior to the surrounding nonagricultural uses. If the agricultural facility complies with applicable state, federal, and local laws, it is presumed to be in accordance with good agricultural practices. NALS, *supra*, at 98.

Because the North Carolina model is the most frequently utilized model, the difficulties in its interpretation meant further analysis. To what extent must the area surrounding an agricultural operation be developed or have competing land uses for there to be "changed conditions" in the locality? Also, the agricultural operation must have been in operation for one year. The statutes ordinarily do not specify whether the operation must be in operation one year before the lawsuit, or one year before the changed conditions in the locality.

One of the few cases interpreting a right-to-farm law, *Herrin v. Opatut*, 248 Ga. 140, 281 S.E.2d 575 (1981), addressed these two issues under the Georgia right-to-farm law was based on the North Carolina model. In *Herrin* the plaintiffs, primarily residents of the area around the offending egg farm, filed suit against the defendants alleging that they were "plagued by flies and offensive odors emanating from the egg farm." The plaintiffs also alleged that the defendants were draining waste from their egg farm into the plaintiff's pond. The plaintiffs requested that the farm be declared a nuisance and enjoined from further activity. The defendants asserted that the only issues in the case were whether they were an agricultural or farming operation within the meaning of the statute, and whether the facility had been in operation for one year prior to the institution of the lawsuit. The Supreme Court of Georgia, however, focused first on whether or not there had been changed conditions within the locality. The court concluded "changed conditions ... in the locality of the facility refers solely to the extension of non-agricultural land uses, residential or otherwise, into existing agricultural areas." According to the court, the legislature had chosen as a matter of policy to exempt an agricultural facility from being declared a nuisance if the facility had been in operation for one year prior to the changed conditions.

An additional problem of interpretation is presented by the exception that the agricultural operation must not have been a nuisance at the time it began. Does the agricultural operation have to demonstrate that it was not a nuisance when it began or does the plaintiff have to demonstrate that it was? Would complaints to state and local agencies about the agricultural operation be sufficient to demonstrate that the agricultural operation was a nuisance when it began?

REVIEW PROBLEM FOR RIGHT-TO-FARM LAWS

Jefferson Ambler, a poultry farmer, resides in an essentially rural county, operating a poultry farm that has been in use since 1954. In 1954, a few neighboring farmers registered complaints with state and local agencies about the odor from the operation, but never pursued the matter further. As a result of a technologically progressive and profitable method of raising chickens developed by the farmer in 1958, he had found it necessary to expand the physical boundaries of his operation substantially in 1965, 1975, and finally in June of 1982. Although the new method results in more air and water pollution than that from more common poultry-raising methods, the farm still complies with all applicable state, federal, and local regulations. No other farm in the state uses this particular method, and each physical expansion has resulted in only a minute increase in air and water pollution.

The area surrounding this farm has been, and still is, essentially rural. Because the area is approximately an hour from a major metropolitan area, more and more city residents have purchased farms there to build "ranchettes." Only two people not engaged in agriculture had moved into the area prior to 1954, and they had maintained a portion of the land for growing crops. By 1956, two farms were divided into three or four lots each, with a residence on each lot. By 1965, one more farm had been similarly divided, and, by 1975, two more farms were divided into three or four lots. In May of 1983, a developer purchased the farm adjacent to the farmer's property to build a residential development. This fifty-acre development would have individual residences on individual one-acre lots. Shortly after the development was completed and occupied in July of 1983, the residents pushed through a local ordinance prohibiting any agricultural operation (defined to include the farmer's operation) from emitting any discharge from any point source into any water source from three to four in the afternoon, the penalty being civil fines. These hours were selected because neighborhood school children had frequently been seen playing in the stream which received the runoff and discharge from the poultry farm. It is impossible for the farm to comply with the ordinance without again changing its method of operation.

If the developer files a suit against the farmer based on nuisance, trespass, and negligence for air and water pollution, what would be the result if the lawsuit seeks an injunction or, in the alternative, damages under the Indiana act? How might the result be different under a state statute based on the New York, Tennessee, or Washington models? For a suggested analysis, see L. MALONE, ENVIRONMENTAL REGULATION OF LAND USE § 6.06[3] (1991).

3. AGRICULTURAL ZONING

Zoning is one of the most commonly used methods for farmland preservation. NATIONAL AGRICULTURAL LANDS STUDY (NALS), THE PROTECTION OF FARM-LAND: A REFERENCE GUIDEBOOK FOR STATE AND LOCAL GOVERNMENTS 21 (1981). To understand agricultural zoning, it is first necessary to have a general overview of how zoning works. Zoning restrictions are an exercise of the state's police power within the inherent power of states. D. KMIEC, ZONING AND PLANNING DESKBOOK § 5.01 (1987). Power to zone must be vested in a local unit of government by the state legislature. The purpose of a local zoning ordinance is to divide the jurisdiction into areas with permitted and special uses for each of those areas. A zoning ordinance consists of two parts, the text and the map. The text creates a variety of districts with certain uses permitted within each of these districts. In addition, in a district there may be special or conditional uses, which may only be utilized in the district upon meeting the conditions set forth in the text. A. RATHKOFF & D. RATHKOFF, THE LAW OF ZONING AND PLANNING §§ 2.02[1], 3.01-3.02, 4.01 (1987). The second part of the ordinance, a zoning map, carves up the county, township, village, or city and assigns use classifications to districts as specified by the text. KMIEC, *supra*, § 3.01. In several jurisdictions, the zoning ordinance must be consistent with the long-term land use plan for the area. *Id.* § 17.05. A land use plan is a long-term plan for growth and development subject to periodic review by the zoning board. *See id.* § 15.01.

There are many ways in which the restrictions of a zoning ordinance may be avoided by a landowner. The party may petition to have the map or the text of the zoning ordinance amended. More commonly, however, a party seeks a use variance from the terms of the zoning ordinance. Ordinarily to do so, the petitioning party must show unnecessary hardship from the ordinance's requirements. Mere economic hardship is not enough to justify a zoning variance. A somewhat simpler way to deviate from the requirements of the zoning ordinance is to get a special use permit or conditional use permit if the anticipated use meets the conditions for special uses set out in the zoning ordinance. *Id.* §§ 6.03 — 6.05. Frequently, constitutional challenges are made to the restrictions imposed by a zoning ordinance. *See id.* §§ 7.02[1]-[7]. Perhaps most commonly, a land use restriction is challenged as a regulatory taking of private property without just compensation. *See id.* § 7.02[5]. In addition, a zoning ordinance may be challenged on the grounds that it is exclusionary, that is, that it is intended to exclude members of a certain economic class, or on the grounds that the zoning ordinance violates the antitrust laws. *Id.* § 7.02[6][d]. Because of the many ways in which a zoning restriction can be challenged, zoning cannot be counted on to provide long-term control over land use or meaningful preservation of agricultural land. Because of the immediate and sometimes extensive profits that can be made from converting agricultural lands to nonagricultural uses, zoning restrictions to preserve agricultural land are subject to constant challenges and political pressure for change.

Agricultural zoning can be exclusive or nonexclusive. Exclusive agricultural zoning is less frequently used than nonexclusive agricultural zoning, because it prohibits nonagricultural use of land within the district and is therefore unpopular with landowners. There are basically three characteristics that are shared by exclusive agricultural zoning ordinances. First, nonfarm dwellings are prohibited. Second, there is a direct focus on preserving farm use rather than defining a farm by a large minimum lot size or other density standard. Third, each proposed farm dwelling usually requires some individual evaluation under the ordinance. The main advantage to exclusive agricultural zoning in preserving farmland is that it ensures there will be no conflict between residential and agricultural uses in those areas where nonfarm dwellings are prohibited. Exclusive zoning ordinances, however, entail higher administrative costs because of the more extensive restrictions and the requirement of review for farm dwellings. The ordinances are more difficult to get adopted than nonexclusive zoning ordinances, because they foreclose residential development to farmland owners who may, at some point in time, wish to sell their farmland to developers. The purpose of exclusive agricultural zoning will, in any event, be undermined if the zoning authority attempts to mitigate its restrictiveness through lax supervision of rezoning and variances. NALS, *supra*, at 122. *See also* Note, *State-Sponsored Growth Management as a Remedy for Exclusionary Zoning*, 108 HARV. L. REV. 1127 (1995).

In nonexclusive zoning ordinances, farmland preservation is accomplished through limiting the density of residential development. Nonexclusive agricultural zoning establishes agricultural use as one of the permitted uses within the district. Commonly, nonexclusive agricultural zoning couples agricultural use with residential use as the permitted uses within the district. *Id.* at 110-11. There are four types of nonexclusive agricultural zoning: conditional use zones, large-lot zones, fixed area-based allocation zoning, and sliding-scale area-based allocation zoning.

With conditional use zones, nonfarm dwellings are a conditional or special use for which a permit must be obtained upon satisfaction of an ordinance's criteria usually designed to direct development to land unsuitable for agricultural use. Conditional use zones are ordinarily combined with a small minimum lot size. *Id.* at 120. This method is a more direct form of regulation of residential development than the other types of nonexclusive agricultural zoning. It is more effective, because it directly limits through a review process in each case the number of residential dwellings that can occur within an agricultural zone. Necessarily, the review process requires administrative and financial resources beyond that required for other types of nonexclusive agricultural zoning. It is not uncommon for controversies over conditional use permits to focus on the validity of criteria and their application. *See, e.g., Thurston v. Cache County,* 626 P.2d 440 (Utah 1981).

With large-lot zoning, the most common form of nonexclusive agricultural zoning, a large minimum lot size is set in an area in which nonfarm development is permitted. This type of restriction limits the density of development by establishing large minimum lot sizes. The lot size generally corresponds to the usual size of farms in the area. NALS, *supra,* at 112. Agricultural large-lot zoning has generally been upheld against constitutional challenges. *See, e.g., Helix Land Co. v. City of San Diego,* 82 Cal. App. 3d 932, 147 Cal. Rptr. 683 (1978); *Sierra Terreno v. Tahoe Reg'l Planning Agency,* 79 Cal. App. 3d. 439, 144 Cal. Rptr. 776 (1978); *Gisler v. County of Madera,* 38 Cal. App. 3d 303, 112 Cal. Rptr. 919 (1971); *Joyce v. City of Portland,* 24 Or. App. 689, 546 P.2d 1100 (1976); *Wilson v. County of McHenry,* 416 N.E.2d 426 (Ill. App. 1981). *See also Judicial Acquiescence in Large Lot Zoning: Is it Time to Rethink the Trend?,* 16 COLUM. J. ENVTL. L. 183 (1991).

With fixed area-based allocation zones, there is a direct linear relationship between the size of the tract and the number of dwelling units permitted on the tract. Frequently, a fixed area-based allocation is coupled with a small minimum lot size. In this way, there can be clustering of residential dwellings in order to leave larger expanses of land free for agricultural use. Thus, the major strength of the fixed area-based allocation zone is that small lots may be used for nonfarm dwelling while the large areas of agricultural land are retained in agricultural use. NALS, *supra,* at 116.

With sliding-scale area-based allocation, the number of dwelling units permitted does not increase in direct linear proportion to the size of the parcel. Thus, a landowner with a small parcel would be entitled to higher density of development than a landowner with a large parcel. The allocation applies to all parcels of record on the date the ordinance becomes effective. Coupled with sliding-scale ordinances, there are ordinarily small minimum lot sizes and other restrictions to allow for clustering of development on the least productive soil.

Sliding-scale zoning was developed in Pennsylvania and is still extensively used in Pennsylvania counties and townships, as the following case indicates.

BOUNDARY DRIVE ASSOCIATES v. SHREWSBURY TOWNSHIP BOARD OF SUPERVISORS

507 Pa. 481, 491 A.2d 86 (1985)

HUTCHINSON, JUSTICE.

This is an appeal from a Commonwealth Court order which affirmed an order entered by the Court of common Pleas of York County. The Court of Common Pleas had affirmed a decision of the Shrewsbury Township Zoning Hearing Board denying appellant's request for a variance and rejecting its challenge to certain provisions of the Township's zoning ordinance designed to preserve agricultural land. On this appeal appellant argues that the provision in question are unconstitutional under the standards set forth in our opinion in *Hopewell Township Bd. of Supervisors v. Golla*, 499 Pa. 246, 452 A.2d 1337 (1982) (plurality opinion), and, additionally, that this Court should order approval of its subdivision plan. We hold that the challenged agricultural preservation provisions of Shrewsbury Township's zoning ordinance are constitutional both facially and as applied to appellant's property and, therefor, affirm Commonwealth Court.

Appellant, Boundary Drive Associates, owns thirty-nine acres of undeveloped prime farmland in Shrewsbury Township, York County, Pennsylvania. The tract originally comprised approximately forty-three acres when appellant purchased it in 1975.[1] At that time Shrewsbury had not enacted a zoning ordinance. However, a land development ordinance then in effect would have permitted appellant to subdivide the tract into half-acre residential lots provided that the new development was connected to New Freedom Borough's public sewer lines.[2]

Appellant submitted a proposal to the Township to develop the tract into seventy-two lots. This proposal contemplated public sewer service and on-site water. It was effectively approved in July, 1976 when the Township failed to act on the plan. In November, 1976 the Township enacted its first zoning ordinance. Under it appellant's land was classified as agricultural. In September, 1978, the Township formally approved the subdivision proposal, at appellant's request. However, it attempted to qualify approval by stipulating that the Township would not assist appellant in securing connection to New Freedom Borough's public sewer system. Appellant was unsuccessful in its negotiations for sewer service with New Freedom Borough. Thereafter, Common Pleas found appellant abandoned efforts to implement this subdivision plan.

---

[1] The entire tract purchased by Boundary Drive consisted of eighty acres, thirty-seven of which are located in adjoining New Freedom Borough.

[2] Shrewsbury's Subdivision and Land Use Ordinance permits 20,000 square foot residential lots only where public water or sewer service is available and requires all subdivision within 1000 feet of any existing public sewerage system to connect to that system.

In 1979 the Township's Zoning Hearing Board approved appellant's proposal, consistent with the zoning ordinance, to sell three one-acre lots from its forty-three acre tract.[4] Those lots were sold. In October, 1981 appellant submitted a second subdivision plan to the Board, proposing to develop its remaining thirty-nine acres into sixty-seven lots having on-site sewer and water systems. The Board determined that the second proposal was inconsistent with Sections 5.03(1)(1), 5.04(1) and 5.04(4) of Shrewsbury's zoning ordinance and refused to grant a validity variance from those provisions. Appellant appealed to the Court of Common Pleas of York County charging that the Board abused its discretion in denying the requested validity variance and, in the alternative, that the provision of Shrewsbury's zoning ordinance are exclusionary and confiscatory and therefore unconstitutional. Common Pleas affirmed the Zoning Hearing Board's substantive determinations.[5] Commonwealth Court likewise held the challenged provisions constitutional, concluding that they "bear a rational relationship to the stated goal of agricultural preservation and do not effect irrational or discriminatory results."[6] *Boundary Drive Associates v. Shrewsbury Township Board*, 81 Pa. Commonwealth Ct. 7, 15, 473 A.2d 706, 710 (1984).

Shrewsbury Township covers 28.6 square miles, seventy-eight percent of which is high quality farmland. Shrewsbury's leading industry is agriculture and, in fact, of all the communities in York County, the Township has one of the highest percentages of prime farmland.

The agricultural preservation provision of Shrewsbury's zoning ordinance are designed to effectuate the Township's policies regarding farmland. These policies are set out in the Township's Comprehensive Plan:

> In planning for agricultural land, it is the Township's policy not to consider agricultural land as "undeveloped farmland awaiting another use." Farmland must be considered as "developed land." It is being used to produce a product. Farming is a land-intensive manufacturing process which converts raw materials into a product, comparable to other industrial operations, with occasional accompanying nuisances of noise, odor and dust. The agricultural zone should not be considered as a holding zone, but as a zone having a positive purpose of utilizing the Township's natural resources for the benefit

---

[4]Under the zoning ordinance petitioner was permitted a total of four dwellings, each on a one-acre residential lot, on the original forty-three acre tract.

[5]The trial court did invalidate Section 14.30 of the zoning ordinance which provides that the Township may charge a party who appeals a decision of the Zoning hearing Board with all the costs associated with the Board's hearing on the matter. Relying on *Appeal of Martin*, 33 Pa. Commonwealth Ct. 303, 381 A.2d 1321 (1978), the court determined that pursuant to Section 1008(2) of the Municipalities Planning Code, 53 P.S. § 11008(2), the Township was required to pay the costs of providing the reviewing court with a transcript of the Zoning Hearing Board's proceedings.

[6]Commonwealth Court also affirmed Common Pleas' ruling that the Township was responsible for paying the cost of providing the court with a transcript of the Board's hearing.

of the entire community and the Township should protect the agricultural zone from interference by incompatible uses which break down the integrity of the zone and also interfere with normal and customary operations within the zone.

Specially, the provisions of the zoning ordinance at issue here designate agricultural districts within the Township and regulate their use. Agricultural districts are further divided into three classifications based on soil capability.

The first category encompasses Class I, Class II, Class IIIe-1 and Class IIIe-2 soils. These soils represent the best farmland in the Township. Pursuant to the zoning ordinance, no non-agricultural use is permitted on such land except that, when necessary, a total of two dwellings may be located on a tract consisting entirely of this highest quality farmland.

The second category consists of soils in Classes IIIe-3 through IVe-4. These too are highly suitable for agricultural use but slightly less productive than soils in the first three classes. Under the applicable zoning provisions, an owner may place on this less productive land the non-farm dwelling units allotted to him by an area-based density schedule. According to this schedule, the number of permissible dwellings increases with the size of the area owned, but not in direct linear proportion to that increase in area.

The third category consists of soils in Classes IVe-5 through VIIs-2. This land is not suitable for agricultural purposes either because of unfavorable topographical features or because the size or shape of contiguous or included suitable farmland precludes efficient use of modern farm equipment. Nevertheless, in order to avoid conflicts between residential and agricultural uses, the Township does not permit unlimited residential development of this type of land. Instead, land in this classification may be used for small farms, large homesites or a variety of uses permitted by special exception.

As stated previously, the Zoning Hearing Board determined that Sections 5.03(1)(1),[7] 5.04(4) of the zoning ordinance precluded appellant's subdivision plan. Section 5.04(1) allocates a permissible number of dwellings on parcels as they existed on November 10, 1976.[8] This provision, in turn, is subject to a qualification contained in Section 5.04(4) which limits the number of dwellings

---

[7]Section 5.03(1)(1) establishes a minimum residential lot area of 40,000 square feet or approximately one acre and a minimum residential lot width of 200 feet. Appellant's proposed lot dimensions range from 20,000 to 35,000 square feet and thus are prohibited by Section 5.03(1)(1). Petitioner's argument that this provision is unrelated to the goal of agricultural preservation has no merit.

[8]The purpose of, in effect, freezing sizes for purposes of this provision is to eliminate the possibility of repeated subdivisions into smaller and smaller tracts each thereafter entitled to its own allotment of dwellings in accordance with the heavier density schedule available to smaller tracts, down to the limit of 40,000 square feet with a 200 foot front as prescribed by Section 5.03(1)(1). This differs from the Hopewell freeze in which all existing tracts were frozen at five residences without regard to tract size.

which can be located on the three classes in the first category of prime farmland. Under Section 5.04(1), dwellings are allotted according to a sliding scale which permits an increased number of homes as the tract size increases:

Size of Parcel	No. of Dwellings Permitted
0-5 acres	1
5-15 acres	2
15-30 acres	3
30-60 acres	4
60-90 acres	5
90-120 acres	6
120-150 acres	7
over 150 acres	8 plus 1 dwelling for each 30 acres over 150 acres

Section 5.04(4) requires that any dwellings constructed in accordance with the schedule set forth in Section 5.04(1) be located in agricultural districts comprised of soils in Classes IIIe-3 through IIIe-6, IVe-1 through IVe-7, VI and VII. However, a maximum of two dwellings may be located in districts comprised exclusively of the best farmland, i.e., soils in Classes I, II, IIIe-1 and IIIe-2.

The report of the Zoning Hearing Board states only that appellant's tract is "good" farmland. Based on the number of houses allotted, the original forty-three acre parcel apparently contained both soils which are first quality and those which are inferior but still highly suitable for farming. Since appellant has already subdivided and sold three one acre lots from its original forty-three acre tract, according to the provisions of the zoning ordinance, it may locate one additional dwelling on the remaining thirty-nine-acre parcel.

Appellant charges that Sections 5.03(1)(1), 5.04(1) and 5.04(4) are unconstitutional both facially and as applied to his property under the standards we enunciated in *Hopewell*, *supra*. Specifically, appellant argues that the fixed scale contained in Shrewsbury's zoning scheme which permits a maximum of two dwellings on tracts comprised exclusively of first quality farmland, regardless of original tract size, is more restrictive than the zoning scheme we struck down in *Hopewell* which allowed five residential lots per parcel without regard to tract size. In addition, appellant contends that the sliding scale set forth in Section 5.04(1) unreasonably discriminates in favor of owners of small tracts. Finally, appellant suggests that the one-acre minimum lot size requirement set forth in Section 5.03(1)(1) thwarts the Township's stated goal of agricultural land preservation; that smaller lot sizes would promote Shrewsbury's efforts to protect the farming industry.

In a zoning appeal, where the court of common pleas has not taken additional evidence, appellate review is limited to a determination of whether the zoning hearing board committed an abuse of discretion or error of law. The reviewing court may not disturb the findings of the board if the record indicates the findings are supported by substantial evidence. 53 P.S. § 11010.

When presented with a challenge to a zoning ordinance, the reviewing court presumes the ordinance is valid. The burden of proving otherwise is on the challenging party.

A zoning ordinance is a valid exercise of the police power when it promotes public health, safety or welfare and its regulations are substantially related to the purpose the ordinance purports to serve. [Citation.] In applying that formulation, Pennsylvania courts use a substantive due process analysis which requires a reviewing court to balance the public interest served by the zoning ordinance against the confiscatory or exclusionary impact of regulation on individual rights. The party challenging the constitutionality of certain zoning provisions must establish that they are arbitrary, unreasonable and unrelated to the public health, safety, morals and general welfare. Where their validity is debatable, the legislature's judgment must control. [Citation.]

Unquestionably, preservation of agricultural land is a legitimate governmental goal appropriately implemented by zoning regulations *Hopewell*, 499 Pa. at 257, 452 A.2d at 1343. In recent years both Congress and Pennsylvania's General Assembly have instituted a variety of measures designed to protect farmland, in particular, and the agriculture industry, generally.[10] Moreover, Section 604(3) of Pennsylvania's Municipalities Planning Code specifically requires that zoning ordinance provisions be designed "to preserve prime agricultural and farmland considering topography, soil type and classification, and present use." 53 P.S. § 10604(3). Accordingly, the question which remains for our decision is whether, as appellant contends, Shrewsbury's agricultural preservation zoning provisions, particularly those which limit the number of permitted dwellings and relate

---

[10]*See, e.g.*, the Farmland Protection Policy Act, 7 U.S.C.A. § 4201 *et seq.* (Supp. 1984) (establishing procedures for maximizing the extent to which federal programs contribute to farmland conversion and for assuring that such programs are compatible with state, local and private efforts to protect such land); I.R.C. §§ 126, 175, 2032A, 6166 (collectively providing tax incentives to inhibit conversion of farmland and to encourage soil conservation). *See also* the Agricultural Area Security Law, Act of June 30, 1981, P.L. 128, No. 43, 3 P.S. § 901 *et seq.* (Supp. 1984-85) (declaring the Commonwealth's policy to conserve, protect and improve its agricultural land and providing various measures to implement that policy); The Right to Farm Law, Act of June 10, 1982, P.L. 454, No. 133, 3 P.S. § 951 *et seq.* (Supp. 1984-85) (limited the circumstances under which a farmer may be subjected to local nuisance regulations); Act of January 13, 1966, P.L. (1965) 1292 ("Act 515"), 16 P.S. § 11941 *et seq.* (Supp. 1984-85) and Act of December 19, 1974, P.L. 973, No. 319, 72 P.S. § 5490.3 (Supp. 1984-85) (authorizing assessment of eligible farmland at current use value for purposes of local property taxation); 72 Pa. C.S. § 1722 (Supp. 1984-85) (providing for the valuation of farmland at its current use value for state death tax purposes); Tax Reform Code of 1971, 72 P.S. § 7602.2 (Supp. 1984-85) (exempting family farm corporations from the ten-mill state capital stock franchise tax).

dwelling sites to soil types, unreasonably restrict appellant's right to use its land as it wishes.[11]

Appellant contends that Shrewsbury's zoning provisions do not pass constitutional muster under our decision in *Hopewell*, *supra*. The agricultural zoning ordinance there at issue essentially froze tract sizes as of June 5, 1974, the enactment's effective date, and permitted an owner of land in Hopewell's agricultural district, regardless of the size of his parcel, to establish up to five contiguous residential lots, each having one single family dwelling on a lot with a maximum size of one and one-half acres.[13]

We ruled this zoning scheme constitutionally infirm on two grounds. First, we determined that:

> By limiting residential subdivisions in the prime agricultural zone of the Township to a maximum of five 1-1/2 acre plots *regardless* of the size of the original tract, an unreasonably severe limitation is placed upon permissible land uses.

499 Pa. at 258, 452 A.2d at 1343 (emphasis in original). Second, we noted that owners of smaller tracts could devote a greater percentage of their total acreage to single-family dwellings than owners of large tracts. We concluded that disparate treatment of large and small landowners was unreasonably discriminatory as it derived "from the mere circumstance of tract size on the effective date of the ordinance and from the limit of five residential lots which may be established without regard to the overall size of the tract." Id. at 259, 452 A.2d at 1344.

Unlike the *Hopewell* zoning scheme, Shrewsbury's ordinance relates residential development to tract size. Appellant suggests that our *Hopewell* decision requires regulation which provides for an increase in allowable dwellings in perfect straightline or linear proportion to tract size, i.e., one dwelling for each X number of acres regardless of tract size. In *Hopewell* we stated that an ordinance permitting "the dedication of one 1-1/2 acre lot to a single-family residence per each X number of acres in the tract ... would have a more equitable effect and would avoid impacting on landowners on an arbitrary basis." *Id.*

We do not read *Hopewell* as requiring a perfect linear relationship between residential lots and acreage. In fact, a zoning scheme requiring such absolute density equality would actually frustrate the objective of farmland preservation. For example, under a zoning scheme employing a strict linear proportion of one dwelling per acre, maximum allowable development would result in the location of 100 houses on every 100 acre tract. Clearly, meaningful preservation of

---

[11]Appellant does not argue that the challenged provisions are exclusionary. In fact, the Zoning Hearing Board determined that sufficient land is available in Shrewsbury for development within the residential districts designated in the zoning ordinance.

[13]These restrictions did not apply to land unsuitable for farming. In addition, a landowner could sell lots larger than one and one-half acres to adjacent farmers.

agricultural land could not be achieved under this type of regulatory scheme. Moreover, a local legislative body could rationally conclude that an ordinance allowing one-half acre lots or so-called "clustering" of residential development would not serve the purpose of farmland preservation on the ground that a fifty-acre development of tract homes with attendant amenities could not co-exist compatibly with an adjacent productive farm. Such a conclusion could be based on the knowledge the members of that governing body had about the odors, noise and dust modern farming methods create.

Alternatively, a regulatory scheme based on dwelling allocation in linear proportion to area could, for example, allow one dwelling for every thirty acres of owned land.[14] However, this linear scheme, if strictly adhered to, might severely and unnecessarily restrict residential and other non-agricultural use of tracts consisting of fewer than thirty acres. Such smaller tracts can be thought of as too small to support an economically viable, independent modern farm. Therefore, a legislative body could rationally conclude it would be unreasonable to prohibit greater densities on these tracts. Thus, while unfettered residential development might interfere with efforts to preserve farmland, the permission given a small landowner to subdivide his relatively small parcel into lots suitable for large homesteads or small, non-working farms is not rationally inconsistent with the legislative purpose of preserving prime farmland.

For the foregoing reasons, we must reject appellant's contention that Shrewsbury's zoning ordinance is unconstitutional because it does not employ a fixed area-based allocation method of regulation.[15]

Appellant offers no additional reasons in support of its contention that Sections 5.03(1)(1), 5.04(1) and 5.04(4) of Shrewsbury's zoning ordinance are unduly restrictive and discriminatory when balanced against the public interest in protecting irreplaceable farmland. The sliding scale set forth in Section 5.04(1), which permits the permissible number of dwellings to increase with tract size, is substantially related to the goal of farmland preservation and is less restrictive than the fixed scale challenged in *Hopewell*. Furthermore, while the two-dwelling

---

[14]In fact, Section 5.04(1) of Shrewsbury's zoning ordinance permits one dwelling for every thirty acres of owned land with respect to parcels exceeding twenty-nine acres. In this regard the regulatory scheme achieves perfect equality of density. As stated above, Section 5.04(1) permits a greater number of dwellings per acre on parcels consisting of fewer than thirty acres. Thus, the provision is non-linear as applied to these smaller tracts.

[15]Similarly, we reject appellant's suggested regulatory scheme which substantially employs straightline proportionality. Specifically, appellant proposes a zoning ordinance which allows one residential lot for every five or ten acres of owned land. In addition, under appellant's scheme, a landowner would be permitted to further divide the agricultural remnant into "reasonably sized smaller parcels." *See* Brief of Appellant at 13-14. As the above discussion illustrates, appellant's zoning scheme would frustrate rather than promote the Township's efforts to preserve farmland. We note, however, that even under Shrewsbury's zoning ordinance, appellant is permitted to locate four dwellings on its original forty-three acre tract which, in terms of density, amounts to approximately one dwelling for every ten acres.

maximum allowed on prime farmland, regardless of tract size, is similar to the fixed scale we struck down in *Hopewell*, it is an integral part of a larger, comprehensive zoning scheme substantially related to the Township's goal of farmland preservation. Therefore, Sections 5.03(1)(1), 5.04(1) and 5.04(4) are not unduly restrictive.[16]

Similarly, the challenged provisions are not unreasonably discriminatory. The sliding scale allotment system does permit greater residential density on smaller tracts but, in so doing, eliminates certain deficiencies inherent in systems based on perfect linearity. Specifically, it accommodates the reasonable expectations of owners of small parcels by placing fewer restrictions on use and, at the same time, promotes the goal of farmland preservation by limiting residential density on larger tracts which can support productive working farms.[17] Therefore, the disparate treatment accorded large and small tract owners under Section 5.04(1) has a rational basis.

Accordingly, Commonwealth Court correctly upheld the Zoning Hearing Board's determination that appellant's subdivision plan is precluded by Sections 5.03(1)(1), 5.04(1) and 5.04(4) of Shrewsbury's zoning ordinance.

Affirmed.

MR. JUSTICE FLAHERTY joins the majority opinion and files a concurring opinion. MR. JUSTICE PAPADAKOS joins the majority opinion and also joins MR. JUSTICE FLAHERTY's concurring opinion.

LARSEN, MCDERMOTT and ZAPPALA, JJ., concur in the result.

FLAHERTY, JUSTICE, concurring.

I join the opinion authored by Mr. Justice Hutchinson. The Shrewsbury Township zoning ordinance, which permits appellant to place upon its original forty-three acre tract a total of four dwellings, does not, *as applied to appellant*, constitute such a severe restriction upon land use as to violate the substantive due process test set forth in *Hopewell Township Board of Supervisors v. Golla*, 499 Pa. 246, 452 A.2d 1337 (1982). Judgment is reserved, however, as to whether the zoning ordinance would be valid when applied to other properties having differing tract sizes and soil compositions, as such properties might arguably, in certain instances, be limited too far in their potential for development under the provisions of the zoning ordinance.

---

[16]Today we hold only that those provisions of Shrewsbury's zoning ordinance at issue her are not unduly restrictive as applied to appellant's land. We, therefore, express no opinion as to whether the same or other provisions of the ordinance would pass constitutional muster when applied to other properties having different tract sizes and soil compositions.

[17]As evident from the discussion on pages 14-16, *supra*, a straightline proportionality zoning scheme would either frustrate the reasonable expectations of owners of small parcels or the stated goal of preservation of agricultural land, depending on the ratio chosen.

In *Hopewell*, this Court made it clear that it will pay heed to traditional concepts of due process in determining the validity of restrictive zoning ordinances. The *Hopewell* decision set forth a further requirement that the extent of permissible residential development bear a reasonable relationship to tract size, though a *per se* requirement that the relationship be a perfect linear one was not imposed. Zoning restrictions, such as the ones which this Court invalidated in *Hopewell*, which constitute examples of governmental capriciousness and which operate to infringe the due process rights to property owners, will not be upheld in their application. As stated in *Hopewell*, 499 Pa. at 255, "The substantive due process inquiry, involving a balancing of landowners' rights against the public interest sought to be protected by an exercise of the police power, must accord substantial deference to the preservation of rights of property owners, within constraints of the ancient maxim of our common law, *sic utere tuo ut alienum non laedas*. 9 Coke 59 — So use your own property as not to injure your neighbors." Further, when the validity of a zoning restriction is challenged, "the function of judicial review ... is to engage in a meaningful inquiry into the reasonableness of the restriction on land use in light of the deprivation of landowner's freedom thereby incurred." *Hopewell*, 499 Pa. at 256. Indeed, a zoning ordinance can be sustained only when the restrictions imposed thereby upon landowner rights are regarded as "clearly necessary" when balanced against the public interest sought to be protected. *Hopewell*, 499 Pa. at 257-258. The important public interest in preserving prime agricultural land supports the restriction that has been placed upon appellant's land, insofar as development has been limited to the creation of four dwellings upon appellant's forty-three acre tract. Thus, the ordinance in question is valid as applied.

NOTES AND QUESTIONS

1. It is correct, as the court states, that the *Shrewsbury* ordinance did have more of a direct relationship between density and tract size than did the ordinance that was successfully challenged in *Hopewell*. However, in *Shrewsbury* was the upheld ordinance in at least one respect more restrictive than the *Hopewell* ordinance?

2. One way in which agricultural land has been protected from local regulatory interference is through insulation of agricultural land from zoning restrictions. Illinois and Iowa take this approach, but judicial interpretations of the two similar statutes, until recently, had taken different paths. The Iowa statute provides that no ordinance adopted under the zoning chapter may apply to land, farm houses, farm barns, farm outbuildings, or other buildings which are primarily adapted, by reason of their nature and area, for agricultural purposes, while so used. Iowa Code Ann. § 358A.2. Under the Illinois statute giving counties the authority to regulate by zoning, permits with respect to the erection, maintenance, repair, alteration, remodeling, or extension of buildings or structures used or to be used for agricultural purposes must be issued free of charge. The powers given to the county to zone cannot be exercised to impose regulations or require permits with respect to land used or to be used for agricultural purposes, or with respect to the erection, maintenance, repair, alteration, remodeling, or extension of buildings or structures used or to be used for agricultural purposes upon such land. The only zoning regulation that can be imposed is that buildings or structures for agricultural purposes may be required to conform to building or setback lines. Ill. Ann. Stat. ch. 34, para. 3151.

The Illinois law provides a very broad exemption from zoning for agricultural land, and this broad exemption has been broadly interpreted in its state courts. In Iowa, by contrast, the statute provides similarly broad protection, but the exemption had been narrowly construed by the Iowa courts. *Compare Tuftee v. Kane Co.*, 31 Ill. Dec. 694, 394 N.E.2d 896 (1979), *County of Lake v. Cushman*, 40 Ill. App. 3d 1045, 353 N.E.2d 399 (1976), *and Soil Enrichment Materials Corp. v. Zoning Bd. of Appeals of Grundy County*, 15 Ill. App. 3d 432, 304 N.E.2d 521 (1973) *with Farmegg Prods., Inc. v. Humboldt County*, 190 N.W.2d 454 (Iowa 1971), discussed in Hamilton, *Freedom to Farm: Understanding the Agricultural Exemption to County Zoning in Iowa*, 31 DRAKE L. REV. 565 (1982). The *Farmegg* decision was overruled in part by *Kuehl v. Cass County*, 555 N.W.2d 686 (Iowa 1996). In *Kuehl*, the court held that proposed hog confinement facilities were primarily adapted for use for agricultural purposes and thus were exempt from county zoning regulations. Thus "[t]o the extent that the *Farmegg Products* engrafted a requirement on exempt agricultural uses not contained in the statute creating the exemption," *id.* at 696, that decision was overruled.

4. AGRICULTURAL DISTRICTING

Agricultural districting programs provide incentives to farmers to join in the voluntary creation of districts to resist the pressures of development. By joining in the voluntary creation of these districts, farmers are eligible for an array of benefits which vary from state to state. Formation of a district is initiated by one or more farmers and approved by an authorized government agency. The districts are created for fixed but renewable periods of time, with the average time for enrollment ranging from four to ten years. The minimum amount of agricultural land acceptable within an agricultural district under these state laws is approximately 350 to 500 acres. The benefits which farmers obtain by inclusion of farmland in an agricultural district may include differential assessment, protection against nuisance ordinances, limits on public investments for nonfarm improvements, prohibitions on eminent domain, limitations on special assessments, limitations on state agency regulations that interfere with farming operations, protection from subdivisions and nonrelated development on adjacent land, programs for purchase of development rights, and agricultural zoning protection. Which protective elements and how many of these protective elements are available depends upon the particular statutory scheme. NALS, *supra*, at 76-77, 82-83.

The somewhat limited Illinois statute for agricultural districting is typical of many state statutes. There are three types of protection provided to landowners under the Illinois Agricultural Districts Act. First, no special assessments may be levied on land within the agricultural district, unless the assessment was made prior to the formation of the district or the assessments are applied on an equal basis to the land. Ill. Ann. Stat. ch. 5, para. 1020. Second, no local ordinance may be passed within an agricultural district that would unreasonably restrict or regulate farm structures or farming practices in violation of the purposes of the Act, unless the regulations or restrictions bear a direct relationship to the public health or safety. *Id.* § 1018. Third, there is a limitation on the power of public agencies with respect to land within a district. The Act declares that it is the policy of all state agencies to encourage the maintenance of viable farming and agricultural districts, and that their regulations and procedures must be modified to serve this end insofar as they are inconsistent with the promotion of public health and safety and any federal law. *Id.* § 1019.

When land is included within an agricultural district, it must remain within the district for a period of ten years. Any owner or owners of land may submit a proposal to the county board for the creation of an agricultural district within such county. An agricultural district shall be not less than 350 acres. No land within the agricultural area can be used for anything other than agricultural production. *Id.* § 1005. In considering formation of an agricultural area, the following factors are to be evaluated by the county board:

1. The viability of active farming within the proposed area and in the areas adjacent thereto;
2. The presence of any viable farmlands within the proposed area and adjacent thereto that are not now in active farming;
3. The nature and extent of land uses other than active farming within the proposed area and adjacent thereto;
4. County development patterns and needs;
5. The existence of a conservation plan approved by the local soil and water conservation district;
6. Any other matter which may be relevant.

Id. § 1008.

5. DIFFERENTIAL ASSESSMENT

As urban sprawl approaches farmland, agricultural land increases in value due to its proximity to places of employment and other urban amenities. Thus, the market value of land no longer reflects its value as agricultural land, but reflects its value for residential development. Most states assess the value of real estate for property taxes on its "highest and best" value, which usually translates into property's market value for development. In addition, property taxes may be raised in urbanizing areas to compensate for the increased need for public services. The result is that agricultural land near urban sprawl is taxed at its value for development, not its current use value for agriculture. The increased property tax burden is one more disincentive for the financially stressed farmer to continue in farming. If farmers are unable to continue farming, the eventual sale of their farmlands leads to increased urban sprawl, with increased property taxes for farmers on the new edge of the urban sprawl. As a result, every state has adopted some form of property tax assessment at the current use value rather than the market value for agricultural lands. F. STEINER & J. THEILACKER, PROTECTING FARMLANDS 184 (1984).

Most states have either preferential assessment or deferred taxation. With preferential assessment, the landowner receives the benefit of assessment at agricultural use value, with no penalty to be paid when the land is withdrawn from agricultural use. NALS, *supra*, at 57. With deferred taxation, a rollback is imposed when the land is converted to a nonqualifying use. *Id*. The deferred tax is equal to the amount of taxes that would have been paid if there had been no preferential assessment during the designated time period. NALS, *supra*, at 57. Rollback periods vary under state laws, with the average rollback period running from four to seven years. *Id*. at 57-58. Thus the rollback taxes are assessed at the fair market value assessed minus farm use value multiplied by the tax rate and the number of years in the rollback period, in some states with the addition of interest. In *Hoffmann v. Clark*, 69 Ill. 2d 402, 372 N.E.2d 74 (1977), the court denied an equal protection challenge to a rollback tax as creating two classes of lands, those converted and those not converted. The court found a rational basis for the distinction deterring conversion of agricultural land. The third form of differential assessment is a restrictive agreement. With restrictive agreements, to obtain the benefit of differential assessment, the landowner must enter into an agreement restricting the land to agricultural use for a designated period of time. If there is withdrawal in contradiction of the terms of the agreement, a penalty is imposed. The penalty for breaking an agreement is essentially a deferred tax, but in most states the statute specifically refers to the penalty as a deferred tax. The principal difference between restrictive agreements and deferred taxation is that withdrawal from restrictive agreements is not automatic. F. STEINER & J. THEILACKER, *supra*, at 189. The fourth form of differential assessment, utilized in only a few states, is the circuit breaker tax credit. If the amount of property tax paid by the farmer or landowner exceeds a certain percentage of income, a tax credit is received against state income taxes. NALS, *supra*, at 60.

BOARD OF EDUCATION v. BOARD OF REVISION OF LAKE COUNTY

57 Ohio St. 2d 62, 11 Ohio Op. 3d 220,
386 N.E.2d 1113 (1979)

The Board of Education brought an appeal challenging the decision of the board of tax appeals that certain property should be assessed for tax purposes at its current agricultural use value rather than its actual value.

PRYATEL, JUSTICE.
Appellant's Proposition of Law No. 2 reads:

> "The ownership and simultaneous dual use of unimproved real property, as a landbank immediately across the street from a major regional shopping center, by persons extensively engaged in the ownership, development and sale of commercial property in the immediate vicinity, is not consistent with an exclusive agricultural use nor the purpose and intent of the current agricultural use valuation classification."

The appellant challenges the propriety of the assessment under the current agricultural use valuation given its use and all the circumstances surrounding it, including: (a) its immediate proximity to a major commercial center; and (b) its ownership by individuals who are actively engaged in major commercial real estate development and sales.[3]

In support of its contention, appellant relies primarily upon language used in rules adopted by the Commissioner of Tax Equalization, 5705-5-01 and 5705-5-02, Ohio Adm. Code. That portion of Rule 5705-5-01(B)(2), which appellant cites as supporting its argument, states:

> "'Current Agricultural Use Value of Land' ... It is the price at which the property would change hands on the open market between a willing buyer and seller, neither being under any compulsion to buy or sell, and both having knowledge of all relevant facts, if the highest and best use was *exclusively agricultural with no other influence being present....*" (Emphasis added.)

Appellant has completely misapplied the rule. This rule has nothing to do with whether the land is found to be "land devoted exclusively to agricultural use," in the first instance, pursuant to R.C. 5713.30(A). That portion of Rule 5705-5-01 cited by appellant deals only with the valuation of the land once it has

---

[3]The issue in this cause is whether the property in question should be classified as land used exclusively for agricultural purposes. The issue of what factors should be considered in determining its value once such a classification is approved is not before the court at this time. Appellant's attorney, Mr. Donald M. Robiner, stated, in his opening comments before the Board of Tax Appeals: "[I]n essence, our challenge is *not a valuation challenge* in the true sense of the word. *It is a legal challenge* ... as to the propriety of the classification...." (Emphasis added.)

been found to be "land devoted exclusively to agricultural use," as defined in R.C. 5713.30(A). Similarly, Rule 5705-5-02 cited by appellant concerns itself only with the valuation of the land.[4]

Section 36, Article II of the Ohio Constitution, adopted to encourage agricultural development, provides:

> "Laws may be passed to encourage forestry and agriculture, and to that end areas devoted exclusively to forestry may be exempted, in whole or in part, from taxation. Notwithstanding the provisions of section 2 of Article XII, *laws may be passed to provide that land devoted exclusively to agricultural use be valued for real property tax purposes at the current value such land has for such agricultural use.*"... (Emphasis added.)

Pursuant to this mandate, the General Assembly enacted R.C. 5713.31, which authorizes property "devoted exclusively to agricultural use" to be valued for property tax purposes at the current value such land has for agricultural use. R.C. 5713.30(A)(1) defines "[l]and devoted exclusively to agricultural use," in pertinent part, as follows:

> "... [P]arcels of land totaling not less than thirty acres which ... were devoted exclusively to commercial animal or poultry husbandry, the production for a commercial purpose of field crops, tobacco, fruits, vegetables, timber, nursery stock, ornamental trees, sod, or flowers or that were devoted to and qualified for payments or other compensation under a

---

[4]It is true that the intent of the constitutional amendment was to give relief to farmers whose land was slowly being engulfed by commercial land through the growth of towns and cities and who were being driven out of business by the soaring real property taxes attendant upon revaluation of their property under the "highest and best use" rule. Admittedly, the landowners herein do not fit cleanly into this category, however, the approach of the appellant would require a determination of the subjective motive of every person applying for the benefits of R.C. Chapter 5713. The results would not comport with the concepts of due process and equal protection of the laws.

Both the drafters of the Constitution and the General Assembly were aware of the possibility of abuse of this provision by speculators (which is obviously the appellant's fear) by providing for recoupment of tax savings. R.C. 5713.34 provides:

> "Upon the conversion of all or any portion of a tract, lot, or parcel of land devoted exclusively to agricultural use a portion of the tax savings upon such converted land shall be recouped as provided for by Section 36, Article II, Ohio Constitution, by levying a charge on such land in an amount equal to the amount of the tax savings on the converted land during the four tax years immediately preceding the year in which the conversion occurs. The charge shall constitute a lien of the state upon such converted land as of the first day of January of the tax year in which the charge is levied and shall continue until discharged as provided by law."

If the landowners convert the property, as defined in R.C. 5713-30(B), the tax savings will be recouped for the four tax years preceding the conversion. In this cause, the amount of that recoupment would be considerable, approaching something close to a half-million dollars.

land retirement or conservation program under an agreement with an agency of the federal government."

The wording of this section is straightforward and its meaning is clear. It is undisputed that the property is used to graze and breed race horses and to grow soybeans, wheat, clover and alfalfa. The board held, and we agree, that this use falls within the definition of land devoted exclusively to agricultural use as defined by R.C. 5713.30(A). If the land is used exclusively for animal husbandry and, or, the production of commercial crops, then the property qualifies for real property tax valuation purposes at the current value such land has for such agricultural use. Accordingly, appellees' property which is used solely to graze and breed race horses and to grow commercial crops is "[l]and devoted exclusively to agricultural use," as defined in R.C. 5713.30(A).

NOTES AND QUESTIONS

1. How is the purpose of farmland preservation served by giving a tax break to these landowners? How could a differential assessment statute be drafted to avoid this situation? Consider in this regard the statutory conditions for differential assessment in *Reiss Greenhouses, Inc. v. County of Hennepin*, 290 N.W.2d 785 (Minn. 1980).

2. What are the advantages and disadvantages to each of the methods of differential assessment for preserving farmland? From a broader social perspective? With respect to the last question, why did the Board of Education bring this lawsuit? One author has suggested that differential assessment would be more effective if more productive land was given a lower value for property tax purposes than other agricultural land. Mark, *A "New" Case for Differential Assessment of Prime Farmlands*, 37 J. SOIL & WATER CONSERV. 210 (July-Aug. 1982). *See also* Currier, *An Analysis of Differential Taxation as a Method of Maintaining Agricultural and Open Space Land Uses*, 30 U. FLA. L. REV. 821 (1978); Malone & Ayesh, *Comprehensive Land Use Control Through Differential Assessment and Supplemental Regulation*, 18 WASHBURN L.J. 432 (1979); Denne, *Explicit Property Tax Policies and the Promotion of Specific Land-Use and Economic Development Objectives: A Review*, 11 ASSESSORS J. 13 (1976).

3. Uniformity clauses in state constitutions are an impediment to differential assessment. Under these clauses, property taxes must be levied uniformly in the state, precluding differing tax treatment for agricultural land. For example, in *Kearney Convention Center, Inc. v. Buffalo County Bd. of Equalization*, 216 Neb. 292, 344 N.W.2d 620 (1984), the court struck down the state's differential assessment program for violating the uniformity clause in the Nebraska constitution that all property be taxed at actual value. Also, in *Banner County v. State Bd. of Equalization*, 226 Neb. 236, 411 N.W.2d 35 (1987), the Nebraska Supreme Court invalidated state preferential assessment statutes for violating the state constitution's uniformity clause.

D. SPECIAL MANAGEMENT TECHNIQUES

Traditionally, land use planning and controls have been the responsibility of local governments. Some states do, however, have state or regional agencies that have supervisory authority over land use planning and regulation by local governments.

In 1963 the American Law Institute (ALI) undertook a comprehensive review of the Standard State Zoning Enabling Act (U.S. Dep't of Commerce Advisory Committee on Zoning, A Standard State Zoning Enabling Act (rev. ed. 1926)), the Standard Planning Enabling Act (U.S. Dep't of Commerce, Advisory Committee Planning and Zoning, A Standard City Planning Enabling Act (1928)), and state legislation based on these models. H. Wechsler, *Foreword to ALI Model Land Development Code* (*Model Code*), at vii-xii (Proposed Official Draft, 1975). This review resulted in the ALI's adoption of the Model Land Development Code in 1975. Bosselman, Raymond & Persico, *Some Observations on the American Law Institute's Model Land Development Code*, 8 URB. LAW. 474 (1976). A significant innovation in the Code was the expanded state role in land use decisionmaking, an innovation which reflected the reform movement in the 1970s to reallocate regulatory power in land use among state, regional, and local planning entities. *See generally* F. BOSSELMAN & D. CALLIES, THE QUIET REVOLUTION IN LAND USE CONTROL (1971).

Article 7 of the Code authorizes state designation of areas of critical concern. *Model Code, supra,* § 7-201. The Code authorizes the state planning agency to designate critical areas "containing or having a significant impact upon historical, natural or environmental resources of regional or statewide importance." *Id.* § 7-201(3)(b). As part of the designation process, the state agency must establish "general principles for guiding development of the area," *Model Code, supra,* § 7-201(1)(d), a broad term that indicates the impossibility of greater specificity in the types of controls needed for the variety of potential critical areas. Another provision of Article 7 authorizes a state agency to review local decisions or developments of regional impact (DRIs). "Development of regional impact" is development which is likely in the judgment of the state agency to present issues of state or regional significance due to the nature or magnitude of the development or the nature or magnitude of its effect on the surrounding environment. *Model Code, supra,* § 7-301(1). This section narrowly focuses on selected programs of regional planning and development controls, critical area regulation, DRI review, and development rights programs for the purpose of environmental preservation. The most comprehensive statewide land use programs are those adopted under the Coastal Zone Management Act, discussed on pages 951-67 *supra*.

1. REGIONAL PLANNING AND DEVELOPMENT CONTROLS

Regional programs ordinarily govern regions contained entirely within a state (the Adirondacks of New York, the Pinelands of New Jersey) but may govern an interstate region (the California/Nevada Lake Tahoe region). As regional programs may vary a great deal, this section briefly outlines three regional programs — for the New York Adirondacks, the New Jersey Pinelands, and the Virginia Chesapeake Bay area — to illustrate the basic mechanisms of regional planning and some of the ways in which such programs may differ.

The Adirondacks Program

In 1968 Governor Rockefeller established a temporary state commission on the future of the Adirondacks in New York. After two years, the Commission recommended the establishment of a state agency for developmental planning for private lands within the Adirondack Park. This recommendation was adopted in 1971 in the Adirondack Park Agency Act. N.Y. Exec. Law §§ 800-820. The Act was unsuccessfully challenged as an unconstitutional delegation of legislative powers, unconstitutional interference with local government, and spot zoning. *Adirondack Park Agency v. Ton-Da-Lay Assocs.*, 61 A.D.2d 107, 401 N.Y.S.2d 903, *appeal dismissed*, 45 N.Y.2d 834, 381 N.E.2d 612, 409 N.Y.S.2d 214 (1978); *Wambat Realty Corp. v. State*, 85 Misc. 2d 489, 378 N.Y.S.2d 912 (1975), *aff'd*, 41 N.Y.2d 490, 362 N.E.2d 581, 393 N.Y.S.2d 949 (1977). The Act created an Adirondack Park Agency which was required by January 1, 1973 to formulate a land use and development plan applicable to the Park, except for those lands owned by the state. N.Y. Exec. Law §§ 805 and 807. In 1973 the New York State Legislature approved the regional land use management plan which had been proposed by the Agency. The plan set permissible density of development on the privately owned lands in the Park and established standards for permitted developments. N.Y. Exec. Law § 805.

Section 805 is the key provision of the Act in setting forth the general requirements for the Adirondack Park land use and development plan. Section 805 requires a plan that consists of a land use intensity area map and accompanying text. The map divides the Adirondack Park into areas and in the accompanying text establishes the intensity (including type, character, and extent) of the land use and development permissible within each area. The text must also state the purposes, policies, and objectives of each area and limitations thereof, which may be in the form of general standards or specific restrictions and conditions, and may vary within an area because of typography, parcel size, or other stated conditions. *Id.*

The applicant for any new land use and development with an impact of regional significance must obtain a permit from the Agency for all Class A regional projects and for any Class B regional projects in any land use area not governed by an approved and validly enacted or adopted land use program. *Id.* § 809. Projects are classified in section 810 of the statute as being Class A regional projects or Class B regional projects based upon the size, nature, and location of a project within each land use area. *Id.* § 810. Permits for all Class A projects must be obtained from the Agency. When a local government adopts an agency-approved local land-use plan under section 807, it may issue permits for Class B projects. Otherwise, permits for Class B projects are also issued by the Agency. The final tier of protection is a procedure for review by the Agency of local land-use programs. Under section 807, the Agency is authorized to review and approve any local land-use program proposed by a local government and formally submitted by the local government to the Agency for approval. *See* Jung, *The Pine Barrens: A New Model of Land Use Control for New York*, 3 BUFF. ENVTL. L.J. 37 (1994).

The Virginia Chesapeake Bay Program

In order to improve water quality protection, the Chesapeake Bay Protection Act creates a state board with the authority to provide assistance to, and establish criteria for, local governments in promulgation of their land use plans. The Act establishes a cooperative state and local program with four objectives: (1) that counties, cities, and towns in Tidewater Virginia incorporate water quality protection measures into their comprehensive plans, zoning ordinances, and subdivision ordinances; (2) that these governments establish programs in accordance with criteria established by the state to define and protect lands designated as Chesapeake Bay preservation areas, which if improperly developed may substantially damage water quality in the Bay; (3) that the state make its resources available to local governing bodies to carry out the Act; and (4) that all agencies of the state exercise their authority in a manner consistent with water quality protection in local plans, comprehensive plans, zoning ordinances, and subdivision ordinances. Va. Code Ann. § 10.1-2100. The Act emphasizes that the state acts primarily in a "supportive role" by providing oversight of local government programs through criteria for those programs. *Id.*

Among the more significant duties of the Board are: (1) to provide information and assistance about land use and development as well as water quality protection to local and regional governments and state agencies; (2) to promulgate criteria for protection of Chesapeake Bay protection areas; (3) to develop procedures for use by local governments for designation of Chesapeake Bay preservation areas; (4) to "ensure" that local governments' comprehensive plans, zoning ordinances, and subdivision ordinances comply with the Act; and (5) to take "administrative and legal actions to ensure compliance" by counties, cities, and towns with the Act. *Id.* § 10.1-2103. Of these powers, none is more important than the authority of the Board to develop criteria for protection of Chesapeake Bay preservation areas. In order to assist counties, cities, and towns in regulating land use and development and protecting water quality, the Board must establish regulations which set criteria for use by local governments to determine the ecological and geographic extent of Chesapeake Bay preservation areas. Regulations must also establish criteria for use by local governments in granting, denying, or modifying requests to rezone, subdivide, or to use and develop land in these areas. The criteria must incorporate measures such as performance standards, best management practices, and other planning and zoning concepts to protect the quality of state waters while allowing use and development of land consistent with the Act. *Id.* § 10.1-2107. These criteria must encourage and promote protection of existing high quality state waters and restoration of other waters to a condition that permits all reasonable public uses and support of aquatic life; safeguard the clean waters of the state from pollution; prevent any increase in pollution; reduce existing pollution; and promote water resource conservation. However, the Board is required to give due consideration to the economic and social costs and benefits which can reasonably be expected to result from the criteria. *Id.*

Counties, cities, and towns in Tidewater Virginia had to use the criteria developed by the Board to establish Chesapeake Bay preservation areas within their jurisdictions by September 20, 1990. *Id.* § 10.1-2109. The Act requires these governments to incorporate protection of water quality into their comprehensive plans. In addition, they must have zoning ordinances that incorporate measures to protect water quality in the Chesapeake Bay preservation areas and that comply with all criteria for zoning in those areas as set by the Board. Similarly, these governments must incorporate protection of water quality in Chesapeake Bay preservation areas into their subdivision ordinances. *Id.*

Local governments must also utilize the Board's criteria to ensure that land development use in Chesapeake Bay preservation areas is accomplished in a way that protects state water quality consistent with the Act. *Id.* § 10.1-2111. The Act provides that "in addition to any other review requirements" of the Act, the Board must review, upon request by any county, city, or town, any application for land development for consistency with the Act. The review must be completed and the report submitted to the requesting government within ninety days of the request. *Id.* § 10.1-2112. State agencies are required to act in a manner consistent with the provisions of comprehensive plans, zoning ordinances, and subdivision ordinances that comply with the Act. *Id.* § 10.1-2114. These protective provisions of the Act, however, are tempered by a provision which states that the Act shall not affect "vested rights of any landowner under existing law." *Id.* § 10.1-2115. *See generally* Liebesman & Singer, *Maryland Growth and Chesapeake Bay Protection Act: The View from the Development Community*, 1 U. BALT. J. ENVTL. L. 43 (1991); Liss & Epstein, *The Chesapeake Bay Critical Area Commission Regulations: Process of Enactment and Effect on Private Property Interests*, 16 U. BALT. L. REV. 54 (1986).

The New Jersey Pinelands Program

In 1979 the State of New Jersey passed the Pinelands Protection Act, N.J. Stat. Ann. §§ 13:18A-1 to 13:18A-29. The New Jersey Act divided the Pinelands Reserve into two areas, a highly protected "preservation area" and a "protection area" designed to buffer the preservation area with very specific statutory delineation of the boundaries of each area. *Id.* § 13:18A-3.

To administer the entire Pinelands area, the state established the Pinelands Commission. The Pinelands Commission was responsible for preparing and adopting the Comprehensive Management Plan for the Pinelands area, and is responsible for making necessary revisions to that plan. *Id.* § 13:18A-8. The Commission is directed to identify land management techniques to preserve the region, such as purchase of land for resale or leaseback, permit systems, acquisition of conservation easements, fee simple acquisition of public recreational areas, sensitive environmental areas, and historic sites, and public access agreements. *Id.* § 13:18A-8(d). The statutory goals for the comprehensive management plan differ for the preservation area and the protection area. For the protection area, development is to be allowed, but it is to be encouraged to proceed in a planned fashion that is designed to preserve the nature of the Pinelands as well as accommodate the economic growth of the area. *Id.* § 13:18A-9(b). Limits on construction and development in the preservation area are much more severe, with no development allowed that is incompatible with the preservation of the area. *Id.* § 13:18A-9(c). Agricultural and recreational uses are encouraged in the preservation area and development is discouraged. *Id.* The Commission has the authority to review any application for development in the Pinelands area which has been approved by municipalities or counties within that area. The Commission may reject the applications for nonconformance with the management plan or for substantial danger to the Pinelands' resources. *Id.* § 13:18A-15.

No development required to receive state or local approval or other authorization can receive such approval or authorization without complying with the requirements of the plan. *Id.* § 13:18A-10(c). Municipalities and counties are required to submit to the Commission master plans and zoning ordinance revisions for review for consistency with the provisions of the comprehensive plan. *Id.* § 13:18A-12. If a county or municipality fails to adopt or enforce a suitable plan or ordinance, the Commission may enforce the plan's standards directly. *Id.*

To counteract somewhat the effects of the restrictions on development that were included in the Pinelands comprehensive management plan, a program for Pinelands development credits was implemented by the plan. *Id.* §§ 13:18A-30 to 13:18A-49. Pinelands development credits are awarded based on land ownership and are transferable. Thus credits may be purchased from landowners by those wishing to develop a particular area. *Id.* § 13:18A-31. Landowners who sell their development credits must record restrictive covenants that limit the use of their land to uses allowed by the comprehensive management plans. *See Matlack v. Board of Chosen Freeholders of County of Burlington*, 191 N.J. Super. 236, 466 A.2d 83 (1982), *aff'd*, 194 N.J. Super. 359, 476 A.2d 1262, *cert. denied*, 99 N.J. 191, 491 A.2d 693 (1984) (explaining the development credit system in a case where the county board had instituted a program for purchase of those credits). A state credit bank has been established to facilitate the sale and purchase of development credits, as well as loan money against these credits. N.J. Stat. Ann. § 13:18A-33.

2. FLORIDA'S CRITICAL AREA REGULATION AND DRI REVIEW

Florida is the only state that has adopted both the critical area regulation and DRI review program of Article 7 of the Model Code. The Florida Environmental Land and Water Management Act of 1972, Fla. Stat. Ann. §§ 380.012 to 380.12, was heralded as "one of the most significant advances in state land use legislation in this country's history." Pelham, *Regulating Developments of Regional Impact: Florida and the Model Code*, 29 U. FLA. L. REV. 789, 793 (1977). It is the state program which most closely resembles the Model Code provisions for critical area regulations. De Grove, *Critical Area Programs in Florida: Creative Balancing of Growth and the Environment*, 34 J. URB. & CONTEMP. L. 51, 59 (1988). *See also* Spahn, *The Beach and Shore Preservation Act: Regulating Coastal Construction in Florida*, 26 STETSON L. REV. 353 (1995).

The Administration Commission, a state agency consisting of the Florida governor and cabinet, is authorized by the Act to designate critical areas. Fla. Stat. Ann. §§ 380.031(1), 380.05(1)(b). As a mandatory prerequisite to designation of a critical area, a resource planning and management committee composed of local elected and planning officials and relevant state and regional agency appointees must be appointed by the governor for the area under consideration. *Id.* §§ 380.045(1) and 380.045(2). Within twelve months after appointment, the committee must either adopt a proposed voluntary resource planning and management program for the area or recommend that such a program not be adopted. *Id.* § 380.045(3). The "major objective" of the program is coordination of state, regional and local planning, program implementation, and regulation of resource and management. Any proposed program must be submitted to the state land planning agency, which in turn transmits it to the Administration Commission. *Id.* The Commission then approves or disapproves of the proposed program. If it approves, the Commission must request each state or regional agency responsible for implementing the program to conduct its programs and regulatory activities consistent with the program, and the agencies must "cooperate to the maximum extent possible in ensuring that the program is given full effect." *Id.* § 380.045(4).

Unlike the Model Code, the Act as amended in 1985 does not exempt DRI in critical areas from the DRI process. *Id.* § 380.06(13). To enforce the Act, if the state agency determines a development order issued by a local government is inconsistent with local land development regulation, the state land planning agency may appeal the order to the state adjudicatory board (which is the Administration Commission) with final recourse to judicial review. *Id.* § 380.07(2). If the agency concludes that local administration of development regulation in the critical area "is inadequate to protect the state or regional interest," the agency may bring judicial proceedings to compel adequate enforcement. *Id.* § 380.05(13).

The most serious challenge to Florida's critical area regulation resulted in substantial amendment to the law in 1979. The Florida Supreme Court concluded in *Askew v. Cross Key Waterways*, 372 So. 2d 913 (Fla. 1978), that the Act's original language for designation of critical areas was an unconstitutional delegation of legislative power to the executive branch because the Administration Commission had been given the "legislative task of determining which geographic areas and resources are in greatest need of protection." *Id.* at 919. Crucial to the court's holding was the broad statutory description of critical areas at that time and the lack of any statutory guidelines for choosing among the resources that qualified. For the original language of the Act and the amendments in response to the *Cross Keys* decision, see Pelham, *supra*. In this respect and others, Florida's implementation of its critical area legislation has had its difficulties, many of which were addressed in the 1979 amendments. Its experience has demonstrated many of the weaknesses in the Model Code critical area program, including the potential for long delays, lack of administrative coordination, and political resistance to designation of critical areas by an administrative agency. In the future, the Florida program will similarly be a testing ground for critical area regulation against a background of comprehensive planning that goes far beyond the approach of the Model Code.

3. DEVELOPMENT RIGHTS PROGRAMS

The right to develop property is one of the strands in the bundle of rights known as property. Restrictive zoning limiting the right to develop has two basic infirmities as a method of environmental preservation. First, zoning restrictions are only as forceful as the zoning board which applies them. Variances, amendments, rezonings, and other exceptions to zoning regulation, if freely provided, can undermine whatever limitations on development a zoning regulation provides. Secondly, the more restrictive the zoning restriction, the more susceptible it is to a challenge under the takings clause.

Programs for the purchase and transfer of development rights developed in response to these deficiencies in zoning as a preservation tool. In a program for purchase of development rights (PDRs), a state or local planning agency purchases the development rights to hold them in abeyance indefinitely (referred to as "land banking") or until a decision is made to release the rights for development. Programs for transferable development rights (TDRs) differ from purchase of development rights programs in that with PDR programs development rights are retired, but with transferable development rights the rights are purchased by private buyers to be transferred for use in another area. A standard TDR program establishes a preservation district and a development district. Landowners in the preservation district are not allowed to develop their rights. These landowners may sell their development rights to landowners in the development district who can use the rights to build at a higher density than that ordinarily allowed under the applicable zoning guidelines.

How do PDR and TDR programs avoid the two shortcomings of zoning for environmental preservation? What drawbacks might TDR and PDR programs have themselves in protecting environmental resources?

WEST MONTGOMERY COUNTY CITIZENS ASSOCIATION v. MARYLAND NATIONAL CAPITAL PARK & PLANNING COMMISSION

309 Md. 183, 522 A.2d 1328 (1987)

McAuliffe, Judge.

A county enjoys no inherent power to zone or rezone, and may exercise zoning power only to the extent and in the manner directed by the State Legislature. The Regional District Act, Md. Code (1957, 1983 Repl. Vol.) Art. 28, § 8-101(b) grants zoning power to the Montgomery County Council sitting as a District Council. By that section, the Legislature specifically defines zoning power to include the right to regulate "the density and distribution of population" and authorizes the District Council to exercise that power by "amend[ing] the text of the zoning ordinance and ... by ... amend[ing] the map or maps accompanying the zoning ordinance text...." By using the process of amending a Master Plan to effect a significant increase in the permissible density of development of residential zones, the District Council has run afoul of the state mandate that zoning changes be made by zoning procedures. Moreover, the alternative argument, that the density decisions were not made by the District Council but were made by the Planning Board pursuant to a valid delegation of legislative power, is unavailing because of the breadth of the power involved and the failure of the District Council to establish sufficiently precise standards.

In October, 1980, the Functional Master Plan for the Preservation of Agriculture and Rural Open Space in Montgomery County ("Agricultural Preservation Plan") was approved and adopted. This plan recommended broad and innovative changes in the zoning text of Montgomery County, to be followed by dramatic zoning map changes that would directly affect one-fourth of the land in the County. The principal purpose of the plan was to preserve open space and agricultural land in the upper part of the County by restricting development of the land. An important adjunct of the plan was the recommendation that Montgomery County adopt and implement a system of transferable development rights ("TDRs"), to provide a form of compensation to owners whose rights to develop their properties would be significantly impaired by down-zoning, and to help ensure long term preservation of the agricultural use of the land.

The concept of TDRs is simple and straightforward. Ownership of land carries with it a bundle of rights, including the right to construct improvements on the land. These rights are subject to governmental regulation where reasonably required to accommodate public health, safety, or general welfare, and ordinarily these limitations of use may be imposed without the necessity of paying compensation to the land owner. There may arise situations, however, where the limitation of use imposed for the public good inflicts an economic impact on the landowner that, while not confiscatory, is so substantial as to prompt the government to provide some type of compensation. Cases involving the preservation of scenic easements and historic or architecturally valuable landmarks, preserving as they do benefits to the public that are largely cultural or aesthetic, yet concentrating the burden upon relatively few, have moved government officials to find ways to compensate the affected property owners. Maryland, recognizing the importance of agricultural land, and the efficacy of restricting the right to develop land as a means of accomplishing that objective, has developed a system for purchasing agricultural land preservation easements. *See* Md. Code (1974, 1985 Repl. Vol.) Agriculture Article, §§ 2-501 thru 2-515. Purchasing development rights with public funds is not the exclusive method of providing compensation, however. Other jurisdictions have accomplished the desired objective by permitting the transfer of development rights from the burdened property to certain other properties in the political subdivision, and have given the value to this right by permitting a greater than normal intensity of development of the transferee or "receiving" property.

Montgomery County chose the latter course — the creation of a system of transferable development rights. In accordance with the recommendation of the Agricultural Preservation Plan, the District Council amended various provisions of the zoning text to provide for a new Rural Density Transfer zone ("RDT zone") having a base density of one single family dwelling unit for each 25 acres, and to create TDRs in favor of the owners of property placed in that classification. Montgomery County Code, 1984, §§ 59-C-11.2 thru 59-C-11.5. The owners of property down-zoned to the RDT zone are granted one TDR for each five acres, less one TDR for each existing dwelling unit. Other amendments to the zoning text provide that if the owners execute a covenant not to develop their land at its base density, the TDRs can be transferred to any property within a properly designed receiving zone, and under certain circumstances can be used to increase by one dwelling unit per TDR the density of development of the receiving property. The text provides that any property in six designated single family residential zones is eligible for designation as a receiving areas for TDRs. The actual designation of the properties that would constitute the "receiving zone," i.e. those designated as available for more intense development through the use of TDRs, is to be made through the planning, rather than the zoning process. Section 59-C-1.39 provides:

> Any property in the RE-2C, RE-2, R-200, R-150, R-90 and R-60 zones that is located in a receiving area designated in an approved and adopted general, master, sector or functional plan may be developed at an increased density by the transfer of development rights in accordance with sections 59-A-6.1, and 59-C-11....

Section 59-C-11.4 provides:

> In accordance with § 59-A-6.1 and in conformance with an approved and adopted general, master, sector or functional plan, residential density may be transferred at the rate of one development right per five (5) acres less one development right for each existing dwelling unit, from the rural density transfer zone to a duly designated receiving zone, pursuant to § 59-C-1.39.

The zoning text imposes no limitation on the ultimate density of development possible for a property placed in the receiving zone, but leaves this decision to the planning process as well. Thus, by General, Master, Sector or Functional Plan, the determination is to be made as to which single family residential properties will be placed in the receiving zone, and what limit of intensification of density will be assigned to each property so designated.

Finally, the zoning text provides that an owner of a designated receiving area property who wishes to intensify development through the use of TDRs must submit a preliminary subdivision plan and site plan detailing the proposed development of the property. These individual plans must conform to the development standards of the zone permitting a density nearest to the TDR density designated by the Master Plan Amendment. Upon approval of the site plan and preliminary plan of subdivision, an easement is recorded in favor of the County, restricting development of the property or properties from which the TDRs were obtained.

In addition to making the zoning text changes recommended by the Agricultural Preservation Plan, the District Council adopted a sectional map amendment, down-zoning 88,000 acres of land to the RDT zone, and thereby creating nearly 17,000 TDRs.[2] It is the attempt by Appellees to utilize some of these TDRs to achieve increased density development of their property that has generated this controversy.

The principal questions presented by this appeal involve the validity of the process legislated by District Council for the classification of properties within the TDR receiving zone and the determination of the density limitation that shall apply to each property within the zone. Appellants also present two questions relating to alleged procedural irregularities in the granting of the preliminary plan of subdivision and the approval of the site plan. In view of the conclusion we reach concerning the substantive questions, we do not reach the procedural matters.[4]

---

[2] The action of the District Council in down-zoning property to the RDT zone was appealed to the Circuit Court for Montgomery County in 1981. Affected property owners argued, among other things, that the down-zoning amounted to a constitutionally impermissible taking of their land, and that the text amendment establishing the RDT zone violated the requirement of uniformity. Their appeal was unsuccessful at the circuit court level, and was not pursued.

[4] Appellants also included in their petitions filed in support of their administrative appeals (later consolidated) allegations of violations of their constitutional rights, and a demand for attorneys fees

We shall first address the question of whether the District Council validly exercised its zoning authority when it approved for adoption amendments to a master plan. At the outset, we state a basic proposition that is not contested by any of the parties — that the regulation of the density and distribution of population is a part of the zoning power and ordinarily is to be exercised by the District Council.

Next, we point out the very substantial distinction between the planning and zoning functions.

> A "Master Plan" is not to be confused as a substitute for a comprehensive zoning or rezoning map, nor may it be equated with it in legal significance.... The zoning as recommended or proposed in the Master Plan may well become incorporated in a comprehensive zoning map for this area, but this will not be so until it is officially adopted and designated as such by the District Council.

Chapman v. Montgomery County, 259 Md. 641, 643, 271 A.2d 156 (1970).

A third major premise is that the County enjoys no inherent power to zone or rezone, and may exercise that power only to the extent and in the manner directed by the Legislature. That power has been granted to the County Council of Montgomery County, sitting as a District Council, and not to the Planning Commission or Planning Board. Art. 28, § 8-101. Thus, say Appellants, the classification and density decisions with respect to receiving area properties cannot be made by the adoption of a Master Plan because that plan is adopted by the Planning Commission and not the District Council. Appellees counter by arguing that enabling and implementing legislation places ultimate control of the Master Plan in the hands of the District Council, and thus the District Council's approval of a Master Plan constitutes the legislative decision required for the exercise of zoning power. Appellants dispute this, contending the District Council is without the necessary authority to initiate or complete the planning process, and that in any event the planning process fails to afford due process to those who might be aggrieved by the decision. Furthermore, they contend the enabling legislation that grants zoning power to the County specifically limits the manner of exercise of that power to the adoption and amendment of the zoning text and the accompanying zoning map.

We conclude, however, that this chartered county is precluded, by the express and unequivocal language of the statute that granted it zoning power, from exercising that power in any manner other than that specifically authorized — namely, by the zoning map and zoning text amendment procedures. Art. 28, § 8-101(b) provides in pertinent part that:

---

and expenses pursuant to 42 U.S.C. §§ 1983 and 1988. We need not consider whether such a claim may be included in an administrative appeal because Appellants appear to have abandoned this claim, and in any event we find no violation of their constitutional rights.

> Each district council, respectively, in accordance with the conditions and procedures specified in this article, may by ordinance adopt and amend the text of the zoning ordinance and may by resolution or ordinance adopt and amend the map or maps accompanying the zoning ordinance text to regulate, in the portion of the regional district lying within its county ... (iv) the density and distribution of population....

The authority "to regulate ... the density and distribution of population" is expressly to be accomplished by adoption and amendment of "the text of the zoning ordinance" and adoption and amendment of "the map or maps accompanying the zoning ordinance text." Thus, where the District Council purports to act in the exercise of its zoning authority, it must do so by adopting or changing the zoning text or zoning map.

> As with all legislative grants, the zoning authority is circumscribed by any limitations established by the General Assembly in the enactment.... *Harbor Island Marina v. Calvert Co.*, 286 Md. 303, 309, 409 A.2d 738 (1979).

Because approval of amendments of the Master Plan does not come within the mandated procedures for legislative zoning action, this process cannot constitute a valid exercise of zoning authority. Accordingly, unless the procedure employed in this case can qualify as a valid delegation of zoning authority to the Planning Board, it cannot be sustained.

This Court has not been hesitant to approve a delegation of legislative power where that delegation is for the purpose of implementing a prior, specific legislative determination, and is accompanied by standards sufficient to limit and direct the exercise of discretion on the part of the agency or official to whom the power is delegated. We have applied these criteria to sustain carefully limited and directed delegations of zoning authority in a variety of cases.

Applying the established criteria to the facts of this case, we find the delegation of authority impermissible. No legislative determination was made to limit or define the optional densities that could or should be assigned to any property in the vast area involved. Nor did the Legislature establish precise standards by which the Planning Board might determine which properties should be placed in the TDR receiving zone, or what TDR density should be assigned to each.[7] By contrast, the Planning Board in this case was given unlimited

---

[7]We are unable to find in the Montgomery County zoning text any standards for the designation of receiving areas, or for classification of properties within the receiving areas according to optional density development opportunities. The 1982 amendment to the Master Plan recites that it followed four guidelines first recommend by the 1980 Agricultural Preservation Plan. These guidelines are very general, requiring only that: 1) the base density of receiving area property should be "reasonable from a planning perspective"; 2) the optional density assigned "should not exceed the ability of the planned public facilities to serve the area or the ability of the land and the environment to accommodate [it]," and should be "compatible with the density and uses planned for the surrounding area"; 3) property proposed for down-zoning should not be included in the

authority to select from a vast pool of residentially zoned property spread over the entire lower portion of the County, and to assign increased density potential to those properties without limitation.

In this case we note the absence of any effective zoning action by the District Council to generally classify properties within the TDR receiving zone. Virtually all of the single family residential properties in three-fourths of the County were declared eligible for that classification, but the ultimate decision of classification was left to the Planning Board. Additionally, there was no valid legislative action to assign different density classifications to properties within the receiving area, nor was there any ceiling on density established so as to leave the Planning Board with but limited authority to fix reduced densities.

The major deficiency in this entire process is the absence of the final step in the planning and zoning process — the amendment of the zoning map, and where necessary the zoning text, to implement the changes recommended by the Master Plan. Certainly comprehensive planning should form an integral part of the process of identifying TDR receiving areas and assigning density classifications. Once the planning has been accomplished and the recommendations made, however, it becomes the duty of the legislative authority to make any necessary changes in the zoning law. Ordinarily, these change are accomplished through a sectional map amendment, which once proposed enjoys a strong presumption of validity and correctness, and requires no showing of change or mistake.

These deficiencies, although perhaps easily remedied by appropriate changes in the zoning text, are fatal to the designation and classification of TDR receiving areas in this case.

NOTES AND QUESTIONS

1. As the main case indicates, TDR programs necessitate difficult determinations of the market for development rights in the designated receiving area. *See generally* Merriam, *Making TDR Work*, 56 N.C.L. REV. 77 (1978). That difficulty raises a related question — what impact does the receipt of TDRs by landowners in the preservation district have on a takings clause challenge to the restriction on development? The saving grace of TDRs is that they may permit an owner of property that has been restrictively zoned to recoup any economic loss on the restricted property by selling the property's severed development rights to receiving properties authorized for increased density of development. In theory at least, the use of TDRs precludes takings clause objections. Does the

---

receiving area; and 4) no property should be recommended for both TDR and "planned development" density options. Additionally, the 1980 Agricultural Preservation Plan noted that "[t]he purchase of development rights must be very attractive to developers. If receiving zones are well located from a marketing standpoint, and the density bonuses are sufficient to justify the purchase of development rights, the TDR concept will work." The 1982 amendment to the Master Plan lists six "plan guidelines" that were followed in the development of the plan, but these guidelines cannot take the place of standards established by a legislative body.

receipt of TDRs go to the issue of whether there is a taking *ab initio*, or only to the issue of whether just compensation has been provided if there has been a taking? Recall the discussion, on pages 126-28 *supra*, of the TDRs provided under the landmark ordinance in *Penn Central*.

In note 2 of the *West Montgomery* case, the court refers to a decision of the Circuit Court for Montgomery County in which landowners challenged the downzoning of agricultural land. The county ordinance rezoned much of the agricultural land as "agricultural reserve," downzoning the reserve from one dwelling per five acres to one dwelling per twenty-five acres. Each landowner in the agricultural reserve, the sending zone, was assigned transferable development rights of one residential unit per five acres which could be sold to developers in designated receiving areas. The county established a development rights bank to purchase and sell development rights until sufficient receiving areas are designated to establish a strong private market. Holding that an exercise of police power could effectuate a taking for which compensation must be provided, the Montgomery County Circuit Court concluded, even without consideration of the TDRs, that the downzoning was not tantamount to denial of "all reasonable use" of the property. In an alternative finding, the *Dufour* court determined that the TDRs buttressed its holding that a taking had not occurred, even though at the time of the downzoning no receiving areas had been designated, no interim development rights bank had been established, and the value of the TDRs was in all likelihood "substantially below 'just compensation' for the diminution in value." Noting the apparent controversy over whether TDRs should be evaluated as an alleviation of the property owner's burden or as just compensation, the court accepted without further analysis Justice Brennan's reasoning in *Penn Central* that TDRs were relevant to the impact of the regulation. (Discussed on pages 126-27 *supra*.) Relying on its holding that even without reference to the TDRs no taking had occurred, the court decided not to receive evidence on the fair market value of the TDRs. *Dufour v. Montgomery County Council*, No. 56964 (Montgomery County Cir. Ct. Md., Jan. 30, 1983). Clearly, the court felt a need for further guidance from the appellate courts in computing the value of TDRs. If, indeed, recent Supreme Court cases demonstrate a movement toward Justice Rehnquist's approach to the takings issue, TDRs may be deemed irrelevant to the threshold issue of whether a taking has occurred. Even the most carefully planned TDR ordinance may run afoul of the strictly interpreted mandate of just compensation. From an economic, legal, and public policy perspective, does the value of TDRs fit more comfortably within the rubric of "just compensation" or within that of a "taking"?

2. Assume a landowner owns two or more contiguous parcels of property in an area of growing development, and the land has been zoned for commercial or residential use. One of the parcels of property is undeveloped — that is, the property provides agricultural, aesthetic, or ecological benefit to the rapidly developing community. The county zoning board then rezones the landowner's property so that the undeveloped parcel must remain undeveloped, but the landowner's other contiguous parcels of property are to retain the same density of development as under the prior zoning ordinances. To compensate for the restrictions on the undeveloped parcel, the county zoning ordinances provide that the parcel's unused development rights may be transferred: (a) to the owner's other contiguous and noncontiguous property or (b) to other designated, contiguous and noncontiguous lots under different ownership. The landowner subsequently submits a development plan for the undeveloped parcel to the zoning board, but the board disapproves the plan in accordance with the newly passed ordinance. The landowner then files suit in state court claiming damages for inverse condemnation and seeks a declaratory judgment that the ordinances have effectuated a taking of property without just compensation.

Assume for purposes of the hypothetical that the restrictions imposed on the undeveloped parcel deprive it of all or almost all of its economic value. Should the court compare the value of *all* of the landowner's contiguous property to the value of the TDRs and conclude that the restrictions on the one parcel do not constitute a taking, because they do not sufficiently deprive the landowner of the economic return on the property as a whole? Could the court even take into consideration the owner's noncontiguous property on which the TDRs might be used? Or should the court focus only upon the economic detriment to the restricted parcel and conclude that the conferral of the TDRs salvages the constitutionality of the ordinance from a takings challenge even if the ordinance would otherwise be a taking of the restricted parcel? Alternatively, again focusing only on the restricted parcel, could the court find, without considering the value of TDRs, that there had been a taking? Would the TDRs satisfy the constitutional requisites for just compensation? *See generally* Malone, *The Future of Transferable Development Rights in the Supreme Court*, 73 KY. L.J. 759 (1985).

3. The hurdles to implementation of a PDR program are cost and lack of administrative resources. Because it is financially impossible to purchase the development rights on all property within the preservation area, a successful PDR program depends upon purchase of rights on key parcels. The selection of which development rights to purchase can lead to litigation by disappointed applicants. *See, e.g., Appeal of John MacEachran*, 438 A.2d 302 (N.H. 1981).

4. An owner of environmentally sensitive land who wants to preserve it may donate a conservation easement to a governmental agency or charitable organization and receive a charitable deduction under the Internal Revenue Code. The deduction is available for donations of easements and sales at less than the market value of the easement.

A gift of partial interests in real property does not qualify for a charitable deduction, unless it is a "qualified conservation contribution." I.R.C. § 170(f)(3)-(B)(iii). A "qualified conservation contribution" must be of a "qualified real property interest" to a "qualified organization," exclusively for "conservation" purposes. *Id.* § 170(h). A qualified real property interest encompasses a restriction *in perpetuity* on the uses which may be made of the property. *Id.* § 170(h)(2)(C). To be enforceable in perpetuity, the recipient of the easement must have the resources to enforce the restrictions of the easement and demonstrate a commitment to protect the conservation purposes. Treas. Reg. § 1.170A-14(c)(1). A qualified organization "includes public agencies and private, tax-exempt nonprofit organizations" under section 501(c)(3) of the Internal Revenue Code. I.R.C. § 170(h)(3).

"Conservation purpose" is defined as:

> (i) The preservation of land areas for outdoor recreation by, or the education of the general public,
>
> (ii) The protection of relatively natural habitat of fish, wildlife, or plants, or similar ecosystem,
>
> (iii) The preservation of open space (including farmland and forest land) where such preservation is —
>
>> (I) For the scenic enjoyment of the general public, or
>>
>> (II) Pursuant to a clearly delineated Federal, State, or local governmental conservation policy, and will yield a significant public benefit, or
>>
>> (iv) The preservation of an historically important land area, or a certified historic structure.

I.R.C. § 170(h)(4)(A).

5. Scholarly writings on the constitutionality of TDRs as a general matter are extensive. For a basic introduction to the debate, compare Costonis, *Development Rights Transfer: An Exploratory Essay*, 83 YALE L.J. 75 (1973-74) and Costonis, *Fair Compensation and the Accommodation Power: Antidotes for the Taking Impasse in Land Use Controversies*, 75 COLUM. L. REV. 1021 (1975) with Berger, *The Accommodation Power in Land Use Controversies: A Reply to Professor Costonis*, 76 COLUM. L. REV. 799 (1976) and Note, *The Unconstitutionality of Transferable Development Rights*, 84 YALE L.J. 1101 (1974-75).

E. HABITAT PRESERVATION REQUIREMENTS FOR PRIVATE DEVELOPMENT UNDER THE ENDANGERED SPECIES ACT

The prohibitions of the Endangered Species Act, 16 U.S.C. §§ 1531-1544, extend beyond federal agency actions and federally funded or approved projects. Section 9 prohibits all "takings" of endangered species by any "person." *Id.* § 1538(a)(1). "Persons" is defined to include private individuals and entities, and "taking" is defined to include adverse impacts on an endangered species habitat. *Id.* § 1532(13) & (19). Section 9 has become a significant control on land use. Arnold, *Conserving Habitats and Building Habitats: The Emerging Impact of the Endangered Species Act on Land Use Development*, 10 STAN. ENVT'L L.J. 1 (1991). For additional viewpoints, compare Cheever, *An Introduction to the Prohibition Against Takings in Section 9 of the Endangered Species Act of 1973: Learning to Live With a Powerful Species Preservation Law*, 62 U. COLO. L.

REV. 109 (1991), with Shaheen, *The Endangered Species Act: Inadequate Species Protection in the Wake of the Destruction of Private Property Rights*, 55 OHIO ST. L.J. 453 (1994), and Harrison, *The Endangered Species Act and Ursine Usurpations: A Grizzly Tale of Two Takings*, 58 U. CHI. L. REV. 1101 (1991).

Section 10(a) authorizes incidental taking permits if the applicant takes certain mitigation measures to protect the species, including preparation of a habitat conservation plan (HCP). *Id.* § 1539(a)(1)(B). For a discussion of HCPs *see* Thornton, *Searching for Consensus and Predictability: Habitat Conservation Planning Under the Endangered Species Act of 1973*, 21 ENVT. L. 605 (1991); *see also* Ruhl, *Regional Habitat Conservation Planning Under the Endangered Species Act: Pushing the Legal and Practical Limits of Species Protection*, 44 SW. L.J. 1393 (1991) (addressing larger-scale Regional Habitat Conservation Plans (RHCPs)). The San Bruno Mountain Area HCP at issue in the following case was the first HCP to be challenged in court.

FRIENDS OF ENDANGERED SPECIES, INC. v. JANTZEN
760 F.2d 976 (9th Cir. 1985)

PREGERSON, CIRCUIT JUDGE.

Friends of Endangered Species, Inc. (Friends) appeals from a summary judgment in favor of public and private appellees. Friends had challenged a decision of the United States Fish and Wildlife Service (the Service) to issue a permit that authorized the "taking" of Mission Blue butterflies from areas of the San Bruno Mountain.

Facts

San Bruno Mountain (the Mountain), an area rich in wildlife, contains about 3,400 acres of undeveloped land located on the northern San Francisco Peninsula. Throughout the early 1970's, appellees Visitation Associates and the Crocker Land Company, a co-owner of Visitation, purchased virtually all the land on the Mountain. In 1975, they proposed to develop approximately 7,655 residential units and 2,000,000 square feet of office and commercial space on the Mountain.

Appellee's proposal generated intense controversy over the appropriate level of development of the Mountain. A local environmental group, the Committee to Save San Bruno Mountain, led the opposition to Visitation Associates' development proposal. In response to this controversy, in March 1976, the San Mateo County Board of Supervisors (the County) adopted the San Bruno Mountain General Plan Amendment (the General Plan Amendment), which permitted construction of only 2,235 residential units, as well as some office and commercial space. The General Plan Amendment designated the remainder of the land on the Mountain as open space.

In 1980, litigation between Visitation Associates and the County over the General Plan Amendment was settled. Under the settlement, Visitation Associates and the Crocker Land Company sold or donated to the County and the State of California over 2,000 acres of the Mountain for parkland. The County and Visitation Associates also agreed to designate about one-third of the Mountain for development and two-thirds for parks.

Shortly after the settlement was reached, the Service found that the Mission Blue butterfly, which was on the endangered species list, inhabited the Mountain.

In May 1980, various individuals and entities formed the San Bruno Mountain Steering Committee (the Committee) to formulate a plan that would both protect the endangered species and allow some development of the Mountain. The Committee consisted of representatives of the County, the cities of Brisbane, Daly City, and South San Francisco (the Cities), Visitation Associates, other prospective developers, landowners, the Service, the California Department of Fish and Game, and the Committee to San Bruno Mountain (the citizens' group which had opposed Visitation Associates' 1975 development proposal).

The Steering Committee initiated a two-year Biological Study of, among other species, the Mission Blue butterfly, to determine its population and distribution on the Mountain and whether development would conflict with the butterflies' continued existence. The study technique employed was a mark-release-recapture of the butterflies.

The Biological Study concluded that the Mission Blue inhabited most of the grassland portions of the Mountain, including areas planned for development. The Study also determined that if development did not occur, the butterflies' grassland habitat would inevitably be lost to encroaching brush, and the butterflies' continued existence would be seriously threatened.

In October 1981, the Steering Committee began developing a Habitat Conversation Plan (the Plan), based on the Biological Study. The Plan was to provide an approach by which habitat protection and real estate development on the Mountain would take place at the same time. The Steering Committee incorporated the final Plan into an implementing document, called the "Agreement with Respect to the San Bruno Mountain Area Habitat Conservation Plan" (the Agreement). The County, the Cities, the major landowners and developers, the California Department of Fish and Game, and the California Department of Parks and Recreation executed the implementing agreement.

The Agreement dedicated 793 privately owned acres to local agencies as permanent open space, preserved 81% of the open space to be restored after temporary disturbances during construction. The Agreement also required lot owners on the Mountain to contribute $60,000 annually to finance a permanent habitat conservation program. The County agreed to supervise the program. According to the Plan, the development would disturb only 14% of the present habitat of the Mountain's population of Mission Blue butterflies.

To effectuate the Agreement, section 10(a) of the Endangered Species Act (ESA), 16 U.S.C. § 1539 required the Service to issue a Permit. Because the Service's approval of the Permit required compliance with federal and California environmental statutes, San Mateo County and the Service agreed in February

1982, to prepare jointly a combined Environmental Impact Report (EIR), required under state law, and an Environmental Assessment (EA), required under federal law. In July 1982, the Service published notice of the draft EIR/EA on the Plan and proposed Permit and made the EIR/EA public for hearing and comment. The Service received both favorable and adverse comments and, in its Permit Findings and final EIR/EA, considered and responded to these comments.

In November 1982, the Service received a formal application for a Permit from the County and the Cities for the incidental taking of Mission Blue butterflies, San Bruno Elfin butterflies, and San Francisco garter snakes. The Service then published notice of its receipt of the Permit application and requested public comments.

In March 1983, the Service issued a Biological Opinion concluding that, pursuant to section 7(a)(2) of the Endangered Species Act (ESA), 16 U.S.C. § 1536, the planned development under the Permit would not jeopardize the continued existence of various species on the Mountain, including the Mission Blue butterfly. The Service also issued a Finding of No Significant Impact (FONSI) stating that issuance of the Permit would not significantly affect the quality of the human environment. This finding obviated the need for an Environmental Impact Statement.

Also in March, the Service issued the Permit, conditioned upon implementation of the Agreement and the Plan.

In August 1983, Friends filed an action in the district court for declaratory and injunctive relief. Friends contended that because the field studies were methodologically flawed, the Service's findings that relied on the field data were arbitrary and capricious, and that approval of the Permit based on such findings constituted an abuse of the agency's discretion. Friends also alleged that the EIR/EA's discussion of environmental impacts and alternatives to development on the Mountain was insufficient under the National Environmental Policy Act (NEPA), 42 U.S.C. § 4321 (1982), to enable the Service adequately to assess the environmental impacts of the Permit and the Plan. Friends alleged that EPA, therefore, required the Service to prepare a full-blown Environmental Impact Statement in this case.

The issues presented on appeal are: (1) whether appellant raised a genuine issue of material fact in alleging that the Service violated the ESA in issuing the Permit allowing incidental "taking of" various species including the Mission Blue butterfly from San Bruno Mountain; (2) whether appellant raised a genuine issue of material fact in alleging that the service failed to comply with NEPA.

Discussion

I. *Violation of the Endangered Species Act*

Appellant first contends that in issuing the Permit, the Service failed to comply with sections 10(a) and 7(a)(2) of the ESA. As the following discussion demonstrates, Appellant's contention is erroneous.

A. *Standard of Review — Administrative Decisions Under the ESA*

Section 706 of the Administrative Procedure Act (APA), 5 U.S.C. § 706 (1982), governs review of the Service's actions concerning the ESA.

Under the APA, the appropriate standard of review for administrative decisions involving the ESA is the "arbitrary, capricious, an abuse of discretion, or otherwise not in accordance with law" standard. 5 U.S.C. § 706(2)(A). Under this standard, administrative action is upheld if the agency has "considered the relevant factors and articulated a rational connection between the facts found and the choice made." We review the district court's granting of summary judgment de novo. And in doing so, we need to determine whether appellant raised a genuine of material fact as to whether the Service acted arbitrarily and capriciously in issuing the Permit under the ESA.

B. *The Service Complied with Section 10(a) of the Endangered Species Act*

Section 10(a) of the ESA allows the Service to permit an applicant to engage in an otherwise prohibited "taking" of an endangered species under certain circumstances. The applicant first must submit a comprehensive conservation plan. The Service then must scrutinize the plan and find, after affording opportunity for public comment, that: (1) the proposed taking of an endangered species will be "incidental" to an otherwise lawful activity; (2) the permit applicant will minimize and mitigate the impacts of the taking "to the maximum extent practicable"; (3) the applicant has insured adequate funding for its conservation plan; and (4) the taking will not appreciably reduce the likelihood of the survival of the species. Appellant challenges the sufficiency of the Permit findings relating to the second and fourth of these section 10(a) requirements.

1. *The field study adequately supported the Service's findings that "the taking will not appreciably reduce the likelihood of the survival of the species."*

The Service went beyond the statutory requirement and concluded that the Permit, coupled with the Plan, was likely to *enhance* the survival of the Mission Blue butterfly.[6]

Appellant contends that the Service's determination that issuing the Permit would not reduce the likelihood of the Mission Blue butterfly's survival was arbitrary and capricious because of alleged scientific shortcomings in the Biological Study upon which the decision was based. Specifically, appellant

---

[6]The Service concluded that the plan would enhance the butterflies' survival because it would result in the conveyance of a substantial amount of critical habitat to public ownership as well as establish a permanent program to protect the grassland habitat, eliminate gorse and some eucalyptus that encroach on the habitat in the San Bruno Mountain Area, regulate recreation and development activities, and insure uniform management of conserved habitat within the area. Gorse is any evergreen shrub or tree of the genus Juniperus.

argues that low recapture rates and allegedly mistaken recaptures by the field crew in the mark-release-recapture phase of the field study invalidated the Study's conclusions, and that the Service abused its discretion in relying upon such data to approve the Permit. With respect to this contention, appellant fails to raise a genuine issue of material fact.

As the district court determined, the legislative history to section 10(a)'s 1982 amendments suggests that Congress viewed appellees' conduct in the present case as the paradigm approach to compliance with section 10(a):

> *In some cases, the overall effect of a project can be beneficial to a species, even though some incidental taking may occur. An example is the development of some 3000 dwelling units on the San Bruno Mountain near San Francisco.* This site is also habitat for three endangered butterflies.... *Absent the development of this project these butterfly recovery actions may well have never been developed.* The proposed amendment should lead to resolution of potential conflicts between endangered species and the actions of private developers, while at the same time encouraging these developers to become more actively involved in the conservation of these species.

Senate Rep. No. 97-418, 97th Cong., 2d Sess. 10 (1982) (emphasis added). The House Conference Report indicates, in stronger terms than the Senate Report, that the Service acted properly in relying upon the Biological Study to comply with section 10(a):

> Because the San Bruno Mountain plan is the model for this long term permit and because the adequacy of similar conservation plans should be measured against the San Bruno plan, the Committee believes that the elements of this plan should be clearly understood.... Prior to developing the conservation plan, the County of San Mateo conducted an independent exhaustive biological study which determined the location of the butter-flies.... The biological study was conducted over a two year period and at one point involved 50 field personnel.
>
> The San Bruno Mountain Conservation Plan is based on this extensive biological study.

H.R. Rep. 97-835, 97th Cong., 2d Sess. 31-32 (1982).

In addition, appellant failed to bring many of these purported field data "errors" and "inconsistencies" to the attention of the Service until after the district court denied appellant's motion for summary judgment. Clearly, the Service did not act arbitrarily in failing to consider criticisms not presented to it before issuing the Permit. Review of the reasonableness of an agency's consideration of environmental factors is "limited ... by the time at which the decision was made." *City and County of San Francisco v. United States*, 615 F.2d 498, 502 (9th Cir. 1980) (citations omitted).

The Service did, however, extensively solicit and consider expert and public comments on the Biological Study before issuing the Permit. And, the Biological Study itself acknowledged methodological limitations.[8]

Thus, there is no evidence that the Service issued the Permit either in ignorance or deliberate disregard of the Biological Study's limitations. Moreover, the Service responded in good faith in its Permit Findings to the criticisms which it sought out and received concerning the Biological Study, and acted reasonably in relying upon the Biological Study to conclude that the Plan would not reduce the likelihood of survival of the Mission Blue butterfly. Again, the Service cannot be said to have acted arbitrarily by not responding to criticisms not received when it approved the Permit.

We also consider it relevant that the Permit was expressly made subject to revocation and reconsideration based upon data that might be revealed from the continuing monitoring called for under the Plan. Thus, the Service complied with section 10(a)'s mandate by determining that "the incidental taking" of the Mission Blue would enhance the survival of the species. In light of the clear declaration of legislative intent and the Service's efforts to consider all criticisms of the Biological Study before relying upon it, we hold that the district court was correct in concluding that there were no genuine issues of material fact that would preclude it from determining that the Service did not act arbitrarily or capriciously in relying on the Biological Study.

2. The Service did not act arbitrarily or capriciously in concluding that the Plan complied with section 10(a)'s requirement to minimize and mitigate the impact of the taking upon endangered species.

The Plan at issue contains various measures to "minimize and mitigate" the impact of the project upon the Mission Blue butterfly. The Plan and the Agreement provide for the permanent protection of 86% of the Mission Blue's habitat. Moreover, funding for the Plan would yield $60,000 annually, which would be used to halt the apparent incursion of brush and gorse into the habitat and permit the re-establishment of grasslands for the butterfly.

In addition to provisions to halt advancing brush and gorse, the Plan contains continuing and comprehensive restrictions on land development and significant financial incentives. Regardless of whether brush and gorse continue to spread, these additional mitigating measures should play a significant role in enhancing the protection of endangered species on the Mountain.

Appellant also contends that the Saddle Area of the Mountain, now publicly owned for parkland and consisting of 75% brush, should be substituted for one of the grassland parcels currently proposed for development. Appellant suggests

---

[8]The Biological Study acknowledged that population estimates had a "high variance" where the recapture rate fell below 50%, but stressed that, while extrapolation to "predict the actual total population is subject to high uncertainty (variance), a comparison of the census ... between similar areas provides a sense of the overall population."

that this Saddle Area alternative would more effectively mitigate the Plan's effects. The EIR/EA authors considered and rejected this Saddle Area development alternative. They concluded, among other things, that development of the Saddle Area would have secondary impacts including a biological impact greater than that produced by the Saddle's proposed use as a county park. The Saddle Area allegedly contains unique wetlands and endangered plants, and its development could meet with stiff environmental opposition.

Thus, the district court correctly concluded that there is simply no genuine factual dispute as to whether the Service acted arbitrarily or unreasonably in determining that the Plan complied with section 10(a)'s mitigation requirement.

> 3. *Appellant does not raise a genuine issue of material fact in alleging that the Service failed to comply with section 7(a)(2) of the ESA.*

Section 7(a)(2) of the ESA states:

> Each Federal agency shall ... insure that any action authorized, funded, or carried out by such agency ... is not likely to jeopardize the continued existence of any endangered species or threatened species or result in the destruction or adverse modification of habitat of such species which is determined by the Secretary ... to be critical.... In fulfilling [these] requirements ... each agency shall use the best scientific and commercial data available.

16 U.S.C. § 1536(a)(2). An action would "jeopardize" a species if it "reasonably would be expected to reduce the reproduction, numbers, or distribution of a listed species to such an extent as to appreciably reduce the likelihood of the survival and recovery of that species in the wild." 50 C.F.R. § 402.02 (1984).

Pursuant to section 7(a)(2), the Service determined that the Permit would not likely jeopardize the continued existence of the Mission Blue butterfly. In so determining, the Service relied upon a variety of information including the Biological Study, the Plan, the Agreement, the EIR/EA, public comments received on the Permit Application, peer reviews of the Biological Study, and file materials on the Mission Blue butterfly.

Appellant erroneously contends that these sources did not represent the best scientific data available because of "the uncontroverted evidence from [the two experts upon whom it relies] revealing major mistakes in the field study."

Again, the low recapture rate realized in the mark-release-recapture phase of the Biological Study was a limitation that the Study itself and the Service acknowledged. And, several peer reviews took note of the limitations inherent in low mark-release-recapture rates. Thus, the Service was aware of all relevant limitations on the Biological Study and the field data, and the Service addressed those limitations in its Permit Findings. During the administrative process, appellant and its two experts did not direct the Service to any better available data. Moreover, the Service considered whatever data and other materials appellants provided. "[T]he issue for review is whether the [agency's] decision was based on a consideration of the relevant factors and whether there has been a clear error of judgment." There is no genuine issue of material fact to dispute the district court's determination that the Service did not act unreasonably or capriciously, or in violation of section 7(a)(2), by considering all the data it received in the present case.

II. *Violation of the National Environmental Policy Act*

[The court concluded that no EIS had to be prepared, alternatives had been considered in the environmental assessment and no "worst case" analysis was required.]

NOTES AND QUESTIONS

1. How does the protection of fish and wildlife differ from that for plants under section 9?

2. Can a private citizen challenge a private development project for violating section 9? *See* 16 U.S.C. § 1540(g)(1). Who has the burden of proving a taking of a species? *See Sierra Club v. Block*, 614 F. Supp. 488, 492 (D.D.C. 1985). Who has the burden of proving or disproving an exemption? *See* 16 U.S.C. § 1539(g). *See also* des Rosiers, *The Exemption Process Under the Endangered Species Act: How the "God Squad" Works and Why*, 66 NOTRE DAME L. REV. 825 (1991). How would application of section 9 to a development project arise? *See* Arnold, *Conserving and Building Habitats: The Emerging Impact of the Endangered Species Act on Land Use Development*, 10 STAN. ENVT'L L.J. 1, 13 (1991).

3. Can an incidental takings permit be issued for projects that reduce the likelihood that a species will survive? That reduce the likelihood of the species' recovery from endangered status? What must an applicant for an individual takings permit do to demonstrate the impacts will be mitigated "to the maximum extent practicable"? For a general discussion of the interrelationship between nuisance law, species preservation, and takings jurisprudence, see Murray, *Private Takings of Endangered Species as Public Nuisance:* Lucas v. South Carolina Coastal Council *and the Endangered Species Act*, 12 UCLA J. ENVTL. L. & POL'Y 119 (1993).

4. The principal case is discussed in Arnold, *supra* note 2, at 17-24, and White, *Where Have All the Butterflies Gone? Ninth Circuit Upholds Decision to Allow Incidental Taking*, 16 GOLDEN GATE U.L. REV. 93 (1986).

BABBITT v. SWEET HOME CHAPTER OF COMMUNITIES FOR A GREAT OREGON

115 S. Ct. 2407 (1995)

JUSTICE STEVENS delivered the opinion of the Court.

The Endangered Species Act of 1973, 87 Stat. 884, 16 U.S.C. § 1531 (1988 ed. and Supp. V) (ESA or Act), contains a variety of protections designed to save from extinction species that the Secretary of the Interior designates as endangered or threatened. Section 9 of the Act makes it unlawful for any person to "take" any endangered or threatened species. The Secretary has promulgated a regulation that defines the statute's prohibition on takings to include "significant habitat modification or degradation where it actually kills or injures wildlife." This case presents the question whether the Secretary exceeded his authority under the Act by promulgating that regulation.

I

... "The term 'take' means to harass, harm, pursue, hunt, shoot, wound, kill, trap, capture, or collect, or to attempt to engage in any such conduct." 16 U.S.C. § 1532(19).

The Act does not further define the terms it uses to define "take." The Interior Department regulations that implement the statute, however, define the statutory term "harm":

> "Harm in the definition of 'take' in the Act means an act which actually kills or injures wildlife. Such act may include significant habitat modification or degradation where it actually kills or injures wildlife by significantly impairing essential behavioral patterns, including breeding, feeding, or sheltering." 50 CFR § 17.3 (1994).

This regulation has been in place since 1975.

A limitation on the § 9 "take" prohibition appears in § 10(a)(1)(B) of the Act, which Congress added by amendment in 1982. That section authorizes the Secretary to grant a permit for any taking otherwise prohibited by § 9(a)(1)(B) "if such taking is incidental to, and not the purpose of, the carrying out of an otherwise lawful activity." 16 U.S.C. § 1539(a)(1)(B).

In addition to the prohibition on takings, the Act provides several other protections for endangered species. Section 4, 16 U.S.C. § 1533, commands the Secretary to identify species of fish or wildlife that are in danger of extinction and to publish from time to time lists of all species he determines to be endangered or threatened. Section 5, 16 U.S.C. § 1534, authorizes the Secretary, in cooperation with the States, see 16 U.S.C. § 1535, to acquire land to aid in preserving such species. Section 7 requires federal agencies to ensure that none of their activities, including the granting of licenses and permits, will jeopardize the continued existence of endangered species "or result in the destruction or adverse modification of habitat of such species which is determined by the Secretary ... to be critical." 16 U.S.C. § 1536(a)(2).

Respondents in this action are small landowners, logging companies, and families dependent on the forest products industries in the Pacific Northwest and in the Southeast, and organizations that represent their interests. They brought this declaratory judgment action against petitioners, the Secretary of the Interior and the Director of the Fish and Wildlife Service, in the United States District Court for the District of Columbia to challenge the statutory validity of the

Secretary's regulation defining "harm," particularly the inclusion of habitat modification and degradation in the definition. Respondents challenged the regulation on its face. Their complaint alleged that application of the "harm" regulation to the red-cockaded woodpecker, an endangered species, and the northern spotted owl, a threatened species, had injured them economically.

Respondents advanced three arguments to support their submission that Congress did not intend the word "take" in § 9 to include habitat modification, as the Secretary's "harm" regulation provides. First, they correctly noted that language in the Senate's original version of the ESA would have defined "take" to include "destruction, modification, or curtailment of [the] habitat or range" of fish or wildlife, but the Senate deleted that language from the bill before enacting it. Second, respondents argued that Congress intended the Act's express authorization for the Federal Government to buy private land in order to prevent habitat degradation in § 5 to be the exclusive check against habitat modification on private property. Third, because the Senate added the term "harm" to the definition of "take" in a floor amendment without debate, respondents argued that the court should not interpret the term so expansively as to include habitat modification.

The District Court considered and rejected each of respondents' arguments, finding "that Congress intended an expansive interpretation of the word 'take,' an interpretation that encompasses habitat modification." 806 F. Supp. 279, 285 (1992)....

A divided panel of the Court of Appeals initially affirmed the judgment of the District Court. 303 U.S. App. D.C. 42, 1 F.3d 1 (CADC 1993). After granting a petition for rehearing, however, the panel reversed. 305 U.S. App. D.C. 110, 17 F.3d 1463 (CADC 1994)....

The Court of Appeals' decision created a square conflict with a 1988 decision of the Ninth Circuit that had upheld the Secretary's definition of "harm." *See Palila v. Hawaii Dept. of Land and Natural Resources*, 852 F.2d 1106 (1988) (*Palila II*). The Court of Appeals neither cited nor distinguished *Palila II*, despite the stark contrast between the Ninth Circuit's holding and its own. We granted certiorari to resolve the conflict. Our consideration of the text and structure of the Act, its legislative history, and the significance of the 1982 amendment persuades us that the Court of Appeals' judgment should be reversed.

II

....

The text of the Act provides three reasons for concluding that the Secretary's interpretation is reasonable. First, an ordinary understanding of the word "harm" supports it. The dictionary definition of the verb form of "harm" is "to cause hurt or damage to: injure." In the context of the ESA, that definition naturally encompasses habitat modification that results in actual injury or death to members of an endangered or threatened species.

Respondents argue that the Secretary should have limited the purview of "harm" to direct applications of force against protected species, but the dictionary definition does not include the word "directly" or suggest in any way that only direct or willful action that leads to injury constitutes "harm." Moreover, unless the statutory term "harm" encompasses indirect as well as direct injuries, the word has no meaning that does not duplicate the meaning of other words that § 3 uses to define "take." A reluctance to treat statutory terms as surplusage supports the reasonableness of the Secretary's interpretation. [Citation]

Second, the broad purpose of the ESA supports the Secretary's decision to extend protection against activities that cause the precise harms Congress enacted the statute to avoid. In TVA v. Hill, 437 U.S. 153, 98 S. Ct. 2279, 57 L. Ed. 2d 117 (1978), we described the Act as "the most comprehensive legislation for the preservation of endangered species ever enacted by any nation." Id., at 180, 98 S. Ct. at 2294....

....

Third, the fact that Congress in 1982 authorized the Secretary to issue permits for takings that § 9(a)(1)(B) would otherwise prohibit, "if such taking is incidental to, and not the purpose of, the carrying out of an otherwise lawful activity," 16 U.S.C. § 1539(a)(1)(B), strongly suggests that Congress understood § 9(a)(1)(B) to prohibit indirect as well as deliberate takings. [Citation] The permit process requires the applicant to prepare a "conservation plan" that specifies how he intends to "minimize and mitigate" the "impact" of his activity on endangered and threatened species, 16 U.S.C. § 1539(a)(2)(A), making clear that Congress had in mind foreseeable rather than merely accidental effects on listed species. No one could seriously request an "incidental" take permit to avert § 9 liability for direct, deliberate action against a member of an endangered or threatened species, but respondents would read "harm" so narrowly that the permit procedure would have little more than that absurd purpose....

The Court of Appeals made three errors in asserting that "harm" must refer to a direct application of force because the words around it do. First, the court's premise was flawed. Several of the words that accompany "harm" in the § 3 definition of "take," especially "harass," "pursue," "wound," and "kill," refer to actions or effects that do not require direct applications of force. Second, to the extent the court read a requirement of intent or purpose into the words used to define "take," it ignored § 9's express provision that a "knowing" action is enough to violate the Act. Third, the court employed noscitur a sociis to give "harm" essentially the same function as other words in the definition, thereby denying it independent meaning. The canon, to the contrary, counsels that a word "gathers meaning from the words around it." [Citation] The statutory context of "harm" suggests that Congress meant that term to serve a particular function in the ESA, consistent with but distinct from the functions of the other verbs used to define "take." The Secretary's interpretation of "harm" to include indirectly injuring endangered animals through habitat modification permissibly interprets "harm" to have "a character of its own not to be submerged by its association." [Citation]

Nor does the Act's inclusion of the § 5 land acquisition authority and the § 7 directive to federal agencies to avoid destruction or adverse modification of critical habitat alter our conclusion. Respondents' argument that the Government lacks any incentive to purchase land under § 5 when it can simply prohibit takings under § 9 ignores the practical considerations that attend enforcement of the ESA. Purchasing habitat lands may well cost the Government less in many circumstances than pursuing civil or criminal penalties. In addition, the § 5 procedure allows for protection of habitat before the seller's activity has harmed any endangered animal, whereas the Government cannot enforce the § 9 prohibition until an animal has actually been killed or injured. The Secretary may also find the § 5 authority useful for preventing modification of land that is not yet but may in the future become habitat for an endangered or threatened species. The § 7 directive applies only to the Federal Government, whereas the § 9 prohibition applies to "any person." Section 7 imposes a broad, affirmative duty to avoid adverse habitat modifications that § 9 does not replicate, and § 7 does not limit its admonition to habitat modification that "actually kills or injures wildlife." Conversely, § 7 contains limitations that § 9 does not, applying only to actions "likely to jeopardize the continued existence of any endangered species or threatened species," 16 U.S.C. § 1536(a)(2), and to modifications of habitat that have been designated "critical" pursuant to § 4, 16 U.S.C. § 1533(b)(2). Any overlap that § 5 or § 7 may have with § 9 in particular cases is unexceptional, and simply reflects the broad purpose of the Act set out in § 2 and acknowledged in *TVA v. Hill*.

We need not decide whether the statutory definition of "take" compels the Secretary's interpretation of "harm," because our conclusions that Congress did not unambiguously manifest its intent to adopt respondents' view and that the Secretary's interpretation is reasonable suffice to decide this case. *See generally Chevron U.S.A. Inc. v. Natural Resources Defense Council, Inc.*, 467 U.S. 837, 81 L. Ed. 2d 694, 104 S. Ct. 2778 (1984). The latitude the ESA gives the Secretary in enforcing the statute, together with the degree of regulatory expertise necessary to its enforcement, establishes that we owe some degree of deference to the Secretary's reasonable interpretation.

III

Our conclusion that the Secretary's definition of "harm" rests on a permissible construction of the ESA gains further support from the legislative history of the statute. The Committee Reports accompanying the bills that became the ESA do not specifically discuss the meaning of "harm," but they make clear that Congress intended "take" to apply broadly to cover indirect as well as purposeful actions....

Two endangered species bills, S. 1592 and S. 1983, were introduced in the Senate and referred to the Commerce Committee. Neither bill included the word "harm" in its definition of "take," although the definitions otherwise closely resembled the one that appeared in the bill as ultimately enacted....

The definition of "take" that originally appeared in S. 1983 differed from the definition as ultimately enacted in one other significant respect: It included "the destruction, modification, or curtailment of [the] habitat or range" of fish and wildlife. Respondents make much of the fact that the Commerce Committee removed this phrase from the "take" definition before S. 1983 went to the floor. We do not find that fact especially significant. The legislative materials contain no indication why the habitat protection provision was deleted. That provision differed greatly from the regulation at issue today....

The history of the 1982 amendment that gave the Secretary authority to grant permits for "incidental" takings provides further support for his reading of the Act. The House Report expressly states that "by use of the word 'incidental' the Committee intends to cover situations in which it is known that a taking will occur if the other activity is engaged in but such taking is incidental to, and not the purpose of, the activity." This reference to the foreseeability of incidental takings undermines respondents' argument that the 1982 amendment covered only accidental killings of endangered and threatened animals that might occur in the course of hunting or trapping other animals. Indeed, Congress had habitat modification directly in mind: both the Senate Report and the House Conference Report identified as the model for the permit process a cooperative state-federal response to a case in California where a development project threatened incidental harm to a species of endangered butterfly by modification of its habitat. Thus, Congress in 1982 focused squarely on the aspect of the "harm" regulation at issue in this litigation. Congress' implementation of a permit program is consistent with the Secretary's interpretation of the term "harm."

IV

....

... The proper interpretation of a term such as "harm" involves a complex policy choice. When Congress has entrusted the Secretary with broad discretion, we are especially reluctant to substitute our views of wise policy for his. *See Chevron*, 467 U.S. at 865-866. In this case, that reluctance accords with our conclusion, based on the text, structure, and legislative history of the ESA, that the Secretary reasonably construed the intent of Congress when he defined "harm" to include "significant habitat modification or degradation that actually kills or injures wildlife."

....

The judgment of the Court of Appeals is reversed.

It is so ordered.

JUSTICE O'CONNOR, concurring.

My agreement with the Court is founded on two understandings. First, the challenged regulation is limited to significant habitat modification that causes actual, as opposed to hypothetical or speculative, death or injury to identifiable protected animals. Second, even setting aside difficult questions of scienter, the regulation's application is limited by ordinary principles of proximate causation, which introduce notions of foreseeability. These limitations, in my view, call into question *Palila v. Hawaii Dept. of Land and Natural Resources*, 852 F.2d 1106 (CA9 1988) (*Palila II*), and with it, many of the applications derided by the dissent. Because there is no need to strike a regulation on a facial challenge out of concern that it is susceptible of erroneous application, however, and because there are many habitat-related circumstances in which the regulation might validly apply, I join the opinion of the Court.

....

... Building upon the regulation's use of the word "breeding," JUSTICE SCALIA suggests that the regulation facially bars significant habitat modification that actually kills or injures hypothetical animals (or, perhaps more aptly, causes potential additions to the population not to come into being). Because "impairment of breeding does not 'injure' living creatures," JUSTICE SCALIA reasons, the regulation must contemplate application to "a population of animals which would otherwise have maintained or increased its numbers."

I disagree. As an initial matter, I do not find it as easy as JUSTICE SCALIA does to dismiss the notion that significant impairment of breeding injures living creatures. To raze the last remaining ground on which the piping plover currently breeds, thereby making it impossible for any piping plovers to reproduce, would obviously injure the population (causing the species' extinction in a generation). But by completely preventing breeding, it would also injure the individual living bird, in the same way that sterilizing the creature injures the individual living bird. To "injure" is, among other things, "to impair." One need not subscribe to theories of "psychic harm," to recognize that to make it impossible for an animal to reproduce is to impair its most essential physical functions and to render that animal, and its genetic material, biologically obsolete. This, in my view, is actual injury.

In any event, even if impairing an animal's ability to breed were not, in and of itself, an injury to that animal, interference with breeding can cause an animal to suffer other, perhaps more obvious, kinds of injury. The regulation has clear application, for example, to significant habitat modification that kills or physically injures animals which, because they are in a vulnerable breeding state, do not or cannot flee or defend themselves, or to environmental pollutants that cause an animal to suffer physical complications during gestation. Breeding, feeding, and sheltering are what animals do. If significant habitat modification, by interfering with these essential behaviors, actually kills or injures an animal protected by the Act, it causes "harm" within the meaning of the regulation. In contrast to JUSTICE SCALIA, I do not read the regulation's "breeding" reference to vitiate or somehow to qualify the clear actual death or injury requirement, or to suggest that the regulation contemplates extension to nonexistent animals.

....

By the dissent's reckoning, the regulation at issue here, in conjunction with 16 U.S.C. § 1540(1), imposes liability for any habitat-modifying conduct that ultimately results in the death of a protected animal, "regardless of whether that result is intended or even foreseeable, and no matter how long the chain of causality between modification and injury." Even if § 1540(1) does create a strict liability regime (a question we need not decide at this juncture), I see no indication that Congress, in enacting that section, intended to dispense with ordinary principles of proximate causation. Strict liability means liability without regard to fault; it does not normally mean liability for every consequence, however remote, of one's conduct. [Citation] I would not lightly assume that Congress, in enacting a strict liability statute that is silent on the causation question, has dispensed with this well-entrenched principle. In the absence of congressional abrogation of traditional principles of causation, then, private parties should be held liable under § 1540(1) only if their habitat-modifying actions proximately cause death or injury to protected animals....

In my view, then, the "harm" regulation applies where significant habitat modification, by impairing essential behaviors, proximately (foreseeably) causes actual death or injury to identifiable animals that are protected under the Endangered Species Act. Pursuant to my interpretation, *Palila II* — under which the Court of Appeals held that a state agency committed a "taking" by permitting feral sheep to eat mamane-naio seedlings that, when full-grown, might have fed and sheltered endangered palila — was wrongly decided according to the regulation's own terms. Destruction of the seedlings did not proximately cause actual death or injury to identifiable birds; it merely prevented the regeneration of forest land not currently inhabited by actual birds.

This case, of course, comes to us as a facial challenge. We are charged with deciding whether the regulation on its face exceeds the agency's statutory mandate. I have identified at least one application of the regulation (*Palila II*) that is, in my view, inconsistent with the regulation's own limitations. That misapplication does not, however, call into question the validity of the regulation itself....

JUSTICE SCALIA, with whom THE CHIEF JUSTICE and JUSTICE THOMAS join, dissenting.

I think it unmistakably clear that the legislation at issue here (1) forbade the hunting and killing of endangered animals, and (2) provided federal lands and federal funds *for the acquisition of private lands*, to preserve the habitat of endangered animals. The Court's holding that the hunting and killing prohibition incidentally preserves habitat on private lands imposes unfairness to the point of financial ruin — not just upon the rich, but upon the simplest farmer who finds his land conscripted to national zoological use. I respectfully dissent.

I

....

In my view petitioners must lose — the regulation must fall — even under the test of *Chevron U.S.A. Inc. v. Natural Resources Defense Council, Inc.*, 467 U.S. 837, 843, 81 L. Ed. 2d 694, 104 S. Ct. 2778 (1984), so I shall assume that the Court is correct to apply *Chevron*.

The regulation has three features which, for reasons I shall discuss at length below, do not comport with the statute. First, it interprets the statute to prohibit habitat modification that is no more than the cause-in-fact of death or injury to wildlife. Any "significant habitat modification" that in fact produces that result by "impairing essential behavioral patterns" is made unlawful, regardless of whether that result is intended or even foreseeable, and no matter how long the chain of causality between modification and injury....

Second, the regulation does not require an "act": the Secretary's officially stated position is that an *omission* will do. The previous version of the regulation made this explicit....

The third and most important unlawful feature of the regulation is that it encompasses injury inflicted, not only upon individual animals, but upon populations of the protected species. "Injury" in the regulation includes "significantly impairing essential behavioral patterns, including *breeding*," 50 CFR § 17.3 (1994) (emphasis added). Impairment of breeding does not "injure" living creatures; it prevents them from propagating, thus "injuring" a *population* of animals which would otherwise have maintained or increased its numbers....

None of these three features of the regulation can be found in the statutory provisions supposed to authorize it. The term "harm" in § 1532(19) has no legal force of its own. An indictment or civil complaint that charged the defendant with "harming" an animal protected under the Act would be dismissed as defective, for the only operative term in the statute is to "take." If "take" were not elsewhere defined in the Act, none could dispute what it means, for the term is as old as the law itself. To "take," when applied to wild animals, means to reduce those animals, by killing or capturing, to human control. [Citations] This is just the sense in which "take" is used elsewhere in federal legislation and treaty. [Citations] And that meaning fits neatly with the rest of § 1538(a)(1), which makes it unlawful not only to take protected species, but also to import or export them (§ 1538(a)(1)(A)); to possess, sell, deliver, carry, transport, or ship any taken species (§ 1538(a)(1)(D)); and to transport, sell, or offer to sell them in interstate or foreign commerce (§§ 1538(a)(1)(E), (F). The taking prohibition, in other words, is only part of the regulatory plan of § 1538(a)(1), which covers all the stages of the process by which protected wildlife is reduced to man's dominion and made the object of profit. It is obvious that "take" in this sense — a term of art deeply embedded in the statutory and common law concerning wildlife — describes a class of acts (not omissions) done directly and intentionally (not indirectly and by accident) to particular animals (not populations of animals).

.... "Harm" is merely one of 10 prohibitory words in § 1532(19), and the other 9 fit the ordinary meaning of "take" perfectly. To "harass, pursue, hunt, shoot, wound, kill, trap, capture, or collect" are all affirmative acts (the provision itself describes them as "conduct," see § 1532(19)) which are directed immediately and intentionally against a particular animal — not acts or omissions that indirectly and accidentally cause injury to a population of animals. The Court points out that several of the words ("harass," "pursue," "wound," and "kill") "refer to actions or effects that do not require direct *applications of force*." That is true enough, but force is not the point. Even "taking" activities in the narrowest sense, activities traditionally engaged in by hunters and trappers, do not all consist of direct applications of force; pursuit and harassment are part of the business of "taking" the prey even before it has been touched. What the nine other words in § 1532(19) have in common — and share with the narrower meaning of "harm" described above, but not with the Secretary's ruthless dilation of the word — is the sense of affirmative conduct intentionally directed against a particular animal or animals.

....

I would call it *noscitur a sociis*, but the principle is much the same: the fact that "several items in a list share an attribute counsels in favor of interpreting the other items as possessing that attribute as well." The Court contends that the canon cannot be applied to deprive a word of all its "independent meaning." That proposition is questionable to begin with, especially as applied to long lawyers' listings such as this. If it were true, we ought to give the word "trap" in the definition its rare meaning of "to clothe" (whence "trappings") — since otherwise it adds nothing to the word "capture." In any event, the Court's contention that "harm" in the narrow sense adds nothing to the other words underestimates the ingenuity of our own species in a way that Congress did not. To feed an animal poison, to spray it with mace, to chop down the very tree in which it is nesting, or even to destroy its entire habitat in order to take it (as by draining a pond to get at a turtle), might neither wound nor kill, but would directly and intentionally harm.

....

The broader structure of the Act confirms the unreasonableness of the regulation. Section 1536 provides:

> "Each Federal agency shall ... insure that any action authorized, funded, or carried out by such agency ... is not likely to jeopardize the continued existence of any endangered species or threatened species or *result in the destruction or adverse modification of habitat* of such species which is determined by the Secretary ... to be critical." 16 U.S.C. § 1536(a)(2) (emphasis added).

The Act defines "critical habitat" as habitat that is "essential to the conservation of the species," §§ 1532(5)(A)(i), (A)(ii), with "conservation" in turn defined as the use of methods necessary to bring listed species "to the point at which the measures provided pursuant to this chapter are no longer necessary." § 1532(3).

These provisions have a double significance. Even if §§ 1536(a)(2) and 1538(a)(1)(B) were totally independent prohibitions — the former applying only to federal agencies and their licensees, the latter only to private parties — Congress's explicit prohibition of habitat modification in the one section would bar the inference of an implicit prohibition [*63] of habitat modification in the other section....

In fact, however, §§ 1536(a)(2) and 1538(a)(1)(B) do not operate in separate realms; federal agencies are subject to *both*, because the "persons" forbidden to take protected species under § 1538 include agencies and departments of the Federal Government. *See* § 1532(13). This means that the "harm" regulation also contradicts another principle of interpretation: that statutes should be read so far as possible to give independent effect to all their provisions. [Citation] By defining "harm" in the definition of "take" in § 1538(a)(1)(B) to include significant habitat modification that injures populations of wildlife, the regulation makes the habitat-modification restriction in § 1536(a)(2) almost wholly superfluous. As "critical habitat" is habitat "essential to the conservation of the species," adverse modification of "critical" habitat by a federal agency would also constitute habitat modification that injures a population of wildlife.

... If the Secretary's definition of "harm" under § 1538(a)(1)(B) is to be upheld, we must believe that Congress enacted § 1536(a)(2) solely because in its absence federal agencies would be able to modify habitat in currently unoccupied areas. It is more rational to believe that the Secretary's expansion of § 1538(a)-(1)(B) carves out the heart of one of the central provisions of the Act.

II

The Court makes four other arguments. First, "the broad purpose of the [Act] supports the Secretary's decision to extend protection against activities that cause the precise harms Congress enacted the statute to avoid." *Ante*, at 10. I thought we had renounced the vice of "simplistically ... assuming that *whatever* furthers the statute's primary objective must be the law."...

Second, the Court maintains that the legislative history of the 1973 Act supports the Secretary's definition. Even if legislative history were a legitimate and reliable tool of interpretation (which I shall assume in order to rebut the Court's claim); and even if it could appropriately be resorted to when the enacted text is as clear as this; here it shows quite the opposite of what the Court says....

Both the Senate and House floor managers of the bill explained it in terms which leave no doubt that the problem of habitat destruction on private lands was to be solved principally by the land acquisition program of § 1534, while § 1538 solved a different problem altogether — the problem of takings....

Third, the Court seeks support from a provision [§ 10(a)(1)(B), 16 U.S.C. § 1539(a)(1)(B)] which was added to the Act in 1982, the year after the Secretary promulgated the current regulation.... This provision applies to the many otherwise lawful takings that incidentally take a protected species — as when fishing for unprotected salmon also takes an endangered species of salmon....

... I must acknowledge that the Senate Committee Report on this provision, and the House Conference Committee Report, clearly contemplate that it will enable the Secretary to permit environmental modification. [Citation] But the *text* of the amendment cannot possibly bear that asserted meaning, when placed within the context of an Act that must be interpreted (as we have seen) not to prohibit private environmental modification. The neutral language of the amendment cannot possibly alter that interpretation, nor can its legislative history be summoned forth to contradict, rather than clarify, what is in its totality an unambiguous statutory text....

Fourth and lastly, the Court seeks to avoid the evident shortcomings of the regulation on the ground that the respondents are challenging it on its face rather than as applied. The Court seems to say that even if the regulation dispenses with the foreseeability of harm that it acknowledges the statute to require, that does not matter because this is a facial challenge: so long as habitat modification that would foreseeably cause harm is prohibited by the statute, the regulation must be sustained. Presumably it would apply the same reasoning to all the other defects of the regulation: the regulation's failure to require injury to particular animals survives the present challenge, because at least some environmental modifications kill particular animals. This evisceration of the facial challenge is unprecedented. It is one thing to say that a facial challenge to a regulation that omits statutory element x must be rejected if there is any set of facts on which the statute *does not require x*. It is something quite different — and unlike any doctrine of "facial challenge" I have ever encountered — to say that the challenge must be rejected if the regulation could be applied to a state of facts in which element *x happens to be present*. On this analysis, the only regulation susceptible to facial attack is one that not only is invalid in all its applications, but also does not sweep up any person who could have been held liable under a proper application of the statute. That is not the law....

III

In response to the points made in this dissent, the Court's opinion stresses two points, neither of which is supported by the regulation, and so cannot validly be used to uphold it. First, the Court and the concurrence suggest that the regulation should be read to contain a requirement of proximate causation or foreseeability, principally because the statute does — and "nothing in the regulation purports to weaken those requirements [of the statute]." I quite agree that the statute contains such a limitation, because the verbs of purpose in § 1538(a)(1)(B) denote action directed at animals. *But the Court has rejected that reading.* The critical premise on which it has upheld the regulation is that, despite the weight of the other words in § 1538(a)(1)(B), "the statutory term 'harm' encompasses indirect as well as direct injuries."...

... The only other reason given for finding a proximate-cause limitation in the regulation is that "by use of the word 'actually,' the regulation clearly rejects speculative or conjectural effects, and thus itself invokes principles of proximate causation." *Non sequitur*, of course. That the injury must be "actual" as opposed to "potential" simply says nothing at all about the length or foreseeability of the causal chain between the habitat modification and the "actual" injury. It is thus true and irrelevant that "the Secretary did not need to include 'actually' to connote 'but for' causation"; "actually" defines the requisite injury, not the requisite *causality*.

The regulation says (it is worth repeating) that "harm" means (1) an act which (2) actually kills or injures wildlife. If that does not dispense with a proximate-cause requirement, I do not know what language would....

The second point the Court stresses in its response seems to me a belated mending of its hold. It apparently concedes that the statute requires injury to particular animals rather than merely to populations of animals. The Court then rejects my contention that the regulation ignores this requirement, since, it says, "every term in the regulation's definition of 'harm' is subservient to the phrase 'an act which actually kills or injures wildlife.'" As I have pointed out, this reading is incompatible with the regulation's specification of impairment of "breeding" as one of the *modes* of "killing or injuring wildlife."

....

The Endangered Species Act is a carefully considered piece of legislation that forbids all persons to hunt or harm endangered animals, but places upon the public at large, rather than upon fortuitously accountable individual landowners, the cost of preserving the habitat of endangered species. There is neither textual support for, nor even evidence of congressional consideration of, the radically different disposition contained in the regulation that the Court sustains. For these reasons, I respectfully dissent.

NOTES AND QUESTIONS

1. "Take" is defined as "to harass, harm, pursue, hunt, shoot, wound, kill, trap, capture or collect, or to attempt to engage in such conduct." 16 U.S.C. § 1532(19). After *Sweet Home*, what constitutes "harm" to wildlife? Is there harm if the development will only cause an overall decline in the population of the species? *See Palila v. Hawaii Dep't of Land & Natural Resources*, 852 F.2d 1106, 1108-09 (9th Cir. 1988) (yes, if it precludes recovery of the species from endangered status). Is *delay* in recovery sufficient to constitute harm? How definite or imminent must the harm be? *See North Slope Borough v. Andrus*, 486 F. Supp. 326 (D.D.C. 1979), *aff'd in part & rev'd in part*, 642 F.2d 589 (D.C. Cir. 1980) (harm must be certain or imminent).

2. The definition of "take" includes "harass." Could whale-watching boats constitute harassment of an endangered species? *See* 50 C.F.R. § 17.3 (harassment is an "intentional or negligent act or omission which creates the likelihood

of injury to wildlife by annoying it to such an extent as to significantly disrupt normal behavioral patterns which include, but are not limited to, breeding, feeding or sheltering"). Many, if not all, of the Justices were concerned in *Sweet Home* about the potential breadth of the regulatory definition of "harm." How is the definition of "harass" even broader? Could this definition withstand a legal challenge along the lines of the challenge made in *Sweet Home*?

Glossary

AEA   —   Atomic Energy Act

AFT   —   American Farmland Trust

ALI   —   American Law Institute

ALJ   —   administrative law judge

APA   —   Administrative Procedure Act

AQMA   —   Air Quality Maintenance Area under the Clean Air Act

ASCS   —   Agricultural Stabilization and Conservation Service

BACT   —   best available control technology, usually referring to the standard for major sources in prevention of significant deterioration areas under the Clean Air Act (*see also* BAT and BADT)

BADT or BADCT   —   best available demonstrated control technology, usually referring to the standards for new sources under the Clean Air Act or Clean Water Act (*see also* BAT and BACT)

BAT   —   best available control technology, usually referring to the standard for nonconventional and toxic pollutants under the Clean Water Act (*see also* BADT and BACT)

BCT   —   best conventional pollutant control technology applicable to conventional pollutants under the Clean Water Act

BDAT   —   best demonstrated available technology, treatment standard for hazardous waste under the Resource Conservation and Recovery Act

BLM   —   Bureau of Land Management

BMP   —   best management practices for control of nonpoint sources under the Clean Water Act

BOD   —   biochemical oxygen demand, a conventional pollutant under the Clean Water Act

BODS   —   biochemical oxygen-demanding substances (*see also* BOD)

BPCTCA   —   best practicable control technology currently available under the Clean Water Act, also referred to as BPT

BPJ	—	best professional judgment, a standard utilized in permit issuance in the absence of national effluent limitations under the Clean Water Act
BPT	—	best practicable control technology currently available under the Clean Water Act, also referred to as BPCTCA
CAA	—	Clean Air Act
CBRA	—	Coastal Barrier Resources Act
CCA	—	California Coastal Act
CERCLA	—	Comprehensive Environmental Response, Compensation and Liability Act, also referred to as the Superfund Act
CEQ	—	Council on Environmental Quality, established under the National Environmental Policy Act
CO	—	carbon monoxide, air pollutant and one of the criteria pollutants under the Clean Air Act
CPSC	—	Consumer Product Safety Commission
CRP	—	Conservation Reserve Program under the 1990 Farm Bill
CV	—	contingent value under the Comprehensive Environmental Response, Compensation and Liability Act
CWA	—	Clean Water Act, or the Federal Water Pollution Control Act
CZEG	—	Coastal Zone Enhancement Grant under the Coastal Zone Management Act
CZMA	—	Coastal Zone Management Act
DER	—	Department of Environmental Resources
DMC	—	de minimis classification under the Comprehensive Environmental Response, Compensation and Liability Act
DNA	—	deoxyribonucleic acid
DO	—	dissolved oxygen, an indicator of water quality
DOE	—	Department of Energy
DOI	—	Department of the Interior
DOL	—	Department of Labor
DOT	—	Department of Transportation

DRI	—	development of regional impact
EA	—	environmental assessment under the National Environmental Policy Act
EAJA	—	Equal Access to Justice Act
ECARP	—	Environmental Conservation Acreage Reserve Program under the 1990 Farm Bill
EDF	—	Environmental Defense Fund
EIA	—	environmental impact assessment under the National Environmental Policy Act
EIS	—	environmental impact statement under the National Environmental Policy Act
EPA	—	Environmental Protection Agency
ESA	—	Endangered Species Act
EUP	—	experimental use permit under the Federal Insecticide, Fungicide, and Rodenticide Act
FAA	—	Federal Aviation Administration
FDF	—	fundamentally different factor variance under the Clean Water Act
FEISS	—	Final Environmental Impact Statement Supplement under the National Environmental Policy Act
FEMA	—	Federal Emergency Management Act
FIFRA	—	Federal Insecticide, Fungicide, and Rodenticide Act
FLPMA	—	Federal Land Policy and Management Act
FOIA	—	Freedom of Information Act
FONSI	—	finding of no significant impact under the National Environmental Policy Act
FPPA	—	Farmland Protection Policy Act
FSA	—	Food Security Act (Farm Bill)
FWPCA	—	Federal Water Pollution Control Act, commonly referred to as the Clean Water Act
g/BHR-hr	—	grams per brake horsepower hour under the Clean Air Act
GSA	—	General Services Administration

GVWR	—	gross vehicle weight rating under the Clean Air Act
HAP	—	hazardous air pollutant under the Clean Air Act
HC	—	hydrocarbon, air pollutant and one of the criteria pollutants under the Clean Air Act until 1982
HCP	—	habitat conservation plan under the Endangered Species Act
HRS	—	Hazard Ranking System under the Comprehensive Environmental Response, Compensation and Liability Act
HSWA	—	Hazardous and Solid Waste Amendments to the Resource Conservation and Recovery Act
ICC	—	Interstate Commerce Commission
ICS	—	individual control strategy for toxic pollutants under the Clean Water Act
I/M	—	vehicle emission inspection and maintenance under the Clean Air Act
ITC	—	Interagency Testing Committee under the Toxic Substances Control Act
LAER	—	lowest achievable emissions rate for major sources in nonattainment areas under the Clean Air Act
LDT	—	light-duty truck under the Clean Air Act
LEV	—	low emission vehicle under the Clean Air Act
LMFBR	—	liquid metal fast breeder reactor
LVW	—	loaded vehicle weight under the Clean Air Act
MACT	—	maximum achievable control technology for hazardous air pollutants under the Clean Air Act
MSHA	—	Mine Safety and Health Administration
MY	—	model year under the Clean Air Act
NAAQS	—	National Ambient Air Quality Standard under the Clean Air Act
NAD	—	non-applicability determination for preconstruction review in prevention of significant deterioration areas under the Clean Air Act
NALS	—	National Agricultural Land Study
NBAR	—	non-binding allocations of responsibility under the Comprehensive Environmental Response, Compensation and Liability Act

NCP	—	National Contingency Plan under the Comprehensive Environmental Response, Compensation and Liability Act
ND	—	non-detectable value of a water pollutant
NEPA	—	National Environmental Policy Act
NFIP	—	National Flood Insurance Program
NFMA	—	National Forest Management Act
NGPRP	—	Northern Great Plains Resources Program
NIH	—	National Institute of Health
NMHC	—	non-methane hydrocarbon, air pollutant regulated under the Clean Air Act
NMOG	—	non-methane organic gas, air pollutant regulated under the Clean Air Act
NO_x	—	nitrogen oxides, air pollutant
NO_2	—	nitrogen dioxide, air pollutant and one of the criteria pollutants under the Clean Air Act
NPDES	—	National Pollutant Discharge Elimination System under the Clean Water Act
NPL	—	National Priorities List under the Comprehensive Environmental Response, Compensation and Liability Act
NRDC	—	Natural Resources Defense Council
NSPS	—	new source performance standard under the Clean Air and Clean Water Acts
NWF	—	National Wildlife Federation
NWP 26	—	Nationwide Permit Number 26 under the Clean Water Act
O_3	—	ozone, air pollutant and one of the criteria pollutants under the Clean Air Act
OCPSF	—	organic chemicals, plastics, and synthetic fibers, an industrial classification
OCRM	—	Office of Ocean and Coastal Resource Management under the Coastal Zone Management Act
OCS	—	outer continental shelf
OCSLA	—	Outer Continental Shelf Lands Act
OMB	—	Office of Management and Budget

OPA	—	Oil Pollution Act
OSHA	—	Occupational Safety and Health Administration
PCBs	—	polychlorinated biphenyls, regulated under the Toxic Substances Control Act and other environmental statutes
PDR	—	purchase of development rights
pH	—	quantitative measure of the acidity of water and a conventional water pollutant under the Clean Water Act
PM	—	particulate matter, air pollutant (*see also* PM-10 and TSP)
PM-10	—	particulate matter of 10 micrometers or less, the particulate standard which replaced in 1987 the National Ambient Air Quality Standard for total suspended particulates
lb/MBtu	—	pounds per million British thermal units, a measurement of heat energy
POM	—	polycyclic organic matter, air pollutant regulated under the Clean Air Act
POTW	—	publicly owned treatment works under the Clean Water Act
ppb	—	parts per billion
ppm	—	parts per million
PRA	—	Paperwork Reduction Act
PRP	—	potentially responsible party under the Comprehensive Environmental Response, Compensation and Liability Act
PSD	—	prevention of significant deterioration under the Clean Air Act
PSES	—	pretreatment standard for existing sources under the Clean Water Act
PSI	—	pounds per square inch
RA	—	regional administrator of the Environmental Protection Agency
RACT	—	reasonably available control technology for existing sources in nonattainment areas under the Clean Air Act
RCA	—	Soil and Water Resources Conservation Act
RCRA	—	Resource Conservation and Recovery Act
RDT	—	rural density transfer
RHA	—	Rivers and Harbors Act

RVP — Reid vapor pressure

SARA — Superfund Amendments and Reauthorization Act

SDWA — Safe Drinking Water Act

SIP — state implementation plan under the Clean Air Act

SO$_x$ — sulfur oxides, air pollutant

SO$_2$ — sulfur dioxide, air pollutant and one of the criteria pollutants under the Clean Air Act

SS — suspended solids, a conventional water pollutant under the Clean Water Act (*see also* TSS)

TCDD — 2, 3, 7, 8-tetrachlorodibenzo-p-dioxin (dioxin), toxic byproduct covered by the Comprehensive Environmental Response, Compensation and Liability Act

TCP — 2, 4, 5-trichlorophenol, toxic byproduct covered by the Comprehensive Environmental Response, Compensation and Liability Act

TDR — transferable development rights

TDML — total maximum daily load set as part of state water quality standards under the Clean Water Act

TOSCA or TSCA — Toxic Substances Control Act

TSP — total suspended particulates, air pollutant (*see also* PM-10 and particulates)

TSS — total suspended solids, a conventional water pollutant under the Clean Water Act (*see also* SS)

TVA — Tennessee Valley Authority

UCA — Uniform Contribution Act

UCAJTA — Uniform Contribution Among Joint Tortfeasors Act

UCFA — Uniform Comparative Fault Act

USDA — United States Department of Agriculture

USLE — universal soil loss equation

VOC — volatile organic compound, air pollutant which is precursor to ozone

WEE — wind erosion equation

WQA — Water Quality Act of 1987, amending the Clean Water Act

WQM   —   water quality management under the Clean Water Act

WQS   —   water quality standard under the Clean Water Act

Table of Cases

References are to pages. Principal cases and the pages
on which they appear are in italics.

Index

A

CONSTITUTIONAL LIMITS ON STATE ACTION —Cont'd
Takings clause limitations —Cont'd
  Compensatory damages as appropriate remedy, p. 130.
  Constitutional basis, pp. 126 to 130.
  Defining property rights.
    State law as dispositive, pp. 139, 146.
  Denying owner of economically viable use of his land, pp. 149 to 164.
  Diminution of value, pp. 135 to 144.
  Flood protection areas.
    Building restrictions, pp. 130, 177, 178.
  General rule, p. 126.
  Historical development of regulatory takings, pp. 126 to 130.
  Mining rights.
    Lands subsidence regulations, pp. 130 to 149.
  Nuisance exception, pp. 160 to 164.
  Public purpose test, pp. 126 to 135.

COSTS OF LITIGATION.
Attorneys' fees, pp. 220 to 232.
  See ATTORNEYS' FEES.

COWBOY ECONOMY, p. 7.

CWA.
See CLEAN WATER ACT.

D

DAMAGES.
Abatement of nuisances.
  Adequacy of remedy, pp. 74 to 83.
Cancer and other diseases.
  Increased risk and fear of increased risk.
    Common law measurement of damages, pp. 54, 55.
Common law, pp. 49 to 73.
  Generally, pp. 49, 50.
Comprehensive Environmental Response, Compensation and Liability Act.
  Limitation of actions, pp. 65, 66.
  Natural resource damages, pp. 850 to 866.
Diminution in market value rule, pp. 66, 67.
Economic harm.
  Common law, pp. 68 to 73.
Groundwater contamination.
  Common law measurement, pp. 59 to 68.
Indemnification for cleanup or restoration costs, pp. 67, 68.
Medical monitoring damages.
  Common law remedy, p. 56.
Permanent-temporary distinction.
  Common law, pp. 59 to 68.
Prejudgment interest.
  Common law, pp. 58, 59.
Punitive damages.
  Common law, pp. 57, 58.
Statutory enhancement of common law rule, pp. 66, 67.
Takings of private property.
  Appropriateness of remedy, p. 130.
Temporary-permanent distinction.
  Common law, pp. 59 to 68.
Toxic substance exposure.
  Common law measurement of damages, pp. 50 to 55.

ENVIRONMENTAL IMPACT STATEMENTS.

N

Z

ZONE OF INTERESTS TEST.
Standing, pp. 219, 220.

ZONING.
Agricultural zoning, p. 999.

Kurtz&Boone

15

Principles of
Contemporary
Marketing

Kurtz&Boone

15

Principles of
Contemporary
Marketing

DAVID L. KURTZ

Distinguished Professor of Marketing and

R.A. and Vivian Young Chair of Business Administration

University of Arkansas

SOUTH-WESTERN
CENGAGE Learning

Australia • Brazil • Japan • Korea • Mexico • Singapore • Spain • United Kingdom • United States

SOUTH-WESTERN
CENGAGE Learning

Principles of Contemporary Marketing, 15th Edition

David L. Kurtz

Vice President of Editorial, Business:
   Jack W. Calhoun

Editor-in-Chief: Melissa Acuña

Acquisitions Editor: Mike Roche

Developmental Editor: Erin Guendelsberger

Editorial Assistant: Kayti Purkiss

Marketing Coordinator: Leigh Smith

Content Project Manager: Scott Dillon

Media Editor: John Rich

Frontlist Buyer, Manufacturing:
   Miranda Klapper

Print Buyer: Arethea Thomas

Sr. Marketing Communications Manager:
   Jim Overly

Marketing Manager: Gretchen Swann

Project Management:
   Elm Street Publishing Services

Composition:
   Integra Software Services Pvt. Ltd.

Sr. Art Director: Stacy Jenkins Shirley

Internal Designer:
   KeDesign, Mason, OH

Cover Design: Patti Hudepohl

Photo Credits:

B/W Image: Getty Images/Hisham Ibrahim

Color Image: Shutterstock Images/Dan Collier

Rights Acquisitions Specialist: John Hill

For product information and technology assistance, contact us at
Cengage Learning Customer & Sales Support, 1-800-354-9706

For permission to use material from this text or product,
submit all requests online at **www.cengage.com/permissions.**

Further permissions questions can be emailed to
permissionrequest@cengage.com.

Exam*View*® is a registered trademark of eInstruction Corp. Windows is a registered trademark of the Microsoft Corporation used herein under license. Macintosh and Power Macintosh are registered trademarks of Apple Computer, Inc. used herein under license.

© 2012 Cengage Learning. All Rights Reserved.

Cengage Learning WebTutor™ is a trademark of Cengage Learning.

Library of Congress Control Number: 2010929381

International Edition:

ISBN-13: 978-0-538-48177-9

ISBN-10: 0-538-48177-3

Cengage Learning International Offices

Asia
www.cengageasia.com
tel: (65) 6410 1200

Australia/New Zealand
www.cengage.com.au
tel: (61) 3 9685 4111

Brazil
www.cengage.com.br
tel: (55) 11 3665 9900

India
www.cengage.co.in
tel: (91) 11 4364 1111

Latin America
www.cengage.com.mx
tel: (52) 55 1500 6000

UK/Europe/Middle East/Africa
www.cengage.co.uk
tel: (44) 0 1264 332 424

Represented in Canada by Nelson Education, Ltd.

tel: (416) 752 9100/(800) 668 0671
www.nelson.com

Cengage Learning is a leading provider of customized learning solutions with office locations around the globe, including Singapore, the United Kingdom, Australia, Mexico, Brazil, and Japan. Locate your local office at:
cengage.com/global

For product information: **www.cengage.com/international**
Visit your local office: **www.cengage.com/global**
Visit our corporate website: **www.cengage.com**

Printed in China by China Translation & Printing Services Limited
1 2 3 4 5 6 7 14 13 12 11 10

AVAILABILITY OF RESOURCES MAY DIFFER BY REGION. Check with your local Cengage Learning representative for details.

To Fred and Tami Bock, two of the best marketers I ever met.

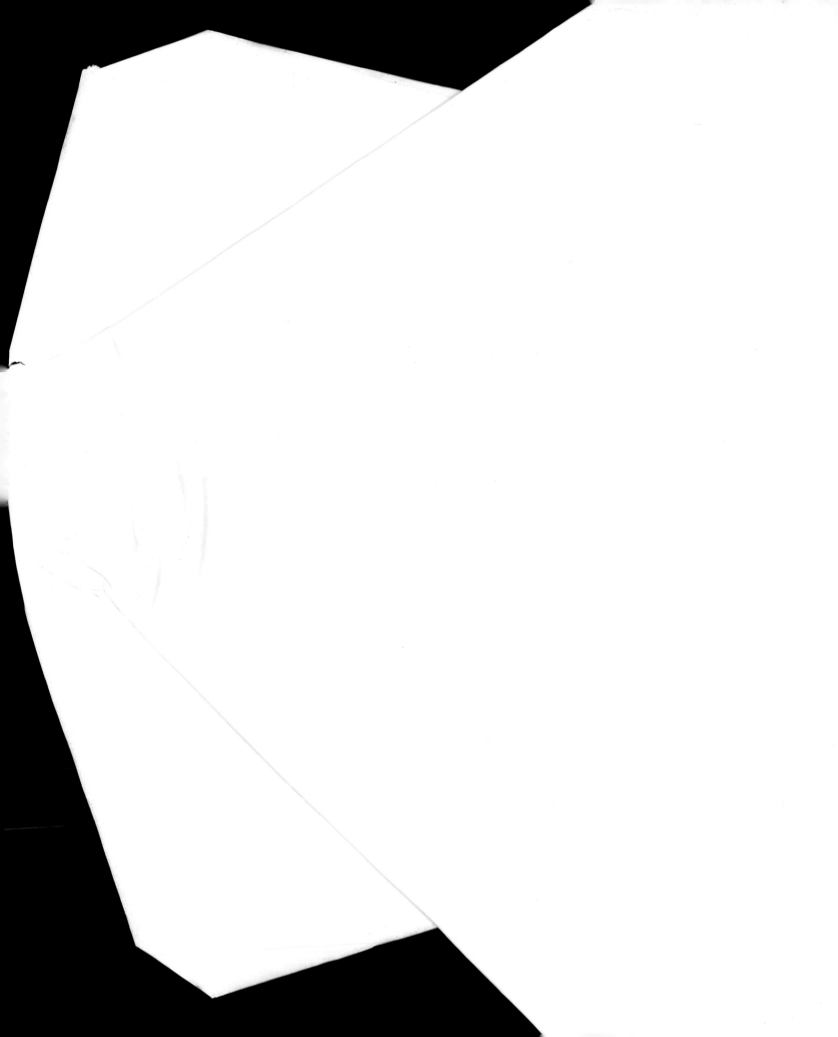

about the author

Dave Kurtz

During **Dave Kurtz's** high school days, no one in Salisbury, Maryland, would have mistaken him for a scholar. In fact, he was a mediocre student, so bad that his father steered him toward higher education by finding him a succession of backbreaking summer jobs. Thankfully, most of them have been erased from his memory, but a few linger, including picking peaches, loading watermelons on trucks headed for market, and working as a pipefitter's helper. Unfortunately, these jobs had zero impact on his academic standing. Worse yet for Dave's ego, he was no better than average as a high school athlete in football and track.

But four years at Davis & Elkins College in Elkins, West Virginia, turned him around. Excellent instructors helped get Dave on a sound academic footing. His grade point average soared—enough to get him accepted by the graduate business school at the University of Arkansas, where he met Gene Boone. Gene and Dave became longtime co-authors; together they produced more than 50 books. In addition to writing, Dave and Gene were involved in several entrepreneurial ventures.

Today, Dave is back teaching at the University of Arkansas, after tours of duty in Ypsilanti, Michigan; Seattle, Washington; and Melbourne, Australia. He is the proud grandfather of six "perfect" kids and a sportsman with a golf handicap too high to mention. Dave, his wife, Diane, and four demanding canine companions (Daisy, Lucy, Molly, and Sally) live in Rogers, Arkansas. Dave holds a distinguished professorship at the Sam M. Walton College of Business in nearby Fayetteville, home of the Arkansas Razorbacks.

brief contents

contents

PART 1

Designing Customer-Oriented Marketing Strategies

ch1 Marketing: The Art and Science of Satisfying Customers   2